Commercial Real Estate Analysis and Investments

David M. Geltner

Norman G. Miller

University of Cincinnati

SOUTH-WESTERN
™
THOMSON LEARNING

Australia · Canada · Mexico · Singapore · Spain · United Kingdom · United States

Commercial Real Estate Analysis and Investments
by
David M. Geltner
Norman G. Miller

Printed in the United States of America
5 04

For more information contact South-Western Publishing, 5191 Natorp Blvd., Mason, Ohio, 45040. Or you can visit our Internet site at http://www.swcollege.com

For permission to use material from this text or product contact us by
• **telephone: 1-800-730-2214**
• **fax: 1-800-730-2215**
• **web: http://www.thomsonrights.com**

ISBN

0-324-13676-5

This book is dedicated to our parents, our wives, and our children, and to all the students we have known who wanted to know not just what, *but* why.

Brief Contents

Contents

9   Measuring Investment Performance: The Concept of Returns   180

23   Macrolevel Valuation I: Static Property Portfolios   590

24   Macrolevel Valuation II: REITs   623

Appendix: Real Estate Transaction Price Indices Based on Regression Analysis   839

Answers to Selected Study Questions   847

Index   881

Preface

What This Book Is About

What is real estate? You could say that it is land. In that sense real estate is the quarter of the earth's surface on which all 6 billion human beings live. Or you could say it is built space, the structures in which we live and work and play, that shape and define our cities, and shelter our dreams. Or you could say that real estate is one-third of the value of all capital assets in the world, over $10 trillion worth of assets in the United States alone. No matter how you define real estate, you can't ignore it. Real estate is important, no matter what line of work you are in.

But think a bit more about what real estate is. What is the "nature of the beast"? Perhaps most obviously, it is not called "real" for nothing. Real estate is *real*. It is dirt and bricks and concrete and steel. Like any major aspect of the real world, real estate can be studied academically from several different perspectives, bringing to bear several different academic and professional disciplines. So if you ask someone, *What is real estate?* the answer you get will likely depend on the profession of the person you are asking. While an architect will describe real estate from an aesthetic and functional perspective, an engineer will describe it from a physical structural perspective. An environmental scientist will describe it from an ecological perspective, and a lawyer will describe it as a bundle of rights and duties associated with "real property," that is, land and the permanent structures on it. All of these answers would be correct, and a complete study of real estate requires a very comprehensive *multidisciplinary* approach.

Yet this book, while not ignoring these various perspectives, is not intended to be a complete multidisciplinary text. In order to provide sufficient depth and rigor to our study, this book will have to concentrate on one of the major disciplines for studying real estate. The discipline we will be using is that of economics. Indeed, we need to be more precise even than that. Within the economic study of real estate there are two major branches: urban economics and financial economics. The former is the branch of economics that studies cities, including the spatial and social phenomena relevant to understanding real estate. The latter is the branch that studies capital markets and the financial services industry. These are the two major branches of economics we will be using in this text because they are the most relevant for understanding commercial property from an investment perspective. Our major emphasis, however, will be on the second of these two branches, the financial economic aspects of real estate.

Why is the financial economic study of real estate so important? To answer this question, let's go back to our original question, *What is real estate?* Just as the architect's or engineer's answer to this question emphasizes the physical (bricks and mortar) aspects, and the lawyer's answer emphasizes the legal (bundle of rights) aspects, the successful real estate business professional's answer is likely to emphasize the financial economic aspects. The investor's fundamental answer to the question is, *Real estate is potential future cash flows.* The nature of these cash flows, their magnitude, time, and risk, will fundamentally be determined in the rental market, which is where urban economics comes in. But whatever is the specific nature of the potential stream of future cash flows generated by real estate, any such stream is, more generally, nothing more and nothing less than what is called a *capital asset.* And capital assets trade in capital markets. So that is where financial economics takes over.

Capital markets determine the opportunity costs and values of capital assets, and allocate the flow of financial capital (aka "money") to and among the underlying physical assets, which in turn produce the future real benefit flows that are the defining characteristic of capital assets. But perhaps more to the point for those with a more public policy or urban planning perspective, financial capital ultimately determines what real estate assets will be built, where, and when, in an entrepreneurial capitalist society such as that of the United States. The physical structures and aesthetic properties studied by the engineer or architect would not and cannot exist in reality without the financial capital to command the resources to produce them. Therefore, the academic discipline that studies financial capital is of vital importance to any real estate professional. As noted, this discipline is financial economics.

Once again, we should be more precise. Within the discipline of financial economics, two major fields are typically covered in graduate-level business schools: corporate finance and investments. Corporate finance concentrates on applications relevant to the financial and strategic management of large corporations whose equity is usually traded on the stock exchange. The investments field studies applications relevant to individuals and institutions making investment decisions about the wealth they own or manage. Both of these fields are relevant to analyzing commercial property from an investment perspective. Indeed, more so than in the classical (or "mainstream") presentations of these two fields, in real estate the topics and applications addressed in corporate finance and investments are more closely interwoven. In real estate we need to integrate these two fields that have grown apart in the mainstream literature and pedagogy.

To do this, we must address a number of features that make real estate unique—different from both the typical corporate finance and the securities investment contexts. For example, most commercial property is not held by publicly traded, taxed corporations. It may be held directly by taxed individuals or tax-exempt institutions, or it may be held by real estate investment trusts (REITs), which are publicly traded corporations that are not taxed at the corporate level. But only relatively rarely is commercial property actually owned (as opposed to rented or used) by the taxed corporations that dominate the stock market. Commercial property assets themselves also differ from the underlying assets held by the typical publicly traded, taxed corporation in that there is almost always a well-functioning market for commercial property. (When was the last time you hired a broker to sell an operating semiconductor manufacturing or automobile assembly plant for you?) In this respect, real estate assets are more like the assets studied in the mainstream investments field, primarily stocks and bonds. But the commercial property market is not as liquid or efficient in its operation as the securities markets dealt with in mainstream investments. (When was the last time you called up or modemed into your broker and ordered the sale of half of your ownership of 1000 North Main Street "at market" before close of business that day?)

Another fascinating difference between real estate and the mainstream corporate and securities environment is the simultaneous existence of two parallel asset markets in which real estate trades. Commercial properties are traded directly in the private property market, and they are traded indirectly in the stock market through the equity shares of REITs and other real estate firms. (Imagine what it would be like if you could buy pharmaceutical laboratories both directly and indirectly through the purchase of drug company stocks.)

These and other differences require a specific, real-estate-oriented treatment and synthesis of the topics covered in mainstream corporate finance and investments. This treatment can be, and needs to be, consistent with, integrated with, and built on the mainstream financial economic fields. A seamless intellectual continuum should exist from the typical finance course taught in the MBA core to the typical graduate course in Real Estate Finance or Real Estate Investments, an intellectual continuum from "Wall Street" to "Main Street." After all, since capital and information flow freely between these loci in the real world, real estate investment knowledge and practice should be built on the same principles that underlie the corporate and securities world.

The real estate treatment we need must also present an intellectually coherent framework, rigorous from an academic perspective, built on a few solid underlying concepts and principles, not a hodgepodge of vaguely connected, semirootless methodologies and rules of thumb. Modern real estate is crying out for a "body of knowledge," an "articulated corpus." The student needs a solid foundation in order to develop fundamental understanding. Yet such an elegant framework should include practical procedures and methodologies that can be applied directly to help answer typical real estate investment decision-making questions in the real world. Built on fundamental understanding, such methods will allow the student to apply creatively the real estate investment analysis framework she learns in academia to the infinite variety of situations she will no doubt encounter in the real world.

The purpose of this book is to present such a framework, a body of knowledge, at a level that the typical American graduate student can readily understand (with a little time, effort, and study, of course). Our intention and hope is that, whether you are pursuing an MBA, MSRE, or MSUP, whether or not you already have some background in mainstream finance or in real estate or in urban economics, you will find this book useful.

One final point: We know that some people claim that real estate is too complex, or lacking in hard data, to study "scientifically"—that it is an art, not a science. The implication is that we can do no better than to support real estate decision making with purely ad hoc analytical techniques. In effect, the implication of this claim is that real estate decision making should be "shot from the hip," or based on vaguely articulated intuition, even though this decision making governs one-third of the world's assets.

But as time thrusts us into the new millennium, such an attitude truly is ignorance. We can do much better than "seat-of-the-pants" decision making. Yes, real estate is complex, data is less than perfect, and decision making will always be somewhat of an art. Real estate is neither rocket science nor heart surgery, and we will never outgrow our need to always apply common sense. But both financial and urban economics are highly developed, sophisticated fields of study. They contain a very impressive corpus of knowledge and toolkit of methodology, as rigorous as any branch of the social sciences. They encompass a long history and a vast body of scientific literature, both at the theoretical and empirical levels, and have several Nobel laureates to their credit. Financial and urban economics are out there waiting to be applied to real estate investment decision making. Read this book and *do it!*

Organization of the Book

This book is designed to be useful for several types of students, in several types of graduate courses. The most typical users will be business students who already have some basic finance background, or urban studies or real estate students who already have (or will elsewhere receive) a background in urban economics. With this in mind, students should be able to use this book somewhat flexibly.

In general, as is typical of textbooks, this book progresses from basic underlying concepts and principles to more specific and specialized considerations and applications. More specifically, the book is organized into eight parts.

Part I. This is a brief two-chapter introductory overview designed to be especially useful to students who have little or no previous experience or exposure to the commercial real estate industry. A number of terms and basic practices that are widely used in real world practice are described here, as well as the fundamental real estate markets, and the parts and articulation of the overall "real estate system."

Part II. This is the urban economics part of the book: four chapters introducing the fundamental concepts and principles of that branch of economics as they relate to commercial property investment analysis. This is the part of the book that deals directly and in some depth with the "space market," as opposed to the asset market, including rental market analysis. This topic is fundamental, underlying the cash flow generation potential of all commercial property assets. Because this is not an urban economics textbook, however, we confine our coverage to a practical level, focused sharply on issues relevant to investment analysis. Students in urban studies programs may skim or even skip Part II and still be able to follow the remainder of the text.

Part III. This part begins the in-depth presentation of financial economics for the study of real estate from an investments perspective. It contains three introductory chapters presenting a brief overview and history of real estate in the capital markets; the fundamental mathematical tools and formulas of present value analysis; and the basic definitions and measures of investment performance, periodic, and multiperiod return measures. These are the fundamental building blocks of the rigorous study of real estate as an application of the financial economics discipline. Most of the material in Part III (along with Chapter 10, the first chapter in Part IV) should already be familiar to graduate business students who have passed through the core finance courses in their curriculums. Such students can skip or skim Chapters 7 through 10 and still be able to follow the rest of the book. However, concepts and applications particularly relevant to real estate are emphasized in these chapters, and some real-estate-specific terminology is introduced, so students without prior real estate exposure should at least skim these chapters.

Part IV. This part presents the fundamental principles, concepts, and methods of microlevel real estate valuation investment analysis, that is, the analysis of individual properties and transactions. The three chapters in Part IV present the core and basic foundation of the entire book, including the wealth-maximization principle, the DCF and NPV methodologies, and the concept of investment value and its relation to market value. As noted, this core framework is entirely consistent with and based on classical financial economics as taught in mainstream graduate-level corporate finance and securities investments courses. However, the implications of real estate's unique features and context are explicitly addressed and incorporated into the framework.

Part V. The three chapters in this part complete the coverage of basic investment analysis concepts and procedures begun in the previous part, extending them from the property level to the owner level. Thus, Part V treats the role of debt and income taxes in real estate investment, including the capital structure question. In a nutshell, while Part IV addresses the question of how to analyze the decision of *which* microlevel properties or projects to invest in, Part V addresses the question of *how to finance* those investments.

Part VI. This is the mortgage part of the book, in which we examine real estate debt primarily from the perspective of the lender (debt investor). The focus is primarily on commercial mortgages, including mortgage analysis fundamentals, commercial loan underwriting, and some basic mortgage economics and investment considerations. Part VI concludes with a brief introduction to commercial mortgage-backed securities (CMBS). Our treatment in Part VI remains at the introductory level, however, because the primary focus of this book is on equity investment.

Part VII. This part presents the basic macrolevel concepts and methods for dealing with real estate from a "top-down" perspective, that is, from a perspective encompassing aggregates of many individual properties, such as portfolios, funds, and REITs. Part VII thus complements Parts IV and V (which present a more "bottom-up view"). The seven chapters in Part VII deal with many of the more recent developments in the real estate investment industry. They cover topics such as modern portfolio theory and capital markets equilibrium pricing theory as these relate to real estate, property portfolio and REIT valuation, unique characteristics of real estate investment performance data (such as the "smoothing" problem in appraisal-based return indices), and issues related to real estate investment management.

Part VIII. This last part of the book is a bit of a "grab bag," a collection of selected topics that are important and useful in professional real estate investment analysis. The chapters in this part deal particularly with leasing and real estate development financial feasibility analysis, including the application of the branch of financial economic option valuation theory known as *real options*. (Option theory is also introduced briefly where it is relevant elsewhere in the book, most notably in Part II's treatment of land value and property life cycle, and Part VI's treatment of mortgage default and refinancing.) A technical appendix on the application of statistical regression analysis to the development of transaction-price-based indices of real estate periodic returns closes the book.

A final word on how this book "reads" is in order. Economics is a very technical subject with heavy emphasis on analysis and quantitative techniques (i.e., *lots of math and formulas*). Because this is an economics text, we can't get around it, even though we know it makes this subject tough for many students. We do sympathize, however, and we have tried to address the problem in several ways.

First, we have tried to clarify concepts intuitively whenever possible, and we have tried to present lots of simple numerical examples. Second, we have tried to identify sections of the text that are particularly advanced or difficult from an analytical or technical perspective and to set these aside to some extent. They are indicated by a preceding asterisk (*) in their section numbers. Less advanced or more "analytically challenged" students may want to skim these sections and not worry too much about the analytical details. While the points covered in these sections are important (or we would have left them out altogether), the overall implication of the point is more important than the technical details.

Finally, we have tried to systematize the presentation of all the material in this book, so as to clarify the underlying structure of the knowledge presented here. The concepts and tools presented in this book are essentially all based on a few relatively simple foundational economic principles, including wealth-maximization, market equilibrium, rational behavior, present value mathematics, and basic probability and statistics. This gives this material an underlying unity. If you look carefully, we hope you will see some beauty and elegance in the material covered in this book.

Acknowledgments

This book would not have been possible without the contributions of a number of individuals who helped in a variety of ways. The original germ of the idea for this project goes back to Christopher Will in 1994. But this project would have died without fruition if it were not for the enthusiasm of Elizabeth Sugg, our acquisitions editor at Prentice Hall, combined with the opportunity provided by Tim Riddiough of MIT for Dr. Geltner to teach the Real Estate Finance & Investments course at MIT in the fall of 1998. This book is a direct outgrowth of that teaching project. We have also had high quality assistance from a number of reviewers and class-testers of the working drafts of this book. Most notable in this regard are David Ling and Wayne Archer at the University of Florida, who class-tested most of this book and provided us with detailed and in-depth feedback. Excellent review and class-testing feedback was also provided by Brent Ambrose, Tony Ciochetti, Terrence Clauretie, Jim Clayton, Ron Donohue, Richard Knitter, David C. Ling, Jianping Mei, Tim Riddiough, and Tony Sanders. We would also like to acknowledge the contribution of the real estate investment professional staff at the State Teachers Retirement System of Ohio, and the members of the research committee of the National Council of Real Estate Investment Fiduciaries (NCREIF). These leading professional practitioners provided us with an invaluable real-world perspective for the microlevel and macrolevel portions of this book, respectively. Commendable administrative and production support for this project was provided by Delia Uherec at Prentice Hall, Laura Cleveland and Linda Zuk at WordCrafters, and Gail Farrar at PD&PS. Finally, much of the underlying inspiration and character of this book is owed to Stewart Myers, the lead author's Ph.D. dissertation supervisor at MIT, and a mentor to more people than he probably realizes.

Introduction to Real Estate Economics

In subsequent parts of this book we are going to be navigating some pretty narrow (and steep) paths. So let's begin with the big picture, with an overview of the real estate system from an economic perspective. The main purpose of Part I is to provide this overview. But we will also present here some of the fundamental nuts and bolts and tools useful in the economic study of real estate. These will help to bring the big picture down to everyday business practice, and be useful in subsequent chapters.

As noted in the preface, two major branches of economics bear on the analysis of commercial property from an investment perspective. The first is what is usually referred to in the United States as *urban economics*, and the second is *financial economics*. In later parts of this book we will explore real estate from one or the other of these two perspectives, separately. In this first part, in contrast, we will attempt to provide some integration and overview, bringing both of these perspectives together. The first chapter introduces the two major types or levels of markets relevant to commercial property analysis. The second chapter then discusses the development industry that links these two markets in a dynamic system, and presents some tools for understanding and analyzing this system.

1 Real Estate Space and Asset Markets

Learning Objectives

After reading this chapter, you should understand:

◆ How to apply the basic economic concepts of supply and demand to real estate markets.

◆ The difference between the real estate space and asset markets.

◆ The concept of market segmentation within the space market.

◆ Why the long-run supply function in the space market is "kinked" and what that means to future rents.

◆ The difference between, and relative magnitudes of, the public versus private asset markets, and the difference between equity and debt capital.

◆ What a cap rate is and what determines cap rates prevailing in real estate markets.

Markets are perhaps the most basic of all economic social phenomena. In essence, a **market** is a mechanism through which goods and services are voluntarily exchanged among different owners. In this chapter we will present a basic introduction to the two major markets that are relevant for analyzing commercial real estate: the space market and the asset market.

1.1 SPACE MARKET

The **space market** is the market for the usage of (or right to use) real property (land or built space). This type of market is also often referred to as the real estate **usage** market or the rental market. On the demand side of this market are individuals, households, and firms that want to use space for either consumption or production purposes. For example, a student renting an apartment is using space for housing consumption. A law firm renting an office is using space for production. Both these types of users are on the demand side of the space market. On the supply side of the space market are real estate owners who rent space to tenants.

The price of the right to use space for a specified temporary period of time is commonly called the rent. It is usually quoted in annual terms, per square foot (SF), though other methods are also used (such as monthly per apartment). The rental price (determined by supply and demand in the space market) thus gives a signal about the current value of built space and the current balance of supply and demand for that space. If usage demand grows and space supply remains constant, rents will tend to rise, and vice versa.

1.1.1 Segmentation of Space Markets

Users in the market for built space generally need a rather specific type of space in a rather specific location. A law firm needs an office building, not a restaurant or retail shop or warehouse, and it may need the building to be in downtown Cleveland, for example. If so, office space in downtown Detroit, or even office space in suburban Cleveland, will probably not satisfy the firm's needs.

The supply side of the space market is also location and type specific. Buildings cannot be moved. A vacant office building in downtown Detroit may be architecturally perfect for the Cleveland law firm, but it is not in the relevant location. Similarly, buildings generally cannot change their type, for example, from shop to office, or office to apartment. While some buildings have been converted from one usage type to another (for example, the warehouses that have been turned into "loft" apartments in New York and other large cities), such conversions are relatively rare and often require considerable construction expenditure.

Because both supply and demand are location and type specific, real estate space markets are highly segmented. That is, space markets tend to be local rather than national, and specialized around building usage categories. The market for warehouses in Dallas exists as a functioning market. A market for warehouses in the United States does not really exist as a single space market. This is in contrast to nationally "integrated" markets, such as that for gasoline, for example, or steel, or financial capital. These latter are homogeneous commodities that can be moved easily from place to place.

Because of space market segmentation, rental prices for physically similar space can differ widely from one location to another, or from one type of building to another in virtually the same location. For example, office rents on new leases in Chicago's Loop can be $23 per square foot while space in similar office buildings in Midtown Manhattan is not available for less than $33/SF. Similarly, apartment buildings can provide their owners with annual rents of $7/SF in suburban Dallas when retail buildings there are yielding $13/SF on new leases.[1] The office buildings in Chicago cannot be picked up and moved to Manhattan to earn a higher rent, nor can the apartments in suburban Dallas readily be converted into shopping centers.

---

[1] These were the actual average rents reported in late 1992 by the National Real Estate Index.

In real estate the primary geographic units of space market segmentation are **metropolitan areas** (also known as MSAs, short for "metropolitan statistical areas"). An MSA, encompassing a central city and its surrounding suburbs, tends to be relatively integrated economically, culturally, and socially. By definition, most points within a metropolitan area are more or less within automobile commuting distance of most other points in the area. The entire metropolitan area is largely built on the same economic base, although that base may be diverse in some areas. However, even within the metropolitan area important geographic submarkets exist. For example, the **downtown** (or **central business district—CBD**) is a different submarket from the suburbs, and individual suburbs will differ from one another. So even within a single metropolitan area considerable geographic segmentation of space markets exists.

In addition to geographical segmentation, real estate space markets are segmented by **property usage type**. The major types of space markets for rental property include office, retail, industrial, and multifamily residential. Other smaller and more specialized markets also exist, such as hotels, health facilities, self-storage facilities, golf courses, and a wide variety of others. Because each of these markets has different types of firms or individuals on the demand side, and different physical, locational, and architectural requirements on the supply side, the real estate industry serving these various space markets also tends to be segmented. Individual real estate professionals tend to specialize in serving one market segment or another. Real estate firms, such as national brokerage businesses, that do encompass more than one market segment tend to be organized in divisions that focus on the various segments.

1.1.2 Supply, Demand, and Rent in the Space Market

Let us "zoom in" on a specific, historic real estate space market and see how the economist's basic concepts of supply and demand and market equilibrium can help us to understand what goes on in a typical functioning space market. We will consider (a somewhat stylized version of) the market for class A office space in downtown Cincinnati, Ohio, during the late 1980s and early 1990s.[2]

From the 1970s to the 1980s office employment grew substantially in downtown Cincinnati. From roughly 24,000 office workers in class A buildings in downtown Cincinnati in the 1970s, by the mid-1980s there were 30,000 such workers. This growth in office usage demand was due partly to national factors, such as a structural shift in the U.S. economy (out of manufacturing and into services) that increased the number of office jobs. The growth was also due to local factors, as several national firms relocated their headquarters from other cities to Cincinnati. The 30,000 workers in the mid-1980s were occupying some 5 million square feet (SF) of space in about a dozen office towers typically 20 to 30 stories tall which defined the skyline of the city. The average rent being charged in these buildings was about $16/SF (per year).

This growth in demand is pictured in Exhibit 1-1. The underlying source of the space demand was the need of office workers for space in which to work. As the

---

[2]Real estate markets are often divided into classes: A, B, and C, to distinguish the physical and locational quality of the buildings, and therefore the levels of rent and types of tenants that are in the market on the demand side. Class A refers to the upper end of the market, where in the case of office buildings typical tenants would include prestigious law firms, corporate headquarters, and financial service firms. The particular historical period in this example is selected because of its educational value in illustrating a classic boom and bust cycle in the space market.

number of office workers increased, this need grew. The need for office space also grew because technological change, such as the rise in the office use of personal computers and fax machines, made more space necessary per worker. The growth in class A office demand is represented in Exhibit 1-1 by the movement out to the right of the demand function line, for example, from a previous time when there were 24,000 workers to the time (by the mid-1980s) when there were 30,000 workers. Notice that if the underlying need for office workers in downtown Cincinnati increased further, to 36,000 workers, for example, then demand in the market would support an additional 1 million SF of space (a total of 6 million SF would be needed) at the same $16 rent.

The demand functions pictured in Exhibit 1-1 look essentially like the classical demand functions of economic theory—downward-sloping continuous lines that move out and to the right as demand grows. This is typical of demand functions in

Exhibit 1-1 Office Demand as a Function of Employment

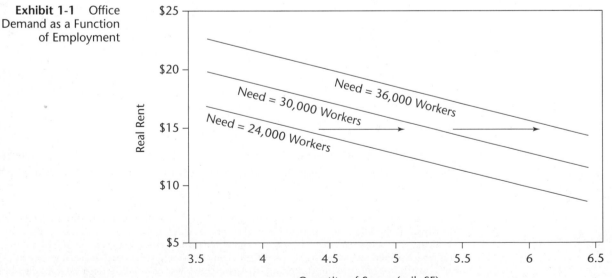

the space market. The supply side is a different story, however. The supply function in the real estate space market does not look like the upward-sloping continuous line depicted in the classical supply/demand diagrams. Instead, the possible supply function shapes shown in Exhibit 1-2 give a better representation of the supply side of most real estate space markets. This uniquely shaped supply function has important implications for understanding the functioning of the space market.

1.1.3 Supply Is "Kinked"

Economists often depict the typical real estate supply function as being "**kinked**"— that is, it is not continuous, but has a "corner" or break in it. The supply function starts out as a nearly vertical line at the current quantity of space supply in the market (in this case 5 million SF). This reflects the fact that the supply of office space is almost completely inelastic; if demand falls, office space cannot be reduced (at least in the short to medium term, even for a number of years). This is a consequence of the extreme longevity of built space. Indeed, compared to most other products, buildings last much longer. Rarely is a building torn down within less than 20 or 30 years from the time it is built, and it is much more common for buildings to endure 50 years or more (especially large-scale structures such as class A downtown office buildings). While some buildings can be converted to different uses, this is expensive and takes time. So at least for several years the market will maintain pretty much the quantity of supply it already has, in the case of a fall in demand.

The kink (or corner) in the supply function occurs at the current quantity of built space at a rent level that equates (on a capitalized present value basis) to the long-run marginal cost of supplying additional space to the market. Recall that the supply function for any competitively supplied product is simply the marginal cost function for producing additional increments of the product. In the case of built space, the marginal cost is the cost of developing new buildings, including the site acquisition cost as well as the construction cost and necessary profit for developers.

Exhibit 1-2 Real Estate Space Market Supply Function

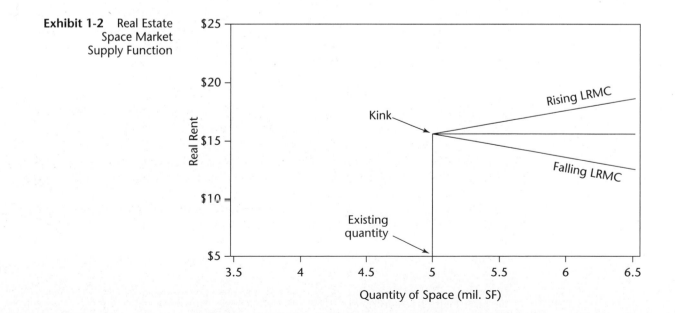

The level of rent that is just sufficient to stimulate profitable new development in the market is called the **replacement cost** level of rent, and this tends to be the long-run **equilibrium rent** in the market. If rents are said to be "below replacement cost" in a market, it means that developers cannot profitably undertake new development in that market. If rents rise above the replacement cost level, new development will be very profitable and will normally occur quickly in most U.S. cities, forcing rents back down to the long-run equilibrium level within a few years at the most.

1.1.4 Relation among Supply, Development Cost, and Rent

To understand the preceding point more clearly, let us return to our numerical example of the Cincinnati class A office market. Suppose that in the mid-1980s it would have cost $200/SF to develop a typical new class A office building in downtown Cincinnati, counting site acquisition cost as well as construction and other development costs, and including sufficient profit for the endeavor to be worthwhile to the developer. Thus, $200/SF was the marginal cost of adding additional office supply into the downtown market.

If we could sell new buildings for $200/SF, then additional development would be feasible. But the price at which one can sell buildings depends on what investors are willing to pay for them. This in turn depends on how much income the investors can expect to obtain from the buildings in the future. The income a building can earn depends on the rents it can charge in the space market. This link between expected future rents and present building values, compared to the current cost of development, determines the replacement cost rent at which the space supply kink point occurs.

It is helpful in this context to quote property prices in terms of how much investors are willing to pay per dollar of annual net rent they would initially receive from their investment. Suppose, for example, that in the mid-1980s investors were willing to pay $12.50 to purchase a class A Cincinnati office property for each dollar of current annual net rent the property could produce. Then if a building could charge $16/SF annual net rent for office space, and expect to keep that space rented, the building would be worth $200/SF (as $16 \times 12.5 = 200$). Using typical real estate terminology, we would say office buildings were selling at an 8% **cap rate**, as the net rent, $16/SF, divided by the building value of $200/SF, equals 8%. In these circumstances the net rent that equates (after dividing by the cap rate prevailing in the market) to the marginal cost of adding office supply into the Cincinnati market is $16/SF. So $16 would be the replacement cost rent level. According to Exhibit 1-2, this was indeed the case, as indicated by the kink point at the $16 rent level.

The rest of the supply function in Exhibit 1-2 consists of a line moving out to the right away from the kink point. This part of the line will exhibit one of three possibilities—rising, level, or falling. A rising supply line results when the development cost of new buildings is greater as more total stock of supply is added into the market. Roughly speaking, if it would cost more to develop the next office building than it did to develop the last one (in real terms, after subtracting general inflation, and including the cost of site acquisition and any necessary demolition), then the supply function is rising beyond the kink point.[3] If it would cost less, then the supply func-

---

[3] In general the term *real prices* refers to prices quoted in constant purchasing power dollars, after removing general inflation (or deflation).

tion is falling. If it would cost the same, then the function is level beyond the kink point.

1.1.5 Forecasting the Future Direction of Rents

One of the most basic and important things you must have in the real estate business is an intelligent idea about the future direction of rents in the space market. The shape of the supply function is important, for it fundamentally determines the level of real rents as demand changes over time. In general, the kink means that if a space market is currently in equilibrium, future growth in demand will result in very little (if any) real increase in rent levels in most markets in the long run.

On the other hand, the kink implies that declines in demand will cause relatively rapid and severe reductions in market rents due to the inelasticity of supply reduction. Such reductions may be expressed, particularly at first, not so much in a reduction in the rents landlords ask for, but in an increase in vacancies and in the offering of "concessions" to potential tenants, such as months of free rent up front, as an inducement to sign a long-term lease.

The kink in the supply curve is one reason real estate space markets have often tended to be cyclical, with periods of excess supply followed by periods of tight markets. A modest example of this occurred in the Cincinnati office market of the 1980s and 1990s. In the late 1980s developers in that market, apparently anticipating further growth in office demand, built an additional 1 million SF of new office space, expanding the supply from 5 million to 6 million SF. This change in supply is indicated in Exhibit 1-3 by the movement of the supply function to the right, from S_1 to S_2, assuming a flat long-run supply function.

Had the demand continued to grow, from D_1 to D_2 for example, this expansion of supply would have been justified, and rent levels in the market would have remained at the long-run equilibrium level of $16/SF. However, as happened in many real estate markets in the late 1980s and early 1990s, the supply overshot the demand.

Exhibit 1-3 Change in Supply and Demand and Rent over Time

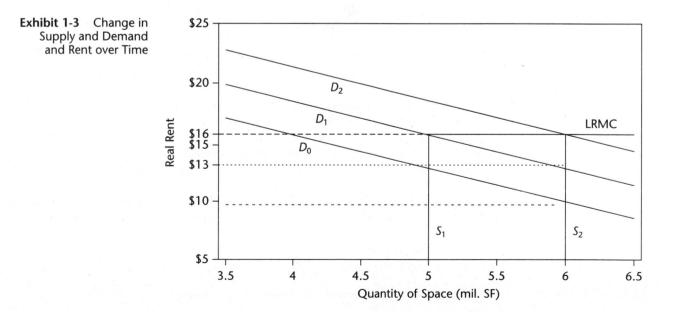

The demand growth did not materialize. The market remained stuck essentially with the same demand function, D_1. Combined with the new supply function of S_2, this caused market rents to plummet to levels around \$13/SF. Indeed, during the general economic recession of 1990–91 and the subsequent corporate downsizing, demand for class A office space in downtown Cincinnati probably actually fell, at least temporarily, from its previous level, perhaps to the level indicated by D_0, resulting in market rents temporarily in the \$10/SF range.

With demand at a level such as D_0 or D_1 and supply at a level such as S_2 in Exhibit 1-3, the market rents are below their long-run equilibrium level. That is, rents are below the level that can support new development, below replacement cost. At such a point, the space market is poised for a substantial surge in real rents if demand begins to grow again. Until rents rise back up to the long-run equilibrium level, the inelasticity of supply works in favor of landlords when demand is growing, enabling substantial hikes in real rents. (These may manifest at first as the filling up of vacancy and disappearance of widespread rent concessions in the market.) By the late 1990s the class A office market in downtown Cincinnati was back up to long-run equilibrium rents.

1.1.6 Is the Supply Function Rising, Level, or Falling?

The principal cause of a rising supply function is land scarcity in the presence of growing usage demand. This results in increasing **location rent**, as space users are willing to pay more real dollars per year for use of the same location.[4] The real cost of building structures does not usually increase over time or from one site to another. If demand keeps growing in the face of fixed land supply, the real price of site acquisition will rise, and this will add to the cost of development.

While location rent is usually the main source of such increased cost, it is also true that as more space is built in the market, the remaining supply of good buildable sites becomes scarcer. Construction will be more expensive on remaining unbuilt land sites that are hilly or swampy or less desirable for other reasons. Also, when new construction is undertaken on a site that already has a major existing structure on it, this greatly adds to the site acquisition cost. Not only must the existing structure be demolished, but the opportunity cost represented by the present value of the potential future income that the existing structure could otherwise generate is a major component of the site acquisition cost. For these reasons, it is possible for the supply curve to rise to the right of the kink point, as indicated by the upper line in Exhibit 1-2.

It is also possible, however, for the supply curve to decline to the right of the kink point. This will occur in areas where the location rent is declining over time in real terms. This occurs when a location is losing its relative **centrality**. For example, during the last half of the 20th century the traditional CBDs of many metropolitan areas in the United States lost value relative to suburban locations. In general, the development of the automobile and telecommunications has reduced the relative value of central locations compared to peripheral ones. This has caused a reduction in the real level of long-run equilibrium rents for some types of commercial property in the United States.

Evidence suggests that in "typical" or "average" space markets in the United States the long-run supply function has tended to be nearly level beyond the kink

---

[4] The term *location rent* will be discussed in more depth in Chapter 4.

Exhibit 1-4 CPI General Inflation Index (solid line) and CPI Housing Rent Index (dashed line) since 1947

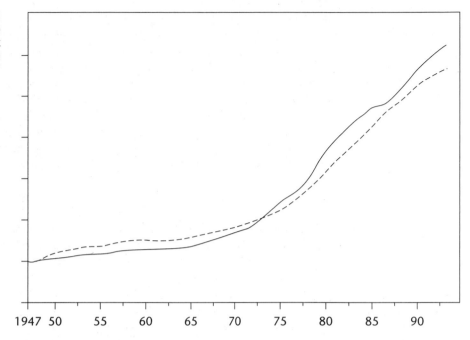

point, perhaps slightly rising or slightly falling. How do we know this? We can observe that rent levels in the economy have not generally tended to rise faster than inflation even as the total supply of built space has greatly expanded. For example, Exhibit 1-4 traces the history of the government's residential rental price index compared with the general inflation index (the Consumer Price Index—CPI) since the end of World War II. The solid line is the CPI, the number of current dollars it would take to purchase the same typical market basket of consumer goods and services at different points in time. The dashed line is the rental housing component of the CPI. Observe that the two curves are very nearly parallel, which indicates that residential rents, on average across the country, have risen at about the same rate as inflation. This means that real rents have not been increasing. This is in spite of the fact that the demand for rental housing over this half-century period has grown, and supply has been added.[5]

   In judging the likely shape or change in level of the long-run supply curve in U.S. real estate markets, several general historical and geographical factors must be kept in mind. A fundamental consideration is that the United States is, relative to many other nations, a "land rich" country, or anyway perceives itself as such as part of our social and political culture. As a result, in the United States urban land use expansion is relatively lightly controlled . A fundamental historical factor that must also be kept in mind is that during the last half-century period pictured in Exhibit 1-4, massive transportation and telecommunications infrastructure investments occurred, including the development of the urban expressways that serve virtually all U.S. cities. This opened up vast tracts of land for urbanization by making all points readily accessible.

[5]As noted, the location value of central locations has been declining relative to that of peripheral locations during this historical period. In U.S. cities, rental housing tends to be less centrally located than commercial property, but more centrally located than single-family (owner-occupied) housing. So its performance may represent an approximate "overall average" in regard to the long-term trend in real rents over the historical period shown.

As a result, the supply of urban land has not been at all fixed in most cities, but able to grow and expand with the demand. As we move into the 21st century, large quantities of lightly used land remain in and around many cities.

As noted, the effect of this physical expansion of urban land has been pronounced in the traditional CBDs. For example, in the downtowns of most U.S. cities, surface parking lots are not uncommon. These represent a ready supply of unbuilt, lightly used land available for development. The historical evidence is that real rents in U.S. downtowns have not generally risen over the past half century, and indeed have fallen in many cities. Exceptions to this rule are generally found only in severely space-constrained areas such as islands or peninsulas like Manhattan, Honolulu, and San Francisco.

In general, unless you have a good and specific reason to believe otherwise, it is probably safest to assume that the shape of the supply function is similar to the middle line portrayed in Exhibit 1-2 in most of the space markets you will probably be dealing in, at least in the United States. This may not be true in some other countries, however.

1.2 ASSET MARKET

While the space market is the most fundamental type of market relevant to the real estate business, the **asset market** is of equal importance. The real estate asset market is the market for the ownership of real estate assets. Real estate assets consist of real property, that is, land parcels and the buildings on them. Therefore, this market is often referred to as the **property market**.

From an economic perspective, such assets consist essentially of claims to future cash flows (e.g., the rents the buildings can generate for their owners). As such, these real estate assets can be compared to, and indeed compete in the capital market with, other forms of capital assets, such as stocks and bonds.[6] So the real estate asset market must be viewed as part of the larger **capital market**, the market for capital assets of all types.

1.2.1 Capital Markets

Broadly speaking, the capital markets can be divided into four categories according to whether they are public or private markets, and according to whether the assets traded are equity or debt. (See Exhibit 1-5.) **Public markets** are those in which small homogeneous units (or "shares") of ownership in assets trade in public exchanges in which many buyers and sellers are generally simultaneously participating in the market with price quotes available for all to observe. The stock market is the classic example of a public capital market. In such markets, transaction prices at which the units of the assets trade are typically reported publicly on a daily or more frequent basis. Public markets are characterized by a relatively high degree of **liquidity** in that it is generally possible to quickly sell units of the assets at or near the last quoted price. This liquidity is both a cause and effect of the fact that in public markets asset share prices can adjust rapidly to relevant news about their value. This ability of asset

---

[6]The net rents generated by a building are analogous in this respect to the dividends paid out by stocks or the interest paid out by bonds, and property competes for investors' capital against these other forms of investments.

	Public Markets	**Private Markets**
Equity Assets	Stocks REITs Mutual funds	Real property Private firms Oil and gas partnerships
Debt Assets	Bonds MBS Money instruments	Bank loans Whole mortgages Venture debt

prices to respond quickly to relevant news is known as asset market **informational efficiency**.

In contrast, **private markets** are those in which the assets are traded in private transactions arranged between individual buyers and sellers who have "found" each other, often through the aid of brokers. In private markets it is common (though not necessary) for **whole assets** (e.g., an entire company or property or oil well or mortgage) to be traded in a single transaction. The average size of the individual transactions therefore tends to be larger in the private markets.

Private markets generally are less liquid than public markets, as it takes longer for sellers to find buyers, and it is more difficult to ascertain a fair price for a given whole asset. Transaction costs (the cost of buying and selling) are typically higher in private asset markets (as a fraction of the value of the asset being traded). As a result of transaction and search costs, privately traded assets are generally traded less frequently than publicly traded assets. The fact that whole assets are traded in private deals between (typically) one buyer and one seller also has consequences for the nature of the asset price information that is available to the public.

In private asset markets it will generally be more difficult (or expensive) to observe the prices at which assets are trading. Furthermore, as whole assets are generally unique (such as a piece of art or a parcel of land), it is difficult to know how relevant an observed transaction price is for judging the value of any other asset. This problem is compounded by the fact that the parties to each trade are also typically unique, so the observed price represents only the agreement of two parties, not a broad market consensus. The same assets are not usually sold repeatedly very frequently, which makes even the trend in prices over time difficult to observe. For all these reasons, asset values in private markets tend not to incorporate or reflect news and information as quickly as do prices in public asset markets. In other words, *private asset markets tend not to be as informationally efficient as public markets*.

Perhaps a quick example will be useful to make this point more concrete. Suppose you own an apartment complex near Los Angeles International Airport. You think the property is worth about $10 million, but of course you are not sure. Now you hear news that should affect the value of your property in a negative way. The FAA has announced new regulations that control the flight patterns approaching the airport, causing more noise and safety problems for your neighborhood. Logically, this reduces the value of your property, other things being equal, below the $10 million you previously thought it was worth. But by how much does it reduce the value? Is it now $9 million, or $9.9 million?

If another similar property near yours would sell, and you could observe that transaction price, this might give you some idea about how the value of your property has changed, but even this would not give a very clear or definitive picture. The other property is not just like yours, and the buyer or seller in that deal may not have nego-tiated the way you would. And anyway, there may be no other similar property nearby that sells anytime soon. In short, you don't know how much to mark down your appraisal of your property's value as a result of the FAA news.

Contrast this situation with that of publicly traded assets. Suppose, for example, ownership of your apartment complex was divided into thousands of small homoge-neous shares that were constantly being traded by numerous buyers and sellers at pub-licly quoted prices on the stock exchange. In that case, you would know very quickly and certainly the effect of the FAA news on the value of your shares, simply by observing the change in the share price.[7]

Now let's move from a comparison of the columns in Exhibit 1-5 to a compari-son of the rows, to consider debt versus equity. Debt and equity are two different types of capital assets, both of which can be traded in either public or private types of asset markets.

Debt assets are essentially the rights to the future cash flow to be paid out by bor-rowers on loans they have taken out (e.g., interest payments and retirement of prin-cipal). The characteristic feature of debt assets is that they give their owners (e.g., the lenders or bondholders) a relatively "senior" or "preferred" claim for obtaining the cash which the *underlying asset* (the source of the cash flow) can generate. Also, debt cash flows are contractually specified, so the recipients know more precisely with rel-ative certainty how much future cash flow they will be receiving, and when. Debt assets are therefore less risky than equity assets. Debt assets also typically have spec-ified "maturity," that is, finite lifetimes after which there will be no further cash flow. For example, a bond might pay 8% of its stated (par) value in interest each year for 20 years, and then be retired by payment of the par value.

In contrast, **equity** assets are those that give their owners the "residual," or "sub-ordinated," claim on the cash flows generated by the underlying asset (e.g., a company or a property). Because equity claims are the residual (the amount that is left over after senior claims, including those of any debtholders), equity tends to be more risky than debt. But the equity owners also typically have more control over managing the underlying assets, and more ability to benefit from growth or "upside" potential in the cash flows generated by the underlying assets. Equity assets, such as stocks and real property are typically infinite-lived. Infinite life means that owners of an equity asset must sell the asset in order to "cash out" or liquidate their holding. It also means that more of the present value of the asset derives from the expectation of cash flows in the distant future, where there is the most uncertainty. This is another reason that the value of equity assets tends to be more volatile than the value of debt assets.

Capital asset products based on real estate have been developed for, and are traded in, all four of these branches of the capital markets. For example, REITs (Real Estate Investment Trusts) offer publicly traded common stock shares in companies that essentially do nothing but own (and manage, and buy and sell) income-producing properties and mortgages.[8] Mortgage-backed securities (MBS) are publicly traded

---

[7]On the other hand, it may be easier for public market asset prices to *overreact* to news, resulting in a sub-sequent "correction" to the price.

[8]In fact, most REITs primarily own equity interests in real property, as opposed to mortgages. To be more specific, a REIT is a corporation or trust that has elected REIT tax status. As long as the REIT conforms to certain government requirements, the REIT is exempt from corporate income tax. These requirements essentially limit the REIT to real estate investment and development type activity and require that the REIT pay out 90% of its earnings each year as dividends to its stockholders. For the most part, REITs

bondlike products that are based on underlying pools of mortgages, which are real-estate-based debt products. There are both residential MBSs and commercial MBSs (the latter known as CMBS). On the other hand, many mortgages, especially large commercial mortgages, are held privately as "whole loans," and these would be traded privately (if at all).

But the most fundamental form of real estate asset, the direct ownership of whole properties, is traded in a private market known as the property market, in which individual commercial buildings, single-family homes, and land parcels are bought and sold among parties who have often found each other through the services of real estate brokers. Ultimately, all the other forms of real-estate-based capital asset products are based on privately traded property as the underlying assets. That is to say, property assets produce the cash flow that is the ultimate source of any income or value for any real estate investment products or vehicles, including REITs and mortgages.

The demand side of the property market is made up of investors wanting to buy property. The supply side consists of other investors (or developers or owner users) who want to sell some or all of the property they currently own. Investors in the property market fall generally into two main types: individuals and institutions. The major types of institutions include REITs, pension funds, life insurance companies, and mutual funds or opportunity funds of various types. Private individuals invest in the property market both directly and also through funds or syndications. In addition to U.S. institutions, many investors in the United States real estate asset market today are foreign individuals and institutions.

In a modern highly developed economy such as that of the United States, the capital markets are highly integrated and sophisticated, well-functioning arenas in which vast quantities of money and information are managed. The capital markets determine how the wealth and capital resources of the society are allocated, which in turn determines the future growth rate and economic production patterns in the economy. For example, if investors decide that the future earnings potential of, say, airplane manufacturers looks relatively good, while that of office buildings looks relatively bad, then airplane stocks will rise and capital will flow to that industry, while office building prices will fall and developers will find it hard to obtain the funds necessary to build new office buildings. In this way, the capital markets govern the real physical allocation of the productive resources of the economy.

Because real estate makes up a large and important part of the overall capital market, the real estate components of the capital markets are quite important in this overall allocation process. In fact, the value of all real estate assets is comparable to that of the stock market in the United States.

1.2.2 Pricing of Real Estate Assets

As noted, the supply side of the property market consists of property owners wanting to sell or reduce their holdings of real estate assets, while the demand side of the market consists of other investors wanting to buy or increase their holdings of real estate assets. The balance between supply and demand determines the overall level of real

must hold for at least four years properties that they develop or purchase, which prevents merchant builders, such as home developers, from electing REIT status. The original idea behind the law that established REITs in 1960 was that REITs would be a vehicle through which small investors could invest in commercial real estate through the stock market, much the same way mutual funds allow small investors to hold diversified portfolios of individual stocks.

estate asset values relative to other forms of physical capital in the country. Within this overall general valuation context, the specific values of individual properties or buildings is determined by the perceptions of potential investors regarding the level and riskiness of the cash flows that each individual property can generate in the future.

As individual properties and buildings differ greatly in size and magnitude, when speaking of property prices and values in general it is common to think in terms of property value *per dollar of current net rent or income*. This way, one can more easily compare prices across properties of different sizes. In fact, in real estate, especially in commercial property markets, a measure that is the *inverse* of this price/earnings multiple is most widely used to describe property prices and values. This measure, known as the **capitalization rate** (**cap rate** for short, also known as an **overall rate**—or **OAR**), is simply the property earnings divided by the property asset price or value.[9] The cap rate is similar to a **current yield** (the amount of current income the investor receives per dollar of current value of the investment). So while the cap rate is an inverse measure of asset value (per dollar of earnings), it may be thought of as a direct measure of the current component of the return on the investment.

Thus, *property values can be represented as earnings (i.e., essentially, net rents) divided by the cap rate*.[10] The cap rate is determined by capital investment supply and demand in the asset market, based on three major factors.

1. Opportunity Cost of Capital. First, the prevailing interest rates and opportunities for earning returns in other forms of investments in the capital markets (e.g., stocks, bonds, money market instruments) is a major determinant of how much investors are willing to pay for any property per dollar of its current income. As noted, real estate assets are in competition for the investor's dollar in the capital market, competing not only with other properties but also with other forms of assets. When interest rates and yields on bonds and stocks are low, for example, investors cannot earn as much return from these alternative investments. At such times investors will tend to be more eager to put their money into property, and they will not expect to earn as high a return from property as they otherwise would. This will raise the price they are willing to pay for the property per dollar of its current income, and reduce the cap rate.

2. Growth Expectations. Second, potential investors will be "forward-looking," considering the likely amount of growth (or decline) in the net rent they can expect the property to generate in the future. Of course, the net rent the property will be able to produce in the future depends on what the balance between supply and demand will be in the *space* market in the future. So to consider the growth question, investors must, in effect, try to forecast the future of the space market in which the property is

---

[9]By convention, cap rates apply to property income and property value (i.e., as if there were no mortgage), not the equity investor's income or equity value if there is a mortgage.

[10]This is merely a conventional way to quote asset prices. It is not a statement of causality. That is, it would be too simplistic to suggest that property values are *caused by* the current income generated by the property and the current cap rate prevailing in the asset market for similar properties. As will be discussed in more depth in Chapters 9 and 10, property investors are more interested in total return (income and capital appreciation) than in current income alone, and such investors take a multi-year, long-run view of the potential and risks in the property's future income and value.

situated. The greater the expected growth in future net rent, the more investors will be willing to pay for the property today per dollar of current net rent, and hence, the smaller the cap rate. (For example, if investors were willing to pay $15.00 instead of $12.50 per dollar of current net income, then the cap rate would be 6.67% instead of 8.00%, as 1/15 = 6.67%.)[11]

As described previously, growth prospects for rents in a market depend on the current state of the market (e.g., are rents currently below the long-run equilibrium level?), on how usage demand will change in the future (will it grow or stagnate?), and the shape of the long-run supply function in the market (is it flat or rising?). In addition to marketwide considerations, each individual property may have unique attributes that affect its own growth prospects, such as existing leases, need for capital improvements, and so forth.

3. Risk. Third, if investors regard the future potential net income from the property as less risky and more certain (perhaps because they view the space market as relatively stable and easy to forecast), then they will be willing to pay more per dollar of current income for the property, also reducing the cap rate. Other things being equal, investors do not like risk and will pay more for less risky assets. Of course, investors' aversion to risk and their preferences for certain types of investments may change over time. For example, some investors may want certain types of assets or properties in order to diversify or balance their overall investment portfolios. The more investors prefer the type of asset that a given property is, the more they will pay for it and the lower will be its cap rate.

1.2.3 Is the Asset Market Segmented Like the Space Market?

Now that you are familiar with both the real estate space market and asset market and the role of the capital market in the latter, we may draw an important distinction between the real estate asset and space markets. While the building users who make up the demand side of the space market require the *physical* characteristics of real estate assets (i.e., they are looking for built space of a particular type in a particular location), this is not generally the case with the investors who make up the demand side of the real estate asset market. Asset market investors are seeking future cash flows—*financial* rather than *physical* assets. Fundamentally, they do not care how or from where the cash is generated. "Money is fungible," is how this point is often expressed. Cash generated from rents in Chicago warehouses is the same as cash generated from rents in Los Angeles shopping centers and as cash generated from General Motors Corporation stock dividends or bond coupons. This means that real estate asset markets are much more integrated than real estate space markets.

Recall that an important consequence of the lack of integration in the real estate space markets is that prices (in the form of rents) can differ greatly among cities or among types of property, even for properties that are physically similar. Similarly, the

[11]Note that this does not imply that investors are willing to settle for a lower *total* return, only that more of that return is expected to come in the form of appreciation or capital growth, and less in the form of initial income.

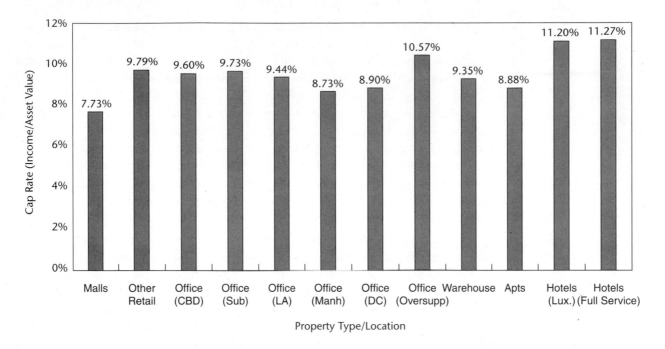

Exhibit 1-6 Cap Rates (OARs) for Commercial Property as of Third Quarter, 1994

much greater degree of integration in the real estate asset markets has the opposite effect. Two properties with cash flows perceived as having similar risk and growth potential will sell at very similar cap rates, even if the properties are physically very different and their space rents out at very different rent levels.

To demonstrate this point more concretely, Exhibit 1-6 shows typical cap rates for a range of different types and locations of commercial property in 1994.[12] This is an interesting year to examine because at that time there were wide disparities in the level of risk perceived by investors in different space markets. Notice that the cap rates for office, retail, warehouse, and apartment properties were very similar (roughly around 9% or 10% per year), and this was true even across different cities. Where cap rates differed, it was not necessarily because rent levels differed or buildings were physically different, but rather because risks or growth prospects were perceived as being different.

This is seen in the cap rates reported for several types or locations of property in particular. For example, the "oversupplied office market" refers to office buildings in markets experiencing particularly high vacancy. Investors perceived such markets as being more risky than markets that were more in balance. So they required a higher expected return for investing in overbuilt markets, which equates to their being unwilling to pay as much per dollar of current income for such properties. In this case we can see that the 10.57% cap rate indicates investors were generally not willing to pay more than about $9.46 per dollar of current income for office buildings in over-built markets, whereas in more typical CBD and suburban office markets they would pay over $10 per dollar of current income.

[12]Exhibit 1-6 is based on the *Korpacz Real Estate Investor Survey*, a widely used survey of professional investors and brokers published by the Korpacz Company, Frederick, Maryland.

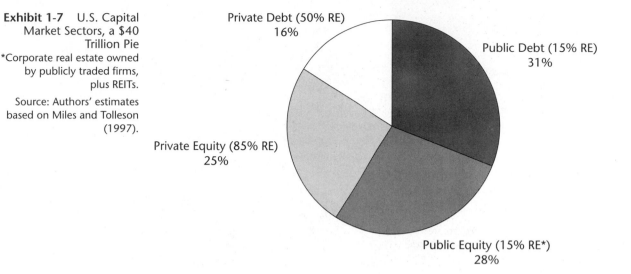

Exhibit 1-7 U.S. Capital Market Sectors, a $40 Trillion Pie
*Corporate real estate owned by publicly traded firms, plus REITs.
Source: Authors' estimates based on Miles and Tolleson (1997).

Private Debt (50% RE) 16%

Public Debt (15% RE) 31%

Private Equity (85% RE) 25%

Public Equity (15% RE*) 28%

Hotel properties were perceived as being even more risky due to the lack of long-term leases from tenants and the volatile and highly competitive nature of the hotel business. In 1994 hotels were selling at cap rates in excess of 11% (price/earnings multiples less than 9). At the other extreme, regional shopping malls were perceived in 1994 as being relatively low risk, with relatively good growth prospects. Malls had average cap rates of only 7.73% in 1994, indicating property values of $12.94 per dollar of net income.

1.2.4 Magnitude of Real Estate Assets in the Overall Capital Market

Exhibits 1-7 and 1-8 give some idea of the absolute and relative magnitude of real estate assets in the capital markets in the United States as of the late 1990s. Exhibit 1-7 shows the approximate proportion of the total market value of all U.S. assets found in each of the four sectors of the capital markets—public and private, debt and equity. Exhibit 1-7 also indicates the percentage of each of these sectors represented by real estate assets.[13] Altogether, real estate represents over one third of the value of the investable capital assets in the United States. Real estate is particularly dominant in the private capital markets. Although similar data is more difficult to find for most other countries, evidence suggests that these proportions are typical of most other advanced economies, with the real estate and private market shares being larger in less developed countries.

Exhibit 1-8 presents a more detailed breakdown of the capital asset "pie" by category of assets. The categories roughly between four o'clock and eight o'clock on the pie chart are real estate categories. The largest value categories include single-family housing equity (over $4 trillion in value), commercial real estate equity (almost $4 trillion including about $200 billion held by REITs and another $1 trillion of corporate real

---

[13] The figures in Exhibits 1-7 and 1-8 have been adjusted as far as possible to eliminate overlap. For example, a $100,000 house with an $80,000 mortgage would be counted as $20,000 of housing equity and $80,000 of residential mortgages (public debt if the mortgage was part of an MBS pool, or private debt if the mortgage was still held by the bank).

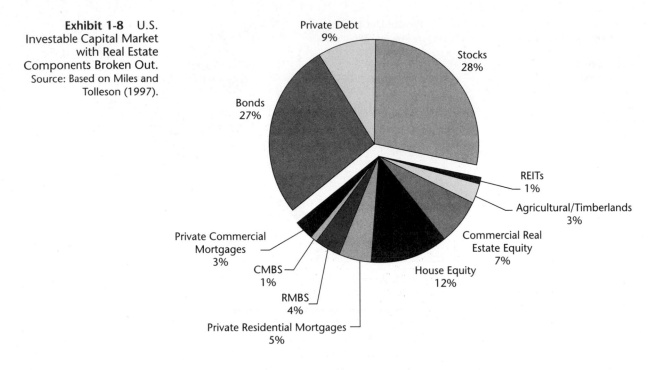

Exhibit 1-8 U.S. Investable Capital Market with Real Estate Components Broken Out. Source: Based on Miles and Tolleson (1997).

estate held by publicly traded non-real estate firms, which is categorized as part of the value of the stock market), residential mortgages (over $3.5 trillion, about half of which is included in publicly traded MBS products), and commercial mortgages (about $1 trillion of whole loans plus over $200 billion in publicly traded CMBS). Agricultural and timber lands represent about $1 trillion in assets.

1.3 CHAPTER SUMMARY

This chapter has described the two major types of markets relevant to the analysis of commercial property: the space market and the asset market. While the space market is the more fundamental of the two in the sense that it determines the cash flows property can generate, and these cash flows underlie any value the property asset can have. However, the asset market is of equal importance because it determines the valuation of property assets, and this in turn governs the flow of financial capital to real estate. Also, the asset market is most directly relevant to the analysis of investment in commercial property, which is the main subject of this book. In introducing these two real estate markets, this chapter has also presented a few of the most basic analytical tools and measures that are widely used in real estate investment practice, including such concepts as the kinked space market supply curve and the cap rate shortcut measure of real estate pricing in the asset market.

KEY TERMS

market
space market
usage market
rental market
demand
supply
rent
segmented markets
metropolitan areas (MSAs)
downtowns, CBDs

property usage type
kinked supply function
replacement cost
equilibrium rent
location rent
centrality
asset market
property market
capital market
public markets

liquidity
informational efficiency
private markets
whole assets
debt
underlying assets
equity
capitalization (cap) rate
overall rate (OAR)
current yield

STUDY QUESTIONS

1.1. If a property has a net rent of $120,000 per year and is selling at a cap rate of 10.5%, what is the price of the property?

1.2. If demand for built space is growing, does this imply that rents will rise? Why or why not? (Hint: Explain the conditions necessary for real rents to rise in a market.)

1.3. If demand for built space is declining, does this imply that real rents (that is, rents measured net of inflation) will fall in the market? Why?

1.4. Draw a picture of the shape of the typical long-run supply curve for real estate (income property). Explain why it has this shape.

1.5. What are typical causes of a rising long-run marginal cost function in the market for built space?

1.6. Exhibit 1-9 traces an historical pattern similar to that of downtown U.S. office property net rents, as compared to inflation. More precisely, the exhibit shows the CPI as in Exhibit 1-4, along with an index of the level of the net cash flow earned by downtown office properties. When the two lines in the exhibit are roughly parallel, they are growing at about the same rate, indicating constant real rents. When the NOI line is falling below the CPI line (a widening gap), that indicates declining real net rents, that is, net rent after subtracting inflation. How could you explain the real rent history apparent for commercial properties in Exhibit 1-9 using a space market supply and demand diagram (with kinked supply, as in Exhibit 1-3)? Draw what the space market supply/demand picture might have looked like in the late 1970s and again in the late 1990s, and then draw another picture to represent built space supply and demand during the late 1980s or early 1990s.

1.7. What are the three major factors influencing property prices or cap rates (OARs) in the real estate asset market? How (i.e., in which direction) does each of these influence the rate?

Exhibit 1-9 Consumer Price Index (solid line) and Downtown Office Property Net Income (similar to net rent): 1978–98.

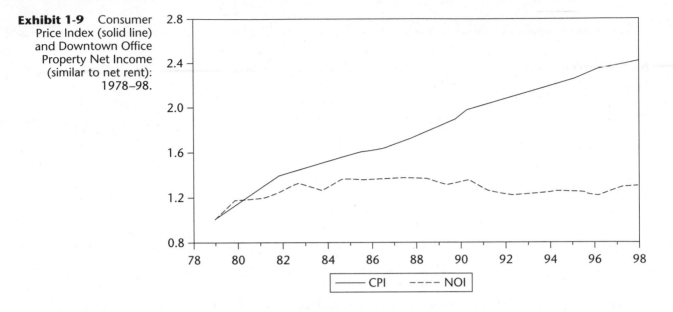

1.8. Use the definition of the cap rate (income/value) and the data on prevailing market cap rates for early 1994 presented in Exhibit 1-6 to estimate the value of (a) a typical high-quality downtown office building with a net operating income of $10 million per year and (b) a large apartment complex with a net operating income of $3.5 million. [Note: This method of valuing income property, dividing the current net income by the cap rate, is known as direct capitalization, a widely used shortcut valuation method which is discussed in greater depth in Chapter 10.]

1.9. Draw a four-quadrant table showing on one dimension the two major types of capital asset products, and on the other dimension the two major types of capital markets in which these assets are traded. [Hint: See Exhibit 1-5.] In which panel of this table would an individual commercial mortgage that is held by an insurance company fall? In which panel would ownership of a commercial building fall? In which panel would real estate investment trust stock (REIT) shares fall? In which panel would mortgage-backed securities (MBS) traded on the bond market fall?

1.10. Approximately what percentage of the total market value of investable assets in the United States is made up of real estate or real-estate-based assets? [Hint: See Exhibit 1-8.]

2 Real Estate System

Chapter Outline

Learning Objectives

After reading this chapter, you should understand:

◆ The real estate system and how it relates to investment analysis of commercial property.

◆ The short- and long-run linkages among the real estate space market, asset market, and the development industry that converts financial capital to new physical supply in the space market.

◆ How negative feedback loops keep the system in balance in the long run.

◆ The role of forward-looking behavior on the part of participants in various aspects of the real estate system, in keeping the system in balance.

◆ How cycles or periods of imbalance between supply and demand can occur in the absence of perfect foresight.

The previous chapter introduced the two basic markets relevant to commercial property investment analysis: the space market and the asset market. These two markets are linked and related in ways that are vital for real estate professionals to understand. In addition to the direct short-run relationship that translates current property cash flow to current property asset value, the two markets are structurally linked over the medium to long run by the commercial property development industry. This industry converts financial capital into physical capital, thereby governing the stock of supply in the space market. This overall system, consisting of these two markets and the industry linking them, is the subject of this chapter.

2.1 COMMERCIAL PROPERTY DEVELOPMENT INDUSTRY

The real estate development industry is the engine of entrepreneurial activity that assembles and applies the financial and physical resources to construct new built space (including the major rehabilitation or conversion of existing buildings). Development is a complex and creative function that at its best displays great vision, at its worst enormous greed, but in almost all cases, considerable risk-taking on the part of the developer. Development often requires intense interaction and cooperation between government officials in the public sector and sources of capital in the private sector.

While literally thousands of firms are involved in the real estate development industry, large-scale commercial development is dominated by a few dozen firms of national scope and a number of regional firms. During the 1990s, a number of REITs became highly active in commercial development, generally specializing in one or two property types. Traditionally, and even still, however, most development firms are privately held, often dominated by one or a few partners typically consisting of the first or second generation of the firm's founders. Private entrepreneurial development firms typically have specialized expertise in the local space markets, but may lack the connections to "deep pocket" sources of capital held by larger developers. Joint ventures are common in the development industry, especially for large projects, combining the strengths of entrepreneurial firms with that of financial institutions, or combining the abilities of specialized local experts with those of large national firms.

Even an economy in recession needs large quantities of existing built space just to continue to function. But the addition of new *increments* to the stock of built space is primarily required only by economic growth, or by structural changes in the economy and activity patterns. As noted in Chapter 1, built space is an extremely long-lived commodity. Buildings do not wear out fast. It is only the demand for *new* built space that supports the development industry. For this reason, development is the most cyclical of all branches of the real estate industry. This is seen graphically in Exhibit 2-1, which traces the level of development activity during the boom and bust and recovery of the 1980s and 1990s.

From the perspective of commercial property investment analysis, the development industry is best viewed in its role as a converter of financial capital into physical

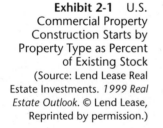

Exhibit 2-1 U.S. Commercial Property Construction Starts by Property Type as Percent of Existing Stock (Source: Lend Lease Real Estate Investments. *1999 Real Estate Outlook.* © Lend Lease, Reprinted by permission.)

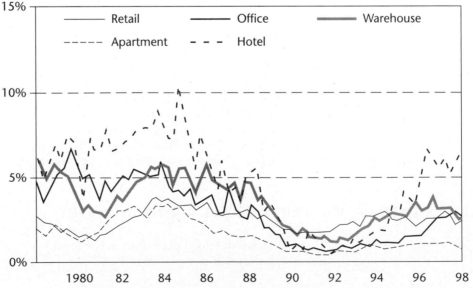

capital, as a feedback link from the asset market to the space market, adding to the supply side of the space market.

2.2 OVERVIEW OF THE REAL ESTATE SYSTEM

You have now been introduced to the three major components of what may be called the **real estate system**: the space market, the asset market, and the development industry. Exhibit 2-2 presents a visual overview of this system, including the major elements in and linkages among these three major components. The exhibit also

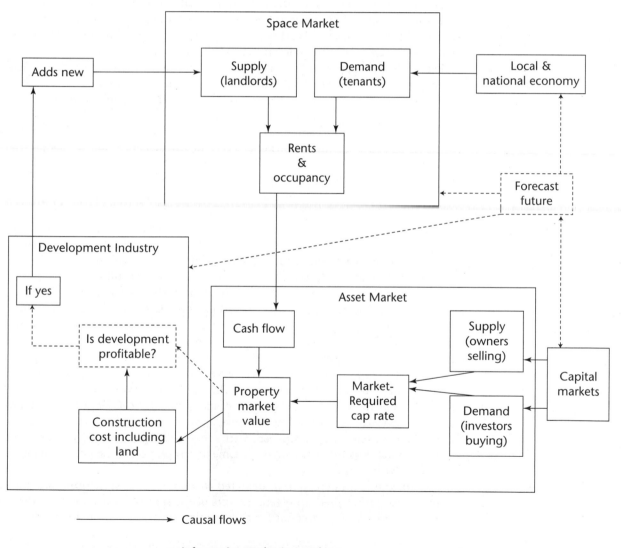

——————▶ Causal flows

- - - - - - - - - -▶ Information gathering and use

Exhibit 2-2   The Real Estate System: Interaction of the Space Market, Asset Market and Development Industry

shows how this system is linked to other, exogenous systems, including the national and local macroeconomies, and the national and international capital markets. Let's briefly "walk through" the real estate system depicted in Exhibit 2-2.[1]

The three large boxes in the exhibit represent the three main elements of the real estate system: the space market, the asset market, and the development industry. Within the space market, we see the interaction of usage demand with the current stock of physical space supply, which determines current rents and occupancy levels in the space market. Underlying the demand side of the space market are the national and local economies, which determine the need for certain quantities of physical space of various types, as a function of the cost (rent) for such space. Governing the amount of physical space on the supply side are the past and current activities of the development industry.

Moving down to the asset market, we see that the space market determines the current operating cash flows produced by the real estate assets, which are the fundamental subjects of the asset market. This operating cash flow interacts with the cap rates required by investors to determine current property market values in the asset market. Both the supply and demand sides of the real estate asset market consist of investors, those currently on the "buy" side and those currently on the "sell" side, either in general or for specific assets. All of these real estate investors are operating within the broader capital markets, which encompass other forms of asset and money markets. Investors' desires and perceptions about the investment risks and returns of real estate assets, as compared to other types of investment opportunities available elsewhere in the capital markets, determine the current market cap rates investors require in real estate deals. A key determinant of cap rates is also investors' forecasts about the future of the relevant space market, both the demand and supply sides, so as to predict the likely future course of rents.

Thus we see how the space and asset markets, reflecting the underlying economic base and the capital markets, interact to produce current real estate asset market values. These values represent the key signal, or output, from the asset market—input into the development industry, the third major box in the exhibit.

Within the development industry component of the system a crucial comparison is made. Current development costs, including construction and land costs (incorporating necessary profit for the developer), are compared against current asset values. If asset values equal or exceed development costs, then development will proceed, thereby adding to the physical stock on the supply side of the space market. As noted in Chapter 1, a key component of development costs is the opportunity value of the land (including all site acquisition costs). This opportunity value is determined in the real estate asset market, as land is a type of real estate asset. Of course, development takes time, and this requires that the development industry be somewhat forward-looking. The developer only succeeds if the newly completed built property's value exceeds its total development cost at the time of completion of the project, which may take several years.

Indeed, the real estate system depicted in Exhibit 2-2 is, in principle, forward looking to varying degrees in several aspects of the system. Not only must developers be forward looking to account for construction time, but the space market is also

---

[1]Exhibit 2-2 has two types of elements: boxes and arrows. The solid boxes represent decision-making agents and empirically observable phenomena. The dashed boxes represent key decisions or actions that drive the system. The solid arrows represent causal linkages and the direction of causality. The dashed arrows represent information flow or information gathering and usage activity.

forward looking in that many users of space require long-term planning for their space needs, and much space is rented out under long-term leases lasting typically from two to ten years. But the greatest incentives for peering into the long-run future probably reside in the asset market part of the system.

Asset market participants are inherently forward looking. Investors make or lose money depending on how their investments do *subsequent to* their purchase. Even when an investor sells relatively quickly to another investor, the price the second investor is willing to pay depends on her perception about the future. Fundamentally, when you "unfold" each subsequent sale transaction of a given asset, you realize that the present value of the asset depends ultimately on the entire future stream of cash flow the asset can generate into the infinite future. To forecast future income streams from the real estate assets they are holding or considering buying, investors must forecast both the local economic base underlying the demand side of the space market and the activity of the development industry on the supply side of the space market. They must also attempt to forecast capital market and national macroeconomic factors such as interest rates, inflation, and investor preferences, all of which affect the opportunity cost of capital and therefore the future values of assets.

It is important to note that within the real estate system depicted in Exhibit 2-2 there exist what are called **negative feedback loops**. These are dampening mechanisms that tend to make a system self-regulating, preventing it from spiraling out of control. The principal negative feedback loop in the real estate system is the ability of the asset market to regulate the flow of financial capital to the development industry. If either supply or demand threaten to get out of balance in the space market, the resulting effect on assets' operating cash flows will trigger a pricing response in the asset market. For example, if new development threatens excess supply in the space market, investors will expect lower future rents, which will cause a reduction in property market asset values today. If this reduction is sufficient, it will make additional development unprofitable. On the other hand, if usage demand for space grows without addition of supply, occupancy and rents will be pushed up in the space market, increasing current cash flow in the asset market, pushing up prices there until new development is triggered. This new development will eventually service the growth in demand and bring rents down to their long-run equilibrium level.

If the participants in the system are sufficiently forward looking and quick in their reactions, the negative feedback loop in the real estate system can keep built space supply and demand in pretty good balance most of the time. Of course, the real estate system has not always operated exactly like a well-oiled machine in this regard. Commercial property markets have been subject to pronounced boom and bust cycles. However, during the 1990s improvements in asset market efficiency, related to the increased role of the more informationally efficient public capital markets, gave hope that the system may work better in the future.

2.3 FOUR-QUADRANT MODEL

A graphical representation of the real estate system we just described, which is useful for performing some basic analyses of the system, has been developed by DiPasquale and Wheaton.[2] This model consists of a **four-quadrant (4Q)** graph, as

[2]See DiPasquale and Wheaton (1992). A similar four-quadrant depiction of the link between the space and asset markets was presented by Fisher (1992).

shown in Exhibit 2-3. The four quadrants depict four binary relationships that together complete the linkages between the space and asset markets.

The four-quadrant graph is most useful for examining the effect on the long-run equilibrium simultaneously both within and between the space and asset markets. The concept of **long-run equilibrium** in real estate involves allowing the markets sufficient time for the supply of built space to adjust to the demand. Equilibrium in the four-quadrant graph is represented by a rectangle whose sides are vertical and horizontal connections between four points, one lying on each of the four binary relationship lines in each of the four quadrants. Where the sides of this rectangle cross the four axes represent the equilibrium stock of built space, rent, asset prices, and rate of new construction in the market. In Exhibit 2-3 the rectangle is indicated by dashed lines and the equilibrium prices and quantities by the points Q^*, R^*, P^*, and C^*.

The northeast quadrant depicts the determination of rent in what we have been calling the space market. The horizontal axis in this quadrant is the physical stock of space in the market (e.g., in square feet), and the vertical axis is the rent (e.g., in \$/SF per year). Thus, the axes of this quadrant are those of the classical price/quantity diagram in the space market, and the space usage demand function is represented in the northeast quadrant by the downward-sloping DD line. If we draw a vertical line from the point on the horizontal axis representing the existing supply of space

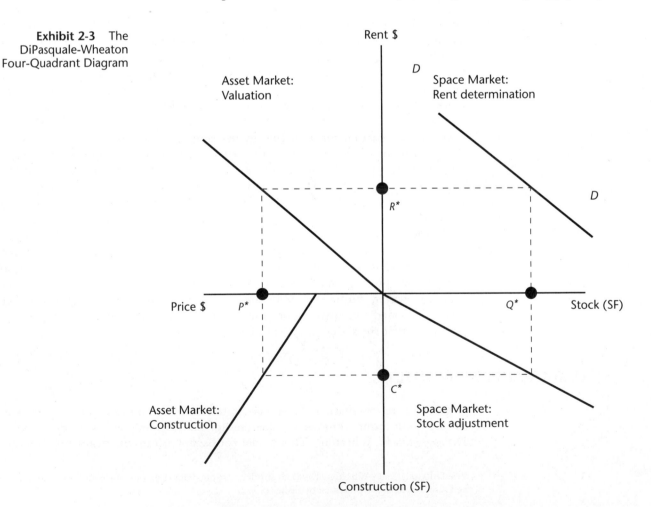

Exhibit 2-3 The DiPasquale-Wheaton Four-Quadrant Diagram

in the market (Q^*), the point at which that line intersects the demand function will tell us the current equilibrium rent, given that amount of space in the market. The equilibrium rent with Q^* amount of space in the market is R^*.

The northwest quadrant depicts the asset market valuation process, relating the equilibrium property prices (on the horizontal axis, in $/SF) to the level of current rent (on the vertical axis, shared with the northeast quadrant, also in $/SF). (Note that in the four-quadrant diagram the point in the center where the axes cross is the "origin" of all four graphs, so that in the northwest and southwest quadrants the horizontal axis values increase as one moves from right to left.) The line in the northwest quadrant represents the cap rate or OAR, which we described in Chapter 1. The steeper the line, the higher the cap rate (lower property price per dollar of current rent). By continuing a horizontal line from the current rent point R^* on the vertical axis to the cap rate line in the northwest quadrant, and then drawing a vertical line down from that point to the price axis, we determine the property price (per SF) implied by the current rent. The point P^* represents the property price. Thus, the two top (or "northern") quadrants depict the short-run or immediate price link between the asset and space markets.

The two bottom (or "southern") quadrants depict the long-run effect of the real estate development industry, by showing the impact of construction on the total stock of built space in the market. The southwest quadrant depicts the operation of the development industry—physical asset production process. The relationship in the southwest quadrant is between property prices and the annual amount of construction activity (including rehabilitation and redevelopment as well as new development). The line in this quadrant relates a given level of property prices to a given rate of construction. The vertical (upside-down) axis represents the physical amount of construction (e.g., in square feet per year). The farther down the vertical axis you go, the greater the level of the construction activity.

The construction function line in the southwest quadrant is outward sloping (down and to the left) indicating that higher property prices will stimulate greater amounts of new construction, as higher prices enable more costly sites to be developed and/or development to proceed at a faster pace due to greater availability of capital. The outward slope of this line therefore represents rising long-run marginal costs in the supply of built space. Greater long-run supply elasticity (i.e., a flatter long-run marginal cost curve for real estate development) would be represented by a more steeply falling line in the southwest quadrant.[3] The construction function line intersects the property price axis at a positive value rather than at the origin, because when property price is below some threshold level, no construction will occur. A vertical line dropped down from the horizontal (asset price) axis at the current asset price P^* will intersect the construction function line at a point that corresponds on the vertical axis (drawing a horizontal line over to it) to the amount of new construction in the market per year (point C^*).

[3] The line in the southwest quadrant is not exactly the same as the long-run supply curve presented in Chapter 1 because the southwest quadrant determines the *rate* of construction *per year*, rather than the accumulated total stock of built space supplied in the market. The interaction of the two bottom quadrants fully depicts the long-run supply function in the space market. The long-run supply function "kink" described in Chapter 1 does not appear in the four-quadrant diagram because this diagram shows purely long-run steady-state relationships. However, the equivalent of Chapter 1's kink could be represented in the 4Q diagram by placing a kink in the stock adjustment line in the southeast quadrant at its corner of the initial rectangle so that the line bends vertically up to the horizontal axis at Q^*.

"Leaving Las Vegas"

The following article appeared in the Wall Street Journal *on August 6, 1997, under the above caption, which played on the name of a popular movie of the time.**

OASIS RESIDENTIAL INC. gambled on the Las Vegas apartment market until its luck ran dry. Now some outside shareholders say they are pressing for a takeover.

The real-estate investment trust is the dominant apartment owner and developer in one of the fastest growing cities in the U.S., but heavy new construction in Las Vegas has slowed rent increases and hurt the company's returns. The result: Its stock price has remained flat for the last year and long-term debt has ballooned to 47% of market value. Oasis is struggling to fund projects in more promising markets such as Reno, Nev., Denver and Southern California.

Oasis is also hounded by speculation about its chief executive, Robert Jones, who analysts complain is "invisible." Mr. Jones, a 48-year-old high-school dropout and son of a Kansas farmer, began building apartments in Las Vegas 21 years ago. He also owns a closely held Las Vegas home-building company that analysts say competes for his time and for Oasis's potential tenants.

Mr. Jones concedes he dislikes speaking in public, including to analysts and investors. But he insists that he spends 90% of his time on Oasis, leaving day-to-day management of his home-building operation to others. With about 6% of Oasis' stock, Mr. Jones says he is one of its largest shareholders.

He wants to lower the firm's Las Vegas exposure—from 83% of its portfolio to 50%—in the next five years. But he also remains sanguine about the local market. "Building permits are becoming much harder to get, and there are almost no locations inside the city left," he says.

Still, some shareholders want a merger. "Oasis would be a good candidate for acquisition by a company with deeper pockets," says Keith Pauley, a portfolio manager at Baltimore investment company ABKB LaSalle Securities Ltd., the company's largest outside shareholder, with about 6% of its stock. Only a very large company could handle the exposure to Las Vegas, he says, and more and more apartment companies are big enough to handle it.

Says Mr. Jones: "We're interested in anything that will make our shareholders money."**

Discussion Questions

1. How does the story here about Oasis Residential demonstrate some of the points you have learned in this chapter about space markets and asset markets?

2. In what space market was Oasis primarily involved in 1997?

3. What does the article suggest about the relative supply and demand balance in the Las Vegas apartment market in 1997?

4. What does the article suggest was the effect on equilibrium rents (and therefore on Oasis's earnings potential) caused by the relatively abundant growth in the supply side of the Las Vegas apartment market?

5. How did the capital markets (in this case, the stock market in particular, as Oasis is a publicly traded REIT) react to this information?

6. Do you suppose Oasis's flat stock price and continued apartment building program could be one reason the firm's debt increased prior to the time the article was written?

7. Does the article suggest that other apartment markets in different cities in the Southwest were facing a different balance between supply and demand from what existed at that time in Las Vegas?

8. Do you see how the reaction of the capital markets works to move financial capital (and thereby ultimately physical capital via the construction and development process) away from overbuilt space markets and toward markets that need more supply?

9. Do you suppose the stock share price of a company in a market with stronger rental growth prospects (i.e., less built space supply relative to demand in the space market, perhaps Reno or Southern California as suggested in the article at that time) would be higher than Oasis's (other things being equal), resulting in that company having an easier time raising capital for construction?

* © Dow Jones & Co., reprinted by permission.

**As it turned out, Oasis was acquired by Camden Property Trust in December of 1997 in a stock transfer valued at about $500 million.

Finally, the southeast quadrant completes the long-run integration of the space and asset markets by linking the rate of construction to the total stock of built space available in the usage market.[4] The line in the southeast quadrant relates the average rate of space construction per year to the total stock of space that can be indefinitely maintained in the market. The concept behind the southeast quadrant is that, in the long run, in the absence of new construction, older space will be removed from the stock as it "wears out" and old buildings are either abandoned and demolished or converted to other uses. Thus, on average over the long run, a certain amount of new construction per year is necessary just to maintain a given stock of space available in the market.[5] The greater the total stock, the greater the annual new construction rate necessary just to maintain that stock in the long run (hence, the outward sloping line from the origin). The line in the southeast quadrant thus links the C^* level of construction activity to the Q^* level of total supply of built space. The four-quadrant picture thus depicts a long-run steady-state equilibrium.

2.4 USING THE 4Q DIAGRAM TO HELP UNDERSTAND BOOM AND BUST IN REAL ESTATE MARKETS

Historically, real estate markets have often experienced boom and bust periods. By this we mean that space markets have exhibited extended periods of rise in building occupancy and rents followed by extended periods of falling or low occupancy and rents. In many commercial property markets the total period of this **real estate market cycle** (e.g., from peak to peak) has been in the neighborhood of 10 to 20 years, which is noticeably longer than the traditional macroeconomic business cycle in the decades after World War II. In addition, property prices in the real estate asset markets, along with liquidity and volume of sales transactions in that market, often appear to go through extended periods of rise and fall, related to the ups and downs in the space market.

In the present section we will apply the four-quadrant diagram presented in the previous section to gain some insight and understanding of the famous boom and bust that occurred in commercial real estate during the 1980s and 1990s.

In seeking to understand this cycle, it is important to recognize that the first half of the 1980s was characterized by two economic phenomena in the United States: a sharp increase in user demand for commercial space, and an increase in investor demand for real estate assets. While it is not surprising that such phenomena would stimulate new construction of commercial space, our question is whether these phenomena caused not only the rise but also the subsequent fall in the real estate markets. In other words, did the boom contain the seeds of the subsequent bust? If so, why and how was this so, and will this behavior tend to repeat in real estate in other times and places?

---

[4]The line in the southeast quadrant is not a continuation of, or related in any way to, the line in the northwest quadrant.

[5]For example, in a market where there are 100,000 apartment units, one or two thousand units per year will likely be lost (generally older units) due to conversion into other uses, demolition to make way for public projects, or simple abandonment. So to maintain 100,000 apartments in the market, one or two thousand new units must be built per year. This reveals how the 4Q diagram depicts long-run average relationships. In particular, the construction function in the southwest quadrant does not represent the amount of construction in any single year, but rather an average rate of construction maintained across a long span of time.

To explore this question we will use the 4Q diagram in a slightly extended way. In the previous section we noted that the rectangle in the 4Q diagram depicts a long-run steady state. In the present exercise we will use the diagram to examine both the long run and the short run, and the relation between the two. In this way the 4Q perspective can show us one way in which the boom could indeed have contained the seeds of the subsequent bust. We will first consider the effect of growth in usage demand holding the capital market constant. Then we will consider the effect of a growth in investor demand for real estate, holding space usage demand constant. Finally, we will put these two phenomena together, as in fact they both occurred simultaneously in the United States during the latter half of the 1970s and first half of the 1980s.

First consider the effect of an increase in demand for space usage, holding the real estate asset market constant. This is depicted in Exhibit 2-4a, where we see the demand function in the northeast quadrant moving out to the right, from D_0 to D_1. In the 1980s a booming economy, an aging population, and a pronounced structural shift in the economy away from traditional manufacturing and toward high-technology and service jobs, all fueled growth in demand for several types of commercial property. This growth was especially pronounced on the East and West Coasts and in some southern states. Some of this growth was certainly anticipated in advance by some in the real estate and capital markets, but the exact magnitude and specific nature and location of the space demand growth was no doubt to some extent unanticipated, and indeed unanticipatable (as no one can have a true crystal ball).

In the short run (say, a year or two) there is not time for new space to be built in response to an unanticipated surge in usage demand, so unless developers and the capital markets have adequately anticipated the demand growth, rents might initially rise to levels that cannot be supported in the long-run equilibrium. This is indicated in Exhibit 2-4a by the movement of rent on the vertical axis from the original level of R^* to a temporary high level of R_1, found by relating the original stock of space (Q^* on the horizontal axis) to the new demand function D_1. The long-run equilibrium effect of the growth in demand, however, results in rents that are not as high as the R_1 level.

The new long-run equilibrium based on the new D_1 demand function is indicated by the rectangle traced in the heavy dashed lines, which lies entirely outside the old four-quadrant rectangle. The new equilibrium is represented by the points with the double asterisks, where the new rectangle crosses the axes. Note that while the new equilibrium rent (R^{**}) is above the old equilibrium rent (R^*), it is below the temporary R_1 rent level. The fact that R^{**} is above R^* indicates that this space market is characterized by at least a slightly upward sloping long-run marginal cost function (i.e., increasing real development costs). Also, note that while the long-run equilibrium quantity of built space is higher than it was at the old demand level ($Q^{**} > Q^*$), the "absorption" (increased occupancy) of space is not so great as would have occurred if rents had been maintained at the old R^* level. This is due to the effect of usage demand sensitivity to rent (price elasticity of demand), indicated by the downward slope of the demand function in the northeast quadrant.

A little experimentation with the four-quadrant graph will demonstrate an important point. It will indeed *always* be the case that the new equilibrium rectangle will lie *outside* the old one as a result of growth in underlying usage demand (holding the capital market in the northwest quadrant constant), provided the asset construction function in the southwest quadrant is outward sloping (rising marginal costs). Rents, property prices, and stock of space must all increase under these circumstances.

But the increase need not be proportionately the same across all of these variables. The amount of increase will depend on the relative elasticities of supply and demand and the capital market's appetite for more investment in real estate. The key to whether rents must rise with a growth in demand lies in the shape of the construction function in the southwest quadrant. As we noted in Chapter 1, if development costs are constant (completely vertical construction function in the southwest quadrant), then rents will remain constant even with growth in demand. In that case the long-run equilibrium rectangle will expand only to the right in its width dimension, and only downward in its height dimension.

Next, consider the effect of an increase in demand for real estate investment assets among investors in the capital markets. By this we mean a relative shift in preferences among investors so that they are willing to pay higher price/earnings multiples for real estate assets than they previously were. Such a shift might occur because investors now perceive real estate to be less risky relative to other investment asset classes (such as stocks and bonds). Or perhaps investors for some reason don't mind or care about real estate's risk as much as they did previously (maybe because their investment holdings are more diversified). Or perhaps investors now tend to expect more future growth in real estate rents than they previously had been expecting, so they don't require as much current return. The point is, for some reason investors are now willing to pay more for real estate assets, per dollar of current real estate rental income, than they were willing to pay before.

Exhibit 2-4a   Effect of Demand Growth in Space Market

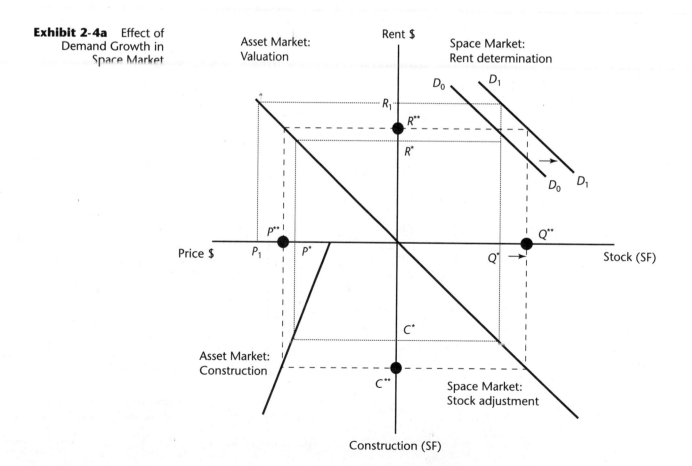

Evidence suggests that something like this did in fact happen in the period from the late 1970s to the mid-1980s in the United States. Several historical phenomena occurring during this period could have been instrumental in this regard. One was the enactment of the Employee Retirement Income Security Act (ERISA) by Congress in 1974. This required that pension funds be "funded" by investing pension contributions. ERISA put explicit emphasis on the benefits of diversified investment portfolios, including diversification out of traditional reliance on the stock market, to consider alternatives such as real estate. This steered a large flow of capital toward real estate from investors who were less concerned about risk in their real estate investments, at least to the extent that risk was not correlated with the bulk of the rest of their portfolios, which were invested largely in stocks and bonds. Another relevant phenomenon of the 1970s and early 1980s was a rise in inflation and increased uncertainty about inflation on the part of investors. Real estate was perceived as providing better protection against inflation than other traditional investments, most notably bonds. During this period, commercial real estate was also granted large tax breaks. Any or all of these phenomena could have increased price/earnings multiples in the real estate asset market.

This type of capital market shift is indicated in Exhibit 2-4b, by the movement down (to a shallower slope) of the valuation line in the northwest quadrant. For example, suppose that prevailing cap rates had been 11% (on average, for typical

Exhibit 2-4b Effect of Demand Growth in Asset Market

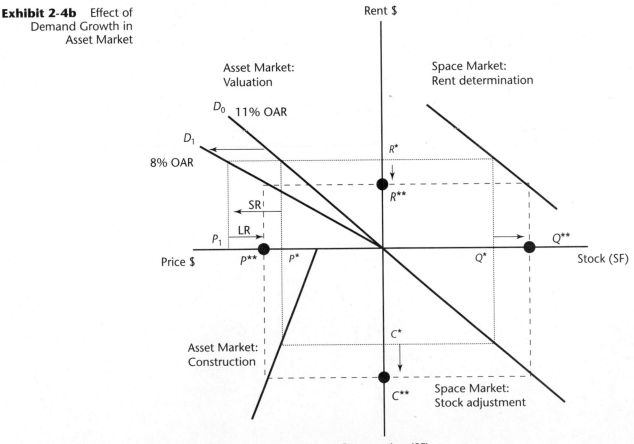

properties in a given real estate market), and now they have moved down three points to 8%, as indicated in Exhibit 2-4b. This represents a substantial upward revaluation of property. Indeed, property values would rise some 37.5% if rents remained constant (from 1/0.11 to 1/0.08 per dollar of rent). And of course, at first rents *would* remain constant, holding supply and usage demand constant in the space market in the northeast quadrant. Thus, if investors are somewhat **myopic** and cannot foresee what the surge of financial capital into the real estate asset market will do to stimulate new construction, then property prices could rise temporarily to a level above what is sustainable in the long run. This is indicated in Exhibit 2-4b by the short run price rise to the P_1 level from the original P^* level.

The new long-run equilibrium is found, as always in a 4Q diagram, by the new rectangle connecting the four quadrants based on the new 8% OAR line in the northwest quadrant. This equilibrium is shown in Exhibit 2-4b by the heavy dashed lines, which intersect the axes at the new equilibrium prices and quantities indicated by the double asterisks. Note that this new equilibrium involves a substantial increase in the amount of built space, which reflects the effect of a real estate development boom that brought the stock of space up to the new Q^{**} level. This is the **physical capital** result of the flow of **financial capital** into the real estate asset market caused by the shift in investor preferences toward real estate assets.

Note that the new equilibrium involves lower rents ($R^{**} < R^*$), and therefore more use of space ($Q^{**} > Q^*$) than the original equilibrium (holding usage demand constant in the space market). The lower rents mean that the lower cap rates in the asset market do not result in as high a long-run rise in property prices as you might have thought at first. The new equilibrium property market prices of P^{**}, although higher than the old P^* prices, may not be much higher.

Experimentation with the four-quadrant diagram should satisfy you that the nature of this result is general. An increase in investor demand for real estate assets (as represented by a drop in prevailing cap rates in the property market) will *always* result in property prices and quantities of built space that are both *greater* than the original levels, with rents for space users that are *lower* than the original levels.[6] The extent of the changes may not be proportional across these variables and will depend on the elasticities (or relative sensitivities) of supply and demand in the four quadrants.

Finally, how do the previous examples using the four-quadrant graph shed light on the question of what could explain the great rise and fall in commercial property prices in the United States in the 1980s and early 1990s? As noted, both the usage demand growth and the investor demand growth phenomena described earlier occurred during the 1975–85 period in the United States. We have seen how both of these phenomena can individually cause a temporary overshooting of real estate asset repricing, in the absence of perfect foresight by market participants. The simultaneous occurrence of demand growth in both the top two quadrants would exacerbate this danger of asset price overshooting. This would cause real estate prices to at first rise and then fall back, even without a subsequent reduction in underlying demand for

---

[6] The only exception would be if the long-run marginal cost function is declining (line sloping inward to the right in the southwest quadrant). What if development costs are flat (construction function in the southwest quadrant would be a vertical line dropped from the P^* point)? Then the new long-run equilibrium rectangle would expand from the old one only to the right in the width dimension, leading to a greater reduction in rent, greater space construction, and a larger long-run stock of space, as compared to the case pictured in Exhibit 2-4b. (The bottom of the rectangle would be determined in the southeast quadrant alone, when the construction function in the southwest is a vertical line.)

The Ground Floor: Speculative Juices Flow in Some Office Markets, Sooner than Seemed Likely

ABI-Inform carried the following abstract of an article by Peter Slatin with the above title, in the March 17, 1997, issue of Barron's *(v77n11, p. 45). In reading this abstract, keep in mind that the office sector was probably the hardest hit of all real estate markets in the boom and bust of the late 1980s and early 1990s. Also, keep in mind that "speculative construction" refers to developers building projects without substantial preleasing commitments, that is, without agreements from major future tenants that they will lease space in the buildings that are being built.*

There has been a slow but steady re-emergence of speculative construction in office markets across the US. In the past year or two, in Denver, Atlanta, Dallas, Portland, and some other cities, developers have managed to line up capital to create pockets of construction that have been unthinkable since the 1980s rolled into the 1990s. Although the wave of new office towers threatens to flood any market, evidence is mounting that much of the last deluge has been absorbed, perhaps faster than

expected, and some areas are even beginning to feel somewhat parched. Meanwhile, financing sources and builders are watching each other warily.[*]

Discussion Questions

1. What does the "absorption" of the "deluge" (that is, the previous oversupply) and subsequent rise of speculative construction tell about what must have happened in the northeast quadrant of the 4Q diagram in some markets by 1997?
2. What does the last sentence in this abstract tell you about the relations between the players in northwest (financing sources) and southwest (builders) quadrants of the 4Q diagram?

either space usage or real estate investment. The fall back in prices would of course only be deepened as a result of a subsequent reduction in demand (particularly given a kinked supply function, which is not pictured in Exhibits 2-4a and b). Such a reduction in demand did in fact happen in the early 1990s as a result of economic recession and financial shifts.[7] Do booms in general contain the seeds of a subsequent bust? Clearly there is no iron-clad law. Cycles can be dampened by the ability of the asset market to react quickly with foresight to relevant new information. Nevertheless, the four-quadrant model allows us to see how cycles can happen.[8]

[7]Among other things, the tax breaks that were given to owners of commercial real estate in the early 1980s were removed (and then some) in 1986. By the late 1980s it was also clear that the economy had moved into a period of disinflation.

[8]For additional discussion of real estate cycles and theories to explain them, see Section 6.2.2 in Chapter 6 and Section 28.2.2 in Chapter 28.

2.5 CHAPTER SUMMARY

This chapter has completed our overview of the big picture of the real estate industry as it relates to investment decisions. In Chapter 1 we presented the two major markets, the space market and the asset market. In this chapter we introduced the development industry as the third major component in the overall system, and we sketched the dynamic linkages among these three components in what can be called the "real estate system". We introduced the four-quadrant model as a simple visual tool to begin to analyze this system. We showed how the four-quadrant model can shed light on the traditional concept of the real estate cycle and suggested something about how such a cycle may be caused by differences between short-run and long-run perturbations of equilibrium in the absence of perfect foresight by market participants.

KEY TERMS

real estate system
negative feedback loop
four-quadrant model

long-run equilibrium
real estate market cycle
myopic price forecasts

physical capital/assets
financial capital/assets

STUDY QUESTIONS

2.1. What are the three major components of the real estate system? How does the development industry link the asset market to the space market?

2.2. Describe three ways in which participants in the real estate system must be forward looking, that is, anticipating future responses to current changes in the system, in order for the system to maintain the balance between supply and demand in the space market.

2.3. Suppose user demand for space in a certain market grows from 4 to 5 million square feet (MSF) at $10/SF net rent. Assuming property market cap rates remain constant at 10%, show on a four quadrant diagram such as Exhibit 2-4a the short- and long-run effects of this change in user demand. [Hint: You can answer qualitatively, or recognize that specific quantitative answers will depend on the shapes and slopes of the curves (i.e., the elasticities) in each quadrant.]

2.4. Suppose investor demand for real estate assets grows in the sense that prevailing cap rates (OARs) in the property asset market fall from 10% to 8%. Assuming usage demand remains constant in the space market, show on a four-quadrant diagram such as Exhibit 2-4b the short- and long-run effects of this change in investor demand. [Hint: You can answer qualitatively, or recognize that specific quantitative answers will depend on the shapes and slopes of the curves (i.e., the elasticities) in each quadrant.]

Exhibit 2-5 Consumer Price Index (solid line) and Downtown Office Property Net Operating Income (similar to net rent): 1978–98

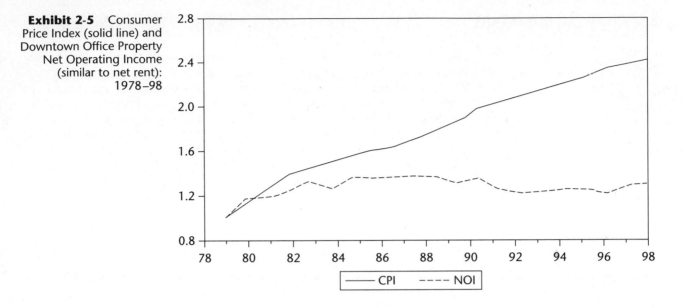

2.5. How could you explain the real rent history depicted in Exhibit 2-5 using a four-quadrant graph such as Exhibit 2-4b? What could have happened in the northwest quadrant in the early to mid-1980s that would result in the pattern seen in this chart of the approximate history of U.S. downtown office property rents? [Note: Exhibit 2-5 is the same as Exhibit 1-9. See question 1.6 and the answer given at the end of the book for additional explanation.]

References and Additional Reading

Archer, W. and D. Ling. "The Three Dimensions of Real Estate Market: Linking Space, Capital, and Property Markets." *Real Estate Finance* 14(3): 7–14, fall 1997.

Case, K. and R. Shiller. "The Efficiency of the Market for Single-Family Homes." *American Economic Review* 79(1): 125–137, 1988.

DiPasquale, Denise and Willian Wheaton. "The Markets for Real Estate Assets and Space: A Conceptual Framework." *Real Estate Economics* (formerly *AREUEA Journal*) 20(2): 181–198, summer 1992.

DiPasquale, Denise and Willian Wheaton. "Housing Market Dynamics and the Future of Housing Prices." *Journal of Urban Economics* 35(1): 1–27, 1994.

DiPasquale, Denise and William Wheaton. *Urban Economics and Real Estate Markets*. Englewood Cliffs, NJ: Prentice Hall, 1996.

Fisher, Jeffrey. "Integrating Research on Markets for Space and Capital." *Real Estate Economics* (formerly *AREUEA Journal*) 20(2): 161–180, summer 1992.

Fisher, J., D. Geltner, and R. B. Webb. "Value Indices of Commercial Real Estate: A Comparison of Index Construction Methods." *Journal of Real Estate Finance & Economics* 9(2): 137–164, 1994.

Grenadier, Steven. "The Persistence of Real Estate Cycles." *Journal of Real Estate Finance & Economics* 10: 95–119, 1995.

Gyourko, J. and D. Keim. "What Does the Stock Market Tell Us About Real Estate Returns?" *Real Estate Economics* 20(3): 457–486, 1992.

Korpacz Real Estate Investor Survey (various issues), The Korpacz Company, Frederick, MD.

Miles, M. and N. Tolleson. "A Revised Look at How Real Estate Compares with Other Major Components of the Domestic Investment Universe." *Real Estate Finance* 14(1), spring 1997 (Institutional Investor Inc., publisher).

Mueller, Glenn. "Understanding Real Estate's Physical and Financial Market Cycles." *Real Estate Finance* 12(3): 47–52, fall 1995.

Pyhrr, Stephen, Waldo Born, and James Webb. "Development of a Dynamic Investment Strategy under Alternative Inflation Cycle Scenarios." *Journal of Real Estate Research* 5(2): 177–194, summer 1990.

Urban Economics and Real Estate Market Analysis

Just as financial economics is the primary branch of economics useful for studying the real estate asset market, so urban economics is the primary academic discipline for studying the space market. We saw in Part I the fundamental importance of the space market in the overall real estate system, both to the asset market and to the development industry. The focus of Part II, therefore, is to introduce some topics of urban economics that are most relevant to commercial property investment analysis. We will include some topics in related fields as well, such as urban geography and real estate space market analysis. The objective is to gain a depth of understanding of the spatial and temporal patterns of urban development, that underlie the functioning of real estate space markets.

The first three chapters in Part II present the principles and tools of urban economics and other related academic disciplines that are useful for understanding cities and making informed real estate decisions. A particular focus of these three chapters that is important in real estate investment analysis is the fundamental determinants of land value within a metropolitan area, how land value changes over time in different parts of the city. Recall that land values are the key determinant of the shape of the long-run supply function in the space market, which in turn governs the long-run trend in rents. The last chapter in Part II focuses on the practical application of urban economics in the analysis of specific real estate space markets.

3

Central Place Theory and the System of Cities

Chapter Outline

Learning Objectives

After reading this chapter, you should understand:

◆ Why cities form, grow, and decline.

◆ The centralizing and decentralizing forces that explain the number and sizes of cities.

◆ What constitutes a "system" of cities, and the essential characteristics of the U.S. system of cities.

◆ The key practical insights and principles of central place theory and urban hierarchy theory, and how real estate decision makers can use these.

◆ What is meant by the economic base and export base of a city.

◆ Employment and population multipliers.

It would not be a great oversimplification to say that in a modern society real estate is an urban phenomenon. While most of the value of real property throughout most of history was based on agricultural production, in the United States today over 90 percent of the value of all real estate is in urban areas, even though these comprise only a small percent of the total land area of the country. An understanding of cities is therefore basic to an educated perspective on commercial property investment analysis.

In this chapter we will begin with an overview of the big picture, the "system of cities." In the process of doing this, we will introduce one of the most fundamental concepts of urban geography and spatial economics, central place theory, together with related concepts including urban hierarchy and regional economic base. The basic objective is to understand the forces that underlie the rise and fall of cities, and, related to that, to gain an understanding of the basic determinants of successful locations for various types of activities.

3.1 PATTERN OF CITY SIZE

Cities do not exist as isolated or purely random phenomena. Rather, each city has a place and a role as an element in a **system of cities**, which serves a functioning economy and geographic region. The nature of the system of cities has implications for the nature of the space markets underlying the real estate assets in those cities. To take a simple example, if you try to place in a regional center such as Des Moines a high-rise upscale apartment building such as would work in a large financial center such as New York, you probably will not succeed. The type of real estate that works in the space market depends on the size and economic characteristics of the city in which it is located.

Perhaps the most basic physical characteristics describing cities are size (in terms of population) and location. Of these two, city size is perhaps the simplest characteristic to describe and measure. Yet the population of a city, and how that population changes over time, has important impacts on its space markets. Larger, more rapidly growing cities will generally be able to sustain higher real rents, other things being equal. With this in mind, let us begin our examination of cities with a look at the patterns that exist in the sizes of cities.

In fact, the sizes of cities follow a pattern that is one of the most striking phenomena in all of social science. This pattern is known as the **rank/size rule** (also referred to as Zipf's Law). The rank/size rule can be expressed as follows:

$$City\ population = \frac{Largest\ city's\ population}{Rank\ of\ city}$$

In other words, if you rank all the cities in a system of cities (that is, all the cities in a coherent geographical region), such that the most populous city has a rank of 1, then the population of each city will approximately equal the largest city's population divided by the rank of the city.

If you plot Zipf's Law on a bar graph, it results in the theoretical pattern of population and rank shown in Exhibit 3-1a. Note the exponentially declining pattern in the length of the bars representing population as we go down the rankings of the cities. Now examine the population/rank bar chart for the actual 1996 population of U.S. cities in Exhibit 3-1b. Notice the similarity between the actual empirical pattern and the theoretical pattern. The rank/size rule describes the distribution of U.S. city sizes remarkably well. This phenomenon is found to hold across a wide variety of countries and regions.

3.2 PATTERN OF CITY LOCATION

Now let's bring location into the picture. Look again at the rank/size chart of U.S. cities in Exhibit 3-1b. Notice that the three largest cities are far apart, each in a different region of the country: New York in the East, Chicago in the Midwest, and Los Angeles in the West. With some exceptions, *cities of similar size are not located near each*

Exhibit 3-1a   Theoretical
Rank/Size Rule

Exhibit 3-1b   Rank/Size
Rule in U.S. Cities

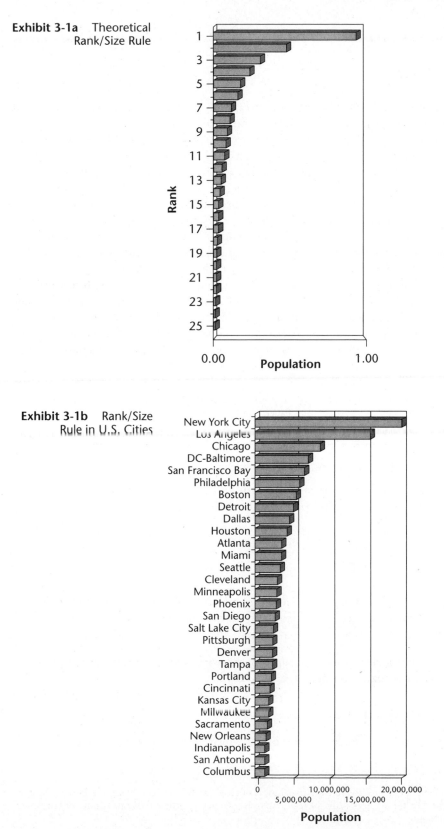

What Causes the Rank/Size Rule?

What causes the rank/size rule? Geographers and economists have long puzzled about the answer to this question, and proposed various theories. Perhaps the simplest explanation has been offered recently by Xavier Gabaix.[*]

Suppose we begin with any arbitrary distribution of city sizes. Now suppose each city grows randomly over time, but with all cities tending to grow at the same common mean annual percentage rate over the long run, and with the same "volatility," that is, the same relative randomness of actual annual growth around the long-run average. Over time the distribution of city sizes will converge toward Zipf's Law, and the convergence will be pretty rapid. This is simply a consequence of mathematics. But why would cities all tend to grow at the same rate on average over the long run? Perhaps because the number of new jobs is proportional to the number of existing jobs. Why would all cities tend to have the same volatility in their annual percentage growth? Perhaps because once a city is large enough, it will have a relatively diversified economic base, and this diversification will reduce

volatility to a common level. Smaller cities may lack sufficient diversification in their economic bases, and may therefore have greater volatility in their growth. If there is a minimum "critical mass" for city size, below which a city will tend to wither and die away, then the volatility in smaller cities' growth will cause many of them to sink below the critical size at some point. This will result in fewer "small cities" than there should be according to Zipf's Law. This is what we observe in the real world. There are fewer small towns than would be predicted by the theoretical rank/size rule. What this mathematical model cannot explain is why the ranking is relatively stable over time. Rarely do cities significantly change rank, and most such changes are systematic (such as the rise of western and southern cities at the expense of eastern cities). Thus, to understand the size pattern of cities, we must also consider location.

See "Zipf's Law for Cities: An Explanation," Harvard/MIT Working Paper, 1998.

---

other geographically.[1] This is seen graphically in the map in Exhibit 3-2 showing the 20 largest metropolitan areas in the country.

3.3 FACTORS UNDERLYING THE PATTERN: CENTRIPETAL AND CENTRIFUGAL FORCES

The rank/size rule and the geographical regional dispersion noted earlier together suggest a hierarchical structure of cities and a division of the U.S. territory into zones of influence. This in turn suggests two points:

1. **Centralizing** city-causation (**centripetal**) **forces** are counterbalanced by opposing **decentralizing** (**centrifugal**) **forces**.
2. The relative strength of the centralizing and decentralizing forces differs for different functions and activities.

The centralizing forces cause cities to form in the first place and to tend to agglomerate into fewer and larger cities over time. The decentralizing forces tend

---

[1] The major exceptions to this rule are the clusters of cities in the northeast along the Boston-Washington corridor, the Great Lakes Milwaukee-Pittsburgh corridor, and the relative proximity of Los Angeles and San Francisco.

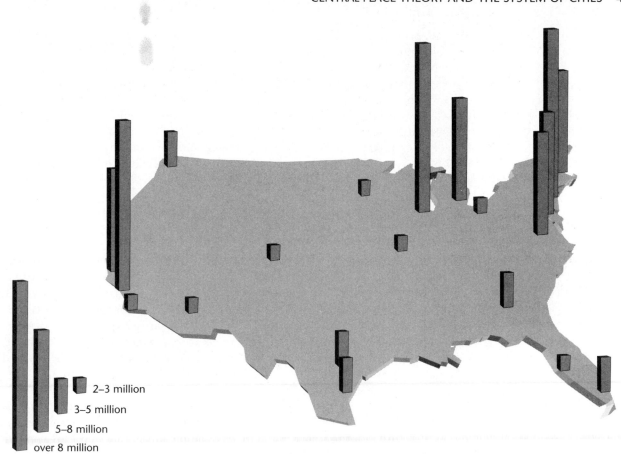

Exhibit 3-2   The 20 Largest U.S. Metropolitan Areas
(Source: U.S. Census estimates for 1996.)

2–3 million

3–5 million

5–8 million

over 8 million

to limit the growth of city size and tend to make more, smaller cities dispersed throughout the territory.

3.3.1 Centripetal Forces

Three primary centralizing forces cause cities to coalesce:

1. Economies of scale
2. Economies of agglomeration
3. Positive locational externalities

Operating together, these three forces underlie an important characteristic of urban growth dynamics known as cumulative causation. What is meant by these fundamental principles of urban dynamics?

Economies of scale refers to the phenomenon whereby it is cheaper and more efficient to produce more of a good or service in larger volume at fewer sites. Fundamentally, economies of scale are caused by fixed production costs at a given site. The fixed costs are independent of the quantity produced at that site. The physical plant and equipment in an automobile factory are examples. As a result of scale economies it is typically more efficient to produce 200,000 automobiles per year in one factory than to produce 50,000 automobiles per year in each of four factories at different locations.

Economies of agglomeration are cost or productivity advantages to the clustering of firms or work sites physically near each other. Unlike scale economies, which require increasing quantity of production to obtain greater efficiency, agglomeration economies do not require increased quantity of production per se, but merely the clustering of production work sites. Agglomeration economies result from the ability of different types of workers and production processes to help each other if they are physically near each other. This may result from "vertical linkages" ("upstream" and "downstream" linkages in production processes) or from "horizontal linkages" ("synergy" across firms or work sites, such as the sharing of a common pool of skilled workers, or the existence of a critical mass of experts in a given field resulting in a creative cross-fertilization and stimulation of individuals).

A closely related economic concept is that of **positive locational externalities**. This occurs when one firm benefits from the nearby location of another firm without the first firm being able to capture all of these benefits for itself. This concept is similar to agglomeration economies. The difference is that locational externalities may occur between as few as two firms or plants, not necessarily requiring a critical mass of firms or workers. An example of a positive locational externality would be the benefit obtained by a trucking firm whose operations are centered, say, in Nashville when a major airline establishes an airfreight hub in that city. The airfreight operations will increase demand for the trucking company's services.

A more subtle example of external economies occurs in the interaction of scale economies and agglomeration economies, and the interaction of supply and demand. As more firms cluster together, the local population and production swells, providing a larger local market for all manner of goods and services. This allows larger-scale production, which, in the presence of scale economies, allows lower cost and more efficient production. This in turn stimulates further demand for additional production. Thus, in the presence of scale economies firms can experience external benefits merely from their proximity to each other, even if they are not directly technologically and physically related to one another. In other words, scale economies can integrate the notions of agglomeration economies and positive locational externalities.

The sort of growth spiral just described has been referred to as **cumulative causation**. It suggests that there can be *momentum* in the growth (or decline) of cities and regions. Growth breeds growth (and, decline breeds decline). If we look at the overall system of cities in the United States, and we define *growth* and *decline* relatively speaking, by the rank of a city's population, we see that when a city commences growing, it tends to continue growing for at least a few decades, and vice versa: when a city begins to decline, the decline tends to persist for at least a few decades.

3.3.2 Centrifugal Forces

The decentralizing forces that put a brake on urban agglomeration and result in a larger number of smaller cities include factors that make it less efficient or more costly to produce goods and services in large cities, or that reduce the quality of life of the inhabitants. For example, congestion, pollution, crime, high intraurban transportation costs, as well as high rents and urban land costs are some of the negative features of large cities that tend to get worse as cities increase in size (at least beyond some critical limit).

Also, a larger average size of cities relative to the total population of a country implies that the number of cities in the population must be fewer. For example, a country with 100 million city dwellers can have at most only 10 cities with 10 million inhabitants, but it could have as many as 100 cities with 1 million inhabitants. Spread out over the same geographical territory, the 10 "super-cities" would be on average much farther apart from each other and from the average rural point in the territory than would 100 cities of 1 million inhabitants each similarly evenly spaced throughout the same territory. Thus, larger (and therefore fewer) cities will tend to increase total transport costs (due to greater average transport distances).

3.3.3 Balance of Forces

When centralizing forces become more powerful or more important in a society, one or a few large cities tend to siphon population and grow faster than smaller cities. For example, reductions in transport and communication costs and the rise of highly centralized governmental and administrative institutions resulted in the development of dominant capital cities in imperial nations, such as London, Paris, and Moscow during the 19th and first half of the 20th centuries. These cities often had larger populations than the rank/size rule would predict. When decentralizing forces become more powerful or important, small- or medium-size cities will capture most of the population growth in a society. For example, in the United States in the late 20th century medium-size cities generally grew faster than the largest cities.

A fundamental key point about the role of centralizing and decentralizing forces in shaping the system of cities is that centralizing forces are relatively stronger than decentralizing forces for some types of activities. For example, upper-level national governmental functions and international financial services are highly concentrated in only a few of the largest and most expensive cities. For these functions the centralizing forces must be relatively strong, or they would not concentrate in such high-cost locations. In contrast, light manufacturing, distribution, corporate and governmental research, lower-level governmental, and corporate managerial functions are widely spread out among cities, including many small- to medium-size cities. For these activities the centralizing forces must be relatively weak, and/or the decentralizing forces relatively strong.

3.3.4 Central Place Theory and the Urban Hierarchy

The empirical geographic observations and economic intuition described earlier have been developed into a body of geographic theory known broadly as **central place theory** (CPT), including an extension known as the **theory of urban hierarchy**. Perhaps the most famous names associated with the development of CPT are the German geographers August Losch and Walter Christaller.

Losch developed CPT by examining the problem of location on a homogeneous "featureless plain." In such a land homogeneous agricultural products are produced everywhere but must be marketed at a number of identical dimensionless points (i.e., the "cities") where, incidentally, the industrial population lives and needs to use the agricultural products while producing the homogeneous industrial goods that the farmers need. The greater the economies of scale in industrial production are, the fewer and farther apart will be the cities, other things being equal, for this will allow the factories to be larger scale. The greater the transportation costs are, the more numerous and closer together will be the cities in the optimal configuration, for this will allow minimization of transportation distances (since any farmer can be served by any city, and any city by any farmer).

Losch's key geometric insight was that city "service areas" or **hinterlands**, would assume a hexagonal shape (like a honeycomb) on such a homogeneous plane, because this is the shape that minimizes the average distance from each city to all points in its service area and still covers all the territory. But while the hexagonally shaped service areas are visually striking in the abstract, the key practical insight of central place theory is the resulting *even spacing* of cities. *Even spacing is what minimizes total transportation costs*, given the total number of cities in the region (e.g., given the scale of industrial production).

Christaller enriched the picture presented by Losch by considering different economic functions or types of production, each of which might be characterized by different degrees of scale economies in production and by different transportation costs in distribution. The optimal configuration of cities on the featureless plain now includes a geographical *urban hierarchy*, in which *higher-order* cities (those containing functions that require more centralization) are fewer and farther apart than *lower-order* cities. But the tendency toward even spacing between cities suggested by Losch's basic CPT still comes through, only now the even spacing applies within each rank or "order."

The larger the population is that is needed to support an efficient production process the larger we would say is the minimum or **threshold market** for that product or activity. The larger the threshold market population, the fewer the number of suppliers.

Cities with more specialized and larger-scale producers that require a larger threshold market, such as steel and aerospace manufacturers, national government, international financial services, as examples, are the higher-order cities, supplying

Prove Central Place Theory to Yourself

This even-spacing rule is very fundamental to urban geography. To prove it to yourself, look at a 12-inch ruler and imagine that it is the space or territory that must be served. Suppose there are 13 "inhabitants" (i.e., the people or sites needing to be served by transportation to and from a single point) spaced evenly across the ruler, located one on each inch mark (including the 0-inch point at the end of the ruler). Suppose the "city" to and from which the inhabitants must travel or be served is located in the exact center, at the 6-inch mark. The person living right on the 6-inch mark has no transport costs; the people living at the 5- and 7-inch marks have costs of one inch each, because they are located one inch from the city, and so on. The total transport costs of the society is the sum across all 13 inhabitants, which equals 42 "person-inches." Now imagine locating the city one

inch mark away from the center, moving it, say, to the 7-inch mark. This will increase the transport costs of some people and decrease those of others, but the number of people whose costs increase exceeds that of the people for whom the costs decrease. In particular, all seven people living below the 7-inch mark (those at 0, 1, 2, . . . , 6) suffer an increase in costs of one person-inch each. Only six people (those on marks 7, 8, . . . ,12) see a cost decrease, also of one person-inch each, as their distance to the city is reduced by one inch. So the total transport costs of the society is now 43. By induction, you can see that if we move the city to any other point farther away from the center, we will only further add to the total costs, in the same manner as has been described here. So the cost-minimizing location for the city is in the center. This is the essence of central place theory.

such unique and specialized goods and services to the more numerous and ubiquitous lower-order cities. Lower-order cities contain less specialized and more ubiquitous producers of goods and services that are characterized by either denser markets, lower-scale economies, or higher transportation costs relative to the value of the product. A city's hinterland now includes the territories served by all the lower-order cities that depend on the higher-order city for the higher-level functions and goods or services. Higher-order hinterlands are thus superimposed over the smaller lower-order hinterlands. (See Exhibit 3-3.) Higher-order cities tend to be, but are not necessarily, larger in population than lower-order cities. In the modern economy higher-order cities are characterized not so much by large-scale manufacturing production, but by major *control* functions, such as corporate headquarters, governmental capitals, and major financial markets or service centers. Large-scale manufacturing and physical distribution services are more characteristic of mid-level cities.

In a nutshell, let us summarize CPT and hierarchy theory with the following statement:

In order to reduce "spatial friction," places of similar size, rank, or function will tend to be evenly spaced *across geographical space and/or population.*

Exhibit 3-3   Central Place Theory and Urban Hierarchy. The diagram shows the theoretical configuration of 39 lower-ordered cities (single dots) and 5 higher-order cities (circled dots), with their "hinterland" territories indicated as on a "featureless plain." The hexagonal shapes minimize aggregate transportation costs. The even spacing of the central points is the key point.

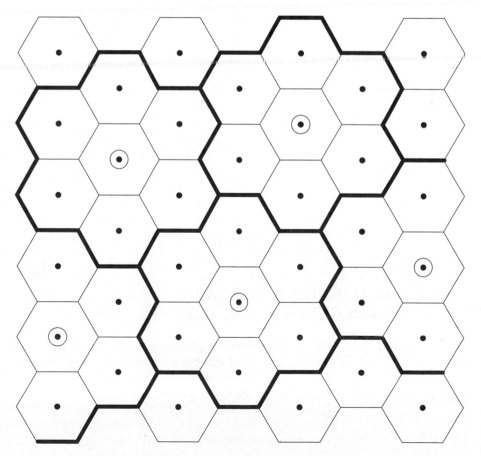

3.3.5 Why Does CPT Matter?

Geographical theories such as CPT may seem rather academic and removed from the real world. But in fact this stuff is very practical and underlies the most basic decision making in real estate development and the operation of the space market. Ignorance of these fundamental geographical principles can spell disaster in the real estate business. Insightful application of these principles is the hallmark of the successful real estate entrepreneur. In this regard it is important to note that while we have introduced CPT and hierarchy theory to explain the location patterns of cities, this theory also applies to the spatial dimension of any economic activity.

In practical real estate terms, the implication of CPT is therefore that every territory must be covered (or served) by at least one central service point. Just as every hinterland needs a city, every market area needs a store or franchise, and every production region needs a branch office to manage it. This gives you the broad outlines of the nature of where it is reasonable to locate certain sites, that is, where sufficient demand for real estate of various types may exist. The emphasis is on the word *where*, for fundamentally, CPT is *location theory*, and the oldest cliché in the real estate business is that what matters is: *location, location, location.*

From a practical perspective, central place theory suggests two important principles, each of which is really the opposite side of the same coin, so to speak. The two principles are:

1. If a territory is underserved there is room for a new central site.
2. If a central site is already effectively located to serve a territory, it is going to be very hard to develop a new such site nearby.

Combined with the hierarchy theory, these principles apply at various levels, ranging from location of retail sites within a metropolitan area to predicting which cities in a country have better potential to grow and develop faster over the long run. The second principle can be thought of as implying that existing central places cast **agglomeration shadows** around themselves, making it difficult for other similar size or similar rank places to develop within that shadow. For example, it would be difficult for another city the size of Atlanta to develop anywhere near Atlanta. Based on the same principle, it would be difficult to develop successfully a second regional shopping mall near an already successfully and functioning mall (unless the market has grown sufficiently to support a second mall, and/or the second mall differentiates itself sufficiently from the first).

3.4 ECONOMIC BASE AND THE GROWTH OF CITIES AND REGIONS

While the broad perspective on the overall system of cities examined in the previous section offers important insights, it still paints a very broad-brush-stroke picture, without paying much attention to the specific details that characterize individual cities. CPT cannot explain why two cities equally ranked and equally well located may fare differently over time as some industries rise and others fall in the economy. To explain this, we need to know more about the specific differences in the local economies of the two cities.

By looking more specifically at the microlevel of individual cities, urban economists have developed perspectives and tools that can increase greatly our understanding of individual cities and how they function economically. The theory that explains what industries are important to a city's growth starts with a deeper investigation of the economic base, the engine that drives a city's sources of income. Understanding which businesses or industries are important to an area has obvious and direct implications for the economic growth prospects for the area.

3.4.1 Definition of Economic Base

Broadly speaking, the **economic base** of a city or region can be thought of as the sources of its income. As such, this is the engine that drives and underlies all real estate activity and values in the region. Economic base analysis is thus a tool to help

- identify which cities or regions will grow,
- characterize what kind of growth (e.g., blue collar versus white collar) will take place, and
- quantify how much growth will occur.

Conceptually, the economic base of a region has three major potential components: (1) the local production of goods and services both for local needs and for export beyond the local urban area; (2) the investment returns to or of capital owned in the local area, such as investment returns on the stored financial wealth of retirees; and (3) government transfers such as Social Security payments. Of these, the production of goods and services is by far the most important in most urban areas.

3.4.2 Export Base

When we examine the local production of goods and services, we can make an important distinction between goods and services that are produced in excess of the needs of the local area, and those that are produced only in quantities equal to or less than local usage. Excess production is exported outside of the local regional market, and this brings income that can be used by the local population to buy goods and services either locally or from other areas. Such production is referred to as export production. It seems reasonable that this type of production would be most important in determining the growth or decline of the local area.

Recognition of the importance of export production provides the rationale for the most widely used urban economic theory of local economic growth, **export base theory**. The key principle of export base theory states that

> *Economic growth of the city or region is dependent entirely on growth in the export (so-called "basic") sector of the local economy.*

All employment is classified as being part of either the **export (basic) sector** or the **service (nonbasic) sector**. Industries that produce more goods and service than are likely to be consumed locally are presumed to be part of the export sector. Thus, according to export base theory, forecasting the growth of a metropolitan area consists of two steps:

1. Identifying the export base industries in the local region
2. Forecasting employment growth in those industries

This process is facilitated by the fact that there are not many major export industries in most local areas.[2]

3.4.3 Location Quotients and SICs

While the export base theory is intuitively reasonable, to apply it in practice we need a way to identify which industries and businesses are part of the export sector for a given region. The most widely used tool for doing this is a quantitative measure known as the **location quotient** (often referred to as the **LQ** for short). The LQ is defined as the proportion of total local employment in a given industry divided by the proportion of total national employment in that same industry. City m's LQ for industry i is given by the following formula:

$$LQ_{mi} = \frac{N_{mi}/N_m}{N_i/N}$$

where N_{mi} = Employment in city m in Industry i
  N_m = Total employment in city m in all industries
  N_i = National employment in industry i
  N = Total national employment in all industries

A location quotient of 1.0 indicates that the same proportion of local workers work in a particular industry as work in that industry in the nation as a whole. A location quotient greater than 1.0 indicates that the local area is more heavily concentrated in that industry than is the average city or region across the country. In practice, it is usually considered that a location quotient must be significantly greater than 1.0 in order to indicate that the industry is part of the export sector of the local economic base.

As an example, suppose that the figures in the following table represent the employment statistics for the Anytown metropolitan area and the nation as a whole regarding total employment and employment in the beverage manufacturing industry.

Total U.S. employment	130,000,000
U.S. beverage industry employment	130,000
Total Anytown employment	750,000
Anytown beverage employment	3,000

We would compute the location quotient for the beverage industry in Anytown as follows:

[2]A general trend in economic development has been for production and trade to become more geographically integrated, taking advantage of technological advance and economies of scale. This results in industries that were once purely local becoming part of the export sector in some cities. For example, dairies traditionally provide milk for a specific city. As the industry developed and storage and transportation technology improved, the concentration of activity has greatly increased, with the dairy industry becoming a part of the export base of some regions, while retaining its traditional service-sector character in others.

$$\textit{Anytown beverage LQ} = \frac{3,000 \ / \ 750,000}{130,000 \ / \ 130,000,000} = \frac{.004}{.001} = 4.0$$

This means that there are four times the typical proportion of beverage industry workers in Anytown as in the nation as a whole. As the Anytown beverage LQ of 4.0 is considerably greater than 1.0, we would presume that the beverage industry is indeed part of Anytown's export base. Growth in the beverage industry in Anytown will increase the total number of jobs in the Anytown region, implying growth in the region.

When combined with an analysis of large employers in a region, location quotients are an excellent way of determining the importance of a particular industry or firm to an area. Location quotients are readily calculable using employment data from the Bureau of Labor Statistics available from the federal government as well as most state governments.[3] Industries are classified in hierarchical layers of aggregation known as the **standard industrial classification** system, or **SIC** code. SIC codes are available in many areas to a five-digit depth of disaggregation, as illustrated in the following table in increasing subcategorization for Cleveland, Ohio, as an illustrative city.

SIC #	Descriptions	Number of Employed Persons
20000	Professional, paraprofessional & technical occupations	200,000
21000	Management support professionals	28,000
21100	Accountants & financial specialists	13,000
21111	Accountants specializing in tax preparation	480

The table gives an example of the branching indicated by one-digit, two-digit, three-digit, and five-digit levels of disaggregation within the SIC code scheme. (The four-digit level was left out of this example.) You can see how the definition of the employment sectors or industries becomes narrower as the number of digits in the SIC code increases.[4]

3.4.4 Service Sector and Export Multiplier

Workers that are not part of the export sector (non-basic jobs) serve the local population, as grocery clerks, divorce attorneys, child care workers, utility line repairpeople, and so on. All of these jobs depend ultimately, directly or indirectly, on the export base of the region. The location quotient for nonbasic occupations will tend to be near 1.0 in most cities. The nonbasic sector is also known as the service sector of

[3] Reports are available monthly on the Internet or through the mail.

[4] It should be recognized that some industries do not classify well under the SIC system. For example, we might suspect that tourism would be important to economic growth in Hawaii, but there is no tourism grouping in the SIC codes. Rather, workers within the industry of tourism are classified as aircraft pilots, retail suppliers, food servers, housekeepers, bartenders, travel agents, taxi drivers, and so on, which do not group together easily. For this reason, location quotients based simply on SIC codes alone will not always suffice for a thorough analysis of the economic base of an area. But LQs do serve well to indicate which jobs are more or less important in predicting economic growth.

the region. If the export sector declined, there would be less need for the service sector. Since the service sector depends on the export sector, the change in the demand for service sector jobs is a function of the change in the number of export sector jobs.

An important feature of regional economies is that the *number of jobs in the nonbasic or service sector generally greatly exceeds the number of jobs directly in the export sector.* As a result:

> *Expansion in the export sector creates an* **employment multiplier effect** *on total local employment.*

As an example, suppose that in the town of Metropolis a new biotech research center needs 1,000 scientists, lab workers, administrators and facility managers, and maintenance workers. Most of the scientists, lab workers, and managers are brought in from around the country, while a few people are simply hired away from other local firms, who must then replace these workers with new workers, most of whom come from outside the region. First, the new research facility has to be built. This will create some temporary jobs. Then the research center must be maintained, which creates permanent new jobs. Most of the 1,000 new workers have families, which means a population increase of at least 2,000 in the metropolitan area, directly related to the new lab. These 1,000 new households (2,000 people) spend much of their paychecks on local goods and services, such as housing, food, entertainment, and so forth. This expands the demand for local goods and services. Local business retailers expand or new retailers move into the area and add employees as a result of this new business, resulting in more employees, more paychecks, and more people moving into the area. After the market has worked through the entire chain of effects, the net population increase due directly and indirectly to the original 1,000 research facility workers might be 5,000 people, a **population multiplier** ratio of 5.0.

Every net new job in an area within the export sector creates a multiplier effect on the total employment including the export and service sectors. Two types of multipliers are often considered in forecasting the growth effects of changes in the export base:

1. Employment Multiplier:

$$\frac{\textit{Net total employment increase}}{\textit{Export employment increase}}$$

2. Population multiplier:

$$\frac{\textit{Net total population increase}}{\textit{Export employment increase}}$$

Typical employment multiplier ratios are in the range of 2.0 to 4.0. Population multipliers are of course higher than employment multipliers. Typical population multiplier ratios range from 2.5 to 9.0 depending on the pay rate or income level of the net new jobs and the business income of the newly expanding export sector firms. Higher-paying export sector jobs have larger population multipliers.

It is important to note that the multiplier effect goes both ways. If jobs within the export sector are lost, the effect is the eventual loss of many indirect service sector jobs and eventually population as well. Since people do not immediately move into or out of an area when jobs increase or decrease, the population effects lag behind the employment changes by several months to a few years.

Several steps are involved in using the export base approach to economic base analysis for the purposes of forecasting future city growth or decline. One first performs an analysis of location quotients on SIC classified workers in an area, relative to the United States, focusing on those high location quotient groupings that also have a significant number of local employees. The next step is to forecast the future employment prospects in each of these groups, both positive and negative, and to use these to suggest a population or total employment growth impact (after considering the multiplier, depending on the income levels of the key industry workers). Such forecasts should take into consideration broad national and international trends, as well as possible unique local firms and situations. Employment forecasts by occupation and SIC group are available from many state government economic agencies, such as state-level employment or economic planning agencies, as well as from professional economic consulting firms.

3.4.5 Classification of Cities by Economic Base

The concept of the economic base, and especially the notion of the export base, suggests a useful way to classify and group individual cities within the overall system of cities in the United States. Such analyses can be used to identify **economic clusters**—cities that are similar in the nature of their economic bases, and which might therefore be expected to have similar growth patterns over time.

The most straightforward way to identify economic clusters is to compare the industrial concentrations of the economic bases, particularly the export sectors, across the cities. In this approach, industries are grouped into similar or related categories, such as heavy industry, high technology, government, and so forth. Using location quotients, one then groups cities into those whose export bases appear to be relatively dominated by one industry group or another. Typically, some cities' export bases will be highly diversified across the industry groups. Thus, one ends up with groups such as heavy-industry-dominated cities, high-technology-dominated cities, government-dominated cities, diversified cities, and so on.

An example of this approach is shown in Exhibit 3-4. This study's author, Glenn Mueller (1993), classified cities into nine groups:

Farm

F.I.R.E.[5]

Government

Manufacturing

Military

Mining (including oil & gas)

Service

Transportation

Diversified

---

[5] Stands for "Finance, Insurance, and Real Estate," a category of professional business occupations characteristic of office employment.

Economic Base Classifications*

Diversified	Farm	FIRE	Government	Manufacturing
Albuquerque	Bellingham	Anaheim	Albany	Akron
Alton & Granite	Chico	Bloomington, IL	Ann Arbor	Allentown
Baton Rouge	Dubuque	Des Moines	Austin	Aurora & Elgin
Beaver County	Eau Claire	Hartford	Baltimore	Bridgeport
Birmingham	Johnson City	New York	Columbia, SC	Charlotte
Boulder	Joplin	Phoenix	Columbus	Cincinnati
Buffalo	Lexington	San Francisco	Dayton	Cleveland
Du Page	McAllen		Galveston	Detroit
Fort Lauderdale	Merced		Raleigh & Durham	Gary & Hammond
Fort Worth	Modesto		Richmond	Grand Rapids
Hamilton	Ocala		Sacramento	Greensboro
Harrisburg	Oxnard		Salt Lake City	Greenville
Indianapolis	Richland		Trenton	Milwaukee
Joliet	Santa Rosa		Washington	Minneapolis
Kansas City, KS	Stockton			New Bedford
Little Rock	St. Cloud			Providence
Los Angeles	Yakima			Rochester
Louisville	Yuba City			San Jose
Manchester				Scranton
Middletown				Seattle
Mobile				St. Louis
New Haven				Wilmington
Oakland				Worcester
Orlando				Youngstown
Portland				
Riverside				
Springfield				
Syracuse				
Tampa				
Toledo				
Tucson				
Vancouver				

Military	Mining	Service	Transportation
Charleston	Bakersfield	Atlantic City	Atlanta
El Paso	Dallas	Boston	Bergen & Passaic
Honolulu	Denver	Las Vegas	Chicago
Jacksonville	Houston	Philadelphia	Essex & Union
Lake County	New Orleans	Pittsburgh	Jersey City
New London	Oklahoma City	Reno	Kansas City, MO

Exhibit 3-4   Example of U.S. City Classification by Dominant Economic Base

Military	Mining	Service	Transportation
Norfolk	Tulsa		Memphis
Omaha	Wichita		Miami
Orange County			Middlesex
San Antonio			Nashville
San Diego			Nassau
Tacoma			

*Location quotients do change over time causing cities to move from one EBC to another—however, this is infrequent.

Source: Mueller, G. "Refining Economc Diversification Strategies for Real Estate Portfolios." *Journal of Real Estate Research* 8(1), winter 1993.

Exhibit 3-4   Continued

Mueller examined employment data for each city and calculated location quotients for each of the nine industrial classifications, based on SIC codes. The highest location quotient in each city determined its classification. If no industry group had an LQ much greater than 1.0, then the city was classified in the diversified group. Notice that the economic clusters identified in Mueller's study do not particularly correspond to geographic regions. For example, manufacturing-based cities are not all in the Northeast or Midwest, but include at least some cities in the South and West, such as Charlotte, San Jose, and Seattle. Mueller's analysis indicated that a real estate investment strategy using economic-based categories such as those listed would provide better diversification than a purely physical geographic diversification strategy, such as putting investments in each major geographic region of the country (like: Northeast, Southeast, Southwest, and so on).

3.5 CLASSIFICATION OF CITIES FOR REAL ESTATE INVESTMENT ANALYSIS

Characterizing groups of relatively similar cities in terms of how their real estate markets will tend to perform over time is problematic if one limits the focus to the economic bases, or even to the growth rates, of the cities. The demographic and economic base characteristics of a city reflect the demand side of the real estate usage market, but not the supply side. A city may have strong growth in demand for real estate usage based on its economic growth and still not produce good real estate investment performance (in the sense of growth in rents or property values). If the city's real estate demand growth is eagerly matched by equal or even greater supply growth from new construction and development, rents will not increase in the long run. (See Part I.) To deal with this problem, one needs to work with data that reflect the long-run equilibrium in the space market, including the effect of new development. Examples of data reflecting the equilibrium in the space market would be data on effective rental rates, or vacancy rates. Data reflecting the property asset market would include data on property price changes (period-by-period capital returns).[6]

[6]Property market period-by-period return data used to be very difficult to obtain at the level of individual metropolitan areas. However, now the Federal National Mortgage Association (FNMA) and Federal Home Loan Mortgage Corporation (FHLMC) publish indices of metropolitan-level housing returns

Exhibit 3-5 Three Major Groups of Cities with Similarly Performing Real Estate Markets in the Late 20th Century

Group I Main Group	Group II Energy	Group III Bicoastal
New York	New Orleans	Boston
Philadelphia	Houston	Atlanta
Washington, D.C.	Dallas	Ft. Lauderdale
Baltimore	Oklahoma City	Phoenix
Chicago	Denver	Los Angeles
Detroit		
Kansas City		
Miami		
Orlando		
Memphis		
Austin		

Source: W.Goetzmann and S.Wachter, "Clustering Methods for Real Estate Portfolios." *Real Estate Economics* 23(3): 271–310, fall 1995, Table 1, p. 279.

A study by William Goetzmann and Susan Wachter (1995) addresses this problem and demonstrates a sophisticated statistical cluster analysis technique to identify groups of cities that performed relatively similarly based on effective rental rates and vacancy rates during the 1980s. This study suggests that three main groups of cities can be distinguished fairly robustly from a statistical perspective as of the late 20th century. Of the 21 major metropolitan areas examined, 11 fall into a "main" cluster consisting primarily of northeastern and midwestern industrial cities but also including Washington, D.C., Memphis, Miami, and Orlando. The second group consists of the five oil- and energy-based cities of Houston, Dallas, Denver, Oklahoma City and New Orleans. The third group is a somewhat polyglot bicoastal collection of cities oriented toward technology-, military-, and retirement-based economies, including Boston, Los Angeles, Phoenix, Atlanta, and Ft. Lauderdale, (the study did not include data on some major cities such as San Francisco, Seattle, and Tampa which, one guesses, might also have fallen in this last group). The Goetzmann-Wachter groups are summarized in Exhibit 3-5.

Finally, it must be noted that the economic bases of cities evolve over time, sometimes surprisingly quickly (witness the transformation of the economic base of Pittsburgh from steel production to medical technology and services during the 1980s). Furthermore, the relations among various segments of the economy change over time. In the 1970s and 1980s high oil prices caused the oil sector to be supply driven, which gave it a countercyclical effect in a national economy that was a net oil importer. As a result, oil-based cities such as Dallas and Houston tended to move opposite the rest of the country, economically speaking, during the 1970s and 1980s. But in the 1960s and 1990s, with oil supplies plentiful, the oil sector was demand driven, which resulted in oil-based cities tending to move with the rest of the economy.

based on transaction prices, and the National Council of Real Estate Investment Fiduciaries (NCREIF) publishes indices of commercial property returns for a number of metropolitan areas based on appraised values. Several commercial firms provide rent and vacancy data for U.S. cities. (For a review of this type of data as of the late 1990s, see Guilkey [1999].)

For all of these reasons, the economic relationships among cities tend not to be stable over time, making it difficult to predict future group behavior based on past history. However, certain features of a city are relatively constant or immutable and have important effects on real estate performance. These include the basic concepts from central place theory discussed earlier in this chapter. The geographic location or "centrality" of a city and the availability of developable land in and around the city tend to change relatively slowly. Also, certain important cultural or social aspects of a city, such as its business climate and the related degree of support for real estate development, change only slowly if at all.

3.6 CHAPTER SUMMARY

This chapter presented a brief introduction and overview of the major theories and principles that have come from geography and spatial economics to explain the rise and fall of cities. This is obviously knowledge fundamental to making rational and informed real estate investment decisions. Some of the concepts covered in this chapter, such as central place theory and economic base theory, are relevant not only at the big picture level of understanding the overall system of cities, but also at the more applied level at which real estate professionals make specific location analyses and decisions.

KEY TERMS

system of cities	central place theory (CPT)	service (nonbasic) sector
rank/size rule (Zipf's law)	theory of urban hierarchy	location quotient (LQ)
centralizing (centripetal) forces	hinterlands	standard industrial classification
decentralizing (centrifugal) forces	threshold market	(SIC)
economies of scale	agglomeration shadows	employment multiplier effect
economies of agglomeration	economic base	population multiplier
positive locational externalities	export base theory	classification of cities
cumulative causation	export (basic) sector	economic cluster of cities

STUDY QUESTIONS

3.1. Explain how the three major centripetal, or centralizing, economic forces can interact to create the phenomenon known as cumulative causation.

3.2. In 1996 the Census Bureau's estimate of the population of the New York City Consolidated Metropolitan Statistical Area (CMSA) was 19,938,492. Boston was 5,563,475. According to the rank/size rule and Boston's rank as indicated in Exhibit 3-1b, what should Boston's population have been?

3.3. Look at the rank/size chart of cities in the European Union (EU) shown in Exhibit 3-6. Do European cities' rank/sizes appear to conform to the exponential shape predicted by Zipf's Law as well as U.S. cities, seem to do? Why do you suppose the rank/size rule might not apply as well for Europe? [Hint: Has Europe historically

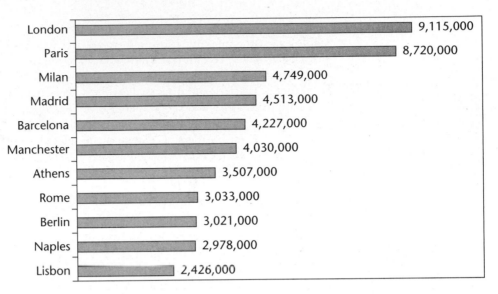

Exhibit 3-6 Population of Major European Cities (Source: U.S. Census estimates, 1992, based on common definition of contiguous built-up area of density 5,000 inhabitants per square mile.)

City	Population
London	9,115,000
Paris	8,720,000
Milan	4,749,000
Madrid	4,513,000
Barcelona	4,227,000
Manchester	4,030,000
Athens	3,507,000
Rome	3,033,000
Berlin	3,021,000
Naples	2,978,000
Lisbon	2,426,000

been a single system of cities like the United States, based on a geographically integrated economy?] Suppose that the EU is far along the way to becoming a geographically integrated economy. What implications does this hold for the system of cities in Europe, the rank/size rule, and the likely growth pattern of European cities in the 21st century?

3.4. Draw a diagram of the essential implication of central place and urban hierarchy theories. [Hint: Can you draw hexagons?]

3.5. What would you say are the implications of central place theory and hierarchy theory for a developer contemplating building a new shopping center at a site in a metropolitan area where there is already a similar size shopping center nearby?

3.6. Which of the following are examples of a basic industry in a city

a. Grocery store

b. Motel serving primarily traveling salesmen

c. Aircraft engine factory

d. Large hotel serving primarily out-of-town convention business

Explain your answer.

3.7. The following are local and national employment figures for three industrial sectors. Calculate the location quotients for each industry and state which industries are part of the export base of the local economy.

Industry	Local Employment	National Employment
Automobile assembly	10,000	1,500,000
Legal services	3,500	2,000,000
Alcoholic spirits production and distribution	2,500	400,000
Total all employment	300,000	120,000,000

Inside the City I:
Some Basic Urban Economics

Learning Objectives

After reading this chapter, you should understand:

◆ What determines land rents in a city.

◆ Why and how a freely functioning, competitive land market will lead to land being used at its "highest and best use" (i.e., most productive use).

◆ What determines how big spatially or how dense a city is.

◆ What determines the relative land values at different locations within a city, and the relative growth rate of these values at different locations.

◆ Why different land uses and densities occur at different locations within a city.

$\mathbf{A}$gain we come back to the old cliché, that only three things matter in real estate: location, location, and location. We might say that Chapter 3 dealt with the first level of location in this cliché, the big picture: why cities or other "central places" (such as shopping centers within cities) locate where they do, and why some such places grow more than others. The "places" treated in Chapter 3, however, were essentially dimensionless points on the plain, just dots. In this chapter and the next we will address the second level of location in the cliché, to consider the nature of land use spatial patterns *within* cities.

Land use spatial patterns and dynamics exert tremendous influence on neighborhood property values and on what types of buildings and land uses are feasible and most productive at a given location at a given time. The study of location value we will embark on in this chapter (and continue in the next) is also of crucial importance in linking the space market to the asset market through the development industry, a link that is of vital importance in real estate investment performance. Keep in mind that location value is the major component in land value, and recall from Chapter 1 that land value plays the key role in determining the shape of the long-run supply function, which in turn governs the trend in rents.

A Threshold Concept: Urban Form

The general subject of both this chapter and the next is what is often called **urban form**. This term refers to the physical spatial characteristics of a city.[1] How big is the city spatially? What is its overall density and geographical dimensions? How does this density vary across different parts of the city? What are the patterns of the locations of different land uses, such as residential, commercial, and industrial, within the city? Where do high-income and low income neighborhoods tend to locate? Obviously, urban form, and how this form changes over time, vitally affects land values and rents, and therefore a whole range of real estate business decisions within any city.

4.1 SOME BASIC ECONOMIC PRINCIPLES OF URBAN LAND VALUE AND USE

Land is the most fundamental defining characteristic of real estate. If you want to deepen your understanding of real estate, a good place to start is by considering what determines the value of land.

4.1.1 Location and the Residual Nature of Land Value

Land derives its value from the fact that it is a necessary input, or **factor of production**. The real estate value of land therefore comes from what is known as derived demand: people are willing to pay for land not because of the value land has in and of itself, but because land is necessary to obtain other things that have consumption or production value. Urban land value derives from the fact that land is necessary to construct buildings, and buildings are necessary for most types of production of goods or services, and also directly for some types of consumption, such as housing. What makes one urban land parcel worth more than another is, primarily, location. Indeed, when you are buying a piece of urban land, what you are usually buying primarily is a particular location relative to other points of attraction.

Let's consider a specific example. A factory produces clothing from bolts of cloth by combining inputs from labor, machines, energy, and land. The machines actually produce the articles of clothing from the raw cloth, but labor and energy are needed to operate the machines and move the output. Land is necessary because the machines and people and inventory take up space and need somewhere to locate. Indeed, where the factory is located will affect how profitable the manufacturing operation is because it will determine the costs of getting the raw material (bolts of cloth) to the factory and the finished products (articles of clothing) from the factory to the ultimate points of retail sale. The cost of the labor and energy to operate the machines will also likely be affected by the location.

---

[1] The term *urban spatial structure* is also used to describe this topic.

Now consider all of these four basic types of inputs in the production process, known as production factors: land, labor, capital (i.e., physical capital, such as machines), and raw materials (including energy). All of these factors of production must be paid for by, and will therefore derive their value from, the value of the finished product. In dividing up the value of the finished product among the four factors of production, the defining characteristic of land that differentiates it from the other three factors is that land is fixed in location, even in the long run. If you own a parcel of land, you can never move it. You can never take it away to some other site where it might be able to earn more rent. The three more **mobile factors** have to get paid first, in order to keep them from "running away" if they don't get paid an amount equal to what they could earn elsewhere, something the land cannot do. The gross value of the production on the site, measured by the total revenue earned by the clothing factory, will therefore go first to the mobile inputs. Only what is left over after the mobile factors have been paid the necessary prevailing market costs will be available to the landowner. This is known as the **residual theory of land value**.

Let's consider this theory in our clothing factory example. Suppose the factory earns gross sales revenues of $10 million per year. We can see that the raw materials must be paid for first based on their market values, or else the sellers of those materials simply would not sell to this factory but rather take their goods elsewhere in the market. Let's suppose these raw materials cost $4 million, leaving $6 million of value to be added by the factory. Next, the factory labor has to get paid the prevailing market wage, or else the workers will quit and take jobs elsewhere. Let's suppose the workers (including the factory management team) earn $5 million. This leaves $1 million per year in profit after subtracting the $9 million cost of goods sold and management overhead from the gross revenues.

But in the long run this profit must provide a return on investment to the financial capital that was contributed to establish the factory. In particular, the physical capital—the machines, plant, and equipment (including the building)—must be paid for in the form of return on and return of the financial capital that was invested. Otherwise the financiers and investors who provided this capital will take it back (or anyway in the long run they will not replace it when it wears out). Suppose this cost of built physical capital is $900,000 per year. (You can think of this $900,000 per year as rent for machines that are leased or as an annual mortgage payment to pay off a loan of the financial capital invested in the plant and equipment.) In the long run, all of this total $9,900,000 cost per year must be paid first to these more mobile factors, before the landowner can get her share, which we can see is only $100,000 per year, the "residual" that is left over after the other factors have been paid. This $100,000 is the amount potentially available from the factory operation to pay rent for the land itself, for the location and space that it provides to the production process.[2]

While we have used the example of a clothing factory, it should be easy to see that we could have picked any other type of factory. Indeed, any type of urban land use can be seen as producing some output of goods or services of value, by combining some more mobile inputs with that of land (space and location). For example, a corporate

---

[2]How do the owners of the factory get their profits? They have not really been left out of the model. The factory owners would typically either be owners of the machines and/or the land, or they can be viewed as providing some of the labor, in the form of the managerial and entrepreneurship services necessary to run the business. Apart from their possible role as landowners, the factory owners are therefore part of the mobile factors of production that must be paid prior to the landowner, in the long run, or they will take their contributions elsewhere.

headquarters office provides executive and control services for the rest of the corporation, a law office provides legal services for its clients, a shopping mall provides a convenient or stimulating environment for people to buy goods they need, and a house or apartment provides shelter and a conducive environment for the abode of a household.

The land is last in line to get paid among the inputs because it is "trapped"; it cannot go elsewhere. Of course the residual theory of land value is a simplified model. The real world is a bit more complicated. But this model captures most of the essence of reality, at least in the long run, in a world where exchange of ownership is governed by free markets.

It is important to keep in mind that there is a flip side of the coin regarding the residual basis of land value. Land may get only, but it also gets *all of*, the residual after the mobile factors have been paid their market values. In a well-functioning market system, competition among providers of the mobile factors of production ensures that no such factor need be paid more than its market value. This means that, at least in the long run, land can receive as rents all of any increase in profit that would occur, either from an increase in the market value of production (holding the market values of the mobile input factors constant) or from a decrease in the cost of the mobile factors (holding the value of the output constant).

For example, if the factory in our previous example could sell its clothing output for $11 million instead of $10 million and the mobile factor costs remained the same, the land could claim $1,100,000 per year. The same would occur if the costs of the mobile factors could be reduced to $8,900,000 instead of $9,900,000, holding the output value at $10,000,000.

How would the landlord "capture" the extra profit from the tenant? In the long run (which is what we are talking about here), the tenant's lease would expire, and the present tenant would then be in competition with other potential tenants for the land. That competition would lead the potential tenants to bid up their offered land rent to a level at which the tenants will just be making sufficient profit for themselves, that is, just covering their own costs including normal profits. All other remaining revenues from production on the site would be included in the land rent offer.[3]

4.1.2 Competition, Equilibrium, and Highest and Best Use

In a well-functioning land market competition exists both among providers of the mobile factors of production and also among landowners. While each parcel of land is unique to some extent, usually a number of parcels are similar enough that they could substitute well for one another for the purposes of most potential users. So there is competition in the land market among alternative sites. Similarly, while each potential land user may be unique in some respects, usually a number of potential users provide competition on the other side of the market as well. Of course, the long-lived nature of buildings means that land uses have limited flexibility to change quickly, but in the long run land use can and does change, so that the urban form we observe does tend to reflect basic economic forces and values.

---

[3] The picture presented here is simplified by the assumption of "perfect competition." That is, we are assuming that there are sufficient numbers of potential tenants for the land competing with each other so that they bid away any excess profit. A more realistic rule of thumb that is often applied in the practice of valuing specific land parcels is to say that the land value is determined by the "second best" developer of the land. The very best developer (or tenant, in the present model) for the land may have unique abilities to make profitable use of the site. This uniqueness could allow the very best user to capture and retain for themselves much or all of the value they add above the "second best" use for the site.

Exhibit 4-1 Highest and
Best Use Example

	Site 1		Site 2	
	Clothing Factory	Grocery Store	Clothing Factory	Grocery Store
Revenues	$10,000,000	$4,600,000	$10,000,000	$5,000,000
Mobile Factor Costs	9,900,000	4,550,000	9,990,000	4,625,000
Residual (Land Rent)	100,000	50,000	10,000	375,000

Among the most powerful of economic forces is the tendency of markets to move toward equilibrium between supply and demand. A characteristic condition of equilibrium in a well-functioning competitive market is that no participant on either side of the market can be made better off by a change away from the equilibrium without making someone else worse off. In other words, any benefits to gainers from a change away from the equilibrium would not be able to offset the losses to the losers from that change. This condition is known as Pareto optimality. In the case of the land market, such equilibrium will be reflected in the fact that each landowner will rent to the user who is willing to pay the highest rent for the land. Otherwise, at least in the long run, the dissatisfied landowners would kick out their current users and rent or sell to those who are willing and able to pay more. This maximizes the total rent earned by all the land (thereby maximizing the productivity of the society). Equivalently, from the perspective of the other side of the market, equilibrium is characterized by the condition that no land user would rather be located at a different place, given the cost or rent they would have to pay for another location. Otherwise, they would simply move to that other place and pay the rent charged there.[4]

Because of its importance, let us consider a bit more concretely what the concept of equilibrium in the land market means, by extending our previous example of the clothing factory. Suppose there are two alternative potential uses for the site in question, either the clothing factory or a grocery store. Let us further suppose that there are two possible different locations, the one previously described and an alternative site located a bit closer to most residences in the neighborhood but a bit farther from the main interstate highways. Exhibit 4-1 summarizes the revenues and mobile factor costs for each use at each site.

As described previously, the clothing factory at site 1 can earn revenues of $10 million per year, with mobile factor costs of $9.9 million, implying that the clothing factory could pay $100,000 per year in rent to the landowner at site 1. The same factory at site 2 could still earn $10 million in revenue, but would face $90,000 in additional transport costs getting the raw material to the factory and shipping out the finished product, due to the greater distance from interstate highway access. The result is that, located at site 2, the clothing factory would have only $10,000 residual left over with which to pay land rent.

The grocery store faces a somewhat different situation. While it too would experience lower transport costs by locating at site 1, it would be less conveniently located to

[4]Once again, we are simplifying by describing "perfect markets." Pareto optimality in land markets requires not only perfect competition on both sides, but also a lack of locational externalities, also known as spillover effects. Recall from Chapter 3 that externalities occur when what is done on one land parcel affects the value of adjacent or nearby land parcels. Such spillover effects can be either positive or negative. The existence of spillover effects in the real world is the major reason for land use control and regulation by communal authorities, such as zoning ordinances enacted by local governments.

serve its retail customers in the residential neighborhood, and so would have to discount its prices and therefore would earn less revenue at site 1. Indeed, the loss in revenue more than offsets the delivery cost reduction for the grocery store. At site 1 the grocery store would earn revenues of $4.6 million with mobile factor costs (including delivery costs for receiving its merchandise) of $4.55 million, leaving only $50,000 residual available to pay rent. At site 2 the grocery store would earn $5 million in revenues, with $4.625 million mobile factor costs, leaving $375,000 left over to pay land rent.

The grocery store can pay more than the clothing factory for site 2 ($375,000 vs. $10,000 annual rent), while the clothing factory can pay more for site 1 ($100,000 vs. $50,000 annual rent). In the long run both the factory and the store could move, and both the site 1 owner and the site 2 owner could remove any tenant (and redevelop the site). Therefore, only one result can be consistent with long-run equilibrium in the land market: the factory must locate at site 1 and the store at site 2.

The equilibrium described in this example results in each location being used at its **highest and best use (HBU)**. This means that each site is used in the way that is most productive for that location. Note that productivity in this sense is represented by the *net* difference between the value of what is produced on the site and the costs of the mobile factors of production, that is, the land residual as we have defined it. Thus, equilibrium in the land market tends to result in land parcels being used at their highest and best use in the long run.[5]

4.1.3 Role of Transport Costs: The Bid-Rent Curve

From the preceding section you can see that land rent (and hence land value) differs from one place to another because the HBU residual value differs from one place to another. And the HBU residual value differs from one place to another primarily as a result of differences in transportation costs. When the transportation costs faced by the users of the site are lower, the residual value is higher, other things being equal. For example, the clothing factory could make more profit located nearer to the highway, so the delivery cost of both its inputs and outputs were lower. The grocery store could make more profit located nearer its customers, who then would not incur as much transportation costs getting to and from the store.

To understand the importance of transport costs, you must conceptualize these costs broadly. Transport costs include the costs of moving both inputs and outputs, costs borne both directly by the sellers and indirectly by the buyers. Of particular importance for the value of nonindustrial land, transport cost is not limited to the direct monetary outlay for transportation, such as gasoline cost. For passenger transportation, travel *time* is usually the most important component of transport cost. In our grocery store example, it is likely not gasoline cost, but rather the value of the time wasted in travel to and from the store, the inconvenience of shoppers having to travel farther, that would force the store to discount its prices at site 1. The implication is that land market equilibrium, the highest and best use of land, will be characterized by the *minimization of aggregate transportation costs* for the society as a whole.

The role of transport costs in determining HBU and land value leads to a key concept in classical urban economics, the **bid-rent curve** (or **bid-rent function**).

---

[5] The social desirability of preserving undeveloped some land parcels can be represented in this model by recognizing that some parcels may have, due to their aesthetic or environmental qualities, a *direct* demand value (i.e., value in "consumption" as undeveloped land) exceeding any *derived* demand value in production, which they would have under development.

The bid-rent is the maximum rent that a potential user would "bid," or be willing to pay, for a site or location. This bid-rent is essentially the same thing as the residual value discussed previously. Each potential user of land has a bid-rent curve (or function), which relates the user's bid-rent to the location of the land site, showing in particular how the bid-rent changes as a function of the user's distance from some **central point**. The central point is the point at which the **transportation costs are minimized** for that use, the point at which the bid-rent or residual value is maximized.

Each potential land use has its own bid-rent function. We might imagine the entrance to a nearby interstate highway as being the central point for the clothing factory, because the highway reduces travel time and cost for its inputs and outputs. If site 1 is one mile from this highway entrance and site 2 is four miles from it, then the value of the bid-rent function for the clothing factory is $100,000 at one mile, and $10,000 at four miles from this central point. The relevant central point for the grocery store would be different, perhaps the intersection of two arterial streets at the center of the residential neighborhood it serves. Suppose site 2 is at this intersection and site 1 is three miles from it. The grocery store's bid-rent function would be valued at $375,000 at site 2 and $50,000 at site 1.

Graphically, a bid-rent function is depicted on a chart with the vertical axis located at the central point and the horizontal axis representing distance from that point. At the central point transportation costs are minimized, and the bid-rent is therefore maximized. The amount of the bid-rent at the central point (the height of the intercept on the vertical axis in the graph) depends on the inherent productivity or value of the land use when transportation costs are minimized. Land uses that are more productive (when transport costs are minimized) will have higher bid-rents at the central point. As you move away from the central point, the bid-rent falls as the transportation costs rise due to the less central location. The rate at which the bid-rent falls, the slope of the bid-rent function, depends on the magnitude of transportation costs in the production process of the given land use, and on how sensitive these transportation costs are to distance from the central point. Land uses that are more sensitive to transport costs will have bid-rent curves with steeper slopes, bid-rents falling more quickly with distance from the central point.

This is depicted in Exhibit 4-2, which shows the bid-rent function for three different land uses, labeled A, B, and C. Use A has the greatest productivity when transportation costs are minimized, and so has a higher bid-rent at the central point. Use C has the lowest productivity in general, but also the least sensitivity to transport

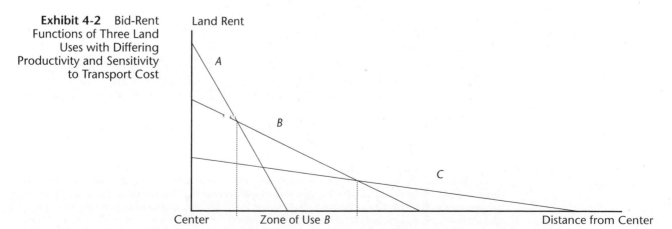

Exhibit 4-2 Bid-Rent Functions of Three Land Uses with Differing Productivity and Sensitivity to Transport Cost

costs, and so has the "shallowest" bid-rent function. Use *B* is between the other two in both respects. The result is that, *in equilibrium* in the land market, assuming all three uses have the same central point, use *A* will prevail closest to that center, being able to outbid the other uses, followed by use *B* a bit farther out from the center, followed by use *C* farthest out.

4.1.4 Summary of Basic Urban Land Value and Land Use Principles

The preceding section presented several of the basic economic principles of land value and use determination. Because the underlying demand for land is a derived demand, and other more mobile factors are required to produce value from land, land value is based on the residual available after the other factors (labor, capital, energy, etc.) have been paid their going market rates. This residual is strongly influenced by transportation costs, which in turn are strongly influenced by location, making land value largely a function of location. Different types of land uses have different productivities, different sensitivities to transportation costs, and different relevant geographical central points, that is, locations where their relevant transportation costs would be minimized. Therefore, different land uses have different residual values, or bid-rents they would be willing and able to pay for any given site. In long-run equilibrium in a well-functioning, competitive land market (when, in principle, even built structures can be changed through the development or redevelopment process), each land site will be used for its highest and best use, the use that can pay the highest bid-rent. This will maximize the aggregate land value (residual value) and minimize the aggregate transportation costs of the society.

4.2 CLASSIC MONOCENTRIC CITY MODEL

The basic economic principles and concepts regarding land value and use described in the previous section have been combined in a very simple and elegant model of urban form known as the **monocentric city**. While this model greatly simplifies and abstracts from the complicated reality of modern cities, it captures enough of the essence to offer useful insights. Indeed, the monocentric model is a classic example of how theory, by simplifying reality, reveals important insights into the nature of that reality.[6]

In the monocentric city model only one central point exists in the whole city, and this central point applies to all potential uses of the land. Indeed, in the simplest version of the model, which we will consider here, there is only one type of land use in the city, housing. The simple monocentric city is a circle of a certain radius extending out from the central point. The central point might be thought of as representing the downtown or central business district (CBD), to which all the households

---

[6] The following discussion draws heavily from DiPasquale and Wheaton (1996), to which the reader is recommended for a more detailed and in-depth treatment of this topic. In general, the monocentric city model, as well as much of the location theory described in the previous section, has its origins in the theories developed by German economist Johann Von Thunen early in the 19th century. While Von Thunen focused on an agricultural state, much more recent extensions of the city model (of which the monocentric model described here is only a very simple version) have been attributed to such American economists as William Alonso, Edwin Mills, Richard Muth, and Dennis Capozza. (See the references and additional reading for Part II for some specific references.)

must commute every day to produce some good that enables them to earn the income they must use to meet their housing as well as all their other consumption needs. From this income they also must pay the transportation costs for their daily commute. These transportation costs, of course, are a function of the distance of their houses from the CBD.

4.2.1 Circlopolis, the Quintessential Monocentric City

To make this model a bit more concrete, let us quantify a stylized example city we will call Circlopolis, which exists in the land of Agricolia. Outside the city, the land is farmed; inside the city, all land is residential, built to a density of 2 persons per acre, or 1,280 per square mile. The metropolitan population of Circlopolis is 1 million, which gives Circlopolis an area of 1,000,000/1,280, or 781 square miles. This determines the **radius to the urban boundary**, recalling that the formula for the area of a circle is π times the radius squared, so the radius is the square root of the area divided by π, or in this case about 16 miles.

Now consider the annual rent for housing at the edge of the city, 16 miles from the center at the boundary between the urban and agricultural land use. In order to induce a farmer to sell his land to enable it to be converted from agricultural production to urban housing, you must pay the farmer the opportunity value of the land in its agricultural use. This would be the agricultural use residual (bid-rent) for the land, equal to the net profit per acre from agricultural production after all the mobile factors have been paid. Suppose this **agricultural rent** is $500 per acre per year. In addition, you must pay the annualized cost of building a house. Suppose there is one resident per house, and houses cost $50,000 to build, which can be paid for by a permanent mortgage at 10% per year, giving an annual **construction cost rent** of $5,000 per house. With two houses per acre, that makes the total annual housing rent per acre at the city edge $10,500, consisting of $10,000 to pay for the construction and $500 to pay for lost agricultural rent.

How does this land rent change as we move in from the urban boundary toward the city center? The residents of houses at more central locations will not have to pay as much in commuting costs, so they will be able to pay more rent for housing and still maintain the same overall level of welfare. In fact, the *housing rent must rise as we approach the center at exactly the rate that the transportation costs fall*. This condition is required by equilibrium.

To see this, suppose this condition did not hold. Suppose, for example, that the housing rent rose by less than the decrease in transportation cost as you moved toward the center. Then residents living closer to the center would be better off than those living farther out. This would cause everybody to want to move closer to the center. Demand would then outstrip supply for more central locations, while houses near the periphery would go searching for residents. Competition among residents bidding for centrally located lots, and among landlords owning peripheral lots trying to find tenants, would force the rent for the more centrally located lots up and the rents for the peripheral lots down until the relative levels were such that everybody is equally well off, considering both their housing rents and their commuting costs. A symmetrical argument would apply if housing rents rose more than the decrease in transportation costs as one moved closer to the center. In that case everyone would want to live farther out, bidding up the rents there until the incentive for peripheral houses was eliminated. In equilibrium, therefore, the rents must be such that the total of housing and commuting costs is the same across all distances from the center.

This tells us that the bid-rent curve for housing in Circlopolis must have a slope equal to the transportation cost per mile, per acre. This slope is known as the **rent gradient**. It tells you how much the equilibrium land rent per acre declines per mile of additional distance from the center of the city. *The rent gradient equals the transportation cost per mile per person times the number of people per acre.*

Suppose in Circlopolis the transportation cost per person is $250 per year, per mile of distance from the CBD (round-trip commuting cost). Then with two inhabitants per acre, the rent gradient must be $500 per mile. Housing located one mile from the urban boundary will rent for $250 more per year than housing on the boundary, or $500 more per acre of land. By the time we get to the center of the city, 16 miles from the edge, where there is no transportation cost, the housing rent will be $4,000 more per house (or per person), or $8,000 more per acre, than it is at the periphery. So the total land rent per year at the center will be some $18,500 per year, including $500 in agricultural opportunity cost rent, $10,000 in construction cost rent, and $8,000 in **location rent**. Note that the location rent per acre at the center exactly equals the transportation cost per acre at the periphery.

Now that we know the housing and transport costs for the inhabitants of Circlopolis, we can see how they are using their income. Suppose they have annual incomes of $50,000 each. They are spending $9,250 each on the combination of housing and transportation. (Recall that there are two persons in the form of two single-individual households per acre.) So they must each be spending $40,750 per year on "other consumption" besides housing and transportation.[7] We have "backed into" this observation about other consumption expenditure, but in reality the direction of causality may go both ways in the long run. How much the Circlopolites want to spend on other consumption (given their income level) also determines how much they have available to spend on housing and transportation, and this, in turn, will in the long run determine the size and density of Circlopolis. This can explain why we see such different densities in cities in different countries, as income levels and culturally based preferences for different types of housing differ widely across countries.

The simple monocentric city model represented by Circlopolis in the land of Agricolia is depicted graphically in Exhibit 4-3. The exhibit depicts a cross-section of property rents from the agricultural hinterland just beyond the urban boundary through the center of the city.

4.2.2 Using the Model: Some Principles about How Rents and City Size Change

The usefulness of the monocentric city model is that it reduces a very complex phenomenon, a city, down to a simple interaction among a few basic economic forces. This allows us to see easily what causes some of the essential features of the urban form. This in turn enables us to examine how rents and urban form may be affected by changes that can happen over time in an economy or society, such as growth in population or income, or changes in transport costs. These changes can have very important effects on real estate opportunities. So let us now use the monocentric city model to examine these effects in our Circlopolis example by changing one variable at a time and seeing how this affects the land rents and urban form variables within the model.

[7]In the magical city of Circlopolis there are no taxes!

Exhibit 4-3 Cross-Section of Land Rents in Circlopolis and Agricolia

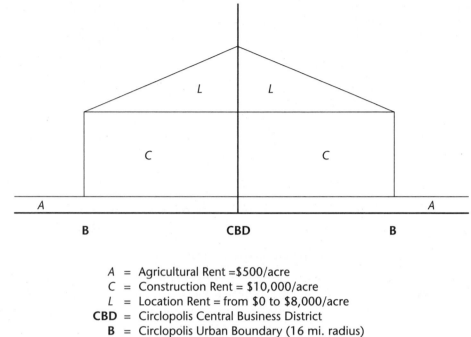

A = Agricultural Rent = $500/acre
C = Construction Rent = $10,000/acre
L = Location Rent = from $0 to $8,000/acre
CBD = Circlopolis Central Business District
B = Circlopolis Urban Boundary (16 mi. radius)

Population. We begin by examining the effect of an increase in the population of Circlopolis, holding density and transportation cost per mile constant. With density constant, the area of the city, and hence the radius, must expand. In particular, for every percent increase in population the area must increase by an equal percent (for constant density), and the radius must increase by about half that percent.[8] The housing rent at the new periphery must equal the construction cost rent plus the agricultural rent, based on the same arguments as before, and these have not changed. Likewise, the rent gradient as we move in from the new periphery must still be the same $500 per mile (because transport cost and density are the same as before), again based on the same equilibrium argument. So this means that population increase, holding density and other prices constant, must increase rents all over Circlopolis. This is depicted in Exhibit 4-4.

We can summarize the analysis up to now in an important principle:

Principle 1:
Other things being equal, larger cities will have higher average rents.

This basic principle, derived from such a simple model of urban form and land values, is no doubt a major reason that land prices, rents, and housing costs are so much higher in the nation's largest cities, such as New York, Chicago, Los Angeles,

---

[8] If the area of the circle increases by p percent (that is, $AREA_{NEW}/AREA_{OLD} = 1 + p$), then

$$\frac{RADIUS_{NEW}}{RADIUS_{OLD}} = \frac{\sqrt{AREA_{NEW}/\pi}}{\sqrt{AREA_{OLD}/\pi}} = \sqrt{1+p} \approx 1 + p/2$$

for relatively small values of p. For example, if $p = 10\%$, then the exact value of $\sqrt{1.1} - 1$ is 4.9%.

Exhibit 4-4 Effect of Population Growth with Density and Transport Cost Constant

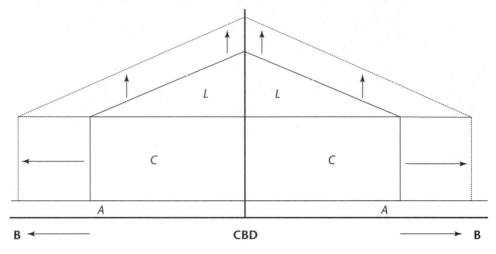

and San Francisco. (For example, in 1990 the median house price in San Francisco was $258,000, while in Cincinnati it was $71,000.)

Perhaps this size principle seems intuitively obvious. But the monocentric city model allows you to deepen your understanding of why larger cities have higher rents. In particular, notice what caused the higher rents when we considered the growth in population in Circlopolis. In our simple model we were holding density constant. Thus, land rents (per acre of land) would tend to be higher in larger cities even if such cities were no denser than smaller cities. This suggests that if larger cities are to keep rents per housing unit at the same level as those in smaller cities, then some combination of higher density and/or lower construction cost must prevail in larger cities. This, in turn, means that, holding rent per housing unit constant across cities of different sizes, larger cities must be characterized by some combination of greater density and/or smaller housing units. The 500-square-foot efficiency apartment in Manhattan, stacked 40 on top of each other, might rent for the same as a 1,000 square-foot garden apartment in central Atlanta.

In fact, we can say more than this. We can see that what caused the higher rents in the population example was *not* the population per se, or even the area of the city, but the *length of the radius*, the distance of the urban boundary from the CBD. The rent gradient is fixed based on transportation costs and density. The rent at the urban boundary is fixed based on the agricultural opportunity cost and the building construction cost. Therefore, what governs the change in the average rent is the change in the distance each point finds itself from the urban boundary.

This is important because, for a given population and density, the radius of the city (i.e., the distance from the CBD to the urban edge) must be greater if the city cannot avail itself of an entire 360-degree arc. In reality, geographic constraints on the urban arc are quite common, as for example with a city on a coastline or peninsula. Most of the largest U.S. cities are on coasts or are cut by waterways or mountain ranges that effectively prevent the use of a large proportion of the arc around the CBD. This no doubt extends the radius of cities such as New York, Chicago, Los Angeles, and San Francisco, further adding to their tendency to support high rents.[9]

---

[9] When the arc around which a city can expand is limited by, say, bodies of water or mountain ranges, the same total area must fit into a fraction of a circle. The radius equals $\sqrt{A/(\pi F)}$, where A is the area and F is the fraction (less than or equal to 1) of the full 360° arc around the CBD that can be used for growth.

It is also interesting to note that if incomes were constant across cities of different sizes, then inhabitants of larger cities would either have to consume less housing (live in smaller houses and/or have less land per house) or spend more on transport costs, compared to residents of smaller cities. Either way, inhabitants of larger cities would have less income left over for other consumption, and therefore less economic welfare than inhabitants of smaller cities. Over time, such an imbalance in economic welfare between citizens of smaller and larger cities would not be tenable. People would migrate from larger to smaller cities, *unless the larger cities offered higher incomes*, on average. But this is exactly what happens in the real world. Larger cities do tend to have higher average per capita incomes than smaller cities. Put the other way around, cities that are able to offer higher incomes tend to attract migration and over time grow larger in population relative to other cities, until an equilibrium across cities is reached. Although we residents of medium-size midwestern cities might not like to admit it, the average resident of New York or Los Angeles is in fact more productive than the average resident of Cincinnati or Cleveland.[10]

If we consider population changes within one city over time, then the monocentric city model can give some insight into how much, or how fast, rents may change over time, and how such changes may differ in different parts of the city. For example, it is not uncommon for a metropolitan area to increase 10% in population over a 10-year period, or indeed over a 5-year period in many Sunbelt cities. Holding density constant as before, such a population increase will result in approximately a 5% increase in the urban radius, from 16 miles to 16.8 miles in our Circlopolis example. All locations now have 0.8 mile additional location rent, or an increase in rent of $400 per acre per year.[11] Notice that the increase in rent is constant across all the preexisting points in the city, but the base rent was higher for more centrally located points. This implies that the *percentage* increase in rent due to urban growth will be greater closer to the periphery of the metropolitan area. For example, at the old boundary the rent grows from $10,500 per acre to $10,900 per acre, a 3.8% increase. At the center the increase from $18,500 to $18,900 is only 2.2%.

Now suppose that instead of holding density constant we held the area of the city constant, as might occur through regulatory or geographic constraints on land use (zoning or "green belts," islands or mountains, for example). Not surprisingly, the model reveals that population growth would still result in higher land rents. But in this case the reason is different. The radius is fixed, so the reason for the higher location rents cannot be greater distance from the urban edge. However, with the

---

This is consistent with our point in Chapter 1 that a rising long-run marginal cost curve (increasing development costs including land cost), implying increasing real rents in equilibrium in the space market, would tend to occur in areas where land supply is constrained in the face of growing demand. Growing demand may be thought of as population growth in the present example. Keep in mind that the radius is the distance from the CBD to the edge of the developed urban area, for example, from Manhattan north up the Hudson Valley.

[10] Hey, we know they're not smarter than us. They must just be taking advantage of the agglomeration and scale economies we talked about in Chapter 3, and of all the capital that's accumulated in those big cities. And of course, small town residents would all agree that big city dwellers are far too "workaholic."

[11] Recall that the additional rent occurs because there are more total people now in the city competing for (i.e., bidding for) the locations within the city, including some people who are farther from the center than anybody used to be when the periphery was not as far out. In order for all these competing citizens to be indifferent between their present location and any other location (the characteristic of equilibrium), rents must settle at a level so that the people at the periphery are satisfied to live that far out considering the amount of location rent they are saving by doing so.

Exhibit 4-5   Effect of
Population Growth
with Area Constant

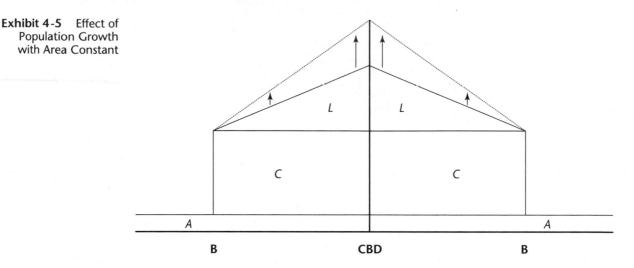

radius fixed and the population growing, the density must increase. Now recall that the land rent gradient in equilibrium must equal the difference in transportation cost per mile, *per acre.* We are holding the transportation cost *per person* constant, but with more persons living per acre, the transportation costs per acre must increase. So the rent gradient would increase. For example, if Circlopolis's population increased by 50% to 1,500,000, there would be three inhabitants per acre instead of two, and this would increase the rent gradient from $500 per mile to $750 per mile. The rent at the urban boundary would still be the same, but land rent everywhere else would increase due to the increased location premium. The new peak rent at the center would be $22,500 (including $12,000 per year of location rent) instead of the old center rent of $18,500 (a 22% increase). This is depicted in Exhibit 4-5.[12]

Thus, while population growth will always tend to increase land rents in a city, *how* the city grows will affect the nature and geographic distribution of those increases. This can be expressed in a second basic principle derived from the monocentric city model:

Principle 2:
If a city grows by increasing area rather than density, property rent growth will be relatively greater closer to the periphery; but if a city grows by increasing density instead of area, property rent growth will be relatively greater the closer to the center of the city.

Transport Costs.   Population growth is not the only basic phenomenon that typically affects the modern city. A second important focus to consider is what would happen as a result of a reduction in transport costs per person per mile, holding population and income constant. This could occur, for example, through improvements in transportation technology or infrastructure. In fact, the 20th century witnessed almost continual such improvements. It is likely that such improvements will continue well into the 21st century, especially if one considers the partial substitutability between telecommunications

---

[12]Note, however, that in this example the rent *per person* would actually decline in the center, from $18,500/2 = $9,250/year, to $22,500/3 = $7,500/year. This is because we are holding construction cost constant per acre (e.g., 1.5 persons per room instead of 1.0).

and transportation.[13] The advent of cell phones, laptop PCs, the Internet, and other telecommunications developments will allow more flexible location and timing of work and shopping activity, which effectively reduces transport costs. Technological improvements in the automobile and mass transit, including greater fuel efficiency, greater safety and reliability, more efficient traffic control, and a more pleasant or productive travel environment (such as is provided by vehicle air-conditioning, stereo sound systems, cell phones, etc.) all act to effectively reduce transport costs.[14]

We know that a reduction in transport costs per person per mile will reduce the rent gradient.[15] This can have various effects on land values and urban form. The two extreme alternatives are depicted in Exhibits 4-6 and 4-7. In the first case (4-6), the residents of Circlopolis have elected to spend at least some of the transport cost savings on purchasing more urban land. Such urban-density-reducing behavior might be reflected in the purchase of houses with larger lots farther out in the countryside, or neighborhoods with more parkland and golf courses, or even shopping centers with more parking spaces, for example. Such a density-reducing result of transport improvements would have the effect of increasing land rents near the periphery and reducing land rents at the center.

Indeed, the pure effect of a density reduction of the city, even without a reduction in transport costs, is to reduce the *absolute* land rents in the center of the city.[16] Transport cost reduction will only magnify this reduction.

The second alternative possible effect of transport improvements occurs if the inhabitants of Circlopolis elect to keep their same level of residential density, that is, not to expand the spatial area of the city in spite of the transportation improvements. This would tend to happen only in cities that face severe physical or governmental constraints on spatial expansion (or perhaps in cultures where there is a positive preference for urban residential density, as might be the case in some Mediterranean countries, for example). Then the transport cost reduction causes land rents to decline everywhere in the city (except on the very periphery). But even in this case rents decline more for locations closer to the center of the city, as depicted in Exhibit 4-7.

It may seem counterintuitive that a technological improvement that increases the overall welfare and productivity of society, namely transport cost reduction, would

[13] Even in the absence of any reduction in transport cost per person-mile of movement, telecommunications and computing developments may allow a reduction in the number of commuting or shopping trips per capita per year, for example, by working at home or shopping on the Internet. This reduces transport costs per acre, at a given density and given distance from the central node. Transport cost per acre is what affects the land rent gradient.

[14] As noted previously, we need to think of transport costs as not merely the monetary outlay for travel, but also all forms of "disutility" and inconvenience associated with travel. Even if average speeds do not increase (and travel time therefore does not decrease per mile), transport cost may fall if the disutility of the travel time decreases as a result of added comfort, productivity, or utility during the time traveling.

[15] Recall that the rent gradient is determined as the transport cost per mile per person times the density, and it would not make sense for transport cost reductions to increase the urban density. Therefore, transport cost reductions must reduce the rent gradient.

[16] This is because the location rent at the center of the city equals the rent gradient times the radius, and the rent gradient equals the transport cost per capita times the density. Thus, the rent gradient is directly proportional to the density, which in turn is inversely proportional to the area of the city. But the area of the city is not directly proportional to the radius, but rather to the *square* of the radius. Therefore, a decrease in density holding all else constant will result in a less-than-proportional increase in city radius, but a fully proportional reduction in rent gradient. For example, if density (and therefore rent gradient) were reduced by half, the radius would only increase by a factor proportional to the square root of two. Location rent at the center would be $\sqrt{2}/2$ times the previous location rent.

Exhibit 4-6 Effect of Transport Cost Reduction Savings Applied to Greater Purchase of Land

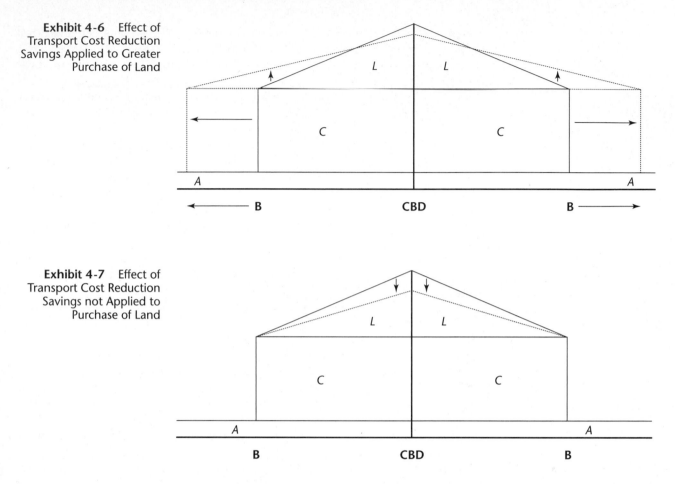

Exhibit 4-7 Effect of Transport Cost Reduction Savings not Applied to Purchase of Land

result in an absolute *decrease* in total aggregate land value in the city, which is what is implied by the real rent reduction possibility in the spatially constrained case depicted in Exhibit 4-7. To understand this, keep in mind that the value of urban land inside the urban boundary is due in part to its "location premium." This premium only exists because of each location's ability to save transport costs. As improved transport technology or infrastructure reduces those costs, the value of this savings is reduced. Moreover, if the inhabitants choose not to spend the transport cost savings on using more land, then the only way those savings can increase welfare is by reducing land rents and thereby increasing real productivity in the city and/or making more income available to the city's inhabitants for the purchase of other goods and services.[17] So it is possible, at least in principle, for transport cost improvements to reduce absolutely the aggregate value of all the land in the city, though such a result would probably be associated only with rather severe external constraints, such as no population increase or spatial expansion of the city.

---

[17]Note that increased productivity or living standards in Circlopolis would naturally tend to draw more population to the city in the long run (from other cities or rural areas, unless they too were experiencing similar increases), which might then allow rents to rise as in the case displayed in Exhibit 4-5. Our assumption of constant population is made for analytical convenience to observe the pure or direct effect of transport cost improvement.

More broadly, transport cost reductions reduce the value of geographic centrality of location, making all locations more equal. Even if this results in an expansion of the urban area, this greater equality across locations must reduce the value of more central locations, at least relatively speaking.

This leads to a third important principle derived from the monocentric city model:

Principle 3:
Declining transport costs (per person, per mile) holding population and income constant, will always reduce the absolute *value of land rent in the center of the city, and always increase the* relative *value of land rent near the periphery of the metro area; the effect on the* absolute *land rent near the periphery is generally ambiguous, depending on changes in density.*

This third principle can probably go a long way to explaining why we have not seen much increase in real rents over time in most U.S. cities during the 20th century in spite of tremendous population and income growth. It may clarify especially how rents have typically declined in real (inflation-adjusted) terms in the central parts of many cities throughout the last half of the 20th century, including in the traditional CBDs.[18]

Income. The third and final phenomenon to examine is income growth, holding population constant. Income growth is more pervasive than population growth, as some cities are not growing in population, but per capita incomes have increased virtually everywhere and are likely to continue to do so. The effect of income growth is more complicated to examine because people can elect to spend their additional income in various ways, and income growth can have secondary effects on transport costs.

Normally, we would expect that people would elect to spend at least some of any additional income on purchasing more urban land (such as houses on larger lots, neighborhoods with more parkland and golf courses, more houses per capita—that is, smaller households due to people living on their own more, etc.). Thus, a rise in incomes would spread the city out spatially, reducing its density and thereby decreasing its rent gradient. This would have the effect of increasing land rents near the periphery and reducing them at the center, as discussed in the case of transport improvements shown in Exhibit 4-6.

This gradient-decreasing, city-expanding result of income growth would be offset at least to some extent, however, by the indirect effect that higher incomes have on per capita transport costs. Recall that a major component of urban transport cost is the value of people's time wasted in traveling or commuting. This value per hour or per mile of travel is normally a positive function of per capita income. (Higher-income individuals are able and willing to pay more to save travel time, because their opportunity cost of wasted time, in terms of forgone income, is greater, as is their ability to pay for leisure time.) So this indirect effect of income growth will (if density were held constant) act to steepen the rent gradient, thereby offsetting at least to some extent the previously noted gradient-decreasing effect of a rise in incomes.

---

[18] We noted in Chapter 1 that the LRMC (development cost, including land cost) curve in most U.S. cities appears to be only slightly upward-sloping, if at all, as evidenced by a lack of significant increase in real rents over time. Of course, many other factors are involved in real cities, including social and political considerations not contemplated in the monocentric city model.

Normally we would expect at least some expansion in city area (hence, reduction in density) to result from income growth. However, if there are severe constraints on the ability of the city area to expand, then the transport cost effect of income growth would dominate. This would result in a steeper rent gradient and greater percentage increases in land rent nearer to the center of the city. This has probably not occurred in most U.S. cities, but may have been a noticeable phenomenon in some other countries.

We can summarize this income effect in a fourth principle:

Principle 4:
Increasing real income per capita (holding population constant) will tend to decrease rent gradients, with a possible result of absolute reductions in land rent at the center of the city, although a secondary transport cost increase effect of higher incomes may mitigate this result or even reverse it, especially if the spatial expansion of the city is constrained.

4.2.3 Summarizing the Monocentric Model

Although greatly simplified, the monocentric model of urban form we have examined here has clarified some basic and very important points about location rents in cities. Other things being equal, larger populations, or geographic constraints on the arc of growth which add to the radius of the city, will be associated with higher land rents. This in turn will require the city's inhabitants to spend larger amounts on the combination of transportation and housing costs, or else accept smaller houses in denser neighborhoods. In general, equilibrium among cities (reflecting the results of people's free ability to move among cities) means that larger cities in a country must be characterized by higher average per capita income levels for their citizens. Transportation improvements will tend to reduce the value of geographic centrality of location, tending to equalize land values throughout the city. Income increases have a more ambiguous effect, depending on how spatially constrained the city is and on the degree to which income increases result indirectly in an increase in transport cost.

Circlopolis may seem unrealistically simple. Yet the principles of location value it demonstrates are realistic and all-pervading. Students often criticize academic theories as being excessively simplified, too abstractly removed from the real world. But the beauty of a good academic theory lies precisely in its simplicity, in its ability to eliminate aspects of reality that are less important to the subject at hand, so that the aspects of reality that are more important can be clearly seen, and thereby understood. This is why the monocentric model—indeed, the monocentric model in its simplest form as presented here—holds such enduring value.

Almost everywhere in real estate there are "centers" and "peripheries." For a given real estate decision, the center that matters (and the associated periphery) may not be the downtown of a metropolis. The relevant center for an apartment development expected to house university students may be the location of the university campus. The relevant center for the clothing factory in our previous example might be a highway node. The point is, you can apply the monocentric model in a variety of ways to obtain useful insights.

As an example, consider the very practical question of whether real rents for commercial properties will tend to increase over time in a growing U.S. city (or the related question of whether commercial property values will tend to grow faster or slower in the long run than single-family home values). At first glance, many people would say yes, commercial rents should grow in a growing city. But the monocentric city model should give you pause before answering so quickly. Commercial property tends to be located at or near central locations. We have seen in the monocentric city model two major conditions that can cause absolute real location rent levels to decline in central areas: transport improvements or (possibly) growth in real per capita income. If these phenomena dominate over the pure population growth effect, location rents in central areas, such as where most commercial buildings are built, could decline in absolute terms over the long run (after adjusting for inflation), even in a growing city. On the other hand, the monocentric model suggests that low-density housing values might tend to grow over time, at least the land value component of their values, even in cities that are not growing in population. This is because low-density housing tends to locate near the periphery, where the monocentric model suggests location values tend to rise over time in a spatially expanding city.

4.3 CHAPTER SUMMARY

This chapter presented the basic determinants of urban form, how cities are shaped and configured. Urban form is intimately linked to land values and to basic real estate business activities such as building construction location and investment decisions. In this chapter we described the fundamental economic principles and concepts that underlie the joint determination of land value and urban form. Concepts such as the residual value of land, bid-rent functions, land market equilibrium, the highest and best use principle, and rent gradients are basic to understanding how cities grow and develop and change over time. These economic fundamentals therefore can be used to inform real estate business decisions.

KEY TERMS

urban form	bid-rent function (curve)	construction cost rent
factors of production	central point	rent gradient
mobile factors	transportation cost minimized	location rent (location premium)
residual theory of land value	monocentric city	
highest and best use (HBU)	radius to the urban boundary	
principle	agricultural rent	

STUDY QUESTIONS

4.1. What is meant by a *factor of production*? Name four categories or types of production factors. How does land differ from the other factors?

4.2. Explain the residual theory of land value. Why is land value only the residual after other factors have been paid?

4.3. What is bid-rent and what is the relationship between the bid-rent and the residual value of land?

4.4. Suppose the most productive use of a particular site is as a high-volume, upscale restaurant, which can generate revenues of $600,000 per year. The operating expenses, including labor, food, and utilities (everything except rent) are $450,000 per year. The building can be built and equipped for $1 million, which can be paid for by a perpetual loan with interest of $100,000 per year. According to the residual theory, how much is the land parcel worth in terms of annual land rent?

4.5. Consider two uses of a site. Use *A* is more sensitive to transportation costs, while use *B* is less profitable apart from transportation costs. Which use is likely to prevail near a transportation node such as a highway intersection?

4.6. How does the highest and best use principle result from long-run equilibrium in the land market?

4.7. Why are denser or more intensive land uses typically found closer to central locations?

4.8. What is the relationship between the rent gradient and transportation costs in a homogeneous monocentric city?

4.9. Describe the two possible effects of population growth on both relative and absolute land values within a monocentric homogeneous city.

4.10. Consider a simple, homogeneous monocentric city with a circular shape. If the location rent premium at the center is $6,000 per year per acre, and the density is three persons per acre, what is the annual transportation commuting cost per capita for residents at the outer edge of the city? Supposing that the annual transportation cost per person per mile of distance from the CBD is $200 (round-trip), how big is the radius of the city?

4.11. Describe the two possible effects of transportation cost reduction (per mile, per person) on both relative and absolute land values within a monocentric homogeneous city.

4.12. Describe the two possible effects of income growth on both relative and absolute land values within a monocentric homogeneous city, considering both direct and indirect effects.

4.13. If there are no constraints on the area of a city, what does the monocentric city model say about the relative growth of land rents in the center versus the edge of a city that is growing either in population or in income?

4.14. What does the monocentric city model say about the relative level of rents in two cities that are otherwise identical except that one city is located on a coastline and so cannot expand around all points of the compass?

4.15. Holding density constant, for every 1% growth in population, approximately what will be the percent growth in city radius?

5 Inside the City II: A Closer Look

Chapter Outline

Learning Objectives

After reading this chapter, you should understand:

◆ The difference between land value and land rent, and the key determinants of land values in and around a city.

◆ Why uncertainty can result in higher land values but less land development in a city.

◆ Why different land uses and densities occur at different locations within a city.

◆ How neighborhoods grow and mature and sometimes decline and rise again.

◆ The concept of property life cycle and its implications for real estate investors.

◆ The nature and cause of the major characteristics of the urban form of the typical U.S. city, and how this form has been changing.

The previous chapter presented just the basics, the bare bones of economic theory for understanding what shapes urban form and the pattern of land value changes over time and space within a city. The simple monocentric city model we explored in Chapter 4 was not only very simple spatially, but it was essentially only a long-run or static model, with little consideration of the dynamics of growth. This chapter presents some more advanced concepts and introduces some broader considerations which are important in real world cities. The first two parts of this chapter deal with land asset value, as distinguished from the annual land rents that were the focus of the previous chapter. This will clarify two very important concerns of real estate investors; growth expectations and uncertainty. The remainder of this chapter will then enrich the simple monocentric model of the previous chapter by introducing some important features of real world cities.

5.1 FROM LAND RENT TO LAND VALUE: THE EFFECT OF RENT GROWTH EXPECTATIONS

Land value is not the same thing as land rent, although the two are closely related. Land value is the present value of the expected future rents the land could receive. Therefore, other things being equal, land value will be greater where land rents are greater. But two other factors also affect land value in addition to the current level of rent the land can earn. The first factor is the expected future *growth rate* of the land rents. The second is *uncertainty*, or risk, in the future level of land rents, in effect, the risk in the growth rate of land rents. In this section we consider the effect of the first of these two factors.

A higher growth rate in future rents will increase the present value of those rents, thereby increasing land value, other things being equal. As we saw previously, usually land rental growth within a city will be associated with outward expansion of the boundary of the city, implying that any fixed location will eventually obtain location rent premiums that grow over time. The potential for city expansion will cause the value of agricultural land just beyond the current boundary of the city to exceed the mere present value of future agricultural rents. This is because the present value of the expected future urban location rent premium is incorporated in the current undeveloped land value. The closer a location is to the boundary of the city (and the more rapidly that boundary is expanding), the greater will be this **growth premium** in the value of the agricultural land.

As a result of this growth premium, land will be more expensive in areas that are expecting greater future growth in rents. Of course, the cost of the land is part of the cost of development, as noted in Chapter 2. Thus, higher land prices require higher expected rents from a developed urban use, in order to justify construction. Therefore, greater future growth prospects for the rent the developed property could earn cause development of raw land to be delayed until the current rent that could be initially charged by the built project is higher than would otherwise be necessary.

Consider a simple example for now. The building will cost $1 million to construct, excluding land cost. If the land costs $200,000, then the total development cost is $1,200,000, whereas if the land costs $500,000 the total cost will be $1,500,000. If buyers of the built property will pay no more than 10 times the current rent that property can earn, then the development project breaks even when $120,000 annual rent can be charged in the first case but only when $150,000 rent can be charged in the second case. This example is overly simplistic, because it ignores the effect of future rental growth on the current rent-multiple that buyers of the property would be willing to pay, and it ignores the effect of uncertainty.[1] Nevertheless, this general point about higher rents associated with faster future rent growth rates remains valid in a more complete model, as described in the next sections.

---

[1] Recall from Chapter 1 that the cap rates that prevail in the property asset market will be lower the greater the future growth expectations in the rent, other things being equal. For example, suppose the greater growth expectations that caused the land to be worth $500,000 instead of $200,000 also enabled an 8% cap rate instead of a 10% cap rate in the pricing of the built property. Then an initial net rent of $120,000 would suffice to enable development even with the $1,500,000 cost (as 0.08 × 1,500,000 = 120,000).

5.2 EFFECT OF UNCERTAINTY ON SPECULATIVE LAND VALUE

In addition to the *expected* rate of future land rent growth, the risk or uncertainty surrounding that growth rate is a key determinant of land value and city size. The effect of this uncertainty is more difficult to analyze than the effect of growth per se. However, in recent years mathematical techniques first applied by financial economists to valuing stock options have helped investors analyze the effect of uncertainty on land values and urban form.[2] Titman pointed out that in the presence of uncertainty it is rational for developers to wait longer than they otherwise would before starting construction, but that such uncertainty actually tends to increase land value.[3]

This is because land provides its owner/developers with a "call option." The owner of a land parcel has the *right without obligation* to develop the land at any time. When development is undertaken, this option is surrendered, the cost of construction is incurred, and in return the value of the developed property is obtained.[4] This optionlike characteristic allows the owner/developer to profit from uncertainty in the following way. Uncertainty in the real estate market can be thought of as the possibility of the occurrence of unexpected upswings and downswings in the real estate market.[5] The option characteristic of land ownership allows the owner/developer to take advantage of the "upside" of uncertainty while avoiding full exposure to the "downside." If and when an upswing occurs in the property market, the owner can choose to develop the property and make particularly large profits. If a downswing in the market occurs, the owner can simply choose not to develop for the time being, thereby avoiding potential losses.

Capozza and Helsley (1990) integrated this options analysis approach into the classical monocentric city model and showed that uncertainty results in a smaller, denser city with higher rents than would prevail in the absence of uncertainty (other things being equal). The key reason for this is the irreversibility of construction. Once a structure is built on a land parcel, it is normally very difficult and expensive to remove or significantly alter it. In the analogy with stock options, once the option is exercised, you no longer have the option. This is why, in the presence of uncertainty, it makes sense to wait longer than one otherwise would to develop a parcel of land. Like surfers waiting for that perfect wave, it makes sense to wait for at least somewhat of an upswing or at least to wait out any likely downswings in the market.

[2]In fact, the option model has a number of applications in real estate that are of interest to commercial property investment analysts. Some of these applications will be described later in this book, in Parts VI and VIII.

[3]See Titman (1985). Note that in this regard uncertainty has a similar effect to that of expected future growth in rents. The implication of option value theory for optimal development timing will be discussed in more depth in Part VIII of this book, where we will discuss the relationship of the "real options" literature to development decision making. A widely used summary is contained in Dixit and Pindyck (1994).

[4]The analogy with stock options is that upon surrendering the option and paying the "exercise price," you receive the underlying stock shares.

[5]The upswings and downswings are unexpected, not in the sense that people don't expect there to be upswings and downswings, but rather in the sense that these changes in the market cannot be perfectly forecast.

This is reflected in the fact that landowners demand a premium in the rent the developed property must be able to charge (over and above the construction cost rent and the agricultural opportunity cost rent) before they are willing to develop agricultural land and thereby convert it to urban use at the boundary of the city. Capozza and Helsley labeled this extra rent the **irreversibility premium**. This premium is necessary because the present value of the urban rents must compensate not only for the construction cost and for the forgone agricultural rents, but also for the value of the call option that is being surrendered, the value of the fact that the landowner could wait and possibly develop the property even more profitably at a later date.

The implications of growth and uncertainty on land rent and land value within the city and in the as yet unurbanized region just beyond the city boundary are shown in Exhibits 5-1 and 5-2. Exhibit 5-1 shows the land rents, and Exhibit 5-2 shows the land values. The land values depicted in Exhibit 5-2 are, as we have noted, based on investor projections regarding the future levels of (and uncertainty surrounding) the land rent components shown in Exhibit 5-1, in particular regarding the behavior of the urban boundary over time. Each component in the land values has a corresponding component in the rents with the exception of the growth premium. This is because the rents modeled in Exhibit 5-1 are current "spot" rents, reflecting purely the current balance between supply and demand in the space market for the indicated locations in relation to the urban boundary.[6]

Notice in Exhibit 5-2 that both the growth premium and the irreversibility premium in the undeveloped land value grow dramatically as the urban boundary approaches. For likely realistic situations, almost all of the market value of undeveloped land parcels just beyond the urban boundary of a growing city consists of these two premiums. The irreversibility premium associated with uncertainty likely will be a significant part of the total undeveloped land value near the boundary.

The growth and irreversibility premiums represent what is often called the speculative value of undeveloped land. We can see from the discussion in this section that, in principle, such land value is based on real and rational considerations. While the irreversibility premium results in higher rents and higher urban densities, this is a rational response to uncertainty in real estate markets, leading to the efficient use of scarce construction capital, transportation resources, and (most of all) land.

Depending on how fast the urban boundary is expanding outward, the growth and irreversibility premiums can cause undeveloped land values just beyond the current boundary of urban development to grow at very high rates, making very high investment returns possible for speculative landowners.[7] But such returns will also be quite risky and volatile, as a slight downturn in the urban growth rate can undercut the basis of the growth and irreversibility premiums that underlie the speculative land value.

[6]The rent one observes empirically in long-term leases does indeed often include a growth premium (depending on the lease terms; it is usually relatively small compared to the growth premium in land value).

[7]During the 1990s, for example, with inflation in the neighborhood of around 3% per year, average returns of 15 to 30 % per year were typically expected by land speculators.

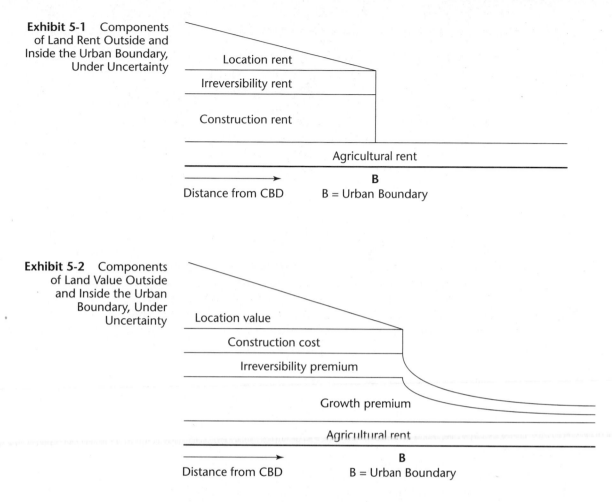

Exhibit 5-1 Components of Land Rent Outside and Inside the Urban Boundary, Under Uncertainty

Location rent

Irreversibility rent

Construction rent

Agricultural rent

Distance from CBD

B

B = Urban Boundary

Exhibit 5-2 Components of Land Value Outside and Inside the Urban Boundary, Under Uncertainty

Location value

Construction cost

Irreversibility premium

Growth premium

Agricultural rent

Distance from CBD

B

B = Urban Boundary

Extending the lessons of the simple monocentric city model we began in Chapter 4, we can summarize the effect of growth and uncertainty in a fifth principle, adding to the four already discussed in Chapter 4:

Principle 5:
Faster urban growth and greater uncertainty in that growth will tend to increase urban land values, with the uncertainty also suggesting that a smaller, denser city is optimal, as rational development is postponed longer than it otherwise would be.

5.3 LET'S GET REAL: NEW TWISTS TO THE OLD MODEL

The classical monocentric city model is great for developing a basic understanding of urban spatial economics. (Recall the description of Circlopolis in Chapter 4.) But real world cities are much richer, more varied places than the homogeneous town of Circlopolis. Now that you have some of the basics down, let's consider some of these more realistic effects.

5.3.1 Density Variations and Heterogeneous Land Use

In the simple monocentric city model we assumed a single, homogeneous land use, such as housing of a uniform density, throughout the city. Real world cities have a variety of land uses (housing, commercial, industrial, etc.) and a range of densities (e.g., high-rise, low-rise, spread-out). What is the most productive way for these various land uses to locate and distribute themselves within the city?

The answer to this question is easy to observe. In most cities we observe denser, more intensive land uses closer to the center. Taller buildings, packed closer together, are found in or near central points (such as the CBD or other major transportation nodes where transportation costs are minimized). But you now have the tools to understand *why* this is the case and how this happens.

Freely functioning land markets result in denser development and more productive use of land located closer to central points where transportation costs are minimized. Such a result makes sense from the perspective of maximizing profits or incomes, because it minimizes the aggregate transportation costs of the society.

How such a result comes about in long-run equilibrium in the land market can be seen in Exhibit 4-2 in Chapter 4, reproduced here as Exhibit 5-3. Recall that this exhibit depicts the bid-rent curves of three different land uses around a single central point. The equilibrium land rent gradient around a central point will be determined by the highest bid-rent curve at each location, as indicated by the thick line tracing out the highest bid-rent functions. The more productive land use with the greatest sensitivity to transportation costs (use *A* in the exhibit) will outbid other land uses near the center. Other things being equal, denser development will indeed be more productive per acre, because greater density means that more labor and physical capital (structures and machines) are applied to the production process, per acre of land. Also, recall from our discussion of the monocentric city that the rent gradient is proportional to density, other things being equal, because transportation costs *per acre* are proportional to density. Thus, higher-density land uses will tend to be both more productive (at the central point) and characterized by steeper rent gradients.

For example, assuming the same transportation costs per person per mile, if there are more persons located per acre, there will be more total transportation costs per

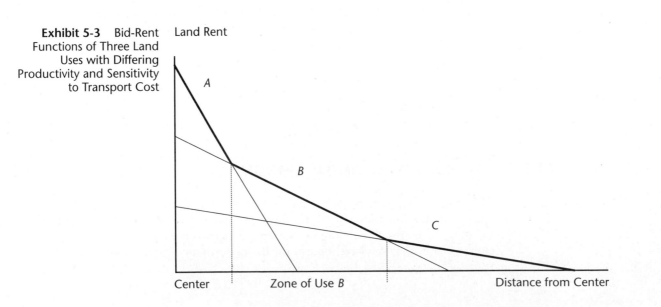

Exhibit 5-3   Bid-Rent Functions of Three Land Uses with Differing Productivity and Sensitivity to Transport Cost

acre. So denser, more intensive land uses will have steeper bid-rent curves that are higher near central locations. Such land uses will therefore be able to outbid other land uses close to central points where transportation costs are minimized.

So it is not just a coincidence that the density of development tends to decline as one moves away from a geographically central point or transportation node. It is a reflection of the fundamental economic principle that in a production process the input factors that are relatively scarce (and hence more expensive) should be used more sparingly and more productively. It is a basic fact of geometry (as well as geography) that central locations are scarcer than noncentral locations. For example, in a circle or a square there are many locations, but only one location is at the exact center of the circle or the square. Greater density near centers reflects the fact that central locations are relatively scarcer than less central locations, and so the land in such locations should be used more intensively. Greater density of land use is virtually synonymous with more intensive and productive land use.

If we combine this density result with the monocentric city model, we get the classical **concentric ring model of urban form**. First suggested by Ernest Burgess, of the famous Chicago School of Urban Geography, which flourished at the University of Chicago in the 1920s and 1930s, the concentric ring model is depicted in Exhibit 5-4. This model suggests that similar types of land uses will tend to locate at similar distances from the center of the city, resulting in concentric rings of similar land uses around the CBD. For example, denser, lower-income housing would tend to be located closer to the center than lower-density, higher-income housing.

Exhibit 5-4   Concentric Ring Model of Urban Land Use Structure (Burgess)

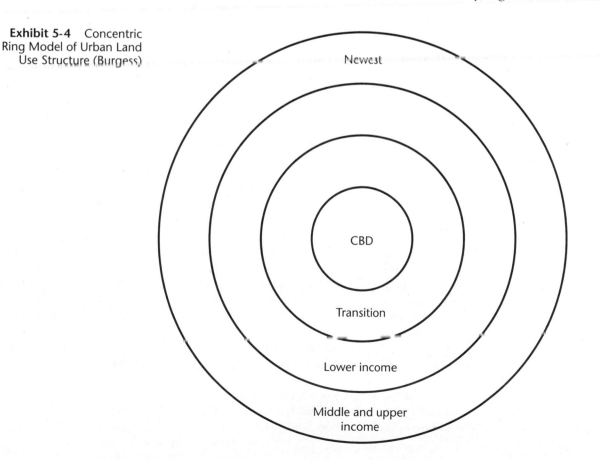

The Burgess concentric ring model was a geographic model rather than an economic model like the monocentric city model. As such, Burgess's model was more complicated but less rigorous in some respects, including considerations other than just transportation costs and long-run equilibrium in the land market. In particular, the Burgess model considered the *dynamics of development*, including the effect of the chronological order in which different sections of the city are developed and the effect of the age of structures. His model also considered social factors such as the preference for greater lot sizes (lower residential densities) with increasing household income.

In the Burgess model the inner ring just outside the CBD is a transition zone or "gray area." This zone consists of warehouses and industrial plants, uses that require good access to transportation, especially rail transport, which tend to be focused in or near the CBD. This inner ring is viewed as a zone in transition, evolving into the expanding CBD at its inner edge, and merging with low-income, high-density housing for the factory workers on its outer edge. As the city expands outward, this second ring consists of older and therefore less desirable houses than those in the outer, newest ring of the city, which consists of the lower-density middle and upper-income housing.

The Burgess model explained many of the major features of the typical industrial city of mid-20th century America. Most notable was the tendency of higher-income residential neighborhoods to be located farther from the center. This is a somewhat curious phenomenon not found in many other countries. As noted in the previous chapter, higher-income households should have higher value of time and therefore greater transportation costs per mile per person, leading to a steeper rent gradient. Higher-income households should also have a greater ability to pay for housing. These two facts by themselves would lead higher-income neighborhoods to tend to be located closer to the center of the city, as is indeed typical in the cities of many other countries. So how does it happen that higher-income residential neighborhoods tend to exist farther from the center in U.S. cities?

Here is a basic answer. Recall that lower densities reduce the transportation cost per acre and thereby reduce the rent gradient. If upper-income people desire enough larger lot sizes or have a strong enough preference for low-density neighborhoods, then this density effect can more than offset the transportation cost effect, resulting in an equilibrium location of higher-income households farther from the center. Furthermore, if higher incomes lead households to want to purchase newer houses, then this will also tend to force the higher-income neighborhoods farther from the center, at least in a city that has been growing rapidly for some time (as most 20th-century cities were). This is because development proceeds from the center outward, leaving inner neighborhoods full of older housing stock. (Of course, in time that stock may be renewed, and if the city ceases population growth and household formation, eventually all neighborhoods could have similar-age housing structures.) Social and political issues related to crime, quality of education, and racial or ethnic diversity have also been factors affecting U.S. cities, which are characterized by municipal political boundaries that separate central cities from their surrounding newer suburbs.

While the concentric ring model captures some important elements of urban form, it also leaves much unexplained. Not long after Burgess came up with his model another Chicago geographer came along with an alternative model, which is pretty much the opposite of the Burgess model. Homer Hoyt was not only a first-rate academic, but also a successful real estate investor, and he is famous for developing the **sector model of urban land use**.

According to the sector model, similar land uses do not all lie at a similar distance from the center of the city, but rather cluster along rays or in pie-shaped wedges emanating from the center. Again, the theory is based on the phenomenon of cities growing outward from their centers. Hoyt noted that once a particular type of land use becomes predominant in a particular direction from the center, or on a particular "side of town," then new development tends to continue that land use in the same direction outward from the center as the city grows. For example, early on it became established in such East Coast cities as Boston and Philadelphia that the west side of town was the fashionable side where the upper-income residents tended to locate. As those cities grew in all directions, the west side continued to be the fashionable and upper-income side, extending farther and farther from the center.

The Hoyt model is depicted in Exhibit 5-5. Hoyt's theory was that some land uses are more compatible with each other and tend to be found in adjacent sectors. Thus, lower-income housing would more likely be found adjacent to industrial development than would high-income housing. He also suggested an environmental cause of some location patterns, with high-income residential areas tending to be located upwind from heavy industrial zones.

The concentric ring model and the sector model are diametrically opposite one another in their view of urban structure. Yet both clearly contain some of the essence of the truth. Most cities are partly explained by both perspectives.

Exhibit 5-5 Sector Model of Urban Land Use Structure (Hoyt)

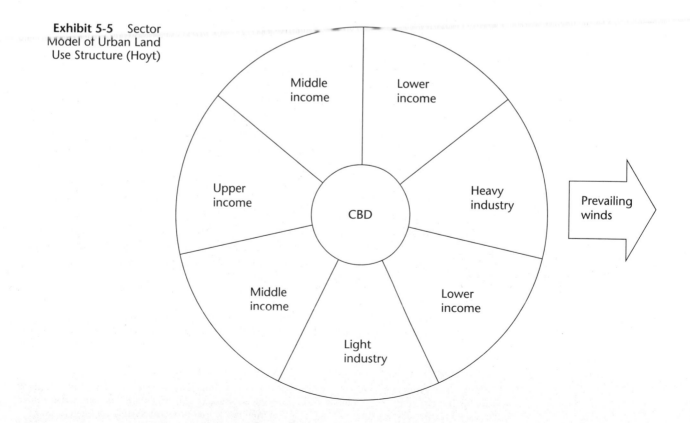

5.3.2 Effect of Land Use Boundaries

Both the concentric ring model and the sector model of urban form and land use recognize that similar land uses tend to "clump together" in cities. For example, we speak of residential neighborhoods, commercial districts, and industrial zones. And we speak of high-income neighborhoods, medium-income neighborhoods and low-income neighborhoods. In part this is because similar land uses face similar transportation cost and locational needs. So if one land use is the highest and best use at a particular site or location, that same general type of use will typically also be the highest and best use at nearby locations as well. The natural tendency of similar land uses to coalesce is often reinforced by land use regulations in most cities, such as zoning regulations in U.S. cities. It is important to recognize that a natural consequence of districts that are relatively homogeneous in land use means that there will be land use boundaries between such districts. These boundaries affect the location rent and land value of the sites adjacent to them and nearby.

Certain types of land uses tend to be compatible and mutually supporting, bringing a synergy or increase in value to each district and use. Other types of land uses are incompatible and detract from the value of each other if they are located too closely. These are examples of what are known as spillover effects or locational externalities, as defined in Chapter 3. For example, residential neighborhoods benefit from having shopping opportunities nearby so that the residents do not have to travel too far to shop. There is thus a benefit in having certain types of commercial districts (those with stores useful to the residents, such as grocery and convenience stores) near or within residential districts. On the other hand, heavy industrial zones—containing air or noise pollution generators such as airports, or large commercial centers that generate high traffic volumes—are generally not compatible with most types of residential land use. Such land uses will tend to reduce the value of nearby residential homes.

Both a freely functioning land market and well-crafted zoning regulations will tend to separate incompatible land uses and draw compatible uses together, at least over the long run.[8] Recognition of such differences underlies both the concentric ring and the sector model of urban form (especially the latter).

Even **compatible land uses** may have local boundary effects that differ from the general effect, however. For example, residents may generally prefer to be located closer to shopping opportunities, as long as they are not so close that traffic congestion and noise reduces the quality of residential life. It may be nice to have a convenience store a block or two away, but not so nice to have the store right next to your backyard. Similar points may be made about schools and churches, or even parks, if the park presents safety or privacy concerns. This is an example of a **negative locational externality**. As a result of boundary effects such as these, location rents often are depressed near to a land use boundary, at least for one of the land uses (the one that is unfavorably affected, such as the residential use in the previous examples).[9]

---

[8] Because these spillover effects involve externalities, a type of market imperfection, a completely free laissez-faire land market will generally not result in optimal land use, although it may come pretty close. In theory, a profit-maximizing monopolist owning all the land might do a better job, as all the spillover externalities would be internalized. Zoning and community land use controls are ways to improve upon the laissez-faire result while reflecting broader social and political concerns of the community and avoiding the dangers of power concentration in the hands of a monopolist.

[9] While location rent may be depressed by location near the boundary, location value may in some cases actually be increased, if the neighborhood is growing, as sites adjacent to the existing commercial center, for example, may offer the prospect of conversion from residential to more valuable commercial use.

This phenomenon is depicted in Exhibit 5-6, which shows the bid-rent function of a land use that benefits from accessibility to another land use at a boundary on the left edge of the horizontal axis of the graph. For example, the exhibit might depict the bid-rent of residential land use around a commercial center whose boundary is at the left edge of the graph. The bid-rent is lower near the land use boundary, then rises as distance eliminates the negative externality, then falls as further increasing distance reduces accessibility to the commercial center.

5.3.3 Polycentric Cities

Up to now, our discussion of urban form has focused largely on single central locations or "monocentric" cities. While most cities do have a single dominant center known as the central business district (CBD) or downtown, real world cities also have other important centers (often referred to as *urban subcenters* in the urban economics literature). For example, most metropolitan areas of a million or more population in the United States have other **major activity centers (MACs)** besides the CBD, which serve metropolitan-wide needs, such as airports, major medical centers, and sports or educational complexes. In addition, traditional cities are sprinkled with **neighborhood business districts (NBDs)**, which serve the needs of local communities. In the last half of the 20th century all U.S. cities have also developed large regional shopping malls in the suburbs, serving large segments of the metropolitan area. By the late 20th century, some of the largest suburban commercial centers, particular those located on beltways and major interstate highway nodes, had developed into what Joel Garreau dubbed "edge cities," activity centers almost as large and multifaceted as many a traditional CBD.

Furthermore, some metropolises have never had a single very dominant CBD in the center. **Polynuclear cities** have not only subcenters, but also multiple major centers. Such cities range from "twins" such as Minneapolis-St.Paul, to multicentered conglomerates like the Los Angeles area, to clusters such as the Ruhr region in Germany.

Fundamentally, cities in the real world could never be perfectly monocentric because *different land uses have different and multiple central points* (locations where their relevant transportation costs are minimized). For example, recall the bid-rent example at the beginning of Chapter 4 regarding two land uses, a clothing factory and a grocery store. The clothing factory's central point (the maximum point of its bid-rent

Exhibit 5-6 Effect of Negative Externalities near a Land Use Boundary

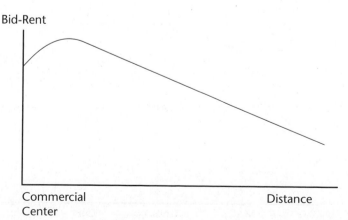

function) might be at the intersection of two interstate highways outside the center of town. The central point for the grocery store could be at the intersection of two commercial streets in the center of a residential neighborhood. Neither of these two central points is in the CBD of the metropolitan area. In fact, there might be several sites in the metropolitan area where either the factory or the store could be located with maximum productivity (minimum transport costs).

Thus, real cities are collections of major and minor central points within the metropolitan area. These tend to be related to one another in a more or less hierarchical manner much like Christaller's urban hierarchy model described in Chapter 3. Land values and rent gradients are, as always, determined in equilibrium by the usage with the highest bid-rent curve at each location, leading to land being used at its highest and best use in the long run. This is depicted schematically in Exhibit 5-7 for a cross-section through a city that has a dominant CBD but also major outlying centers as well. The land rents (which determine and reflect the land uses) are given by the heavy solid lines, the highest bid-rent functions over each point.

In summary, a good, practical way of viewing urban land value would recognize that there are multiple centers of attraction for most economic land uses, and that transportation costs to all of these multiple areas affect land rent and value. For a residential user, the centers of attraction are work, school, shopping, friends, relatives, recreation areas, and so on, and the more accessible the site to all of these attractions the more valuable the site, due to overall transport cost minimization. For a retail vendor, minimization of the transportation costs for all potential customers makes the site more valuable. For an industrial land user, distribution costs and raw material transport costs are the critical costs affecting land value. Sites that are highly accessible to desired attractions (i.e., work, customers, suppliers) will naturally become more intensely used in a freely functioning competitive land market. More accessible land must be used more intensely because it is more valuable, but it is more valuable because it is highly accessible. The two factors, accessibility (minimization of transport costs) and productivity are interrelated, and both influence value.

5.3.4 Neighborhood Dynamics and Life Cycle

The simple monocentric city model considers only transport costs in a long-run equilibrium in which there is complete flexibility to change the built structures on the land. The age of the built structures or of the neighborhoods of the city is ignored in this simple model. On the other hand, both the Burgess and Hoyt models described in the previous section recognized that land value and land use are indeed affected by the age of the built structures on the land. Older structures tend to be less productive,

Exhibit 5-7 Rent Gradients in a Polycentric City

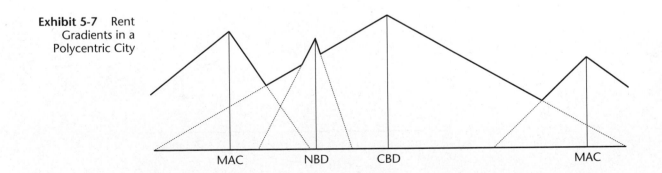

MAC   NBD   CBD   MAC

less desirable for users, and more expensive to operate or maintain. Yet even old structures usually have some value, and tearing them down is costly. It is usually cheaper to build new buildings on undeveloped land, or land on which the existing buildings are so old or outmoded that they have almost no further value (and by the time buildings get that old, there may be a stigma attached to the neighborhood). Undeveloped land, by its nature, tends to be located near or beyond the existing periphery of the urban area. Thus, neighborhoods on or near the periphery of the metropolitan area tend to have structures that on average are much newer than those in centrally located neighborhoods.

This unequal distribution of structural age in a city tends to be more pronounced in decades during and after major expansion, such as almost all U.S. cities experienced in the 20th century. On the other hand, as we saw in Chapter 4, urban growth, especially if combined with growth in real incomes, should tend to increase the absolute value of all locations within the city. This includes the old, central neighborhoods, unless transportation cost reductions or social and political problems offset the advantages of centrality of location.[10]

This suggests a natural dynamic, or process of evolution, of neighborhoods within a city. Borrowing terminology from biology, this process is sometimes referred to as **neighborhood succession theory**. This theory differs from those we have previously examined in that it considers changes in land values and land uses in a single location (or part of a city, a neighborhood or district) across time. The previous models we have looked at focused on such changes across different locations within the entire city as of a single point in time. The typical life cycle of a neighborhood according to succession theory is depicted in Exhibit 5-8. Let us trace this model for a typical district, that of West Side in Anytown, USA.

At first a bucolic agricultural zone just beyond the edge of the expanding urban area of Anytown, West Side experiences an initial growth phase characterized by rapidly rising land values as the area becomes ripe for urban development. This phase begins at point *I* in time, represented on the horizontal axis in Exhibit 5-8. The West Side area is initially developed with low-density housing, and within a generation is fully built up with such new houses. As development is completed, West Side's growth period and rapid rise in undeveloped land values ends, but the neighborhood enters a long period of maturity, in which values generally are maintained. Starting from point *II* in time, this mature period could continue indefinitely, with structures gradually being refurbished or replaced by new buildings as the original structures age but the neighborhood retains its low-density residential character.

However, the evolution of the metropolitan area of Anytown as a whole may tend to put pressures on West Side that could cause it to evolve in either of two possible directions away from this stable maturity. This occurs at point *III* in time in Exhibit 5-8.

The happier possibility is that land value in West Side could rise again significantly. This might be caused by expansion of the overall geographic area of the Anytown metropolis, which could give West Side a greater location premium as the neighborhood becomes, relatively speaking, more centrally located in the metropolitan area. This would tend to make redevelopment to more productive land uses profitable in the neighborhood, such as development of higher-density housing and/or

---

[10]In the long run a stable city or one whose area is constrained would tend to have mixtures of new and old structures more evenly distributed across all neighborhoods, or might even have more new structures in the inner neighborhoods.

Exhibit 5-8
Neighborhood
Succession Model

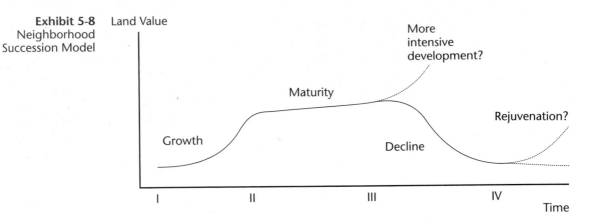

commercial buildings.[11] Zoning or other political constraints might be applied to hold off such redevelopment, maintaining the original density but now with higher-valued houses, making the neighborhood over time a more exclusive, upper-income area. The profit incentive would argue strongly for redevelopment, however. This might cause dissension within the neighborhood between those favoring and those opposed to rezoning and new development. But we might view such dissension as a "good problem," which (we can hope) would be resolved through a fair and democratic process.

Alternatively, the unhappy possibility would see West Side entering into a period of decline. The Anytown metropolitan area might evolve in a manner that reduces West Side's value. Various economic, geographic, and sociopolitical factors could cause such decline. For example, intraurban transportation improvements could result in transport cost reductions that could reduce the location value of West Side. (Recall Exhibits 4-6 and 4-7 in Chapter 4.) As its structures age relative to newer neighborhoods, lower-income residents may move into West Side. Political boundaries based on historical accident may place West Side in a municipality with tax burdens that are high relative to income, with relatively poor-quality schools and social problems such as a high crime rate. Disinvestment may then ensue, in which West Side's buildings are allowed to age and deteriorate without capital replenishment. A negative spiral in terms of land value and property value could result.

But this is not the end of the story. Of course, the decline could continue and gradually play out with West Side permanently stuck in a low-value status. However, it is also possible that in the decline in value lie the seeds of a turnaround. This is represented at point *IV* in time in Exhibit 5-8. With structures virtually completely deteriorated and land values depressed by the stigma of the neighborhood, redevelopment may now be rather inexpensive. If West Side has some favorable attributes that it can capitalize on, or if the Anytown metropolis evolves in a direction favorable for West Side, redevelopment or refurbishment of West Side could become profitable. For example, in the 1970s and 1980s many old, centrally located neighborhoods were revitalized through new investment (the term *gentrification* was coined).

---

[11]Our previous discussion in sections 5.1 and 5.2 of land value just beyond the boundary of an expanding city is relevant to the value of property in West Side in this circumstance. West Side is now just beyond the boundary of an expanding higher-density or higher-value (per acre) land use, for example, just beyond the boundary of an expanding Burgess model "ring." In such a circumstance, much of the value of property in West Side will be due to land value rather than the value of the existing structures. This land value will contain the growth and irreversibility premia described in sections 5.1 and 5.2.

From the perspective of real estate investors, neighborhood succession theory holds an important implication. Succession theory suggests two things about the course of land rents and land values over time. First, land rents and values will tend to remain nearly constant, in real terms, over long periods of time, possibly indefinitely (once urban development has occurred in a neighborhood). But second, the possibility exists of occasional sharp, sudden changes in land rent and land value, due to changes in the optimal role and function of the neighborhood within the metropolitan area (that is, changes in what might be called the neighborhood HBU). These changes may or may not be very easy to predict, and they can conceivably go in either a positive or negative direction. As described in section 5.2, to the extent that a change in land rent is predictable, it will be reflected in advance by corresponding changes in land values.[12] Normally, there will be at least one, but perhaps only one, positive "pop" in land value for a given location, occurring at (and just prior to) the time when that location is reached by the expanding urban boundary, when development of urban land uses first becomes feasible on the site.

5.4 PROPERTY LIFE CYCLE AND THE EFFECT
OF STRUCTURAL DEPRECIATION

Just as neighborhoods may be characterized by a succession of HBUs over time, individual properties (or sites) within the neighborhood experience their own characteristic life cycles. Even if the neighborhood is very stable, with an essentially constant characteristic HBU for the neighborhood, individual properties will pass through a repeating life cycle as the built structure on the site ages and eventually is replaced or rehabilitated. Like the neighborhood life cycle, the **property life cycle** is important for real estate investors to be aware of, as it is fundamental to the nature of the investment returns that can realistically be expected from a given property.

Real estate investors should bear in mind that there are two components of property value: land value and structure value. The relationship between these two components is shown in the simple model of property life cycle presented in Exhibit 5-9. The model shown in the exhibit is consistent with the model of land value as a development option, as put forth by Titman (1985), Capozza and Helsey (1990), Williams (1991), and others (introduced in section 5.2). Exhibit 5-9 presents a picture of a single location in the city across an entire history of continuous time, which is represented on the horizontal axis.

The discrete points in time when construction or major reconstruction of the structure on this site takes place are represented by the C symbols along the time axis. At those points in time the structure is built or rebuilt to best serve the highest and best use (HBU) of the site as of that point in time. This value of the newly developed or redeveloped property just after each development may be seen as tracing out the evolution of the usage value of the site over time, based on its HBU. This trend, indicated

---

[12] Exhibits 5-1 and 5-2 need not apply only to the advance of the outer boundary of the urbanized area of an expanding city into the agricultural zone. The boundary shown in these exhibits may refer to any expanding boundary of more intensive land use within the city, such as the expansion of a commercial zone into residential areas, or the expansion of a higher-density residential zone into a lower-density residential zone.

Exhibit 5-9 Components of Property Value over Time

Property Value Components

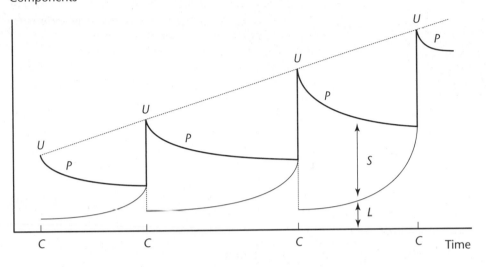

C = Construction / reconstruction points in time
U = Usage value at highest and best use at time of reconstruction
P = Property value
S = Structure value
L = Location and redevelopment option value

by the dashed line and the *U* symbols, is a good way to conceptualize the trend in the location value of the site.[13]

As depicted in Exhibit 5-9, the location value of the site is growing continuously over time, as evidenced by the upward trend in the *U* values. Of course this would not necessarily be the trend for any given site in the real world, especially if we measure value in real terms, that is, in dollars of constant purchasing power (i.e., net of general inflation). We have seen both in this chapter and the previous chapter how location value can either increase or decrease over time, or remain constant for long periods.

The market value of the property at any point in time consists of the structure value plus the land value. **Structure value** is indicated by *S* in Exhibit 5-9. Just after reconstruction, structure value makes up the bulk of the property value. But the structure value declines over time as the building depreciates, both from physical obsolescence and "**economic obsolescence**," the latter reflecting the fact that the nature of the structure may become unsuited to the HBU of the site as the HBU evolves over time. For example, the HBU may evolve from low-density to higher-density residential use, or from residential to commercial use. Obsolescence also reflects the effect of changing technology and changing tastes on the optimal physical design of a new structure for the relevant HBU—what is referred to in the appraisal profession as **functional obsolescence**. For example, suppose class A office buildings need to have optical fiber wiring in the 2000s, whereas copper wiring was

[13] What we are calling "location value" reflects what the appraisal industry terms the "HBU as if vacant," the highest and best use to which the site would be developed if there were no existing structure on it.

sufficient in the 1970s. Then a structure with copper wiring, built as a class A building in the 1970s, will lose its class A status by 2000 (and be forced to reduce its asking rents accordingly), purely due to functional obsolescence.

The other component of the property value is the **land value** (labeled *L*). The land value component consists of the value of the **redevelopment option**, including the growth and irreversibility premia described in sections 5.1 and 5.2.[14] The land value component is very small just after redevelopment, because the building is then at the HBU for the site, so the profitability of further redevelopment, if any, is a long way off in the future.[15] Over time, the land value component will grow if the structure depreciates physically or functionally, or if the HBU of the site as if vacant evolves and changes over time away from that which the current structure can serve (this latter is economic obsolescence, as described above).

The total of land value plus structure value equals the property value at any point in time, labeled *P* in the exhibit. That is, $P = S + L$. The optimal time for redevelopment will not occur until the entire value of the site equals its land value component alone; that is, the current structure has become worthless as such (S = 0) due to the value of the redevelopment option on the site.[16] (In the exhibit, *C* is depicted as occurring when the old value of *L* equals the old value of *P*.)

Typically, the structure value and the land value are bundled together and cannot be purchased separately.[17] Indeed, the breakout between these two components of property value at any point in time is practically and empirically difficult. But the combination of structure value and land value can be observed at any point in time as the total

---

[14] As described in section 5.1, the growth premium component of the land value reflects the expected value of the location premium in the future rent from a new or redeveloped structure, beyond the redevelopment point in time. Note, however, that the value of any location premium associated with the *current* structure is reflected in the structure value component of the property value as opposed to the land value component, as these concepts are being defined here. (This may appear to be inconsistent with the definition of land value in the context of the monocentric city model discussed in Chapter 4 and sections 5.1 and 5.2. But in fact structural depreciation and redevelopment were not included in the basic monocentric city model, so this is a fine point that was not contemplated in the definition of land value employed in that model.) It should also be noted that the value of the current structure *as if* it would never be torn down represents an "opportunity cost" in any redevelopment of the site that would involve demolishing the existing structure. Even if this structure is no longer the HBU of the site, it would still typically be able to provide some future benefit flows. If the building is torn down, the future net cash flow it could have earned is forfeited. Analysis of option value in real estate will be discussed in more depth in Part VIII. For the case of redevelopment (as opposed to initial development on vacant land), the option model has been refined by Amin and Capozza (1993) and Childs, Riddiough, and Triantis (1996).

[15] In financial option valuation terminology, the redevelopment option is *deeply* "out of the money" when the structure is new.

[16] Note that this does not necessarily (or usually) imply that the existing structure could no longer earn positive net rents, only that such rents are insufficient to justify further delay of a more profitable redevelopment. The perspective taken here is consistent with traditional appraisal practice of charging against the structure any loss in property value due to economic obsolescence or divergence of the existing structure from the HBU as if the site were vacant. It should also be noted that in some cases it may be optimal to hold a site for some time purely for speculation before beginning redevelopment, even after the existing building on it becomes essentially worthless. The new HBU for the site may evolve further in a favorable direction. If you develop too soon, you may miss such opportunity. This is analogous to the fact that it is not always optimal to exercise a call option as soon as it is "in the money." Also, we are ignoring here the demolition cost for the existing structure. Demolition is an additional cost of redevelopment that can delay the optimal timing of construction.

[17] Some portion of the structure value may be "purchased" in the form of a long-term leasehold. The existence of long-term leaseholds encumber the property to the potential detriment of the redevelopment option value component of the property value.

property value, the value of the bundle, P, indicated by the heavy line in the exhibit. The continuous change in P over time (between the reconstruction points) essentially determines the capital gain or loss that would be faced by an unlevered investor in the property during its period of operation between redevelopment events.[18]

Exhibit 5-9 shows how **depreciation of the structure** renders the growth rate of the property value (P) generally less than the growth rate of the location value (U). This result is guaranteed by the fact that the value of the newly redeveloped property includes the construction cost component, over and above the site acquisition cost component. (In Exhibit 5-9 we observe that the value of U at C, which equals the new P at that point in time, exceeds the value of the old P at C, which equals the old L at that point. This difference is the capital expenditure on construction.[19]) This leads to a principle that is of fundamental importance in real estate investment analysis:

> The Depreciation Principle:
> *Over the long run, the change in location value provides a theoretical ceiling to the average capital gain of the unlevered investor in already-built property (that is, property that is fully operational).*

As an example, suppose that redevelopment occurs once every 50 years, and at the time of redevelopment the old property (essentially just land value) is typically worth 20% of what the new, redeveloped property will be worth. This is equivalent to saying that site acquisition costs are 20% of the total project development costs. This means that during the 50 years between redevelopment events, built property value grows at an average rate of 3.2% per year *less* than the growth in location value of the site during that time.[20]

The preceding principle regarding property value carries an implication for the rents that can be charged by a property owner between major redevelopment events. To the extent that rents remain an approximately constant percent of property value, rents must also grow at a rate less than (or decline at a rate greater than) that of the location value of the site. In fact, the more fundamental direction of causality flows in the other direction. Property value declines below that of the potential HBU (that is, the HBU as if the site were vacant) fundamentally because the rent that the market will bear for the existing structure falls farther and farther below the rent of the potential HBU.

---

[18] The discontinuous jumps in property value at the points in time of the reconstructions reflect the injection of new capital into the property via the construction process. Therefore, these jumps do not in themselves represent a capital gain for any investor. It is important to recognize that the capital gain (or loss) experienced by an investor in the property is represented by the change in P only *between* reconstruction points, not across construction points, in Exhibit 5-9.

[19] If there were no depreciation of the structure, then P would indeed run right along the dashed line connecting the Us, and the usage or location value change would continuously equal the property value change.

[20] Calculated as follows: $0.2 = 1 \times (1 + x)^{50} \rightarrow x = 0.2^{1/50} - 1 = -0.032$. If acquisition costs are 50% of development project value, and redevelopment occurs only every 100 years, then we have: $x = 0.5^{1/100} - 1 = -0.007$. Keep in mind that this refers to depreciation *only relative* to the evolution of the location value of the site, and applies on average over the entire property life cycle between redevelopment events. Although Exhibit 5-9 does not depict such a case, it is possible for property value to increase over time in real terms prior to redevelopment, if the land value component rises fast enough to more than offset the depreciation of the structure component. This will occur primarily only when either: (a) the structure is nearly worthless, so that virtually the entire value of the property is in its redevelopment option value; or (b) there is a rapid positive change in the location value of the site.

Office Market Finds Shortcut to Recovery Through the Suburbs

ABI-Inform® carries the following abstract of an article by Geoffrey Richards with the above title, in the October 1996 issue of National Real Estate Investor *(v38n11, pp. 92–101). As you read this abstract, think about how it reflects both the simple monocentric city model, as well as some of the additional factors discussed in section 5.3. It should also bring to mind some of the points raised in Chapter 3 about the system of cities in the United States.*

US suburban office markets have captured about 75% of the office demand since 1990. The suburban migration trend is fueled by companies seeking to be closer to where employees live. While most of the national markets have improved substantially, several suburban markets are well ahead of the rest and should attract the most development and investment activity in the next few years. Atlanta leads the way in the Southeast region. The city's total suburban office inventory is more than 64 million square feet. In the Midwest, Chicago's suburban office market continues to improve rapidly with the East-West Corridor and the Northwest submarkets leading the way. In the Southwest, the markets of Las Vegas and Phoenix are experiencing a great deal of activity. On the West Coast, San Francisco is absorbing space, and the Los Angeles suburbs of Burbank, Century City and Santa Monica are bouncing back due to new opportunities in the entertainment industry. In the Pacific Northwest, Portland has single-digit office vacancy rates and is seeing some new construction, as is Seattle.*

Discussion Questions

1. What feature of the Burgess concentric ring model may be reflected in the greater relative growth of office demand in the suburbs? [Hint: Are residential real estate users the only ones who want new buildings with the latest architectural and landscape amenities at a reasonable price?]

2. Does the growth of office development in suburbs suggest that the polycentric model is becoming more relevant to U.S. cities than the monocentric model? [Hint: Would you say that office buildings are characteristic of "central places," defined as places where the land rent level is higher than that of the surrounding area?]

3. What does this abstract suggest about the regional distribution of growth in office employment in the United States? [Hint: Does the list of cities in the second half of the abstract reflect a random or equal representation of U.S. geographic regions, or are some regions left out?]

5.5 CHAPTER SUMMARY

This chapter and the previous chapter have taken you on an introductory tour through the inside of cities and into the basic structure of property value. This inside tour has complemented the overview tour of the system of cities presented in Chapter 3. The academic discipline primarily at work here, conducting these tours, has been urban economics, assisted ably by geography, and sociology to some extent. The principles, tools, and insights raised in these tours are obviously important to making well-informed commercial property investment decisions. They relate especially to the ability to obtain a realistic impression of the long-run prospects for the space market relevant to particular locations. In the remaining chapter of Part II we will zero in on commercial property market analysis at a less theoretical, more applied level typical of real estate business practice.

KEY TERMS

growth premium
irreversibility premium
concentric ring model of urban
    form
sector model of urban land use
compatible land uses
negative locational externality

major activity center (MAC)
neighborhood business district
    (NBD)
polycentric city
polynuclear city
neighborhood succession theory
property life cycle

structure value
functional obsolescence
economic obsolescence
land value
redevelopment option value
structural depreciation

STUDY QUESTIONS

5.1. How does the expected future growth rate of land rent affect the relationship between current land value and current land rent?

5.2. How does uncertainty in the future land rent affect current land value and land rent, other things being equal? What are the implications for city size?

5.3. Consider two undeveloped land sites. At site 1 the highest and best use (HBU) is a warehouse that would cost $1 million to build (exclusive of land cost) and would then generate annual net rents of $150,000, which are expected to grow at 3% per year. At site 2 the HBU is an apartment building that can generate net rents of $800,000, projected to grow at 1% per year, with construction cost of $5 million. Suppose investors buying built properties (that is, properties already developed and in operation) require an initial annual return (in the form of current net income) of 12% minus the expected annual growth rate in the net income, as a percent of the investment cost. For example, they would want an initial yield or cap rate of 9% for the warehouse (12% − 3% = 9%). Suppose the land value for site 1 is $1 million and the land value for site 2 is $2 million. On which of these sites (1, 2, both, or neither) is it currently profitable to undertake construction? Show your reasoning.

5.4. Compare and contrast the Burgess concentric ring model with the Hoyt sector model of urban form. Which, if either one, do you think better describes most cities?

5.5. Draw a schematic picture of what the rent gradient looks like in a polycentric city.

5.6. What is meant by the term "edge city"?

5.7. What does neighborhood succession theory say about the rate land values or rents will tend to grow over time within a given neighborhood?

5.8. Discuss the effect of land use boundaries on bid-rents and land values. Give an example of two land uses with negative locational externalities for at least one of the uses when the two uses are adjacent to one another.

5.9. According to property life cycle theory, property value is the sum of the values of what two components? Describe each of these two components.

5.10. How do you know that property value must grow at a rate less than the growth rate in the location value of the site (on average over the long run between major redevelopment projects)?

5.11. Suppose site acquisition costs typically equal 30% of total development project costs, and 30 years typically elapse between major redevelopment on a given site. By what percent per year does the property value grow *less than* the growth rate of the location value of the site?

6 Real Estate Market Analysis

Chapter Outline

6.1 **General Features of Real Estate Market Analysis**
    6.1.1 Purpose of Market Analysis
    6.1.2 Market Supply and Demand Variables and Indicators
    6.1.3 Defining the Scope of the Analysis
    6.1.4 Trend Extrapolation versus Structural Analysis
    6.1.5 Major General Tasks in Conducting a Basic Short-Term Structural Market Analysis
*6.2 **Formal Model of Space Market Equilibrium Dynamics and Cyclicality**
6.3 **Chapter Summary**

Learning Objectives

After reading this chapter, you should understand:

◆ What is meant by real estate market analysis, and what types of business decisions it is useful to assist.

◆ The key elements and quantitative variables involved in market analysis.

◆ Some of the major types of data sources for conducting market analyses.

◆ The difference between simple trend extrapolation and a structural market analysis.

◆ The major steps in conducting a structural analysis of the real estate space market.

◆ The implications for space market dynamics and cyclicality when market participants cannot or do not base decisions on forward-looking forecasts of the space market.

The preceding chapters discussed the underlying economic and geographic forces that govern urban land values and location patterns. Successful real estate professionals base their decisions on knowledge of these fundamental patterns. In addition to such general and fundamental knowledge, however, real estate professionals typically use a set of practical analytical tools and procedures that relate fundamental principles to the decision at hand. These practical research procedures are often collected under the label of **real estate market analysis,** the subject of this chapter. Market analysis is typically designed to assist in such decisions as:

▪ Where to locate a branch office
▪ What size or type of building to develop on a specific site
▪ What type of tenants to look for in marketing a particular building

- What the rent and expiration term should be on a given lease
- When to begin construction on a development project
- How many units to build this year
- Which cities and property types to invest in so as to allocate capital where rents are more likely to grow
- Where to locate new retail outlets and/or which stores should be closed

Broadly speaking, to assist in making such decisions, market analysis has as its objective the quantitative or qualitatitive characterization of the supply side and demand side of a specific space usage market that is relevant to the given decision. For example, we might perform a market analysis for retail space in the Boston CBD, or for luxury apartment units south of Market Street in downtown San Francisco.

Real estate market analysis techniques and data sources differ somewhat by market sector, or property type. For example, the specific types of data and analytical procedures used in analyzing the market for office space differ from those used in determining the feasibility of developing a new shopping mall. Nevertheless, all real estate market analysis shares some basic features. This generic core is the focus of the present chapter.

6.1 GENERAL FEATURES OF REAL ESTATE MARKET ANALYSIS

As noted, real estate market analysis seeks to quantify and forecast the supply and demand sides of specific space usage markets. Practical market analysis must be simple enough, and based on realistic data, so that it can be applied relatively quickly and inexpensively, and easily communicated and understood in the real world of business practice. Most market analysis is thus characterized by rather direct, common sense procedures. This section will sketch some typical market analysis considerations and procedures.

6.1.1 Purpose of Market Analysis

Real estate market analysis is performed for a wide variety of purposes and in varying contexts, to assist with different types of real estate decisions. Some market analyses focus on specific microlevel decisions, while others focus on broader and more general characterizations of real estate markets. Specific microlevel analyses focus on individual building sites or individual users of real estate. For example, a developer might want to examine the feasibility of building a particular type of development on one or more specific sites. This is sometimes referred to as "feasibility analysis" or "site analysis" for a real estate development.[1]

The second type of analysis, general characterization of a real estate market, has as its purpose quantifying and forecasting the supply of and demand for space, typically including the forecast of future rents and vacancies in a particular geographic real estate **market segment**. You may recall from Chapter 1 that real estate space usage markets are segmented by both property type and geographic location. Thus, the definition of a relevant real estate market normally specifies a geographic scope

[1]Development project feasibility analysis will be discussed further in Part VIII.

and property type. For example, a market analysis might focus broadly on the office market in metropolitan Chicago, or more narrowly on the market for class A office buildings in downtown Chicago. Such general market characterizations provide information that is useful for making a number of different decisions having to do with that market, or comparing that market with other markets.

Clearly, the purpose of the market analysis will strongly dictate the type of analysis approach to be taken. The variety of typical uses of market analyses makes it impossible to present an exhaustive or general procedure. Rather, we will here consider a general framework that is applicable for most examples of general market characterization.

6.1.2 Market Supply and Demand Variables and Indicators

The typical general market analysis will focus on a few variables, or indicators, that quantitatively characterize both the supply and demand sides of the real estate space market, as well as the balance between these two sides (the market equilibrium). Following is a typical list of the market descriptive variables:

- Vacancy rate
- Rent level
- Quantity of new construction started
- Quantity of new construction completed
- Absorption of new space

The **vacancy rate** refers to the percentage of the stock of built space in the market that is not currently occupied. To compute the vacancy rate, one must know two more fundamental quantities: the total stock of space in the market and the amount of space that is currently vacant. For current and historical data these quantities are determined by inventorying and surveying public records and landlords and are often compiled by brokerage firms and consulting firms or data firms that sell real estate market information.[2]

To be more accurate, the vacancy rate should include all space that is currently unoccupied and available for occupancy, including space that may be currently under lease but available for subleasing. The vacancy rate is one indicator that reflects the current balance between supply and demand in the market (the other is the current market rent level). Vacancy is thus an equilibrium indicator rather than an indicator of either the supply side or the demand side alone. Vacancy rate data is usually more widely available and more reliable than the other equilibrium indicator, rents.

It is important to keep in mind that in a typical real estate market it is normal for some vacancy to exist. Fundamentally, this is because it does not make economic sense for landlords to rent space to the first potential tenant that comes along, no matter how low the rent that tenant is offering to pay. Similarly, it does not make sense for tenants to rent space in the first building they find no matter how high the rent there or how suboptimal the location. Both the space owner (landlord) and space user

[2] For a review of space market supply and demand data and forecasting sources at the MSA level as of the late 1990s, see Guilkey (1999).

(tenant) suffer costs when tenants move (such as lost rent incurred by the landlord when the space is vacant and moving expenses incurred by the tenant who moves). This is why leases are typically signed committing both parties for some period of time (especially in commercial property markets, where leases are often for multiple years). Therefore, for both the supply and demand sides of the market, profits will be maximized if firms take some time to search for better deals. This search time results in space being held vacant, waiting (in effect) for better deals to show up. Thus, zero vacancy in a market would probably indicate suboptimal behavior on the part of decision makers.[3]

Another rational reason for vacancy in a market is due to growth in the demand side, and the variable and unpredictable nature of that growth. Supply typically has to be added in a "lumpy" manner, because buildings must be built of a certain size in order to be economical considering construction and land costs. Because of the time it takes to build, construction decisions must be made in the absence of perfect information about the future balance of supply and demand in the market at the time when the building will be completed. This also leads naturally to some excess space being provided in the typical real estate market from time to time. This growth-based source of rational vacancy tends to be more important in markets where demand is growing faster, and with more volatility, or ups and downs in the growth rate.

For these reasons real estate markets are characterized by what is sometimes called a **natural vacancy rate**, which is the vacancy rate that tends to prevail on average over the long run in the market, and which indicates that the market is approximately in balance between supply and demand. When vacancy is below the natural rate, it is said that the market is a sellers' market or landlords' market, or that the rental market is tight, with demand exceeding supply in some sense. When the vacancy rate is above the natural level, the market is said to be a buyers' market or tenants' market (or overbuilt), with the supply of available space exceeding the current level of demand. *When vacancy is below the natural rate, rents will tend to be driven up (and new development will tend to occur). When vacancy is above the natural rate rents will tend to be driven down.*

The natural vacancy rate is not the same for all markets. As noted, it tends to be higher in faster-growing, more volatile markets, and also in markets where there are fewer regulatory or geographical constraints on new development. Whatever the natural vacancy rate (and it is usually difficult to know precisely what it is in any given market), the actual vacancy rate will tend to cycle over time around this natural rate.

The second market indicator of great importance is the current **market rent,** which refers to the level of rents being charged on typical new leases currently being signed in the market. Of course, rents on specific leases will vary according to the specific nature of the site and space being rented, and also according to the terms of the lease. It is therefore important to control for such variations when trying to measure trends in rents across time. This makes reliable quantification of market rents rather difficult. It is also usually important to control for the effect of general inflation, to examine the trend in *real rents*. This is because real rents are what really matters (reflecting purchasing power or opportunity cost), and because real rents reflect the actual physical balance between supply and demand in the space market. Another factor to keep in mind is that *asking rents*, which may typically be reported in surveys of

[3] See Part VIII for additional discussion of this topic.

landlords, may differ from the *effective rents* actually being charged new tenants. The concept of effective rent (discussed more fully in a later chapter) includes the monetary effect of concessions and rent abatements that landlords may sometimes offer tenants to persuade them to sign a lease. For example, a landlord may quote a rent of $10 per square foot, but then offer the first year rent-free if the tenant signs a five-year lease. Yet the rent may be reported in a survey or a casual inquiry as $10.

The quantity of new **construction starts** and/or **completions** is another important indicator of real estate markets. As described in Chapter 2, construction represents the addition of new supply to the stock of space available in the market. Of course, construction takes time, typically anywhere from a few months to build a simple house to a few years to build a large commercial complex. The new supply does not enter the market until the construction is complete, although preleasing may commit tenants in advance. In some older markets it is also important to consider demolition or conversion of old structures as well as construction of new buildings to arrive at the net addition of space supply in the market.

The final general market indicator that is widely used is space absorption. This refers to the amount of additional space that is occupied per year. Absorption can be thought of as an indicator of the activity on the demand side of the space market, just as construction is an indicator of activity on the supply side. It is useful, however, to distinguish between gross and net absorption in the market.

Gross absorption measures the total amount of space for which leases were signed during the year, regardless of where the tenants came from. This is a good measure of the volume of rental transaction activity, a very relevant measure of the demand for leasing brokerage services. However, some tenants would be moving from one site to another within the same market, so the signing of their lease would imply vacating one space in the market as well as occupying another space in the same market. This would not imply a growth in the overall amount of occupied space in the market and thus would not signify growth in the overall demand for space in the market.

A better measure of demand growth is **net absorption**, which is simply the net change in the amount of occupied space in the market. This is the more relevant number to compare to the net amount of construction completed during the same period of time. Comparing net construction completed to net absorption indicates whether demand and supply are growing at the same rate, with resulting implications for changes in the balance between demand and supply in the market. When net absorption exceeds net construction completions, vacancy declines in the market, and when construction exceeds absorption, vacancy must rise. The relationship between the quantity of vacant space at the end of a period and the quantity of net construction completions and net absorption during the period, is indicated by the following equation:

$$(vacant\ space)_t = (vacant\ space)_{t-1} + (construction)_t - (net\ absorption)_t$$

The five variables described in this section form a basic quantitative overview of the space market, including how the balance between supply and demand in the market is changing and the sources of those changes on both the supply and demand sides. Exhibit 6-1 shows the results of a typical market analysis. This analysis was conducted by the research staff of a large real estate investment advisory firm. The market analysis depicted in the exhibit shows the U.S. national office market at the national aggregate level, including construction, absorption, and vacancy. The analysis was done in

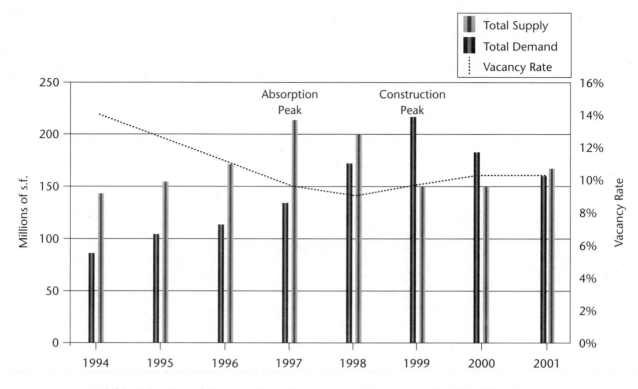

Exhibit 6-1   Annual Construction, Absorption, and Vacancy in the U.S. Office Market. 1994–98 are historical figures; 1999–2001 are forecasts. (Source: LaSalle Advisors Investment Research, *1999 Investment Strategy Annual Report*. Reproduced by permission. © LaSalle.)

1999 based on historical data through 1998, presenting a three-year forecast for the years 1999–2001. Although a national aggregate analysis like this is too broad to be very useful for specific real estate project planning, it is useful for examining broad trends. In this case we see clearly the recovery in office demand during the late 1990s, with absorption exceeding construction every year from 1994 through 1998, bringing vacancy down from over 15% to under 10% on average.

The five basic variables described in this section can often be combined or added to other data to provide indicators that are useful for gazing into the future and attempting to draw some conclusions about where the market is headed. For example, if you take the current amount of vacant space in the market, plus the amount of any new construction started but not yet complete, and divide that sum by 1/12th the annual net absorption, you get an indicator known as the **months supply**. The formula is presented here:

$$MS = \frac{Vacancy + Construction}{Net\ absorption\ /\ 12}$$

The months supply (MS) is an indicator of how long it will take (in months) for all of the vacant space in the market to be absorbed (driving the market down to a zero vacancy rate). The MS formula assumes that (1) the rate of new demand growth continues as indicated by the net absorption rate; and (2) there is no new construction in the market other than what has already been started. The months supply can be compared to the length of time (in months) that it takes to complete the typical construction project. If the months supply is less than the construction time, then this indicates that the market can support additional new construction. If (as we suggested earlier) it is not practical for the market to go all the way down to zero vacancy, or if there is likely to be demolition or abandonment of existing occupied space in the market, then the market can handle additional new construction even when the months supply is somewhat greater than the average construction project duration. However, if the months supply extends far beyond the average construction project duration, then the indication is that the market is oversupplied and there will be continued downward pressure on real effective rents.

6.1.3 Defining the Scope of the Analysis

The definition of the relevant real estate market is typically the threshold task in any real estate market analysis. For example, at one extreme are analyses of the overall national market, such as that shown in Exhibit 6-1. Such analyses would be based on aggregate national statistics that can be obtained from government and commercial sources. But to be relevant to specific business decisions it is usually necessary to define the market more specifically and functionally. Generally market analysis focuses at the metropolitan level or even narrower, such as a quadrant or neighborhood of a metropolitan area (e.g., the North Dallas Market or the South Atlanta/Hartsfield Airport Market). A metropolitan region forms an overall functional market area that can usually be usefully subdivided into several submarkets. The CBD of the metropolitan area is typically considered one market area and the suburbs are divided into several markets by geographic sector, sometimes including inner and outer rings. Typically, each market area has one or a few major transportation nodes and major activity centers.

As an example, Exhibit 6-2 shows a schematic map of the metropolitan area of Atlanta divided into nine local office markets. While many potential office tenants would need to be located specifically in one of these market areas, other tenants—for example, a large national firm moving an initial branch office to Atlanta from out of the metropolitan area—might consider several different submarkets to be equally appropriate for their needs. So to some extent, one must consider the entire metropolitan area as a single market, although the geographically distinguishable submarkets within the metro area are also relevant.

Apart from geographical scope, the temporal range of the analysis must also be defined—that is, what period of time is to be covered. Historical analysis can give important insights into and perspective regarding the dynamics of a market. In addition, most market analyses must address future forecasts, for decisions are forward looking in time. A five- to ten-year future horizon is usually desirable, although data problems and random events often make forecasting much beyond three years rather unreliable.

6.1.4 Trend Extrapolation versus Structural Analysis

Another threshold issue in defining a market analysis is to decide the type of analysis approach. In this regard it is useful to distinguish two broadly different types of approaches (but keep in mind that often a hybrid involving elements of both is most useful). The two approaches may be labeled **simple trend extrapolation**, and

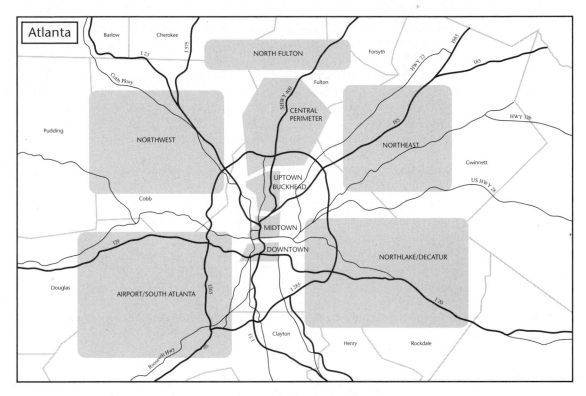

Office Submarket Profile

Selected Atlanta Office Submarkets	Class A					Class B				
	Stock (sf)			1Q-3Q	Effective	Stock (sf)			1Q-3Q98	Effective
	3Q98 (000)	Share	Vacancy	Absorp.	Rent/sf	3Q98 (000)	Share	Vacancy	Absorp.	Rent/sf
Downtown	10,951	19.1%	11.1%	143,000	$21.32	4,550	9.9%	35.0%	(57,000)	$13.14
Midtown	5,526	9.7%	3.4%	150,000	$24.37	3,693	8.0%	17.4%	19,000	$13.44
Buckhead	7,939	13.9%	6.7%	369,000	$24.84	1,829	4.0%	8.5%	22,000	$19.20
Northwest	10,538	18.4%	10.7%	533,000	$22.76	9,070	19.8%	8.8%	249,000	$16.42
Central Perimeter	13,049	22.8%	9.3%	236,000	$23.57	7,385	16.1%	6.4%	60,000	$17.90
North Fulton	4,771	8.3%	25.2%	1,330,000	$21.05	2,557	5.6%	8.1%	514,000	$17.60
Northeast	2,802	4.9%	16.8%	328,000	$19.27	5,085	11.1%	15.9%	335,000	$13.61
Northlake/Decatur	1,200	2.1%	3.7%	163,000	$19.26	9,806	21.4%	6.3%	50,000	$14.12
Airport/South Atlanta	424	0.7%	5.2%	9,000	$16.52	1,935	4.2%	20.3%	33,000	$10.38
Overall	57,200	100.0%	10.5%	3,260,000	$21.44	45,909	100.0%	12.4%	1,225,000	$15.09

Exhibit 6-2   Atlanta MSA Office Submarkets, 1998
(Source: Lend Lease Real Estate Investments, *Real Estate Outlook: 1999*,
based on data from Jamison Research and Lend Lease Investment Research.
© Lend Lease, Reproduced by permission.)

structural analysis. With simple trend extrapolation one looks directly at the market supply and demand variables of interest and extrapolates these variables into the future based purely on their own past historical trends. For example, one would obtain data on the historical vacancy rate and rents in the market and project the future vacancy rate and rents based on the historical trend.

This approach can take advantage of time-series statistical techniques. As noted in Chapter 2, real estate space markets tend to have a lot of inertia and to be rather cyclical. This potentially allows for considerable ability to forecast at least a few years into the future, based just on past trends. Indicators such as the months supply described earlier can be useful for making near-term forecasts. Formal time-series econometric techniques also can often be usefully applied to this type of forecasting.[4] However, in common business practice more informal or heuristic procedures are often used to make the projection, or the formal models are combined with more intuitive judgment.

The structural approach to market analysis, on the other hand, attempts to model the *structure* of the market by identifying and quantifying the underlying determinants of the variables of interest. This requires explicit quantification and forecasting of both the supply side and the demand side of the market, so that equilibrium indicators such as the vacancy rate and rent can be projected by forecasting the supply and demand sides separately and comparing the two forecasts. Depending on the depth at which the structural analysis is done, this may include developing a model of the determinants of space usage demand in the market (a demand model), and forecasting these underlying sources of demand. For example, demand for office space usage is driven fundamentally by the amount of office employment in the area, while the demand for retail space is driven by the level of real per capita disposable income and the regional population. A structural model should also consider the supply side of the market. At a minimum this must include an examination of current new and planned construction and demolition in the market.[5]

6.1.5 Major General Tasks in Conducting a Basic Short-Term Structural Market Analysis

Here we review the major steps and tasks involved in conducting a structural market analysis at a very basic level, a level that will often suffice for short- to medium-term forecasts of space market conditions (up to about three years in the future). Exhibit 6-3 presents an overview of the tasks involved in a typical analysis of this type. Eight separate tasks are identified. Notice that the tasks involve analysis of both the supply and demand side of the market, with three tasks focusing on each side of the market separately, and two tasks integrating across the two sides.

The first steps in the structural market analysis are to inventory the existing supply of space and to identify the fundamental sources of the demand for space usage in the relevant market. Supply inventories are available from local brokerage firms, local

---

[4] The most basic techniques include autoregression, in which the market variable of interest (such as the vacancy rate) is regressed on its own past values to estimate a relationship across time. Autoregression, and more general univariate models such as autoregressive integrated moving average (ARIMA), can capture cyclicality and lagged effects. Relatively user-friendly statistical software packages for personal computers are available to facilitate this type of forecasting. If data permits, more sophisticated techniques such as transfer function analysis, vector autoregression, or vector error correction models can be employed, potentially encompassing variables from the asset market, such as property yields and capital market factors, as well as structural variables from the space market itself.

[5] A more sophisticated structural analysis would include a formal system of models of market equilibrium between supply and demand. This requires estimating formal models of both demand and supply, including some representation of the **price elasticities** of both supply and demand, and the response **lags** in both these sides of the market. Price elasticity relates how much the amount of space supplied (or demanded) responds to a given change in the rental price in the market. The lags relate to how much time elapses between a rental price change and the resultant change in demand or supply responding to that price change. This type of formal structural analysis will be described in more detail in section 6.2.

Exhibit 6-3   Generic Framework of a Basic Short-Term Structural Market Analysis for Real Estate

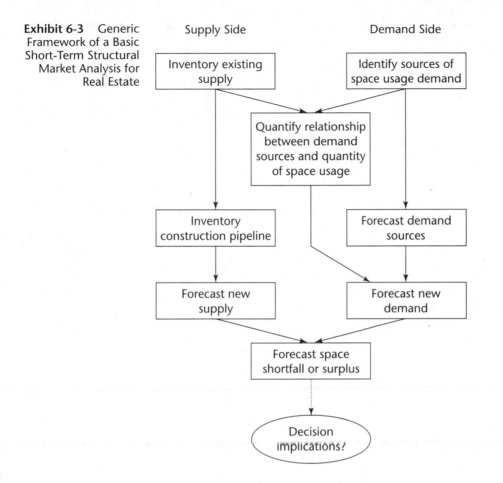

planning agencies, and commercial firms specializing in providing this type of data. The fundamental sources of demand are the drivers of the need for space usage in the market. Some typical indicators of these **demand drivers** that are relatively easy to quantify and are often used in demand studies for different types of property are indicated in the table in Exhibit 6-4. Population projections are published by the Census Bureau. Employment data by occupation is published by the Bureau of Labor Statistics and Bureau of Economic Analysis of the federal government, including regional breakdowns and future projections.[6] Most state governments also publish such data, as do many local planning commissions and chambers of commerce. Income information by type and region is published by the Bureau of Economic Analysis and the Census Bureau, as well as state and local sources and private commercial sources. Geographic Information Systems (GIS) technology makes possible more geographically precise use of such information.

The next step in the structural market analysis is to relate the underlying demand sources to the amount of real estate space usage demand. In some cases this will be straightforward because of the nature of the market. For example, there should be approximately a one-to-one correspondence between the number of households and the

[6] The Standard Industrial Classification (SIC) system for classifying industries was discussed in Chapter 3 and may also be useful here.

Exhibit 6-4 Major
Demand Drivers by
Property Type

Property Type	Demand Drivers
Residential single family (Owner occupied)	■ Population ■ Household formation (child-rearing ages) ■ Interest rates ■ Employment growth (business & professional occupations)
Residential multifamily (Apartment renters)	■ Population ■ Household formation (non-child-rearing ages) ■ Local housing affordability ■ Employment growth (blue collar occupations)
Retail	■ Aggregate disposable income ■ Aggregate household wealth ■ Traffic volume (specific sites)
Office	Employment in office occupations: ■ Finance, Insurance, Real Estate (FIRE) ■ Business & professional services ■ Legal services
Industrial	■ Manufacturing employment ■ Transportation employment ■ Airfreight volume ■ Rail & truck volume
Hotel & convention	■ Air passenger volume ■ Tourism receipts or number of visitors

number of housing units demanded (except for special markets such as student housing). But in other markets it will be necessary to relate, for example, the number of square feet of space required to the number of employees of a given occupation. This can be done by comparing the square footage of various types of space identified in the supply stock inventory to the number of employees of various occupations identified in the demand side analysis. For example, it might be determined that the average office worker uses 200 square feet of space under typical market conditions.[7]

Next, one must develop forecasts of future demand for, and supply of, space in the relevant market. On the demand side, the sources of demand previously identified must be projected based on the extrapolation of past trends or judgment about the evolution of the local economic base.[8] Combined with the relationship between demand sources and space usage, this will result in a projection of the amount of space demand at various times in the future.

On the supply side this step involves inventorying the construction pipeline, that is, identifying all projects currently under construction as well as projects that are in various stages of planning. This information could be found by researching construction permits issued by local governments, which are public information. Also, local business and financial newspapers typically announce major construction projects that receive financing. However, not all projects that are planned will actually be built, so

[7]Keep in mind that when markets are soft and rents are low, tenants expecting growth may lease more space than they need, inflating the apparent square feet of space per employee, while the reverse may happen when markets are tight and rents are high.

[8]See Chapter 3, section 3.4.

the quantification of the construction pipeline will involve some judgment or estimation. In older neighborhoods or regions, it will be important to also estimate the amount of demolition and abandonment of existing occupied space in this step of the analysis. The result of this step is a projection of net new space to be added to the market at various times in the future.

The end result of a basic structural analysis such as we are describing here is some projection of the future relationship between supply and demand in the market. In the near term (say, ond to three years in the future), this type of analysis can be fairly accurate and result in a quantitative projection of the magnitude of space supply shortfall or surplus. Such supply/demand balance projections may have various decision implications. For example, it might appear that within three years there will be a demand for a million more square feet of office space in a certain market than is currently in the construction pipeline. If typical projects are around 500,000 square feet, then this would suggest a possible need for two new such projects. Alternatively, the projection might indicate that excess supply will continue in the market even after three years, with no need for new projects.

In general, projected tightening of the market (as indicated by a growing space shortfall) should lead to higher rents and lower vacancy rates, and a projected surplus of supply will lead to rising vacancy rates and falling rents. This relates not only to construction and development decisions but also to other types of real estate decisions. Investment in existing structures will appear more profitable the greater the projected future space supply shortfall (other things being equal, in particular, the price of the property), for this would imply better prospects for future rental growth or greater ease of leasing currently vacant space.[9] Leasing decisions can be enlightened by such a market analysis as well. For example, a landlord may hesitate to commit to a long-term lease at a low rent if the market is projected to tighten.

*6.2 FORMAL MODEL OF SPACE MARKET EQUILIBRIUM DYNAMICS AND CYCLICALITY[10]

To help the interested reader gain a basic familiarity with formal space market equilibrium forecasting, this section will present a simplified numerical example of a system of articulated supply, demand, and construction models with price response elasticities and lags.[11] Such a system of models is useful not only to help you get an

---

[9] The ability to predict space market variables such as rents and vacancy does not necessarily imply an ability to predict property investment total returns, as asset prices may already reflect predictable movements in the space market. However, real estate asset markets are not perfectly efficient, and practitioners widely believe that those who can predict the space market best will have greater opportunities to earn higher investment returns. (See, for example, Miles [1997] and Miles & Guilkey [1998].) In any case, a space market in its "cycle" does affect the nature of the investment performance of real estate assets (such as the relative magnitude of current income versus capital growth) even if it does not affect the ex ante total return. Specific space markets are often at different places in their cycles at the same time, so there is clearly a rationale to use space market analysis to help guide investment allocation among alternative markets.

[10] Sections indicated with a preceding asterisk in the section number cover more advanced or analytically difficult material. Students with relatively little economics or quantitative background may want to skip or skim these sections.

[11] The model presented here is simple enough for a student with only basic computer spreadsheet skills to enter the formulas into a spreadsheet and play around with the parameters of the model, to see the effect on the resulting dynamic behavior of the market.

idea of how more sophisticated real estate market forecasting is done, but also to derive some classical principles of real estate market dynamics, such as the potentially cyclical nature of many real estate space markets.[12] Formal modeling of the type described here can allow a more rigorous and explicit quantitative forecast of future rents and vacancies, and facilitate longer-term forecasts.

Our dynamic model of a space market is represented by a system of six linked equations that reflect the relationship among supply, demand, construction, rent, and vacancy over time. The equations are linked by the fact that the output from each equation represents input in another equation, to form across all six equations a complete representation of the market equilibrium over time. The system will allow the simulation and forecast of rents, vacancy, construction, and absorption in the market each year.

The first two equations reflect the supply side of the market. Equation (1) is a model of the development industry, relating construction completions (new additions to the supply of space in the market) to rents prevailing in the market at the time when the construction projects are started.

$$C(t) = \begin{cases} \varepsilon(R(t-L) - K), \, if \, R(t-L) > K, \\ 0, \, otherwise \end{cases} \tag{1}$$

$C(t)$ is the amount of new space completed in year t. $R(t-L)$ is the rent prevailing in the market in year $t-L$. Because construction takes time, there is a lag between when construction decisions are made (when the rents that trigger that decision are observed) and when new supply is completed.[13] This lag is expressed in the model by the parameter L, which is the length of time it takes to complete the typical construction project in the market. There is also a "trigger rent" (like the replacement cost rent discussed in Chapter 1), above which new construction will be started and below which there will be no new construction starts. This trigger rent level is indicated by K. The supply elasticity is reflected by the parameter ε, which determines the amount of new construction started per dollar by which the current rent exceeds the trigger rent. Greater values of ε indicate that development responds more elastically to rents; that is, more new supply will be built for each dollar that rents rise above the trigger level.

Equation (2) simply states that the total stock of space supply in year t, labeled $S(t)$, equals the previous year's stock, $S(t-1)$, plus the new construction completed in year t.

$$S(t) = S(t-1) + C(t) \tag{2}$$

Two more equations portray the demand side of the space usage market. Equation (3) is the demand model, relating the amount of space that potential users would

[12] The general model examined here is often called a **stock-flow model**. The development of this type of model for real estate markets has been associated with researchers such as Kenneth Rosen, William Wheaton, and more recently, Patric Hendershott, among others. Though first developed for office markets, these types of models can be applied to any real estate market sector. While a comprehensive literature review is beyond the scope of this book, some seminal articles are cited in the reference list at the end of Part II.

[13] Note that this model thus assumes that developers are unable to forecast changes in rents.

currently *like* to occupy, $D(t)$, to the current rent level, $R(t)$, and the current level of underlying need, $N(t)$.[14]

$$D(t) = \alpha - \eta R(t) + \tau N(t) \qquad (3)$$

The measure of need reflects the fundamental sources of space usage demand discussed in the previous section. For example, for office markets, $N(t)$ might be measured by the number of office employees working in the market. The three parameters, α, η, and τ calibrate the demand model. The parameter α is a constant or "intercept" for the model. The response sensitivity parameter η reflects the price elasticity of demand, while the parameter τ reflects the "technology" of space usage, reflecting the quantity of space usage demanded per unit of underlying need. For example, if $N(t)$ is the number of office employees, then τ would represent the number of square feet per employee.

We assume it takes one year for space users to implement or realize the level of space usage demand they desire (due, for example, to time required to find the necessary space and move into it, or to vacate space and get out of leases in the case of reductions in space demand). So equation (4) simply equates the amount of space actually occupied at time t, $OS(t)$, to the demand in the previous year, $D(t-1)$. The previous year's demand is just the output of equation (3) applied in the previous year.

$$OS(t) = D(t-1) \qquad (4)$$

The fifth equation in the system simply reflects the definition of the vacancy rate, $v(t)$, as the fraction of the currently available stock of space that is currently unoccupied.

$$v(t) = [S(t) - OS(t)]/S(t) \qquad (5)$$

Note that the variables on the right-hand side of equation (5) are outputs from equations (2) and (4).

Finally, the system is made complete by equation (6), which represents landlord rental pricing behavior. Landlords are assumed to raise or lower rents in response to perceived contemporaneous vacancy rates.[15] In particular, if current vacancy rates are above the natural vacancy rate for the market, labeled V, then landlords will reduce rents. If current vacancy rates are below the natural rate, then landlords will raise rents. The sensitivity of rental response to vacancy rate deviations from the natural rate is reflected in the response parameter λ. It is assumed that it takes a year for landlords to respond effectively to changes in the market (perhaps due to difficulty of accurately observing the market, or sluggish response to the market).

$$R(t) = R(t-1)(1 - \lambda\{[v(t) - V]/V\}) \qquad (6)$$

The above six equations present a complete dynamic system of the real estate space market, including market supply, demand, and construction. By quantifying

[14] Thus, space users also do not forecast rents in this model.

[15] As with the other actors in this model, landlords do not forecast future rents.

the parameters in the equations, the decision-relevant characteristics of the market equilibrium can be simulated through time. In a realistic application, such a model would be specified and calibrated using econometric techniques. It is also possible to build explicit links to the capital market into the model, for example by relating the trigger rent, K, to capital market parameters such as real interest rates (see Hendershott [1995]).

To see how such a model of the real estate space market can simulate the functioning of the market over time, consider an office market that starts off with an employment level of 70,000, a stock of 20 million SF of built space, a vacancy rate of 10% (equal to its natural vacancy rate), and a rent level of $20/SF.

Now suppose this market is characterized by system parameters with the following numerical values:

- Supply sensitivity $\varepsilon = 0.3$
- Demand sensitivity $\eta = 0.3$
- Technology $\tau = 200$ SF/employee
- Demand intercept $\alpha = 10$ million SF
- Rent sensitivity $\lambda = 0.3$
- Construction lag $L = 3$ years

Exhibit 6-5 shows the 50-year evolution of rents, vacancy rate, and construction in such a market if the employment level grows steadily at a rate of 1% per year. The left-hand vertical scale in the exhibit shows the equilibrium level of rent (in $/SF), the vacancy rate (in percent), and the level of office employment in the market. The right-hand vertical scale measures the amount of new construction in millions of square feet. The graph traces the annual levels of each of these variables starting from the steady state described earlier.

The cyclical nature of the resulting market dynamics is obvious in this model. With the response and lag parameter values cited, this space market has a cycle of approximately 11 years. This **real estate cycle** exists even though there is no cycle, just steady growth, in the underlying source of the demand for space usage (employment), and even though there is no "lumpiness" in the provision of new space (buildings can be built in any size). The example depicted in Exhibit 6-5 demonstrates several features that tend to characterize real estate space market cycles.

- The real estate cycle may be different from and partially independent of the underlying business cycle in the local economy.
- The cycle will be much more exaggerated in the construction and development industry than in other aspects of the real estate market, such as rents and vacancy.
- The vacancy cycle tends to lead the rent cycle slightly (vacancy peaks before rent bottoms).
- New construction completions tend to peak when vacancy peaks.

The existence of a "built-in" cycle in the real estate space market, and indeed the specific features of the cycle noted, can be seen to result from several characteristics of the model described here. The particular response sensitivities and lags determine the cyclicality of the market, and more fundamentally, the myopic or adaptive nature of the behavior of the market participants tends to produce cyclicality. In this model,

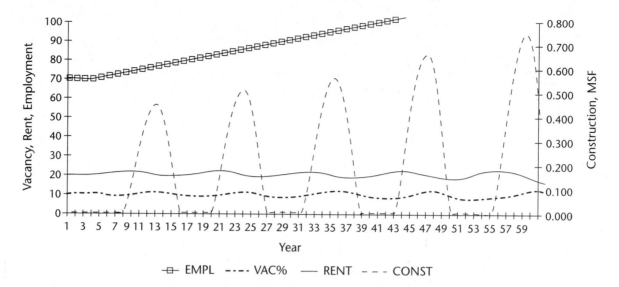

Exhibit 6-5 Simulated Space Market Dynamics

the market participants (developers, landlords, and tenants) base their decisions on present and past information rather than on forecasts of the future. Actual behavior in realistic markets is not as simple as that depicted in this model. As noted in Chapter 2, market participants do try to forecast the future, especially through the role that the real estate asset market plays in the overall system. Nevertheless, the simple model shown here probably does capture an important part of real estate market behavior, for market participants may not always put as much effort into basing decisions on future forecasts as they should, and even if they did, those forecasts would never be perfect.[16]

6.3 CHAPTER SUMMARY

This chapter presented the objectives, scope, and major elements involved in real estate space market analysis, as this type of analysis can help in making specific real estate decisions, including investment decisions. The elements and tools used in market analysis are based on the more fundamental urban economic and geographic principles discussed in the previous chapters. But market analysis needs to focus at a more specific level. Market analysis of this type is designed above all to be practical in a business or public policy decision-making environment. This means the analysis procedures must be simple enough to be understood and applied by practitioners, and they must be usable with realistic data availability. In this closing chapter of Part II, we left the more academic or theoretical realm of the preceding three chapters. If real estate market analysis does not help decision makers in a timely manner, it will not usually be useful in the real world. However, in this chapter we also saw how an articulated system of supply and demand models of the space market (including the construction industry) can be used to reveal some general patterns in the dynamics of these markets.

[16]See Chapter 28, Section 28.2.2, for a discussion of an alternative theory of real estate cycles that does not involve myopic or irrational behavior.

This chapter concludes Part II, the part of this book that is based primarily on urban economics and focuses primarily on the space market component of the real estate system defined in Chapter 2. The remainder of this book will focus primarily on topics most relevant to the asset market component of the system, and will be based primarily on financial economics as the major underlying academic discipline.

KEY TERMS

real estate market analysis
market segment
vacancy rate
natural vacancy rate
market rent
construction starts

construction completions
gross absorption
net absorption
months supply
simple trend extrapolation
structural analysis

price elasticity
lags
demand drivers
stock-flow model
real estate cycle
submarkets

STUDY QUESTIONS

6.1. What is the difference between a microlevel market analysis and a general characterization of a real estate market?

6.2. What are the two dimensions normally involved in defining a relevant real estate market?

6.3. Name and define the major supply and demand variables and indicators of market balance for real estate space usage markets.

6.4. In computing the market vacancy rate, how should one treat space that is leased but unoccupied and available for sublease?

6.5. Why is it normal for there to be some vacancy even in a healthy, well-functioning real estate market?

6.6. What is the relationship among the current market vacancy rate, the natural vacancy rate, and the direction of change in market rents?

6.7. What characteristics of a market are associated with a higher natural vacancy rate?

6.8. What is the difference between asking rent and effective rent?

6.9. Why is net absorption a better measure of demand growth in a market than gross absorption?

6.10. Discuss how you can use the months supply measure of vacant space in a market, combined with knowledge of the typical length of time to complete construction projects, to judge whether the market is likely to be able to absorb additional new construction.

6.11. Suppose a certain market has 1 million SF of currently vacant space, 2 million SF of space under construction, and annual absorption of 1.5 million SF. What is the months supply in this market? If the average project takes two years to complete, would you say this market is oversupplied, meaning that there is no need to pursue any new development projects?

6.12. Discuss the following statement: In a complete market analysis one must always consider an entire metropolitan area, even if one is really only interested in one part or subregion within the metropolis.

6.13. Discuss the differences between, and relative merits of, trend extrapolation and structural analysis as a way of conducting a market analysis.

6.14. Describe the eight basic tasks typically required in a structural analysis of a real estate space usage market.

6.15. Describe the major quantifiable drivers of demand for the principal types of real estate.

*6.16. Use a spreadsheet to build the simple stock-flow model of a real estate market described in section 6.2. Extend the simulation out for at least 50 years. Assume a constant rate of growth of underlying need. (You can access such a spreadsheet in this book's Web site.) Now vary the parameters that calibrate the system (elasticities, sensitivities, lags) and see how the resulting dynamics of the market change. Discuss your findings.

*6.17. What are the major features characterizing cycles in the real estate space usage market according to the basic stock-flow model?

*6.18. What is meant by myopic or adaptive behavior by market participants in the stock-flow model?

PART II

References and Additional Reading

Chapter 3: Central Place Theory and the System of Cities

Christaller, W. *Central Places in Southern Germany* 1933. English translation by C. W. Baskin. London: Prentice-Hall, 1966.

Gabaix, X. "Zipf's Laws for Cities: An Explanation," Harvard/MIT Working Paper, 1998 (presented at the Allied Social Sciences Association annual meeting, New York, January 1999).

Goetzmann, W. and S. Wachter. "Clustering Methods for Real Estate Portfolios." *Real Estate Economics* 23(3): 271-310, fall 1995.

Guilkey, D. "How Good Are MSA Forecasts?" *Real Estate Finance*, 15(4): 27–42, winter 1999.

Krugman, P. *Development, Geography, and Economic Theory*. Cambridge, MA: MIT Press, 1995.

Losch, A. *The Economics of Location* (1940). English translation by Fischer, Yale University Press, New Haven, 1954.

Mueller, G. "Refining Economic Diversification Strategies for Real Estate Portfolios." *Journal of Real Estate Research* 8(1): 55–68, winter 1993.

Chapters 4 and 5: Inside the City

Alonso, William. *Location and Land Use*. Cambridge, MA: Harvard University Press, 1964.

Amin, K. and D. R. Capozza. "Sequential Development." *Journal of Urban Economics* 34: 142–158, 1993.

Burgess, Ernest. *The City*, Chicago: University of Chicago Press, 1925

Capozza, Dennis and Robert Helsley. "The Stochastic City." *Journal of Urban Economics* 28: 187–203, 1990.

Childs, P. D., T. J. Riddiough, and A. J. Triantis. "Mixed Uses and the Redevelopment Option." *Real Estate Economics* 24: 317–339, 1996.

DiPasquale, Denise and William Wheaton. *Urban Economics and Real Estate Markets*. Englewood Cliffs, NJ: Prentice Hall, 1996.

Dixit, A. and R. Pindyck. *Investment Under Uncertainty*. Princeton, NJ: Princeton University Press, 1994.

Garreau, Joel. *Edge City: Life on the New Frontier*. New York: Doubleday, 1994.

Hoyt, Homer. *The Structure and Growth of Residential Neighborhoods in American Cities*. Washington DC: Federal Housing Administration, 1939.

Muth, Richard. *Cities & Housing*. Chicago: University of Chicago Press, 1969.

Titman, Sheridan. "Urban Land Prices Under Uncertainty." *American Economic Review* 75: 505–514, 1985.

Williams, J. "Real Estate Development as an Option." *Journal of Real Estate Finance & Economics* 4(2): 191–208, June 1991.

Chapter 6: Real Estate Market Analysis

Clapp, John. *Dynamics of Office Markets* AREUEA Monograph Series No.1, Washington, DC: Urban Institute Press, 1993.

ERE-Yarmouth Investment Research. *Real Estate Outlook: 1997.*

Guilkey, D. "How Good Are MSA Forecasts? A Review of the Major Supply- and Demand-Side Information Providers." *Real Estate Finance* 15(4): 27–42, winter 1999.

Hendershott, Patric. "Real Effective Rent Determination: Evidence from the Sydney Office Market." *Journal of Urban Economics* 12: 127–135, 1995.

Miles, M. "A Foundation for the Strategic Real Estate Allocation: The Space Market Index." *Real Estate Finance* 14(3): 23–30, fall 1997.

Miles, M. and D. Guilkey. "A Tactical Look at the Space Market Index." *Real Estate Finance* 14(4): 39–46, winter 1998.

Miller, Norman and M. Sklarz. "A Note on Leading Indicators of Housing Price Trends." *Journal of Real Estate Research* 1(1): 99–109, fall 1986.

Mueller, Glenn and Steven Laposa. "The Paths of Goods Movement." *Real Estate Finance* 11(2), summer, 1994.

Rosen, Kenneth. "Toward a Model of the Office Sector." *Journal of the American Real Estate & Urban Economics Association (AREUEA)* 12(3): 161–169, fall 1984.

Shilling, James, C. F. Sirmans, and John Corgel. "Natural Office Vacancy Rates: Some Additional Evidence." *Journal of Urban Economics* 31: 140–143, 1991.

Wheaton, William. "The Cyclic Behavior of the National Office Market." *Journal of the American Real Estate & Urban Economics Association (AREUEA)* 15(4): 281–299, winter 1987.

Basic Financial Economic Concepts and Tools

Perhaps the most fundamental characteristic of real estate is that it is long-lived. After all, land underlies all real estate, and land lives forever, practically speaking. When we combine this longevity with the fact that real estate can generally produce benefits of some type for some people, we arrive at the essence of why financial economics is important for understanding real estate. Financial economics is the branch of economic science that focuses on the capital markets, that is, markets for capital assets. Capital assets are claims to potential future benefit flows that can be measured in monetary terms. Real estate assets are therefore capital assets. So knowledge of financial economics is vital for understanding real estate.

The heart of financial economics is the systematic study of how markets for capital assets function and thereby determine the prices of capital assets, giving monetary value to such things as real estate assets. Fundamentally, financial economics is concerned with how capital markets weigh the timing, risk, and other attributes of the possible future cash flows from different types of assets to determine what these assets are worth in the market today, that is, at what price they trade or could be traded. Closely related to this issue (indeed, a part of it) is the matter of how these asset market values change over time.

In Part III we begin the in-depth study of the financial economics of real estate that is the main focus of this book. Orienting ourselves within the real estate system presented in Chapter 2, in Part III (and the remainder of this book) we will be focusing primarily on the real estate asset market and the broader capital markets of which it is a part. Part III covers some very basic background material and fundamental building blocks. If we may permit ourselves a real estate analogy, Parts III and IV together will present the building blocks and the foundation out of which, and on which, the rest of the structure will be built.

Chapter 7 presents an introduction and overview (continuing from the introduction in Chapter 1), situating real estate in the context of the broader capital markets, and giving the reader some perspective of the recent history of real estate as an investment asset class. Chapter 8 presents the major mathematical formulas used in converting multiyear cash flow streams to present value and computing returns on investments, essential tools in the study and practice of financial economics applied to real estate. Chapter 9 presents the fundamentals of the measurement of investment performance.

Real Estate as an Investment: Some Background Information

Learning Objectives

After reading this chapter, you should understand:

◆ The basic structure and functioning of the investment industry.

◆ The nature of investor objectives, constraints, and concerns.

◆ The major types of investment products and vehicles, and the difference between an underlying asset and an investment product.

◆ The major similarities and differences in the investment products based on real estate as opposed to other classical industrial or service corporations as underlying assets.

◆ The four major traditional investment asset classes and their characteristic differences.

◆ The investment performance of the major asset classes in recent decades, at a broad-brush and general level.

◆ Some of the major historical trends and events that have influenced real estate investment performance in recent decades.

How much do you already know about the investment industry in general? How much do you already know about commercial real estate in particular as an investment? Unless you can answer *quite a bit* to both of these questions, this chapter will provide some useful background for you, background that will help you to understand the subsequent chapters in this book. We won't cover any very deep academic theories or methods in this chapter, but we will present some very basic background information, the type of thing practitioners deal with every day, directly or indirectly, in the investment business. This chapter is divided into two major parts. The first part discusses the investment industry, beginning with the most basic underlying consideration—investors' objectives and concerns. The second part presents real estate as one investment asset class among several major such classes. It compares real estate investment performance to that of the other major asset classes at a broad-brush level, including a brief history of recent real estate investment trends.

7.1 INVESTMENT INDUSTRY, AND REAL ESTATE'S ROLE THEREIN

The word *industry* carries a variety of specific meanings. We often think of factories and the production or distribution of physical goods when we hear the word *industry*. In this sense, you may not think of investment activity, and the professional management of investments, as an industry, because you don't see any smokestacks or physical products. But this would be misleading. More broadly, the word *industry* refers to purposeful work and diligence, and in economics the term is used to refer to a branch of economic activity or trade. In this sense the investment business is a major industry in the United States. An introduction to some aspects of this industry is a very good place to begin a serious study of commercial real estate as an investment, and that is the purpose of this first section of this chapter. We begin with the most fundamental element in that industry: investors.

7.1.1 Investor Objectives and Concerns

Investors buy and sell capital assets, thereby making up both the demand and supply side of the capital markets. Through the process of buying and selling, investors determine the market values of capital assets, that is, the prices at which these assets trade. In deciding the prices at which they are willing to trade, investors consider the fundamental characteristics of the assets' future cash flow prospects. Investors also consider the nature of the capital markets in which the assets trade and how the functioning of those markets may affect the prices at which assets can trade. In Part I of this book we introduced you to these basic considerations when we presented the space and asset markets and the real estate system. Now let's focus in more depth on the players in this game, the investors. Naturally, investors view considerations about real estate cash flow and asset values keeping in mind their own objectives and constraints, the things they care about and worry about in making their investments. These objectives and constraints are therefore fundamental to understanding how real estate values are determined.

So, a good place to begin the study of real estate from an investment perspective is to consider the question; *Why do people invest?* Investment is the act of putting money aside that would otherwise be used for current consumption expenditure.[1] Why would someone do that? At the individual level, people may find themselves with more money than they currently need for consumption, or they may have a future objective for which they are willing to sacrifice some current consumption.

Consider a dual-income couple in their 20s. They may want to save for a down payment on a house. This might involve an investment horizon of, say, three to five

[1] In this context, we could use the word *save* as well as the word *invest*. But of course, money that is saved "goes somewhere." In effect, savings *is* investment, and it is the investment aspect that is of concern to us in this book.

years. Now consider a couple in their mid-30s. They may want to begin saving for their children's college tuition. This might involve a horizon of 10 to 15 years. Another couple in their mid-40s might want to save for their own retirement, with an investment horizon of over 20 years. Finally, consider a retired couple in their 60s or 70s. They may have assets they have accumulated over their working lives and now may want to begin drawing current income out of these assets, or even drawing down the principal value of the assets, to bolster their spendable income during their retirement years.

All of these individuals may differ not only in their investment time horizons, but also in their preferences for risk-taking in their investments. Virtually all investors would prefer a safe investment to a risky one, other things being equal. But investments vary in their risk. Therefore, risky investments must offer investors the prospect of a higher return; otherwise, no one will want to put their money there. But while this is true in general, investors differ in their preferences regarding the trade-off of risk and return. Some investors have a stronger preference for low-risk assets. They would require a greater increment in expected return in order to be willing to invest in a more risky asset.

Because of the importance of investors in the capital markets, let us refine and systematize our understanding of their motivations a little bit by defining the major **objectives**, and the major constraints or concerns faced by most investors. At a fundamental level, it is useful to distinguish two different and mutually exclusive types of investment objectives:

- The **growth** (or **savings**) **objective**, which implies a relatively long time horizon with no immediate or likely intermediate need to use the cash being invested
- The **income** (or **current cash flow**) **objective**, which implies that the investor has a short-term and ongoing need to use cash generated from the investment

Investors with the growth objective can put money away for a relatively long period of time. The investment need not pay out any cash unless and until it is sold, and need not be sold in the near term. If the investment does generate income in the meantime, this might be plowed back into investment so as to maximize the growth of the accumulated capital over the investment time horizon. This objective is typical of young to middle-aged individuals, of wealthy individuals of all ages, and of institutions such as pension funds of growing companies that expect to experience more cash inflow than outflow liabilities for many years into the future.

Investors with the income objective need to consider how much cash the investment will generate initially, as well as how this cash flow stream may change over time. Normally, an investor with a current income objective would tend to look for an investment with a high current cash payout rate, that is, the fraction of investment value that is typically paid out to the investor each year (e.g., in the form of interest coupons, dividends, or net rental payments). Investors with an income objective would typically include retired individuals and institutions such as endowment funds or pension funds with more retired members than current contributors.

It may be said that all investors have either a savings or income objective. In some cases the same investor may define both of these objectives for different parts of a wealth portfolio. But in addition to these objectives, investors all also face one or more of a set of typical constraints or concerns. The following list summarizes the major constraints and concerns that affect most investors, particularly in the real estate asset market:

- **Risk:** The possibility that future investment performance may vary over time in a manner that is not entirely predictable at the time when the investment is made.
- **Liquidity:** The ability to sell and buy investment assets quickly at full value and without much affecting the price of the assets.
- **Time Horizon:** The future time over which the investor's objectives, constraints, and concerns are relevant.
- **Investor Expertise and Management Burden:** How much ability and desire the investor has to manage the investment process and the investment assets.
- **Size:** How "big" the investor is in terms of the amount of capital in need of investment.
- **Capital constraint:** Does the investor face an absolute constraint on the amount of capital they have available to invest, or can additional capital be obtained relatively easily if good investment opportunities are available?

Some of these issues have already been mentioned. We noted that investors dislike risk. Real estate investors are no different from other investors in that, other things being equal, they will prefer less risky investments.

Similarly, investors like liquidity. Other things being equal, investors will pay more for (or equivalently, accept lower returns from) assets that are more liquid. Liquidity gives investors flexibility to move capital in or out of the investment and to respond to news and perceived opportunities. Different investors have different needs for, or preferences for, liquidity, just as they do for risk avoidance. Liquidity is potentially a major constraint or concern in real estate investment because property assets can require a long time to sell at full value, compared to publicly traded stocks and bonds, for example. As noted in Chapter 1, private asset markets are generally less liquid than public markets.

Investors' time horizons obviously affect both their ability to bear risk and their need for liquidity, or tolerance for illiquidity. Another particular concern in traditional real estate investment, as distinguished from securities, is the need for specialized expertise and the ability to bear some management burden when investing in property assets. Finally, in real estate investment, as in other types of investment, the nature of the opportunities and challenges differs according to the size of the investor. For example, larger investors may face lower costs per dollar invested due to economies of scale, and they may face a broader range of alternatives. They may also face greater ability to hire professional managers, both for their investments in general and for the operation of any properties they own. On the other hand, larger investors may have less liquidity, as the weight of their capital may tend to influence asset prices when they move it around.

Many large investors, and virtually all small investors, typically face some sort of "capital constraint", a limit to the amount of funds they can invest in any period of time. This means that they may sometimes have to forego investing in profitable opportunities, and it means that anything they do invest in prevents them from investing in something else. Such investors need to make certain they are ordering their priorities correctly so as to choose the best overall combination of investments available to them at a given time.

7.1.2 Implications of Investor Heterogeneity

A key implication of the range of differing investment objectives and constraints is that *investors are heterogeneous*—they have different personal goals and lifestyles, they are at different points in their life cycles, and they have different amounts of wealth and earned income. The ideal investment for one investor will not be the same as the ideal investment for another investor. Furthermore, many investment decisions are not made by individuals as such, but by institutions. Although all money in the private sector ultimately is owned by individuals, much investment activity that is important in real estate is made by investment institutions, such as banks, life insurance companies, pension funds, and mutual funds. Like individuals, investment institutions also are a heterogeneous lot. They have different constituencies, different liabilities, different levels or types of expertise, and they are subject to different types of regulations and legal constraints. Institutions also come in all sizes, from small to very large. All of this affects their investment objectives and constraints, as described previously.

One implication of **investor heterogeneity** is that this lays the foundation for a market in investment products. Some investors will want to buy when other investors want to sell. Another implication of heterogeneity is the need for a variety of different investment products and vehicles.

Fortunately, a modern capitalist society presents a wide variety of underlying investment opportunities in the form of different types of long-lived productive physical assets. An office building presents a very different likely future cash flow and value risk pattern than that of a biotech startup firm or a large industrial corporation. The matching of heterogeneous investors with heterogeneous physical assets is the key opportunity and function of the *investment industry*. The conception and construction of investment institutions, products, and vehicles that match sources of money with potential users of capital goes back to the Renaissance, lies at the root of the Industrial Revolution, and stimulates the heart of modern capitalist economies. How does this process work for real estate?

7.1.3 General Structure of Investment Products and Vehicles

As noted, at a broad-brush level, the investment industry matches heterogeneous investors (sources of financial capital) with heterogeneous productive assets (physical capital). This is done by the development of investment institutions, products, and vehicles. In this system, it is useful to distinguish underlying assets from investment products or vehicles. **Underlying assets** refers to the directly productive physical capital, such as an office building or an industrial or service corporation. Such a corporation is in fact a collection of physical, human, and legal assets and relationships organized into a system that can produce net cash flow over time through the production and sale of goods or services. In contrast to underlying assets, **investment products** or **vehicles** are typically (though not necessarily) one or more levels removed from the underlying assets, but they are based on the underlying assets. While investment products and vehicles are not themselves directly productive in the physical as opposed to purely financial sense, they have direct or indirect claims on, and sometimes commitments to, the directly productive underlying physical assets. Investment vehicles may or may not have governing authority over the underlying assets.

Perhaps the best way to understand this system is to look at a picture. Exhibit 7-1 schematically depicts the way the investment industry works in the classical

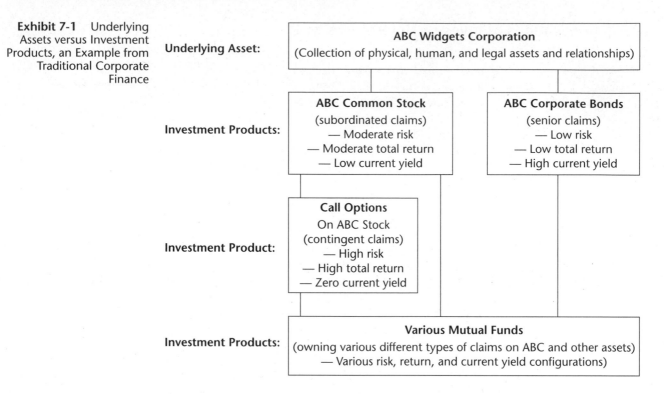

Exhibit 7-1 Underlying Assets versus Investment Products, an Example from Traditional Corporate Finance

and traditional structure of U.S. industry, using a fictitious industrial corporation, ABC Widgets, as the underlying asset. The box at the top of the diagram depicts ABC Widgets, the underlying asset, a collection of physical and human resources that generates a cash flow stream by the production and sale of widgets. For the investment industry, underlying assets such as ABC Widgets Corporation are the "raw material" on which investment products are based. The "finished products" are vehicles in which investors can directly place their money, or financial capital.

The first layer of investment products are those based most directly on the cash flow of the underlying asset. Traditionally, this layer would be represented by common stocks and corporate bonds issued by the underlying corporation. In traditional corporate finance for large industrial and service corporations, these basic investment products are usually publicly traded in a relatively liquid secondary market, such as the stock exchange. In essence, the claims to ABC's cash flows are partitioned into two classes of investment products that have different risk and return characteristics.

ABC corporate bonds are the senior claims, meaning that they will be paid first, and they are for a fixed contractual amount with a finite expiration or maturity.[2] All of these features make ABC bonds relatively low risk for most investors. Traditional bonds provide a relatively high current income yield to their investors, as this represents the entire expected total return to the bonds.

In contrast, ABC's common stock is the residual (subordinated) claim on ABC's cash flow, with no contractual guarantee of the amount the stockholders will receive. ABC's stock represents the equity in the ABC Corporation, perpetual-lived claims

---

[2] Corporations also make use of privately held debt, such as bank debt or privately placed bonds, but we assume ABC has no such debt as it is not depicted in Exhibit 7-1.

with governing authority over the corporation, and they present the typical investor with more risk, but the prospect of higher returns on average over the long run, than ABC's bonds. If ABC is a large, well-established firm, then its stock may be viewed as having moderate investment risk. Such a firm would normally pay regular dividends, providing stockholders with at least a small current yield on their investment, with the bulk of their total return coming in the form of expected growth in share price over time. This share price represents the present value of the expected future stream of dividends.

This first level of investment products—stocks and bonds—has been the mainstay of corporate finance and the investment industry in the United States since the 19th century. But particularly in recent years, additional layers and types of investment products have been developed, based on the stocks and bonds. Some of these secondary products are specialized claims, such as contingent claims, that pay off only under certain circumstances and otherwise expire worthless.

The archetypal examples of this type of product are the standardized "call and put options" that are publicly traded on the Chicago Options Exchange and elsewhere. Options are an example of a derivative investment product, in that they are derived from other products, in this case common stocks. For example, an ABC call option would allow its holder to purchase a certain number of shares of ABC stock at a specified price on or prior to a specified date. For such a product, the underlying asset is another investment product, namely the common stock of ABC Corporation. Call options are typically very high risk, because they are effectively levered to a high degree and they may end up being worthless if the underlying asset's share price never rises above the exercise price at which the option allows purchase of the stock. The expected return on options is very high, but that is because the risk is very high, and there is no income yield at all while holding the option.

Another type of investment product that has become very important in recent decades is the mutual fund. A typical mutual fund is a diversified pool of stocks and/or bonds. Mutual funds allow investors to invest indirectly in a large number of different stocks or bonds simply by purchasing a share in the mutual fund. Mutual funds are quite varied, with different objectives and different risk and return profiles.

The main point of the system of investment products built upon the underlying asset of ABC Widget Corporation, as depicted in Exhibit 7-1, is to allow investors with different risk and return objectives to all be satisfied investing, directly or indirectly, in the same underlying asset. By defining different types of claims on future cash flows, ABC Widget can offer investors products with very different risk and return characteristics, indeed, risk and return characteristics that can be quite different from those of the underlying asset itself. ABC Widget's future cash flow stream may be a perpetual, low-risk, slightly variable stream, while its bonds are very low-risk, finite-lived, fixed streams; its stock shares are moderate-risk, perpetual assets with substantial price volatility; and its call options are very high-risk, short-lived "bets." An investor in a mutual fund owning some shares of ABC will barely notice the individual or unique effect of ABC in his returns.

We see how investor heterogeneity drives the investment industry. We also see how the entire system is built ultimately on underlying physical assets, producers of cash flow streams from the production and sale of goods and services, the "raw material" in the investment industry.

Let's carry this analogy a bit further. If the only type of ore that existed were iron ore, we could produce quite a variety of different types of finished products out of steel, but we could not produce any products of aluminum or copper or tin. The existence of a variety of different ores (raw materials) allows the production of a much broader variety of finished products. This is so also in the investment industry. A greater variety of underlying physical assets allows a greater variety of investment products, with a greater range of risk and return characteristics and potential for diversification of investment portfolios. This allows more types of investors to be served through the investment process and increases the effectiveness and efficiency of the allocation of financial capital to underlying physical assets.

This is where real estate comes into the picture. Real property assets are underlying assets in the investment industry, comparable to, but different from, the industrial and service corporations that characterize traditional corporate finance and investments.[3] Because real estate is different, it presents unique opportunities. The investment industry based on real estate underlying assets, and the variety of real estate investment products and vehicles, is growing and evolving rapidly. Traditionally, the investment system for real estate has been a bit different from that of industrial corporations, although recent evolution has brought the two systems closer together.

Exhibit 7-2 depicts the investment system for a typical collection of real estate underlying assets, say, a group of shopping centers developed and owned by a single family, the Grump brothers. Like underlying physical assets of any type, these real properties produce a stream of cash flow from the production and sale of goods or services, in this case, built space and location for operations by retail tenants.

Unlike the situation for the typical large industrial corporation, however, in the traditional real estate system it is possible for investors to *own directly the underlying physical assets*. This is indicated in Exhibit 7-2 by the line linking the underlying asset at the top with the investors represented by the box at the bottom of the diagram. But note that this box is divided into two types of investors, large and small. Underlying physical assets are large entities, typically worth millions of dollars each.[4] It is generally not possible for small individual investors who are not very wealthy to own whole commercial properties directly.[5] But it is possible for wealthy individual investors, as well as investment institutions (such as pension funds or life insurance companies), to own large commercial properties or portfolios of properties directly. This is a key difference between the investment system for real estate and that for typical industrial and service corporations.

As with the stocks and bonds that form the backbone of corporate finance, a "first layer" of traditional real estate investment products has been around for a long

[3] Real estate is "different," in the most fundamental sense, in the same way that each type or class of underlying physical asset is different. In a mathematical sense, real estate values and cash flows are *statistically independent*; that is, they do not change over time in ways that are perfectly correlated with any one or combination of other classes of underlying assets. More specific aspects of real estate's uniqueness have been mentioned in Part I of this book, and will be covered in more depth in this and subsequent chapters.

[4] In fact, individual real estate assets are usually not worth as much as individual whole corporations, which is one reason that it is possible to have direct ownership of whole real estate assets. In the example in Exhibit 7-2, we are talking about a collection or portfolio (perhaps a "chain") of numerous individual shopping centers managed as a single underlying asset, and this, of course, greatly builds up the value. This portfolio or chain of centers may easily be worth as much as a typical medium-size corporation traded on the stock exchange.

[5] Of course, small commercial properties and apartments are not that expensive, and it is possible for individuals of modest wealth to get into real estate investment at this so-called "mom and pop" end of the business.

Exhibit 7-2 Real Estate Example of the Investment System

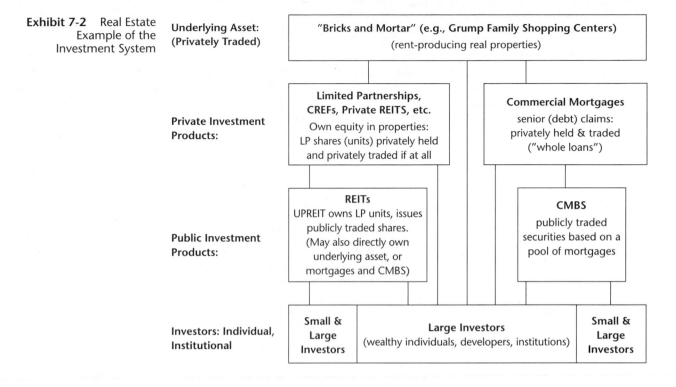

time. Best known of these are the commercial mortgages, which are debt products, loans secured by the underlying real property assets. Commercial mortgages are comparable to corporate bonds in that they represent senior claims on the property cash flows and they provide investors with a finite-lived, contractually fixed cash flow stream. Unlike typical corporate bonds, commercial mortgages traditionally have not been broken up into small homogeneous shares or units that are traded in public exchanges. Instead, the traditional procedure has been to keep each mortgage as a "whole loan," which is typically held to maturity by the originating institution (such as a life insurance company or bank) or occasionally traded privately in a negotiated deal for the whole loan in its entirety.

There are also investment products designed to enable **passive investors** to invest in real estate equity. Passive investors are those who do not wish to be deeply or directly involved in the management and operation of the underlying real estate assets. They may lack the necessary specialized expertise or the time and resources required by such management, yet they value the risk and return characteristics of commercial real estate equity. For example, passive investors in real estate equity are often interested in real estate's ability to diversify an investment portfolio that otherwise consists largely of traditional corporate stocks and bonds. A variety of real estate passive equity investment products have been developed over the years. Some of the most prominent include real estate limited partnership units (RELPs), **comingled real estate funds (CREFs or unit trusts)**, and **private REITs (real estate investment trusts** whose shares are not traded publicly). These investment vehicles are similar to corporate stock in that they provide their investors with an ownership interest in the underlying asset, sometimes leveraged. However, these real estate equity vehicles differ from corporate stock; in in some cases they have rather limited governance authority over the assets, and they are not traded in liquid public exchanges.

Indeed, a common and prominent feature of the first level of real estate investment products shown in Exhibit 7-2, the traditional level, is that these products are privately traded, if they are traded at all, not traded on public exchanges like stocks and bonds. While secondary markets do exist to some extent in which some of these products can be traded, such secondary markets are not highly developed and generally lack liquidity.

In fact, if we go back to the underlying physical assets themselves, we note that these assets are also directly traded privately in the property asset market. This is possible because, as noted, investors can own the underlying physical assets in real estate directly, and because most individual real estate assets are smaller than typical industrial corporations. In fact, the major traditional market for trading real estate equity is the property market in which the underlying physical assets are traded, rather than secondary markets for the first-level equity and debt products shown in Exhibit 7-2. Although the property market is a **private market**, in which individual buyers and sellers have to "find" each other and negotiate deals privately, this is a highly developed and well-functioning asset market. The existence of this direct market for underlying whole assets is another important difference between real estate and mainstream corporate finance and investment.

As with the corporate side of the investment industry, recent decades have seen the development of significant new real estate investment products and vehicles. Most notable for commercial property was the "securitization revolution" of the 1990s, which saw a tremendous development of publicly traded investment vehicles, represented by the second level of investment products shown in Exhibit 7-2, the REITs and **CMBS (commercial mortgage-backed securities)**. This has linked Wall Street (traditional mainstream corporate finance and investment) to Main Street (traditional real estate finance and investment) much more closely than ever before, and provided a major new source of capital for commercial real estate. CMBS and REITs were introduced and briefly described in Chapter 1, and we will say only a little bit more about them here.

In essence, CMBS are debt products, while REITs are equity products.[6] CMBS are typically based on pools of commercial mortgages. Different classes of securities are usually issued from the same underlying pool. Some classes are more risky than others, and different classes have different typical maturities. This allows a variety of risk and return patterns to be created for the different CMBS classes based on the same underlying pool of mortgages. In this way investors with different risk preferences and investment horizons can be served.

REITs, on the other hand, are usually perpetual ownership vehicles that typically specialize in investing in, and often actively developing and managing, portfolios of commercial property equity. They are usually levered, issuing either "entity-level debt" backed by the REIT as a whole (such as bonds) or mortgages backed by specific properties owned by the REIT ("property-level debt"). Traditional REITs directly own underlying physical real estate assets. In the 1990s a new type of REIT structure known as the umbrella partnership REIT, or UPREIT, was pioneered. By the end of the 1990s, many of the largest REITs were UPREITs. As depicted in Exhibit 7-2, an UPREIT does not directly own the underlying "bricks and mortar,"

---

[6] However, REITs can invest in mortgages, and some REITs specialize in this acitivity, or in buying CMBS. These are known as mortgage REITs. However, even mortgage REITs typically behave like equity rather than debt, in part because they tend to be highly leveraged, so the debt on the liability side of their balance sheets largely offsets the debtlike characteristics on the asset side of their balance sheets.

but rather owns units in a partnership, which in turn owns the underlying physical properties either directly or indirectly. The purpose of this complicated arrangement is to allow property owners to "sell" their properties to the REIT without incurring a taxable event.[7]

REITs typically present their investors (stockholders) with risk and return characteristics similar to those of levered investment in the underlying physical real estate, but with some important differences. First, REIT shares are small, enabling small individual investors to participate in commercial property investment.[8] Second, REIT shares are usually publicly traded and so provide the typical investor with more liquidity than direct investment in privately traded underlying real estate assets. Third, unless the investor purchases a large proportion of all the REIT shares, the investor will have little management burden, as the job of managing the properties will be done by the REIT's professional management. (This is analogous to buying stock in an industrial firm but not having to be actively involved in the management of that firm, as the firm has a full-time professional management team.) Fourth, REITs are typically rather actively managed firms that may engage in buying and selling of properties as well as property development, not just passively holding and operating a static portfolio of properties.[9] Thus, the risk and return characteristics of the REIT reflect the risk and return characteristics of the REIT's management, including the stock market's perception of their abilities and future opportunities, as well as the nature of their existing portfolio of properties.

A final difference between the investment performance of REITs and direct investment in underlying real estate assets is due simply to the fact that REITs trade in the stock market. As a result, REIT share values reflect the functioning and valuation of the stock market rather than that of the direct property asset market. It is unclear to what extent this affects REIT risk and return, but as noted in Chapter 1, the stock market is likely more informationally efficient than the private property market. Thus, REIT share prices probably respond more quickly and completely to news relevant to their value. Some researchers also believe that the stock market is subject to fads or overreaction, leading to excess volatility, at least in the short run.

As a result of the development of the REIT industry during the 1990s, commercial real estate equity is now traded in two major asset markets, the private property

---

[7] Successful individual real estate developers and investors own many properties that are worth much more than they cost them. If they sold these properties, they would realize a large capital gain and owe large income taxes on that gain. This is what would happen if they sold their properties to a REIT either for cash or common equity shares of the REIT. However, if you exchange an interest in one partnership for an interest in another partnership, the form of ownership does not change, and the IRS considers that no taxable event has occurred. An UPREIT can "pay" for properties it acquires by giving the seller units in the umbrella partnership, rather than cash or common shares. These umbrella partnership units may be convertible over time into equity shares in the REIT, giving their owner flexibility over when and whether to realize the taxable event.

[8] This was the original purpose Congress had in mind in establishing the REIT investment vehicle as a tax status in 1960. As noted in Chapter 1, REITs avoid corporate-level income tax by conforming to certain requirements that ensure that REITs remain, in essence, a purely real estate investment vehicle.

[9] REITs are encouraged by the tax code not to be too "active." They must pay out 90% of their accrual accounting-based earnings (not their cash flow) each year as dividends, or they will lose their REIT tax status and be forced to pay corporate income tax. This may put some constraint on their ability to retain cash for discretionary activity without having to go to the capital market. Also, REITs must typically hold most of their assets for at least four years, which prevents rapid turnaround and "merchant building." Nevertheless, these provisions effectively do not prevent most REITs from considering a substantial range of rather active management strategies. (See Chapter 24 for more discussion.)

asset market in which the underlying physical assets are traded directly, and the public stock exchange in which REIT shares are traded. Both of these asset markets are well-functioning, very highly developed markets. This situation is rather unique to real estate. It would be as if, in addition to being able to buy shares in automobile manufacturing companies, investors could also directly buy and sell stamping plants, engine factories, and vehicle assembly plants, or perhaps even individual machines, parts inventories, and design labs—in short, all the physical assets of an automobile company.[10]

There are some implications of this unique double-market environment for real estate investment, which we will come back to in subsequent chapters in this book. For now, the main point is simply for you to realize that this dual market situation exists. Exhibit 7-3 shows one way to depict these two parallel markets. The exhibit traces the implied values of commercial property assets in the two markets. It shows two indices of asset value. The NAREIT index is based on the share prices of REITs. The NCREIF index is based on the appraised values of large commercial properties held directly by institutional investors.[11] The two indices trace broadly the same picture over time. However, the REIT share prices seem to have some tendency to lead the private market valuations in time, by registering turning points and trends a bit sooner. On the other hand, the REIT-based index appears a bit more volatile in the short run, with some ups and downs that prove to be transient. Sometimes one market seems to value real estate more than the other market, although which one has the higher valuation varies over time.

Let us now summarize the modern real estate investment system depicted back in Exhibit 7-2. The defining characteristic of this system is that the underlying assets are real properties. Real property is unique, presenting risk and return characteristics not exactly like those of the whole industrial and service corporations that form the underlying assets in traditional corporate finance.[12] Unlike typical corporate finance,

[10] If REITs were only very passive investors in existing fully operational properties, then they would be comparable to closed-end mutual funds that invest in portfolios of stocks, with the closed-end fund's shares trading separately in the stock market. To some extent, REITs are indeed like closed-end stock funds, only they invest in real estate assets instead of stocks. But most of the newer and larger REITs, especially those formed during the 1990s, are much more actively managed, deeply and directly involved in the operation and management of their properties, and often in the development of new buildings as well. Such firms are more similar to a vertically integrated industrial or service corporation specializing in providing built space to tenants than they are like mutual funds that simply buy and sell existing assets.

[11] Exhibit 7-3 is based on the NAREIT index of share price capital returns and the NCREIF index property appreciation returns, with some minor alterations by the authors. The NAREIT index has been "unlevered" using aggregate REIT industry balance sheet statistics provided by NAREIT (the National Association of Real Estate Investment Trusts, Washington). The NCREIF Index (published by the National Council of Real Estate Investment Fiduciaries, Chicago), which is already unlevered, has been "unsmoothed" to remove the effect of appraisal lag. (The problem of "appraisal lag" is discussed in Chapter 25. The unsmoothing procedure employed here is the annual "one-step" reverse-engineering method described in section 25.3.3.) Because the starting value of an index is arbitrary, no generality is lost by setting the starting values of these two indices so that their average value levels across time are equal. One would expect a relationship like this to hold on average over the long run, or else all the assets would tend to be held in only one form or the other (whichever provided the highest valuation). The result is pictured in Exhibit 7-3. Thus this is only an approximate and broad-brush picture: it demonstrates the basic nature of the relationship between the two types of asset markets for real estate equity investment.

[12] At the level of the underlying physical assets, this same statement could probably be made about any major segment or class of assets; for example, airlines are different from banks.

Exhibit 7-3 End-of-Year Public versus Private Asset Market Commercial Real Estate Values (Indexes set to have equal average values—1974–98)

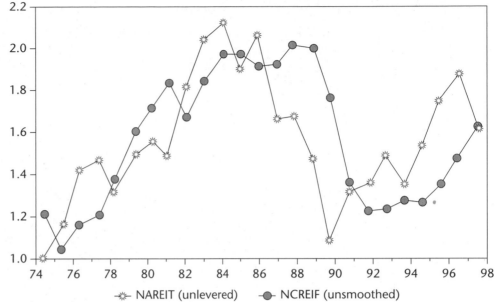

—☀— NAREIT (unlevered) —●— NCREIF (unsmoothed)

real estate underlying physical assets trade directly in a well-functioning, albeit private, asset market. As always, the investment industry creates investment products and vehicles that enable a variety of risk and return patterns to be carved out of the same underlying assets, so that heterogeneous investors can be better served, and capital can flow more efficiently and effectively to real estate. As always, equity products and debt products are prominent in the investment system. In recent years, publicly traded vehicles have been developed that significantly increase the liquidity, and perhaps the informational efficiency, in the real estate industry. By the late 1990s approximately 10% of the value of commercial real estate in the United States was held directly or indirectly by these public market debt and equity vehicles, REITs and CMBS, including a larger percentage of some higher-end property types. This creates a unique double-market environment for real estate, unlike what prevails for other types of underlying assets.

7.2 REAL ESTATE AS AN ASSET CLASS

Do you recall what we said about the importance of having different types of underlying physical assets, so that greater variety and range of alternatives can be offered to heterogeneous investor groups? We noted that commercial real estate is a unique class of underlying assets. What we want to do in the remainder of this chapter is to put ourselves in the shoes of investors, scanning the big picture of the investment universe available to them to see the nature and role of real estate as one of several major investment asset classes. We will review the historical, empirical investment performance of the major asset classes. To simplify matters at this broad-brush level, we will consider the main traditional form of institutional real estate investment, that is, the direct unlevered investment in large scale commercial property.

7.2.1 Four Major Investment Asset Classes

Traditionally, **four major asset classes** are identified in the investment universe and portfolio planning.

- Cash (T-bills)
- Stocks
- Bonds
- Real estate

Although classification at this level is necessarily somewhat stylistic and simplified, these four classes make a useful taxonomy for several reasons. First, each presents unique typical characteristics regarding the objectives and constraints that typically concern investors. Second, substantial empirical historical data is publicly available regarding the investment performance of each of these asset classes. Third, each of these four classes is large enough in magnitude to support substantial capital flow into or out of the asset class without great disruptions to markets and industries. Fourth, each of these asset classes is "investable." That is, asset markets and investment vehicles exist enabling institutions and/or individuals to buy and sell assets in each of these classes.[13] The approximate aggregate value of the assets in each of the four classes is shown in Exhibit 7-4, as of the late 1990s.[14] Real estate equity represented about a quarter of the total $33 trillion investable asset pie.[15]

The table in Exhibit 7-5 presents a qualitative characterization of the typical investment performance expectations of each of the four asset classes. The table qualitatively describes each of the asset classes along five dimensions of investment performance.

- Risk
- Average total return on investment
- Average current yield (current income as a fraction of investment value)
- Average growth (capital return or growth in investment principal value)
- Relative degree of inflation protection (positive correlation of investment returns with unexpected changes in inflation)

Exhibit 7-5 clarifies what we mean when we say that each asset class offers investors unique investment performance attributes. None of the four classes substantially duplicates any of the others in what it provides for investors. Together, they present a wide range of possibilities.

---

[13] Other, less "investable," asset classes can be defined conceptually, such as "human capital" and small privately held businesses. But it is difficult to invest in such other classes, and difficult to quantify their magnitude.

[14] The real estate asset class total value of approximately $8 trillion depicted in Exhibit 7-4 includes residential as well as commercial property, but it includes only "pure-play" equity value. The value of mortgages and of corporate real estate (held by publicly traded, non-real-estate companies) is excluded in the real estate share, but included in the bond and stock shares, respectively. The total value of underlying real estate assets including these components would be nearly $14 trillion. Commercial property in the United States is only about one-third the total of the underlying real estate asset value, on the order of $3 to $4 trillion. The source of the estimates in Exhibit 7-4 is Miles & Tolleson (1997), adjusted and updated by the authors' estimates. Exhibit 7-4 differs from Exhibit 1-8 in Chapter 1 primarily because private debt (other than mortgages) is not classified as "investable" in Exhibit 7-4, and so is not included in the "pie."

[15] Lists of asset classes often include international equity as a fifth asset class. However, from a broader perspective, *all* of the three risky asset classes (stocks, bonds, and real estate) may include international as well as domestic investment.

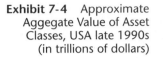

Exhibit 7-4 Approximate Aggegate Value of Asset Classes, USA late 1990s (in trillions of dollars)

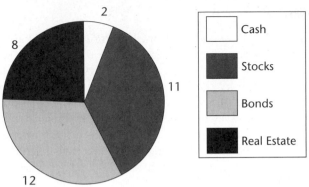

Exhibit 7-5 Stereotypical Characterization of Major Investment Asset Classes

Investment Concern	Stocks	Real Estate*	Long-Term Bonds**	Cash (T-Bills)
Risk	High	Moderate to Low***	Moderate to Low***	Lowest
Total Return	High	Moderate	Moderate	Lowest
Current Yield	Low	High	Highest	Moderate
Growth	High	Low	None	None****
Inflation Protection	L. R. Good	Good	Bad	Best (if reinvested)

*Unlevered institutional quality commercial property (fully operational).

**Investment grade corporate or government bonds.

***Low risk for investors with long-term horizons and deep pockets, so they can hold the assets to maturity or until prices are favorable. Moderate risk for investors fully exposed to asset market price volatility.

****Unless the investment is rolled over (reinvested), in which case there is no current yield.

Real estate has an important role in the overall picture, as one of these four major asset classes. Note in particular that in the risk and return dimensions unlevered investment in real estate tends to fall between stocks at one extreme and cash (or short-term bonds such as T-bills) at the other extreme. In this regard, real estate is much like long-term bonds. Unlike bonds, however, real estate provides some capital growth and relatively good inflation protection. On the other hand, the contractual and finite nature of bond cash flows enables investors who can buy and hold bonds to maturity, without having to sell them in the bond market, to greatly reduce the risk in their investment (at least in nominal terms).[16]

Another important and defining characteristic of the four major asset classes is that they do not all "move together" in their investment performance. That is, they do not always tend to all do well at the same time, or all do poorly at the same time. The correlation among their periodic returns is at most only moderately positive, and in some cases less than that. This means that investors can diversify their portfolios by allocating across the four asset classes.

[16] Real estate investors who can have a long-term and flexible holding horizon also can greatly reduce the risk. Most of the return for such investors will come in the form of the relatively stable and predictable real estate rents. Such investors may also be able to take advantage of the greater degree of asset price predictability in the real estate market.

7.2.2 Historical Investment Performance

Exhibit 7-6 presents a broad-brush historical, empirical picture of the investment performance of the four asset classes over the last three decades of the 20th century. The exhibit shows what one dollar of investment, placed at the end of 1969, would have grown to by the end of each of the following years, in each of the four asset classes. Exhibit 7-6 assumes that any income generated by the investment was plowed back into the investment, so that the values shown represent the compounded accumulation of the total returns. In addition to the four asset classes, Exhibit 7-6 shows the effect of inflation by tracing the Consumer Price Index (CPI), indicating the number of dollars necessary in each year to purchase what one dollar could have bought in 1969.

Over the historical period shown in Exhibit 7-6, the champion performer was clearly the stock market. For every dollar invested at the beginning of 1970, the investor in the stock market would have $39.14 by the end of 1998. The lowest return was provided by U.S. Treasury Bills, that is, a continuously rolled-over reinvestment in the short-term notes of the government, similar to a typical money market fund. Such investment would have grown to only $6.67 per dollar of original investment. Intermediate performance was turned in by long-term bonds and real estate ($14.32 and $14.91, respectively). All four of the asset classes "beat inflation;" that is to say, they provided their investors with a positive "real" return, increasing the purchasing power of their invested dollars. The CPI indicates that it would have taken $4.34 to buy at the end of 1998 what $1.00 bought at the beginning of 1970.[17]

While the historical results shown in Exhibit 7-6 are broadly consistent with the relative total return expectations noted in Exhibit 7-5, it is important to realize that investment performance is always risky to some extent. This means that performance, both absolutely and in relative terms comparing across the asset classes, varies over time in ways that are never perfectly predictable. For example, during roughly the first half of the historical period shown in Exhibit 7-6, it was not the stock market, but rather real estate that posted the best overall performance, as seen in Exhibit 7-7a. During the 1970–83 period, each dollar invested at the outset would have grown to $4.75 in real estate, but to only $3.31 in stocks, or $2.83 in T-bills. During that

---

[17]Quantitative performance histories such as those portrayed in Exhibit 7-6 must be interpreted cautiously. It is difficult to measure investment performance in a way that is exactly comparable across asset classes, and there is always a question of what "index" best represents the specific investments or opportunities faced by a given investor. The numbers in Exhibit 7-6 are based on the following indexes. For the stock market we have used the Standard & Poor 500 Index, which consists of 500 relatively large stocks. For bonds we have used an index of long-term U.S. Treasury Bonds. Both the stock and bond index returns, as well as the Treasury Bill returns, are as computed by Ibbotson & Associates in their annual *Stocks, Bonds, Bills & Inflation Yearbook*. The real estate returns are more problematical. The returns shown here are based on the NCREIF index, published by the National Council of Real Estate Investment Fiduciaries. However, unlike the other indices, the NCREIF index is based on appraised values rather than actual transaction prices or market values, and many of the appraisals in the NCREIF index are slightly "stale." Most researchers feel that this would make the NCREIF index appear artificially lagged in time and smoothed in a graph such as Exhibit 7-6 comparing the asset classes. Therefore, as in Exhibit 7-3, the real estate index shown in Exhibit 7-6 has been modified slightly from the official NCREIF index, to attempt to correct for the appraisal problem and provide an index that is more comparable to the other three. Also, we have used other sources similar to the NCREIF index to extend the real estate series farther back in time, as the NCREIF index does not begin until 1978. The measurement of periodic real estate returns, and the nature and use of the NCREIF Index, will be discussed in some depth in Part VII later in this book.

Exhibit 7-6   Historical Performance of Major Investment Asset Classes, Compared to Inflation (CPI), 1969–98

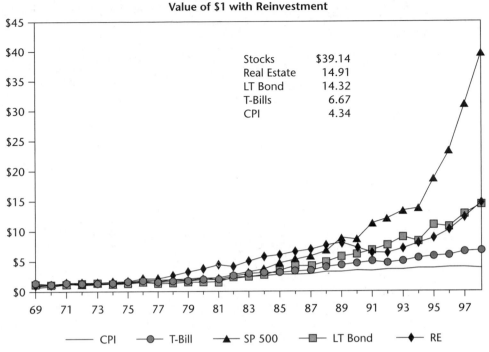

Value of $1 with Reinvestment

Stocks	$39.14
Real Estate	14.91
LT Bond	14.32
T-Bills	6.67
CPI	4.34

—— CPI   ——●—— T-Bill   ——▲—— SP 500   ——■—— LT Bond   ——◆—— RE

period long-term bond investments would have grown only to $2.36, less than the CPI of $2.69,[18]

On the other hand, during the second half of the period, depicted in Exhibit 7-7b, the stock market greatly dominated all the other asset classes. For each dollar invested at the end of 1983, the stock market investor would have $11.83 by the end of 1998, versus $6.05 for the bond market investor, $2.97 for the real estate investor, and only $2.36 for the T-Bill investor. This period saw the worst fall in commercial real estate values in the United States since the 1930s. Even so, real estate during this period beat inflation and T-bills, thanks to a strong recovery in the latter half of the 1990s.

The table in Exhibit 7-8 summarizes the 1970–98 annual investment performance history shown in Exhibit 7-6, in the form of some basic statistical measures. The first column of Exhibit 7-8 indicates the average annual total return, the growth in investment value from both capital value appreciation as well as income paid out to the investor (such as dividends, interest, or rent). The second column indicates the annual standard deviation in these yearly total returns during the 29-year history considered. This standard deviation is a measure of the variability across time in the returns, also

---

[18] This indicates a negative real return in long-term bonds over the 1970–83 period. This was due to rising inflation over most of that historical period. As noted in Exhibit 7-5, bonds are negatively affected by inflation. However, it must also be recognized that the historical periodic returns examined in this section assume, in effect, that investors sell and reinvest their portfolios at the end of each year. This results in an investor in long-term bonds being subject annually to the vagaries of the bond market, which was generally unfavorable during the 1970s. In reality, many investors in long-term bonds would not sell their investments so frequently, but would instead hold onto their bonds until maturity, taking in the coupon interest income as their return on investment. Such investors would not have fared as poorly during this period as is indicated in Exhibit 7-7a.

Exhibit 7-7a
Performance of the Major
Asset Classes, 1969–83

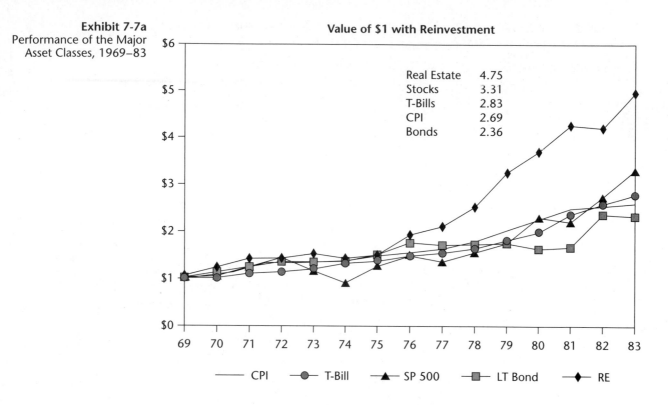

Value of $1 with Reinvestment

Real Estate	4.75
Stocks	3.31
T-Bills	2.83
CPI	2.69
Bonds	2.36

CPI — T-Bill — SP 500 — LT Bond — RE

Exhibit 7-7b
Performance of the Major
Asset Classes, 1983–98

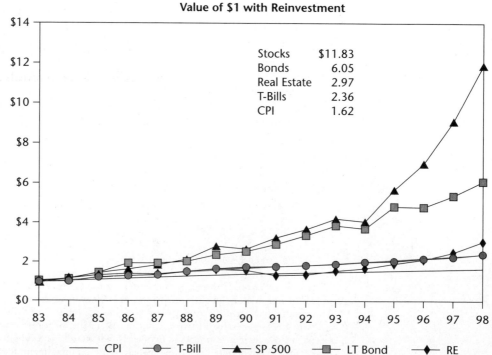

Value of $1 with Reinvestment

Stocks	$11.83
Bonds	6.05
Real Estate	2.97
T-Bills	2.36
CPI	1.62

CPI — T-Bill — SP 500 — LT Bond — RE

Exhibit 7-8 Historical
Statistics on Annual
Returns, 1970–98

Asset Class	Average Total Return	Standard Deviation	Average Income Return	Average Appreciation Return
T-Bills	6.80%	2.66%	6.80%	0.00%
G Bonds	10.20%	11.80%	9.18%	1.01%
Real Estate	10.22%	9.92%	6.60%	3.62%
Stocks	14.68%	16.21%	4.70%	9.98%
Inflation	5.24%	3.24%		

known as the volatility of the investment. This is a basic way to measure the risk in the investment asset class. The last two columns on the right in the table break the average total return into two components. The income return is the average current income paid out to the investor each year by the investment, as a fraction of the investment value at the beginning of the year. The appreciation return is the average annual capital gain or percentage growth in asset value.[19]

The historical statistics presented in the table in Exhibit 7-8 are depicted graphically in the bar charts in Exhibits 7-9a and 7-9b. Exhibit 7-9a shows the average total return, and breaks out the two components: average current income and average capital appreciation. Notice that the bulk of the return on investment in stocks comes typically in the form of capital gain, or share price appreciation. In contrast, virtually all of the return to bonds was typically from the current income paid by the bond interest.[20] Commercial real estate typically derives its return from both asset value appreciation and current net rental income, although the bulk of the return to unlevered investments in fully operational properties comes from net rental income.[21]

Exhibit 7-9b shows the standard deviation in the asset periodic returns across time, the volatility. We noted that this is a basic way to measure the risk in an investment because it indicates the range of variability in the investment performance outcomes across time. Comparing Exhibits 7-9a and b reveals an important point. Note that the average total return shown in Exhibit 7-9a corresponds closely to the magnitude of volatility shown in Exhibit 7-9b. This is the classical relationship between *risk and return*, in which *greater risk is associated with greater average returns over time*, and lower average returns are associated with more stability in those returns across time.

[19] These various measures of investment performance will be defined more rigorously and discussed in more depth in a subsequent chapter. The allocation of the entire total return of T-bills to the income component is somewhat arbitrary, as T-bill investors can easily convert current income to growth by rolling over the maturing T-bills into the purchase of new bills.

[20] This is because, prior to the maturity of the bonds, bond values vary inversely with currently prevailing market interest rates, and these interest rates are generally as likely to go up as down over time. However, during the particular historical period covered in the exhibit, interest rates went down a bit more often than they went up, giving bonds a slight positive average appreciation return for that period.

[21] Capital appreciation would be a larger component of real estate return during periods of higher inflation. On average over the historical period represented in Exhibit 7-9, inflation was not sufficiently high to cause the appreciation return component to approach the income return component in magnitude. As noted in previous chapters, average appreciation is generally slightly below the inflation rate for typical commercial property in the United States, reflecting the real depreciation of the structure.

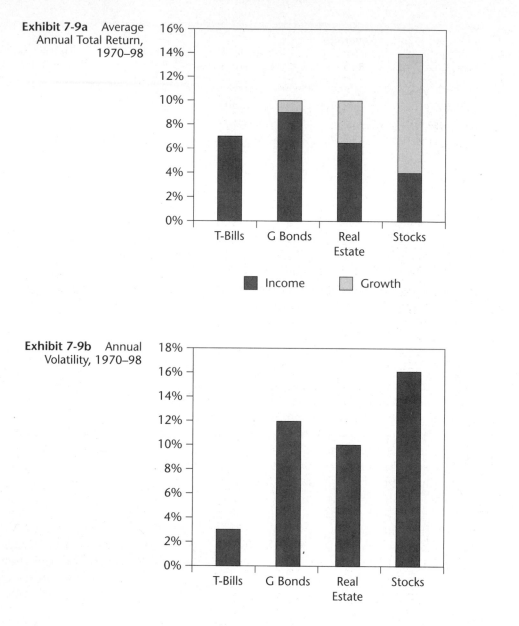

Exhibit 7-9a Average Annual Total Return, 1970–98

Exhibit 7-9b Annual Volatility, 1970–98

Exhibits 7-9a and 7-9b reveal the actual realization of these expectations during the 1970–98 period, at the broad-brush level of the four major investment asset classes.

7.2.3 Brief History of Commercial Real Estate Investment during the Last Quarter of the 20th Century

Exhibit 7-10 depicts the "roller coaster ride" in commercial property values in the United States over the 1970–98 period. The somewhat cyclical-looking picture presented in the exhibit is annotated to indicate some of the major events that affected institutional investment and asset valuation in the commercial property market.

Exhibit 7-10 The "Roller Coaster Ride" in Commercial Property Prices over the Last Quarter of the 20th Century

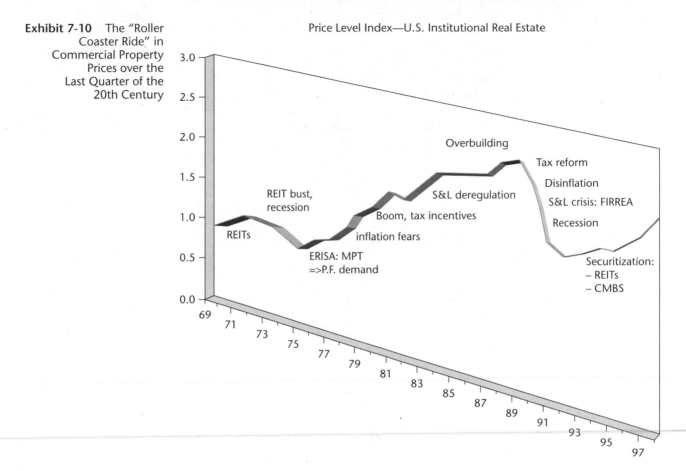

Price Level Index—U.S. Institutional Real Estate

Exhibit 7-10 indicates only the capital value level over time, without including income reinvestment. As such, it traces a rough picture of average property market values over time for large commercial properties of the type invested in by institutions such as life insurance companies, banks, and pension funds.

The history begins with strong commercial property performance during the 1960s, including a boom fueled in part by REIT investment in the late 1960s and first years of the 1970s. The typical REIT in this early period was a mortgage REIT, highly levered by borrowing short-term money at low interest rates and investing in long-term mortgages at higher fixed interest rates. Then deficit spending during the Vietnam War combined with the first Arab Oil Embargo of 1973–74 to lead to an unprecedented take-off of inflation combined with a simultaneous economic recession. This was the beginning of the so-called **stagflation** of the 1970s.[22] This cut demand for commercial property space usage just as short-term interest rates soared in response to the new inflation, placing the mortgage REITs in a deadly squeeze that resulted in many bankruptcies and a crash in commercial property prices during 1973–75.

---

[22] Normally, it was more common for higher inflation to be associated with economic boom times rather than recessions, and for recessions to be associated with declines in inflation. The 1974 recession was different because it was caused largely by real cost increases on the supply side of the macroeconomy, due to the U.S. economy's dependence on imported oil, rather than by a reduction in aggregate demand. The ugly combination of recession and inflation was dubbed *stagflation*.

With the economic recovery of the mid- to late 1970s, commercial property really took off as an investment. Stagflation kept the stock and bond markets in the doldrums (and the stock market had a long memory with regard to its experience with REITs in the early 1970s), but inflation fears actually helped fuel investor demand for real estate, which was perceived as a good hedge against the inflation danger. Furthermore, 1974 saw the passage by Congress of the **Employee Retirement Income Security Act (ERISA)**, which stimulated a boom in institutional investment in commercial property. ERISA required that pension funds be "funded"—that is, capital had to be invested for the long term so that there would be sufficient money in the funds to cover future pension benefit liabilities promised by the pension plans. ERISA took account of some theoretical developments in financial economics of the 1950s and 1960s known as Modern Portfolio Theory (MPT). This theory suggested that investors should diversify their investments broadly, so as to minimize risk and maximize return per unit of risk. This led ERISA to suggest, in effect, that pension fund investments should be broadly diversified, including consideration of real estate as an alternative investment in addition to the traditional pension asset classes of stocks and bonds. This resulted in a vast new source of capital flowing into commercial property investment, as pension fund contributions mushroomed with the bulge of the baby boom generation entering the labor force.

With inflation fears and institutional investment demand bolstering it, the commercial property markets barely skipped a beat with the sharp back-to-back recessions of 1980–81. (Unlike those in the early 1970s, property markets were not significantly overbuilt in the early 1980s; there was then little excess supply of built space.) Yet more real estate investment incentives were provided by the tax cut ushered in by the new Reagan administration in 1982. This tax law enhanced previous provisions that provided generous depreciation allowances and tax shelters for wealthy investors. Also during the 1980s, the deregulation of the savings and loan industry allowed these institutions to invest in commercial mortgages for the first time, thus opening up another new (and inexperienced) source of capital for commercial property. Deregulation and tax incentives combined with the economic recovery of the mid-1980s and the continued flow of institutional capital into real estate, resulting in a continuation of the boom in commercial property prices through the mid-1980s.

By the late 1980s the huge accumulated flow of capital to commercial real estate had stimulated a building boom of historic proportions. Financial capital was converted to physical structures by the development industry. Much of this development was driven or supported by tax incentives that distanced the investor from the underlying economic costs and benefits of the physical real estate that was being built, resulting in some bad projects that found themselves with few tenants. Furthermore, the savings and loans and commercial banks that financed much of the new construction operated in an environment of "moral hazard," in which government deposit insurance divorced their source of capital from the risks of its investment.[23]

In 1986 a sweeping tax reform act removed virtually all of the special tax incentives from which real estate had benefited. Also, by the late 1980s the inflation rate was down sharply, and inflation appeared to be under control, undercutting the "inflation fear" source of real estate investment demand. And by the late 1980s the extent

---

[23] The term *moral hazard* was coined in the insurance industry to describe a situation in which one party controls the risks (in this case the financial institutions), while another party pays the price of the downside outcome from a risky decision (in this case the U.S. government, via the Deposit Insurance Corporations).

of overbuilding in the space market was obvious, as was the financial crisis in the over-extended savings and loan industry, which had loaned vast sums in commercial mortgages backed by economically weak building projects. The commercial real estate asset market began to falter. The stock market drop and economic recession of 1990 were the straws that broke the camel's back. Amid crumbling financial institutions awash with bad mortgages, the bottom fell out of the commercial property market in the early 1990s. Traditional sources of capital for commercial real estate, such as banks, life insurance companies, and pension funds, dried up completely. Indeed the capital flow from such sources turned negative, with lenders refusing to refinance loans that came due and even trying to sell existing mortgages. Commercial real estate asset prices fell 30 to 50% in the span of two years in most of the major property markets, the largest drop in property values in the United States since the Great Depression.

The bottom was finally reached in 1992 and 1993, with a flood of new capital coming into real estate. The money came first from opportunistic "vulture funds" and "grave-dancers" financed by wealthy individuals. This was followed rapidly by the public capital markets as a new source of money in the form of an unprecedented expansion of the REIT industry, as well as the development of an entirely new industry in the form of commercial mortgage-backed securities (CMBS). In 1993 alone, 50 new REITs issued initial public offerings (IPOs) of stocks, raising over $9 billion, more than three times the largest previous annual total.[24] During this period it was not uncommon to be able to buy large new commercial properties for a small fraction of their construction cost.[25]

The remarkable development of the public capital market as a source of real estate investment money during the 1990s powered the recovery of the commercial property market during most of that decade and greatly changed the real estate investment industry, as described in section 7.1. The development of both the debt and equity sides of this market was stimulated by government actions. For example, the development of CMBS had its roots in the **Financial Institutions Recovery, Reform, and Enforcement Act** of 1989 **(FIRREA)** passed by Congress to bail out the savings and loan industry. FIRREA set up a government corporation, the Resolution Trust Corporation (RTC), charged with rapidly selling huge quantities of bad commercial mortgages. FIRREA also imposed risk-adjusted capital requirements on financial institutions, giving them an incentive to hold assets in a publicly traded ("securitized") form, such as CMBS, rather than as whole loans. Necessity being the mother of invention, the means to tap the public debt market was found via the CMBS vehicle.

REITs also were given a boost by tax reforms in the late 1980s and early 1990s that gave them greater management flexibility and facilitated institutional investment in REIT stock. This, combined with the invention of the Umbrella REIT (UPREIT) structure and the great need for liquidity among commercial property owners in the early 1990s, led to the takeoff of the REIT Revolution in 1993.[26] For the first time in history, large quantities of prime commercial property equity were being transferred from traditional private ownership to ownership by publicly traded real estate corporations.

---

[24] Of the total of $147 billion raised through the public capital markets by REITs in the first 37 years of their history from 1961 through 1997, $108 billion was raised during the five years from 1993 through 1997.

[25] Of course, the typical such property was largely devoid of tenants.

[26] The pioneering UPREIT IPO was that of Taubman Centers, Inc, a chain of regional shopping malls run by the Taubman brothers, in the fall of 1992.

By the mid-1990s the traditional sources of capital, especially the pension funds and commercial banks, were also back in the real estate investment business in a big way. With the long economic boom of the 1990s, excess supply in the space markets was gradually filled up with tenants, further bolstering the confidence of conservative investors. By the late 1990s the commercial property market was fully recovered, at least for the time being. There was also some evidence that the REIT and CMBS markets were improving the efficiency of the capital markets in playing their role as a negative feedback loop, or regulator of overall capital flow to the real estate system, as we described in Chapter 2. A sharp pull-back in the REIT and CMBS markets during 1998 temporarily cut off a part of the money flow to new development projects, thereby heading off what had begun to appear to some as the beginning of a new round of overbuilding in some markets.[27]

7.3 CHAPTER SUMMARY

This chapter presented some very basic background information about commercial real estate assets as an investment class. We highlighted the similarities and differences between real estate and the other major traditional investment asset classes, stocks and bonds in particular. We noted important recent developments in the public capital markets, the REIT and CMBS industries in particular. We put this information in some historical context and provided some summary quantification of typical investment performance in recent decades based on empirical evidence. You should now have a working knowledge of the basic commercial real estate investment products and vehicles, and the recent history that sets the stage for today's real estate investment world. This knowledge will be useful as you pursue subsequent chapters in this book.

KEY TERMS

investment objective
growth (savings) objective
income (current cash flow) objective
risk
liquidity
investment horizon
investor expertise
investor management burden
investor size

investor heterogeneity
underlying asset
investment product/vehicles
passive investors
comingled real estate funds
   (CREFs)
private REITs (real estate
   investment trusts)
private markets

commercial mortgage-backed
   securities (CMBS)
four major asset classes
stagflation
Employee Retirement Income
   Security Act (ERISA)
Financial Institutions Recovery,
   Reform, and Enforcement Act
   (FIRREA)

[27] During the early to mid-1990s REITs had been able to purchase existing properties in the property market at prices that appeared to be "bargains" from the perspective of the stock market where REITs trade. So capital flowed rapidly into REITs and through them into the property market as REITs purchased existing buildings. By around 1997 property market values had recovered to the point that there were no longer "bargains" from a REIT valuation perspective. This removed the easy growth opportunities that REITs had enjoyed, and REIT investors in the stock market reacted accordingly, repricing REITs as income stocks rather than growth stocks. This resulted in a fall in REIT share prices and a temporary cutoff of capital flow as new REIT stock issues were canceled. This type of process will be discussed further in Chapters 12, 20, and 24.

STUDY QUESTIONS

7.1. Describe the two major, generally mutually exclusive, objectives of investors.

7.2. Characterize the following investors as to whether their major investment objectives are likely to be savings or income. What would be a likely typical investment horizon for each investor?

   a. A graduate student in her mid-20s

   b. A fading rock star in his mid-20s who has saved several million dollars over the past five years

   c. A dual-income professional couple in their mid-30s, with two children

   d. A 40-year-old just-retired major league baseball player who never went to college but has saved up several million dollars and owes large annual alimony payments

   e. A retired couple in their late 60s.

7.3. What are the major constraints and concerns faced by most investors?

7.4. What are the major differences between real estate and traditional industrial corporations regarding the structure and nature of the investment products and vehicles based on these underlying assets, and the asset markets in which these entities trade?

7.5. In the traditional commercial real estate investment structure, what is the significance of the fact that it is possible for investors to own the underlying physical assets directly, and that these assets are not too large? Suppose there were a well-functioning, highly active market for blast furnaces, or automobile stamping plants. How would this help, say, Inland Steel, or Ford Motor Company, to know whether it makes sense to build a new blast furnace or stamping plant?

7.6. Describe two types of private investment products or vehicles based on commercial property as the underlying asset.

7.7. Describe two types of publicly traded investment products or vehicles based on commercial property as the underlying asset.

7.8. Describe two ways (investment products or vehicles) for passive investors to invest in commercial real estate equity.

7.9. What are the four major traditional investment asset classes? Based on typical examples of each class, rank-order the classes by

   a. expected total return

   b. current income yield

   c. capital value growth

   d. risk

   e. inflation protection ability

   (When considering risk, assume that the investor is fully exposed to the asset price volatility in the periodic returns to the asset class.)

7.10. Which asset class gave the best historical (ex post) investment performance (based on average total return) during the 1970s? Which class gave the best performance during the 1980s?

7.11. Suppose an investor placed $5 million into each of two investment funds at the beginning of 1970. All investment earnings were reinvested. One fund invested in commercial real estate and produced a performance like that portrayed for real estate in Exhibit 7-7. The other fund invested in common stocks and produced a performance like that indicated for the stock market in Exhibit 7-7.

    a. How much did the investor have in each of the two funds at the end of 1983?

    b. What was the real purchasing power in each of the two funds, measured in dollars of 1969 purchasing power?

    c. Now repeat your answers to (a) and (b) only assuming the initial $5 million investment was made at the beginning of 1984 until 1998 and use 1983 dollars as the measure of constant purchasing power.

7.12. What is the apparent historical relationship between average investment performance (total return) and the riskiness of the investment as measured by volatility?

7.13. The crash in prices of institutional grade commercial property in the United States during 1989–92 was the worst since the Great Depression. Make an argument that this crash was due to unique historical events during the preceding decade. Now make a counterargument suggesting that such swings are likely to recur.

7.14. What are the major institutional sources of capital for commercial real estate in the United States today? How has the relative importance of different sources been changing in recent years?

8 Present Value Mathematics for Real Estate

Chapter Outline

Learning Objectives

After reading this chapter, you should understand:

◆ The basic formulas and procedures for converting typical real estate future cash flow and risk patterns to present value, given the appropriate discount rates.

◆ The origin or derivation of these formulas, in such a way that you can apply them with some flexibility to new situations.

◆ How to invert the present value formulas to compute the implied return or the time until a future value is received.

◆ How a typical business or financial calculator works to make these calculations quick and easy.

If someone offered you a choice between $10,000 today or $10,000 one year from now, which would you choose? It is a fundamental fact of financial economics that dollars at one time are not equivalent to dollars at another time. This is not just because of inflation. Due to the real productivity of capital, and due to risk, future dollars are worth less than present dollars, even if there were no inflation. In real estate investment analysis we constantly need to compare dollars at different points in time. Present value mathematics consists of the formulas, procedures, and techniques for making such comparisons and evaluations. This chapter will present some of the most basic and commonly used of these tools.

Please keep in mind that the focus of this chapter is on the mechanics, the formal mathematical formulas. In order to know how to use these formulas properly in real estate investment analysis, you need to know the right numbers to plug into the formulas. This requires combining economics with mathematics, a combination we will explore in later chapters.

For the purposes of this chapter, present value formulas can be grouped into two classes: single-sums and multiperiod cash flows. The single-sum formulas are the most basic building blocks, as the multiperiod formulas are all built up as sums of the single-sum formulas. So we will begin this chapter with single-sum formulas, and then advance to multiperiod formulas in the second half.[1]

8.1 SINGLE-SUM FORMULAS

Single-sum formulas refer to situations in which only two points in time are considered. Typically, one of these two points is the present. A single cash flow or monetary value is posited at one of the two points in time, and the task is to determine the value it equates to at the other point in time.

8.1.1 Single-Period Discounting and Growing

The simplest sort of present value problem is single-period discounting or growing. Let's go back to the choice between $10,000 today versus one year from today. We no doubt agree that we would all choose the $10,000 today. But suppose the choice is $10,000 today versus $11,000 in one year, or $12,000, and so on. Clearly there is some value greater than $10,000 that we would prefer to take in one year. How high that "indifference point" is depends on several things. For example, we would want to consider how much interest we could earn on a one-year deposit in a bank. If we could earn 5% simple interest on a one-year CD, then $10,500 in one year would be equivalent to $10,000 today, because 10,000 × 1.05 = 10,500. However, we might require a promise of more than $10,500 in a year in exchange for our $10,000 today if we view the future promise as being more risky than a bank CD. In effect, we might want more than a 5% expected return to get us to forgo the present cash. Suppose we wanted a 10% expected return "risk premium" on top of the 5% we could earn at the

---

[1]If you are already familiar with these formulas and procedures, you can safely skip this chapter. The only thing we do here that is a little different from the typical coverage is that we present the underlying geometric series formula from which the regular multiperiod (annuity and perpetuity) present value formulas are derived. This will give the reader some additional depth and flexibility and enable us to show how to develop formulas for the present values of buildings with long-term leases, a common problem in commercial real estate.

bank, for a total expected return of 15% in order to entice us to forgo our $10,000 today in exchange for a cash sum promised next year. Then $11,500 is our indifference point, because

$$\$10,000 + (15\% \times \$10,000) = \$11,500$$

or equivalently

$$\$10,000 \times (1 + 0.15) = \$11,500$$

Now suppose that we know our required expected return percentage (say 15% as in the previous example), and we know the amount that is being promised one year from now. So the question is, how much are we willing to forgo today in exchange for the promised sum in one year? We can find this present value by simply inverting the previous formula and solving for the present value rather than for the future value. For example, if $11,500 is being offered in one year, then we could determine that we are willing to pay $10,000 today by dividing the expected future amount by one plus the expected return, as follows:

$$\$10,000 = \frac{\$11,500}{1 + 0.15}$$

Assuming that 15% is our required expected return (opportunity cost of capital), any offer of more than $11,500 next year would be preferred over holding on to our $10,000 today, while any offer of less than $11,500 would be rejected in favor of keeping our $10,000 today.

In the previous example, the $10,000 amount is the *present certainty equivalent*, often more simply referred to as the **present value,** of the *future expected sum* (or **future value**) of $11,500 in one year, based on a simple annual expected return of 15%. In general, if we let PV represent the present value, FV represent the future value, and r represent the simple expected return, then the formula for discounting future values to present value is

$$PV = \frac{FV}{1 + r} \tag{1a}$$

and the corresponding formula for growing a present value to its future equivalent is

$$FV = (1 + r)PV \tag{1b}$$

Using formula (1a) you could answer the question of how much cash in the present would equate to $10,000 promised money in one year, under the 15% required return assumption of the previous numerical example. The answer would be $PV = \$8,695.65 = 10,000/1.15$. When solving for present value given the future value, the problem is one of **discounting** rather than **growing**, and the required expected return percentage in the denominator acts as the **discount rate**. Discounting is merely the inverse of growing.

8.1.2 Single-Sums over Multiple Periods of Time

The problem in the previous section involved only a single period of time, with the return or discount rate expressed as a simple rate per the amount of time in that period. For example, if everything in the earlier numerical example were the same except that the waiting period between the present cash and the future payment were two years instead of one year, then the formulas would still apply only we would have to interpret the 15% return as a simple biennial rather than annual return, that is, a return over two years instead of one year.

Now suppose there is more than one period of time between the time of the *PV* amount and the time of the *FV* amount, yet we want to express the return per unit of time in each period. For example, suppose the future payment is promised in two years and we want to obtain 15% simple annual return *each* year. If you put, say, $100 in a one-year CD at 15% simple annual interest, you would have 1.15 × $100 = $115 after one year. If you took that $115 and put it in another 15% CD again the second year, your $115 would grow to 1.15 × $115 = $132.25 after the second year. In other words, $100 growing at 15% simple annual interest compounded annually for two years is

$$(1.15)(1.15)100 = (1.15)^2 \, 100 = 132.25$$

Note that this is more than the $130 you would have if you simply took the original $15 interest and multiplied by two. This is because you earn interest on interest (or return on return) whenever the interest or return is compounded (that is, computed and credited to the principal in the account). This process is known as **compounding** or compound growth.

It is easy to see by extension of this reasoning that if we were dealing with three years instead of two, we would have

$$(1.15)(1.15)(1.15)100 = (1.15)^3 \, 100 = 152.09$$

So, by inductive reasoning, we can see that the general formula for equating present and future value across multiple periods with compounding once per period is given by

$$PV = \frac{FV}{(1 + r)^N} \tag{2a}$$

for discounting a future sum to present value and:

$$FV = (1 + r)^N PV \tag{2b}$$

for compounding a present sum forward to its future equivalent, where *r* is the simple interest or discount rate (or expected return) *per period*, and *N* is the number of periods between the present and the future time when the future sum is to be received.

The previous formulas are the building blocks for classical present value and mortgage mathematics. In modern practice these formulas are normally applied using an electronic calculator or computer spreadsheet. For example, in a typical computer spreadsheet (such as Lotus or Excel), the right-hand side of (2a) would be keyed in as $FV/(1 + r)\text{^}N$, where *FV*, *PV*, *r*, and *N* represent the cell addresses of the relevant future sum, present value, simple interest rate per period, and number of periods, respectively.

In case you need to solve for the compound growth rate or the length of time until the future value will be received, the previous formulas can be algebraically inverted to solve for r or N:

$$r = \left(\frac{FV}{PV}\right)^{1/N} - 1 \tag{2c}$$

$$N = \frac{\ln(FV) - \ln(PV)}{\ln(1 + r)} \tag{2d}$$

where $\ln(.)$ refers to the natural log. Of course, modern calculators and computer spreadsheets allow these types of problems to be solved without your actually having to remember formulas such as these!

8.1.3 Simple versus Compound Interest

From the discussion in the previous section you can see that there is more than one way to define how the interest rate (or equivalently, the rate of return, or the discount rate) is measured per period when there is more than one period between the PV cash flow and the FV cash flow. For example, go back to the example in the previous section in which we started out with $100 in the present and grew this to $132.25 after two years. We saw how this growth could be expressed as a per annum (or annual) rate of 15%, using annual compounding, because $(1 + 0.15) \times (1 + 0.15) = 1.3225$. But it would also be possible to take the total return increment over the two years, the 32.25%, and simply divide this by two and express the return as 16.125% per annum. This latter definition is called simple interest, because it does not include the effect of compounding.

The important point to remember is that how we define the interest or return per period does not affect the actual dollars that we have at the two points in time. The definition is merely a matter of convention. Whether we call it 15% per year compounded annually, or 16.125 percent per year simple interest, it is still $132.25 starting out from $100 two years earlier. You do have to be careful to understand the definition being used in a given context, and you must be consistent (e.g., don't compound simple interest in formulas to compute future sums).

8.1.4 Effective versus Nominal Rates

In the example in the previous section the compound interest rate was computed assuming the interest was compounded once per year (annual compounding). But in fact interest may be compounded at any **frequency**. Often, interest is compounded more frequently than once per year. For example, suppose 7.5% semiannual interest were compounded over a year (i.e., twice). After one year you would have $(1.075)(1.075) = 1.155625$ times whatever amount you started with. As you can see, 7.5% compounded semiannually would be equivalent to a little over 15.56% simple annual interest or interest compounded annually. Nevertheless, in terms of the conventions of measurement and quoting of interest rates, the 7.5% compounded semiannually would usually be referred to as 15% per annum interest, compounded semiannually. The term **effective annual rate** (or **EAR**) would be used to refer to the 15.5625% actual yield.

In real estate applications, cash flows often occur at monthly intervals. For example, rents and mortgage payments are usually scheduled at monthly intervals. As a result, monthly interest rates are often actually applied in calculations, but rates are quoted in what is called nominal per annum terms. Under the convention of quoting rates in nominal per annum terms, the simple per-period rate (which is the rate that is actually applied in calculations) is multiplied by the number of periods in a year for the purpose of quoting the rate in per annum terms. For example, a simple interest rate of 1% per month would typically be referred to as a 12% per annum rate (i.e., the nominal per annum rate), even though the effective rate or EAR is $(1.01)^{12} - 1 = 12.6825\%$. The EAR is defined as the actual annual yield corresponding to the nominal rate defined previously, given the simple per-period rate compounded at the end of each period. The relationship between effective and nominal rates is shown in the following formulas:

$$EAR = (1 + i/m)^m - 1 \qquad (3a)$$

$$i = m[(1 + EAR)^{1/m} - 1] \qquad (3b)$$

where i is the nominal annual rate, m is the number of compounding periods per year, and $i/m = r$ is the actual simple interest rate being applied per compounding period. In the previous example we had $i = 12.00\%$, $EAR = 12.6825\%$, $r = 1.00\%$, and $m = 12$. The nominal annual rate i is sometimes referred to as the **equivalent nominal annual rate (ENAR)**.

As a result of this naming convention when applying the present value and future value formula (2) described previously, one usually works in nominal terms by expanding the simple per-period interest rate compounded once per-period (r) and the number of basic periods of time (N) as follows, consistent with the earlier definitions:

$$r = i/m$$

$$N = m \times T$$

where i is the nominal annual rate of interest (e.g., 12% in the previous example), m is the number of compounding periods per year (e.g., 12 in the example of monthly compounding), and T is the length of time between when the PV and FV cash flows occur *measured in years*. Recast in nominal per-annum terms (allowing for a compounding frequency different from yearly), the present value formulas for single-sums become as follows:

$$PV = \frac{FV}{\left(1 + \dfrac{i}{m}\right)^{mT}} \qquad (4a)$$

$$FV = PV\left(1 + \frac{i}{m}\right)^{mT} \qquad (4b)$$

$$i = m \left[\left(\frac{FV}{PV} \right)^{1/(mT)} - 1 \right] \tag{4c}$$

$$T = \frac{\ln(FV) - \ln(PV)}{m \ln(1 + i/m)} \tag{4d}$$

Most calculators designed especially for business applications allow the user to set the value m so the calculator knows the number of compounding periods per year, and the user can then enter the interest rate in its nominal annual form (that is, you enter i and T rather than r and N; e.g., in the previous example you would enter 12 for the interest rate rather than 1 or .01, and enter the number of years between the PV and FV cash flows, rather than the number of months). The calculator then automatically divides i by m to determine the rate per period to apply in the formulas.

On the other hand, microcomputer spreadsheet financial formulas typically require as direct inputs the rate per period (r) and the number of periods (N). In order to work in nominal annual terms, the user must therefore have the spreadsheet calculate r and N from i, m, and T in other cells of the worksheet, and have these other cells serve as the inputs to the present value formulas.

8.1.5 Bond Equivalent and Mortgage Equivalent Rates

As noted, rent is usually collected monthly and mortgage payments are usually made monthly, so nominal rates (i, or the ENAR, using the earlier labels) based on the previous formulas with $m = 12$ is the most common way interest rates or yields are quoted in real estate. Nominal rates defined this way are sometimes referred to as **mortgage equivalent rates**.

Meanwhile, over on Wall Street, traditional corporate bonds and long-term government bonds are designed to pay interest semiannually, that is, twice per year.[2] In fact, classical bonds had coupons corresponding to each of the promised semiannual interest payments, which the bondholder would clip off and turn in at a bank to receive the payment in cash. Because of this, in the bond market rates are typically quoted with $m = 2$ in formula (3). Nominal rates based on $m = 2$ are thus referred to as **bond equivalent** or **coupon equivalent** rates.

Thus, real estate rates and bond rates are quoted in different ways. This was fine as long as Wall Street and Main Street did not interact very directly. But nowadays many mortgages are combined in pools and sold in the bond market, and bond market yields largely determine mortgage market yields. People dealing with mortgages need to be able to convert readily between mortage equivalent and bond equivalent yields. This is done by *equating the effective annual rate (EAR)*. For example, we noted that a bond equivalent rate of 15% corresponds to an EAR of 15.5625%, found by plugging $i = 0.15$ and $m = 2$ into formula (3a). Now plug this 15.5625% EAR into formula (3b) with $m = 12$ to find that the mortgage equivalent rate of 14.551655% corresponds to the bond equivalent rate of 15%. Mortgage equivalent rates are lower than their corresponding bond equivalent rates because the increased frequency of

---

[2] The terms *semiannual* and *biannual* are equivalent, both referring to twice per year. The term *biennial* is different, referring to once every two years.

compounding results in faster growth. If the mortgage equivalent rate were 15%, this would correspond to a bond equivalent rate of 15.4766% and an EAR of 16.07545%. (Plug $i = 0.15$ and $m = 12$ into formula [3a] to obtain the EAR, which you then plug into formula [3b] with $m = 2$.)

As always, this type of operation is easily done using financial calculators by changing the value in the "periods per year" register, without need to memorize the formulas. You simply substitute the appropriate value for m in the "periods per year" register. (See practice problems 11–20 at the end of this chapter.)

*8.1.6 Continuously Compounded Interest Rates

The extreme limit of frequent compounding of interest is **continuous compounding**. Many bank accounts, CDs, and other financial instruments employ continuous compounding, and many interest rates are quoted in continuously compounded terms. Continuous compounding is also mathematically convenient for many types of analyses, especially those involving advanced mathematics, and so is often used in sophisticated studies.[3] In continuous compounding, the interest is literally compounded every instant.

Computing continuously compounded interest rates and continuously compounded growth or discounting is easy using the natural logarithm and the base of natural logs (the latter is known by the mathematical symbol e, which stands for a value approximately equal to 2.7183, and is available as a special key on most business calculators and in all spreadsheet software). The continuously compounded equivalents corresponding to the various forms of formulas (2) or (4) are shown as formula (5), where T is the amount of time in years (including fractional parts of a year) between the PV and FV cash flows, and k is the *per-annum* continuously compounded rate (of growth or discount, i.e., the continuously compounded interest rate).

$$PV = FV/e^{Tk} \tag{5a}$$

$$FV = PVe^{Tk} \tag{5b}$$

$$k = \frac{\ln(FV) - \ln(PV)}{T} \tag{5c}$$

$$T = \frac{\ln(FV) - \ln(PV)}{k} \tag{5d}$$

[3] Continuous compounding enables one to convert complex multiplicative expressions into simple additive expressions using natural logs. Additive expressions are much easier to work with mathematically. For example, if r_t is the simple rate of return in period t, then at the end of two periods, $FV = (1 + r_1)(1 + r_2)PV$, but if r_t is the continuously compounded rate of return in period t, then $\log(FV) = \log(PV) + r_1 + r_2$, where $\log(.)$ is the natural log. The ending log value is simply the beginning log value plus the sum of all the continuously compounded periodic returns.

8.2 MULTIPERIOD PROBLEMS

The formulas described in section 8.1 are the basic building blocks. They deal with only one future cash flow. Of course, real estate is a long-lived asset that typically produces cash flows for many periods, or indeed infinitely into the future. The present value of any stream of discrete cash flows can be computed using the previous formulas by simply computing the present value of each future sum and then adding all these present values together. For example, suppose $10,000 will be received in two years and another $12,000 will be received in three years. Suppose the interest rate applicable to the payment two years from now is 10%, and the rate applicable to the payment in three years is 11% (all compounded annually). Then the present value of the future cash flow stream consisting of these two payments is $17,038.76, computed using formula (2) as follows:

$$PV = \frac{\$10,000}{(1 + 0.10)^2} + \frac{\$12,000}{(1 + 0.11)^3} = \$8,264.46 + \$8,774.30 = \$17,038.76$$

Of course, such a procedure gets tedious when there are many future cash flows. This is one reason it is often useful in real estate investment analysis to be able to express the present value of a multiperiod future cash flow stream using a simplified formula. Another reason is that such simplified formulas may enable interesting relationships to become apparent. For example, they can reveal the basic nature of the relationship among the current yield or income return, the expected average future growth rate of the cash flows, and the discount rate or required expected total return on a long-lived commercial property with a regular pattern of cash flow generation.

Relatively simple formulas for present value relationships can usually be found if the future cash flow stream has a regular pattern. While the cash flow streams of real buildings will not usually be so regular, they can often be well approximated (or "modeled") by regular patterns that enable simple present value formulas to be computed. These simple multiperiod formulas are the subject of this section of this chapter.

*8.2.1 Geometric Series Formula

In the real world, cash flow streams often all occur at equal intervals of time and all change over time at a constant rate (even if that rate is zero). Such a regular stream of cash flow is known as an **annuity** if the stream has a finite life (finite number of cash flows), or a **perpetuity** if the stream is infinite. Many important real estate cash flows are of this type (such as mortgages and leases). Other real estate cash flows can be reasonably approximated by annuities or perpetuities (e.g., the net cash flow from an apartment building may be modeled as a constant-growth perpetuity). So these are very important.

In order to explain how to value annuities and perpetuities, we think it is best to begin with first principles: a famous mathematical formula known as the **geometric series formula**. This is not just for your cultural benefit. If you understand the geometric series formula, you will have a greater depth of knowledge that will give you more flexibility to solve a wider range of real estate problems in the real world. For example, you will be able to develop a simple analytical formula for the value of a building that rents out its space in long-term leases, a typical and fundamental situation in commercial real estate. This will enable you to analyze such issues as the optimal lease term, or the trade-off between lease term and rent levels or rent growth rate. So bear with us a moment as we delve into some classical mathematics. At first this may seem complicated and abstract, but we will soon get to a very simple formula that you will be able to apply in a variety of practical real estate situations.

Suppose we have a sum consisting of N terms, each of which is exactly d times the value of the preceding term, and whose first term has the value a. Another term for d is the **common ratio**. Label the value of this sum S.

$$S = a + ad + ad^2 + \cdots + ad^{N-1}$$

Now multiply this sum by the common ratio, d:

$$Sd = ad + ad^2 + ad^3 + \cdots + ad^N$$

Now subtract Sd from S:

$$S = a + ad + ad^2 + \cdots + ad^{N-1}$$

$$-Sd = -ad - ad^2 - \cdots - ad^{N-1} - ad^N$$

The intermediate terms all cancel out in the subtraction, leaving:

$$S - Sd = a - ad^N$$
$$= (1 - d)S = a(1 - d^N)$$

Thus

$$S = a(1 - d^N)/(1 - d) \tag{6a}$$

Formula (6a) is the geometric series formula. It says that the sum of the series equals the first term times the quantity one minus the common ratio raised to the power of the number of terms, all divided by the quantity one minus the common ratio.

Now note that if $d < 1$, then $d^\infty = 0$, so if the series is infinite (as in a perpetuity), then the value of the sum simplifies to

$$S = a/(1 - d) \tag{6b}$$

These simple formulas can be used to address a wide range of real estate problems. Some of the most important examples are discussed in the following sections.

8.2.2 Present Value of a Level Annuity in Arrears

Perhaps the most widely used application of the geometric series formula is to compute the present value of a **level annuity** in arrears, which is a series of equal payments made at the *end* of every period starting one period from the present. This type of cash flow stream defines the classical mortgage, with monthly payments. For example, a 30-year mortgage is a level annuity in arrears with $N = 360$.

To see how this problem is an example of the geometric formula, let's take a specific example. Suppose there are 240 payments left on a mortgage that has monthly payments of $1,000 each. How much is the mortgage worth today if the opportunity cost of capital (discount rate) is 12% per year (actually, 1% per month) and the next payment on the mortgage is due one month from now?

We can set up this present value as the sum of a sequence of present values of single sums, using formula (2):

$$PV = \frac{\$1000}{1.01} + \frac{\$1000}{1.01^2} + \frac{\$1000}{1.01^3} + \cdots + \frac{\$1000}{1.01^{240}}$$

So here, the first term is $a = 1,000/1.01$. The number of terms is $N = 240$. And the common ratio is $d = 1/1.01$, because each term is that factor times the previous. Now if we substitute these values of a, d, and N into the geometric formula (6a) we arrive at

$$PV = \frac{a(1 - d^N)}{1 - d} = \frac{(\$1,000 / 1.01)\,[1 - (1 / 1.01)^{240}]}{1 - (1 / 1.01)}$$

$$= \frac{\$1000[1 - (1 / 1.01)^{240}]}{0.01} = \$90,819$$

This famous case of the geometric formula is often written as

$$PV = PMT\,\frac{1 - 1/(1 + r)^N}{r} \tag{7a}$$

or alternatively as

$$PV = PMT\left(\frac{1}{r} - \frac{1}{r}\,\frac{1}{(1 + r)^N}\right)$$

where PMT is the level cash flow payment amount, and r is the effective simple interest rate *per payment period*.

The ratio of the present value of the annuity to the amount of each payment, PV/PMT, is often referred to as the "annuity factor," or the "present value interest factor for an annuity" (PVIFA).[4] As we can see from formula (7a), the annuity factor is a function only of the interest rate r and the number of payment periods N: $[1 - 1/(1 + r)^N]/r$. You multiply the periodic payment amount by this factor to arrive at the present value of the cash flow stream.

---

[4] For constant-payment mortgages this is also known as the mortgage constant, the ratio of the mortgage payment to the initial principal loan amount.

Keep in mind that the underlying formula that is equivalently expressed in (7a) is

$$PV = \frac{PMT}{1+r} + \frac{PMT}{(1+r)^2} + \frac{PMT}{(1+r)^3} + \cdots + \frac{PMT}{(1+r)^N} \tag{7}$$

From this expansion we can see that the annuity formula is an application of the geometric series formula, with $a = PMT/(1 + r)$ and $d = 1/(1 + r)$. We also see how formula (7) is built up as a series of applications of formula (2). It should be clear that an underlying assumption is that the simple effective interest rate per payment period (r) is being compounded at the end of every payment period. Thus, for example, if the payment period is monthly and $r = 1\%$, then the nominal interest rate would typically be quoted as 12%, and the effective annual rate would actually be 12.6825%, based on formula (3a).

Expressed in terms of the nominal annual rate, the annuity formula becomes

$$PV = PMT \frac{1 - \left(\dfrac{1}{1 + \dfrac{i}{m}}\right)^{(Tm)}}{\dfrac{i}{m}} \tag{7b}$$

where the variables are all defined as before.

8.2.3 Present Value of a Level Annuity in Advance

Sometimes the cash flows arrive at the *beginning* of each period, rather than at the end. This is particularly common for rent payments in long-term leases. For example, suppose a 20-year ground lease has a fixed net rent of $1,000 per month paid at the beginning of the month. What is the value of this lease when it is signed if the opportunity cost of capital is 12% per year (1% per month)? We have

$$PV = \$1,000 + \frac{\$1,000}{1.01} + \frac{\$1,000}{1.01^2} + \cdots + \frac{\$1,000}{1.01^{239}}$$

This is the same as the previous problem only multiplied by 1.01. Here, the first term is $a = 1,000$, but otherwise this problem is identical to the previous one (N is still 240, the number of terms on the right-hand side, or the total number of payments, and the common ratio, d, is still $1/1.01$). So the lease is worth

$$PV = \frac{a(1 - d^N)}{1 - d} = \frac{(\$1,000)[1 - (1/1.01)^{240}]}{1 - (1/1.01)}$$

$$= \left(\frac{1.01}{0.01}\right) \$1,000 [1 - (1/1.01)^{240}] = \$91,728$$

To convert formula (7a) to give present value with payments in advance, you simply multiply the right-hand side of (7a) by the factor $(1 + r)$, or equivalently by

$\{1 + (i/m)\}$, to remove one period's discounting from the present value calculation. Thus, the annuity present value formula for payments in advance is given by formula (8a) (keeping in mind that $r = i/m$ and $N = mT$ in the usual convention).

$$PV = PMT \, (1 + r) \frac{1 - 1/(1 + r)^N}{r} \tag{8a}$$

The annuity formula is much more commonly used assuming payments in arrears than in advance. Business calculators typically have a button that allows one to set the calculator for payments either in arrears or in advance (the default setting is normally payments in arrears). Spreadsheet software formulas also typically provide an optional indicator to convert present value formulas to payments in advance, with the default being for payments in arrears.

8.2.4 Present Value of a Constant-Growth Annuity in Arrears

The annuities we have just considered were level payment annuities; that is, all their periodic cash flows were equal. Now let's relax that assumption by allowing all the periodic cash flows to grow (or shrink) at the same rate. That is, each cash flow is the same multiple of the previous cash flow. The present value of such a stream of cash flow will clearly also be an application of the geometric series formula. For example, consider a 10-year lease providing for annual payments at the ends of the years. The initial rent is $20/SF but that rent will grow at a rate of 2% per year each year thereafter. What is the present value of the lease, per SF, assuming an opportunity cost of capital of 10% per year?

To solve this problem, first set up the underlying present value problem as a series of formula (2) type single-sums:

$$PV = \frac{\$20}{1.10} + \frac{(1.02)\$20}{1.10^2} + \frac{(1.02)^2\$20}{1.10^3} + \cdots + \frac{(1.02)^9\$20}{1.10^{10}}$$

This allows us to see clearly that the first term is $a = 20/1.1$, the number of terms on the right-hand side (number of periodic payments) is $N = 10$, and the common ratio is $d = (1.02/1.10)$. Plug these values into formula (6a) to get

$$PV = \frac{a \, (1 - d^N)}{1 - d} = \frac{(\$20 / 1.10) \, [1 - (1.02 / 1.10)^{10}]}{1 - (1.02 / 1.10)}$$

$$= \$20 \frac{1 - (1.02 / 1.10)^{10}}{0.10 - 0.02} = \$132.51$$

So the lease is worth $132.51/SF.

This case of the geometric formula is referred to as the **constant-growth annuity**, and in general it is often written as

$$PV = CF_1 \left(\frac{1 - [(1 + g)/(1 + r)]^N}{r - g} \right) \tag{9}$$

where CF_1 is the value of the *initial* cash flow (periodic payment), g is the growth rate *per period* in the cash flows, and r is as always the discount rate per payment period.[5] Note that in the special case where $g = 0$, the constant-growth annuity formula collapses to the level payment annuity formula, as it should.

8.2.5 Present Value of a Constant-Growth Perpetuity

Now consider an infinite sequence of cash flows, a perpetuity in which each periodic payment is a constant ratio times the previous payment. For example, suppose an apartment building has 100 identical units that rent at $1,000 per month with building operating expenses paid by the landlord equal to $500 per month. On average, there is a 5% vacancy. You expect both rents and operating expenses to grow at a rate of 3% per year (actually, 0.25% per month). The opportunity cost of capital is 12% per year (actually, 1% per month). How much is the property worth?

Once again, to solve this problem we first set it up as a fundamental series of single-sums based on formula (2). The initial monthly net cash flow is $500 \times 100 \times 0.95 = \$47,500$. Thus, the underlying present value problem is

$$PV = \frac{\$47,500}{1.01} + \frac{(1.0025)\,\$47,500}{1.01^2} + \frac{(1.0025)^2\,\$47,500}{1.01^3} + \cdots$$

This allows us to see clearly that the first term is $a = 47,500/1.01$ and the common ratio is $d = 1.0025/1.01$. As this is a perpetuity, we apply the simpler version of the geometric formula (6b) instead of (6a), so we have

$$PV = \frac{a}{1 - d} = \frac{\$47,500\,/\,1.01}{1 - (1.0025\,/\,1.01)} = \frac{\$47,500}{0.01 - 0.0025} = \$6,333,333$$

The building is worth $6,333,333.

This case of the geometric formula is written in general notation as

$$PV = \frac{CF_1}{r - g} \tag{10}$$

with the variables defined as before, and it is referred to as the **constant-growth perpetuity** formula.

---

[5] Standard business calculators typically do not have a g key to compute growing annuities. However, you can "trick" your calculator to do this type of problem using the standard keys, by simply defining the interest rate as $1/d - 1$ (that is, $(1 + r)/(1 + g) - 1$). You then enter the initial cash flow (undiscounted) as PMT, set the calculator to assume payments in advance (beginning-of-period payments, as if the problem were not in arrears, even though it is), compute the PV, and then divide the answer by $1 + r$ to get it back in arrears. For example, in the previous problem, enter the interest rate as 7.84314% (= 1.10/1.02 − 1), enter 20 into PMT, 10 into N, 0 into FV, and compute $PV = 145.76$, which when divided by 1.10 will give 132.51.

8.2.6 Some Basic Economic Implications of the Perpetuity Formula

The constant-growth perpetuity formula is often taught in introductory finance as a famous and simple way to compute the fundamental value of a share in a company's common stock. The formula is referred to as the *Gordon Growth Model*, in which CF_1 is the current annual dividend payment per share, g is the expected long-term average annual growth rate in the company's dividends (presumably the growth rate in the company's earnings per share), and r is the stock market's required expected annual total return from investing in the stock (including consideration of how risky the stock is). For example, if a company currently pays \$1 per share in quarterly dividends (\$4/year), has a track record of providing consistent long-term average growth in dividends of 5% per year, and the market requires an average annual total return (including both dividends and capital gain) of 12%, then the stock should be worth \$4/(0.12-0.05) = \$4/0.07 = \$57.14 per share. Presumably (according to the model), if the stock is currently selling for less than that, then it is a good buy.

In general, the constant-growth perpetuity model represents a basic way to understand the value of any infinitely lived income-producing asset, as a relationship among the current level of net cash flow produced by the asset, the likely long-term average rate of growth in that cash flow, and the expected annual total return required by investors in the asset. As such, this model is broadly applicable to commercial property and provides a basic understanding of the cap rate, defined as the current annual income divided by the value of the property. For example, the constant-growth perpetuity model reveals that the apartment building described earlier would have a cap rate of 12% − 3% = 9% (this is $r - g$ on a per-annum basis). In other words, the apartment would sell for a price approximately 11 times its annual net income (that is, 1/0.09). In fact, the building's annual net income is \$47,500 × 12 = \$570,000. Dividing this by the \$6,333,333 estimated value implies the cap rate of 9%. Thus, the perpetuity model reveals that the cap rate for a building like this equals investors' expected total return minus their expected annual long-term growth rate in the building's net income.

*8.2.7 Introducing Long-Term Leases

While some types of commercial real estate, such as apartment buildings, do not make much use of long-term leases, most types of commercial property use leases that last several years or more. For example, leases in office or warehouse buildings are often 3 to 10 years long. Within each lease, once the lease is signed, the cash flows specified in the lease have relatively low risk because the tenant is contractually obligated to make the lease payments. (From the perspective of the risk of the rental cash flows, once the lease is signed, it is much like a loan to the tenant, or a bond issued by the tenant.) On the other hand, prior to the signing of any given lease, the cash flows that the building can earn under such future leases are less certain, which makes them more risky, for it is not known exactly what rent a landlord will be able to charge. Furthermore, within each lease the growth rate in the rent will often be known for certain, while between leases the growth rate will depend on conditions in the rental market.

Thus, to model the cash flows of a building subject to long-term leases, we really need to consider two different growth rates and two different discount rates. One set of rates applies *within* leases (the **intralease rates**), and the other set of rates applies *across* leases (the **interlease rates**). At first glance this would seem to complicate the present value calculation greatly. However, the geometric series formula enables us to obtain a relatively simple formula for the present value of such a building. The present value calculation is broken down into two steps. Each lease is a constant-growth annuity whose present value as of the time of lease signing can be determined using formula (6a), and the building as a whole is a constant-growth perpetuity whose value can be determined using formula (6b). In effect, the building is a "perpetuity of successive annuities". Consider the following example.

A space will lease out in 10-year leases successively in perpetuity. The leases have annual rent payments at the beginnings of the years. Each lease will be for a constant rent once that lease is signed, but new leases will be signed at rent levels reflecting annual growth in market rent. This growth is expected to be 1% per year, but this is an uncertain, risky growth expectation. So the expected rent in each successive lease will be 1.01^{10} times the previous lease's rent, although this is not guaranteed. Once a lease is signed, the opportunity cost of capital for computing the PV of that lease as of the time of its signing is 6% per year, reflecting the relatively low risk of the contractually fixed rental payments. However, between leases or prior to lease signings, the opportunity cost of capital is 11% per year, reflecting the greater risk associated with not knowing for certain what the future market rent will be. The initial lease is expected to be signed (and first rent received) one year from now, with an annual rent of $10/SF. What is the value of this property per SF?

In the first step of solving this problem, we compute the present value of the first lease when it is signed, as a level annuity in advance. We have $a = 10$, $N = 10$, $d = (1/1.06)$:

$$PV(Lease\ 1) = \frac{a\,(1 - d^N)}{1 - d} = \frac{\$10\,(1 - 1/1.06^{10})}{1 - 1/1.06}$$

$$= \$10\left(\frac{1.06}{0.06}\right)(1 - 1/1.06^{10}) = \$78.02\,/\,SF$$

The present value of this first lease as of today is this expected value at signing (one year from now) computed above, divided by 1.11 (because this is a risky value—we do not know for sure the lease will be signed with a rent of $10/SF). Thus, the present value of the first lease as of today is $78.02/1.11 = $70.29/SF. This is the value of the first term in the perpetuity of successive annuities that represents the present value of the property as a whole. Thus, this is the value of a in the perpetuity formula (6b) for calculating the building's value.

In the second step of solving this problem we need to identify the common ratio, d, to apply in the perpetuity problem. In this case, $d = (1.01/1.11)^{10}$, because there are 10 years (the lease term) between each expected lease signing, and we expect market rents to grow at a rate of 1% per year in this rental market. In other words, if we let PVL_j represent the value of the jth lease at the time of its signing, then the perpetuity that represents the building value is given by the following infinite series of single-sums:

$$PV\ (building) = \frac{PVL_1}{1.11} + \frac{(1.01)^{10}PVL_2}{1.11^{11}} + \frac{(1.01)^{20}PVL_2}{1.11^{21}} + \cdots$$

Note that the larger interlease discount rate of 11% is used here because we are discounting *across leases*, that is, across time prior to the signings of the future leases we are evaluating. (This is in contrast to the computation of the values, at signings, of each lease, in which the smaller intralease discount rate is applied in the annuity formula.) Thus, the value of the property is

$$PV\ (building) = \frac{a}{1-d} = \frac{PVL_1/1.11}{1-(1.01/1.11)^{10}} = \frac{\$70.29}{1-(1.01/1.11)^{10}} = \$115.05/SF$$

So the building is worth $115.04/SF.

Note that this is a substantially different value than if we employed the simple constant-growth perpetuity formula to the initial $10/SF rent level as if there were no long-term leases: $PV = CF_1/(r - g) = \$10/(0.11 - 0.01) = \$10/0.10 = \$100/SF$.

The use of the long-term leases, while delaying the growth in cash flow to only once every 10 years, reduces the risk of the cash flows sufficiently in this case so that the present value of the space is substantially greater than it would be if only short-term leases were employed. The ability to apply the underlying geometric series formula flexibly as in this problem enables one to analyze questions involving long-term leases, such as the trade-off between lease term, rental level, and building value.

8.2.8 Summarizing the Present Value of Geometric Cash Flow Streams

All of the previous problems have really only used a single underlying formula, the geometric series formula (6). The general procedure has been to set up the underlying present value problem as a sequence of single-sums, so that it is clear what is the first term on the right-hand side of the equation (the value *a*), what is the common ratio between those terms (*d*), and what is the number of terms (*N*). In complex problems, such as when more than one long-term lease is involved, this procedure should be applied in more than one step, building up the overall present value problem. The following list summarizes the application of formula (6) to the basic simple cases:

- For the level perpetuity or annuity, $d = 1/(1 + r)$ where r = interest rate per period.
- For constant-growth perpetuity or annuity, $d = (1 + g)/(1 + r)$.
- For cash flows in arrears (at ends of periods), $a = CF_1/(1 + r)$.
- For cash flow in advance (at beginnings of periods), $a = CF_1$.
- For annuities, N = number of periods.
- For perpetuities, N = infinity and d must be <1 (so, $d^N = 0$).

8.2.9 How to Convert Annuities to Future Values

All of the previous examples were present value problems in which we were converting a future cash flow stream to present value. In some cases it is useful to do the reverse, converting a stream of cash flows into a future value as of a terminal point in time, by growing the cash flows to the terminal point. In fact, this can be done still using the same geometric formula. For example, consider the future value of an annuity of

$100/month in arrears (paid at the ends of the months) for 12 months at 12% per annum (compounded monthly, actually 1% per month). As always, the first step is to set the problem up as a sequence of single-sums based on formula (2), in this case formula (2b). Here we have

$$FV = \$100(1.01)^{11} + \$100(1.01)^{10} + \cdots + \$100$$

So the first term is $a = 100(1.01)^{11}$, the number of terms is $n = 12$, and the common ratio is $d = 1/1.01$. Thus

$$FV = \frac{\$100\,(1.01)^{11}[1 - (1/1.01)^{12}]}{1 - (1/1.01)} = \$1,268.25$$

In general, the future value problem simply represents $(1 + r)^N$ times the present value problem. For example, if the following gives the present value:

$$PV = \frac{CF_1}{1 + r} + \frac{CF_2}{(1 + r)^2} + \cdots + \frac{CF_N}{(1 + r)^N}$$

then multiplying both sides of the equation by $(1 + r)^N$ will give the future value as in formula (11):

$$(1 + r)^N PV = (1 + r)^N \frac{CF_1}{1 + r} + (1 + r)^N \frac{CF_2}{(1 + r)^2} + \cdots + (1 + r)^N \frac{CF_N}{(1 + r)^N} \quad (11)$$

$$= CF_1 (1 + r)^{N-1} + CF_2 (1 + r)^{N-2} + \cdots + CF_N = FV$$

8.2.10 Solving for the Cash Flows

If the present value can be expressed as a function of a single periodic payment amount, such as the level payment in an annuity or the initial cash flow in a growth annuity or perpetuity, then it is straightforward to invert the present value formula to solve it for the cash flow. For example, the following formula inverting (7a) tells the level payment amount (PMT) that is required to produce a given present value, given the number of payments and the interest rate:

$$PMT = PV \frac{r}{1 - 1/(1 + r)^N} \quad (7c)$$

For example, a borrower wants a 30-year, monthly-payment, fixed-interest mortgage for $80,000. As a lender, you want to earn a return of 1% per month, compounded monthly. You agree to provide the $80,000 up front (i.e., at the present time), in return for the commitment by the borrower to make 360 equal monthly payments in the amount of $822.89 each, starting with the first payment due in one month. The required monthly payment of $822.89 is found as

$$822.89 = 80,000 \frac{.01}{1 - 1/(1.01)^{360}}$$

8.2.11 Solving for the Number of Payments

Similarly, it is possible to invert the previous formulas to find the number of payments or length of time required for a given cash flow stream to produce a given present value. For example, to find the number of specified level payments required to pay off a given amount at a given interest rate, formula (7) can be solved for Tm:

$$Tm = -\frac{\ln\left(1 - \frac{i}{m}\frac{PV}{PMT}\right)}{\ln\left(1 + \frac{i}{m}\right)}$$

(7d)

where $\ln(.)$ is the natural logarithm. In the case of the growth annuity, formula (9) is solved for N:

$$N = \frac{\ln\left(1 - \frac{PV}{CF_1}(r - g)\right)}{\ln\left(\frac{1 + g}{1 + r}\right)}$$

(9a)

8.2.12 Combining the Single Lump Sum and the Level Annuity Stream: Classical Mortgage Mathematics

The typical calculations associated with classical mortgage mathematics can be solved using one or the other or a combination of the single-sum formulas described in section 8.1 and the annuity formulas just described. This is because the classical mortgage is constructed as an annuity with the contractual principal as the PV amount.[6] To calculate the monthly payments on a loan of a given amount, you simply apply the annuity formula solved for the payment as in (7c). To calculate how much you can borrow given a specified level of monthly payments for a specified number of years, you apply the present value annuity formula (7a). To calculate the remaining outstanding loan balance (OLB) at any point in time (i.e., after a given number of payments), the annuity formula also applies. The OLB equals the present value of the remaining loan payments discounted at the loan's contractual interest rate, so you apply the annuity formula (7a) to determine the PV with N equal to the number of payments not yet made. The PV amount so determined equals the OLB on the loan. In other words, after q payments have been made on a loan that has a monthly payment amount of PMT and originally was for T years at a rate of i, the OLB is given by

---

[6] Note that the contractual principal of a loan is not necessarily exactly equal to the amount of cash the borrower will receive from the lender at the time the loan is disbursed. This is due to the possible presence of discount points of prepaid interest or loan application fees and other expenses that may be taken out of the loan disbursement. Nevertheless, the borrower's debt obligation at the time the loan is taken out equals the entire contractual principal amount.

$$OLB = PMT \, \dfrac{1 - \left(\dfrac{1}{1 + \dfrac{i}{m}} \right)^{(mT-q)}}{\dfrac{i}{m}}$$

(7e)

For example, the $80,000, 12%, 30-year mortgage we noted earlier with the monthly payments of $822.89 would have an outstanding loan balance after 10 years of payments equal to $74,734.40, based on the following calculation:

$$74,734.40 = 822.89 \, \frac{1 - 1/(1.01)^{240}}{.01}$$

The classical mortgage is "fully amortizing," meaning that the regular monthly payments completely and exactly pay off the entire contractual principal over the course of the maturity of the loan. But many loans are not fully amortizing. They may amortize, for example, at a 30-year rate but have a maturity of only 10 years, which means that the outstanding loan balance is due after 10 years. An extreme version of this would be a loan that does not amortize at all, also known as an interest-only loan. Interest-only loans are common particularly among commercial mortgages.

In the case of partially amortizing or nonamortizing loans, the cash flow stream from the mortgage consists of the combination (or sum) of an annuity plus a single lump sum payment at the end. The annuity portion consists of the interest plus any partial amortization, while the single sum at the end consists of the remaining principal at the time of maturity of the loan. In the case of an interest-only loan the annuity is purely interest (each payment equaling the per-period simple interest rate times the contractual principal), while the single-sum liquidating payment at the end equals the entire contractual principal amount.

Using our previous labels and formulas (i.e., *FV* represents the single-sum amount and *PMT* represents the regular periodic payment amount), a wide variety of mortgages can be represented by the following formula.

$$PV = \left(\frac{PMT}{(1+r)} + \frac{PMT}{(1+r)^2} + \cdots + \frac{PMT}{(1+r)^N} \right) + \frac{FV}{(1+r)^N}$$

(12)

where, as always, $r = i/m$, the simple per-period interest rate, and $N = Tm$, the total number of periods in the maturity of the loan. In formula (12) the first part on the right-hand side in the parentheses is the annuity part, and the last term on the right is the single sum. For example, a 12% interest-only loan for $80,000 would have $PMT = \$800$ and $FV = \$80,000$, which would give $PV = \$80,000$ at the 12% nominal annual rate ($r = 12\%/12 = 1\%$), for any loan term (any value of N).

8.2.13 How the Present Value Keys on a Business Calculator Work

Business calculators typically have two sets of keys or functions that are useful in solving present value problems: the mortgage math keys and the discounted cash flow (DCF) keys. The former are designed specifically to deal with the type of level annuity and single-sum problems discussed in section 8.2.12 and represented by formula (12). The DCF keys are designed to enable present value and **internal rate of return (IRR)** calculation of a more general stream of future cash flows. The IRR and DCF valuation will be defined and discussed in Chapters 9 and 10, while mortgages will be discussed further in Part VI. The focus of the present chapter is only on the mathematical mechanics and the functioning of the typical business calculator.

The mortgage math keys are the quickest way to solve problems that can be set up with some combination of a stream of level regular cash flows plus at most one additional lump-sum cash flow at the end of the level stream. There are typically five mortgage math keys corresponding to the five variables in formula (12): PV, FV, PMT, N, and r.[7] The mortgage math keys work by solving formula (12) for the value of the variable whose key has been pressed, given the values that currently reside in the registers of the other four variables in the Formula. Note that, as per formula (12), the calculator assumes that the last one of the regular annuity cash flows whose amounts are specified in the PMT register occurs at the same time (N periods in the future) as the single lump-sum amount represented in the FV register.

Note also that formula (12) can be rewritten to equate to zero as follows:

$$0 = -PV + \left(\frac{PMT}{(1 + r)} + \frac{PMT}{(1 + r)^2} + \cdots + \frac{PMT}{(1 + r)^N} \right) + \frac{FV}{(1 + r)^N}$$

In this form it is seen clearly that the sign of the PV amount will normally be opposite to that of the PMT and FV amounts. From the lender's perspective, the PV amount represents an up-front cash outflow, while the other amounts are the future debt service payments that provide cash inflows. Thus, it makes sense that calculators represent amounts entered into the PMT and FV registers as being of opposite sign to amounts calculated in the PV register, and vice versa.[8]

8.2.14 IRR and Multiperiod DCF Formula

The DCF keys on the calculator are designed to solve a more general present value problem. If the future cash flows are not well described by the equal payments of a level annuity plus at most one lump sum at the end, then the DCF keys must be used to compute present values or internal rates of return (IRR). The DCF keys allow all the future cash flow amounts to be different.

Consider an arbitrary stream of cash flows occurring at the ends of each of a consecutive sequence of uniform-length time periods (net cash flow amounts labeled CF_0, CF_1, CF_2, etc., occurring in time periods labeled 0, 1, 2, and so on, where period 0 is the present). These cash flow amounts are entered into the calculator

---

[7]As noted, in many cases you can enter the payment frequency per year in the calculator, and then you can enter the interest in nominal annual terms, and the calculator will automatically compute $r = i/m$.

[8]An exception is when using the mortgage math keys to compute the terminal value (FV) of a level stream, as in formula (11). For such problems, set $PV = 0$ in the calculator and solve for FV. The FV amount represents the terminal (compound growth) value of the payments, with FV being opposite in sign to PMT, as in formula (11) set equal to zero. Note that in general there is no algebraic analytical formula to solve formula (13) for the IRR. The calculator must find the answer by a repetitive trial-and-error process through which it iterates to an answer that is acceptably close to solving the equation.

cash flow registers, which are often labeled something like CFj or C0, C1, and so on. The DCF keys solve the equation in formula (13) for either the *NPV* value or the *IRR* value:

$$NPV = CF_0 + \frac{CF_1}{(1 + IRR)} + \frac{CF_2}{(1 + IRR)^2} + \cdots + \frac{CF_T}{(1 + IRR)^T} \tag{13}$$

where T is the number of future periods encompassed in the analysis (beyond the present).[9]

To solve for the *IRR*, the *NPV* is by definition assumed to be zero, and the amount in the CF_0 register must be of opposite sign to the bulk of the values in the other CF_j registers ($j = 1, \ldots, T$). For example, you would typically enter the up-front investment amount as a negative number representing cash outflow in register CF_0, such as the price of the property, while the subsequent cash flows would be largely positive representing the net cash dividends or rental payments received from the investment. If the discount rate were then specified (typically in the interest key of the calculator), then this discount rate would be used in place of the *IRR* rate in formula (13) and the formula would be solved to determine the net present value (*NPV*) of the project. Alternatively, if you press the *IRR* register, the calculator will compute the value of the IRR.[10] Finally, if you specify an amount of zero for the CF_0 register, then pressing the *NPV* key will compute the present value (corresponding to the *PV*, or gross present value) of the future stream of cash flows (in arrears). Note that in this case the *NPV* register does not in itself compute a *net* present value, as we have 0 in the present cash flow.

---

[9] Note that equation (13) is the most general formula for the present value of an arbitrary stream of discrete future cash flows assuming a constant discount rate. (If the cash flows occur at irregularly spaced points in time, one can simply define the smallest common time divisor as the period, and have $CF_t = 0$ between the cash flow receipts.) An even more general formula would allow for time-varying discount rates, as follows:

$$NPV = CF_0 + \frac{CF_1}{(1 + r_1)} + \frac{CF_2}{(1 + r_2)^2} + \cdots + \frac{CF_T}{(1 + r_t)^T}$$

where r_t is the time-weighted average multiperiod return from time zero to time t. It is useful to note that even in this most general form, the present value equation is "homogeneous of degree one" in the cash flows. That is, if all the cash flow amounts on the right-hand side of the equation are multiplied by any constant a, then the left-hand side NPV is also multiplied by that same constant. More formally: if $NPV = f(CF)$, then $aNPV = f(aCF)$, where $f( )$ is the present value equation, CF here is an arbitrary vector of cash flows, and a is a scalar constant. This is simply a consequence of the distributive law of multiplication and addition: $a(b + c) = ab + ac$, but it allows great computational convenience in working with present values. For example, the ability to use tables of "annuity factors," and the ability of lenders to publish loan interest rates applicable to loans of varying amounts, is a consequence of this homogeneity property.

[10] In some calculators the IRR may be reported on a per-period basis, so that, for example, if the periods were months, you would have to multiply the computed IRR by 12 to obtain the nominal per-annum rate.

8.3 CHAPTER SUMMARY

This chapter has presented the major formulas and procedures that are most useful for the calculation and analysis of the present value of the types of cash flow streams most commonly found in commercial real estate. Included in this are the important inverses of the present value formulas, that is, formulas for calculating implied returns, terminal values, and the time (or number of payments) until a certain present or future value is achieved. We have focused on the formal mechanics of the basic formulas, leaving the economic reasoning and analysis necessary for the correct application of these formulas largely to be covered in later chapters.

KEY TERMS

Single-sum formulas
present value
future value
discounting
growing
discount rate
interest rate
compounding
growth rate
compounding frequency

effective annual rate (EAR)
equivalent nominal annual rate
 (ENAR)
mortgage equivalent rate
bond equivalent (coupon
 equivalent) rate
continuous compounding
annuity
perpetuity
geometric series formula

common ratio
level annuity
constant-growth annuity
constant-growth perpetuity
intralease rate
interlease rate
internal rate of return (IRR)
calculator registers
 (N,I,PV,PMT,FV,NPV,IRR,CF)

STUDY QUESTIONS

8.1. What is the present value of an offer of $15,000 one year from now if the opportunity cost of capital (discount rate) is 12% per year simple interest?

8.2. What is the present value of an offer of $14,000 one year from now if the opportunity cost of capital (discount rate) is 11% per year simple interest?

8.3. What is the present value of an offer of $15,000 two years from now if the opportunity cost of capital (discount rate) is 12% per year compounded annually?

8.4. What is the present value of an offer of $14,000 two years from now if the opportunity cost of capital (discount rate) is 11% per year compounded annually?

8.5. What is the future value of $20,000 that grows at an annual interest rate of 12% per year for two years?

8.6. What is the future value of $25,000 that grows at an annual interest rate of 11% per year for two years?

8.7. What is the present value of an offer of $15,000 one year from now if the opportunity cost of capital (discount rate) is 12% per year nominal annual rate compounded monthly?

8.8. What is the present value of an offer of $14,000 one year from now if the opportunity cost of capital (discount rate) is 11% per year nominal annual rate compounded monthly?

8.9. What is the future value of $20,000 that grows at a nominal annual interest rate of 12% per year, compounded monthly, for two years?

8.10. What is the future value of $25,000 that grows at a nominal annual interest rate of 11% per year, compounded monthly, for two years?

8.11. What is the effective annual rate (EAR) of 8% nominal annual rate compounded monthly?

8.12. What is the effective annual rate (EAR) of 6.5% nominal annual rate compounded monthly?

8.13. What is the effective annual rate (EAR) of 8% nominal annual rate compounded semiannually?

8.14. What is the effective annual rate (EAR) of 6.5% nominal annual rate compounded semiannually?

8.15. If the bond equivalent rate is 10%, what is the corresponding mortgage equivalent rate?

8.16. If the bond equivalent rate is 6%, what is the corresponding mortgage equivalent rate?

8.17. If the mortgage equivalent rate is 10%, what is the corresponding bond equivalent rate?

8.18. If the mortgage equivalent rate is 6%, what is the corresponding bond equivalent rate?

8.19. What is the effective annual rate (EAR) of 8% nominal annual rate compounded continuously?

8.20. What is the effective annual rate (EAR) of 6.5% nominal annual rate compounded continuously?

8.21. If you invested $15,000 and received back $30,000 five years later, what annual interest (or growth) rate (compounded annually) would you have obtained?

8.22. If you invested $40,000 and received back $100,000 seven years later, what annual interest (or growth) rate (compounded annually) would you have obtained?

8.23. In question 8.21, what nominal annual rate compounded monthly would you have obtained?

8.24. In question 8.22, what nominal annual rate compounded monthly would you have obtained?

8.25. In question 8.21, what continuously compounded rate would you have obtained?

8.26. In question 8.22, what continuously compounded rate would you have obtained?

8.27. If you invest $15,000 and it grows at an annual rate of 10% (compounded annually), how many years will it take to grow to $30,000?

8.28. If you invest $20,000 and it grows at an annual rate of 8% (compounded annually), how many years will it take to grow to $40,000?

8.29. In question 8.27, suppose the 10% is a nominal annual rate compounded monthly.

8.30. In question 8.28, suppose the 8% is a nominal annual rate compounded monthly.

8.31. In question 8.27, suppose the 10% annual rate is compounded continuously.

8.32. In question 8.28, suppose the 8% annual rate is compounded continuously.

8.33. A real estate investor feels that the cash flow from a property will enable her to pay a lender $15,000 per year, at the end of every year, for 10 years. How much should the lender be willing to loan her if he requires a 9% annual interest rate (annually compounded, assuming the first of the 10 equal payments arrives one year from the date the loan is disbursed)?

8.34. A real estate investor feels that the cash flow from a property will enable her to pay a lender $20,000 per year, at the end of every year, for eight years. How much should the lender be willing to loan her if he requires a 7.5% annual interest rate (annually compounded, assuming the first of the eight equal payments arrives one year from the date the loan is disbursed)?

8.35. In question 8.33, suppose the lender wants the 9% as a nominal annual rate compounded monthly?

8.36. In question 8.34, suppose the lender wants the 7.5% as a nominal annual rate compounded monthly?

8.37. In question 8.33, suppose that not only will the interest be compounded monthly, but the payments will also arrive monthly in the amount of $1,250 per month (the first payment to arrive in one month)?

8.38. In question 8.34, suppose that not only will the interest be compounded monthly, but the payments will also arrive monthly in the amount of $1,666.67 per month (the first payment to arrive in one month)?

8.39. In question 8.37 (with 120 equal monthly payments of $1,250) suppose the borrower also offers to pay the lender $50,000 at the end of the 10-year period (coinciding with, and in addition to, the last regular monthly payment). How much should the lender be willing to lend?

8.40. In question 8.38 (with 96 equal monthly payments of $1,666.67) suppose the borrower also offers to pay the lender $90,000 at the end of the eight-year period (coinciding with, and in addition to, the last regular monthly payment). How much should the lender be willing to lend?

8.41. You are borrowing $80,000 for 25 years at 10% nominal annual interest compounded monthly. How much must your monthly payments be if you will completely retire the loan over the 25-year period (i.e., what is the level payment annuity with a present value of $80,000)?

8.42. You are borrowing $125,000 for 30 years at 9% nominal annual interest compounded monthly. How much must your monthly payments be if you will completely retire the loan over the 30-year period (i.e., what is the level payment annuity with a present value of $125,000)?

8.43. At a nominal annual interest rate of 10% compounded monthly, how long (how many months) will it take to retire a $50,000 loan using equal monthly payments of $500 (with the payments made at the end of each month)?

8.44. At a nominal annual interest rate of 8.75% compounded monthly, how long (how many months) will it take to retire a $100,000 loan using equal monthly payments of $750 (with the payments made at the end of each month)?

8.45. A tenant offers to sign a lease paying a rent of $1,000 per month, in advance (i.e., the rent will be paid at the beginning of each month), for five years. At 10% nominal annual interest compounded monthly, what is the present value of this lease?

8.46. A tenant offers to sign a lease paying a rent of $2,500 per month, in advance (i.e., the rent will be paid at the beginning of each month), for seven years. At 9% nominal annual interest compounded monthly, what is the present value of this lease?

8.47. A building is expected to require $1 million in capital improvement expenditures in five years. The building's net operating cash flow prior to that time is expected to be at least $20,000 at the end of every month. How much of that monthly cash flow must the owners set aside each month in order to have the money available for the capital improvements, assuming the equal monthly contributions placed in this "sinking fund" will earn interest at a nominal annual rate of 6%, compounded monthly?

8.48. A building is expected to require $4,250,000 in capital improvement expenditures in three years. The building's net operating cash flow prior to that time is expected to be at least $200,000 at the end of every month. How much of that monthly cash flow must the owners set aside each month in order to have the money available for the capital improvements, assuming the equal monthly contributions placed in this "sinking fund" will earn interest at a nominal annual rate of 5%, compounded monthly?

8.49. A landlord has offered a tenant a 10-year lease with annual net rental payments of $30/SF in arrears. The appropriate discount rate is 8%. The tenant has asked the landlord to come back with another proposal, similar in every way except with rent that steps up annually at a rate of 3% per year, in return for a lower starting rent. What should the landlord's proposed starting rent be?

8.50. A landlord has offered a tenant a five-year lease with annual net rental payments of $20/SF in arrears. The appropriate discount rate is 10%. The tenant has asked the landlord to come back with another proposal, similar in every way except with rent that steps up annually at a rate of 5% per year, in return for a lower starting rent. What should the landlord's proposed starting rent be?

8.51. An apartment building can be well represented as producing net rent of $10/SF annually in arrears, with expected annual growth over the long run of negative 1% per year (that is, a decline of 1% per year). Use the constant-growth perpetuity formula to estimate the apartment building's value (per SF) if the required annual expected total return from the investment is 10%.

8.52. An apartment building can be well represented as producing net rent of $7.50/SF annually in arrears, with expected annual growth over the long run of 1% per year. Use the constant-growth perpetuity formula to estimate the apartment building's value (per SF) if the required annual expected total return from the investment is 12%.

8.53. Suppose a certain property is expected to produce net operating cash flows annually as follows, at the end of each of the next five years: $15,000, $16,000, $20,000, $22,000, and $17,000. In addition, at the end of the fifth year we will assume the property will be (or could be) sold for $200,000.

   a. What is the NPV of a deal in which you would pay $180,000 for the property today assuming the required expected return or discount rate is 11% per year?

b. If you could get the property for only $170,000, what would be the expected IRR of your investment?

8.54. Suppose a certain property is expected to produce net operating cash flows annually as follows, at the end of each of the next five years: $35,000, $37,000, $45,000, $46,000, and $40,000. In addition, at the end of the fifth year we will assume the property will be (or could be) sold for $450,000.

a. What is the NPV of a deal in which you would pay $400,000 for the property today assuming the required expected return or discount rate is 12% per year?

b. If you could get the property for only $375,000, what would be the expected IRR of your investment?

*8.55. A 100,000-SF space is expected to rent in five-year fixed-rent leases successively in perpetuity (annual payments at the beginnings of the years). You expect the first lease will be signed one year from now, with the first rent payment to be received at that time. The second lease will begin five years after that, the third five years later, and so on. The rent in each lease is constant, but between new lease signings the rent is expected to grow at a rate of 2% per year. The rent on the first lease is expected to be $20/SF per year. To compute the present value of each lease as of the time of its signing, use a low discount rate of 8% per year, reflecting the fact that the cash flows under the lease are contractually fixed. However, prior to the signing of each lease, the amount of the rent for that lease is uncertain and risky, so a 12% rate is appropriate for discounting lease values back to present value prior to lease signings. Use the level annuity formula embedded in a constant-growth perpetuity formula to compute the present value of this 100,000-SF space. [Hint: Recall the $S = a(1 - d^n)/(1 - d)$ geometric sum formula. This is a level annuity in advance embedded in a constant-growth perpetuity.]

*8.56. A 250,000-SF space is expected to rent in 10-year fixed-rent leases, successively in perpetuity (annual payments at the beginnings of the years). You expect the first lease will be signed one year from now, with the first rent payment to be received at that time. The second lease will begin 10 years after that, the third 10 years later, and so on. The rent in each lease is constant, but between new lease signings the rent is expected to grow at a rate of 1% per year. The rent on the first lease is expected to be $15/SF per year. To compute the present value of each lease as of the time of its signing, use a low discount rate of 6% per year, reflecting the fact that the cash flows under the lease are contractually fixed. However, prior to the signing of each lease, the amount of the rent for that lease is uncertain and risky, so a 10% rate is appropriate for discounting lease values back to present value prior to lease signings. Use the level annuity formula embedded in a constant-growth perpetuity formula to compute the present value of this 250,000-SF space. [Hint: Recall the $S = a(1 - d^n)/(1 - d)$ geometric sum formula. This is a level annuity in advance embedded in a constant-growth perpetuity.]

9 Measuring Investment Performance: The Concept of Returns

Learning Objectives

After reading this chapter, you should understand:

♦ What is meant by investment returns and how to quantify both period-by-period total returns and IRRs.

♦ The two major components of the total return, and why these are important.

♦ The characteristic features of the main types of returns, and when it is best to use each type.

♦ What is meant by risk in investment, how to quantify risk, and how it relates to returns.

♦ How to account for inflation in return measures.

♦ The NCREIF Property Index (NPI), and how the NPI return formula is derived.

Now that you are equipped with some basic background information and tools from the two preceding chapters, you are ready to begin mastering the basic building blocks of real estate investment analysis, beginning in this chapter with a consideration of how return and risk are measured. Of course, the problem of measuring investment performance is common to all types of investment, not just real estate, so much of what we will cover in this chapter is identical to what you will find in any introductory corporate finance or investments textbook. Here, we will make sure the application of these concepts to real estate is made clear, and we will cover some considerations and conventions that apply uniquely or particularly to real estate investment analysis.

9.1 INVESTMENT RETURNS: BASIC DEFINITIONS AND CLASSIFICATION

Recall from Chapter 7 that underlying the variety of investors and investment goals are two fundamental types of objectives, what we called income and growth (or savings). We also noted several typical constraints and concerns investors have, including most prominently the question of *risk* in the investment. What we want to do now is to build on these concepts to define a way to *quantify investment performance*: how well is the investment doing for the investor? To this end, the concept of investment **returns** is very useful. Returns are the fundamental measure of investment performance both at the microlevel of individual properties and deals, and at the macrolevel of the big picture of overall investment strategy and real estate as an asset class among others in the capital markets. Indeed, we will see how this concept may be defined and measured in ways that will allow us to quantify not only the overall end result or average investment performance over time, but also the nature and amount of risk in the investment.

Fundamentally, return is how we measure profit in an investment endeavor. In essence, the return on an investment is *what you get, minus what you started out with, expressed as a percentage of what you started out with.*

For example, if you invest $100 and end up a year later with $110, then you have made a 10% return. If you end up with only just your original $100, you have a 0% return, and if you end up with only $95, you have a negative return of 5%.

Investors typically quantify measures of return either by looking backward or forward in time.

1. Looking backward in time, **ex post** (i.e., historical) returns are used to measure past performance, which is useful

   - to estimate future performance (to the extent the future can be predicted from the past);

   - to judge the past performance of investment advisors or managers; and/or

   - to understand the current investment environment and "mood," as it is a product of recent past experience.

2. Looking forward in time, **ex ante** (i.e., expected) returns are used to quantitatively express future performance expectations, which are directly relevant for making investment decisions in the present, for these decisions will have their wealth impact for the investor as a result of what transpires in the future.

9.1.1 Two Fundamental Types of Return Measures

It is useful to distinguish two major types of return measures: **period-by-period** (or **periodic**) **returns**, and **multiperiod returns**. We will consider each of these in turn.

Periodic returns are usually quantified as simple **holding period returns (HPR)**. They measure what the investment grows to *within* each single period of time, assuming that all cash flow (or asset valuation) occurs only at the *beginning* and *end* of the period of time (i.e., no intermediate cash flows). Periodic returns are measured separately over each of a sequence of regular and consecutive (relatively short) periods of time (typically daily, monthly, quarterly, or annually). For example, in 1993 the return on the S&P 500 index of stocks was 10.00%, followed by a rather disappointing

1.33% return in 1994, and then a very pleasing 37.50% return in 1995. Periodic returns can be averaged across time to determine the **time-weighted** multiperiod **return**, so called because a rate of return that is earned over more periods or during a larger fraction of the overall time interval will figure more strongly in the overall average return.

The second general type of return measure, the multiperiod return, gives a single inherently multiperiod return number for a relatively long-term period of time during which there can be cash flows into or out of the investment at intermediate points in time. The most widely used multiperiod return measure is the **internal rate of return (IRR)**. Unlike period-by-period returns, the IRR can be computed without having to know the capital value of the investment at intermediate points in time. This makes the IRR more convenient to compute for real estate investments that are not regularly and frequently reappraised. Although the multiperiod return usually covers more than one year, it is generally quoted as a per-annum (i.e., per-year) rate. For example, we might determine that a certain investor earned a 12% return per year over the three-year period from the beginning of 2000 through the end of 2002. The IRR is a **dollar-weighted** (or money-weighted) **return** because it reflects the effect of having different amounts of money invested at different periods of time during the overall lifetime of the investment.

9.1.2 Advantages and Disadvantages of Periodic and Multiperiod Return Measures

In modern real estate investment analysis both period-by-period and multiperiod return measures are widely used. Each type of return measure has several advantages and disadvantages, or strengths and weaknesses for different applications.

In real estate, period-by-period returns are more relevant at the macrolevel and in examining portfolios of investments. Periodic returns allow real estate investment performance to be quantified on the same type of metric that is used for the main components of most institutional portfolios, stocks and bonds. Investment classes that do not have good measures of their periodic returns are traditionally considered marginal or "noncore" components of such portfolios. Periodic returns also facilitate the measurement of the risk in investment performance by making possible the quantification of the variability of returns over time (asset "volatility"). For macrolevel and portfolio analysis, real estate performance must be compared with that of other types of assets over the same interval of time, both in regard to risk and return, and it is important to observe the **comovement** of different assets. That is, we need to know how different asset classes tend to move either together or differently over time. Periodic returns allow this type of analysis to be done. Similarly, periodic returns are particularly useful for tracing the historical ups and downs of asset markets, identifying turning points, and discerning time trends in the markets.

Period-by-period returns are also more appropriate for evaluating or comparing the performance of investment managers who have no control over the timing of capital flow into or out of the investments they manage. This is because periodic returns and the time-weighted averages computed from them are insensitive to the timing of capital flows into or out of the investments whose returns are being measured. (This is not true of dollar-weighted returns.) Many investment managers or institutions lack control over capital flow timing. For example, a pension fund must invest all the money that flows into it from active employee member contributions each year, and it must draw out each year sufficient money to pay the pension benefit liabilities it faces for retired members. These are functions of demographics and employment policies of the pension plan sponsor and are not under the control of the investment manager.

On the other hand, the IRR is the classical measure of investment return at the microlevel of individual properties and development projects. For this purpose the IRR has two great advantages. First, it does not require knowledge of market values of the investment asset at intermediate points in time. (This is in contrast with the periodic return, which cannot be computed without such intermediate asset value knowledge.) In real estate, the typical investment is held for several years, and we typically do not know the exact capital value of the investment asset except at the beginning and end of the investment holding period when the property is bought and sold. But we do know the cash flows generated by the asset each period, which is what we need to compute the IRR. In such circumstances, a dollar-weighted multiperiod return such as the IRR may be the only type of total return that can be quantified.

The other advantage of the IRR is just the opposite of that of the periodic return regarding the effect of the timing of capital flow. Just as there are times when one does not want the return measure to be influenced by the timing of capital flow into or out of the investment, so there are times when one does want precisely this. In particular, a dollar-weighted, purely internal return measure such as the IRR will give a fairer and more complete picture of the performance of an investment manager who does have responsibility and control over the timing and amounts of cash flow into and out of the investment vehicle.

In the remainder of this chapter we will develop your understanding of each of these two types of return measures in greater depth, with particular emphasis on real estate investment applications.

9.2 PERIODIC RETURNS

In traditional real estate investment analysis, and even today at the "mom and pop" level of small commercial properties, periodic returns are not computed or considered. Yet modern real estate investment at the institutional level could not function without the widespread use of periodic returns. These types of returns are the bread and butter of the world of Wall Street. The ability to compute real estate periodic returns is fundamental to the linking of Wall Street and Main Street, which has been the hallmark of the last decades of the 20th century in the real estate investment industry. Periodic returns for real estate are necessary to elevate real estate to the status of an investment asset class that can compete in the multiasset institutional portfolio alongside the classical investment classes of stocks and bonds, asset classes for which a wealth of periodic return data exists.

There is another reason for learning how to relate the periodic return measure to real estate in some depth, even at the microlevel. Because of the simplicity of its definition and construction, the simple HPR is a powerful conceptual tool and an elegant pedagogical device. It can be very useful for building your understanding of the nature of real estate investment performance. For all of these reasons, in this section we will present the periodic return measure formally and in some depth and relate its computation to a basic definition of investment risk.

9.2.1 Formal Definition of the Periodic Return

It is time to introduce the most widely used quantifiable definition of the period-by-period return, the simple holding period return (HPR), and describe how this return measure may be broken out into various components that are separately important to investors.

The most basic and complete measure of periodic return is called the **total return**, because it includes both the change in the capital value of the asset during the period and any income paid out by the asset to the investor during the period. We will use the symbol r_t to refer to the total return during period t. (The periods most commonly used for real estate period-by-period returns are quarters, with some use also of either monthly or annual periods.) The formula for the total return during period t is

$$r_t = (CF_t + V_t - V_{t-1})/V_{t-1} \tag{1}$$

In formula (1), CF_t represents the net amount of cash flow or income paid out to the investor in (owner of) the asset during period t, and V_t represents the market value of the capital asset as of the end of period t. Note that formula (1) can also be written as

$$r_t = [(CF_t + V_t)/V_{t-1}] - 1$$

In formula (1), the assumption is that CF_t occurs entirely at the *end* of period t. The HPR assumes a passive, zero cash flow investment *within* each period of time, with valuations at the beginning and end of each period. It is as though the asset were bought at the beginning of each period and then sold at the end of each period. The lack of cash flow prior to the period end may not exactly match reality, however. For example, a stock may pay out its quarterly dividend in the middle of the calendar quarter. In practice, the periods used for computing the sequence of periodic returns are defined as intervals of time short enough so that the exact timing of the cash flow within the period makes little numerical difference. Usually, quarterly or shorter intervals will do the trick in this regard. If not, then approximations are typically employed, such as time-weighted investment, which will be described shortly.

The period-by-period total return can be broken down into two components, known as the **income return** and the **appreciation return**. These are relevant for the two major types of investment objectives we noted in Chapter 7, income and growth.

The income return, which is also often referred to as the **current yield**, we will label y_t for period t, and define it as

$$y_t = CF_t/V_{t-1} \tag{2}$$

Thus, the income return equals the cash flow paid out to the asset owner during period t, as a fraction of the value of the asset at the beginning of the period.

The appreciation return is also referred to by a variety of other labels, such as **capital return**, capital gain, price-change component, or growth. We will symbolize it by g_t for period t, as given by

$$g_t = (V_t - V_{t-1})/V_{t-1} \tag{3}$$

Thus, the appreciation return is the change in the asset market value during period t, as a fraction of the asset market value at the beginning of period t.

Numerical Example of Period-by-Period Return Components in Real Estate

Property value at end of 2000 = $100,000
Property net rent during 2001 = $10,000
Property value at end of 2001 = $101,000

What is 2001 r, g, y?

$$y_{2001} = \frac{\$10,000}{\$100,000} = 10\%$$

$$g_{2001} = \frac{\$101,000 - \$100,000}{\$100,000} = 1\%$$

$$r_{2001} = 10\% + 1\% = 11\%$$

Note that the income and appreciation return components sum to the total return, during the period:

$$r_t = y_t + g_t \tag{4}$$

Thus, the income and appreciation returns represent components of the total return. Clearly, *the income return component is more directly relevant to the income objective of investors*, while *the appreciation return component is more directly relevant to the growth objective.*

The total return is the most important measure of the periodic return because it is more complete than either the growth or income component alone. Furthermore, it is generally possible to convert growth into yield or vice versa within the total return, *but it is not possible to increase the sum of the two components* (that is, the total return). For example, to convert growth into yield, one sells a portion of the investment, thereby "cashing out" some or all of the capital gain. To convert yield into growth, one reinvests some or all of the received income, either in the same asset or in a different asset.

The total return is thus the fundamental statistic for measuring period-by-period investment returns. However, it is important to realize that in the case of direct investment in real property assets, it may be more difficult or expensive to convert between yield and growth than is the case with investments in financial securities such as stocks and bonds (or REITs). For example, it may be difficult or unwise to reinvest income from a property back into improvements in that property, as the property may not need improvement, or improvement of the property would not yield sufficient future payback in the form of rental increases or building operating expense reductions. (Of course, income from the property could be invested in other assets.) Similarly, it may be difficult or impossible to sell a part of a property or a partial interest in a property, in order to convert capital gain into realized income.

A Note on Return Terminology

Unfortunately, return terminology can get confusing, as different branches of the investment industry use the same terms to mean different things.

Income return (CF_t/V_{t-1}) is typically called current yield or dividend yield or just yield in stock market terminology. However, particularly in the bond market (but also in real estate), the word *yield* (often clarified as *total yield* or *yield to maturity*) is also used to refer to the internal rate of return (IRR), which is a multiperiod measure of the *total* return.

In real estate, people often define the income return as: NOI_t/V_{t-1}, where *NOI* is the net operating income generated by the property. This is the definition employed in the NCREIF index. On an annualized basis, such an NOI-based income return is essentially equivalent to what is often referred to as the OAR or cap rate (short for overall rate, or capitalization rate.) But in principle (and

to be more comparable to stock market definitions), the income return should be defined based on cash flow distributable to the investor. This would normally be the NOI less any (non-scale-expanding) capital improvement expenditures necessary to keep the building competitive. That is, $CF_t = NOI_t - CI_t$, where CI_t is the capital improvement expenditures during period *t*. For example, a \$100,000 property with net operating income of \$10,000 and capital expenditures of \$2,000 would have a cap rate of 10% but current cash yield of 8%. Sometimes this problem is dealt with by "expensing" the average level of capital improvement expenditures as a "capital reserve" expense item, so the NOI is then computed net of normal capital expenditures. Capital improvement expenditures typically average 1 to 2% of property value per year, over the long run, for most types of buildings.

(Another possibility would be to borrow against the increased equity the property provides as a result of gain in value, but this will increase the risk of the remaining investment.) Because conversion between yield and gain is more difficult or costly for real estate assets, investors often are more concerned about the individual return components in the case of real estate assets than they are for financial securities such as stocks.

The formulas given previously make it clear that in order to calculate the period-by-period returns and components, one must know (or estimate) the value of the property at the beginning and end of each period of time, with the periods defined as fairly short intervals, such as years or quarters. While most individual investors do not go to the trouble or expense to reappraise and record property values so frequently, institutional investors and fiduciaries such as pension funds may indeed require frequent reappraisals, precisely for the purpose of tracking the period-by-period returns. Indices of period-by-period capital returns may also be computed statistically using transactions price data from a large sample of individual properties at least some of which are bought and sold each period.[1] As a result, a growing amount of period-by-period return data is available for real estate.

---

[1] Statistical techniques for such computations, such as repeat-sales regressions, will be discussed in a later chapter.

9.2.2 Time-Weighted Investment

The simple HPR formula described earlier, which assumes all cash flow occurs at the ends of the periods, works well enough in the securities market where public asset price quotes enable periodic returns to be computed typically on a monthly or daily frequency. In fact, it usually works fine as a very close approximation even for quarterly returns, the common frequency for the major real estate indices. But the longer the period, the greater the inaccuracy caused by the fact that not all cash flows actually occur only at the ends of the periods. A method is needed to deal with intermediate cash flows (e.g., monthly cash flows within quarterly periodic returns).

The general approach to address this problem is to compute the internal rate of return (IRR) within each period assuming the asset was bought at the beginning of the period and sold at the end, with other cash flows occurring whenever they actually occurred within the period. As the exact computation of the IRR is inconvenient, in practice this approach is implemented for our present purposes by an adjustment to the simple HPR, known as time-weighted investment. This involves the replacement of the simple V_{t-1} denominator in the HPR formula with a time-weighted denominator.[2] The time-weighted adjustment to the HPR formula is shown in formula (5), for the return within each period (the subscript t is omitted for simplicity).

$$r = \frac{EndVal - BegVal + \sum CF_i}{BegVal - \sum w_i CF_i} \tag{5}$$

where: $\sum CF_i$ refers to the sum of all net cash flows occurring in period t, and w_i is the proportion of period t remaining at the time when net cash flow i was received by the investor. (Note that cash flow from the investor to the investment is negative; cash flow from the investment to the investor is positive.)

For example, consider an asset that was worth $100 at the beginning of the calendar quarter, still worth $100 at the end of the quarter, and paying out $10 to the investor only at the end of the first month of the quarter. The simple HPR would be computed as $(100 - 100 + 10)/100 = 10.00\%$. The exact IRR for the quarter is 10.70%, computed as

$$0 = -100 + \frac{10}{1 + IRR/mo} + \sum_{j=2}^{3} \frac{0}{(1 + IRR/mo)^j} + \frac{100}{(1 + IRR/mo)^3}$$

$$\Rightarrow IRR/mo = 3.4469\%$$

$$\Rightarrow IRR/qtr = (1.034469)^3 - 1 = 10.70\%$$

The HPR computed with the time-weighted denominator is 10.71%, computed as

$$r = \frac{100 - 100 + 10}{100 - (2/3)10} = \frac{10}{93.33} = 0.1071$$

[2] The derivation of this adjustment is explained in Giliberto (1994).

9.2.3 NCREIF Index Return Formula

The most widely used index of institutional commercial property periodic returns in the United States is the NCREIF Property Index (NPI). The NPI is published quarterly by the National Council of Real Estate Investment Fiduciaries, an industry association whose data-contributing members include the major real estate investment advisory firms providing management services to tax-exempt investors, primarily pension and endowment funds. The NPI is based primarily on regular appraisals of the properties in the index, which by the late 1990s included approximately 2,500 properties worth some $70 billion.[3] The index represents property level (that is, unlevered) total returns, including breakdowns of the income and appreciation components as described earlier. It is published at both the aggregate level and with numerous sectoral and market breakdowns, by both property type and geographic region.[4] The historical series begins in 1978 for the aggregate index and major subindices.[5]

The NPI uses a time-weighted investment formulation to compute its quarterly returns, which are value-weighted aggregates across all the properties in the index each quarter. The exact NCREIF formula uses a time-weighted denominator that is based on the assumption that one-third of the quarterly NOI is received at the end of each month within the quarter, and that any capital improvement expenditures (CI) or partial sales receipts (PS) occur at the midpoint of the quarter. The formula is presented as:

$$r_{NPI} = \frac{End\ Val - Beg\ Val + (PS - CI) + NOI}{Beg\ Val - (1/2)(PS - CI) - (1/3)NOI} \tag{6}$$

Note that one third of the quarterly NOI is subtracted out of the denominator as a result of the time-weighting process. This term actually derives from the following calculation of the $\sum w_i CF_i$ term

$$(1/3)NOI = (2/3)(1/3)NOI + (1/3)(1/3)NOI + (0)(1/3)NOI$$

reflecting the three assumed monthly payments of the NOI.[6]

---

[3] The NPI and data issues relating to its use will be discussed in depth in Part VII.

[4] NCREIF publishes major subindices for office, retail, industrial, and apartment properties, broken down by geographic region and division. The NCREIF geographic regions break the country into four groups of states: East, Midwest, South, and West, while the geographic divisions comprise eight finer groupings, dividing each region into two divisions. NCREIF also publishes finer subindices, including more subdivisions of property types as well as state and metro area breakdowns, as long as there are at least 20 properties in each index. Further breakdowns down to the level of four properties per index are offered on a custom basis. Data on net operating income and capital improvement expenditures are also reported at similar levels of aggregation.

[5] Similar indices are published in other countries, particularly anglophone and some continental European countries. For example, the Investment Property Databank (IPD) in London publishes indices for the United Kingdom and several other countries. In Canada, the International Council of Real Estate Asset Managers publishes an index, while the Property Council of Australia publishes an Australian index.

[6] A more typical assumption is that operating income is received uniformly throughout the period, or at the midpoint of the period (or the midpoint of each month within the period). This results in the coefficient on the NOI term in the denominator being (1/2) rather than (1/3). The (1/2) coefficient is used, for example, by the IPD index in England and the PCA index in Australia. All such return formulas (based on simplifications of the time-weighted investment formula) are referred to generally as "modified Dietz" return measures, named after Peter Dietz, a pioneering financial economist.

NCREIF reports the quarterly NPI returns broken down into income and appreciation components. These are defined as follows:

$$g_{NPI} = \frac{End\ Val - Beg\ Val + (PS - CI)}{Beg\ Val - (1/2)(PS - CI) - (1/3)NOI}$$

$$y_{NPI} = \frac{NOI}{Beg\ Val - (1/2)(PS - CI) - (1/3)NOI}$$

(6a)

Note that NCREIF defines the income return based on the NOI without subtracting capital improvement expenditures. Instead, NCREIF subtracts capital improvement expenditures from the end-of-period asset value in computing the numerator of the appreciation return.[7] Assuming that most capital expenditure is internally financed from the net operating income generated by the properties, this causes the NCREIF appreciation return to typically understate the amount of price appreciation in the property market, and to overstate the current cash yield. (It does not affect the total return.) The NPI income return is more like a quarterly "earnings/price" ratio, and the appreciation return reflects purely property market pricing effects (as estimated by appraisers) net of capital improvement effects.[8]

9.2.4 Real versus Nominal Returns

In order to understand fully the meaning of the return measures we have just described, you need to understand the role of **inflation** in return measures, and the difference between a real and a nominal return.

Inflation is the gradual loss of purchasing power of the dollar (or any currency unit) as prices of the same goods and services rise over time. When we speak about inflation we usually are referring to general inflation, which describes the rise in prices across an average "market-basket" of all goods and services in the economy. The most widely employed measure of general inflation in the United States is the Consumer Price Index (CPI), which is published monthly by the Bureau of Labor Statistics in Washington. If the CPI rises from 150 in December 2000 to 155 in December 2001, then we would say there was 3.33% inflation in 2001 (as (155 − 150)/150 = .0333). This means that, on average (or, for the "average" consumer), prices are 3.33% higher in December 2001 than they were a year earlier. Put another way, the real purchasing power of the dollar shrank by 3.33% in 2001. That is, it requires $1.0333 in 2001 to buy what $1.00 bought in 2000.

What matters to investors is the **real return**, which is defined as the return net of inflation. A real return is a return measured in constant-purchasing-power dollars. On the other hand, returns are generally actually observed and reported using "current" dollars, that is, dollars of whatever purchasing power prevails at the time when the dollars are transacted. Returns in current dollars are often called **nominal returns**, to distinguish them from real returns. Thus, nominal returns include inflation, while real

---

[7] This convention is typical in the computation of private real estate market periodic returns. It is also employed by the IPD in England, Russell-Canada, and the PCA in Australia.

[8] However, NCREIF reports the detailed component information that goes into computing the returns (the *BegVal, EndVal, NOI, CI,* and *PS* each quarter), so it is possible for users of the NPI to "reconstitute" the income and appreciation components at their own discretion.

Example of Real versus Nominal Return

2000 property value = $100,000
2001 net rent = $8,000
2001 property value = $102,000
2001 inflation = 3.33%

What is the *real r, y,* and *g* for 2001?

Real *g* = (102,000/1.0333)/100,000 − 1 = −1.29% ≈ 2% − 3% = −1%
(versus nominal *g* = +2%)

Real *y* = (8,000/1.0333)/100,000 = +7.74% ≈ 8%
(versus nominal *y* = 8% exactly)

Real *r* = (110,000/1.0333)/100,000 − 1 = +6.46% ≈ 10% − 3% = 7%
(versus nominal *r* = 10%)

= *y* + *g* = +7.74% + (−1.29%) = 6.46% ≈ 8% − 1% = 7%

returns are adjusted for inflation so that they reflect the actual purchasing power return net of inflation. Unless it is clearly stated otherwise or obvious from the context, returns are normally quoted and reported in *nominal* terms. It is up to the user of the return information to make the inflation adjustment.

Let's go back to our hypothetical example in which the CPI at the end of 2000 is 150 and at the end of 2001 it is 155, so there was 3.33% inflation during 2001. Suppose a property that was worth $100,000 at the end of 2000 (in current 2000 dollars) is worth $102,000 at the end of 2001 (in current 2001 dollars). The property also generated $8,000 in net cash flow during 2001 (assume all of this cash flow occurred at the end of the year). In nominal terms, the total return would be computed as

$$r_{2001} = \frac{8,000 + (102,000 - 100,000)}{100,000} = 10.00\%$$

which includes 8.00% income component and 2.00% appreciation. To get the real return, we divide the 2001 dollar amounts by the ratio of the 2001 to 2000 cost of living, 1.0333, so as to express all components of the return in dollars with the same purchasing power, namely year 2000 dollars. The computation of the real returns is shown in the box above.

You should note several points about this computation. First, the real growth or appreciation is negative, reflecting a real depreciation (negative appreciation) of 1.29%; the property value would have had to increase to $103,330 just to keep pace with inflation. Second, the real total return is some 3.55% less than the 10.00% nominal return. This difference is greater than the 3.33% inflation, because of the effect inflation has not only on the $100,000 base capital as of the beginning of the period, but also on the incremental earnings represented by the $8,000 income and

$2,000 nominal capital gain. Third, note that the effect of inflation is much smaller in the income return component than it is in the appreciation return component or total return, in percentage terms. This is because the income is generally at least an order of magnitude smaller than the property value when measured in dollar terms over a short interval of time (such as a year). Thus, inflation is often ignored in the current yield component of real estate investment. Fourth, note that the commonly used shortcut of simply subtracting the inflation rate from the nominal appreciation or total return gives answers that are approximately correct, to the nearest whole percent.

Finally, you should note that inflation can be negative, during periods of deflation, when the purchasing power of the currency increases over time. All of the previous procedures still apply, only with negative percentages for the inflation (subsequent CPI levels lower than prior levels).

9.2.5 Measuring Risk in Returns

One of the things investors are most concerned about in making investments is *risk*. As real estate is well known to involve risk, understanding how risk is related to returns is a basic part of understanding real estate investment. In traditional real estate investment analysis and at the "mom and pop" level, risk is largely ignored quantitatively and addressed only qualitatively. Such an approach will not work in the modern institutional investment environment, however. We need to be able to quantify the risk in real estate investment, and to quantify it in a way that is comparable to the way risk is measured in the other major investment asset classes. In recent decades this is beginning to be done with increasing sophistication, based on the use of real estate periodic returns data.

In principle, we can think about investment risk and define it formally in various ways. For example, one intuitive definition would be that risk is the probability that the investors will lose all of the capital they invest. For example, if you take out a mortgage to buy a property, and later you cannot make the mortgage payments and the bank forecloses on your loan and fails to sell the property for more than you owe on the loan, then you would have lost all the capital you put into the property. This, however, is a rather extreme and narrow definition of risk, relevant only to the specific problem of default risk on levered investments. We might also consider risk as the possibility of losing *any* of the original invested capital. For example, if you pay $100,000 for a property free and clear of any debt, and a year later the property has earned $5,000 in net income, but you cannot then sell the property for more than $90,000, then you would have lost 5% of your investment value (at least on paper, as of that point in time). Or we could define risk as some combination of the probability of loss and the likely severity of loss if it occurs.

All of these notions of risk are related to the range in the possible future returns that the investment might earn, or to the degree of deviation or dispersion of those returns around the ex ante expected return. The most widely used statistical measure to quantify such dispersion is known as the **standard deviation** of the probability distribution of the future return possibilities. This measure of investment risk is also known as **volatility**. The greater is the standard deviation in the possible return (for a given future time horizon), the greater will usually be the risk defined in any of the previous ways. Thus, a good general way to think about and quantify risk in investments is depicted in Exhibit 9-1. The horizontal axis represents all the possible values that the return on some investment could have over some given future time horizon.

Exhibit 9-1 Risk and Expected Return as Future Return Probability Distributions: Three Assets

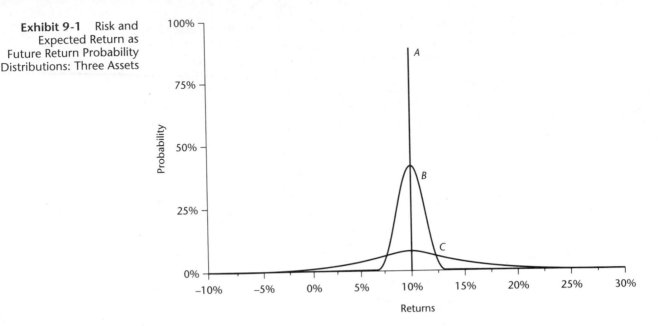

The vertical axis measures the probability associated with each possible future return value.

If the future return could be known exactly in advance, then there would for certain be only one point on the horizontal axis, the known certain future return, which would have a probability of 100%. In this circumstance, the subsequently realized return (ex post) would for certain exactly equal the expected return (ex ante). This would be a *riskless* asset, and is depicted in Exhibit 9-1 for the asset labeled *A* which has a sure return of 10%. The standard deviation of the probability distribution of asset *A*'s return is zero.

The asset labeled *B* depicts an investment asset with a little bit of risk. The future return is not known for certain in advance; there is some range of possible values. The ex post realized return will not necessarily exactly equal the ex ante expectation. For asset *B*, the expected return is again 10%, but now the standard deviation is 1%. The probability distribution pictured in Exhibit 9-1 has the typical bell shape of what is called the normal (or Gaussian) distribution. Most analysts consider that this shape is not a bad approximation of the general shape of the typical return distributions of real estate and other major capital assets.[9]

The normal distribution is symmetrical, which means the realized returns are as likely to be above as below the mean or expected value, which is also the single most likely value. With the normal distribution there is about a two-thirds chance that the realized return will lie within one standard deviation of the mean. So in the case of asset *B* this means there is only about one chance in three that the realized return would fall outside the range of 9 to 11%. Although no extreme return value is completely ruled out by the normal distribution, as you can see in the graph,

[9] However, this is a somewhat controversial topic. There is some evidence that investment returns tend to have "fat tails," with more probability of extreme events than is indicated by the normal distribution. See Young and Graff (1995). Nevertheless, the normal distribution is still widely used for analytical purposes.

there appears to be effectively no chance of asset *B*'s return falling below 7 or above 13% during the given time interval covered in this example.

The asset labeled *C* in Exhibit 9-1 depicts a more risky investment asset. The expected return is again 10%, but now the standard deviation is 5%, implying a one-third chance that the return could fall below 5% or above 15%, and we see that the effective outer range of future possibilities appears to extend from –3% (a loss), to +23%. There is only a 1% chance that the realized return would lie beyond this range.

To place this quantitative measure of investment risk in some practical perspective, there is good evidence that the standard deviation of the return distribution of a typical individual real estate investment (say, a fully leased income property) is in excess of 10% per year, probably over 15%. A diversified portfolio of many individual real estate assets would have a smaller standard deviation, but may still be around 8% per year, or more, depending on how the returns are measured. (See box, page 194.) This compares to annual volatility of around 30% for a typical individual stock, and around 15% for diversified investments in large stocks as represented by an index such as the S&P 500.[10]

We are thus able to quantify both the expected return and the risk in that return for investments by using statistics about the probability distributions of their future return possibilities. The expected return is represented by the mean of the distribution, and the risk is represented by the standard deviation of the distribution. Although sophisticated analyses usually work with continuous probability distributions such as the normal distribution shown in Exhibit 9-1, in making forward-looking investment decisions we are in fact dealing with subjective impressions of future probabilities for which simpler discrete probability distributions may suffice. In such cases the mean is computed by multiplying each possible future return value by its probability of occurrence, and then summing over all these possibilities. The standard deviation is computed by taking the difference between each future return possibility and the mean, squaring these differences, multiplying by the probability associated with the future return value, summing these, and then taking the square root.

The quantitative meaning of the mean and standard deviation are best seen through a simple numerical example, which will also serve to illustrate their computation. Suppose there are only two possible future return scenarios, both equally likely. The return will either be +20% or –10%, and the probability is 50% for the occurrence of each possibility. Then

Expected (Ex Ante) Return:
= (50% chance) × (+20%) + (50% chance) × (–10%)
= +5%

Risk (Standard Deviation) in the Return:
= $[(0.5)(20 - 5)^2 + (0.5)(-10 - 5)^2]^{(1/2)}$
= ± 15%

The expected return is 5%, the midpoint between the two return possibilities, and the risk in the return is plus or minus 15%, reflecting the fact that in this case the actually realized return can deviate 15 points either above or below the expectation (to –10% or +20%).

[10] Some recent historical quantitative evidence on volatility was presented in Chapter 7.

How Volatile Are Commercial Property Assets?

Volatility is a very basic measure of the risk of assets from an investment perspective. It is very easy to observe empirically and measure the volatility of assets that are traded as securities on public exchanges, such as stocks and bonds (including REITs). It is much more difficult to measure the volatility of assets that are rarely (and privately) traded, such as commercial properties. Nevertheless, research undertaken in the academic community starting in the late 1980s has given us a pretty clear idea about the quantitative magnitude of real estate volatility measured in a manner roughly comparable to that of stocks and bonds.

The evidence regarding the magnitude of real estate volatility is of various types. For individual property volatility, the main evidence has come from studies applying option pricing theory to real estate. Option theory allows the implied volatility of built property assets to be derived from the prices of mortgages or land. Studies of this nature include Quigg (1993); Ciochetti and Vandell (1999); and Holland, Ott, and Riddiough (1998), among others. Additional evidence is in Geltner, Graff, and Young (1994). These studies all estimate individual property annual volatility approximating, or effectively in excess of, 15%.

Evidence on the volatility of diversified portfolios of many properties, or the volatility of aggregate indices of commercial real estate, comes primarily from studies of the historical periodic returns to such portfolios or indices. During the 1978–98 period, the annual volatility of the periodic total returns was 6.9% in the NCREIF index of unlevered commercial property, 8.0% in the Giliberto-Levy Commercial Mortgage Price Index (GLCMPI), and 16.4% in the NAREIT index of REIT returns. These are the most widely used indices of commercial property, commercial mortgages, and REITs, respectively. As noted in Chapter 7, the NCREIF Index is based on appraised values, and most academic researchers are convinced that it tends to artificially "smooth" the true property returns, suggesting that the actual volatility was greater than the 6.9% indicated by that index. It also seems likely that underlying properties should be at least as volatile as the mortgages secured by them. This suggests that unlevered property returns should be at least as volatile as the 8.0% indicated by the GLCMPI. This is supported in studies such as Fisher, Geltner, and Webb (1994) and Geltner (1993). On the other hand, the use of leverage and other characteristics of REITs suggests that passive holdings of diversified portfolios of individual properties should be less volatile than the NAREIT index. Furthermore, the effect of diversification would lead portfolios or aggregate indices of many properties to be less volatile than individual properties, which we said may have typical volatilities as low as 15% per year. In summary, diversified property annual volatility almost certainly lies in the range between 8% and 15%, but probably toward the lower end of that range.

For practical purposes, most business calculators and all electronic spreadsheets can automatically calculate these statistics for a list of equally likely returns. For example, if you think the return can either be 10%, 15%, or 20%, with 10% and 20% equally likely and 15% twice as likely as either 10% or 20%, then enter 10 and 20 each once and enter 15 twice into the list (in the calculator, or into a contiguous range in a spreadsheet) and apply the mean (or average) and standard deviation formulas to the list.

While volatility can be estimated subjectively, it is often useful to examine what the volatility has actually been during recent history. This gives some idea about what may be reasonable to assume for the future. This is where periodic returns data come in handy. With a historical time-series of periodic returns data, one can compute the historical volatility using this data. The formula for the standard deviation of a historical series of periodic returns is

$$s = \sqrt{\frac{\sum_{t=1}^{T}(r_t - \bar{r})^2}{T-1}} \tag{7}$$

where T is the number of periods of time in the sample of period-by-period returns, r_t is the return in period t, and $\bar{r}$ is the mean return across the T-period history. In this case, the historical data is treated as a sample of time, possibly representative of what could happen in the future as well.

The main point to understand in this definition of risk and return is that risk is represented by the range or deviation of the possible future return outcomes around the prior expectation of the return, which may be thought of roughly as a best guess (that is, an unbiased guess, neither optimistic nor pessimistic). This definition of investment risk therefore raises an interesting corollary: the more risky (higher standard deviation) the asset, the greater also is the "upside" possibility. That is, given two assets with the same expected return, the more risky asset will typically have a greater chance of returning a larger profit than the less risky asset could. This may partly explain why more trading and investor interest surrounds more volatile assets.

9.2.6 Relationship between Risk and Return

Investors are *risk averse*. For example, suppose two assets are available to investors, both identical in every respect (including, in particular, the fact that they have the same expected return ex ante), except that asset A is less risky (has a lower standard deviation of return), while asset B is more risky (as in the depiction in Exhibit 9-1). No investors would want to buy asset B faced with this choice, and indeed any investors holding B would prefer to sell it and buy A. Thus, the price of asset A would be bid up, and the price of B would be bid down. This process would act to increase the expected return on B and decrease the expected return on A (relative to the prices one would have to pay to obtain them).[11] In equilibrium (that is, when supply and demand balances for both assets), the riskier asset must offer a higher mean return (ex ante) than the less risky asset.

This is perhaps the most fundamental point in the financial economic theory of capital markets: that expected returns are (and should be) greater for more risky assets. This point is depicted in Exhibit 9-2. This same point is also described algebraically in the following equation:

$$E[r_t] = r_{f,t} + E[RP_t] \tag{8}$$

where $E(r_t)$ is the expected total return of a given asset over future period t, $r_{f,t}$ is the return one could earn during period t from investing in a riskless asset (such as U.S. Government Treasury Bills), and $E(RP_t)$ is the expected **risk premium** that investors require on an ex ante basis for investing in the given asset. The expected risk premium is proportional to the amount of risk investors perceive to be involved in investing in the given asset.

---

[11] We will have more to say about the link between asset prices and returns in the next chapter. Suffice it to say here that a lower price for an asset implies, other things being equal, a higher expected return for the investor.

Exhibit 9-2 Financial Economics in a Nutshell: Risk and Return

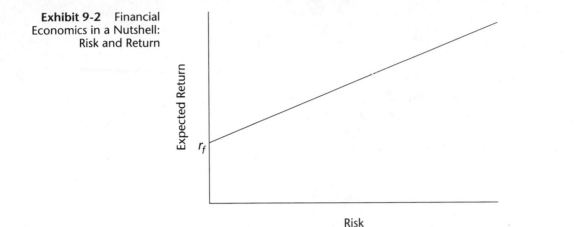

In Exhibit 9-2, risk (as perceived in the investment marketplace) is measured on the horizontal axis, and expected total return (ex ante, going forward) is measured on the vertical axis. The idea is that by investing in a riskless asset, investors can achieve a sure return equal to the rate labeled r_f. This **riskfree interest rate** compensates investors for the pure **time value of money**, the fact that investors are allowing someone else (in this case the government) to use their money for some period of time. Risky assets must offer a higher expected return in order to compensate investors for taking on risk when they buy these assets. The difference between the riskfree interest rate and the expected return on a risky asset is the expected risk premium, which is seen in the graph to be proportional to the amount of risk in the asset.

The picture presented in Exhibit 9-2 might be called financial economics in a nutshell. It is perhaps the single most important idea to remember from this book. It is an idea that is so simple and obvious that it never evokes arguments from students in an academic setting, yet it seems to be much more difficult for people to keep in mind when they get out in the real world. People investing in real estate commonly believe, implicitly if not explicitly, that they are getting a higher ex ante return *without* assuming greater risk. We will see how the risk/return trade-off depicted in Exhibit 9-2 enters at a fundamental level into almost every aspect of investment analysis and decision making as the later chapters of this book unfold. So, always keep Exhibit 9-2 in mind.

With this in mind, let us say a little more about the horizontal axis before we leave Exhibit 9-2, that is, the measurement of risk *as perceived in the investment marketplace*. We have noted that one widely used way to measure risk is by the volatility, or standard deviation of the asset's periodic returns across time. As a first approximation, the horizontal axis in Exhibit 9-2 could therefore be thought of as quantified, at least approximately, by the volatility. However, there are other important considerations, and in fact the exact measurement of risk in a way that completely explains the expected returns investors require of all assets is very difficult. We will mention only one other major consideration at this point, because it is particularly important for real estate, and leave a more in-depth and sophisticated discussion for later in this book.

Consider the effect caused by the fact that most investors do not put all their money into only a single investment asset. Rather, they diversify their investments by putting some of their money in a number of different assets. The total of all of an investors' various assets may be called the investor's wealth portfolio. Naturally, an investor wants to maximize the expected return and minimize the risk within his or her entire wealth portfolio. It is at this wealth portfolio level that risk and return really matters to the investor. Other things being equal, an asset that tends not to "move together" with the other assets in the portfolio (i.e., the asset's return tends to be low when the other assets have high returns, and high when the others are low) will be more valuable for diversification. Such an asset can be used to help reduce the volatility of the entire wealth portfolio, even though this asset by itself may have a relatively high volatility.

Thus, the risk that matters to most investors is not just the standard deviation of an asset's return over time, but also the comovement of that asset's returns with those of other assets. Such considerations, often referred to as Modern Portfolio Theory (MPT), will be examined in more depth in Chapter 21. Suffice it to say at this point that one of the appealing characteristics of real estate as an asset class is precisely that it tends to have relatively low comovement with most of the other major types of assets found in the typical investor's portfolio, such as stocks and bonds.

9.2.7 Summarizing Periodic Returns: Synthesizing the Three Ways to Break Down the Total Return

This is perhaps a good time to pause and step back, to synthesize some of what we have learned about periodic returns. The HPR is an elegant measure of investment performance, capturing a rich depth of attributes that matter to investors in a simple way that allows quantitative measurement. Notice in particular that we have identified three different ways in which the periodic or time-weighted average total return can be broken down into two components: income plus growth, riskfree rate plus risk premium, and real return plus inflation premium. These are summarized here:

$$r = y + g$$
$$r = r_f + RP$$
$$r = R + (i + iR) \approx R + i$$

where i refers to the inflation rate and R refers to the real total return.

Whenever one has more than one way to determine a single item, the scope for analysis is greatly enhanced. By setting up simultaneous mathematical identities such as the previous, one can solve for as many as three unknown variables (across the three identities) given the other four. Deductive logic can then be applied to solve decision problems rigorously. Although we are at a very basic and simple level here, it is surprising how useful this knowledge about returns can be to help us in realistic decision-making situations. Following is an example.

Suppose a certain real estate market is characterized by prevailing cap rates on fully operational built properties of around 10%. That is, income return components (y) are around 10% for built properties. Now suppose you own a vacant piece of buildable land in this market. (Perhaps you just inherited it from a rich uncle.) Inflation is running about 3% per year, but after some research you think your vacant land will grow in value a little faster than inflation, probably more like 5% per year. You feel that vacant land is more risky than investments in fully operational buildings. What should you do?

We can use the previous identities to answer this question quite rigorously. First, use the $y + g$ identity to quantify the likely expected total returns for built property and for the vacant land. If inflation is around 3%, then g is likely to be at least non-negative, so the total return on built property investments, call it r_B, is probably at least 10%, since $y_B \approx 10\%$ all by itself. The vacant land produces no income (indeed, it may produce a negative income, due to property taxes and upkeep), so the total return to the land, r_L, is at most 5%. Of course, the riskfree rate, r_f, is based on government bonds and so it is the same for both types of investment. This means that the risk premium on the land investment is at least 5%, or 500 basis points, below the risk premium on built property investment: $RP_B - RP_L > 5.00\%$. Yet, the land is *more risky* than operational buildings. Clearly, the land is not a good investment.

What does this imply? It would make sense to sell the land immediately and take the proceeds and buy operational buildings, or some other type of investment, even government bonds. But who would buy the land? Perhaps a developer, someone who would develop the land immediately and make a substantial profit in the development process itself. To a developer, the land might be worth the value we think it has, the value that we expect to grow at only 5% per year. But obviously, the land would not be worth that value to anyone else. Anyone other than a developer would face the same expected return and risk comparison that convinced us that the land was not a good investment. Thus, either we must sell the land to a developer, or it is not really worth what we were thinking it was worth. Because it is really worth much less, from this lower base, its value might indeed grow over the coming years at a rate much greater than 5%.

The only theory we have applied in this analysis is represented in the basic periodic return formula decompositions described in this section. This has allowed us to gain some relevant investment insight about our land parcel. It suggests that we should sell the land immediately; the type of buyer we should look for; and if we cannot find such a buyer then it suggests a sharp downward revision of our estimate of the land value.

9.3 MULTIPERIOD AND DOLLAR-WEIGHTED RETURNS

Suppose you want to know the return earned over a multiperiod span of time, expressed as a single average annual rate? There are two widely used approaches for computing such a measure. One is simply to take the average of the periodic returns across the time span in question. This will produce a *time-weighted* average return. The other approach is to compute an inherently multiperiod return, most often the IRR, which is a *dollar-weighted* average return. These two approaches will be discussed in this section.

9.3.1 Time-Weighted Average Return

The average of consecutive period-by-period returns across time is referred to as a time-weighted average return for the overall interval of time. The term *time-weighted* comes from the fact that, for example, if an asset produces a given rate of return twice as long or twice as frequently across time as it does another different rate of return, then the former rate will be weighted twice as much as the latter in the computation of the average return across the entire span of time. For example, if the periodic returns are 10%, 10%, and 13% in each of three consecutive years, then the arithmetic average return across the three periods is 11% per year (the 10% is weighted twice as much as the 13%). As noted, the time-weighted average return is *independent of the magnitude of capital invested at each point in time*. It is therefore *not affected by the timing of capital flows into or out of the investment.*

We can compute the time-weighted average return from a series of periodic returns in two ways. The simple or **arithmetic average** indicates the central tendency of the individual periodic returns, and is computed as the sum of the individual periodic returns divided by the number of periods. In the previous example, $(10\% + 10\% + 13\%)/3 = 11.00\%$. In contrast, the **geometric average** reflects the effects of **compounding**, or the earning of return on return. This is also referred to as **chain-linking** the returns. In the previous example the geometric mean would be computed as follows:

$$(1.10 \times 1.10 \times 1.13)^{(1/3)} - 1 = 10.99\%$$

Each of these methods of computing the time-weighted average has some advantages and disadvantages that make it more appropriate than the other for certain purposes. The arithmetic mean is characterized by the following attributes:

- The arithmetic mean is *always* greater than the geometric mean (e.g., if the geometric mean is -5%, the arithmetic mean might be -4%), the more so the greater is the volatility in the periodic returns series.
- The arithmetic mean has "superior statistical properties" in the sense that it provides the best estimator of the true underlying return tendency each period, and therefore provides the best forecast of the return for any one future period.
- The arithmetic mean return components (income and appreciation) sum to the arithmetic mean total return.

These attributes of the arithmetic mean can be contrasted with the following attributes of the geometric mean:

- Because the geometric mean reflects compounding of returns, it better represents the average growth rate per period during the overall time span so as to reflect the relation between the amount of value the investor ends up with and the amount they started with.
- The geometric mean is unaffected by the volatility of the periodic returns.
- The geometric mean return components (income and appreciation) do not sum to the geometric mean total return. (A complicated "cross-product" term involving interaction of the two components is left out of the compounding of the individual components.) Indeed, the geometric mean income return is of questionable economic meaning, although the geometric mean appreciation return can represent the average growth in asset value or price.

Considering the previous attributes, it is not surprising that the arithmetic mean is most widely used in forecasts of future expectations and in portfolio analysis. On the other hand, because of the geometric mean's direct relation to ending value as a multiple of beginning value, it is not surprising that the geometric mean is most widely used in historical performance measurement and in the evaluation of investment managers. For this purpose, it is also an advantage of the geometric mean that it is unaffected by the volatility of the periodic returns.[12] In general, the geometric mean tends to be used more often by professional practitioners and accounting professionals, while the arithmetic mean tends to be used more often by academics and economists.[13] The arithmetic and geometric means are more similar

- the less volatility there is in the periodic returns, and
- the more frequent the returns (shorter the return periods)

In the extreme, if there is no volatility at all (constant returns), or the length of the return periods approaches zero (continuous compounding), the arithmetic mean will exactly equal the geometric mean across time.

9.3.2 Internal Rate of Return (IRR)

The IRR is the classical and traditional measure of investment performance in real estate. It is needed in two situations. Since investments in real property are usually held for a long period of time, several years at least, most property owners do not want to go to the expense of regularly appraising the value of their property when they are not planning to sell it. Thus, at the microlevel of individual properties and deals, it is often impossible to calculate the period-by-period returns necessary to compute a time-weighted average. In contrast, the IRR can be calculated easily with data that the property owner will almost always have available. It requires only (1) the price the property was bought for, (2) the net cash flow generated by the property during each period since it was bought, and (3) an estimate of what the property is currently worth (or what it was sold for).

The IRR is also useful because it is a dollar-weighted average return, as contrasted with a time-weighted average. As noted earlier, a dollar-weighted return reflects the effect of the magnitude of capital invested during each period. As a result, it captures the effect of capital flow *timing*. If an investor tends to enter an investment just before it does well and exit the investment just before it does poorly, the IRR earned by that investor will improve accordingly, above the time-weighted average return on the underlying investment. The reverse occurs if the timing is unfavorable. Thus, if it is appropriate to measure the effect of capital flow timing on the investment performance, then the IRR is a better measure than the time-weighted average return. Similarly, if it is not appropriate to include such effects (such as when the manager being evaluated does not have responsibility or control over timing), then the IRR is not an appropriate performance measure. In the real world, many situations are rather ambiguous in this regard. An investment manager may have some influence over capital flow timing, but not complete freedom. In classical investment analysis in the securities industry, the time-weighted average return has been generally considered

---

[12] For a given geometric mean performance, the arithmetic mean will be larger the greater is the volatility in the periodic returns. Thus, an investment manager can make the arithmetic mean look better simply by investing in more volatile assets. Obviously, this is not the type of incentive an investor wants to give to his money manager.

[13] Academics are prone to avoid the whole issue of geometric versus arithmetic means by simply working with continuously compounded returns (log differences), in which the distinction between the two types of means effectively disappears. (The sum of the log differences divided by the number of return periods is the same as the log of the ratio of ending to beginning value levels divided by the length of time between them.)

to be more appropriate in most investment management situations. However, each case may be considered on its own merits.

The formal definition of the IRR is as follows. Let PV represent the amount that was invested in year 0 (e.g., 1997), and let CF_t refer to the net cash flow in year t (e.g., $t = 1$ refers to 1998, $t = 2$ refers to 1999, and so on). It is important to note that the net cash flow during intermediate years may be generated either from operation of the asset or partial sales, that is, disposition of part of the asset. Intermediate cash flows may also reflect subsequent investments after the initial purchase or construction of the property (for example, capital improvement expenditures are negative cash flows from the investor/owner's perspective). The sign of cash flows must be defined consistently. For example, cash outflows (from the investment to the investor) are positive, while cash inflows (from the investor to the investment) are negative. Now define an investment holding period or "horizon" such that in year N the investment is assumed to be completely liquidated (i.e., sold). Then CF_N includes both any net operating cash flow during year N as well as the "salvage" value or net sale proceeds from the final disposition of the property (this latter cash flow is usually referred to as the "reversion" in real estate parlance). Then the IRR is defined by the following equation:

$$PV = \frac{CF_1}{(1 + IRR)} + \frac{CF_2}{(1 + IRR)^2} + \cdots + \frac{CF_N}{(1 + IRR)^N} \qquad (9)$$

In general, it is not possible to solve an equation such as (9) algebraically to determine the IRR analytically. It is necessary to solve the equation "numerically," that is, by trial and error. For some patterns of cash inflows and outflows across time it will be mathematically impossible to compute an IRR (the IRR will not exist), or the IRR may not be unique (more than one value may solve the equation). Such cases are pretty rare in practice, generally involving situations in which there is more than one reversal of sign in the cash flow stream. This may occur in redevelopment or turnaround projects, for example, in which an initial investment is followed by positive cash flow which is then followed by large cash outflows for redevelopment and then more positive cash inflow after the redevelopment.[14]

To better understand how the IRR is a dollar-weighted average return across the time span it covers, consider our previous numerical example in which we postulated three consecutive years in which an investment produces periodic returns of 10%, 10%, and 13%. We noted previously that this gives the investment a time-weighted average return of 11%. Now suppose you put $100 into the asset earning these returns at the beginning of the first year. At the end of the first year you would have $110, and by the end of the second year your investment would have grown another 10% to $121 (equal to $110 × [1 + 10%]). At that point in time suppose you decide to put an additional $200 of new capital into the asset. So you have $321 in the investment at the beginning of the third year, when it earns 13%. You end up with $362.73 at the end of the third period ($321 × [1 + 13%]). Your net cash flows are −$100 at the beginning of year 1, −$200 at the beginning of year 3, and +$362.73 at the end of year 3. This cash flow stream can be computed using the previous

---

[14] In such cases, while a unique IRR may not be determinable, there will often (though not always) exist only one IRR that is reasonable. In any case, a reasonable "cost of capital" can always be posited by the analyst and a single net present value (NPV) determined for the project at that capital cost. (More about this in the next chapter.)

formula to have an IRR of 11.69%. The IRR is higher than the time-weighted return because more capital was tied up in the investment during the year when the higher (13%) periodic return was earned.

On the other hand, suppose instead of investing more at the beginning of year 3 you had disinvested part of your capital at that point in time, say, by selling half of your $121 investment. Then the cash flow stream would have been −$100 at time zero, +60.50 two years later, and then +68.37 at the end of year 3. This stream has an IRR of 10.60%, which is not only less than the IRR with the previously considered favorable cash flow timing, but also less than the underlying investment's time-weighted return of 11%.

Finally, suppose you were completely passive after your initial $100 investment, taking nothing out and putting no more into the investment. Your cash flow stream would then have been −$100 at time zero and +$136.73 at year 3 ($100 \times 1.1 \times 1.1 \times 1.13$). This stream has an IRR of 10.99%, exactly equal to the geometric mean time-weighted average return for the underlying investment during those three years.

The IRR is referred to as an *internal* rate because it includes only the returns earned on capital *while it is invested in the project* (or with the manager who is being evaluated). Once capital is withdrawn from the investment, it no longer influences the IRR. This is in fact what makes the IRR a dollar-weighted return.

It is also important to note that the IRR gives a measure of the total return that was achieved by the investment: from initial income flow, subsequent growth (or decline) in income flow, and finally capital value appreciation (or decline) as reflected in the sale price (or terminal value) of the asset at the end. The IRR reflects both the initial cost of the investment and any subsequent capital invested, as the IRR is based on *net* cash flows in each period. It is a purely cash-flow-based measure that does not differentiate between investment and return on or return of investment. The IRR does not indicate *when* the return was generated within the overall span of time the investment was held (e.g., would the return per annum have been higher or lower if the asset had been held half as long?). It is therefore not useful for computing statistics such as comovements among assets or volatility of returns across time.

Some other aspects of the IRR may help to build your intuition about it, particularly in relation to the time-weighted return. First, as we saw in the previous example, *if there are no intermediate cash flows, the IRR will exactly equal the time-weighted geometric mean return* (no cash placed into or taken out between the beginning and end of the investment). Second, there is a special theoretical case of regularity in both the space and asset markets in which the IRR and periodic return are the same. Suppose (1) regular intermediate cash flows grow at a constant rate every period, and (2) the asset value always remains a constant multiple of the current periodic cash flow. Then the IRR will exactly equal the sum of the initial cash yield rate plus the growth rate ($IRR = y + g$), and the IRR will exactly equal both the arithmetic and geometric time-weighted mean return ($IRR = r$).[15] (The growth rate, g, here applies identically to both the cash flows and the asset capital value.) This special case is equivalent to a constant-growth perpetuity, which we saw in Chapter 8 has a present value of $PV = CF_1/(r − g)$, and a current yield equal to the inverse of the constant multiple: $y = CF_1/PV$.

---

[15] The combination of constant-growth cash flows and constant-multiple asset value implies that the periodic returns are constant across time, so there is no volatility, allowing the arithmetic and geometric means to equate in the periodic returns.

A Note on Terminology

In the real estate appraisal business, the IRR is often called the "total yield". In real estate investment and appraisal, the expected IRR looking forward into the future when making an investment is often called the "going-in IRR". In the bond business, the IRR is simply called the bond yield. The yield to maturity (YTM) is the IRR assuming the bond is held to maturity.

9.4 CHAPTER SUMMARY

This chapter has continued to develop your basic set of tools and building blocks for real estate investment analysis by defining investment returns in some depth and detail. We defined two types of returns at a specific, quantitative level: periodic returns (the HPR) and dollar-weighted multiperiod returns (the IRR). The strengths and weaknesses, and the major uses, of each of these types of returns were described. We also showed how the periodic return could be used to define investment risk in a way that can be measured quantitatively, as the volatility, or range of variability, in these returns over time. The next chapter will use what we have presented here to show how real estate investments can be analyzed and evaluated quantitatively at the *micro*, or individual deal, level.

KEY TERMS

returns	comovement	standard deviation
ex post	total return	volatility
ex ante	income return	risk premium
period-by-period (periodic) returns	appreciation return	riskfree interest rate
multiperiod returns	current yield	time value of money
holding period returns (HPR)	capital return (gain, growth)	arithmetic average return
time-weighted return	inflation (general, CPI)	geometric average return
internal rate of return (IRR)	real return	chain-linking (compounding)
dollar-weighted return	nominal returns	returns

STUDY QUESTIONS

9.1. Suppose the Sam Sell Select Fund buys a property at the end of 1998 for $11,250,000 on behalf of its wealthy investor clients. At the end of 1999 the fund sells the property for $12,500,000 after obtaining net cash flow of $950,000 at the end of 1999. Suppose inflation during 1999 was 3.5%, and government bonds yielded 5%. Consider the simple holding period returns for the 1999 calendar year period. Compute the following return measures (to the nearest basis point).

  a. The nominal income return

  b. The nominal appreciation return

  c. The nominal total return

  d. The ex post risk premium

  e. The real appreciation return (using the exact definition)

  f. The continuously compounded nominal total return

  g. What was the continuously compounded nominal appreciation return?

9.2. The real estate investment advisor to the Tired Old Firemen's Pension Fund is faced with a possible property acquisition that will cost $4,200,000. The advisor feels that in one year this property will face the following subjective probabilities. There is a 25% chance for an optimistic scenario or "upside" outcome, in which case the property will be worth $5,000,000. There is a 25% chance of a pessimistic scenario or "downside" outcome, in which case the property would be worth $3,750,000. And there is a 50% chance of an expected scenario or "most likely" outcome, in which case the property will be still be worth $4,200,000 next year. Using simple HPRs, compute the following.

  a. The expected appreciation return

  b. The standard deviation of the possible appreciation return [Note: if you use Excel on this, use STDEVP rather than STDEV because this is not a sample: it is your complete subjective probability distribution. The range on which to apply STDEVP would include four cells, two for the "most likely" outcome.]

9.3. In the second quarter of 1998, the NCREIF Property Index (NPI) total return for the Boston metropolitan area was 3.75% (this is a quarterly return, not per annum). This was based on 48 properties having an aggregate appraised value of $2,422,231,157 as of the beginning of the quarter, which grew to $2,472,997,756 by the end of the quarter, while producing $45,627,584 in net operating income and absorbing $6,062,426 in capital improvement expenditures. (There were no partial sales.) Using the NCREIF formula given in the chapter, consider the following questions.

  a. What would the quarterly total return for Boston have been if the NPI used the simple HPR formula (with just the beginning asset value in the denominator) instead of a time-weighted investment value in the denominator? [Note how little difference this would make in basis points, even multiplying by four to factor up to annual from quarterly rates.]

  b. Recall that NCREIF defines the income return based on the NOI without subtracting capital improvement expenditures. Instead, NCREIF subtracts capital improvement expenditures from the end-of-period asset value in computing the numerator of the appreciation return. Thus, NCREIF reported an income return for Boston in 1998.2 of 1.893% and an appreciation return of 1.855%. Now compute how different these two return components would be if the income return were defined on a cash flow basis with capital expenditures subtracted, and if appreciation return were defined on an asset price change basis using just ending asset value without subtracting capital expenditures. How big a difference would this change have made in Boston in 1998.2 if you factored your answer up by a multiple of four, to put it in per annum instead of quarterly terms? (Report your answer in basis points.)

9.4. The following table gives the NPI total return for a 10 quarter period for Boston and San Francisco. Compute the following quarterly statistics for both cities to the nearest basis point, and answer the subsequent questions. (Hint: We suggest using a computer spreadsheet.]

   a. The arithmetic average return (use the AVERAGE function in Excel)

   b. The standard deviation of the return ("volatility," use STDEV in Excel)

   c. The geometric mean return (you can use the Excel statistical function GEOMEAN, but you have to add unity to each return in the series, and then subtract unity from the GEOMEAN result, or just apply the geometric mean return formula directly by compounding the returns in the spreadsheet)

   d. Why are the arithmetic means higher than the geometric means, and why is this more so for San Francisco?

   e. Based on the geometric mean, and factoring up to a per-annum rate, by how many basis points did San Francisco beat Boston during this period?

   f. Now compute the quarterly Sharpe ratio for each city based on the geometric mean you computed in (c) and the volatility you computed in (b). The Sharpe ratio is a measure of risk-adjusted return performance, defined as the risk premium divided by the volatility. Assume that the average quarterly return to Treasury Bonds during the period in question was 1.50%. Which city had the better Sharpe ratio?

YYQ	BOS	SF
1996.1	0.0486	0.0242
1996.2	0.0303	0.0298
1996.3	0.0310	0.0323
1996.4	0.0236	0.0680
1997.1	0.0324	0.0291
1997.2	0.0329	0.0438
1997.3	0.0464	0.0371
1997.4	0.0429	0.1000
1988.1	0.0582	0.0730
1998.2	0.0375	0.0793

9.5. A common type of real estate investment vehicle used by institutional investors is known as a "unit fund" or "open-end" commingled fund (CREF). Investors can put capital into, and withdraw capital out of, such funds on the basis of the appraised value of the assets in the fund, which are regularly and frequently reappraised. Thus, if the assets are appraised at $10 million, and you invest $100,000, you have a 1% share, entitling you to 1% of the net cash flow and proceeds from sales within the fund. Now consider a "passive" buy-and-hold strategy over a three-year period in such a fund. Suppose you invest $200,000 in the fund at the end of 1995, to obtain two "units" (i.e., shares). During 1996 the fund pays $5,000 per unit from net rental income, and at the end of 1996 is reappraised to a net asset value of $98,000 per unit. During 1997 the fund pays $10,000 per unit in net rental income, and the appraised value at the end of 1997 surges to $112,000 per unit. Finally, during 1998 the fund pays out $7,000 in net income and at the end of 1998 the assets of the fund are sold in the real estate market and liquidated for net cash proceeds of $118,000 per unit. Use your calculator or a computer spreadsheet (the latter will be faster and more reliable) to answer the following questions, reporting your answers to the nearest basis point.

a. Assuming that appraised value accurately reflects market value (opportunity cost) of the assets at intermediate points in time, what are the period-by-period total returns for each of the three years the investment was held (1996, 1997, 1998)?

b. Based on these period-by-period returns, what is the geometric average annual total return during the three-year holding period of the investment (1996–1998)?

c. What is the internal rate of return (IRR, per annum) of the investment over its three-year holding period?

d. Which of these two average returns over the three-year life of the investment tells exactly what the profit would have been per original dollar invested if the investor had taken the cash paid out plus proceeds from liquidating his units at the end of each year and used all (and only) this cash to immediately purchase units (and fractions thereof) in the fund again for the following year (i.e., so that there was no cash flow into or out of the investment except at the beginning and end of the three-year period)?

9.6. Suppose that the investor in the above question 9.5 at first was cautious, buying only one unit at the end of 1995. Then a year later he felt that the market would rebound in 1997 after its poor performance in 1996. So he made an additional capital contribution to buy one more unit at that time. Then, with the great performance of the fund in 1997, he decided to cash out one of his units at the end of 1997 (assume the fund would purchase the unit back for its appraisal-based value as of the end of 1997).

a. Calculate the investor's IRR.

b. Why is this IRR higher than that calculated in the previous question, and also higher than the mean period-by-period return to the fund over the 1996–98 period?

c. Why is the time-weighted HPR a better measure for judging the performance of the fund, and the IRR a better measure for judging the performance of the investor in this case?

d. Under what conditions would the IRR not be a fair measure of the investment decision maker's ex post performance?

9.7. Describe three ways to break the total nominal return down into two components. (Provide formulas, and label your variables.)

9.8. Consider two assets: an apartment building in town and a raw land parcel on the fringe of the metropolitan area. Assume the raw land produces no income but owes 1% of its value per year in property taxes, while the apartment has a current yield (cap rate) of 8%. Assume also that the value of the raw land is more risky than that of the apartment building. Which of these two assets is likely to have a higher appreciation return component? Why? Now prove (using simple algebra and basic investment economic logic) that the raw land must have an ex ante expected appreciation rate at least 9% greater than that of the apartment building. [Hint: Use your answer to question 9.7.]

9.9. Using the standard deviation, quantify the risk in a property investment whose total return one year from now will be either +20% or –5%, with equal probability. What is the mean or expected return?

9.10. Consider two real estate investments. One offers a 10% expected return with volatility of 10%, the other offers a 15% expected return with volatility of 20%. Is it possible to say, from just this information, which one is the better investment? [Hint: Consider Exhibit 9-2.]

PART III

References and Additional Reading

Bank Administration Institute. *Measuring the Investment Performance of Pension Funds for the Purpose of Inter-Fund Comparison*, Bank Administration Institute, Park Ridge, Illinois, 1968.

Brealey, R. and S. Myers. *Principles of Corporate Finance*, 5th ed. New York: McGraw-Hill, 1996, Chapter 3.

Ciochetti, B. A. and K. Vandell. "The Performance of Commercial Mortgages." *Real Estate Economics* 27(1): 27–62, spring 1999.

Fisher, J., D. Geltner, and R. B. Webb. "Value Indices of Commercial Real Estate: A Comparison of Index Construction Methods." *Journal of Real Estate Finance and Economics* 9(2): 137–164, 1994.

Geltner, D. "Estimating Market Values from Appraised Values Without Assuming an Efficient Market." *Journal of Real Estate Research* 8(3): 325–346, 1993.

Geltner, D., R. Graff, and M. Young. "Random Disaggregate Appraisal Error in Commercial Property: Evidence from the Russell-NCREIF Database." *Journal of Real Estate Research* 9(4): 403–419, fall 1994.

Giliberto, M. "The Inside Story on Rates of Return." *Real Estate Finance* 11(1): 51–55, spring 1994.

Giliberto, M. "The Inside Story on Rates of Return II: Commercial Mortgages." *Real Estate Finance* 11(2): 10–13, summer 1994.

Holland, S., S. Ott, and T. Riddiough. "Uncertainty and the Rate of Commercial Real Estate Development." MIT Center for Real Estate Working Paper, 1998.

Mahoney, J., J. Murphy, and S. Keogh. "The Internal Rate of Return and Institutional Performance Measurement for Real Estate Portfolios." *Real Estate Finance* 15(2): 63–72, summer 1998.

Miles, M. and N. Tolleson. "A Revised Look at How Real Estate Compares with Other Major Components of the Domestic Investment Universe." *Real Estate Finance* 14(1), spring 1997 (Institutional Investor Inc., publisher).

Quigg, Laura. "Empirical Testing of Real Option-Pricing Models." *Journal of Finance* 48: 621–639, June 1993.

Young, M. et al. "Defining Commercial Property Income & Appreciation Returns for Comparability to Stock Market-Based Measures." *Real Estate Finance* 12(2): 19–30, summer 1995.

Young, M. and R. Graff. "Real Estate Is Not Normal: A Fresh Look at Real Estate Return Distributions." *Journal of Real Estate Finance and Economics* 10(3): 225–260, May 1995.

Real Estate Valuation and Investment Analysis at the Microlevel

Part IV continues our presentation of the basic building blocks of real estate investment analysis begun in Part III. In Part IV we are going to focus very intensely at what we will call the microlevel. To see what we mean by this, consider an analogy between real estate and rain forests. Two types of scientists study rain forests. At the microlevel biologists study the individual species of plants and animals, learning how individual species live, reproduce, and evolve over time. At the macrolevel ecologists study the big picture—how all the individual species relate to one another. In Part IV we are going to be like the biologists, studying how individual real estate assets get their values in the asset market, and how investors may view and evaluate individual deals. From a decision-making perspective, Part IV is about the most fundamental microlevel decision: what properties or projects you should invest in.

The basic plan is as follows. Chapter 10 will present the fundamental concepts and tools of the evaluation of microlevel investment decisions, the basics of risk and return in the context of the analysis of individual investment transactions, projects, and deals. Chapter 11 will cover the nuts and bolts of real estate cash flow proformas, or projections of future expected cash flows generated by real estate assets. Chapter 12 will discuss some issues unique to real estate, issues that begin to bridge the micro- and macrolevels, such as the implications of the simultaneous existence of the REIT market and the direct property market for real estate assets. But our focus in Chapter 12 will still be at the microlevel. These are topics that are at the same time advanced because of their subtlety and complexity, yet still basic because of their omnipresence and importance in making rational real estate investment decisions.

10 The Basic Idea: DCF and NPV

Chapter Outline

Learning Objectives

After reading this chapter, you should understand:

◆ The relationship between investor return expectations and asset prices.

◆ The DCF valuation procedure, and how to use it.

◆ The relationship between DCF and ratio shortcut procedures such as direct capitalization.

◆ The NPV investment decision rule (including the hurdle rate).

At the microlevel of real estate investment activity, the level at which deals are made, the primal question can usually be summed up as, How much is the asset worth? Each side in a potential deal will almost always be willing to "do the deal" at some price. So the question boils down to, at what price? In other words, how much is the asset worth? What we want to do in this chapter is to answer this question in a way that gives you a fundamental understanding, a solid basis from which you can use your reasoning abilities to deal with the range of situations the real world may present. To do that, we begin with the link to the fundamental investor objectives and concerns we talked about and learned how to quantify in Part III.

10.1 RELATION BETWEEN RETURN EXPECTATIONS AND PROPERTY VALUES IN THE ASSET MARKET

Here we are at the beginning of Chapter 10 saying that the focus of the action in the deal is on the asset value. Yet, we just devoted the entirety of Chapter 9 to a description of investment *returns*, and we made a big deal about how earning returns is the objective of investment. Do we have a disconnect here?

Not really. But it is clear that in order to understand fundamentally what is going on at the microlevel in most real estate activity, we need to establish the link between the expectation of returns, which motivates investors, and the prices or values of assets, which is the issue they are most directly grappling with in the day-to-day business of real estate investment. In essence, this "missing link" can be summed up in the following precept:

> *The prices investors pay for properties determine their expected returns, because the future cash flow the properties can yield is independent of the prices investors pay today for the properties.*

To make this point more concrete, consider the following simplified example. Suppose it is reasonable to expect that a certain property can produce in the upcoming year a net rental income of $10,000, and will be worth $105,000 at the end of the year. Then, if we pay $100,000 for the property today, our expected total return at the time of the purchase is 15%. This is determined as the $10,000 rent plus the $5,000 capital gain ($105,000 less the $100,000 price we paid), expressed as a fraction of the amount invested (i.e., the price we paid). On the other hand, if we pay $105,000 today, the expected return is only 9.52% ($10,000, plus no capital gain, divided by the $105,000 investment amount). If we could get the property today for $95,000, our expected return would be 21.05% over the coming year ($10,000 rent, plus $10,000 gain in investment value from $95,000 to $105,000, as a fraction of the $95,000 initial investment).

Thus, the expected return is inversely related to the price of the asset, because the expected future cash flows from the asset (including the resale), *remain the same*, no matter how much you pay today for the asset. They remain the same *because they are determined by factors that are independent of how much you pay today for the asset.* Future rents are determined by supply and demand in the space market. The resale price you can reasonably expect is determined by the future rents the next buyer can expect going forward, and by the opportunity cost of capital (the next buyer's required expected return) at the time of your resale. Neither of these factors, neither the equilibrium in the space market nor that in the capital market, is influenced by the price you pay today for the property.

> ### Don't play the "Greater Fool."

In the classroom, this precept may seem terribly elementary and obvious. Students never argue against it when we teach it in an academic environment. But out there in the real world, a kind of "fog of war" descends over the field of the deal-making battle. There is often pressure to close a deal, and that makes participants susceptible to wishful thinking. The seller won't budge below $10 million. I know the first year's income will be $1 million, and I know I want a 12% return, so it must be reasonable to expect that the property will be worth $10,200,000 a year from now (as that will give me the 12% return).

This type of reasoning is so tempting, and so easy to slip into in the heat of battle, that it is not at all uncommon. Indeed, it is sometimes even put forth as an explicit principle of real estate investment, known as the **Greater Fool Theory**. According to this theory, you don't need to worry about paying too much for a property because, even if you have been foolish and paid too much, it is unlikely that you are the stupidest person in the market. Thus, you can always count on finding a greater fool who will pay at least that much again and rescue your ex post return!

In truth, we cannot deny that it may sometimes be possible to "luck out" in this manner. But if you have gone to the trouble to get this far in this book, then you probably already agree with us that the Greater Fool Theory is hardly a sound systematic basis on which to make good real estate investment decisions.

Apart from its hazards at the individual level, widespread application of the Greater Fool Theory would lead, by definition, to a disconnection between asset prices and the underlying fundamental cash flow generation potential of those assets. Such a disconnection is the definition of an asset price "bubble," in which prices grow over time only because each buyer expects such growth, unrelated to the underlying physical productive potential of the assets. Most finance students have heard about the famous Tulip Bulb Bubble in 17th century Holland, in which the equivalent of hundreds of thousands of dollars were paid for single tulip bulbs. Of course, bubbles have a tendency to burst. When they do, it is the practitioners of Greater-Fool-Theory investing who get burned, who prove themselves to have been the greatest fools after all.

10.2 DISCOUNTED CASH FLOW VALUATION PROCEDURE

Remembering the fundamental link between asset prices and returns, based on underlying operating cash flow potential as described in section 10.1, can help prevent you from becoming the latest victim of the real estate market's famous boom and bust cycles. To apply this pricing principle in practice, the basic investment valuation framework known as multiperiod **discounted cash flow** valuation (or just **DCF** for short) has gained wide acceptance in recent decades, both in academic circles and in professional practice.

DCF is probably the single most important quantification procedure in microlevel real estate investment analysis. In essence, the procedure consists of three steps:

1. **Forecast the expected future cash flows.**
2. **Ascertain the required total return.**
3. **Discount the cash flows to present value at the required rate of return.**

Mathematically, these three steps can be summarized in the following equation, letting V represent the value of the property today:

$$V = \frac{E_0[CF_1]}{1 + E_0[r]} + \frac{E_0[CF_2]}{(1 + E_0[r])^2} + \cdots + \frac{E_0[CF_{T-1}]}{(1 + E_0[r])^{T-1}} + \frac{E_0[CF_T]}{(1 + E_0[r])^T} \qquad (1)$$

where CF_t = Net cash flow generated by the property in period t

$E_0[r]$ = Expected average multiperiod return (per period) as of time zero (the present), also known as the **going-in IRR**[1]

T = The terminal period in the expected investment holding period, such that CF_T would include the resale value of the property at that time, in addition to normal operating cash flow

To clarify the basic mechanics of this procedure, consider the following simple numerical example. The subject property is an office building with a single lease. Suppose the present time is the end of the year 2000. The building has a six-year net lease which provides the owner with $1,000,000 at the end of each year for the next three years (2001, 2002, 2003).[2] After that, the rent steps up to $1,500,000 for the following three years (2004 through 2006), according to the lease. At the end of the sixth year (2006) the property can be expected to be sold for 10 times its then-current rent, or $15,000,000. Thus, the investment is expected to yield $1,000,000 in each of its first three years, $1,500,000 in each of the next two years, and finally $16,500,000 in the sixth year (consisting of the $1,500,000 rental payment plus the $15,000,000 "reversion" or sale proceeds). In this way we have quantified an *expectation* of the multiperiod future cash flow stream this property can generate.

Now suppose that, after considering the relative risk and current expected returns of real estate versus stocks and bonds, and of this particular office building versus other types of real estate, you figure that 10% per year would be a reasonable expected average total return (the "going-in IRR") for an investment in this property. Then the value of the property is found by applying the DCF formula (1) as follows:

$$13,757,000 = \frac{1,000,000}{(1.10)} + \frac{1,000,000}{(1.10)^2} + \frac{1,000,000}{(1.10)^3} + \frac{1,500,000}{(1.10)^4}$$

$$+ \frac{1,500,000}{(1.10)^5} + \frac{16,500,000}{(1.10)^6}$$

We see that the estimated market value of the property is $13,757,000 as of the present time (year 2000). This price will yield an expected average total return of 10% for the buyer. If the price were less than this, say, $12 million, the buyer would get an ex ante (going-in) return greater than 10% (namely, 13% at the $12 million price, computed as the IRR on the $12 million investment, assuming the given expected future cash flow stream). This would be a better deal for the buyer but a bad deal for the seller, assuming the 10% going-in IRR well reflects capital market expectations for returns on this type of investment. If the price were greater than the indicated value, say, $15 million, then the expected return for the buyer would be less than

---

[1] Note the similarity in form between equation (1) and the equation that defined the internal rate of return (IRR), equation (9) in Chapter 9. Thus, the IRR is indeed the type of return measure that is usually used in DCF analysis. However, this does represent a simplification.

[2] A net lease is one in which the tenants pay the operating expenses of the building, so in this example we will assume the rent equals the net cash flow to the landlord. Note more generally that the cash flow for each period is the *net* difference between any cash flowing from the investment to the investor, minus any cash flowing from the investor to the investment.

10%, indeed only 8.14% at the $15 million price, and this would presumably be a bad deal for the buyer and a good deal for the seller.

With the basic idea of the DCF procedure in mind, let us spend a little time refining your understanding of how to apply this procedure to real estate, and honing your ability to use this tool in a practical way.

10.2.1 Match the Discount Rate to the Risk

In the DCF valuation procedure, the discount rate serves to convert future dollars into their present value equivalents. This requires accounting for both the time value of money and the risk in the expected future cash flows. Recall from Chapter 9 that the total return (which we labeled r) can be broken into a riskfree interest component and a risk premium component: $r = r_f + RP$. The riskfree interest rate component accounts for the time value of money, and the risk premium component accounts for the risk. This means that a higher discount rate should be applied to more risky cash flows.[3]

An important application of this principle to commercial property investment analysis relates to properties with long-term leases. When existing long-term leases are present in the property, it usually makes sense to discount the future cash flows already fixed by contract under the existing leases at a lower rate than the cash flows that are projected for the property beyond the expiration of the existing leases. The residual or reversion value of the property based on the projected future resale price also would normally be more risky than contractual base rent from existing leases.

To clarify this point, let us extend our previous numerical example of the office building with a single lease. When applying DCF analysis in the real world of commercial property analysis, it is more common to use a 10-year projection of future cash flows than the 6-year projection we used before. Suppose that the existing net lease in the building expires at the end of the sixth year, but we wish to do a 10-year DCF valuation. Suppose further that our expectation as of today about the net rent this property can earn for the four years following expiration of the existing lease (years 7 through 10) is $2 million per year, and that we expect the property would sell at the end of year 10 for $20 million. Thus, the 10-year expected cash flow projection for this property is given by the table in Exhibit 10-1.

The first six of these annual cash flows are relatively low risk because they are already contracted for with an existing tenant. The last four cash flows, corresponding

---

[3] The use of the discount rate to account for risk implies a certain regularity in the relationship between risk and time. Roughly speaking, the risk measured in dollars is assumed to compound at a constant rate per unit of time until the cash flow will be received. More precisely, consider the number of risky expected dollars at time t that would equate in present value to a certain number of riskless dollars at the same future time t. Then the use of the discount rate in the DCF procedure implies that the number of risky expected time t dollars that equate today to each riskless time t dollar is K^t where K is a constant greater than one, equal to $(1 + r_f + RP)/(1 + r_f)$. This is equivalent to saying that the investor would be indifferent in trading each risky expected time t dollar for $1/K^t$ time t riskless dollars. Thus, the greater the risk premium, the more rapidly future risky dollars diminish in present value proportionately to future riskless dollars, as the time to cash receipt moves farther out into the future. But no matter what the risk premium, this relationship between future risky and certain dollars is a constant exponential function of the time until the cash flow will be realized, hence the regularity assumption. In any case, it should be clear that it is not necessary to use a larger discount rate merely because a risky cash flow will be received further in the future. The discounting process itself accounts for the fact that risk compounds over time. The risk premium in the discount rate should reflect the amount of risk per unit of time.

Exhibit 10-1
Hypothetical Office
Building Net Cash Flows

Year	1	2	3	4	5	6	7	8	9	10
CF_t	$1	$1	$1	$1.5	$1.5	$1.5	$2	$2	$2	$22

to years 7 through 10, are more risky as of the present time. It might make sense to discount the first six cash flows at, say, 8%, and the last four at 15%, for example. For now, let's not worry too much about where these rates come from.[4] The point is that, in principle, discount rates should correspond to the risk of the cash flows they are being applied to. Using the 8% and 15% rates would give a present value of $13,058,000, for our property, computed as

$$\$13,058,000 = \sum_{t=1}^{3} \frac{\$1}{(1.08)^t} + \sum_{t=4}^{6} \frac{\$1.5}{(1.08)^t} + \sum_{t=7}^{10} \frac{\$2}{(1.15)^t} + \frac{\$20}{(1.15)^{10}}$$

10.2.2 Intralease and Interlease Discount Rates

In fact, to demonstrate the principles of risk-adjusted discounting (as opposed to typical current practice), we should make a further refinement in our DCF valuation of this simple property. As this property apparently rents in a market that is typically served by long-term leases, it is likely that the new lease that is signed in year 7 will be a long-term lease, covering all four of the remaining years. When we say that $2 million is the expected rent, we mean that is the most likely annual rent that would be signed in year 7 for a *multiyear lease beginning at that time*. Once that lease is signed, the risk within the years covered by the lease will be low, like the risk in the first six cash flows.

Because of this, the four annual $2 million expected cash flows from the second lease, covering years 7 through 10, should really be discounted at the low (e.g., 8%) discount rate back to a "future present value" as of the beginning of year 7 (the time the second lease is expected to be signed). This low discount rate is what might be called an **intralease discount rate**. It reflects only the risk that the tenants might default on their contractual lease obligations. Once the second lease is signed, this is the only risk the landlord will face regarding the projected rents in years 7 through 10. Once the "future present value" of the second lease is calculated as of its signing at the beginning of year 7, then this amount should be discounted back to time zero at a higher rate (e.g., the 15% rate). The higher rate might be termed an **interlease discount rate**. It reflects rental market risk. Prior to the signing of the second lease, we do not know for certain what the rent in the second lease will be. The landlord is thus fully exposed to the rental market prior to the signing of the lease. After the lease is signed, however, the landlord is insulated from rental market risk over the period covered by the lease.

With this more sophisticated perspective, applying the 8% discount rate as the intralease rate and the 15% rate as the interlease rate, we arrive at a present value of $13,453,000 as our value estimation for our office property, as follows:

---

[4] The 8% rate might be based on the rate at which the existing tenant can borrow money, while the 15% rate might be based on average returns to REITs in the stock market, or some other analysis. Discount rates, or the "opportunity cost of capital," will be discussed in more depth in the next chapter.

$$\$13,453,000 = \sum_{t=1}^{3} \frac{\$1}{(1.08)^t} + \sum_{t=4}^{6} \frac{\$1.5}{(1.08)^t} + \left(\frac{1}{(1.15)^6}\right)\left(\sum_{t=1}^{4} \frac{\$2}{(1.08)^t}\right) + \frac{\$20}{(1.15)^{10}}$$

10.2.3 Blended IRR: A Single Discount Rate

At this point we should pause and point out that the matching of discount rates to cash flows is not always done in current practice. It is more typical to apply a single blended discount rate to all the property's projected net cash flow. In part, this may be due to laziness on the part of practitioners. But there is often some justification for this practice. For one thing, many buildings with long-term leases have many different spaces all with leases that expire at different times. It gets quite tedious and time-consuming to rigorously apply the approach described in the preceding section. Another consideration is that it is often not precisely clear what the different discount rates should be. For one thing, property net cash flows may not be entirely fixed even during periods covered by leases. The leases may be "gross leases" that only fix the rental revenue, leaving the landlord exposed to risk in the operating expenses of the property. Or the leases may include percentage rents or indexed rent which will vary according to future contingencies. Uncertainty over the correct discount rates takes some of the motivation out of the desire to be methodologically correct. Finally, if a property has a pattern of lease expirations over time, which is typical for buildings of its type, then one may apply a single **blended IRR** rate as a legitimate shortcut, provided that rate has been derived from observation of the values of buildings similar to the subject property.

To see how this works, let's return to our numerical example. We can compute a single blended rate of return that discounts the 10 expected future cash flows in Exhibit 10-1 to the "correct" present value of $13,453,000, simply by computing the IRR for this cash flow stream. The IRR is 13.13%. If our building were typical of a class of similar buildings regarding the time and risk pattern of its lease expirations and cash flows, then we would tend to observe a blended rate of around 13% being widely applied in the market, as a shortcut to value buildings such as ours, using the DCF procedure. We could then take that blended rate observed in the market and apply it to our building's projected future cash flows to arrive at the same value estimation of $13,453,000, as follows:

$$\$13,453,000 = \sum_{t=1}^{3} \frac{\$1}{(1.1313)^t} + \sum_{t=4}^{6} \frac{\$1.5}{(1.1313)^t} + \sum_{t=7}^{10} \frac{\$2}{(1.1313)^t} + \frac{\$20}{(1.1313)^{10}}$$

10.2.4 Unbundling Cash Flows: An Example

As noted, the use of separate, explicit interlease and intralease discount rates is not widespread in current DCF valuation practice. We have introduced the concept here partly for pedagogical reasons, to deepen your understanding of the fundamental sources of commercial property value and to build your intuition about how to apply the DCF technique. How precisely it is necessary or possible to match discount rates with different risks in the cash flow components is always a judgment call. In the real world, separate rates are typically used only when special circumstances exist, such as when a building has a long master lease or other atypical lease expiration pattern. However, as the capital markets develop for real estate, it becomes more and more possible to **unbundle** real estate cash flow components and sell different components in the capital markets.[5] This suggests that differential discounting may become more widespread in property valuation. For example, in the 1990s securities backed by leases began to be sold in the bond market. (These were often called LOBS, for Lease Obligation Backed Securities.) In the modern investment industry, one person's shortcut can be another person's gold mine, and a lost opportunity to the "shortcutter." Consider the following example.

Suppose there is another office building just like the one we valued earlier, except that its existing lease has seven years left on it rather than only six years. In other words, the expected cash flows in this second building are the same as the expected cash flows in the previous building (including a contractual net rent step-up to $2 million in year 7 of the existing lease in the second building). The only difference is the time of lease expiration, and therefore the risk in the year 7 cash flow projection. Now suppose the original building is more typical of what prevails in the market, so that a familiarity with the market for these types of buildings would suggest that a blended rate of 13.13% would be applicable in a 10-year DCF valuation of the property.

Now we will suppose that the second building, the one with the longer lease, is owned by an old investor by the name of Peter Shortcut. Mr. Shortcut applies the typical blended rate to his building's projected cash flows to arrive at his value estimation of $13,453,000, as in the formulation in the previous section. Mr. Shortcut is now approached by a young whippersnapper investment ace named Sue Marketwise, who offers Shortcut $13,500,000 for the property. Peter Shortcut snaps up the offer, thinking he's copped a bargain from a young, inexperienced investor. Meanwhile, Ms. Marketwise takes the property and sells the existing lease for $6,813,000 to investors who are glad to accept an 8% expected return on these low-risk cash flows, and who therefore compute the value of the lease as follows:

$$\$6,813,000 = \sum_{t=1}^{3} \frac{\$1}{(1.08)^t} + \sum_{t=4}^{6} \frac{\$1.5}{(1.08)^t} + \frac{\$2}{(1.08)^7}$$

Ms. Marketwise then sells the property (subject to the lease assignment) to other investors who are glad to accept a 15% expected return for the rental market and residual value risk (with an 8% return on the second lease payments once that lease is signed). These investors therefore pay Marketwise $6,881,000 for the property, based on the following calculation:

$$\$6,881,000 = \left(\frac{1}{(1.15)^7}\right)\left(\sum_{t=1}^{3} \frac{\$2}{(1.08)^t}\right) + \frac{\$20}{(1.15)^{10}}$$

Marketwise realizes $13,694,000 in total from unbundling and selling the property ($6,813,000 + 6,881,000). Her investment was only $13,500,000. She therefore nets a profit of $194,000. Had Peter Shortcut been less lazy, and applied the appropriate risk-adjusted discount rates to his property's actual projected cash flows, instead of using the blended rate, he would have realized that the property was worth $13,694,000, based on the following calculation:

[5] See, for example, R. Graff (1999).

$$\$13,694,000 = \sum_{t=1}^{3} \frac{\$1}{(1.08)^t} + \sum_{t=4}^{6} \frac{\$1.5}{(1.08)^t} + \frac{\$2}{(1.08)^7}$$

$$+ \left(\frac{1}{(1.15)^7} \right) \left(\sum_{t=1}^{3} \frac{\$2}{(1.08)^t} \right) + \frac{\$20}{(1.15)^{10}}$$

Armed with this knowledge, old Mr. Shortcut might have bargained a bit more shrewdly with Ms. Marketwise and obtained a higher price from her.

10.3 RATIO VALUATION PROCEDURES: DIRECT CAPITALIZATION AND GIM AS SHORTCUTS

The use of a single blended discount rate in the DCF procedure may be considered a bit of a shortcut. But if you are interested in shortcut valuation techniques, an even *shorter* shortcut is widely used in practice. This is known as **direct capitalization**, which we defined and described way back in Chapter 1. Now that you understand the DCF approach, let's revisit this shortcut and see how it relates to multiperiod analysis.

With direct capitalization, the property's initial year net income alone is divided by the cap rate to arrive at an estimate of the property value. The *multiyear cash flow projection is skipped.* As an example, consider again our previous $13,453,000 office property. If this property were typical of a class of similar properties whose current income and sales prices could be observed easily in the market, then we would tend to observe cap rates for sales of such properties around 7.43%, as this is our property's first year net income divided by its current value ($1/13.453 = 7.43\%$). Thus, we could estimate our property's value by inverting this equation, dividing the $1 million initial year's income by 0.0743, a shortcut to arrive at our value estimate of $13,453,000.

Another shortcut valuation procedure is to apply the **gross income multiplier (GIM)** to the gross income of the property rather than applying the cap rate to the net income.[6] The GIM is particularly useful for valuing small properties where one can estimate the gross revenue with relative ease and reliability, based simply on observation of the prevailing gross rents in the relevant space market, combined with knowledge about the size and rentable space in the subject building. Information on the building's operating expenses, and hence net income, may be more difficult to obtain, or viewed with more suspicion, as its only source may be the current property owner who is trying to sell the building.

Both the cap rate and the GIM are examples of **ratio valuation**; in which a single year's income or revenue from the property is multiplied (or divided) by a ratio to arrive at an estimate of the current asset value of the property.

---

[6]As an example, suppose that the $13,453,000 property we have been previously talking about charged the tenants in the current lease a *gross* rent of $1,500,000, with $500,000 annual operating expenses, to result in the current net income of $1,000,000. Then this property would have a GIM of $13,453,000/$1,500,000 = 8.97. If this were typical of the market, we could observe this GIM in the marketplace and estimate our building's value by multiplying its current gross income by the GIM.

10.3.1 Relationship of the Cap Rate to the Total Return

Shortcut procedures certainly have their place in practice, but as *causal* models of asset value they tend to be simplistic and awkward, or incomplete and sometimes misleading, compared to the multiperiod DCF procedure. For example, even though our example property's value of $13,453,000 may be estimated by the use of, or expressed in terms of, a 7.43% cap rate, this does not imply that its value is *caused by* investors' simply wanting an initial current income yield of 7.43%. Rather, investors care about a more complete multiperiod total return perspective on their future investment performance, as represented in the DCF procedure. It is more accurate to think of the longer-term total return perspective represented by DCF as *causing* the property value of $13,453,000. The cap rate of 7.43% is then best viewed as merely a reflection of the more fundamental DCF valuation. Don't mistake the reflection for *the real thing!*[7]

For example, consider the two buildings whose 10-year future expected cash flows (including resale) are portrayed in the table in Exhibit 10-2. Building A and building B both have the same current net annual cash flow of $1 million, and we will assume that they both have the same risk. Should they both be valued using the same cap rate? As their current incomes are the same, this would imply that the two buildings have the same current value. But surely no investor would be foolish enough to pay the same price for these two buildings. Any rational investor would be willing to pay more for building B because its future cash flows are expected to grow more than building A's. But how much more would you pay for B than for A? In order to answer this question, you would undoubtedly prefer to consider your expected *total* return, and to apply a multiyear DCF valuation.

Since these two buildings have identical risk, investors would require the same expected total return, $E[r]$, for each building. Suppose this required return is 12% per year. Then applying the multiyear DCF formula (1) tells us that building A is worth $8,333,333, while building B is worth $10,000,000. In other words, building A has a cap rate of 12% while building B has a cap rate of 10%. This is fundamentally because the investor requires a 12% total return for the multiperiod investment, given the amount of risk involved. Thus, both buildings' values, and hence their cap rates, are determined by application of the multiperiod procedure.

This example also points out the relationship among the cap rate, the expected long-term growth rate in the building's cash flow and value, and the investor's required total return. The two buildings in Exhibit 10-2 happen to be perfect examples of constant-growth perpetuities with constant valuation multiples, where the cash flows grow at a constant rate (2% in the case of Building B) and the asset value is always a constant multiple of the current cash flow. Recall from Chapter 9 that this corresponds to the

[7]As an historical aside, the term *cap rate* has its origins in the appraisal profession, where it was originally viewed as something more akin to the discount rate in the multiperiod DCF, hence the term *capitalization rate*. In the days before personal computers, appraisers needed a mathematical shortcut to collapse the multiperiod problem into a simple calculation. In effect, ways were devised to calculate cap rates so they would equate to a full-blown multiperiod DCF valuation, with some regularity assumptions. A famous and widely used example was the Ellwood Formula. In this traditional appraisal use, cap rates were indeed viewed as causal, determining the market values of properties given their initial (or stabilized) NOIs. More commonly nowadays, even appraisers simply observe cap rates empirically in the marketplace, by observing property NOIs and transaction prices. As such, cap rates clearly are caused by market value, rather than themselves causing value, especially in a world in which PCs make solving the explicit multiperiod problem very easy for anyone to do.

	Year	1	2	3	4	5	6	7	8	9	10
Exhibit 10-2 Annual Net Cash Flow Projections for Two Identical-Risk Buildings ($ millions)	A	$1.000	$1.000	$1.000	$1.000	$1.000	$1.000	$1.000	$1.000	$1.000	$11.000
	B	$1.000	$1.020	$1.040	$1.061	$1.082	$1.104	$1.126	$1.149	$1.172	$13.385

regularity assumptions in which the IRR equates to the time-weighted average total return, which can be broken down exactly into the sum of a current yield component and a capital gain or growth component. In other words, Exhibit 10-2 corresponds to the case in which $V = CF_1/(r - g)$. For building A, $g = 0\%$, so its value is $V^A_0 = \$1/0.12 = \$8.333$ million. For building B, $g = 2\%$, so its value is $V^B_0 = \$1/(0.12 - 0.02) = \$1/0.10 = \$10$ million. The cap rate in both cases is given by the current yield component of the total return: $y = r - g$.

Real world buildings do not exactly match the regularity assumptions of the constant-multiple, constant-growth perpetuity, although they often come close, making this a decent model to build intuition about property value. Thus, the model of the cap rate as approximately equaling the investor's required total return less the expected long-run growth rate (in both income and property value) is useful as a basic conceptualization. We applied this model in Chapter 1 when we presented the cap rate as being largely determined by three factors: interest rates, expected growth, and risk. Expanding the previous model of the cap rate, using the breakdown of r described in Chapter 9, we see that $y = r - g = r_f + RP - g$, where r_f is the riskfree interest rate and RP is the risk premium in the required total return.[8]

Note that there is a case in which the cap rate and the total return discount rate in the DCF are indeed the same: when $g = 0$, that is, when the building is expected to have essentially level nominal cash flows and level nominal value. This situation will be widespread, at least as an approximation, when the inflation rate approximately equals the real annual rate at which buildings depreciate.[9]

10.3.2 Empirical Cap Rates and Market Values

If the cap rate is not by itself the fundamental determinant of property value, it is nevertheless quite useful as a way of measuring empirically observed property prices in the real estate asset market. The cap rate is, in effect, a way of quoting the price of the property as its value per dollar of current income, except that the inverse of this ratio is used.

[8] This relationship holds either in nominal or real terms. Expected inflation is a component of both the expected total return (r) and the expected growth rate (g). Thus, inflation largely cancels out in the $r - g$ formula. This model therefore suggests that cap rates, or property price/income multiples, should be relatively insensitive to changes in inflation expectations. This relates to the fact noted in Chapter 7 that real estate is generally perceived as a good hedge against inflation risk.

[9] The real depreciation rate of built property in the United States is typically 1% to 3% per year, largely due to aging and obsolescence of the built structure. The factors determining the growth rate in land or location value were discussed in Part II. Care must also be taken regarding how the cap rate is measured. As noted in Chapter 9, the cap rate is often measured as NOI/V, without subtracting realistic long-run capital expenditure requirements from the NOI. This will overstate the cap rate defined strictly as the net cash flow yield (y).

Viewed from this perspective, the direct capitalization procedure is just a way to translate the observable net income of a subject property into its current expected market value, under the prevailing conditions in the real estate market, with no fundamental causality implied. While this approach is quite handy and very widely employed, two dangers must be kept in mind, both due to the skipping of the explicit multiyear cash flow forecast for the subject property.

First, buildings may appear superficially similar, yet have different long-run future cash flow forecasts in relation to their current income. We saw this in our previous example of building A and building B. The cap rate that is empirically observed in the marketplace must be taken from buildings that are similar to the subject property not only regarding risk, but also regarding the occupancy and rental growth expectations, lease histories and expiration patterns, and need for capital improvement expenditures. One property may be dominated by leases that were signed five years ago and are about to expire, while the similar property that sold last month across the street has all new leases. In short, anything that could cause the DCF valuation to differ between the subject building and the buildings whose cap rates are observed in the market could cause direct capitalization to be misleading as a method of valuing the subject property.

Another consideration is that by allowing the investor to skip the multiyear forecast of operating cash flows, direct capitalization exposes the investor to greater danger of being swept up in an asset market bubble. In a bubble, asset market prices get disconnected from realistic consideration of the underlying ability of the assets to generate operating cash flow. If direct capitalization simply divides current income by the ratio of current income to price in the existing market, it will yield implied asset values that simply reflect any current bubble in the market. Recall that part of the benefit of the DCF procedure lies precisely in forcing the analyst to go through the exercise of thinking realistically about the property's fundamental ability to generate net cash flow from its operation over the *long-term* future.[10]

10.4 TYPICAL MISTAKES IN DCF APPLICATION TO COMMERCIAL PROPERTY

A few mistakes are quite common in the application of DCF to commercial real estate. Generally, the mechanics of the DCF procedure are carried out correctly (that is, the "math all adds up"). The problem is that the analysis has fallen into the **GIGO** mistake. This stands for "Garbage In, Garbage Out." The point is, a valuation result can be no better than the quality of the cash flow and discount rate assumptions that go into the right-hand side of the DCF valuation formula (1).

Forecasted cash flows and the required return should be *realistic* expectations, neither optimistic nor pessimistic. In principle, the cash flow forecast should come

---

[10] This danger in direct capitalization is related to the difference between market value and investment value. These differing concepts for valuing real estate assets will be discussed in Chapter 12. For now it suffices to recognize that direct capitalization based on empirically observed market prices, when applied correctly, yields an estimate of the property's market value. This value may differ from the investment value the property would have to a given investor who would hold the property for a long time without selling it in the property market. To quantify investment value, a long-term approach such as DCF is necessary. In most cases, however, the two concepts of value should be approximately the same, as market values should reflect investment values, which in turn reflect the long-term DCF perspective.

from a careful examination of the space market in which the property is situated, as described in Parts I and II of this book, as well as consideration of the existing leases and vacant space in the building. The required return (the **discount rate**) should generally be found by considering the capital markets, including the likely total returns and risks offered by other types of investments competing for the investor's dollar. The required expected total return ($E[r]$) should be thought of as the **opportunity cost of capital** and should represent the going-in IRR investors could expect from alternative investments of similar risk.

In practice, time and resource limitations will often prevent in-depth, formal analysis of these inputs. But there is no excuse for using unrealistic or biased numbers, given the available and relevant public information. Let us briefly consider two types of GIGO mistakes that are prevalent in the application of DCF to commercial real estate. The first is intentional misleading, and the second is excessive laziness.

10.4.1 If Your Case Lacks Merit, Dazzle Them with Numbers

The full-blown DCF procedure tends to look rather fancy to unsophisticated audiences, simply because it involves a lot of numbers and mathematical formulas (with exponents, yet!). The procedure itself can sometimes be used as a smoke screen to draw attention away from the underlying assumptions, or the reasonableness of the input numbers on the right-hand side of the equation. Here is a typical scenario. Joe Broker presents the Tired Old Firemen's Pension Fund Investment Committee with a property acquisition brief that contains 10 pages of DCF number-crunching in the appendices, so it must represent a sophisticated and in-depth analysis, right? Wrong. Hidden in the fine print (or not printed at all) are assumptions such as the following:

- The existing leases will all renew with 100% probability, implying no need to forecast an expected revenue loss from vacancy between leases and no need to forecast needed capital improvement expenditures to retain or attract tenants.
- Inflation is projected at 5% per year even though recent inflation experience, and average economic forecasts, has inflation running at less than 3% per year.
- The current market rent is based on leases recently signed for buildings that are newer than the subject property, and which have greater appeal in the space market than the subject property, or on leases that contained concessions offered to the tenants that are not reflected in the subject property cash flow projections.

The point is that it is easy for analysts with a vested interest in one side or the other of a valuation argument to purposely develop their DCF analysis with a view through rose-tinted lenses. The idea is to hide their bias in the sheer mass of numbers and formulas presented in the analysis. The lesson: don't be taken in by this intentional form of GIGO.

10.4.2 Excessive Laziness

A second widespread form of GIGO in the application of DCF to commercial property occurs when overly simplistic (or downright incorrect) assumptions get taken up into the conventional wisdom and then are applied pretty much as a matter of course in the typical DCF valuation (e.g., We all know cash flows grow with inflation, don't we?). If it would require expensive and time-consuming custom-tailored studies to debunk these assumptions, one could forgive their use in routine work (such as regular appraisal of properties) or in the heat of battle (when the pressure is on to "do a deal"). But in many cases it would take no such expensive or time-consuming studies, just an application of common sense and some basic urban economics (as described in Parts I and II of this book) to improve upon (or debunk) the conventional assumptions.

What is particularly insidious about these types of mistakes is that they could never become widespread or endure so long, except that, in the right-hand side of the DCF valuation formula (1), *the mistakes in the numerators and denominators cancel out!* The result is a reasonably accurate indication of the present value of the property. This is important, because in a well-functioning property market, DCF assumptions that give unrealistic present values would be easy to spot as silly assumptions: the implied property values would seem unrealistic.

In essence, here is what goes on in a typical form of conventional-wisdom GIGO. The property net cash flow in the numerators is forecasted either too high on average, or to grow over time at a rate that is unrealistically high. For example, forecasted capital improvement expenditures will be unrealistically low, or the projected resale price may be unrealistically high, or the rent the building can charge will be assumed to grow at the expected rate of general inflation. This last assumption is often easy to pass off as being reasonable, until you realize that it ignores the likely real depreciation of the building as it ages in its life cycle. Such excesses in the cash flow forecasts would lead to obvious overvaluation of the property, except that they are offset by the use of an unrealistically high expected total return as the discount rate in the denominators. For example, 3% per year expected growth in rents along with a 12% discount rate will typically give about the same property valuation as 1% annual growth with a 10% discount rate.[11]

So what?, you say. If we get the right present value for the property anyway, then what's the problem? In fact, there are two problems, and both of them are serious. For one thing, investors develop false expectations about returns. The discount rate is the multiperiod expected total return on the investment. If it is unrealistically high, investors are living in a fairy tale world in which they think they are going to get higher returns than they actually will, on average. They may also be misled into expecting greater growth in their capital over time than is in fact realistic. Unrealistic return expectations could cause investors to make incorrect allocations of capital between alternative types of investments, or to make financing decisions that do not have the effect they think they will.[12]

A second problem is that the use of "fairy tale numbers" undercuts the credibility of the DCF valuation framework. Market participants and analysts lose faith in the

---

[11] Recall the constant-growth perpetuity model: $V = CF_1/(r - g)$.

[12] Suppose an investor thinks a property presents an expected return of 10%, and the investor can take out a long-term mortgage on the property at an 8% interest rate. One reason the investor might be interested in the mortgage is because he believes he will have "positive leverage," due to the 200 basis-point spread between the expected return on the underlying property and the contractual cost of the debt. But if the realistic expected return on the property is only 8% instead of 10% (reflecting more realistic cash flow growth assumptions), then the positive-leverage argument is not realistic, or greatly exaggerated. (The issue of positive leverage will be discussed further in Chapters 13 and 19.)

ability of DCF to tell them anything useful, because they corrupt it with misinformation. You wouldn't buy a good car and then run it on impure gasoline that will corrode the engine. So, don't use GIGO assumptions on the right-hand side of the DCF valuation equation, even if you can (apparently) get the "right" property valuation.[13]

10.5 IS DCF REALLY USEFUL IN THE REAL WORLD?

With the GIGO danger in mind, it is appropriate to return now to the classical complaint professors hear at this point from graduate students who have some real world experience in commercial real estate. The students complain that, in their experience, successful real estate investment decision makers may go through the motions of DCF analysis for the sake of proforma requirements of outside investors, but they do not really *use* the DCF procedure in actually making their own investment decisions. Rather, these decisions seem to be made on the basis of much more ad hoc or seat-of-the-pants analyses and calculations, where nonquantifiable or barely quantifiable intuition reigns supreme.

While such questions are understandable, a few moments of thought should reveal that they miss the point. The question does not claim that the DCF procedure is wrong or incorrect, only that it is not used in practice. In fact, if the DCF procedure is correct in principle, yet not used in practice, then surely its use in practice holds the potential to improve decision making. In essence, the DCF procedure differs from simpler, more ad hoc approaches in that it makes *explicit* the long-term, multiperiod, total return perspective of investment performance. Few commercial real estate investors would admit to not being really interested in this perspective.

Use of DCF does not preclude or supersede the application of insight and intuition. Quite the contrary. The correct and careful application of DCF should generally be able to provide insight and enlighten intuition. Consider a simple example. Suppose a successful real estate investor claims that he has a criterion different from DCF, a simple ad hoc criterion of investing only when he is satisfied that he can make back his investment outlay purely from the net operating cash flow of the property in less than four years. As stated, such a criterion is not explicitly a property valuation procedure but rather an investment decision rule. But investment decision rules cannot be separated logically from implicit asset valuation procedures.

Now suppose this investor is presented with the opportunity to buy the office building that we examined previously, with the expected cash flows as indicated in Exhibit 10-1, for the previously discussed price of $13,453,000. We saw that at this price this building would provide the investor with an expected return of 13.13% per year over an anticipated 10-year holding period. To be consistent with his stated criterion, our intuitive investor would have to pass up this opportunity, because the office building's expected operating cash flows during the first four years total only $4.5 million, far below the $13,453,000 asking price. But a clever broker has found a good deal for this investor. For the same $13,453,000 price he can buy a property

---

[13] Notice that in this context the property valuation is "right" only in the sense that it seems consistent with the current property market, typically as indicated primarily by observed transaction price cap rates. If the market is currently overvalued, this GIGO-based way of using DCF will not protect you from investing at the wrong time. Recall that one reason for using the multiperiod analysis is to provide some check against the possibility of an overheated asset market that is likely to suffer a correction or fall back in the near to medium-term future.

that presents net cash flow of $3,500,000 per year for each of the next four years, a total of $14 million. This property clearly exceeds the investor's criterion. However, after the first four years, this property will provide no further cash flow or value at all, for it is located on a flood plain that is scheduled to be flooded by a reservoir behind a dam that is currently under construction.

According to this investor's stated decision criterion, he would pass up the opportunity to buy the first office building, meaning that he implicitly values the office building at less than the $13,453,000 price. Yet his stated decision criterion gives him no basis to reject the offer of the flood property at the same price, suggesting that he must believe it is indeed worth that price. Application of the DCF procedure could reveal to this investor that the going-in IRR on the flood property would be only 2.23% per year, no doubt less even than an investment in government bonds would provide.

Surely such DCF analysis would bring some insight to this investor, perhaps even help him to clarify his intuition. Indeed, it is not hard to see that either our "successful" investor has not really thought through his *true* decision criterion, or else he will not be a successful investor for very long. Similar types of arguments can be applied to virtually all property valuation procedures other than the DCF approach. When procedures other than DCF give a different result than DCF, it is usually clear that the DCF result makes more sense.

But let us return to the students' question. *Why* is DCF apparently not seriously used more widely in real world decision making? Perhaps an important answer to this question lies in the way DCF is applied in practice. The GIGO mistakes described in the previous section can easily eviscerate the usefulness of the DCF procedure. If people do not know how to use DCF properly, then obviously it will not be very useful to them in practice. But that means that those who do know how to use DCF properly will have an advantage out there in the competition.

10.6 CAPITAL BUDGETING AND THE NPV INVESTMENT DECISION RULE

The DCF valuation procedure described in the preceding sections can be combined naturally with a very simple and intuitive investment decision rule known as the **Net Present Value** (or **NPV**) rule.

In this section we will consider in some depth the application of the NPV rule to commercial real estate investment decisions. Let's begin by making sure we have a clear definition of what is meant by this decision rule. The NPV of an investment project or a deal is defined as the present dollar value of what is being obtained (the benefit) minus the present dollar value of what is being given up (the cost).[14]

For example, recall once again the office building described in section 10.2 that was worth $13,453,000. If the present owner offered the property for sale at $10 million, then from the seller's perspective the NPV of the deal would be −$3,453,000. This is computed as the $10 million cash that would be received in the present from the sale (the benefit of the deal for the seller) minus the $13,453,000 present value of the asset, which is being given up in the sale (the cost of the deal to the seller).

---

[14] In the public sector this type of analysis is often referred to as benefit-cost analysis. The idea is the same, only the benefits and costs are measured in terms of their social values rather than private wealth.

From the buyer's perspective, the NPV would be exactly the opposite, +$3,453,000, as the $10 million sale price is what is given up, and the property worth $13,453,000 is obtained from the deal.

To make good microlevel investment decisions, here is what the NPV Rule says to do:

NPV Investment Decision Rule

1. Maximize the NPV across all mutually exclusive alternatives.
2. Never choose an alternative that has: NPV < 0.

Following this rule, combined with careful (*realistic*) application of the DCF valuation procedure (avoiding the GIGO mistakes) would protect the seller in the previous example from making the mistake of offering the property for sale for $10 million. It would also clarify and quantify the value of the deal from the buyer's perspective.[15] The first part of the rule would help the potential buyer to choose, for example, between two mutually exclusive investments in which, say, the other alternative was a project worth $2 million whose cost was $1 million. It would make more sense to buy the $13,453,000 property at $10 million (NPV = +$3,453,000) than the $2 million property at $1 million (NPV = +1,000,000), provided one has to choose between these two.[16]

---

[15] The second part of the rule (never choose investments that have NPV < 0), is actually encompassed in the first part of the rule. It is virtually always possible to do something with NPV = 0 no matter how much money you have available to invest (including the possibility of "doing nothing," e.g., buying Treasury Bills), so that there is practically always a zero-NPV alternative that is mutually exclusive to any investment. Hence, maximizing the NPV across mutually exclusive alternatives logically implies never doing a deal with NPV < 0.

[16] Note that this is in spite of the fact that the second project offers a 100% "profit" while the first project only offers a 34.5% "profit" on the invested capital. Remember, the two projects here are *mutually exclusive*: you have to do one *or* the other; you cannot do both. This type of absolute mutual exclusivity arises, for example, between two alternative ways to develop the same land parcel, or between developing the land today versus waiting and developing it next year. With this absolute type of mutual exclusivity, the wisdom of the NPV rule is obvious: would you rather have $3,453,000 or $1,000,000? But hold on, you say, the first project uses up $10,000,000 of my capital; the second project only $1,000,000, leaving me with $9,000,000 more still available to invest. You may have a good point there, but *only* if you face a rigid capital availability constraint. We will argue in Chapter 15 that rigid capital constraints are less widespread than often appears at first. If you've really found a positive-NPV opportunity, you can probably raise the capital to finance it. (In other words, if you've got another positive-NPV investment you can make that needs $9,000,000, you can probably raise the $9,000,000 in ways that allow you to keep all or most of the positive NPV for yourself.) If you really do face a rigid capital constraint, then optimal investment decision making can be quite complicated, although the NPV rule as we have stated it here is still valid. Look at it this way. If the investment decision maker faces a capital constraint, then every microlevel investment is *potentially* mutually exclusive with *every* other possible investment. The NPV rule would then imply that all possible combinations of investments exhausting the available capital would have to be considered, so we could pick the combination that maximizes total NPV. Of course, it is not practical to reconsider the whole world just to make each investment decision. Furthermore, who knows what positive-NPV opportunities may come along in the near future that we cannot see as yet? Fancy decision-making tools, such as linear programming, integer programming, and stochastic optimal control, can

The beauty of the NPV rule lies in its elegance and simplicity, and its intuitive appeal. The power of the NPV rule derives from the fact that it is based directly on the fundamental **wealth maximization** principle. In effect, the NPV rule says nothing more, and nothing less, than Maximize your wealth. The corollary to this is that any rule other than the NPV rule will violate the wealth maximization principle. In effect, if you do not follow the NPV rule, you will be "leaving money on the table." This is expressed symbolically here:

Wealth Maximization → NPV rule

To clarify the link between the DCF valuation procedure and the NPV decision rule, it may be helpful to express the NPV for the typical commercial property investment decision as follows:

> If buying: $NPV = V - P$
>
> If selling: $NPV = P - V$

where V = Value of property at time zero (e.g., based on DCF)
P = Selling price of property (in time-zero equivalent \$)

This makes it easy to see that the NPV rule is simply saying that you should maximize the value of what you are getting minus the value of what you are giving up, assuming these values are computed in an "apples versus apples" manner, adjusting for time and risk. The role of the DCF procedure is to make the necessary adjustment for time and risk.[17]

10.6.1 NPV Rule Corollary: Zero-NPV Deals Are OK

The following corollary to the NPV decision rule is often overlooked in practice:

Zero-NPV deals are OK!

A deal does not have to have a large positive NPV to make sense. Zero-NPV deals are not zero-profit deals, in the sense that, if the discount rate accurately reflects the opportunity cost of capital, it includes the necessary expected return on the investment. This return is the normal amount of "profit" that would be required for an investment of this nature. Zero NPV simply means that there is not supernormal profit expected. A zero-NPV deal is only "bad" if it is mutually exclusive with another deal that has a positive NPV.

---

be applied, in principle, to guide decision making in such circumstances. But in practice data is often lacking or too "fuzzy" to make such elaborate techniques worthwhile. As always, reason and common sense must be given the last word.

[17] DCF will not always be the best way to make this adjustment. While the DCF procedure is usually coupled with the NPV decision rule, it is important to realize that these two decision tools are distinct, and need not necessarily go together. For example, in cases in which the investment has important "option-like" characteristics, option valuation theory may work better than DCF to ascertain the present value of the benefits and costs of the project, and hence to quantify the NPV. We will see examples of this in later chapters. Nevertheless, for most typical decision situations, DCF and NPV make a powerful and useful combination.

Related to this point, notice that, if the NPV is defined on the basis of the *market value* of the asset in question, then the NPV on one side of the deal (e.g., that of the seller) is just the negative (or opposite sign) of the NPV on the other side of the deal (e.g., that of the buyer). **Market value**, which we will label *MV* for short, is by definition *the price at which the property is expected to sell in the current asset market*. This is therefore also the price a buyer must expect to pay to obtain the property. Thus, from this perspective:

$$NPV(Buyer) = V - P = MV - P$$

$$NPV(Seller) = P - V = P - MV = -NPV(Buyer)$$

Now if both the buyer and the seller are applying the NPV rule, then they both require $NPV \geq 0$. But as we see in the earlier equations, this requirement can only be satisfied simultaneously on both sides of the deal if $NPV = 0$. That is

(i) $NPV(Buyer) \geq 0 \rightarrow -NPV(Seller) \geq 0 \rightarrow NPV(Seller) \leq 0$

(ii) $NPV(Seller) \geq 0 \rightarrow -NPV(Buyer) \geq 0 \rightarrow NPV(Buyer) \leq 0$

(i) & (ii) together $\rightarrow NPV(Buyer) = NPV(Seller) = 0$

Thus, as long as we are evaluating the NPV on the basis of market values, then a zero NPV is actually what we would expect.

In practice, investment decision makers often only like to do deals that appear to have a substantial positive NPV going forward. This desire may not be very realistic, however, when the deal is evaluated from a market value perspective, and the impression of widespread achievement of large positive NPVs may be more illusory than real in typical commercial real estate investing.

Several factors may make it appear that real estate investments have large positive NPVs when they do not actually. For example, the discount rate or cost of capital may be taken to be the cost of borrowed funds, which is lower than the full opportunity cost of capital because it ignores the higher risk (hence higher required return) equity component. Another common mistake is that cost components are left out of the equation. For example, the investor's own time and resources spent finding the deal and managing the project, or the property ownership responsibility, may be left out of the analysis or not fully priced. In development projects, the true opportunity cost of the land may be ignored in the NPV calculation, or included only at its historical cost rather than current market value. Yet the use of the land is clearly an opportunity cost of the development (due to the irreversibility of the construction project), and the value of that opportunity cost is the current market value of the land, not its historical cost.

Sometimes an investor obtains a good deal by using private information that she is not legally required to reveal—for example, knowledge about development plans on adjacent sites. But to the extent that such information is truly private, it cannot affect market values, because *MV* is based on public information. Thus, if we are computing the NPV on the basis of market values, private information would not move the NPV away from the expected value of zero. For these and other reasons, it is likely that deals with substantial positive NPV are less common than is widely perceived, at least as long as we are measuring the NPV based on market value.

Can Sellers Take Advantage of "Inside Information" to Get Positive NPVs?

Property owners sometimes claim that they know more about a building they have owned for a number of years than any potential buyer could know, and this gives them an information advantage in negotiating a sale price, enabling them to earn a positive NPV in the sale transaction. The problem with this reasoning is that it falls into the well-worn *the-other-guy-is-stupid* thought trap. Sure, a seller knows more about his building. But potential buyers are well aware of their information disadvantage in this regard. They discount the price they are willing to offer accordingly, based on the likely or average level of "unseen problems" for buildings like the subject property. They also build contingencies into the offer and employ their own inspectors of various types,

and may demand covenants or warranties in the sale. The situation is much like that in the used-car market. "Lemons" are more common in the used-car market than in the car population as a whole. Buyers are aware of this and discount the prices they are willing to pay accordingly, or require warranties from the seller. Furthermore, with long-lived assets such as real estate, any buyer (or seller) at one point in time will be (or was) a seller (or buyer) of the same property at another point in time. This does not mean that owners are never able to take advantage of their inside information, but it does mean that, on average over the long run, sellers do not earn positive NPVs any more than buyers do.

The fact that the expected NPV of a typical real estate investment deal is approximately zero has an important practical implication. It suggests that if you analyze a deal and find that it appears to offer a large positive NPV based on market values (relative to the amount of investment involved), then you should first double-check your analysis and information. An apparently large positive NPV would typically imply that either you or the opposite party in the transaction has made a serious mistake. Make sure it is not you![18]

10.6.2 Hurdle Rate Version of the Decision Rule

An alternative version of the NPV decision rule—preferred by many decision makers—expresses the decision rule in terms of the investment's expected return (typically a single blended IRR rate) rather than in terms of its NPV. The IRR version of the investment decision rule is as follows:

1. Maximize the difference between the project's expected IRR and the required return.
2. Never do a deal with an expected IRR less than the required return.

[18] The conditions under which it would be reasonable to expect a large positive NPV are discussed in Chapter 12. An obvious filter that is widely employed in practice is to ascertain how long an apparent bargain has been available in the market. One would not expect substantially positive NPV opportunities, measured on the basis of market value, to wait around very long in a well-functioning market. By definition, such opportunities should get snapped up quickly. If you have found a deal that is abnormally good-looking but has been available for quite a while, your suspicions should rightly be raised. Presumably, a lot of other people have shied away from the deal for some reason. What is the reason? That reason is probably that the deal does not really present an NPV bargain.

Do Investors Use the Hurdle Rate Rule instead of the NPV Rule?

Sometimes investors claim that they use the hurdle rate rule instead of the NPV rule. If this is really true, then they are not maximizing their wealth. As successful investors in the long run are, virtually by definition, those who maximize their wealth, it is probably not really true that these investors use the hurdle rate rule instead of the NPV rule. It is likely that they routinely employ the hurdle rate rule, but in those rare circumstances in which the hurdle rate and NPV rules would give a different answer, the most successful investors probably implicitly apply the NPV rule instead, due to its wealth implications. Although it is intuitive to think in terms of returns, ignoring the NPV can lead to muddled thinking. When you focus uniquely on the return, it is tempting to want to allocate your money to investments that provide the highest return. But this may be unwise if the high-return investments are also of greater risk, or prevent you from making larger investments that would actually increase your present wealth more.

As always, the required return is the total return including a risk premium reflecting the riskiness of the investment, the same as the discount rate that would be used in the DCF valuation of the investment described in section 10.2. This required return is referred to as the **hurdle rate**. The first part of the rule assures that projects with the highest returns will be selected first. The second part assures that no projects will be selected that do not at least cover their opportunity cost of capital on an ex ante basis.

In most typical circumstances, the IRR version of the investment decision rule will give the same decision result as the NPV version of the rule. That is, if the investment under consideration passes the NPV test with NPV ≥ 0, then it will also pass the IRR test with IRR $\geq E_0(r)$.[19] However, the two versions of the rule will not necessarily give the same rank-ordering of potential investment projects, and this can be important for decision making if some of the projects are mutually exclusive. Mutual exclusivity occurs if the investor cannot do both projects: implementing one project rules out the possibility of implementing the other. A typical situation in which this occurs is with real estate development on a particular parcel of land. Preclusion may also occur if the investor faces an overall constraint on the amount of capital available to invest. The general rule in these cases is that one should select whatever feasible combination of projects has the highest NPV, as this will maximize the wealth of the investor.

10.7 CHAPTER SUMMARY

This chapter presented the basic concepts and procedures for commercial property valuation and investment analysis at the microlevel, that is, the level of individual properties or projects. In this chapter we started with the concept of investment returns

---

[19]Recall from Chapter 8 that in some circumstances the IRR of an investment cannot be calculated, or is not unique. In such cases, it may be impossible to apply the hurdle rate rule based on the IRR. Modifications of the IRR (such as the financial management rate of return—FMRR) have been promoted to deal with this problem, but such procedures require additional assumptions. The simplest recourse is to apply the NPV rule, as the NPV can always be calculated and will always give the correct answer.

from Chapter 9 and related the returns investors are interested in to the asset values they are grappling with in microlevel deals. We presented the multiperiod DCF method as the basic tool in this process, although we also discussed shortcuts in the valuation context such as direct capitalization. Finally, we related asset valuation to investment decision making by considering the NPV rule. The following chapters will elaborate on the basic concepts introduced here.

APPENDIX 10: MICROLEVEL INVESTMENT PERFORMANCE ATTRIBUTION: PARSING THE IRR

One of the salient characteristics of investment in the private property market is that individual assets are typically held by investors for relatively long periods of time. For example, investors typically hold income properties five to ten years. This is due in part to the relatively high transaction costs in buying and selling property. It is also due to the ability and desire of many direct real estate investors to earn investment returns through successful operational management of the properties they invest in, rather than simply from "trading" (that is, buying and selling assets). Real estate, with its long individual asset holding periods, contrasts with investment in the stock market, for example, where so-called "active" portfolio managers often change their positions in individual assets (that is, the stocks of individual firms) much more frequently.

Another feature of real estate assets is that they tend to be "cash cows" compared to the typical stock market investment. This feature interacts with the long holding period to magnify the importance of operational income generation in the overall investment return.

Both of these features, long individual asset holding periods and income-based returns, make the internal rate of return (IRR) typically a more interesting investment performance measure in real estate than in stock market investing. Recall from Chapter 9 that the IRR can be calculated over a long, multiyear holding period for an investment in a given property, and it provides a meaningful quantification of the investment performance of that asset. The IRR thus can be computed either *ex ante* (at the outset of the investment), where it measures *expected* performance, or *ex post* (at the end of a holding period), where it measures the realized return on the investment.

In either use of the IRR, it is sometimes of interest for diagnostic or analytical purposes to break the IRR down into components that add up to the total IRR, and represent different "sources" of the total return, formally speaking. This process is sometimes called "parsing" or "partitioning" the IRR, and it may be viewed as a type of microlevel **performance attribution**, because it attributes the overall investment performance to the components that make up the IRR.[20]

IRR attribution is usually broken down into three components: (1) initial cash flow yield, (2) subsequent cash flow growth, and (3) yield change (or "valuation change") between the beginning and end of the holding period. IRR attribution is not an exact science, in part because there are interaction effects among the return components, and also because the attribution result is sensitive to the length of the holding

---

[20] Macrolevel performance attribution, that is, analysis of the performance of a professional investment manager or of an actively managed portfolio of many individual properties, will be discussed in Chapter 27.

period. Nevertheless, microlevel return attribution can provide interesting insights into the source and nature of the overall multiperiod return.

To see how IRR attribution can be done, consider the following simple example. A property is bought at an initial cash yield of 9% and held for 10 years. Net cash flow generated by the property grows at a rate of 2% per year for each year during that holding period, at the end of which the property is (or could be) sold at a yield of 10% based on the upcoming (year 11) operating cash flow projection. The cash flows from this 10-year investment are presented in the first three rows of the table in Exhibit 10A-1. The first row is the net operating cash flow (net of capital expenditures); the second row is the capital flow; and the third row is the overall cash flow (the sum of the two previous rows).[21]

The first step in performance attribution is to compute the overall actual IRR and the initial yield. These act as the two reference points on which the cash flow growth and yield-change components will be defined. The overall actual IRR is based on the actual operating and capital cash flows depicted in the third row of the exhibit. The actual IRR is 10.30%. The **initial yield component** is then defined simply as the net cash flow yield that obtained in the first year of the investment, based on the purchase price. As noted, this is 9.00% ($1,000,000/$11,111,100). Note that it is equivalent to compute the initial yield as the IRR over the holding period based on the actual purchase price but holding the cash flows constant at the initial level, and assuming the terminal yield remains the same as the initial yield. This is seen in row 6 in the exhibit, which is the sum of rows 4 and 5.

The next step is to compute the **cash flow growth return component** defined on the initial yield. This is done by computing what the IRR would have been given the actual operating cash flows (in row 1) but with a terminal capital cash flow based on the initial yield of 9% rather than the actual terminal yield of 10%. A 9% terminal yield would have produced the capital cash flow indicated in row 7 in the exhibit. That is, if it were possible to sell the property at the end of year 10 for the same 9% yield as the property obtained at the beginning of the holding period, then the resale price would be $13.544 million, instead of the $12.190 million price that reflects the 10% yield actually obtained. This results in the 11.00% IRR indicated in row 8 (which is the sum of the row 1 and row 7 cash flows).[22] Then, the cash flow growth component is computed as 11.00% − 9.00% = 2.00%, the row 8 IRR minus the initial yield (row 6 IRR).[23]

---

[21] The initial capital outflow of $11.11 million reflects the initial yield of 9%. The terminal capital inflow is the proceeds from property resale at a price reflecting the 10% yield on the projected year-11 operating cash flow.

[22] The row 8 IRR in Exhibit 10A-1 happens to be an example of the special case noted in Chapter 9 in which the IRR exactly equals the sum of the initial yield and the constant growth rate (of both the cash flows and the asset value). This is a peculiarity of the simple numerical example depicted here. In general, of course, property cash flows will not necessarily grow at a constant rate every year during an investment holding period (either ex post or ex ante, due in part to the effect of long-term leases and capital expenditures). So the equating of the IRR to the sum of initial yield and the overall growth rate is the particular result in this example.

[23] Note that the cash flow growth component thusly defined is based on the initial yield. From a theoretical perspective, this definition is somewhat arbitrary. For example, we could alternatively define the cash flow growth effect based on the terminal yield by modifying the initial purchase price to reflect the actual terminal yield. In this example, this would result in a cash flow growth IRR component of +2.00%, found by subtracting the 10.00% terminal yield from the 12.00% IRR indicated in row 11. However, basing the component measurement on the initial yield makes intuitive sense, as returns are defined relative to the original capital investment.

	IRRs	0	1	2	3	4	5	6	7	8	9	10	11
								Year					
1. Actual Operating CF			1.0000	1.0200	1.0404	1.0612	1.0824	1.1041	1.1262	1.1487	1.1717	1.1951	1.2190
2. Actual Capital CF		−11.1111										12.1899	
3. Actual Total CF (1 + 2)	10.30%	−11.1111	1.0000	1.0200	1.0404	1.0612	1.0824	1.1041	1.1262	1.1487	1.1717	13.3850	
4. Initial Operating CF Constant			1.0000	1.0000	1.0000	1.0000	1.0000	1.0000	1.0000	1.0000	1.0000	1.0000	1.0000
5. Capital CF @ Initial Yield on 4												11.1111	
6. Initial CF @ Initial Yield (4 + 5)	9.00%	−11.1111	1.0000	1.0000	1.0000	1.0000	1.0000	1.0000	1.0000	1.0000	1.0000	12.1111	
7. Capital CF @ Initial Yield on 1												13.5444	
8. Actual Operating CF @ Initial Yield (1 + 7)	11.00%	−11.1111	1.0000	1.0200	1.0404	1.0612	1.0824	1.1041	1.1262	1.1487	1.1717	14.7395	
9. Capital CF @ Actual Yield on 4												10.0000	
10. Initial CF @ Actual Yield (4 + 9)	8.32%	−11.1111	1.0000	1.0000	1.0000	1.0000	1.0000	1.0000	1.0000	1.0000	1.0000	11.0000	
Initial Yield Component ([6]IRR)	9.00%												
CF Growth Component* ([8]IRR – [6]IRR)	2.00%												
Yield Change Component** ([10]IRR – [6]IRR)	−0.68%												
Interaction Effect ([3]IRR – sum [components])	−0.02%												
11. Actual Operating CF with Purchase Price @ Terminal Yield	12.00%	−10.0000	1.0000	1.0200	1.0404	1.0612	1.0824	1.1041	1.1262	1.1487	1.1717	13.3850	
12. Constant Terminal CF @ Actual Yield	8.32%	−13.2788	1.1951	1.1951	1.1951	1.1951	1.1951	1.1951	1.1951	1.1951	1.1951	13.1460	
Alternative Definition of CF Growth Component***	2.00%												
Alternative Definition of Yield Change Component****	−1.68%												

Exhibit 10A-1 Example Property Investment Cash Flow

*Based on initial yield: 11%–9%.

**Based on initial CF level: 8.32%–9%.

***Based on terminal yield instead of initial yield: 12%–10%.

****Based on terminal CF level and terminal yield: 8.32%–10%.

Finally, we compute what the overall property cash flows would be if the initial net operating cash flow remained constant throughout the holding period, but the yield changed as it actually did between the initial purchase and the resale. In that case, the operating cash flows would remain at their initial level of $1,000,000 per year (as indicated in row 4), and the resale price of the property at the actual terminal yield of 10% would be $10,000,000 (as indicated in row 9). This would result in the overall cash flows indicated in row 10 (the sum of rows 4 and 9), which provide an IRR of 8.32% on the initial purchase price of $11.11 million. This is the IRR that would result if there were no growth in property net operating cash flow, but the yield changed as it actually did from 9% to 10% between the initial purchase and the subsequent resale. The **yield-change component** is then computed as −0.68% = 8.32% −9.00%, the difference between the row 10 IRR and the initial yield (or row 10 IRR minus row 6 IRRs).[24]

Now note that the three IRR components defined earlier do not exactly add up to the overall total IRR: 9.00% initial yield + (−0.68%) yield-change effect + 2.00% cash flow growth effect = 10.32%. This is two basis points more than the total IRR of 10.30%. This difference may be thought of as an "interaction effect," or a combined effect of the cash flow growth and the yield-change effect based on the initial yield and cash flow level.[25]

Property-level investment performance attribution analysis can be defined in other ways than that presented here, and can be taken to deeper levels of analysis, defining additional components besides the three examined here.[26] In general, it is a useful diagnostic tool. However, it is important to keep in mind that the attribution of IRR components represents only a *formal* breakdown of the sources or determinants of the IRR. That is, they are simply a mathematical decomposition of the overall IRR, with no necessary correspondence to, or implication regarding, what the investor did, or what the property market did, over the period covered by the IRR computation. For example, the reasons the yield increased from 9% to 10%, or the property operating cash flows grew an average of 2% per year, are not addressed by the formal analysis.

[24] Note that this definition of the yield-change effect is based on the initial cash flow level of $1,000,000. Once again, this definition is somewhat arbitrary from a theoretical perspective, although it makes the most intuitive sense. (An alternative definition based on the terminal cash flow level would give a yield-change effect of −1.68%, as seen based on the difference between the row 12 IRR and the 10% terminal yield.)

[25] The interaction effect will not always be as small as it appears in the numerical example in Exhibit 10A-1. However, within the property-level IRR the yield change and cash flow growth interaction effect is a second-order effect and therefore tends to be less important than it often is in macrolevel portfolio performance attribution as described in section 27.1.3 of Chapter 27.

[26] For example, the effects of the various cash flow components of potential rent, vacancy, operating expenses, and capital expenditures can be broken down and examined in various ways. In general, however, the deeper one goes, and the more components one identifies, the more complex the analysis becomes, with the potential for arbitrary classifications and more serious interaction effects. At some point it makes more sense simply to examine the cash flow components directly rather than attempt to attribute IRR components to the various sources.

KEY TERMS

returns and values
expected cash flows (numerators)
Greater Fool Theory
discounted cash flow (DCF)
going-in IRR
reversion cash flow
expected returns (denominators)
intra-/interlease discount rates
blended IRR

Unbundled cash flows
direct capitalization
gross income multiplier (GIM)
ratio valuation
empirical cap rate
GIGO
discount rate
opportunity cost of capital
net present value (NPV)

wealth maximization
market value
hurdle rate
performance attribution
initial yield component
cash flow growth return
  component
yield-change component

STUDY QUESTIONS

Conceptual Questions

10.1.   What is the relationship between the ex ante return on an investment and the price for the asset paid by the investor?

10.2.   What is the Greater Fool Theory? How can the multiperiod DCF valuation procedure help to protect investors from falling victim to this theory?

10.3.   What is the relationship between the discount rate that should be used in the DCF procedure and the cash flows that are being discounted?

10.4.   When is it most important to "unbundle" a property's cash flows to apply different discount rates to different cash flow components?

10.5.   What is wrong with the following statement: Property X is worth $10 million in the market today because it produces $1 million of annual net income, and cap rates in the relevant property asset market are currently 10%.

10.6.   What is meant by the term *GIGO* in reference to the practical application of the DCF valuation procedure for commercial property? What are some typical mistakes in the numerators? What about in the denominators?

10.7.   What is the approximate relationship among the cap rate, the discount rate, and the long-run average growth rate in property cash flow and value?

10.8.   What is wrong with the following statement: Investors typically overstate both the numerators and denominators in applying the DCF approach to commercial property, with the two types of errors largely canceling each other out, so that there is really no harm done by this type of mistake.

10.9.   What fundamental principle underlies the NPV investment decision rule? [Hint: What is the relation between NPV and the investor's wealth?]

10.10. Why is a zero-NPV deal OK? Where is the profit for the investor in a deal in which NPV = 0?

10.11. Why is the NPV of the typical deal zero when evaluated from a market value perspective?

10.12. Describe at least two problems that can be encountered in using the hurdle rate version of the NPV investment decision rule, and how those problems can be resolved.

Quantitative Problems

10.13. Consider a property with expected future net cash flows of $25,000 per year for the next 5 years (starting one year from now). After that, the operating cash flow should step up 20%, to $30,000, for the following 5 years. If you expect to sell the property 10 years from now for a price 10 times the net cash flow at that time, what is the value of the property if the required return is 12%?

10.14. In the previous question, suppose the seller of the building wants $260,000.

   a. Should you do the deal? Why or why not? [Hint: What would be the net present value of the deal for the buyer at $260,000?]

   b. What is the IRR if you pay $260,000? How does this compare to the required return of 12%?

   c. What is the IRR if you could get the seller to accept $248,075 for the property? What is the NPV at that price?

10.15. Suppose that the required return on the property in question 10.13 is 11% instead of 12%. What would the value of the property be? By what percentage has this value changed as a result of this 100-basis-point change in the required return? [Note the sensitivity of property value to small changes in the expected return discount rate used in the denominators of the right-hand side of the DCF valuation equation.]

10.16. Go back to the property in question 10.13 with the 12% required return. What is the value of the property if the cash flow steps up 25% in year 6, to $31,250, instead of the original assumption of 20%? By what percentage has this roughly 1% per year change in the rent growth assumption (25% over five years instead of 20% over five years) changed the property value? [Note the sensitivity of property value to small changes in the percentage growth in expected cash flows in the numerators of the right-hand side of the DCF valuation equation.]

10.17. An apartment complex has 1,000 units of which on average 100 are vacant at any given time. Per unit, the rent is $400 per month, and the operating expenses are $1,800 per year (per occupied unit). If you expect both rents and expenses to grow at 3% per year, the required return is 12.5%, and the building value is expected to remain a constant multiple of its net income, then what is the NPV of a deal to buy the property for $25 million? [Hint: Use the perpetuity formula: $PV = CF_1/(r - g)$.]

10.18. What is the IRR of the deal in question 10.17? [Hint: Just invert the perpetuity formula and solve for r.]

10.19. The following table shows two 10-year cash flow projections (in $ millions, including reversion) for the same property. The upper row is the projection that will be presented by the broker trying to sell the building, and the bottom row is the realistic expectations. Suppose that it would be relatively easy for any potential buyers to ascertain that the most likely current market value for the property is about $10 million.

a. What going-in IRR (blended rate) will equate the presented cash flow projection to the observable $10 million present value (as of year 0)?

b. What rate will equate the realistic projection to that same present value?

c. What is the most likely amount of "disappointment" in the ex post rate of return earned by an investor who buys this property believing the broker's cash flow projection (i.e., the difference in presented versus realistic return)?

Year	1	2	3	4	5	6	7	8	9	10
Presented	$1.0000	$1.0300	$1.0609	$1.0927	$1.1255	$1.1593	$1.1941	$1.2299	$1.2668	$14.7439
Realistic	$1.0000	$1.0100	$1.0201	$1.0303	$1.0406	$1.0510	$1.0615	$1.0721	$1.0829	$12.1399

10.20. The buildings in a certain warehouse market are characterized by net cash flow projections like the one shown in the following table, based on net leases of five-years' duration. In this market properties are typically evaluated using a going-in IRR of 10.50% (blended rate). Thus, the typical property sells for a cap rate of about 8.25%. You have the opportunity to purchase a property with these same typical cash flow projections, at the typical cap rate or going-in IRR. However, your building is entirely covered by a 10-year lease with a AAA-credit tenant who can borrow money at 6%.

a. How much is this lease worth (for example, if it could be sold into a LOBS pool)?

b. Assuming that the appropriate interlease and reversion discount rate is 12%, what is your NPV from this deal?

Ten-Year Cash Flow Projection ($ millions)

Year	1	2	3	4	5	6	7	8	9	10
Operating	$1.0	$1.0	$1.1	$1.1	$1.2	$1.2	$1.3	$1.3	$1.4	$1.4
Reversion										$14.0
CF	$1.0	$1.0	$1.1	$1.1	$1.2	$1.2	$1.3	$1.3	$1.4	$15.4

10.21. Suppose a property worth $10 million in the marketplace provides an initial annual gross income of $2 million and a net income of $1 million. What is the GIM, and what is the cap rate prevailing in the property market for this type of property?

10.22. The projected cash flows (including reversion) are shown in the following table for property A and property B.

a. If both properties sell at a cap rate (initial cash yield) of 10%, what is the expected total return on a 10-year investment in each property?

b. If the 10% cap rate represents a fair market value for each property, then which property is the more risky investment (and how do you know)?

c. What is the annual growth rate in operating cash flows for each building during the first nine years?

d. How is this growth rate related to the cap rate and the investor's expected total return (IRR) in each property?

Annual Net Cash Flow Projections for Two Properties ($ millions)

Year	1	2	3	4	5	6	7	8	9	10
A	$1.0000	$1.0100	$1.0201	$1.0303	$1.0406	$1.0510	$1.0615	$1.0721	$1.0829	$12.0305
B	$1.0000	$0.9900	$0.9801	$0.9703	$0.9606	$0.9510	$0.9415	$0.9321	$0.9227	$10.0487

*10.23. In a certain market the typical lease is net to the landlord with a term of five years, and rents typically grow 1% per year, both within leases (due to built-in step-ups) and in the prevailing market rents charged on new leases. Properties typically have a single tenant and are sold with a new lease just signed (i.e., five years of contractual cash flows). Tenants typically can borrow at 8%, and the going-in cap rate prevailing in the property market is 9% (initial cash yield). Assuming annual cash flows in arrears and no vacancy between leases, what is the implied interlease and reversion discount rate?

*10.24. (based on Appendix). A 10-year property investment is characterized by the net cash flow stream indicated in the following table (including initial investment and reversion at the end of year 10). Compute the following:

a. Overall total IRR

b. Initial cash yield component

c. Cash flow growth component

d. Yield-change component

e. Interaction effect (Hint: Base your answers to (c) and (d) on the initial yield and initial cash flow level.)

Year	0	1	2	3	4	5	6	7	8	9	10	11
1. Actual Operating CF		$1,000	$1,005	$950	$1,010	$1,015	$1,020	$800	$1,025	$1,030	$1,036	$1,041
2. Actual Capital CF	−$12,500	$0	$0	$0	$0	$0	$0	$0	$0	$0	$12,244	
3. Actual Total CF (1 + 2)	−$12,500	$1,000	$1,005	$950	$1,010	$1,015	$1,020	$800	$1,025	$1,030	$13,279	

11 Nuts and Bolts for Real Estate Valuation: Cash Flow Proformas and Discount Rates

Chapter Outline

Learning Objectives

After reading this chapter, you should understand:

◆ The components and terminology of the typical commercial property investment cash flow projection proforma.

◆ Some major practical considerations in making realistic commercial property cash flow projections.

◆ Some major practical considerations in estimating the appropriate opportunity cost of capital to use as the discount rate in DCF valuation of commercial property.

Chapter 10 laid out the basic framework for investment valuation at the microlevel. In this chapter we will explore the details of how these tools are typically applied to commercial real estate. The DCF valuation problem can be thought of conceptually as involving two major analytical steps: (1) forecasting the future expected net cash flows from the property; and (2) determining and applying the appropriate opportunity cost of capital as a discount rate. We will treat each of these steps in turn in this chapter.

All of the discussion in this chapter is at what may be called the "property-before-tax" (PBT) level. That is, we are examining cash flows and valuation at the property level, as distinguished from the level of the owner of the property equity. Thus, the analysis here does not consider funds borrowed against the property, debt service payments, or income taxes. These matters will be treated in subsequent chapters.

11.1 PROFORMAS AND CASH FLOW PROJECTION

In this section we turn to the first task: forecasting of the property cash flows. This task is so basic that a special term has evolved to describe the document that lays out the cash flow projection. It is called a **proforma**. The Latin origin of this word (it means "for form") suggests that this cash flow forecast document may be produced more for appearance's sake than as a serious step in analysis and evaluation. Indeed, we would be less than honest if we did not admit that this is often the case in practice, as lenders and outside investors will typically require a proforma as a matter of course before a deal can be considered. But the proforma, or the cash flow forecast that makes it up, should be taken seriously. While nobody has a crystal ball, going through the exercise of trying to estimate unbiased, realistic forecasts of a property's future cash flow generation potential is fundamental to sound decision making. With this in mind, let's look at the nuts and bolts of a typical real estate proforma.

Cash flows are typically projected for a reasonably long period of time (10 years is the most common). This is because real properties are long-lived and most investors hold properties for long periods (in part due to the costs of transactions). Even if the owner expects to sell the property shortly, the resale value of the property (i.e., the price any potential buyer would be willing to pay for it) is fundamentally dependent on the ability of the property to generate operating income over the long term, so a long horizon is still necessary for rational evaluation. Long-horizon forecasts also have the salutary effect of forcing the analyst to grapple with difficult issues regarding where the rental market is headed. (Most of the value of most buildings is derived from the building's earning potential *after* the current leases expire.)

The importance of going through the proforma construction exercise is particularly obvious in the case of commercial properties with long-term leases. It may also be useful for apartment properties, however, as it makes explicit the long-term rental and expense growth rate assumptions that underlie the value of the property.

Broadly speaking, two categories of cash flows should be represented in a complete proforma for real estate investment analysis: the **operating cash flows** and the **reversion cash flows**. The former refers to cash flows that result from normal operation of the property and therefore accrue to the owner of the property regularly throughout the period the property is held as an investment. In contrast, reversion cash flows occur only at the time of, and due to, the sale of all or a portion of the property asset.

The table in Exhibit 11-1 shows in general form the typical line items in a proforma for an income-producing property. A brief discussion of each of these items will be helpful.

11.1.1 PGI and Market Rent Projection

The top line item in the operating cash flows is the primary potential source of property revenue, the cash it could earn if it were fully rented. This item is typically labeled potential revenue or **potential gross income**, abbreviated **PGI**. In practice,

Exhibit 11-1 Typical
Line Items in a Proforma
for Income Property

Operating (all years):

Potential gross income (PGI) = (Rent/SF) × (Rentable SF) =	PGI
– Vacancy allowance = – (Vacancy rate) × (PGI) =	– v
+ Other Income (e.g., parking, laundry) =	+ OI
– Operating expenses* =	– OE*
Net operating income =	NOI
– Capital improvement expenditures** =	– CI**
Property-before-tax cash flow =	PBTCF

Plus reversion (only last year and when partial sales occur):

Property value at time of resale =	V
– Selling expenses (e.g., brokers' fees) =	– SE
Property-before-tax cash flow =	PBTCF

*Major operating expense categories:

- Largely fixed costs (insensitive to occupancy level):
  Property taxes
  Hazard insurance
  Property security
  Property management
- Largely variable costs (sensitive to occupancy level):
  Utilities
  Building and grounds maintenance and routine repairs

[Note: Some or all of the expenses may be reimbursed from tenants to landlords or paid directly by tenants based on "net" or "expense stop" leases. In this case, an additional revenue line item for the landlord, typically entitled "expense reimbursements," may appear in the proforma.]

**Major capitalized expenditures:

- Leasing costs:
  Tenant build-outs or improvement expenditures
  Leasing commissions to brokers
- Property improvements:
  Major repairs
  Replacement of major equipment (e.g., HVAC, elevators)
  Major remodeling of building, grounds, and fixtures
  Expansion of rentable area

this item is also often referred to as the **rent roll**, especially in properties with long-term leases. This refers to the fact that in properties with long-term leases the current PGI is often enumerated by explicitly listing each lease and potentially leasable space in the property. The PGI is determined by multiplying the amount of rentable space (e.g., square feet) by the rent per unit of space (e.g., rent per SF).[1]

For space covered by existing long-term leases, projection of the PGI will involve two rather different sorts of calculations. As long as an existing lease will be in effect, the revenue is a function of the contractual rent terms in that lease. Once the existing lease expires, and for any space not covered by existing leases, the revenue will be a function of future leases that will likely be signed. Thus, projecting the rent roll in the proforma becomes primarily an exercise in examining and forecasting the rental market in which the property is situated. As noted in previous chapters, this requires consideration of both supply and demand in the space market, as well as the subject building's particular circumstances.

Estimating the current and future market rent levels applicable to the space in the subject building is crucial to property valuation. Because of their importance, these rental assumptions are often listed explicitly in the proforma table. They are often presented in a "supra line item" placed above the PGI line in the table to emphasize the fact that much of the PGI projection, especially in future years, is derived from the market rent level projection.

In any proforma projection, it is important to recognize that the future is inherently uncertain. We cannot predict the relevant future rent levels with anything like perfect accuracy. For an analysis to be well done, forecasts need only be realistic and unbiased.

The realism of the assumption about current market rent can be checked by examining recent leases signed for the building and comparing them with recent leases signed in similar buildings. This is known as a **rent comps analysis** (short for "comparable" buildings) and is a standard procedure of commercial appraisers.

Projection of future change in market rents going forward involves analysis of supply and demand in the relevant space market, as discussed in Parts I and II of this book. However, in typical current practice, the initial market rent relevant to the subject building is often simply projected to grow at the general inflation rate, treated as a constant percentage growth each year. This may be modified if the local rental market is perceived as being temporarily "out of equilibrium."[2]

The simplistic assumption that rents will grow at the inflation rate will often be unrealistic, however. It tends to ignore the effect of economic depreciation of the building, especially if the structure is not old and it is located in a stable or growing market in which new structures are built from time to time. The subject building must compete against these newer structures in the same market, and this may force it to lower its rents relative to the "top of the market" rent level. Because of this, in many cases it is more realistic to assume that the market rent effective for a

---

[1] In the case of apartment properties, the apartment unit itself is often the spatial unit used. For example, the rent roll for a building with 100 similar apartment units would be calculated by multiplying the average expected rent per unit times the 100 units in the building.

[2] Recall our discussion in Parts I and II about supply and demand in the space market, and the interaction of the space and capital markets via the development industry. Market rents may temporarily rise above or fall below long-run equilibrium levels, making it realistic to expect them to fall back or pop up to the long-run equilibrium level in real terms.

given (i.e., *aging*) building will tend to grow typically at annual rates one to three percentage points *less than* inflation, over the long run.[3]

A good way to check this assumption is to examine the past rental history of the subject building, and also of other existing buildings in the market. Compare the rents charged in otherwise similar leases that were signed 5 to 10 years ago against the rents charged in more recent leases, *within the same buildings*.[4] Compute the average annual rental growth rate indicated by these comparisons. For example, if typical rent in leases signed 5 to 10 years ago was $10/SF, and the typical rent in leases signed within the last 3 years was $11/SF, then this suggests an average annual growth rate of approximately 1.6%, computed as $(11/10)^{[1/(7.5-1.5)]} - 1 = 1.6\%$.[5] Then compare this average nominal growth rate with the average inflation rate over the same historical period. For example, if inflation averaged 3% per year during the period covered by the leases examined in the previous example, then the average *real* growth in rents was *negative* 1.4% per year, computed as $1.6\% - 3\% = -1.4\%$. In the real world, the result of such comparisons often indicates negative real growth in rents charged by existing buildings, especially in central locations.

Another approach to examine this same question is to compare the *current* rents charged by buildings of *different ages*, in the local space market relevant to the subject building.[6] Try to compare buildings that were all considered "top of the market" at the time they were built. Notice the relationship between the rents charged by the newer buildings and those charged by older buildings. Suppose, for example, that

---

[3] For the institutional quality commercial properties held in the NCREIF database, the average annual growth rate in net operating income (NOI) was 38 basis-points *less than* the average annual inflation rate, during the 1978–99 period, in spite of the fact that capital improvement expenditures on these properties averaged over 30% of NOI per year.

[4] In identifying the leases to examine, you will want to compare apples to apples as much as possible. Try to control for differences in the spaces or leases that might have significantly affected the rent, such as amenities, location within the building, size and contiguity of the space, length of the lease term, provisions for rent concessions, step-ups or expense pass-throughs, and so forth. No comparison will be perfect, but this exercise can be enlightening.

[5] The formally correct method to compute the average annual growth rate is to regress the natural log of the rents onto the number of years in the past in which the leases were signed. That is, for each comparable lease i in the same building, estimate the coefficient β in the following regression equation:

$$LN(Rent_i) = \alpha + \beta t_i$$

where $Rent_i$ is the annual rent per SF in lease i; t_i is the number of years between the signing of lease i and the signing of the oldest lease in the analysis; and α is a constant to be estimated by the regression. This equation is equivalent to

$$Rent_i = Rent_0 e^{\wedge}(\beta \times t_i)$$

where α is the natural log of the rent in the oldest lease, $Rent_0$, and e is the base of natural logs. A more sophisticated analysis would include additional explanatory variables on the right-hand side of the regression equation, quantifying characteristics of the space and of the lease terms other than rent, which might affect the rent. But the simple bivariate model described here is often sufficient, combined with common sense, to provide useful insight about what sort of rental growth is realistic to expect.

[6] The easiest way to conduct such a comparison is to use the current asking rents quoted by property managers and leasing brokers. As always, try to control for lease term and quality of space.

buildings built within the past 5 years charge an average rent of $12/SF, while buildings over 10 years in age charge an average rent of $10/SF. Suppose the newer buildings average 3 years in age, and the older buildings average 15 years in age. Then this implies a decline of about 1.5% per year of age of the building in the market *real* rent relevant to a given building.

A rough method of computations is as follows. Take the ratio of the old building rents divided by the new building rents, in this case 10/12 = 0.833. This represents the cumulative falloff in rent associated with number of years of age difference between the new and old buildings, in this case 12 years, the difference between the 15-year average age and the 3-year average age. Thus, the annual percentage falloff in rent (below the top of the market, that is, the newest buildings in the market) is computed as $0.833^{1/12} - 1 = 0.015 = 1.5\%$.[7] One typically finds results like this in U.S. markets for class A commercial properties in central locations.

11.1.2 Vacancy Allowance and EGI

Generally we cannot realistically expect a property always to be fully leased and generating its entire PGI every year. The second line item in Exhibit 11-1, the **vacancy allowance**, accounts for the expected effect of vacancy in the net cash flow of the property. This line item is usually quantified in one of two ways. For properties with many short-term leases, such as apartment buildings, the vacancy allowance is typically accounted for as a percentage of the PGI. For example, suppose the average tenant remains in an apartment for five years, and the average apartment unit is vacant for three months between tenants. Then the total cycle for a unit is 63 months (60 months occupied, followed by 3 months vacant), so the average apartment is therefore vacant 3/63, or 4.8%, of the time, which could be rounded off to 5%. The vacancy allowance in the proforma would be computed as 5% of the potential gross revenue projection in each year.[8]

The second method of computing the vacancy allowance is to forecast explicitly the likely vacancy period that will be associated with each rental unit or space in the building, considering the expiration of each lease currently in the building. This method is more appropriate for buildings with long-term (i.e., multiyear) leases, or buildings that currently have substantial vacancy that is expected to be filled up over some projected schedule.

With either method of vacancy calculation, the resulting projected overall long-term average vacancy percentage should be compared to available information about typical vacancy in the local market for similar buildings. If the projected vacancy rate for the subject building differs much from the typical vacancy in its market, this discrepancy should be either explained or corrected.

[7] More formal analysis would use regression, as described in the previous note. In this case regress the log of the rent of building i onto the age of building i (and a constant). The β coefficient is interpreted as the *real* growth rate in rents (a negative β indicates depreciation, or a fall-off of rents with age) *relative to* the rent charged by the top of the market.

[8] If the apartment market is currently oversupplied, a larger vacancy allowance percentage might be applied in the near-term years of the proforma projection. Similarly, if the apartment building currently has a vacancy level different from the long-term average, the first few years of the proforma projection should reflect this fact.

Subtracting the vacancy allowance line item amount from the PGI provides a projection of what is often referred to as the **effective gross income (EGI)** for the property in each year in the proforma. However, many properties have other sources of earning income besides the rental of their space for the occupancy of tenants, for example, revenue from the operation of vending machines or laundry machines in apartment buildings, and revenue from parking operations or billboard or antenna rental in office or retail buildings. These sources of income are typically referred to as **other income**, represented by the third line- item in Exhibit 11-1.

11.1.3 Operating Expenses

The next major category in the proforma is **operating expenses**. This heading will include a number of regularly occurring, specific expense line items associated with the ongoing operation of the property. Typical major categories include property management and administration, utilities, insurance, regular maintenance and repair, and property taxes. Note that charges for depreciation expenses are *not* included among the operating expenses. This is because the property proforma statement is a cash flow statement rather than an accrual income statement, and depreciation expenses are not a cash outflow per se. The occurrence of real depreciation of the property over time (whether due to physical or economic obsolescence) will be reflected in the cash flows (and hence in the proforma statement) in one or a combination of several possible ways. These include: (1) lower real rents over time (as previously noted); (2) higher operating expenses; (3) higher capital improvement expenditures; or (4) lower resale value (higher terminal cap rate applied) in the reversion cash flow at the end of the period covered by the proforma.[9] Also, income taxes are not included in the operating expenses, as such taxes are attributable to the owner/investor, not to the property itself.

It should also be noted that property management expenses should be identified and charged as an operating expense (i.e., *above* the NOI bottom line), *even if the owner/investor will be managing the property itself*. Property management is an opportunity cost, absorbing the time and energy of whoever is performing this job. In the case of owner/managers (or "self-management"), it is important not to confuse return on the *financial* capital invested in the property with return on *human* capital or labor invested in property management. After all, investment in other forms of capital such as stocks or bonds would not generally require a management input on the part of the investor. So comparisons among investment alternatives will be biased in favor of real estate if this cost is not subtracted from the real estate yield.

---

[9] While depreciation per se is never deducted from the income reported in the property NOI, in some cases, as noted earlier, a "reserve for capital improvement expenditures" is deducted as a regular amount each year. Fundamentally, of course, capital improvement expenditures act to mitigate the effect of depreciation in a real physical sense. Deduction of a capital reserve from the operating income is particularly common in the appraisal profession when attempting to arrive at a "stabilized NOI" that is meant to reflect a (forward-looking) typical amount of net cash flow the property can provide per year, on average over the long run. In contrast, property managers often work with operating budgets and capital budgets that are deliberately separate and distinct, with capital expenditures not "reserved" out of the NOI bottom line in the operating budget. In part this is because the owner may choose to finance capital improvements "externally" rather than from the cash flow generated by the property's operations. Care must be taken in working with proforma statements and NOI figures to ascertain whether the NOI is net of such a capital reserve deduction, and if so, whether the deduction is realistic and complete.

In general, the cost of property management in cases of self-management can be quantified by the opportunity cost defined by the fee that would be charged by a professional property manager to manage the subject property. For small properties this is often in the range of 5% to 10% of the EGI per year. Management costs are usually lower on a percentage basis for larger properties, due to economies of scale. For example, management costs of large-scale class A office properties are typically in the 2% to 3% range.

It is often useful to describe a property's operating expenses in terms of either **fixed** or **variable costs** (or, some line items may be best described as a combination of the two). Fixed expenses, in principle, are unaffected by the level of occupancy in the building. They will remain at the same level (at least in the short run, say, for a year or so) no matter how vacant or full the building may be. Property taxes and insurance charges are typically in this category. Variable expenses occur in direct proportion (more or less) to the level of occupancy. For example, in a building that is half vacant, utility expenses will often be only about half what they would be when the building is full.

Class A properties often have so-called **net leases** in which the tenants pay all or most of the operating expenses. Other leases provide for partial reimbursement of some or all operating expense line items. For example, landlords and tenants often negotiate **expense stops**, in which tenants pay all operating expenses above an agreed-on base level, which typically reflects the level of operating expenses per SF when the lease was signed. When operating expenses are expected to be reimbursed by tenants, these reimbursements will typically appear as additional cash flow line items in the proforma, as positive inflows in the landlord's favor, partially offsetting the operating expense outflows.

11.1.4 Net Operating Income

The **net operating income (NOI)** results from the subtraction of the operating expenses from all the sources of revenue previously discussed (rental revenue, other income, and expense reimbursements). NOI is the most widely used indicator of the net cash flow or operating profit generation ability of the property.

There are several reasons for the primary focus on NOI as the bottom line of property level operating net cash flow. A more complete and accurate measure of net cash flow would subtract capital improvement expenditures made on the property. However, because of the irregular and discretionary nature of the timing of many capital improvement expenditures, the NOI is typically a more stable and easily quantified number than the actual net cash flow after capital expenditures. Also, at least to some extent from an accrual accounting perspective (as opposed to a purely cash flow perspective), NOI is an appropriate bottom line indicator of operating profit, as capital expenditures presumably add to the value of the asset. While depreciation expenses are not subtracted from NOI, in real estate the depreciation of the building is relatively minor compared to short lived assets and should in any case be reflected in other aspects of the proforma projection, as noted earlier.

As a result, in common usage NOI is often treated as virtually the same thing as the property's net cash flow, and property investment current yield or income return measures (such as the cap rate) are often quantified as the current NOI divided by the current property value. While convenient and often sufficient, such a practice does risk ignoring the potentially important impact of capital improvement expenditures.

11.1.5 Capital Improvement Expenditures

This brings us to the next line item in Exhibit 11-1, **capital improvement expenditures**. In general, this item refers to major expenditures providing long-term improvements to the physical quality of the property, required to maintain or add to the value of the property.[10] Examples would be replacing the heating, ventilation, and cooling (HVAC) system; replacing a roof; adding a parking lot or repaving an existing one; adding new landscaping; or other such investments.

So-called **tenant improvement expenditures (TIs)** are a major category of capital expenditures in many buildings with long-term leases. This refers to customized physical improvements, including finishings and decorations, provided at the time of lease signing to the space the tenant will occupy. These are often viewed as **concessions** the landlord offers the tenant to get the tenant to sign the long-term lease. Sometimes TIs are necessary even just to get an existing tenant to stay and sign a new lease when an existing lease expires. TIs may be managed and paid for directly by the landlord, or the landlord may simply provide the tenant with an allowance amount, which the tenant then spends as it deems fit.

From a cash flow timing perspective, the characteristic of capital improvement expenditures that distinguishes them from regular operating expenses is that capital expenditures occur less frequently, at irregular intervals of time. Capital expenditures are also characterized by considerable flexibility and discretion on the property owner's part as to exactly when to make the expenditure and how much to spend.[11] In the property management business, projected capital expenditures will typically be presented in a separate proforma, as part of a capital budget for the property. But for investment analysis purposes, capital expenditures must be consolidated into the overall property proforma.

Even though the NOI is often thought of as the operating bottom line in property level analysis, it is important to recognize that capital expenditures are in fact neither a minor nor a trivial determinant in the net cash flow of the property. On average over the long run, capital improvement expenditures typically equal 1% to 2% of the property value per year (typically around 10% to 20% of the NOI).[12] This percentage will of course tend to be less in new buildings and greater in middle-aged buildings. (Very old buildings may be nearing redevelopment and so are not worth major capital improvement expenditures.)

It is also important to recognize that accounting procedures vary as to what is classified as a capital improvement as opposed to operating expense. For example, commissions paid to leasing brokers are often classified as capital improvement

---

[10] If a capital expenditure does not add to the value of the property *relative to* what that value would be without the expenditure (as of the time of the expenditure), an increment in value at least equal to the cost of the expenditure, then there is no rational business justification for making the expenditure at that time. (The usual NPV rule applies.) Generally, capital improvements add to property value either by increasing the future rent that can be charged or by decreasing the future operating expenses (or both).

[11] It is often possible to borrow much or all of the expenditure amount. However, such financing considerations are usually left out of the property proforma, as they represent a separate issue from the valuation of the property. The method in which capital improvements are financed does not generally change the value of the property because such financing transactions rarely have a significantly nonzero NPV.

[12] For all properties in the NCREIF index, during the 1978–98 period, capital expenditures averaged 33% of NOI. However, the NCREIF properties are weighted heavily toward types of property that require particularly large capital expenditures, such as shopping malls and class A office buildings.

expenditures, even though such expenditures are generally not rare or discretionary and they are typically financed from the cash flow generated by the building.[13]

11.1.6 The Bottom Line: PBTCF

Viewing the NOI as the bottom line of cash flow available for distribution from building operations can be somewhat misleading. The more realistic picture of the free-and-clear cash flow available to the owners of the property (before debt service and income taxes are taken out) is represented by the NOI less the capital improvement expenditures, the **property-before-tax cash flow (PBTCF)**. This is identified in Exhibit 11-1 as the overall operating bottom line.

11.1.7 Reversion Cash Flows

In addition to the operating cash flows described previously, reversion cash flows must be included in the proforma in any year when all or part of the property is expected to be sold. In most cases, reversion cash flows will appear only in the last year of the proforma, as the entire property is expected to be sold at once. Indeed, for investment analysis purposes a proforma should always include reversion cash flows in the last year of the proforma; otherwise, a major part of the value of the property will be left out of the analysis. At the property-before-tax level, the reversion cash flows consist simply of the expected resale price of the property at the projected future point in time, net of selling expenses (such as brokers' fees and transaction costs).

An often-heard complaint is that the projection of future selling price is an exercise in "crystal ball gazing." But remember that cash flow projections are not expected to be without error, only unbiased. The fact that future cash flows will differ from prior projections is merely a reflection of the fact that real estate is risky, and this risk is treated in the denominator of the DCF procedure by the use of the risk-adjusted discount rate. With this in mind, clearly the projection of future resale value is one of the most important and useful exercises in the proforma analysis. In a typical 10-year DCF valuation, the projected reversion accounts for well over one third of the total present value of the property.

Generally, the best, as well as most widely used, method for forecasting the resale price of the property is to apply direct capitalization to the end of the proforma projection period. Typically, the analyst projects the NOI of the property one more year beyond the proforma horizon. For example, in a 10-year analysis the NOI would projected for an 11th year. The year-11 NOI would then be divided by an assumed **reversion cap rate** (also known as the **going-out cap rate**, or **terminal cap rate**) to project the expected market value of the property at the time of reversion at the end of the 10th year.[14] If the NOI projection is realistic, and the cap rate assumption is realistic, then this should provide a realistic projection for the selling price.

This procedure helps protect the investor against temporary real estate market bubbles and the Greater Fool fallacy, as described in Chapter 10. In the first place, by placing the reversion fairly far into the future (e.g., 10 years), the relative magnitude

---

[13] Another problem is that rental concessions such as rent rebates and rent holidays are sometimes "accrued," that is, spread out over the life of the lease rather than reflected in the years when the rent cash flows are actually reflected.

[14] In direct capitalization, the cap rate is divided into the upcoming year's NOI, that is, the first year of NOI subsequent to the valuation date of the property.

of the reversion value component in the overall present value of the property is sharply reduced. (It is usually well below one-half the total present value.) This serves to mitigate the effect of mistakes or bias in the projected reversion value. Second, by using projected direct capitalization based on NOI, the reversion forecast is based on a projection of the fundamental ability of the property to earn operating cash flow in the rental market, rather than a simple extrapolation of the current investor's purchase price of the property.[15]

In applying this procedure, the projected reversion will be quite sensitive to the assumed going-out cap rate. It is normally most realistic to project a going-out cap rate at least equal to, or slightly higher than, the going-in cap rate (that is, the cap rate at the time of purchase), based on typical market cap rates. This is because, as buildings age, they usually become more risky or less able to grow the rents they can charge (or more prone to needing capital improvement expenditures). So cap rates of older buildings tend to be higher than those of otherwise similar newer buildings. However, prevailing cap rates will depend on the nature of the market at the time, and the cap rate relevant to a given building will depend on its particular circumstances regarding, for example, existing tenants and leases, and need for capital improvements.

For example, if the asset market is particularly "exuberant" at the time of purchase, the going-in cap rate will tend to be abnormally low, and such a low rate should probably not be projected for the reversion.[16] Alternatively, consider the case in which a building has a large existing lease that was signed when the rental market was "hot" several years ago, but that lease will soon expire in a space market characterized by lower rents. The building's going-in cap rate will appear abnormally large, reflecting the large initial revenue from the vintage lease divided by a present asset value that reflects the likely lower rents in the future. In such circumstance it might be appropriate to project a going-out cap rate lower than the going-in rate.

11.1.8 Numerical Example

Exhibit 11-2 presents a simple example 10-year proforma for the Noname Building, a 30,000 SF office building consisting of three 10,000-SF spaces each of which rents out separately under a five-year lease. The current and projected market rent for the building is shown in the first row. The market rent in year 1 is estimated to be $10/SF, meaning that leases signed today (at the beginning of year 1) would be expected to have this rent. The market rent is then projected to grow at a constant rate of 1% per year. Such a projection might be based, for example, on a judgment that the space market is currently in, and expected to remain in, its long-term equilibrium, with expected inflation of 2% per year and building depreciation of 1% per year in real terms. (Such depreciation would presumably be due to economic obsolescence, even after sufficient capital expenditure for reasonable upkeep of the building.) This results in a net 1% per year expected growth rate for the rent the building could charge on new leases.

The next section of the proforma presents the rent roll for the three spaces, totaling the PGI of the building. Space 1 is currently occupied by a tenant that has an

---

[15] An alternative procedure for forecasting reversion value, growing the initial purchase price of the property at some specified growth rate, obviously does not protect the investor in this respect. Any mistake in the initial purchase price would simply be projected onto the reversion forecast, as per the Greater Fool Theory.

[16] Recall that cap rates tend to be largely insensitive to changes in inflation.

Item		Year										
		1	2	3	4	5	6	7	8	9	10	11
Market rent/SF:		$10.00	$10.10	$10.20	$10.30	$10.41	$10.51	$10.62	$10.72	$10.83	$10.94	$11.05
Potential revenue:												
Gross rent space 1 (10,000 SF)		$105,000	$105,000	$105,000	$103,030	$103,030	$103,030	$103,030	$103,030	$108,286	$108,286	$108,286
Gross rent space 2 (10,000 SF)		$100,000	$100,000	$100,000	$100,000	$100,000	$105,101	$105,101	$105,101	$105,101	$105,101	$110,462
Gross rent space 3 (10,000 SF)		$100,000	$101,000	$101,000	$101,000	$101,000	$101,000	$106,152	$106,152	$106,152	$106,152	$106,152
Total PGI		$305,000	$306,000	$306,000	$304,030	$304,030	$309,131	$314,283	$314,283	$319,539	$319,539	$324,900
Vacancy allowance:												
Space 1		$0	$0	$0	$51,515	$0	$0	$0	$0	$54,143	$0	$0
Space 2		$0	$0	$0	$0	$0	$52,551	$0	$0	$0	$0	$55,231
Space 3		$100,000	$0	$0	$0	$0	$0	$53,076	$0	$0	$0	$0
Total vacancy allowance		$100,000	$0	$0	$51,515	$0	$52,551	$53,076	$0	$54,143	$0	$55,231
Total EGI		$205,000	$306,000	$306,000	$252,515	$304,030	$256,581	$261,207	$314,283	$265,396	$319,539	$269,669
Other income		$30,000	$30,300	$30,603	$30,909	$31,218	$31,530	$31,846	$32,164	$32,486	$32,811	$33,139
Expense reimbursements												
Space 1		$0	$1,833	$2,003	$0	$1,651	$964	$1,118	$2,870	$0	$1,823	$329
Space 2		$0	$2,944	$3,114	$1,814	$3,465	$0	$153	$1,905	$469	$2,292	$0
Space 3		$0	$0	$170	$0	$260	$0	$0	$1,752	$316	$2,139	$645
Total revenue		$235,000	$341,078	$341,891	$285,238	$340,624	$289,075	$294,324	$352,974	$298,667	$358,602	$303,781
Reimbursable operating expenses:												
Property taxes		$35,000	$35,000	$35,000	$35,000	$35,000	$36,750	$36,750	$36,750	$36,750	$36,750	$36,750
Insurance		$5,000	$5,000	$5,000	$5,000	$5,000	$5,250	$5,250	$5,250	$5,250	$5,250	$5,250
Utilities		$16,667	$25,500	$26,010	$22,109	$27,061	$23,002	$23,462	$28,717	$24,410	$29,877	$25,396
Total reimbursable expenses		$56,667	$65,500	$66,010	$62,109	$67,061	$65,002	$65,462	$70,717	$66,410	$71,877	$67,396
Management expense		$6,150	$9,180	$9,180	$7,575	$9,121	$7,697	$7,836	$9,428	$7,962	$9,586	$8,090
Total operating expenses		$62,817	$74,680	$75,190	$69,684	$76,182	$72,699	$73,298	$80,146	$74,371	$81,463	$75,486
NOI		$172,183	$266,389	$266,701	$215,554	$264,442	$216,376	$221,026	$272,828	$224,295	$277,139	$228,295
Capital expenditures:												
TI			$50,000		$50,000		$55,000	$55,000		$55,000		$55,000
Leasing commissions			$15,150		$15,455		$15,765	$15,923		$16,243		$16,569
Common physical improvements						$100,000						
Net cash flow (operations)		$172,183	$201,248	$266,701	$150,100	$164,442	$145,611	$150,103	$272,828	$153,053	$277,139	$228,295
Net cash flow (reversion)											$2,282,951	
IRR @ $2,000,000 price: 10.51%												

Exhibit 11-2   Noname Building: Cash Flow Projection

existing lease signed two years ago at a higher rent of $10.50/SF. (Perhaps the space market was abnormally tight at that time, or that tenant negotiated a "bad deal" for itself.) This lease is set to run three more years and will expire at the end of year 3. Space 2 has just leased out in a new five-year lease at the current market rate of $10/SF. This lease will expire at the end of year 5. Space 3 is currently vacant and not expected to lease up until the beginning of year 2. At that time the market rent is projected to be $10.10/SF, which is the projected rent for space 3 from years 2 through 6.

In the proforma, the PGI is calculated for all three spaces as though each were fully occupied every year. Note that when a lease is projected to expire, the space "rolls over" at the projected market rent prevailing at the beginning of the next lease period. Thus, for example, after space 1's current lease expires at the end of year 3, the rent roll for that space is "marked to market" as of the next year, at the projected year-4 market rent of $10.30/SF. (Actually, this is a rounded estimate. The precise estimate is $10.303, which is why the PGI for 10,000 SF is projected at $103,030 based on the year 4 market rent.)

The next section of the proforma computes the vacancy allowance that must be subtracted from the PGI to arrive at the effective gross income. Space 3 is expected to be vacant for the entire first year, so its entire PGI for year 1 is attributed to vacancy allowance. The assumption for the remainder of the proforma is that when leases expire, there is a 50% chance the existing tenant will renew, resulting in no vacancy. However, if the existing tenant does not renew, the expectation is that the space will remain vacant for an entire year.

Recall that the proforma is supposed to forecast the *expected* cash flows, that is, the mean of the subjective ex ante probability distribution of the possible cash flows for each year. To compute this mean, we multiply the probability of each scenario by the cash flow resulting from that scenario, and sum over all the scenarios. In this case, we have two scenarios: tenant renews or tenant does not renew. Thus, we compute the expected vacancy allowance for a given space during the year following its lease expiration as follows:

$$(1 - Probability\ of\ renewal) \times Market\ Rent$$

For example, the market rent is projected to be $10.51/SF in year 6. Space 2's lease expires at the beginning of year 6. So the projected vacancy allowance for year 6 for space 2 is[17]

$$(1 - 0.5) \times (\$10.51/SF) \times 10,000\ SF = \$52,551$$

After adding other income to the EGI, the next section of the proforma computes expense reimbursements. Although the typical leases for this building are gross leases, that is, leases in which the landlord is responsible for paying the operating expenses of the building, there are nevertheless some provisions here for tenants to reimburse some of these expenses to the landlord.

[17] Suppose the renewal probability was estimated to be 75%, and the expected vacant period in the event of nonrenewal was four months. Then the projected (expected) vacancy loss for space 2 for year 6 would be

$$(1 - 0.75)(\$10.51)(10,000\ SF)(4/12\ mo.) = \$8,758$$

In particular, the leases here have expense stops, requiring the tenants to reimburse the landlord for certain operating expenses *in excess of a specified base level per SF*. For example, the current lease in space 1 has a "stop" of $2/SF. The tenant must reimburse the landlord for his pro rata share of the reimbursable operating expenses in excess of that amount. Look down at the total reimbursable expenses line in the next section. These are projected to be $56,667 in year 1. As there are 30,000 SF in the building, this works out to reimbursable expenses of $1.89/SF. This is less than the $2/SF expense stop for space 1, so that tenant is not projected to pay any expense reimbursement in year 1. On the other hand, in year 2 the reimbursable expenses are projected to be $65,500, or $2.1833/SF. Thus, space 1 is projected to reimburse the landlord for $1,833 in year 2, computed as the $0.1833/SF projected excess over his stop times his 10,000 SF.[18]

After adding the EGI, the other income, and the expense reimbursements to arrive at the total revenue, the next section in the proforma projects the operating expenses.[19] Four categories of operating expenses are enumerated here: property tax, hazard and liability insurance, utilities, and management (which includes administration, cleaning, routine service and upkeep, etc.). Of these four expense categories, only management is not subject to the expense stop tenant reimbursement provisions. Some of these expense items, such as utilities, are projected to be less in years when there is some expected vacancy (in a probability sense, in keeping with the cash flow projection being a statistical "expectation" of a probability distribution). Some expenses tend to grow with inflation, while others tend to remain relatively fixed, at least over intervals between adjustments. For example, property taxes tend to remain a roughly constant proportion of property value, but taxes may only be adjusted once every several years (based on new property value assessments).

The NOI is computed as the total revenue minus the total operating expenses. Then, *below* the NOI line, capital expenditures are projected. Three categories are included here: TIs, leasing commissions, and general capital expenditures for common areas or structural improvements. TI expenditures are projected whenever a new lease is expected to be signed. These are initially projected at $5/SF, growing to $5.50/SF later. In reality, TI allowances will vary from market to market and as a function of the state of the space market (whether the market tends to favor tenants or landlords). Leasing commissions in this example are projected at 3% of the total PGI amount associated with the lease. A single major common area physical improvement costing $100,000 is projected for year 5, midway through the proforma period. This might be an accumulation of repairs and upgrades that would be necessary by that time. In reality, specific capital items might be budgeted, or a general reserve amount might be taken out every year.

A key point to note is that the cumulative capital expenditures of all types projected for years 1–10 is about 18.5% of the cumulative NOI during that period, in our example building. This is a plausible percentage. (Recall that the typical range for this figure is between 10% and 20%, and over 30% for some types of class A properties.) Projections of capital expenditure substantially below 10% of NOI in a 10-year proforma should be suspect, unless a reasonable explanation is provided, or a correspondingly reduced resale value is projected for the reversion.

[18] In some cases there may be provisions to adjust the expense stop based on the amount of *occupied* space in the building.

[19] Obviously, the computation order requires projection of reimbursable expenses prior to projection of reimbursement revenue.

The overall bottom line in our example proforma is labeled "net cash flow," and is broken down between operational and reversion components. The reversion in this case was projected by applying a 10% going-out cap rate to the year 11 NOI projection. Note that the operating net cash flow bottom line is somewhat "lumpy" across time. For example, the projected net cash drops from $267,000 in year 3 to $150,000 in year 4. This is typical of years in which the leases will expire covering a large portion of the building's space. Because of releasing capital costs such as TIs and leasing commissions, the net cash bottom line will typically be more affected by lease expirations than the NOI. Thus, realistic net cash flow projections are typically "choppier" than NOI projections, as is the case in the Noname Building.[20]

If the Noname Building could be bought at the beginning of year 1 for $2 million (with end-of-year annual cash flows thereafter), the going-in IRR would be 10.51% per year over the 10-year projection. The going-in cap rate would be 8.61%, which may seem a bit low until you realize that the year-1 NOI reflects one third of the space being vacant. A fully occupied NOI, as represented by the year-2 projection, would imply a cap rate of 13.32%, which seems high. However, neither of these cap rates reflects the necessary capital expenditures. This demonstrates why cap rates can be tricky to use for judging property value. The IRR applied to the net cash flow (net of capital expenditures) is a more meaningful and reliable measure. As there is only slight overall growth projected for this property, we would expect the $E[r]$ expected total return (**going-in IRR**) to be only slightly higher than a long-run **stabilized cap rate**. Thus, if 10.5% is a reasonable expected total return for this property, then our projected going-out cap rate of 10%, applied to estimate the reversion value, is reasonable and consistent with a $2 million current valuation.

11.2 DISCOUNT RATES:
THE OPPORTUNITY COST OF CAPITAL

Recall that the DCF valuation procedure consists of numerators and denominators on the right-hand side of the valuation equation (formula [1] in Chapter 10). The preceding section focused on the numerators, the cash flow projection. To complete the picture, we need to give some more attention now to the denominators. In particular, we need to consider the "discount rate" used in property level valuation, what we labeled $E[r]$ in the formula.

The basic conceptual idea behind the DCF discount rate was already discussed in Chapter 10. The discount rate is the multiperiod, dollar-weighted average *total* return expected by the investor, in the form of a going-in IRR. It is therefore an ex ante return measure. As it is a total return, the discount rate includes a risk premium (which we labeled RP) on top of the **riskfree rate** (which we labeled r_f). This risk premium should reflect the amount of risk in the cash flows that are being discounted. There must always be this relationship between the denominators and numerators in a DCF valuation: the denominators must reflect the risk that is in the numerators. For this reason we noted that in some cases it is desirable to separate the property's cash

---

[20] In extreme cases, this can result in projected years of negative net cash flow for a property that is generally profitable. Obviously, the building owner needs to plan in advance for income volatility, and especially for possible years of negative cash flow, when the property's income will have to be supplemented by external sources. It will often be possible to finance major capital improvement expenditures using borrowed money.

flows into components that are characterized by different risk, for example, existing lease cash flows versus residual cash flows. More often, however, at least in current practice, a single "blended" discount rate is applied to the entire net cash flow of the property, especially if the property has a typical occupancy and lease expiration pattern. What we want to do in this section is to focus at a more practical level, to provide some guidance about how to determine what is a reasonable rate to use in the DCF valuation of typical commercial properties.

A good place to begin is to recall the answer to the basic question, Where do discount rates come from? The DCF discount rate is meant to be the **opportunity cost of capital (OCC)** for the subject investment. It is the return investors could typically expect to earn (on average) in other investments of similar risk to the subject investment. This is what is required to get investors to be just willing to invest in the subject property. If the expected return in the subject property is lower than that of similar-risk investments, no one would want to invest in the subject property. If the expected return in the subject property is higher than that in similar-risk investments, then there will be a stampede of investors wanting to sell other investments and use the money to buy the subject property, which would drive up the price of the subject property until this price offered a return similar to the other investments. (Recall the inverse relationship between the current price of the asset and its expected return.) As "other investments," by definition, are traded in the capital markets, we can therefore say that discount rates "come from" the capital markets (including both public and private asset markets).

11.2.1 General Observations About Real Estate Discount Rates

This concept of the OCC is all well and good in principle, but what can we say in practice about how to determine the specific numbers to use in analyzing real estate investments? Two steps are involved in answering this question. First, we need to be able to draw empirical conclusions about the typical rates of return investors expect from different types of investments. Second, we need to make some judgment about the relative risk of the property we are interested in, as compared to other investments whose ex ante returns we think we can observe.

Two of the characteristics that define a well-functioning asset market is that there is sufficient volume of trading of assets and sufficient information about transaction prices and asset income yields so that investors can make reasonably informed judgments about ex ante returns. Clearly, public stock and bond markets provide a wealth of historical information that helps investors to estimate reasonable return expectations. As stocks and bonds are part of the overall investment universe in which real estate competes, information about stock and bond returns is also relevant for forming real estate return expectations. In addition, the private real estate asset market functions sufficiently well to provide direct empirical evidence about expected returns in real estate.

Information about current ex ante returns in the asset markets is relevant for discount rates in two ways. First, this information tells potential investors what their alternatives are. Suppose we observe, as we did in Chapter 7 (Sect. 7.2), that (unlevered) total returns on institutional quality commercial property tend to be intermediate between stock market returns and Treasury Bill returns. At a broad-brush level, this sets out some basic alternatives. You can invest in the stock market and probably earn a higher return over the long run than you would through unlevered investment in good-quality commercial property. Or, if you just keep rolling over your money in Treasury Bills, you will probably earn a lower return.

These ex ante return alternatives suggest, in turn, that the capital markets view such real estate as having a level of risk that is intermediate between that of stocks and Treasury Bills. This is the second way in which observed returns inform the choice of discount rate. They tell you something about the risk in the subject investment, at least the *relative* risk, at a broad-brush level, as perceived by the market. In other words, the observation of return expectations tends to inform our judgment about the relative risk of different types of assets.

11.2.2 Putting in Some Numbers: Historical Evidence on the OCC for Institutional Commercial Property

With these general considerations in mind, let's begin by building on what we learned in Chapter 7 about the historical returns to different broad classes of assets, to shed some light on what are typically appropriate rates to use in discounting real estate cash flows. Exhibit 11-3 reproduces a part of Exhibit 7-8 and computes the historical **risk premiums** ("excess returns") associated with the total returns on stocks, bonds, and real estate. This has been done in Exhibit 11-3 by treating the return to Treasury Bills (short-term government debt) as the riskfree rate (r_f) and subtracting this from the average total returns earned by each of the other three asset classes over the same period of time.

From this exhibit we see that, during the 1970–98 period, the risk premium on the sorts of institutional quality commercial properties represented by the NCREIF index averaged 3.42% (or 342 basis points). The risk premium on long-term bonds was similar, while the risk premium on stocks, at nearly 800 basis points, was more than twice the real estate risk premium.

If these historical risk premiums represent current expectations, then we can apply them to current Treasury Bill yields to derive current expected total returns. For example, in the late 1990s Treasury Bill yields were typically around 5%. Adding an approximately 3.5% risk premium to this riskfree rate would suggest an expected total return for institutional quality commercial real estate of about 8.5%, going forward on investments made in the late 1990s.

The problem with this approach is that the historical results in Exhibit 11-3 are *ex post* risk premiums, not **ex ante** expectations. They represent the realization of what actually did happen during one sample of time (1970–98), not necessarily what investors were expecting *would happen* when they made their investments, nor necessarily what investors currently are expecting. Nevertheless, the future is unlikely to be

Exhibit 11-3 Historical Return, Risk, and Risk Premiums, 1970–98

Asset Class	Total Return	Volatility	Risk Premium
T-Bills	6.80%	2.66%	NA
G Bonds	10.20%	11.80%	3.40%
Real estate	10.22%	9.92%	3.42%
Stock (S&P 500)	14.68%	16.21%	7.88%

Source: NCREIF, Ibbotson Assoc. data as modified by the authors in Exhibit 7-8 (see Sect. 7.2.2 in Ch. 7).

too radically different from the past, so historical results such as those in Exhibit 11-3 do provide some information relevant to forming current expectations.

Another perspective from the historical information can be gained by examining the risk directly, rather than the average returns. Recall that data on historical periodic returns allows us to compute the historical **volatility**, which is often viewed as an indication of the amount of risk in an investment.[21] Exhibit 11-3 suggests that a large portfolio of institutional commercial properties would have displayed a volatility somewhat more than half that of a diversified investment in the stock market during the 1970–98 period. This suggests that real estate was more than half as risky as the S&P 500 stock index, at least if we measure risk by portfolio volatility. This approximately agrees with the way professional investors typically respond to surveys that ask them questions such as, How risky would you say real estate is relative to the stock market? During the 1980s and 1990s the answers to this question typically suggested that investors viewed real estate as having between one half and two thirds of the stock market risk.[22]

If such relative risk perceptions are stable over time, this suggests that investors would generally want to be able to expect an *ex ante* risk premium for institutional quality real estate investments equal to about one-half that for large capitalization stock investments. This roughly agrees with the historical *ex post* real estate risk premium we observed during the 1970–98 period.

The specific number we have estimated here, 8.5%, is less important than the reasoning process it reveals. We have used historical market-based information, together with common sense and current perceptions, to make a judgment about the *relative* risk of real estate compared to other asset classes. We combined this with information about reasonable expected returns from those other asset classes. Based on this, we developed our estimate of what is a reasonable current return expectation for real estate, going forward.[23] This type of reasoning will never give a precise or definitive answer, but it is a rational process for putting some plausible bounds on the correct OCC, at least at a broad-brush level. In short, it is a useful exercise.

The problem of estimating the OCC is made more interesting by the way things change over time. For example, risk relationships may not be stable over time, either

---

[21] Finance theory argues that the volatility of an asset is not a good measure of the risk that investors care about because investors can diversify their holdings to eliminate much of this volatility. Instead, investors may care only about the "covariance" (or comovement) between the asset and some broad index of wealth or welfare, such as national consumption, because such comovement cannot be diversified away for the typical investor. However, volatility is still a good *relative* measure of risk for any assets that tend to have about the same correlation with such a broad wealth index.

[22] Recall that the real estate volatility indicated in Exhibit 7-8 (and 11-3) is corrected for "appraisal smoothing." Without this correction, the real estate volatility would be a bit less, around 7% instead of 10%, as measured by annual returns. This still indicates a volatility around one-half that of large capitalization stocks. We will discuss appraisal smoothing and other considerations regarding real estate periodic returns data in Part VII.

[23] In the previous exercise we compared T-bills and stocks to real estate. We might also have used long-term bonds. As noted, the ex post historical risk premium in long-term bonds was similar to that in unlevered institutional quality commercial property equity during the 1970–98 period. By the late 1990s long-term government bond yields were down to around 6%, considerably below our 8.5% estimate for real estate. However, most investors perceive real estate as being more risky than government bonds. The ex post bond performance during 1970–98 may reflect particular historical circumstances during that period, such as abnormally high inflation risk during the early part of that period, and declining interest rates driving ex post bond returns above their ex ante expectations during the latter part of the period.

in empirical statistics or in investors' subjective perceptions. There is much evidence that investors' expected risk premiums change over time, and that these changes are responsible for much of the volatility and value changes in asset markets. When investors are relatively "bullish," they tend to require relatively small risk premiums in their investment return expectations, which drives up asset values. (Keep in mind the inverse relationship between asset values and ex ante returns.) Thus, contrary to popular intuition, when assets are valued relatively highly (as evidenced, for example, by high price/earnings multiples), there are usually relatively low total return expectations going forward.[24]

Other relevant evidence comes from the yield curve in the bond market. The yield curve reflects the current difference between the ex ante return expectations on long-term versus short-term government bonds. Usually the yield curve is slightly upward-sloping, with long-term bond yields 100 to 200 basis points above short-term bond yields. But sometimes it is steeply upward-sloping, with a spread more like 300 to 400 basis points. When the yield curve is steeply upward-sloping, real estate risk premiums are more likely to be higher, measured as a spread over T-bills. After all, real estate assets are long-lived, while T-bills are short-term. A steep yield curve often corresponds to a weak current economy and low current demand for capital, factors often associated with depressed real estate prices. But the steep upward slope of the curve implies that the capital markets are expecting better times in the future, which suggests greater than average price appreciation for real estate assets going forward. For example, the early 1990s were characterized by a steep upward-sloping yield curve, and also by relatively high ex ante risk premiums in real estate looking forward from that time (which corresponded to the bottom of the real estate cycle).

11.2.3 Another Perspective: Survey Evidence

In such a changing world, one way to get an idea about investors' expected returns on real estate investments is simply to *ask them*, at frequent intervals. Several national real estate information firms regularly survey the investment community and publish the average stated returns investors say they expect going forward. In addition, brokerage and appraisal firms, as well as commercial mortgage underwriters, usually have a working familiarity with the discount rates that are currently being used for specific types of property in specific types of locations.

The results of a widely used national survey of investor return expectations, presented in Exhibit 11-4 for the 1992–98 period, will serve to illustrate this type of survey-based evidence about investor return expectations. Exhibit 11-4 shows the reported values of the Korpacz Yield Indicator (KYI), a national survey-based measure of professional investors' expected total returns (free-and-clear going-in IRRs) on unlevered investments in institutional quality commercial property.[25]

The KYI pertains to the same types of property, and is based on the same types of investors, as the **NCREIF Property Index (NPI)** we considered previously for the

---

[24] This is obvious in the current yield component of the return, as high price/earnings multiples imply low current yields. But the total return will also be relatively low unless *realistic* earnings growth expectations are abnormally high.

[25] The KYI is published quarterly in the *Korpacz Real Estate Investor Survey*, by the Korpacz Company, Inc., Frederick, MD. Similar information is published by other firms.

Exhibit 11-4 Backward-Looking versus Forward-Looking Total Returns in the Property Market: NCREIF versus Korpacz

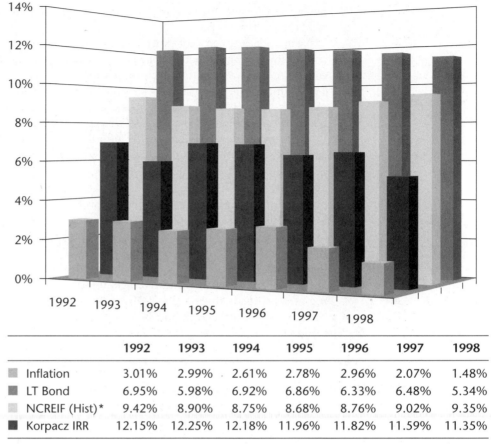

	1992	1993	1994	1995	1996	1997	1998
Inflation	3.01%	2.99%	2.61%	2.78%	2.96%	2.07%	1.48%
LT Bond	6.95%	5.98%	6.92%	6.86%	6.33%	6.48%	5.34%
NCREIF (Hist)*	9.42%	8.90%	8.75%	8.68%	8.76%	9.02%	9.35%
Korpacz IRR	12.15%	12.25%	12.18%	11.96%	11.82%	11.59%	11.35%

*All indicators are for current year except NCREIF, which is cumulative average return since inception in 1977.

historical record. For purposes of comparison, Exhibit 11-4 also shows the historical cumulative average annual total return to the NPI since its inception (at the end of 1977) up to each year indicated in the exhibit. Thus, in Exhibit 11-4 the KYI indicates that investors stated *expected* returns as of the year indicated, while the NPI indicates actual average *ex post* property performance as of that same year (since 1978). The KYI is forward looking and subjective; the NPI is backward looking and objective. Exhibit 11-4 also shows current long-term government bond yields, and the current inflation rate, as of each year. The bond yield, like the KYI, is a current ex ante measure, although the nature of bonds enables this to be an objective measure based on current bond market prices and the yields to maturity implied by those prices.

Several points bear noticing in Exhibit 11-4. One is the stability of the stated ex ante real estate returns from the survey. This is characteristic of survey-based measures of investors' stated return expectations. However, a stable expected total return does not necessarily imply a stable ex ante risk premium, as the riskfree interest rate varies over time. In fact, survey-based stated real estate returns for institutional investment remained near 12% for much longer than the period covered in Exhibit 11-4, reaching well back into the 1980s. During the early part of that period, Treasury Bills were typically yielding slightly over 8%, implying an ex ante real estate risk premium of around 300 to 400 basis points. By the early 1990s, with interest rates down to the 6% to 7% level, the stated 12% real estate return implied a risk premium of 500 to 600 basis points.

Thus, a nearly constant expected total return has not implied such a constant ex ante risk premium. This reported change in investors' required risk premium was broadly consistent with commercial real estate's temporary "fall from favor" during the early 1990s among the major institutional investors who had supported the real estate bull market of the 1980s. The same types of investors who were satisfied with a 300-basis-point risk premium in the mid-1980s required almost twice that by the early 1990s.

Other aspects of the data reported in Exhibit 11-4 raise questions about the realism of the subjective returns investors state in surveys, however, at least at some points in time. For example, the KYI appears to be consistently at least 200 basis points higher than the objective evidence about real estate total return performance provided by the NPI. Of course, the NPI is backward-looking history, while the KYI is forward-looking expectations, so the two need not equate exactly. Nevertheless, by the mid-1990s the NPI covered an entire property market cycle, including bull markets in the early 1980s and late 90s as well as the bear market of the early 1990s. Furthermore, the historical period covered by the NPI return in Exhibit 11-4 was characterized by much higher average inflation than investors were generally expecting going forward during the 1990s. Thus, measured on a real basis (net of inflation), the gap between the KYI and NPI would be even wider.[26] It also seems difficult to reconcile the stability of the KYI with the fall in interest rates and rise in property values during the late 1990s.

11.2.4 Getting an Indication of Total Return Expectations by Observing Current Cap Rates in the Property Market

It seems likely that investors tend to put on rose-tinted glasses when they publicly state the expected returns they have for their real estate investments, at least sometimes. A 12% return sounds nicer than a 10% return. Realistic ex ante IRRs are very difficult to observe directly or empirically. Thus, both historical return statistics and contemporary survey measures have their drawbacks (although both are useful). Fortunately, there is a third way to get an idea about investor ex ante return expectations.

It is easier to observe empirically the cap rates (or current yields) at which properties trade in the market than it is to observe the ex ante total returns investors are expecting. All you need to observe cap rates empirically is information about transaction prices and the likely net operating income (NOI) of the traded properties. Because of this, investors polled in surveys may tend to state their going-in cap rate expectations more realistically than their going-in IRRs. Or you can compute your own estimate of current average cap rates if you have access to transaction price data.

The cap rate is not the same as the going-in IRR we need for the DCF denominators. But the cap rate and the IRR are closely related, as noted in Chapter 10. In particular, at least as an approximation, we can invoke the **constant-growth perpetuity**

---

[26] For example, the average annual inflation during 1978–98 was 4.6%. During the late 1990s investors' ex ante annual inflation expectations were typically down to around 3%, which was still slightly above the actual current inflation rate during this period. If we subtract a 3% inflation expectation from the 1998 KYI, we get an implied ex ante real return expectation of 8.35%. If we subtract the historical 1978–98 inflation from the 1978–98 average annual NPI return of 9.35%, we get an average ex post real return performance of only 4.75% per year, 360 basis points below investors' 1998 stated ex ante expectation in real terms.

model (introduced in Chapter 8). Recall that this implies that the current yield equals the long-run expected total return minus the long-run expected average growth rate in the property net cash flow. Turning this relationship around, we can derive at least an approximate indication of the expected *total* return (or discount rate) from observations about current cap rates, by adding realistic growth expectations onto the cap rates:

$$E[r] = E[y] + E[g] \approx (Cap\ rate) + E[g]$$

With this in mind, Exhibit 11-5 presents both IRR and cap rate information from the Korpacz survey. Stated cap rates, as indicated by the reported **OAR (over-all rate)** are even more stable than the stated IRR expectations. The differences between the stated OAR and IRR expectations closely match the contemporaneous inflation rates. According to the approximate relationship in the previous equation, $E[r] - (Cap\ rate) \approx E[g]$. Thus, Exhibit 11-5 suggests that investors typically avow going-in IRRs and cap rates that imply that they expect property cash flow and value to grow, going forward on average over the long run, at the current rate of inflation. Yet such expectations would not generally be realistic, for the reasons we have noted previously, as buildings age and depreciate in real terms, resulting generally in long-run growth rates lower than inflation.[27]

Let us suppose now that the cap rate expectations stated in the Korpacz survey are reasonably realistic, as they are probably based on empirically observable cap rates for typical transactions that occur in the current property market. This implies that the rose-tinted glasses are being applied to the stated total returns, the IRR expectations, not to the cap rates. Accordingly, we can modify the stated IRR expectations downward to reflect more realistic growth expectations on top of the stated OAR expectations. This suggests that we trim 100 to 300 basis points off the KYI during the 1990s to reflect realistic depreciation and/or capital expenditures. This would imply realistic ex ante IRRs during the 1990s averaging around 10% for the types of institutional quality commercial property covered by the Korpacz survey.[28]

The technique we applied to the OAR numbers in Exhibit 11-5 can be applied generally wherever the "current typically prevailing" cap rates can be observed for a property asset market. By adding *realistic* long-run growth expectations onto the cap rates (net of average capital expenditures), one can arrive at a realistic indication of the

---

[27] If the OARs reported in the Korpacz survey are not net of a realistic average annual reserve for capital expenditures (as cap rates are often defined on NOI before such a reserve is removed), then the previously described discrepancy is only exacerbated. As noted, realistic capital improvement expenditures over the long run typically average at least 100 to 200 basis points of property value per year. If the OARs investors are thinking of when they report their expectations are not net of such reserves, then the equivalent true net cash yield expectations ($E[y]$) would be at least 100 to 200 basis points *below* the OARs shown in Exhibit 11-5, implying that much larger gap between the current yield and the stated IRR total return expectations.

[28] It seems likely that realistic ex ante total returns to commercial property were trending generally downward during most of the 1990s. They were probably typically at least one or two points higher than 10% during the early part of the decade when construction was at a standstill (implying greater-than-average rent and value growth potential going forward from that point in time for existing properties), and the perception of real estate risk was heightened in the aftermath of the commercial property crash (implying higher-than-average ex ante risk premiums). By the end of the decade, realistic going-in IRRs were probably at least one or two points lower than 10%, as long-term government bond yields fell below 6% and large-scale construction of new space had resumed in many markets.

Exhibit 11-5 Stated
Going-in IRRs, Cap Rates,
and Inflation

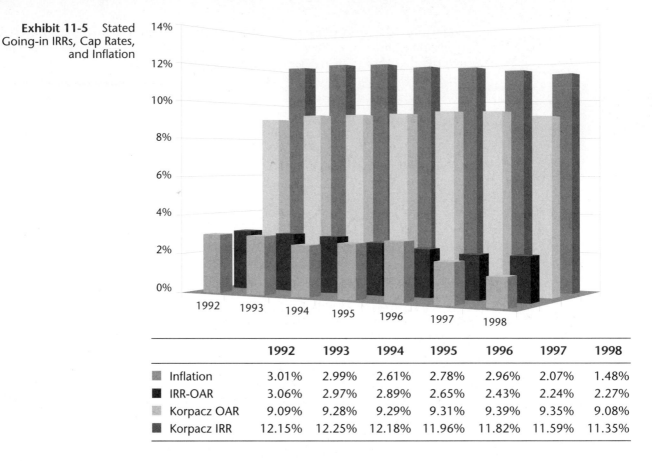

	1992	**1993**	**1994**	**1995**	**1996**	**1997**	**1998**
Inflation	3.01%	2.99%	2.61%	2.78%	2.96%	2.07%	1.48%
IRR-OAR	3.06%	2.97%	2.89%	2.65%	2.43%	2.24%	2.27%
Korpacz OAR	9.09%	9.28%	9.29%	9.31%	9.39%	9.35%	9.08%
Korpacz IRR	12.15%	12.25%	12.18%	11.96%	11.82%	11.59%	11.35%

currently prevailing long-run total return expectations for the type of property in question.[29] This is the opportunity cost of capital for investment in such property, at least from the current perspective of the property asset market in which such assets are trading, and therefore the appropriate discount rate to employ to estimate market values by the DCF procedure.

11.2.5 Variation in Return Expectations for Different Types of Property

The preceding section gave some idea about how to quantify realistic discount rates at a broad-brush level, that is, for typical **institutional quality commercial property**. This has traditionally been considered to include large, fully operational, income-producing properties of high-quality construction in high-quality locations (so-called

---

[29] If the observed cap rates are defined based on NOI, before subtracting realistic average capital expenditures, then the growth rate to add onto the thusly defined cap rate should be low enough to reflect NOI and property value growth without capital improvements. Alternatively, if the observed cap rates are defined based on property net cash flow after subtracting realistic capital expenditures, then the growth rate to add onto this smaller cap rate can be correspondingly higher, reflecting the value-preserving and value-enhancing effects of capital improvements on the property. In principle, both of these two approaches should end up giving the same total return expectation.

class A or premium properties). But, as different types of commercial property have different amounts of investment risk, the appropriate discount rate should differ accordingly across property types. In this regard, the type and location of the property, though not to be ignored, is generally less important than two other dimensions that govern the perceived ex ante risk and return of the property: the *size* of the property (as measured by its value) and its operational or life cycle status.

As far as perceived risk and return are concerned, "large" properties may be defined as those that typically interest major institutional equity investors. For example, by the late 1990s the average individual property in the NCREIF index was worth close to $30 million. Large institutions (including REITs) are the primary equity investors in such properties, and these institutions have traditionally perceived such properties, when they are "fully operational" (that is, fully leased, or nearly so), as being relatively low risk. As many of these institutions tend to be conservative regarding their risk preferences, such properties are viewed as real estate investment **portfolio core properties.** Smaller, older, or less fully utilized properties, as well as development or redevelopment projects, have traditionally been viewed as being more risky by these investors and as such are often referred to as noninstitutional or noncore properties.[30]

Exhibits 11-6a and b show the typical differences in expected total returns and cap rates across different types of commercial property in the late 1990s, once again based on the Korpacz survey. Notice that the differences across property markets (defined by property type and geographic location) are generally rather minor, and less than the difference between the institutional and noninstitutional property classes. Expected returns and stated cap rates for noninstitutional properties are typically at least 100 to 200 basis points greater than those for otherwise similar institutional properties. This difference reflects a greater ex ante risk premium applied by investors in noninstitutional property.

There is some debate as to whether this differential in risk premiums is justified by the actual difference in the amount of investment risk. It is not clear, for example, why size per se should affect the risk. On the other hand, properties that are less fully occupied, or in need of major development or redevelopment investment, or that are occupied by tenants that are less creditworthy, will clearly carry greater uncertainty about the range or volatility in their future net cash flow generation potential.[31]

It also seems likely that the private property asset markets are somewhat **segmented,** or characterized by different investor **clienteles.** Smaller-scale individual investors tend to dominate the asset market for noninstitutional properties, while large financial institutions and REITs dominate in the institutional asset market. These different investor clientele may have different risk perceptions and preferences. For example, small investors may not be able to diversify their portfolios as well as large institutions can, exposing them to more risk from property investments.

---

[30]Institutions may still invest in such noninstitutional properties, but they are often considered as opportunistic investments, aimed at earning high returns. Recognizing the higher risk, such investments usually receive relatively small allocations of capital compared to the core real estate portfolio.

[31]This is not just greater purely random volatility. It is likely that the greater downside in noninstitutional property would tend to coincide temporally with slumps in the macroeconomy, while the upside would coincide with economic booms. Thus, it may be difficult to fully diversify away the added risk in noninstitutional property. A similar effect is noted in the so-called small-cap and the book/market equity ratio factors in the stock market. Small stocks and those with relatively high book/market equity ratios tend to require higher expected returns, on average. This issue is discussed in more depth in Chapter 22.

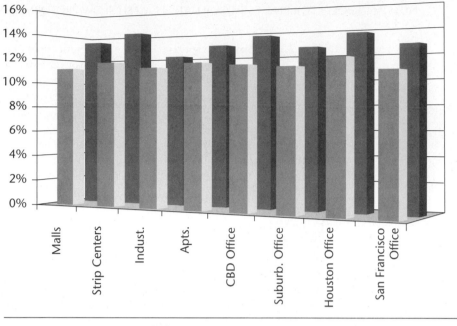

Exhibit 11-6a Investor Total Return Expectations (IRR) for Various Property Types (Source: Korpacz Investor Survey, 1st quarter 1999.)

	Malls	Strip Centers	Indust.	Apts.	CBD Office	Suburb. Office	Houston Office	San Francisco Office
▪ Institutional	11.14%	11.61%	11.14%	11.48%	11.28%	11.11%	11.78%	10.71%
▪ Noninstitutional	13.50%	14.20%	12.18%	13.01%	13.69%	12.73%	13.75%	12.46%

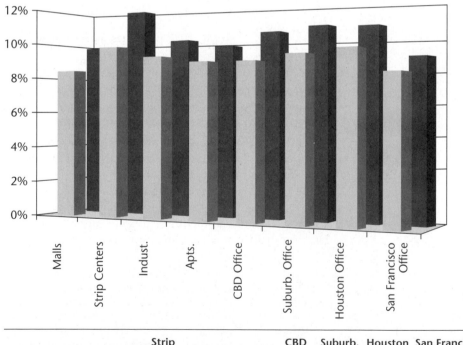

Exhibit 11-6b Investor Cap Rate Expectations for Various Property Types (Source: Korpacz Investor Survey, 1st quarter 1999.)

	Malls	Strip Centers	Indust.	Apts.	CBD Office	Suburb. Office	Houston Office	San Francisco Office
▪ Institutional	8.41%	9.76%	9.14%	8.83%	8.82%	9.17%	9.43%	8.42%
▪ Noninstitutional	9.88%	11.97%	10.21%	9.83%	10.56%	10.83%	10.75%	9.58%

If this is so, and the typical clientele investors are the marginal investors in each market segment, then asset market prices in that segment will reflect each clientele's risk perceptions and preferences. This could explain higher expected returns for noninstitutional properties.

Certain types of property investments are traditionally considered more risky than the major core types of commercial properties portrayed in Exhibit 11-6. For example, hotel properties, especially if they are not luxury hotels in prime locations, will typically command risk premiums 100 to 300 basis points above those of the four major core property types (office, industrial, retail, and apartment). In part, this may be due to the lack of leases governing their rents. At the extreme for real estate return expectations (on unlevered investments), raw land is reputed to command total return expectations typically in the 15% to 30% range. Such real estate generally produces little or no current positive cash flow, and its value depends entirely on the NPV of future construction that can be built on it. As noted in Part II, this gives raw land investment performance characteristics like those of call options, similar to that of a highly levered investment in the underlying asset (the future building on the site).

11.3 CHAPTER SUMMARY

Chapter 11 put the flesh on the bones of the microlevel investment valuation framework laid out in Chapter 10, by getting down to the specifics of cash flow projection and discount rate determination in the DCF process. Keep in mind that at this level of specificity, things change over time, and each deal must be considered anew. Nevertheless, in this chapter we tried to present a way of approaching the quantification of real estate valuation parameters, and showed how to characterize realistic default assumptions. The burden of proof lies with those who claim assumptions significantly different from these.

KEY TERMS

proforma
operating cash flows
reversion cash flows
potential gross income (PGI)
rent roll
rent comps analysis
vacancy allowance
effective gross income (EGI)
other income
operating expenses
property management opportunity
   cost
fixed and variable costs
net leases

expense stops
net operating income (NOI)
capital improvement expenditures
tenant improvement expenditures
   (TIs)
concessions
property-before-tax cash flow
   (PBTCF)
reversion cap rate
going-out cap rate
terminal cap rate
going-in IRR
stabilized cap rate
discount rate

riskfree rate
opportunity cost of capital (OCC)
risk premium
ex post and ex ante risk premiums
volatility
NCREIF property index (NPI)
constant-growth perpetuity model
overall rate (OAR)
institutional quality commercial
   property
portfolio core properties
capital market segments and
   clienteles

STUDY QUESTIONS

11.1. Define the net operating income (NOI) for commercial real estate assets (formula), and state the three typical recipients of this cash flow.

11.2. What is the difference between the net operating income and the property's before-tax cash flow?

11.3. Consider the projection of the reversion value in a multiyear DCF valuation.

   a. What should be the typical expected relationship between the going-in cap rate and the going-out (reversion or terminal value) cap rate projected for the resale of the property at the end of the expected holding period (i.e., should you usually expect the going-out to be less than, equal to, or greater than the going-in)?

   b. Why?

   c. How is your answer related to projected capital improvement expenditures during the holding period?

   d. How is your answer related to the state of the property market at the time of purchase of the property at the beginning of the holding period (factors that affect the going-in rate)?

11.4. What items should be included in the operating expenses but taken out before computing the property NOI?

11.5. Why should you subtract management expenses before determining the property NOI even if you are managing the property yourself?

11.6. Show a 10-year proforma projection of the operating NOI and net property-before-tax cash flow (PBTCF) for a three-unit apartment house in which (a) each unit currently (year 1) rents for $300/month; (b) rents are projected to grow at 3% per year; (c) the average tenant will remain three years, and then the apartment will be vacant an average of three months before the next tenant moves in; (d) operating expenses are currently estimated at $1,500 per unit per year (including management expenses), expected to escalate at 3% per year; (e) you anticipate needing to replace kitchen appliances for $1,000 per unit in year 3; and (f) you anticipate having to replace the shingle roof for $2,500 in year 5.

11.7. A 150,000-SF office building has a triple-net lease providing a constant rent of $20/SF per year. (With a triple-net lease you can assume the rent equals the net operating cash flow.) The lease has five years before it expires (i.e., assume the next payment comes in one year, and there are four more annual payments after that under the present lease). Rents on similar leases being signed today are $22/SF. You expect rents on new leases to grow at 2.5% per year for existing buildings. You expect to release the building in year six after the current lease expires, but only after experiencing an expected vacancy of six months, and after spending $10/SF in tenant improvements (TIs). After 10 years you expect to sell the building at a price equal to 10 times the then-prevailing rent in new triple-net leases. Based on survey information about typical going-in IRRs prevailing currently in the market for this type of property, you think the market would require a 12% expected return for this building.

   a. What is the NPV of an investment in this property if the price is $30 million? Should you do the deal?

     b. What will be the IRR at that price?

     c. What is the cap rate at the $30 million price?

11.8. Consider the building described in question 11.7. Suppose everything is the same except that, since the time the current lease was signed, the market for office space has softened. Rents on new leases are lower now and will only be $18/SF next year instead of the $20/SF that prevailed when the current lease was signed. Furthermore, suppose that the current lease has only one more year until it expires, instead of five. You expect to release in year 2, and again in year 7, with six months of vacancy and $10 in capital expenditures each time, as before. You still expect growth of 2.5% per year in new-lease rental rates, starting from the expected year-1 level of $18.

     a. What is the value of the property under the required return assumption of question 11.7?

     b. What would be the NPV of the deal from the buyer's perspective if the owner wants to sell the building at a cap rate of 10% based on the existing lease?

     c. What would be the cap rate for this building at the zero-NPV price?

     d. Why is the market value cap rate so different in this case than in the case presented in question 11.7?

12 Advanced Microlevel Valuation

Chapter Outline

12.1 **Market Value and Investment Value**
12.1.1 How to Measure Investment Value
12.1.2 Joint Use of IV and MV in Decision Making
12.1.3 Watch Out for the IV Sales Pitch
12.1.4 Marginal and Intramarginal Investors: How to Get Positive NPV
12.2 **Danger and Opportunity in Market Inefficiency**
12.2.1 Valuation Noise
12.2.2 Asset Market Predictability
*12.3 **Dueling Asset Markets: REIT Market versus Property Market**
12.3.1 Valuation at the Microlevel
12.3.2 Microlevel Differential Valuation: Cash Flow Expectations
12.3.3 Microlevel Differential Valuation: Opportunity Cost of Capital
12.3.4 What about Informational Efficiency?
12.3.5 Microlevel Risk Is in the Property, Not in the REIT
12.3.6 Summarizing the Dueling Markets: Going from the Micro to the Macro Perspective
12.4 **Chapter Summary**

Chapter 12 Appendix: Basic Valuation Concepts: Transaction Prices and Market Values

Learning Objectives

After reading this chapter, you should understand:

◆ The difference between investment value (IV) and market value (MV), and how to use both of these concepts in real estate investment decision making.

◆ The circumstances that make substantially positive NPV investment opportunities realistic.

◆ The investment implications of a lack of informational efficiency in the real estate asset market.

◆ The implications, for investors at the microlevel, of the simultaneous existence of two types or levels of real estate asset markets: the property market and the REIT market.

◆ The difference between firm-level REIT cost of capital and the microlevel opportunity cost of capital applicable to REIT valuation of individual properties at the microlevel.

Chapters 10 and 11 introduced you to the basics of doing investment analysis and evaluation at the microlevel of individual deals, or transactions, involving commercial property. The material presented there is essentially standard corporate finance and investments fare applied to real estate. However, to be a more sophisticated user of such methods in the real estate arena, you should be aware of some additional issues and concepts relating to the unique situation of real estate.

In particular, the commercial real estate investment environment has three salient characteristics that differ from the typical corporate capital budgeting environment or the typical securities investment environment, the focus of most mainstream finance textbooks.

1. Unlike the typical corporate environment, a well-functioning market usually exists for the underlying physical assets that are being considered, namely, commercial buildings (as opposed to, say, assembly lines or microchip plants).

2. Although the commercial real estate asset market is a well-functioning market, it is not as informationally efficient as the market for publicly traded securities, such as the stock market in which most industrial corporations trade (and in which REITs trade as well).

3. In addition to the private real estate asset market, there also exists a large market for publicly traded REIT shares in the stock exchange. Thus, parallel asset markets, or two levels of asset markets, are both relevant for real estate investment.

The major issues raised by these three differences are the subject of the present chapter. These are rather subtle issues, relating to basic economic and valuation theory, and their subtlety makes them worthy of advanced students, such as yourselves. So, fasten your seatbelts!

12.1 MARKET VALUE AND INVESTMENT VALUE

Up to now, we have been defining and measuring NPV on the basis of the market value of the assets involved in the deal, with market value defined as the expected price at which the assets would sell in the current real estate market. We noted that such a definition of NPV is possible because of the existence of the property market. Now we need to think about this in a little more depth.

In some sense, we have been treating real estate asset values in much the same way as stock market analysts treat stock values.[1] But investors in stocks can buy and sell very quickly and easily, at very low transaction costs, without assuming any management burden of the assets they are purchasing. As a result, stock market investors typically hold onto a given stock for a relatively short period of time. On the other hand, when you buy a commercial property, it is typically something you are investing in for the long haul.

In this respect, real estate investing is more like corporate capital budgeting than it is like stock market investing. Corporations make decisions to allocate their capital to long-lived projects to produce real goods and services over a long period of time, such as a new steel mill or chemical plant. But the corporate capital budgeting situation is a bit different from the real estate situation, too, for the previously noted reason that there is typically no well-functioning market for the underlying assets in which the corporation is investing.

Because real estate straddles these two worlds (securities investments and corporate capital budgeting), we need to be careful in how we apply the classical principles and methodologies developed in these two fields. In this regard, the first thing we must do is pursue the concept of *value* in a bit more depth.

---

[1] The stock market analogy helps us to see why the NPV of a typical deal is zero. When investors buy and sell stocks, such trading is not generally perceived as involving positive or negative NPV for the participants.

To begin, let us be clear what we mean by **market value** (which we will sometimes abbreviate as **MV**), and why this concept is important and useful in real estate investment analysis. Market value is the *expected price* at which the asset can be sold in the current property market. In other words, if we put a property up for sale, we don't know for sure exactly what price we can get. It depends in part on who we find as an opposite party in the deal. We may find someone who is particularly enthusiastic about the property, or, on the other hand, we may end up having to deal with a really tough negotiator. The market price can be thought of as the most likely price at which we will do a deal, prior to a deal actually being done. It is the ex ante expectation (or the mean of the probability distribution) of the possible prices.[2]

As thusly defined, the market value is a very important and useful measure of value because it reflects the opportunity cost or **opportunity value** of the investment in the asset. That is, any investor has the ability at any time to either purchase or sell the asset for a price close to its market value (and with the actual ex post transaction price as likely to be above as below the market value). In effect, as well as any single number can represent, the investor gives up the opportunity to retain or receive the MV in cash when she decides instead to purchase or continue holding the asset.

Although market value, and an NPV estimation based on MV, is always useful and of fundamental importance in decision making, one can conceptually define and measure commercial property value another way, and calculate an NPV based on this second concept of value. This second definition of value is what is referred to in the real estate profession as the **investment value** (which we will sometimes abbreviate as **IV**).[3] The investment value of a property is its value *to a particular owner*, who would be owning and operating the asset *for a long period of time*, and explicitly not planning to sell the asset for a long period of time. As IV is defined with respect to a specified investor, and investors differ in their ability to generate and use future cash flow and value from the asset, so IV values may differ for different investors for the same asset as of the same point in time. In contrast, the MV is, in principle, the same for a given asset for all investors as of a given point in time.[4] In rough terms, you can think of the distinction between MV and IV as follows:

MV = *What you can sell the asset for today*
IV = *What the asset is worth to you if you don't sell it for a long time*

[2] The concept of market value also must entail a commitment to sell (or buy) the property reasonably quickly, regardless of the current market conditions. Otherwise, we could make MV out to be unrealistically high (or low), and just say we will wait as long as it takes to find someone willing to pay (or accept) that price. In effect, we would be saying that we will wait until the *market moves* in our favor. This would be analogous to a stock market investor placing a limit order to sell (buy) a given stock at a specified price above (below) the current market price of the stock. The real estate concept of MV is meant to be analogous to the market price of the stock, not some investor's limit order price.

[3] Investment value is especially well defined in the appraisal profession, where it is closely related to such other definitions of value as inherent value or usage value. The appraisal industry distinguishes these concepts carefully from those of market value or exchange value. Another term sometimes used in a manner similar to investment value is intrinsic value. Like inherent value, intrinsic value highlights the value placed on real property by users of the property, in contrast to investment value, which highlights more explicitly the value of the property for a non-user owner. However, there is considerable overlap in meaning across all the "i" valuation concepts: inherent, intrinsic, and investment. (See the appendix at the end of the chapter for further elaboration on concepts of value.)

[4] Although two people may disagree in their estimate of MV, conceptually only one true MV exists at any given time.

In classical corporate capital budgeting, because there is typically no well-functioning market for the underlying physical assets, IV is the *only* way one can measure the value of these assets, and the only basis on which one can calculate the NPV of proposed projects.[5] In real estate, the property market enables the MV perspective also to be quantified (for individual physical assets). However, we can still define the IV perspective for real estate deals as well. Indeed, some real estate deals involve assets or financial arrangements so unique that it would be very difficult to estimate accurately the relevant market values. Even when we can estimate MV accurately, the IV perspective is still relevant to investment decision making in real estate, as we will see in the following sections.

12.1.1 How to Measure Investment Value

In quantifying investment value, one should use the same multiperiod DCF technique described in Chapters 10 and 11. Indeed, in practice the multiperiod perspective is often more important in quantifying IV than MV. Although, in principle, multiperiod DCF analysis underlies the determination of MV at a fundamental level, estimating the current MV for a given type of property may often be done by the shortcut of simply observing the transaction prices of similar assets. But IV, which is based on the assumption of a long-term holding of the asset, can only be determined by going through a full long-term projection of net cash flows.[6]

Because IV is specific to a particular owner or user of the asset, the cash flows should reflect how that owner or user would manage and operate the asset, as well as the particular owner/user's income tax situation. Thus, the actual cash flow amounts forecasted on the right-hand side of the DCF formula may differ from one investor to another in computing IV. In principle, the investor's after-tax cash flows are discounted at market after-tax discount rates.[7]

In theory, the discount rate applied in the denominators of the DCF calculation may also differ from one investor to another in the computation of IV. However, care must be taken not to abuse this theoretical possibility in practice. Discount rates for computing IV should not be "pulled from the air" or made up on an ad hoc basis on the claim that a given investor has "unique risk preferences." Remember that discount rates reflect the time value of money and the price of risk. All investors have access to the capital markets, and so all investors face the prices of time and risk available in that market. Going beyond the market in this regard is stepping out on very soft sand.[8] Therefore, even when we are computing IV, discount rates should still reflect

---

[5] In classical capital budgeting theory it is assumed that IV at the level of the corporation's underlying assets will be reflected rapidly in the MV of the corporation's stock, due to the informational efficiency of the stock market. Thus, for a publicly traded firm, IV at the level of the firm is traditionally taken to be virtually equivalent to MV at the level of the firm's investors. While this classical conception ignores such issues as asymmetric information between managers and investors, it probably provides a useful approximation of reality for most publicly traded firms most of the time (including REITs).

[6] An exception to the need for a long horizon in the analysis sometimes occurs in the case of raw land and development projects. It is sometimes appropriate for an IV analysis horizon to end with a projected sale of the completed new structure.

[7] Income tax considerations will be treated in more depth in Part V.

[8] For example, to apply a "personalized" risk premium, in principle it is necessary to quantify the investor's utility function or risk preferences, given his overall wealth portfolio and consumption patterns. Such analysis is rare in practice and usually considered beyond the reasonable scope of the definition of investment value. Indeed, for an investment entity that has more than one individual owner, there is fundamental theoretical ambiguity about how to aggregate preferences across the different owners.

an **opportunity cost of capital (OCC)** based essentially on the capital market. Thus, we should always analyze the capital market (including the property market) in order to determine the relevant price of risk and time value of money.

In practice, the best policy is usually to limit the use of personalized risk premiums to the situation in which the given investor would (realistically) operate the subject property in a unique way, so that its cash flows would be perceived *by the capital market* to be of different risk than that of the typical operation of such a property. Such a situation is rare and difficult to quantify with rigor. Thus, the main focus in questions of IV differing from MV should normally be on the numerators of the DCF valuation, the expected future cash flow generation, rather than on the denominators.[9]

12.1.2 Joint Use of IV and MV in Decision Making

As it is common in real estate to be able to compute reasonable estimates of both IV and MV, we need to consider how these two perspectives of value relate to each other in making rational investment decisions. The basic principle is to apply the NPV decision rule to the NPV computed *both* ways. In other words, an acceptable deal will have to pass the **NPV investment criterion** both when the NPV is computed on the basis of MV and when the NPV is computed on the basis of IV. Recall from Chapter 10 that the NPV criterion requires the maximization of NPV across mutually exclusive alternatives, and the absolute avoidance of negative-NPV deals.

For a typical deal, the NPV from an IV perspective will simply equal IV minus MV if you are buying (or holding) the asset, and MV minus IV if you are selling the asset. This is because the asset can be expected to be bought or sold for the MV amount, by definition. Although IV in principle differs from one investor to another, if the two investors on the opposite sides of a deal are similar in their ability to use and profit from the asset over the long run, then their IVs will be similar. In this case the previous point implies that the NPV of successfully consummated deals between similar types of investors will typically be approximately zero both from the IV and MV perspectives. This also implies that IV and MV will be approximately equal in such situations.[10]

---

[9] In traditional corporate capital budgeting the investment decision-making entity is a publicly traded corporation, acting on behalf of its shareholders. In such circumstances the derivation of the appropriate discount rates purely from the capital market is obvious, because the capital market will determine the corporation's share price, and hence its shareholders' wealth impact of any corporate investment decisions, based on the market for the firm's equity shares. This same argument applies in real estate to the case of investment by publicly traded entities such as REITs. However, in real estate investment, property assets can be held directly by individuals or private entities. It is in such circumstances that personalized IV discount rates can be contemplated, at least theoretically. For example, a private investor whose personal wealth is uniquely and necessarily tied to Chicago apartment property may place a low investment value on the purchase of an additional Chicago apartment due to its failure to provide any diversification in her constrained portfolio. In effect, an additional Chicago apartment is a more risky investment to her than to the typical investor. However, such considerations are normally addressed at the macrolevel of investment strategy, as part of the investor's portfolio policy, as they are difficult to quantify at the microlevel of investment in terms of the investment value of specific assets. (Portfolio theory will be addressed in Part VII.)

[10] The seller is requiring $NPV = MV - IV \geq 0$. The buyer is requiring $NPV = IV - MV \geq 0$. The only mutually acceptable solution (in which IV is the same for both parties) is $IV = MV$, at which point $NPV = 0$ for both parties.

Although deals between similar types of investors will typically have NPV near zero from both the MV and IV perspectives, deals can have substantially positive (or negative) NPV when computed from the IV perspective. This could occur even though the deal is done at market value so that it has a zero NPV from the MV perspective. Indeed, a deal can produce a positive NPV for both sides of the transaction, due to unique circumstances affecting one or both parties. This is because IV is personal, in the sense that it relates to a specific owner or investor and is divorced from the market in the sense that the asset is presumed to be held off the market for a long period of time. In fact, finding situations in which the IV-based NPV is positive for both sides of the deal is one of the main objectives of much real estate investment activity.

Unique characteristics of the investor and the property, or the relationship between the two, can cause IV to differ from MV for a given investor. Let's look at an example. KrazyLoPrices Inc. Discount Warehouse has built a booming business at their store at 9999 Consumption Boulevard and is now in need of expansion space and more parking capacity. They would also hate to see their main competitor, EvenLowerPrices Ltd., open up one of their megastores across the street. In such a situation, the vacant lots adjacent to and across the street, at 9997 and 9998 Consumption Boulevard, are likely worth more to KrazyLo than they are to anyone else. In other words, IV > MV for those lots, for KrazyLo.

In general, when IV > MV, it makes sense to buy, build, or hold (whichever is relevant). On the other hand, when IV < MV, it makes sense to sell if you already own, and not to buy if you don't yet own the property, as would be the case, for example, if KrazyLo somehow lost its ability to make a profit at the Consumption Boulevard location.

Usually IV- and MV-based NPV calculations lead to consistent decision recommendations even when they differ in magnitude. However, if the IV and MV perspectives seem to lead to different recommendations, remember that the underlying objective is wealth-maximization, and apply *common sense*. For example, suppose project A has a higher IV-based NPV and project B has a higher MV-based NPV, but they both have nonnegative values for both ways of computing the NPV. Then it would generally be most logical to select whichever alternative has the overall highest NPV (that is, the higher of the two best NPVs), bearing in mind that realization of the IV-based NPV requires a long holding period.[11]

---

[11] Note that the risk involved in the slow realization of the wealth through the long holding or operational period has presumably already been fully accounted for in the discount rate employed to determine the IV-based NPV. Thus, we do not have a "one in the hand versus two in the bush" comparison here: the IV- and MV-based NPVs are in theory "apples-to-apples" comparisons of present wealth. As another example, suppose an investor has somehow obtained the opportunity to buy a property at a price that is clearly below market value. (Perhaps he holds some option or right-of-first-refusal.) Yet the unique circumstances of the property and this investor prevent this investor from being able to make good use of the property himself, so his acquisition of the property would be a negative-NPV deal from his own IV-based perspective. In this case common sense suggests that the investor should exercise his option to acquire the property at the below-market price, and then quickly sell it to (or enter into a joint venture with) another buyer who can make profitable use of the property at the market price. The IV perspective can be ignored here because the investor is not compelled to hold the property for the long term, and he can sell it in the market at a profit (net of transaction costs, presumably).

Always bear in mind the following implication of the basic principle that the NPV in any deal should generally make sense from both the IV and MV perspectives.

- *Avoid paying more than MV, even when your IV > MV.*
- *Avoid selling for less than MV, even when your IV < MV.*

Of course, the nature of MV is that it should be possible to either buy or sell at a price near MV. However, the "lumpiness" of real estate tends to qualify this rule in practice. Because of the uniqueness of properties and investors, a notion that is often used to help conceive of MV in real estate practice is that of the **second-most-motivated buyer**. The maximum price this buyer would be willing to pay (the IV to this buyer) is taken to be the MV for the property. The most motivated buyer is the one who has the highest IV for the property. For example, the most creative and entrepreneurial developer with the greatest expertise regarding how to use a given site can probably purchase that site for a positive NPV viewed from his own IV-based perspective. The IV of the site for this "best" developer is greater than it is for any other developer, and hence greater than the MV of the site.

If there is not much uniqueness in the property or the potential investors, then the IV of the most motivated and second-most-motivated buyers will be very similar. But if the most motivated buyer would place a much higher IV on the property than would the second-most-motivated buyer, then it may be possible to sell the property for more than its market value.

One implication of the difference between IV and MV is that you need to be aware that the opposite party in a transaction may have some idea about the magnitude of *your* IV in the deal. They will naturally try to negotiate a price above MV, closer to your IV, in order to take advantage of this knowledge if they can. For example, the owner of 9997 and 9998 Consumption Boulevard will certainly know that her lots are worth more to KrazyLo than to anyone else, that is, more than their MV. The question is, how much more? This is where careful investigation and negotiating skill can pay off (on either side). If you are dealing with unique assets or financial arrangements, then you may have little recourse to competing players as alternative opposite parties in the deal. But the other side may have little recourse as well. Obviously, it is important to keep IV information confidential and to apply sound negotiation principles when dealing in such a situation.

This brings us back to our starting point about the difference between real estate and securities investment on the one hand, and between real estate and corporate capital budgeting investment on the other hand. The more lumpiness and uniqueness there is among assets and investors, the more difficult it will be to estimate market values accurately, and the more likely it will be that investors' IVs could greatly differ from any estimate that could be made of MV. This is the situation in which real estate investment analysis converges toward corporate capital budgeting analysis in some respects, and IV tends to become the only relevant value perspective.[12] The more homogeneous the assets and the investors are, the easier it will be to estimate market values, and the less likely it will be that IV differs much from MV for most of the

---

[12] An important difference between classical corporate capital budgeting and real estate investment is that real estate investment typically operates in a very different income tax environment. This will be treated in subsequent chapters.

active participants in the market.[13] This is the situation in which real estate investment analysis converges toward classical securities investment analysis, and MV becomes the dominant valuation perspective.[14] Much commercial real estate investing occurs somewhere between these two extremes.

12.1.3 Watch Out for the IV Sales Pitch

Because investment value is defined only in relation to a specific investor/owner, and because an estimate of IV is not necessarily subject to verification by comparison to market transaction prices of similar properties, IV tends to be a more subjective measure than MV. This often makes it relatively easy to abuse the IV concept and its application in the NPV rule. It is tempting to compute IV in a way to make the NPV of a favored property or project look good, or to support whatever position one is in.

To avoid falling victim to the abuse of the IV concept, you should carefully estimate MV as well, whenever a relevant market can be identified. If someone claims that IV differs from MV (in a way that supports his sales pitch), it is best to be skeptical. He may be right. But we suspect that more often than not IV and MV are pretty similar, if they are both estimated properly. Most real estate asset markets function pretty well, in the sense that obtaining reasonably accurate estimates of current market value is fairly easy. And remember that a deal should normally make sense from both the IV and MV perspectives separately.

12.1.4 Marginal and Intramarginal Investors: How to Get Positive NPV

We noted that the investment value NPV of a given deal for a given investor is typically determined by the relationship between the MV and IV of the asset for the investor. We can deepen our understanding of both IV and MV and derive some additional practical insight by examining how these two valuation measures operate in a well-functioning property market. A useful concept in this regard is the distinction between **marginal** and **intramarginal investors** in the market.

The chart in Exhibit 12-1 presents a schematic picture of a well-functioning property market. The horizontal axis represents the annual volume of trading in the asset market (e.g., number of properties bought and sold). The vertical axis represents the prices of properties (e.g., per square foot). The downward-sloping demand function shows the amount of assets potential buyers would like to purchase, based on their perceived investment values. Investors with the highest IVs would become active in the market first, even at relatively high prices. At lower prices additional buyers would enter the market. The upward-sloping supply function shows the amount of assets potential sellers (that is, existing owners of the assets) would like to sell, based on their

---

[13] Competition in the asset market drives MV to equal IV when there are large numbers of similar investors and assets. If IV were greater than MV, large numbers of investors would compete against each other to bid up market prices until MV = IV. If IV were less than MV, large numbers of sellers would compete against each other until price was driven down to MV = IV.

[14] An important difference between classical securities investment analysis and real estate investment analysis is that the real estate asset market, at least the private market for directly held property, is less informationally efficient than the securities market, as we noted previously.

Exhibit 12-1 Relation between Investment Value (IV) and Market Value (MV) in a Well-Functioning Asset Market

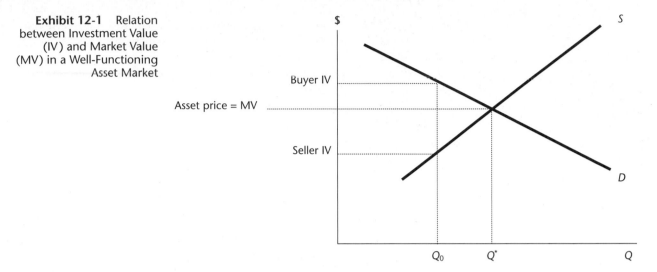

$ = Property prices (vertical axis)

Q = Volume of investment transaction per unit of time

Q_0 = Volume of transactions by investors with more favorable circumstances, hence would enter market at less favorable prices (i.e., intramarginal market participants, e.g., investors with different tax circumstances than marginal investors in the market)

Q^* = Total volume of property transactions, including marginal investment (investors on margin are indifferent between investing and not investing in property)

Note: Prices, and hence market values (MV), are determined by the IV of the marginal investors (the investors for whom NPV = 0 on both an IV and MV basis).

perceived investment values. At low prices only a few sellers would be willing to do deals. More sellers enter the market at higher prices.

Market value (per SF) is determined by **asset transaction market equilibrium**. The equilibrium price is that which equates supply and demand. This is the price at which IV is the same for both buyers and sellers who are on the margin. By definition, marginal participants are those with NPV = 0 computed on both an IV and MV basis. Exhibit 12-1 shows how the IV of the marginal investors determines or underlies the market prices. *MV equals the IV of the marginal participants in the asset market.*

IV will differ from MV (and this will enable positive-NPV deals to be done, measured on the basis of IV) *only for intramarginal market participants*, those that are to the left of the equilibrium point in the diagram. These are market participants for whom (and deals in which) the IV for the buyer differs from the IV for the seller, for the same asset. By definition, this requires that the sellers and buyers in these deals are different from each other in some way that is important to the investment value of the asset.

Exhibit 12-1 points out another characteristic of a well-functioning asset market, one that is in equilibrium. Such a market is characterized by many deals in which *the same types of investors are observed on both sides of the transactions.*[15] For example, if we

[15] In particular, the existence of observable MVs enables any type of investor that would be on the buy side of the market to also be on the sell side. The converse is not true, however, as potential owners for whom IV < MV would generally not want to purchase an asset. On the other hand, it is not generally irrational for intramarginal buyers, for whom IV > MV, to also be sellers of *individual* assets, as long as they are not *net* sellers in the aggregate. For example, a tax-exempt pension fund would be a typical intramarginal buyer due to its tax-advantaged situation. It might be on both sides of the market for purposes of rebalancing its portfolio or pursuing what it perceives to be superior return prospects in

observed REITs buying, we would also expect to observe REITs selling. Different types of investors could still be active in the market, of course, but all deals would tend to be done at or near the MV price. Intramarginal investors could be making substantial positive NPVs from *net* adjustments in their holdings, measured on the basis of IV rather than MV.

We can distill from this analysis some practical conclusions about how you can know whether you are likely to be able to do a substantially positive NPV deal measured on the basis of your IV, in a well-functioning market. We see that positive-NPV deals are *intramarginal* deals. Such deals are easy to recognize. A necessary characteristic of intramarginal deals is that the principal parties on the two sides of the deal must be *different* in some important way regarding their ability to profit from the asset, at least on an after-tax basis. This type of difference is a necessary, although not sufficient, condition of positive investment value NPV deals. (Such a difference by itself is not sufficient to ensure a positive NPV because you still have to make sure you are not making a pricing mistake.)

In practice, the two most common sources of positive investment-value NPVs are probably income tax status and operational advantages in controlling the real productive capacity of the property. Often the latter source involves some sort of quasi-monopolistic position that gives the investor some advantageous market control. For example, a developer's ownership of adjacent sites might give it unique ability to profit from a certain type of development on a given parcel of land, due to synergy and spillover effects. Another typical type of potentially profitable situation occurs when the owner of the property would also be the primary user of the property, and the property has a unique fit in the real productive process of this owner (as in our KrazyLo example earlier).

In fact, the type of uniqueness associated with substantially positive NPV opportunities often requires some sort of construction or redevelopment of a property. The market tends to reward, at least temporarily, those who are first with a good idea. **Entrepreneurial profits** are the supernormal return on successful business creativity, in real estate as in any other industry. Be the first to invent and produce a "triple-A" quality rental apartment complex in a market that has latent demand for such a product and you will make a bundle, at least for a while (until other copy cat developers build enough competing apartments to drive rents and prices down to the normal profit level).

12.2 DANGER AND OPPORTUNITY IN MARKET INEFFICIENCY

The necessity to deal simultaneously with IV and MV measures of value in making investment decisions is one result of real estate's unique asset market characteristics. Now we want to consider the implications of the fact that the real estate asset market is not as informationally efficient as the public exchanges on which securities such

---

one market as compared to another. It might sell an office building in Chicago (incurring a theoretical loss of IV − MV on that deal) and immediately take the proceeds from that sale (MV) and buy a retail mall of equivalent MV in Los Angeles (reaping a positive-NPV of IV − MV in the second deal). The two transactions cancel out in NPV, but result in a rebalancing of the portfolio. Of course, liquidity demands could conceivably force an intramarginal owner to make a net sale and thereby incur a negative NPV, but such transactions would normally be rare and are certainly to be avoided.

as stocks and bonds are traded. Two aspects of this type of **informational inefficiency** are important in this regard. One is the presence of **random noise** in the asset valuation and pricing process. The other is the presence of considerably more inertia and predictability in real estate's periodic investment returns than one finds in securities returns.

12.2.1 Valuation Noise

Real property markets are characterized by infrequent, privately negotiated deals in which whole, unique assets are traded. In this type of market it is difficult to know at any given time the precise market value of any given real estate asset. A potential buyer or seller of the office building at 100 North Main Street cannot simply get on the Internet and look up the latest trade price for a share of ownership in the building. He would have to do some research to estimate the current market value of a real estate asset, or pay someone else to do such research for him. And even then he wouldn't be sure of the exact MV.

In this scarcity of price information lies both danger and opportunity of a type not present in stocks or bonds investing. We can define this danger and opportunity in terms of the NPV and valuation concepts we have been using. In investing in real estate, while the *expected* NPV is approximately zero when measured on an MV basis, *this is not guaranteed*.

> *In real estate investment in the direct (private) property market, it is* possible *to do deals with substantially* positive, *or* negative, *NPVs, measured on the basis of market value.*

In part, this is because parties to transactions sometimes make mistakes. They may fail to discover or consider adequately some knowable information relevant to the market value of the property. But even when neither side in a deal makes a mistake, the nature of the real estate market is somewhat random. Market values can never be observed definitively, but only estimated. Both sides in a deal may have done their homework adequately and equally well. Neither party may have made any mistake in the sense that they both made reasonable use of all the information and resources available to them at the time when the deal was made. Yet one side gets the better deal. If we could step back after the dust settles and have the deal reviewed by an impartial panel of experts (individually or collectively), with all the information available to the panel, the judgment of the panel would sometimes be that one side got the better deal, relative to the market value at the time.[16]

How can this happen? In some cases, one party will have better information. They may not have investigated the deal any harder or more diligently than the other side, but they just "lucked out" by happening to discover something about, say, expansion plans of a potential tenant or an adjacent property owner. If such information is not private (in the sense that it can be verified by anyone), then it is arguably relevant to the market value of the property, particularly as it may be revealed once the deal is closed. In other cases, one side will simply be a better negotiator than the other side. A third possibility is that one side may be under some sort of duress, or greater

---

[16] It is important to recognize that individual transaction prices are not the same as market values. The appendix at the end of this chapter describes in more depth the difference between transaction prices and market values.

How Big Is Random Noise?

How much "randomness" is there in commercial property prices or estimates of market value? Are individual transaction prices or appraisal estimates of individual property values widely dispersed around the "true" property market values? Or is the distribution very tight, with little randomness?

This question is difficult to answer because it is essentially an empirical question, yet a key ingredient we need for the answer is empirically unobservable, *in principle*, namely, the true market value. However, we can say something. First, statistical and experimental techniques do allow indirect estimation of the relative magnitude of the random valuation component, the "standard error" in property value estimates. For example, two academic researchers, Julian Diaz and Martin Wolverton, conducted an experiment in which professional appraisers independently estimated the market value of the same asset, as of the same point in time, based on the same information about the property and its market. The resulting value estimates had a standard deviation of around 5% of the average estimate of property value. This agrees with statistical estimates of the magnitude of transaction price noise in the housing market, published by Professor Goetzmann of Yale. Statistical analysis of

the NCREIF Property Database suggests an average error magnitude in the range of 5% to 10%.* Second, theory tells us something about what to expect about the magnitude of random noise. In particular, we believe that noise should be greater for assets that are more unique, and for assets trading in "thinner," less active markets. In such circumstances, there is less information on which to base estimates of value.

---

*The Diaz-Wolverton experiment is reported in Diaz and Wolverton (1998). Goetzmann's estimates are found in Goetzmann (1993). The 10% estimates are described in Geltner (1998). A much lower estimate of average error (around 3%) comes from a study by Richard Graff and Mike Young of simultaneous "external" and "internal" appraisals of the properties in a major investment advisor's portfolio. (See Graff and Young [1999].) However, it is likely that the external and internal appraisals in the Graff-Young study were not completely independent of one another, as they both may have had access to the prior appraised values of the properties. This could provide a common anchor for the two appraisals, which would reduce the apparent dispersion in value estimations. Additional evidence on random dispersion in appraisal estimates was reviewed in England by Crosby, Lavers, and Murdoch (1998). They suggested an average error magnitude on the order of 10%.

---

pressure to close the deal. Perhaps a seller is in need of cash to pay creditors. Perhaps an investment manager on the buy side of a deal will lose credibility if she is unable to place all the capital her client wants invested by the end of the year.

To guard against the danger of substantially negative NPV deals evaluated from an MV perspective, financial institutions engaged in commercial real estate investment, as well as investment managers acting as fiduciaries, mandate specific predeal investigation and analysis procedures, often referred to as **due diligence**. Investors typically also try to learn something about the motivations of the parties on the other side in the deal, as best they can. But remember that the flip side of the negative-NPV danger is the positive-NPV opportunity. Because MV is the same for everyone, in principle, whenever one side does a negative-NPV deal from an MV perspective, the other side of the deal gets a positive-NPV deal from the MV perspective (by definition). Part of the uniqueness and excitement of real estate investing lies in the presence of this danger and opportunity. This is different from investing in stocks and bonds. And it is different from corporate capital budgeting. Real estate investors can often reap a reward for individual investigation and research efforts more easily than can investors in more efficient markets.

12.2.2 Asset Market Predictability

To the extent that MV-based nonzero NPVs are an essentially random occurrence, their effect on the investor may be greatly reduced if the investor is well diversified. Random errors (on both the positive and negative side) tend to average out over the long run and across many deals. But another result of market inefficiency can have a more systematic effect. As noted in previous chapters, informational efficiency in asset markets refers to the tendency of prices to reflect quickly and fully all relevant information or news. The converse of this, informational inefficiency, implies that asset prices move more slowly in response to the arrival of news, only **partially adjusting** within a given short to medium time horizon. This results in future asset market price movements being more predictable in less efficient markets.[17]

As with random noise, the **predictability** result of inefficiency brings both danger and opportunity. The opportunity is that investors can take advantage of the predictability to attempt to buy low and sell high. Investors in real estate probably have a greater opportunity for **market timing** than do investors in securities.

Taking advantage of real estate asset market predictability is not as easy or profitable as it may first appear, however. For one thing, real estate asset markets are far from completely predictable. While they are almost certainly not as informationally efficient as the securities market, and hence more predictable than such markets, real estate asset markets are not terribly inefficient either, and hence cannot be fully predicted.

Second, **transaction costs** in buying and selling property are much greater than those in the securities market. Such costs remove much of the profit investors could otherwise obtain from trading on predictable asset movements.[18] Transaction costs can be mitigated by holding real estate investments for long periods of time because this spreads out the transaction costs over many periods of return. But long holding periods also mitigate the per-annum percentage profit that can be earned from timing the ups and downs of the market. This is because long holding periods also spread out over more years of investment the "windfall" gain from successful timing, and also because the farther in the future one tries to predict, the less accurately it is possible to predict, even for relatively predictable markets. Investment returns over long holding periods will often be more sensitive to how well the property is managed during the holding period than to the timing of when the property was bought or sold.

Finally, at least at the individual property level, the randomness of transaction noise, as described in the preceding section, may swamp much of the advantage of market timing, or in any case can add greatly to the risk of short-term investments.

---

[17]Some studies documenting and quantifying the predictability in private real estate asset market returns include the following: Barkham and Geltner (1995), Case and Shiller (1990), Case and Quigley (1991), Gyourko and Keim (1992), among others.

[18]Typical "round-trip"(i.e., buying and selling) transaction costs in real estate are on the order of 5% to 10% of asset value. Costs include brokerage, legal, and administrative fees, as well as the cost of any research and investigation undertaken by the investor directly. In contrast, transaction costs for dealing in the securities market are on the order of one-third to one-tenth this magnitude (sometimes much less, and moving down with technological developments and deregulation in securities trading).

Can Predictability Cause IV to Differ from MV?

It is sometimes suggested that predictability in the real estate asset market can cause investment value to differ from current market value for assets and investors in general. The idea is that if the property market is somewhat predictable, then it will at least sometimes be possible to predict, not with certainty but with relatively high probability, that asset MVs will be headed in one direction or the other over the medium to long run. For example, when asset price/earnings multiples appear to be very high or very low by historical standards, this may be an indication that the asset market is either "overheated" (as in a bubble), or temporarily excessively depressed. As IV is based on long-run holdings, the long-run forecast of MV (together with the future operating cash flows the asset will generate) is more relevant to IV than the current prevailing MV. This is a different concept of IV than the traditional definition, which is based on differences among individual investors. In this case, the argument is that IV in general differs from MV in the same way for *all* investors in the market as of a given time. In this conception, the current market is viewed as "mispricing" assets, viewed from a long-run perspective.

While this conception of IV and MV is interesting, it raises questions that are very difficult to answer rigorously, from both a conceptual and empirical perspective. For example, it suggests not only that the asset market is inefficient, but also that market participants are acting generally irrationally in paying prices equal to the current market values. But asset prices may be abnormally low because risk is abnormally high, from an ex ante perspective. It is also not clear what the practical implications of this concept of IV should be. For example, bubbles are always much easier to perceive in retrospect than at the time, and as noted, predictability is much less in the long run than in the short run. Most academic real estate scholars would probably advise considerable caution in the use of this type of conception of IV.

For all these reasons, real estate investors cannot generally or systematically make **supernormal profits** due to the predictability of real estate asset market prices. Indeed, we can be almost certain that supernormal profits are not widespread because there are no major barriers to investors of many types entering the real estate market, either directly or indirectly.[19] If supernormal profits were widely and easily available, investors would be drawn toward real estate and would reallocate their investments toward real estate and away from other asset classes. This would bid up real estate asset prices (and bid down other asset prices) to levels at which supernormal profits were no longer generally available in real estate.[20]

But this does not mean that, as a real estate investor, you can afford to ignore the predictability of real estate returns. That would be foolish, not only because you might miss upside opportunities, but because you could get stuck on the losing end of the cyclical swings in the property market. Inertia in the property markets means

[19]Recall our discussion in Chapter 7 about the variety of real estate investment products and vehicles, and the incentives facing the investment industry to develop new such products and vehicles to allow investors to place capital directly or indirectly in real estate assets.

[20]Even if it is possible to earn high ex ante returns by using the predictability in the private property market, such returns would not necessarily represent supernormal profits. Property prices may be depressed because the market perceives real estate as being more risky than usual, or prices may be inflated because the market perceives real estate to be less risky than usual. Who is to say the market is wrong, ex ante?

that when asset prices start rising, they often have a tendency to continue to rise for several years. Similarly, when prices start to fall, they may have a tendency to continue to fall for several years. Wary investors try to avoid buying near the peaks of such cycles, and selling near the troughs. In traditional real estate practice, probably the single greatest cause of investors being forced to sell into a down market is the use of large amounts of debt to finance real estate investment. Investors with low to moderate levels of debt can usually ride out prolonged downswings.[21]

*12.3 DUELING ASSET MARKETS: THE REIT MARKET VERSUS THE PROPERTY MARKET

This brings us to the third characteristic feature of real estate asset markets that holds implications for the application of basic investment analysis tools at the microlevel. This is the existence of not one, but two types, or levels, of asset markets that are relevant for real estate asset valuation: the private direct property market and the public market for REIT shares. This situation was noted in Chapter 7, but up to now (since Chapter 10) our microlevel valuation discussion has focused on the private direct property market alone. What are the implications of the simultaneous existence of the REIT market?

Broadly speaking, at least three major questions of interest to real estate investors are raised by the existence of parallel asset markets. One is the question of which asset market to use in making real estate investments: public, private, or both (and how to manage the allocation between the two). A second question is the possibility of "arbitrage": could it be possible to trade between the two asset markets to make seemingly (or nearly) "riskless" profits on real estate investments?[22] The third question concerns asset valuation. Do the two asset markets value differently the same underlying physical assets as of the same point in time, and if so, which market's value is "correct"?

Obviously, all three of these questions are related to one another, and all are important. However, the third question most directly concerns us at the microlevel of individual asset valuation and investment analysis at the level of individual property transactions. As this is our focus in the current chapter, we will largely put off the other two questions until Part VII. Thus, our focus here is on the third question, and in particular on its first part: Do the REIT market and the private direct property market value the same underlying physical assets differently as of the same point in time?

---

[21]The causes of large amounts of net real estate investment just prior to and during the peak of the cycle are more of a mystery. Of course, it is always easier to identify the peak *after* the market has turned, but even so, behavioral and institutional problems may cause excess investment around the market peak. For example, analysts have identified a phenomenon labeled the Santa Claus effect, in which investment and financial institutions tend to reward asset classes that have performed well in the recent past by increasing capital allocations to those types of investments, and punish investment managers who have done poorly in the recent past by removing capital allocation from them. (See Mei [1996]).

[22]We place the term *arbitrage* in quotes here because it is not generally possible to construct rigorous arbitrage trades in real estate as it is in the bond or options markets, for example. Strictly speaking, arbitrage refers to trades in which profit is achieved immediately from trading, with no risk at all. Transactions involving the direct property market cannot possibly be executed fast enough, or at prices certain enough in advance, to allow completely riskless trading. The term *arbitrage* as employed here is thus an approximation.

In common parlance and on the basis of the casual empiricism frequently heard among practitioners in the real estate investment industry, the answer to this question would clearly be yes. Industry investment analysts commonly refer to price/earnings multiples as being different in the REIT market versus the private property market, and this is typically taken as evidence that the two markets are evaluating the same properties differently. More careful analyses attempt to quantify the **net asset value (NAV)** of REITs by evaluating REIT property holdings in the same way that appraisers value properties in the private market. Then this NAV (per share) is compared to REIT share prices in the stock market, and a **premium** or **discount** to NAV is computed, implying (or at least suggesting) a **differential valuation** of the same assets in the two markets.

Exhibit 12-2 presents one way to picture the empirical relationship between the two markets' valuations during the last two decades of the 20th century. The chart shows four indices, two for cash flow levels and two for asset values, based on the **NCREIF and NAREIT indices.** The solid lines are the asset valuation indices, and the dashed lines are the cash flow indices. The triangles are the NCREIF indices and the squares are the NAREIT indices. NCREIF presents property level statistics for commercial properties held directly in the private market. The NAREIT indices are based on the share prices and dividends of all publicly traded REITs.

The main point in Exhibit 12-2 that concerns us at present is that the valuation indices for NCREIF and NAREIT do not move together exactly over time. Nor do these differences appear to be fully explained by the relationship between the asset valuations and their corresponding current cash flow levels. For example, in the late 1980s REIT share values were relatively low compared to REIT current dividends, at the same time as NCREIF property values were relatively high compared to NCREIF current NOI. The opposite occurred during most of the 1990s, as REIT share values were relatively high compared to dividends while NCREIF property values were relatively low compared to NOIs. Roughly speaking, Exhibit 12-2 suggests that REIT share values tended to be below their NAVs during the late 1980s, while the opposite relationship characterized most of the 1990s.

12.3.1 Valuation at the Microlevel

Although interesting at the macrolevel, the type of broad-brush aggregate relationships depicted in Exhibit 12-2 can be misleading if you attempt to apply them directly at the microlevel to individual asset valuation. We need to be more careful in order to answer the question of whether, or to what extent, the two asset markets imply differential valuation at the microlevel.

To begin, we need a more precise definition of our question. What do we mean when we ask whether the REIT market and the private direct property market could imply different valuations of the same physical assets at the same point in time? Individual physical assets are traded directly in the private property market, so such assets are valued directly in that market. Individual physical assets do not trade in the market for REIT shares. Therefore, REIT share values only provide *indirect* indications or implications about underlying physical asset valuation. A more precise statement of our question would be based on the following conception of differential valuation. If REITs can generally purchase and sell properties at prices equal to the prevailing market value in the private property market without such actions causing any change in REIT share prices, then there is no differential valuation between the two markets at the microlevel. If, on the other hand, REIT purchase or sale of assets at the prevailing

Exhibit 12-2 NAREIT versus NCREIF Asset Values and Cash Flows (all indices set to average value = 1) (Source: Authors' estimates are based on NAREIT index and NCREIF index.

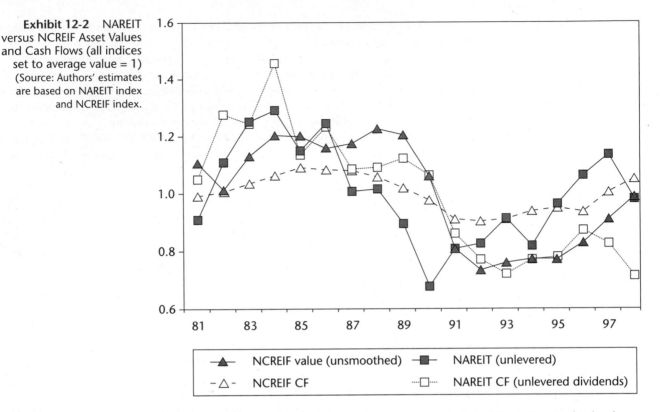

Notes on Exhibit 12-2: Valuations are based on appraisals, but the NCREIF value level index portrayed in Exhibit 12-2 has been "unsmoothed" to approximately correct for the smoothing and lagging effect of the appraisal process and the presence of "stale appraisals" in the NCREIF Index. The NCREIF cash flow index represents the relative change in cash flow (within the same buildings), based on the NCREIF index income and appreciation return components. The NAREIT value level index portrayed in Exhibit 12-2 has been "unlevered" to make a more direct comparison to NCREIF property-level statistics. The NAREIT cash flow index is based on dividends paid out to shareholders, with relative levels derived from the NAREIT index capital gain and dividend yield return components. Each index depicts the relative change in value across time based on an arbitrary starting value for the index. Without loss of generality, each index in the chart has been set to have a starting value such that the average value of the index over the two decades is unity.

private property market MV would cause a change in REIT share prices, then a valuation differential currently exists.

With this concept in mind, we can specify the following definition of a microlevel valuation differential:

$$(IV_R = MV_P) \Leftrightarrow \text{No valuation differential}$$

$$(IV_R \neq MV_P) \Leftrightarrow \text{Valuation differential}$$

Here, IV_R refers to the investment value of a given property for a given REIT, and MV_P refers to the market value of that property in the private property market. The IV_R value is the value of the property for the REIT's shareholders. IV_R equates to MV_R, the (indirect) market value of the property in the REIT market, in the sense that if the

REIT owns the property then the REIT's share price in the stock market will reflect this IV_R value of the property (along with all the REIT's other assets and liabilities). Thus, the NPV of a microlevel property market transaction for the REIT, based on the impact for the REIT's preexisting shareholders, is

If REIT is buying: $NPV_R = IV_R - MV_P$

If REIT is selling: $NPV_R = MV_P - IV_R$

This definition helps to clarify when, and under what conditions, we are likely to observe differential valuation at the microlevel. Differential valuation implies positive-NPV opportunities for REITs based on investment value. As noted in section 12.1, such opportunities can only occur when the relevant REITs are intramarginal participants in the private property asset market. Although such opportunities may occur idiosyncratically for any given REIT at any given point in time, in order for such opportunities to imply general, marketwide differential valuation between the REIT and property markets, such positive opportunities would have to be widespread, accruing generally to all (or most) REITs at the same time. In such circumstances, we would typically observe REITs very actively trading in the private property market, and on *only one side* of the property market, either tending only to buy or tending only to sell.

On the other hand, lack of marketwide differential valuation would be characterized by REITs being marginal participants in the property market. Recall that for marginal participants, IV equals MV (transactions are generally at NPV = 0). Property asset markets in which REITs are marginal participants will be characterized by REITs being about equally common on both the buy and sell sides of the market for existing properties. In such a market, REITs would be among the least advantaged investors on the buy side of the market. That is, they would typically not be able to profit from property investment any more than other investors (on an after-tax basis, considering shareholders' personal taxes as well as entity-level taxation). They would also be among the most advantaged property investors on the sell side of the market. That is, REITs would generally be able to profit as much or more from continuing to hold their property assets as any other sellers typifying the sell side of the property market.

Another way of stating the previous result is to say that differential pricing exists at the microlevel only in markets and for properties in which the investment value for REITs differs from the investment value for the *marginal* participants in the private market: $IV_R \neq IV_P$.

Let us clarify how the two markets work in tandem in this regard by considering a simple example. Suppose that at some point in time REIT market valuation exceeds private property market valuation such that, in general, $NPV_R = IV_R - MV_p > 0$. That is, such positive opportunities for REITs arise not just idiosyncratically for a few properties or a few REITs, but are widespread. Stock market investors will in such circumstances recognize that REITs face widespread positive-NPV opportunities simply from buying existing properties in the property market. The stock market will capitalize this expected positive NPV "growth opportunity" in the share prices of REITs, driving up share prices to reflect the value not only of the REITs' existing in-place assets but also of the expected future NPVs the REITs will obtain from future property purchases. The result will be a high price/earnings multiple for REIT shares, making it easy for REITs to raise additional equity capital in the stock market to finance property market purchases.

But this process, of course, contains the seeds of its own destruction, for this is how speculative markets work to provide a negative feedback loop in the real estate system and development cycle. As REITs raise capital that they apply to making purchases in the property market, competition among REITs drives prices in the private property market up to the level at which $NPV_R = IV_R - MV_P = 0$, in other words, until $MV_P = IV_R$. At this point, REITs are no longer intramarginal participants in the property market, and their positive-NPV growth opportunities are gone. The stock market will recognize this (perhaps even foresee it coming in advance), and will down-value REIT shares accordingly, so that REIT share prices now only reflect the value of the REITs' in-place assets. (The present value of a future $NPV_R = 0$ opportunity is, of course, just zero.) This will result in REIT price/earnings multiples falling to levels more typical of their long-run historical average.[23] There they will remain until something changes either in the REIT market or the private property market to perturb the equilibrium again.

12.3.2 Microlevel Differential Valuation: Cash Flow Expectations

The previous definition of **microlevel differential valuation** enables us to clarify the possible general sources of such differences. As we know from section 12.1, investment value is determined by the DCF valuation model based on both numerators and denominators on the right-hand side of the equation. The numerators reflect the future cash flow expectations from operation of the property. The denominators reflect the opportunity cost of capital (OCC). Thus, fundamentally two potential sources of differential valuation exist between the REIT and private property asset markets. Differential valuation results from differential market perceptions either regarding the expected level of future cash flows the property will generate, or regarding the opportunity cost of capital.

This can be depicted symbolically as follows:

$$\textit{Differential valuation} \Leftrightarrow IV_R \neq IV_P$$

$$\Leftrightarrow DCF(E\{CF_R\}, E\{r_R\}) \neq DCF(E\{CF_P\}, E\{r_P\})$$

where the P subscript refers to the marginal participant in the private property market.

Consider first the $E\{CF\}$ potential source of differential valuation, the market's expected future cash flows from the property. There are various ways in which it might

---

[23]Let MV_R be the market value of a REIT's existing in-place assets as valued by the stock market. Let $NPV_R = IV_R - MV_P$ be the value of the REIT's growth opportunities, and let D_R be the value of the REIT's existing debt liabilities. Then if there are N shares of the REIT's equity outstanding, the share price of the REIT in the stock market is $(MV_R + NPV_R - D_R)/N$. If the growth opportunities disappear (i.e., $NPV_R = 0$), then the REIT's share price must adjust to $(MV_R - D_R)/N$. If NPV_R had been positive and now is zero, then this adjustment represents a fall in share price. Note that such adjustment in share price occurs even though the expected total return required by stock market investors for investing in the REIT has not necessarily changed at all. The disappearance of positive-NPV_R opportunities, for example, may have resulted purely from a bidding up of prices in the property market, that is, a rise in MV_P. In this sense, the adjustment in REIT share prices may reflect *no change at all in the REIT's opportunity cost of capital*. What has changed is the allocation of the expected total return between the expected growth (or capital gain) component and the current cash yield component.

be realistic to expect that a given REIT could obtain greater future cash flows from a given property than the best private owner of the property could obtain. For example, the REIT may have superior property management ability, or it may have economies of scale that enable it to save on operating expenses.[24] Perhaps the REIT has name-recognition or a brand identity among potential tenants that allows it to generate greater revenue.[25] Furthermore, the cash flows that matter to the REIT from owner-ship of a given property may not be limited to just the cash flow from that subject property. What matters to the REIT are all of the incremental cash flows caused by the ownership of the subject property, including any synergistic or spillover effects on the REIT's other property holdings.[26]

On the other hand, a given REIT may have disadvantages in any of these respects as well. The key point to recognize here is that idiosyncratic abilities or circum-stances will not cause differential valuation between the REIT and private property markets as a whole. Idiosyncratic factors are those that relate to a given REIT or a given property only. Such factors will motivate specific REITs to make specific trans-actions and may be reflected in those REITs' stock prices, but will not cause general, marketwide differences in valuation because they will affect only a few properties or a few REITs and will tend to cancel out at the aggregate level. In order for differences in $E\{CF\}$ to be a source of general differential valuation between the REIT and pri-vate property markets, such differences must be systematic across a large number of individual REITs and applicable to numerous individual properties, or indeed to vir-tually all properties of a given type.

Suppose such systematic differences existed. Suppose, for example, that REITs in general (or many REITs, or several very large REITs) were able to generate greater $E\{CF\}$ prospects than private owners for a given type of property.[27] This could cause genuine differential valuation between the two asset markets for that type of property, but only for a while. The relevant REITs would be the intramarginal purchasers of the type of property in question, dominating the buy side of the market for those proper-ties, until they bought (or built) virtually all such properties in existence. Then only REITs would own such properties, and REITs would then be the marginal participants in the private property market for the type of assets in question. Thus, while $E\{CF\}$ can be a source of genuine differential valuation, this can only occur temporarily. It is important not to forget about the built-in **negative feedback loop** or **regulatory mechanism** that operates in the functioning of the two markets in tandem.

Just how temporary are such valuation divergences between the two asset mar-kets? This depends on how many REITs have the relevant unique $E\{CF\}$ prospects, and how fast they can access capital. More REITs will be able to access more capital, and provide greater competition among themselves for the purchase of the relevant type of property assets, thereby driving up MV_P more quickly to the point at which

---

[24]If property management ability and economies of scale in management are the extent of a firm's advan-tage, there is no need for the firm to actually own the properties it manages. Rather, it might specialize in selling its management services to third parties. (See Vogel [1997].)

[25]This type of advantage is often called **franchise value**.

[26]This is sometimes referred to as economies of scope. For example, a REIT with sufficient property holdings in a given geographical space market may be able to exercise market power within that space market, thereby increasing its rental profits.

[27]Widespread existence of *unexhausted* economies of scale or scope could be a source of such systematic $E(CF)$ differentials, for example. "Unexhausted" scale economies means that the REITs have not yet reached their optimal, most efficient size: they are still too small.

$MV_P = MV_R$. The stock and bond markets are very efficient at providing capital where positive NPV opportunities appear, and it does not require a great number of REITs to ignite sufficient competition to rapidly bid up the price of a specific type of asset in the property market. It would probably be foolish to assume that either private property owners or REITs have any sort of monopoly on smart, well-informed asset managers looking for profitable deals. Asset prices in the private property market are no doubt more sluggish than REIT share prices, but they are not likely to be terribly far behind.

12.3.3 Microlevel Differential Valuation: Opportunity Cost of Capital

Now consider the other potential source of differential asset valuation between the REIT and private property markets: the opportunity cost of capital (OCC), or $E[r]$. Indeed, if one defines valuation as *the way in which an asset market converts future cash flow expectations into present value*, then this is the *only* potential source of a true valuation differential. Such a concept of valuation no doubt lies behind the popular notion that valuation differences are reflected in **price/earnings multiples** and that the **cost of capital** is represented by the inverse of the price/earnings multiple, or by **current cash yield** (what we have previously labeled $E[y]$). But now you can see that such a view can be misleading. The true cost of capital is not just the price/earnings ratio or the current cash yield. It is the entire expected total return. As you recall from Chapter 9:

$$E[r] = E[y] + E[g] = r_f + E[RP]$$

The OCC includes both current yield plus expected growth, and it includes both the time value of money (the riskfree interest rate) and an expected risk premium.

With this in mind, let's take a more sophisticated view of the OCC as a potential source of asset market valuation differences between the REIT and property markets. Let's begin by recalling three basic points about the OCC at the microlevel of individual property valuation. First, the OCC derives essentially from the capital markets, even for purposes of computing investment value. Second, the relevant risk for determining the risk premium in the OCC at the microlevel is the risk in the subject asset's future cash flows. In other words, *risk resides in the asset, not in the investor*. Third, capital markets are substantially integrated. Vast quantities of money can move rapidly from one place to another in response to perceived differentials in expected risk-adjusted returns (i.e., in response to perceived positive-NPV opportunities).[28] Electronic information technological development has greatly improved information flow as well. The result is that, while the private property markets and public securities markets are not perfectly integrated, they are largely so, and becoming more so all the time.[29]

---

[28]In Chapter 7 we described how the real estate investment industry employs a variety of investment products and vehicles (and constantly develops new ones) to facilitate such capital flow.

[29]We will qualify and elaborate on the capital market integration point shortly, and also in Part VII.

These considerations mitigate against large differentials existing in the OCC for very long between the REIT and private property markets, *for the same underlying physical assets as of the same point in time.* The argument is the same as we described previously regarding $E\{CF\}$-based differences in valuation. Large valuation differentials, whether based on differences in $E\{CF\}$ or in the relevant OCC, would be "arbitraged" away by investors seeking superior returns across the two markets.

Now the astute reader may ask how even small or transient differences could exist in the $E[r]$ between the two asset markets, given that, unlike $E\{CF\}$, $E[r]$ derives from the capital markets, not from the property asset itself. Don't all investors face the same capital markets, and hence the same "price" of time and of risk as reflected in the OCC? Therefore, shouldn't the same asset always face the same OCC for all investors, whether they be in the private property market or the stock market?

This is a good question, and it merits some discussion. First, suppose all capital markets were perfectly efficient and completely integrated. In that case there would be only one way in which REIT OCC could differ from private OCC for the same asset, and this way is akin to the difference in $E\{CF\}$ described previously. REITs might be able to manage properties in such a way that the risk in their future cash flows is different. For this to result in a general valuation difference among REITs as a class, such differential ability to manage cash flow risk would have to be systematic, across many REITs and properties, not just an idiosyncratic ability of a given REIT with respect to a given specific property.

Now consider the real world in which capital markets are neither perfectly efficient nor completely seamless. In reality, the REIT (i.e., stock market) portion of the capital market differs in structure and functioning from the private property market. This may allow additional sources of systematic differences in OCC between the public and private asset markets, even for the same underlying assets as of the same point in time. In particular, there are nontrivial costs and institutional barriers in "moving" assets from private ownership to REIT ownership and vice versa.[30] Furthermore, although there is considerable overlap, the investor population active on the margin in the stock market differs somewhat from that which is active in the private property market.[31] These two investor populations may face different tax circumstances, and more fundamentally, they may not always share the same risk preferences and perceptions.

For example, investors with a greater preference or need for liquidity would presumably not require as high a risk premium for owning property assets in a REIT as in a private vehicle (such as a limited partnership or unit trust). REITs, being more

---

[30]However, as noted in Chapter 7, such costs and barriers fell substantially between the mid-1980s and the early 1990s. The special income tax advantages of private ownership of real estate were largely eliminated in the tax reform of 1986. At the same time, restrictions on the ability of REITs to manage themselves and engage in less passive types of activities were removed. In the early 1990s a "look-through" provision made it easier for large institutions to invest in small REITs without violating regulations on share ownership concentration. Also, in the early 1990s the UPREIT structure was developed, which enabled REITs to acquire assets with low-cost bases from private owners without necessarily triggering a capital gains tax event for the private owner. Nevertheless, some restrictions remain, in addition to normal transaction costs. For example, REITs lose their tax status if they sell large numbers of properties without holding them at least four years.

[31]For example, there are many more small individual investors in the stock market than there are in the market for large-scale institutional quality commercial properties.

liquid for small investors, would presumably not need to compensate such investors for illiquidity in their investments.[32] On the other hand, the greater liquidity in the stock market is also reflected in greater short-run volatility in stock prices, which may be of concern to short-horizon investors.

The basic point here is that the risk and return performance of an asset, as faced by the investors in that asset, is influenced to some extent by the nature of the market in which the investors trade the asset (directly or indirectly). The risk and return performance that matters to investors is not entirely determined purely by the fundamental characteristics of the underlying physical asset itself. As the OCC is determined by investors' expectations about the risk and return performance they face, so the relevant OCC can differ in different trading environments. The previously described incentive to "arbitrage" away differences in value caused by such differences in OCC tends to keep these differences to a minimum in the long run, and probably makes substantial differences rare and short lived, but it does not eliminate them altogether.[33]

12.3.4 What about Informational Efficiency?

We noted previously that the stock market in which REIT shares trade is more informationally efficient than the private property market in which whole individual properties trade directly. Thus, apart from permanent or quasi-permanent differences in valuation between the REIT and private property markets discussed earlier, temporary differences may occur due purely to this difference in informational efficiency between the two asset markets. In particular, REIT share prices may respond more quickly to news relevant either to $E\{CF\}$ or to $E[r]$ (for example, news about the real macroeconomy or about interest rates). Such price changes do not

[32]In this regard, differences in liquidity between small REITs and large REITs within the stock market may be at least as important as differences between the private and public asset markets. It has been argued that REITs face economies of scale in cost of capital at the firm level, due at least in part to the greater liquidity that large-capitalization REIT stocks provide for large institutional investors. (See, for example, Linneman [1997].)

[33]This amounts to saying that two branches of the capital markets—the private property market and the stock market in which REITs trade—are segmented, or not fully integrated. This issue will be discussed further in Part VII of this book. For now, a brief note is in order for the interested reader. When markets are fully integrated, the same "price of risk" (expected return risk premium per unit of risk) must prevail across the two markets. If two markets are not fully integrated, the OCC can reflect different prices of risk, reflecting the differing risk preferences of the (different) marginal participants in the two markets. Several studies have found evidence supporting the idea that the market values of private real estate and stocks reflect essentially the same price of risk. (See, for example, Geltner [1989], Liu et al. [1990], and Mei and Lee [1994].) However, a more recent study by Ling and Naranjo (1999) rejects the hypothesis that the private property markets were integrated with the stock market (in the sense of having the same price of risk) during the 1978–94 period. Ling and Naranjo did find, however, that REITs were integrated with the rest of the stock market. The Ling-Naranjo study does not specifically test whether private property and REITs were integrated during that period. The question of integration across the capital markets remains on the cutting edge of academic research. At this point, it is probably advisable to exercise caution in attempting to draw definitive practical conclusions from the work to date. Short histories and data problems (especially with the measurement of private property returns in a manner that is comparable to stock returns) cloud the results. While it seems likely that REIT and private property markets are not *fully* integrated, resulting in some differential pricing of risk on average, it is not clear *how large* such differential pricing is, particularly in the long run. On the other hand, innovations in the investment industry, technological improvements, and deregulation all tend to improve market integration over the long run.

in themselves reflect fundamental differences in valuation between the private and public markets. The two markets would (in principle) agree about the value implications of the news. The private market merely takes longer to reflect these (same) value implications.[34]

This possibility bears upon the second part of the question we set out to answer at the beginning of section 12.3, namely, if the two asset markets do imply a different value for the same asset as of the same point in time, *which valuation is "correct"?* In truth, there may be no complete or definitive answer to this question. In a sense, both markets are "correct" from their own perspectives, or from the perspective of their marginal investors. Nevertheless, to the extent that the value difference is due purely to differences in informational efficiency, it is tempting to conclude that the REIT valuation is, shall we say, "more correct" (in the sense that it reflects more up-to-date information). On the other hand, we noted that the stock market may overreact to news, leading to subsequent price "corrections." This can result in the two markets sometimes presenting a tortoise and hare relationship to each other. In short, it is wise to be cautious about making judgments as to which market valuation is "more correct" in this sense.[35]

12.3.5 Microlevel Risk Is in the Property, Not in the REIT

Before leaving this section we should probably return to a point we skimmed over rather quickly in section 12.3.3. We noted that *risk resides in the asset, not in the investor.* This simply reflects the point we made first in Chapter 10 that the relevant OCC for evaluating a given property is an OCC that reflects the risk in that property. This point no doubt seemed innocuous enough when we presented it in Chapter 10, where we were thinking purely in terms of a private property market perspective. But now suppose we have two REITs: REIT A has an average cost of capital of 10%, while REIT B has an average cost of capital of 12%, in both cases based on their total return performance history in the stock market. To simplify this illustration, we will also assume that neither of these REITs has ever employed any debt.[36] Does REIT A's lower average cost of capital imply that it can use a lower discount rate in estimating its present investment value for property X, an office building in San Francisco? In other words, can REIT A "afford to pay" a higher price for property X than REIT B can, because of REIT A's lower average cost of capital?

The answer is, probably not. Any REIT's overall cost of capital reflects the average risk of all of its assets. This may or may not be the same as the risk of property X. In general, the *marginal* (or incremental) cost of capital relevant to investment in a given asset may differ from the *average* cost of capital of the firm as a whole. The most likely explanation for REIT A's lower historical cost of capital is that REIT A's assets have historically been less risky than REIT B's. This may be because REIT A

---

[34]The reason is the previously noted difficulty in equating general publicly available news to its exact quantitative implications for the values of specific individual real property assets in the absence of a continuously functioning "auction" market for each individual property. Private markets have less ability to aggregate information across individuals and "learn from themselves" through the observation of transaction prices. (See the appendix to this chapter for additional elaboration.)

[35]The relation between public and private markets at the macrolevel, including implications for tactical investment policy, will be discussed further in Part VII.

[36]In subsequent chapters we will see how such firm-level cost of capital estimates can be calculated as a weighted average cost of capital (WACC) for the firm.

invests in less risky properties, or it may be because REIT B tends to undertake more new construction and development projects. (Development is inherently more risky than in-place bricks and mortar, even though the type of property may be the same once built.)

In general, REIT A's lower historical cost of capital *at the firm level* does not imply that it can afford to pay more for property X *at the property level*. Assuming both REIT A and B face the same incremental future cash flow stream from property X, the investment value of property X is the same for both REITs. If either REIT pays more than this value, its stock price per share will be diluted. If either REIT can get property X for less than this IV, its stock price will be enhanced. For either REIT, the OCC relevant for evaluating the investment value of property X is the property X OCC, not the REIT's average OCC. Of course, the REIT's firm-level average OCC may give a good indication of property X's OCC, but only to the extent that the REIT's other assets (on average or in the aggregate) are similar in risk to property X.

If you follow this reasoning, then you should be able to see even easier through the following two fallacies that are common in real world practice. (1) REIT A can borrow money at 6% while REIT B has to pay 8% interest on its debt. Therefore, REIT A can afford to pay a higher price for property X. (2) REIT A has a price/earnings multiple of 12 while REIT B's multiple is only 10. Therefore, REIT A can afford a higher price for property X. You should now realize that neither the interest rate on a firm's debt, nor its price/earnings ratio, is generally equivalent to the expected total return on the firm's underlying assets (the firm's average OCC). Furthermore, as we just noted, even the firm's average OCC is not necessarily the relevant OCC for computing its investment value for a given asset.[37]

12.3.6 Summarizing the Dueling Markets: Going from the Micro to the Macro Perspective

To summarize the discussion in this section, we can make a couple of qualitative generalizations about the microlevel valuation implications of the existence of real estate's two "dueling" asset markets. First, asset valuation differences at this level are not impossible, and indeed are probably not uncommon, based on differences both in cash flow expectations and in the opportunity cost of capital. Second, at least at the microlevel, such differences will probably generally be small, with large differences tending to be very transient. Third, at least over the very long run, valuation differences should tend to average out so that neither market structure provides permanently higher or lower values. Otherwise, all assets would tend to gravitate toward one ownership form or the other.

A final question that we should touch briefly on relates back to Exhibit 12-2 and the professional practitioners' focus on short-run measures such as current yields and price/earnings ratios. If microlevel differences in valuation are small and transient, why do we see relatively large differences in macrolevel valuations such as those portrayed in Exhibit 12-2? The answer to this question obviously lies in the difference between the micro- and macrolevels. For one thing, REITs in general do not tend to hold exactly the same types of properties as are represented in the general population

---

[37]A firm's debt is usually, by construction, less risky than the firm's underlying assets. (See Chapter 13 and Part VI.) A firm's earnings/price ratio is akin to its current cash yield, $E[y]$, except that some of the earnings are typically held back to finance growth and not paid out in dividends, resulting in the earnings/price ratio typically being larger than the current dividend yield.

of commercial properties, or in particular samples of such properties, such as the NCREIF index. Furthermore, as noted in section 12.3.1, REIT share prices reflect not only their existing in-place assets, but also their entity-level capital structure (such as the degree of leverage), and their future **growth opportunities** as represented by their ability to make positive-NPV acquisitions, developments, and dispositions. Financial management and growth opportunities are highly sensitive to the nature and quality of entity-level REIT management. REIT share prices, and REIT risk and return, reflect these macrolevel variables as well as the aggregate of all their existing microlevel asset holdings. This could explain much of any apparent discrepancy between REIT and private property market valuation statistics.

12.4 CHAPTER SUMMARY

You can now unfasten your seatbelts. We have landed. Chapter 12 dealt with some very deep and subtle issues. This is the kind of thing you have to read more than once, and think about for a while. We sympathize. From a purely pedagogical perspective, we would have been very happy if we could have left out this chapter. But the topics addressed here are obviously important and fundamental. Although they are of academic interest, they also carry important implications for real world investment decision making. Furthermore, it is in these unique characteristics of real estate that some of the most exciting opportunities in real estate investment can be found. If you study this chapter carefully, you should come away with a deeper and more accurate understanding of and insight into microlevel real estate investment decision making and how real estate asset markets work. Smart people can make use of such a level of knowledge in the real world!

APPENDIX 12: BASIC VALUATION CONCEPTS: TRANSACTION PRICES AND MARKET VALUES

Valuation theory has a long history in economics and the appraisal profession. Becoming familiar with some of the basics of this theory should help to build your intuition and understanding of value in real estate. In this appendix we will define and distinguish between several different concepts of value and price.

The most primal concept of value is what is often termed **inherent value**. This refers to the value of an object (in our case, a commercial property) to a given owner or user of the object, in the absence of any consideration of the market value or exchange value of the object. Inherent value represents the maximum amount a given person would be willing to pay for a good *if he had to*. From the perspective of a *user* of the property, inherent value is the **usage value** of the property. This would apply, for example, to owner/occupiers as in the case of some corporate real estate, in which ownership and usage are not separated. From the perspective of an *investor* in a property, defined as a non-user owner, inherent value is essentially the same as what we have been calling investment value (IV).[38]

---

[38] As noted, the terms *inherent value*, *intrinsic value*, and *investment value* have a fair amount of overlap in common usage. But in general, the former two terms have more of a usage value connotation, while investment value refers more specifically to values for non-user owners, landlords rather than owner/occupiers.

Now consider two populations of potential user owners or investors for a given type of property. One population already owns such property, while the other population does not. These two populations are represented in Exhibit 12-3a. The left-hand distribution consists of potential buyers of this type of property (current nonowners), and the right-hand distribution is that of potential sellers (current owners of such property).[39] The horizontal axis measures inherent value (say, per square foot) for the type of property in question, while the vertical axis shows the number of people in each population having the inherent value indicated on the horizontal axis.

Now suppose these two populations are able to interact and trade examples of this type of property among themselves. For a price corresponding to any given value on the horizontal axis, we would have a number of willing buyers equal to the area underneath the buyer curve to the right of the given price. We would also have a number of willing sellers equal to the area underneath the seller curve to the left of the given price. The entire potential buyer population would be willing to pay at least the amount A for this type of property, while no buyer would be willing to pay more than D. No current owner of this type of property would be willing to sell for less than B, while all owners would be willing to part with their property for the amount E.

If potential buyers and potential sellers randomly find each other, we would observe some transactions, for there is some overlap of the two distributions. All transactions would occur within the price range between B and D. **Transaction prices** are the prices at which deals are actually done, the prices at which examples of the type of property in question change hands. While inherent values are very difficult if not impossible to observe empirically, transaction prices can be observed empirically, and can thus be thought of as objective information (in contrast to inherent values, which may be more subjective in nature). If we observe many transactions, we would expect that the frequency distribution of transaction prices would have a shape similar to the triangular region that is simultaneously underneath both curves between B and D.[40]

If the property market functioned as a well-ordered double auction, with the auctioneer calling out prices and bidders (both buyers and sellers) revealing their true inherent values, C is the price at which the market would clear, the "equilibrium price." C is thus the value at which there are as many willing buyers as there are willing sellers (the area to the right of C under the buyer curve equals the area to the left of C under the seller curve). In a well-ordered auction market with perfect inherent value information revelation, *all* the transactions for this type of property would take place at the price C, and this price would maximize the aggregate consumer or producer surplus from the usage of this type of property.[41]

In real property markets, however, we do not have perfect auction markets to reveal the equilibrium value C. But we do usually have reasonably active and well-functioning asset transaction markets. The potential buyers and potential sellers of a given type of property can observe (more or less easily and accurately) the prices at which transactions of that (or similar) type of property occur from time to time. Such observation gives potential market participants some information about the

[39]For the potential sellers, the inherent value may be interpreted as the *minimum* price at which they would be willing to sell the property *if they had to* sell that low.

[40]That is, the transaction price frequency distribution is the intersection of the areas underneath the two inherent price distributions.

[41]Economic "surplus" in this context refers to the net value or utility obtained by the producer or consumer as a result of trade.

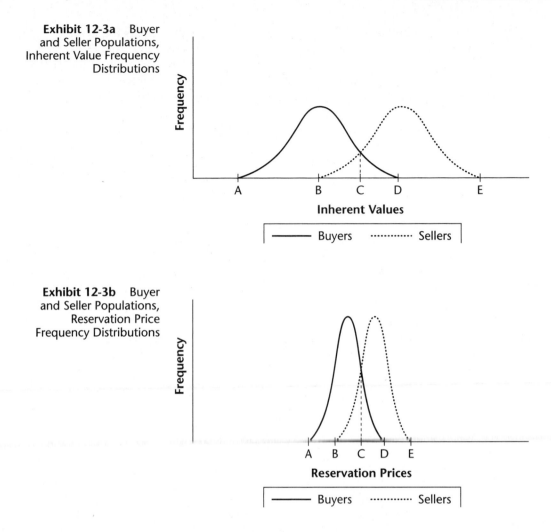

Exhibit 12-3a Buyer and Seller Populations, Inherent Value Frequency Distributions

Exhibit 12-3b Buyer and Seller Populations, Reservation Price Frequency Distributions

equilibrium value (C in our diagram). While observation of transaction prices does not fully reveal the equilibrium value, it does gives some indication, putting some range around the likely equilibrium value. Potential buyers and sellers rationally use such transaction price information in determining their **reservation prices**, the prices at which they will stop searching any further for a willing partner and will agree to trade. Reservation prices are based on inherent values but also incorporate information about the market, the perceived likely equilibrium value.[42]

Buyer reservation prices will be no higher than, but in some cases may be lower than, inherent values. Seller reservation prices will be no lower than, but in some cases may be higher than, inherent values. Potential buyers who see evidence from the market that their inherent values are above the equilibrium value will tend to reduce their reservation prices below their inherent values, because no one wants to pay more than necessary, and because the market informs people about values. Sellers who perceive the equilibrium price to be above their inherent values will tend to raise their

---

[42] Reservation prices are also based on the cost of the searching process. The more difficult and costly it is to find potentially suitable properties (or buyers), the higher (lower) will be the optimal reservation price for buyers (sellers) of a given type of property, other things being equal.

reservation prices above their inherent values, because no one wants to sell for less than necessary. At the other end of the inherent value distributions, nonowners whose inherent values are well below the range of observable transaction prices will effectively drop out of the potential buyer pool. Owners whose inherent values are well above the observed transaction price range will similarly drop out of the potential seller distribution.[43]

This causes reservation price distributions to be tighter, less spread out, and closer to the true equilibrium value C than the underlying inherent value distributions. This difference between the reservation price distributions of the effective potential market participant pool on the one hand, and the underlying inherent value distributions on the other hand, is the effect of the market "teaching itself about itself" through the information *revealed by transaction prices observable through the functioning of the market itself.*[44] In the financial economics literature this process is often called **price discovery**. The more numerous and frequent the transactions, the more alike or homogeneous the individual properties or assets in the market, and the easier it is to observe accurately the transaction prices, the tighter and closer to C will be the reservation price distributions. This is because the information revealed by the observed transactions will be more directly relevant to the valuation of the other properties in the market. This is sometimes referred to as the effect of **market density**.

Let's consider an extreme case, in which homogeneous shares of the same asset are traded continuously in a double-auction market open to the public and always full of numerous buyers and sellers, and in which all transaction prices are reported immediately and publicly, similar to what goes on in a public stock exchange. In such an extreme case, buyer and seller reservation price distributions would effectively collapse onto the single value of C, the market-clearing equilibrium value. Then (but only then, in such a hypothetical extreme case), the unique observed transaction price would exactly equal the equilibrium value of the asset, as of the time of the transaction.

Exhibit 12-3b illustrates a more realistic case of reservation price distributions for property markets. The scale on the horizontal axis is meant to be the same as that in Exhibit 12-3a, so that the narrower frequency distributions in Exhibit 12-3b indicate that the reservation price distributions shrink the transaction price distribution range from what it would be with no market information available to buyers and sellers. The observable transaction price range from B to D around C is narrower in Exhibit 12-3b than it is in 12-3a based only on the inherent value distributions. This is the effect of market density. But in the typical property market situation depicted in Exhibit 12-3b some dispersion of observed transaction prices around the equilibrium value still occurs because the market is not sufficiently dense to eliminate all such dispersion.

---

[43]In other words, in both cases they will simply stop searching for opposite parties to a potential transaction.

[44]The astute reader will realize that this mechanism of market self-learning through transaction price observation holds implications for our previous assertion at the beginning of Chapter 10: that the price at which an investor can expect to sell a property in the future is *independent* of the price paid for the property in the past by the investor. In fact, in a market of thinly traded unique assets, the price paid by the current owner may indeed have some relevance in the future as an indication of value for the property. However, this relevance diminishes rapidly with the passage of time, and in any case would be far from determinative. What we asserted in Chapter 10 is *essentially* true in the context of that chapter, and provides the best guidance for investment decision making.

Now it is important to recognize that the value C in this model is what is normally defined as the **market value**, or the exchange value of the type of property in question.[45] Recognizing that Exhibit 12-3b represents a snapshot of the property market as of one point in time, we see that even if several transactions were occurring at precisely that point in time, these observable transaction prices would be merely "drawings" from the transaction price distribution (which ranges between B and D). No single transaction price necessarily equals C, nor is there even any guarantee that the average among the observed transaction prices will necessarily equal C. We thus arrive at a fundamental principle of the valuation of thinly traded objects:

Observed transaction prices are disbursed around the contemporaneous market value.

This principle underlies the application of modern statistics to the empirical study of market values in real estate. It suggests a statistical-based definition of market value as the mean of the ex ante (i.e., potential) transaction price distribution as of a given point in time. This allows us to employ basic statistical inference and sampling theory, for example, to enlighten the process of estimating market values. In particular, we may assume that the arithmetic average of randomly observed transaction prices is a statistic whose ex ante mean is the market value (C).[46] The standard deviation of this statistic is $(1/\sqrt{n})$ times the standard deviation of the potential transaction price distribution, where n is the number of transaction price observations.[47] This is sometimes referred to as the square root of n rule. The general implication of this statistical perspective is that the average of the observed transaction prices, at a single point in time, is a statistically unbiased estimate of the true market value, C, as of that point in time, and the more transaction observations we include in computing this average, the more precise will be our estimate.[48]

[45]Recall that, as we are talking about a type of property, this value would probably be measured in some normalized units, such as dollars per square foot or dollars per dollar of current income (the inverse of the cap rate or current yield).

[46]Here we are assuming that all observed transactions occur as of a single point in time (a snapshot of the market). Obviously, as market values change over time, a sample of observed transaction prices occurring at different points in time will each be drawn from the potential price distribution centered around the (varying) market value as of the time each transaction occurred. Such a sample mean would then represent a type of "moving average" of market values across time. The implications this holds for real estate time-series return and risk statistics will be discussed in Part VII.

[47]For the mean of the potential transaction price distribution to equal exactly the equilibrium value C, we require that the mean of that distribution equal its median, that is, that the distribution be symmetrical, which in turn requires that the buyer and seller reservation price distributions are symmetrical in their relevant tails. In this case the mode of the transaction price distribution, or single most likely price, will also coincide with C.

[48]We assume here that each transaction is independent of the others, and that the transacting properties are all identical, or that errors induced in adjusting the observed prices for differences in the properties are independent. Vandell (1991) presented a more detailed analysis of optimal selection and weighting of comparable property transactions. A statistical procedure known as hedonic regression can also be used for this purpose, as will be described in Chapter 23.

KEY TERMS

market value (MV)
opportunity value
investment value (IV)
opportunity cost of capital (OCC)
NPV investment criterion
second-most-motivated buyer
marginal investors
intramarginal investors
asset transaction market equilibrium
entrepreneurial profit
informational inefficiency (in asset markets)
random noise (in asset valuation)
due diligence
partial adjustment (of asset prices to news)

predictability (inertia in asset price movements)
market timing
transaction costs
supernormal profits
cycles
arbitrage
net asset value (NAV)
discount/premium to NAV
differential valuation (across asset markets)
NCREIF and NAREIT indices
microlevel differential valuation
negative feedback loop (regulatory mechanism)
franchise value (brand recognition)

price/earnings multiples (P/E)
cost of capital (denominator)
    sources of value
current cash yield
growth opportunities (for REITs)
inherent value
usage value
transaction price
reservation price
price discovery
market density

STUDY QUESTIONS

12.1.   Why is market value (MV) an important way to conceive of, and measure, asset value for investors in commercial real estate?

12.2.   Why is investment value (IV) an important way to conceive of, and measure, asset value for investors in commercial real estate?

12.3.   Suppose a certain site has a McDonald's restaurant on it (equipped with the usual golden arches, etc.). As a McDonald's, the site can generate $50,000 per year, net cash. In any other use it can only generate at most $40,000 per year, and it would cost $20,000 to remove the golden arches. Assuming a 10% required return:

   a.   What is the market value of this property?

   b.   What is its investment value to McDonald's? [Hint: Use the perpetuity formula: $V = CF/r$.]

12.4.   In question 12.3, assume that the property is currently owned by McDonald's.

   a.   What is McDonald's expected NPV from selling the property, evaluated from an MV perspective?

   b.   What is McDonald's expected NPV from selling the property, evaluated from an IV perspective?

12.5.   Now assume that the property described in question 12.3 is owned by someone other than McDonald's, a "typical" real estate investor by the name of Bob.

   a.   What is Bob's expected NPV from selling the property, evaluated from an MV perspective?

b. What is Bob's expected NPV from selling the property, evaluated from an IV perspective?

c. What if Bob tries to sell the property to McDonald's?

12.6. What are the general (and defining) characteristics of marginal participants in an asset market?

12.7. Describe a characteristic indicator that a property market is currently in equilibrium?

12.8. What are the general necessary conditions for a real estate investment transaction to involve substantial positive NPV for at least one side of the deal without involving negative NPV for the other side?

12.9. If a certain property is put up for sale, there is a 50% chance it will sell for $900,000 and a 50% chance it will sell for $1,100,000.

a. What is the market value of this property?

b. What is the standard deviation of the random noise in this property's price as a percentage of its market value?

c. If the property sells for $900,000, what was the ex post NPV from the market value perspective for the seller and the buyer?

d. If the property sells for $1,100,000, what was the ex post NPV from the market value perspective for the seller and the buyer?

e. What is the ex ante NPV from the market value perspective?

12.10. Name at least three sources or causes of real estate transaction prices deviating around the market value of the asset.

12.11. Suppose two identical properties are traded in two different asset markets: property A in a relatively inefficient or sluggish market and property B in a more efficient market. When news arrives relevant to asset value, property A's market value will move only halfway to the new value in the first period, and the rest of the way in the next period. Property B's value will move all the way to the new value in the first period. At the beginning of period 0 both properties are worth $1000. Then news arrives that implies they should be worth 10% more.

a. In the absence of any further news, how much will property A and property B be worth at the end of period 1 and period 2?

b. In the absence of transaction costs, and assuming you can borrow $1,000 for two periods at $50 interest, how much money could you make (and how could you make it) by trading between the two properties across the two markets? (Assume that at the beginning of the dealing you do not own either property, and at the end you cash out completely, paying back any loaned money.)

c. Suppose the transaction costs are 3% of property value each time you either buy or sell a property (but loan transactions are free). Now what is your profit or loss from the same transactions as in (b)?

12.12. Why is it difficult for real estate investors to make supernormal profits from market-timing investments even though the property market is somewhat sluggish with relatively predictable short-run movements in asset prices?

*12.13. Describe a general indicator of the existence of differential valuation of (the same) real estate assets between the private property market and the REIT market. [Hint: What would we expect to see in the nature of the parties to the transactions in the private property market?]

*12.14. a. What are the two fundamental sources of possible differential valuation of real estate assets between the private property market and the REIT market?

b. How might REITs in general be able to influence property cash flows in ways that private owners could not?

c. How might the risk perceptions and preferences of the average investor in the stock market differ from those of the average investor in the direct private property market?

*12.15. Why is it unlikely that large differences in valuation would persist for long periods of time between the private property market and the REIT market?

*12.16. (from the appendix) What is the difference among inherent value, reservation prices, transaction prices, and market values? Define and contrast each of these conceptions or measures of value.

*12.17. (from the appendix) What is meant by the term *price discovery*? Why is price discovery likely to be more efficient in "denser" asset markets?

PART IV

References and Additional Reading

Adams, P., B. Kluger, and S. Wyatt. "Integrating Auction and Search Markets: The Slow Dutch Auction." *Journal of Real Estate Finance and Economics* 20(3): 239–254, September 1992.

Barkham, R. and D. Geltner. "Price Discovery in American and British Property Markets." *Real Estate Economics (formerly AREUEA Journal)* 23(1): 21–44, spring 1995.

Brealey, R. and S. Myers. *Principles of Corporate Finance*, 5th ed., New York: McGraw-Hill, 1996, Chapters 2, 4–6.

Case, B. and J. Quigley. "Dynamics of Real-Estate Prices." *Review of Economics and Statistics* 73(1): 50–58 February 1991.

Case, K. and R. Shiller. "Forecasting Prices and Excess Returns in the Housing Market." *AREUEA Journal* 18(3): 253–273, fall 1990.

Crosby, N., A. Lavers, and J. Murdoch. "Property Valuation Variation and the 'Margin of Error' in the UK." *Journal of Property Research* 15(4): 305–330, December 1998.

Diaz, J. and M. Wolverton. "A Longitudinal Examination of the Appraisal Smoothing Hypothesis." *Real Estate Economics* 26(2), summer 1998.

Downs, A. "Public, Private Market Valuations Do Diverge." *National Real Estate Investor*, December 1994, p. 20.

Geltner, D. "Estimating Real Estate's Systematic Risk from Aggregate Level Appraisal-Based Returns." *Real Estate Economics* 17(4): 463–481, winter 1989.

Geltner, D. "Estimating Market Values from Appraised Values Without Assuming an Efficient Market." *Journal of Real Estate Research* 8(3): 325–346, 1993.

Geltner, D. "The Use of Appraisals in Portfolio Valuation & Index Construction." *Journal of Property Valuation & Investment* 15(5): 423–447, 1997.

Geltner, D. "How Accurate is the NCREIF Index as a Benchmark, and Who Cares?" *Real Estate Finance* 14(4), winter 1998

Giliberto, S. M. and A. Mengden. "REITs and Real Estate: Two Markets Reexamined." *Real Estate Finance* 13(1): 56–60, spring 1996.

Goetzmann, W. "The Single Family Home in the Investment Portfolio." *The Journal of Real Estate Finance & Economics* 6(3): 201–222, May 1993.

Graff, R. "Changing Leases into Investment-Grade Bonds." *Journal of Real Estate Portfolio Management* 5(2): 183–194, 1999.

Graff, R. and M. Young. "The Magnitude of Random Appraisal Error in Commercial Real Estate Valuation." *The Journal of Real Estate Research* 17: 33–54, 1999.

Gyourko, J. and D. Keim. "What Does the Stock Market Tell Us About Real Estate Returns." *Real Estate Economics* 20(3): 457–486, fall 1992.

Ling, D. and A. Naranjo. "The Integration of Commercial Real Estate Markets and Stock Markets." *Real Estate Economics* 27(3): 483–516, fall 1999.

Linneman, P. "Forces Changing the Real Estate Industry Forever." *Wharton Real Estate Review*, spring 1997.

Liu, C., D. Hartzell, T. Grissom, and W. Grieg. "The Composition of the Market Portfolio and Real Estate Investment Performance." *Real Estate Economics* 18(1): 49–75, spring 1990.

Mei, J. "Assessing the 'Santa Claus' Approach to Asset Allocation." *Real Estate Finance* 13(2): 65–70, summer 1996.

Mei, J. and A. Lee. "Is There a Real Estate Factor Premium?" *Journal of Real Estate Finance & Economics* 9(2):113–126, September 1994.

Vandell, K. "Optimal Comparable Selection and Weighting in Real Property Valuation." *AREUEA Journal (Real Estate Economics)* 19(2): 213–239, summer 1991.

Vogel, J. "Why the New Conventional Wisdom about REITs Is Wrong." *Real Estate Finance* 14(2), summer 1997.

Completing the Basic Investment Analysis Picture

In Parts III and IV we introduced the fundamental financial economic principles and procedures underlying the valuation of real property, including the basics of investment analysis at the micro (individual property) level. In Part V we will add to that picture by introducing two additional considerations that are often important in considering commercial real estate investments: debt and income taxes. These topics are a bit more advanced, in the sense that they build on the basic foundation presented in the previous chapters. However, these topics are not any more difficult to master than what we have already come through, and our treatment here will remain at a practical level. With the incorporation of debt and taxes we address the necessary concomitant to the investment decision covered in Part IV. There, you learned how to decide what to invest in. Here, you learn how to finance such investment.

The topics considered in Part V differ from our previous focus in that they relate to the *owners* of properties, rather than to the properties themselves per se. That is, we are shifting focus from the property level to the investor level, the individuals or institutions who are considering real estate investments. One implication of the owner perspective is that the issues addressed in Part V sometimes go beyond the consideration of a single property to encompass a broader perspective of the investor's decision making, based upon the investor's overall financial position, which may include a portfolio of many properties as well as different types of investments such as stocks and bonds. Nevertheless, our primary focus in Part V will remain at the microlevel, on the analysis of individual properties and deals. (We will reserve most of our treatment of broader, macrolevel issues for Part VII.)

Use of Debt in Real Estate Investment (Part I): The Effect of Leverage

13

Learning Objectives

After reading this chapter, you should understand:

◆ What is meant by the term *leverage*, and how the use of debt financing affects the leverage of the equity investment.

◆ How leverage affects the equity investor's expected total return, and the income and appreciation components of that return.

◆ How leverage affects the risk in the total return to equity, and therefore the market's required risk premium in the ex ante return.

◆ The weighted average cost of capital formula (WACC) and how this formula can be useful in quantifying leverage effects in theory, and in making practical approximations.

◆ What is meant by the term *positive leverage*, and the conditions that result in such leverage.

◆ How the use of debt, and its effect on leverage, enables the same underlying real property asset to serve investors with different objectives and concerns.

The use of debt financing is very widespread in real estate investment. Indeed, real estate is famous as a source of collateral for vast amounts of debt. During the 1990s there was well over $1 trillion in commercial mortgage loans outstanding in the United States, as well as additional real estate debt in the form of entity-level bank loans, bonds issued to REITs, and CMBS. Indeed, individual investors and REITs typically use large amounts of debt, and even tax-exempt institutions sometimes purchase property subject to mortgage loans.

In order to help you develop a sophisticated understanding of the use of debt in real estate investment, we have divided this topic into two parts, corresponding to

Chapters 13 and 15. (In between, Chapter 14 will introduce the effect of income taxes.) Both of these chapters will consider the role of debt in real estate investment primarily from the borrower's perspective, although this will occasionally require consideration of what is happening to the lender as well. (Real estate debt viewed primarily from the lender's, or debt holder's, perspective will be the main focus of Part VI.)

The present chapter will focus on the effect of **leverage** on the investment performance of the equity position. The use of debt to finance an equity investment creates what is called "leverage" in the equity investment, because it allows equity investors to magnify the amount of underlying physical capital they control (which may also magnify the risk and return performance of the equity). It is important to understand this effect thoroughly. In this chapter we will largely ignore income tax considerations related to debt, to focus on the pure effect of leverage.

After taxes are introduced in Chapter 14, Chapter 15 will then step back and view the role of debt from a broader perspective, that of optimal capital structure for real estate investment. Capital structure refers to the relative proportion of equity and debt in real estate investment, and Chapter 15 will integrate leverage and income tax considerations to view capital structure from a more comprehensive perspective.

The topic of the present chapter, the effect of leverage on equity investment, is fundamental to all investment analyses, not just real estate analyses. However, this topic is often skimmed rather lightly in corporate finance textbooks because it is argued that stockholders can lever up or down (either by borrowing money or investing in bonds) "on their own account." They do not need the corporation in whose stock they are investing to do their levering for them.

This argument is as applicable to REITs as it is to other publicly traded firms, but REITs control only a fraction of all commercial property investment. In real estate it is not uncommon for individual investors to own the underlying productive assets directly, with effectively no corporate-level entity involved in the investment decision-making process. Furthermore, even when the direct owner of the real estate equity is a corporate or partnership entity, it is important to understand how leverage affects the risk and return performance of that investment entity. The effects of leverage at the entity level are likely to have important implications for the strategic and tactical management of the entity. In addition, the ultimate individual investor/owners of a real estate investment entity need to understand leverage in order to determine whether to adjust their personal leverage on their own account in response to the entity leverage. With this in mind, the present chapter will start out at a very elementary level and take you up through a level at which you can apply some basic analytical tools that are quite useful in real world practice.

THE BIG PICTURE

Before we get into the nuts and bolts of leverage, however, let's step back for a minute and introduce the use of debt in its broader context in real estate investment, to consider the forest rather than the individual trees. Do you recall the point we made early in Chapter 7 about **heterogeneous investors?** This fundamental fact permeates all aspects of investment, including the issue of debt financing for real estate investments. Indeed, at a broad-brush level, it may be said that a fundamental reason for the widespread use of mortgage debt in income-property investment is the diversity among investors.

Recall that different individuals, as well as different types of institutional investors, have different objectives and constraints governing their investment decisions. Some investors want growth, while others want income. Some are willing to take on considerable risk in pursuit of high returns, while others are willing to sacrifice high returns in order to keep their investments safe and liquid. Also, access to capital, and the resulting availability of funds to invest, varies greatly across investors. This variety among investors results in a need for a variety of **investment products**, as we called them in Chapter 7.

In this chapter we will see how leverage provided by mortgage debt allows the same underlying income-generating physical asset to offer very different types of investment products that can satisfy the needs of investors with very different types of objectives and constraints. A moderate-risk, underlying real estate asset presenting moderate growth and moderate yield may support high-risk equity investment with high growth and a low current yield, as well as low-risk debt investment with zero growth and a high current yield. In fact, mortgages are distinguished from real estate equity not only, or not necessarily, by differences in risk and return. Mortgages allow "passive" investment, in which the investor does not have to manage the property. And mortgages provide a contractually fixed, finite maturity cash flow stream that may be ideal for an investor with a fixed investment horizon.

Because of the various ways in which mortgages differ from real estate equity from an investment perspective, the pool of investors who are potentially able and willing to invest (directly or indirectly) in real estate (i.e., to provide capital toward the purchase of property) is increased. This tends to increase property values and/or the efficiency of the allocation of capital to real estate. At a very fundamental and big-picture level, this is what is going on in the widespread use of debt in real estate investment. Now with this in mind, let's get down to the nitty-gritty of understanding how leverage works.

13.1 BASIC DEFINITIONS AND MECHANICS OF LEVERAGE

A good way to understand the effect of leverage on the real estate equity investor's (that is, the debt borrower's) position is by analogy to the physical principle of the lever. This principle was first explicitly formulated by the ancient Greek mathematician and mechanical engineer Archimedes (287–212 B.C.E.) who lived in Syracuse on the island of Sicily and was famous for his designs of catapults and siege machines, among other clever devices. To illustrate the principle of the lever, Archimedes supposedly made the statement: "Give me a place to stand, and I will move the Earth." He meant this literally, although he would also need an incredibly long-armed lever and a place to put the fulcrum!

In fact, the analogy between financial and physical leverage is very helpful. This analogy is depicted in Exhibit 13-1. The upper panel depicts a physical lever. The weight that can be balanced or lifted at the end of one arm of the lever equals the weight at the end of the other arm times the ratio of the lengths of the two arms. In the example shown, a 200-pound man balances a 500-pound weight by standing at the end of an arm that is two and one-half times longer on his side of the pivot point than it is on the other.

The analogy to financial leverage is direct and provides important insight into the effect on investment. This is represented in the bottom panel in the exhibit. An investor purchases a $10 million apartment property using, say, $4 million of her

Exhibit 13-1 Analogy of Physical Leverage and Financial Leverage

Physical Lever

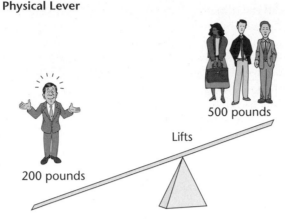

Leverage Ratio = 500/200 = 2.5

Financial Leverage

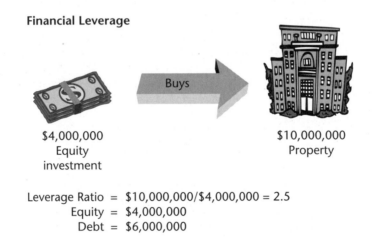

$4,000,000
Equity
investment

$10,000,000
Property

Leverage Ratio = $10,000,000/$4,000,000 = 2.5
Equity = $4,000,000
Debt = $6,000,000

own money and $6 million borrowed in a mortgage backed by the property as collateral. The leverage ratio in this case is $10 million divided by $4 million, or 2.5. Just as physical leverage enables 200 pounds of force to lift 500 pounds of weight using a lever with a leverage ratio of 2.5, so financial leverage enables the investor to purchase (and "own" or *control*) an asset whose value is 2.5 times greater than the amount of money invested. With financial leverage, the **leverage ratio (LR)** is defined as the total value of the underlying asset divided by the value of the equity investment: $LR = V/E = (L + E)/E$, where V is the asset value, L is the loan value, and E is the equity.

The word **equity** actually has its roots in the notion of balance, and thereby recalls the physical leverage analogy. Investors' equity is their ownership share, and it normally gives them primary governing control over the underlying asset, as long as they live up to their requirements under their debt obligation. On the other hand, the debt receives a senior, or preferred, claim on the underlying asset's cash flow and

Leverage Ratio versus Loan-to-Value Ratio: A Note on Terminology

It is important to recognize that the term, *leverage ratio* as we are here defining it (labeled *LR*) is not the same as the **loan-to-value ratio (LTV)**, though the two are related. In particular, if V is the value of the underlying property, E is the value of the equity, and L is the value of the loan (such that $V = E + L$), then the *LR* is $V/E = V/(V - L)$, while the *LTV* is L/V. The greater the *LTV*, the greater the *LR*, but the relationship is not linear: $LR = 1/(1 - L/V) = 1/(1 - LTV)$; $LTV = 1 - (1/LR)$.

For example, an *LTV* of 50% corresponds to an *LR* of 2, while an *LTV* of 75% corresponds to an *LR* of 4. Increasing the *LTV* by a factor of one-half in this case results in a doubling of the leverage ratio. It is important to keep the difference between *LR* and *LTV* in mind, because in real estate practice leverage is typically spoken of in terms of the *LTV*, whereas investment risk and return performance is most directly related to the *LR*, as we will see.

value. As a balancing compensation for giving up the senior position, the equity gets the **residual claim,** that is, the claim to the entire residual value in the investment, or all the remaining cash flow and value after subtracting the debt holder's claim.[1] Thus, equity value equals the underlying property value minus the outstanding mortgage balance. In the case shown in Exhibit 13-1, the property value is $10 million and the debt is worth $6 million, so the equity is worth $4 million.

Management Incentive Effects

It is important to note that this arrangement generally results in a *compatible matching of governance and incentive.* Equity's governance of the asset gives it the greater ability to influence the total value of the underlying asset (e.g., by management actions), while its residual claim causes any increment in this value to accrue to the value of the equity. If the equity owners manage the property well, they will reap the benefit; if they manage it poorly, they will suffer the loss (at least up to a point). Thus, by giving the equity owner the primary management control, the value of the underlying asset (the property) will likely be maximized, thereby maximizing the productivity of the physical capital.[2]

[1] We are speaking here of *private sector* claims on the property. Of course, the government gets the first claim, in the form of property taxes.

[2] Obviously, maximization of the underlying property value is also in the interest of the debt holder, as it minimizes default risk. While the equity/debt incentive alignment works well in normal circumstances (e.g., when the debt is not too large relative to the current property value), there are circumstances in which the incentives can get out of alignment and cause a conflict of interest between equity and debt holders to the detriment of overall underlying property value. Such "agency costs" are ignored in the present chapter, but will be treated in Chapter 15.

13.2 EFFECT OF LEVERAGE ON THE RISK AND RETURN TO EQUITY

Now let's consider the effect leverage has on the expected return and the risk of the investment from the perspective of the equity investor. We will consider the expected return first, and then the risk.

13.2.1 Effect on the Expected Return

We can see the essence of the effect of leverage on the equity investor's expected return by continuing the previous example for another year. Suppose, in particular, that by the end of the subsequent year our $10,000,000 apartment property has increased 2% in value, to $10,200,000, and meanwhile also has provided $800,000 in net cash flow during the year. Thus, the underlying property has provided a 2% appreciation return or growth, and an 8% income return, for a total return of 10%. This is the return applicable to an all-equity investment in the property free and clear of debt, that is, an *unlevered* investment ($LR = 1$; $LTV = 0$).

But what about the levered investor? Suppose the mortgage is an interest-only loan at 8% (no amortization of principal), so $480,000 of interest must be paid as "debt service" from the $800,000 cash flow generated by the property, ($8\% \times \$6,000,000 = \$480,000$). This leaves only $320,000 cash flow remaining for the equity investor ($800,000 − $480,000 = $320,000). The capital position of the equity investor at the end of the year consists of the asset, which is now worth $10,200,000, minus the $6,000,000 liability still owed to the mortgage lender, for a net capital value of $4,200,000. However, the equity investor only invested $4,000,000 of her own money; the rest was obtained from the mortgage. Thus, the return on the leveraged equity investment is 13%, consisting of 8% in the income component ($320,000/$4,000,000) and 5% in the appreciation component (the $200,000 increase in equity value from $4,000,000 to $4,200,000, as a fraction of the $4,000,000 invested).

These results are summarized in the table in Exhibit 13-2. Notice that the substantial leverage used in this case ($LR = 2.5$; $LTV = 60\%$), has the effect of substantially increasing the expected return.[3] This is because the equity investor has been able to borrow money at an interest rate lower than the expected return on the property (8% is less than 10%). It is also important to note that, in this case anyway, the increase in the expected return has come entirely in the form of an increased appreciation component, with no change in the income component.

At first, this sounds great. It sounds like a free lunch: the investor has increased her total return expectation simply by using other people's money! But rarely do we get something for nothing in the real world. In fact, this brings us to the other side of the effect of leverage on the equity investment.

---

[3] When considering the effect of leverage on the risk and return performance of the investment, we are implicitly holding constant the total amount of capital to be invested by the equity investor. This is why we typically measure the effects of leverage using return percentages rather than absolute dollar amounts. For example, in the case of our apartment building example, we are implicitly assuming, in effect, that the equity investor has a total net wealth of $4,000,000 available to invest at the present time. Thus the benchmark of comparison for the equity investor is the levered $4,000,000 investment in the $10,000,000 property versus an unlevered (all-equity) investment in a similar but smaller $4,000,000 property. The expected total return for the unlevered investment is thus $10\% \times \$4,000,000 = \$400,000$; while that for the levered investment is $13\% \times \$4,000,000 = \$520,000$.

Exhibit 13-2 Typical Effect of Leverage on Expected Investment Returns

	Property	Levered Equity	Debt
Initial value	$10,000,000	$4,000,000	$6,000,000
Cash flow	$800,000	$320,000	$480,000
Ending value	$10,200,000	$4,200,000	$6,000,000
Income return	8%	8%	8%
Appreciation return	2%	5%	0%
Total return	10%	13%	8%

13.2.2 Effect on the Risk in the Return

We have seen an example of how leverage can increase the equity investor's expected return, but we need now to consider its effect on the risk of the equity investment. The fact is, under normal circumstances, *if leverage increases the ex ante return on the equity, then it will also increase the risk in that equity.* How does leverage increase the equity investor's risk? To answer this question, let us continue our previous numerical example based on the $10 million apartment building.

Suppose at the time the investment decision must be made we do not know exactly what the future will bring for this property. This is a realistic assumption reflecting the fact that the underlying asset is risky. To simplify the picture for purposes of illustration, let us say that we can represent the risk in the property by defining two possible future scenarios, each of which is equally likely to occur. We will call the first scenario the optimistic scenario. If this scenario unfolds, the property will increase in value over the coming year to $11,200,000, a 12% increase in value (10% more increase than the expected growth of 2%), and the property will also generate $900,000 in net cash flow for the year ($100,000 more than the expected amount of $800,000). The pessimistic scenario envisions a reduction in property value over the coming year to $9,200,000, a decline of 8% (which would be 10% lower growth than the +2% expectation), and the generation of only $700,000 in net cash flow by the building during the year ($100,000 less than expected).[4] These are the only two possible future eventualities. Let us furthermore assume that, *no matter which of these two scenarios actually occurs, if the investor has taken out the 8% loan, she will still owe $480,000 in interest and $6,000,000 in principal on the loan.*

Exhibit 13-3 then quantifies the return components that would prevail in each of the two scenarios under these assumptions, and it indicates the range in these returns between the optimistic and pessimistic outcomes. This range is a way to quantify the risk in the investment. Greater range indicates more uncertainty about the future returns, including a potentially worse downside outcome. For example, without leverage the pessimistic scenario will result in a total return on the property equity over the coming year of −1%. But with the 60% LTV loan, the levered equity total return would be −14.5% if the pessimistic scenario occurs. Thus, leverage magnifies the downside loss by 13.5% in this case.

---

[4] Note that if each of these scenarios is viewed as having a 50% chance of occurring, then the ex ante means, or expected values of the returns (looking forward in time), equal the returns discussed in Exhibit 13-2.

	Property (LR = 1)			Levered Equity (LR = 2.5)			Debt (LR = 0)		
	OPT	PES	RANGE	OPT	PES	RANGE	OPT	PES	RANGE
Initial value	$10.00	$10.00	NA	$4.0	$4.0	NA	$6.0	$6.0	NA
Cash flow	$0.9	$0.7	±$0.1	$0.42	$0.22	±$0.1	$0.48	$0.48	0
Ending value	$11.2	$9.2	±$1.0	$5.2	$3.2	±$1.0	$6.0	$6.0	0
Income return	9%	7%	±1%	10.5%	5.5%	±2.5%	8%	8%	0
Appreciation return	12%	–8%	±10%	30%	–20%	±25%	0%	0%	0
Total return	21%	–1%	±11%	40.5%	–14.5%	±27.5%	8%	8%	0

OPT = Outcome if optimistic scenario occurs.
PES = Outcome if pessimistic scenario occurs.
RANGE = Half the difference between optimistic scenario outcome and pessimistic scenario outcome.
Note: Initial values are known deterministically, as they are in present, not future, time, so there is no range.

Exhibit 13-3 Sensitivity Analysis of Effect of Leverage on Risk in Equity Return Components, as Measured by Percentage Range in Possible Return Outcomes ($ values in millions)

Exhibit 13-3 indicates that the ranges in the equity return components increase by a factor of 2.5 as we move from the unlevered (underlying property) to the levered equity position.[5]

For example, the range in the total return between the optimistic and pessimistic scenarios is ±11% with no leverage, and ±27.5% with the 60% LTV loan. The 2.5 factor magnification of the outcome range holds not only for the total return but also for *each component* of the total return (current income as well as appreciation). The factor 2.5 is also the leverage ratio for a 60% LTV loan. It is not a coincidence that the underlying property risk is magnified by a factor equal to the leverage ratio in this case. In this example the debt is effectively riskless because the debt investor gets the same return (8%) no matter which future scenario occurs. *When debt is riskless, the risk in the equity return is directly proportional to the leverage ratio (LR).*

Of course, debt in the real world, especially long-term debt, is not riskless. We saw in Chapter 7 that long-term bonds may have a periodic return **volatility** as high as that of unlevered property equity. However, treating the debt as though it were riskless can often be a useful analytical device from the perspective of the borrower, for the purpose of seeing how the debt affects the risk in the levered equity position. This is because the borrower is contractually obligated to pay the debt service amounts specified in the loan, no matter what happens to the property value or the rents it can earn. Furthermore, the equity investor often intends to hold the property investment and its debt at least until the maturity of the loan.[6] In that case, the volatility in the market value

[5]Recall from Chapter 9 that, under the 50/50 probability assumption, the range in the return over the coming year is identical to the standard deviation of the probability distribution of the future return. The ranges depicted in Exhibit 13-3 are centered around the mean (or expected) returns shown in Exhibit 13-2. Recall also that to see the dollar effect of leverage, we must hold constant the total amount being invested. Holding the amount invested by the equity investor constant, the ranges in the absolute dollar outcomes would be magnified by the same multiple as the percentage returns (in this case, 2.5).

[6]This is particularly true for commercial mortgages, which often have a maturity of only 5 to 10 years. Transaction costs often make it inadvisable to sell property more frequently than that.

Who Bears Default Risk?

In our discussion of the effect of leverage on the risk in the borrower's equity, we have noted only the effect of leverage on the *range* of investment outcomes for the borrower. Of course, from the perspective of periodic returns, this effect is closely related to volatility. The volatility in the equity's periodic returns will generally be increased with more leverage. What we have not mentioned, however, is **default risk**. Some people claim that when equity investors borrow more money, they increase their default risk, and that this is a separate form of risk from what we described here by the effect of leverage on the range or volatility in the future equity return. If the equity investor is levered, she can lose *all* of her investment (that is, a capital return component of −100%), if she defaults on the loan. The greater the leverage, the greater the probability of such default.

If you think it through carefully, however, you should see that this type of default risk is either already included in (the downside of) the range effect we described previously, or else it is actually a risk born by the lender, not the borrower. Thus, it is not correct, conceptually, to think of default risk as an additional component of risk borne by the borrower, apart from the range-magnification effect we described.

To see this, consider once again the $10,000,000 apartment building. Suppose the range of outcomes was ±$5,000,000 in the property value and ±$500,000 in the cash flow, instead of ±$1,000,000 and ±$100,000 as before. In this case the downside scenario leaves the equity investor holding a property worth $5,200,000 generating $300,000 of income, against a mortgage on which $6,000,000 of principal and $480,000 of interest is owed. Suppose first that the equity investor could not default on the loan (presumably because the loan allows the lender "recourse" to other assets the borrower has,

which are sufficient to cover the debt obligation). In that case the equity investor would be subject to the full downside capital loss of $4,800,000 (compared to the initial property value of $10,000,000), which would represent a levered capital return of −120%, computed as ($5,200,000 − $6,000,000 − $4,000,000)/$4,000,000. This is just the effect of leverage on risk that we already described, because the 120% loss is 2.5 times the 48% loss in the (unlevered) property value. (It fell in value from $10,000,000 to $5,200,000.)*

Now suppose the equity investor can effectively default on the loan, giving up the property to the lender (who has no further recourse to the borrower's other assets). In that case the equity investor loses (shall we say "only") 100% of her initial capital. The ability to effectively default has actually reduced the magnitude of the equity investor's loss, from 120% to 100% of her original investment (the loss is reduced from $4,800,000 to $4,000,000, a savings of $800,000 for the borrower). The ability to default allows the borrower, at her option, to pass some of the potential loss (in some scenarios) over to the lender. That is why default risk is a risk borne by lenders, not by borrowers.**

---

*There would also be a −4.5% return in the income component, compared to +3% without leverage. Compared with the ex ante income return expectation of 8%, the downside result in the income return is 5 points less without leverage, but 12.5 points less with leverage.

**In addition, $180,000 additional cash outflow in interest payments would also be avoided by the borrower: a total savings to the borrower of 24.5% of her original equity is passed on as loss to the lender through the default process (with limited liability, as in a "nonrecourse" loan). Default risk from the perspective of the lender will be discussed in Part VI.

of the debt (usually due primarily to fluctuations in interest rates) would not be relevant to the equity investor. The situation faced by the equity investor is then indeed similar to what is depicted in Exhibit 13-3.[7]

13.2.3 Risk and Return: Putting the Two Effects Together

We have now seen, at least for our simple apartment building example, the effect of leverage on both the expected return and the risk in the return for the equity investor.[8] Exhibit 13-4 puts these two effects together and demonstrates the effect on the risk premium in the ex ante equity return, under our previous assumption that the mortgage is riskless. Consistent with that assumption, the 8% return on the mortgage includes no risk premium. In that case, the risk premium in the levered equity return is directly proportional to the leverage ratio, LR. The unlevered property equity has a leverage ratio of 1, and a risk premium of 2% (the difference between the property's 10% expected return and the mortgage's 8% return). With the 60% LTV loan, the levered property equity has a leverage ratio of 2.5 and a risk premium of 5% (the difference between the 13% expected return on the levered equity and the 8% mortgage return), which is 2.5 times the 2% risk premium on the unlevered property.

This proportionality of the risk premium and the leverage ratio makes sense when the debt is riskless because, as we saw previously, in that case the equity risk is also directly proportional to the leverage ratio. Thus, the equity risk premium is simply remaining proportional to the risk.

Note that the expected total return, $E[r]$, does *not* increase proportionately with the risk. (The 13% expected total return on the levered equity is only 1.3 times the 10% expectation on the unlevered investment, even though there is 2.5 times the risk.) This is because the ex ante total return includes the riskfree rate (compensation for the time value of money) as well as the risk premium (compensation for risk). Only the risk premium component of the total return need increase with the added risk brought on by the leverage.

Now let us suppose, more realistically, that the mortgage is not riskless. In this case the 8% interest rate on the mortgage includes a risk premium for the debt investor. For example, suppose that T-bills are yielding 6%, the riskfree rate of return. Then the 8% mortgage has a 2% risk premium, the 10% expected return on the unlevered property represents a 4% risk premium, and the levered equity with the 60% LTV loan has a 7% risk premium, based on the difference between its expected return of 13% and the 6% riskfree rate. This situation is depicted in Exhibit 13-5.

When the debt is not riskless, the equity risk premium is no longer directly proportional to the leverage ratio. (The 7% risk premium on the levered equity is only

---

[7]The main simplifications in our numerical example are the existence of only a single period of time (the present and next year), and of only two possible future scenarios. In the real world, one would want to consider a multiperiod measure of return (the IRR) and a probability distribution of possible future outcomes. This requires a more involved mathematical analysis, often referred to as *sensitivity analysis*. Nevertheless, the general qualitative impacts on risk will normally be quite similar to what is depicted in Exhibit 13-3 (as measured by the standard deviation of the equity investor's IRR).

[8]It should be noted that in some types of real estate investment the above-described effects of leverage are inherent in the operational characteristics of the investment even without the use of financial leverage (in the form of debt financing). See, in particular, our discussion of land and development investment in Chapters 28 and 29.

Exhibit 13-4   Effect of Leverage on Investment Risk and Return

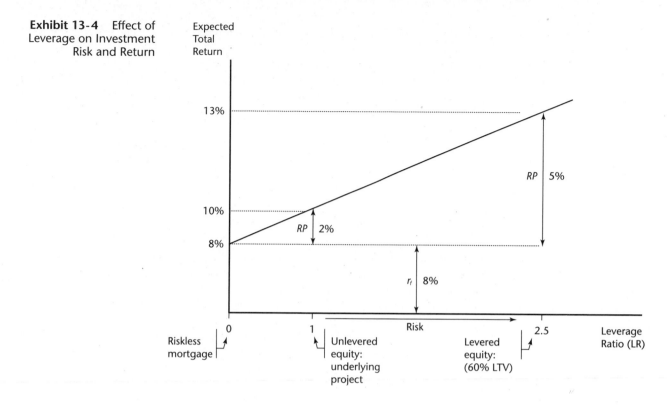

Exhibit 13-5   Effect of Leverage on Investment Risk and Return: A Risky Debt Example

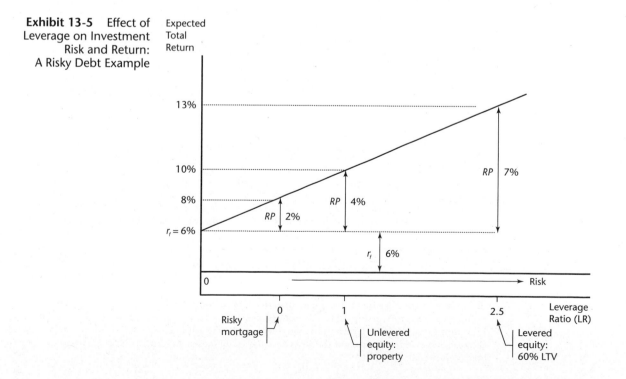

1.75 times the 4% risk premium on the unlevered property, even though the leverage ratio is 2.5 times that of the unlevered property.) However, the equity risk premium is still a linear function of the leverage ratio. The nature of that function will be discussed in the next section, in which we introduce the WACC formula. For now, the important point is that, regardless of whether the debt is riskless, the ex ante equity risk premium will normally be *directly proportional* to the amount of risk in the equity, where risk is defined *in the way that the asset market cares about it*. This is indicated by the second horizontal axis in Exhibit 13-5, parallel to and above the axis measuring the leverage ratio. This top horizontal axis measures risk as defined by the capital markets. By definition, the zero point on this axis corresponds to the 6% risk-free rate of return, the rate of return that includes zero risk premium. If we assume that the property and debt are both obtained at prevailing market rates, then this guarantees that the ex ante equity risk premium will be directly proportional to its risk as defined by the capital market.

Another way of saying this is to say that the equity ex ante risk premium *per unit of risk* (as defined by the capital market) will remain constant no matter how large or small a loan the equity investor takes out to buy a property. This result holds as long as the loan is unsubsidized and the property is bought at fair market value. By definition, this equity risk premium per unit of risk equals the **market price of risk**.[9] This is another way of saying that there is no free lunch in the normal use of leverage. Leverage affects the ex ante equity risk premium in just such a way that the benefit of the additional expected return is exactly offset by the cost of the additional risk.[10]

13.3 A USEFUL FORMULA: THE WACC

To quantify the effect of leverage on equity risk and return, a formula known as the **weighted average cost of capital (WACC)** is often useful. The WACC formula is given here:

$$r_P = (LTV)r_D + (1 - LTV)r_E \tag{1}$$

where r_P is the return on the underlying property free and clear; r_D is the return to the debt on the property; r_E is the return on the levered equity in the property; and LTV is the loan-to-value ratio: L/V.[11]

---

[9]The market price of risk is, by definition, the ex ante risk premium per unit of risk implied in the market prices of assets.

[10]If the property is purchased at below market value, providing a positive NPV to the buyer, then the ex ante equity risk premium will be more than proportional to the leverage ratio (assuming market rate debt). However, the debt transaction itself will still be zero NPV as long as the debt is at market interest rates. In other words, leverage at market interest rates leaves the dollar magnitude of the equity investment NPV unaffected. This results in any nonzero NPV being a larger fraction of the equity investment as the amount borrowed is increased.

[11]In many corporate finance texts the WACC is defined on an after-corporate-income-tax basis, in which the return to the corporation's debt, r_D, is multiplied in the WACC formula by $(1 - T_c)$, where T_c is the marginal corporate income tax rate. However, in most real estate applications there is effectively no double taxation, either because the real estate investment is made directly without a (taxable) corporate ownership layer (e.g., partnership, LLC, etc.), or because the investment is being made by a corporation that is exempt from corporate-level income tax, such as a REIT. Thus, in effect, $T_c = 0$ for most real estate applications, so our definition of the WACC is not really inconsistent with the corporate finance textbook definition.

For example, suppose the LTV ratio is 60%, and the return to equity is 13% while the return on the debt is 8%. Then the previous formula provides a return on the underlying property equal to 10%. These numbers should seem familiar. Our numerical example in the previous section was simply an example of the WACC formula.

The WACC formula is derived directly from the basic accounting identities and the definition of the simple holding period return (HPR):

Assets = Liabilities + Owners' equity
Property cash flow = Debt cash flow + Equity cash flow

Thus, the WACC is valid for the HPR whenever these identities hold. However, in practice the formula is applied over positive spans of time over which a multiperiod return measure is used, such as the IRR. In this case the WACC formula holds exactly only if all the variables in it, the LTV ratio and the returns, remain constant, which is rarely ever the case.[12] This causes the formula to lose exactness in typical applications. It will be less exact when it is applied over longer periods of time, during which there can be greater fluctuations in the variables. Nevertheless, the WACC formula is a useful approximation when applied with common sense to periodic returns and to ex ante multiperiod returns over time horizons when the variables are not expected to fluctuate too greatly.

One of the nice things about the WACC is that it is quite intuitive and therefore easy to learn. Since the claims on the property net cash flow consist of the debt claim and the equity claim, the property value, and hence the return on the property, must consist of a debt share and an equity share. In the WACC formula the return to each component is simply weighted by that component's share of the property value.

13.3.1 The WACC and REIT Cost of Capital

The WACC formula as expressed in equation (1) shows the return to the underlying asset isolated on the left-hand side of the equation, and the LTV and returns to debt and equity on the right-hand side. This is the convenient way to memorize the formula, and also the convenient way to apply the formula when it is easier to observe empirically the return on the levered equity than it is to observe the return on the underlying physical assets. This is in fact the typical situation in corporate finance, in which we can empirically observe the return on corporate equity by examining the history of the corporation's stock returns. This situation is also relevant to applying the WACC formula to REITs, whose equity is publicly traded. The return on a REIT's stock is the return to its levered equity, r_E.

For example, suppose REIT A can borrow at 6%, while REIT B has to pay 8% interest on its debt. Doesn't this imply that REIT A has a lower cost of capital than REIT B? We can use the WACC to answer this question. Suppose REIT A has a debt/equity ratio of 3/7 (implying LTV = 30%), while REIT B has a debt/equity ratio

---

[12]For example, the LTV changes as the market value of the property and of the debt change over time. Changes in the LTV also cause changes in the expected returns to debt and equity (ceteris paribus), as changes in the LTV affect the relative risk of the equity and debt.

of unity (LTV = 50%). Suppose both REITs have an expected return to their equity of 15%. Then formula (1) tells us

$$WACC(A) = (0.3)6\% + (0.7)15\% = 12.3\%$$
$$WACC(B) = (0.5)8\% + (0.5)15\% = 11.5\%$$

The weighted average cost of capital for REIT A's assets is 12.3%, compared to only 11.5% for REIT B's assets. Apparently, REIT B holds less risky property assets than REIT A does (or REIT B tends to be less involved in risky development projects, for example). REIT B's debt is more costly probably because REIT B is more highly levered than REIT A, causing its debt to have more default risk. REIT B's lenders must be compensated for this risk by obtaining a higher interest rate on their loans.[13]

13.3.2 Use of the WACC in Direct Property Investment

In applying the WACC formula to the property market and to direct investments in commercial real estate, it is often more convenient to turn formula (1) around and solve it for the equity return. This is because it is often easier in practice to observe empirically or estimate the return on the underlying property than it is to estimate directly the return on the levered equity. So we would invert the WACC formula to solve for the return on the levered equity:

$$r_E = (r_P - LTV r_D) / (1 - LTV) \tag{2}$$

In this way the more observable parameters are all on the right-hand side of the equation.

For example, suppose we can observe in the property market that the expected total return on a certain type of property is 10%, and that mortgages are available at 8% interest and a 75% LTV ratio. Then the expected total return on the equity invested in such property using a 75% LTV ratio mortgage would be 16%:

$$16\% = [10\% - (0.75)8\%] / [1 - (0.75)]$$

13.3.3 The WACC and Return Components

The WACC formula can be applied to any additive components of the total return, such as the yield (y) and the growth (g), or the **risk premium (RP)**. You just have to be consistent, applying the formula to only one component at a time within the equation. For example, if we apply the WACC to the current yield component of the return, then we can obtain the following formula for the **equity cash yield**:

$$y_E = (y_P - LTV y_D) / (1 - LTV) \tag{3}$$

This is sometimes known as the equity yield formula. If the current yield on the property is 8%, and the cash yield on the debt is 9%, then with an LTV ratio of 50%

---

[13]REIT B's debt may also be more costly if it is has a longer-term average maturity than REIT A's debt and the yield curve in the debt market is upward-sloping. Indeed, quantifying the cost of debt capital is a bit more complex than suggested in this simple example. The yield curve, as well as default risk premiums and the relationship between stated yields and expected returns on debt, will be discussed in Part VI.

the initial cash yield on the levered equity investment will be 7%. This is often referred to as the **cash-on-cash return** on the investment. Note that in applying the formula in this way, the current yield on the loan may not be exactly the same as the interest rate on the loan. The loan's current yield is its annual debt service as a fraction of the loan amount, so if the debt service includes amortization of principal then the loan current yield will be greater than its interest rate.[14]

13.3.4 The WACC and Risk

As the WACC formula is applicable to any additive component of total return, we can apply it to the risk premium (RP). For example, expressing the WACC formula in terms of the leverage ratio instead of the LTV ratio, the ex ante risk premium in the levered equity investment is given by the following formula:

$$RP_E = RP_D + LR(RP_P - RP_D) \qquad (4)$$

The equity risk premium equals the debt risk premium plus the leverage ratio times the difference between the property and debt risk premiums. Formula (4) specifies the linear relationship between the risk premium and the leverage ratio noted in the previous section.[15] It also demonstrates that if the debt is riskless ($RP_D = 0$), the equity risk premium is directly proportional to the leverage ratio, as formula (4) then reduces to:

$$RP_E = (LR)(RP_P)$$

As noted, risk in the equity investment (as measured by the capital market) will be directly proportional to the equity risk premium if both the property and debt are obtained at prevailing market prices.

13.4 POSITIVE AND NEGATIVE LEVERAGE

In the real estate investment industry the term **positive leverage** is often used. It refers to the situation in which leverage will increase the equity investor's return. **Negative leverage** is less widely spoken of (perhaps because it is a less happy circumstance), but it would imply the opposite: leverage decreasing the equity investor's return. These terms are most often applied in an ex ante sense, referring to return expectations going forward for the investor.

---

[14]The loan interest rate (or "yield to maturity") represents the total return to the loan. We can represent the appreciation return component of the loan as the percentage change in the loan balance due. (This is a "book value" definition, ignoring changes in the market value of the debt as might be caused, for example, by changes in interest rates or in the LTV.) The loan appreciation rate would therefore be negative for an amortizing loan. As the appreciation rate plus the current cash yield rate always sum to the total return, this implies that the current yield in an amortizing loan will exceed its contractual interest rate or total yield. For a classical constant-payment amortizing loan, the cash yield is given by the "mortgage constant," or annuity factor, described in Chapter 8.

[15]Note that this linearity assumes that the debt risk premium, RP_D, remains constant over the relevant range in the leverage ratio. As high values of LR will result in greater default risk in the loan, typically implying a higher risk premium in the debt, formula (6) must be adjusted accordingly.

The condition for positive leverage is the following:

Whenever the return component is higher in the underlying property than it is in the mortgage loan, there will be positive leverage in that return component.

The condition for negative leverage is of course just the opposite: whenever the property return component is lower than the corresponding debt component. When the property and debt have the same expected return, leverage is neutral, leaving the equity return unaffected. These conditions follow directly from the WACC formula, as seen clearly in the leverage ratio version of the formula:

$$r_E = r_D + LR(r_P - r_D) \tag{5}$$

The equity return equals the debt return plus the leverage ratio times the difference between the property return and the debt return.[16] If this difference is positive (property return is greater than debt return), then more leverage will increase the equity return. If this difference is negative, then just the opposite will occur. As noted in the previous section, formula (5) can be applied to any component of the total return.

Consider the previous apartment building investment as an example. The income return component was 8% in both the underlying property and the debt, so leverage was neutral in the income return component, leaving the equity investor's expected income return unchanged by the amount of leverage. The property appreciation was 2%, which was greater than the zero appreciation in the loan amount (recall that the loan was interest-only, with zero amortization), so there was positive leverage in the appreciation return component. The total return in the underlying property was 10%, and the total return to the loan investor was 8%, resulting in positive leverage in the total return.

13.5 EFFECT OF LEVERAGE ON GROWTH AND YIELD

We can apply the WACC formula to examine the differential effect of leverage on the income and appreciation components of the expected return. This is shown in Exhibit 13-6 based on the WACC, for typical numerical values. The major point to notice is that, for typical values of the relevant return variables, leverage *shifts the investor's return relatively away from current income and toward capital gain.* This occurs whether the cash-on-cash leverage is positive or negative. The fundamental reason is that the property-minus-loan differential is usually greater in the appreciation return than in the income return. In other words, usually,

$$g_P - g_D > y_P - y_D$$

[16]Once again, we are simplifying by treating the debt return as a constant over the relevant range of the leverage ratio. In reality, sufficiently higher LR will result in a higher r_D. At the extreme, a 100% LTV ratio (infinite LR) must imply that r_D equals r_P and r_E is then undefined, for at that point the debt-holder effectively owns the property as the equity holder has no value at all. This is clearly seen by substituting 100% for LTV in formula (1):

$$r_P = LTVr_D + (1 - LTV)r_E = 1r_D + (1 - 1)r_E = r_D$$

Is There Always Positive Leverage in the Total Return?

Investors usually assume that positive leverage will exist, at least on an ex ante basis in the total return. In fact, such positive leverage is not guaranteed, for two reasons.

First, the equity investor may overpay for the property. As noted in Chapter 12, real estate markets are "thin" and not perfectly efficient, so such pricing mistakes are possible. If the equity investor pays more than fair market value for the property, his realistic ex ante return (on an unlevered basis) will have a risk premium less than what the market requires, and possibly less than that in the mortgage, even though the mortgage may be less risky than the property.

Second, it is possible for the mortgage to be riskier than the underlying property, when risk is defined by the capital markets. It is thus possible for the ex ante return on the mortgage to exceed that on the underlying property, even though both the mortgage and property are obtained at market value. Particularly when dealing with more than one asset class (here we have two: real estate and debt), the relevant definition of "risk" as it matters in the capital markets (and hence, as it is reflected in return expectations) is probably not well represented by a one-dimensional measure such as the volatility. The mortgage clearly has *different* risk from the underlying property, but not necessarily *less* risk from this perspective. For example, suppose the major source of risk that the market cared about was uncertainty in the future inflation rate. The nominally fixed cash flows in a fixed rate mortgage would then make such a mortgage riskier, in terms of real (inflation-adjusted) value, than the property whose rent and value will likely be able to adjust to unexpected increases in future inflation.

In fact (as is discussed in more depth in Chapter 19), empirical evidence in the form of historical periodic returns suggests that, from the perspective of the capital markets, long-term fixed rate commercial mortgages may be about as risky as typical institutional quality commercial property. During the 1972–98 period the volatility in the Giliberto-Levy Commercial Mortgage Price Index (GLCMPI) was about the same as that of the NCREIF Index of commercial property, after adjusting for inflation and "smoothing."[*] The "beta" of the GLCMPI with respect to the stock market was greater than that of the NCREIF index.[**] Also, the average total return in the GLCMPI was 9.51% per year (net of credit losses), while that in the NCREIF index was only 9.16%. Of course, such average ex post historical returns may not coincide exactly with typical ex ante expectations. The general

downward trend in interest rates during this period, and the historically severe property slump in the early 1990s, may have caused the historical results in the 1972–98 period to overstate mortgage return expectations and understate property return expectations.

On a going-forward basis, most investors view mortgages as less risky than the underlying property, and on an ex ante basis mortgage yields usually appear to be lower than realistic IRRs on commercial property, although not necessarily much lower. Ex ante yields on mortgages are relatively easy to observe, and they typically give long-term fixed rate commercial mortgages realistic risk premiums on the order of 150 to 300 basis points above T-bills, when the yield curve has its most common slightly upward-sloping shape.[†] While *realistic* ex ante returns on commercial property are more difficult to observe (as we noted in Chapter 11), a typical reasonable range for institutional quality commercial properties is on the order of 300 to 400 basis points above T-bills. The ex ante return spread between property and mortgages (the degree of positive leverage) will tend to be greater in noninstitutional property, or with shorter-term or adjustable rate loans.[††] On the other hand, positive leverage will tend to be less, other things being equal, when long-run inflation expectations are rising.

In summary, the existence and degree of positive leverage in the ex ante total return depends on the specifics of the loan, the property, and the state of the capital markets and the macroeconomy.

---

[*]The GLCMPI is the most widely used index tracking the periodic total returns to long-term commercial mortgages in the United States. "Smoothing" here refers to the effect of appraisals and lagged valuations in artificially damping the apparent risk in the NCREIF index.

[**]As will be discussed in Part VII, "beta" is a measure of nondiversifiable risk for an investor whose wealth is invested in the stock market.

[†]The yield curve reflects the difference between interest rates on long-term versus short-term debt. As will be explained in Chapter 18, realistic ex ante returns on mortgages are a bit less than their stated yields or interest rates, as one must take into account of the probability of credit losses as a result of default. Mortgage risk and ex ante risk premiums will be discussed further in Chapter 19.

[††]In principle, the spread should also be increased for sufficiently low LTV ratios, as this should lower the market's required default risk premium in the mortgage ex ante return. The advent of the CMBS market in the 1990s provided increased possibility for low-credit-risk loans to obtain low interest rates, as a result of CMBS "tranching" and explicit yield stratification in the debt market. This will be discussed further in Chapter 20.

In the example in Exhibit 13-6 $g_P - g_D$ is +3%, and $y_P - y_D$ is either +1% (in the top panel, with the 6% loan) or −1% (in the bottom panel, with the 8% loan). In either case the growth differential exceeds the yield differential. Let us review how these differentials are computed.

The property growth rate of 2% equals the difference between the 10% total return and the 8% current yield or cap rate on the property ($g_P = r_P - y_P$). The loan growth rate is the negative of its amortization as a fraction of the current outstanding loan balance. This can be seen as the difference between the loan's current cash yield and its total return as represented by the loan interest rate ($g_D = r_D - y_D$).[17] The current cash yield of the loan is its annual debt service as a fraction of its outstanding loan balance. Initially, this will equal the **mortgage constant (MC)**, the annual annuity factor used to compute the loan payments.

In Exhibit 13-6 we have two loan scenarios, one in which the loan interest rate is 6%, resulting in positive leverage in the cash-on-cash yield for the equity investor, and the other in which the loan interest rate is 8%, resulting in negative leverage. In both cases, however, the loan amortizes initially at a rate of 1% per year, as indicated by the difference between the mortgage constant and the loan interest rate. (The 6% loan has a 7% MC, while the 8% loan has a 9% MC.) Thus, the initial growth rate differential between the property and the loan is +3% (computed as: $g_P - g_D = 2\% - [-1\%] = 2\% + 1\% = 3\%$).[18]

The difference between the property yield (or cap rate) of 8% and the loan current cash yield (or mortgage constant), which is either 7% or 9%, determines whether the loan will present the equity investor with positive or negative leverage in the cash yield. With the 6% loan the leverage is positive, while with the 8% loan the leverage is negative. Thus, we see that in the top panel of Exhibit 13-6 the equity yield (y_E) rises the more leverage is applied (as indicated by the leverage or loan-to-value ratios shown in the left-hand columns). In the bottom panel the equity cash yield falls the more leverage is applied. In both cases, however, the equity appreciation return increases with leverage, and rather substantially.[19]

The return component effects of leverage indicated in Exhibit 13-6 have been computed using the WACC formula presented in section 13.3. For example, in the case of a 67% LTV with the 6% loan in the top panel, we have

Total:	10%	=	(67%) ×	6%	+	(33%) × 18%
Yield:	8%	=	(67%) ×	7%	+	(33%) × 10%
Growth:	2%	=	(67%) ×	(−1%)	+	(33%) × 8%

The levered equity total return is 18%, consisting of 10% current yield and 8% growth.

---

[17]For our purpose here we can ignore origination fees and other sources of the loan's total yield, and we can assume market value equals book value for the loan. Returns to debt investment will be discussed in more detail in Part VI.

[18]In the absence of refinancing, assuming a standard constant-payment amortizing mortgage, the loan balance will decline gradually over time while the loan payments remain the same, so the loan amortization rate as a fraction of the remaining loan balance will grow over time.

[19]In Exhibit 13-6 the equity appreciation return increases more than proportionately with the leverage ratio, because the loan amortization results in negative growth in the loan value.

Exhibit 13-6   Typical Relative Effect of Leverage on Income and Growth Components of Investment Return (numerical example)

Property total return (r_P): 10:00%
Cap rate (y_P): 8:00%

Positive cash-on-cash leverage:
Loan interest rate (r_D): 6.00%
Mortgage constant (y_D): 7.00%

		Equity return component:		
LR	LTV	y_E	g_E	r_E
1	0%	8.00%	2.00%	10.00%
2	50%	9.00%	5.00%	14.00%
3	67%	10.00%	8.00%	18.00%
4	75%	11.00%	11.00%	22.00%
5	80%	12.00%	14.00%	26.00%

Negative cash-on-cash leverage:
Loan interest rate (r_D): 8.00%
Mortgage constant (y_D): 9.00%

		Equity return component:		
LR	LTV	y_E	g_E	r_E
1	0%	8.00%	2.00%	10.00%
2	50%	7.00%	5.00%	12.00%
3	67%	6.00%	8.00%	14.00%
4	75%	5.00%	11.00%	16.00%
5	80%	4.00%	14.00%	18.00%

Note that, even in the case of positive cash-on-cash leverage, where the equity yield rises with leverage, the equity appreciation return rises even faster, resulting in a *relative* increase in the growth component within the equity total return. Thus, leverage has the effect of shifting the total return relatively away from current income and toward growth, even when income leverage is positive. While this will not necessarily always be the case, it is typical.

13.6 CHAPTER SUMMARY

Let us summarize what we have learned in this chapter about leverage and the use of debt to finance the equity real estate investment. In general, we see that debt financing, and the resulting leverage, has three major effects:

1. Under the typical assumption that the loan is less risky than the underlying property, leverage will increase the ex ante total return on the equity investment by increasing the risk premium in that return.

2. Under the same relative risk assumption, leverage will increase the risk of the equity investment normally proportionately with the increase in the risk premium noted in (1).

3. Under the typical situation of nonnegative price appreciation in the property and nonnegative amortization in the loan, leverage will usually shift the expected return for the equity investor relatively away from the current income component and toward the growth or capital appreciation component.

We have also seen how all three of the effects noted qualitatively here can be quantified, at least to a useful approximation, by use of the WACC formula. The trade-off implied by the first two points implies that the use of leverage does not normally affect the NPV of the equity investor's position, assuming the debt is unsubsidized. The previously-noted risk and return effects of leverage allow underlying real estate property assets to attract capital from a variety of investors. Some investors prefer equity's management control and growth potential even though it may have greater risk. Others prefer the more passive role, contractually fixed cash flows, and finite maturity of mortgages. In the big picture, this differentiation improves the choices available to investors and the overall efficiency of the capital markets.

KEY TERMS

leverage	management incentive effects	equity cash yield
heterogeneous investors	volatility	cash-on-cash return
investment products	default risk	positive leverage
leverage ratio (LR)	market price of risk	negative leverage
equity	weighted average cost of capital	mortgage constant (MC)
loan-to-value ratio (LTV)	(WACC)	
residual claim	risk premium (RP)	

STUDY QUESTIONS

Conceptual Questions

13.1.   What is the difference between the leverage ratio (LR) and the loan-to-value ratio (LTV)? How much greater property value can be purchased with a 75% LTV than with a 50% LTV? What is the LR associated with each of those two LTVs?

13.2.   What is meant by the preferred or senior claim of debt?

13.3.   How does the equity investor's ability to control property management align the interests and incentives of the debt and equity investors in normal circumstances, so as to maximize total property value? [Hint: What are the implications of the fact that equity has the "residual" claim on property value?]

13.4.   What is wrong with the following statement: Only a fool would invest in real estate without financing most of the purchase with a mortgage; borrowing allows you to increase your expected return by using other people's money!

13.5. If we assume the debt is riskless, then what is the relationship between the leverage ratio and both the risk and the risk premium in the equity investor's return?

13.6. Without assuming riskless debt, what is the relationship between the ex ante equity risk premium and the amount of risk in the equity investment, measuring risk as it is defined by the capital markets and assuming that both the property and debt are obtained at market value? How is this relationship affected by the degree of leverage (amount of debt)?

13.7. a. How does leverage affect the equity investor's ex ante risk-adjusted return, or the expected risk premium per unit of risk, assuming the property is bought at fair market value and the debt is unsubsidized?

   b. How does leverage affect the NPV of the equity investor's investment if the property is bought at a price *different from* its fair market value, assuming the loan is at the market interest rate and the investor has unlimited equity capital available to invest?

13.8. Why doesn't the equity investor's expected total return increase proportionately with risk?

13.9. That famous real estate investor, Bob, has $1,000,000 of his own equity capital available to make a real estate investment. He finds a bargain, a property with a market value of $1,100,000 that he can buy for $1,000,000.

   a. By how much can Bob enhance his net wealth by leveraging his purchase of this bargain property using borrowed money to finance at least part of his investment?

   b. Now suppose the bargain property is twice as large, worth $2,200,000, and Bob can buy it for $2,000,000, but he still has only $1,000,000 of his own capital available. In these circumstances how much more can Bob increase his net wealth by using leverage, assuming he could borrow at least up to a 50% LTV ratio?

13.10. What is the underlying conceptual basis of the WACC formula?

13.11. Discuss the following statement: There is *always* positive leverage with respect to the *total* return (ex ante).

13.12. With respect to the *income component* of the before-tax ex ante return, when will there be positive leverage and when will there be negative leverage?

13.13. How is the expected income return component related to the LTV ratio, the property cap rate, and the mortgage constant on the loan (on a before-tax basis)?

13.14. Suppose you want to increase the income component of your return from your real estate equity portfolio, but you do not want to sacrifice the appreciation component. What must you look for? If you can't find a loan with positive leverage in the equity yield, what trade-off must you accept?

13.15. How does leverage usually affect the relative magnitude of the income and appreciation components in the equity investor's expected return?

13.16. How does leverage enable the same underlying asset to serve the investment objectives of different types of investors? What are the two types of investment products that result from the use of debt financing of real estate investment?

Quantitative Problems

13.17. Suppose you expect that one year from now, a certain property's before-tax cash flow ($PBTCF = NOI - CI$) will equal only $15,000 per year under a plausible pessimistic scenario or as much as $25,000 per year under a plausible optimistic scenario. If you borrow an amount such that the loan payments will be $10,000 per year (for certain), then what is your *range* of expected income return component (equity yield) under the no-leverage and leverage alternatives, assuming that the property price is $200,000 and the loan amount is $100,000?

13.18. Does increasing leverage (borrowing a larger fraction of the property value) usually primarily increase the expected income component of the return or the appreciation component? Why? [Hint: Use the WACC formula and assume that $E[g_D]$ is usually either zero or negative, less than $E[g_P]$, while $E[y_D]$ is usually positive and around the same magnitude as $E[y_P]$.]

13.19. a. Assuming riskless debt, if the loan-to-value ratio is 80%, approximately how much more risk will there be in the equity return than if the LTV ratio were 60%? Put another way: If the return to equity can vary per year within a range of $\pm 20\%$ with a 60% LTV ratio, then within what range can it vary with an 80% LTV ratio?

   b. How much larger should the market's required risk premium be in the required return to equity with 80% debt as compared to 60% debt?

13.20. A certain real estate limited partnership (LP) advertises that it has a target of matching the stock market in total return for its limited partner investors, before taxes. (Suppose that the stock market risk premium is expected to be 7%.) The conservative office and warehouse properties that the partnership plans to acquire typically command risk premiums in their before-tax expected returns of about 3%. Assuming riskless debt, what loan-to-value ratio must the LP plan to maintain in its property investments in order to have a good chance of meeting its stated target?

13.21. Answer question 13.20 assuming the riskfree interest rate is 5% and the debt would have an interest rate of 7%.

13.22. a. If the cap rate on a certain property is 12% and loans are available at a 11% mortgage constant, then approximately what is the expected income component of your before-tax return if you borrow 80% of the property price?

   b. What if you only borrow 50%?

13.23. a. Answer part (a) of question 13.22, only now with respect to the growth component of the equity return, assuming the loan interest rate is 10% and the expected total return on the property is also 10%.

   b. What if the property cap rate were 9% instead of 12%?

Income Tax Considerations
and After-Tax Cash Flows
for the Equity Investor

Chapter Outline

Learning Objectives

After reading this chapter, you should understand:

◆ How to extend the microlevel commercial property cash flow proforma projection to the level of the equity investor's after-tax cash flows.

◆ The major impacts income taxes have on the investor's cash flows, including the basic effects of tax shields on the after-tax cash flows and investment returns of the levered equity investor.

◆ The major issues and procedures involved in after-tax equity investment valuation at the microlevel.

In the last chapter we began to step beyond pure property level analysis to investor level analysis by considering the effect of leverage on the equity investment. In this chapter we extend this progression with a basic consideration of how the owner's income tax obligations may affect the cash flows and investment valuation decisions discussed in Part IV. We will see how income tax effects interact with the possible use of debt financing in the equity investment, although we will not assume that debt financing will necessarily be employed.

14.1 GENERAL EFFECTS OF INCOME TAXES AND DEBT

To begin, it is important to understand how a property owner's income tax obligation reduces the net after-tax cash flow received by the investor, and how certain expenses can provide what is termed a tax shield for taxable investors. To see how this works, we need to consider the difference between **property-level before-tax cash flows** and **owner-level after-tax cash flows**.

This requires consideration of some basic differences between accrual accounting and cash flow accounting. Accrual accounting is designed to register income and expenses when they are "accrued," that is, when they are legally owed.[1] On the other hand, cash flow accounting is designed to register cash inflows and outflows when they actually occur for the property owner. Even though we are interested, as always, in cash flows, the owner's accrual-based income statement for the property is relevant, because the income tax obligation on commercial property income is based on accrual accounting. Income taxes are themselves, of course, a cash flow item.

Recall first from Chapter 11 that the typical property-level before-tax cash flow statement identifies the net operating income (NOI) from the property, as well as a bottom-line property-level before-tax net cash flow (PBTCF), which consists of the NOI less any capital improvement expenditures. This cash flow statement differs in several respects from the accrual statement on which the owner's income tax obligations are computed. Three differences are most important: depreciation, capital expenditures, and debt amortization.

Depreciation. **Depreciation expense** is not deducted from the cash flow bottom line because depreciation expense is not a cash outflow, but rather reflects (in theory) the presumed accrual of losses in property value over time. While in reality property often does not lose nominal value over time (typically due largely to the effect of inflation), IRS tax rules still allow property depreciation expenses to be accrued for purposes of calculating net income from the property for the purpose of computing the owner's income tax obligation. On the other hand, at the time of property resale, the capital gains income tax obligation will be based on the difference between the sale price and the book value of the property, with the latter reflecting the accumulated depreciation expenses during the period of ownership.[2]

Capital Expenditures. **Capital expenditures** are deducted from the cash flow bottom line because these are cash outflows. In contrast, on an accrual basis such expenditures would not be fully charged as expenses in the year they are made, but rather would be capitalized into the book value of the asset and then depreciated gradually over the life of the improvement. Thus, capital expenditures do not (much) reduce the income tax obligation of the property owner in the year they are made, even though they do reduce the owner's net cash flow that year.

---

[1] *Accrual accounting* is simply the standard type of accounting taught in basic accounting courses and used in corporate accounting.

[2] Note, however, that the capital gains tax may be deferred by using the sale proceeds to buy a similar property.

Debt Amortization. If the owner has financed the property by taking out a mortgage, the cash flow to the owner is reduced by the entire amount of the debt service payments to the lender. From an accrual perspective, however, only the interest portion of the debt service payment is charged as an expense against the owner's taxable income, as any portion of the debt service that is used to pay down principal is viewed as a reduction of the owner's debt liability, which is not an expense.

All three of these general effects of income taxes and debt on the property owner's operating cash flow are depicted in Exhibit 14-1a. Starting from the property NOI, the exhibit shows two branches of further calculations. The right-hand branch is accrual based, and the left-hand branch is cash flow based. In the right-hand branch, the owner's income tax obligation is calculated based on taxable income, which removes the accrual items of debt interest and depreciation expenses from the NOI. The income tax obligation thusly calculated from accrued income is itself a cash outflow item, which is removed from the NOI along with the entire debt service (principal amortization as well as interest) and any capital improvement expenditures, to arrive at the equity-after-tax cash flow (EATCF) at the bottom of the left-hand branch in the diagram. The EATCF is the bottom line that is of ultimate interest to the property owner.[3] The right-hand branch simply shows how the tax item is computed.

In addition to these effects on operating income, during years when there is reversion cash flow (e.g., typically when the property is sold), the owner must pay **capital gains tax** (CGT) on the difference between the net sale proceeds and the book value (or adjusted basis) of the property. This is shown in Exhibit 14-1b.[4]

Exhibit 14-1a   Equity-After-Tax Cash Flows from Operations

PGI
− Vacancy
= EGI
− OEs
= NOI

Cash Flow
− Capital improvements
  expenditures
= PBTCF
− Debt service (interest & principal)
− Income tax
= EATCF

Taxes
Net operating income (NOI)
− Interest (I)
− Depreciation expense (DE)
= Taxable income
× Investor's income tax rate
= Income tax due

---

[3]As a finance professor of ours once said when explaining why cash flows are more relevant for investment analysis than accounting-based income: "You can't buy beer with accrued net income."

[4]The capital gains tax will be discussed in more detail in the numerical example that follows.

Exhibit 14-1b
Computation of CGT in
Reversion Cash Flow

Net sale proceeds (NSP)
– Adjusted basis
= Taxable gain on sale
× CGT rate
_____
= Taxes due on sale

where the adjusted basis or net book value is calculated as

Original basis (total initial cost)
+ Capital improvement expenditures
– Accumulated depreciation
_____
= Adjusted basis

14.2 NUMERICAL EXAMPLE OF AFTER-TAX PROFORMA

The effect of these accrual-based income tax considerations can best be seen by recourse to a simple numerical example. Exhibit 14-2 depicts a 10-year proforma statement for an apartment property investment being contemplated by an individual investor who faces a 40% marginal tax rate for ordinary income and a 20% rate for long-term capital gains income (including both federal and state taxes). The property could be purchased for $1 million, with a depreciable cost basis of $800,000, reflecting the fact that IRS rules allow only the building structure, equipment, and fixtures on the property to be depreciated, not the land component of the property value. The rationale behind the nondepreciability of land is that land does not physically "wear out" as a structure does, and "location value" (as described in Part II) is traditionally considered to be at least as likely to increase as decrease over time.

14.2.1 Basic Equity Cash Flow Calculations

The cash flow projection in Exhibit 14-2 picks up largely where our description of property cash flow proformas left off in Chapter 11. In this example, the NOI of the apartment property is projected to start out at $90,000 in the first year, and then grow at a rate of 2.5% per year to a level of $112,398 in year 10. As described in Chapter 11, this NOI is a property-level operating income figure net of all operating expenses, including property taxes and management expenses.

Depreciation of the property value over time is not considered an operating expense (and, as noted, may not actually occur for a properly maintained building in an environment with even modest inflation). However, the IRS allows depreciation expense to be charged against taxable income. As of the late 1990s the IRS rules for residential income property such as this apartment building allowed **straight-line depreciation** based on a 27.5-year lifetime for the building.[5] This means that the property owner can charge an annual expense against the property's NOI equal to 1/27.5 of the cost basis of the property. In this case, this allows a depreciation expense of $29,091 per year, as seen in the next line in the proforma, as 800,000/27.5 = 29,091.[6]

---

[5] The IRS **depreciable life** for nonresidential commercial buildings was 39 years as of the late 1990s.

[6] Some components of the property equipment such as HVAC or kitchen appliances may be depreciated more rapidly (and in buildings with long-term leases, leasing expenses may be depreciated over the life of the lease). These subtleties are ignored for clarity of exposition in this example.

Property purchase price year 0:	$1,000,000									
Depreciable cost basis:	$800,000						Unlevered	Levered		
Ordinary income tax rate:	40.00%			Before-tax IRR:			10.60%	11.86%		
Capital gains tax rate:	20.00%			After-tax IRR:			7.45%	10.76%		

TRADITIONAL FORMAT

Operating Accrual Items	Year: 1	2	3	4	5	6	7	8	9	Oper. Yr. 10	Reversion Item	Rever. Yr. 10	Total Yr. 10
NOI	$90,000	$92,250	$94,556	$96,920	$99,343	$101,827	$104,372	$106,982	$109,656	$112,398	Sale Price	$1,280,085	
− Depr. Exp.	$29,091	$29,091	$29,091	$29,091	$29,091	$29,091	$29,091	$29,091	$29,091	$29,091	− Book Val.	$809,091	
− Int. Exp.	$75,000	$74,800	$74,600	$74,400	$74,200	$74,000	$73,800	$73,600	$73,400	$73,200			$481,100
= Net Income (BT)	($14,091)	($11,641)	($9,135)	($6,571)	($3,948)	($1,264)	$1,481	$4,291	$7,165	$10,107	= Book Gain	$470,994	
− Inc. Tax	($5,636)	($4,656)	($3,654)	($2,628)	($1,579)	($506)	$593	$1,716	$2,866	$4,043	− CGT	$94,199	
= Net Income (AT)	($8,455)	($6,985)	($5,481)	($3,942)	($2,369)	($759)	$889	$2,574	$4,299	$6,064	= Gain (AT)	$376,795	$382,859

Adjusting Accrual to Reflect Cash Flow

	Year: 1	2	3	4	5	6	7	8	9	Oper. Yr. 10	Reversion Item	Rever. Yr. 10	Total Yr. 10
− Cap. Imprv. Expdtr.	$0	$0	$50,000	$0	$0	$0	$0	$50,000	$0	$0	+ Book Val.	$809,091	
+ Depr. Exp.	$29,091	$29,091	$29,091	$29,091	$29,091	$29,091	$29,091	$29,091	$29,091	$29,091	− Loan Bal.	$730,000	
− Debt Amort.	$2,000	$2,000	$2,000	$2,000	$2,000	$2,000	$2,000	$2,000	$2,000	$2,000	= EATCF	$455,886	
= EATCF	$18,636	$20,106	($28,390)	$23,148	$24,722	$26,332	$27,980	($20,335)	$31,390	$33,155			$489,041
+ Inc. Tax	($5,636)	($4,656)	($3,654)	($2,628)	($1,579)	($506)	$593	$1,716	$2,866	$4,043	+ CGT	$94,199	
= EBTCF	$13,000	$15,450	($32,044)	$20,520	$23,143	$25,827	$28,572	($18,618)	$34,256	$37,198	= EBTCF	$550,085	$587,282

CASH FLOW COMPONENTS FORMAT

Operating Accrual Items	Year: 1	2	3	4	5	6	7	8	9	Oper. Yr. 10	Reversion Item	Rever. Yr. 10	Total Yr. 10
NOI	$90,000	$92,250	$94,556	$96,920	$99,343	$101,827	$104,372	$106,982	$109,656	$112,398	Sale Price	$1,280,085	
− Cap. Imprv. Expdtr.	$0	$0	$50,000	$0	$0	$0	$0	$50,000	$0	$0			
= PBTCF	$90,000	$92,250	$44,556	$96,920	$99,343	$101,827	$104,372	$56,982	$109,656	$112,398	= PBTCF	$1,280,085	$1,392,482
− Debt Svc.	$77,000	$76,800	$76,600	$76,400	$76,200	$76,000	$75,800	$75,600	$75,400	$75,200	− Loan Bal.	$730,000	
= EBTCF	$13,000	$15,450	($32,044)	$20,520	$23,143	$25,827	$28,572	($18,618)	$34,256	$37,198	= EBTCF	$550,085	$587,282
− tax NOI	$36,000	$36,900	$37,823	$38,768	$39,737	$40,731	$41,749	$42,793	$43,863	$44,959	Tax Mkt. Gain	$36,017	$80,976
+ DTS	$11,636	$11,636	$11,636	$11,636	$11,636	$11,636	$11,636	$11,636	$11,636	$11,636	− Acc. DTS	$58,182	$46,545
+ ITS	$30,000	$29,920	$29,840	$29,760	$29,680	$29,600	$29,520	$29,440	$29,360	$29,280			$29,280
= EATCF	$18,636	$20,106	($28,390)	$23,148	$24,722	$26,332	$27,980	($20,335)	$31,390	$33,155	EATCF	$455,886	$489,041

Exhibit 14-2   Example After-Tax Income and Cash Flow Proformas

The proforma in Exhibit 14-2 assumes that the investor will take out a loan to finance 75% of the purchase price of the property. This $750,000 mortgage will have an interest rate of 10%, and requires that $2,000 of the principal balance be paid back ("amortized") each year in annual payments in arrears (that is, at the ends of the years). Thus, as the initial loan balance is $750,000, the 10% interest rate requires $75,000 in interest to be paid in year 1. The total **debt service** payment owed by the property owner to the bank that year, however, is $77,000, including the $2,000 principal amortization, which will bring the new loan balance down to $748,000 at the beginning of year 2. Thus, in year 2 the interest owed is $74,800 (calculated as 10% of $748,000), and the total debt service is $76,800. For income tax purposes, the property owner (debtor) may charge against taxable income the *interest component only* of these debt service payments, as **interest expense**, as indicated in the third line of the proforma.

14.2.2 Accrual-Based Income and Tax Shelter

This brings us to the fourth line, which is the owner's net income from this property investment as recorded by the owner for income tax reporting purposes. Note that in year 1 (and indeed for most of the projected years) this taxable net income is a negative number. The $90,000 NOI from the property is reduced first by the $29,091 depreciation expense and then by the $75,000 interest expense to leave a net taxable income of −$14,091. If the property owner has other positive taxable income from other sources, then this **tax loss** of $14,091 on the apartment building can be deducted against this other income, thereby reducing the owner's overall taxable income. This will save the owner income taxes in the amount of her income tax rate times the taxable income deduction, in this case $5,636 (calculated as 40% times $14,091). This is referred to as a **tax shield** or **tax shelter**, because it allows other income that would otherwise be taxable to avoid paying taxes.

The IRS has put some limits on the ability to use property tax losses to shelter other income. These limits change as tax rules change, but they tend to apply most severely to higher income investors. In any case, *property income* (from other properties the investor might own that are producing positive taxable income) can always be sheltered by tax losses on a given property. Tax losses can also be carried forward from one year to the next when the investor's total taxable income is negative.[7]

The proforma in Exhibit 14-2 assumes that the investor can use all of the tax shelter this apartment property can provide in each year. The tax shelter from this investment appears to be considerable because, as noted earlier, the projected taxable income from this property investment looks to be quite negative. Positive net income is not projected until year 7, and then it is small. Even on an after-tax basis, reflecting any savings from tax shelter, the net income is negative by $8,455 in the first year and does not turn positive until year 7. (After-tax net income is simply the before-tax income minus the income tax, but as tax shelter is counted as "negative taxes" because it saves that amount in taxes, after-tax income will be greater, that is, less negative, than before-tax income whenever taxable income is negative.) Due to the depreciation expense and (even more so in this case) to the interest expense, positive

---

[7] Property rental income is classified by the IRS as "passive" income, and all sources of a taxpayer's passive income are pooled for tax reporting purposes. However, above certain overall income limits, losses from passive income cannot be deducted from "active" income (e.g., from wages) or "portfolio" income (e.g., from financial investments).

income is not projected until far in the future, and then it is much smaller in magnitude than the earlier projected negative income.

So why would the investor even contemplate such an investment? Part of the answer lies in the potential for profit in selling the property later. But the more important and more fundamental reason lies in the difference between accrual-based taxable income and actual current cash flow. The importance of this difference is seen in the rest of the proforma in Exhibit 14-2. In the lines below the Net Income (AT) line in Exhibit 14-2 we adjust the accrual-based accounts to reflect current cash flow, in the traditional format.

14.2.3 After-Tax Operating Cash Flow

First, we subtract any capital improvement expenditures that were not expensed. These typically include expenditures for large physical improvements to the building or its equipment, such as installing a new roof or new windows.[8] These are cash outflows. In the example apartment building in Exhibit 14-2, the owner is projecting such expenditures of $50,000 in year 3 and year 8.[9]

The next step in going from accrual to cash flow accounting is to add back the depreciation expense we previously subtracted, because (as noted) this is not a cash outflow. On the other hand, we must subtract the debt principal amortization, which is indeed a cash outflow.

This brings us to the **equity-after-tax cash flow (EATCF)** to the levered equity owner in Exhibit 14-2. This is the most important bottom-line number for the property owner, assuming that the tax shelter is indeed useful. To arrive at the **equity-before-tax cash flow (EBTCF)**, we simply add the income tax back into the EATCF. This is the last line in the traditional format in Exhibit 14-2. In years when there is negative income tax payment from the property (i.e., when the property is a net tax shelter), which will occur when there is a tax loss from the property (the property's taxable income is negative), the EATCF will be larger than the EBTCF. In the example, this is projected to occur until year 7.

Below the traditional format in Exhibit 14-2 we have presented an alternative method of calculating the same cash flows. This cash flow components format is simpler than the traditional format in some respects and illustrates more clearly the components of the after-tax cash flows. In particular, this presentation explicitly highlights the tax shield components of the cash flow, including a separation of the

---

[8] See the discussion of capital improvement expenditures in Chapter 11. In some cases, especially for commercial buildings with long-term leases owned by tax-exempt investors, a variety of regularly occurring leasing costs are capitalized. Note that capital expenditures may, but do not necessarily, increase the size (or rentable area) of the building. All capital expenditures should increase the value of the building *relative* to what it would be *without* the expenditures, or it would not make sense to spend the money on the "improvement." Such value increments will result from either greater rents or lower operating expenses in future years (and/or greater resale value for the property), compared to what would occur without the improvements.

[9] Because major capital improvement expenditures are "lumpy" across time, that is, occur at somewhat infrequent and irregular intervals and amounts, many proforma operating statements include a regular, relatively constant amount each year as a "reserve" item, instead of projecting the specific lumpy expenditures. This stabilizes the annual cash flow, making it easier to work with the numbers. However, the annual reserve is not really a cash outflow to the owner, as even if such cash is actually placed aside in a separate sinking fund account, it is still owned by the investor and earns interest for the investor. On the other hand, large capital expenditures may be financed with borrowed funds, which will smooth the cash flow impact over time.

portions of the tax shields attributable to depreciation and to interest expense. In this approach the EBTCF is calculated first, directly from the PBTCF and the capital expenditures. Then the income tax as if there were no tax shields is computed by applying the ordinary income tax rate to the NOI. Finally, the **depreciation tax shields (DTS)** and **interest tax shields (ITS)** are directly and separately computed and added back in to arrive at the EATCF. For operating cash flows, the DTS equals the depreciable cost basis divided by the depreciable life times the owner's ordinary income tax rate.[10] The ITS equals the loan interest expense times the owner's ordinary income tax rate.[11]

Notice that the cash flows in Exhibit 14-2 look to be quite a bit more positive, and much sooner so, than the accrual-based net income figures described previously. The first year's after-tax cash flow is $18,636, which is 7.45% of the equity investment of $250,000 (the $1,000,000 purchase price less the $750,000 loan). The impact of the tax shields combined with the fact that the depreciation expense is not a cash outflow causes the net cash flow from the property to be larger than the accrual-based net income.

While the cash flows are generally larger than the net income, they are also less smooth over time. As noted in Chapter 11, this is because of the effect of capital expenditures, which tend to be "lumpy," occurring in large amounts at irregular and occasional points in time. However, this lumpiness effect is magnified in the equity bottom line, due to the effect of debt adding financial leverage to the operating cash flow of the building. In the case of our example apartment building, the cash flow proforma reveals years in which the equity owner will experience substantial negative net cash flow, much larger negative amounts in a single year than appear in the accrual-based net income figures. (Note that this is in some contrast to the unlevered PBTCF bottom line indicated in the lower panel of Exhibit 14-2, as no projected negative years occur prior to debt service payment.) The owner must plan for and budget for such negative years, and the lender should also be aware of the stress such years can put on the borrower's ability to service the debt, unless adequate precautions and preparations are made.

While some types of capital expenditures are somewhat discretionary and can be postponed, or perhaps financed with loans or paid for gradually, other types of capital expenditures cannot be delayed and must be paid for up front. For example, the expiration of long-term leases may require major expenditures to bring in a new long-term tenant.

14.2.4 After-Tax Reversion Cash Flow

Recall from Chapter 11 that the last year of a proforma cash flow projection for investment analysis must include not only the normal operating line items for that year but also the so-called reversion items associated with the (presumed) resale of the property at the end of the year. Hence, in year 10 Exhibit 14-2 depicts both operating and reversion components, which are then summed to present the year-10 total bottom-line figures for net income and net cash flow (in the far right-hand column). The reversion items are labeled and quantified in the two columns immediately to the left of the last column in the exhibit.

---

[10]$11,636 = (0.40) \times ($800,000/27.5)

[11]For example, for the first year, $30,000 = (0.40) \times $75,000.

Reversion calculations begin with the projected resale price (net of projected selling expenses such as broker and legal fees). In the apartment building example in Exhibit 14-2, this projected sale price is $1,280,085. (This is a 2.5% per year increase from the $1,000,000 initial purchase price, based on the assumption that the net operating income is projected to grow at that rate, and that the asset market's required yield, or cap rate, will remain the same for this building, that is, at 9% based on NOI, reflecting a mature, stable market and good upkeep of the building.)

To calculate the projected capital gains tax owed upon sale, we subtract from the sale price the projected **book value** of the property at the time of sale. The book value equals the original purchase price plus any (as yet undepreciated) capital expenditures made on the building during the period of ownership, less the **accumulated depreciation** expenses. Ten years of annual depreciation expenses of $29,091 will have reduced the book value of the property by $290,910, while the $100,000 of capital expenditures will have increased it by that much (here, for simplicity, we ignore depreciation of the capital improvements). So the book value is projected at $809,091 (found as $1,000,000 less $290,910, plus $100,000, including rounding). The difference between the $1,280,085 sale price and the $809,091 book value gives the projected (book) capital gain of $470,994. The owner's projected capital gains income tax rate of 20% is applied to this figure to obtain the CGT obligation of $94,199, leaving a book-value net after-tax gain of $376,795.

Once the CGT is determined, the reversion cash flows are straightforward to calculate. The before-tax reversion for the equity owner is simply the projected property sale proceeds of $1,280,085 less the projected outstanding loan balance on the mortgage, which in this example is $730,000 (the original $750,000 loan amount less 10 years' worth of annual $2,000 amortization payments). This leaves an equity-before-tax reversion cash flow of $550,085. If we then subtract the projected capital gains income tax obligation of $94,199 (as calculated previously), we arrive at the equity after-tax reversion cash flow of $455,886 (including rounding). As noted, the complete year-10 cash flow includes both the operating and reversion components, as shown in the last column.[12]

It should be noted that the total CGT of $94,199 can be thought of as comprising two components, $36,017 attributable to the actual or "economic" gain in the property's market value (from $1,000,000 to $1,280,085), plus $58,182 attributable to the accumulated depreciation on the property. As of the year 2000 this distinction did not matter for tax-computation purposes, although it may have some economic interest. However, the IRS has sometimes made a distinction between these two components of the capital gain and has applied a higher CGT rate to the component attributable to accumulated depreciation. This is typically referred to as the "recapture" component, as this part of the CGT attempts to capture back for the IRS at least part of the DTS of previous years. These two components of the capital gains tax are identified separately in the cash flow components format calculations shown below the traditional format in Exhibit 14-2. The CGT component based on the economic gain in the property is computed in the line that represents what the income tax would be

---

[12] The reversion EATCF is also found from the accrual-based gain by adding back the non-cash-flow item (book value) and subtracting the cash outflow item (loan balance), as shown in the traditional format in the upper panel of Exhibit 14-2.

in the absence of any tax shields.[13] The recapture component of the CGT is then computed in the DTS line item.[14]

14.2.5 Projected Total Return Calculations

Using the net cash flow figures in the proforma, it is possible to calculate the projected internal rate of return (IRR) for the investment in the apartment building depicted in Exhibit 14-2. Assuming an up-front investment of $1,000,000 in cash and ignoring the debt-based components of the cash flow projection, one can calculate the unlevered returns, also known as property-level or free-and-clear returns. (This can be done by recalculating the figures in Exhibit 14-2 as if there were no loan.) To calculate the levered equity return based on the $250,000 up-front cash investment and the $750,000 loan, we use the EBTCF and EATCF lines depicted in Exhibit 14-2, for before-tax and after-tax returns, respectively.

The calculated IRRs are reported at the top of Exhibit 14-2. On an unlevered basis, the projected returns are 10.60% before tax and 7.45% after tax. The levered return expectations are higher: 11.86% before tax and 10.76% after tax. Note that the after-tax return expectation for the levered equity is not as much reduced below the before-tax return as is the case without leverage. This reflects the levering of the tax shield effects, primarily the depreciation tax shields. In particular, without leverage the after-tax return is 70% of the before-tax return (7.45%/10.60%), reflecting an "effective" tax rate of 30% in the 10-year going-in IRR in this case. This is a blend of the 40% **ordinary income tax** rate and the 20% capital gains tax rate, reflecting the fact that some of the total return is achieved through the receipt of ordinary income, and some through the realization of capital gain. It also reflects the effect of the depreciation tax shield.

With leverage, the effective tax rate is reduced in this example to only 9% (comparing the 10.76% return to the 11.86% return). This occurs for two reasons. For one thing, the leverage shifts the composition of the investor's IRR relatively away from ordinary income and toward the capital gain component. More important, however, the leverage magnifies the effect of the depreciation tax shields.[15]

14.3 NOTE ON THE VALUE OF LEVERAGE AND TAX SHELTER

The numerical example in Exhibit 14-2 illustrates how leverage can increase the equity investor's expected total return on a before-tax basis, and reduce the effective tax rate on her investment returns. Although the interaction of leverage and tax effects will

---

[13] $36,017 = (0.20) \times [\$1,280,085 - (\$1,000,000 + \$100,000)]$. Note that in the absence of any income tax shields, there would be no depreciation tax shields. Thus, it is consistent with this assumption to define this line item based on *economic* gain rather than *book* gain.

[14] $58,182 = (0.20) \times (10 \times \$29,091) = (0.20) \times [10 \times (\$800,000/27.5)]$. Note that this line item thus reflects both the original DTS cash flows from the operating years and the recapture by the IRS of whatever portion of those DTS is permitted by the recapture tax rate in the reversion year.

[15] In this numerical example we have presented the cash flow proforma as a future projection, an *ex ante* proforma. Thus, the investment returns we have calculated here are *expected* (going-in) returns. The relationship of such IRR expectations to NPV and the investment decision will be discussed later in this chapter. As far as the mechanics of the after-tax cash flow and IRR computations are concerned, of course, they are the same whether the cash flow proforma is ex ante or ex post (historical data).

be addressed more fully in the next chapter, we should pause briefly here to put these results in some context.

Consider first the leveraging up of the expected before-tax return. We have already explained in Chapter 13 how this does not necessarily imply that the equity investor who uses debt financing is getting something for nothing. The point we raised there was that in such circumstances the leverage also normally increases the *risk* in the equity investor's position, such that, viewed from a market value perspective, there is no net gain in value to the borrower. (In other words, borrowing at the market interest rate is a zero-NPV transaction.)

Now we see that there may be additional magnification of equity returns on an after-tax basis, as leverage magnifies the effects of tax shelter. But once again, the fact that the effective tax rate in the levered after-tax return is lower than the effective tax rate in the unlevered after-tax return does not necessarily imply any "free lunch" for the borrower. For example, there is no necessary implication that the increase in the after-tax risk premium is more than proportional to the increase in risk faced by the equity investor. If the risk premium in the expected after-tax return is merely increasing proportionately with the extra risk the investor takes on through the added leverage, then no value is created (or lost) for the borrower as a result of the use of leverage.

Consider a numerical example to illustrate this point. Suppose the interest rate on riskless debt is 6% before tax and 4% after tax, and suppose the unlevered return on property is 8% before tax and 6.5% after tax.[16] Thus, the unlevered risk premium is 2% before tax (8% − 6%) and 2.5% after tax (6.5% − 4%). Now suppose that the use of leverage doubles the risk faced by the equity investor. With twice as much risk, the risk premium faced by the levered equity investor in his expected total return would have to grow to 4% before tax ($2 \times 2\%$) and to 5% after tax ($2 \times 2.5\%$) in order to make the leverage worthwhile on a risk-adjusted basis. This implies that the levered investor would have to be able to expect a total return going-in of 10% before tax ($r_f + RP = 6\% + 4\%$) and 9% after tax ($r_f + RP = 4\% + 5\%$). Thus, the effective tax rate on equity returns is only 10% with leverage (1 − 9%/10%), but 18.75% without leverage (1 − 6.5%/8%). Yet there is no necessary implication of value creation in these return numbers, as the risk premium per unit of risk is the same with and without the leverage.

Ultimately, in principle, a sufficient amount of leverage could be applied so that levered after-tax returns could equal or even exceed levered before-tax returns, implying a zero or negative effective tax rate on the returns. This is possible because of the effect of depreciation and interest tax shields obtained by the equity investor, presuming his ability to use all such shields. In practice, debt underwriting restrictions on the part of the lender, and a lack of ability to use tax shields on the part of the borrower, tend to put a limit on this ability. In any case, there is no necessary implication of a free lunch (i.e., positive NPV) for the borrower resulting from these tax effects.[17]

---

[16]The effective tax rate would likely be lower on property than on riskless debt due to the effect of capital gains and depreciation tax shields in the return. In this example the effective tax rate on property returns is 18.75% = (8% − 6.5%)/8%, while that on riskless debt is 33.3% = (6% − 4%)/6%.

[17]See Chapter 15 for an in-depth discussion of the tax benefits of borrowing for the equity investor.

14.4 AFTER-TAX EQUITY VALUATION AND CAPITAL BUDGETING

In Chapter 10 we described the basic DCF method for valuing income-producing commercial property and the NPV decision rule for making investment or capital budgeting decisions. Our application of these procedures in Chapter 10 was at the property level (prior to considering the use of debt) and on a before-tax basis (prior to considering the property owner's income tax).[18] Our focus in Chapter 10 was (rather implicitly then) on the estimation of market value (MV), a term we defined more explicitly in Chapter 12. Of course, the DCF and NPV procedures can also be applied at the after-tax level for specified equity investors who may or may not use debt financing. Indeed, we noted in Chapter 12 that the concept of investment value (IV), as distinct from market value, is applied in principle at the after-tax level of a specified owner of the given property.

14.4.1 After-Tax DCF in General

To compute investment value, the first step is to discount the projected equity-after-tax bottom line from the after-tax proforma (the EATCF row in Exhibit 14-2). This results in an estimate of the present value of the investor's levered equity in the property, including consideration of the income tax shield effects. (Don't forget to include the after-tax equity reversion in the terminal year.) Add this equity present value to the amount of any loan the equity investor will be receiving for the property purchase to arrive at an estimate of the total investment value of the property to the equity investor. This represents the maximum price the investor would be willing to pay for the property, if he had to. (Don't forget our injunction in Chapter 12 against paying more than MV, even if your IV exceeds MV.) The value for the property computed in this way may then be compared to the price at which the property can be obtained (or sold for) in the property market, to arrive at the NPV of the deal for the equity investor from an investment value perspective.

In evaluating the investor's equity in this way, it is important to be consistent in the treatment of the numerator and denominator within the basic DCF operation. The following rule must be heeded carefully:

> *Discount* equity-after-tax *cash flows*
> *at the appropriate* equity-after-tax *discount rate.*

The appropriate discount rate for levered equity cash flows will normally be greater than that for property-level free-and-clear cash flows, for the previously noted reason that the levered position is normally more risky for the equity investor and so requires a greater risk premium in the expected total return. On the other hand, the discount rate for after-tax cash flows is usually less than the discount rate

---

[18]In corporate finance textbooks DCF valuation and capital budgeting analysis are applied at the after-tax level. However, in the typical corporate context, the taxes being considered are corporate-level income taxes only. The typical textbook application is actually at a before-tax level from the perspective of the ultimate investors, the shareholders of the corporation. In real estate, taxed corporate-level entities rarely hold the property, so our before-tax presentation in Chapter 10 was actually consistent with the typical corporate finance textbook presentation.

for before-tax cash flows because the after-tax opportunity cost of capital reflects the paying of income taxes on investment returns.

Correctly quantifying the effect of equity leverage and the effect of income taxes in the opportunity cost of capital can be quite difficult in practice. We know that the amount one must add to the before-tax risk premium in the required expected total return is usually greater, the greater the leverage. *But how much greater?* [19] We know that the after-tax required return is likely to be lower than the before-tax required return for a taxable investment. *But how much lower?* For example, the effective tax rate on the total return is a function of the proportion of the return that will be received as ordinary income as opposed to capital gains income, and also of the likely holding period of the investor. [20] It is often difficult in practice to explicitly and properly take account of all of these considerations to estimate an appropriate after-tax discount rate for the levered equity cash flows.

Can we get around this problem simply by focusing on the expected return rather than the NPV of a deal, by "backing out" the IRR implied by a given price? In the apartment building investment we considered earlier, for example, we computed a levered after-tax return to equity of 10.76%, given the $1 million price for the property. But what are we to make of this 10.76%? Is it a good return or not? What should the hurdle rate be, given the leverage, the tax rate, and the investment holding horizon?

Most investors would want to answer such questions by reference to the typical market return expectation for such an investment. Is 10.76% above or below the market return? [21] The answer to this question depends on the relation between the fair market value of the property and the $1 million price (and loan terms) we used to compute the 10.76% return. Unless we knew through other analysis that $1 million is the market value of the property, we may find ourselves simply staring at the 10.76% return and not knowing what to make of it.

14.4.2 Shortcut for Marginal Investors

The preceding discussion has pointed out a fundamental practical difficulty in computing investment value. It is often difficult to know the correct discount rate to apply to a levered position. Fortunately, a shortcut is often possible. As noted in Chapter 12, in many cases it may be safe to assume that investment value and market value are virtually identical. In particular, this is true by definition for marginal investors in the property market, who would typically be types of investors who

---

[19] The WACC formula described in Chapter 13 gives some idea of the effect of leverage on the required equity return, but remember that the WACC formula is only an approximation over positive spans of time. For an investor looking at a 10-year holding horizon, the WACC approximation may not be accurate enough.

[20] The *effective* capital gain tax rate is less than the nominal rate due to the effect of deferral of the capital gains tax until the gain is actually realized at the time of the resale of the property (or even later with like-kind reinvestment). This effect in turn is a function of the growth rate in property value and the length of time the property is held before its resale. Suppose investment value grows at 10% for 10 years. With a capital gains tax rate of 20% (and ignoring depreciation for exposition), the after-tax capital available is $(1.10)^{10} - 0.20[(1.10)^{10} - 1] = 2.274994$, which is equivalent to $(1.08567)^{10}$. Thus, the effective after-tax growth rate is 8.57% per year, which is 85.7% of the before-tax growth rate, implying an effective tax rate of $100 - 85.7 = 14.3\%$, instead of 20%.

[21] Recall that we argued in Chapter 12 that, even for computing investment value, the appropriate opportunity cost of capital should normally be obtained, if possible, from the capital market (see section 12.1.1).

are about evenly distributed on both the buy and sell sides of the market. In such cases, one can work with property-level before-tax cash flows (PBTCF) rather than the equity-after-tax cash flows (EATCF) when doing valuation and capital budgeting analysis. This shortcut approach, in effect *assuming* that IV – MV, is widely used in the real world of real estate investment practice. We will label this approach the **property-before-tax (PBT) approach**.

For purposes of estimating market value explicitly, the PBT shortcut is doubly sound. Not only is this approach simpler, but by avoiding the need to estimate the marginal tax rates and the holding periods and leverage of the marginal investors in the property market, it avoids the danger of making mistakes in estimating these parameters. In a well-functioning property asset market it is generally easier to make reliable empirical observations regarding the market values of the before-tax numbers (both the cash flows and the expected returns), so mistakes are less likely at the PBT level.

As an example of this approach, consider again our apartment property in Exhibit 14-2. Suppose we can reliably estimate through observation of the property market that the current market return (10-year going-in IRR) for such properties is 10.60% on a before-tax, property-level basis. Then working at the PBT level we can ascertain that $1 million is the current market value for the property. Now suppose our example investor in Exhibit 14-2 is typical of the type of investor on the margin in the market for that type of property. Then we know by definition that $1 million is the investment value of the property for this investor. We do not need to estimate the after-tax levered opportunity cost of capital for this investor. Indeed, we do not even need to estimate the investor's EATCFs. Had we somehow known that 10.76% was the investor's after-tax levered opportunity cost of capital, we could have applied this rate to the investor's EATCFs (and added in the loan value) to arrive at the same $1 million investment value. But this would be a longer and more difficult route, especially because, as noted previously, we would not know that 10.76% was the correct discount rate.[22]

Notice that what enables us to use this PBT shortcut is the fact that a well-functioning market exists for the underlying physical assets involved in real estate investment decisions. In our apartment example, the fact that we can "observe" (directly or indirectly) that $1 million is the current market value of this property enables us to avoid having to work at the after-tax level.

Although the PBT shortcut is very useful and widely applied, remember that in principle it applies to market value, and therefore to investment value only for the typical marginal investor in the market for the type of property in question. You should be careful about applying the PBT shortcut to analyses of investment value for investors who differ from typical marginal investors in the relevant property market.

14.4.3 Value Additivity and the APV Decision Rule

The PBT shortcut may be viewed as an application of a more general valuation and investment decision procedure often referred to as **adjusted present value**, or **APV**. The APV procedure is an extension of the basic NPV analysis procedure described in Chapter 10. APV allows the NPV procedure to include explicitly the effect of financing in evaluating a real estate investment deal. From the equity investor's perspective, the deal may be considered the *combination* of the property purchase as if it were free and clear of debt, and the financing arrangements.

---

[22]Of course, once we determine that $1 million is the MV of the property, we could then "back out" the implied 10.76% levered-equity after-tax IRR. The importance of this possibility will be discussed later in this section.

More formally, the APV of a deal is defined as follows:

$$APV = NPV(Property) + NPV(Financing) \tag{1}$$

In equation (1), *NPV(Property)* is the NPV of the property transaction as if there were no debt. *NPV(Financing)* is the net value of the financing arrangements. Typically, financing involves the use of debt, and we can think of the *NPV(Financing)* term as the NPV of the borrowing transaction, from the perspective of the equity investor (the borrower).

The APV investment decision rule states that the traditional NPV decision criterion should be applied to the APV, that is, to the NPV of the deal as a whole including its financing component. This APV must be maximized across mutually exclusive alternatives and always be nonnegative in order for the deal to make sense from a wealth-maximization perspective. The APV concept is based on the **value additivity principle**, the notion that the value of the property must equal the sum of the values of all the claims on the property's cash flows, the equity investor's plus the debt investor's claims.[23]

As the debt market is usually rather competitive and efficient, the *NPV(Financing)* term will usually have a value of zero since it is an MV-based valuation, assuming unsubsidized, market-rate financing (as would typically be obtained, for example, from a bank or other private financial institution, or by issuing bonds in the public market). In these conditions, therefore, the NPV of the equity investment (using debt) is the same as the NPV of an all-equity investment in the property without using debt, evaluated from the perspective of market value, that is, *APV = NPV(Property)*. This is the condition in which the PBT shortcut described in the previous section is typically applied.

On the other hand, if subsidized financing is involved in the deal, such as some seller-provided loans or government-assisted financing, then the NPV of the financing part of the deal can be substantially positive to the buyer/investor. In this case the APV can exceed the NPV to an all-equity investment in the property.[24] The PBT shortcut may still be useful for quantifying the *NPV(Property)* component of the APV, but the *NPV(Financing)* component must be valued separately and added to the *NPV(Property)* to obtain the total deal value for the equity investor.[25]

14.4.4 Evaluating Subsidized Financing

One implication of the APV rule is that a seller who offers cut-rate financing should do so only if it would otherwise be impossible to sell the property at as high a price (in the same period of time). In other words, from the perspective of a seller offering

[23]The value additivity principle has a long tradition in the appraisal profession. In corporate finance its roots go back to the development of arbitrage pricing theory and the famous 1958 work by Modigliani and Miller on the value of corporate debt financing. (See also Myers [1974].)

[24]Apart from subsidized loans, there may be additional benefits from the financing part of the deal in cases in which the equity investor faces a particularly high effective income tax rate (e.g., corporate real estate owned by tax-paying corporations, which effectively subject their shareholders to double taxation on corporate income). In such cases the tax shelter debt can provide may be valuable even without a subsidized interest rate. However, this is not common in most real estate deals, as will be discussed in Chapter 15.

[25]Indeed, for the reasons noted in the previous section, it will often be easier, and less prone to error, to quantify *NPV(Property)* and *NPV(Financing)* separately and add these two components, rather than attempting to quantify directly the NPV of the levered equity. At a minimum, the APV approach provides a good check on any direct quantification of the levered equity value. In particular, direct evaluation of *NPV(Equity)* should not generally imply violation of the APV = 0 rule for MV-based valuations, unless there is a clear reason to believe that this rule does not apply. (See section 14.4.5.)

The Relationship between APV and Value Additivity

The value additivity principle can be expressed by the following equation:

$$V = E + D \qquad (2)$$

where V is the value of the property, E is the value of the equity, and D is the value of the debt. Now define P as the price paid for the property, and let L be the amount of the loan (the cash received by the borrower from the lender). Thus, $P - L$ is the cash paid by the equity investor (not necessarily the same as E, because value and price may differ), and $D - L$ is the MV-based NPV of the loan transaction from the lender's (mortgage issuer's) perspective. Now if we subtract P from both sides of equation (2) we have

$$
\begin{aligned}
V - P &= E + D - P \\
&= E + D - [(P - L) + L] \\
&= E - (P - L) + D - L \\
&= E - (P - L) - (L - D)
\end{aligned}
$$

Thus,

$$E - (P - L) = (V - P) + (L - D)$$

This demonstrates that equation (2) is equivalent to equation (1), the APV formulation, because $E - (P - L)$ is the NPV of the deal for the equity investor as financed, defined as the APV in equation (1). On the right-hand side of the equation, $V - P$ is the MV-based NPV of the property transaction for the buyer in an all-equity deal, labeled $NPV(Property)$ in equation (1). Similarly, $L - D$ is the MV-based NPV of the loan transaction from the equity investor's perspective, labeled $NPV(Financing)$. Thus, assuming neutral debt, the APV > 0 whenever the value of the equity exceeds the equity investor's cash outlay. It should be noted that the arbitrage basis of value additivity applies to market value only, but the common sense of value additivity as a first principle (or as an accounting rule) can be applied to investment value as well.

a low-interest loan, the $NPV(Financing)$ term is negative, so for the overall deal to make sense, the property component of the transaction would have to have a positive NPV: $NPV(Property) > 0$. Otherwise, $APV = NPV(Property) + NPV(Financing)$ would be negative.[26]

To quantify the NPV of the loan transaction to the borrower, that is, the $NPV(Financing)$ term in the APV formula, you compute the present value of the benefits minus the present value of the costs, as in any NPV computation. In this case the PV of the benefits is just the up-front cash or cash equivalent obtained by the borrower from the lender. The PV of the cost is the present value of the liability the borrower incurs, measured by the loan's contractual cash flows discounted at the *market* interest rate (not the contractual interest rate in the subsidized loan), because the loan market provides the opportunity cost of capital.

As an example, suppose you estimate that the market value of a certain property, V, is $20,000,000. The seller, however, will not budge below a $20,500,000 price. The $NPV(Property)$ is thus: $V - P = -\$500,000$. However, the seller offers you a 5-year $10,000,000 interest-only loan at 5% (with annual payments in arrears). If the market interest rate on such a loan were 8%, then this financing package from the seller would be worth $1,197,813, computed as follows from a market value perspective:

---

[26]Evaluated from a market-value perspective (before tax), the NPV of the loan transaction from the borrower's perspective is just the negative of the NPV of the loan transaction from the lender's perspective, as the two sides of the transaction face the same cash flows only with opposite signs.

$$NPV(Financing) = \$10,000,000 - \left(\sum_{n=1}^{5} \frac{\$500,000}{(1.08)^n} + \frac{\$10,000,000}{(1.08)^5} \right)$$

$$= +\$1,197,813$$

Note that the cash flows of the loan reflect the loan's stated contractual interest rate of 5% on $10,000,000 (equal to $500,000 per year), but these future cash flows are discounted to present value at the current market interest rate. Thus, calculated on a market value basis, the overall APV of the proposed deal is positive, and the deal is made feasible by the seller loan:

$$APV(Deal) = -\$500,000 + \$1,197,813 = +\$697,813$$

The method just described, using the before-tax cash flows and before-tax interest rate for the loan, is the way an appraiser would typically calculate the "cash equivalency" of the subsidized loan. It reflects the opportunity value of the loan as if, for example, the loan were sold into the secondary mortgage market. If the seller attempted to sell the loan into such a market just after the loan were issued, she would receive $8,802,187 for the loan, as this value reflects the prevailing mortgage market interest rate of 8%. In this sense the above procedure reflects an MV-based evaluation.

Suppose, however, that the equity investor faces a different tax rate than that of the typical marginal investor in the bond market whose IV determines the MV of the debt. In that case an after-tax investment value perspective would logically be most relevant for valuing the *NPV(Financing)* component of the APV for the equity investor. In fact, *for non-market-rate loans*, the IV of debt will differ from its MV even for an investor whose tax rate is the same as that of the marginal investor in the bond market.

Suppose, for example, that all investors face a marginal income tax rate of 40% on debtlike investments. Then the value of the *NPV(Financing)* term for the equity investor due to the subsidized loan is only $783,633 from an after-tax investment value perspective, not the $1,197,813 calculated earlier. The present value of the after-tax future loan payment liabilities faced by the equity investor is $9,216,367, not the $8,802,187 market value of the loan.[27]

$$NPV = \$10,000,000 - \left(\sum_{n=1}^{5} \frac{(1 - 0.4)(\$500,000)}{[1 + (1 - 0.4)(0.08)]^n} + \frac{\$10,000,000}{[1 + (1 - 0.4)(0.08)]^5} \right)$$

$$= +\$783,633$$

[27] Note, however, that if the loan were not subsidized (so that the annual interest payments were $800,000 instead of $500,000), then the loan would be worth $10,000,000 evaluated on either a before-tax or after-tax basis. In the after-tax valuation the cash flows are lower due to the interest tax shield, but the after-tax discount rate is also lower. These two effects cancel each other out in the PV when the tax rate applied is the same in the numerator and denominator, provided the numerator reflects the same interest rate as that in the denominator. However, if the discount rate is greater in the denominator than the interest rate reflected in the numerator, then the tax effect will be proportionately greater in the denominator than the numerator. This is exactly what occurs in subsidized loans. Assuming equal tax rates, subsidized loans provide after-tax NPVs converging to $(1 - T)BTNPV$ as the loan term approaches zero, and to $BTNPV$ as the loan term approaches infinity, where T is the borrower's tax rate and $BTNPV$ is the before-tax NPV of the loan.

This after-tax IV-based valuation of the subsidized loan is more relevant for an investor who is wondering how much more she should be willing to pay for the property than the amount she otherwise would without the loan deal.[28] For example, suppose the property buyer takes the $10,000,000 cash from the seller loan and uses this money to purchase a similar loan in the secondary mortgage market at the same time. The loan she buys will carry the market rate of 8%, thereby providing interest income of $800,000 per year. So her net cash flow up front from the two loan transactions is zero, followed by five annual net cash flows of $300,000 each ($800,000 − $500,000). On an after-tax basis these five cash flows are worth $180,000 each (after paying 40% taxes on the net interest income of $300,000). Discounting these after-tax cash flows at an after-tax opportunity cost of capital of 4.8% (equal to [1 − 0.4] times the market rate of 8%) gives the present value of $783,633.[29]

14.4.5 Another Implication of the APV Rule: Discovering Market Returns to Equity

Recall from Chapter 10 that NPVs are normally expected to be approximately zero when evaluated from a market value perspective, unless one side in the deal is making a mistake. This implication holds also for the APV, and this leads to a useful practical implication. If we can assume that the MV-based APV for a deal is zero, then this fact can be used to "back out" the market's implied expected return for levered positions.[30]

For example, suppose that a levered position in a certain deal will provide the expected before-tax equity cash flow stream depicted in the bottom line of the table on the next page. The equity investment consists of the $1,100,000 price of the property less the $800,000 loan. These may or may not be the market values of the individual components of the deal.[31] But if we can assume that neither side in the deal would be allowing the market value of their net wealth to be reduced, then the APV = 0 rule allows us to determine that the market's expected return on the levered equity position in the property is 19.18%. This is the IRR of the bottom line in the table, the sum of the property and financing cash flows. In other words, a 10-year IRR expectation of 19.18% provides the expected risk premium required by the market for the amount of risk contained in this type of levered position.

---

[28] In principle, if we are evaluating the NPV(*Financing*) term from an investment value perspective, then we should also evaluate the rest of the APV, namely the NPV(*Property*) term, from the IV perspective. However, if the investor is typical of marginal investors in the property market, then the NPV(*Property*) term will be the same whether valued from the MV or IV perspective. Furthermore, it may be argued that only the NPV(*Financing*) term is relevant for the purpose of ascertaining how much more than market value the investor should be willing to pay for the property as a result of the subsidized loan, for in the absence of the subsidized loan the seller can only expect to sell the property for its market value anyway.

[29] The alternative of immediately selling the claim on the net cash flow difference in the secondary loan market is not as good for the property investor, after tax. The claim on five annual $300,000 payments would sell in the secondary market for $1,197,813 (PV of a $300,000 annuity at 8%). But the immediate realization of this income from the arbitrage transaction would be taxed at 40%, so the net left over after taxes to the property purchaser would be 0.6 × $1,197,813 = $718,688.

[30] Of course, the WACC formula can also be used to derive the levered equity return from the returns to the underlying property and the mortgage. But as noted, the WACC is only an approximation when it is applied to multiperiod return measures such as the IRR. Thus, the technique presented here is useful as an additional perspective.

[31] For example, the market value of the property might actually be $1,000,000, and the market value of the debt might be $700,000.

Year	0	1	2	3	4	5	6	7	8	9	10
Prop. Inc.		100,000	102,000	104,040	106,121	108,243	110,408	112,616	114,869	117,166	119,509
Debt Svc.		−49,000	−49,000	−49,000	−49,000	−49,000	−49,000	−49,000	−49,000	−49,000	−49,000
Prop. Sale	−1,100,000										1,000,000
Loan	800,000										−700,000
Equity CF	−300,000	51,000	53,000	55,040	57,121	59,243	61,408	63,616	65,869	68,166	370,509

14.4.6 Implications for the After-Tax Levered OCC and the "Art of the Deal"

In fact, we can go further than what is implied in the preceding analysis. It is true that the technique just described for determining market returns to levered equity is based on the APV = 0 rule and therefore applies generally to MV-based valuation, which is defined on a before-tax basis. However, recall that, by definition, MV = IV for marginal investors, and IV is defined on an after-tax basis. Thus, expected after-tax equity returns for marginal investors may also be derived using the APV = 0 rule in the manner described earlier. But recall that, even for computing investment value, the relevant OCC should be derived based on the capital market. Therefore, the OCC of the marginal investors in an asset market normally provides the relevant OCC for computing investment values for *all* investors in the given market, including intramarginal investors.[32]

As an example, consider our apartment building in Exhibit 14-2 again. Suppose the investor in that exhibit is typical of marginal investors in that apartment market. Suppose further that we know that $1 million is the market value of the property (e.g., from a PBT-level analysis) and that the debt is unsubsidized. Then we could ascertain that marginal investors' after-tax required expected return to levered equity in such investments is 10.76% for 10-year expected holding periods with leverage as in our example. This is the IRR of the investment to such investors, hence the return that implies APV = 0 on both an MV and IV basis to such investors. Thus, 10.76% would represent a good estimate of the after-tax levered OCC for all investors in the market for such apartment properties (assuming the risk leverage and holding period in the example).[33]

The APV technique and its use in "backing out" the implied after-tax levered-equity OCC is not presented in most traditional real estate investments textbooks. Why have we decided to present it here? This technique can be very valuable to avoid confusion in the real world. In particular, it can help to cut through the smoke screen presented by complicated leveraged deal structures, to allow you to see whether (or in what way) you are getting a good deal.

---

[32] Recall section 12.1.1 in Chapter 12. Intramarginal investors generally have different expected future cash flows than marginal investors, perhaps due to a different tax status or a unique ability to manage the investment entrepreneurially, not because they have a different OCC.

[33] This point is further developed in Chapter 15, in which an appendix to Part V is presented for additional illustration. One caveat is that leverage may not affect the risk of all investors in the same way. Nevertheless, the technique suggested here is generally useful for practical purposes.

Real estate investment at the microlevel is a haven for "deal artists" who are expert at putting together complicated financial arrangements. A variety of parties in several levels of investment products results in a slicing and dicing of claims to the underlying property cash flows but, lo and behold, the bottom line gives *you* a really great expected return on your part of the deal: 20%, after tax! How can you pass it up? Without benefit of the APV perspective, you may be easy prey. You have no good reason to pass up such a deal. In fact, although 20% sounds good, you really have no solid basis for accepting the deal.

Using the APV perspective you can analyze such a deal by beginning with a very fundamental question. Does the overall deal structure create any real value? Does it enhance the future net operating cash flows of any underlying physical asset or group of assets, that is, either increase their expected value or reduce their risk? Does it cause a *net* reduction in taxes paid (at all levels, considering all the parties to the deal)? If not (and often the answer is obviously not), then, according to the value additivity principle, the *overall net* APV of the deal (across all the participants, buyers and sellers) must be zero.

Now proceed by assuming that everybody else in the deal is *not* doing anything stupid. This implies that their components of the deal all must have a zero APV, at least from a market value perspective.[34] The necessary implication is then that your part of the deal also has a zero APV viewed from the market value perspective. (This is value additivity again.) This implies that your 20% after-tax return is just a "fair return." It compensates you only for the amount of risk you are taking on, as the market would evaluate that risk, nothing more.

This means that if the 20% return at first looked great to you, then you may not have been understanding how much risk you were taking on, at least, as evaluated from a capital market perspective. What is that risk? Do you indeed want to take it on? If the deal still looks great to you, does that imply that some party in the deal structure is indeed doing something stupid, that is, receiving a negative APV evaluated from a market value perspective? If so, who is it? If not, where and how is value being created?

14.5 CHAPTER SUMMARY

Chapter 14 extended the basic microlevel investment analysis and evaluation framework of Part IV to the equity-after-tax level, going from PBTCFs to EATCFs. While after-tax equity analysis is in principle a straightforward extension of the framework presented in Part IV, in practice it is often complicated and difficult to know exactly the correct cash flow and discount rate assumptions to apply. Fortunately, the widespread existence of a well-functioning property market often makes it possible in real estate practice to take a shortcut around these difficulties by working at the PBT level and using the APV rule. In any case, Chapter 14 continued our progression, begun in Chapter 13, from the property level to the owner level of analysis, by adding the basics of income tax considerations in the investment analysis. The next chapter will build on both this chapter and the previous to focus on the big picture of the role of debt financing in real estate equity investment.

---

[34]The definition of "doing something stupid" is, in the present context, agreeing to something that reduced the present market value of your net wealth.

KEY TERMS

property-level before-tax cash
   flows vs. owner-level after-tax
   cash flows
depreciation expense
capital expenditures
debt amortization
capital gains tax
straight-line depreciation
depreciable life

debt service
interest expense
tax loss
tax shield or tax shelter
equity-after-tax cash flow
   (EATCF)
equity-before-tax cash flow
   (EBTCF)

depreciation tax shields (DTS)
interest tax shields (ITS)
book value
accumulated depreciation
ordinary income tax
PBT approach
adjusted present value (APV)
value additivity principle

STUDY QUESTIONS

14.1. What is the difference between the property's before-tax cash flow and the equity-before-tax cash flow?

14.2. How can your after-tax cash flow be higher than your before-tax cash flow in a real estate investment?

14.3. Approximately what percentage is nondepreciable land in the total property value of the typical income property in the Midwest of the United States? What is the depreciable life of nonresidential commercial property, according to the IRS? What is the depreciable life of residential income property?

14.4. The NOI is $850,000, the debt service is $600,000 of which $550,000 is interest, the depreciation expense is $350,000. What is the before-tax cash flow to the equity investor (EBTCF) if there are no capital improvement expenditures or reversion items this period?

14.5. In question 14.4, what is the after-tax cash flow to the equity investor if the income tax rate is 35%?

14.6. A nonresidential commercial property that cost $500,000 is considered to have 30% of its total value attributable to land. What is the annual depreciation expense chargeable against taxable income?

14.7. Consider an apartment property that costs $400,000, of which $300,000 is structure value (the rest is land). Suppose an investor expects to hold this property for five years and then sell it for at least what he paid for it (without putting any significant capital into the property). If the investor's marginal income tax rate is 39%, and the capital gains tax rate is 28%, what is the present value, as of the time of purchase, of the depreciation tax shields obtained directly by this investor during the five-year expected holding period (including the payback in the reversion)? Assume taxes are paid annually, with the first tax payment due one year from present, and assume that DTS for this investor are effectively riskless, and the investor's after-tax borrowing rate is 5%.

14.8. Use the following information and the APV decision rule to answer the following questions. A seller has offered you a $1,500,000 interest-only seven-year loan at 6% (annual payments), when market interest rates on such loans are 7%. You face a 35% marginal income tax rate.

   a. Basing your decision on market values, how much more should you be willing to pay for the property than you otherwise think it is worth, due to the financing offer?

   b. Answer the same question only now basing your answer on investment value rather than market value. You may assume that the investor is typical of the marginal investors in the property market, and faces a tax rate similar to that of marginal investors in the bond market.

14.9. What is meant by the adjusted present value (APV) approach to extending the NPV rule to encompass project financing? What is the relationship of the APV technique to the value additivity principle?

14.10. The figures in the following table depict the before-tax cash flow projection for a typical 10-year holding period for a levered investment in a property whose current market value is $5 million, for which a $3 million interest-only 10-year mortgage would be the typical financing mechanism at a market interest rate of 8%. What is the market's implied required going-in 10-year IRR for the levered equity investment?

Year	0	1	2	3	4	5	6	7	8	9	10
Prop. Inc.		450,000	454,500	459,045	463,635	468,272	472,955	477,684	482,461	487,286	492,158
Debt Svc.		−240,000	−240,000	−240,000	−240,000	−240,000	−240,000	−240,000	−240,000	−240,000	−240,000
Prop. Sale	−5,000,000										5,523,111
Loan	3,000,000										−3,000,000
Equity CF	−2,000,000	210,000	214,500	219,045	223,635	228,272	232,955	237,684	242,461	247,286	2,775,269

14.11. Consider a commercial (nonresidential) property that costs $1 million with an initial before-tax yield of 9% (based on NOI) and an expected growth rate of 2.5% per year (in income and value). Ignoring capital improvements and selling expenses, develop a 10-year proforma for before-tax and after-tax property and equity cash flows. Assume a 40% income tax rate (28% for capital gains), and financing of 75% of the property price with a 10% interest-only loan, and that land is worth 20% of the property value.

   a. Use the proforma to determine the ex ante before-tax IRR of the unlevered property investment.

   b. Use the proforma to determine the after-tax IRR of the unlevered property investment.

   c. Use the ratio of the ATIRR calculated in (b) divided by the BTIRR calculated in (a) to determine the after-tax borrowing rate for the investor (by applying this ratio to the loan rate).

d. Apply the after-tax borrowing rate you just calculated to determine the present value of the DTS during the projected 10-year holding period (including the payback of the DTS in the reversion).

e. Compute the implicit PV(DTS) component in the reversion resale price of the property by treating the present value of the DTS you computed in (d) as a constant-growth perpetuity that recurs once every 10 years with a growth rate of 2.5% per year and a discount rate to present value equal to the ATIRR you calculated in (b).

f. Add the answers to (d) and (e) to arrive at the total component of DTS in the value of the property, as a percentage of the property value.

g. Compute the before-tax ex ante IRR of the levered investment in this property.

h. Compute the after-tax ex ante IRR of the levered equity in this property.

i. Compute the ratio of the AT/BT in the levered IRR, and note the difference between this ratio and the unlevered equivalent. Do you think this is an argument for debt financing for this property investment for this investor?

Use of Debt in Real Estate Investment (Part II): Capital Structure

15

Chapter Outline

Part V Appendix
Practical Mechanics for Calculating After-Tax NPVs and OCCs

Learning Objectives

After reading this chapter, you should understand:

◆ What is meant by capital structure, and the major pros and cons for the use of debt financing of real estate equity investments for different types of investors.

◆ What is meant by an equity capital constraint and how this can affect the value of debt financing.

◆ The relationship between income tax considerations and the value of debt financing for different types of investors in the typical real estate context.

◆ The relationship between the use of debt financing and such considerations as management incentives, investor liquidity, and inflation.

◆ The costs of financial distress and how these are affected by the use of debt.

Chapter 15 continues our exploration of the role of debt in the real estate equity investment, begun in the preceding two chapters. In this chapter we will step back a bit from the nuts and bolts perspective of the previous chapters, in which we quantified the effects of leverage and taxes. Here we will focus on the big picture, including a more comprehensive consideration of why different types of investors might want to, or not want to, borrow money, that is, employ debt capital to finance their real estate investments. This question is traditionally considered in corporate finance under the topic of **capital structure**, the relative use of debt versus equity financing of publicly traded corporations. Our purpose in the present chapter is to examine this topic particularly from the perspective of real estate investment and real estate investors.

As usual, some of the peculiar aspects of real estate, and the context in which real estate investment typically occurs, bring some unique considerations regarding capital structure. For example, much real estate investment is made directly, that is, by **ultimate investors**, individuals who hold real estate directly or through small partnerships. Much real estate equity investment also is made by tax-exempt institutions such as pension funds, who simultaneously hold large investments in debt instruments such as bonds and mortgages. Even when real estate investment is made by publicly traded equity corporations, it is often done through the REIT tax status, which differs from the typical corporate situation in the automatic avoidance of corporate-level income taxes. Also, the nature of the underlying physical assets—which are relatively easy for outsiders to observe, understand, and evaluate (thanks in part to a well-functioning direct market for these assets)—has implications for the use of secured debt.

These and other considerations make it worthwhile to examine the capital structure issue, and more broadly the role of debt, from a real estate perspective. While we will attempt to be somewhat comprehensive in this examination, we will not claim to tie all the loose ends together completely. Capital structure is a bit of a puzzle to economists, not only in real estate but also as it relates to mainstream corporate finance. Our attempt to be comprehensive will necessitate some loss in rigor and in the ability to quantify all the relevant considerations. Our basic approach in this chapter will be to discuss the major pros and cons associated with debt financing of real estate equity investment. The basic question before us is, why would various types of equity investors want to, or not want to, borrow money to make their real estate investments?

Keep in mind that the role of debt is an investor-level topic rather than a property-level topic. Some of the issues we treat in this chapter are not relevant to all investors, and some of the issues cut one way for some investors and the other way for other investors. Obviously, the exact answer to the question of optimal use of debt will differ from one investor to another and will be difficult to entirely resolve quantitatively. We never outgrow our need to apply common sense. The discussion in the present chapter is meant only to add some depth and breadth to the knowledge and understanding you can bring to bear in applying your common sense.

The overall plan of attack in Chapter 15 is to survey the major issues relevant to the use of debt in real estate investment. We have already discussed some of the important issues in this regard in our discussion of the big picture in Chapter 13. There we noted that real estate equity is a very different investment product from real estate debt, and some of these differences are magnified by the use of leverage. For example, the use of debt financing will typically increase the risk and average total return in the equity investment, especially the growth component of that return. These characteristics may be appealing to certain investors.

In this chapter we will introduce some further considerations. We will begin with a consideration of the implications of equity capital constraints. This topic is often skipped or lightly passed over in corporate finance textbooks. Large publicly-traded corporations do not usually face a constraint on their availability of equity capital for financing good investments. But this topic is worthy of consideration for many real estate investors. The second topic we will consider is the classic mainstay of corporate finance capital structure analysis: debt and taxes. However, as we will see, the real estate context is typically rather different in this regard. Finally, we will introduce several other issues that can be important, such as the costs of financial distress and the roles of liquidity, management incentives, and inflation. An appendix at the end of this chapter shows how to use some of the macrolevel considerations discussed in Part V to help quantify microlevel investment values.

15.1 DEBT WHEN THERE IS AN EQUITY CAPITAL CONSTRAINT

Large publicly traded corporations can almost always raise capital rather easily to finance positive-NPV investment opportunities, and they usually have a choice of raising either equity capital or debt capital. For example, equity capital can be raised in the public markets through new stock issuance, or it can be raised privately through joint ventures. Individual investors and tax-exempt institutions, on the other hand, may not have this kind of freedom. If they want to expand their investments beyond what their own equity can provide, debt may effectively be their only alternative. Even their ability to borrow money may be sharply constrained unless the debt is secured by tangible assets such as real estate.

In such cases, debt financing represents a way to break through an **equity capital constraint**. But why would this be valuable? Why should investors *want* to invest more capital than they already own by themselves? Broadly speaking, there are two reasons: (1) to take advantage of positive-NPV investment opportunities, and (2) to diversify their holdings of risky assets. Let's consider each of these in turn.

15.1.1 Debt to Obtain Positive Equity NPV

Although positive-NPV opportunities may be rare when evaluated from a market value (MV) perspective, we suggested in Chapter 12 that positive-NPV opportunities may be available from an investment value (IV) perspective for entrepreneurial or tax-advantaged developers and investors. Furthermore, the "lumpiness" of real estate investment, typically requiring the purchase of "whole assets," often presents investors with capital requirements greater than their available equity. In short, but for the use of debt financing, they would have to forgo positive-NPV opportunities.

Related to this point is a consideration that is often particularly important at the level of small- to moderate-scale individual real estate entrepreneurs. This is the possibility of *leveraging the investor's own "human capital."* The point is that for some investors, the effect of leverage can extend beyond the leveraging of their financial capital invested in commercial property. It can also leverage their human capital in the form of their property management or development abilities.

In general, the term **human capital** refers to productive abilities and skills, or valuable expertise, that individuals have acquired that can be used to generate income. Such income, the "return" on human capital, is typically in the form of wages or salaries or other earned income, but in general it may come in any form of wealth enhancement. Some individuals possess human capital in their ability to manage or develop commercial property. For such individuals, acquisition of such property is not only an investment of their financial capital, but also a means to obtain a return on their human capital. By owning or developing property, they effectively guarantee themselves some degree of employment as property managers or developers. In the presence of the previously noted constraints and difficulties involved in the acquisition of equity capital, the use of debt financing allows such individuals to purchase larger physical quantities of property than would otherwise be the case. This allows them to perform more property management or development services and thereby obtain more return on their human capital.

How would the leveraging of human capital show up in the quantitative DCF and NPV mechanics we described in previous chapters? In practice, it may be difficult to distinguish this component. However, in principle, the present value of the return on human capital should show up as a component in a positive-NPV calculation of an appropriate deal at the micro-level, evaluated from the IV perspective. Investor's human capital gives them a unique ability to profit from a given investment.

Recall from our discussion of IV and MV in Chapter 12 that the NPV of a property acquisition equals IV − MV when evaluated from an IV perspective. And recall that, at the level of individual deals, it is often most practical to think of MV as being determined by what the second-most-motivated buyer is willing to pay. In this circumstance, it may be the human capital of the first-most-motivated buyer that elevates her IV above the MV cost of the acquisition. In this framework, the cost of acquiring the relevant human capital has already been paid (i.e., it is a "sunk cost" in economics terminology). Thus, the return on this capital in the form of the unique ability to earn additional income from the property investment represents a positive component in the investor's NPV.[1]

Now assuming this human capital return (measured in dollars) is proportional to the physical size or dollar value of the property investment, the positive NPV component due to human capital will be greater the larger the underlying property investment. Hence, to the extent that equity capital availability is constrained below the level of exhaustion of the investor's human capital, debt financing enables additional positive NPV to be realized.

15.1.2 Debt and Diversification

It can be valuable to break through a capital constraint on real estate equity investment for another important reason. The use of debt financing may be the only way equity-constrained investors can *diversify their real estate investments*. Due to the previously noted lumpy nature of direct real estate investment in the private property market, where whole assets must be purchased, even a moderately large amount of equity capital may only be sufficient to purchase one or a few individual properties. However, mortgages can typically be obtained for large fractions of the total value of the underlying property, enabling debt capital to stretch the investor's equity significantly, facilitating diversification across a greater number of individual properties. For example, without the use of debt, $10 million worth of equity can only purchase two $5 million properties. With the use of 75% LTV ratio debt, the same $10 million equity can be diversified across eight different $5 million properties.

Diversification is theoretically a desirable part of any investment strategy, no matter how risk averse or aggressive the investor is. Diversification is a rare phenomenon in economics in that it offers a type of free lunch. Diversification allows you to increase your expected return without increasing your risk, or vice versa, to reduce your risk exposure without reducing your expected return.

[1] This "sunk cost" aspect of human capital gives it much the same nature as that of a call option, including the ability of its owner to exercise the option when it is favorable to do so as we described in Chapter 5. Option theory applications to real estate will be discussed further in Part VIII.

An important point should be kept in mind regarding the diversification argument for the use of debt. Any diversification financed by debt should generally be in the form of equity investments in *risky* assets, such as property or stocks. In general, it does not make sense to finance "diversification into bonds" by the use of debt. Do not "*borrow in order to lend.*" If you are simultaneously borrowing money to finance a real estate investment while you are investing in bonds or mortgage-backed securities, then you are just canceling out one position with the other, while paying the **bankers spread** (the difference between the borrowing and lending interest rate).

15.1.3 Limitations on the Equity Constraint Argument for the Use of Debt

Clearly there is a powerful argument for the use of debt financing in real estate equity investment if that is the only way the investor can realize a positive-NPV equity opportunity or diversify his equity investments. But how widespread are genuine constraints on the supply of equity capital, particularly when positive-NPV equity investment opportunities are available? The existence of such constraints would seem to reflect a shortcoming in the capital markets. Getting rid of such shortcomings provides profit opportunities in the investments industry. Has somebody missed an opportunity here?

In fact, constraints on equity capital are probably not as widespread as is often assumed in real estate, even for relatively small individual investors. Open-end real estate investment funds, and both private and public REITs, are vehicles that are widely used to funnel equity capital into commercial real estate.[2] Real estate entrepreneurs are adept at setting up partnerships and corporations of various types, including limited partnerships in which the "outside" equity capital providers have very little control over property or asset management. This may be difficult for very small individual investors just starting out, but once a track record of successful investment can be shown, it is much easier to obtain equity partners.

REITs and large publicly traded firms are not the only ones with virtually unconstrained access to equity capital, especially if positive-NPV equity opportunities are available. Indeed, access to equity capital may depend more on the track record of the seeker than on the way in which its equity is traded, although there is probably a bias in favor of large size. Unsuccessful REITs have little ability to raise equity by issuing new shares, but large firms can probably make more small mistakes before investors sour on them.

Nor is it necessary even for small real estate investors to use debt in order to diversify their real estate investments across numerous individual properties. Diversified real estate equity investment vehicles, ranging from publicly traded REITs to private unit trusts and partnerships, exist as alternatives to debt-financed diversification. Therefore, the diversification argument for debt financing is not a "pure" argument in favor of the use of debt. It must involve other considerations, such as control or information sharing. This suggests once again that positive-NPV equity opportunities and human capital considerations are likely to be involved.

---

[2] Open-end real estate funds allow their investors to buy into and sell out of the funds on the basis of the appraised values of the properties in the fund. Private REITs are corporations or trusts electing REIT tax status whose ownership shares are not traded in public exchanges. These investment vehicles are often called commingled investment funds, or CREFs.

To summarize, equity capital is rarely completely constrained in an absolute sense when positive-NPV opportunities are available. Rather, there may be issues of management **control and governance**, and of information revelation and sharing that may convince some investors not to look for additional equity partners at a time when they face a given positive-NPV opportunity. This may be perceived as an "effective equity constraint." In other circumstances, however, an absolute equity constraint may indeed be said to exist. Pension funds may be an important example of this, as they represent a major class of investors in commercial property. To see how pension funds may face an important equity constraint, we need to turn to a consideration of debt and taxes.

15.2 DEBT AND TAXES IN THE REAL ESTATE CONTEXT

In classical corporate finance the capital structure debate is dominated by income tax considerations. Corporate-level income tax shields provided by debt are advanced as a major argument in favor of the use of debt to finance the corporation. Similarly, in real estate conventional wisdom the most common argument one hears for why debt financing makes sense is that it brings income tax advantages for taxed investors. Indeed, we saw in Chapter 14 how to quantify the **interest tax shields (ITS)** associated with debt financing of a real estate investment. We saw how debt can lever the effect of the tax shields to create after-tax levered equity returns that have lower **effective tax rates** than the corresponding unlevered returns. Classical corporate finance and real estate conventional wisdom seem to be reinforcing each other on this point: surely debt financing of real estate must have tax advantages for taxed investors.

15.2.1 Neutrality of Taxes for Most Real Estate Borrowers

Alas, superficial appearances can be deceiving. We took pains in Chapter 14 to point out that the tax shelter provided by debt does not necessarily imply that debt adds a positive-NPV component to the borrowing transaction for most taxed investors in real estate. Tax shelter as a rationale for borrowing is largely an illusion for most real estate investors because it ignores the other side of the debt market. Lenders have to pay taxes on the interest income they receive. Interest rates on loans are therefore sufficiently high to enable lenders to pay their taxes and still receive a sufficient after-tax return. This means that borrowers are effectively paying taxes on debt interest, as lenders **pass through** the taxes to the borrowers.

It is true that many investors in the bond market are tax-exempt institutions. But such institutions are **intramarginal investors**. The **marginal investors** in the debt market are taxed investors. The tax rate of these marginal investors governs the price of debt and therefore gets reflected in the interest rates borrowers face. Only borrowers who are subject to a higher effective tax rate than that reflected in debt market interest rates will obtain a positive-NPV component (on an after-tax, investment value basis) due to tax shelter effects in the borrowing transaction. In other words, only borrowers whose effective tax rates are higher than that of the marginal investors in the debt market will obtain a tax advantage from borrowing.

What is the effective marginal tax rate embodied in debt market interest rates? This can be seen by comparing market yields on **tax-exempt municipal bonds** to otherwise similar **corporate bonds** and mortgages whose interest is subject to income taxation. The yields in these two markets must leave the marginal investors indifferent between the two markets on an after-tax basis; otherwise, the corporate and municipal bond markets will not be in equilibrium. That is, capital would be flowing rapidly out of one of these two markets and into the other, unless the market yields equilibrated the after-tax yields of the marginal investors.

During the 1990s the difference between municipal and corporate bond yields suggested that the effective marginal income tax rate of the marginal investors in the bond market was in the neighborhood of 25% to 30%. For example, in mid-1999 typical tax-exempt long-term bond mutual funds were yielding around 4.9%, while funds of long-term corporate bonds of similar risk and maturity were yielding around 6.8%. This suggests that the marginal effective tax rate on the marginal suppliers of capital to the debt market was about 28% (1 − 4.9%/6.8%). This ratio tends to remain pretty stable over time.

Although the marginal tax rate implied by comparisons of municipal and corporate bond yields is lower than the top tax bracket on individual income, it must be recognized that the effective tax rate on investment income is lower than this top bracket. For example, recall our examination of a typical 10-year apartment investment in Chapter 14. There we assumed that the investor faced a marginal tax rate on ordinary income of 40% and a capital gains tax rate of 20%. Yet the difference between this investor's before-tax and after-tax 10-year IRR on the apartment investment implied that she would face an effective tax rate of only 30% on that investment, even without any use of debt financing.[3] Property income this investor uses to pay the interest on a loan financing her equity investment in the property would otherwise produce the unlevered property return that faces this effective tax rate of 30%. Thus, it is this type of *effective* tax rate on investment returns that the potential borrower should compare with the lender's tax rate implied in the spread between corporate and municipal bond yields.

For most typical individual investors making direct investments in commercial property, this type of comparison does not result in a significant positive-NPV component in the borrowing transaction, based on the tax shelter. Another way to state this point is that there is usually very little net tax shelter, or net loss of tax revenue to the government, as a result of a taxed-investor taking out a mortgage. One more mortgage issued implies just that much more debt capital invested on the margin in the debt market, where the investors are taxed effectively at a 25% to 30% rate on their investment returns.

This bottom line of debt neutrality with respect to taxes is probably pretty accurate for most real estate investors, most of the time. Tax shelter considerations do not, in themselves, provide a good reason to borrow money to finance a real estate investment. Income tax considerations also typically do not argue against the use of debt. Taxes are neutral.

15.2.2 Investor Heterogeneity with Respect to Taxes

Although taxes are probably about neutral for the typical taxed investor in real estate, they are not neutral for all real estate investors. As we have noted repeatedly in this book, all investors are not the same. In particular, much real estate investment is made by multiowner investment entities such as corporations or pension funds, rather than

---

[3] The 30% effective tax rate resulted from comparing the 10.60% before-tax IRR with the 7.45% after-tax IRR (1 − 7.45/10.60 = 30%).

by individuals directly. In computing the tax benefits of debt financing, we need to consider all levels of taxation, both corporate and personal.

In fact, in most cases this still does not change the neutrality result described in the previous section. Most corporate-level real estate investment entities are **tax-exempt institutions** or tax pass-through vehicles, such as REITs, limited partnerships, and LLCs. As a result, only the ultimate investor's personal tax rate matters in most cases for real estate investment anyway, even when that investment is made by a corporate entity.[4]

On the other hand, consider profitable taxed corporations, such as the typical industrial or service firms traded on the stock exchange. It is not uncommon for such firms to make major real estate investments. It is estimated that over 10% of the value of the stock market is attributable to corporate real estate. Yet profitable corporations present their equity investors with a double layer of income taxation. Corporate earnings are subject to **corporate income taxes,** and then shareholders' earnings on their equity investments in these corporations are also subject to personal income taxes **double taxation**. The investment returns to equity in taxed corporations are therefore more highly taxed than other types of investment returns. Even though taxed corporations can use a variety of tax sheltering devices (such as depreciation expenses), the effective tax rate on their equity returns is almost certainly higher than the 25% to 30% faced by marginal debt investors as implied by the spread between corporate and municipal bond yields. Thus, there is probably a positive-NPV component to borrowing for profitable taxed corporations, due to the tax shelter effect.

At the other extreme of the tax spectrum are tax-exempt institutions such as pension funds and life insurance companies. Life insurance benefits are tax exempt, as are the investment earnings of **whole life policies** prior to the receipt of the benefits.[5] The capital contributions into pension funds are tax deductible up front, and earnings on pension investments are completely tax-free until they are paid out to the ultimate investor. Whether after-tax investments are tax exempt (whole life), or tax-deductible investments are tax deferred (pensions), the result is an effective tax rate of zero on the investor's capital invested in whole life or pension vehicles. This implies that borrowing has a negative-NPV consequence for life insurance and pension institutions, in the absence of an equity capital constraint, as the ultimate borrower (the beneficiary) faces a lower effective tax rate (zero) than the marginal lender in the debt market. On the margin, the government will surely gain revenue as a result of borrowing by tax-exempt institutions.[6]

---

[4] If anything, the effective tax rate on the returns of taxed investors' holdings of REIT stocks is likely to be less than that on their bond holdings because REIT total returns usually include a larger growth component than bond total returns. As noted in Chapter 14, the effective tax rate on the growth component of the total return is much lower than that on the current income (either dividend or interest) component not only because the capital gains tax rate is lower than the ordinary income tax rate, but also because capital gains can be deferred in time, thereby reducing the effective tax rate. Thus, if anything, it is likely that REIT borrowing has a slightly negative NPV component associated with the income tax effect of the debt transaction. In other words, the government probably gains a little revenue whenever a REIT borrows money.

[5] The beneficiary's contributions into his whole life policy (i.e., his premium payments) are made from after-tax personal income or wealth, as distinct from pension contributions, which are tax deductible up front.

[6] The exception would be if the tax-exempt institution could borrow at tax-exempt municipal bond interest rates. This is not usually possible, however.

15.2.3 The Case of Pension Funds

The previous result is complicated if the tax-advantaged institution effectively faces an equity capital constraint. In fact, this is virtually always the case for pension funds. Such funds are a major provider of commercial property equity investment in the United States, especially for so-called institutional quality property.[7] Yet the supply of capital available to pension funds is limited and effectively fixed within any given period of time. A pension fund cannot, for example, issue stock to raise equity capital to invest. Thus, for pension funds the tax effect of borrowing interacts with a capital constraint alleviation effect. We noted in section 15.1 that a major use of debt is to break a capital constraint for an investor who faces unexhausted positive-NPV investment opportunities. This may occur for pension funds because their tax-advantaged status tends to make them intramarginal investors in the property equity market. Thus, from an after-tax investment value perspective, pension funds can make positive-NPV investments simply by purchasing property assets at their current market values.

This possibility, combined with the constraint on their equity capital supply, may provide a tax-based argument in favor of the use of debt financing for pension fund real estate investment.[8] Although the borrowing transaction in and of itself does indeed have a negative-NPV tax component for the fund, the resulting debt expands the capital available to invest in opportunities that have positive-NPV tax components. These two effects may more or less offset each other, or the tax benefits on the investment side may even outweigh the tax loss on the borrowing side. In this way we could view borrowing as a net positive-NPV transaction for the pension fund because it relieves the institution's capital constraint and allows a levering of its tax-advantaged equity investment opportunities.

*15.2.4 Numerical Example of the Tax Effects of Debt

To make more concrete the previous points about the tax-based value of debt for different types of investors, consider the following simplified numerical example in the framework illustrated in Exhibit 15-1a and b.

In the world depicted in the exhibit there are only two points in time, the present and one year from now. There are three types of assets—property, taxed debt, and tax-exempt debt—and assets may be held either directly by individuals or indirectly by multiowner entities. The three types of multiowner entities are corporations subject to corporate-level income tax, zero-tax entities such as REITs and partnerships, and tax-sheltered entities such as pension funds and life insurance companies. Property assets are expected to pay $110 next year, at which time taxed debt will pay $106 and tax-exempt debt will pay $104 for sure. All three types of assets have a current market value of $100. In other words, the market interest rate on debt is 6% for taxed debt and 4% for tax-exempt debt, while the expected return in the property market is 10%. The income tax rate is 33.3%, applicable at both the corporate and individual levels. However, we will assume that the effective personal tax rate on returns on equity

---

[7] By the late 1990s it was estimated that pension funds directly held over $150 billion in commercial property equity, according to Institutional Real Estate Inc. and the Roulac Group, Inc.

[8] This same argument applies to pension investment in other forms of equity as well.

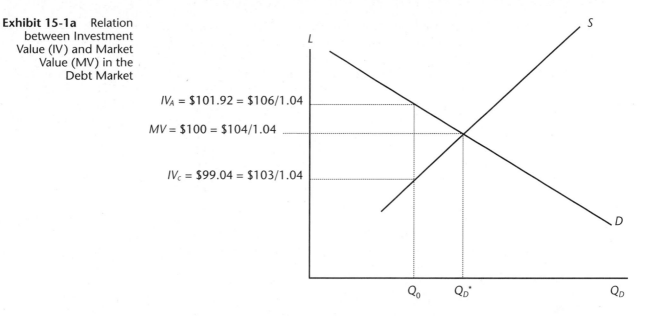

Exhibit 15-1a   Relation between Investment Value (IV) and Market Value (MV) in the Debt Market

$IV_A = \$101.92 = \$106/1.04$

$MV = \$100 = \$104/1.04$

$IV_c = \$99.04 = \$103/1.04$

investment (in either property or corporations) is a bit less at the level of the ultimate individual investors, only 25%. This reflects the ability of equity investors to defer some taxes by taking some of their investment return in the form of capital gain.[9]

Exhibit 15-1a depicts the debt market for taxed debt. The vertical axis represents the present value price of debt, L. The horizontal axis represents the volume of debt transactions, labeled Q_D, the total amount of capital placed into debt assets. Buyers of debt are lenders; they have long positions in the debt assets. Sellers of debt are borrowers; they have short positions in the debt assets. Debt transactions, of course, involve parties on both sides of the deal.

The demand function in Exhibit 15-1a, indicated by the line labeled D, shows how much money investors would be willing to invest in debt assets (Q_D) as a function of the current price of debt (L). It traces the investment value (IV) of debt for investors facing different tax situations. At higher prices (lower interest rates) only the most tax-advantaged investors would be willing to buy debt. At lower prices (higher interest rates) other investors would enter the market.

The line labeled S represents the supply function for debt, the amount potential borrowers are willing to borrow as a function of the price (interest rate). At lower debt prices (i.e., lower loan issuance proceeds per dollar of future par value that must be paid back, in other words, at higher interest rates) only borrowers who can obtain the greatest tax shelter advantage from debt will enter the market. The supply function traces the IV of the debt liability the borrowers will incur as a function of their tax status.

The point at which supply and demand are equal determines the equilibrium in the debt market and produces the market prices and yields that are empirically

---

[9] The specific numbers used in this example are only illustrative. Although they are in the ball park of what would be realistic, the world depicted here is highly simplified. The reader may wish to plug in alternative numerical assumptions to see how implications would change.

observable in the debt market.[10] This occurs at the Q_D^* volume of debt issuance, corresponding to the $100 market value of debt per $106 of par value due one year from now. Thus, the before-tax market interest rate on taxed debt is 6%. This is consistent with the 33.3% tax rate and the 4% yield in the market for tax-exempt debt noted previously. Otherwise, the markets for taxed and tax-exempt debt would not be in equilibrium across the two markets, and capital would flow one way or the other until they reached equilibrium, with taxed investors being indifferent between investing in taxed debt and tax-exempt debt.

The $100 market value (MV) of the debt can be computed in either of two ways. We can apply the before-tax market interest rate of 6% to the before-tax debt cash flows of $106 (both of which are directly empirically observable in the taxed-debt market): $106/1.06 = $100. Alternatively, we can apply the after-tax opportunity cost of capital (OCC) of 4% to the after-tax debt cash flows of the marginal investors in the debt market, those who face the 33.3% tax rate on interest income: [$106 − 0.333 × ($106 − $100)]/1.04 = $104/1.04 = $100. As noted in Chapter 12, after-tax investment value and before-tax market value equate (IV = MV) for marginal participants in a capital asset market.

Intramarginal transactions are possible in the debt market when one or both sides of the deal face an effective tax rate different from that of the marginal participants in the market. For example, at Q_0 we might have a debt investor (lender) who is a tax-exempt institution such as a pension fund or life insurance company. To this investor, the debt is worth more than $100, since, unlike the marginal investors in the debt market, this investor doesn't have to pay taxes on the $6 of interest income the debt will provide next year. Thus, discounting after-tax cash flow at the after-tax discount rate of 4%, we can compute the investment value of the debt for such "advantaged" investors, labeled IV_A in the exhibit, equal to $101.92 (computed as $106/1.04).[11] It makes sense for such investors to buy taxed debt

---

[10] The demand and supply functions in Exhibit 15-1 are drawn as continuous lines for purposes of clarity of illustration. In fact, the simplified world we have described would have discontinuous "step functions" corresponding to the three tax-status classes of investors (double-taxed corporations; single-taxed individuals, partnerships, and REITs; and tax-exempt pension funds and life insurance companies). The real world, however, is more complicated, so that continuous functions may be a better representation.

[11] Note that the OCC used as the discount rate is taken from the capital market, for the reasons described in section 12.1.1 in Chapter 12. This is why the tax-exempt investor's after-tax discount rate is 4%, not 6%, even though such an investor does not have to pay taxes on corporate bond returns. Chapter 12's injunction against "personalized" risk premiums is also valid regarding "personalized" tax rates in the OCC. Thus, the OCC of *all* investors (including intramarginal ones) reflects the tax rate of marginal investors in the relevant asset market, in this case the bond market. The common sense in this methodology can be seen by recourse to a counter-example. If the tax-exempt investor used a "personalized" tax-free OCC as her discount rate (in this case, 6%), then she would perceive no tax-based positive NPV from investment in corporate debt, as such debt would be evaluated at $100 = $106/1.06. This would be no more value than is perceived by taxed investors in such debt: $100 = $104/1.04. Such evaluation would make sense from an MV perspective, but not from an IV perspective, as the IV perspective should reflect the value of tax advantage. Similarly, a 6% OCC would falsely lead tax-exempt investors to perceive negative IV-based NPV from investment in tax-exempt debt even in the absence of a capital constraint, as such debt would be evaluated at $98.11 = $104/1.06, which is less than its $100 price. Yet, in the absence of a capital constraint, there is no reason for tax-exempt investors not to invest in tax-exempt debt, for such investment would not then preclude their investment in higher-yielding taxed debt. Only with a capital constraint does investment in taxed and tax-exempt debt become mutually exclusive, and in that case the maximization of the IV-based NPV would dictate avoidance of lower-yielding tax-exempt debt investment by tax-exempt investors. With a capital constraint, the opportunity cost of investment in municipal debt must include the forgone positive NPV of any displaced investment in corporate debt: ($104/1.04 − $100) − ($106/1.04 − $100) = −$1.92. But note that this is not the same as $104/1.06 − $100 = −$1.89.

rather than tax-exempt debt. In fact, on an after-tax IV basis, the NPV of the loan transaction for such a lender is +$1.92 for every $100 it lends, as it receives future cash flow commitments with a present value of $101.92 but only has to pay $100 to purchase the debt from the borrowers, since all deals are done at the market price. This is consistent with the basic NPV computation for buyers of an asset: NPV = IV − MV.

On the borrowing side of the market, the intramarginal players will be profitable taxed corporations, for their investors face a double layer of taxation. To the equity investors in such corporations, the present IV of the future debt service obligation is only $99.04, even though they receive $100 in current loan proceeds. (This is labeled IV_C to indicate it is the IV of debt for corporate investors.) The IV_C value is found by discounting the after-tax cash flows at the after-tax OCC of 4%, recognizing that the cash flows must pass through two levels of taxation, at both the corporate and personal levels.

As the corporate tax rate is 33.3%, and the effective personal tax rate is 25% on corporate shareholder equity earnings, this leads to a total two-layer effective tax rate of 50%, computed as $1 − (1 − 0.333) × (1 − 0.25) = 1 − 0.5 = 0.5$. Thus, $6 of corporate pretax earnings (or of tax-deductible expenses) equates to $3 of after-tax earnings (or expenses) at the personal level, after passing through both levels of taxation. In effect, the after-tax present value of the $106 future pretax debt obligation for the corporate shareholders is thus $103/1.04 = $99.04.[12] The NPV of the debt transaction for sellers of debt (borrowers) is computed as $MV − IV$. Thus, for the double-taxed equity investors in profitable taxed corporations, the NPV of the corporate borrowing transaction is $100 − $99.04 = +$0.96, for each $100 that is borrowed.[13]

Exhibit 15-1b depicts the property market in a manner similar to what we have just described for the debt market. The vertical axis measures the price of underlying property assets (V), and the horizontal axis measures the volume of property market transactions. The demand curve (D) reflects the amount of property investment as a function of property price, based on the investment value of property for different investors.[14]

---

[12] The $6 of interest expense to the corporation equates to $4 after corporate taxes because the interest expense is deductible from corporate income that faces the 33.3% tax rate. This $4 of corporate after-tax expense offsets an equivalent amount of corporate after-tax earnings which, when finally received by the corporation's equity shareholders would face the 25% effective personal tax rate on equity earnings. Thus, at the ultimate investor level, the $6 interest expense equates to $3 of reduced earnings after both layers of taxes are considered, as $3 = $4 × (1 − 0.25).

[13] Note that the magnitude of the positive NPVs available on an after-tax basis to intramarginal participants appears relatively small in this numerical example, per dollar of current transaction value. This is because we are dealing with a very short investment horizon of one year in this simplified example. The longer the investment horizon is, the larger will be the absolute magnitude of any nonzero NPV available per dollar of current transaction value. For example, at the other extreme, suppose the debt was a perpetuity paying $6 of interest per year forever. Then its IV for the tax-exempt institutions would be $150 = $6/0.04. This would provide the tax-exempt investor with a positive NPV of $50 for every $100 of debt it buys. However, the investment horizon does not affect the *sign* of the NPV, which is why we can ignore this issue to simplify the present illustration.

[14] In the real world, intramarginal investors in the property market are advantaged not necessarily just by tax advantages. Some investors may have unique location or management advantages or entrepreneurial abilities regarding specific properties, as described in Chapter 12 and in section 15.1.1. If we were to model such general investment value considerations in the present framework, we would have to allow that some investors would be able to generate greater than $110 of expected future property income. However, our focus at present is purely on tax effects, so we assume all property owners face the same $110 prospects.

The supply function in the property market (labeled S) depicts the willingness of existing owners to sell their property, based on their investment value for the property. The more advantaged owners would be less willing to sell and would only enter the market if property prices got high enough. Less advantaged owners would enter the market on the sell side even at relatively low prices. From a tax perspective, profitable taxed corporations are less advantaged owners because earnings from their property investments are subject to two layers of income taxation. However, they can often sell their corporate property and still retain a large amount of control over it for purposes of using the property by engaging in "sale-leaseback" arrangements with more tax-advantaged investors wanting to own property.[15]

In Exhibit 15-1b we see that the equilibrium in the property asset market results in a Q_P^* volume of transactions at a market value (MV) of \$100 for every \$110 of expected future value in one year (including both asset value and net operating income). This reflects (and actually determines) the expected before-tax return of 10% prevailing in the property market. As noted, taxed investors in property assets face an effective tax rate of 25% on property investments, less than the full 33.3% due to their ability to shelter some income and defer some tax obligations. Thus, the relevant after-tax OCC in the property market is 7.5%. By definition, MV = IV for marginal participants, so we can calculate property market value using either the before-tax figures observable directly in the property market (\$110/1.10 = \$100) or after-tax figures for the marginal participants ([\$110 − 0.25(\$110 − \$100)]/1.075 = \$107.5/1.075 = \$100). (The latter is actually determinative in a causal sense, but the former is easier to observe empirically.)

In the real world, the marginal investors in the typical property market are probably taxed individuals investing after-tax income through tax-exempt or tax pass-though vehicles such as REITs and partnerships. Thus, the marginal investors in the property market face one (but only one) layer of taxation, and this layer probably is mitigated to some extent (but not entirely) by the ability to shield equity earnings and defer tax obligations. This is why our assumption of a marginal effective tax rate of 25% in Exhibit 15-1b is probably reasonable at a ballpark level for a typical property market in the real world.

Now consider intramarginal investment in the property market. As our focus here is on tax considerations, the intramarginal buyers will once again be tax-advantaged institutions such as pension funds and life insurance companies, just as they were when we discussed the debt market in Exhibit 15-1a. Similarly, tax-disadvantaged investors such as the double-taxed shareholders of profitable taxed corporations will be the intramarginal sellers of property, often via sale-leaseback types of arrangements so that the corporation can retain control and use of the property.[16]

---

[15] The exhibit does not mean to imply that the number of advantaged buyers must necessarily equal the number of disadvantaged sellers, or that these two types of investors must trade with each other. All types of investors can trade with anyone at the market price of MV. The exhibit merely indicates that if properties could only be sold for prices no higher than IV_C, only Q_0 number of owners would be willing to sell, and these would be relatively disadvantaged owners of property. Similarly, if property could only be bought for prices no lower than IV_A, then only Q_0 quantity of investors would be willing to buy, and these would all be advantaged investors.

[16] If no REITs or taxed individuals are actively buying properties, but tax-exempt institutions are buying, then this would suggest that property market prices have been bid up to the level at which tax-exempt institutions are the marginal participants in the market. In such circumstances even the tax-advantaged investors would face little or no positive NPV from buying properties. Such a circumstance is probably

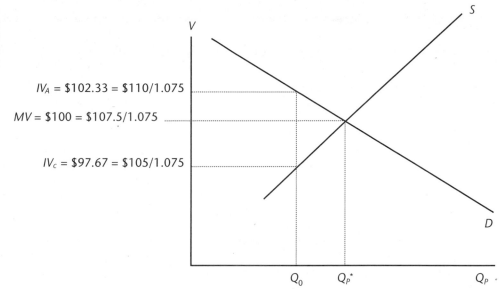

Exhibit 15-1b Relation between Investment Value (IV) and Market Value (MV) in the Property Market

$IV_A = \$102.33 = \$110/1.075$

$MV = \$100 = \$107.5/1.075$

$IV_c = \$97.67 = \$105/1.075$

Using the example numbers in our illustration, tax-advantaged intramarginal property buyers such as pension funds have a present investment value for property equal to the IV_A value of $102.33 for every $110 of future expected cash flow. They therefore achieve a positive NPV ($IV_A - MV$) of $2.33 for every $100 worth of property they buy, computed as $110/1.075 − $100 = $102.33 − $100. Tax-disadvantaged intramarginal sellers also obtain a positive NPV of $2.33, calculated as: $MV − IV_C = $100 − $97.67, for every $100 worth of property they sell.[17]

Finally, consider the situation faced by capital-constrained tax-exempt investors in the property market. They can make a positive NPV of $2.33 for every $100 worth of property they buy. But they face a fixed limit on the amount of equity capital they have available to invest in property (or in anything else for that matter). By borrowing money to finance their property investments, however, they can increase the amount of property they own. For every additional $100 worth of property they buy using borrowed funds, they obtain the $2.33 positive NPV due to their tax advantage being on the long side of the property investment. But they lose the $1.92 that we saw in Exhibit 15-1a as the difference between their IV and MV in debt transactions. The net result is a small but positive NPV of $0.40 ($2.33 − $1.92, with round-off) for every $100 of property they buy using funds borrowed at the 6% market interest rate.

rare, as it would not likely be a stable equilibrium, for all non-tax-exempt property owners would then face a positive-NPV opportunity (measured on an IV basis) simply from selling properties at market value. As the supply of tax-exempt capital is relatively limited and constrained, and the weight of REITs and directly taxed property owners is large in most markets, the scramble to realize such positive-NPV opportunities on the sell side would tend to drive prices back down to the more typical equilibrium level.

[17] The $10 of pretax corporate property earnings equates to $6.667 after the 33.3% corporate income tax. The $6.667 of after-tax corporate property earnings equates to $5.00 of after-tax earnings for the corporation's equity shareholders after the effective personal income tax rate of 25% on equity earnings is applied. Discounting the $105 future expected value at the 7.5% after-tax OCC gives $97.67 present value of the property for the corporation's shareholders, computed on an after-tax IV basis: $105/1.075 = $97.67.

How Are Pension Fund Contributions Effectively Tax-Exempt?

Consider $1,000 of pretax (i.e., gross) income at time zero. You first have to pay taxes on this income at time zero before you can do anything with it. If the tax rate is 30%, you have $700 of disposable income left over to invest. Suppose you can invest at a pretax rate of return of 10% (e.g., you buy a government bond that yields 10%). If your investment is not tax sheltered, then you have to pay taxes of 30% each year on your investment earnings that year. This makes the effective after-tax rate of growth of your money $(1 - 0.3) \times 10\% = 7\%$, not 10%. Therefore, after N years you will have $700(1.07)^N$ of disposable cash available to spend, with no more taxes owed at that time. On the other hand, if you could have invested your $700 time-zero disposable income in a vehicle that was tax sheltered, then you would have been able to earn the entire 10% return without paying taxes, so your disposable cash in year N would have been $700(1.10)^N$, which is obviously greater than $700(1.07)^N$ (and this difference is more, the greater is N). Now consider the way pension fund contributions work. We start with the same $1,000 of pretax gross income at time zero.

If you put that in a pension fund at time zero you won't have to pay taxes on it at time zero because pension contributions are deductible from your taxable income. So you can invest the entire $1,000 rather than just $700. Furthermore, earnings in the fund are tax exempt as long as you leave them in the fund. So your money will grow at the full 10% rate during the N years, after which time you will have $1,000(1.10)^N$ in the fund. However, when you take your money out of the pension fund in year N, you do then have to pay taxes on all the money you withdraw from the fund. Thus, your after-tax disposable cash in year N from your pension investment is $(1 - 0.3) \times \$1,000(1.10)^N = \$700(1.10)^N$, which is the same as if you had been able to make a time-zero investment of your regular after-tax disposable income in a tax-sheltered vehicle that did not have to pay taxes on its investment returns. Thus, the combination of tax-deductible contributions up front, plus tax-sheltered growth while the investment is in the fund, makes pension investments effectively tax exempt, as though the investment returns were not taxed.

This illustrates how it is possible for the use of market-rate taxed debt to be a positive NPV decision for tax-exempt institutions. This results from these institutions' equity capital constraint combined with their ability to make tax-based positive-NPV property acquisitions at market prices (due to their tax-advantaged situation). The interaction of these two circumstances results in the tax-based argument for debt financing in this case. However, the magnitude of the tax benefits of debt financing for tax-exempt institutions is likely to be relatively small, as the tax advantage on the long (property) side of their position is at least partially offset by the tax disadvantage on the short (debt) side.[18]

15.3 OTHER CONSIDERATIONS REGARDING THE ROLE OF DEBT IN REAL ESTATE INVESTMENTS

In addition to the previously described considerations of risk-matching, dealing with capital constraints or management control concerns, and income taxes, several other considerations are important in the overall picture of the role of debt in real

[18]The practical mechanics for calculating relevant after-tax NPVs are reviewed in more depth in the appendix attached to this chapter.

estate investment. Some of the major such considerations will be described in the present section.[19]

15.3.1 Debt as an Incentive and Disciplinary Tool for Management

One argument for the use of debt in real estate investment is that leverage can actually be a tool to help give incentive or discipline to property asset managers (**management incentive**).[20] This argument differs in a fascinating way from our previous discussion in that it is based on human behavioral considerations that go beyond the classical economic assumption of rational behavior. In particular, the idea is that real estate equity investors, as owner/managers of property, behave irrationally (or anyway, suboptimally) when they are faced with lower levels of risk and reward in their investment. Here is how the argument goes.

You have seen how debt increases the risk and return potential in the property equity owner's position. Indeed, as it is typically possible to borrow large fractions of the underlying property value, risk and reward can be greatly magnified through the use of debt. At least as an approximation, an equity investment with a 75% LTV loan will have *four times* the risk and reward potential of an unlevered position in the property, and *twice* the risk and reward even of a 50% LTV investment (100% debt/equity ratio). Yet property investments with 75% LTV ratios are not considered abnormally risky, and they are not at all uncommon in the real world.[21] If such highly levered equity is not abnormally risky, imagine how little is the risk in the underlying property assets free and clear of debt. Without debt, much commercial property apparently presents very low risk, with correspondingly low reward potential.

Property's low level of risk and reward potential is particularly noticeable in comparison with other productive underlying physical assets that require active management, such as the typical industrial and service corporations that trade on the major stock exchanges. Furthermore, the argument continues, it is relatively easy and straightforward to manage properties. Compared to managing, say, a high-tech firm or multinational industrial corporation, there is limited scope to the creative possibilities of what can be done, or how the income-earning capability of the underlying assets can be made to grow. Managers can't usually make major mistakes, apart from doing obviously stupid things. Indeed, this characteristic of real estate is probably a major reason lenders are willing to loan such a high percentage of the underlying asset value in real estate.

---

[19] Some considerations that are prominent in corporate finance are left out of the following discussion, such as the possible "signaling" roll of the use of debt finance, and the resulting "pecking order" theory suggesting a preference for debt finance over external equity. It is not clear that such considerations are as important for real estate due to the different tax and investment holding environments, as discussed earlier. Empirical evidence regarding the pecking order for REITs is mixed. Ghosh, Nag, and Sirmans (1997) found some evidence that REITs prefer external equity to debt, contrary to the traditional pecking order in taxed corporations. On the other hand, an earlier study by Howe and Shilling (1988) found evidence of a preference for debt.

[20] The argument presented here lacks widespread support in the academic literature, although it is hinted at in such articles as Jensen (1986).

[21] Mortgages with 75% LTV ratios are regularly issued on institutional commercial properties by conservative lending institutions such as life insurance companies and pension funds, without recourse to the borrower guaranteeing the loan (that is, the loan is backed only by the property collateral).

In short, in the absence of leverage, the argument goes, real estate is a bit *boring*. Properties by themselves are not likely to attract the best and brightest management talent, people willing to work hard and take risks in order to advance up a long-run career path. With so little risk and so little scope for management impact, this argument suggests that property owner/managers would get a bit lazy over time. They might tend to let opportunities to improve the profitability of the underlying properties slip by. They might not notice or pursue an opportunity that only improves returns by, say, 1% or they might overlook or fail to correct a mistake that damages returns by only 1%.

But sufficient leverage can change this picture, according to the argument. Leverage (and lots of it) can make these stodgy underlying assets very interesting, even exciting. As we have seen in Chapter 13, sufficient leverage can turn low-risk, low-growth underlying assets into high-risk, high-growth investments from the perspective of the equity owner/manager of the property. This can turn those 1% impacts into 4% impacts (e.g., with 75% LTV ratio debt). Little things start becoming more noticeable. Managers start facing much more incentive to pay attention to details and opportunities. If you "borrow to the hilt," gearing the equity up to leverage ratios of three or four, then those cozy cash flow margins become much thinner. Managers have to stay on their toes and occasionally get quite creative to make the necessary profits and avoid losing their equity by default. In other words, *debt is what makes real estate exciting!* (at least for fully operational, up-and-running properties). And this excitement makes property owner/managers do their jobs more efficiently and effectively. This, in turn, enhances the productivity and the value of the underlying real physical assets. In short, through the use of debt, real value is potentially created. If the amount of debt is right, not too little and not too much, this could increase the size of the total pie, for both debt and equity investors.[22]

This argument in favor of debt applies in principle both to small individual entrepreneurs and to large corporations and institutions such as REITs. It is relevant both in the management of individual property assets and portfolios of assets, at both the property management and asset management levels.

15.3.2 Debt and Liquidity

We have shown how the WACC model can be used to quantify how debt increases the risk of the equity investment. But there is another cost of debt that is closely related to the increase in risk, but more difficult to quantify, although it is no less real. Debt generally results in a *loss of liquidity* by the equity investor.

Why is this a problem? Well, it may not be, for an investor who is very liquid overall, or for one who only borrows a small fraction of the underlying property value. But it is often possible to borrow large fractions of the value of income-producing properties. Such debt can result in a serious loss in liquidity for the borrower. **Liquidity** in this context refers to one's ability to convert one's net worth quickly into cash without suffering a loss of value. Investors have liquidity when the value of their assets, especially of their readily marketable assets such as cash and securities (sometimes called "liquid assets"), comfortably exceeds the value of their liabilities.

---

[22]Although it would be very difficult to quantify this effect in practice, in principle this argument implies the existence of a general positive-NPV component to the use of debt to finance real estate equity investment (or perhaps a negative-NPV result from failure to use debt). But this argument may apply only up to a point, for it is counteracted by the potential costs of financial distress, as we will discuss shortly.

Liquidity is desirable for investors because it provides **decision flexibility.**

In general, lack of liquidity, or illiquidity, is one of the major concerns about direct real estate investment in comparison with stocks and bonds, for example. While the typical investor can sell stocks or bonds virtually immediately at full value, it may take months to sell a commercial property at full value. However, *provided you have not already borrowed much against a property you own*, you can generally convert much of the equity value of a real estate investment into cash relatively quickly and at relatively little transaction cost without selling the property at all by taking out a mortgage on it. Thus, one way to at least partially "cure" the illiquidity problem in real estate investments is not to lever the initial purchase of the property, holding the debt capacity "in reserve" for a time when it is more needed. In other words, *if you don't borrow now, you can borrow later.*

Keeping debt as low as possible gives the investor strategic and tactical decision flexibility and control. This is particularly important in the case of real estate investing because of the relatively inefficient nature of property markets compared to securities. We have noted how the lack of informational efficiency in property markets means that real estate prices sometimes "bubble up" above their fundamental values, and sometimes "crash" below their true value. Such cyclicality makes property markets more predictable than security markets.

As we noted in Chapter 12, there is both danger and opportunity in real estate market inefficiency and predictability. Those who maintain liquidity are likely to be more able to take advantage of the opportunity and are less likely to fall victim to the danger. The principal danger, of course, is that one may pay too much for a property and then be forced to sell it at the bottom of the cycle. The most likely reason an investor would be forced to sell when the market is bad is that his creditors are demanding payment and the investor lacks sufficient cash (i.e., liquidity) to come up with the money owed. On the other hand, a more liquid investor will be able to take advantage of bargain buys when the market is down. Indeed, this point applies even apart from cyclical opportunities in real estate markets. Favorable investment opportunities in the form of individual positive-NPV opportunities do not tend to wait around for long, and even with the use of debt the investor still must typically come up with some equity cash. Taking advantage of such opportunities requires liquidity. This, in turn, requires keeping indebtedness low.

While the liquidity argument against the use of debt applies to all investors in principle, it is certainly less important for investors who by their very nature tend to be highly liquid, such as pension funds of growing corporations, for example. Also, this argument is not very applicable to individual investors making real estate investments via relatively liquid vehicles such as REITs. On the other hand, the liquidity argument does apply at the entity level of the REITs themselves, as they are investing directly in the relatively illiquid private property market.

15.3.3 Cost of Financial Distress

The argument in section 15.3.1 about the incentive benefits of debt suggests that a quirk of human behavior may cause debt to actually add real value to the underlying property investments. This is a controversial idea because it is difficult to quantify or prove, and it goes against the classical economic assumption of rational human behavior (in some sense). On the other hand, another argument, which is much less controversial, points out that debt, at least at a sufficiently high LTV, brings deadweight costs onto the underlying property investment. This potential cost of debt is often referred to as the **costs of financial distress**, or **COFD** for short.

There are two fundamental sources of COFD. One is the deadweight burden of **third-party costs**, such as legal and administrative fees, in the event of default, **foreclosure**, or **bankruptcy** caused by the existence of the debt. These legal and administrative costs are a burden to both the equity and debt investor. The second source of COFD is the **agency cost** associated with conflicts of interest that can arise between the equity and debt investors at high LTV ratios. This cost is well described in most corporate finance texts. Because of the existence of **limited liability**, equity investors with highly levered positions face little downside risk from highly risky investments on the part of the corporation, thereby exposing the corporation's debt holders to most of the downside. The result can be a skewing of incentives to the detriment of the overall value of the firm (that is, to the sum of both debt and equity value). In the case of real property, for example, equity investors may lose their incentive to seek good long-term tenants and to maintain or upgrade the property in the optimal manner.

Both the third-party costs of default and foreclosure, and the agency costs, arise in an expectational or probabilistic sense ex ante, well before they might materialize in actuality. The mere probability of their occurrence affects the present value of the debt and equity. Although such costs fall largely on debt holders ex post (when and if they ever actually occur), their ex ante impact at the time a loan is taken out falls on the equity investor, as lenders factor in the expected COFD in the interest rates and origination fees they charge to issue debt.

As a result of these considerations of the cost of financial distress, we can say for certain that 100% debt financing (even if it were possible) would *never* be optimal, even for the borrower (at least in a well-functioning debt market).[23] How much less than 100% is the optimal level of debt depends on the relative strengths and importance of the likely costs of financial distress and the other pros and cons of debt we have been discussing in this chapter.

In this regard it is important to note that fully operational commercial real estate assets are probably able to take on higher levels of debt than other more management-intensive or more volatile underlying assets without raising a significant expectation of financial distress costs. As we noted in section 15.3.1, fully operational real estate assets are relatively low in volatility and their management is relatively straightforward, presenting managers with relatively little opportunity to make major mistakes. The relative simplicity of property and asset management also makes it easy for outside investors, such as debt holders, to observe and monitor the quality of such management. This reduces the potential conflict of interest between equity and debt investor, and enables a larger fraction of underlying asset value to be borrowed before COFD becomes significant.

This is probably a major reason debt/equity ratios are higher for mortgage loans secured by real property than for debt backed by the typical publicly traded industrial or service corporation. This point is illustrated in Exhibit 15-2, which traces the

[23]One hundred percent financing for individual projects is generally a sort of illusion. Either a significant (hidden) equity contribution is in fact being made (perhaps "in kind"), or the lender is counting on recourse to the borrower's other assets and income-earning ability. Otherwise, why would the lender accept relatively low debtlike returns for an investment that contains at least as much risk for the lender as an all-equity position in the underlying asset, which offers higher risky-asset return expectations. If the apparent 100% financed project actually displaces borrowing capacity on the part of the owner of the project, then effectively only a portion of the project debt is actually backed by the project itself; the rest is backed by the borrower/owner of the project. In this sense, the financing is not really 100%.

Exhibit 15-2 Effect of Expected Costs of Financial Distress (COFD) on the Value of the Firm and on Property Value

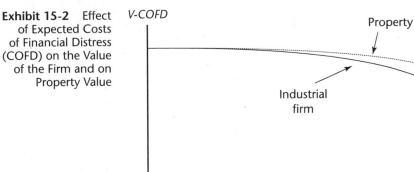

total "value of the firm" (or value of the underlying asset) as a function of the ratio of debt value divided by total firm value (or LTV ratio). The solid line represents the typical industrial or service corporation traded on the stock exchange, while the dashed line represents a typical fully operational real property asset. The value of the firm equals the underlying asset value free and clear of debt, minus the present value of any expected future costs of financial distress: $V - COFD$. Real estate typically allows a greater LTV ratio before the COFD factor becomes important.

15.3.4 Debt and Inflation

During the 1970s and early 1980s, when the investment community was very concerned about inflation, the popular "get-rich-quick" literature on real estate investment touted the benefits of debt financing as a way to make money off of inflation. The more you borrow, the more money you make just from inflation, and real estate provides more ability to borrow than any other type of investment. After all, when you borrow money in an inflationary environment, the dollars you pay back to the lender are worth less than the dollars you originally borrowed, due to the effect of inflation eating away the purchasing power of the dollars.

You probably already see the fallacy in this argument. Like the simplistic conventional wisdom about the tax advantages of debt, this inflation-based argument for debt ignores the lender side of the debt market. It implicitly assumes either that lenders are stupid, or that they don't have as good ability to forecast inflation as borrowers do. Neither of these assumptions is true. Lenders factor the expected rate of inflation into the interest rate at which they are willing to lend. The total dollars you pay back to the lender are more than the dollars you borrow, due to the interest you pay. The market interest rate in the debt market, whether it be for mortgages or bonds, is sufficient to cover the expected level of inflation and still provide lenders with a real return.

Now, once the loan is made, it is indeed true that if inflation turns out to be higher than had been expected, the borrower will be rendered better off, and the lender worse off. But this is *ex post*, not ex ante, and the borrower has no ability to control or influence the subsequent inflation rate. Inflation is just as likely to turn out to be lower than had been expected at the time when the loan was made, which would make the borrower worse off and the lender better off. It is the ex ante expectations that are relevant for making the decision about the use of debt, and those expectations do not favor either the borrower or the lender in the debt transaction.

Nevertheless, it is important to understand the effect of inflation on the borrower's ex post position, and how this alters real estate's natural inflation-hedging ability. In general, rents and property values tend to move with inflation. When inflation turns out to be greater than had been previously expected, rents and property values are able to be greater than they otherwise could be, *measured in nominal terms*. This makes real estate act as an inflation hedge, protecting the investor against unanticipated increases in inflation.[24]

This inflation-hedging quality of real estate equity is magnified by the use of fixed rate debt, to the point that inflation can actually become a positive risk factor in the levered equity. That is, unanticipated surges in inflation may actually *improve* the levered equity real estate return net of inflation. This can be a valuable effect for investors who are particularly exposed to possible harm from unanticipated increases in inflation. For example, if the investor is likely to lose her job as a result of a surge in inflation, or if her wealth is trapped in assets that tend to be particularly negatively affected by inflation, then the "inflation-reversing" effect of financing real estate investment with fixed rate debt could be attractive.[25]

Of course, the inflation effect cuts the other way when inflation turns out to be less than previously expected. Then nominal real estate equity returns turn out to be lower than previously expected, and the use of fixed rate debt will magnify this effect, leading to a lower real return than had been expected.

These effects are illustrated numerically in Exhibit 15-3. The exhibit portrays a property initially worth $100 in an environment in which inflation over the next year is anticipated to be 2% and the property is expected to depreciate 1% in real terms. The middle column of figures reflects these ex ante expectations. The two other columns show alternative inflation scenarios, one in which inflation turns out to be 2% less than anticipated, and the other in which inflation turns out to be 2% greater than anticipated. The property itself is assumed to be a "perfect" inflation hedge, in the sense that it retains its same *real* value no matter what happens to inflation. The exhibit shows the effect on the levered equity of the presence of a 60% LTV ratio one-year loan whose principle is payable at the end of the first year.[26]

Notice that the property value grows 1% less than the inflation rate in all scenarios, producing a –1% real return. The real deviation of the ex post return from the ex ante expectation is zero in all scenarios for the unlevered property, as seen in the second-to-last row in the table. This reflects our "perfect hedge" assumption. On the other hand, the property growth is magnified in the levered equity, allowing

---

[24]Remember: real estate is a risky asset, even measured in real terms, net of inflation. Thus, real estate is not a "perfect" hedge against inflation. Real estate returns in the private property market tend to be positively correlated with inflation, but not perfectly correlated. Also keep in mind that unanticipated changes in inflation are usually correlated with events in the real macroeconomy and in monetary policy. These events often have an impact on the real value of property. For example, an unanticipated upsurge in inflation may trigger tighter monetary policy and signal slower-than-anticipated future real growth in the economy. Such "news" would be negative for most real estate values, in real terms.

[25]On the other hand, don't forget our dictum: Don't borrow in order to lend, as the net result is the payment of the banker's spread. If the investor's portfolio is overly sensitive to inflation due to heavy concentration in long-term fixed rate bond investments, it would generally make more sense to reduce the bond exposure rather than to borrow money while still holding onto the bonds.

[26]We may assume the loan interest is paid from the property operating cash flow, which is not depicted in the exhibit.

Exhibit 15-3 Example of Effect of Inflation on Ex Post Levered Equity Appreciation Returns with One-Year Loan

Scenario:	Ex Post–	Ex Ante	Ex Post+
Inflation:	0%	2%	4%
Values*			
Property			
Yr. 0	$100	$100	$100
Yr. 1	$99	$101	$103
Debt balance payable:			
Yr. 0	$60	$60	$60
Yr. 1	$60	$60	$60
Levered Equity:			
Yr. 0	$40	$40	$40
Yr. 1	$39	$41	$43
Appreciation %			
Nominal Returns			
Property:	–1.0%	1.0%	3.0%
Levered equity:	–2.5%	2.5%	7.4%
Nominal Deviation from Ex Ante			
Property:	–2.0%	0.0%	2.0%
Levered equity:	–5.0%	0.0%	5.0%
Real Returns			
Property:	–1.0%	–1.0%	–1.0%
Levered equity:	–2.5%	0.5%	3.3%
Nominal Deviation from Ex Ante			
Property:	0.0%	0.0%	0.0%
Levered equity:	–2.9%	0.0%	2.8%

*Real depreciation rate = 1%/yr.

it to provide a slightly positive real return under the ex ante scenario, and magnifying its positive covariance with inflation. The levered equity will lose 2.5% in real value if the low-inflation scenario materializes, or gain 3.3% if the high-inflation scenario occurs. In real terms, the levered equity loses (or gains) when inflation turns out to be lower (or higher) than anticipated, even though the unlevered property real return is invariant across inflation scenarios. The levered equity's real deviation from its ex ante expectation is approximately ±3%, positively correlated with the inflation outcome.[27]

Thus, the example in Exhibit 15-3 shows how leverage can increase the covariance between the ex post nominal return and inflation, and introduce positive correlation between the ex post real return and inflation. This **reverse-inflation risk** may be useful to some investors, or a needless increase in risk to other investors. It is a factor to consider, but not a general argument in favor of debt financing applicable to all investors.

[27] Note that the results portrayed in Exhibit 15-3 are well approximated by the WACC formula described in Chapter 13. Slight deviations from this formula reflect the fact that a positive span of time (one year) is covered in Exhibit 15-3, during which time the LTV ratio changes, which makes the WACC formula an inexact approximation.

15.4 CHAPTER SUMMARY

This chapter reviewed the value of debt financing of real estate equity investments from the perspective of the equity investor. In attempting to treat this issue comprehensively, we broached the question of optimal capital structure (the share of debt versus equity) in real estate investment, but we did not attempt to offer a definitive answer to this question. We instead sought to clarify the major issues and considerations that are important for designing finance strategy for various types of real estate investors. These issues lie on both sides of the argument for the use of debt and affect different types of investors in different ways. We went into particular depth regarding income tax considerations, as these can be quite important, yet the conventional wisdom seems to be excessively simplistic and perhaps misleading about the tax advantages of debt.

The obvious overall result of a comprehensive consideration of the pros and cons of debt is that, on balance, some investors find it more profitable to borrow, while others find it more profitable to lend. This result applies both to real estate investors and to investors at large. The debt market equilibrates these two positions in the aggregate, with the resulting interest rates and yields that are observed in that market. (In Part VI we will move to a consideration of mortgages from the lender's perspective.)

To summarize Chapter 15 and Part V, clearly no single "correct" capital structure exists for all real estate investments or all investors. However, it does appear likely that relatively "transparent" and stable, low-volatility investments such as most class A income-producing properties can optimally support higher levels of debt than can more managerially complicated, higher-risk underlying assets such as many industrial and service corporations. The widespread use of large amounts of debt in real estate investment (over $1 trillion outstanding) suggests that this is so. On the other hand, casual empiricism suggests that the major reason why real estate investors get into trouble usually has to do with excessive debt (at least, with the advantage of hindsight). Both the equity investors (borrowers) and the debt investors (lenders) suffer in this repeating play. Perhaps the conventional wisdom "hypes up" the advantages of debt a bit more than is really warranted. So, be careful!

KEY TERMS

capital structure
ultimate investors (individuals)
equity capital constraint
human capital
IV-based NPV
diversification (and debt)
banker's spread
control and governance issues
interest tax shields (ITS)
effective tax rates (on investment returns)
pass-through of taxes
marginal and intramarginal investors

municipal (tax-exempt) bonds and yields
corporate (taxed) bonds and yields
before-tax and after-tax opportunity cost of capital
heterogeneity of investors
tax-exempt institutions
corporate income taxes
double taxation
whole life policies
management incentives
liquidity
decision flexibility

cost of financial distress (COFD)
third-party costs
foreclosure
bankruptcy
agency costs
limited liability
ex ante costs (probabilistic expectations)
inflation
hedging inflation risk
real returns
reverse-inflation risk

STUDY QUESTIONS

15.1. Believe it or not, Bob has amassed quite a lot of human capital in the form of his property management expertise. For every 100,000 SF of property Bob manages, he can earn $20,000 per year of net "wages," over and above what he could earn doing anything else with his time. Over Bob's expected remaining active lifetime these earnings amount to a present value of $200,000 for every 100,000 SF he manages permanently. Bob has the capacity to manage up to 1,000,000 SF of property at any given time. However, Bob likes to work on his own, so he prefers to manage his own properties rather than hiring himself out as a third-party manager. (This is more efficient and allows Bob more freedom and flexibility to use his expertise to the maximum.) The types of properties Bob knows how to manage cost $50/SF, and come in buildings of 100,000 SF each. Suppose Bob has access to over $100 million of equity capital, consisting of his own wealth and that of some partners whom he feels comfortable with in that he knows they will not interfere with his property management practices.

    a. What is the value to Bob of being able to borrow up to 80% of the value of any properties he buys?

    b. Now suppose Bob can access only $10 million of equity without jeopardizing his ability to control management. What is the value to Bob of being able to borrow up to 60% of the value of any properties he buys? What is the value to him of being able to borrow up to 80% of property value?

15.2. Why does the ability to leverage positive-NPV opportunities and the ability to diversify property investments make an argument in favor of borrowing for investors that face a constraint on their supply of equity capital, but not for investors that are not so constrained (such as REITs or open-end funds)?

15.3. Discuss the following statement: One reason to borrow money to finance a real estate investment is to reduce your risk exposure. If you borrow $80,000 and only put up $20,000 of your own money to buy a $100,000 property, you have less of your own money at risk, particularly if you take the extra money that you would otherwise have put in the property and put it in a safe investment such as CDs or Treasury Bonds instead.

15.4. What types of investors or investment entities are likely to truly face a serious equity capital constraint? How does the issue of governance and control of the underlying asset interact with the capital structure question so that it may appear to some investors that they face an equity constraint?

15.5. True or False and *why*: One reason to borrow money to finance a real estate investment is that you obtain valuable interest tax shields that save you from paying some taxes you would otherwise owe.

15.6. **a.** Why do the interest tax shields associated with debt financing have a positive value for the typical profitable corporation but not for the typical taxed individual investing directly in the property market?

    b. Answer the same question for REITs.

15.7. If income taxes were the only consideration, would you expect to find profitable taxed corporations owning much of their own real estate? Why not?

15.8. How can it make sense for a pension fund, which is tax exempt, to borrow money to finance a real estate equity investment?

15.9. Describe the management incentive argument for the use of debt financing in real estate.

15.10. What is the relationship between debt and liquidity, and why is liquidity valuable for investors? Are there considerations peculiar to real estate that affect the value of liquidity? If so, what are they?

15.11. Describe the two fundamental sources of the costs of financial distress (COFD). How is the COFD related to the ex ante cost of debt capital faced by the borrower at the time of the financing decision?

15.12. Is the expectation of future inflation a reason for real estate equity investors to borrow money to finance their real estate investments? Explain why or why not.

15.13. Discuss the pros and cons of borrowing to finance real estate investments. Describe at least two considerations that would always be negative about debt for any investor, and at least two considerations that would always be positive for virtually any investor. Explain how leverage, taxes, and inflation considerations might lead some investors to prefer borrowing and others to avoid borrowing.

15.14. How do REITs differ from the typical profitable taxed corporation in the effect of income taxes on the value of borrowing? How do REITs differ from the typical tax-exempt investor (such as a pension fund) in the effect of income taxes on the value of borrowing? Consider all levels of taxation in your answers.

Practical Mechanics for Calculating After-Tax NPVs and OCCs

This appendix illustrates with a simple numerical example how microlevel after-tax NPV calculations may be applied consistent with macrolevel market equilibrium assumptions. The appendix demonstrates how such macrolevel assumptions can facilitate the quantification of microlevel investment values through the use of the APV = 0 rule for market values and marginal investment values, introduced in Chapter 14. In effect, the procedure demonstrated here can be used to deal with one of the trickiest problems in microlevel real estate investment analysis, namely, how to determine the appropriate after-tax opportunity cost of capital for a levered position by an intramarginal investor. Here we apply this procedure to the example of the after-tax evaluation of the levered equity position of taxed and tax-exempt investors with and without capital constraints, as described in the numerical example used in Chapter 15.[28]

The basic assumptions in this appendix duplicate those in section 15.2.4 and Exhibit 15-1. The underlying property investment has a 10% expected return, taxed debt yields 6%, and tax-exempt debt yields 4%. These values are empirically observable in the marketplace as MV-based values. The APV = 0 (or IV = MV) rule is then applied to marginal investors to derive the after-tax opportunity cost of capital rate of 4% for riskless debt. (This implies a 33.3% effective marginal tax rate on returns on debt investment for marginal investors in the debt market.)

Next, we consider the situation faced by the marginal investor in the property market, who we assume is a taxed investor subject to an effective tax rate of 25% on property equity investment returns. The base-case microlevel NPV calculation for this investor is presented in Table A1 for a $100 all-equity property investment, discounting after-tax cash flows at after-tax discount rates. The after-tax OCC of 7.5% is derived once again by application of the APV = 0 rule for marginal investors (IV = MV). We know from the nature of the equilibrium in the property market that for this type of investor, the NPV (or APV) of this investment must be zero.

Table A2 shows the microlevel NPV calculation for the marginal investor using debt financing with a 50% LTV and the same $100 equity capital as in the base case. Two hundred dollars worth of property is purchased using $100 of debt. This results in $20 of property earnings and $6 of debt interest, or a net return to the levered equity of $14 (which equals 14%) on a before-tax basis. As the equity earnings are subject to the 25% tax rate, this results in after-tax levered equity earnings of $10.50, or 10.5%.

The levered equity cost of capital in this case is seen to be 14% before tax and 10.5% after tax. We know this because we know the above calculation is for a marginal investor. This enables us to invoke the APV = 0 (IV = MV) rule to "back out" the cost of capital from the APV = 0 criterion. In effect, we are using our macrolevel assumption of equilibrium in the property market to "discover" the relevant cost of capital. This is an example of how it is often less confusing to work with NPVs rather

---

[28] This appendix demonstrates principles introduced in Chapters 12–15, although material from Chapters 14 and 15 (sections 14.4 and 15.2) are most directly illustrated.

Table A1   Marginal Taxed Investor Base Case (no leverage)

Item	Yr. 0 Principal	Yr. 1 Principal	Yr. 1 Interest or Return	Yr. 0 PV (Yr. 1 CF)
Property BTCF	−100	+100	+10	110/1.10 = 100
Tax (25%)			−2.5	
Property ATCF	−100	+100	7.5	107.5/1.075 = 100

NPV	PV Cost	PV Benefit	NPV
BT (MV)	−100	+100	= 0
AT (IV)	−100	+100	= 0

Table A2   Taxed Investor Expansion Using Debt

Item	Yr. 0 Principal	Yr. 1 Principal	Yr. 1 Interest or Return	Yr. 0 PV (Yr. 1 CF)
Property BTCF	−200	+200	+20	220/1.10 = 200
Debt BTCF	+100	−100	−6	−106/1.06 = −100
Equity BTCF	−100	+100	+14	114/1.14 = 100
Income tax (25%)			−3.5	
Equity ATCF	−100	+100	+10.5	110.5/1.105 = 100

NPV	PV Cost	PV Benefit	NPV
BT (MV)	−100	+100	= 0
AT (IV)	−100	+100	= 0

than with hurdle rates when dealing with after-tax valuations. Apart from the implication of our macrolevel equilibrium assumption, it might be difficult to know the correct cost of capital relevant to the levered equity position.[29]

Now consider the base-case microlevel NPV calculation for the tax-exempt investor, presented in Table B1, for a similar $100 all-equity property investment. Note that because the investor is tax exempt (such as a pension fund or life insurance company), the after-tax cash flows are identical to the before-tax cash flows. The result is a positive NPV of $2.33 on an IV basis, due to the investor's tax-advantaged situation. (By definition, the NPV computed on an MV basis is zero, as the property is purchased at fair market value.)

Table B2 expands the investment to $200 worth of property investment under the assumption that the tax-exempt investor does not face an equity capital constraint. Naturally, the after-tax NPV doubles to $4.65.

Finally, Table B3 presents the calculations for a $100 levered equity position on the part of the tax-exempt investor facing a $100 constraint on the availability of

[29] More typical real world calculations would involve multiyear cash flow projections and IRRs. The single-period world of the present example is adopted for ease of illustration.

Table B1   Tax-Exempt Investor Base Case (no leverage)

Item	Yr. 0 Principal	Yr. 1 Principal	Yr. 1 Interest or Return	Yr. 0 PV (Yr. 1 CF)
Property BTCF	−100	+100	+10	110/1.10 = 100
Tax			0	
Property ATCF	−100	+100	+10	110/1.075 = 102.33

NPV	PV Cost	PV Benefit	NPV	
BT (MV)	−100	+100	= 0	
AT (IV)	−100	+102.33	= +2.33	

Table B2   Tax-Exempt Investor Expansion to $200 Investment, All Equity

Item	Yr. 0 Principal	Yr. 1 Principal	Yr. 1 Interest or Return	Yr. 0 PV (Yr. 1 CF)
Property BTCF	−200	+200	+20	220/1.10 = 200
Tax			0	
Property ATCF	−200	+200	+20	220/1.075 = 204.65

NPV	PV Cost	PV Benefit	NPV	
BT (MV)	−200	+200	= 0	
AT (IV)	−200	+204.65	= +4.65	

Table B3   Tax-Exempt Investor Expansion Using Non-Tax-Exempt Debt (taxed lender)

Item	Yr. 0 Principal	Yr. 1 Principal	Yr. 1 Interest or Return	Yr. 0 PV (Yr. 1 CF)
Property BTCF	−200	+200	+20	220/1.10 = 200
Debt BTCF	+100	−100	−6	−106/1.06 = −100
Equity BTCF	−100	+100	+14	114/1.14 = 100
Levered equity ACTF	−100	+100	+14	114/1.1097 = 102.73

NPV Levered Equity	PV Cost	PV Benefit	NPV	
BT (MV)	−100	+100	= 0	
AT (IV)	−100	+102.73	= +2.73	

equity capital. Thus, we are back to the base-case amount of equity, but now with a 50% LTV, borrowing at the 6% interest rate of taxed debt.

Once again, the after-tax levered discount rate of 10.97% is determined by what we already know about the APV. In particular, we know that the NPV of the property component of the investment alone (on an all-equity basis) is +$4.65, as seen in the previous calculation. We also know that the NPV of the financing component of the deal in itself for the tax-exempt investor is −$1.92, computed as in Chapter 15: *NPV(Financing)* = +$100 − ($106/1.04) = $100 − $101.92 = −$1.92. Thus invoking value additivity in the IV we have

$$APV = NPV(Property) + NPV(Financing)$$

$$= +\$4.65 + (-\$1.92) = +\$2.73$$

This implies that the relevant after-tax levered-equity OCC for the tax-exempt investor is 10.97%, the discount rate that produces the $2.73 APV that is consistent with equilibrium in both the property and debt markets.[30]

The NPV of $2.73 for the tax-exempt investor is much less than the $4.65 that could be obtained from an all-equity investment in the same amount of underlying property without an equity constraint. But it is $0.40 greater than the $2.33 NPV the tax-exempt investor obtains in the base case without the use of debt financing and only $100 of equity available. Thus, in this case, the net value of the debt financing is +$0.40, as described in Chapter 15.[31]

---

[30] We can approximate the after-tax levered equity OCC by applying the WACC formula discussed in Chapter 13 to the after-tax returns. Applying formula (2) from Chapter 13 with LTV = 50%, r_P = 7.5%, and r_D = 4%, we obtain

$$r_E = (r_P - (LTV)r_D)/(1 - LTV) = [7.5\% - (0.5)4\%]/0.5 = 11\%$$

This approximately equals the 10.97% we derived for the tax-exempt investor in Table B3. However, recall that the WACC formula gives only an approximation of the exact equity return, and this approximation will not generally be as accurate as it is in this simple example in which there is only one period of time. Note also that the market-based levered OCC relevant for the tax-exempt investor (10.97%) is not exactly the same as that for the marginal taxed investor (10.50% = 14% × [1 − 0.25]). In equilibrium, we would not necessarily expect these two rates to be equal, as the effect of leverage on risk may differ as a function of the tax status of the investor. This type of fine-tuning of discount rates would be practically impossible if we had to estimate these rates without recourse to our macrolevel market equilibrium assumptions and APV-based analysis, as demonstrated in this appendix.

[31] It will not necessarily always be the case that the use of debt financing will have a positive NPV for an equity-constrained tax-exempt investor. The result depends on the specific ex ante returns and marginal tax rates prevailing in the relevant capital markets.

PART V

References and Additional Reading

Ahern, T., Y. Liang, and N. Myer. "Leverage in a Pension Fund Real Estate Program." *Real Estate Finance* 15(2): 55–62, summer 1998.

Brealey, R. and S. Myers. *Principles of Corporate Finance*, 5th ed. New York: McGraw-Hill, 1996, Chapters 13–14,17–19.

Cannaday, R., and T. Yang. "Optimal Leverage Strategy: Capital Structure in Real Estate Investment." *Journal of Real Estate Finance & Economics* 13(3): 263–271, November 1996.

Childs, P., S. Ott, and T. Riddiough. "Leasing Risk, Financing Risk and Capital Structure Decisions." Real Estate Research Institute (RERI) Working Paper (WP–64), 1997.

Gau, G., and K. Wang. "Capital Structure Decisions in Real Estate Investment." *Real Estate Economics* (formerly AREUEA Journal) 18(4): 501–521, winter 1990.

Geltner, D. "Debt and Taxes: A Pension Fund Investment Perspective." *Real Estate Finance* 16(3), fall 1999.

Ghosh, C., R. Nag, and C. F. Sirmans. "Financing Choice by Equity REITs in the 1990s." *Real Estate Finance* 14(3): 41–50, fall 1997.

Howe, J. and J. Shilling. "Capital Structure Theory and REIT Security Offerings." *Journal of Finance* 43: 983–993, September 1988.

Jaffe, J. "Taxes and the Capital Structure of Partnerships, REITs, and Related Entities." *Journal of Finance* 46:401–407, March 1991.

Jensen, M. "Agency Costs and Free Cash Flow, Corporate Finance & Takeovers." *American Economic Review* 26: 323, May 1986.

Maris, B. and F. Elayan. "Capital Structure and the Cost of Capital for Untaxed Firms: The Case of REITs." *Real Estate Economics* (formerly AREUEA Journal) 18(1): 22–39, spring 1990.

McDonald, J. "Optimal Leverage in Real Estate Investments." *Journal of Real Estate Finance & Economics* 18(2): 239–252, March 1999.

Modigliani, F. and M. Miller, "Cost of Capital, Corporation Finance and the Theory of Investment." *American Economic Review* 48: 261–297, June 1958.

Myers, S. "Interactions of Corporate Finance and Investment Decisions: Implications for Capital Budgeting." *Journal of Finance* 29: 1–25, March 1974.

Mortgages from an Investment Perspective

In Part V we discussed real estate debt from the perspective of the equity investor, the borrower. We pointed out that, from the broader perspective of the capital markets and the investment industry as a whole, the borrowing transaction creates two different types of "investment products" from the same underlying real asset: levered property equity and debt secured by the property. Each of these two products appeals to different types of investors. Investors who are more risk averse (and more tolerant of inflation risk) and who need more current income from their investments, or who want an asset with a specified finite lifetime and do not want to be involved in property management, find real estate debt to be an appealing type of investment product. The debt market equates the supply (borrowers wanting debt capital) and demand (debt investors) in the market for debt products of all types, including mortgages, which are debt products backed by real estate assets.

The debt market as a whole is arguably the largest, deepest, and most technically sophisticated of all the branches of the capital markets. It includes both short and long-term U.S. government debt, international bonds, corporate and municipal bonds, commercial paper, both residential and commercial mortgages, and asset-backed securities, including both residential and commercial mortgage-backed securities (MBS). In the United States alone, by the end of the 1990s, there were over $15 trillion worth of tradable debt assets outstanding, over a quarter of which were based directly or indirectly on real estate. These included approximately $1 trillion worth of directly held commercial mortgages (whole loans), plus several hundred million dollars' worth of commercial mortgage-backed securities (CMBS). In a typical year, close to half a trillion dollars of commercial mortgages are issued in the United States.

Even if your primary focus is on equity investment in real estate, you need to have some depth of familiarity with the debt side of the picture, that is, with real estate debt from the perspective of the debt investor. Not only is such perspective necessary to deepen and round out the understanding of the equity investor, but also real estate debt provides a large and important set of professional career opportunities for graduate students in the real estate field. Many major real estate investors, such as pension funds and life insurance companies, deal simultaneously in both equity and debt products as investors.

With this in mind, the five chapters in Part VI will introduce the basic concepts, terminology, and methodologies useful for understanding and dealing with real estate debt from the debt investor's perspective. We have two primary specific objectives in this part. First, we want you to understand enough of the debt investor's typical perspective and concerns so that you, as an equity investor (or working for an equity investor), can be an effective partner, either on the same or opposite side of a deal with a debt investor. Second, we want to extend your understanding of real estate debt sufficiently, including some nuts and bolts, so that you can be somewhat creative in putting together real estate financing packages, whether you are working from the equity or debt investment side. To this end, Chapters 16 and 17 will present mortgage fundamentals (most of which are in fact relevant to both residential and commercial loans). Chapters 18 and 19 will then delve in more depth into the underlying economics of the debt market in general, and commercial mortgage investment and underwriting in particular. Finally, Chapter 20 introduces some basic concepts and tools used in the CMBS industry.

16 Mortgage Basics I: An Introduction and Overview

Chapter Outline

Learning Objectives

After reading this chapter, you should understand:

◆ The legal and financial structure of mortgages.

◆ The major different types of real estate mortgages in the United States, and how the mortgage industry works.

◆ The major legal terms and legal characteristics of mortgages.

◆ The nature and costs of the foreclosure process and the workout process as a way to avoid foreclosure.

The classical form of real estate debt is the **mortgage**, a loan secured by real property as collateral. The word *mortgage* comes from two Middle English words (which are actually French in origin): *gage* meant an obligation or commitment (as in our modern word *engaged*), while *mort* referred to death or dying. Hence, a "dying commitment," that is, a commitment that was not permanent, but had a finite lifetime. In return for present value obtained, a landowner committed himself to pay compensation in money or kind over a period of time in the future. As land was the direct source of most wealth in medieval times, it was natural to secure the mortgage with a pledge of real property. Thus, mortgage lending is one of the oldest forms of debt recognized in Anglo-Saxon law.

In the present chapter we will focus on the basic legal and financial structure of the mortgage; fundamental terminology and concepts that apply to virtually all mortgages, residential as well as commercial; and standard fixed rate and adjustable rate loans as well as other more exotic species. As always, our focus is primarily on loans on commercial property, although at the basic level of this chapter, all mortgages have much in common. We begin with an introductory overview of the different types of mortgages and branches of the mortgage industry.

16.1 BASIC TYPOLOGY OF MORTGAGES AND OVERVIEW OF THE U.S. MORTGAGE INDUSTRY

While we can categorize mortgages in many ways, Exhibit 16-1 presents a simple typology useful for characterizing the mortgage industry in the United States in the late 20th century. Broadly speaking, mortgages are divided into **residential mortgages** and **commercial mortgages**. The former are secured by owner-occupied single-family homes, the latter by income-producing property.[1] Residential and commercial loans make up two distinct branches of the industry and are typically administered separately. These two sides of the business differ in several respects:

- Individual residential loans are much smaller on average, but much more numerous, than commercial loans.
- Residential properties generate no income, so the lender depends on the individual borrower's income to service the loan, while commercial loans can be serviced from the income produced by the property securing the debt.
- Residential borrowers are usually not financial or business professionals and are typically in the market for a loan only occasionally (on average about once every 5–10 years), while commercial borrowers are typically commercial or financial entities staffed by business professionals with much greater financial expertise than the typical homeowner.
- Commercial properties tend to be more unique, while single-family homes tend to be more homogeneous.
- Social and political concerns, and the resulting government involvement, are much greater regarding residential loans than commercial loans, including different statutory and common laws governing foreclosure and bankruptcy for residential versus commercial loans.

As a result of these differences, the residential mortgage business has become a "mass production" industry, while commercial mortgages (particularly for larger loans) remains more of a "custom shop," where individual loans are crafted and negotiated, to some extent, one deal at a time. Also, the federal government established an extensive regulatory oversight and has helped to standardize the residential mortgage business.

Within each of these branches of the industry are further subbranches and categories of loans. For example, residential mortgages are traditionally divided into government-insured and conventional loans. The former category includes Federal Housing Administration (FHA) and Veterans Administration (VA) loans, in which

[1] In fact, most lenders include in the residential category loans backed by multifamily dwellings up to four units per apartment. Loans on larger apartment buildings and complexes are usually treated as commercial mortgages.

Exhibit 16-1 Typology of U.S. Mortgages

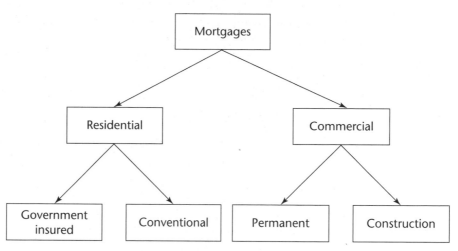

the federal government insures the lender against loss in the event of default and fore-closure. This enables these loans to be made for larger fractions of the underlying asset value (indeed, VA loans may be for 100% of the house value). Conventional loans have no government-provided default insurance. However, private mortgage insurance is often purchased, enabling loan-to-value (LTV) ratios up to 95% of the house value. (Without insurance, conventional loans are typically limited to no more than 80% LTV.)

Loan standardization and the widespread availability of default insurance, and the related efforts of the federal government starting in the 1930s and continuing into the 1970s, helped to establish an extensive and well-functioning **secondary market** for residential mortgages in the United States. A secondary market is one in which mortgages are bought and sold by third parties. The **primary market** is where the loans are **originated** or issued initially. In the primary market the lending institution or mortgage company issuing the mortgage is the buyer, in the sense that it is providing the money up front in return for the promised future cash flows (i.e., taking the long position in the mortgage as an investor). The borrower is the seller, in the sense that it is receiving the money up front, in effect taking a short position in the mortgage as an investor. Once issued, however, the mortgage itself is a capital asset, a claim on a stream of future cash flows, and this asset (if properly constructed legally) can be traded, that is, sold by the original issuer to a third party, who may then sell it again to another party, and so forth. This is the secondary market.

In the case of residential mortgages, the secondary market has experienced extensive **securitization** since the early 1970s. That is, large numbers of individual mortgages are pooled and large numbers of small homogeneous securities (like shares of stock, or "units") are sold in the public securities market, based on the underlying mortgage pool. Holders of these securities receive shares of the cash flows received by the pool of underlying mortgages. In fact, most residential mortgages are not retained by their original issuing institution, but rather are sold into the secondary market to be securitized largely as MBS.

In contrast, the lack of standardization and default protection inhibited the development of a secondary market for commercial mortgages for many years. However, in the early 1990s widespread securitization of commercial mortgages took off with the development of the **commercial mortgage-backed securities (CMBS)** industry, though with some notable differences from residential loan securitization. As commercial loans lack default insurance, bond-rating agencies had to develop the ability to classify CMBS securities according to their default risk in a manner that enabled the bond market to price such securities effectively. The growth of CMBS has led to more standardization in commercial mortgages, but still not so much as in residential loans. At the end of the 1990s a larger proportion of commercial than residential mortgages was still held by originating institutions or privately placed to investors as **whole loans**, that is, without being pooled or securitized.

Within the commercial mortgage industry, an important division occurs between so-called **permanent loans** and **construction loans**. The latter are made specifically for the purpose of financing a construction project (which may be either to build single-family homes or income-producing buildings). Once the building is complete, the loan is supposed to be paid off. Permanent commercial mortgages are long-term loans designed to finance a completed, fully operational income property.

Both the real estate economics and the financial nature of these two branches of the business are quite distinct. Construction loans are relatively short term, typically one to three years in duration, while permanent commercial mortgages are typically five to ten years in duration (sometimes much longer). In construction loans the cash is disbursed from the lender to the borrower gradually, as the project progresses, with no payments back from the borrower to the lender until the project is complete, when the entire loan is due. In permanent loans, the cash is disbursed from the lender to the borrower all at once up front and paid back with interest gradually over the life of the loan.

Construction loans have extensive default risk, as the underlying building does not yet exist when the loan is made. However, they have relatively little **interest rate risk**, which is the risk that the value of the loan will fall in the secondary market as a result of a rise in interest rates in the bond market. The fact that construction loans are of short duration, and often made at **floating interest rates** (interest rates that move with the prevailing interest rates in the bond market), protects construction loans from interest rate risk. On the other hand, permanent loans have less default risk (as they are secured by a fully operational property), but they often have considerable interest rate risk for the investor (unless they are **adjustable rate mortgages**, or **ARMs**).

As a result of these differences, construction loans are traditionally issued largely by commercial banks and thrift institutions, while permanent loans are often placed with life insurance companies and pension funds. Banks and thrifts are **depository institutions** whose liabilities are of short duration (depositors can remove their money largely on demand). They need to match these short-term liabilities with short-term assets, such as construction loans. Life insurance companies and pension funds tend to have liabilities of much longer duration (based on life insurance policies and pension benefit obligations), often with a high degree of predictability in their future cash outflow requirements. Such institutions need to match these long-term liabilities with stable and dependable long-term cash inflows, such as permanent mortgages can provide.

Because of the extensive default risk in a construction project, the construction lender must be very familiar with the local real estate space market and the local real estate developers and construction firms that do much real estate development in the United States. Commercial banks and thrift institutions have extensive systems of local branch offices that can develop this kind of expertise. Permanent lenders buying whole loans are often large national and international institutions, far removed from Main

> *A Note on Terminology: EE versus OR*
>
> Mortgage terminology is often rather arcane. Two widely used terms that are often confusing to new students are *mortgagee* and *mortgagor*. The mortgagee is the lender, and the mortgagor is the borrower. Here's a way to help remember these: the borrower is the property *owner*. *Owner* begins with an *O*, so the *or* ending is appropriate. The same trick works for the terms *lessor* (the landlord, or property owner) and *lessee* (the tenant or renter).

Street. However, they usually work through **mortgage bankers** and **mortgage brokers** who have local expertise in the real estate industry in specific space markets, in order to place their mortgage capital.[2]

In the traditional functioning of the commercial mortgage industry, construction and permanent lenders often work as a team to provide construction finance. The construction lender will not commit to provide the construction loan until a permanent lender has agreed to provide a permanent loan on the completion of the project. In this case, the permanent loan is referred to as a **take-out loan**, as it is used to pay off (or "take out") the construction loan.[3]

16.2 BASIC LEGAL CONCEPTS AND TERMINOLOGY FOR MORTGAGES

Whether residential or commercial, permanent or construction, all mortgages are based on certain fundamental legal concepts and structures. Mortgages also typically involve a number of specific provisions and terms that may sound rather like legaleze, but you must be familiar with them in order to work with real estate debt at a practical level. In this section we will introduce some of these basic considerations.

16.2.1 Legal Structure of Mortgages

A mortgage is **secured debt**, which means that specified collateral can be used by the debt holder, or **mortgagee**, to obtain the funds owed if the borrower, or **mortgagor**, fails to pay what is owed under the loan. In a real estate mortgage, the collateral is real property. The mortgage consists technically of two separate but connected legal documents: a **promissory note** and a **mortgage deed**.

---

[2] Mortgage bankers issue loans but do not generally hold onto them as long-term investments, rather selling them immediately to long-term investors such as life insurance companies and pension funds. Mortgage brokers do not issue loans, but screen loan applicants and bring candidates to the issuing institutions.

[3] Sometimes a third type of loan is used to bridge the construction loan and the permanent loan. This may be necessary for projects built "on spec," that is "speculative" developments, in which few if any tenants for the building have committed themselves in advance to lease space in the completed building. For such projects, there may be an extensive lease-up period between the completion of the construction and full or nearly full occupancy of the building. The construction lender may want to be paid when the project is physically complete, but the permanent lender may not be willing to disburse funds until the building is substantially occupied. Bridge financing is sometimes referred to as a "mini-perm" loan, especially if it is provided by the permanent lender. Construction finance, and the analysis of the financial feasibility of development projects, will be treated in more depth in Part VIII of this book.

The promissory note establishes the debt. It is a written, signed contract between the borrower and lender. In this contract one legal person (the mortgagor) promises to pay another legal person (the mortgagee) the cash flow amounts specified in the loan, in return for the loan.

The mortgage deed, also known sometimes as a **security deed** or a **deed of trust**, secures the debt by conveying, or potentially conveying, the ownership of the collateral from the borrower to the lender. In essence, if the borrower fails to live up to the terms and conditions specified in the promissory note, then the mortgage deed enables the lender to acquire the collateral property for purposes of obtaining what is owed. The mortgage deed should be recorded in the title recording office appropriate to the specified property. The date it is recorded will, in the absence of contravening factors, establish the priority that the lender has in his claim to the collateral property.

There are two types of legal bases for the lender's claim on the collateral property. In most states mortgages are governed by what is called the **lien theory**: the mortgagee holds a lien on the collateral property. This gives her the right to take the property to force a foreclosure sale in the event the borrower fails to perform under the promissory note, but it does not give the lender the title to the property. In contrast, in a few states mortgages are governed by what is called the **title theory**.[4] Under this theory the mortgagee holds the ownership title to the collateral property until the borrower is released from the promissory note commitment (normally by the loan being paid off). The borrower technically only retains the right of use and possession of the property, as long as the provisions of the promissory note are kept. In title theory states the lender can generally take possession of the property more quickly and easily in the event of default.

The essential relationship between the borrower and lender regarding the note and deed is portrayed in Exhibit 16-2. In return for cash up front the borrower gives the lender a note and deed. When the loan is paid off, the lender releases the borrower from the note and returns the deed.

In some states the legal structure of the mortgage is more complicated, based on a deed of trust, as depicted in Exhibit 16-3. In this case a third party known as the trustee is involved in the mortgage, in addition to the borrower and lender. When the money is loaned, the borrower gives the ownership title of the property to the trustee, who holds the title for the benefit of the lender during the time the loan is in effect. If the loan is paid off, the trustee returns the title to the borrower. If the borrower defaults, the trustee has the power to sell the property on behalf of the lender, using the proceeds of the sale to compensate the lender for what is owed under the loan. In this case, the trustee has what is called the **power of sale**. In some states, the mortgagee has the power of sale even without the deed of trust arrangement. In other states, only a court can actually sell the collateral property in foreclosure, in what is called a **judicial sale**.[5] In general, the foreclosure sale process tends to be a bit quicker and less administratively costly in power-of-sale states.

---

[4] The title theory states are Alabama, Georgia, Maine, Maryland, Mississippi, New Hampshire, Pennsylvania, Rhode Island, and Tennessee.

[5] The major states in which judicial sales predominate for commercial mortgages are Connecticut, Delaware, Florida, Illinois, Indiana, Kansas, Kentucky, Louisiana, New Jersey, New York, North Dakota, Ohio, Pennsylvania, South Carolina, and Wisconsin.

Exhibit 16-2   Mortgage Deed Relationships

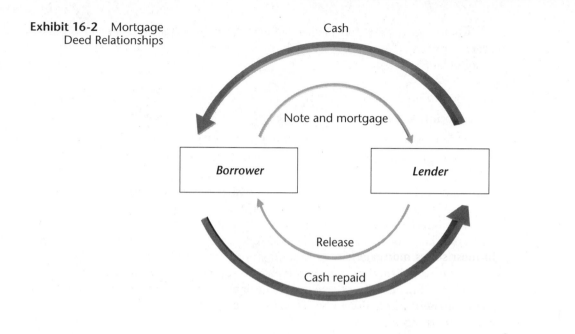

16.2.2 Priority of Claims in Foreclosure

As noted, if the borrower defaults on his obligations under the promissory note, the lender can force a foreclosure sale of the collateral property and use the proceeds from that sale to obtain what is owed. But there may be more than one claimant to the fore-closure sale proceeds. Anyone with a lien on the collateral property has a claim. There may be more than one mortgage on the property, and there may be others with liens apart from mortgage lenders. For example, the local property tax authority can place a lien on a property if its owner has not paid the property tax due on the property. Also, a construction firm that has done work on the property can place a lien on the property if it was not paid in full for the work performed.

Exhibit 16-3   Deed of Trust Relationships

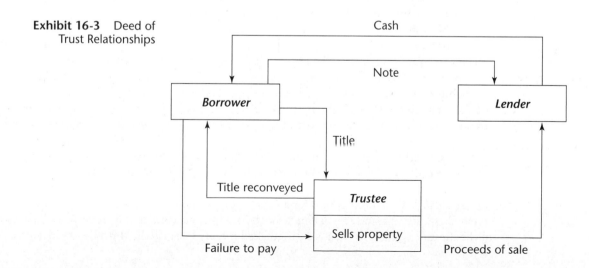

When property has multiple lien holders, the claimants are arranged in a "pecking order" of priority that is generally established by the date of recording of the lien, with the following exceptions:

- Property tax liens come first.
- Sometimes mechanics' liens can take priority over others.
- Explicit subordination clauses can reduce priority.
- Bankruptcy proceedings may modify debt holder rights.

Property tax liens are entitled to take first position no matter when they were recorded. Statutory provisions often give construction firms a certain window of time in which to record mechanics' liens after work was performed and not paid for. These liens can take priority over other liens recorded prior to the end of the relevant window of time. A loan may have a subordination clause that explicitly subordinates it to other loans issued later. This is common in second mortgages provided by sellers, for example. Finally, if the borrower has declared bankruptcy, even secured creditors may have their claims altered by the bankruptcy court, especially in the case of commercial mortgages.

Apart from these exceptions, the priority of claims in foreclosure goes according to the date of the recording of the lien, which would normally be the date when the mortgage was issued. The first mortgage is the most **senior debt** in position, and would normally be the outstanding loan that was made first. If the owner subsequently took out a second mortgage, it would be subordinate to the first mortgage, an example of **junior debt**. There could be a third mortgage, a fourth, and so on. Senior claims must be fulfilled completely before any remaining available proceeds from the foreclosure sale are applied to the next highest claimant in the pecking order.

For example, suppose $9 million is owed on a first mortgage, $2 million is owed on a second mortgage, and $1 million is owed on a third mortgage. The collateral property sells in foreclosure for $10 million. The first mortgagee will receive the entire $9 million she is owed. The second mortgagee will receive the remaining $1 million from the sale, half of what he is owed. The third mortgagee will receive nothing.

It is important to note that this pecking order prevails no matter which lien holder actually brought the foreclosure suit in court. Subordinate lien holders will have their liens extinguished by the foreclosure suit, provided they are included in the suit and properly notified thereof in advance. For this reason, junior lien holders who stand to gain or lose the most in the foreclosure process are most likely to actually bring the foreclosure suit. This is described by the dictum: Redeem up, foreclose down.

Take the previous example as a case in point. If it is known that the current market value of the property is approximately $10 million, then the foreclosure suit would most likely be brought by the second mortgage holder, as he is most on the margin regarding whether he will obtain his full principal or not. Lien holders can bid for the property in the foreclosure sale and use their claim as payment. For example, the second mortgagee could bid $11 million for the property and use his claim to pay $2 million of this. He would then have to pay the first mortgagee the full $9 million owed on the first mortgage, but the second mortgagee now controls the property and can make sure it is sold for as high a price as possible. The first lien is extinguished by the suit and the payment of the $9 million (this is the "redeem up" part of the dictum). The third lien is extinguished merely because the third lien holder was included in the suit and properly notified in advance (this is the "foreclose down" part of the dictum). If the second mortgagee sells the property for $10 million, he would be left with $1 million, or half of what he was owed under his loan.

The lien holder bringing the suit must identify any junior lien holders and include them in the foreclosure suit. The suit will not extinguish any validly recorded liens not included in the suit. The purchaser of the property in the foreclosure sale could end up owning the property subject to a lien that had been junior and now is senior, a danger any astute bidder would be aware of.

16.2.3 Typical Mortgage Covenants

The deed and note in a mortgage will typically include a number of clauses and **covenants** detailing the agreement between the borrower and lender at the time the mortgage is issued. The rights and duties of both parties should be specified clearly. Over the years, a number of clauses and covenants have become common in many mortgages. Familiarity with these terms will increase your practical understanding of how mortgages work.

Promise to Pay. This clause is in every mortgage and means just what it says. The borrower promises to pay the lender the principal, interest, and penalties specified in the promissory note.

The Order of Application of Payments. This clause establishes the order in which any payments received from the borrower will be applied to the various components of the debt. In particular, the standard order is as follows:

> 1st: Expenses
> 2nd: Penalties
> 3rd: Interest
> 4th: Principal

If the lender has had to incur any expenses to which he is entitled to be recompensed by the borrower, the borrower's payments will be used for this purpose first. Any funds left over from the borrower's payments will next be applied to pay off any penalties the borrower has incurred under the agreed terms of the debt. Then, interest owed will be paid. Finally, if any money from the payment is left over, it will be applied to reduce the outstanding principal balance of the loan.

Good Repair Clause. This clause requires the borrower to maintain the property in reasonably good condition. This clause is usually coupled with another: the lender's right to inspect, which enables the lender to enter and inspect the property from time to time (generally with prior notice and at the borrower's convenience) to verify that the property is being properly kept up. These clauses help the lender to make sure that the value of their collateral is being maintained.

Joint and Several Liability. This clause provides that, when there is more than one signatory to the loan, each individual signing the debt is completely responsible for the entire debt.

Acceleration Clause. In general, an **acceleration clause** allows the lender to "accelerate" the loan, that is, to make the entire outstanding principal balance due and payable immediately under certain conditions. Acceleration clauses may be used for several purposes in the mortgage agreement. One is in case of default by the borrower, such as if the borrower fails to make the payments required in the loan. This enables the lender to obtain the entire remaining loan balance through the foreclosure sale process, rather than just the delinquent payments, penalties, and expenses. Another common use of the acceleration clause is to effect a due-on-sale provision.

Due-on-Sale Clause. This enables the lender to accelerate the loan whenever the borrower sells the property.[6] This is particularly valuable to the lender if market interest rates have risen since the time the loan was issued, enabling the lender to reinvest at a higher yield the capital that had been tied up in the loan. In any case, without such a clause, the lender could end up with a borrower responsible on the note who no longer owns the property securing the loan. This could cause a loss of incentive by the borrower to repay the loan. The **due-on-sale clause** does not force the lender to accelerate the loan on the sale of the property; it merely gives the lender that right. There may be times when the lender would be pleased to have the loan continue in effect after a sale, perhaps with the new property owner taking over the loan.

The process of changing borrowers is known as **loan assumption**.[7] In the absence of a due-on-sale clause, the lender will not generally be able to effectively block assumption of the loan by a new buyer of the property.[8] Such assumption can be valuable for both the original borrower and the new buyer of the property if interest rates have risen since the time the loan was issued. In effect, it enables the purchaser of the property to obtain a below-market-interest-rate loan, which should enable the seller of the property to sell it for a higher-than-market price. Most conventional residential mortgages in the United States have due-on-sale clauses in them, but FHA and VA loans do not, and many commercial mortgages do not.

Borrower's Right to Reinstate. This clause allows the borrower to stop the acceleration of the loan under default, up to a point in time just prior to the actual foreclosure sale, upon the curing of the default by the borrower (that is, the payment of all sums due).

Lender in Possession Clause. This clause gives the lender the automatic right of possession of the property in the event the borrower defaults on the loan. This enables the lender to control the leasing and maintenance of the building prior to completion of the foreclosure process. Sometimes this can help the lender to mitigate the "running down" or loss in value of the property during a prolonged foreclosure process.

---

[6] Usually the due-on-sale clause is written such that any transfer of a substantial beneficial interest in the property triggers the acceleration provision. Thus, the due-on-sale requirement cannot be avoided by use of land contracts or other such procedures in which the title does not initially change hands.

[7] One situation in which assignment is useful is when the original borrower is having trouble servicing the debt, not due to problems with the collateral property, but to problems from other sources. By selling the property and assigning the loan to the new owner, the health of the debt can be restored.

[8] Even without a formal assumption of the mortgage, the borrower (seller of the property) will often be able to keep the original loan in effect through the use of a "wraparound" second mortgage. The seller issues a second mortgage to the buyer for an amount that covers the payments on the first mortgage.

Release Clause. In all loans, the borrower will be released from the debt and the lender is required to return the mortgage deed and extinguish his lien on the property when the loan is paid off according to the terms of the promissory note. (This is referred to as defeasance or reconveyance.) In some cases, there will be additional specific release clauses, for example, freeing specified parts or amounts of the original collateral property upon the paying off of portions of the debt principal. This is useful when the original collateral will be sold off gradually in parts or parcels, as in the case of housing tract developments and subdivisions. In another use, an original borrower may be released from the debt when the mortgage is assumed by another debtor.

Prepayment Clause. This provision gives the borrower the right (without obligation) to pay the loan off prior to maturity.[9] This can be valuable for the borrower when interest rates fall below the contract rate on the loan, as it enables the borrower to refinance the mortgage at lower interest rates by paying off the old loan with the proceeds from a new, lower-interest-rate loan. (Of course, lenders understand this possibility when they issue the mortgage in the first place and charge an interest rate sufficiently high to compensate for the value of this option they are giving the borrower.) Unless a prepayment clause is explicitly stated in the mortgage agreement, the borrower does not have the right to pay the loan off early, that is, prior to its originally stated maturity. Virtually all residential mortgages in the United States have prepayment clauses.[10]

Many commercial mortgages do not have prepayment clauses. (This is often referred to as a "lockout" loan or, confusingly, as the borrower being "locked in" to the loan.) Often, commercial loans technically permit prepayment, but set prepayment penalties so high as to effectively eliminate the value for the borrower of refinancing the loan.[11] This eliminates prepayment risk for the lender, which is the risk that the loan will be paid off at the borrower's discretion before the loan's contractual maturity. This is an important consideration because many debt investors want to use their investments precisely for the purpose of matching the maturity of liabilities with that of their assets, and so they buy debt assets with a view toward holding them to maturity.[12]

Subordination Clause. As noted previously, this is a provision making the loan subordinate to other loans that the borrower obtains, that is, lower in claim priority for the lender in the event of foreclosure, even though the other loans may have been recorded subsequent to the loan in question.[13] Subordination clauses are often used in

---

[9] This is the same type of option that exists in callable corporate bonds. In effect, it gives the borrower a *call option on a bond*, in which the bond has cash flows equivalent to the remaining cash flows on the callable debt, and the exercise price of the option is the outstanding loan balance (plus prepayment penalties, i.e., what one would have to pay to retire the debt).

[10] Government regulations require that adjustable rate residential mortgage permit prepayment without penalty. Most fixed-rate residential loans also allow prepayment with little or no penalty.

[11] This still gives the borrower some flexibility, but removes the interest rate risk for the lender. For example, the prepayment penalty may be specified to be sufficient so that the lender's original contract yield is maintained over the original contract maturity of the debt, even though the lender would have to reinvest the prematurely prepaid principal at market interest rates below that contractual yield for the remainder of the original loan's lifetime.

[12] If they can do this, they also avoid exposure to interest rate risk in the sense that they would have to reinvest their capital at lower interest rates prior to the end of their investment target horizon.

[13] Recall that claim priority is normally established by the date of recording of the mortgage deed. The subordination clause overrules this priority.

seller loans and subsidized financing to enable the recipient of such financing to still obtain a regular first mortgage from normal commercial sources.

Lender's Right to Notice. This is a provision in junior loans (i.e., subordinate loans, such as second mortgages) requiring the borrower to notify the lender if a foreclosure action is being brought against the borrower by any other lien holder. Junior lien holders may wish to help to cure the borrower's default on the other loan or help work out a solution short of foreclosure. This is because junior lien holders will stand to lose much more in the foreclosure process than senior lien holders, due to their being lower in the pecking order for the foreclosure sale proceeds.[14]

Future Advances Clause. This provides for some or all of the contracted principal of the loan to be disbursed to the borrower at future points in time subsequent to the establishment (and recording) of the loan. This is common in construction loans, in which the cash is disbursed as the project is built. Even though some of the loan principal is not disbursed until later, the priority of the lien applying to all of the principal is established based on the time of the initial recording of the mortgage.

Exculpatory Clause. This removes the borrower from responsibility for the debt, giving the lender no recourse beyond taking possession of the collateral that secures the loan. Without an exculpatory clause, the lender can obtain a deficiency judgment and sue the borrower for any remaining debt owed after the foreclosure sale (i.e., in the event the foreclosure sale proceeds are insufficient to recompense the lender for all that is owed). Loans containing exculpatory clauses are known as **nonrecourse loans**. They are common in the commercial mortgage business in the United States, especially for borrowers that have a solid track record of past performance.[15]

16.3 DEFAULT, FORECLOSURE, AND BANKRUPTCY

Although the majority of real estate loans are repaid in full without incident, problems are not uncommon. On average, over 15% of long-term commercial mortgages in the United States end up facing serious default, and a foreclosure, bankruptcy, or workout situation, at some point before the maturity of the loan.[16] Technically, a **default** occurs

---

[14] This provision would enable the junior mortgagee to find out about the foreclosure action earlier than would necessarily occur when she is officially joined in the foreclosure suit. Recall our example in the previous section in which there were three lien holders. The third lien holder might want to cure the borrower's default on the other loans to prevent the foreclosure sale in which the third lien holder stands to lose his entire claim. Perhaps the property market will turn around or the property itself can be turned around so that it would be worth more than $12 million, instead of the current expected value of $10 million. At $12 million there would be enough value to make whole even the third lender.

[15] Even in the absence of an explicit exculpatory clause, commercial mortgages can often be made effectively nonrecourse by use of "single-asset" borrowing entities that have limited liability, such as a corporation that owns nothing other than the property that is being financed by the mortgage. However, astute lenders wanting to avoid a nonrecourse loan situation can require the parent holding company or an individual with large net worth to sign the note with joint and several liability, or they may require additional collateral for the loan.

[16] Data on permanent loans issued by life insurance companies between 1972 and 1992 indicate a lifetime cumulative default rate roughly between 10% and 25%, depending on the nature of the property asset market in the years subsequent to the issuance of the loan. Default is most likely during the third through seventh year of the loan's lifetime. See Esaki, l'Heureux, and Snyderman (1999). Their working definition of a serious default is payment delinquency greater than 90 days. The incidence and cost of commercial mortgage foreclosure will be discussed in more depth in Chapter 18.

whenever the borrower violates any clause or covenant in the mortgage agreement. However, many defaults are not serious in that they do not pose a threat to the lender's yield-to-maturity and are ignored by the lender. Serious defaults generally have to do with failure to make the stipulated loan payments.

When faced with a default by the borrower, lenders have a number of possible actions they can take. Broadly speaking, these can be categorized as being either **litigious** or **nonlitigious** in nature. The former involve the courts and formal legal proceedings that can lead ultimately to foreclosure. If lenders delay or avoid this course of action, they are said to be exercising **forbearance**. As a general rule, lenders prefer to resolve problems without recourse to litigious actions, if possible, thereby saving legal expenses and retaining more flexibility to deal with the borrower in a less formal, less adversarial, and often more expeditious manner.

When nonlitigious options are insufficient, lenders face several types of judicial actions they can take through the courts. As a first step, they can *sue for specific performance* under the promissory note. This involves getting a court to officially require the borrower to perform some specific act (such as fix a default). This is often used as a "shot across the bow," warning the borrower how seriously the lender views the default.[17] A second level of recourse is for the lender to sue for damages under the promissory note, without invoking the mortgage deed. This is less expensive and administratively involved than the third step, which is to invoke the mortgage deed to bring a foreclosure action.

The foreclosure process allows a forced sale of the collateral property, with the proceeds being used to compensate secured creditors for what is owed them, insofar as possible. Any remaining proceeds from the foreclosure sale, after payment of debts and expenses, go to the borrower, but there is normally nothing left over by that point. Foreclosure is generally regarded by both lenders and borrowers as a last resort because it is expensive and slow and represents a rather public type of failure of the loan for both parties.

If the foreclosure sale does not provide funds sufficient to pay the secured debt holders all that they are owed, the holders of remaining nonextinguished debts can obtain a **deficiency judgment**. This allows the lender to sue the borrower for the remainder of the debt, provided the mortgage did not contain an exculpatory clause (as previously described). However, in practice deficiency judgments are often of limited value, as the borrower may by this time have little other assets or income that can be attached, or the borrower may declare **bankruptcy**.

Bankruptcy on the part of the borrower is in fact a major danger to commercial mortgage lenders prior to foreclosure, even if the collateral property securing the loan contains sufficient value and income-generating ability to service the debt. The most serious threat to secured lenders such as mortgage holders is what is known as **cramdown**, which may occur under a **Chapter 11** filing by the borrower for protection from creditors.[18] The idea behind Chapter 11 is to allow a potentially salvageable business to continue operating while it works itself out from under excessive debt. Under Chapter 11 all of the borrower's creditors are lumped together, and they all may be forced to accept a restructuring of their debts, including secured lenders whose collateral might

---

[17] To some extent, the litigious and nonlitigious tracks can be pursued in parallel, in a kind of "good cop/bad cop" routine.

[18] A declaration of bankruptcy under Chapter 7 is of less concern to secured lenders, as this involves complete liquidation of all of the borrower's assets, with secured debt holders obtaining the proceeds of any sale of collateral assets in much the same manner as under the foreclosure process.

be sufficient to service their loans by themselves. In effect, healthy properties could be used to bail out sick properties or businesses at the expense of the holders of mortgages on the healthy properties. In effect, a restructuring of the mortgage is forced by the bankruptcy proceeding onto the lender (crammed down the lender's throat, as it were). Because of this, the mere possibility or threat of bankruptcy can be a weapon used by borrowers against lenders.[19]

16.4 NONLITIGIOUS ACTIONS AND WORKOUTS

As noted, lenders generally view foreclosure as a last resort and prefer to address loan problems before they get to that point (and before a Chapter 11 declaration can cause them to lose negotiating leverage). If applied in a timely and deft manner, nonlitigious actions can often obtain the most successful resolution of loan problems.

16.4.1 Costs of Foreclosure

The value of nonlitigious solutions to debt problems may be viewed as the avoidance of the costs of foreclosure. Foreclosure involves a variety of costs, nearly all of which are **deadweight burdens**, that is, a loss to one or the other side of the loan without a commensurate gain on the other side. These costs can be quite large as a fraction of the property value and the loan balance. They include the following:

- Third-party costs in the form of legal and administrative expenses such as court costs will typically be on the order of 10% of the loan balance, and can be much more.
- Deterioration of the property during the foreclosure process is common. The borrower has little incentive to maintain the property well during this period, and lenders and courts lack property management skills. The problem with commercial property is not just the physical maintenance and repair, but also tenant relations and leasing.
- Revenue may be lost by the property, and interest payments lost to the lender, while capital is still tied up in the loan, during the time taken by the foreclosure process, which is typically close to a year in length, sometimes more.[20]
- Both the borrower and the lender can suffer negative reputation effects from the foreclosure process, which is a very public procedure.
- Lenders will usually have to write down officially the value of the assets on their books as a result of a foreclosure, whereas book values may be maintained to some extent, at least for a while, if foreclosure can be avoided. Writing down assets can cause lenders problems with reserve requirements and other regulations.

---

[19]Cramdown is of sufficiently widespread concern among commercial mortgage lenders that an industry exists providing insurance specifically against the possibility of cramdown. In some cases lenders require borrowers to pay for this type of insurance before they will commit to the loan, or as part of a workout agreement restructuring a loan.

[20]Studies by Brian Ciochetti (1996) of foreclosures on permanent commercial mortgages issued by insurance companies indicate an average length of the formal foreclosure proceeding of 9.1 months, after an average of 3.5 months of payment delinquency, for a total of 12.6 months.

The magnitude of these and other costs can easily exceed 25% to 35% of the outstanding loan balance in total.[21]

16.4.2 Nonlitigious Actions

To avoid such costs, lenders commonly employ several nonlitigious actions when faced with problem loans. One such option is a transfer of the loan to a new borrower. This solution is most common when there is no major problem with the property, but only with the original borrower, perhaps due to problems in the borrower's other holdings or business ventures.

Another common type of nonlitigious resolution to a mortgage problem is the procedure known as **deed in lieu of foreclosure**. In this case, the borrower simply gives the property to the lender in return for the lender releasing the borrower from the debt. The result is virtually the same as a foreclosure, but without the legal expense and delay. This benefits the lender, who stands to lose most from such expense and delay. On the other hand, the borrower benefits because a deed-in-lieu is not as public and does not stain the borrower's reputation as much as a formal foreclosure. The deed-in-lieu is a useful device when both sides agree that nothing can be done to save the loan.

A third approach is for the lender and borrower to work together to **restructure** the loan, to bring new equity partners into the deal, or otherwise creatively "work out" the problem. Indeed, this process is sufficiently common that the verb has become a noun: it is referred to as a **workout** of the loan.

16.4.3 Workouts

Workouts occur in infinite varieties, with varying degrees of good or bad feelings among the parties, and with the possibility of litigious action always waiting in the wings. The basic ingredients are typically some combination of a rescheduling or forgiveness of some debt, often in return for the lender obtaining either some equity participation in the property or a greater yield in the long run. For example, the loan term may be extended, or a repayment "holiday" provided. Sometimes a nonrecourse loan may be restructured with more recourse or use of additional capital, or new equity or debt partners may be brought into the deal. This may involve an assumption of all or part of the debt by the new partner. Some firms and individuals specialize in helping with real estate loan workouts, acting as advisors, brokers, and mediators to the principal parties. There is even scope for entrepreneurial profit in the workout process, provided the underlying property has good long-term potential.

An important consideration for the lender in mortgage restructurings is the presence of other lien holders on the property. If the subject loan is modified sufficiently, it may be deemed by the courts to be a new loan and may thereby lose its seniority among the other preexisting liens. Also, courts may invalidate a restructuring of one loan that excessively burdens other lien holders on the same property. The cooperation of all lien holders is usually necessary in a major workout.

---

[21] The Esaki-l'Heureux-Snyderman study (1999) found an average loss severity of almost 38% as a fraction of the outstanding loan balance, among loans that were liquidated in foreclosure. This figure includes lost interest as well as principal and expenses.

16.5 LIMITED LIABILITY AND FORECLOSURE COSTS: THE BORROWER'S PUT OPTION AND STRATEGIC DEFAULT

Now that you understand basically how mortgages work, let's draw on financial economics to deepen your understanding of mortgages as investments. Obviously, the basic idea in a mortgage is to provide the investor with a reliable cash flow stream, and this is normally what happens—a bit boring perhaps, but useful. When borrowers or loans get into trouble, however, the nature of the investment can change drastically. Investors are aware of this as a possibility (with some probability of occurrence) long before it occurs in reality. Two features of the typical commercial mortgage are of particular importance in this regard and can interact to cause additional ramifications. We are speaking of **limited liability** on the part of the borrower and the existence of significant costs associated with the foreclosure process.

16.5.1 Limited Liability and the Borrower's Put

Many commercial mortgages are nonrecourse loans. In effect, the only thing the lender can take in the event of default and foreclosure is the property collateral securing the debt. The fact that this property may be worth less than the outstanding balance on the loan gives the borrower a type of option known as the **borrower's put option**. Options always have a positive value to their holders, so this option has some value to the borrower. However, this value is taken from the lender.

In general, a put option gives its holder the right without obligation to sell a specified underlying asset at a specified price. In the case of a nonrecourse mortgage, the underlying asset is the collateral property, and the borrower's ability to default on the loan effectively gives him the ability to sell the property to the lender at a price equal to the outstanding loan balance.[22] By defaulting on the loan, the borrower is said to "put" the property to the lender, thereby ridding himself of a liability equal, at least in book value, to the outstanding loan balance. The lender loses an asset with this same book value. Of course, the borrower loses, and the lender gains, the value of the property.

This situation is depicted in Exhibit 16-4 as of the time of maturity of a $100 loan. The horizontal axis represents the value of the underlying property securing the loan. The vertical axis represents the value of what the lender obtains. If there were no limited liability, the lender would receive $100 no matter what the value of the property, as depicted in Exhibit 16-4a. With the existence of limited liability (as with the nonrecourse loan), the lender faces the situation depicted in Exhibit 16-4b. As long as the property is worth more than the outstanding loan balance, the lender will receive the whole amount due ($100). If the property is worth less than the loan balance, the borrower would maximize her own wealth by defaulting on the loan and putting the property back to the lender. The lender then receives only the value of the property, which is less than the loan balance. For example, if the property were worth $90, the lender would receive value that is $10 less than the $100 owed. If the property were worth only $80, then the gap would be $20.

---

[22]To be more precise, the exercise price equals the current market value of a default-free version of the mortgage. This may differ from the outstanding loan balance ("par value" of the loan) if market interest rates have changed since the loan was issued. To simplify the basic point here, however, we can ignore this interest rate effect.

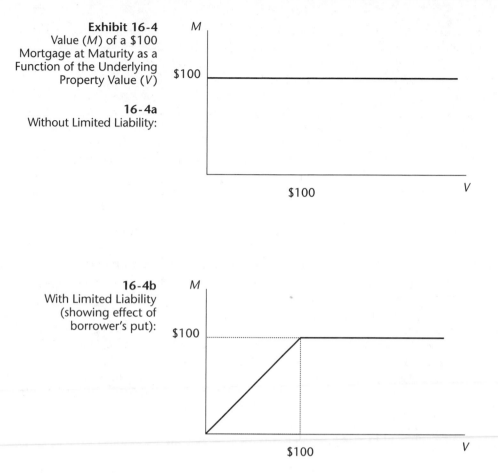

Exhibit 16-4
Value (*M*) of a $100
Mortgage at Maturity as a
Function of the Underlying
Property Value (*V*)

16-4a
Without Limited Liability:

16-4b
With Limited Liability
(showing effect of
borrower's put):

The difference between the loan value to the lender without limited liability (as in Exhibit 16-4a) and its value with limited liability (Panel 16-4b) is the value of the put option to the borrower. To the lender, this is obviously a negative value, or cost. Of course, lenders are aware of this possibility when they issue the loan, and mortgage investors in general are aware of the borrower's put option whenever they make investments. Mortgage prices, and the resulting yields in the mortgage market, reflect the existence of the borrower's put option. This is why mortgage yields are higher than equivalent-maturity U.S. government bonds, which lack default risk. On a probabilistic basis, the greater are the expected losses from the borrower exercising the put option (i.e., the greater the **credit risk** or expected **credit losses** in the loan), the higher will be the contractual yield the mortgage lender or investor will require.

16.5.2 Foreclosure Costs and Strategic Default

In the previous example there were no costs of foreclosure. If the property was worth $90 when the borrower defaulted, then the lender obtained $90 worth of value on his $100 debt. In reality, the lender can only take the property by going through the legal process of foreclosure. As noted, this is a time-consuming and expensive process. This gives the nonrecourse borrower additional potential leverage over the lender and suggests the possibility of the borrower engaging in **strategic default** behavior.

This refers to the borrower deliberately defaulting on the loan for the purpose of forcing the lender into a workout to the borrower's advantage, even though the collateral property is generating sufficient income to service the debt and has a current market value likely in excess of the outstanding loan balance.[23]

How can such behavior be in the borrower's interest? The presence of the dead-weight burden of foreclosure costs can make it so. Consider a simple numerical example involving a nonrecourse mortgage. There is only one cash flow left on the loan, due one year from now, in the amount of $10,600,000. The value of the underlying property at that time is currently uncertain, but has the following three possibilities:

- Scenario I: $13 million
- Scenario II: $11 million
- Scenario III: $9 million

If foreclosure occurs, the costs of foreclosure will amount to $2 million of deadweight burden (legal and administrative expenses paid to third parties). As the loan is nonrecourse, the lender would have to bear all of these costs in the event of foreclosure, although they could be recouped from the property sale proceeds.

Considering only the previous facts, it is easy to see what a wealth-maximizing borrower would do in each scenario. In scenario I the borrower would not default. To default on the loan would be irrational because the lender could take the $2 million costs of foreclosure plus the debt balance from the foreclosure sale proceeds, leaving the borrower with a net of only $400,000 ($13,000,000 − $10,600,000 − $2,000,000). On the other hand, by not defaulting, the borrower nets the full $2,400,000 difference between the property value and the loan balance. Thus, the NPV consequence of a decision to default would be −$2,000,000. In effect, the borrower would needlessly pay the costs of foreclosure if he defaulted.

Now skip to scenario III, the case in which the property is worth only $9 million, which is less than the outstanding loan balance. (Such a circumstance is referred to as the loan being "under water" or an **underwater loan**.) In this case it would be rational for the borrower to default, exercising his put option as described previously. If the borrower does not default, then he must pay the full $10,600,000 loan balance. As the property is only worth $9,000,000, the decision not to default would have a negative NPV consequence of $1,600,000. (Alternatively, you can view the decision to default as having a positive-NPV impact of $1,600,000 relative to its only alternative.)

This would be an example of classical **rational default**, when defaulting on the loan is a positive-NPV action that maximizes the NPV to the borrower across all the mutually exclusive alternatives available to him and hence satisfies the basic microlevel investment decision rule presented in Chapter 10.[24] Note that under scenario III default would be rational even if there were no deadweight costs of foreclosure. The borrower might simply give the lender a deed in lieu of foreclosure in these circumstances. Otherwise, the $2,000,000 foreclosure costs would be

---

[23] The term *strategic default* was used in a 1994 article by Riddiough and Wyatt, demonstrating how such borrower behavior could be consistent with equilibrium pricing in the mortgage market.

[24] In general, it is not necessarily rational for the borrower to default as soon as the loan is under water if the loan is not yet mature. However, in the present simple example, the loan is due.

absorbed by the lender, paid out of the property sale proceeds as the loan is non-recourse, and the lender would net only $7,000,000 of the $10,600,000 owed.

Finally, consider the intermediate case, scenario II, in which the property is worth $11 million. In this case the loan is not under water: the property is worth more than the outstanding loan balance. However, it is not worth more than the sum of the outstanding balance plus the foreclosure costs. This is the situation in which strategic default becomes a possibility. The borrower can credibly threaten the lender with default, given the nonrecourse nature of the loan, and probably force the lender into a workout deal in which the debt is restructured to the borrower's advantage. Suppose, for example, that the borrower defaults on the loan and offers the lender the following workout deal. If the lender refrains from foreclosing on the property, the borrower will pay the lender $9,100,000, instead of the $10,600,000 owed. Why would the lender take such a deal? Because by avoiding the $2,000,000 deadweight burden of the foreclosure costs, the lender will be better off by $100,000. The borrower, of course, ends up $1,500,000 better off than if he did not default. In effect, the two parties have split the $1,600,000 difference between the loan balance and the net value of the property in foreclosure, with the borrower getting the bulk of this difference because of his ability to force the lender to absorb up to $1,600,000 worth of foreclosure costs if he defaults.

The action described for the borrower in scenario III would be an example of a strategic default. In this case the borrower did not have to default on the loan. The property was generating sufficient cash and value to service the debt. But by defaulting (or credibly threatening default), the borrower was able to improve her position by forcing the lender into a workout.

Of course, the real world is more complicated than the simple example described here. For one thing, both sides have **reputation effects** to consider. If the lender accepts the borrower's offer, the word may get out, and other borrowers with other loans may be tempted to play the same game with the lender. If instead the lender calls the borrower's bluff and forecloses, he may develop a reputation as a "tough guy" who will not play such games. After all, if the lender forecloses in response to the borrower's default, the lender may lose up to $1,600,000 compared to what was owed under the loan, but the borrower also would lose $400,000 compared to the case in which the borrower did not default. The borrower would also suffer the negative reputation effects of foreclosure, which could harm her future ability to borrow funds.[25] So the borrower may indeed be bluffing. In any case, the borrower would probably agree to pay quite a bit more than $9,100,000 to the lender in order to avoid formal foreclosure.

In practice, borrowers and lenders address workout situations in a variety of ways in the commercial mortgage business. While problem loans raise the specter of the deadweight costs of foreclosure, once a loan or borrower is in trouble, both opportunities and further dangers are presented from that point, with the resulting scope for creativity and entrepreneurship. Even as a mere possibility, actions such as strategic default need to be considered by lenders and mortgage investors in a probabilistic sense, for they can affect investment prospects and values.

---

[25]Ciochetti and Vandell (1999) estimated that typical default transaction costs in permanent commercial mortgages average 5% and 15% of the outstanding loan balance for the borrower and lender, respectively.

16.6 CHAPTER SUMMARY

This chapter introduced the real estate mortgage and the U.S. mortgage industry. Although our focus was primarily on commercial loans, we presented underlying legal and financial structures, terminology, and salient features that are common to most mortgages in the United States. Although the majority of loans never cause problems, we discussed the nature of the default, foreclosure, and workout processes, as these possibilities always exist in a probabilistic sense and must be considered by investment decision makers.

KEY TERMS

mortgage	mortgagee	default
residential mortgage	mortgagor	litigious and nonlitigious actions
commercial mortgage	promissory note	forbearance
secondary mortgage market	mortgage deed	deficiency judgment
primary mortgage market	deed of trust (security deed)	bankruptcy
origination (issuance) of loans	lien theory	cramdown
securitization	title theory	chapter 11
commercial mortgage-backed securities (CMBS)	power of sale	deadweight burden
	judicial sale	deed in lieu of foreclosure
whole loans	foreclosure	restructuring loans
permanent loans	senior and junior debt	workout of loans
construction loans	covenants	limited liability
interest rate risk	order of application of payments	borrower's put option
floating interest rates	acceleration clause	credit risk (credit loss)
adjustable rate mortgages (ARMs)	due-on-sale clause	strategic default
depository institutions	loan assumption wraparound loan	underwater loans
mortgage bankers	prepayment clause	rational default
mortgage brokers	subordination clause	reputation effects
take-out loan	exculpatory clause	
secured debt	nonrecourse loans	

STUDY QUESTIONS

16.1. What determines whether a mortgage is classified as residential or commercial in the United States?

16.2. What are the major differences between the residential and commercial mortgage business in the United States?

16.3. Why is it that large commercial mortgage borrowers can often negotiate a customized loan from the issuer, while us small-fries trying to buy a house have to take a standard model?

16.4. When Bob takes out a mortgage to buy a $10 million apartment building, is that transaction occurring in the primary or secondary mortgage market? Is Bob's position short or long in the debt asset?

16.5. Why are commercial banks predominant in the issuance of construction loans, while life insurance companies and pension funds are a larger presence in the permanent loan market? [Hint: Recall the maturity-matching principle.]

16.6. What are the two parts (or legal documents) required in any mortgage? Under what circumstances does the mortgage deed convey title to the property?

16.7. a. Which states would you expect to have slightly lower mortgage interest rates: title theory states or lien theory states? Why?

b. Answer the same question regarding power of sale versus judicial sale.

16.8. Bob is the mortgagee in a mortgage recorded on 1/31/1996 on the property at 1000 North Main Street in the amount of $7,500,000. Sue has a mortgage on the property for $1,000,000, recorded on 2/28/1998. Piet has a third mortgage for $500,000, recorded on 3/31/2000. The property sells in foreclosure for $9,000,000, and there are $1,000,000 in costs to third parties.

a. How much does each lien holder receive?

b. Which of the three lien holders is most likely to bring the foreclosure suit, and why?

c. How do your answers to (a) and (b) change if Sue's mortgage has a subordination clause in it and Piet's does not?

16.9. Why might a first mortgage holder not have the first priority on the proceeds from a foreclosure sale?

16.10. What is meant by the expression, "Redeem up, foreclose down"?

16.11. a. What is the normal order of application of payments in a mortgage?

b. How does this order affect the remaining balance after an annual $1 million payment is made (on time) on a mortgage with 10% simple annual interest and an outstanding balance of $8 million just prior to the payment (i.e., what is the new balance after this payment is made)?

c. Suppose the payment was late by one day, and the loan provisions call for a late-payment penalty fee of $10,000?

16.12. Bob and Piet are 50/50 joint venture partners in a property investment in which they have borrowed $10 million and both signed the mortgage. Apart from the real estate investment, Bob has a net worth of $10 million, while Piet's net worth is 50 cents. They default on the loan when the property is worth $8 million. Assuming foreclosure expenses of $1 million, what are Bob's and Piet's respective net worths after the foreclosure, assuming the loan had a joint-and-several-liability clause but no exculpatory clause?

16.13. What is meant by acceleration of a loan? Name two common applications of acceleration clauses in a mortgage agreement.

16.14. When (and why) is it most valuable to the borrower for a loan *not* to have a due-on-sale clause in it?

16.15. Bob is the mortgagor on a $5 million, 6%, interest-only first mortgage on the property at 1000 North Main. The loan has another five years to run before it comes due, and it has no due-on-sale clause. Since Bob bought the property, it has increased in value from $7 million to $10 million, while interest rates have increased from the 6% that had prevailed to 8% today. Sue now wants to buy the property from Bob for $10 million, but she has only $2 million available for a down payment and can only afford 7% interest on an $8 million loan. Describe how Bob can clench this deal by extending Sue a wraparound loan as a second mortgage.

16.16. Other things being equal, would you expect a lender to demand a higher interest rate on a loan with an exculpatory clause in it? Why?

16.17. What is cramdown? When does it occur?

16.18. Why might a lender employ forbearance, or avoid instituting a formal foreclosure procedure with a borrower in default?

16.19. Describe the nature and magnitude of the typical deadweight costs of foreclosure for commercial properties.

16.20. What are some of the specific options available to borrowers and lenders in a workout process? [Hint: Describe various ways in which loan terms can be altered and/or additional equity capital injected into the property.]

16.21. Why are deficiency judgments often of relatively little value to the lender, even though the borrower has no exculpatory provision?

16.22. Why might a borrower give the lender a deed in lieu of foreclosure?

16.23. What is the relationship between the borrower's limited liability and the value of the borrower's put option?

16.24. What is strategic default, and how is it related to limited liability and the costs of foreclosure?

16.25. Suppose $10,600,000 is due and payable on a nonrecourse mortgage, and the property securing the loan is only worth $9,000,000. What is the value to the borrower of her put option?

16.26. Consider a nonrecourse mortgage with one payment of $10,600,000 due one year from now. The uncertain future is characterized by the following scenarios and probabilities:

Scenario I (70% probability): Property worth $13,000,000

Scenario II (20% probability): Property worth $11,000,000

Scenario III (10% probability): Property worth $9,000,000

If foreclosure occurs, the costs paid to third parties will be $2 million. U.S. government bonds maturing in one year are yielding 6%. If investors would require an expected return risk premium of 1%, what would this loan sell for today if scenario III would result in a deed-in-lieu and scenario II would result in a strategic default in which the difference between the borrower's and lender's extreme positions is split 50/50? What would be the loan's nominal yield, and what would be the present value cost of the credit risk?

17 Mortgage Basics II: Payments, Yields, and Values

Learning Objectives

After reading this chapter, you should understand:

◆ How to compute mortgage payments and balances for a variety of different types of loans, and how to creatively design your own customized loans.

◆ How to compute mortgage yields, and how to use mortgage yields to evaluate mortgages.

◆ The nature of the refinancing and prepayment decision, including the ability at some level to quantitatively evaluate this decision from a market value perspective.

$\mathbf{T}$he preceding chapter introduced you to the basic legal structure of the mortgage, how mortgages work. In this chapter we will pick up from there, and also from the present value mathematical principles introduced in Chapter 8. Our objective here is to hone your understanding of how to compute loan payments, values, and yields, so that you can use this ability to creatively design and structure loans and effectively analyze debt investments. While the material in this chapter is rather technical and quantitative, it is also extremely practical and useful. Furthermore, it is much more fun than it used to be because much of the drudgery of formula memorization and number-crunching is automated nowadays through the use of electronic calculators and computer spreadsheets. This makes it easier for you to concentrate on the (more important) underlying economics.

17.1 CALCULATING LOAN PAYMENTS AND BALANCES

The most basic thing you need to be able to do to handle a mortgage (whether as borrower, lender, or investor) is to know how to compute loan payments and balances given the loan terms. In fact, you already have the tools to do this, based on what you learned in Chapter 8 and Chapter 16. Chapter 8 presented the relevant present value mathematical formulas and gave you some practice with the basic calculations. Chapter 16 presented the relevant legal structure. Now let's put the two together and see how we can be more creative.

17.1.1 Four Basic Rules

You may recall from Chapter 16 that one of the basic clauses present in all mortgages is the order of application of payments clause. This clause stipulates that payments received are applied to interest before principal. From this clause and the basic terms of the mortgage agreement we derive the **four basic rules** for calculating loan payments and balances.

- Rule 1: The interest owed in each payment equals the applicable interest rate times the outstanding principal balance (i.e., the **outstanding loan balance**, or **OLB** for short) at the end of the previous period: $INT_t = (OLB_{t-1})r_t$.

- Rule 2: The principal amortized (paid down) in each payment equals the total payment (net of expenses and penalties) minus the interest owed: $AMORT_t = PMT_t - INT_t$.

- Rule 3: The outstanding principal balance after each payment equals the previous outstanding principal balance minus the principal paid down in the payment: $OLB_t = OLB_{t-1} - AMORT_t$.

- Rule 4: The initial outstanding principal balance equals the initial contract principal specified in the loan agreement: $OLB_0 = L$.

The following abbreviations are being used:

$$L = \text{Initial contract principal amount (the loan amount)}$$
$$r_t = \text{Contract simple interest rate applicable for payment in period } t$$
$$INT_t = \text{Interest owed in period } t$$
$$AMORT_t = \text{Principal paid down in the period } t \text{ payment}$$
$$OLB_t = \text{Outstanding principal balance } after \text{ the period } t \text{ payment has been made}$$
$$PMT_t = \text{Amount of the loan payment in period } t.$$

The first of these rules derives from the basic nature of the mortgage agreement, that the borrower agrees to compensate the lender for the use of the lender's money by paying interest. The second rule is the order of applications clause. (Under normal circumstances we can ignore the expenses and penalties portion of the clause.) The third and fourth rules follow directly by definition. Together, these four rules define a complete mathematical system for determining all payments and the outstanding balance due on the loan at any point in time.[1]

---

[1]The four rules as stated here assume simple interest compounded on the dates each payment is due. This is the typical way interest is computed in mortgages in the United States. In principle, it is possible to use other methods. For example, interest could be compounded continuously even though payments are due only at one or more discrete points in time. Whenever interest is compounded, the principal balance on the loan is adjusted to include the compounded interest. If interest is compounded more frequently than it is paid, the resulting compound growth in principal is known as "accretion of principal."

It is important to note that the first rule refers to the **contract interest rate**, that is, the rate stipulated in the loan agreement, applied as a simple interest rate *per payment period* specified in the mortgage. Thus, if the mortgage specifies monthly payments, then the applicable interest rate is the simple monthly rate, which is conventionally defined as the nominal per-annum rate stipulated in the loan, divided by the number of payment periods per year specified in the loan. For example, a 12% loan with monthly payments actually applies a simple interest rate of 1% due at the end of each month.[2] Using the notation from Chapter 8: $r = i/m$, where i is the nominal annual rate and m is the number of payment periods per year. Also, keep in mind that the contract interest rate in the loan does not necessarily equal the yield prevailing in the current mortgage market.

Similarly, the "initial principal" referred to in rule 4 is not necessarily equal to the net cash flow proceeds obtained by the borrower from the lender at the time the loan is made. For example, prepaid interest (points) or origination fees may be deducted from the cash paid up front by the lender to the borrower.

17.1.2 Applying the Rules to Design Loans

The four rules described earlier practically cry out to be entered as formulas in the cells of a computer spreadsheet, from which you can use your creativity in designing a loan with payment and repayment patterns to your liking. Let's examine a few of the more famous patterns.

Interest-Only Loan. ($PMT_t = INT_t$, or equivalently: $OLB_t = L$, or $AMORT_t = 0$, for all t) This is the oldest and most basic pattern of loan payments. In the **interest-only loan** there is no amortization of principal: the outstanding loan balance remains constant throughout the life of the loan, and the entire original principal must be paid back by the borrower in a lump sum at the loan's maturity date. As a result, the regular loan payments consist purely of interest. If the interest rate is fixed at a constant rate, then the regular payments will be fixed and level. This is the classical payment pattern of long-term corporate and government bonds, and it is not uncommon in commercial mortgages in the United States (with the difference that bond payments are traditionally semiannual whereas mortgage payments are monthly).

The payment and interest profile of the interest-only loan is depicted graphically in Exhibit 17-1, for an example $1 million, 30-year loan at 12% interest with monthly payments. The table below the chart shows the first and last scheduled payments. As 12% nominal annual interest equates to a simple monthly interest rate of 1%, the interest and payment amounts due each month on this loan are $10,000. The last payment (at the end of month number 360) is $1,010,000, including the last

---

Prior to payment due dates, interest not yet compounded to principal accrues on a pro rata basis as simple interest owed proportionate to the fraction of the time between the last and next compounding date. Interest accrued but not paid at the time a payment is due is generally added to the principal balance at the time the payment is due (as implied by rules 2 and 3, considering that $AMORT_t$ can be a negative number). Thus, the four rules can be applied to the case in which interest is compounded more frequently than payments are due, simply by treating the payment periods defined here (indexed by the t subscripts) as corresponding to the interest-compounding periods in the loan, rather than as the actual payment-due periods.

[2] Recall from Chapter 8 that this implies an effective annual rate (EAR) of $(1.01)^{12} - 1 = 12.68\%$, compounding the simple monthly rate at the monthly frequency.

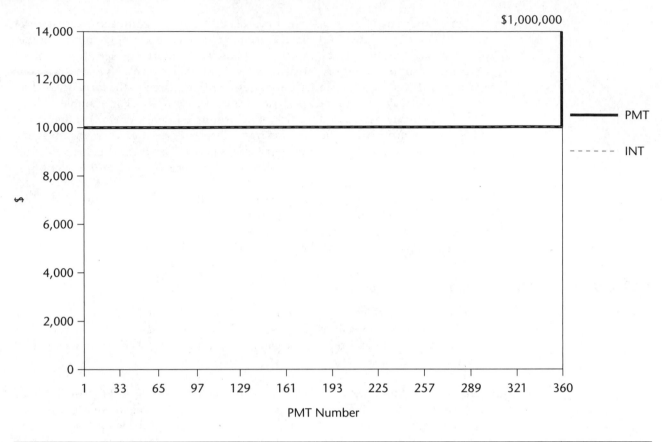

Month	Rules 3 & 4 OLB (Beg)	PMT	Rule 1 INT	Rule 2 AMORT	Rules 3 & 4 OLB (End)
0					$1,000,000.00
1	$1,000,000.00	$10,000.00	$10,000.00	$0.00	$1,000,000.00
2	$1,000,000.00	$10,000.00	$10,000.00	$0.00	$1,000,000.00
3	$1,000,000.00	$10,000.00	$10,000.00	$0.00	$1,000,000.00
. . .	. . .	. . .	. . .	. . .	. . .
358	$1,000,000.00	$10,000.00	$10,000.00	$0.00	$1,000,000.00
359	$1,000,000.00	$10,000.00	$10,000.00	$0.00	$1,000,000.00
360	$1,000,000.00	$1,010,000.00	$10,000.00	$1,000,000.00	$0.00

Exhibit 17-1 Interest-Only Mortgage Payments and Interest Component
($1,000,000, 12%, 30-year, monthly payments)

month's interest and the entire original principal. The amounts in the cells of the loan schedule table are computed using the appropriate formulas from the previously described four basic rules, as indicated at the top of the table columns.[3]

The interest-only loan is very straightforward and easy to understand. It has the advantage to the borrower of regular payments that are less than those of an otherwise equivalent amortizing loan. Some borrowers may view as an advantage the fact that the entire regular payment is tax-deductible.[4]

On the other hand, because principal is not paid down, the interest-only loan maximizes the total dollar magnitude of interest paid over the lifetime of the loan, as compared to amortizing loans. Because of the repayment spike at the loan's maturity, the weighted average time until the loan payments are made is greater than that for an amortizing loan of the same maturity. This may have some negative implications for some debt investors. For example, if the loan has a fixed interest rate, it will make the present market value of the loan more sensitive to movements in market interest rates.[5] The repayment spike at the end also confronts the borrower with the need to either refinance the loan or sell the property when the loan matures. This can cause problems if either the property or the debt market is not favorable at that time. Indeed, this is the major problem with the interest-only loan, and the major motivation for the development of amortizing loans.

Constant-Amortization Mortgage (CAM). ($AMORT_t = L/N$, all t) The simplest way to solve the problem of the repayment spike at the end of the interest-only mortgage is to pay down a constant amount of principal in each loan payment. This results in a **constant-amortization mortgage**, or **CAM**. Such loans were used for a time in the 1930s when interest-only loans were causing havoc during the Great Depression (many a family farm was lost when the mortgage came due) and when persistent deflation resulted in declining rents and land values. As can be seen in Exhibit 17-2, the CAM is characterized by a declining payment pattern. As the loan balance is reduced by a constant amount each period, the interest owed falls by a constant amount as well.

The payments on a CAM are computed by dividing the initial principal by the number of payments to compute the amortization amount per period, and then applying rule 2 to compute the total payment due each period as the sum of the amortization

---

[3] Note that the four rules are applied as formulas in *three* of the four necessary columns in the spreadsheet (one column corresponding to each of the four variables: OLB, PMT, INT, and AMORT). If the rules were applied in formulas in *all four* columns, the system would be "circular." Instead, one of the four columns is defined based on the defining characteristic of the loan type. For example, in Exhibit 17-1, we have chosen to define the PMT column based on the $PMT_t = INT_t$ (for all t) criterion of the interest-only mortgage. (Alternatively, we could have chosen to define any one of the other three columns based on the loan type definition, such as $AMORT_t = 0$ or $OLB_t = OLB_{t-1}$.)

[4] Recall from Chapter 14 that only the interest portion of the debt service payment is tax deductible. However, recall from Chapter 15 that the tax-shelter value of debt to the borrower is often largely illusory, as much (if not all) of the taxes saved through the deduction are paid indirectly by the pass-through of the marginal lender's taxes in the form of the difference between the market yield on taxed bonds and that on tax-exempt bonds.

[5] In general, the present values of cash flows that are more distant in the future are more sensitive to the average per-period discount rate than are the present values of more near-term cash flows. For example, the PV of $110 one year from now declines only from $100 to about $99 if the interest rate increases from 10% to 11% ($110/1.10 versus $110/1.11). However, the PV of a perpetuity of $10 per year declines from $100 to about $91 with the same change in the interest rates ($10/0.10 versus $10/0.11).

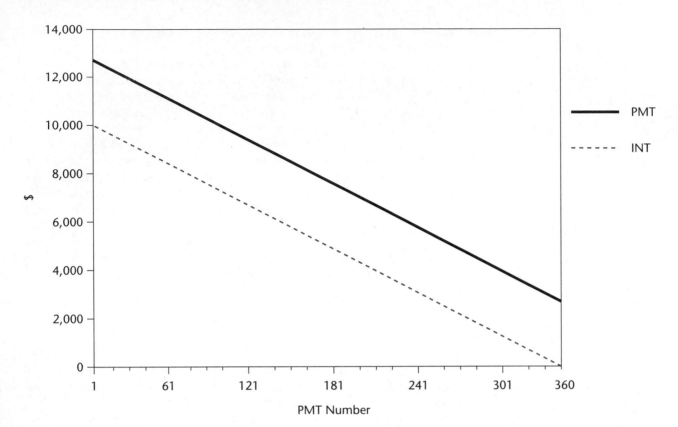

Month	Rules 3 & 4 OLB (Beg)	Rule 2 PMT	Rule 1 INT	AMORT	Rules 3 & 4 OLB (End)
0					$1,000,000.00
1	$1,000,000.00	$12,777.78	$10,000.00	$2,777.78	$997,222.22
2	$997,222.22	$12,750.00	$9,972.22	$2,777.78	$994,444.44
3	$994,444.44	$12,722.22	$9,944.44	$2,777.78	$991,666.67
...	...	...	...	...	...
358	$8,333.33	$2,861.11	$83.33	$2,777.78	$5,555.56
359	$5,555.56	$2,833.33	$55.56	$2,777.78	$2,777.78
360	$2,777.78	$2,805.56	$27.78	$2,777.78	$0.00

Exhibit 17-2 Constant-Amortization Mortgage (CAM) Payments and Interest Component ($1,000,000, 12%, 30-year, monthly payments)

and the interest computed based on rule 1. Thus, for our $1,000,000, 30-year example loan, the amortization each month is $2,777.78, computed as $1,000,000/360. Therefore, the first payment is $12,777.78, considerably higher than the $10,000 interest-only payment. After the first payment the loan balance is reduced to $997,222.22 by the application of rule 3, which in turn slightly reduces the amount of interest owed a month later in the second payment. This pattern continues until, after the 100th payment in our example, the CAM payment is less than that of the interest-only loan and continues to decline linearly to the end of the loan maturity. The outstanding loan balance also declines linearly.

In an economy free of persistent deflation, the declining payment pattern in the CAM is an undesirable characteristic for many borrowers, and for many debt investors as well. From the borrower's perspective, it causes the initial loan payment to be excessively high, and does not well match the loan payment pattern with the likely income generation pattern of the underlying property that is being financed with the mortgage. From the perspective of the typical mortgage investor, the CAM likely requires an inconvenient (and possibly expensive) reinvestment of capital each period as the mortgage is amortized. For this reason, CAMs are not widely used in the United States today, although there may be unique circumstances in which such loans would be appropriate.

The Constant-Payment Mortgage (CPM). ($PMT_t = PMT$, a constant, for all t) This brings us to the classic. The **constant-payment mortgage** solves many of the problems of both the interest-only loan and the CAM. Its constant payments make budgeting easy for both the borrower and lender, and tend to match well the typical pattern of rent growth in mature income properties. It provides flexibility in the trade-off among payment level, amortization rate, and maturity. If the loan is fully amortizing (as is typical with residential mortgages), the CPM avoids the problem of the repayment spike at the loan's maturity, and if the amortization rate is slow enough, the payments are not much higher than with an interest-only loan (although this requires very long-term debt). A "hybrid" payment pattern can be obtained by setting the maturity of the loan shorter than the amortization rate. This results in a **balloon payment** at maturity, but the size of the balloon can be reduced by increasing the payment level (faster amortization).[6] Although a CPM need not necessarily have a fixed interest rate (the amortization can vary according to rules 2 and 3), it is most common to combine the CPM payment pattern with a contractually fixed interest rate for the life of the loan.

The payments on the CPM are determined using the annuity formula applied with the contractual interest rate, the initial contractual principal, and the number of payment periods specified in the contractual amortization of the loan: $PMT = L/[(1 - 1/(1 + r)^N)/r]$. Then rule 1 is applied to determine the interest components and rule 2 is applied to back out the amortization component each period.

Continuing our $1,000,000, 12%, 30-year example in Exhibit 17-3, this results in a constant monthly payment of $10,286.13. This is barely more than the $10,000 payment on the interest-only loan, although it fully pays off the debt. Of course, 30 years is a long time, and if the loan is paid off prior to that time, a large liquidating payment may be required. As evident in the chart in Exhibit 17-3, in the early years of the CPM almost all of the payment consists of interest, so the outstanding loan balance declines very slowly. (The dashed line showing the interest component in the chart traces a pattern corresponding to that of the outstanding loan balance, as with any fixed interest rate loan the interest is always a constant fraction of the outstanding balance.) In our example, after 15 years (180 payments), the remaining balance is still $857,057.13, less than 15% of the principal having been paid down in the first half of the loan life. In the later years of the fully amortizing CPM the principal is paid

---

[6]A basic trade-off in all mortgages is between the payment level and the amortization rate. Other things being equal, faster amortization implies higher payments.

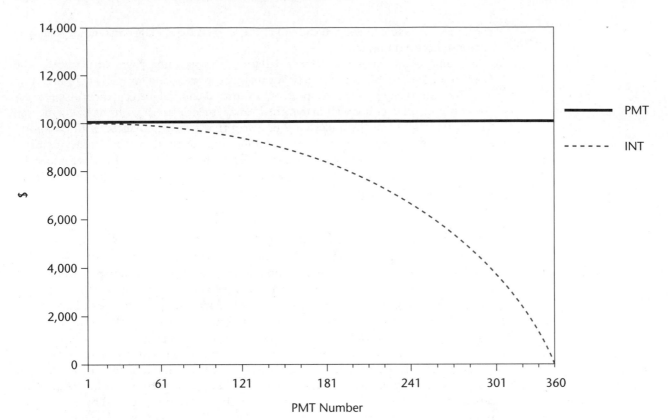

Month	Rules 3 & 4 OLB (Beg)	PMT	Rule 1 INT	Rule 2 AMORT	Rules 3 & 4 OLB (End)
0					$1,000,000.00
1	$1,000,000.00	$10,286.13	$10,000.00	$286.13	$999,713.87
2	$999,713.87	$10,286.13	$9,997.14	$288.99	$999,424.89
3	$999,424.89	$10,286.13	$9,994.25	$291.88	$999,133.01
. . .	. . .	. . .	. . .	. . .	. . .
358	$30,251.34	$10,286.13	$302.51	$9,983.61	$20,267.73
359	$20,267.73	$10,286.13	$202.68	$10,083.45	$10,184.28
360	$10,184.28	$10,286.13	$101.84	$10,184.28	$0.00

Exhibit 17-3 Constant-Payment Mortgage (CPM) Payments and Interest Component ($1,000,000, 12%, 30-year, monthly payments)

down rapidly, as indicated by the sharp falloff in the interest line in the chart. As a result, in the later years of a CPM, only a fraction of the payment consists of interest expense, which sharply reduces the tax-deductibility of the debt service.

Graduated Payment Mortgage (GPM). ($PMT_{t+s} > PMT_t$, for some positive value of s and t) Just as the declining payment pattern of the CAM was appropriate for a deflationary environment, a loan with a growing payment pattern would often be most appropriate in a strongly inflationary environment.[7] Such a loan is represented by the **graduated payment mortgage (GPM)**. The typical GPM has a fixed interest rate, but its payments increase over time. This is done in order to allow the initial payments to be lower than they otherwise could be. The GPM is useful not only in inflationary environments in which high interest rates make CPM mortgage payments hard to afford, but also for dealing with loans on income properties that are in turnaround, development, or workout situations, in which their ability to generate net rent is expected to increase over time. GPMs may also be useful for first-time home buyers, whose incomes can be expected to grow.

The most straightforward way to set up a GPM would be to simply use the constant-growth annuity formula introduced in Chapter 8, rather than the level annuity formula.[8] However, in practice it is inconvenient to have the payment changing every month. It makes more sense to have the payment step up at regular intervals, such as once per year. Also, it is often not necessary or practical to have the payment growing throughout the entire life of the mortgage. Four or five annual steps during the first part of the life of the loan usually accomplish the desired objective of improving the affordability of the loan for the borrower and matching the loan payment pattern with the ability of the underlying property or borrower to service the debt.

Exhibit 17-4 depicts our standard example $1,000,000, 12%, 30-year loan as a GPM with four step-ups of 7.5% each. Thanks to the GPM structure, the initial monthly payment can be reduced to $8,255.76, well below the $10,286.13 of the equivalent CPM. However, after three step-ups the payment in the fourth year, at $10,256.10, exceeds that of the interest-only loan, and after the fourth step-up the payments level off for the remainder of the loan at $11,025.31, considerably above the CPM payment level.

An important feature of GPMs is revealed by the arc of the interest component line in the chart in Exhibit 17-4 (the dashed line). Notice that this line rises first, before it begins to fall. As the interest is a constant proportion of the outstanding loan balance, the curve of this line indicates that the OLB rises for a while in the GPM. Initially, the payments are less than the interest owed ($PMT_t < INT_t$), resulting in **negative amortization** ($AMORT_t = PMT_t - INT_t < 0$). This may be of concern to lenders, as it runs some risk that the loan-to-value ratio (LTV) could rise above its initial level, unless the property value increases as fast as the loan balance.[9]

---

[7] Another approach for dealing with inflation is the price level adjusted mortgage (PLAM). In a PLAM the value of the outstanding balance is adjusted periodically using an index of purchasing power such as the CPI. This enables the interest rate charged on the loan to approximate the real interest rate, rather than the nominal interest rate which includes an inflation premium.

[8] If g is the growth rate per payment period, then recall from Chapter 8 that the constant-growth annuity formula relates the initial payment (PMT_1) to the initial principal (L) as follows:

$$PMT_1 = L \left/ \left(\frac{1 - [(1 + g)/(1 + r)]^N}{r - g} \right) \right.$$

[9] Recall from Chapter 16 that lenders can get into trouble when a loan threatens to go "under water" (LTV > 100%), or even when it is still slightly "above water." Presumably the danger of negative amortization causing an increase in the LTV is less of a concern in inflationary times, as with sufficient inflation the nominal value of the property would tend to rise even if its real value were remaining the same or falling.

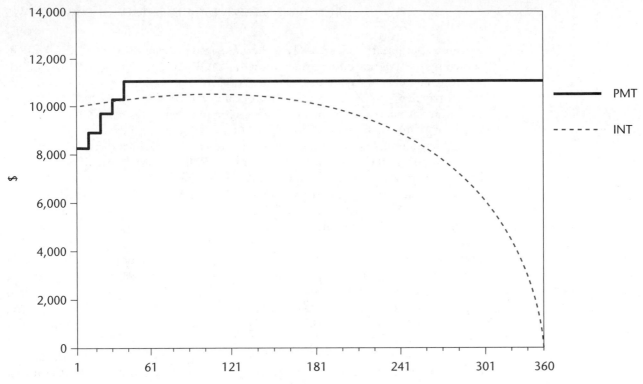

Month	Rules 3 & 4 OLB (Beg)	PMT	Rule 1 INT	Rule 2 AMORT	Rules 3 & 4 OLB (End)
0					$1,000,000.00
1	$1,000,000.00	$8,255.76	$10,000.00	($1,744.24)	$1,001,744.24
2	$1,001,744.24	$8,255.76	$10,017.44	($1,761.69)	$1,003,505.93
3	$1,003,505.93	$8,255.76	$10,035.06	($1,779.30)	$1,005,285.23
. . .	. . .	. . .	. . .	. . .	. . .
12	$1,020,175.38	$8,255.76	$10,201.75	($1,946.00)	$1,022,121.38
13	$1,022,121.38	$8,874.94	$10,221.21	($1,346.28)	$1,023,467.65
14	$1,023,467.65	$8,874.94	$10,234.68	($1,359.74)	$1,024,827.39
. . .	. . .	. . .	. . .	. . .	. . .
24	$1,037,693.53	$8,874.94	$10,376.94	($1,502.00)	$1,039,195.53
25	$1,039,195.53	$9,540.56	$10,391.96	($851.40)	$1,040,046.92
26	$1,040,046.92	$9,540.56	$10,400.47	($859.91)	$1,040,906.83
. . .	. . .	. . .	. . .	. . .	. . .
36	$1,049,043.49	$9,540.56	$10,490.43	($949.88)	$1,049,993.37
37	$1,049,993.37	$10,256.10	$10,499.93	($243.83)	$1,050,237.20
38	$1,050,237.20	$10,256.10	$10,502.37	($246.27)	$1,050,483.48
. . .	. . .	. . .	. . .	. . .	. . .
48	$1,052,813.75	$10,256.10	$10,528.14	($272.04)	$1,053,085.79
49	$1,053,085.79	$11,025.31	$10,530.86	$494.45	$1,052,591.34
50	$1,052,591.34	$11,025.31	$10,525.91	$499.39	$1,052,091.95
. . .	. . .	. . .	. . .	. . .	. . .
358	$32,425.27	$11,025.31	$324.24	$10,701.05	$21,724.21
359	$21,724.21	$11,025.31	$217.24	$10,808.07	$10,916.15
360	$10,916.15	$11,025.31	$109.16	$10,916.15	$0.00

Exhibit 17-4 Graduated Payment Mortgage (GPM) Payments and Interest Component
($1,000,000, 12%, 30-year, monthly payments; 4 annual steps of 7.5%)

To compute the payment and balance schedule of a GPM, you apply the loan graduation terms to the initial payment to compute each subsequent payment once the initial payment is known (e.g., step-ups of 7.5% once every 12 months for the first four years). Once the payment in each period is determined in this manner, you proceed as usual using the four rules: deriving the interest component from the application of rule 1, backing out the amortization using rule 2, and going forward with the outstanding balance using rule 3.

The only trick is determining the amount of the initial payment. This is done by repetitive application of the level annuity formula, recognizing that each step in the GPM is a level annuity, and the present value of all the GPM payments is just the sum of the present values of all of the steps. In our example, each step has a periodic payment value 7.5% higher than the previous step, and the present value of the annuity corresponding to that step must be discounted back to time zero from the point at which the step begins, one year later than the previous step.

For example, let $PV(r,N,PMT)$ represent the present value of the N-period level annuity with periodic payment amount PMT and simple periodic discount rate r. Then the present value as of time zero of the first annual step in our 12% example loan is $PV(0.01,12,PMT_1)$ where PMT_1 is the initial payment level. The time-zero value of the payments in the second step is: $PV(0.01,12,PMT_2)/1.01^{12}$, where PMT_2 is the second payment level. But we know that $PMT_2 = 1.075(PMT_1)$. Now recall that the annuity formula is proportional to the payment level, that is, $PV(r,N,PMT) = PV(r,N,1) \times (PMT)$. Thus, the present value of the second step is: $(1.075PMT_1/1.01^{12})PV(0.01,12,1)$. Therefore, the present value (as of time zero) of the entire GPM in our example can be written as

$$
\begin{aligned}
L = PMT_1[&PV(0.01,12,1) \\
&+ (1.075/1.01^{12})PV(0.01,12,1) \\
&+ (1.075^2/1.01^{24})PV(0.01,12,1) \\
&+ (1.075^3/1.01^{36})PV(0.01,12,1) \\
&+ (1.075^4/1.01^{48})PV(0.01,312,1)]
\end{aligned}
$$

where L is the initial contract principal ($1,000,000). It suffices merely to invert this formula to solve for the initial payment value, PMT_1 ($8,255.76 in our example). While this formula may seem a bit daunting, it is easily built up in steps, and easily typed into the appropriate cell in a computer spreadsheet.

Adjustable Rate Mortgage (ARM). ($r_t \neq r_{t+s}$ for some s and t) Another way to improve the affordability of a mortgage for a borrower is to allow the contract interest rate in the loan to adjust periodically to changes in the interest rates prevailing in the debt market. This reduces the interest rate risk for the lender (or mortgage investor), making a lower interest rate possible.

The advantage of the ARM in reducing the initial interest rate is particularly strong for long-term mortgages during times when a steeply upward-sloping **yield curve** is prevailing in the bond market. The yield curve depicts the yield on bonds as function of their maturity. With a steeply upward-sloping yield curve, short-term bonds are priced with a much lower yield than long-term bonds. This tends to occur when inflation is expected to increase in the long term, or when short-term real interest rates are temporarily depressed due to stimulative government monetary policy and/or low current demand for short-term capital (as during a macroeconomic recession). Although the ARM may be a long-term mortgage, it is like a chain of short-term fixed rate loans linked together, because the interest rate can be adjusted at relatively short intervals.[10] The ARM can therefore be priced similar to short-term debt, with an interest rate based on the short-term end of the yield curve.

Continuing our previous numerical example, Exhibit 17-5 depicts a hypothetical $1,000,000, 30-year ARM that might be available at the same time as the 12% loan we examined in the previous examples. This ARM has an initial interest rate of 9%, and the applicable interest rate adjusts once every year (12 payments), based on the prevailing interest rates on U.S. Treasury Bonds with a one-year maturity, plus a constant **margin** to reflect the greater default risk in the mortgage.[11] In this case the one-year government bond is serving in the role of what is called the **index** for the ARM because it is governing the applicable interest rate on the ARM.[12]

Ex ante, it is impossible to know for certain what the future payments on the ARM will be beyond the initial year because it is impossible to forecast with certainty what the prevailing market yields will be for the index on the loan. Of course, a forecasted payment schedule can be computed based on an *assumed* forecast of future bond rates. Ex post, the actual payment and balance history of the ARM is likely to look jagged, as in Exhibit 17-5, which assumes a particular (hypothetical) history for the government bond rate.

The interest rates applicable over the life of an ARM are likely to vary both up and down over time; however, they may tend to be higher on average than the initial interest rate, for two reasons. First, if the yield curve is steeply upward-sloping when the loan is issued, market yields even on short-term debt (such as the loan index) will tend to rise in the years after the loan is issued.[13] Second, the initial rate on the ARM may be what is called a **teaser rate**. A teaser rate is an initial rate less than the current value of the index-plus-margin for the loan at the time the loan is issued. If the initial rate is a teaser, then the applicable rate on the loan will rise even if market interest rates (as represented by the rate on the loan index) remain the same.[14]

Although the applicable contract interest rate may vary unpredictably in the ARM, the loan will certainly fully amortize over its 30-year lifetime because the four rules will always be applied to determine the payments. To see how this works in prac-

---

[10] Short-term commercial loans, such as construction loans, often have a "floating" interest rate, which may adjust frequently. Long-term ("permanent") loans typically adjust no more frequently than once per year.

[11] ARMs also often have "caps" or "ceilings," placing limits on how far the applicable interest rate in the loan can adjust in any one move, or over the lifetime of the loan.

[12] The index on an ARM must be a publicly observable rate that is not subject to manipulation by the lender. The most widely used index for residential loans is the U.S. Treasury Bond with maturity corresponding to the adjustment interval in the ARM. Other widely used indexes include cost of funds indices (COFI) relevant to the lender, and the London Interbank Borrowing Rate (LIBOR).

[13] An abnormally steep yield curve is usually an indication that the capital markets are predicting a rise in future short-term interest rates. On the other hand, if the yield curve is slightly upward-sloping, with long-term rates, say, 100 to 200 basis points above short-term rates, then it will usually be approximately correct to forecast future short-term interest rates at a constant level equal to the current short-term rates. (See Chapter 19 for an explanation of the yield curve.)

[14] For example, suppose the current one-year T-bond is yielding 8% and an ARM with a one-year adjustment interval has a 2% margin. If the initial interest rate on the ARM were 9%, this would be a teaser rate, 1% below the fully indexed rate. In this case, even if the market interest rate remains at 8% for the T-bond, the ARM rate will rise to 10% at the first adjustment time.

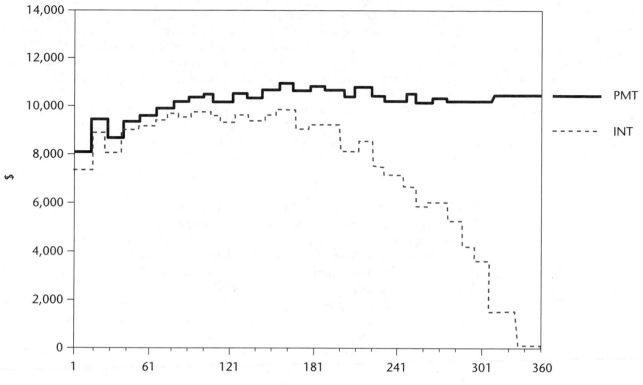

Month	Rule 3 & 4 OLD (Beg)	PMT	Rule 1 INT	Rule 2 AMORT	Rule 3 & 4 OLB (End)	Applied Rate
0					$1,000,000.00	
1	$1,000,000.00	$8,046.23	$7,500.00	$546.23	$999,454	0.0900
2	$999,454	$8,046.23	$7,495.90	$550.32	$998,903	0.0900
3	$998,903	$8,046.23	$7,491.78	$554.45	$998,349	0.0900
. . .	. . .	. . .	. . .	. . .	. . .	. . .
12	$993,761	$8,046.23	$7,453.21	$593.02	$993,168	0.0900
13	$993,168	$9,493.49	$9,095.76	$397.73	$992,771	0.1099
14	$992,771	$9,493.49	$9,092.12	$401.37	$992,370	0.1099
. . .	. . .	. . .	. . .	. . .	. . .	. . .
24	$988,592	$9,493.49	$9,053.81	$439.68	$988,152	0.1099
25	$988,152	$8,788.72	$8,251.03	$537.68	$987,614	0.1002
26	$987,614	$8,788.72	$8,246.54	$542.17	$987,072	0.1002
. . .	. . .	. . .	. . .	. . .	. . .	. . .
358	$31,100	$10,605.24	$356.61	$10,248.63	$20,852	0.1376
359	$20,852	$10,605.24	$239.09	$10,366.14	$10,485	0.1376
360	$10,485	$10,605.24	$120.23	$10,485.01	0	0.1376

Exhibit 17-5   Adjustable Rate Mortgage (ARM) Payments and Interest Component ($1,000,000, 9% initial interest, 30-year, monthly payments; one-year adjustment interval, possible hypothetical history)

tice, consider the payment and balance history depicted in the lower panel of Exhibit 17-5. The initial interest rate on the loan is 9%. This gives the loan an initial monthly payment of $8,046.23, found by applying the level annuity formula, $PMT(r,N,PV)$, with $r = 9\%/12 = 0.75\%$, $N = 30 * 12 = 360$, and $PV = L = \$1,000,000$, the initial principal. After 12 payments and the application of the four basic rules, this leaves a remaining balance of $993,168.

Now at the one-year anniversary of the loan, suppose that the one-year U.S. Treasury Bond yield turns out to be 8.99%. If the ARM has a margin of 200 basis points, then the applicable interest rate on the ARM will adjust from its previous 9% rate to a new rate of 10.99%. This is computed as the observed index rate on the anniversary date (8.99%) plus the 2% margin.[15] The payment for the second year of the ARM is then computed as $PMT(r,N,PV)$ with $r = 10.99\%/12 = 0.9158\%$, $N = 29 * 12 = 348$, and PV = $993,168, the outstanding loan balance at the beginning of the second year. This gives a monthly payment during the second year of $9,493.49. This type of procedure is applied at each anniversary date or adjustment time in the loan.[16]

ARMs typically have at least slightly lower overall average expected yield-to-maturity than otherwise similar **fixed rate mortgages (FRMs)**. This is because the yield curve is typically at least slightly upward-sloping, even in the absence of inflation fears or expansionary monetary policy. Of course, this does not imply that the borrower is getting something for nothing, for the borrower absorbs the interest rate risk that the lender avoids.[17]

In our numerical example, the initial interest rate and payment is considerably lower in our 9% ARM than in the traditional fixed rate CPM. (Recall that the fixed rate loan was at 12%, with the CPM payment at $10,286.13, versus an initial payment of $8,046.23 for the ARM.) However, with this much of a difference between their initial interest rates, it is not unlikely that the applicable interest rate and payment on the ARM will rise to levels above that of the equivalent FRM at some point during the life of the loan. For example, the bottom of the lower panel in Exhibit 17-5 reveals that in the last year of the life of our example ARM the applicable interest rate turned out to be 13.76%, which resulted in monthly payments that year of $10,605.44, considerably above those on the corresponding FRM.[18]

---

[15] Sometimes the relevant rate is specified as the *average* yield observed on the index during some window of time, such as the month prior to the anniversary date of the loan. This reduces the borrower's risk somewhat, as it tends to mitigate the danger associated with the anniversary date of the loan happening to fall at the time of a brief spike in market interest rates.

[16] In principle, it is possible for the payments in the ARM to be fixed even though the applicable interest rate varies. In this case changes in the interest rate cause changes in the amortization of the contractual principal remaining on the loan, resulting either in changes in the loan maturity or the size of the balloon payment due at maturity. Fixed-payment ARMS are rare, however, in part because of the danger of "negative amortization" noted previously.

[17] Indeed, as will be discussed in Chapter 19, interest rate risk is fundamentally *why* the yield curve is most commonly slightly upward-sloping.

[18] The ARM may have a prepayment clause in it entitling the borrower to refinance. (Government regulations require residential ARMs to have the prepayment option.) However, the ARM payments will tend to fall when prevailing market interest rates fall, which reduces the value to the borrower of refinancing at that time. When market interest rates fall, the ARM rate will tend to automatically adjust downward as well. Thus, the prepayment option is typically less valuable in an ARM than it is in an FRM. As this option is less valuable to the borrower, so it is less costly to the lender. This is another aspect of the lender's reduced interest rate risk, which enables the ARM interest rate to be lower than rates on otherwise identical FRMs.

Your Customized Loan. The types of mortgages and payment patterns previously described include the most common ones prevailing in the United States during the 1990s, but they obviously do not exhaust the possibilities. With a computer spreadsheet and the four basic rules you can easily become a creative "financial engineer" and develop your own type of loan and payment pattern. Such creativity may not do you much good in trying to get a mortgage on your house, but remember that the commercial mortgage business is less standardized and often allows more customization and negotiation. Particularly in dealing with unique properties or investment circumstances, such as developments, turnarounds, and workouts, it may be useful to be able to be creative in designing loan terms and financing packages.

17.2 LOAN YIELDS AND MORTGAGE VALUATION

Investors, as we know, are interested in returns. This is no less true for debt investors than it is for equity investors. In the debt market in general, and in the mortgage market in particular, investment returns are generally referred to as **yields**.[19] Now that you know how to compute loan payments and balances, you can easily learn how to compute loan yields. From there, it is a short step to loan valuation.

17.2.1 Computing Mortgage Yields

The yield of a loan generally refers to its internal rate of return (IRR). Most commonly, this IRR is computed over the full remaining potential life of the loan, as if the loan would not be prepaid and the investor would hold the loan to maturity. To be more precise, this should be referred to as the **yield-to-maturity (YTM)** of the loan, although in common parlance, unless it is specified otherwise, the simple word *yield* usually refers to the YTM.

As an example, consider a $1,000,000, 30-year CPM with an 8% annual interest rate. Such a loan would have monthly payments of $7,337.65. The IRR of this loan computed as a simple monthly rate is found by solving the following equation for r.

$$0 = -\$1,000,000 + \sum_{t=1}^{360} \frac{\$7,337.65}{(1+r)^t}$$

Of course, the answer is $r = 0.667\%$, which equates to the nominal annual rate of $i = rm = (0.667\%)(12) = 8.00\%$. We know this because of how we determined the payment amount of $7,337.65, by using the annuity formula with a nominal annual rate of 8%.[20] In this case, therefore, the YTM of the loan is identical to its contract interest rate.

[19] Recall from Chapter 9 that terminology in the bond and mortgage market is a bit different from that in the stock and equity market. Yield in the equity market typically refers to the income component of the periodic total return, or the current income or dividend value as a fraction of the current asset value. "Yield" in the debt markets typically refers to a multiperiod measure of the total return.

[20] In this book we will round monthly payments to the nearest cent, and present or future lump-sum values to the nearest dollar. A more exact monthly payment computation for a precise 8.00% yield is $7,337.645739. In practice the final payment on the loan would be adjusted slightly to make up for the effect of rounding.

The yield on a mortgage will not always equal its interest rate. Suppose the previous $1,000,000 loan had a 1% **origination fee**. This means that the lender charges the borrower 1% of the loan amount up front, just to grant the loan. Such charges may also be referred to as prepaid interest or discount points (or just points, for short). They are normally quoted in **points** (a point in this sense refers to a percentage point of the outstanding loan balance).[21] With a one-point origination fee the lender will actually disburse to the borrower only $990,000, even though the contractual principal (L) and the initial outstanding loan balance (OLB_0) is $1,000,000.[22] In this case, the YTM on the loan is found by solving the following equation for r.

$$0 = -\$990,000 + \sum_{t=1}^{360} \frac{\$7,337.65}{(1+r)^t}$$

The answer is $r = 0.6755\%$, or a nominal annual rate of 8.11%. The effect of the origination fee is to increase the mortgage YTM by 0.11% (or 11 **basis points**) over the stated contract interest rate in the loan.

Another way in which the YTM of a loan can differ from its contract interest rate is through the effect of the mortgage market on the value of the loan. Suppose the originator of this mortgage got the commitment and terms to this loan locked in a month before the closing of the loan transaction. During that month yields dropped in the mortgage market, so that the loan originator has an offer to sell this mortgage as soon as it closes for a value of $1,025,000. The buyer of the loan in the secondary market is, in effect, offering to pay more for the loan than its current contractual outstanding balance ($1,000,000), or **par value**. In effect, the mortgage market has caused the market value of the loan to differ from its par value or contractual OLB. The loan originator can make an immediate profit of $25,000, or $35,000 including the one-point origination fee. The buyer of the mortgage is, in effect, offering to make an investment in this mortgage with a YTM of 7.74%, found by solving the following equation for r (and multiplying by 12).

$$0 = -\$1,025,000 + \sum_{t=1}^{360} \frac{\$7,337.65}{(1+r)^t}$$

Contractual Interest Rates versus YTMs. In general, the YTM of a loan will differ from the loan's contractual interest rate whenever the current actual cash flow associated with the acquisition of the loan differs from the current outstanding loan balance (or par value) of the loan. At the time of loan origination in the primary market, this will result from discounts taken from the loan disbursement. In the resale of

---

[21]The term *basis points* refers to one hundredth of a percent. One hundred basis points equals one point or 1%.

[22]As soon as the borrower signs on the dotted line, he legally owes $1,000,000, even though he only receives $990,000.

the loan in the secondary market, the YTM will reflect the market value of the loan regardless of the par value or contractual interest rate on the loan.

APRs and Effective Interest. The YTM from the lender's perspective at the time of loan origination is often referred to as the **annual percentage rate**, or **APR**. This term is used in consumer finance and residential mortgages, where it has an official definition based on the Truth-in-Lending Act.[23] In common parlance the YTM at the time of loan issuance is also often referred as the **effective interest rate** faced by the borrower. However, it is important to recognize that the borrower may face additional transaction costs associated with obtaining the loan that are not reflected in the APR or YTM. In particular, costs for items that are required by the lender but paid to third parties, such as appraisals and title insurance, are not included in the APR calculation. These costs may differ across lenders, so the actual lowest cost of capital for the borrower will not necessarily come from the lender with the lowest APR.

YTMs and Expected Returns. The YTM of a loan may differ from the investor's expected total return (and therefore also from the borrower's expected cost of capital) for two reasons. First, the YTM computed as before ignores the possibility of default on the loan by the borrower. The contractual cash flows specified in the loan agreement are assumed in computing the yield. More realistically, there is normally some ex ante probability that default will occur at some point in the life of the loan. This causes the realistic ex ante mean return faced by the investor to be less than the default-free YTM, which is the way loan yields are measured and quoted in the market.[24]

Second (even ignoring the possibility of default), if the loan has a prepayment clause or a due-on-sale clause, then the borrower may choose to pay the loan off before its maturity. This is common in residential mortgages, and not uncommon in commercial mortgages. The yield (IRR) over the realistic expected life of the loan (until the borrower prepays) will differ from the YTM whenever there is a prepayment penalty and whenever the YTM differs from the contractual interest rate on the loan.

At the time of loan origination in the primary market, the YTM differs from the contractual interest rate only due to disbursement discounts, so the expected yield to the lender (or effective interest rate to the borrower) generally *increases* the shorter the time until the realistic prepayment horizon. This effect is magnified if there is also a prepayment penalty.

As an example, let's return to our previous $1,000,000, 30-year, 8% loan with the one-point origination fee. We saw that its YTM at origination was 8.11%. Now suppose the borrower is expected to prepay the loan after 10 years. The yield of the loan

[23] See Federal Reserve Board, Regulation Z, 12 CFR 226 as amended. This regulation does not apply to most commercial mortgages. Note that the APR is generally rounded to the nearest eighth of a point.

[24] Default risk will be discussed in more depth in the next chapter. Keep in mind, however, the basic principle introduced in Chapter 16, that the value of the loan to its holder equals the value of an otherwise equivalent default-free loan (such as a government bond) minus the value of the borrower's put option represented by the borrower's limited liability. Thus, option valuation theory can be used to value default-risky debt, and the YTMs observed in the debt market reflect such valuation.

with an expected prepayment horizon of 10 years is 8.15%, computed by solving the following equation for r (and multiplying by 12).[25]

$$0 = -\$990,000 + \sum_{t=1}^{120} \frac{\$7,337.65}{(1+r)^t} + \frac{\$877,247}{(1+r)^{120}}$$

The resulting 8.15% yield is more realistic than the 8.11% YTM if this loan would in fact more likely be repaid in 10 years. The 8.15% yield is also the YTM of a 10-year mortgage with a 30-year amortization rate. Such a loan would have a mandatory balloon payment of \$877,247 at the end of its 10-year maturity.[26]

The shorter the prepayment horizon, the greater the effect of the disbursement discount on the realistic yield of the mortgage. Prepayment penalties cause a similar (though slightly smaller) effect. The effect is hyperbolic, not linear, with the impact on the yield much greater the shorter the prepayment horizon. This is seen in Exhibit 17-6, which shows the effect on the yield of a 30-year, 8% mortgage caused by various different prepayment horizons and loan terms. For example, with one point of disbursement discount the yield would be 8.25% over a five-year horizon, or 8.55% over a two-year horizon. If the loan had two points of disbursement discount instead of one, its yield over the 10-year horizon would be 8.31% instead of 8.15%. If it had one point of prepayment penalty instead of the additional point of disbursement discount, the 10-year yield would be 8.21%.[27]

---

[25]Recall from Chapter 8 that a business calculator solves the following problem (equation [12] in Chapter 8):

$$0 = -PV + \sum_{t=1}^{N} \frac{PMT}{[1 + (i/m)]^t} + \frac{FV}{[1 + (i/m)]^N}$$

Thus, to solve the problem on a business calculator, first enter the contractual loan terms ($N = 360$, $i = 8\%$, $PV = 1000000$, $FV = 0$, and compute $PMT = -7337.65$). Then change the number of payments to that in the expected horizon ($N = 120$) to compute the OLB as $FV = -877,247$, *before* changing the amount in the PV register to reflect the fee: $PV = 990000$. It is important to change the amount in the PV register last, just before computing the yield using the i register. This is a general rule. For example, if the loan had also had a prepayment penalty, it would be important to compute the amount of the prepayment penalty with the original contract principal in the PV register, and include the prepayment penalty in the FV register amount, before changing the value in the PV register to reflect any disbursement discount.

[26]The OLB on the loan can be computed on a business calculator in either of two ways. You may enter the number of payments *already made* in the N register and then compute the future value (FV) of the loan (with the initial principal amount in the PV register). Alternatively, with the loan's original liquidating payment at maturity in the FV register (zero for a fully amortizing loan), it is equivalent to enter the number of payments *yet to be paid* in the N register, and then compute the present value (PV). That these two approaches are mathematically equivalent can be seen by manipulating the mortgage math calculator equation (equation [12] in Chapter 8). Letting q be the number of previous payments and Tm be the original number of payments in the fully amortizing loan maturity, it is equivalent to solve this equation either for PV with $N = Tm - q$ and $FV = 0$, or for FV with $N = q$ and $PV = P$, the original contract principal.

[27]It is computationally useful to note that when the disbursement discount and prepayment penalty are quoted in points, that is, as a fraction of the outstanding loan balance or par value of the loan, then there is no need to know the dollar magnitude of the loan or its payments in order to compute its yield. You can substitute any convenient loan amount (such as \$1) to compute the yield for any loan so described. This is a consequence of the fact that the present value equation is homogeneous of degree one in the cash flows, as noted in Chapter 8.

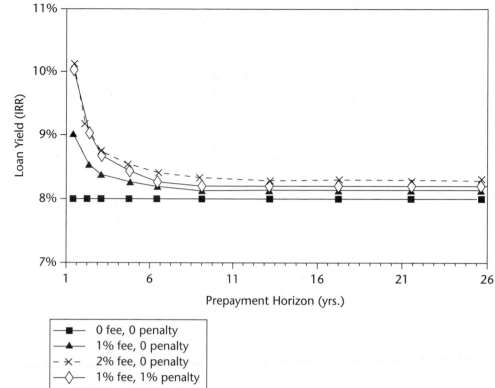

Exhibit 17-6a Effect of Prepayment on Loan Yield (8%, 30-year)

Exhibit 17-6b Yield (IRR) on 8%, 30-year CP-FRM

Loan Terms	Prepayment Horizon (yrs.)						
	1	2	3	5	10	20	30
0 fee, 0 pen	8.00%	8.00%	8.00%	8.00%	8.00%	8.00%	8.00%
1% fee, 0 pen	9.05%	8.55%	8.38%	8.25%	8.15%	8.11%	8.11%
2% fee, 0 pen	10.12%	9.11%	8.77%	8.50%	8.31%	8.23%	8.21%
1% fee, 1% pen	10.01%	9.01%	8.67%	8.41%	8.21%	8.13%	8.11%

17.2.2 Why Points and Fees Exist

In the commercial mortgage industry origination fees are often charged to compensate mortgage brokers who find and filter loan applications for the financial institutions who supply the long-term capital. In general, loan originators face overhead and administrative costs that may be attributed to the loan origination process per se, and which therefore differ from the opportunity cost of the capital that is being invested in the loan. While the latter cost accrues over the life of the loan, the former cost is sunk at the time the loan is issued. Up-front fees are a way for the loan originator to make some profit while providing some disincentive against early prepayment of the loan by the borrower. (Recall the hyperbolic relation between the yield and the prepayment horizon when there is a disbursement discount.) Up-front fees can also be used as a trade-off against the level of the regular loan payment: greater origination fees and discount points allow lower regular loan payments for the same yield. This results in the familiar **mortgage menu** typically offered by residential lenders, in which discount points are traded off against the interest rate on the loan.

For example, suppose the originator of the previously described $1,000,000 mortgage with the 30-year amortization rate expects (or requires) that the loan will be paid back in 10 years (i.e., with a balloon payment and no penalty). The following combination of disbursement discount points and contract interest rate will all provide the same 8.15% 10-year yield, with the resulting indicated difference in the monthly payments.

Discount Points	Interest Rate	Monthly Payment
0	8.15%	$7,444.86
1	8.00%	$7,337.65
2	7.85%	$7,230.58
3	7.69%	$7,124.08

At the other end of the loan's lifetime, prepayment penalties are rare in residential mortgages in the United States, but are more widespread in commercial mortgages. They are used to discourage prepayment, in effect, by reducing the net value of the borrower's prepayment option. In the extreme, prepayment penalties may be set so high as to effectively eliminate the value of this option.

17.2.3 Using Yields to Value Mortgages

Now that you know how to compute mortgage yields, you can use this knowledge as a valuation tool. Investors buy mortgages (or issue them as loan originators) in order to earn returns, as with any other investment. We have seen how the mortgage yield is related to the return the mortgage investor can expect. As with any investment, the return (and therefore the yield) is an inverse function of the price of the asset (holding the future cash flows constant). For a given loan (i.e., a given set of contractual future cash flows), a given yield will therefore correspond to a certain price, and vice versa. In effect, yields become a convenient way to measure and quote the prices of mortgages prevailing in the debt market. By applying the relevant market yield to a given mortgage, you can ascertain the market value of that mortgage, what it is likely to sell for in the secondary market. In general, for a given required yield, you can determine how much a specified mortgage is worth.

As an example, consider once again our $1,000,000, 8%, monthly-payment, 30-year-amortization, 10-year-maturity balloon loan. How much is this loan worth at closing if the market yield at that time is 7.50%? The answer is $1,033,509, computed as [28]

$$\$1,033,509 = \sum_{t=1}^{120} \frac{\$7,337.65}{(1.00625)^t} + \frac{\$877,247}{(1.00625)^{120}}$$

---

[28] Here, the market yield (discount rate) has been quoted as a **mortgage equivalent yield (MEY)**, so the nominal annual rate of 7.50% corresponds to a simple monthly rate of 7.5%/12 = 0.625%. In practice, the mortgage market and bond market are tightly integrated, and market yields are usually quoted in

This is just the inverse of the yield calculation problems we did in the last section. There, we knew the present cash flow value (the PV amount), and solved for the implied return. Now we know the required return, so we must solve for the implied present value. This is nothing more (or less) than a DCF valuation problem similar to those we introduced in Chapter 10, only now we are valuing a debt asset rather than an equity asset.[29] The discount rate is the yield observed in the debt market for loans with similar risk and payment timing patterns as the subject loan. The implied loan value is that at which the loan can be traded with NPV = 0 based on market value.[30]

Similarly, if both the yield and the worth of the mortgage are specified, you can determine the required payments and hence the contract interest rate and/or discount points that are required for a given par value or contractual principal amount. For example, suppose the market yield on the day of closing of the 8%, $1,000,000 loan is 8.5% instead of 7.5%. How much must the loan originator charge the borrower in the form of discount points if the lender is not to do a negative-NPV deal from her perspective, based on market value?

To answer this question we solve the same type of loan valuation equation as before, to see that the loan will be worth $967,888 on closing:[31]

$$\$967,888 = \sum_{t=1}^{120} \frac{\$7,337.65}{(1.0070833)^t} + \frac{\$877,247}{(1.0070833)^{120}}$$

As this value is $32,112 less than the initial principal, that is the amount by which the lender must discount the up-front disbursement. In other words, 3.2112 points of prepaid interest or origination fees must be charged.[32]

17.3 REFINANCING DECISION

If a loan has a **prepayment option**, the borrower can choose to pay the loan off early to take advantage of favorable interest rate movements, **refinancing** the old loan with a new, cheaper loan. This refinancing decision can be evaluated by comparing two loans, the existing ("old") loan and a "new" loan that would replace it. Traditionally, this comparison is made using the classical DCF methodology we have just

bond or **coupon-equivalent** terms (**BEY** or **CEY**). Yields quoted in bond terms must be converted to MEY before application to monthly cash flows. In the previous example, if the market yield is 7.5% MEY, then the observed market yield in the bond market (for a bond of equivalent risk and maturity) must be 7.62% BEY, as $[1 + (0.0762/2)]^2 = [1+(0.075/12)]^{12}$. See Chapter 8 for a discussion of mortgage-equivalent and bond-equivalent yields and effective annual rates (EARs).

[29] As noted, one difference here is that the contractual cash flows are used in the numerators on the right-hand side of the valuation equation. In Chapter 10 the realistic *expectations* of the cash flows in each period were used in the numerators. Considering the probability of default, the contractual cash flow amounts are generally higher than the realistic expectations of these cash flows. Thus, the discount rate (the market yield) in the corresponding denominators is gross of the expected credit loss to the lender in the event of default.

[30] With reference to Chapters 12 and 15, note that the valuation described here computes the market value (MV) of the loan, which equates to the investment value (IV) only for marginal investors.

[31] 8.5%/12 = 0.70833%

[32] This shows how leaving the final determination of the loan origination fee flexible until the closing can enable the latest changes in the secondary mortgage market to be reflected in the loan terms.

been describing. In this section, we will first present this traditional approach, then we will explore something important that is left out of the traditional picture, namely, the prepayment option value in the old loan.

17.3.1 Traditional Refinancing Calculation

The traditional approach involves a simple DCF valuation of the two loans. Here we will label the DCF-based present values of the two loans $PV(CF^{OLD})$ and $PV(CF^{NEW})$, for the old and new loans, respectively. The $PV(\ )$ function here refers to the DCF procedure, and CF^{OLD} represents the *remaining* cash flows in the old loan. CF^{NEW} represents the future cash flow stream in the new loan (after its initial disbursement to the borrower). In order to make an apples-to-apples comparison, both loans must be evaluated over the same time horizon, and for the same loan amount.[33] Furthermore, both loans must be evaluated using the current opportunity cost of capital as the discount rate. With the two loans evaluated in this manner, the **NPV of refinancing** for the borrower is defined as the value of the old liability minus the value of the new liability, quantified as $PV(CF^{OLD}) - PV(CF^{NEW})$, less any transaction costs the borrower faces in the refinancing deal.

This procedure is equivalent to calculating the net incremental difference in cash flows each period under the new loan compared to the old, and summing the present values of these periodic savings to the borrower. Using the same discount rate (the current opportunity cost of capital), the difference in the present values of the cash flows equals the present value of the differences in the cash flows:[34]

$$PV(CF^{OLD}) - PV(CF^{NEW}) = PV(CF^{OLD} - CF^{NEW})$$

Normally, the savings from refinancing will occur in the regular monthly payments, while the last cash flow in the analysis time horizon may involve an incremental cost to the borrower, as the new loan may at that time have a larger outstanding balance than the old loan would have had.

To implement this DCF procedure in practice, we need to define specifically how to determine the common time horizon applied to both loans, the amount of the new loan, and the discount rate. The common time horizon should be the expected time until the old loan would be likely to be paid off in the absence of refinancing, which at the latest is the maturity date of the old loan.[35] This may be earlier than the maturity of the replacement loan, in which case the replacement loan must be evaluated with expected cash flows corresponding to such early prepayment of the replacement loan. In order to keep the amount of debt constant, the new loan should be evaluated

---

[33] This condition is necessary in order to avoid mixing two distinct decisions: the refinancing decision and a decision to change the degree of leverage on the equity investment. The importance of keeping these two decisions separate can be seen by recourse to an extreme example. Suppose a $1,000,000 loan is to be refinanced with a $500,000 loan. The borrower will be getting rid of an old liability that has twice the magnitude of the new liability. Simply comparing the values of the two liabilities, it would appear that the borrower would be approximately $500,000 better off no matter what the difference in interest rates! Obviously, this would be misleading from the perspective of evaluating the refinancing decision per se. To isolate the NPV of this decision alone, we hold constant for analysis purposes the amount of debt in comparing the old loan with its replacement loan. Of course, in practice the investor may choose to change the amount of debt at the same time as the refinancing.

[34] This identity follows directly from the distributive law of multiplication and addition: $ab + ac = a(b + c)$.

[35] It may be earlier than the maturity if the loan has a due-on-sale clause.

for an amount such that the actual cash disbursement the borrower receives is just sufficient to pay off the old loan exactly. Thus, if the new loan has a disbursement discount, then the contractual principal borrowed on the new loan must exceed the current OLB plus prepayment penalty on the old loan. Finally, the opportunity cost of capital used as the discount rate in the analysis should be determined as the yield on the new loan, computed over the common time horizon. If the new loan has any disbursement discounts, or if the new loan has a prepayment penalty and the common time horizon is prior to the new loan's maturity, then this discount rate will, of course, exceed the contract interest rate in the new loan.

Shortcut Procedure. The preceding conditions on the discount rate and the amount of the new loan imply that a shortcut exists to quantify the difference between the new and old loan values. In effect, *we do not need to quantify the amount of the new loan or its payments*. Defining the opportunity cost of capital as the yield on the new loan assures that $PV(CF^{NEW})$ equals the cash disbursement to the borrower on that loan. And the condition on the new loan amount requires that this cash disbursement must equal the amount required to pay off the old loan, an amount we will label OLB^{OLD}. Thus, the conditions described above imply $PV(CF^{NEW}) = OLB^{OLD}$. The refinancing NPV can thus be redefined (apart from transaction costs) as: $PV(CF^{OLD}) - OLB^{OLD}$.

This result has an important conceptual implication. Fundamentally, the refinancing decision *is not a comparison of two loans*. Rather, it is a decision simply regarding the old loan: *Does it make sense to exercise the old loan's prepayment option?* It does not matter whether the old loan would be paid off with capital obtained from a new loan, or additional equity, or some combination of debt and equity. Thus, the refinancing decision is simply a comparison of the current liability value of the old loan with the cash that would currently be required to pay off the old loan. A new loan is necessary in the analysis only as a (possibly hypothetical) source for ascertaining the current relevant opportunity cost of capital.

An Example NPV Calculation. The best way to understand the traditional refinancing valuation is to consider a specific numerical example. Let's go back to our previously described 8%, $1,000,000 mortgage with 30-year amortization and 10-year maturity at origination. Suppose this loan was issued four years ago and has a prepayment option with a penalty of two points. Suppose that if not refinanced, this loan would probably be held to its maturity, six more years. Now suppose that new loans are available today with a maturity of six years at an interest rate of 7%, with one point of disbursement discount up front, and an amortization rate of 30 years. What is the net value of refinancing the old loan at this point in time (apart from transaction costs)? . . .

Step 1: Old Loan Liquidating Payment. Let's begin by calculating what it would take to pay off the old loan today. The outstanding balance on the old loan after four years (48 payments) is $962,190, and when we add two points of prepayment penalty this gives a liquidating payment of $1.02 \times 962,190 = \$981,434$.[36] This is the amount we labeled OLB^{OLD}.

Step 2: Opportunity Cost of Capital. Now let's compute the relevant cost of capital as the yield on the new loan over the remaining maturity on the old loan. We don't

[36]$962,190 = PV(0.08/12,26*12,7337.65) = FV(0.08/12,48*12,7337.65)$, where $7,337.65 = PMT(0.08/12,30*12,1000000)$

need to know the loan amount to do this. The loan would have monthly payments based on a 360-month level annuity at a simple interest rate of 7%/12 = 0.5833% per month. For every dollar of loan amount this is a monthly payment of 0.006653 dollars: $PMT(0.07/12,30*12,1) = 0.006653$. The balloon at the end of the six-year maturity on the new loan would be $0.926916 per dollar of loan amount:

$$PV(0.07/12,24*12, [PMT(0.07/12,30*12,1)]$$

$$= FV(0.07/12,6*12, [PMT(0.07/12,30*12,1)] = 0.926916$$

Considering the one-point disbursement discount up front, this gives the new loan a yield over the six-year horizon of 7.21%, as[37]

$$\$0.99 = \sum_{t=1}^{72} \frac{\$0.006653}{[1 + (0.0721/12)]^t} + \frac{\$0.926916}{[1 + (0.0721/12)]^{72}}$$

This would be the yield (or effective interest rate) no matter what the amount of the new loan. Thus, 7.21% is the current opportunity cost of capital (OCC) relevant to our refinancing calculation.

Step 3: Present Value of the Old Loan Liability. Now let's compute the present value of the old loan's remaining cash flows using the 7.21% OCC we just computed in step 2 as the discount rate. The old loan has regular monthly payments of $7,337.65 and a balloon payment of $877,247 at its maturity six years from now (10 years from the issuance of the loan).[38] Thus, the present value of this liability to the borrower is now $997,654, computed as[39]

$$\$997,654 = \sum_{t=1}^{72} \frac{\$7,337.65}{[1 + (0.0721/12)]^t} + \frac{\$877,247}{[1 + (0.0721/12)]^{72}}$$

This is the value we labeled $PV(CF^{OLD})$. Traditionally, this amount is viewed as the present value of the benefit of the refinancing to the borrower, as it is taken to represent the current value of the liability that would be removed by paying off the old loan.

Step 4: Computing the NPV. Now we can compute the traditional NPV of refinancing to the borrower before considering transaction costs. This is simply the present value of the benefit computed in step 3 less the amount of the liquidating payment computed in step 1:

$$NPV = \$997,654 - \$981,434 = \$16,220$$

This is the value of $PV(CF^{OLD}) - OLB^{OLD}$, including the prepayment penalty in OLB^{OLD}.

---

[37] $0.0721 = 12*RATE(6*12,0.006653,0.99,0.926916)$

[38] $\$877,247 = PV(0.08/12,20*12,7337.65) = FV(0.08/12,10*12,7337.65)$

[39] $\$997,654 = PV(0.0721/12,6*12,7337.65,877247)$

The Long Route: Specifying the New Loan. Let's confirm that this shortcut gives us the same NPV as if we specified the replacement loan amount. From step 1 we know we need $981,434 of cash disbursement from the new loan in order to pay off the old loan. As the new loan has a one-point disbursement discount, we would have to borrow $991,348 as the initial contractual principal in the new loan, computed as $981,434/0.99. At 7% interest, this gives the new loan a monthly payment of $6,595.46 and a balloon of $918,896 after six years.[40] We already know from step 2 that the yield on this new loan, over the six-year horizon, is 7.21%, including the effect of the one-point disbursement discount. Now, what is the present value of this new loan discounted at the 7.21% rate? Of course, it is $981,434! The yield, by definition, is the discount rate that causes the loan's future cash flows to have a present value exactly equal to its time-zero cash disbursement.[41] Thus, we can immediately confirm that the difference in the two loan values is $997,654 − $981,434 = $16,220. In other words, $PV(CF^{OLD})$ − $PV(CF^{NEW})$ = $PV(CF^{OLD})$ − OLB^{OLD}. We don't need to deal with the new loan, except as a means to ascertain the relevant current cost of capital.[42]

*17.3.2 What Is Left Out of the Traditional Calculation: Prepayment Option Value

According to the traditional analysis performed earlier, our example loan should be prepaid, as long as the transaction costs involved in obtaining the necessary capital are less than $16,220. Suppose, for example, that such transaction costs would be $10,000 (approximately 1% of the amount of capital required).[43] Then the NPV of paying off the old loan would be $16,220 − $10,000 = $6,220. However, something important has been left out of this analysis. We have ignored the value to the borrower of the prepayment option in the old loan. The DCF-based valuation of the old loan liability, $PV(CF^{OLD})$, did not account for the positive value of this option as an asset to the borrower.

That the prepayment option has a positive value to the borrower can be seen in the previous calculations. We have determined that by exercising this option today the borrower could increase the market value of its net wealth by $6,220, even after transaction costs. Clearly, the prepayment option is worth *at least* this much. But in paying off the old loan, the borrower extinguishes this prepayment option. An option

---

[40]$991,348 = PV(0.07/12,6*12,6595.46,918896)

[41]$981,834 = PV(0.0721/12,6*12,6595.46,918896)

[42]We also arrive at the same answer if we evaluate the incremental savings of the new loan versus the old within each period. The old-loan minus new-loan monthly payment is $7,337.65 − $6,595.46 = $742.19. The old-loan minus new-loan balloon payment after six years is $847,247 − $918,896 = −$41,649. The present value of these incremental cash flows is $16,220:

$$\$16,220 = \sum_{t=1}^{72} \frac{\$742.19}{[1 + (0.0721/12)]^t} - \frac{\$41,649}{[1 + (0.0721/12)]^{72}}$$

[43]These transaction costs would typically include third-party fees such as appraisal and title insurance costs that might not be included in the loan origination fee, or investment banker fees (in the case of equity capital). In addition, the borrower should consider their own costs involved in searching for replacement capital.

no longer exists after it is exercised.[44] The loss of this option is therefore a cost to the borrower if they prepay the old loan. How much is this option worth?[45]

To develop some basic intuition about the nature and value of the prepayment option, let's extend our previous example. In that example, current market interest rates are 7%. But what will interest rates be a year from now? We don't know for sure. But suppose we can characterize the future of interest rates one year from now by the following probabilities:[46]

5% with 50% probability
9% with 50% probability

We can calculate what the NPV of paying off the old loan would be under each of these two future interest rate scenarios. This is done simply by repeating the traditional DCF valuation procedure described in the previous section, only with the old loan advanced one more year into the future, and using the future interest rate scenarios as the basis for determining the OCC in each case. With five years paid off on the old loan its outstanding balance would be $950,699, and its required liquidating payment including prepayment penalty would be $969,713. Under the 5% market interest rate scenario the yield on a new loan would be 5.24% (with five years' maturity instead of six, and a 30-year amortization rate). Applying this discount rate to the old loan's five years of remaining cash flows to maturity gives a $PV(CF^{OLD})$ value of $1,062,160. This results in an NPV of loan prepayment of $1,062,160 − $969,713 = $92,448 prior to transaction costs, or $82,448 net of these costs, under the 5% interest rate scenario.

Similar calculations reveal that under the 9% interest scenario, prepaying the old loan would have a *negative* NPV to the borrower of $75,078 (including the $10,000 transaction cost). With market interest rates at 9%, it would obviously not make sense for the borrower to pay off an 8% loan. However, a basic characteristic of options is that they provide their owner with a *right without obligation*. The borrower does not have to prepay the old loan just because he has the option to do so. Obviously, if the 9% interest rate scenario occurred, the borrower would not exercise the prepayment option on the 8% loan.

Considering the previous analysis, we can see that the prepayment option in the old loan provides the borrower with the following **contingent values** one year from now:

$82,448 in the 5% scenario
$0 in the 9% scenario

[44] It is true that a new loan used to replace the old loan might also have a prepayment option. But this option will have very little current value because the new loan is at the market interest rate. Furthermore, the borrower would have to pay for a prepayment option in a new loan (the presence of such an option is one reason the yield on a new loan would be as high as it is), whereas the borrower already owns the option in the old loan.

[45] As noted in Chapter 16, the prepayment option is a call option on a bondlike asset whose value is $PV(CF^{OLD})$ and whose exercise price is OLB^{OLD}. (Call options give their holders the right without obligation to acquire an underlying asset upon the payment of an exercise price.) The rigorous and complete valuation of such an option requires a very technical analysis that is beyond the scope of this book.

[46] Historically, the annual standard deviation of the yield on long-term government bonds has been on the order of 200 basis points, the standard deviation our interest rate probability function assumed here. Thus, this numerical example, though crude, is not out of the ballpark for realistic implications.

These values are contingent because they depend on which interest rate scenario actually occurs. However, given the 50% probability for each scenario, we can compute the expected value, as of today, of the prepayment option next year. It is[47]

$$(50\%) * (\$82,448) + (50\%) * (0) = \$41,224$$

How much is this expected future value worth today? To find out, we must discount it to present value using a risk-adjusted discount rate that reflects the amount of risk in the prepayment option value. Such options tend to be quite risky. Witness the large range in possible value outcomes next year between the two scenarios: $82,448 versus nothing. Thus, we should use a high discount rate. Suppose, for example, the market would require a 30% expected return for investing in such an option.[48] Then the present value of the prepayment option today (given our future interest rate scenario) is $31,711 = $41,224/1.30.

If the prepayment option is worth anything like this much, then clearly it would not make sense to pay off the old mortgage today. Prepayment today, when interest rates are 7%, has an NPV of $6,220, as we have seen, ignoring the option value. Not prepaying today, but rather waiting until next year to see what happens with interest rates, has an NPV of $31,711, ignoring the current payoff value. These two possibilities are mutually exclusive. We cannot both pay off the old loan today and wait until next year and see if we prefer to pay it off next year instead. Each course of action rules out the other. Recall the basic NPV investment decision criterion: *Maximize the NPV across all mutually exclusive alternatives*. Thus, the classical NPV criterion tells us that we should choose the wait-and-see alternative, given the interest rate scenario we have assumed here. The $31,711 NPV is preferable to the $6,220 NPV.

We can also obtain this same result by properly including the prepayment option value in the valuation of the old loan. The prepayment option value is positive to the borrower, but negative to the lender.[49] Labeling *C(Prepay)* as the market value of the prepayment option, and *D(Old)* as the market value of the old loan, we have

$$D(Old) = PV(CF^{OLD}) - C(Prepay) \tag{1}$$

The market-value-based NPV of old loan prepayment, from the borrower's perspective, is therefore:

$$NPV(Prepay) = D(Old) - OLB^{OLD} - TC \tag{2}$$

where *TC* is the borrower's transaction costs in the deal.

Equation (2) simply says that when the market value of the existing loan exceeds the cash that would be required to pay off that loan (including the transaction costs), then refinancing will have a positive impact on the borrower's net wealth.

---

[47] Actually, the expected value of the option next year is at least this great, as we have ignored any possibility that the option might be even more valuable if it were not exercised in the 5% scenario.

[48] Rigorous option value theory uses arbitrage arguments to avoid having to estimate this discount rate. However, it is not uncommon for call options to provide expected returns well in excess of 20% even when they are "in the money."

[49] The holder of the short position in the loan holds the long position in the prepayment option. Similarly, the holder of the long position in the loan holds the short position in the prepayment option.

As the market value of the old loan already incorporates the value of the prepayment option (which reflects the possible value of waiting to prepay the old loan later), paying off the old loan will be currently optimal for the borrower whenever equation (2) is positive. Combining (1) and (2), we see that

$$NPV(Prepay) = PV(CF^{OLD}) - C(Prepay) - OLB^{OLD} - TC \tag{3}$$

This makes it clear that the $C(Prepay)$ component is left out of the traditional refinancing analysis. Because option value is always positive, the traditional, purely DCF-based approach will be biased in favor of refinancing, tending to give too high a value for the NPV in equation (3). In fact, because of the value of the prepayment option, it will never be optimal to pay off a loan as soon as market yields drop just a little bit below the interest rate on the old loan.

It is important to recognize that in a highly liquid debt market, $D(Old)$ could be observed empirically from the prices (yields) of traded bonds or mortgage-backed securities, and these prices would include the value of the $C(Prepay)$ component. However, most commercial mortgages are unique and held privately as whole loans, not securitized or traded on the bond market. It is often difficult to find a liquid asset closely comparable to a given mortgage.[50] This makes it necessary to evaluate the prepayment option component explicitly in order to obtain a precise computation of the market-value-based NPV of loan prepayment.

In practice, a simplistic rule of thumb is often applied to deal with the prepayment option value effect. When yields on new loans get to around 200 basis points below the interest rate on the old loan, prepayment likely makes sense even considering the prepayment option value. However, if not much maturity is left on the old loan, or if one has good reason to believe that market interest rates may fall further in the near future, then it may still not make sense to pay off the old loan.[51] On the other hand, if the loan has a long time remaining before maturity, or if one has good reason to believe that interest rates are about as low as they will go, then it may make sense to refinance even if current interest rates are less than 200 basis points below the old loan rate.

17.4 CHAPTER SUMMARY

Building on Chapters 8 and 16, this chapter presented the basic nuts and bolts for quantifying mortgage cash flows and yields. We saw how to apply this knowledge in loan valuation and in addressing related decisions such as refinancing. The procedures and methods presented here are as relevant for residential loans as for commercial loans, and as important to borrowers as they are to lenders.

---

[50] What is needed is comparability in the contract interest rate, maturity, prepayment ability (including penalties), and default risk. Similar size of the loan may also be important if there are economies of scale in prepayment transaction costs.

[51] Also, a substantial prepayment penalty or abnormally large transaction costs can eliminate the value of prepayment to the borrower.

KEY TERMS

four basic rules of payments and
   balances
outstanding loan balance (OLB)
contract principal (L)
interest owed (INT)
amortization of principal (AMORT)
payment amount (PMT)
contract interest rate (r)
interest-only loan
constant-amortization mortgage
   (CAM)
constant-payment mortgage (CPM)
balloon payment

graduated payment mortgage
   (GPM)
negative amortization
adjustable rate mortgage (ARM)
yield curve
margin (in ARM)
index (in ARM)
teaser rate
fixed rate mortgage (FRM)
yield (IRR)
yield-to-maturity (YTM)
origination fee
discount points

basis points
par value
prepayment penalty
annual percentage rate (APR)
effective interest rate
mortgage menu
mortgage-equivalent yield (MEY)
bond- or coupon-equivalent yield
   (BEY, CEY)
prepayment option
refinancing
NPV of refinancing
contingent value

STUDY QUESTIONS

Conceptual Questions

17.1.   Describe the four basic rules for computing loan payments and balances. How would you implement these rules in a computer spreadsheet?

17.2.   How is rule 2 derived from the order of application of payments clause?

17.3.   In what sense is a mortgage with a 12% annual interest rate really a 1% mortgage when it has monthly payments?

17.4.   What are the major advantages and disadvantages of interest-only loans for both borrowers and lenders, as compared to amortizing loans?

17.5.   In what type of economy might a CAM be most useful? What are the major problems with CAMs in a nondeflationary economy?

17.6.   What advantages do CPMs have over CAMs and interest-only loans?

17.7.   Describe the general relationship among the amortization rate, maturity, regular payment, and balloon payment in a CPM.

17.8.   What are the advantages and disadvantages (for both the borrower and lender) of a GPM, as compared to an otherwise similar CPM? Under what circumstances (economic and property-specific) will a GPM be most useful?

17.9.   What are the major advantages and disadvantages of ARMs from the borrower's and lender's perspective? How does an ARM subject the lender to less interest rate risk than does a CPM? In what economic circumstances (e.g., interest rate environment) will ARMs be most useful?

17.10. What are the conditions in which the YTM will equal the contract interest rate on the mortgage?

17.11. At the time of loan issuance in the primary market, what can we say in general about the relationship between the YTM and the contract interest rate if the loan has disbursement discount points?

17.12. **a.** What is the difference between the quoted YTM and the expected return (going-in IRR) for the typical mortgage investors? [Hint: Describe two sources of difference.]

b. When will the expected return (over the realistic prepayment horizon) exceed the YTM in a default-free loan?

17.13. What is the APR, and how is it related to the YTM?

17.14. **a.** What are some of the major reasons up-front points and fees are so common in the mortgage business?

b. What is the major reason for the existence of prepayment penalties?

17.15. What is a mortgage menu, and how can it be advantageous to borrowers (and therefore to lenders trying to attract borrowers)?

17.16. **a.** How can the refinancing decision be evaluated as a comparison of two loan values?

b. How must you define the new loan (or replacement loan) in such an analysis.

c. Why is the refinancing decision not, fundamentally, a comparison of two loan values?

d. What is it instead?

17.17. What is the relevant opportunity cost of capital to use as the discount rate in a refinancing evaluation?

17.18. Why is it important to keep the loan amount constant between the old and new loan in a refinancing analysis?

17.19. What is left out in the traditional DCF-based valuation of the refinancing decision?

17.20. **a.** Why might it not make sense to refinance a loan with a prepayment option as soon as the market yield on new loans dips below the contract rate on the old loan?

b. How is the prepayment option value incorporated in the classical NPV investment decision criterion applied to the refinancing decision?

17.21. Describe the rule of thumb commonly applied in practice to deal with the effect of the prepayment option on the refinancing decision.

Quantitative Problems

17.22. Consider a $2 million, 8%, 30-year mortgage with monthly payments. Compute the first three payments and the loan balance after the third payment for each of the following loan types: (a) interest-only, (b) CAM, (c) CPM.

17.23. Consider a $2 million, 8%, 30-year GPM with monthly payments and two annual step-ups of 10% each (one after the first 12 payments, and the other after the 24th payment).

a. What is the initial monthly payment on this loan (prior to the first step-up)?

b. What is the final monthly payment level (after the second step-up)?

17.24. Consider a $2 million, 30-year ARM with monthly payments and annual interest adjustments. The initial interest rate is 6%. The index for the loan is one-year U.S. government bonds, currently yielding 5.5%. The loan has a margin of 250 basis points.

　　a. Is the loan's initial interest rate a teaser rate? How do you know?

　　b. If one-year T-bonds remain at 5.5%, what will be the applicable interest rate for this mortgage after the first year?

　　c. What are the initial monthly payments on this loan?

　　d. Assuming T-bonds remain at 5.5%, what will be the monthly payments after the first year?

　　e. Under that assumption (and assuming no discount points), what is the forecasted yield-to-maturity on this loan at the time it is issued, assuming it has no discount points?

17.25. Consider a $2 million, 8% CPM with monthly payments. What is the regular monthly payment and the balloon payment amounts in each of the following cases:

　　a. Fully amortizing, 25-year loan

　　b. 25-year amortization, 10-year balloon

　　c. 15-year amortization, 10-year balloon

　　d. What is the major disadvantage, and advantage, of the 15-year amortization-rate 10-year loan in (c) as compared to the 25-year amortization-rate 10-year loan in (b)?

17.26. Consider a $2 million, 7.5%, 30-year mortgage with monthly payments. What is the YTM of this loan under the following circumstances:

　　a. No points, fully amortizing

　　b. Two points of disbursement discount, fully amortizing

　　c. Two points of disbursement discount, 8-year maturity with balloon.

17.27. Consider a $2 million, 7.5%, 30-year mortgage with monthly payments and an expected realistic prepayment horizon of eight years. What is the contractual yield (effective interest rate) at issuance over the expected life of the loan under the following circumstances:

　　a. No points or penalties

　　b. One point of disbursement discount

　　c. Two points of disbursement discount

　　d. Two points of disbursement discount plus one point of prepayment penalty

17.28. Consider a $2 million, 7.5%, 30-year mortgage with monthly payments and an eight-year maturity with balloon.

　　a. How much is this loan worth at issuance if the market YTM for such loans is 7.125% BEY?

　　b. If instead the market yield is 7.875%, how many disbursement discount points must the lender charge to avoid doing a negative-NPV deal?

17.29. A lender wants to achieve a 7.5% yield (MEY) on a 30-year amortization, monthly-payment loan with an eight-year maturity with balloon. How many disbursement discount points must the lender charge under the following circumstances:

    a. Contract interest rate is 7.25%

    b. Contract interest rate is 7.0%.

17.30. **a.** As a borrower, which of the following two 25-year, monthly-payment loans would you choose if you had a 15-year expected prepayment horizon: 6% interest rate with four points, or 6.75% interest with one-half point?

    b. Suppose your prepayment horizon was five years?

*17.31. Three years ago you obtained a 10%, $6 million, monthly-payment mortgage with 20-year amortization and an eight-year maturity. (The loan thus matures five years from now, with a balloon payment.) This loan has a prepayment clause, but stipulates a three-point prepayment penalty on the outstanding balance. Today, it would be possible to obtain a similar mortgage at 8% interest with a one-point origination fee up front and 20-year amortization.

    a. Assuming transaction costs would be $60,000, and the current value of the prepayment option in the old loan is $150,000, what is your NPV for paying off the old loan today?

    b. If you could reduce the transaction costs to $50,000, should you pay the loan off immediately?

*17.32. Consider the same old loan as in question 17.31, only now suppose interest rates have risen instead of fallen, so that similar loans today would carry a 12% interest rate. Suppose further that the old loan has no due-on-sale clause, and you want to sell the property that is collateral on the loan. A buyer is willing to pay $10 million for the property, but has only $2 million available, and does not feel comfortable with the payments on an $8 million mortgage at 12%, although he would do the deal at 11.5% with a 30-year amortization rate and a 10-year balloon.

    a. What would be your yield on your investment in a wraparound loan meeting the seller's specifications?

    b. Why are you able to get an expected return on this investment so much in excess of the current market rate of 12%?

*17.33. A commercial mortgage is written for $1 million at 8% with 30-year amortization and a 10-year balloon payment. A yield-maintenance prepayment penalty is included as follows. If the borrower pays the loan off early, she must pay the lender an amount such that if the lender reinvests the proceeds (including the prepayment penalty) in U.S. Treasury Bonds maturing on the same date as the original maturity of the mortgage, the lender will receive the same 8% mortgage-equivalent YTM on the loan's outstanding balance as she would have received in the mortgage over the remaining time until the loan's original maturity. Now suppose the borrower prepays the loan after seven years. Suppose that on that date three-year government bonds are yielding 6% (bond-equivalent yield). How much prepayment penalty must the borrower pay? (Compute your answer based on coupon-equivalent yield, converting the mortgage MEY to its equivalent BEY.)

*17.34. A commercial mortgage is written for $1 million at 8% with 30-year amortization and a 10-year balloon payment. A yield-maintenance prepayment penalty is included as follows. If the borrower pays the loan off early, he must pay the lender the present value of the remaining contractual payments on the loan discounted at the then-prevailing rates on T-bonds of a maturity equivalent to the remaining time on the loan, plus a margin of 50 basis points. (The difference between MEY and BEY is ignored, that is, the BEY T-bond rate plus margin is applied directly, to the remaining monthly cash flows in the loan as if it were a MEY rate.) Now suppose the borrower prepays the loan after seven years. Suppose that on that date three-year government bonds are yielding 5.50%. How much prepayment penalty must the borrower pay?

Commercial Mortgage Analysis and Underwriting

Learning Objectives

After reading this chapter, you should understand:

◆ How to quantify the effect of default risk on the expected returns to commercial mortgages.

◆ How commercial mortgage underwriting procedures are related to default risk.

◆ The major traditional procedures and measures used in commercial mortgage underwriting in the United States.

◆ What is meant by a participating mortgage, and how such loans can be useful.

The previous two chapters familiarized you with the fundamentals of mortgages, basic concepts and considerations that are relevant to both borrowers and lenders, for both residential and commercial mortgages. In this chapter we will focus more specifically on issues that are most relevant to commercial mortgage lenders and investors. (Of course, an appreciation of the lender's perspective can also be very useful to borrowers who must negotiate with lenders.) This chapter is divided into two main parts. After an introduction discussing some quantitative aspects of default risk, we will describe the nuts and bolts of typical commercial mortgage underwriting. A third section at the end introduces an important type of commercial mortgage, the participating loan.

18.1 EXPECTED RETURNS VERSUS STATED YIELDS: MEASURING THE IMPACT OF DEFAULT RISK

The previous chapter described in depth how to compute the yield-to-maturity (YTM) for a mortgage. We noted that the yield computed in this way is a **contract yield**, or what is often referred to as a **stated yield**, as distinct from a realistic **expected return**. The former is based on the contractual cash flow terms of the mortgage, while the latter recognizes the realistic probability of default and foreclosure. To distinguish these two measure of return, in the present chapter we will use the abbreviation YTM to refer to the contract yield, and $E[r]$ to refer to the expected return (which may also be referred to as the expected yield or ex ante yield).[1]

In practice, quoted yields are always contract yields, and people work with contract yields when designing and evaluating mortgages. However, for mortgage *investors*, whether they are loan originators or buyers in the secondary market, realistic expected returns are the more fundamental measure for making investment decisions. The difference between the stated yield and the expected return quantifies the impact of the default risk in the ex ante return that the lender cares about.

18.1.1 Yield Degradation and Conditional Cash Flows

In the commercial mortgage business, shortfalls to the lender as a result of default and foreclosure are referred to as **credit losses**. The effect of credit losses on the realized yield as compared to the contractual yield is referred to as **yield degradation**. To understand how to quantify the difference between stated and expected yields in mortgage investments, let's begin by examining yield degradation with a simple numerical example.

Suppose an interest-only mortgage is issued by Sue to that famous (and fearless) real estate investor, Bob. The loan is for $100 at an interest rate of 10%, for three years, with annual payments. Thus, the contractual cash flows under the loan call for two annual payments of $10 followed by $110 at the end of the third year. As there are no points or origination fees, the contractual YTM on this loan at origination is 10%. Therefore, at the end of the third year, if Bob has met his contractual cash flow obligations, the realized yield on the loan will also be 10%.

Now suppose that Bob makes his first two payments all right, but when it comes time for the third payment, he defaults. Sue takes the property and sells it immediately, but she is only able to get 70% of what is owed, or $77. In this case, the credit loss is $33, and 70% is referred to as the **recovery rate**. Sue would have experienced a **loss severity** of 30%. The result would be a realized yield on the mortgage of −1.12%, computed as the IRR on the actual cash flows to the lender:

$$0 = -\$100 + \frac{\$10}{1 + (-0.0112)} + \frac{\$10}{[1 + (-0.0112)]^2} + \frac{\$77}{[1 + (-0.0112)]^3}$$

The yield degradation is 11.12%, as the realized yield of −1.12% is this much less than the contract yield of 10.00%. The yield degradation is how much the lender

[1]Note that the use of $E[r]$ in this context is consistent with our previous use of this label in Parts III–V of this book where it referred to the mean of the probability distribution of the future return.

loses compared to what she was supposed to get, measured as a multiperiod lifetime return on the original investment.

From an ex ante perspective, analyzing Bob's mortgage beforehand, we would refer to this 11.12% yield degradation as a **conditional yield degradation**. It is the yield degradation that will occur *if* Bob defaults in the third year, and *if* Sue ends up getting 70% of the OLB at that time. The 70% recovery rate is also a conditional rate, conditioned on the default occurring in the third year. Thus, ex ante, the 11.12% yield degradation is *conditional* on these events or assumptions.

Suppose Bob couldn't even come up with the second payment on the loan, so he defaulted at the end of the second year, and Sue foreclosed immediately and recovered 70% of the OLB. In this case the realized yield would be −7.11%, as

$$0 = -\$100 + \frac{\$10}{1 + (-0.0711)} + \frac{\$77}{[1 + (-0.0711)]^2}$$

The yield degradation would therefore be 17.11%. This points to an important fact. Other things being equal (in particular, the conditional recovery rate), *the conditional yield degradation is greater, the earlier the default occurs in the loan life*. Lenders are hit worse when default occurs early in the life of a mortgage.

Now let's consider the relation among the contract yield, the conditional yield degradation, and the expected return on the mortgage. After all, the expected return is most relevant to the mortgage investor at the time when the decision is made to invest in the loan (i.e., to issue the loan). As the expected return is an *ex ante* measure, we must specify the ex ante probability of default and the expected conditional recovery rate or loss severity. Suppose that at the time the mortgage is issued, there is a 10% probability that Bob will default in the third year of the mortgage and that Sue will then recover 70% of the OLB. Suppose there is no chance of any other default event. Thus, there is a 90% chance Sue will make the contract yield, and a 10% chance she will make that yield less the third-year conditional yield degradation of 11.12%. Under these circumstances, the expected return at the time the mortgage is issued is approximately equal to 8.89%, computed as follows:

$$8.89\% = (0.9)10.00\% + (0.1)(-1.12\%)$$
$$= (0.9)10.00\% + (0.1)(10.00\% - 11.12\%)$$
$$= 10.00\% - (0.1)(11.12\%)$$

In general, the expected return, which we will label $E[r]$, is given by the contract yield (labeled YTM), minus the product of the default probability (labeled $PrDEF$) times the conditional yield degradation (labeled $YDEGR$):

$$E[r] = YTM - (PrDEF)(YDEGR) \qquad (1)$$

*18.1.2 Hazard Functions and the Timing of Default

In this example we simplified the problem of computing the expected return by assuming there is only one point in the life of the mortgage when default can occur. In reality, default conceivably can occur at any point in time. This possibility is represented by what is known as a **hazard function**. The hazard function tells the conditional probability of default at each point in time given that default has not already occurred before then. As an example, let's consider Bob's simple three-year loan again. Suppose that the hazard function representing the conditional probability of Bob defaulting in each year is given in the following table:

Year	Hazard
1	1%
2	2%
3	3%

This means that there is a 1% chance Bob will default in the first year (i.e., at the time of the first payment), a 2% chance that he will default in the second year *if he has not already defaulted in the first year*, and a 3% chance he will default in the third year if he has not already defaulted by then.

Once we know the hazard function for a mortgage, we can compute the cumulative and unconditional default and survival probabilities, as shown in the following table.

Year	Hazard	Conditional Survival	Cumulative Survival	Unconditional PrDEF	Cumulative PrDEF
1	0.01	$1 - .01 = 0.9900$	$0.99 \times 1.0000 = 0.9900$	$.01 \times 1.0000 = 0.0100$	0.0100
2	0.02	$1 - .02 = 0.9800$	$0.98 \times 0.9900 = 0.9702$	$.02 \times 0.9900 = 0.0198$	$.0100 + .0198 = 0.0298$
3	0.03	$1 - .03 = 0.9700$	$0.97 \times 0.9702 = 0.9411$	$.03 \times 0.9702 = 0.0291$	$.0298 + .0291 = 0.0589$

The **conditional survival probability** in each year is 1 minus the hazard for that year. It is the probability the loan will not default in that year, given that it has not defaulted prior to that year. The **cumulative survival probability** is the probability that the loan has survived (not defaulted) through the given year. This is the product of all the previous conditional survival probabilities (including the given year). The **unconditional default probability** is the probability, as of the time of loan origination, that default will occur in a given year. It equals the hazard in that year times the cumulative survival probability through the end of the previous year.[2] This is an unconditional probability because it does not depend on the conditioning assumption of the loan not having yet defaulted prior to the given year. The cumulative default probability is the probability, as of the time of loan origination, that the loan will have defaulted during or prior to the given year. It equals the sum of the unconditional default probabilities up to and including the given year, and it also equals one minus the cumulative survival through the given year.

Thus, the probability that the loan will default at any time during its life is the **cumulative default probability** through the end of the loan maturity, or (equivalently) the sum of all the unconditional default probabilities across all the years in the loan life. With hazards of 1%, 2%, and 3%, the ex ante probability that Bob will default at some point in the life of his three-year loan is 5.89% (computed as $0.0589 = 0.0100 + 0.0198 + 0.0291 = 1 - 0.9411$).[3]

---

[2] The unconditional default probability can also be computed as the difference in the cumulative survival probability at the beginning and end of the given year (e.g., $0.0291 = 0.9702 - 0.9411$).

[3] Note that this is less than the sum of all the individual hazards.

For each year in the life of the loan, a conditional yield degradation can be computed, conditional on default occurring in that year, and given an assumption about the conditional recovery rate in that year. For example, we saw that with Bob's loan the conditional yield degradation was 11.12% if default occurs in year 3, and 17.11% if default occurs in year 2, in both cases assuming a 70% recovery rate. Similar calculations reveal that the conditional yield degradation would be 22.00% if default occurs in year 1 with an 80% recovery rate.[4]

Defaults in each year of a loan's life and no default at all in the life of the loan represent mutually exclusive events that together exhaust all of the possible default timing occurrences for any loan. For example, with the three-year loan, Bob will either default in year 1, year 2, year 3, or never. Thus, the expected return on the loan can be computed as the contractual yield minus the sum across all the years of the products of the *unconditional* default probabilities times the conditional yield degradations. This is simply a generalization of formula (1):

$$E[r] = YTM - \sum_{t=1}^{T} (PrDEF_t)(YDEGR_t)$$

where $PrDEF_t$ is the unconditional default probability in year t, $YDEGR_t$ is the conditional yield degradation in year t, and there are T years in the life of the loan.

For example, given the previously stated hazard function (1%, 2%, and 3% for the successive years) and conditional recovery rates (80%, 70%, and 70% for the successive years), the expected return on Bob's 10% mortgage at the time it is issued would be

$$
\begin{aligned}
E[r] &= 10.00\% - [(.0100)(22.00\%) + (.0198)(17.11\%) + (.0291)(11.12\%)] \\
&= 10.00\% - 0.88\% \\
&= 9.12\%
\end{aligned}
$$

The 88 basis-point shortfall of the expected return below the contractual yield is the **ex ante yield degradation** in Bob's mortgage. This might also be referred to as an **unconditional yield degradation**. It reflects the ex ante credit loss expectation in the mortgage as of the time of its issuance.

18.1.3 Yield Degradation in Typical Commercial Mortgages

How large is the ex ante yield degradation in typical commercial mortgages in the United States? To answer this question we need to know something about the hazard function that is typical of commercial mortgages. Surprisingly enough, there was relatively little publicly available information on this subject until the 1990s.

---

[4] This is computed as (80%) × ($110)/[1+(−.12)] = $100, so −12% is the conditional return, and −12% is 22% less than the contractual yield of 10%. Note that in computing the conditional yield, the conditional recovery rate is applied to the OLB at the time of the default, in this case $110. This reflects the fact that the lender would accelerate the loan in the event of default so that the entire outstanding balance would be due at that time. It is likely that a greater proportion of the loan balance could be recovered from a foreclosure in the first year, as there is less time for the property to have lost value subsequent to loan issuance. So it is plausible to assume a recovery rate of 80% in the first year if the subsequent rate is 70%.

Exhibit 18-1 Typical Commercial Mortgage Hazard Rates (Source: Esaki, l'Heureux, and Snyderman [1999].)

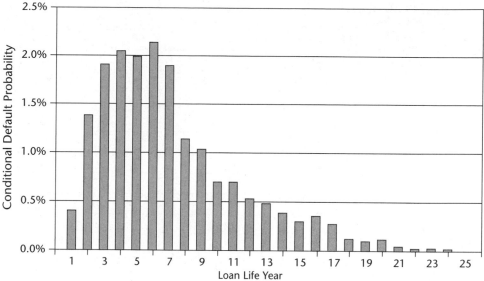

Since then, a growing number of studies have contributed to our ability to analyze commercial mortgages rationally.

Exhibit 18-1 portrays the empirical hazard function found in an influential study by Esaki, l'Heureux, and Snyderman (1999) that examined over 15,000 individual commercial mortgages issued from 1972 through 1992 by major life insurance companies that are members of the American Council of Life Insurers (ACLI).[5] Note that the hazard function is characteristically humpbacked. The probability of default immediately after loan issuance is relatively low, but rises rapidly, peaking in the early-to-middle years of the loan life, before falling off in the later years. Constant-payment loans are most likely to get into trouble roughly during the third through seventh year of the life of the loan.[6] In the ACLI data the hazard probabilities peak at just over 2% in the sixth year and fall off rapidly after the seventh year. The implied mean time until default (if it occurs) is just under seven years.

Exhibit 18-2 portrays the cumulative survival function implied by the hazard probabilities in Exhibit 18-1. The implied cumulative lifetime default probability is slightly over 16%. Roughly one in six commercial mortgages issued by life insurance companies in the United States during the 1972–92 period defaulted.[7]

[5] This study was an update and extension of work begun by Mark Snyderman (1990). The ACLI publishes data on loan defaults in the *ACLI Quarterly Survey of Mortgage Loan Delinquencies and Foreclosures*. In the Esaki, l'Heureux, and Snyderman study, a loan was considered to be defaulted if it was reported as being more than 90 days delinquent.

[6] It would seem reasonable to expect that loans with large balloon payments, such as interest-only loans, would tend to run into trouble when they come due, although the Esaki study finds little historical empirical evidence of this (Esaki et al. [1999]).

[7] Esaki et al. (1999) reported that the default rate on loans with at least 10 years of seasoning (defaults through 1997 on loans issued through 1987) was 18.1%.

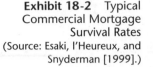

Exhibit 18-2 Typical Commercial Mortgage Survival Rates (Source: Esaki, l'Heureux, and Snyderman [1999].)

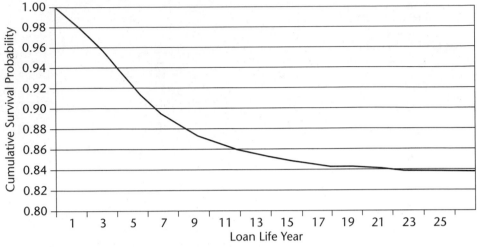

Historical default rates have varied widely depending on when the loans were issued. This is depicted in Exhibit 18-3. The bars in the exhibit indicate the lifetime default rates for loans issued in each of the years 1972–92, based on the Esaki et al. study. The line in the graph traces the relative level of commercial property values, based on the NCREIF index.[8]

The historical lifetime default rates shown in Exhibit 18-3 are relatively low on cohorts of loans issued in years when property values were relatively low. For example, loans issued in the mid-to-late 1970s had lifetime default rates around 10%. Of the loans issued in the early 1990s, only a little over 5% had defaulted through the end of 1997. On the other hand, loans issued when property values were relatively high, such as the early 1970s and mid-1980s, had much higher lifetime default rates, peaking at over 27% for loans issued in 1986. When property values were relatively low, mortgage issuers granted only relatively small loan amounts, and subsequent rises in property values made default relatively rare. When property values were relatively high, larger loans were issued and there was an increased probability that subsequent falls in property market values would put the loans "under water" (i.e., the loan OLB would be greater than the value of the property collateral securing the loan).[9]

Default probabilities are not the only type of information necessary to estimate the typical magnitude of ex ante yield degradation in U.S. commercial mortgages. We also need information on conditional recovery rates or loss severities once default occurs. This type of information is more difficult to obtain, although more is becoming available all the time.

The Esaki et al. study reported an average conditional recovery rate of 62%. This included the effects of foreclosure expenses as well as lost interest and principal based

---

[8] The NCREIF index appreciation value levels in Exhibit 18-3 have been "unsmoothed" by the authors and extended back in time using additional data.

[9] As noted previously, this type of behavior has been described as a "Santa Claus approach," in which borrowers are rewarded (that is, loaned more capital) when they have done well and penalized (given less capital) when they have performed poorly, during the recent past. Indeed, if real estate markets are cyclical, and the LTV ratios at which lenders will grant loans are constant, then this could result in the type of default rate cyclicality suggested in Exhibit 18-3.

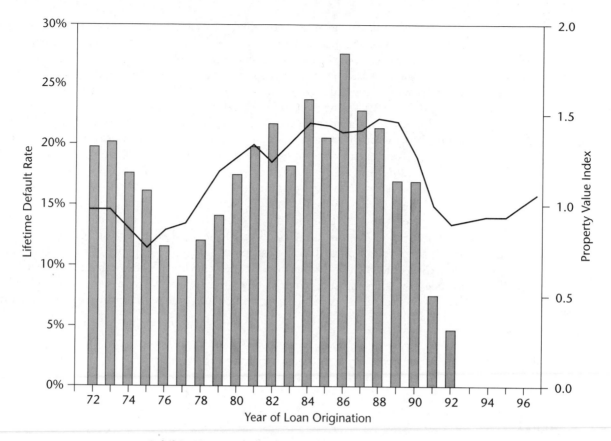

Exhibit 18-3 Lifetime Default Rates and Property Values
(Sources: Esaki, l'Heureux, and Snyderman [1999]; NCREIF index.)

on the *reported* value of the property at the time of foreclosure. However, a more detailed study by Ciochetti (1998) tracked 308 foreclosed mortgages from "cradle to grave," including the period subsequent to foreclosure when the property was owned by the lender (as "real estate owned"—REO). The loans had all originated between 1974 and 1990. Ciochetti found that while the average recovery was 57% based on reported property value as of the time of foreclosure (implying 6.5% conditional yield degradation), the average recovery was only 34% through to the final disposition of the collateral property by the lender (implying 10.6% conditional yield degradation).[10] This suggests that the Esaki et al. conditional recovery statistics may be a bit optimistic. Nevertheless, as of the late 1990s it was widely assumed that conditional recovery rates were typically in the 60% to 70% range.[11]

[10] This does not necessarily imply that the lender lost money on the property during the REO period. It may be that the reported value of the property as of the time of foreclosure (the value at which the lender took ownership) was higher than the true market value of the property at that time.

[11] For example, a 35% loss severity (recovery of 65%) has been assumed in the Giliberto-Levy Commercial Mortgage Price Index. As the Ciochetti statistics were based on the experience of only one lender and covered the effects of the historically severe property market "crash" of the early 1990s, it is possible that they overstate typical loss severity.

Default probabilities and conditional recovery statistics can be combined to provide estimates of conditional and ex ante yield degradation for typical loans.[12] Such information is used in the construction of indices of the periodic returns to commercial mortgages, based on synthetic portfolios of typical mortgages. By the late 1990s the most widely used such index was the Giliberto-Levy Commercial Mortgage Price Index (GLCMPI).[13] The GLCMPI includes estimates of the magnitude of credit losses suffered in the index total return each quarter as a fraction of the OLB of all loans. On an annualized basis these credit losses provide an approximate indication of the magnitude of the **ex post yield degradation** realized by the aggregate portfolio of outstanding loans during each year.

Exhibit 18-4 shows the magnitude of annual credit losses in the GLCMPI over the 1972–98 period (measured in basis points of outstanding par value). As we would expect, credit losses are higher during downturns in the commercial property asset market (mid-1970s, early 1990s). Credit losses peaked at almost 240 basis points in 1992, but were as low as 10–20 basis points during boom years. Ex post realizations of credit loss are certainly more volatile than expectations beforehand. However, averaged across a long span of time, ex post credit losses provide some indication of the typical ex ante yield degradation in permanent commercial mortgages in the United

Exhibit 18-4
Commercial Mortgage
Credit Loss as Fraction
of Par Value
(Source: GLCMPI
(John B. Levy & Co.)

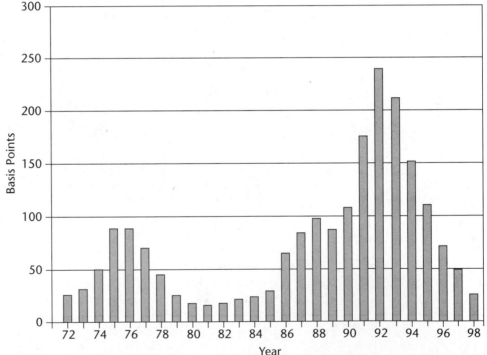

[12] It must be recognized that not all defaulting loans are foreclosed, as some defaults are worked out, as described in Chapter 16. However, lenders usually still suffer losses in such cases. In addition, lenders suffer some losses from loan delinquencies that are not classified as defaults (e.g., delinquencies of less than 90 days).

[13] The GLCMPI is published by John B. Levy & Co., Richmond, VA.

Is It Surprising that So Many Commercial Mortgages Default?

No borrower plans on defaulting on a loan when he takes it out. And lenders go to lots of trouble to try to avoid making loans that will default. So is it surprising that about one out of every six long-term commercial mortgages in the United States defaults? Well, not really, when you go back to fundamentals.

The most fundamental fact is *volatility*. Recall in Chapter 9 that we suggested that the typical individual commercial property probably has an annual volatility in excess of 15%. This means that the annual standard deviation in a typical property's appreciation return (or change in value) is at least about 15% of its initial value. Now recall that the normal probability distribution has about one third of its total probability beyond one standard deviation from its mean. This implies that about one sixth of the probable value outcomes are at or below one standard deviation *below* the mean outcome. Suppose the expected (i.e., mean) property value a year from now is the same as the current property value. Then 15% annual volatility implies that there is about a one-sixth chance that a given property will be worth, one year from now, 85% or less of its current value. Now suppose property values follow a "random walk" through time. In other words, suppose property values change randomly across time, like stock market values. (Whether the value rose or fell during the past year does not tell you anything about whether it will rise or fall next year, like the flipping of a coin.) Then it is a mathematical fact that the volatility grows with the square root of the time over which it is measured. The biennial volatility would be $\sqrt{2}$ times the annual volatility; the decennial volatility would be $\sqrt{10}$ times the annual volatility, and so forth.* Now we know from the Esaki et al. study cited in the text that the typical commercial mortgage default occurs about seven years into the life of the loan. Thus (somewhat simplistically speaking), the relevant volatility for determining default frequency is the seven-year volatility, not the annual volatility. If the annual volatility is 15%, then the seven-year volatility is $\sqrt{7}$ times this amount, or 40%. Without any expected appreciation in the property value, there would be about a one-sixth chance that a given property would be worth, seven years from now, only 60% of its current value, or less. Even if the property is expected to appreciate at, say, 2% per year, this will increase the expected value in seven years only to about 15% above the current value, so there would still be a one-sixth chance that the property would be worth only 75% of its current value, or less, after seven years.

The standard loan-to-value (LTV) ratio required by mortgage issuers has traditionally been 75%. If loans don't amortize much and borrowers tend to default whenever the loan is "under water" (that is, when the property is worth less than the loan balance), then the 75% LTV criterion suggests a typical default probability of about one sixth. (See illustration.)

Of course, this analysis is highly simplified, and many commercial mortgages amortize their principal over time. But on the other hand, in a low-inflation environment many properties may tend to appreciate at less than 2% per year. And while it may not make sense to default on a loan just because its par value is under water, the reason the property has lost value is likely to be because its rental income has dropped, which may force the borrower to default. You can see the basic point. *Empirically observed default rates in commercial mortgages are consistent with empirical evidence about property volatility.*** The average property may not be as risky as the average stock (whose annual volatility is typically around 30%), but when you lend 75% of a property's value, you are asking for, well, about a one-sixth chance of running into a default.

---

*If property values do not follow a purely random walk, but rather have some inertia, as would be the case in a sluggish or informationally inefficient asset market, then the volatility actually increases *more than* the square root of the measurement time interval. So the analysis here would be conservative in that regard.

**Ciochetti and Vandell (1999) studied this question much more rigorously. Their estimate of the individual property annual volatility implied by the empirical evidence on commercial mortgage values and default rates is about 17%, assuming property values follow a random walk.

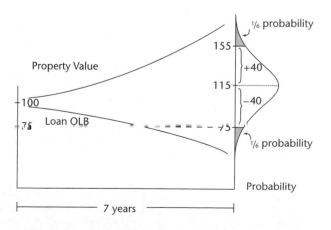

States. The average annual credit loss in the GLCMPI during the 1972–98 period was 73 basis points.[14] Construction loans would be expected to contain greater ex ante yield degradation than permanent loans because of their short maturities and likely greater conditional loss severities.

18.2 COMMERCIAL MORTGAGE UNDERWRITING

Underwriting is the word used to describe the process commercial mortgage originators go through to decide whether to issue a proposed mortgage. As noted in Chapter 16, this process can be much more involved than taking out a typical home mortgage. Commercial mortgages are often negotiated, and the terms of the loan may be customized to reflect the unique circumstances presented by the borrower, the lender, and the collateral property. The larger the loan is, the more it is worthwhile to spend time and energy in this negotiation and customization process. For typical commercial mortgages of several million dollars, procedures are generally fairly standardized. Even for larger loans, in the tens of millions of dollars each, standard underwriting criteria are issued by the institutions supplying the mortgage capital. Although these criteria may be "bent," they provide important policy guidelines. In this section, we will describe typical commercial underwriting criteria and how the underwriting process typically works.

What Underwriting Is All About. To begin, you should recognize the basic purpose of underwriting. Expressed simply, the purpose of underwriting is *to make default a rare event*. We noted in the previous section that, on average, about one in six long-term commercial mortgages in the United States defaults, or at least did so during the last quarter of the 20th century. Is this one-sixth rate "rare enough"? Well, yes, provided lenders are being adequately compensated for the risk. As with all investments, such compensation occurs in the magnitude of the ex ante total returns, or yields, the lenders can realistically expect when they issue the loans. Thus, more broadly and fundamentally, underwriting has as its purpose to ensure that lenders are getting the expected return they want at the time they make the loan. The tighter the underwriting criteria are, the lower will be the probability of default and the lower will be the ex ante yield degradation, thereby raising expected returns toward the contractual yield rates.

Of course, lenders cannot operate outside the market. Suppose a lender tried to set underwriting guidelines so tight that the ex ante yield degradation would be eliminated altogether. This would make the mortgage like a default-free bond. If the lender then tried to charge an interest rate above the yield on default-free government bonds, then she would probably find it difficult to make the loan. Borrowers

---

[14] The GLCMPI also estimates periodic total returns on commercial mortgages both with and without adjustment for credit loss. The average per-annum adjusted return over the 1972–98 period was about 100 basis points lower than the average unadjusted return. This number is greater than the 73 basis-point average credit loss because the denominator in the holding-period returns (HPRs) adjusts over time to reflect changes in the current market value of the mortgage. This value declines prior to loan default, as the current loan-to-value ratio typically rises and debt service coverage ratio typically falls, increasing the loan's default risk and thereby lowering its market value. In contrast, the denominator in the credit loss calculation remains at the par value of the loan (its contractual OLB). For this reason, in principle, the average credit loss over time probably provides a better indication of the magnitude of ex ante yield degradation.

conforming to such tight underwriting criteria could shop around among competing lenders to get a lower interest rate.

In fact, most real estate borrowers cannot (or do not want to) conform to underwriting standards so tight as to eliminate default risk. As a result, mortgage lenders have to monitor the market constantly and modify their underwriting criteria accordingly, if they want to play the game (that is, issue commercial mortgages). Loan originations must satisfy both sides of the deals, and as with any market, prices (that is, ex ante yields) reflect an equilibrium in which, on the margin, both sides are just willing to do business. Thus, in effect, underwriting criteria ensure that the realistic expected return to the lender is high enough, but not too high, so that it includes just the ex ante risk premium required by the market.

The Two Foci of Underwriting—Borrowers and Properties. When examining a mortgage loan application, a lender's attention is naturally focused on two subjects: the borrower and the proposed collateral property. In the commercial mortgage business (in contrast to the residential business), the more important of these two foci is normally the property. As noted, many commercial mortgages are nonrecourse, and even when recourse is technically available beyond the collateral property to the borrower, there is often little of value the lender can get. Furthermore, with a commercial mortgage (unlike a residential loan), the borrower will rely principally on the collateral property itself, being an income property, to provide the cash to service the loan. If the property is sufficiently lucrative in comparison with the loan requirements, then the loan will probably turn out all right even if the borrower is a bit weak.

Nevertheless, the borrower is still an important consideration even in commercial mortgages. On the downside, a borrower who gets into trouble on other businesses or properties other than the collateral property may use the collateral property as a "cash cow" to bail out his other losses, perhaps to the detriment of a loan on the healthy collateral property. Borrowers of commercial mortgages also can wreak havoc on secured lenders by filing for protection under Chapter 11 of the bankruptcy law. So lenders need to examine the nature of the borrowing entity and any parent or related firms and holding companies in order to ascertain the financial health of the relevant borrowing entity.

On the upside, borrowers on commercial mortgages (more so than residential borrowers) are often potential repeat customers. Commercial borrowers are often wealthy individuals, businesses, or institutions that are permanently in the real estate investment business in one way or another. If they are successful, they will be needing capital regularly for other projects and investments. It makes good business sense for lenders to cultivate such customers. Thus, the reputation and future business prospects of the borrower are important considerations for the lender. The mortgage lending business is very competitive in the United States, and a lender may relax underwriting criteria to some extent to cultivate or retain a borrower with good future potential.

18.2.1 Basic Property-Level Underwriting Criteria

Although information about the borrower is important, the primary attention when putting together the nuts and bolts of a specific deal typically focuses on several traditional criteria relating to the property that is to be the collateral in the loan. These criteria focus on two major aspects of the property: asset value and income flow. The value of the property relates naturally to the value of the loan, while the magnitude of the property's income flow is more directly relevant to the amount of periodic debt service that will be required by the loan.

Initial Loan-to-Value Ratio (ILTV). The **initial loan-to-value ratio (ILTV)** is the classical asset-value-based underwriting criterion. It is defined as the initial loan value (the contractual principal amount of the loan) divided by the current market value of the collateral property:

$$LTV = L/V$$

The ILTV ratio is an important underwriting criterion for obvious reasons. Commercial property market values display **volatility**, which means they can go down as well as up over time. A lower initial LTV ratio will reduce the probability that at some point during the life of the loan the property will be worth less than the OLB. Although default will not necessarily occur as soon as the property is worth less than the loan balance, if the property value falls far enough below the OLB, default will certainly be rational (i.e., wealth maximizing) for the borrower. Thus, the initial LTV ratio is directly related to the ex ante default probability in the loan. Indeed, because the current market value of the property reflects the entire future income stream the property can generate, the ILTV is arguably the most fundamental and important single underwriting criteria, as it reflects both asset value considerations (directly) and income coverage considerations (indirectly) in a single summary measure.[15]

For typical levels of commercial property volatility, the relationship between default probability and the initial LTV ratio on a long-term commercial mortgage looks something like the curve shown in Exhibit 18-5. Note that this relationship is highly nonlinear. Default probability is very low and nearly constant over a wide range of low values of the LTV ratio, but then increases sharply over higher LTV ratios.

The greater the volatility in the collateral property value is, the lower will be the initial LTV ratio corresponding to a given ex ante default probability. Typical commercial mortgage underwriting criteria in the United States have traditionally required the ILTV ratio to be equal to or below 75%. ILTV limits on property types that are viewed as more risky, such as raw land, will be set lower than this.[16] As noted in Chapter 15, an LTV ratio of 75% implies a much higher leverage ratio or debt/equity ratio than is typical in the stock market. Nevertheless, during periods of rapid price inflation and during real estate booms there is often strong pressure on lenders to relax this traditional limit. The traditional limit may also be exceeded if extra guarantees and credit enhancements are included in the loan, such as extra collateral, recourse provisions, cramdown insurance, and so forth.[17]

In estimating the market value of the property (V), lenders will generally require their own independent appraisal, and if the loan is to finance a property purchase, they

---

[15] On the other hand, the difficulty of estimating precisely the market value of the property may render the LTV a "fuzzier" measure than income-based measures, as current income can often be observed more reliably than property value.

[16] Although stated limits rarely exceed 75% or 80%, competitive pressures in the property and lending markets have likely on occasion pushed the effective (honestly stated) limit to well beyond 75%, with consequences in terms of subsequent default rates that were discussed in section 18.1.

[17] It should be noted that if property value tends to increase over time in nominal terms due to inflation, and the borrower does not add to the debt on the property, then the average LTV ratio over time will tend to be less than the initial ratio.

Exhibit 18-5 Typical Relationship between Initial LTV Ratio and the Ex Ante Lifetime Default Probability on a Commercial Property Mortgage

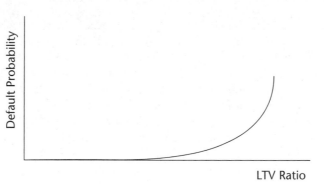

may take the property value to be whichever is lower between the appraisal and the agreed-on purchase price of the property. In practice, the loan terms may be effectively agreed on before an independent appraisal is conducted, and lenders may often rely for decision-making purposes on their own informal estimate of property value. In any case, at least two methods of estimating property value are often employed, direct capitalization and multiyear DCF valuation (as described in Chapter 10). Often, lenders use the lowest of the two values indicated by these two approaches for underwriting purposes. In some cases lenders will set general guidelines governing their in-house valuation procedures, such as placing lower bounds on the capitalization rate and/or the discount rate that can be employed in the valuation.[18]

While the LTV ratio criterion is applied most stringently as of the time of loan issuance, it is also often forecasted over the life of the loan based on a projection of the property NOI and direct capitalization. Of particular concern, of course, is the projected LTV ratio at the time of loan maturity if the loan is not fully amortizing. The lender needs to be able to expect that the property value will well exceed the OLB on the loan at that time.

Debt Service Coverage Ratio (DCR). As the LTV ratio is the basic asset-value-based underwriting criterion, so the DCR is the classical income-based criterion. The **Debt Service Coverage Ratio (DCR)** is defined as the collateral property's annual net operating income (NOI) divided by the annual debt service required by the loan:

$$DCR = NOI/DS$$

The debt service (*DS*), of course, includes both the periodic interest payments and any amortization of principal called for in the loan terms. This ratio clearly makes sense as an underwriting criterion, for the NOI generated by the property is normally the primary source of cash to service the loan.

---

[18] For example, a lender may state that cap rates no lower than 9% must be employed in conducting a direct capitalization valuation. Of course, all such rigid criteria must bend to the market, as noted previously, assuming the lender really wants to be in the mortgage business. In other words, a stated standard of a 9% cap rate floor may look nice on paper, but if the cap rates currently prevailing in the property market are 8%, then the lender will not be able to issue many mortgages unless it either informally relax its cap rate floor or otherwise relaxes its LTV limit.

A typical standard for the DCR would require that this ratio must equal or exceed 120%. To reduce the risk of a cash flow squeeze, the lender wants some buffer, provided by the excess of the required DCR above 100%. The DCR criterion may be raised higher for types of property that appear more risky, or during times when lenders are more risk averse. On the other hand, lower DCR hurdles may be accepted during times of rapid inflation, or when the loan market is "hot." A projected temporary violation of the DCR hurdle for one or two years may be tolerated if there is a solid projection of sufficient debt service coverage during the other years of the loan life. Taken together, the LTV ratio and the DCR are the two most widely used underwriting criteria. However, other measures are also commonly examined.

Break-Even Ratio (BER). The **break-even ratio (BER)** is another widely employed income-based underwriting criterion, that is, usually not used instead of the DCR but as a supplemental requirement that must also be met. The BER is defined as the sum of the annual debt service and property operating expenses divided by the potential gross income:

$$BER = (DS + OE)/PGI$$

The BER gives the occupancy ratio of the building (one minus the vacancy rate) below which there will be insufficient net operating income to cover the debt service. If the BER is greater than 100%, then the property investment will be a net cash flow drain on the borrower (even without considering any necessary capital improvement expenditures on the property). This would obviously be a dangerous situation from the lender's perspective, so underwriting criteria will typically require the BER to be less than some fraction well below 100%. A typical BER limit might be on the order of 85% or less. Sometimes the maximum BER criterion is stated as the average occupancy rate prevailing (or expected to prevail) in the space market in which the property is situated, or that rate less some buffer.

Equity Before-Tax Cash Flow (EBTCF). As noted in Chapter 11, the **equity-before-tax cash flow (EBTCF)** is the cash flow bottom line for the equity investor on a before-tax basis, reflecting the need for capital improvement expenditures on the property. The EBTCF equals the NOI less debt service and capital improvement expenditures:

$$EBTCF = NOI - DS - CI$$

If this measure is projected to be negative for any year during the life of the loan, this raises an obvious underwriting red flag, as the borrower faces a potential negative cash flow in any such year. While the EBTCF measure is arguably more relevant in principle than the DCR, it is often relatively difficult for the lender to estimate and project future CI needs. Furthermore, CI expenditures tend to be somewhat discretionary in their amount and timing, and the property owner may be able to finance some types of CI expenditures by the use of additional debt. As a result, the DCR criterion is more widely employed in practice than the EBTCF measure, although both are often examined. The EBTCF measure is particularly relevant for certain types of property, such as properties in need of improvement and properties that employ long-term leases in which major tenant improvement expenditures (a component of CI) may be required of the landlord whenever a lease expires.[19]

Multiyear Proforma Projection. Although lenders typically scrutinize the ratio criteria described earlier (LTV, DCR, and BER) most carefully for the initial year of the loan, they generally require and examine a multiyear cash flow projection for the property and debt service, extending to the maturity of the loan. Borrowers usually supply such proforma projections, but lenders naturally take these with a grain of salt and attempt to double-check the assumptions. Senders will examine any or all of the criteria noted previously for all the years in the proforma, not just the initial year.[20]

18.2.2 Variables and Loan Terms to Negotiate

Commercial mortgages present a potentially large array of possible loan terms and variables that can be negotiated. A partial list would include the following:

- Loan amount
- Loan term (maturity)
- Contract interest rate
- Amortization rate
- Up-front fees and points
- Prepayment option and back-end penalties
- Recourse vs. nonrecourse debt
- Collateral (e.g., cross-collateralization)
- Lender participation in property equity

All such items can affect the risk and expected return in the loan. The number of these variables presents considerable flexibility and scope for creativity in the loan negotiation process. Typically, one or more of these items will matter more to one side of the deal than to the other side. As with any negotiation, much of the art of putting together a successful deal lies in finding a combination that maximizes both sides' preferences. This requires an understanding of the trade-offs—most fundamentally, how changing the loan terms and variables affects the ex ante risk and return on the loan from the perspective of both the borrower and lender. On the basis of previous discussions in this chapter and Chapters 16 and 17 you should have a good idea about the nature of this trade-off for some of the items listed. For example, we saw in Chapter 17 how reducing the amortization rate in the loan (i.e., longer amortization) can reduce the annual debt service (thereby increasing the DCR ratio) without changing the contract interest rate. Ultimately, the giving and taking in a successful negotiation results in ex ante risk and return expectations in the loan that conform to the market and to the desires of both sides of the deal.

---

[19] In some cases, lenders attempt to define the NOI used in the DCR ratio to be net of recurring capital expenditures, such as leasing costs (commissions and TIs).

[20] See Chapters 11 and 14 for more detailed descriptions and discussion of the proforma.

18.2.3 Numerical Example of the Underwriting Process

It's our favorite real estate investor, Bob, once again. (Don't you just wish he would quit!) This time Bob wants to buy an existing fully operational 100,000-SF single-tenant office building in Iowa, and he has come to your firm, Sioux City Capital (Sioux for short), requesting a $9,167,000 purchase-money mortgage. Bob's mortgage broker has put together a package indicating that Bob will be paying $12,222,000 for the property, so that the requested loan would have an ILTV of 75%. Bob wants a 10-year interest-only nonrecourse loan. He is willing to accept a lock-out loan that does not permit prepayment. You must decide whether to grant this loan as requested, reject it out of hand, or try to negotiate a modified loan.

To begin to answer this question you first look at the capital markets to see what sort of contractual interest rate you would have to charge for a typical loan of this nature. You note that 10-year U.S. Treasury Bonds are currently yielding 6%. You also note that in the commercial mortgage market spreads on nonrecourse 10-year lock-out loans with a 75% ILTV are currently running at 200 basis points CEY. From this information you can compute that the mortgage would have to carry a 7.87% interest rate (MEY).[21]

Next you consider the underwriting criteria Sioux is currently employing for loans of the type Bob wants. Given the fact that Sioux City Capital is actually a mortgage bank rather than a portfolio lender, Sioux will not be investing in Bob's mortgage on a long-term basis themselves. Rather, they will be placing into Bob's mortgage the capital of a large international life insurance company with whom Sioux has an ongoing relationship. It is this ultimate capital provider (who probably does intend to hold Bob's mortgage for the long term) whose underwriting criteria must be met. Unlike Sioux, this life insurance company does not know anything about Bob or the local real estate market, but they do know what sort of risk and return they are looking for in their commercial mortgage portfolio. Based on these considerations, they have specified the following underwriting criteria that Sioux will have to meet in any loans they issue:

1. Maximum ILTV ≤ 75%
2. Maximum projected terminal LTV ≤ 65%
3. In computing LTV: (a) apply direct capitalization with initial cap rate no less than 9%, terminal cap rate no less than 10%; (b) apply multiyear DCF valuation also for ILTV with discount rate no less than 10%; and (c) use the lower of the two ILTVs computed.
4. Minimum DCR ≥ 120%
5. Maximum BER ≤ 85% or average market occupancy less 5%, whichever is lower
6. Consider need for capital improvements and avoid negative EBTCF projections.

---

[21] Note that spreads are quoted on Treasury Bonds of equivalent maturity to the mortgage loan. Also, recall that mortgage and bond market yields must be equated on an effective annual rate (EAR) basis. Thus, the 200-basis-point spread implies that the mortgage must have a bond-equivalent yield of 8.00% (the 6.00% T-bond yield plus the 200-basis-point CEY spread). This equates to an EAR of 8.16%. In this example we have assumed annual payments on the loan, so 8.16% is the loan interest rate that would equate to the current capital market requirements. However, a more typical loan with monthly payments would require a standard mortgage-equivalent yield of 7.87%, computed as $\{[(1 + .08/2)^2]^{(1/12)} - 1\} \times 12 = .0787$. This is the rate we will use in the present illustration.

With these requirements in mind, you examine Bob's loan request in some detail, applying your own knowledge of the space market in which Bob's property is situated. Bob's mortgage broker has submitted a package of information with the loan application including the following information about the property:

1. 100,000-SF fully leased single-tenant office building

2. Good-credit tenant (not a publicly traded corporation) signed 10-year net lease three years ago.

3. The lease has current net rent of $11/SF per year (annual payments at ends of years), with step-up provisions to $11.50 in year 5 (two years from now) and $12.00 in year 8 (five years from now).

4. Current rents in the relevant space market are $12/SF for new 10-year leases (with no concessions), and are expected to grow at a rate of 3% per year (e.g., will be $12.36 one year from now, $16.13 in 10 years).

The broker has also submitted the cash flow proforma projection shown in Exhibit 18-6a. In this proforma the broker has assumed a 75% probability of renewal for the tenant at the beginning of year 8, and has assumed that if the tenant does not renew there will be a three-month vacancy period. The broker has not included any provision for capital improvement expenditures and has assumed a 9% terminal cap rate to estimate the reversion value of the property at the end of year 10.

After examining this proforma and making some inquiries, you develop an alternative proforma projection for Bob's property that you feel is more realistic. You agree that the current market rent is $12/SF, but you decide to reduce the expected rent growth rate assumption from 3% to 1% per year for Bob's building. Even though rents for new buildings in the space market might grow at 3%, Bob's building will be aging and becoming more obsolete in that market, so you feel that 1% is a more realistic expectation. After some investigation, you decide that the tenant, though not a publicly traded corporation, is a stable company that presents good credit risk. You decide to accept the broker's assumptions about this tenant's renewal probability and the vacancy downtime in the event of non-renewal, but you believe that some leasing expenses will be involved even if the tenant does renew. You decide to project year 8 leasing commission fees of $2/SF if the tenant renews and $5 if they do not renew. You also decide that it would be realistic to project tenant improvement expenditures of $10/SF if the existing tenant renews and $20/SF if a new tenant moves in. Finally, you decide that a 10% terminal cap rate would be a more realistic projection than the broker's 9% assumption considering that the building will be 10 years older by then.

Your modified proforma is shown in Exhibit 18-6b, including the implied underwriting income ratios, the DCR and BER, given the $9,167,000 interest-only loan that Bob wants, assuming the 7.87% interest rate currently required by the mortgage market.[22] It appears from Exhibit 18-6b that Bob's loan request will satisfy Sioux's income-based underwriting criteria. The initial DCR is 152%, well above the 120% minimum requirement, and the projected DCR is even higher in future years as the rent in the existing lease steps up and the space turns over at a higher projected

---

[22]The monthly debt service on the interest-only loan is calculated as $(0.0787/12) \times 9,167,000 = \$60,120$. Thus, the annual debt service is $12 \times 60,120 = \$721,443$.

Year	1	2	3	4	5	6	7	8	9	10	11
Market rent (net)/SF	$12.36	$12.73	$13.11	$13.51	$13.91	$14.33	$14.76	$15.20	$15.66	$16.13	$16.61
Property rent (net)	$11.00	$11.50	$11.50	$11.50	$12.00	$12.00	$12.00	$15.20	$15.20	$15.20	$15.20
Vacancy allowance	$0.00	$0.00	$0.00	$0.00	$0.00	$0.00	$0.00	$0.95	$0.00	$0.00	$0.00
NOI/SF	$11.00	$11.50	$11.50	$11.50	$12.00	$12.00	$12.00	$14.25	$15.20	$15.20	$15.20
NOI	$1,100,000	$1,150,000	$1,150,000	$1,150,000	$1,200,000	$1,200,000	$1,200,000	$1,425,116	$1,520,124	$1,520,124	$1,520,124
Reversion @ 9% cap										$16,890,268	

Exhibit 18-6a Broker's Submitted Proforma for Bob's Office Building

Year	1	2	3	4	5	6	7	8	9	10	11
Market rent (net)/SF	$12.12	$12.24	$12.36	$12.49	$12.61	$12.74	$12.87	$12.99	$13.12	$13.26	$13.39
Property rent (net)	$11.00	$11.50	$11.50	$11.50	$12.00	$12.00	$12.00	$12.99	$12.99	$12.99	$12.99
Vacancy allowance	$0.00	$0.00	$0.00	$0.00	$0.00	$0.00	$0.00	$0.81	$0.00	$0.00	$0.00
NOI/SF	$11.00	$11.50	$11.50	$11.50	$12.00	$12.00	$12.00	$12.18	$12.99	$12.99	$12.99
NOI	$1,100,000	$1,150,000	$1,150,000	$1,150,000	$1,200,000	$1,200,000	$1,200,000	$1,218,214	$1,299,428	$1,299,428	$1,299,428
Lease commission	$0	$0	$0	$0	$0	$0	$0	–$275,000	$0	$0	
Tenant improvements	$0	$0	$0	$0	$0	$0	$0	–$1,250,000	$0	$0	
Reversion @ 10% cap										$12,994,280	
Less OLB										$9,167,000	
PBTCF	$1,100,000	$1,150,000	$1,150,000	$1,150,000	$1,200,000	$1,200,000	$1,200,000	–$306,786	$1,299,428	$14,293,709	
Debt service	–$721,443	–$721,443	–$721,443	–$721,443	–$721,443	–$721,443	–$721,443	–$721,443	–$721,443	–$9,888,443	
EBTCF	$378,557	$428,557	$428,557	$428,557	$428,557	$478,557	$478,557	–$1,028,229	$577,985	$4,405,266	
DCR	152%	159%	159%	159%	166%	166%	166%	169%	180%	180%	
BER @ market	60%	59%	58%	58%	57%	57%	56%	56%	55%	54%	

Exhibit 18-6b Sioux's Modified Proforma for Bob's Office Building and Loan Application

market rent.[23] Your familiarity with the space market makes it clear that the initial BER of 60% is well below the average space market occupancy rate less 5%.[24]

Unfortunately, Bob's loan proposal as it stands has several problems. One is apparent in the cash flow projection. It appears that there could well be a sharply negative EBTCF in year 8, the year the existing lease expires. The EBTCF is projected to be negative by over $1,000,000 in that year.[25] This problem can probably be dealt

[23] The initial DCR of 152% is calculated as $1,100,000 NOI for year 1 divided by the $721,443 debt service.

[24] The BER in Exhibit 18-6b has been calculated based on the projected market rent, rather than the property's rent based on the existing lease. This makes sense as the underwriting criterion compares the BER to the average occupancy rate in the market. Thus, the 60% BER for year 1 in the proforma is found as the $7.21443/SF debt service divided by the $12.12/SF projected market rent for that year.

[25] The projected cash flow in year 8 reflects the mean or expectation across the renewal scenarios. It is calculated as follows. The vacancy allowance per SF is $(1 - 75\%) \times (0.25 \times \$12.99) = \$0.81/SF$. This is the nonrenewal probability $(1 - 75\% = 25\%)$ times the conditional loss from vacancy that will occur if the tenant does not renew. This is expected to be three months of vacancy, or 25% of the income from a year that could otherwise earn the projected market rent of $12.99/SF. The expected lease commission is $(75\%)(\$2/SF) + (1 - 75\%) \times (\$5/SF) = \$2.75/SF$. The expected tenant improvement expenditure is $(75\%)(\$10/SF) + (1 - 75\%) \times (\$20/SF) = \$12.50/SF$.

with, however. Single-tenant buildings, or properties in which a large proportion of the space is under leases that all expire near the same time, commonly face this type of occasional negative cash flow. Much of the problem is due to the need for capital improvement expenditures. The borrower may be able to finance some of this need. More to the point, there is ample positive EBTCF projected prior to the projected negative year, and the negative year is in the rather distant future by which time property appreciation should have reduced the danger of default. If necessary, some sort of sinking fund covenant might be included in Bob's mortgage to ensure that sufficient cash will be available to cover the projected shortfall in year 8.

A more serious problem in Bob's application is not apparent from the income analysis alone, but appears in the valuation analysis. If one applies a 9% going-in cap rate to the initial year's NOI of $1,100,000, the implied property value is $12,222,000, the same price Bob is apparently planning to pay for the property, and just sufficient to allow the proposed $9,167,000 loan to meet the 75% ILTV criterion. However, after investigating the relevant property market, you decide that realistic expected returns (going-in IRRs) for this type of property are well approximated by the 10% discount rate in your underwriting criteria. In any case, you do not see how you can apply a discount rate less than that in performing a DCF valuation of the property. At a discount rate of 10%, the 10-year projected property-level cash flows (PBTCF) shown in Exhibit 18-6b (including the projected reversion) give a present value of only $11,557,000, which implies a 79% ILTV.[26] This violates the ILTV underwriting criterion.

As Bob's loan proposal does not fail your underwriting criteria by very much, you decide not to reject it out of hand, but rather to make a counterproposal. To meet the 75% ILTV limit in your underwriting criteria, you could offer Bob a slightly smaller loan of $8,700,000. However, without amortization such a loan would still not meet the **terminal LTV (TLTV)** criterion of 65%. Dividing $8,700,000 into the projected 10-year reversion value of $12,994,000 results in a projected TLTV of 67%. However, the smaller loan could have some amortization and still produce an annual debt service payment similar to what Bob was originally asking for with his larger interest-only loan. For example, if the loan amortized at a 40-year rate, then the balloon payment after 10 years on an $8,700,000 loan would be $8,230,047, which implies a TLTV ratio of only 63%, less than the 65% limit. The annual debt service on such a loan would be $715,740, slightly less than the $721,443 Bob was originally proposing.

This shows how trade-offs among the loan terms can be manipulated to meet underwriting criteria. Bob might accept a counterproposal of a smaller $8,700,000 loan with a 40-year amortization rate. If Sioux's underwriting criteria are competitive, and if your estimate is correct that the property market would not likely accept a realistic going-in IRR of less than 10% on a property like Bob's office building, then it should be difficult for Bob to find another lender that will lend any more than $8,700,000 on the property.[27]

---

[26] $9,167,000/$11,557,000 = 79.3%

[27] Admittedly, these are two rather large ifs. The difficulty of being able to observe or estimate property market values precisely, combined with lenders' desire to be competitive in the mortgage lending business, probably goes some way in explaining why the default rate is as high as it is, and why it has been so much higher on loans issued during boom times.

18.3 PARTICIPATING MORTGAGES

Suppose, in our previous example, that Bob really wants to purchase the property for $12,222,000, and he really needs the full $9,167,000 loan amount he originally requested. One possibility that might then be considered is a **participating mortgage** rather than a conventional straight loan. In a participating mortgage the lender receives some equity-like participation in the property investment. This will increase the lender's expected return above what would be implied purely by the **base contract interest rate** on the loan, and it also may reduce the risk of the loan from the perspective of the lender's *real* return, net of inflation. As a result, participating mortgages are appealing to some lenders and generally offer a base interest rate that is lower than that of a straight mortgage. The lender may also accept a higher ILTV ratio if the participation gives the lender sufficient expected return. From the borrower's perspective, although some upside potential is lost to the lender, the lower base interest rate enhances the positive leverage effect from the debt.

Typical participating mortgages often give the lender some equity **participation** in both the annual operating income and the reversion from the property investment. For example, a lender might be entitled to receive a specified percentage of the annual net operating income of the property above a specified threshold or after the **base** interest debt service is taken out. In addition, the lender might be entitled to a certain fraction of the property resale proceeds above a threshold or after the loan balance is taken out.[28] The equity participation payments are often referred to as **conditional interest**, or **kickers** in popular parlance (because they kick in above the stated threshold or base earnings).

To make this concept more concrete, let's continue the example of Bob's loan application to Sioux. Suppose that, in addition to their life insurance company source of capital for straight loans, Sioux also operates as a mortgage broker for a pension fund, the Sioux Fund (Sioux for short). The Sioux Fund wants to invest in participating mortgages because of the fund's need to match its future cash inflow with its future pension liability obligations that will be adjusted to inflation.[29] Sioux might therefore offer the following deal to Bob.

Sioux will loan Bob his entire original $9,167,000 request in a 6.00% interest-only loan even though such a loan would slightly exceed the standard 75% ILTV criterion, and even though the 6.00% stated base interest rate provides virtually no default-risk premium. In return, however, the loan would specify that, in addition to the 6% base interest, Sioux will receive conditional interest in the form of a 40% participation on any annual NOI in excess of $800,000 and any gross resale proceeds in excess of $12,250,000.

The expected cash flow in this participating mortgage is shown in Exhibit 18-7 for both Bob and Sioux. For example, in year 1 the 6% loan has a base interest debt service of $550,020 (computed as 6% × $9,167,000). This base interest payment is due and payable no matter what the NOI of the property turns out to be. In addition, there is a projected participation payment of $120,000 in the first year, computed as 40% of the $300,000 difference between the projected $1,100,000 NOI and the $800,000

[28] If the property is not sold prior to loan maturity, the reversion value participation might be based on an appraisal of the property as of the time of loan maturity.

[29] The pension payments of the Sioux Fund's beneficiaries have a cost of living adjustment (COLA) that is pegged to the general inflation rate.

Year	1	2	3	4	5	6	7	8	9	10	11
Market rent (net)/SF	$12.12	$12.24	$12.36	$12.49	$12.61	$12.74	$12.87	$12.99	$13.12	$13.26	$13.39
Property rent (net)	$11.00	$11.50	$11.50	$11.50	$12.00	$12.00	$12.00	$12.99	$12.99	$12.99	$12.99
Vacancy allowance	$0.00	$0.00	$0.00	$0.00	$0.00	$0.00	$0.00	$0.81	$0.00	$0.00	$0.00
NOI/SF	$11.00	$11.50	$11.50	$11.50	$12.00	$12.00	$12.00	$12.18	$12.99	$12.99	$12.99
NOI	$1,100,000	$1,150,000	$1,150,000	$1,150,000	$1,200,000	$1,200,000	$1,200,000	$1,218,214	$1,299,428	$1,299,428	$1,299,428
Lease commission	$0	$0	$0	$0	$0	$0	$0	–$275,000	$0	$0	
Tenant improvements	$0	$0	$0	$0	$0	$0	$0	–$1,250,000	$0	$0	
Reversion @ 10% cap										$12,994,280	
Less OLB										$9,167,000	
Participation										$297,712	
PBTCF	$1,100,000	$1,150,000	$1,150,000	$1,150,000	$1,200,000	$1,200,000	$1,200,000	–$306,786	$1,299,428	$14,293,709	
Base interest debt service	–$550,020	–$550,020	–$550,020	–$550,020	–$550,020	–$550,020	–$550,020	–$550,020	–$550,020	–$9,717,020	
Participation	–$120,000	–$140,000	–$140,000	–$140,000	–$160,000	–$160,000	–$160,000	–$167,286	–$199,771	–$199,771	
Loan CFs	$670,020	$690,020	$690,020	$690,020	$710,020	$710,020	$710,020	$717,306	$749,791	$10,214,503	
EBTCF	$429,980	$459,980	$459,980	$459,980	$489,980	$489,980	$489,980	–$1,024,092	$549,637	$4,079,205	
DCR	200%	209%	209%	209%	218%	218%	218%	221%	236%	236%	
BER @ market	45%	45%	44%	44%	44%	43%	43%	42%	42%	41%	

Exhibit 18-7 Participating Mortgage for $9,167,000 at 6% (Interest-Only), with 40% Equity Kickers (over $800,000 NOI and $12,250,000 Resale)

threshold above which the participation kicks in. The exact amount of the participation payment (if any) is less certain than the base interest, because it depends on the uncertain future NOI amount. Similarly, in the reversion cash flow projected for year 10, $297,712 of participation proceeds are projected for the lender in addition to the $9,167,000 loan principal balance. This is computed as 40% of the $744,280 difference between the projected gross sale proceeds of $12,994,280 and the $12,250,000 base for the reversion kicker.[30]

Why does this proposed 6% participating mortgage look advantageous to Sioux? In this case there are at least two reasons. First, the equity participation provides Sioux with an expected yield at least as great as what they could receive from a straight mortgage in the current market. This can be seen by computing the IRR of the loan cash flows, shown in Exhibit 18-7, assuming an initial (year-0) cash disbursement of $9,167,000. The IRR to the expected cash flow stream (including the participation payments) is 7.90%, which is slightly greater than the 7.87% yield prevailing in the market for straight mortgages.

While this slightly greater expected return might not be sufficient to compensate Sioux for the extra default risk in a 79% ILTV mortgage if it were a straight loan, the participating loan actually reduces another type of risk, namely, **inflation risk**. If future inflation turns out to be greater than expected, Sioux's pension liabilities will be greater than expected, because of the COLA adjustment in their beneficiaries' pension plans. With a straight mortgage, Sioux's cash inflows would not change

---

[30] The annual and reversion kicker percentages need not be the same. For example, the kicker might be 30% on the NOI and 50% on the resale. Note also that in a properly constructed participating mortgage the equity participation payments (on both the annual income and reversion proceeds) are tax deductible to the borrower. The IRS classifies participation payments as interest, not dividends, because the lender does not have governing control over the property.

as a function of what future inflation turned out to be. However, with the participating mortgage, if future inflation turns out to be greater than expected, then Sioux's participation cash flows likely will turn out to be greater than expected, at least as regards the pure effect of inflation alone. This is because Bob's office building should be able to increase its nominal rents more in the long run if there is more inflation. This would probably increase both the annual and reversion participation payments to Sioux. Thus, the participating mortgage provides a bit of a hedge against inflation risk.

As a result of the inflation risk consideration, the 6% participating mortgage may well provide Sioux with a sufficient expected return.[31] But should Bob accept the offer? To answer this question, let's examine the expected 10-year IRR on Bob's levered equity investment with the participating mortgage.

The EBTCF figures in Exhibit 18-7 are Bob's expected cash flows after taking out the projected mortgage participation payments. With a $9,167,000 loan and a property price of $12,222,000, Bob's up-front equity investment will be $3,055,000. This results in a going-in levered IRR of 12.97% for Bob. Suppose, instead, Bob got the loan he originally asked for, the interest-only straight mortgage at 7.87%. Under the same underlying property cash flow projection as in Exhibit 18-7, this would result in the EBTCF projection shown in Exhibit 18-6b. Given the initial $3,055,000 investment, this cash flow stream has an expected IRR of 12.83%, slightly less than what Bob could expect with the participating mortgage. This is because the debt component of the participating mortgage, that is, the debt service payments attributable to the 6% base interest rate, provides Bob with greater positive leverage in his equity investment than the 7.87% loan would do.

Of course, this does not mean that Bob is getting something for nothing in Sioux's proposal. The nature of Bob's risk has changed. The other component of the participating mortgage (the equity component) gives away some of Bob's upside expectations, but none of Bob's downside risk. So Bob's overall equity risk under the participating loan is a bit skewed, unfavorably for Bob. Nevertheless, Bob may well find Sioux's proposal agreeable.[32]

Although participating mortgages are often a successful solution to otherwise intractable underwriting problems, they do raise some difficult issues that need to be carefully considered. For one thing, there are legal liability and administrative issues not raised by straight loans that the lender needs to consider carefully. For example, the lender will need to be able to audit the borrower's accounts to make sure income and expenses are being recorded properly so that the lender is getting its fair share. How will the lender know if the borrower is padding expenses so as to effectively reduce the lender's participation? Do participating mortgages exacerbate potential

---

[31] Obviously, Sioux would consider the typical interest rates and kickers that are prevailing in the current market for participating mortgages, so as not to make an offer that is below market. In practice, however, the market for participating mortgages is often quite thin, and it may be difficult to identify loans that are exactly comparable in terms of risk and expected return. Thus, market rates and terms must be estimated approximately.

[32] Although it is not much of an issue in Bob's case, another reason participating mortgages are appealing in some instances is that the lower base interest rate reduces pressure on the initial income coverage, as indicated by the initial DCR, for example. This is most important in situations in which the property net operating income can be realistically expected to grow significantly over the life of the loan. For this reason, participating mortgages are often most appealing when inflation expectations have driven up interest rates, and they may serve much the same purpose as the graduated payment mortgage (GPM) or the adjustable rate mortgage (ARM) with a low initial teaser rate, as was described in Chapter 17.

problems of **moral hazard** for the lender? (Moral hazard is the term used to describe the situation in which the party in control of a decision can benefit from a course of action that harms the other party.) For example, does the participating mortgage give the property owner an incentive to skimp on capital improvement expenditures? Such expenditures may be born entirely by the owner (if the lender's participation is based on NOI, before CI expenditures are taken out), yet they enhance property value and future rents that the owner must share with the lender.[33]

18.4 CHAPTER SUMMARY

This chapter introduced you to the basics of commercial mortgages, largely from the lender's perspective. You should now have a feeling for how to analyze the default risk in such loans and how underwriting is carried out in the commercial mortgage origination industry. In the next chapter we will step back a bit to consider the broader economics of commercial mortgages from the perspective of the ultimate investors in such loans.

KEY TERMS

contract (stated) yield
expected return (ex ante yield)
credit losses
yield degradation
recovery rate
loss severity
conditional yield degradation
hazard probability/function
conditional survival probability
cumulative survival probability
unconditional default probability

cumulative (lifetime) default
   probability
ex ante (unconditional) yield
   degradation
ex post yield degradation
underwriting
initial loan-to-value ratio (ILTV)
volatility
debt service coverage ratio (DCR)
break-even ratio (BER)
equity-before-tax cash flow (EBTCF)

terminal LTV (TLTV)
participating mortgage
base contract interest rate
participation
base (threshold) cash flow
kickers
conditional interest
inflation risk
moral hazard

STUDY QUESTIONS

18.1. What is the difference between the contract (or stated) yield and the realistic expected return (ex ante yield) on a mortgage? Why is this difference important?

18.2. Ignoring multiple periods of time, what is the general relationship among the expected return, the contract yield, the unconditional default probability, and the conditional yield degradation?

---

[33] Riddiough (1994) pointed out that participating mortgages may also raise adverse selection problems.

18.3. In a one-period world, if the conditional yield degradation is 10%, the unconditional default probability is 15%, and the lender wants an expected return of 8%, what contract yield must the loan carry?

18.4. Consider a three-year mortgage with annual payments in arrears. Suppose the probability of default is 1% in the first year and 5% each year thereafter given that default has not occurred previously.

   a. What is the hazard function of this loan?

   b. What is the unconditional default probability in year 2?

   c. What is the cumulative (or lifetime) default probability in this loan as of the time of its origination?

18.5. Suppose the loan in question 18.4 is an 8% interest-only loan. If the conditional recovery rate is 75% in each year, what is the expected return on the loan?

18.6. What is the major purpose of underwriting in the commercial mortgage industry? What is the relationship between underwriting and the market for commercial mortgage assets?

18.7. What are the two major foci of the lender's attention in commercial mortgage underwriting? Which one of these is usually more important, and why?

18.8. What is the difference between value-based and income-based underwriting criteria? In what way could you consider that the value-based criteria are more fundamental or important?

18.9. What is the relationship of the initial loan-to-value ratio (ILTV) to the default risk in the loan? How is this relationship affected by the volatility in the underlying property?

18.10. Suppose 10-year Treasury Bond yields in the bond market are 7.00% CEY, and the mortgage market requires a contract yield risk premium of 175 basis points (CEY). If a property has a net operating income (NOI) of $400,000, and the underwriting criteria require a debt coverage ratio (DCR) of at least 125%, then what is the maximum loan that can be offered assuming a 30-year amortization rate and monthly payments on the mortgage?

18.11. Using the discounted cash flow (DCF) valuation method, what is the maximum loan that can be made on a property with the following annual net before-tax cash flow, assuming an 11.5% discount rate and underwriting criteria that specify a maximum loan/value ratio of 70%? Cash flows: $1 million in year 1, 1.1 million in years 2 through 4, 1.5 million in years 5 through 9, and $12 million in year 10 including reversion.

18.12. Why do lenders need to consider multiyear cash flow projections rather than just the initial income of the property?

18.13. What potential problem would the projected equity-before-tax cash flow (EBTCF) reveal that the DCR or BER would not reveal?

18.14. What are the pros and cons of participating mortgages from both the borrower's and lender's perspectives, as compared to otherwise similar straight debt?

18.15. Bob is thinking of buying a property whose five-year net cash flow projection is shown in the following table (occurring at the end of each year). In addition, at the end of year 5 the property is expected to be worth 10 times its net cash flow that year.

Year 1	$1,000,000
Year 2	$1,100,000
Year 3	$1,100,000
Year 4	$800,000
Year 5	$1,200,000

Bob can purchase this property for its $11,400,000 market value with an $8,000,000 loan. He has two choices of loans (both five-year interest-only loans with annual payments in arrears). Loan 1 is a straight 8% loan. Loan 2 is a participating mortgage with 7% base interest and 45% kickers on any annual cash flow above $1,000,000 and any resale proceeds (or property appraised value at maturity) above $11,400,000.

a. What is the property market's expected return (going-in IRR) to the underlying property?

b. Ignoring default risk, what is the expected return on loan 1?

c. On loan 2?

d. On Bob's levered equity with loan 1?

e. On Bob's levered equity with loan 2?

*18.16. Read the text box on page 447. This box presents a simplified way to compute a rough estimate of the likelihood of mortgage default as a function of property value volatility and the LTV ratio of the loan when it is issued. There it was argued that a 75% LTV ratio lending criterion would lead approximately to a one-sixth lifetime default probability. Use this same simplified approach, and the fact that about 5% of the normal probability distribution lies beyond two standard deviations from its mean, to estimate what LTV ratio lending criterion would be necessary to reduce the default probability to 1/40 (or 2.5%).

19

Commercial Mortgage Economics and Investment

Learning Objectives

After reading this chapter, you should understand:

◆ The importance of the most basic concepts in bond investments and fixed-income portfolio management, such as duration, interest rate risk, and the yield curve.

◆ The economics underlying commercial mortgage yields, that is what drives investors' required expected returns on mortgages.

◆ The nature of recent historical ex post total return (HPR) performance of U.S. commercial mortgages.

The previous chapter covered the nuts and bolts of commercial mortgage lending, focusing on loan origination, the primary market. Underlying this market, however, are the ultimate investors in commercial mortgages, including institutions that hold such loans in their portfolios and investors who deal in the secondary market for loans. In the secondary market commercial mortgages are often securitized in ways that are appealing to different types of investors. Indeed, commercial mortgages are part of the "debt market" broadly defined, which includes all types of bonds.

In this chapter we will consider the underlying economics of commercial mortgages within the context of the bond market and the overall capital market, including the investment performance of commercial mortgages and the roles such assets can play for different types of investors. We begin with a brief description of some fundamental considerations in the bond market, including duration, interest rate risk, the yield curve, and, maturity matching. The second section relates these basic considerations to equilibrium expected returns in the commercial mortgage market, and reviews ex post mortgage investment performance.

19.1 SOME BASIC CHARACTERISTICS OF BONDS

Broadly speaking, commercial mortgages are part of the bond market, the market for finite-lived assets with contractually fixed cash flows. To deepen your understanding of commercial mortgages from an investment perspective, you need to be familiar with a few basic characteristics of the bond market, characteristics that relate to all types of debt products, including commercial mortgages. In this section we will discuss the concepts of duration, interest rate risk, the yield curve, and maturity matching.

19.1.1 Duration and Maturity

Recall that one of the defining characteristics of debt investments is the fact that their contractually fixed cash flows typically give the investor an explicit, finite **maturity** for their investment. For example, a 10-year mortgage will provide income and value for 10 years, and then it will expire.[1] This is a very useful attribute for certain investment purposes, such as servicing a finite-lived obligation the investor may have, as in the case of a pension plan for example. But maturity is also related to the sensitivity of the value of the debt to changes in market interest rates. You have no doubt noted previously that the present value of a more distant future cash flow is more sensitive to the discount rate than is the present value of a more proximate cash flow. Thus, the volatility of bond values, and the magnitude of interest rate risk for bond investors, is directly related to the maturity of the bond investment.

As an example, consider two zero-coupon 6% bonds currently worth $100 each.[2] Both the coupon rate (that is, the contract interest rate) and the current market yield are 6%, for both bonds, so they are selling at par value. Bond A has a maturity of 5 years, promising a single future cash flow of $133.82 in 5 years ($133.82 = $100[1.06]^5). Bond B has a maturity of 10 years, so its single future cash flow is $179.08 in 10 years (equal to $100[1.06]^{10}). Now suppose the relevant market yield suddenly changes to 7%. Thus, 7% becomes the opportunity cost of capital (OCC) at which the bonds' future cash flow must be discounted. However, the future cash flow amount is contractually fixed (as these are fixed rate loans). The present value of bond A therefore falls from $100 to $95.41 = $133.82/1.07^5. But the PV of bond B falls farther, from $100 to $91.04 = $179.08/1.07^{10}. The one-point increase in market yield (from 6% to 7%) caused the 5-year bond to lose less than 5% of its value while the 10-year bond lost almost 9%.

Because the sensitivity of bond values to changes in market interest rates is very important for investors, we need to be able to measure it accurately. While the maturity of the bond gives some idea of this sensitivity, a more accurate measure is the **duration** of the bond. The duration is defined as the weighted average time (in years)

---

[1] Of course, if the debt instrument gives the borrower a prepayment option (callable debt), then the maturity is not precisely specified in the debt contract. However, many commercial mortgages do not permit prepayment (or charge high prepayment penalties).

[2] A "zero-coupon" bond does not pay out interest, but rather accrues interest over time, so that the only cash flow occurs at the maturity of the bond, and this cash flow includes the accumulated compounded interest accrued at the contract interest rate (which is still referred to as a coupon rate, even though the bond actually has no coupons per se). The interest accrual procedure is described in the four rules of loan payment and balance computation discussed in Chapter 17.

until the bond's future cash flows will be received. The weighting is proportional to the component of each future cash flow in the present value of the bond. For zero-coupon bonds the duration and maturity are the same because they have only one future cash flow (which therefore occurs at the maturity date). But for bonds that pay periodic interest, the duration, though generally a positive function of maturity, can differ significantly from the bond's maturity, especially for longer-term loans.

For example, suppose bond A and bond B, our 5-year and 10-year loans from the previous example, were interest-only mortgages with annual payments, instead of zero-coupon bonds. Exhibit 19-1 demonstrates how we would compute the duration of each of these bonds and reveals that the 5-year bond has a duration of 4.47 years, while the 10-year bond has a duration of 7.80 years.

The basic procedure for computing the duration of a mortgage with monthly payments is given in the following formula:

$$Duration = \sum_{j=1}^{N} t_j \left(\frac{CF_j/(1+YTM)^{t_j}}{\sum_{i=1}^{N} CF_i/(1+YTM)^{(t_i)}} \right) \Big/ 12 \qquad (1)$$

Here, t_j is the number of months until the jth cash flow is received, CF_j is the amount of the jth cash flow (including any balloon in the final payment), N is the total number of payments to maturity, and YTM is the current market yield on the loan. The monthly weighted average time until cash flow receipt must be divided by 12 to put the duration in annual terms. Note that the summation in the denominator is just the

		Bond A (5-yr. maturity, 4.47-yr. duration)				Bond B (10-yr. maturity, 7.80-yr. duration)		
Year = t_j	CF_j	$PV(CF_j) =$ $CF_j/(1.06)^{\wedge}(t_j)$	$w =$ $PV(CF_j)/$ $PV(Bond)$	$w \times t$	CF	$PV(CF_j) =$ $CF_j/(1.06)^{\wedge}(t_j)$	$w =$ $PV(CF_j)/$ $PV(Bond)$	$w \times t$
1	$6.00	$5.66	0.0566	0.0566	$6.00	$5.66	0.0566	0.0566
2	$6.00	$5.34	0.0534	0.1068	$6.00	$5.34	0.0534	0.1068
3	$6.00	$5.04	0.0504	0.1511	$6.00	$5.04	0.0504	0.1511
4	$6.00	$4.75	0.0475	0.1901	$6.00	$4.75	0.0475	0.1901
5	$106.00	$79.21	0.7921	3.9605	$6.00	$4.48	0.0448	0.2242
6					$6.00	$4.23	0.0423	0.2538
7					$6.00	$3.99	0.0399	0.2793
8					$6.00	$3.76	0.0376	0.3012
9					$6.00	$3.55	0.0355	0.3196
10					$106.00	$59.19	0.5919	5.9190
Sum		$100.00	1.000	4.4651		$100.00	1.000	7.8017

Exhibit 19-1   Computation of Duration at Par Value for Two Interest-Only, 6% Coupon, Annual-Payment Mortgages

current market value of the mortgage. If the current market yield equals the contract interest rate on the loan, then this market value will equal the current contractual OLB (or par value) of the mortgage.

It should be noted that the measure of duration computed in formula (1) is what is called **Macaulay duration**, named after Frederick Macaulay, who first coined the term in 1938. It is the most intuitive definition of the duration concept. However, a slightly different measure, often referred to as **modified duration**, is more commonly used in practice because it more closely approximates the relative sensitivity of bond values to changes in interest rates. Modified duration equals the Macaulay measure divided by $(1 + YTM)$.

Exhibit 19-2 graphs the modified duration of a monthly-payment, 8% interest, 30-year amortizing mortgage, as a function of the maturity of the loan (that is, the year of its balloon payment or year of prepayment at par value). The solid curve in Exhibit 19-2 is typical of the relationship between maturity and duration for mortgages. The straight dashed line indicates the duration of a zero-coupon bond (which is the same as the maturity). Note that for short-term loans maturity and duration are similar, but the mortgage duration tapers off for loans longer than about five years' maturity, and is less than nine years even for a 30-year maturity mortgage. In general, duration is a function of the loan's maturity, its coupon rate (contractual interest rate), amortization rate, and the current relevant market yield.

The modified duration measure approximates the percentage change in the loan's value caused by a one-point change in the market yield. Thus, if we multiply the change in market yield by the duration, we get the approximate percentage change in loan value, as represented here:

$$\frac{\Delta D}{D} = -(Duration)(\Delta YTM) \tag{2}$$

where ΔD represents the change in current market value of the debt, and ΔYTM is the change in the relevant market yield. The sign is negative because bond values are inversely related to yields.

For example, consider our 6%, 10-year bond B in Exhibit 19-1. We computed its Macaulay duration to be 7.8 years at a 6% market yield. Its modified duration would thus be 7.36 years (7.8/1.06). Now suppose the relevant market yield moves up to 6.5%. Formula (2) would predict a loss of 3.68% in the value of bond B as $-(7.36) \times (0.5\%) = -3.68\%$. The exact new value of bond B is $96.41, found by applying the 6.5% yield in a full DCF valuation.[3] This is a loss of 3.59%, slightly less than what is indicated by formula (2). This is because the modified duration measure precisely indicates the percentage change in bond value only for infinitesimal changes in market yields. The approximation is less exact the greater is the change in the yield. Nevertheless, modified duration gives a useful picture of the sensitivity of bond value to market interest rates.[4]

---

[3]
$$\$96.41 = \sum_{j=1}^{10} \frac{\$6}{(1.065)^j} + \frac{\$100}{(1.065)^{10}}$$

[4] Debt values are nonlinear, declining functions of the relevant market yield. For noncallable debt, the curvature of this value function is convex; that is, it bends up away from the axes in a Cartesian graph. Because of this "convexity," bond values actually lose a bit less value when yields rise, and they gain a bit more value when yields fall, as compared to what is indicated by the modified duration measure in formula (2).

Exhibit 19-2 Duration as a Function of Maturity (30-year amortizing, 8% monthly-payment, at par)

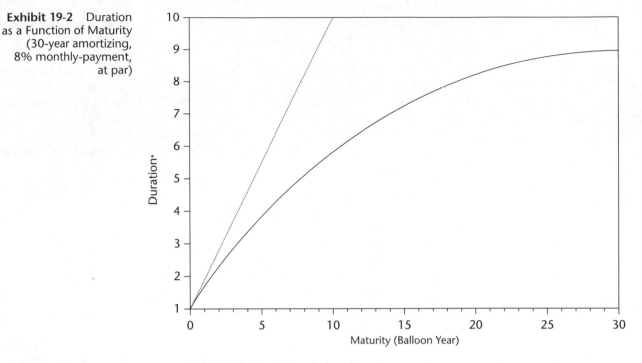

*Modified duration = Macaulay/(1 + r)

19.1.2 Interest Rate Risk and Preferred Habitat

Although bonds have contractually fixed cash flows and are generally perceived as low-risk investments, in fact, bond investors are exposed to several types of risk. We already introduced the concept of default risk in previous chapters. But another type of risk exists to which even default-free government bonds are subject. This is **interest rate risk**. Interest rate risk refers to the effect on the bond investor of changes in the interest rates that prevail in the debt market, known as **market yields**. Both short-term and long-term interest rates change over time in ways that are difficult to predict. This is illustrated in Exhibit 19-3, which shows the history of yields on U.S. government bonds from 1926 to 1998. To better understand interest rate risk, let's consider how changes in interest rates can cause problems for two different types of bond investors.

Bob is our first investor (of course). He likes to trade bonds actively, buying and selling them frequently without waiting for them to mature. He does not have any particular future horizon or target point in time when he needs to cash out of his bond investments. In his manner of investing, Bob is exposed to the volatility of bond market values caused by changes in interest rates. This is the type of volatility we have been dealing with in the previous section, in our discussion of duration. There we noted that longer-duration bonds have greater sensitivity to a given interest rate change. Thus, longer-duration bonds will tend to have more of the type of volatility that Bob must deal with.

Now consider Sue. She has a specific target date at which she needs a specific amount of cash. In particular, Sue knows that she will need $1 million in five years, and she wants to set aside sufficient capital now to provide for that obligation. Sue faces several possible strategies to accomplish this objective.

Exhibit 19-3 Yields on U.S. Government Bonds [Source: Ibbotson Associates (SBBI Yearbook).]

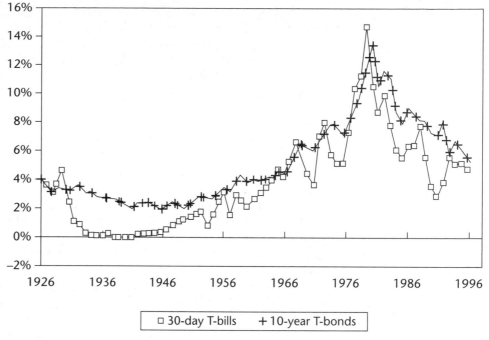

□ 30-day T-bills   + 10-year T-bonds

The most obvious strategy for Sue would be to buy a zero-coupon bond maturing in five years. Suppose the market interest rate on such bonds is 6% (compounded annually). Then such a bond will sell for $1,000,000/1.06^5 = $747,258 today. Sue could invest this amount today and guarantee that she will have exactly the amount she needs in five years. She will face no risk (assuming the bond has no possibility of default). The fact that market interest rates may change between now and her five-year horizon is of no concern to her because she will certainly hold her bond to maturity, when it is contractually obligated to pay $1 million. This investment strategy is called **cash flow matching**. The investor's fixed future cash outflow obligations are exactly matched by future inflows that are contractually fixed.

But Sue faces at least two other alternatives. One would be to buy short-term bonds and plan to reinvest them when they mature. For example, suppose one-year bonds are yielding 6%. If she puts $747,258 into one-year bonds, she will have $792,093 (1.06 × 747,258) in one year. She could then reinvest that amount in a second one-year bond, and so forth, "rolling over" the short-term bonds for five years. With this **roll-over strategy**, however, Sue is exposed to interest rate risk. A year from now, one-year bonds may no longer be yielding 6%. Yields on such bonds may be either higher or lower than 6%. If they are lower, then Sue will have to reinvest at a lower yield. This may cause her to fail to meet her $1 million target in five years. For example, suppose interest rates fall to 5% in one year and remain there for the next four years for all maturities of bonds. Then the $792,093 that Sue got from her first-year investment would only grow to $962,794 by the end of the fifth year (792,093 × 1.05^4). She would fall short of her target by almost 4%.

A second alternative Sue could consider would be to invest in a bond whose maturity is longer than her target horizon, for example, a 10-year bond, and plan to sell this bond in five years, prior to its maturity. For example, if 10-year zero-coupon bonds are currently yielding 6%, then Sue could put $747,258 into such a bond, which promises a single contractual cash flow of $1,338,226 in 10 years. In five years, if yields on five-year zero-coupon bonds are 6% at that time, then this bond will have a market value of $1 million (1,338,226/1.06^5), which Sue could cash out by selling the bond. But this strategy also subjects Sue to interest rate risk. Suppose in five years market yields on five-year zero coupon bonds are higher than 6%. Then the market value of Sue's bond at that time would be less than $1 million. For example, if interest rates are 7%, then her bond will only be worth $954,136 (1,338,226/1.07^5), a shortfall of more than 4%.

Which strategy should Sue employ? If market interest rates are the same on all maturities of bonds, then the answer is obvious. The cash flow matching strategy, buying a five-year zero-coupon bond, is clearly the best strategy because it eliminates the interest rate risk. We would say that a duration of five years is Sue's **preferred habitat** for her bond investments. That is the duration that matches the duration of Sue's liabilities, so it is the duration that she prefers for her bond investments, *other things being equal*.

On the other hand, if interest rates on longer duration bonds were sufficiently higher, then Sue could probably be induced to invest in bonds of longer duration than her preferred habitat. For example, suppose 10-year zero-coupon bonds were offering 7% interest, while 5-year zeros were only offering 6% interest. Sue could either invest $747,258 in five-year bonds and meet her target risklessly, or she could invest a smaller amount in 10-year bonds and expect to meet her target, albeit with some risk.[5] Similarly, if interest rates on short-term bonds were sufficiently higher than those on five-year bonds, then Sue could probably be induced to employ the roll-over strategy of investing in bonds of shorter maturity than her target.

19.1.3 The Yield Curve

You should now be in a position to understand a fundamental phenomenon of the bond market, the **yield curve**. This refers to the difference in the market yields of otherwise identical bonds of different maturities (or, more precisely, different durations). We mentioned the yield curve in previous chapters.[6] Now you can apply your understanding of interest rate risk to deepen your understanding of this important phenomenon. Essentially, the yield curve that is observed between short- and long-term Treasury Bonds is due largely to two considerations: expectations regarding future

[5] For example, suppose Sue expects that in five years the market yield on five-year zeros will be 6%, the same as it is today. Then a 10-year zero that she bought today would have five years left on it, so she would require such a bond with a par value (at maturity) of $1,000,000 × (1.06^5) = $1,338,226. A 10-year zero with such a par value would sell today at a 7% yield for $680,286 (1,338,226/1.07^{10}). Under these expectations, Sue faces a choice between investing $747,258 and meeting her five-year $1 million target for sure, or reducing her current investment by $66,972 dollars (almost 9%), but then facing some possibly sleepless nights as she could not be sure she will exactly meet her target. (Of course, on the upside she might exceed her target if she has a longer-term bond and interest rates fall.)

[6] Most notably, in Chapter 11 (when we discussed the ex ante risk premium in the real estate OCC); in Chapter 13 (when we discussed the relationship of real estate and debt returns regarding the existence of positive leverage); and in Chapter 17 (when we discussed the rationale for adjustable rate mortgages and the forecasting of their YTMs).

short-term nominal interest rates, and concerns about interest rate risk as described in the preceding section.

Consider first the role of expectations about future short-term rates. If investors expect that rates on short-term bonds will be higher in the future than they are now, then they will naturally demand higher yields on long-term bonds than on short-term bonds. Otherwise, they could employ a roll-over strategy, investing only in short-term bonds, and expect to be better off at the end. There would be no investment demand for long-term bonds unless such bonds offered a higher yield than current short-term bonds. Similarly, if investors expect that rates on short-term bonds will be lower in the future than they are now, then borrowers will be able to extract lower interest rates on long-term loans than they could on current short-term loans. Otherwise, borrowers could expect to be better off by borrowing short term and planning to refinance when rates fall. There would be no borrowers willing to take capital from investors trying to issue long-term bonds. Investors would be willing to lend long term at lower rates because they would expect that otherwise they would probably have to roll over their investments at lower yields in the future. Such expectations can account for differences in yields between short- and long-term debt instruments. This is known as the **expectations hypothesis** for explaining the yield curve.

In recent history, a prime driver of differential expectations about short-term interest rates has often been inflation. Short-term interest rates will normally at least equal the current level of inflation prevailing at the time, as short-term lenders want to at least preserve the purchasing power of their capital. But short-term *real* interest rates (net of inflation) are usually pretty low. Thus, when inflation is abnormally high, investors in the United States generally expect inflation to be lower in the long run, so short-term interest rates are expected to fall. This is particularly true if the Federal Reserve Board (FRB or "Fed") can be counted on to adopt tight monetary policy to control inflation. Such policy drives up current short-term interest rates. On the other hand, when inflation is abnormally low, investors may expect that it will rise in the future, leading to higher future short-term interest rates. Also, when the economy is in a recession, the Federal Reserve tends to try to stimulate the economy by driving down current short-term interest rates (which may be low anyway due to lack of demand for capital). The FRB has considerable ability to influence current short-term interest rates, but much less control over long-term rates. If investors believe that the Fed is weak at controlling inflation, then long-term rates may rise due to fear of future inflation.

Expectations about future short-term interest rates are not the only influence on the yield curve. As noted, interest rate risk also plays a role. This role is more prominent when inflation is low and stable. Clearly, investors who actively trade bonds by selling them prior to maturity are subject to volatility that, for a given change in interest rates, is greater for longer-duration bonds. Risk aversion would generally lead such investors to require higher ex ante yields in long-term than in short-term bonds.

Related to interest rate risk, the preferred habitat of bond investors can drive the yield curve to assume various shapes. If more bond investors have short-term preferred habitats (because they have short-term obligations or prefer greater liquidity), then long-term bond yields will have to be higher than short-term bond yields in order to induce such investors to be indifferent between short- and long-term bonds. (Recall in our previous example that yields on 10-year bonds would have to be higher than yields on 5-year bonds to get Sue, with her 5-year horizon, to invest in 10-year rather than 5-year bonds.) The borrowing side of the debt market may also complement this demand, if more borrowers tend to prefer longer-term debt, which puts them under less short-term refinancing pressure.[7]

This interest rate risk and habitat-based explanation for the yield curve is known as the **liquidity preference theory**. It seeks to explain why the yield curve typically is upward-sloping (i.e., long-term yields are typically greater than short-term yields).

Preferred habitat, liquidity preference, and interest rate expectations all interact to produce the yield curve observed in the debt markets. The yield curve constantly changes and is reported graphically in financial newspapers such as the *Wall Street Journal*. Exhibit 19-4 depicts the yield curve during three rather different periods of the 1990s: the spring of 1993, the spring of 1995, and the fall of 1998.

The curve for 1993 would be described as steeply rising, with long-term rates over 300 basis points higher than short-term rates. During that period the economy was still viewed as recovering from a recession. Federal monetary policy was generally expansionary (keeping short-term rates low), while investors expected greater inflationary pressures and/or greater demand for capital in the longer run as the economy recovered.

By 1995 the economy was fully recovered, and the FRB raised short-term interest rates to keep the economy from overheating, thereby reducing the long-run danger of inflation. By this time inflation had been low and stable for some period, lending further credence to lower long-run inflation expectations. The slightly rising yield curve of 1995 is characteristic of a stable economy with stable interest rate expectations.

The 1998 yield curve comes from the fall of that year, at which time there was considerable fear that the U.S. economy was moving toward a recession, caused by an

Exhibit 19-4 Yield Curve U.S. Treasury Strips

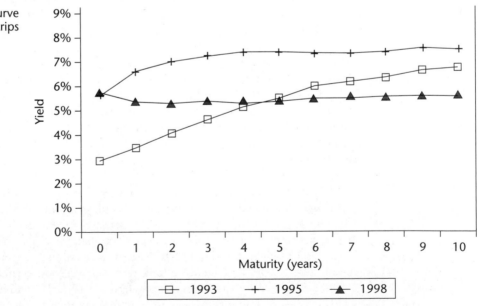

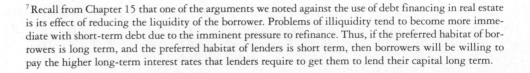

---

[7] Recall from Chapter 15 that one of the arguments we noted against the use of debt financing in real estate is its effect of reducing the liquidity of the borrower. Problems of illiquidity tend to become more immediate with short-term debt due to the imminent pressure to refinance. Thus, if the preferred habitat of borrowers is long term, and the preferred habitat of lenders is short term, then borrowers will be willing to pay the higher long-term interest rates that lenders require to get them to lend their capital long term.

international financial crisis. The result was a flat (or even slightly inverted) yield curve, with long-term rates no higher (or even slightly lower) than short-term rates. If a recession occurred, demand for capital would be reduced, driving down future interest rates.

As noted, the most common type of yield curve is one that is slightly rising, with long-term yields some 100 to 200 basis points above short-term rates. However, a glance back at Exhibit 19-3 shows that there have been (relatively brief) periods when the yield curve has been inverted, with short-term rates above long-term rates. For example, during the late 1970s and early 1980s energy price increases drove inflation to unprecedented peacetime levels, resulting in dramatically inverted yield curves. In fact, inverted yield curves are often good leading indicators of impending recession in the macroeconomy, as they often occur when an overheated economy has driven up inflation. (Recession did follow the inverted yield curves of the late 1970s, but not that of 1998.) More generally, the yield spread, defined as the yield on long-term Treasury Bonds minus the yield on short-term Treasury Bonds, is positively correlated with future real economic growth. Exhibit 19-5 summarizes this discussion by presenting several characteristic yield curve shapes together with what they would typically be saying about the economy.

19.1.4 Maturity Matching and the Management of Fixed-Income Portfolios

What have the yield curve and interest rate risk to do with commercial mortgages? Such phenomena and considerations are basic to the motivations and decisions of the investors who ultimately supply the capital for mortgages, and they underlie or reflect much of the dynamics of the overall debt market. Commercial mortgages are a part of this market. To further your understanding of the roles commercial mortgages can play for investors, we need to consider in more depth some of the concerns of investors in this market.

Exhibit 19-5 Typical Yield Curve Shapes

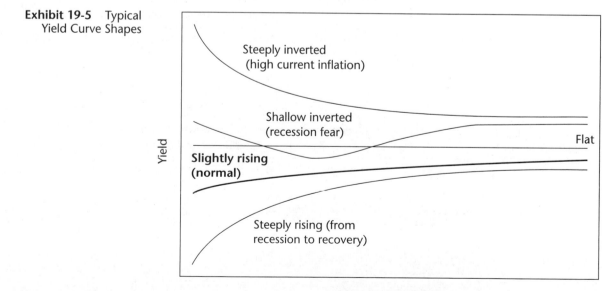

The Maturity-Matching Problem. Let's begin by considering the problem of Simplified National Bank, whose balance sheet as of 6/30/2000 is depicted, in Exhibit 19-6a, with values measured in market values (which may differ from accounting book values). Simplified's assets consist of $100 million of commercial mortgages they have issued. Their liabilities consist of $90 million in deposits, leaving $10 million worth of stockholders' equity.

Simplified's mortgages all happen to be 10-year, zero-coupon loans at 6%. In other words, they provide for a total future cash flow of $179,084,770 on 6/30/2010. Simplified's deposits are all one-year certificates of deposit (CDs) yielding 5%. They promise payments totaling $94,500,000 on 6/30/2001. Now suppose news suddenly arrives that causes the entire yield curve to shift up by one point. One-year yields move from 5% to 6%, while 10-year yields move from 6% to 7%. The result for Simplified's stockholders is depicted in the market value balance sheet for the following day, depicted in Exhibit 19-6b.

Simplified's assets are reduced in value by about $9 million to approximately $91 million, while its liabilities are reduced in value by only about $1 million, to around $89 million.[8] Assets must balance against the total of liabilities and stockholders' equity. Thus, equity value falls by around $8 million, to less than $2 million. A one-point increase in interest rates has led to a 9% fall in asset value, a 1% fall in liability value, and an 80% fall in stockholders' equity value!

This is an example of the danger in what is known as a **maturity gap**. A maturity gap occurs when an investor's assets have greater weighted average duration than his liabilities. The maturity gap problem is exacerbated in lending institutions by the use of leverage. In this case, the initial duration of Simplified's assets was ten years, while

Exhibit 19-6a   Simplified National Bank Balance Sheet as of 6/30/2000

Assets		Liabilities and Equity	
Mortgages:	$100,000,000	Deposits:	$90,000,000
		Equity:	$10,000,000
Total Assets:	$100,000,000	Total L&E:	$100,000,000

Exhibit 19-6b   Simplified National Bank Balance Sheet as of 7/01/2000

Assets		Liabilities and Equity	
Mortgages:	$91,037,616	Deposits:	$89,150,943
		Equity:	$1,886,673
Total Assets:	$91,037,616	Total L&E:	$91,037,616

[8] $179,084,770/1.07^{10}$ = $91,037,616. $94,500,000/1.06$ = $89,150,943.

the duration of its liabilities was one year, giving it a maturity gap of nine years. Simplified's equity value was initially 10% of its asset value, giving it an initial leverage ratio of 10. The combination of a maturity gap and leverage can greatly magnify interest rate risk.

Depository lending institutions tend to be susceptible to maturity gap problems because their deposits are their primary source of capital, and deposits tend to be of short duration.[9] Thus, such institutions tend to be highly levered with short-duration liabilities.[10] The duration of such an institution's equity is approximated by the product of its maturity gap times its leverage ratio.[11] For example, the 80% loss in Simplified's equity value due to a one-point rise in interest rates approximately equals its nine-year duration gap times its initial leverage ratio of 10.

Depository lending institutions are always looking for ways to deal with the maturity gap problem. One way is to make more short-term and fewer long-term loans, thereby reducing the maturity gap. This is one reason banks tend to like to hold construction loans in their asset portfolios more than long-term permanent mortgages. Permanent mortgages are among the longest duration of all bank loans. Another strategy is for banks to issue floating rate or adjustable rate loans. Such loans' values are not as sensitive to changes in market interest rates, because their contractual cash flows rise and fall with these rates. This is one reason banks are usually willing to make adjustable rate loans at lower interest rates than fixed rate loans. The interest rate sensitivity of a long-term adjustable rate loan may be no greater than that of a short-term fixed rate loan.

A third strategy for dealing with the maturity gap problem is to sell long-term loan assets into the secondary market rather than holding them in the institution's permanent asset portfolio. This approach has become very widespread in recent decades, first with residential mortgages and more recently with commercial mortgages. Ultimately, the bank becomes primarily only a loan originator, at least for some types of loans, rather than a long-term investor. The bank then makes its profits in the form of fees for services, rather than from the yield spread between their assets and liabilities. The services may include loan origination and/or loan servicing. The latter refers to the administration of existing loans, including collection and distribution of loan payments.[12]

---

[9] Demand deposits such as checking and savings accounts are effectively near zero duration because depositors can move their funds out quickly if the interest rate offered by the bank on the deposits is not responsive to the market.

[10] High leverage is necessary for lending institutions because they must cover their administrative costs as well as make their profit from the narrow spreads between borrowing and lending rates. For example, suppose there is a 200 basis-point spread between borrowing and lending rates and administrative costs are 150 basis points. This leaves 50 basis points for profit. If the equity investors in the bank require a 10% return, then equity can be no more than 5% of total asset value (as 0.5% is 10% of 5%), implying a leverage ratio of 20.

[11] Using formula (2) and the $A = L + E$ accounting identity, we have

$$dur_E = -(\Delta E/E)/\Delta YTM = [(dur_A)A - (dur_L)L]/E = [dur_L + (dur_A - dur_L)(A/E)] \approx (dur_A - dur_L)(A/E)$$

where dur_A and dur_L are the durations of the firm's assets and liabilities respectively, i.e., $(dur_A - dur_L)$ is the maturity gap.

[12] A fourth strategy for dealing with interest rate risk involves investment in derivative products that have negative interest rate risk, thereby hedging the lending institution's exposure. For example, in Chapter 20 we will describe a class of security known as an interest-only strip (or IO), based on mortgage loans sold into the secondary market. Certain IO securities can be used as interest rate risk hedges in some circumstances.

The maturity gap problem of depository institutions is probably one reason the liquidity preference theory usually works fairly well for explaining the yield curve. But one investor's problem is another investor's opportunity, for other types of financial institutions have long-duration liabilities. Chief among these are life insurance companies and pension funds. Such institutions typically have a long-duration preferred habitat as investors. They can often use long-term mortgages or bonds to implement something close to a maturity-matching strategy. Such institutions are therefore the natural investors in long-term loans, tending to hold such loans in their permanent asset portfolios. Such **portfolio lenders** traditionally provide most of the capital behind permanent commercial mortgages in the United States.[13]

In addition to depository institutions and long-term portfolio lenders, other major categories of investors in the U.S. debt market include endowment funds, wealthy individuals, and foreign investors. Many of these investors have varied or flexible investment holding time horizons. Furthermore, duration habitat preference is not the only concern of bond investors. Although such investors tend generally to be more conservative than equity investors, there is nevertheless considerable range in risk preferences among debt investors. Some investors are willing to trade off interest rate risk and/or default risk for greater expected returns. Also, it must be recognized that investor risk perceptions are determined in many cases by an overall wealth portfolio perspective. Investors' overall wealth is typically invested in other types of assets besides just bonds, notably stocks. Bond risk differs from equity risk, and bonds can be used to diversify a stock portfolio. On the other hand, bonds typically carry more inflation risk than other types of assets, a particular concern to pension funds and others whose liabilities are adjusted to inflation.

Fixed-Income Investment Strategies. Broadly speaking, investment management strategies for fixed-income portfolios can be classified as **trading-oriented** and **immunization-oriented strategies**. The former involve regular buying and selling of bonds prior to maturity. The latter seek to hold bonds to maturity.

Trading-oriented strategies include both active and passive approaches. The former seek to "beat the market," earning superior risk-adjusted returns by employing superior interest rate forecasts or by finding debt products that are mispriced. The objective is to trade in the bond market by buying low and selling high. Passive approaches typically seek to minimize management expenses by investing in bond portfolios that closely replicate major indices of bond holding period returns. Passive strategies still require some bond trading, for example, to keep a constant average maturity, although passive strategies do not require as much trading as active strategies. Depending on the risk aversion of the investor, leverage may be employed in either active or passive trading-oriented strategies, in order to exploit yield spreads (e.g., borrowing at lower short-term rates in order to invest at higher long-term rates, in effect, purposely creating a maturity gap). All trading-oriented strategies are exposed to interest rate risk because in such a strategy bonds are often sold prior to maturity.

In contrast, immunization-oriented strategies seek to avoid interest rate risk. This can be done by avoiding the sale of bonds prior to maturity. Immunization-oriented strategies are more conservative than trading-oriented strategies and generally result

---

[13]In recent years even the traditional portfolio lenders have often sold whole loans into the secondary market and used the proceeds to buy CMBS, a seeming redundancy! However, CMBS provide some advantages over whole loans, as we will discuss in Chapter 20.

in lower average investment returns. The cash flow matching technique described previously is an extreme example of immunization, possible when all future obligations can be predicted exactly in nominal terms (and when appropriate-maturity bonds can be found to match them). More typically, immunization is applied by matching the weighted average duration of assets and liabilities. This protects the investor's net wealth from most of the effects of interest rate swings.[14] It does not, however, protect against unexpected changes in inflation, if the investor's liabilities are adjusted to inflation. Perhaps because of this, immunization strategies are less popular than one might think, even among conservative institutions such as pension funds.

19.2 COMMERCIAL MORTGAGE RETURNS: EX ANTE AND EX POST

With some basic knowledge of bond investment in hand, you can now understand the fundamental determinants of commercial mortgage returns, both ex ante and ex post. The ex ante returns are the market yields (the required return expectations for marginal investors in the debt market), the yields that effectively determine asset prices in that market. Ex post returns are the periodic returns, or HPRs, actually realized by mortgage investors trading in the debt market, reflecting the effect of changes in the market yield (and therefore in asset values) during each holding period. We begin with the former, ex ante returns.

19.2.1 Mortgage Yield: The Components of Ex Ante Returns

In this section we want to integrate the debt investment economics you learned in the previous section with our quantification of default risk in Chapter 18 to summarize the overall components of commercial mortgage yields. This is important for borrowers because such yields represent their cost of debt capital and determine the amount that can be borrowed in return for a given pledge of future income. An understanding of ex ante yields is also important for mortgage investors because such yields represent their expected returns if they hold the mortgage to maturity, and changes in such yields cause either gains or losses in their realized returns if they do not hold to maturity. The better you understand mortgage market yields, the more rationally you can think about how such yields may change over time.

A good way to visualize the determinants of commercial mortgage yields is to build up the total yield as a stack of various components. This is represented in Exhibit 19-7. We will discuss briefly each component shown in the exhibit.

---

[14]As noted, duration is not a perfect measure of interest rate sensitivity. Sophisticated immunization techniques also attempt to take account of convexity, shifts in the yield curve, and other issues. It is worthwhile to note also that a principle similar to duration matching, what is often referred to as **maturity matching**, is often applied to develop sound financing strategies for long-term equity investments. The idea is that assets should be financed with debt whose maturity corresponds to the expected lifetime of the asset (or more properly, the cash outflows for the debt service should correspond in time to the expected cash inflows from the asset). This avoids liquidity problems and interest rate risk for the equity investor.

Exhibit 19-7 Components of Commercial Mortgage Total Yield

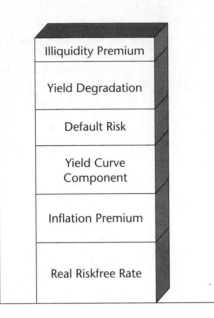

Real Riskfree Rate. This is the most basic part of the yield, the pure short-term time value of money (TVM) for constant-purchasing-power dollars, the real value of what we have been labeling r_f in this book ever since Chapter 9. This component is typically in the neighborhood of 200 to 300 basis points, but it varies with short-term capital supply and demand, and in response to Federal Reserve Board monetary policy.

Inflation Premium. This is the premium due to the expected rate of inflation in the short term. It reflects the need of the investor to obtain the short-term real return measured in constant purchasing power. The inflation premium component is typically close to the recent past average rate of inflation, for example, 200 to 300 basis points during the late 1990s. The sum of the real riskfree rate and the inflation premium equals the nominal riskfree rate, what we have labeled r_f, typically observed as the U.S. Treasury Bill yield.[15] In the late 1990s T-bill yields were typically around 5%.

Yield Curve Component. This component reflects the effect of the yield curve, as discussed in section 19.1.3. It reflects considerations of interest rate risk, liquidity preferences, and expectations about future short-term interest rates. Of course, interest rate expectations include the effect of long-term inflation expectations.[16] This component of the mortgage yield depends on the current shape of the yield curve and

---

[15] Recall from Chapter 9 that $(1 + r) = (1 + R)(1 + i)$, where R is the real rate and i is the inflation rate. Thus, $r = R + i + iR$. The third term is usually ignored as it is very small. If investors require a nominal return sufficient to preserve a target after-tax real return, then we have $[1 + (1 - T)r] = (1 + R)(1 + i)$, which implies $r = (1 + R)(1 + i)/(1 - T)$, where T is the tax rate and R is the *after-tax* target real return.

[16] More precisely, the long-term interest rate expectations component includes the effect of any *difference* between long-run and short-run inflation expectations, as the latter are already included in the nominal T-bill yield that is already on our "stack."

the duration of the mortgage.[17] Usually, the yield curve is slightly upward-sloping, with long-term Treasury Bonds yielding 100 to 200 basis points more than short-term T-bills. Fixed rate long-term (permanent) commercial mortgages are typically priced based on the long-term end of the yield curve (typically based on yields of Treasury Bonds of the same maturity), and so would include a positive yield curve component in their YTMs. Adjustable rate loans can be priced based on the short-term end of the yield curve. Based on our discussion in section 19.1.3, the yield curve component of mortgage market yields varies over time in response to the outlook for the macroeconomy and long-term inflation fears. With a steeply upward-sloping yield curve, this component of mortgage yields may be 300 to 400 basis points or more. With an inverted yield curve, the yield curve component would be negative. During the stable, low-inflation environment of most of the latter half of the 1990s, the yield curve component was typically about 100 basis points.

Default Risk. This component reflects the risk premium investors require in their expected total return due to the *risk* of default. (This is different from the effect of the *expectation* of default, which will be discussed next.) Recall that return risk refers to the phenomenon of realized ex post returns possibly varying *around* their expectation as of the time the investment was made. Risk is thus two-sided. Realized returns can be either above or below their prior expectations. Investors demand a risk premium in their ex ante returns because they dislike this uncertainty (they are risk averse). The risk that matters most to investors is the component of ex post return uncertainty that cannot be diversified away. Default risk is of this nature. Commercial mortgage borrowers tend to default more often when the economy is doing poorly, which is likely to be just when mortgage investors can least afford to experience an unpleasant surprise. Therefore, investors demand a risk premium because of the uncertainty associated with the possibility of loan default.[18] The default risk premium defined in this way, that is, as a component of the *expected return* to commercial mortgages, is probably typically in the neighborhood of 50 to 100 basis points.

Ex Ante Yield Degradation. This component reflects the effect of the *expectation* of default in the commercial mortgage. It is the difference between the *contractual* yield as if there were no possibility of default (the "stated yield") and the *expected return* including the realistic possibility of default. This component of the mortgage yield was discussed extensively in section 18.1 of the preceding chapter. There we noted that for typical long-term commercial mortgages in the United States, the ex ante yield degradation is probably in the neighborhood of 50 to 100 basis points on average.[19] The sum of the default risk-based yield component discussed in the previous

[17] Prepayable mortgages lack definite maturity. This introduces what is known as prepayment risk, a risk that is closely related to interest rate risk, because prepayment is more likely when interest rates fall, forcing the lender to reinvest at a lower yield. As noted in Chapter 17, prepayment risk can be quantified and evaluated using option pricing theory. In general, callable bonds have higher yields than otherwise similar noncallable bonds, reflecting the cost to the investor of the prepayment option given to the borrower. The U.S. Treasury Bonds on which the yield curve is computed are noncallable.

[18] It should be noted that commercial mortgage default rates have more to do with the health of the commercial property sector than with the health of the macroeconomy as a whole. Although commercial property returns are positively correlated with such macroeconomic indicators as national consumption, this correlation is far from perfect. It is not clear how commercial mortgage default risk compares to that of corporate bonds in this regard.

[19] Recall that the average credit loss in the GLCMPI was 73 basis points during the 1978–98 period.

paragraph, plus the ex ante yield degradation, equals the spread between quoted yields of commercial mortgages and those of similar-duration Treasury Bonds. This spread is often referred to as the **default risk premium**. However, as noted, this risk premium really consists of two separate components, one of which is a true risk premium, and the other of which is an adjustment of the contractual yield to reflect realistic return expectations. The two components together have typically averaged in the neighborhood of 150 to 200 basis points for commercial mortgages. This is about the same yield spread as that between Treasury Bonds and lower investment-grade (e.g., BBB- or Baa-rated) corporate bonds.

Illiquidity Premium. The final component of the typical commercial mortgage ex ante yield is an **illiquidity premium**. This is a component of the risk premium necessary to compensate investors for putting their money in a relatively illiquid asset, that is, one that may be difficult to sell quickly at full value. Most commercial mortgages are not securitized, but are held as whole loans. The secondary market for such loans, each of which is unique in some respects (including the nature of the property securing it), is thin, typically less well developed than the underlying property market. Although such illiquidity can pose problems for an investor, the types of investors that hold whole loans typically have deep pockets, that is, they have plenty of liquidity elsewhere in their wealth portfolios. Thus, the illiquidity of commercial mortgages is not of as much concern to them as you might think, and the illiquidity premium in commercial mortgages is typically fairly small, on the order of 20 to 50 basis points. The upper end of this range would apply to loans that are more unique or less appealing to large institutional investors.

The securitization of commercial mortgages, in the form of CMBS, has resulted in whole loans being sliced up into different classes of securities, many of which are traded publicly, thereby acquiring greater liquidity. However, liquidity is far from perfect even for publicly traded corporate bonds, and investors in publicly traded securities may care more about liquidity than holders of whole loans, so they attach a greater premium to it. Furthermore, the securitization process, while it may result in a diminution of the illiquidity premium, brings additional layers of administration and servicing of the debt. This adds to the mortgage administrative costs, which places another layer onto the effective yield faced by loan originators and borrowers in the primary market. As a result, contractual yields on loans that are to be securitized are not obviously lower in general than yields on loans intended to be held whole by portfolio lenders.[20]

The sum of the six components just described gives the contractual yield prevailing in the commercial mortgage market, the yield that reflects the value of the mortgage asset in the debt market and that is used computationally to price mortgage loans. This is referred to simply as the market yield observable in the mortgage market. For example, the table in Exhibit 19-8 shows how the approximate values of these

---

[20] Exact apples-to-apples comparisons are difficult because the loans that are issued to be securitized typically differ in various respects (such as size, credit quality, and loan terms) from those that are not intended to be securitized. In theory, however, if there is an active primary market simultaneously in mortgages to be held whole in portfolios and in mortgages that are to be securitized in the secondary market, then the yields of both types of loans must be equal for the same type of loan. Otherwise, one side of the market would dry up (e.g., if yields were higher in loans not to be securitized, then borrowers would flock to the conduits issuing loans to be securitized, and vice versa—if yields were lower in loans not to be securitized then lenders would not issue such loans, that is, all loans would be securitized).

Exhibit 19-8
Approximate Commercial
Mortgage Market Stated
Yield Components at
Two Historical Periods

	Late 1990s	1993
Real riskfree rate:	2.50%	0.00%
Inflation premium:	2.50%	3.50%
Yield curve:	1.00%	3.50%
Default risk:	0.75%	1.00%
Yield degradation:	0.75%	0.50%
Illiquidity:	0.25%	0.50%
Total stated yield:	7.75%	9.00%

six components totaled up to typical mortgage market contract interest rates during different macroeconomic "climates" prevailing at two periods of time during the 1990s. The table depicts two periods: the latter part of the decade when the economy was relatively stable, and 1993 when the commercial real estate market was still recovering from its recent slump and the Fed had driven short-term interest rates sharply down to stimulate the macroeconomy out of the recession of the early 1990s. The earlier period was also characterized by inflation expectations a bit higher than the latter period.

As seen in the bottom line in Exhibit 19-8, mortgage rates were higher in 1993 than in the late 1990s, typically at around 9% in the former year versus less than 8% in the later years. Particularly striking is the difference in the expected return risk premium between these two periods. The nominal riskfree interest rate was around 3.5% in 1993 and around 5% in the later years of the decade.[21] Removing the yield degradation component from the stated yields, we see that the expected total return was about 8.5% in 1993 and 7% in the later years.[22] Thus, the typical commercial mortgage ex ante risk premium, $RP = E[r] - r_f$, was about 500 basis points in 1993 and about 200 basis points in the later years of the 1990s (8.5% − 3.5% = 5%, and 7% − 5% = 2%). Much of this reduction in mortgage risk premiums during the 1990s reflects the movement in the yield curve from a steeply upward-sloping shape in 1993 to a slightly upward-sloping shape in the late decade. However, there was also a shift in investor perceptions of, and preferences for, commercial property market risk.[23]

[21] As noted, the nominal riskfree rate empirically observable in T-bill yields equals the sum of the first two components in the "yield stack" in Exhibits 19-7 and 19-8.

[22] Recall that the yield degradation component reflects the difference between the realistic expected total return ($E[r]$, the going-in IRR) and the contractual or stated yield for the mortgage.

[23] This point was noted in Chapter 11, in our discussion of the opportunity cost of capital for commercial real estate investment. There it was pointed out that expected return risk premiums were typically in the neighborhood of 300 to 400 basis points for institutional quality commercial property during most of the 1980s and latter 1990s, but probably up to twice that level in the early 1990s during and in the aftermath of the property market crash. In this respect 1993 was an extreme year in which yield curve effects were combined with property market cyclical effects. If realistic commercial property expected returns in 1993 were around 12% (given the low point in the property market cycle), then that would imply a risk premium of around 850 basis points in the going-in IRR for typical institutional property investment at that time, as compared to a 500-basis-point risk premium in commercial mortgages at the same time. If realistic going-in IRRs on unlevered property investments then declined to around

19.2.2 Ex Post Performance: The Historical Record

The yields described in the previous section are the market's ex ante stated yields, the contractual YTMs reflecting the before-tax expectations of the marginal investors in the mortgage asset market. For investors who hold their loans to maturity, these ex ante yields will indeed also equal their ex post realized yields, before taxes and in the absence of default or prepayment. However, for investors who sell mortgages prior to maturity, or for investors who compute the periodic returns to their mortgage portfolios by "marking to market" their portfolio values at the end of each period, realized ex post returns will typically differ from ex ante yields.

Computing HPRs for Mortgages. Ex post **holding period returns (HPRs)** are computed for bonds or mortgages just as they are for properties or stocks. Each periodic return consists of the cash flow within that period plus any change in the market value of the debt asset between the beginning and end of the period, all divided by the market value of the debt asset as of the beginning of the period. The periodic cash flow typically consists of regular debt service (both interest and principal amortization), although it would also include any prepayment of principal or loss recovery through foreclosure in the event of default. The change in market value of the debt asset reflects (1) changes in the contractual OLB (due to regular amortization and to prepayments or balloon payments) and (2) changes in the market value of the debt asset due either to changes in market interest rates or to changes in the perceived default risk of the loan.

The HPR formula for mortgages is represented symbolically in formula (3) below, for the return in period t:

$$r_t = \frac{CF_t + (V_t - V_{t-1})}{V_{t-1}} = \frac{(PMT_t + REC_t) + (D_t - D_{t-1})}{D_{t-1}} \tag{3}$$

where PMT_t is the regular debt service during period t, REC_t is the value of any prepayments or the net recovery in any foreclosures during period t, and D_t is the market value of any remaining debt as of the end of period t. In a mortgage index, this formula is aggregated across a large number of individual loans composing the index portfolio.[24]

Realized periodic total returns, as measured by the HPRs, are much more volatile than ex ante yields. The volatility of ex post mortgage total returns (like those of other bonds) derives primarily from changes over time in the *market value* of the debt asset (changes in $D_t - D_{t-1}$). As noted, such market value changes primarily reflect two effects: (1) changes in market interest rates (that is, changes in the ex ante yields) and (2) changes in perceived default risk (that is, changes in the expected future cash flow from the mortgage).[25] Apart from this volatility effect, the *average* level of ex post

---

8.5% by the late 1990s, then this would imply roughly a 350-basis-point risk premium for property at a time when mortgage risk premiums were on the order of 200 basis points. Thus, both the risk premiums and the degree of positive leverage declined in commercial real estate investment during the 1990s, from levels that were at historical peaks early in the decade.

[24] In an index such as the GLCMPI a simulated portfolio is used, composed of cohorts of typical loans. The loans in the index portfolio typically change from one period to the next, but by definition the HPR within each period is computed on the basis of a "static portfolio" (that is, the same loans) at the beginning and end of the period.

[25] These two effects act on, respectively, the denominators and numerators in the DCF valuation of the mortgage.

returns in a historical index reflects the effect of realized credit losses as a result of defaults in the loans that compose the index portfolio, as well as the general trend in market interest rates over the historical period being measured. Another difference to bear in mind between ex ante and ex post returns is that ex ante yields are multiperiod IRRs, while ex post periodic returns are typically reported as a series of HPRs.

With these differences in mind, we would expect mortgage HPRs to approximately equal ex ante yields on average over the long run, adjusting as appropriate for credit losses and differences between IRRs and average HPRs.[26] Over the very long run, this expectation is indeed probably born out in practice. Although very long-term data is not available for mortgages, Exhibit 19-9 traces ex ante yields and ex post HPRs for long-term U.S. government bonds from 1926 through 1998. The ex ante yields (that is, the current yields observed in the bond market) are represented by the relatively smooth solid line, while the ex post HPRs are represented by the more volatile dashed line that oscillates around the ex ante yield. The striking volatility apparent in the HPRs is a manifestation of interest rate risk. Nevertheless, the average HPR is within a few basis points of the average ex ante yield for these default-free bonds over this long period of history.[27]

Over shorter periods of history interest rates may trend in one direction, often reflecting swings in inflation or government fiscal and monetary policy. Such changes in interest rates may not be completely anticipated by investors and therefore not fully reflected in ex ante yields. As interest rate changes are fully reflected in ex post returns, this can cause average ex post returns to differ from average ex ante returns

Exhibit 19-9 Yields (ex ante) and HPRs (ex post) on Long-Term U.S. Government Bonds, 1926–1998 [Source: Ibbotson Associates (SBBI Yearbook).]

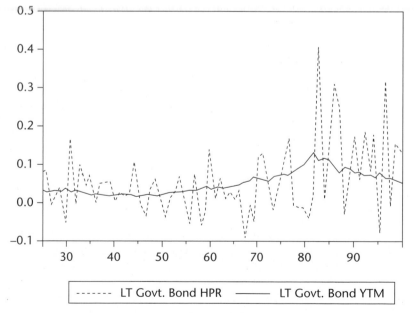

26 Recall that the arithmetic time-weighted average HPR is a positive function of the volatility of the series. For normally distributed returns the arithmetic mean approximately equals the geometric mean plus one-half the variance of the returns series. IRRs are essentially like geometric mean returns in this respect (although they are dollar-weighted rather than time weighted).

27 Over the 1926–98 period, the U.S. Treasury long-term bond geometric mean was 5.24% for the ex ante yield to maturity, and 5.33% for the ex post annual HPR.

Exhibit 19-10 U.S.
Commercial Mortgage
Yields and HPRs

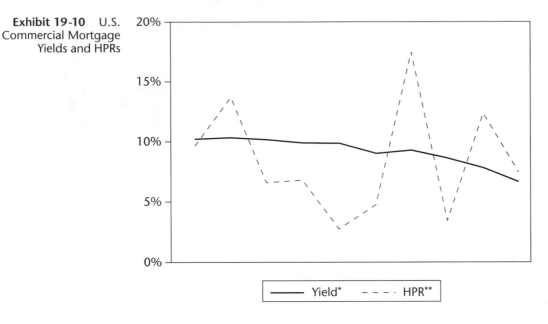

1988	1989	1990	1991	1992	1993	1994	1995	1996	1997	1998
10.21%	10.24%	10.05%	9.89%	9.26%	8.76%	9.00%	8.61%	7.86%	7.94%	6.93%
9.42%	13.93%	6.39%	6.88%	2.54%	6.85%	4.86%	17.23%	4.32%	12.25%	7.25%

*Contract yield, source: Korpacz.
**Ex post total return adjusted for credit losses, source: GLCMPI.

over short to medium length historical periods. During periods of generally declin-ing interest rates, such as the 1980s and 1990s, ex post bond returns tended to exceed ex ante returns (at least for default-free bonds). The opposite was true in the preced-ing period of rising interest rates during the 1970s.

Historical Results for Commercial Mortgages. Exhibit 19-10 shows average prevailing contract yields and the annual ex post periodic total returns for long-term fixed rate commercial mortgages in the United States during the 1988–98 period. Over this period the average stated yield was 8.98% while the average ex post total return was 8.36%, as measured by the Giliberto-Levy Commercial Mortgage Price Index (GLCMPI).[28] The GLCMPI is adjusted to reflect credit losses due to defaults. During the 1988–98 period such losses were substantial due to the commercial property crash in the early part of that period. Without including the effect of credit losses, the average GLCMPI return during 1988–98 would have been 9.91%, con-siderably above the average contract yield. This reflects the effect of the generally declining interest rates during this period.

Exhibit 19-11 presents a longer-term and broader view of ex post periodic return performance, comparing annual GLCMPI total returns (loss-adjusted) with those of

[28]Adjusting for volatility the GLCMPI average was 8.26%. The stated yields in Exhibit 19-10 are taken from the *Korpacz Real Estate Investor Survey*.

Exhibit 19-11
Year-End Value of $1
(income reinvested)

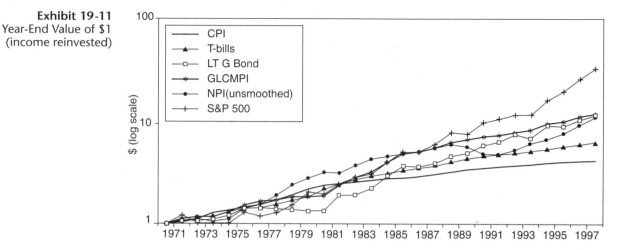

the NCREIF Property Index (NPI, unsmoothed), the S&P 500 Stock Index, long-term U.S. government bonds, and T-bills.[29] The Consumer Price Index (CPI) is also indicated. The chart indicates what one dollar invested at the end of 1971 would have grown to in each of the asset classes at the end of each subsequent year (with rein-vestment of income). Exhibit 19-12 presents the historical statistics for the periodic total returns during this period. Commercial mortgages provided a time-weighted geometric average annual total return of 9.51% during this period, slightly more than the average long-term government bond return of 9.39%.[30]

It is important to note the evidence on the comovement between mortgages and other asset classes apparent in the correlation statistics in Exhibit 19-12. Such comove-ment is important in determining the effect of mortgages in a mixed-asset investment portfolio, and in determining the effect of leverage on real estate equity risk. The most striking correlation in Exhibit 19-12 is between mortgages and long-term bonds. This reflects the fact that mortgages are essentially bondlike assets, whose HPR volatility is driven largely by interest rate movements.[31] Mortgages are also moderately positively

[29]In Exhibits 19-11 and 19-12 the NPI has been "unsmoothed" (or "delagged") using the annual reverse-engineering procedure described in Geltner (1993). (See Chapter 25 for further description.)

[30]This 12-basis-point spread between mortgage and government bond returns does not necessarily imply that average mortgage ex post returns have failed to achieve the typical 50-to-100-basis-point ex ante default risk premium described in section 19.2.1. The long-term government bond index tracked here has a longer average duration than that of the GLCMPI, and the yield curve was upward-sloping on average during the 1971–98 period. The average ex post return differential between mortgages and government bonds of similar duration was greater than 12 basis points during 1971–98. Incidentally, if it were not for the effect of credit losses, the mortgage return would have exceeded the government bond return by about 120 basis points in Exhibit 19-12, measured by the geometric means.

[31]The GLCMPI appears slightly less volatile than the bond index in Exhibit 19-12. Once again, this differ-ence is largely explained by the difference in average duration between the GLCMPI and the Ibbotson long-term government bond index. The bond index's longer average duration makes it more sensitive to interest rates. The GLCMPI duration was over seven years in the 1970s, but less than five years in the 1990s.

	CPI	T-bills	LT G Bond	GLCMPI**	NPI***	S&P 500
Geom. Mean	5.26%	6.86%	9.39%	9.51%	9.16%	13.82%
Arith. Mean	5.31%	6.89%	10.02%	9.75%	9.62%	15.09%
Volatility	NA	2.72%	12.22%	7.54%	10.01%	16.69%
Sharpe*	NA	NA	0.26	0.38	0.27	0.49
Correlations:						
CPI	100%	58%	−50%	−48%	14%	−39%
T-bills	58%	100%	−2%	4%	11%	−10%
LT G Bond	−50%	−2%	100%	81%	−29%	48%
GLCMPI	−48%	4%	81%	100%	−4%	49%
NPI (unsmoothed)	14%	11%	−29%	−4%	100%	17%
S&P 500	−39%	−10%	48%	49%	17%	100%

*The Sharpe Ratio is equal to (*Mean − T-bill Mean*)/*Volatility*. It is a crude measure of return adjusted for risk (see Chapter 21 and 27).
**Net of credit losses.
***Unsmoothed.

Exhibit 19-12 Historical Annual Periodic Total Return Statistics, 1972–1998
(Sources: Ibbotson Associates, John B. Levy & Co., NCREIF.)

correlated with stocks, as represented by the S&P 500 index (approximately +50% correlation), and negatively correlated with inflation (approximately −50%). In both these respects mortgages are very similar to long-term bonds.

It is perhaps a bit surprising that mortgages showed less correlation with real estate during the 1972–98 period than they did with stocks. The annual GLCMPI and unsmoothed NCREIF index were effectively uncorrelated during this period (−4% correlation coefficient). This probably largely reflects the differential response of property and fixed rate mortgages to changes in inflation expectations. As noted in previous chapters, commercial property is considered an inflation hedge, typically responding positively to increases in inflation. The opposite is true of fixed rate long-term debt. Thus, even though mortgages and underlying property might both respond in the same direction to unanticipated changes in *real* interest rates (and to changes in property market fundamentals), their opposite response to unanticipated changes in inflation dampens their correlation. This means that, viewed from a mark-to-market perspective (the perspective represented by periodic returns), leverage with long-term fixed rate debt would tend to increase the volatility of real estate equity proportionately more than stock equity.[32]

[32] The volatility of the levered equity position as a function of the leverage ratio (LR), the volatilities of the underlying asset and the debt (S_P and S_D respectively), and the correlation between these two (C_{PD}) is

$$S_E = \sqrt{[(LR)S_P]^2 + [(LR-1)S_D]^2 - 2C_{PD}[(LR)(LR-1)S_P S_D]}$$

Thus, when the correlation between the underlying asset and the debt is positive ($C_{PD} > 0$, as in the case of stocks), the periodic return volatility of the levered equity is reduced by the effect of the third term subtracted from under the square-root operator. This third term disappears in the case of zero

A Nagging Data Problem in Commercial Mortgage HPR Indices

Regularly published indices of ex post periodic total returns to commercial mortgages did not exist in the United States until the 1990s. Indices such as the GLCMPI provide an invaluable resource for investors, and the quality of such indices is generally good, presenting fewer measurement problems, for example, than appraisal-based indices of underlying property returns, such as the NCREIF Index. Nevertheless, it's more fun to use an index than to learn about what goes into making it.

As of the late 1990s, a nagging weakness plaguing commercial mortgage indices was the difficulty in getting reliable information about conditional loss severity in the event of default. The computation of credit loss effects in the GLCMPI is based on relatively reliable

information regarding default *incidence* (using data from ACLI). But such accurate information on conditional loss *severity* was not accessible by the late 1990s. As a result, the GLCMPI credit loss adjustment generally assumes average conditional loss severities around 30%.

This weakness is relevant for computing the credit loss adjusted returns that are important in the type of comparative performance analysis we have been doing in this section. It is quite possible that the 30% assumption was too low during much of the 1972–98 period, particularly during the slump of the late 1980s and early 1990s. (See, e.g., Ciochetti [1998] and Fabozzi and Jacob [1999].) If so, then true loss-adjusted HPRs would be lower than those indicated in the GLCMPI.

Mortgage versus Property Risk and Return: Is There Positive Leverage? It is interesting to note in Exhibit 19-12 that commercial mortgage ex post total returns have averaged about the same as those of underlying commercial property (as measured by the NCREIF index). This suggests that, from the perspective of average ex post HPRs (as opposed to ex ante expectations), borrowing did not generally provide positive leverage for commercial property investors over the 1972–98 period, at least for the types of institutional real estate represented by the NCREIF index.[33] Of course, the historical period covered by these statistics includes the commercial property market slump of the late 1980s and early 1990s. The 1972–98 period also includes the long secular decline in interest rates from the early 1980s to the late 1990s. These two historical phenomena possibly caused average ex post HPRs to exceed average ex ante expectations in mortgages, and to fall below such expectations

---

correlation ($C_{PD} = 0$, as with commercial property and long-term fixed rate mortgages). Intuitively, this point can be seen as follows. When the market value of the underlying assets of a typical publicly traded corporation declines, there is a likelihood or tendency for the market value of the firm's outstanding bonds to decline at the same time, as suggested by the +50% correlation between stock and bond returns. Thus, the two declines will tend to offset each other to some degree, resulting in less leverage in the equity volatility than would be the case if there were no positive correlation between equity and debt returns.

[33] The ex post average HPR perspective presented here is not exactly the same as the multiperiod return perspective of a borrow-and-hold investor who paid the loan off at par value. Nevertheless, the fact that the mortgage returns here are adjusted for credit losses, and our previous point that such average ex post returns tend to equal average ex ante mortgage return expectations in the long run, does suggest that there was, on average, little or no positive leverage (ex post) in the total return on institutional quality commercial property during the 1972–98 period.

in underlying property. This historical result may account for a lack of positive leverage ex post, without implying that positive leverage did not exist ex ante.[34]

On the other hand, it may be that the capital markets viewed commercial mortgages as being as risky as underlying commercial property during the 1972–98 period. As noted in Chapter 13 (in our discussion of leverage), although debt risk is different from property risk, it is not necessarily of less concern to the relevant marginal investors in the capital markets.[35]

In this regard, several points of comparison between the mortgage and property HPR statistics indicated in Exhibit 19-12 are worthy of consideration. On the one hand, the statistics suggest that commercial mortgages were slightly less volatile than the underlying properties securing them (7.5% mortgage volatility versus 10% property index volatility, unsmoothed). This point appears to suggest slightly less risk in mortgages than in the underlying property. On the other hand, mortgages were more highly correlated with stocks and bonds, and less correlated with inflation, than were the underlying properties. This means that mortgages typically provided less portfolio diversification benefit, and greater exposure to inflation risk, than did underlying property.[36] The 1970s and early 1980s was a period of growing use of portfolio theory by investors, and it was a period of historically high capital market sensitivity to inflation risk. To put this another way, measured in *real* terms (net of inflation), mortgage volatility was virtually the same as unsmoothed property index volatility, but a greater part of the property volatility could be diversified away in a mixed-asset portfolio of stocks and bonds.[37]

Considering the foregoing, it seems plausible that the capital markets might have evaluated the risks of mortgages as highly as those of underlying property, on average during the 1972–98 period. This would imply that even on an ex ante basis, long-term fixed rate debt would not have provided positive leverage for equity investment in institutional quality commercial property.[38] Thus, historical results

---

[34] Comparing ex post and ex ante yields is an inexact art. It is difficult to quantify reliably some of the important counterbalancing considerations. For example, while a greater-than-expected decline in interest rates would tend to push ex post mortgage HPRs above their ex ante expectations, greater-than-expected credit losses have the opposite effect (not only on the HPRs but on the average realized lifetime yields). The period of the 1980s and 1990s probably included both of these types of results. Furthermore, the weakness noted in the text box is relevant in weighing this balance.

[35] It seems likely that immunization-oriented debt market investors who experience buy-and-hold returns tend to be intramarginal, while the marginal investors who determine asset market prices may typically be more concerned with periodic returns, such as those represented by the GLCMPI.

[36] This suggests that levered equity positions in real estate should make better inflation hedges and better diversifiers of a stock portfolio than unlevered property equity. Remember that the borrower has a negative (or short) position in the debt asset, while the lender or mortgage investor has the corresponding positive (or long) position. In a portfolio, the effect of the short position is just the opposite of the effect of the long position.

[37] Portfolio theory will be discussed in Part VII. For now it suffices for you to realize that property's lower correlation with stocks and bonds gives it greater diversification benefit than mortgages in a mixed-asset portfolio that is long in bonds. On the other hand, mortgages are more useful than property for implementing immunization-oriented strategies such as maturity matching of assets and liabilities.

[38] The magnitude of the ex ante expected return risk premium corresponds to the magnitude of risk as perceived by the relevant marginal investors in the capital market, by definition, the market's valuation of risk.

during the latter part of the 20th century cast some doubt on the realism of the traditional assumption that mortgages are less risky than underlying property, at least as regards long-term fixed rate mortgages on institutional quality property equity. This, in turn, raises a question about how widespread is positive leverage in the ex ante total return in such circumstances.[39]

19.3 CHAPTER SUMMARY

In this chapter we stepped back to give you some economic background relevant to the entire debt market, the branch of the capital market in which commercial mortgages are an integral part. By understanding such fundamental phenomena as interest rate risk, maturity matching, and the yield curve, you can better understand commercial mortgages and the role they play in the capital markets. We also completed in this chapter the picture of commercial mortgage investment risk that we began in Chapter 18, so that you now have a more comprehensive picture of what determines prices and yields in the mortgage market. Finally, we reviewed some evidence of the recent historical HPR investment performance of commercial mortgages in the United States. In so doing, we broached some of the macrolevel portfolio concerns of mixed-asset investors, issues that we will pursue further in Part VII. In the meantime, we need to complete our picture of real estate debt by considering CMBS in the next chapter.

KEY TERMS

maturity
duration (Macaulay and modified)
interest rate risk
market yields
cash flow matching
roll-over strategy
preferred habitat
yield curve

expectations hypothesis
liquidity preference theory
maturity gap
portfolio lenders
trading-oriented strategies
immunization-oriented strategies
maturity matching
contractual yield component "stack"

default risk
ex ante yield degradation
default risk premium
illiquidity premium
holding period returns (HPR)
   to debt

[39] But see note #23 at the end of section 19.2.1. The typical mortgage ex ante risk premiums depicted in Exhibit 19-8 appear to be less than contemporaneous underlying property ex ante risk premiums during both of two very different environments in the early and late 1990s.

STUDY QUESTIONS

Conceptual Questions

19.1.   Why is finite maturity important and useful to certain types of investors?

19.2.   Define the term *duration*. What is the general relationship between duration and maturity. How is this relationship different for zero-coupon versus coupon bonds? How is it different for short-term versus long-term debt?

19.3.   What is interest rate risk?

19.4.   Describe the bond investment strategy known as cash flow matching? Give an example.

19.5.   What is meant by the term preferred habitat? How is it related to the duration of a bond investor's liabilities?

19.6.   What is the yield curve, and what are the two principal considerations of bond market investors that underlie the curve?

19.7.   Suppose the bond market expects short-term interest rates to remain constant for the foreseeable future, yet we observe a rising yield curve in the bond market. What can you then say about the preferred habitats of borrowers versus lenders? What is the name for this theory to explain the typical upward-sloping shape of the yield curve?

19.8.   Describe the typical macroeconomic current environment and future expectations associated with the following shapes of the yield curve: (a) steeply upward-sloping, (b) slightly upward-sloping, (c) shallow-inverted or flat, (d) steeply inverted.

19.9.   What is a maturity gap? Why is this problem particularly acute in lending institutions?

19.10. What is a portfolio lender? What types of financial institutions are typically portfolio lenders for permanent commercial mortgages in the United States? What is it about the maturity of such institutions' liabilities that makes them natural candidates for this role?

19.11. What is the difference between trading-oriented and immunization-oriented strategies for managing fixed-income investments? What is the major type of risk trading-oriented strategies are exposed to? What is the major type of risk immunization-oriented strategies are exposed to if the liabilities are adjusted to inflation?

19.12. Describe the six components of mortgage market contractual yields in the "stack" in Exhibit 19-7. Discuss what different historical economic events and environment may have explained the difference between 1993 and the late 1990s in each component of the stack as indicated in Exhibit 19-8.

19.13. Why are ex post mortgage returns so much more volatile than ex ante expectations, as suggested in Exhibits 19-9 and 19-10?

19.14. What were the major statistical characteristics of ex post mortgage returns as represented by the GLCMPI during the last three decades of the 20th century? Compare mortgages to private property equity, stocks, and bonds in regard to average ex post return and volatility.

19.15. What are the implications of the correlation statistics shown in Exhibit 19-12 regarding the role of mortgages, as compared to property equity, in a mixed-asset (stock and bond) portfolio? [Hint: Think about diversification potential and inflation risk.]

19.16. Discuss the following statement: There is some theoretical reason to believe, and some historical evidence to support, the hypothesis that long-term fixed rate mortgages often do not provide positive leverage in the total return to equity investment in institutional quality commercial property. [Hint: Describe the theory and the historical evidence, but also point out countervailing considerations and evidence that goes against the hypothesis.]

Quantitative Problems

19.17. What is the Macaulay duration of an eight-year, 10%, interest-only mortgage with annual payments occurring at the ends of the years? What is the modified duration of this same mortgage?

19.18. What are the Macaulay and modified durations of an eight-year, 10% interest-only, monthly-payment mortgage?

19.19. Suppose market interest rates decline from 10% to 9%. What would the modified duration predict would be the percentage increase in value of the monthly-payment loan in question 19.18? What would be this loan's actual percentage increase in value?

*19.20. Suppose there is no preferred habitat. That is, suppose that the expectations hypothesis is the only explanation for the yield curve. Now suppose the yield on zero-coupon bonds maturing at the end of five years is 6.5%, and the yield of zero-coupon bonds maturing at the end of four years is 6.25%. What is the bond market's implied expected short-term (one-year) interest rate four years in the future (that is, the one-year rate that is expected to prevail from the end of year 4 to the end of year 5)?

19.21. Suppose a certain lending institution's assets have an average duration of five years, and its deposits have an average duration of one and a half years. Suppose the market value of its equity is 5% of that of its assets. What is the approximate duration of the institution's equity?

19.22. Suppose half of a pension fund's liabilities have a duration of 15 years, and half have a duration of 5 years. If the institution wants to immunize its net asset portfolio, what should be the average duration of its bond and mortgage investments?

20 Introduction to Commercial Mortgage-Backed Securities

Chapter Outline

20.1 What Are CMBS?
20.1.1 A Brief History: The Birth of an Industry
20.1.2 Conduits, Seasoned Loans, and Risk-Based Capital Requirements
20.1.3 Magnitude of the CMBS Industry

20.2 CMBS Structure: Tranching and Subordination
20.2.1 A Simple Numerical Example of Tranching
20.2.2 Allocating the Credit Losses

20.3 CMBS Rating and Yields
20.3.1 Bond Credit Rating
20.3.2 Credit Rating and CMBS Structure
20.3.3 Rating CMBS Tranches
20.3.4 Yield Spreads and the Capital Market
20.3.5 CMBS versus Corporate Bond Spreads

20.4 Chapter Summary

Learning Objectives

After reading this chapter, you should understand:

◆ The basic outlines of the U.S. CMBS industry, including the typical structure of CMBS products and the role played by rating agencies.

◆ What is meant by tranching, and how this is used to concentrate and stratify the default risk in CMBS.

◆ What determines the market yields of CMBS, and why these yields may differ from those of corporate bonds.

One of the most important and exciting developments in real estate finance during the 1990s was the emergence of a large and important secondary market for commercial mortgages in the United States, based on commercial mortgage-backed securities, a process referred to as **securitization**. CMBS provide a new and in some respects more efficient source of capital for commercial real estate, and they offer investors in the bond market a variety of new securities that can serve different types of investment needs and concerns. CMBS products, and the industry that produces and services them, are very complex, and in the late 1990s this industry was still young and evolving rapidly. Therefore, the purpose of this chapter is somewhat limited, as we seek here only to introduce you to the basics of CMBS.

20.1 WHAT ARE CMBS?

CMBS are mortgage-backed securities (MBS) based on commercial mortgages. The securities provide claims to components of the cash flow of the underlying mortgages. As with any security, CMBS are issued in relatively small, homogeneous units so as to facilitate trading by a large potential population of investors, including those who do not wish (or are unable) to invest large sums of money in any given security. Many CMBS are traded in relatively liquid public exchanges, in effect, a part of the bond market. As is common with bonds, the market for a given individual security is likely to be rather thin, but the similarity within classes of securities is great enough to allow relatively efficient price discovery and resulting high levels of liquidity in the market. Other CMBS are privately placed initially and only traded privately, if at all, which may make them no more liquid (or even less liquid) than privately held whole loans.

20.1.1 A Brief History: The Birth of an Industry

The CMBS market of the 1990s got its start with the Resolution Trust Corporation (RTC) in the early part of the decade, as a result of the Financial Institutions Reform, Recovery and Enforcement Act of 1989 (FIRREA). The RTC was a federal government corporation that was set up to liquidate the loan portfolios of thrifts and banks that had failed in the commercial property crash at the end of the 1980s. The RTC was faced with the task of selling large quantities of commercial mortgages, many of them nonperforming, very quickly.

Traditional private institutional sources of real estate capital were effectively not available at that time. The traditional institutions (such as commercial banks, life insurance companies, and pension funds) had just been "burned" in the crash (or were still in the process of crashing and burning). On the other hand, Wall Street was thriving and had spent the 1970s and 1980s cutting its teeth on residential MBS, developing various procedures useful for securitizing large pools of mortgages (such as the procedure known as tranching, which we will explain shortly).

Key players and investors in the public capital markets perceived in the early 1990s that the commercial property market had overshot, fallen too far relative to fundamental value. They also saw that the RTC was under great political pressure to sell assets quickly. These "grave-dancers" and bargain-hunters helped the RTC to give birth to a new industry.

The key to this birth was the development by the traditional bond-rating agencies of the ability to rate the default risk of CMBS tranches. Many of the types of investors that are necessary to make a liquid public market function effectively are necessarily passive, particularly in the case of the bond market. Such investors lack the time, resources, and expertise to become involved in the risk assessment and management of either individual mortgages or pools of mortgages. With residential MBS this problem had been solved by the use of mortgage insurance and pool insurance. But with commercial mortgages, bond-rating agencies and Wall Street analysts had to learn how to quantify the default risk of commercial mortgages. When a CMBS tranche obtains a bond rating, investors who know little or nothing about commercial real estate feel comfortable working under the assumption that the default risk of that tranche is very similar to the default risk of any other bond with the same rating. This vastly expands the pool of potential investors and makes the public market for CMBS viable.

20.1.2 Conduits, Seasoned Loans, and Risk-Based Capital Requirements

Many of the loans that back CMBS are originated specifically with the intention of forming CMBS. Entities that originate such loans are called **conduits**, because they do not hold onto the whole mortgages they issue. They are merely a conduit for capital to flow from Wall Street to Main Street. Such loans are referred to as conduit loans. Conduit lenders are often commercial or investment banks, or syndicates of banks, including local mortgage bankers as necessary for local real estate expertise and contacts. Apart from conduit loans, other loans in CMBS pools may have been issued originally by portfolio lenders, such as life insurance companies, who intended to retain the loans in their asset portfolios. For various reasons, they may subsequently decide to sell some of their portfolio loans into the secondary market. Old loans in a CMBS pool are referred to as **seasoned loans**.

During the 1990s an important stimulus for some institutions to sell commercial mortgages into the secondary market was the establishment of **risk-based capital requirements (RBC)** for depository institutions and life insurance companies. These requirements were part of the fallout from the linked crises in the commercial property markets and the financial industry at the end of the 1980s. RBC requirements make it necessary for banks and insurance companies to retain a greater amount of equity backing for investment in types of assets that are viewed as more risky. In effect, regulatory constraints were placed on the leverage of such institutions. The more risky the institution's asset holdings, the tighter the leverage constraint. Throughout the 1990s RBC requirements viewed commercial mortgages in the form of whole loans as being more risky than good-quality debt securities. Such loans could be sold into the CMBS market, and the proceeds of such a sale could be used to buy CMBS securities that had much lower RBC requirements than the original whole loan. (Tranching was a major means to accomplish this trick.)

20.1.3 Magnitude of the CMBS Industry

The circumstances just described led to a very rapid development of the CMBS industry in the United States in the 1990s. Exhibit 20-1 shows this development, contrasting the absolute and relative magnitude, by source, of the outstanding commercial mortgage capital in the United States in 1988 and 1998. Note that CMBS went from virtually nothing to over 20% of the total debt outstanding, accounting, in effect, for virtually all of the overall net growth of some $200 billion in commercial mortgage capital.[1] Based on the history of mortgage securitization in the residential sector nearly two decades earlier, it seems likely that the role of CMBS in the commercial mortgage industry will continue to increase early in the 21st century, although traditional privately held whole loans will also remain a substantial share of the industry.

[1] Keep in mind that much of the commercial bank lending is for construction loans, whereas most of the other loans (including those in CMBS) are permanent loans. Thus, the CMBS proportion of long-term mortgage debt was considerably larger than 20%.

Exhibit 20-1
Commercial Mortgage
Debt* Outstanding by
Source, 1988–1998
(Source: U.S. Federal
Reserve Bank.)

*Excludes loans on
multifamily housing.

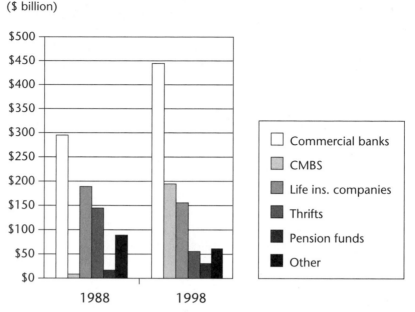

20.2 CMBS STRUCTURE:
TRANCHING AND SUBORDINATION

To begin to understand how CMBS work, we need to get our hands dirty a bit, to learn about how the sausage is made.[2] A typical CMBS issue is backed by a pool of numerous individual loans.[3] Typically, several classes of securities, known as **tranches**, are created from a given underlying mortgage pool.[4] Each tranche is characterized by a different type of claim on the pool's cash flows. In effect, the cash flow from the underlying mortgage pool is "unbundled" and classified into different components, and each tranche gets a certain priority of claim on one or more of these cash flow components.

Tranching cash flow claim priority involves two primary dimensions: loan retirement and credit losses. The former relates to the duration and interest rate risk in the securities; the latter relates to the default risk. In CMBS usually the default risk

[2]Sorry.

[3]This is not always the case. A sufficiently large individual mortgage can be securitized. Alternatively, a number of loans all with the same borrower may be cross-collateralized and packaged together in a CMBS issue. Cross-collateralization means that if one loan is defaulted, all the loans are automatically in default. This gives the borrower an incentive to use performing properties to help out weak ones. Nevertheless, the majority of CMBS are issued on pools of **many** loans issued to numerous borrowers.

[4]The word *tranche* is French for "slice." It should be noted that it is certainly possible conceptually and legally to create CMBS that are not tranched. MBS that are based on the undifferentiated cash flows of the entire pool of underlying mortgages are known as pass-through securities, and they are not uncommon in the residential MBS industry. However, through the 1990s, the CMBS industry was been dependent on tranching as a means to facilitate formal credit rating and to add value in a bond market that was stratified by clientele with different degrees of risk aversion.

dimension is most important. (The opposite is true in RMBS, in which maturity is the prime concern due to the greater prepayment risk in residential loans.) In addition, interest and principal cash flow components may be stripped from each other and assigned differently to the various classes. This can result in some exotic features in some securities, such as negative convexity, and even the ability of some securities to increase in value when market interest rates rise (and decrease when rates fall) in some circumstances.[5] The best way to understand how tranching works is to consider a simple example.

20.2.1 A Simple Numerical Example of Tranching

Consider a pool consisting of 10 commercial mortgages, each with $10 million par value (OLB) and a 10% coupon (contract) interest rate. All 10 mortgages are interest-only loans with annual payments at the end of the year. All of the mortgages are nonrecourse, with lockouts preventing prepayment. Suppose further that five of the loans mature in exactly one year, and the other five in exactly two years. Thus, the underlying pool is characterized by a total par value of $100 million, with a **weighted average maturity (WAM)** of 1.5 years and a **weighted average coupon (WAC)** of 10%.[6] Finally, suppose that the total value of all the properties collateralizing the pool loans is $142,857,000, giving the pool a par value LTV ratio of 70% ($100,000,000/$142,857,000).

Now we will suppose that three tranches of CMBS securities are carved out of this pool and sold into the bond market. The first tranche is a senior class of securities we will call the A tranche. It has $75 million of the par value, three-quarters of the total. It is therefore said to have a **credit support** of 25%. This means that loans containing 25% of the entire par value in the pool would have to default before this tranche would lose any of its par value or claim on the interest income of the pool. The greater the degree of credit support for a tranche is, the less is its default risk. In this case, as the pool LTV ratio is 70%, we can think of the property value underlying the mortgage pool as having to lose 47.5% of its value $(1 - [1 - 0.25][0.70])$ before the value of the collateral underlying the A tranche would be less than that tranche's par value. As the A tranche is the safest $75 million of the pool par value, the underlying property value would have to fall to $75,000,000/$142,857,000 = 52.5% of its initial value before the A tranche would be "under water," in the sense of having less collateral value than its par value. As the A tranche is the senior tranche in the pool, this means that it has default risk similar to a mortgage with a 52.5% LTV ratio.

Another feature of the A tranche is that whenever a loan in the pool matures and pays off its OLB, this cash flow goes to the A tranche and retires a corresponding amount of the A tranche par value. Thus, the A tranche will be the first tranche to be retired. This gives it the shortest weighted average maturity and therefore generally the least interest rate risk of all the securities issued from the pool. For example, the A tranche's WAM is 1.33 years, while the overall pool average WAM is 1.5 years.

---

[5] Negative convexity occurs when a security does not increase in value with a fall in interest rates as much as its duration would indicate, or it decreases in value more than its duration indicates when interest rates rise.

[6] In this simple example all the loans are of equal value, so the "weights" are equal. More generally, the weighting is computed proportional to the par values, which typically vary across the loans in the pool.

The second class of securities issued from our underlying mortgage pool is assigned the remaining $25 million of par value in the pool. This is a junior (or subordinate) class which we will call the B tranche. In our simple example the B tranche is also what is called a **first-loss tranche** because it bears the greatest exposure to credit losses due to default. The par values of any mortgages that default are subtracted from the par value of the first-loss tranche, thereby proportionately reducing its claim on interest cash flow. Only after the first-loss tranche is completely wiped out by defaults will subsequent additional defaults be assigned to another more senior tranche.

At first glance it might seem that our B tranche has about the same default risk as a 70% LTV mortgage, as that is the LTV ratio of the pool. But in fact the B tranche has greater default risk than a 70% LTV whole loan because the B tranche is not the most senior tranche. It is providing credit support for the A tranche, and it valiantly performs this role by potentially sacrificing itself. For example, if a property securing a 70% LTV whole loan is sold in foreclosure for a price 50% of its original value, the loss severity for the loan is only 28.6% (1 − [50%/70%]), but this would be more than sufficient to wipe out the B tranche completely.[7]

Not only is the first-loss tranche first in line to get hit with defaults, but also it is last in line to be retired at par value. Whenever loan balances are paid off, the cash receipts are used to retire more senior tranches. Only after these are all retired will the first-loss tranche be entitled to receive payments of loan balances. Thus, the first-loss tranche has not only the greatest default risk, but also the longest maturity and therefore the most interest rate risk. In our example, the WAM of the B tranche is 2 years, whereas the pool WAM is, as you recall, only 1.5 years.

The third and last tranche carved out of our pool is a residual tranche called the **IO tranche** (for "interest-only"). An IO tranche has no par value assigned to it and is not entitled to receive any cash flow from payments of loan principal balances. What it is entitled to receive is any payments of interest in the pool that are not claimed by other tranches on the basis of their par values and coupon rates. Often, the coupon interest rate assigned to each tranche will be set equal to or less than the *lowest* coupon rate on any mortgage in the pool. This way, no matter which mortgages might default or pay off early, there will be sufficient interest income in the pool to pay the coupon interest owed to all of the par-valued tranches. But this also means that there is usually extra interest in the pool, as the average coupon in the pool is likely to be greater than the coupon rates assigned to the securities. This "extra" interest is paid to the IO tranche.

IO securities lack the balloon payments of the par-value tranches, which gives them relatively short maturities. However, they face considerable risk of loss in value due to premature reduction in the par value of the pool. When loan par value is removed from the pool, the corresponding loans stop paying interest. This typically reduces the overall cash flow to the IO tranche. Indeed, the IO tranche can be very sensitive to reductions in overall pool interest receipts because the IO tranche is subordinated to the par-valued tranches in its claim on the interest payments. The IO tranche

[7] Using the terminology of Chapter 18, the B tranche faces about the same unconditional default probability as a 70% LTV loan, but it faces much greater conditional loss severity. Recall that the ex ante (or unconditional) yield degradation (the expected loss in yield due to default) equals, essentially, the unconditional default probability times the conditional loss severity. Another way to see this is to realize that the B tranche in our example faces a default risk similar to a second mortgage equal to 17.5% of the value of a collateral property that also secures a first mortgage in the amount of 52.5% of property value.

only gets the *residual* interest cash flow after the par-valued tranches have received all that is owed to them. As the total expected future cash flow to the IO tranche is diminished by reductions in pool par value, so the present value of the IO tranche securities is diminished by these reductions.

In general, there are two sources of premature diminution in pool par value: loan prepayments and loan defaults. The former relates to interest rates and interest rate risk. The latter related to default risk in the underlying mortgage pool. Thus, in a fundamental sense, the IO tranche is subject to default risk, defined as the risk of loss in security value due to defaults in the underlying loan pool.[8] Technically, however, this is not considered default risk as such, from the perspective of the IO security holders, because the IO tranche has no par value of its own and hence nothing to be defaulted on.[9]

If the underlying mortgage pool contains a significant number of mortgages with prepayment options, then IO securities can behave in unique ways when market interest rates are sufficiently below the average contract interest rate for the pool. In such circumstances, many of the pool's mortgages have a high likelihood of prepaying in the near future, as borrowers exercise their prepayment options in order to refinance at lower rates. When loans are paid off early, they no longer pay interest, thereby reducing the cash flow expectations of the IO tranche. In such circumstances, if market interest rates rise, future IO tranche cash flow expectations will rise (because of a reduced prepayment tendency in the pool loans), and this can cause the market value of the IO tranche securities to rise. This gives the unique result of a debt-based security whose value increases with a rise in interest rates.[10] Thus, in certain circumstances, IO securities can be used by investors to hedge against increases in interest rates. (The general shape of the value function of IO securities in relation to market interest rates is shown in Exhibit 20-2.)

Now let us suppose that the 10% contract rate on the underlying mortgages in our example is the current market interest rate for such loans. Then it should certainly be possible to sell the A tranche at a yield lower than 10% because of its favorable default risk (and probably also because of its shorter maturity).[11] For example, let us

[8] Note that when loans default, much of the OLB may eventually be recovered, but delinquent interest is usually completely lost.

[9] For this reason, the IO tranche may be given a high credit rating in a technical sense. Do not be misled, however, as this does *not* imply that the IO tranche has little risk or little exposure to default risk in the underlying pool. In effect, what is actually default risk with respect to the underlying mortgages is converted in the IO tranche to maturity risk, which in the case of IO securities involves the risk of loss in tranche value due to a loss in total cash flow to the tranche. Whether premature loss of pool par value is due to loan defaults or to loan prepayments does not matter, mechanically, as far as the IO tranche is concerned. However, from an economic perspective, risk of IO value loss due to underlying loan default is not exactly the same as risk of IO value loss due to loan prepayment. The former tends to occur for any loans when the economy or real estate market is doing poorly, while the latter tends to occur only for loans with prepayment options, when interest rates fall substantially below the contract rates on the loans. While these two "states of the world" (poor economy and falling interest rates) tend to be positively correlated, they are not identical and therefore may hold different value to security holders.

[10] Note that this result obtains only when pool loans contain a prepayment option and market interest rates are sufficiently below the contract rate on the pool loans.

[11] Recall that the yield curve is not always upward-sloping, so shorter maturity will not necessarily always warrant a lower yield. However, lower default risk will always allow bonds to be sold at a lower market yield. The A tranche securities would also typically be more liquid than the underlying whole loans, which would further allow a lower yield on the A tranche securities as compared to the underlying loans.

Exhibit 20-2 The General Shape of IO Securities Value as a Function of Market Interest Rates

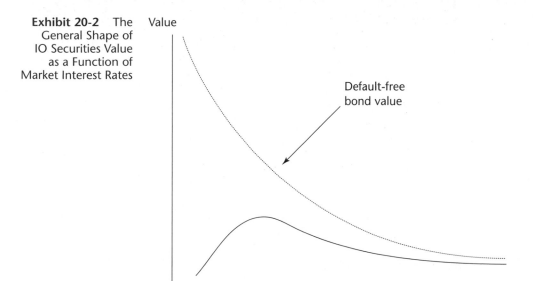

Value

Default-free bond value

Market interest rates

assume that the A tranche is issued with an 8% coupon rate and sells at par value in the CMBS market. We might then assume that the B tranche is given a 10% coupon rate, equal to the minimum coupon in the underlying pool. The B tranche will then certainly sell at a discount to its par value, due to its having greater default risk and longer expected maturity than the underlying pool. For example, suppose the B tranche sells at a 12% yield. Having set the coupon rates on the par-valued tranches, we can quantify the expected cash flows to the IO tranche based on the difference between the 8% coupon in the A tranche and the 10% coupon in the underlying pool. Because it faces considerable value-reduction risk due to the possibility of loan defaults in the pool, we will suppose that the IO tranche sells at a 14% yield.[12]

20.2.2 Allocating the Credit Losses

To make sure you understand how tranching works, let's continue our example forward in time. Suppose that all of the loans perform according to contract in the first year, but in the second year one of the remaining five loans defaults on its $1 million interest payment. The loan is sold in foreclosure for net proceeds of $5 million. Thus, the pool is short $6 million of contractual cash flow in year 2. Exhibit 20-3 shows how the ex post cash flows received compare in this case to the ex ante cash flows that had been scheduled for each tranche. The $5 million loss in principal value would be taken out of the par value of the B tranche, thereby reducing its interest claim by $500,000 in year 2 (based on its 10% coupon rate). Thus, in year 2, the B tranche receives only $22 million cash flow instead of the $27.5 million it was scheduled to receive. There is then no extra interest in the pool, so the IO tranche

---

[12] In our example pool all the loans have lockout provisions, so the only source of value reduction risk in the IO tranche is loan defaults. In the real world, some mortgage pools may be purely lockout loans, but many pools contain some or all loans with prepayment options.

Exhibit 20-3 Ex Ante vs. Ex Post Cash Flows by Tranche and Year

Tranche (par, coupon)		Year 1 Prin. + Int. = Total CF	Year 2 Prin. + Int. = Total CF
A (75, 8%)	Scheduled: Received:	50 + 6 = 56 50 + 6 = 56	25 + 2 = 27 25 + 2 = 27
B (25, 10%)	Scheduled: Received:	0 + 2.5 = 2.5 0 + 2.5 = 2.5	25 + 2.5 = 27.5 20 + 2.0 = 22.0
IO (NA)	Scheduled: Received:	0 + 1.5 = 1.5 0 + 1.5 = 1.5	0 + 0.5 = 0.5 0 + 0.0 = 0.0
Pool (100,10%)	Scheduled: Received:	50 + 10 = 60 50 + 10 = 60	50 + 5 = 55 45 + 4 = 49

receives nothing in year 2 (instead of the $500,000 it was scheduled to receive). The A tranche is unaffected by the default.

The table in Exhibit 20-4 summarizes the three classes of CMBS issued from our simple example mortgage pool. The important thing to notice is how tranching has *stratified and concentrated* the *default risk* and the *maturity* in the pool, resulting in different classes of securities that present investors with a wider variety of different levels and types of risk than is available in the undifferentiated pool of underlying loans. Notice also that *the sum of the parts is worth more than the whole*. The underlying mortgages as whole loans have a current market value of $100 million, yet the CMBS issued from them sell for $100.85 million. How is this possible?

Part of the answer to this question is that the greater variety of securities in the CMBS tranches may be more useful to investors of different types than the undifferentiated whole loans. As noted, the CMBS present investors with a range of different maturities, default risks, and responsiveness to interest rate changes. Another part of the answer lies in the ability of relatively passive or distant investors to place their capital into CMBS. The need for local real estate expertise in order to understand the amount of default risk has been replaced by bond ratings.[13] The need to

Exhibit 20-4 Summary of Example Pool Tranche Characteristics

Class	Par Value (millions)	WAM (yrs.)	Credit Support	Coupon	YTM	Value as CMBS (millions)
A	$75	1.33	25%	8%	8%	$75.00
B	$25	2.00	0% (first-loss)	10%	12%	$24.15
IO	NA	1.25	NA	NA	14%	$1.70
Pool	$100	1.50	NA	10% (WAC)	NA	$100.85

[13]For example, our A tranche securities might receive a bond rating of A, indicating investment-grade securities, while our B tranche securities might get a speculative-grade rating such as B, or perhaps they would receive no rating at all and become so-called junk bonds.

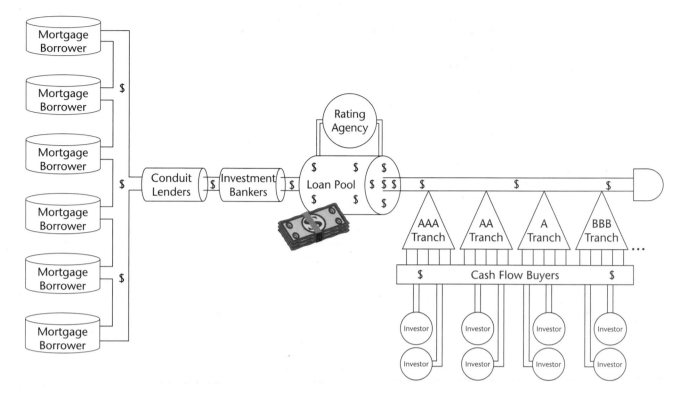

Exhibit 20-5 CMBS Securitization Process

maintain contact with the borrower and administer the collection of loan payments has been taken over by a **pool servicer**. These changes allow investors that could not consider investing in whole mortgages directly to consider CMBS. Yet another source of value, at least for some tranches, is increased liquidity as compared to the underlying whole loans.[14]

Exhibit 20-5 summarizes visually the overall CMBS process. Fundamentally, capital flows from the bond market investors indicated at the bottom right of the figure to the real estate investors indicated at the left side of the figure. In return, interest and principle amortization flows from the real estate investors into the mortgage pool from which it is repackaged into the CMBS tranches that define the securities the bond market investors have bought. Intermediate agents such as investment banks, conduits, and bond-rating agencies (among others) make the whole process work, in effect, linking the underlying capital providers to the real estate investors. Of course, some cash flow and asset value is taken by these intermediaries as their compensation for the services they provide.

---

[14] Of course, the CMBS issue adds another layer of administration that must be paid for. Also, the quality of information available to bond-rating agencies about large mortgage pools is generally not as good as that available to portfolio lenders about individual mortgages. These administrative cost and information disadvantages offset the advantages of CMBS, so that in the real world CMBS are preferable to whole loans in some situations and not in others.

LOBS: A Similar Idea to CMBS

A type of security that is closely related to CMBS is a **LOBS (lease-obligation-backed security)**. Typically, in a LOBS numerous leases from a single tenant are pooled to provide the cash flow to service the securities. LOBS enable property equity investors to cash out the debtlike component of their investment represented by their existing leases (as described in Chapter 10). During the 1990s LOBS were typically secured not only by the specified leases but also by the property equity. The potential advantage of the LOBS over a traditional mortgage is that the interest rate on the LOBS would reflect the bond credit rating of the tenant. But comparing a LOBS to a typical whole commercial mortgage is like comparing apples to oranges. A AAA-rated LOBS would be more comparable to the *part* of the mortgage par value that goes into the AAA-rated tranche of a CMBS.

20.3 CMBS RATING AND YIELDS

Recall that the key to a well-functioning liquid public market in CMBS is the ability of distant, passive investors with no local real estate expertise to feel confident about the magnitude of default risk in the securities they are buying. Without such confidence, such investors will not place their capital into CMBS, and the only market for commercial mortgages would then be investors who have the specialized knowledge and expertise to evaluate the relevant credit risk on their own. The primary means by which nonspecialized bond investors derive confidence in the magnitude of default risk in CMBS is the receipt of a credit rating for the securities from one of the established bond-rating agencies on Wall Street.

20.3.1 Bond Credit Rating

Exhibit 20-6 shows the major credit rating labels of two of these agencies: Moody's and Standard & Poor's. The idea behind the bond credit rating process is to provide investors with an objective and expert assessment of the approximate magnitude of default risk. In principle, any two bonds with the same credit rating (from the same agency) should have similar default risk.[15] The hierarchical labels are traditionally grouped into categories. The top four ranks of labels, from AAA through BBB using the S&P terms, are usually considered to be **investment grade**. Traditionally, this means that bonds of this credit quality are acceptable investments for conservative institutions. Although traditional whole-loan commercial mortgages are generally not publicly traded and do not receive credit ratings, their market yields are often similar to that of corporate bonds rated BBB (or Baa). The next two ranks, BB and B,

---

[15] In this context, the term *default risk* encompasses both the unconditional probability of default and the conditional loss severity in the event of default, in essence, the major factors that determine the magnitude of the ex ante yield degradation as defined in Chapter 18. It is not uncommon for a bond to be rated by more than one agency. In such cases the ratings from the two agencies occasionally disagree. Ratings are reviewed and updated periodically or whenever a major event occurs that could affect creditworthiness.

Exhibit 20-6 Traditional Bond Ratings

Rating		Meaning
Moody's	**S&P**	
Aaa Aa	AAA AA	Highest quality (investment grade)
A Baa	A BBB	High quality (investment grade)
Ba B	BB B	Medium quality (speculative grade)
Caa & lower	CCC & lower	Poor quality, some issues in default (speculative to "junk" grades)
Unrated	Unrated	Too little information or too risky to rate (generally "junk" grade)

are traditionally considered **speculative grade**, meaning that there is substantial probability of default. Ranks lower than B (and unrated bonds) are often termed junk bonds. Many of these bonds are in default, while for others there is simply not enough information for a rating agency to be willing to judge credit quality.

20.3.2 Credit Rating and CMBS Structure

Exhibit 20-7 shows stylistically how a CMBS issue of the late 1990s was typically structured in terms of the credit ratings assigned to its tranches. Note that the structure depicted in Exhibit 20-7 is considerably more complex than the three tranches described in our previous numerical example.[16] There are a variety of intermediate tranches (often referred to as **mezzanine tranches**) that contain varying levels of credit support and subordination. With multiple levels of intermediate tranching, the prepayment exposure cascades from the top while the default exposure cascades from the bottom based on the credit support. For example, in Exhibit 20-7, all prepayments go to the A tranches until they are fully retired, then to the B tranches until they are fully retired, and then to the C tranches, and so forth. All losses of par value due to defaults go first to the D tranche until it is retired, then to the C tranche until it is fully retired, and then to the B5 tranche until it is fully retired, and so forth. In addition, the senior tranches are often differentiated by maturity, sometimes within the same level of credit support.[17] In a typical CMBS issue, which would be worth several hundred million dollars or more, the bulk of the pool par value is typically able to be sold as senior AA- or AAA-rated securities, at yields lower than those on the underlying whole loans.

[16] Even Exhibit 20-7 is simpler than most real world CMBS issues.

[17] Maturity tranching was first developed in the collateralized mortgage obligations (CMO) derivatives based on residential MBS. By concentrating and stratifying the maturity (and hence the interest rate risk) of a pool that contains individual loans of varying maturity and prepayment risk, the usefulness of the securities is increased for certain types of investors, such as those trying to implement maturity-matching or immunization-oriented strategies. This enables the bond issuer to price the various securities at different points along the yield curve.

Tranche	Rating	% of Pool Par	Description	Credit Support %	Tranche LTV Ratio	Yield Spread*	WAM (yrs.)
A1	AAA	25%	Senior (first)	32.55%	47.2%	90	5.7
A2	AAA	41%	Senior (second)	32.55%	47.2%	120	9.4
B1	AA	6%	Mezzanine	26.50%	51.5%	130	9.7
B2	A	6%	Mezzanine	20.50%	55.7%	150	9.8
B3	BBB	7%	Mezzanine	15.50%	59.2%	200	9.9
B4	BBB-	2%	Mezzanine	13.00%	60.9%	250	9.9
B5	BB	6%	Subordinate	7.00%	65.1%	450	10.0
C	B	3%	Subordinate	3.50%	67.6%	650	10.0
D	Unrated	3%	First-Loss	0%	70.0%	900	13.7
IO	AAA	0%	Interest-Only	NA	NA	Various	Not stated

*Over 10-year T-Bonds, in basis points of typical YTM at issuance.

Source: Modified from Fabozzi and Jacob (1999).

Exhibit 20-7 Stylized (Simplified) Tranching Structure of Typical CMBS Issue (Late 1990s)

Not surprisingly, the market yields that reflect the prices at which the securities sell are quite sensitive to the credit rating. Such yields are typically quoted in terms of spread over a similar-maturity benchmark Treasury Bond, most commonly the 10-year bond for CMBS. Senior tranches often sell at yield spreads around 100 basis points, while intermediate tranches (so-called mezzanine debt) sell at spreads ranging to over 200 basis points. Subordinate tranches sell at very large spreads typical of junk bonds. The most risky CMBS tranches, such as first-loss pieces, are clearly more risky than the underlying property equity, even more risky than some levered equity positions. This makes sense, for even if only a small fraction of the mortgages in the pool default, the first-loss tranche will be worthless. In contrast, senior debt and unlevered equity positions will virtually never be completely worthless, for the underlying asset will always have some value.

As noted, the variety in the risk and return attributes of the securities carved out of a mortgage pool allow different tranches to appeal to different types of investors. The CMBS market is another example of how investor heterogeneity drives the investment industry. Typically, the investment-grade tranches that make up the bulk of a typical CMBS issue find ready buyers in the form of conservative institutions such as pension funds, life insurance companies, and bond mutual funds. On the other hand, the market for the more risky speculative and junk tranches (the so-called B pieces) is much thinner. The major buyers and holders of the lower tranches are aggressive investors willing to take on risk for high expected returns, and who typically have specialized knowledge and expertise regarding commercial property risk. Such investors have included, among others, the investment banks and conduits issuing the CMBS, the **special servicers** charged with taking over defaulted loans in the pool to attempt workouts with the borrowers, and specialized mortgage REITs.

The credit rating of a CMBS tranche is a function of the nature and risk of the underlying mortgage pool as well as of the amount of credit support in the tranche.

For example, a mortgage pool consisting of loans that have relatively low and homogeneous LTV ratios will not need as much credit support for a given credit rating. Therefore, a larger proportion of the securities issued from such a pool can have higher credit ratings, which means lower yields, thereby enabling the overall CMBS issue to obtain a higher average price and greater total proceeds. Holding the quality of the underlying mortgage pool constant, greater credit support will result in a higher rating for a given tranche.

For example, an underlying pool with good-quality information and a 60% LTV ratio might require only 20% credit support for a AAA rating, enabling 80% of the issue's total par value to go into senior tranches. In contrast, a more heterogeneous pool with an average LTV ratio of 75% and some questionable appraisals might require 45% credit support for a AA rating, allowing only 55% of the pool to be sold at a high-priced senior level.

The bond-rating agency has the job of figuring out how much credit support is required for a given credit rating for each tranche in a CMBS issue. Often the CMBS issuer works with the rating agency in a somewhat iterative process to design the structure of the issue. For example, if the rating agency requires 35% credit support for a AAA rating and 30% for a AA rating, it is then up to the CMBS issuer to decide whether to structure the senior tranche as a AAA-rated tranche containing 65% of the pool, or as a AA-rated tranche containing 70% of the pool.

20.3.3 Rating CMBS Tranches

Credit rating agencies combine statistical and analytical techniques with less quantitative investigations (such as legal and management assessments) and common sense in order to judge the amount of default risk in a CMBS issue. Traditional underwriting measures such as LTV ratio and DCR are examined for the pool as a whole. However, the use of such measures is a bit tricky in a pool of many mortgages that is being carved into tranches with varying degrees of credit support. In reality, each mortgage is typically unique to some degree. For example, a pool with an average LTV ratio of 70% might contain a few mortgages with LTV ratios in excess of 80%. This may not matter much for the senior tranches, but it would matter very much for the first-loss pieces. Thus, the diversity or heterogeneity of the mortgages within a pool (**pool heterogeneity**) can matter as much as the average characteristics of the pool.[18]

Rating agencies generally cannot consider each mortgage in a large pool individually, nor do they have the local real estate expertise of the primary market issuers, the type of expertise necessary to evaluate individual loans. Instead, the rating agency makes greater use of aggregate statistics about the pool (both its average characteristics and its heterogeneity), as well as information about the underwriting standards and abilities of the loan issuers in the primary market. A list of some of the key variables

---

[18] For example, Childs, Ott, and Riddiough (1996) showed how diversification within the pool (say, by property type or geographical region) reduces the default risk of the higher tranches, but can actually increase the default risk in the lower tranches. Diversification actually makes it more likely that some mortgages will default, but less likely that a very large proportion of the mortgages will default. Higher tranches will be affected only if a very large proportion of the mortgages in the pool default, while lower tranches can be wiped out even if only a few loans default.

and factors that are typically considered to be important in judging the credit quality of a mortgage pool would include the following:

- Overall average LTV ratio and DCR
- Dispersion (heterogeneity) in LTV and DCR
- Quality of LTV and DCR information
- Property types in the pool
- Property ages and lease expirations
- Geographical location of properties
- Loan sizes and total number of loans
- Loan maturities
- Loan terms (e.g., amortization, floating rates, prepayment, recourse)
- Seasoning (age) of the loans
- Amount of pool overcollatalerization or credit enhancement
- Legal structure and servicer relationships
- Number of borrowers and cross-collateralization

Because of the importance of the credit rating function in determining the value and hence financial feasibility of a CMBS issue, the rating agencies play a quasi-regulatory role in the CMBS market.[19] The result is greater standardization of commercial mortgages, especially smaller loans of the type that are most likely to be issued by conduits.

20.3.4 Yield Spreads and the Capital Market

It is important to note that the yield spreads that reflect the capital market's evaluation of default risk in CMBS tranches can change over time, especially for the higher-risk tranches. When the markets perceive a threat to credit quality, such as an imminent recession in the macroeconomy or overbuilding in the commercial real estate sector, spreads will widen, and usually more so for lower-rated tranches.

A dramatic example of this occurred in 1998. Exhibit 20-8 shows the yield spreads on various ratings of CMBS tranches during that year. In August of 1998 Russia defaulted on its international bonds, triggering a financial crisis in an environment in which investors were already jittery about the possibility that a weak global economy could cause a recession in the United States. At that time the U.S. commercial property market had been heating up for several years, and by early 1998 some observers were worried that too much new construction was being started. Suddenly, the possibility of an excess supply of commercial property loomed on the horizon (if construction starts continued to grow and/or a major recession occurred in the U.S. economy). The result was a general "flight to quality" in the capital market as investors pulled out of the stock market and risky bonds, placing their money instead into U.S. Treasury Bills and Bonds. As in other sectors of the bond market, CMBS yields rose and spreads widened, dramatically for the lower-grade securities. As noted

---

[19] This is much like the role played by FNMA, FHLMC, and GNMA as the dominant secondary market buyers and security issuers in the RMBS market.

Exhibit 20-8 CMBS Spreads (basis points over 10-year T-bonds), 1998

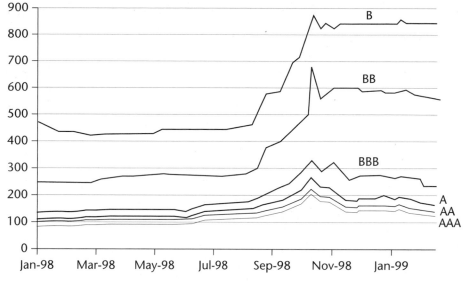

previously, default risk is particularly sensitive to downturns in the real economy, and the lower CMBS tranches are very exposed to such risk.[20]

Though these events were traumatic at the time, they may have been a textbook example of how the capital markets can help to effectively regulate the flow of capital to the real estate sector, the negative feedback loop in the real estate system we described in Chapter 2. The jump in yields for lower-rated CMBS depicted in Exhibit 20-8 effectively eliminated the market for new issues of CMBS by the fall of 1998.[21] As a result, the flow of capital reaching the real estate sector was cut back.[22] This reduction in capital flow put some brakes on new construction, directly or indirectly resulting in less new space supply coming into the system than otherwise would have been the case at that time.

By the end of 1998 the crisis seemed to be under control. In the fall of that year the Federal Reserve Board lowered U.S. short-term interest rates and mounted a rescue operation of a famous and hugely levered hedge fund whose debts had threatened to swamp the markets. The threat of imminent recession receded as the U.S. economy continued to grow strongly with little inflation even in the face of the foreign economic downturn. As in the rest of the bond market, CMBS yield spreads began to come back down, first in the senior tranches, later and more gradually in the junior tranches. By 1999 capital was again flowing to real estate through the CMBS market.

[20] Recall the different types of investors who tend to invest in the different credit risk categories. Investors in low-grade debt tend to be more aggressive investors and speculators. They often take levered positions in high-yield securities, making them even more vulnerable to default risk. Even a relatively faint whiff of bad news can send such investors stampeding.

[21] Commercial property investors and developers who had been planning to borrow money using the CMBS market as an indirect source of funds (e.g., through conduit mortgages) would have to face interest rates so high, and/or LTV ratio limits so low, that the financial feasibility of their investments and developments would be called into question.

[22] As noted in section 12.3 in Chapter 12, REIT share prices also tumbled in 1998, temporarily also eliminating new REIT equity issues as a source of capital for real estate.

But the speed and magnitude of the cutoff of capital flow in 1998, when there were legitimate reasons to see dark clouds on the horizon, was impressive and unprecedented for U.S. commercial real estate. It reflected the new role of the public capital markets in real estate finance, with their informational efficiency so highly touted by financial economists. To some real estate investors, the capital market reactions of 1998 appeared to be a case of jittery nerves. But that may be exactly the kind of nerves lower-tranche CMBS investors should have, and exactly the kind of motivation needed to stimulate informational efficiency in asset markets.

20.3.5 CMBS versus Corporate Bond Spreads

Another interesting phenomenon in the CMBS market through the 1990s was the difference between the market yields of equally rated, equal-maturity CMBS and corporate bonds. As seen in Exhibit 20-9, typical CMBS yields are often observed to contain nearly twice the yield spread (over comparable maturity Treasury Bonds) as that of corporate bonds with the same credit rating.[23] At first glance, this seems surprising, as equal credit ratings are supposed to imply nearly equal default risk. However, CMBS are very "different animals" than corporate bonds. Several unique features of CMBS may explain their greater average spreads.

1. **Prepayment Risk.** Although most commercial mortgages in the United States either have lockout provisions or steep prepayment penalties, some do not. As a result, some CMBS pools have mortgages in them that are more like callable corporate bonds, resulting in a yield premium to reflect the prepayment risk faced by the investor. Such a yield premium would affect spreads for all tranches, but especially for senior tranches, given the typical principal payback priority structure.[24]

2. **Agency and Extension Risk.** In the event of default in CMBS pools, a conflict of interest tends to exist between investors in senior tranches and those in junior tranches. The former want immediate foreclosure, while the latter tend to prefer a workout and extension of the loan term. The authority to decide whether to foreclose or exercise forbearance is normally vested in a special servicer, who is usually effectively controlled by the junior tranche holders (after all, they stand to lose or gain the most from how the default is handled).[25] The result is that the foreclosure/workout decision cannot be expected to be handled optimally from the senior tranche holders' perspective. This adds risk and/or reduces the present value of the mortgage-backed asset for the senior tranche holders, resulting in a higher yield in the senior tranches. No such conflict of interest exists in typical corporate bonds because there is only one class of investors. To the extent that this unique consideration is not captured in credit ratings, this effect can partly explain higher yields in senior tranche CMBS.

[23] Even in the AAA-rated securities, which are the most insulated from default-risk-based features that may be unique in CMBS, corporate bond yields are typically 30 to 40 basis points lower than CMBS yields.

[24] Recall that all payments of principal, whether scheduled or prepayments, are used to retire the most senior tranche first in the typical CMBS structure. With the prepayment option, faster-than-expected retirement of principal would be associated with lower-than-expected market interest rates, forcing the CMBS investors to reinvest their capital at lower interest rates than they had anticipated.

[25] CMBS issues are normally serviced by two types of servicers. The master servicer handles the routine administrative work of collection and distribution of cash flows and reporting. The special servicer handles defaults.

Exhibit 20-9 CMBS versus Corporate Bond Market Yield Spreads in Comparable Maturity AAA-Rated Securities (Source: Snyderman [1999].)

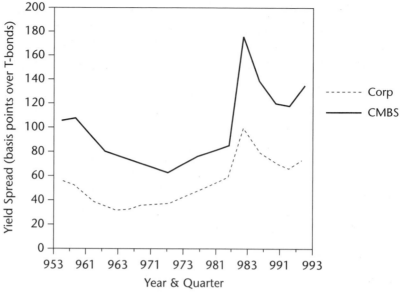

3. Credit Information Quality and Going-Concern Risk and Liquidity Implications. Bonds backed by large publicly traded corporations have available more ongoing information relevant to the credit risk of the borrower. Also, the public corporation is a single going-concern that typically knows it will need to return to the bond market again, probably regularly in the near and long-term future. It therefore must consider carefully its reputation in the bond market, and this makes it less likely to default on its bonds. In contrast, there is typically less publicly available information relevant to the credit risk of the multitude of small, private borrowers and properties that back the typical CMBS pool. As noted, it is also an inherently more complex task to assess the credit risk of a multitude of small borrowers and properties than that of a single large borrower. For both of these reasons, rating agencies and investors are more in the dark about the credit risk of the typical CMBS issue than they are about the risk of the typical corporate bond. In a sense, what we are saying here is that there is not only risk, but also uncertainty about how much risk there is. You could say there is "risk in the risk assessment," and this effectively adds to the magnitude of risk from the investor's perspective. A secondary result of this type of added risk is that it tends to reduce the liquidity of the rated asset. Lack of liquidity in turn also adds to the market's required yield premium. These concerns are especially relevant for the lower-rated tranches.

Such differences as these between CMBS and corporate bonds presumably explain the difference in yields for otherwise similar-maturity bonds with the same credit rating.[26] The higher CMBS spreads cannot be presumed to give CMBS investors something

---

[26]It is also possible that bond investors perceived an agency problem in CMBS rating during the 1990s. At that time credit rating firms were in greater competition for CMBS business than for corporate bond business. (Two rating agencies dominated in the corporate bond business, while four firms competed in the CMBS business.) As rating firm profits are proportional to the volume of ratings done, the CMBS rating business was under more competitive pressure. This could have caused either the reality or the perception of some favorable rating bias among CMBS rating agencies, a bias not present or less present in the corporate bond business.

for nothing, that is, a better risk-adjusted expected return than corporate bonds. On the other hand, remember that CMBS were still a new type of security in the 1990s. The capital markets were still learning about the nature of their risk and return. It may be that yield spreads between corporate bonds and CMBS will tend to narrow gradually over time, possibly in part as a result of innovations in CMBS structuring. If the CMBS industry and markets become more efficient, a larger share of commercial mortgages will likely find their way into the secondary market, and CMBS will provide a larger share of real estate debt capital. If the RMBS experience is any guide, ultimately over half of all commercial mortgages may be securitized. Nevertheless, administrative costs and the problems described earlier will probably continue to give some advantage to whole loans issued by portfolio lenders for some borrowers, especially larger ones.

20.4 CHAPTER SUMMARY

This chapter introduced you to the basics of CMBS, the most important recent development in the commercial real estate finance industry. While much of this chapter was given over to describing the basic nuts and bolts of CMBS structuring and rating, we also stepped back occasionally to present the big picture. In a continuation of a theme that has run throughout the financial economics parts of this book, we saw how CMBS serve the diverse needs of heterogeneous investors in the capital market. In serving such investors, CMBS open up a new source of capital for commercial real estate, a source that promises greater informational efficiency, at least in some respects, than the traditional sources.

With this chapter we complete Part VI, our focus on commercial mortgages. Now it is time to move back to the equity side of the picture, and up to the macro-level of strategic investment concerns, the level we have been dealing with on the debt side in both this chapter and the previous chapter.

KEY TERMS

securitization
conduits
seasoned loans
risk-based capital requirements (RBC)
tranches, tranching
subordination
weighted average maturity (WAM)
weighted average coupon (WAC)

senior tranches
junior tranches
credit support
first-loss tranche
interest-only (IO) tranche
pool servicers
lease-obligation-backed securities
    (LOBS)

bond credit rating
investment grade
speculative grade
special servicers
mezzanine tranches
pool heterogeneity

STUDY QUESTIONS

20.1. Describe the essential structure of the CMBS industry: Who are the ultimate investors in CMBS? What branch of the capital market do CMBS trade in? What is the role of the conduit? The investment bank? The rating agency?

20.2. Why are rating agencies so vital in the CMBS market?

20.3. What is a tranche? Explain how tranching typically works in the U.S. CMBS industry.

20.4. How does tranching stratify and concentrate the default risk in the pooled mortgages, and why is this valuable?

20.5. What is particularly unusual about the IO tranche in some circumstances? How can this be useful?

20.6. Suppose a CMBS mortgage pool has an average LTV ratio of 75%, and the senior tranche in the CMBS issue has 35% credit support. Approximately what LTV ratio in a first mortgage whole loan issuance would correspond to the same credit risk as the senior tranche of this CMBS issue?

20.7. A certain mortgage pool has $1 billion in par value. The senior (A) tranche has 30% credit support, and the next level (B) has 25% credit support. How much par value of securities was issued in the A tranche? How much par value was issued in the B tranche? How much par value will be lost by each tranche in each of the following scenarios:

   a. 20% of the underlying pool par value defaults.

   b. 27% of the underlying pool par value defaults.

   c. 33% of the underlying pool par value defaults.

20.8. In a certain CMBS issue $500 million of senior securities and $100 million of mezzanine securities are issued. The coupon on the senior securities is 7%, and that on the mezzanine is 9%. The average contractual interest rate in the underlying mortgage pool is 10%. Assuming annual interest payments and no par value retired or defaulted, how much residual interest will be available for an IO tranche from these two par-valued tranches at the end of the first year?

20.9. Why is it, and how can it be, that the more junior CMBS tranches command stated yields that are higher than the expected returns to the underlying property equity that backs the credit of these securities? Why are junior CMBS tranches more risky than whole first mortgages with the same LTV ratios?

20.10. What are the credit rating classifications and labels of the two major bond-rating agencies? What types of investors would you typically expect to purchase bonds of the various credit classifications?

20.11. How do bond-rating agencies analyze CMBS issues in order to provide credit ratings for the various tranches? What are some of the important variables they consider? Why is the dispersion or heterogeneity in the mortgage pool as important as the average characteristics of the pool?

20.12. Why do lower-grade CMBS yield spreads tend to react in a more exaggerated fashion than do senior tranches to bad news about the economy or the real estate market?

20.13. Why do corporate bond yields tend to be lower than CMBS yields for the same credit rating and maturity?

PART VI

References and Additional Reading

Childs, P., S. Ott, and T. Riddiough. "Property Diversification, Risk, and Return in CMBS Investment." Real Estate Research Institute Working Paper (WP-49), 1996.

Childs, P., S. Ott, and T. Riddiough. "The Value of Recourse and Cross-Default Clauses in Commercial Mortgage Contracts." *Journal of Banking & Finance* 20: 511–536, April 1996.

B. A. Ciochetti. "Loss Characteristics of Commercial Mortgage Foreclosures." Real Estate Research Institute Working Paper, February 1996.

B. A. Ciochetti. "Investment Loss Characteristics Associated with Commercial Mortgages." Real Estate Research Institute Working Paper, March 1998.

B. A. Ciochetti and K. Vandell. "The Performance of Commercial Mortgages." *Real Estate Economics* 27(1): 27–62, spring 1999.

H. Esaki, S. l'Heureux, and M. Snyderman. "Commercial Mortgage Defaults: An Update." *Real Estate Finance* 16(1): 81–86, spring 1999.

Fabozzi, F. and D. Jacob (eds.). *The Handbook of Commercial Mortgage-Backed Securities*, 2nd ed. New Hope, PA: Frank J. Fabozzi Associates, 1999.

Geltner, D. "Estimating Market Values from Appraised Values without Assuming an Efficient Market." *Journal of Real Estate Research* 8(3): 325–346, 1993.

M. Giliberto. "The Inside Story on Rates of Return II: Commercial Mortgages." *Real Estate Finance* 11(2): 10–13, summer 1994.

Mei, J. "Assessing the Santa Claus Approach to Asset Allocation: Implications for Commercial Real Estate Investment." *Real Estate Finance* 13(2): 65–70, summer 1996.

Polleys, C. "An Empirical Investigation into CMBS Pricing and the Role of the Rating Agency." Real Estate Research Institute Working Paper, 1998.

Riddiough, T. "Incentive Issues and the Performance of Participating Commercial Mortgages." Real Estate Research Institute Working Paper (WP-21), 1994.

T. Riddiough and S. Wyatt. "Strategic Default, Workout, and Commercial Mortgage Valuation." *Journal of Real Estate Finance & Economics* 9(1): 5–22, July 1994.

Snyderman, M. "A Commercial Mortgage Performance Index." *Journal of Portfolio Management* 16: 70–73, 1990.

Snyderman, M. "Public Debt: A New Fact of the Fixed Income World." Presentation to the Association for Investment Management & Research conference, Boston, November 1999.

Sundaresan, S. *Fixed Income Markets and Their Derivatives*. Cincinnati, OH: South-Western College Publishing, 1997.

Vandell, K. "Predicting Commercial Mortgage Foreclosure Experience." *Real Estate Economics* 20(1): 55–88, spring 1992.

Vandell, K., W. Barnes, D. Hartzell, D. Kraft, and W. Wendt. "Commercial Mortgage Defaults: Proportional Hazards Estimation Using Individual Loan Histories." *Real Estate Economics* 21(4): 451–480, winter 1993.

Macrolevel Real Estate Investment Issues

Recall the analogy we made at the outset of Part IV between real estate investment and a rain forest. There we said we were going to be like the botanists looking at individual trees rather than ecologists considering the entire forest. Indeed, most of this book up to now focused primarily at the microlevel of individual properties and deals. While some of the preceding material included broad background information and fundamental building blocks relevant to the macrolevel (and more recent chapters went beyond a strict property-level focus*), nevertheless, the bulk of our attention on real estate equity investment so far has been at the microlevel.

That is about to change. Part VII will focus specifically on the major macrolevel issues, concepts, and analytical tools. Here is where we study the forest as a whole rather than the trees. To be more precise, what we are referring to as the macrolevel in real estate investment concerns the investor's decisions and management regarding many individual properties simultaneously, that is, aggregates of properties. The macrolevel is also the level at which the investor's *overall portfolio* is considered, which is why it is often referred to as the portfolio level. At its broadest this includes the investor's entire net wealth portfolio, including not just real estate but other investment asset classes as well, the so-called "mixed-asset portfolio." Indeed, it is at the macrolevel that the interface between real estate and other asset classes enters most directly into analysis and decision making. The macrolevel is also a good place to talk more about REITs as investments. In a REIT the decision-making entity, the firm, generally controls numerous individual properties.

The concept of a macrolevel of real estate investment analysis and management really only dates from the last third of the 20th century. Traditional real estate investment was effectively a purely microlevel endeavor. Indeed, the distinction between these two levels is somewhat unique to real estate. The concepts of macrolevel investment decisions and activities, and macrolevel valuation, for example, are a bit foreign

---

*For example, the last section in Chapter 12 (on the "dualing asset markets") touched on the relationship between the micro- and macrolevels of real estate investment. The type of financing and capital structure issues addressed in Part V are considered to be largely macrolevel (that is, firm-wide) decisions in traditional corporate finance, although in real estate the prevalence of project-specific financing gives these issues a more microlevel flavor. The last chapters in Part VI addressed the role of mortgages from a broader, portfolio-level perspective.

to the fields of securities investments and corporate finance. Yet during the last two decades of the 20th century the macrolevel of real estate investment analysis and decision making blossomed rapidly into a major component and force within real estate, with its effects permeating down to even small-scale microlevel transactions, not least because the macrolevel is central to the growing link between Wall Street and Main Street. The macrolevel is therefore also the level where we find many of the more modern and rapidly growing real estate professional career paths.

At a broad-brush level, and by way of an initial introduction, it is useful to think of three major types of macrolevel real estate investment decision arenas: *strategic* policy formulation, *tactical* policy formulation, and policy *implementation*. Strategic investment policies define broad, overall allocations and long-run directions and objectives. Tactical policies seek to profit from shorter-term opportunities. Implementation concerns how to carry out policies of both the strategic and tactical type most effectively. For example, an analytical tool widely used at the strategic level is modern portfolio theory (MPT). A major concern at the tactical level is market timing and econometric forecasting of the space and asset markets. Major topics in implementation include the analysis and evaluation of the performance of investment managers, and the crafting of incentive structures that align the interests of such managers with their investor clients. In all three of these decision areas, the macrolevel cannot be divorced from the microlevel. Macrolevel decisions are ultimately implemented at the microlevel, and the quality of the macro–micro link is a key to long-run success in real estate investment.

We will address all three of these macrolevel decision arenas in Part VII, as well as the macro–micro link, by presenting some fundamental macrolevel principles and analytical tools and showing how these relate to investment decision making. The major macrolevel investment principles and analytical tools we will address include portfolio theory, equilibrium asset pricing theory, macrolevel valuation and return measurement issues, and real estate investment management performance attribution and evaluation.

Part VII is organized into seven chapters. Chapters 21 and 22 begin with a presentation of MPT and equilibrium asset pricing models, the classical tools and discipline for "top-down" real estate investment decision making, including particular consideration of the role of real estate in the mixed-asset portfolio. Chapters 23 and 24 treat macrolevel valuation issues from the two extremes of the real estate investment product spectrum: the passive portfolio of properties in the private market and actively managed REIT firms in the public market. Chapter 23 also provides a foundation for Chapter 25, where we get down to a very fundamental nuts-and-bolts problem, that of dealing with the peculiarities and measurement errors inherent in real estate investment performance data, including the so-called appraisal smoothing problem. Finally, Chapters 26 and 27 focus on the investment policy implementation decision arena with a detailed look at the real estate investment management industry, including quantitative performance attribution and evaluation.

21 Real Estate and Portfolio Theory: Strategic Investment Considerations

Learning Objectives

After reading this chapter, you should understand:

◆ What is meant by modern portfolio theory (MPT) and how to apply this theory using computer spreadsheets,

◆ The major strategic investment policy implications MPT holds for real estate at the broad-brush level of the overall mixed-asset portfolio,

◆ The usefulness of the riskless asset assumption and the meaning of the Sharpe-maximizing portfolio,

◆ The nature of institutional investment portfolios in the real world, and the major practical considerations involved in applying portfolio theory to such investors.

Throughout the financial economics part of this book, we emphasized two major concerns of investors: total *return* and the *risk* surrounding that return. In this chapter we take our decision-making focus to the level of the investor's overall wealth, the portfolio level. But return and risk remain the major foci of our attention. In particular, this chapter will introduce you to a sophisticated body of principles and techniques known as **modern portfolio theory (MPT)**, or more generally, portfolio theory.

Portfolio theory deals with the strategic decision of how best to allocate the investor's capital across a range of assets or asset classes. To address this decision in a rigorous way, portfolio theory makes three major contributions: (1) it treats risk and return together in a comprehensive and integrated manner; (2) it quantifies the investment decision-relevant implications of risk and return; and (3) it makes both of these contributions at the portfolio level, the level of the investor's overall wealth.

Before we begin, we should probably say a word or two about the nature of the material in this chapter. Modern portfolio theory (and its offspring, the capital asset pricing model, or CAPM for short) won a Nobel Prize for three of the most famous financial economists of all time: Harry Markowitz, William F. Sharpe, and John Lintner. This is sophisticated stuff. Portfolio theory contains a level of analytical rigor that makes it appear rather technical. If you don't like formulas and math, this will not be your favorite chapter in this book. But theories don't earn Nobel Prizes just for their technical impressiveness. Portfolio theory's elegance allows it to reveal, simply, some fundamental aspects of the world, aspects that cut right to the heart of good strategic investment decision making. This is why, from its inception, portfolio theory was used directly and widely in the real world of investment practice. This is not just ivory-tower academic stuff. It provides insights that are important for investment decision making at the broadest and most fundamental level. These insights are especially important for real estate, as we will see.

21.1 NUMERICAL EXAMPLE OF THE PORTFOLIO ALLOCATION PROBLEM: REAL ESTATE IN THE MIXED-ASSET PORTFOLIO

The best way to begin to learn about portfolio theory in a way that will be usable for you is to walk through a simple numerical example. Let's take the case of our favorite real estate investor, Bob. Bob was given the job of managing the $10 billion portfolio of a pension fund. He was told by the fund's board of trustees to come up with a recommendation on how to allocate their assets between three alternative investment asset classes: common stocks, long-term bonds, and commercial real estate. He was also told to

- "diversify the investments of the fund" so as to minimize risk as measured by the volatility in the fund's total portfolio value; and to

- meet a target long-term overall expected total return of 9% per annum for the fund.

What should Bob have done? (What would you have done in his place?)

In order to begin to answer this question in a rational and quantitative way, Bob realized that he had to ask himself what he expects the long-term average total returns would be in the future for the three asset classes he had to choose among: stocks, bonds, and real estate. In fact, this first step was a tough and very important part of the problem. Not surprisingly, Bob put in quite an effort to come up with what he thought were rather reasonable future average return estimates of 12% per year in the stock market, 8% in the long-term bond market, and 9% in commercial real estate.[1]

---

[1] Bob based his reasoning on an examination of long-term historical return performance relative to "risk-free" Treasury Bills, as well as current projections for inflation and short-term interest rates going forward into the future. In short, Bob conducted an analysis not unlike what we briefly described in

After expending such an effort to come up with ex ante return estimates that he was so proud of, Bob then rushed to a silly allocation recommendation that embarrassed him when he took it to the board of his pension fund client. He suggested a simple equal allocation of 33.3% to each of the three asset classes. The board's independent consultant, Sue, immediately pointed out to Bob the problem with this suggestion. According to Bob's return expectations, his recommended allocation would overshoot the fund's 9% return target by 67 basis points. In particular, the portfolio expected return implied by Bob's suggested allocation was[2]

$$(0.333)12\% + (0.333)8\% + (0.333)9\% = 9.67\%$$

At first Bob protested that such overshooting did not present a problem; after all, wasn't a 9.67% expected return better than a 9.00% expected return? But Sue retorted that the 9% target had been arrived at by considering *how much risk* the board wanted to take on in their investments, recognizing that in the capital markets, one can realistically obtain a higher ex ante return only by investing in assets that have more risk.

With that, Bob went back to the drawing board and came up with an allocation that exactly met the board's 9% target. In particular, Bob proposed to invest 22.5% of the fund in stocks, 67.5% in bonds, and 10% in real estate. The expected return to the fund would then be

$$(0.225)12\% + (0.675)8\% + (0.100)9\% = 9\%$$

But once again Bob was embarrassed by Sue (who actually seemed to take pleasure in his embarrassment). She asked Bob why this particular allocation was any better than the multitude of other possible allocations that would also exactly meet the 9% target.[3] Sue pointed her finger at Bob in front of the board and asked him whether this allocation minimized the expected **volatility** of the fund's overall portfolio ("as directed by the board," she rubbed it in). Bob could only stammer something about his intuitive feeling that it was "probably pretty close" to minimizing the volatility (but in fact he didn't really know). A meeting was scheduled for the following week, a week in which Bob burned a lot of midnight oil.

Bob realized that in order to be more rigorous in his recommendation, he would have to estimate the volatility of each of the three asset classes, as well as the correlation among their returns. This was necessary in order to compute the volatility that any combination of these three assets would have. Estimating these "second moment statistics" was even harder than estimating their expected returns.[4] Nevertheless, Bob

---

Chapters 7 and 11. (See especially the discussion in section 11.2 regarding the estimation of real estate opportunity cost of capital.) To help quantify risk and the price of risk in different asset classes, Bob may also have used some insights from capital asset market general equilibrium pricing theory and practical stock value analysis tools (as will be described in a later chapter), as well as some lessons and tools from bond market economics (as described briefly in Chapters 18 and 19).

[2] Note that the formula used here is essentially the same as the weighted average cost of capital (WACC) formula we described in Chapter 13. This and other formulas useful for computing portfolio statistics are described in the appendix at the end of this chapter.

[3] Technically, what we have at this point is one linear equation with two unknowns: $w_{ST}(12\%) + w_{BN}(8\%) + (1 - w_{ST} - w_{BN})(9\%) = 9\%$, where w_{ST} is the allocation to stocks and w_{BN} is the allocation to bonds. Mathematically, an infinite number of combinations of w_{ST} and w_{BN} would satisfy this equation. The solution $w_{ST} = 0.225$, $w_{BN} = 0.675$ is just one such solution.

came up with the following estimates for annual volatility, or standard deviation in the periodic returns across time:

- **Stock market annual volatility: 15%**, based on the historical investment performance of the S&P 500 index over the past few decades
- **Long-term bond annual volatility: 8%**, also based on historical performance, adjusted slightly downward because Bob expected interest rates might not be quite as volatile in the future as they had been in the last few decades
- **Real estate annual volatility: 10%**, based on the historical performance of the NCREIF index, adjusted slightly to account for the effect of appraisal smoothing
- **Correlation between stocks and bonds: +50%**, based on recent historical evidence and the understanding that both asset classes tended to respond in the same direction to macroeconomic news on such issues as economic growth, inflation, and real interest rates
- **Correlation between stocks and real estate: +25%**, based on historical evidence and the recognition that, although real estate market cycles have often appeared to be independent of the stock market, both real estate and stocks are dependent on the health of the underlying macroeconomy and, as long-term assets, their values respond similarly to changes in real interest rates
- **Correlation between bonds and real estate: 0%**, based on historical evidence and the fact that periodic return volatility in the long-term bond market is very sensitive (in a negative way) to news about inflation, while real estate is relatively unaffected by inflation (or even positively affected in nominal terms)

Bob knew these estimates were "soft," and he was not extremely confident that they were correct. But he also knew that no one has a crystal ball and therefore no one could make perfect estimates. Nevertheless, decisions had to be made based on the best information available. He felt he could defend these estimates (even against Sue) because they were reasonable and realistic in the light of available historical evidence, plausible economic theory, and common sense. Bob's risk and return expectations for the three asset classes are summarized in the table in Exhibit 21-1a.[5] Perhaps more

Exhibit 21-1a   Bob's Risk and Return Expectations

	Stocks	Bonds	Real Estate
Expected Return ($E[r]$)	12.00%	8.00%	9.00%
Volatility	15.00%	8.00%	10.00%
Correlation with:			
Stocks	100.00%	50.00%	25.00%
Bonds		100.00%	0.00%
Real Estate			100.00%

[4] The distinction between "first moment" and "second moment" statistics is described in the chapter appendix.

[5] The actual historical annual correlation statistics for the three asset classes' periodic total returns as described in Chapter 7 for the 1970–98 period were +47% between stocks and bonds, +14% between stocks and real estate, and −27% between real estate and bonds. Bob's adjustments from the historical annual data were meant to reflect likely long-run performance expectations going forward from the present time.

Exhibit 21-1b Bob's
Covariance Expectations

	Stocks	Bonds	Real Estate
Stocks	0.022500	0.006000	0.003750
Bonds	0.006000	0.006400	0.000000
Real Estate	0.003750	0.000000	0.010000

important from a political perspective, Bob actually got Sue to agree before the meeting with the board that these were plausible expectations.

Once Bob had come up with these risk and return expectations, the mechanics of computing the volatility of a portfolio consisting of any allocation across the three asset classes was actually quite easy, using the basic spreadsheet software that Bob had on his laptop computer. The first step was to compute a table of the **covariances** between each pair of possible assets. This was done using the information in Exhibit 21-1a, as indicated in the table in Exhibit 21-1b.

In this table each cell is a covariance (or variance if the cell is on the diagonal).[6] For example, the middle cell in the top row of Exhibit 21-1b (covariance of stocks and bonds) is found from the data in Exhibit 21-1a as 0.006 = (0.15)(0.08)(0.50).[7]

The next step in computing the portfolio covariance was to multiply each of these covariances by the product of the "weights," or proportional shares of the total portfolio value, given to each asset class in Bob's proposed allocation. For example, in Bob's proposed allocation of 22.5% to stocks and 67.5% to bonds, the covariance of 0.006 between stocks and bonds would be multiplied by the product of 0.225 times 0.675. Considering also the 10% allocation to real estate that Bob was proposing, this resulted in the table shown in Exhibit 21-1c.[8]

The final step in computing the volatility of Bob's proposed portfolio was simply to sum all of the **weighted covariances** in the nine cells in Exhibit 21-1c and take the square root of that sum.[9] This resulted in an expected portfolio volatility of 7.84%,

Exhibit 21-1c Bob's
Weighted Covariances

	Stocks	Bonds	Real Estate
Stocks	0.001139	0.000911	0.000084
Bonds	0.000911	0.002916	0.000000
Real Estate	0.000084	0.000000	0.000100

[6] As described in the chapter appendix, the variance in an asset's return is equivalent to its covariance with itself.

[7] In general, $COV_{ij} = S_i S_j C_{ij}$, where COV_{ij} is the covariance between assets i and j, S_i is the volatility (that is, the time-series standard deviation in the periodic total returns) of asset i, and C_{ij} is the **correlation coefficient** between the two assets' periodic returns.

[8] For example, looking again at the middle cell in the top row (stocks and bonds), the computation is 0.000911 = (0.225)(0.675)(0.006). In general, the value in the cell in row i, column j of the weighted covariance table is $w_i w_j COV_{ij}$, where w_i is the proportional allocation to asset i within the portfolio (that is, the share of the total portfolio value invested in asset i).

[9] Of course, this is easily done in a computer spreadsheet simply by selecting the entire table and the range of cells to be summed.

based on Bob's risk and return expectations as indicated in Exhibit 21-1a, and Bob's proposed allocation weights of 22.5% stocks, 67.5% bonds, and 10% real estate.[10]

Once Bob had set up his electronic spreadsheet to compute the portfolio volatility, he realized that he could easily find the allocation that would indeed minimize the portfolio volatility, as the board of the pension fund wanted him to do (and Sue would surely demand). Bob found his ideal allocation using the **solver** utility in his spreadsheet software.[11] He told the solver to select an allocation across the three asset classes so as to minimize the value in the cell that computed the portfolio volatility, subject to the following constraints:

- The target return must be met:

$$\sum_{i=1}^{N} w_i E[r_i] = E[r_P],$$

where $E[r_P]$ is the target long-term return for the portfolio, w_i is the weight (proportion of total portfolio value) allocated to each asset class i, and $E[r_i]$ is the expected long-term return to each asset class.

- The allocation weights must all sum to unity:

$$\sum_{i=1}^{N} w_i = 1.$$

In addition, Bob added constraints requiring each asset allocation to be nonnegative because his pension fund client did not wish to take short positions (such as borrowing money) in any major asset class.[12]

---

[10] The variance of a portfolio is given by the following formula, as presented in the chapter appendix:

$$S_P^2 = \sum_{i=1}^{N} \sum_{j=1}^{N} w_i w_j COV_{ij}$$

where there are N assets in the portfolio, and

$$\sum_{i=1}^{N} w_i = 1$$

[11] Mathematically, the portfolio optimization problem described here is a type of constrained optimization problem that can be solved using a technique called quadratic programming. The solvers in general-purpose computer spreadsheets usually employ more general numerical solution procedures that can handle a wide variety of problems, including the portfolio problem described here. Computer spreadsheet solvers are usually adequate for handling portfolio problems with up to at least a dozen or so possible assets. More specialized software is necessary for handling very large numbers of assets. Keep in mind that spreadsheet solvers iterate numerically to the constrained optimal solution. They may not provide an exact optimum. (In practice, it is sometimes necessary to "zero out" the allocations before running the solver each time in order to get the solver to iterate correctly.) Although solvers generally come standard in spreadsheet packages, they may not load in the "standard install" procedure.

[12] In a short investment position, the asset is sold (cash proceeds obtained) *before* it is bought (cash paid out). To prohibit short positions, constraints in the form of $w_i \geq 0$ must be entered in the solver for each possible constituent asset class i in the portfolio.

As a result of this exercise, Bob found that an allocation of 15% to stocks, 44% to bonds, and 41% to real estate would meet the fund's 9% expected **return target** while minimizing its expected volatility at 6.83%, a full point below the 7.84% volatility in Bob's previously suggested allocation.

Of course, this allocation is only ideal to the extent that Bob's risk and return expectations for the three asset classes, as summarized in Exhibit 21-1a, are accurate. However, Bob's confidence in this regard was raised by the fact that he had already gotten Sue to agree that these expectations were reasonable. Nevertheless, knowing that any such future expectations are only approximate, he thought it prudent to test the effects of changing his expectations within plausible bounds. Such **sensitivity analysis** was easy to do using his computer spreadsheet and solver, simply by changing the values in the input table (Exhibit 21-1a).[13] For example, Bob was a bit unsure about his correlation assumptions for real estate, so he tested the effect of assuming that real estate was more highly correlated with the other asset classes: +50% with the stock market (instead of +25%), and +25% with long-term bonds (instead of 0%). The result was a variance-minimizing allocation of 16% stocks, 47% bonds, and 37% real estate.

Bob went back to the pension fund board with a recommended allocation that was relatively heavy in real estate and bonds and a bit light in stocks. Both the board and Sue seemed a bit uneasy about this suggestion, but they couldn't immediately find any flaw in Bob's approach or his conclusions. They had to admit that, if they didn't like his recommendation, they would have to go back to their own drawing boards and reexamine their stated objectives for the portfolio. For example, perhaps they did not really want to be so conservative as what was implied by their 9% return target. Or perhaps there was something important being left out of the picture, perhaps some element of risk that they weren't considering, or some cost of investment in one or more of the asset classes that was not being reflected in the directives they had given Bob.[14]

21.2 BASIC MEAN-VARIANCE PORTFOLIO THEORY (MPT)

The preceding story of Bob and his three-asset portfolio allocation problem is an example of the application of what is called **mean-variance portfolio theory**. As noted in the beginning of this chapter, this theory is also sometimes referred to as modern portfolio theory (abbreviated as MPT), or Markowitz portfolio theory, for the economist who is largely credited with its development. In this theory the objective of the macrolevel investment decision maker is taken to be the minimization of portfolio volatility (or variance) subject to an expected return target. In fact, this objective is

---

[13] As we pointed out, the subsequent calculations in Exhibits 21-1b and 21-1c leading to the computation of the portfolio volatility, which is minimized by the solver, were all based only on the input values given in Exhibit 21-1a and the proposed portfolio allocation weights.

[14] In reality, most U.S. institutions consider more than just domestic stocks, long-term bonds, and real estate as the major asset classes in the core of their investment portfolios. In particular, "cash" (short-term debt, especially T-bills) and international debt and equity are generally considered as major components. We will expand our consideration to include cash (T-bills) later, and we have left out international investments to simplify this example. However, to be fair, it should be recognized that, if we were to expand stock and bonds to include separate international components, then we could in like manner (at least in principle) also expand real estate to include a separate international real estate component. Some U.S. institutions do invest directly in overseas real estate assets.

mathematically equivalent to its "dual" description: the maximization of portfolio expected return subject to a volatility constraint. The numerical example in the preceding section demonstrated concretely what mean-variance theory does, how it is typically applied in the real world, and the basic mechanical steps for applying the theory using common computer spreadsheet software. Let us now step back and look at this theory from a broader and deeper perspective, so as to derive a more general understanding of how it can be useful to decision makers.

21.2.1 Investor Preferences and Dominant Portfolios

As risk and return are the two main issues portfolio theory is concerned about, a good place to begin is to consider a picture of the risk and return preferences of the investor. Exhibit 21-2 depicts risk and return on the horizontal and vertical axes of a rectangle, respectively. Each point in the rectangle is a different combination of risk and return. The investor's preferences are indicated by the indifference curves shown in the rectangle. These curves show how the investor judges the trade-off between risk and return for her investments. The investor is indifferent among portfolios that provide risk and return combinations that lie on the same indifference curve.

You can think of the indifference curves as contour lines on a map of a ski slope, representing a three-dimensional surface above the risk/return rectangle. Higher points on this surface indicate risk/return combinations that are preferred by the investor. Other things being equal, investors generally prefer greater return and less risk. Thus, the investor preference surface is rising toward the upper left corner of the rectangle. The investor will prefer points farther to the "north" and "west" in the rectangle; points such as P will be preferred over points like Q.

The rectangle in the top panel in Exhibit 21-2 (panel A) depicts a conservative investor, one who is relatively more risk averse (less risk tolerant) in his investment preferences. Such an investor's indifference curves are steeply curved to the north in the risk/return rectangle, indicating that he must be compensated with a lot of additional return in order to be willing to take on a little more risk. This is seen by the fact that the curves move a considerable distance along the vertical (expected return) axis for each small increment along the horizontal (risk) axis.

In contrast, the rectangle in panel B of Exhibit 21-2 depicts a more aggressive investor, one who is relatively more risk tolerant. Such an investor's indifference curves are less steeply rising over the horizontal axis, indicating less need for additional expected return in more risky investments.

Suppose that points P and Q in Exhibit 21-2 represent the expected return and risk of two different portfolios, that is, two different allocations for the investor's wealth. Clearly both the conservative and the aggressive investors depicted in Exhibit 21-2 would prefer portfolio P to portfolio Q. In fact, as long as investors are not actually "risk loving" (that is, as long as they do not actually prefer more risk to less, holding return constant), they will always prefer a point such as P to one like Q.

Now consider Exhibit 21-3. Here, the risk and return possibilities are divided into four quadrants emanating from portfolio Q. Any portfolio (such as P) that provides as much or more expected return than Q with as little or less risk, is said to *dominate* Q. This would be any portfolio providing risk/return combinations above and/or to the left of Q, that is, in the upper-left quadrant. Similarly, any risk/return combination in the lower-right quadrant would be *dominated by* Q. *Any* investor, no matter what her risk preferences (whether she is conservative or aggressive, as long as she is not actually risk loving), will prefer a **dominant portfolio** to a dominated portfolio.

Exhibit 21-2 Utility Preference Surface (indifference curves) of an Investor

Panel A: Conservative (relatively risk-averse) investor:

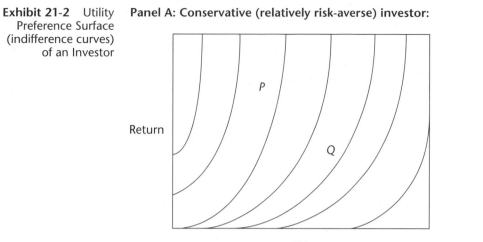

Return

Risk

Panel B: Aggressive (less risk-averse) investor:

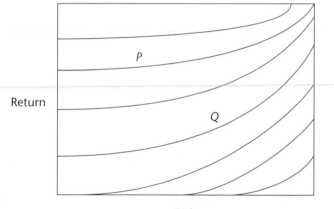

Return

Risk

In practice, and from a quantifiable perspective, mean-variance portfolio theory is used primarily to help investors avoid holding dominated portfolios. Portfolio theory is about moving investors from points such as Q to points such as P whenever possible, that is, moving up and/or to the left (or "northwesterly") in a standard risk/return diagram such as that in Exhibit 21-3.[15] Classical Markowitz portfolio theory has less to say (quantitatively) about choosing between Q and another portfolio that lies in either the quadrant to Q's northeast or the quadrant to Q's southwest. To rigorously make such a

---

[15] For example, back in section 21.1, Sue's criticism of Bob's recommended allocation of 22.5% stocks, 67.5% bonds, and 10% real estate was based on the dominance argument. That allocation achieved no more expected return than the one Bob ultimately came up with (9%), but it had more volatility (7.84% instead of 6.83%).

Exhibit 21-3 Portfolio Dominance

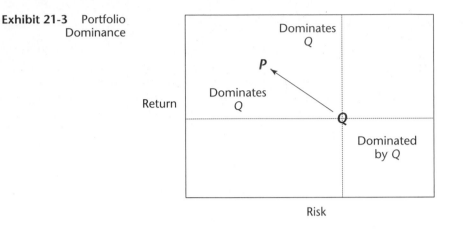

Return

Risk

choice, we would need to know how to quantify the investor's risk preferences more completely than simply knowing that he is not risk loving.[16]

21.2.2 Portfolio Theory and Diversification

The expression: Don't put all your eggs in one basket, has been around a long time. Long before Harry Markowitz published his seminal paper on portfolio theory in 1952, people had an intuitive sense that they should not put too much of their total wealth into a single investment or type of asset. This might be referred to as intuitive diversification.[17] It is common sense that if all (or nearly all) of your wealth is invested in only one type of asset, then you are overly exposed to loss in the event of a down-side event that randomly affects only that one type of asset. Portfolio theory adds to this primitive concept of diversification by quantifying the benefit of diversification in terms of portfolio risk and return, and by providing some rigorous (albeit some-what simplistic) guidance as to exactly how to diversify, that is, *how many* eggs should you put in *which* baskets.

In this regard, it is important to understand that some combinations of assets are more valuable than others as far as their diversification effect is concerned. For example,

---

[16] Some techniques have been developed to attempt to quantify investor preferences more precisely. For example, the investor may be guided through an exercise in which she states her preference for various combinations of stocks and bonds given various different expected returns and historical volatility patterns, in such a way that a "preference map" along the lines of what is depicted in Exhibit 21-2 can be constructed for the investor regarding various risk/return combinations. More commonly in the real world, however, this part of the portfolio allocation decision (that is, movement in a southwesterly or northeasterly direction in the risk/return diagram) is treated "heuristically" or nonquantitatively, which is to say, politically. Implicitly, of course, some indication of the investor's preferences are inevitably revealed in the allocation policy he finally adopts. That the adoption process should be somewhat *political* actually makes *economic* sense. Although a Nobel Prize was given to Harry Markowitz for his development of portfolio theory, another Nobel Prize was given to another economist, Kenneth Arrow, in part for his development of what is called the "impossibility theorem." Arrow proved that it is mathematically impossible to define a so-called social welfare function that can be relied on to aggregate individual preferences into a single rational preference function. In effect, viewed from a very fundamental perspective, any investment decision-making institution that has more than one individual owner or beneficiary must employ some sort of political process to aggregate preferences effectively, so as to arrive at a common decision. Alas (but aren't you really glad), there is a limit to how far technocrats can take us.

[17] The term *naive diversification* is also used, but this seems unnecessarily perjorative.

Exhibit 21-4a shows a scatter-plot and regression line of the total annual returns to stocks and long-term bonds during the 1970–98 period. Each point in the scatter-plot represents the annual periodic returns to stocks and bonds in a given year. As you can see from the upward slope of the regression line, these two asset classes tended more often than not to move together in time. This tendency is quantified by their positive correlation coefficient of 47%.[18] On the other hand, look at the scatter-plot of bond and real estate returns for the same period shown in Exhibit 21-4b. These two asset classes tended more often than not to move in opposite directions during this period, as indicated by their correlation coefficient of −27%.

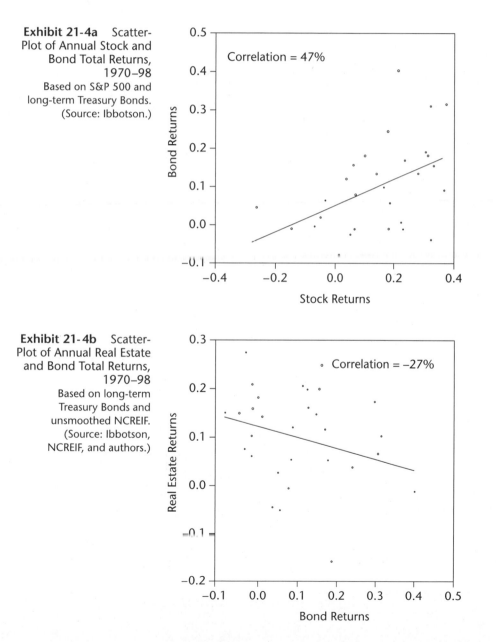

Exhibit 21-4a Scatter-Plot of Annual Stock and Bond Total Returns, 1970–98 Based on S&P 500 and long-term Treasury Bonds. (Source: Ibbotson.)

Exhibit 21-4b Scatter-Plot of Annual Real Estate and Bond Total Returns, 1970–98 Based on long-term Treasury Bonds and unsmoothed NCREIF. (Source: Ibbotson, NCREIF, and authors.)

[18] The definition and meaning of the correlation coefficient is explained in the appendix at the end of this chapter.

Now look at the annual periodic total return histories for 1970–98 shown in Exhibit 21-5. Exhibit 21-5a shows the returns to stocks, to bonds, and to a portfolio consisting of 50% stocks and 50% bonds (the last represented by the solid line in the chart).[19] With the exception of the early years (when stocks and bonds tended not to move together), the diversified (50/50) portfolio is just about as volatile as the undiversified (pure) portfolios. Stocks and bonds were sufficiently positively correlated

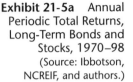

Exhibit 21-5a Annual Periodic Total Returns, Long-Term Bonds and Stocks, 1970–98 (Source: Ibbotson, NCREIF, and authors.)

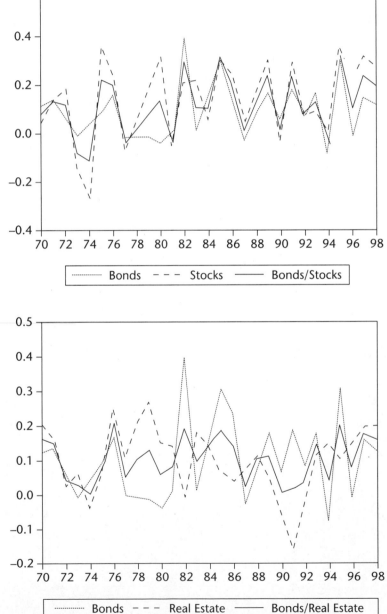

Exhibit 21-5b Annual Periodic Total Returns, Long-Term Bonds and Real Estate, 1970–98 (Source: Ibbotson, NCREIF, and authors.)

[19]Of course, the returns to the 50/50 portfolio simply lie midway between the returns to the two pure portfolios.

during most of the 1970–98 period so that there was only a small reduction in volatility resulted from combining the two in a single half-and-half portfolio.[20] In contrast, Exhibit 21-5b shows that a 50/50 combination of real estate and bonds would have had noticeably less volatility than either pure portfolio alone. Note that the solid line between the two dashed lines jumps around noticeably less than either of the two dashed lines.[21] In general, pairs of assets that do not move together provide greater diversification benefit when they are combined in a portfolio. The volatility of such assets tends to cancel out when they are combined in a portfolio.

21.2.3 Perceived Role of Real Estate in the Mixed-Asset Portfolio

By now it should be obvious that our point about diversification is a very important consideration for real estate investment from a broad, mixed-asset portfolio perspective. Real estate as an asset class tends to be less positively correlated with other major asset classes, such as stocks and bonds, than those other asset classes are with each other, at least when viewed at relatively short frequencies (such as annual periodic returns).[22] This makes real estate in general appear to be a relatively good "diversifier" within the overall portfolio. This **diversification benefit** of real estate is a major reason for substantial inclusion of real estate in many large institutional portfolios.

For example, recall our numerical example in section 21.1. Bob ended up recommending a relatively large allocation to real estate in an "optimally diversified" portfolio (for a given return target). The large allocation to real estate in that example was clearly *not* due to real estate providing an exceptionally large expected return. (Recall that Bob estimated a real estate return of 9%, compared to 12% for stocks and 8% for bonds.) Nor was it because real estate was expected to provide exceptionally stable (that is, low volatility) returns. (Recall that Bob estimated real estate volatility at 10%, compared to 8% for bonds and 15% for stocks.) The reason it made sense to give real estate a large allocation in Bob's portfolio recommendation was primarily that it had a relatively low correlation with the other asset classes. (Recall that Bob estimated real estate's correlation with bonds to be 0%, and with stocks to be 25%, as compared to a stock–bond correlation of 50%.[23])

---

[20] During 1970–98, when the annual correlation between stock (S&P 500) and long-term bond (U.S. Treasury Bonds) returns was +47%, stocks had a volatility of 16%, bonds of 12%, and the half-and-half portfolio's volatility was 12%. If we drop off the decade of the 1970s, the correlation between stocks and bonds was +58% during 1981–98, and the 50/50 portfolio had a volatility of 12% as compared to 13% for each of the pure portfolios.

[21] In fact, the bond volatility was 12%, the real estate volatility was 10%, and the half-and-half portfolio volatility was less than 7%.

[22] Longer-term perspectives will be discussed in the next chapter. Real estate's relatively low correlation at short to middle time intervals probably carries through to the international investments arena as well. For example, evidence suggests that the correlation between international securities and U.S. real estate is lower than the correlation between international securities and U.S. securities. In addition some evidence shows that the correlation between U.S. and overseas investments may be lower within the real estate asset class than within securities such as stocks and bonds. This may reflect the fact that property markets are less integrated across national borders than securities markets are. Also, the fundamental value of property assets may tend to be more narrowly geographically fixed than that of securities. See, for example, Ziobrowski (1995) and Eichholtz (1996).

[23] For example, the real estate share in the optimal portfolio drops to zero (regardless of the return target) if real estate is assumed to have +75% correlation with each of the other two asset classes and the other

Another Role for Real Estate

Mean-variance portfolio theory highlights real estate's role as a diversifier within the portfolio. This role makes sense from the MPT perspective, viewing the mixed-asset portfolio as encompassing the investor's entire net wealth. From the perspective of a pension fund, however, or other such institution managing a portfolio of assets at least in part to meet future liability obligations, a somewhat different perspective is warranted. The net wealth of the investor may be viewed as the asset portfolio minus the present value of future liability obligations (e.g., pension benefit payments to retirees). These obligations are generally largely contractually fixed (in the case of a "defined benefit" pension plan, for example). Managers of the fund must therefore consider two objectives, not only the risk and return optimization of the fund's assets, but also its need to meet obligations on the liability side. Management of the portfolio focusing on the liability rather than asset side of the balance sheet was discussed in Chapter 19, where we noted that immunization-oriented strategies may be more relevant than mean-variance optimization. Although bonds are particularly useful in such strategies, real estate also has a useful role on the liability side. In particular, pension benefit obligations tend to be sensitive to inflation, both because of **cost-of-living adjustments (COLAs)** in the benefits, and because of inflation-driven salary-creep that tends to push up pension entitlements. As noted in previous chapters, real estate is a relatively good inflation hedge, whereas long-term bonds are notoriously exposed to inflation risk. Thus, if real estate's major role on the asset side of the balance sheet is as a diversifier, its major role on the liability side is often as an inflation hedge.

Indeed, real estate's particularly low correlation with long-term bonds was especially useful in our example. By combining large and roughly equal amounts of real estate and bonds, the optimal allocation was able to reduce the portfolio volatility substantially. This is one reason stocks ended up with a relatively small allocation, even though they provided the highest expected return.

21.2.4 The Efficient Frontier

Now let's put together the general point about diversification we made in section 21.2.3 with the idea described in 21.2.2 about avoiding dominated portfolios. This synthesis is one of the most important ideas in portfolio theory, the efficient frontier.

To understand the concept of the efficient frontier, let's go back again to our numerical example from section 21.1. In particular, let's take Bob's risk and return expectations for the three asset classes, but let's ignore for the time being the constraint represented by the 9% return target. First, consider the risk and return opportunities facing Bob if he could only invest in one asset class, that is, if he could not diversify across asset classes but instead had to choose one "pure" portfolio, either stocks, bonds, or real estate. In that case, Bob would face the risk/return combinations indicated by the three points in Exhibit 21-6a. He could either get 8% expected

risk and return expectations remain as in Exhibit 21-1a. On the other hand, real estate's share in the optimal 9% target return portfolio falls only to 33% if we assume real estate's expected return is 8% (as low as the bond return expectation) instead of 9% (holding all other expectations as in Exhibit 21-1a). If we change the Exhibit 21-1a expectations only by giving real estate a 15% volatility (equal to that of stocks) instead of 10%, then the real estate share in the optimal 9% return portfolio falls to 22%.

Exhibit 21-6a Three Assets: Stocks, Bonds, Real Estate (no diversification)

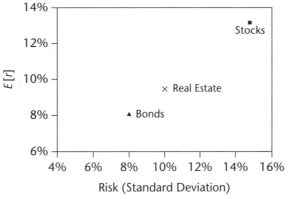

Exhibit 21-6a Three Assets: Stocks, Bonds, Real Estate (no diversification)

return and 8% volatility by investing in bonds, or 9% return and 10% volatility in real estate, or 12% return and 15% volatility in stocks.

Notice that these three possibilities all lie generally in a northeasterly/southwesterly relation to one another in the risk/return diagram. No one possibility is dominated by any other. This is typical of the risk/return relationships we would expect among asset classes. But the possibilities shown in Exhibit 21-6a are highly constrained, not allowing any diversification across asset classes. Suppose we relax this constraint a little by allowing diversification across any *two* asset classes. This expands the risk/return possibilities to the three curved lines indicated in Exhibit 21-6b. Each curve represents the risk/return possibilities from mixing two asset classes, either stocks and bonds, stocks and real estate, or bonds and real estate. For example, the curve on the lower left, connecting the pure bond and pure real estate possibilities, represents risk and return combinations available from various allocations to bonds and real estate.

Now we see that certain pairwise combinations are dominated by others. Some points on each of the three curves lie to the northwest of some points on the other curves. For example, a portfolio containing 75% stocks and 25% real estate dominates a portfolio with 75% stocks and 25% bonds. The former has expected return of 11.3% with volatility of 12.1%, while the latter has expected return of 11.0% and volatility

Exhibit 21-6b Three Assets: Stocks, Bonds, Real Estate (with pairwise combinations)

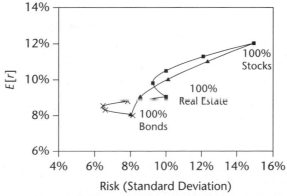

—■— RE & Stocks —▲— Stocks & Bonds ✕ RE & Bonds

of 12.4%, that is, a lower expected return with more risk. An investor with the risk and return expectations presented in Exhibit 21-1a should never hold a portfolio of 75% stocks and 25% bonds if he could invest in real estate instead of bonds.

It is interesting also to notice the shape of the three curves in Exhibit 21-6b. They all curve up and to the left as compared to a hypothetical straight line connecting the two endpoints of the curve (pure investments). This means that diversified mixtures of the two asset classes will provide some additional expected return for a given amount of risk, or less risk for a given expected return, between the risk/return limits implied by the undiversified (pure) investments (the endpoints of the curves). This favorable "bending" of the risk/return possibility curve is a mathematical result between any two assets or asset classes that are not perfectly positively correlated. This is important because in reality no two *underlying* assets (or asset classes) will ever be perfectly correlated. The result we see in Exhibit 21-6b is typical in this regard.[24]

Note also that the curves involving real estate combinations (either with bonds or stocks) are more sharply bent than the curve that represents stock and bond combinations. This is the effect of real estate's relatively low correlation with the other two asset classes, especially with bonds. In fact, among the three pairs depicted in Exhibit 21-6b, the most favorable bending is in the real estate/bond combinations. As you recall, Bob's estimates of the correlations among the asset classes was 0% between real estate and bonds, +25% between real estate and stocks, and +50% between stocks and bonds.

Exhibit 21-6b still represents a constraint on the investor's ability to diversify, as diversification is limited to only two asset classes. Suppose we relax this restriction. With the possibility of diversifying across all three asset classes, many more risk/return possibilities open up. As before, some of those possibilities are dominated by others. As no investor should want to hold any portfolios that are dominated, the set of interesting combinations of the three asset classes consists only those that are not dominated. Such a portfolio is called an **efficient portfolio**, and the risk/return possibilities associated with the set all possible efficient portfolios is called the **efficient frontier**.[25] Any portfolio on the efficient frontier is not dominated by any other portfolio, and any non-dominated portfolio is on the efficient frontier. In other words, the efficient frontier consists of all asset combinations that maximize return and minimize risk.[26]

The efficient frontier for combinations among the three asset classes in our numerical example is shown in Exhibit 21-6c. The heavy curved line marked with diamonds

[24] Only "derivative" assets can be perfectly correlated. As noted in Chapter 7, derivative assets are characterized by having their returns depend completely on the returns to one or more fundamental underlying assets (e.g., a call option on a stock). Underlying assets generate returns directly by the production of real goods or services. Such an asset is never perfectly correlated with any other asset because there is always some possibility of an event that will uniquely or differently affect each asset. For example, even if company A and company B are near clones of each other, A's stock may rise and B's fall when it is announced that A won a contract that B also bid for, or if B's successful president quits unexpectedly, and so forth. Of course, if company A and company B are not near clones of each other, then it is even more obvious that they will not always respond in the same way to the same news. This latter consideration is why broad asset classes cannot be perfectly correlated (or even very highly correlated), as they represent very different types of assets.

[25] **Terminology alert:** Do not confuse efficient in this sense, with *efficient* in the sense we previously used this word to describe the functioning of an asset market, that is, the concept of *informational efficiency*. An efficient portfolio is simply one that is not dominated by any other portfolio in its expected return and risk. This does not carry any implication regarding the informational efficiency of the asset markets in which its constituent assets trade.

[26] More precisely, for a given volatility, the efficient frontier maximizes the expected return, and for a given expected return the efficient frontier minimizes the volatility.

Exhibit 21-6c Three Assets with Diversification: The Efficient Frontier

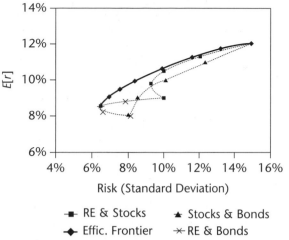

is the efficient frontier for stocks, bonds, and real estate with the risk and return expectations indicated in Exhibit 21-1a. This curved line represents the best risk and return possibilities, those that are farthest northwest in the diagram. Points farther to the north or west of the efficient frontier are not feasible. Now you see why this is called a frontier. The efficient frontier always has this characteristic curved shape, running generally from the southwest toward the northeast in the risk/return diagram, bending upward and leftward relative to a straight line.

Each point on the efficient frontier represents a unique combination of its possible constituent assets. In the case represented in Exhibit 21-6c, each point on the frontier represents a unique proportional allocation among stocks, bonds and real estate.[27] Each point on the efficient frontier also corresponds to a unique risk/return combination. For example, as we saw in section 21.1, the point on the efficient frontier corresponding to an expected return of 9% entails a volatility of 6.83% and represents an allocation of 15% to stocks, 44% to bonds, and 41% to real estate.

21.2.5 Bringing in Investor Preferences

Portfolio theory tells us that all investors should hold portfolios on the efficient frontier. Which portfolio on the efficient frontier any given investor should hold depends on the risk and return preferences of the investor. As noted, the efficient frontier is generally sloped from the southwest to the northeast in the risk/return diagram.[28] A rational choice among different points on the efficient frontier can only be made by consulting the investor's preferences for risk and return. As we saw in the example in section 21.1, in practice these preferences are often expressed in terms of a target long-run

---

[27] In general, some of the efficient portfolios may have zero or negative allocations to one or more constituent assets. In the example we have been considering here, none of the allocations are negative because we have constrained our portfolio to avoid short positions. The "no shorts" constraint is generally realistic for large institutional portfolios when considering allocation strategy across broad asset classes.

[28] This is a mathematically necessary consequence of the way we defined the efficient frontier, as the possibilities that maximize return and minimize risk.

rate of return for the portfolio, and within an institution this target may be selected by a more or less political process. Investors who are more aggressive or risk tolerant specify higher return targets (knowing that this implies greater portfolio volatility), while conservative investors specify lower return targets.

This process is depicted in Exhibit 21-7. Both panels show the efficient frontier we just constructed based on the risk and return expectations in Exhibit 21-1a. The other curve shown in the figure is an indifference curve reflecting the investor's preferences. In particular, the indifference curve reflects the highest level of satisfaction (or "utility") the investor can achieve. Indifference curves that lie parallel to the curve shown would either be infeasible (to the northwest of the depicted curve) or indicative of lower levels of investor satisfaction (to the southeast of the depicted curve). The indifference curve that is just "tangent" to the efficient frontier (i.e., the indifference curve that touches the efficient frontier at one and only one point) is the best the investor can do.

The top panel, 21-7a, shows this result for a relatively conservative investor, indicating a target return of 9%. The bottom panel, 21-7b, shows the result for a slightly more aggressive investor, indicating a target return of 10%. The 10% target implies an optimal portfolio volatility of 8.73% as compared to the 6.83% volatility

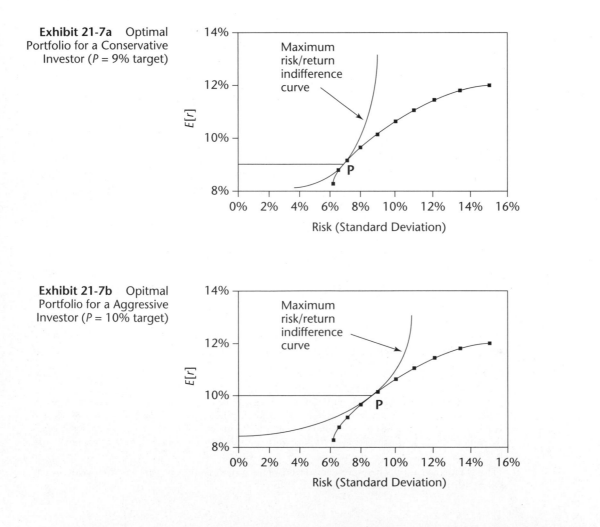

Exhibit 21-7a Optimal Portfolio for a Conservative Investor (P = 9% target)

Exhibit 21-7b Opitmal Portfolio for a Aggressive Investor (P = 10% target)

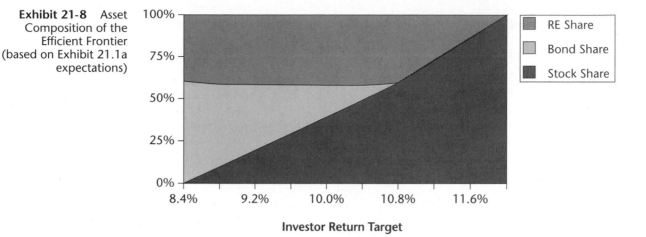

Exhibit 21-8   Asset Composition of the Efficient Frontier (based on Exhibit 21.1a expectations)

implied by the 9% target. While the efficient portfolio for the 9% target had only 15% allocation to stocks, the efficient portfolio for the 10% target would have 40% allocation to stocks, based on the same risk and return expectations (those of Exhibit 21-1a). Interestingly, *both* targets imply a 41% allocation to real estate in this case. (The 10% target reduces the bond allocation to 19%.)

Exhibit 21-8 shows another way to present the efficient frontier. This exhibit shows how the optimal shares of the constituent asset classes change as a function of the investor's expected return target. The portfolio target rate of return is indicated on the horizontal axis.[29] The vertical dimension of the rectangle in Exhibit 21-8 stacks the efficient allocations to each asset class on top of each other to account for 100% of the investor's wealth. As before, Exhibit 21-8 is based on Bob's expectations as stated in Exhibit 21-1a. Notice that the optimal real estate share is rather large (around 40%) and stable for a broad range of relatively conservative return targets. The optimal share allocated to stocks rises steadily with the return target, first at the expense of bonds, and then at the expense of real estate. This makes intuitive sense, as real estate has a slightly higher expected return than bonds (though lower than stocks), and the correlation between real estate and stocks is lower than that between bonds and stocks.

21.3 ALLOWING FOR A RISKLESS ASSET: THE TWO-FUND THEOREM AND THE SHARPE-MAXIMIZING PORTFOLIO

Portfolio theory as described in the preceding section provides an elegant and rigorous framework for thinking about strategic asset allocation at the level of the investor's overall wealth portfolio. It provides insight and builds intuition relevant to all investors. It is widely used in practice, particularly by large institutional investors

---

[29]Note that, the portfolio expected return is on the horizontal axis in Exhibit 21-8, whereas it had been on the vertical axis in the previous figures.

Can Portfolio Theory Be Applied *within* the Real Estate Portfolio?

It is easy to see how, beginning in the 1970s, the real estate investment industry welcomed modern portfolio theory and its ERISA implications for planning capital allocations at the level of the broad, mixed-asset portfolio. For the first time, real estate was included, at least conceptually, as a vital part of the institutional investment picture, along with the traditional mainstays, stocks and bonds. By the 1980s this enthusiasm had carried down to the level of the *real estate component* within the overall portfolio. Advocates argued that MPT could and should be applied *within* the real estate allocation, for example, to find the optimal mixture among different property types (e.g., office, retail, industrial, etc.) and/or geographic regions (e.g., the East, South, West, etc.).* What was being advocated, in effect, was a hierarchical or two-stage process. The investment institution would first use MPT to help decide how much capital to place in real estate as whole, and then use MPT again to help determine the optimal property segment allocation within that the overall real estate budget.

While this type of hierarchical structure may make sense from an institutional management perspective for implementing strategic investment policy, there are a couple of problems in trying to apply MPT in this way. First, little conceptual basis exists for the application of MPT below the level of the entire wealth portfolio of the investor. A key tenet of MPT is that the investor cares about the risk and return in the entire portfolio, rather than any component of the portfolio in isolation. For example, suppose a property segment has little correlation with other property segments but high correlation with stocks and bonds. From the perspective of the real estate portfolio alone, such a property segment would look very appealing in an MPT framework. But from the perspective of the overall wealth portfolio, which includes large allocations to stocks and bonds, such a property segment would be much less appealing.

A second problem is practical in nature. It is very difficult to come up with the kind of highly refined yet reliable risk and return expectations by property segment that are necessary for the rigorous application of MPT within the real estate portfolio. As you can see from our discussion of MPT, one would need good estimates of expected returns, volatility, and correlations among all pairs of property segments. For example, if you wanted to consider four property types in four geographic regions, you would need 16 return estimates, 16 volatility estimates, and 120 correlation estimates. Historical periodic returns data in the property market is just not good enough, nor is our knowledge of the determinants of future real estate returns, to permit very useful analysis at this level of detail.

For these reasons, rigorous application of MPT at the *within-real-estate* level is not very widespread in terms of detailed investment decision making. However, it is sometimes useful for conceptual purposes, for example, to understand the potential role a new type of real estate investment could play within the real estate portfolio. Also, less formal, common-sense based diversification of the real estate portfolio is usually a wise strategy for large institutions.** Portfolio theory builds our intuition about how to think logically about such diversification. For example, portfolio theory suggests that property types whose uses tend to follow different economic cycles, or economic regions whose economic bases are distinct and relatively uncorrelated, would be relatively more valuable for diversification purposes. (Recall our discussion in Chapter 3 about the classification of geographic regions by economic base.) Even in such less formal application of portfolio theory intuition, however, it makes sense to consider the investor's overall wealth portfolio as the context for diversification, rather than just the real estate component of the investor's wealth.

---

*See, for example, Miles and McCue (1984).

**The most important argument *against* diversification in real estate investment is the need for specialized local expertise, both in the acquisition/disposition phases and in the property ownership/management phase. It may be difficult, especially for small investors, to acquire sufficient expertise efficiently in more than one local area or property type. The segmentation of real estate space markets, and lack of informational efficiency in property asset markets, then exposes "novices" or "outsiders" to greater risk at the microlevel, and this may more than offset the macrolevel arguments for diversification.

such as pension funds.[30] However, an important consideration for many investors has not been included in the theory as presented so far. In particular, we have considered only *risky* assets as possible components of the portfolio. By risky assets, we mean investments whose returns cannot be predicted with certainty in advance, investments whose periodic returns are volatile. Yet it is often useful to envision another type of asset, a *riskless* (or *riskfree*) asset.

In principle, a riskless asset's return is known in advance for certain, and it is viewed as having no volatility in the realization of its periodic returns. In reality, of course, there is no such thing as a completely riskless asset. However, the concept of the riskless asset is a useful construct because it provides an interesting extension of the theory described previously.

One reason for the introduction of a riskless asset in portfolio theory is that this construct can *approximate borrowing or short-term lending* by the investor. Borrowing, or the use of debt to finance investment, can be represented by a short position in the riskless asset.[31] When the investor borrows money (in effect *levering* her overall wealth, as described in Chapter 13), she normally intends to pay back the loan without defaulting. Thus, from the investor's perspective, the return on the debt asset appears certain, providing some logic for treating the debt as riskless. On the other hand, many investors hold a certain amount of "cash" in their wealth portfolios, that is, investments in very short-term debt. This is most commonly in the form of U.S. Treasury Bills (T-bills), although private sector "commercial paper" and other instruments are also used. The periodic returns on such short-term lending by the investor have very little volatility and virtually no default risk, and so may be viewed as an approximately riskless investment.

21.3.1 Two-Fund Theorem

While the riskless asset construct is useful as an approximation for borrowing and short-term lending, it has another, more technical use as well in portfolio theory. The riskless asset construct can be used as a sort of mathematical technique to simplify greatly the portfolio allocation problem. This simplification is known as the **two-fund theorem**, and it too is widely used in practice.

To see what the two-fund theorem means and how it works, you need to understand a basic mathematical fact. Recall from our discussion of Exhibit 21-6b that whenever two risky assets are less than perfectly positively correlated, the risk/return possibilities of combinations of those two assets lie along a curve that is bent upward and leftward in the risk/return diagram. But now suppose one of the two assets is riskless, that is, contains no volatility. In this case, the risk/return possibilities of combinations of the two

---

[30]As noted in Chapter 7, MPT inspired some of the language in the Employee Retirement Income Security Act of 1974 (ERISA), a federal law that is fundamental to the management of pension funds in the United States. This is one reason pension funds take MPT so seriously.

[31]Recall that a short position can be represented by a negative investment allocation. In the case of short positions the investor receives cash when the position is taken and gives up cash when the position is closed or retired. This is in direct contrast to long positions, which are characterized by the fact that cash is given up at the time the investment position is taken, and cash is obtained when the asset is sold to close out the position. Thus, you can see how borrowing can be represented as a short position in a debt asset, just as lending is a long position in such an asset.

assets will lie exactly on a straight line connecting the risk/return possibilities of the two assets.[32]

This means that, in a risk/return diagram, the risk/return possibilities from a combination of a riskless asset and *any* portfolio of risky assets will lie along a straight line connecting the riskless asset's risk/return with the risky portfolio's risk/return. This is depicted in Exhibit 21-9a for combinations of a riskless asset with an interest rate of r_f and a risky portfolio with risk and expected return represented by point Q. All the risk/return possibilities lying on the straight line connecting r_f with Q are feasible by holding the portfolio Q combined with either long or short positions in the riskless asset. If the investor puts some of his wealth in the portfolio Q, and some in the riskless asset, then his risk and return will lie on the line segment between points r_f and Q, to the left of Q.[33] (The greater the share of his wealth in the riskless asset, the closer to r_f his expected return will be, and the farther to the left of Q on the straight line his risk and return will lie.) If the investor borrows money, then his risk and return will lie on the straight line to the right of Q.[34]

In Exhibit 21-9 the curved line represents the efficient frontier of risky assets described in the previous section. Thus, the risky portfolio Q is an efficient portfolio, in the absence of the possibility of investing in a riskless asset. Nevertheless, if it is possible to take positions in a riskless asset, no investor would want to combine such positions with Q. All of the risk/return possibilities on the straight line connecting r_f with Q are dominated by possibilities lying on the straight line connecting r_f with P, a different portfolio also lying on the efficient frontier of risky assets. This is depicted in Exhibit 21-9b. In fact, you can see by geometric reasoning that the possibilities on the straight line connecting r_f and P dominate any and all other feasible risk/return possibilities. P lies at the point on the risky asset efficient frontier (the curved line) that is just tangent to a straight line passing through r_f.[35]

---

[32] This is because the riskless asset has, by definition, zero volatility (measured as the standard deviation of its periodic returns). With zero variance, the riskless asset also must have zero covariance with *any* risky asset or portfolio. The formula for the volatility of a combination of two assets is

$$S_P = \sqrt{w^2 S_i^2 + (1-w)^2 S_j^2 + 2w(1-w)COV_{ij}}$$

where S_P is the volatility of the combination of assets i and j, w is the share of wealth in asset i, $(1-w)$ is the share in asset j, and COV_{ij} is their covariance. If j is a riskless asset, then S_j and COV_{ij} are both zero, so this reduces to $S_P = wS_i$. As $r_P = wr_i + (1-w)r_j = r_j + w(r_i - r_j)$, it is clear that both r_P and S_P are linear functions of w, the weight in the risky asset i. (Note that we are measuring risk here by the volatility, or standard deviation of returns, not by the variance.)

[33] This would be short-term lending, that is, taking a long position in the riskless asset.

[34] This would be taking a short position (placing a negative proportion of the investor's wealth) in the riskless asset. As the proportion of the investor's wealth in both the riskless asset and the risky portfolio must sum to unity, this implies that the proportion of the investor's wealth placed in the risky portfolio Q would exceed unity. In other words, borrowing enables the investor to place more than his total wealth in the risky portfolio, his own net wealth plus the amount he has borrowed against it. As the expected return to Q exceeds the riskfree rate of r_f at which he is borrowing, the resulting leverage is "positive" (to use the terminology introduced in Chapter 13), causing the investor's expected return to exceed r_Q, lying therefore to the right of Q on the straight line connecting r_f and Q.

[35] Any line northwest of P would not be feasible, as it would pass entirely through the infeasible region to the northwest of the risky asset efficient frontier. In other words, it would be impossible to find a risky portfolio to combine with the riskless asset to produce risk/return possibilities that lie on such a line. Any straight line through r_f that would run southeast of P would be dominated by the line through P.

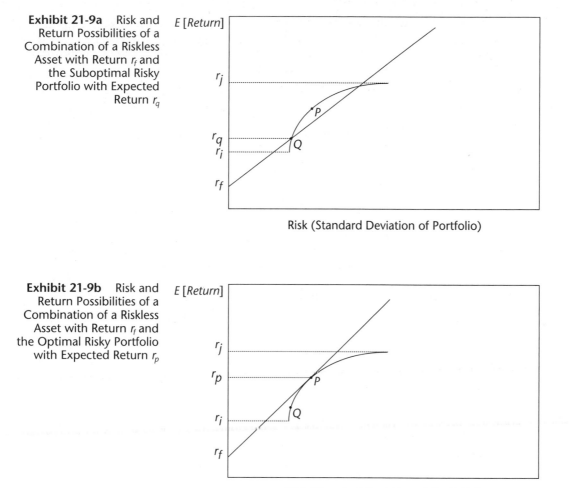

Exhibit 21-9a Risk and Return Possibilities of a Combination of a Riskless Asset with Return r_f and the Suboptimal Risky Portfolio with Expected Return r_q

Exhibit 21-9b Risk and Return Possibilities of a Combination of a Riskless Asset with Return r_f and the Optimal Risky Portfolio with Expected Return r_p

This brings us to the two-fund theorem. According to this theorem, all investors (no matter what their risk preferences) will prefer combinations of the riskless asset and *a single* particular risky asset portfolio, (the point *P* in Exhibit 21-9b). With the possibility of riskless borrowing or lending, the optimal allocation among risky assets, *P*, is determined *not* by the investor's risk preferences, but only by her expectations about asset future returns. The investor's risk preferences can be met by adjusting the position in the riskless asset only, by either borrowing more (for more aggressive preferences) or lending more (for more conservative tastes), so as to meet the appropriate expected return target.

21.3.2 Sharpe-Maximizing Portfolio

How can we determine which combination of risky assets corresponds to the unique optimal allocation represented by point *P* in the two-fund theorem? The answer to this question is obvious in the geometry we just used to discover the theorem. The point *P* is the portfolio that maximizes the slope of a straight line connecting that portfolio's risk and return with the risk and return of the riskless asset. Of course, the riskless asset has zero risk, and its return is r_f. The risk (volatility) of the risky-asset portfolio is S_P, and its' return is r_P. The slope of the line connecting these two points is thus: $(r_P - r_f)/S_P$. This is the risk premium of the risky asset portfolio divided by its volatility. This ratio is known as the **Sharpe ratio**, named after William F. Sharpe, who shared the Nobel Prize for portfolio theory. In the presence of a riskless asset, the optimal combination of risky assets is the one with the highest Sharpe ratio.[36]

While the two-fund theorem has an elegance that appeals to the aesthetic sense of academicians, it also has a simplicity and intuitive appeal that practitioners like. It is thus widely used in practice. As the Sharpe ratio is just the risk premium (what we have been labeling RP) divided by the risk (defined as volatility), it is a natural measure of **risk-adjusted return** and is widely (and somewhat informally) used as such by practitioners. The numerator of the Sharpe ratio measures the investor's compensation for risk, the excess return over what an investment in T-bills would provide. The denominator of the Sharpe ratio is the amount of risk in the investment as measured by the standard deviation of its periodic returns. If the Sharpe ratio is applied at the level of the investor's entire wealth portfolio, volatility is arguably the relevant measure of risk. Furthermore, the Sharpe ratio is unaffected by the investor's position in the riskless asset, either by borrowing or lending risklessly. Thus, it makes intuitive sense to want to find the risky asset allocation that maximizes the Sharpe ratio.

$$\textit{Sharpe ratio of P} = \frac{r_P - r_f}{S_P} = \frac{RP_P}{S_P}$$

In considering the role of real estate in the optimal mixed-asset portfolio, the Sharpe-maximizing perspective sometimes reduces the real estate share for conservative investors, as compared to the perspective from classical MPT without a riskless asset. In general, the Sharpe-maximizing risky asset allocation tends to place lower weights in low-return asset classes, as compared to the variance-minimizing allocation with a conservative target return.

As an example, let us return again to Bob's portfolio allocation problem with the risk and return expectations in Exhibit 21-1a. To meet Bob's (rather conservative) 9% return target, recall that the variance-minimizing shares among the three risky asset classes were: 15% stocks, 44% bonds, and 41% real estate. Now suppose we can approximate the riskfree interest rate as being 6%. The Sharpe-maximizing risky asset allocation (P) would then consist of 35% stocks, 24% bonds, and 41% real estate. The relative proportion of stocks is considerably greater, and long-term bonds smaller, than in the 9% target variance-minimizing portfolio. However, this comparison is a bit misleading because this all-risky-asset Sharpe-maximizing portfolio is too aggressive for Bob's client. This is seen by the fact that, without any investment in T-bills, the **Sharpe-maximizing portfolio** would have an expected return

---

[36] You can use the solver on a spreadsheet to find the Sharpe-maximizing allocation the same way as we described in section 21.1 to find the variance-minimizing allocation. Simply compute the Sharpe ratio of the portfolio in a cell of the spreadsheet using formulas A.1 and A.6 from the chapter appendix, as before. Then, instead of telling the solver to minimize the portfolio variance, tell it to maximize the portfolio Sharpe ratio. You will no longer need the target return constraint in the solver. (The resulting optimal allocation will just be for the risky asset portfolio, P. You will have to lever this portfolio up or down using the risky asset to meet a given target return.) Obviously, somewhere in the spreadsheet you have to input the riskfree rate, r_f. The Sharpe-maximizing allocation will be different for different values of r_f.

Exhibit 21-10
Comparison of Optimal
9% Return Target Portfolio
Allocations, Variance-
Minimization vs. Sharpe
Ratio-Maximization

	Return & Risk Expectations*			Portfolio Allocations	
	Return	Volatility	Sharpe Ratio	Var.-Min.	Sharpe-Max.
Cash (T-bills)	6.00%	NA**	NA	NA	21%
Bonds	8.00%	8.00%	0.25	44%	19%
Real Estate	9.00%	10.00%	0.30	41%	32%
Stocks	12.00%	15.00%	0.40	15%	28%
Var.-Min. Portfolio	9.00%	6.83%	0.44	100%	NA
Sharpe-Max. Portfolio	9.00%	NA**	0.46	NA	100%

*Also includes correlations:
 Stock/Bond +50%, Stock/Real Estate +25%, Bond/Real Estate 0%.

**From the Sharpe-maximization perspective, T-bills are viewed as having zero volatility, but as this is not exactly true in reality, it would be misleading to calculate and show a Sharpe-maximizing portfolio volatility juxtaposed with that of the variance-minimized portfolio.

of 9.81% with 8.31% volatility (compared to 6.83% volatility in the 9% target all-risky-asset variance-minimizing portfolio).

To meet the 9% return target using the Sharpe-maximizing portfolio, we would have to allocate 79% of the investor's wealth to the Sharpe-maximizing risky asset portfolio and 21% to T-bills. The overall allocation would then be 28% stocks, 19% long-term bonds, 32% real estate, and 21% T-bills. The combined long-term and short-term debt allocation (bonds and bills) would be 53%, slightly higher than the 44% allocation to long-term debt alone in the variance-minimizing 9% target port-folio. Thus, the optimal 9% target portfolio from a Sharpe-maximizing perspective allocates considerably more weight to stocks (28% instead of 15%) and less weight to real estate (32% instead of 41%). In a sense, part of the reason the real estate allo-cation is so high in the variance-minimizing portfolio is simply because the investor has specified a conservative return target, and real estate has a relatively low expected return![37] These differences between the Sharpe-maximizing and variance-minimizing perspectives are summarized in the table in Exhibit 21-10.[38] Note that, even though the optimal real estate allocation is reduced in the Sharpe-maximizing portfolio, it still retains a large share, given the indicated expectations.

21.3.3 Summary of the Implications of the Riskless Asset Construct

In this section we have seen how the extension of the original Markowitz portfolio theory to include consideration of a riskless asset can be useful in several ways:

- It allows an alternative, intuitively appealing definition of the optimal risky asset portfolio, the one with the maximum Sharpe ratio.

[37] Some investors may feel uncomfortable with this aspect of the classical portfolio optimization model.

[38] In Exhibit 21-10 T-bills are used as a proxy for the riskfree asset. As an example of the computation of the Sharpe ratio, the real estate ratio is computed as $(9\% - 6\%)/10\%$. Note that the Sharpe ratio of a portfolio is unaffected by its allocation to the riskfree asset.

- It can help to avoid "silly" portfolio recommendations that put too little weight in high-return assets just because the investor has a conservative target return (or vice versa).
- It provides a useful framework for accommodating the possible use of leverage or short-term debt holdings in the portfolio.

On the other hand, the riskless asset construct is an extension of the original model that adds an additional, not-quite-realistic assumption. The use of one form or the other of the portfolio model depends in part on taste, and in part on circumstances. In practice, both versions are widely used in the real world.

21.4 SOME BROADER CONSIDERATIONS IN PORTFOLIO ALLOCATION

The preceding two sections introduced you to classical portfolio theory. Either with or without the riskless asset construct, this is the most widely used conceptual tool for considering macrolevel investment allocation decisions in the framework of risk and return. It is an elegant and powerful theory for developing strategic insight about investment allocation. Furthermore, although the specific numbers we have been working with in this chapter are only examples, they are broadly consistent with typical expectations used in the real world.

With this in mind, it is of more than passing interest to note the similarity between the optimal real estate allocation share suggested in Exhibit 21-10 and the actual proportion real estate represents in the total U.S. investable wealth indicated in Exhibit 7-4, way back in Chapter 7. While all of these numbers are soft, there is an important suggestion here of broad agreement between the normative perspective provided by portfolio theory and the empirical perspective provided by the actual asset class market valuations. Both perspectives seem to suggest that real estate is roughly between one-fifth and something less than one-half of the total pie.[39] This rough agreement suggests, at least at a very broad-brush level, that we have some combination of a good theory of asset allocation and an efficient capital market in the United States.[40]

Yet this brings us to a curious point. The largest centrally managed investment portfolios in the United States, namely, institutional investment portfolios such as those of pension funds, generally allocate a much smaller share to real estate than what has been implied by the (example) numbers in this chapter. In this section we will consider why this is so.

---

[39]Exhibit 7-4 estimates the real estate asset class at around 24% of the total market value of the U.S. investable asset universe. The analysis in the previous sections of the present chapter suggest an optimal real estate allocation typically on the order of one-third (give or take 10% or so, depending on investor expectations and risk preferences) of a portfolio consisting of the same four asset classes: stocks, bonds, real estate, and cash.

[40]If capital markets are efficient, then they should allow investors to implement their allocation goals. If the normative allocation theory is good (i.e., if it makes sense to people), then investors' allocation goals should generally reflect the recommendations of the theory. The conjunction of these two conditions (market efficiency and good normative theory) would therefore lead to the empirical observation that the "average portfolio" (as reflected in aggregate market value shares) resembles the normative recommendation from the theory.

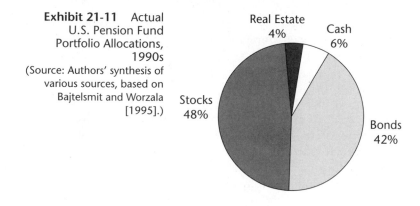

Exhibit 21-11 Actual U.S. Pension Fund Portfolio Allocations, 1990s (Source: Authors' synthesis of various sources, based on Bajtelsmit and Worzala [1995].)

21.4.1 Real Estate Allocations in Real World Institutional Portfolios

Let us begin by noting the typical allocation to real estate in large, professionally managed institutional investment portfolios in the United States, as represented by defined-benefit **pension funds** (PFs for short). Such funds control over $2 trillion of assets in the United States and represent the major source of diversified investment in private real estate equity.[41]

Exhibit 21-11 depicts PF allocation among the four major asset classes we have been considering in this chapter, as of the 1990s. As you can see, PF portfolios are dominated by stocks and bonds, with almost half the total in each of these asset classes.[42] Compared with the normative suggestion of portfolio theory, and indeed, compared with the broader evaluation of the aggregate investable asset universe in the United States, the PF allocation to real estate is quite low. A quarter of a century after the passage of the **ERISA** law, the average pension fund in the United States still has less than 5% allocated to real estate equity. Why is this?

21.4.2 Reasons for the Low Institutional Allocation to Real Estate

To be honest, the short answer to the question of why PF allocation to real estate is so far below the implications of the classical normative theory is: We are not sure. In fact, this question has intrigued (and frustrated) academic real estate researchers for almost

---

[41]Other major investors in commercial property, such as REITs and wealthy individuals, often have more specialized investment objectives that prevent them from considering real estate as one element in a broad, mixed-asset portfolio. For example, REITs can only invest in real estate, and often do so as part of a more active, vertically-integrated real estate management strategy, so as to profit from expertise in a certain property type. In contrast, defined-benefit pension plans are the major locus of passive investment allocation across all the major asset classes through a centralized decision-making process. PFs are therefore an ideal laboratory for viewing portfolio theory in practice.

[42]The "stocks" category in Exhibit 21-11 includes PF investment in REITs. However, investment in REITs was a very small proportion of the total PF stock allocation, and also was small compared with the PF allocation to direct (private) real estate equity (although the PF allocation to REITs grew considerably during the decade of the 1990s). The "bonds" category in Exhibit 21-11 includes both public and private debt instruments, including mortgages and MBS. As noted in Part VI, such real estate-backed debt products are characterized by investment performance generally similar to other debt products, such as corporate bonds, and so should be viewed in the present context as components of the "bonds" asset class broadly speaking. This is consistent with both the normative and empirical depictions of the asset pie in Exhibits 21-10 and 7-4.

two decades. A number of clever theories have been put forth, and no doubt almost all contain some truth. To give you a sample, we will mention two here. In general, all of these approaches argue that something important is left out of classical portfolio theory.

Real Estate Market "Frictions." One of the important things left out of the classical theory is what may be called **market frictions**. In reality, direct investment in privately traded real estate assets faces some difficulties or constraints not present in investment in publicly traded securities such as stocks and bonds. In particular, real estate assets are relatively **illiquid**. That is, they cannot be sold quickly at full market value. In other words, real estate investment faces transaction costs much greater than those involved in trading stocks and bonds (per trade, measured as a percent of the value of the assets being traded). Related to this is the fact that real estate assets are relatively **lumpy**. You generally have to trade whole assets (entire properties) rather than small shares of such assets. Another constraint that applies more to real estate than other asset classes is that it is virtually impossible to take short positions in private real estate equity. Generally no effective mechanism exists for selling a property before you buy it.[43] Depending on how important such frictions and restrictions are to PF investors, the real estate share could be reduced substantially in the optimal portfolio.[44]

Long-Interval Expectations. Another approach to trying to square normative portfolio theory with empirical PF allocations is to take a longer-term perspective on the risk and return expectations for the asset classes. Investors generally think in terms of annual, quarterly, or even monthly statistics on mean returns, volatilities, and correlations among the asset classes. But in reality, PFs have long investment horizons. What should matter to them in making long-term, strategic allocation decisions is long-interval statistics measured at, say, the decennial or at least half-decade frequency, rather than annual or shorter.

In the traditional context of portfolio theory application to the stock and bond market, this consideration does not matter. When all potential constituent assets in the portfolio are traded in informationally efficient markets, their periodic returns are largely uncorrelated across time.[45] This causes mean returns and covariances all to be linear functions of the periodic return frequency used to compute the return statistics.[46] In this case, the optimal portfolio allocation prescribed by the classical theory would be invariant to the periodic return frequency at which the return expectations

---

[43] No law prevents the establishment of such contracts, but in reality they are very rare. Some recent attempts have been made to allow short sales of investment vehicles based on indices of real estate periodic returns, but so far such attempts have not come to much.

[44] An excellent example of this approach to resolving the PF real estate allocation conundrum is presented by Kallberg, Liu, and Greig (1996). Their model reflects such real estate market frictions as lumpy assets and inability to short-sell. Their analysis suggests an optimal real estate allocation around 9%, which is closer to the empirical PF real estate allocation of 5% than to the classical portfolio theory normative real estate allocation which is in excess of 20%. However, the Kallberg-Liu-Greig analysis also indicates an optimal allocation to bonds of less than 2%. Thus, the overall mixed-asset portfolio suggested by their model is at least as different from the empirical PF allocation as is that implied by classical portfolio theory.

[45] That is, there is no autocorrelation and also no lagged cross-correlation.

[46] For example, the mean decennial returns and covariances would be 10 times the mean annual returns and covariances.

are measured. The same optimal portfolio would apply for the long-horizon investor as for the short-horizon investor. But if one or more asset classes do not trade in an informationally efficient market, then return correlations may exist across time.[47] This can cause the optimal long-horizon portfolio to differ from the optimal portfolio computed with, say, annual frequency return and risk expectations.

Suppose private real estate asset markets are sluggish, as we described previously.[48] This would typically cause real estate volatility and cross-correlation with other asset classes to be greater, relatively speaking, when measured in long-interval return statistics. There is probably more positive correlation between real estate and stock returns, in particular, when you measure returns only every decade, than when you measure them every year.[49] The longer the frequency, the greater the dominance of fundamental economic links across underlying risky asset classes such as stocks and real estate. These links tend to be positive in nature, reflecting in the same way broad macroeconomic and structural movements.[50] As a result, when viewed from a long-run perspective, real estate probably brings to the mixed-asset portfolio less diversification benefit (and greater relative volatility) than it does when viewed from the perspective of annual-frequency return statistics. This would cause the optimal real estate share to be less.[51]

The previous are only two examples of academic theoretical approaches attempting to explain the empirical PF allocation to real estate from a normative perspective. There have been others as well (see box). Any one (or a combination) of these approaches could perhaps reconcile PF behavior with economic rationality. After all, there are hundreds of large pension funds, and each one makes decisions through a more or less bureaucratic process typically involving a board of trustees that normally includes

[47] For example, if private real estate markets are sluggish, responding more slowly than the securities markets to relevant news, then there would generally be positive autocorrelation in real estate returns, as well as nonzero lagged cross-correlations between real estate and securities.

[48] See previous discussions in Chapters 1, 7, and 12 (including the Chapter 12 appendix).

[49] Although rigorous historical statistics are difficult to obtain for long histories, the following chronology seems plausible based on general historical knowledge. Both commercial real estate and stocks were up in the 1920s; down in the 1930s; up in each of the 1940s, 1950s, and 1960s; then they diverged in the 1970s and 1980s (real estate was up and stocks down in the 1970s, the opposite was true in the 1980s), before they were both up again in the 1990s. Thus, out of the eight decades since 1920, real estate and stocks probably moved together six times and apart two times (relative to their own long-run trends). This is crude historical analysis, but you get the point. Yet, at the annual frequency these two asset classes show little positive correlation in historical statistics.

[50] However, not all such fundamental economic determinants of asset value would necessarily move stocks and commercial real estate in the same direction. Recall, for example, the monocentric city model of land value we described in Chapter 4. There we showed how technological improvements and real economic growth could actually lead to a reduction in real land values in central locations, where most commercial real estate is located. Yet such technological improvements and real economic growth should generally cause increases in the real value of the stock market. More generally, rents for space usage are profits for real estate assets, but costs of production for the industrial and service corporations that dominate the stock market. Thus, it is unlikely that real estate and stocks are very highly positively correlated even when viewed from a long-run, fundamental economic perspective.

[51] Although the long-run perspective described here can be argued in *principle* to reduce the optimal real estate share, it is not clear how effective this argument is in practice. Geltner, Rodriguez, and O'Connor (1995) performed such an analysis using estimated five-year-frequency return statistics. The optimal mixed-asset portfolios they computed had a private real estate share ranging from %0 to 48%, but generally in the 20% to 30% range for target returns typical of pension funds, still far above the empirical PF real estate allocation.

More Academic Answers to the Pension Fund Real Estate Investment Puzzle

The reasons for the discrepancy between the empirical and theoretical allocations to real estate in pension fund portfolios has been one of the most persistent puzzles to fascinate the academic real estate research community. The explanations describe in the text are only two of a number of theoretical explanations offered by academic research to try to explain the relatively small empirical real estate allocations. Without claiming to be exhaustive, we will briefly mention in this box three of the most intriguing approaches suggested by academics during the 1990s, including studies by Ciochetti and Shilling (1999), and Gatzlaff (1995), and Liang, Myer, and Webb (1996).

Ciochetti and Shilling (1999) argue that PFs should optimize their *net* wealth portfolio, subtracting the present value of their future pension liability obligations from the present value of their asset holdings, rather than optimizing only the asset side of their balance sheet. This consideration reduces the optimal real estate share (in favor of greater allocation to bonds), if it is assumed that the present value of pension liability obligations changes over time more like bond values than like real estate values. This is traditionally the argument for PF managers to follow a bond-based "immunization" type of investment strategy, as described in Chapter 19, rather than a mixed-asset "mean-variance" type of strategy. A key issue in the Ciochetti-Shilling argument has to do with the extent to which future pension liability obligations are sensitive to future inflation. If pension obligations are sensitive to inflation, then real estate's inflation-hedging abilities may still call for a large allocation to real estate, even from a net wealth perspective.

Gatzlaff (1995) takes a completely different approach, arguing that PFs should optimize *not* their *own* (institutional) net wealth portfolios, but rather that of the "average" *individual beneficiary* (member of the plan). A large proportion of the wealth of most pension plan members consists of their home equity. Gatzlaff shows that single-family home equity value is more highly correlated with commercial real estate than it is with stocks and bonds. Hence, the optimal pension fund portfolio places less investment in commercial real estate, given the beneficiary's large positive weight in home equity. However, it is questionable if this perspective makes sense for a *defined benefit* pension plan, in which the benefits received by the plan members are essentially fixed independent of the pension fund portfolio performance, so that portfolio investment return risk falls largely on the plan sponsor rather than the beneficiary [see also Liu, Grissom, and Hartzell (1990), and Geltner, Miller, and Snavely (1995)].

Finally, the approach of Liang, Myer, and Webb (1996) is completely different from any of those described before. They argue that the statistical "confidence bounds" around the efficient frontier allocations (based on historical empirical estimates of risk and return) are very broad. The typical existing pension fund allocation to real estate is well within those bounds. Thus, we cannot say with rigorous "statistical significance" that the existing allocation is suboptimal, even though this allocation does differ from the "point estimate" that represents the best single guess about what the optimal allocation should be.

---

several individuals. Different reasons may motivate different trustees. Indeed, multiple reasons may motivate any one trustee. But a nagging problem with all of these explanations is akin to what Einstein said when confronted with a book published in Nazi Germany arguing against the theory of relativity, entitled *100 Authors Against Einstein*. Einstein's comment was simply, "Had I been wrong, one author would have been quite enough!" An alternative approach to explaining PF allocations might take a more behavioral or political approach combined with an apprehension of the implications of informational inefficiency in the private real estate asset markets.

Recall our discussion in Chapter 12 about the investment implications of such inefficiency. We noted there that real estate markets are not able to provide the kind of protection public securities markets provide against doing negative-NPV deals (measured from a market value perspective). Lack of informational efficiency means that real estate transaction prices are "noisy," that is, they are disbursed around the "true" market value of the properties being traded. There is a real danger of doing a bad deal, paying too much or selling for too little.

Now recall that space markets are segmented by property type and geographic area. And of course, real estate asset values are strongly influenced by what happens in the space market in which the asset is situated (where real estate cash flows are ultimately determined). Therefore, to minimize the danger of "doing a bad deal" (i.e., incurring a negative NPV at the microlevel), you typically need good *local real estate expertise*. Pension funds lack such expertise, and they know it. Sure, they can hire specialized real estate investment managers and local agents, but there may be agency problems in working with such third parties. Because of this, PFs probably tend (rather understandably) to feel that they are at a relative disadvantage when dealing with privately traded real estate as compared to stocks and bonds.[52]

Pension funds also may tend to be at a relative disadvantage regarding the other consequence of informational inefficiency that we described in Chapter 12, the inertia and *predictability* in real estate investment performance. We noted that real estate returns are more predictable than those of other asset classes, and that this predictability presents both an opportunity and a danger. "Quicker" investors, that is, those who can reallocate capital relatively easily in response to perceived opportunities, will be most able to profit from the opportunities presented by this type of predictability. Investors who are more bureaucratic, who must make decisions slowly and deliberately, often by committee, will typically be less able to profit from such opportunities. Indeed, such investors risk finding themselves on the wrong side of predictability.

Institutional investors are often criticized for "herd behavior" and making investment allocation decisions in a more "adaptive" or "reactionary" manner, tending to reward (like Santa Claus) asset classes that have done well in the recent past by allocating more capital to them, without sufficient regard for future prospects.[53] To some extent, the fiduciary responsibilities and organizational structure of pension funds make it difficult for them to avoid these types of problems. The resulting danger is the risk of buying high and/or selling low. This danger is more serious in less informationally efficient asset markets, in which the inertia can extend and exacerbate the effects of poor timing.

PF trustees (and their staff and hired investment managers) often operate in a political and legal (fiduciary) environment where they tend to have more to lose from perceived poor investment performance than they have to gain from good performance. In such an environment, the mere perception or fear of the dangers in real estate market inefficiency may be sufficient to cause PF decision makers to shy away from direct private investment in real estate equity. Perhaps this accounts for the gap between actual PF allocations to real estate and the prescriptions of normative portfolio theory.

---

[52] Williams (1999) put forth a formal equilibrium model arguing along these lines, although his model was applied to a slightly different question, namely, why "noninstitutional" property typically commands higher expected returns than "institutional" property.

[53] See Mei (1996).

21.5 CHAPTER SUMMARY

This chapter introduced you to the most famous and fundamental tool in macrolevel real estate investment analysis, modern portfolio theory. This theory, including its extension using the riskless asset construct, provides the core discipline for rigorous strategic investment decision making. This is the level of decision making relevant to deciding broad, long-run capital allocation policies across the major asset classes. As real estate is one of the major asset classes, the perspective, intuition, and methodology we presented in this chapter is of vital importance to anyone seriously interested in real estate investment.

APPENDIX 21: A REVIEW OF SOME STATISTICS ABOUT PORTFOLIO RETURNS

At its root, portfolio theory is about the risk and expected return in a combination of individual assets. Risk and return are quantified using statistics that describe periodic returns series over time. Therefore, some basic statistics about periodic returns of portfolios are reviewed in this appendix. As portfolios are combinations of individual assets, it is also important to understand the relationship between time-series and cross-sectional return statistics as applied to real estate assets.

Cross-Sectional and Time-Series Return Statistics

Return statistics measure the central tendencies and dispersion in the returns to assets or portfolios (combinations of assets). The two types are defined here:

- *Cross-sectional* statistics are taken *across multiple individual assets, as of a single point in time.*
- *Time-series* statistics are taken *across multiple periods of time* (either for a single asset or portfolio, or for multiple assets or portfolios, but always measuring effects *across time*).

Although classical, formal portfolio theory makes direct use only of time-series statistics, both types of statistics are broadly relevant in the analysis and characterization of real estate portfolios. Furthermore, a good understanding of the distinction between these two types of return statistics is necessary to avoid confusion.

The best way to cement your understanding of the difference between these two types of statistics in practice is to consider a simple but concrete numerical example. Accordingly, let us consider two individual real estate assets (two properties), A and B. We will consider their investment performance as represented by their total periodic returns in each of two consecutive periods of time, year 1 and year 2. (To simplify the numerical example, we will assume that neither property generates any income in either year, so that their total returns are determined entirely by their change in value, or appreciation return.) The following table presents the value of each property at the beginning and end of each year:

Example Property Values

Time	Value Property A	Property B
Beg. Yr. 1	$2,000,000	$1,000,000
End Yr. 1	$2,160,000	$1,060,000
End Yr .2	$2,419,200	$1,123,600

Based on these values, we can compute property A's periodic returns as 8% and 12% respectively for year 1 and year 2.[54] Similarly, property B's return is 6% in both years.[55] Looking *across time* at each property in turn, we can see that property A's average return was 10% and property B's was 6% during the period of history encompassed by years 1 and 2 together.[56] These time-series average statistics present a measure of the "central tendency" of the returns to each of these properties during that period. On the other hand, looking *across properties* within each year, we can see that the average return in year 1 was 7% and the average return in year 2 was 9%.[57] (Note that these cross-sectional average returns are *equally weighted* mean returns. The weight of each property's return in computing the cross-sectional average is identical, namely, 50%.)

We can also compute statistics of dispersion in the periodic returns, either across time or across properties. The simplest statistic of dispersion is the population standard deviation. This is computed as the square root of the equally weighted mean of the squared deviation of each return from its equally weighted mean. For example, by this measure the time-series dispersion in property A's return is ±2% around its mean of 10%, computed as

$$2\% = \sqrt{\{[(8\% - 10\%)^2 + (12\% - 10\%)^2]/2\}}$$

The cross-sectional dispersion in year 1 would similarly be measured as ±1% around its mean of 7%, computed as

$$1\% = \sqrt{\{[(8\% - 7\%)^2 + (6\% - 7\%)^2]/2\}}$$

The following table summarizes the individual periodic returns and the previously described mean and standard deviation statistics for our example. In the top left panel, the rows correspond to the two years, and the columns to the two properties.

[54]($2,160,000 − $2,000,000)/$2,000,000 = 8%. ($2,419,200 − $2,160,000)/$2,160,000 = 12%.
[55]($1,060,000 − $1,000,000)/$1,000,000 = 6%. ($1,123,600 − $1,060,000)/$1,060,000 = 6%.
[56]For property A: (8% + 12%)/2 = 10%. For property B: (6% + 6%)/2 = 6%. Recall from Chapter 9 that these are "arithmetic" means. Arithmetic means tend to be more widely used in portfolio theory. Property A's "geometric" mean return across the two years would be ($2,419,200/$2,000,000)$^{(1/2)}$ − 1 = 9.98%. Property B's geometric mean return is identical to its arithmetic mean, as it has no dispersion in its return over time: ($1,123,600/$1,000,000)$^{(1/2)}$ − 1 = 6%.
[57]For year 1: (8% + 6%)/2 = 7%. For year 2: (12% + 6%)/2 = 9%.

The cross-sectional statistics are presented to the right, and the time-series statistics at the bottom. (Note that property B's returns had 0% standard deviation, indicating no dispersion during these two years, as the return was constant at 6% both years.)

Periodic Returns			Cross-Sectional Statistics		
Year	Property A	Property B	Year	Mean	St. Dev. (Pop.)
1	8.00%	6.00%	1	7.00%	1.00%
2	12.00%	6.00%	2	9.00%	3.00%
Time-Series Statistics					
Mean	10.00%	6.00%			
St. Dev. (Pop.)	2.00%	0.00%			

It is obvious from this simple numerical example that cross-sectional statistics and time-series statistics are very different "animals." They are measuring conceptually different things. For example, you should see that it would be conceptually possible for there to be great cross-sectional dispersion within each period of time, yet the returns across time within all (or a combination of) properties could be constant, lacking any time-series dispersion (i.e., no volatility). Such a result would follow if each property always displayed a constant return, but that return was different for every property. Similarly, it would be possible for there to be no cross-sectional dispersion at all (all properties always having the same return within any given period of time), yet a portfolio consisting of all (or any combination of) such properties could have plenty of dispersion in its periodic returns over time (i.e., lots of volatility). All it would take to accomplish this result would be for each property's returns to vary across time.[58]

Although portfolio theory uses time-series statistics, it is most concerned about such statistics for portfolios consisting of multiple individual assets. If each asset in the portfolio always had the same proportion of the portfolio's total value as every other asset, then the cross-sectional equally weighted mean returns such as those computed earlier would represent the portfolio's periodic returns. In practice, however, the value weights of the individual assets in a portfolio usually vary across the assets. For example, consider the portfolio consisting of property A and property B.

---

[58] In fact, something like this latter scenario is substantively important in understanding the nature of indices of real estate periodic returns. Recall from Chapter 12 (including the appendix to that chapter) that in a market in which assets are "thinly traded," there is a distinction between the market value of an asset, and either the transaction price or any estimate of market value of the asset (including an appraised valuation). As a result, the valuations of the individual properties within each period of time, the valuations on which the periodic return of the index or portfolio is based, typically contain errors. Such valuations generally do not exactly represent the true market value of the property. However, to the extent that such "errors" are purely random (i.e., they lack systematic or common components across properties), they will tend to diversify out of an aggregate index (or portfolio) consisting of many individual properties. Therefore, for purposes of analyzing an index or portfolio of many properties, it may often be a useful simplification to view the constituent properties as effectively having no cross-sectional dispersion in their returns. In effect, we consider only the component of each property's return that is *common* across all properties, the component representing the market as a whole, or the asset class, represented by the index. This type of consideration and analysis will be discussed in depth in a Chapter 25.

The values of this portfolio at the beginning and end of each year are shown in the following table, along with the portfolio's periodic returns. The previously described time-series statistics are also computed for the portfolio, based on its periodic returns. The portfolio's time-weighted arithmetic mean return is 8.68% across the two years, and its volatility during that period was 1.35%.

Time	Property A	Property B	Portfolio	Return
Beg. Yr. 1	$2,000,000	$1,000,000	$3,000,000	
End Yr. 1	$2,160,000	$1,060,000	$3,220,000	7.33%
End Yr. 2	$2,419,200	$1,123,600	$3,542,800	10.02%
T.S. Mean				8.68%
T.S. St. Dev. (Pop.)				1.35%

Note that the portfolio returns of 7.33% and 10.02% in years 1 and 2, respectively, differ from the equally weighted average returns computed previously (7% and 9%). This is because the assets composing the portfolio had different returns and different value-based weights in the portfolio. The portfolio returns may also be referred to as the *value-weighted* average returns across the individual assets. For example, based on the asset values as of the beginning of year 1, property A has two thirds of the port-folio value and property B has one third because property A was worth $2 million at the beginning of year 1, when property B was only worth $1 million. Thus, the value-weighted average return across the two properties in year 1 is (2/3)8% + (1/3)6% = 7.33%.

In general, the return during period t to a portfolio consisting of N component assets is the value-weighted average return across all the assets:

$$r_{Pt} = \sum_{i=1}^{N} w_{it} r_{it},$$

where   (A.1)

$$\sum_{i=1}^{N} w_{it} = 1$$

where w_{it} is the proportion of portfolio value in asset i at the beginning of period t, and r_{it} is asset i's return that period.[59]

Time-Series Statistics Used in Portfolio Theory

As noted at the outset of this appendix, portfolio theory is essentially about the risk and return characteristics of portfolios. Such risk and return is quantified by statistics describing the period-by-period total returns to the portfolio, returns like those we just calculated for the portfolio in the simplified numerical example in the preceding

[59] This is equivalent to the weighted average cost of capital (WACC) formula introduced in Chapter 13. As noted there, it applies to the simple holding period return (HPR).

section.[60] The statistics used directly in portfolio theory are therefore time-series statistics, that is, measures of central tendencies, dispersion, and comovement across time. In practice, any given historical period is normally taken to represent a sample of time. Thus, in practice we usually use sample statistics rather than the population statistics used in the previous numerical example.[61]

Broadly speaking, we can group the statistics used in basic portfolio theory into two types. *First moment* statistics measure *central tendencies*, that is, the overall average or typical value of the return. *Second moment* statistics measure *dispersion* and *comovement*, that is, how returns vary over time and in relation to those of other assets. The classical first moment statistic used in portfolio theory is the mean, usually the arithmetic mean.[62] The major second moment statistics used in portfolio theory are the variance (and its square root, the standard deviation, or volatility) and the covariance (and its normalization, the correlation coefficient). These statistics are described here.

Mean.   This is the average value of the returns across time. It represents expected performance (ex ante) or achieved performance (ex post). In general, for portfolio theory the time-weighted mean is most relevant, for the reasons described in Chapter 9. Assuming the historical period from which the mean is calculated is a representative stretch of history, the historical arithmetic mean is the best estimate of the ex ante return, that is, what the return will be in any given future single period.[63] As noted in Chapter 9, the formula for computing the arithmetic mean of a series of T periodic returns $(r_1, r_2, \ldots r_T)$ is as follows, where $\bar{r}$ is the ex post mean return:

$$\bar{r} = \left(\frac{1}{T}\right)\sum_{t=1}^{T} r_t \tag{A.2}$$

[60] Recall from Chapter 9 that periodic returns are series of consecutive short holding period returns (HPRs) across time.

[61] The distinction between sample and population statistics is normally only a technical fine point in most of the practical applications we will consider. For example, as noted in formula (A.3), the formula for computing historical return variance (or volatility) is modified slightly from what was used in the previous numerical example.

[62] See Chapter 9 for a discussion of the differences between, and the relative advantages and disadvantages of, the arithmetic and geometric means. Recall also that when returns are defined as continuously compounded (or log differences), then the arithmetic mean is effectively the same as the geometric mean.

[63] The time-weighted geometric mean may be a better indicator of multiperiod average performance over an interval of time equal to that in the historical sample. (Recall that if the underlying returns are normally distributed, the arithmetic mean approximately equals the geometric mean plus one-half the variance in the returns.) Note also that if returns are not "memoryless" (i.e., if they have "inertia" or react with a lag to prior observable events), then we may be able to predict the likely future return better than we can simply using the average past return. As noted in Chapter 12, this is probably often the case with real estate assets traded in the private property market. In effect, a given stretch of past history may not well represent what we know about the near to medium-term future, as far as real estate returns are concerned. (In other words, the *ex ante* mean may differ from a given *ex post* mean.) In fact, even in the case of highly efficient asset markets such as the stock market (or REIT market), only the "excess return" (that is, the risk premium or return component in excess of T-bills) is really (approximately) memoryless. Short-term interest rates (hence, T-bill returns or the riskfree interest rate) vary over time in relatively predictable ways. (Recall our discussion in Chapter 19 about the yield curve.)

The ex ante return, or expected return, labeled $E[r]$, may or may not be taken to equal the ex post mean return from a given historical sample.[64]

Variance. This is the most widely-used measure of the magnitude of dispersion about the mean.[65] In theory, it is the central tendency of the squared difference between the realized return and the ex ante mean return, $E[(r - E[r])^2]$. In practice, variance is often estimated statistically from a historical sample of periodic returns, using the following formula, where S^2 represents the variance:[66]

$$S^2 = \frac{\sum_{t=1}^{T} (r_t - \bar{r})^2}{T - 1} \tag{A.3}$$

Standard Deviation. This is the square root of the variance. Applied to a series of periodic asset returns as in portfolio theory, this measure is commonly referred to as the volatility. The advantage of this measure over the variance is that it is measured in units of returns rather than "squared returns." For example, if a return has an expected value of 10% based on a 50% chance that it will turn out to be 15% and an equal chance that it will turn out to be 5%, its standard deviation or volatility is 5%, while its variance is 25 "percent-squared." As you can see, the standard deviation is a more intuitive measure than the variance.

As noted in previous chapters, the volatility is a basic measure of the risk of an investment. In particular, the volatility is often taken as the measure of the *total risk* in an investment (that is, including both the "idiosyncratic" or specific risk that can be diversified away and the "systematic" risk that cannot be diversified away). The volatility of an asset or portfolio is often used to measure the amount of risk an undiversified investor (that is, one who holds only that asset or portfolio) is exposed to.

The formula for estimating volatility from a historical series of periodic returns, labeled S, is as follows:

$$S = \sqrt{\frac{\sum_{t=1}^{T} (r_t - \bar{r})^2}{T - 1}} \tag{A.4}$$

[64] The two most popular models for deriving ex ante return estimates in the stock market are the capital asset pricing model (CAPM) and the Gordon growth model. These will be discussed in a Chapters 22 and 24.

[65] Other measures that are sometimes used in portfolio theory instead of the variance include most prominently the mean absolute difference (MAD) and the semi-variance (based only on the left-hand tail of the return distribution, that is, only deviations *below* the mean are included). The former is less sensitive to a few "outlier" events, while the latter is arguably a better measure of how most investors view risk if returns are not symmetrically distributed. In practice, however, the traditional variance is still the most widely used measure of risk, and for many portfolio applications will give results similar to those obtained from other measures.

[66] Note that the sum of the squared differences from the mean are divided by *one less than* the number of observations in the time-series. This modification is necessary to remove bias from statistical estimators of second moments. In effect, this formulation of the variance estimator is treating the historical time-series as a sample drawn from a larger potential population of returns (including those that will occur in the future). In implementing this formula in an electronic spreadsheet (such as Excel), you need to use the "sample" (as opposed to "population") version of the formula: *VAR( )* as opposed to *VARP( )*.

Covariance. This is the most widely used measure of pairwise comovement, that is, how the returns of two assets (or portfolios) move together across time. What the variance measures for a single asset's returns, covariance measures for a pair of assets.[67] The formula for computing the historical covariance between asset (or portfolio) i whose returns are $(r_{i1}, r_{i2}, \ldots r_{iT})$ and asset (or portfolio) j whose returns are $(r_{j1}, r_{j2}, \ldots r_{jT})$, labeled COV_{ij}, is as follows:[68]

$$COV_{ij} = \frac{\sum_{t=1}^{T} [(r_{it} - \bar{r}_i)(r_{jt} - \bar{r}_j)]}{T-1} \tag{A.5}$$

In terms of its economic significance in portfolio theory, the most important thing about the covariance statistic is the fact that the covariance between an asset and a portfolio is the component of that asset's variance that is not diversified away when the asset is added to the portfolio. Thus, covariance is basic to measuring the "systematic risk" in an asset, the risk that cannot be diversified away. This characteristic of covariance may help you to see the intuition in the following formula, which gives the time-series variance of a portfolio (S_P^2, the "volatility-squared" of the portfolio) as a function of the covariances of the returns to the N constituent assets in the portfolio and the weight (w_i, the share of the total portfolio value) invested in each asset i ($i = 1, \ldots N$):[69]

$$S_P^2 = \sum_{i=1}^{N} \sum_{j=1}^{N} w_i w_j COV_{ij} \tag{A.6}$$

In other words, the variance of a portfolio is the sum of the products of the weighted covariances of the individual constituent assets across all of the pairs of assets in the portfolio.[70] This is the formula that was used in the table in Exhibit 21-1c to compute the volatility of Bob's portfolio.

---

[67]Indeed, covariance is a generalization of the variance measure, as one way to define the variance is as the covariance of an asset with itself.

[68]By comparing formula (A.5) with formula (A.3), you can see that COV_{ii}, the covariance of asset i with itself, is equivalent to the variance of asset i: S_i^2.

[69]Recall from formula (A.1) that the weights sum to one:

$$\sum_{i=1}^{N} w_i = 1$$

[70]This is a summation of N^2 terms. Note, however, that $w_i w_j COV_{ij} = w_j w_i COV_{ji}$, and recall that $COV_{ii} = VAR_i = S_i^2$, the variance of asset i. Thus, Formula (A.6) can also be expressed as a summation of $N + [(N^2 - N)/2]$ terms, including N terms in the variances of the assets and $(N^2 - N)/2$ terms that are twice the covariances of each different pair of assets in the portfolio:

$$S_P^2 = \sum_{i=1}^{N} w_i^2 S_i^2 + 2 \sum_{i=1}^{N} \sum_{j=i+1}^{N} w_i w_j COV_{ij}$$

Cross-Correlation Coefficient. This statistic (referred to simply as the correlation for short) is a normalized measure of comovement. While the covariance is measured in units of "squared return" like the variance, the correlation ranges between negative unity and positive unity. The correlation (labeled C_{ij}) equals the covariance divided by the product of the standard deviations of the two variables:

$$C_{ij} = \frac{COV_{ij}}{S_i S_j} \tag{A.7}$$

Note that the correlation coefficient has the same sign as the covariance, but it is bounded between -1 and $+1$.

Exhibit A21-1 pictures what different correlations would typically look like in scatter-plots of the two assets' returns. Exhibit A21-1a depicts $+90\%$ correlation. Exhibit A21-1b depicts -90% correlation. With *positive* correlation the two assets' returns tend to move *together*: when one is up, the other tends also to be up; when one is down, the other tends also to be down. *Negative* correlation indicates that the two assets' returns tend to move *oppositely*: when one is up, the other is down. Zero correlation indicates a lack of systematic relationship between the two assets' returns. As the correlation approaches positive or negative 100%, the relationship between the two assets approaches a *deterministic* relationship in which the two assets move in lockstep (always either together or oppositely, lying on a perfectly straight line of either positive or negative slope[71]).

The correlation is important in portfolio analysis because it indicates how useful an asset (or a pair of assets) can be for purposes of diversification. The lower the correlation coefficient between two assets is, the better they can "diversify each other," in the sense that the greater will be the potential to reduce volatility by combining the two assets in a portfolio. In the extreme, two assets that are perfectly negatively correlated ($C_{ij} = -100\%$) can be combined to produce a portfolio that is completely riskless, in the sense of having zero volatility.

Autocorrelation. This is simply the correlation of an asset's (or portfolio's, or asset class's) returns with themselves lagged in time. The autocorrelation reflects the nature of the informational efficiency of an asset market, as discussed in previous chapters. For example, in general, zero autocorrelation is an indication of an informationally efficient asset market, in which prices quickly reflect full information (and therefore, returns lack predictability). Positive autocorrelation indicates a sluggish asset market that lacks perfect informational efficiency (prices only gradually incorporate new information). Negative autocorrelation indicates a "noisy" market (excessive short-run volatility, that is, a tendency for price overreactions that are subsequently "corrected").

Evidence suggests that private property markets display positive autocorrelation in the short to intermediate term. Public securities markets (including REITs) tend to show very little autocorrelation in general, though with some tendency toward negative autocorrelation in the intermediate run (perhaps offsetting some positive autocorrelation in the very short run).

[71] The correlation indicates the sign of the slope, but not its magnitude or steepness.

Exhibit A21-1a +90% Correlation

Exhibit A21-1b −90% Correlation

Exhibit A21-1c 0% Correlation

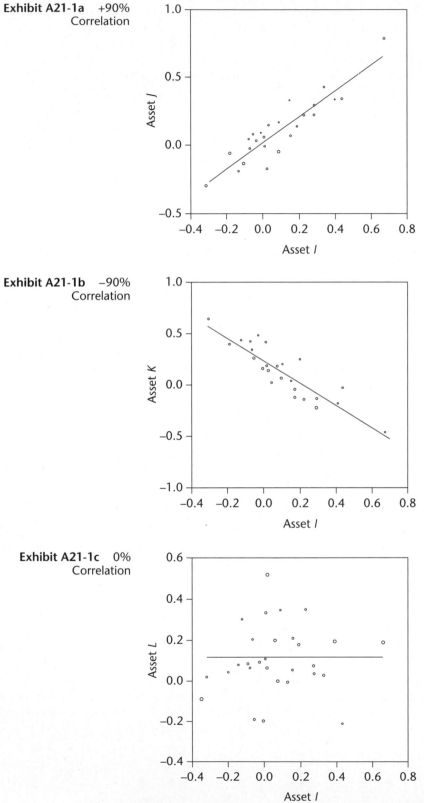

When an asset has zero autocorrelation (over all lags), the variance in its return is directly proportional to the length of the time interval over which the return is measured. For example, annual periodic returns would have four times the variance of quarterly periodic returns. When an asset has positive autocorrelation, the long-run variance is more than proportional to the short-run variance, while the opposite is true with negative autocorrelation. Thus, private real estate volatility tends to increase *relative to* that of securities when returns are measured at lower frequency (longer periodic intervals). For example, quarterly private real estate returns generally appear quite a bit less volatile than quarterly stock market returns, but five-year-interval private real estate returns are probably about as volatile as five-year-interval stock market returns.

KEY TERMS

modern portfolio theory (MPT)
volatility (standard deviation of return)
covariances (between assets)
weighted covariances
correlation coefficient (between returns)
solver (in spreadsheet)
constraints (to portfolio allocation)
target return (for portfolio)
sensitivity analysis

mean-variance portfolio theory (Markowitz)
dominant portfolio (domination)
risk preferences (of investors)
cost of living adjustments (COLAs)
mixed-asset portfolio
diversification benefit
efficient portfolio
efficient frontier
two-fund theorem
Sharpe ratio

risk-adjusted return
Sharpe-maximizing portfolio
pension funds
ERISA
market frictions
illiquidity
lumpy investments
long-interval expectations
informational efficiency

STUDY QUESTIONS

21.1.   In the example of Bob the investment manager in section 21.1, what would you say was the specific objective Bob ended up trying to serve in his portfolio allocation recommendation, and what constraint did he operate within?

21.2.   Why should all investors, regardless of risk preferences, avoid holding *dominated* portfolios?

21.3.   What does modern portfolio theory recommend besides not putting all one's eggs in one basket?

21.4.   Answer the question: Why do investors invest in real estate? from a portfolio theory perspective. [Hint: Consider the trade-off between risk and return. What is the primary role of typical income property real estate within the portfolio? Is it bought to achieve a high average return?]

21.5. How are investor risk preferences reflected in typical portfolio theory application? [Hint: What is the role of the target return specified by the investor?]

21.6. How is the two-fund theorem useful in practical portfolio theory applications? What is the relationship between the two-fund theorem and the Sharpe-maximizing portfolio?

21.7. Consider two portfolios. Portfolio A has an expected return of 10% and volatility of 8%. Portfolio B has an expected return of 9% and volatility of 7%. The interest rate on a riskfree investment is 5%. Which of the two risky portfolios is not on the efficient frontier? [Hint: Use the two-fund theorem.]

21.8. Consider again portfolios A and B from question 21.7. What would be the expected return to a portfolio C that consists of a 50/50 weighting of A and B?

21.9. Consider again portfolio C from question 21.8. Assuming (very reasonably) that portfolios A and B are not perfectly positively correlated, will portfolio C's volatility be greater or less than halfway between A's and B's volatility (that is, 7.5%)?

21.10. Discuss two academic theories for why U.S. pension funds do not allocate nearly as much of their investments to real estate as MPT apparently suggests they should.

21.11. Discuss some political and legal considerations, along with the nature of informational efficiency in the real estate asset market, that could explain pension fund reluctance to invest more in commercial real estate.

22

Equilibrium Asset Valuation and Real Estate's Price of Risk in the Capital Market

Chapter Outline

Learning Objectives

After reading this chapter, you should understand:

◆ What is meant by equilibrium asset pricing models and how these tools are used in practice to aid macrolevel investment decision making.

◆ The classical CAPM and its major theoretical and practical strengths and weaknesses.

◆ How the CAPM can be (or why it should be) applied to real estate and where it falls down in this regard, including a distinction between application at the overall multi-asset-class portfolio level and application at the more specific level within the private real estate asset class.

◆ What is meant by multifactor asset pricing models and how they may be applied to real estate in the future.

The previous chapter introduced you to portfolio theory, the fundamental tool of **strategic investment decision making** at the macrolevel. This chapter will build on portfolio theory to present a topic that is relevant for both strategic and **tactical investment decision making**. Our subject in this chapter will be equilibrium asset pricing models. Such models are typically built on the foundation of portfolio theory, but go beyond portfolio theory to provide a simplified representation of how the capital market perceives and prices risk in the assets that are traded in the market. Intuitively, we know that assets that are riskier, in some sense that the capital market cares about, will trade in equilibrium at lower prices. This discount in asset value due to risk is just the reflection of the fact that investors in the capital market require a higher expected return for riskier assets.[1] Thus, asset pricing models at the macrolevel are, in effect, models of the ex ante risk premium required by investors.[2]

Asset valuation and tactical investment decision making are naturally linked because tactical decision making aims at profiting from short- to medium-term opportunities. This often involves identifying assets (or, more likely, asset classes, or *types* of assets or investment products) that are currently "mispriced" in some sense. Now, in order to know if something is mispriced, you need to have some idea about what its value should be when asset markets are in equilibrium. This is what equilibrium asset pricing models do. They give the investor insight about what asset values and expected returns should be in equilibrium. Thus, it makes sense for equilibrium asset pricing theory, which has traditionally been built on the foundation of portfolio theory, to be our next topic.

22.1 REVIEW OF CLASSICAL ASSET PRICING THEORY

One of the most fundamental endeavors in the field of financial economics is the development of theory explaining how asset prices are determined in the capital market. Although this theory has involved impressive technical accomplishments that give it an academic appearance, in fact **capital asset pricing models (CAPMs)** are of great practical interest.

22.1.1 Practical Uses for Asset Price Theory

Capital asset pricing models are of practical importance for at least three major macrolevel investment decision applications:

1. Equilibrium pricing models can help investors understand what are reasonable expected returns, going forward into the future, on investments in different asset classes or types of investment products.

2. Such models can help to identify specific types of assets or investment products (or "sectors" of the asset market) that are currently mispriced relative to long-run equilibrium.

---

[1] Recall the inverse relationship between asset value and expected return. (See, e.g., Chapter 10.)

[2] To put macrolevel valuation in a broader context, note that the most widely used asset valuation model at the microlevel is the DCF model described extensively in Part IV. There, we noted the importance of the expected return risk premium in deriving the discount rate used in the denominators of the DCF valuation equation, and we noted that this risk premium reflects the opportunity cost of capital (OCC) as this is determined ultimately in the capital market. However, in Chapters 11 and 12 we stopped short of considering in depth *how* the capital market determines the expected return risk premium in the OCC. This is the question we turn to in the present chapter. Note, however, that what is a deep, somewhat academic issue at the microlevel of individual property valuation is a much more practical and decision-relevant issue at the macrolevel of broad-brush strategic and tactical investment decision making across portfolios of many individual assets.

3. By quantifying how the capital market prices risk, asset pricing models can be used to adjust portfolio returns to reflect the amount of risk in the portfolio, thereby helping to control for risk when evaluating portfolio returns or investment performance.

The first of these applications is just another way of saying what equilibrium pricing models do. Recall that asset prices and expected returns are codetermined because, in real estate for example, expected future operating cash flows from an asset are determined by the space market and actions by the property manager. Thus, operating cash flow expectations are exogenous to the capital market. Given these cash flow expectations, the value of the property (or its expected price in equilibrium) is determined by the expected return required by investors in the asset market in which the property trades. Conversely, the prices at which assets trade determine their expected returns, given their future cash flow expectations.

Asset pricing theory generally focuses on the expected returns side of this equation, leaving the forecasting of assets' future operating cash flows to microlevel analysis. Asset pricing models are models of the capital market, not of the space market. Thus, equilibrium asset pricing models are macrolevel tools useful for identifying reasonable expected long-run rates of return for types or categories of assets. Such return expectations have a variety of uses, not the least of which is to enlighten the assumptions used by investors in strategic policy formulation, for example, in applying portfolio theory as described in the preceding chapter.[3]

The second use of capital asset pricing models is oriented more specifically to tactical investment decision making, the identification of short- to medium-term profit opportunities. Suppose theory tells you, for example, that real estate and stocks should be priced so that real estate presents the investor with about half the risk premium of an investment in the stock market. If prices are currently such that real estate seems to present an equally great expected risk premium as the stock market, going forward, then the timing may be right to sell some stocks and buy some real estate, *if the theory is good!* In principle, the investor who acts thusly stands to make some extra profit (on a risk-adjusted basis, or through the use of appropriate leverage, or when market prices move the relative values of the two asset classes back toward their long-run equilibrium relationship).[4] Thus, capital asset pricing theory relates to investment *timing* issues as well.

[3]Recall that in Chapter 21 Bob employed expected returns of 9% for real estate and 12% for stocks, when the riskfree interest rate was 6%. This implied that stocks were expected to provide twice the risk premium of real estate over the long run (12% − 6% = 6%, versus 9% − 6% = 3%). Is this relative difference in stock versus real estate return expectations consistent with equilibrium in the capital market? This is the type of question equilibrium asset price modeling is designed to help answer.

[4]Prior to (or in the absence of) a market correction that moves asset prices back to their long-run equilibrium relationship, the investor stands to make above normal returns from the real estate investment, and/or to avoid below normal returns from investment in the stock market, under the conditions stated here. To see this point better, consider a simplified numerical example. Suppose a certain portfolio of assets is expected to produce $10 million of operating cash distribution per year in perpetuity (in dividends or rental payments, for example). Suppose capital asset pricing theory says this portfolio *should* provide an expected return of 10% per year. Then this portfolio should sell for $100 million in the market. Now suppose you can find such a portfolio selling for $83 million, a price at which it provides a 12% expected return for a perpetual holder. The pricing theory would suggest that you should buy this portfolio. You will get a supernormal return in either one or a combination of two ways. First, as long as you hold your investment, you will (expectationally) continue to receive a 12% yield on your original investment when

The third use of equilibrium asset pricing models noted earlier is to help control for risk in assessing investment performance. A CAPM may allow quantitative adjustment of the return on a given portfolio of assets so as to reflect the amount of risk in the portfolio (as risk matters to the capital market). To allow such quantification, equilibrium asset pricing models must do two things. They must show how to quantify investment risk as it matters in the capital market (that is, as it matters in equilibrium asset prices and expected returns), and they must identify the **market price of risk**, that is, the expected return risk premium per "unit" of risk (as previously defined). If a theory does both these jobs well enough, then it can be used to help control for risk when comparing the investment performance of different portfolios. This helps to make possible apples-to-apples comparisons of the performance of different investment managers or funds.

In the remainder of this section, we will present you with the basics of equilibrium asset pricing theory, with a particular focus on its relevance to real estate investment decision making. We will begin with the "granddaddy" pricing theory, the one that earned a Nobel Prize for William Sharpe and John Lintner, known simply as the capital asset pricing model, or CAPM for short. In subsequent sections we will broaden the perspective to include models and considerations more particularly relevant to real estate.

22.1.2 From Portfolio Theory to the CAPM

The Sharpe-Lintner CAPM is one of the most famous theories in all of financial economics. It grew out of, and is built on, the Markowitz mean-variance portfolio theory that we described in the previous chapter (MPT). So let's pick up where we left off in that chapter and see, in a simplified intuitive way, how we can extend MPT to develop a theory about how all assets in the market are priced. We can do this in four easy steps, as follows.[5]

Step 1: The Two-Fund Theorem. We begin with the basic assumptions of MPT, that investors want to maximize return and minimize risk in their wealth portfolios (i.e., they don't want to hold dominated portfolios), and we add the assumption described in section 21.3 of Chapter 21 that a *riskless asset* exists. Recall that this leads to the two-fund theorem, which demonstrates that *all* investors (no matter what their risk preferences) should want to hold *the same* portfolio (i.e., the same relative weights) of risky assets, as long as those investors have the same risk and return expectations.

---

the risk only warrants a 10% return. Second, when (and if) asset prices move up to their equilibrium level of $100 million, you can then sell the portfolio and also obtain a capital gain "pop" in your realized total return. The sooner this happens, the greater will be your average return over your period of holding the investment. For example, if it happens after just one year, you would receive a total return of 32.5%, equal to the $10 income plus the $17 capital gain (from $83 to $100), as a fraction of your $83 investment. Of course, none of this is for certain, even if the asset pricing model is correct; that is the nature of risk in investment. For example, the future cash flow expectation may change with the arrival of new events or information.

[5] The CAPM can be derived in several different ways, depending on what simplifying assumptions one wishes to make. The approach presented here corresponds closely in spirit (although not in analytical rigor) to the original development of the model.

Step 2: Common Expectations. Remember that asset markets (especially securities markets such as the stock market) are known to be pretty efficient, that is, asset prices are pretty good at reflecting all publicly available information relevant to their values. Thus, any one investor will not usually have better information than the market as a whole concerning the values of assets or their future expected returns. Thus, everyone will converge to having the same expectations regarding risks, returns, and values. Combined with the two-fund theorem, this will lead everyone to want to hold the same portfolio (relative weights) of risky assets, which will therefore be empirically observable as the **market portfolio**, the aggregate of all risky capital assets. The relative weight placed on each asset (or asset class) in this market portfolio corresponds to the current market value of each asset as a fraction of the aggregate market value. This market portfolio thus reflects the overall wealth portfolios of all investors.

Step 3: Only Covariance with the Market Matters. Now recall that a basic tenet of portfolio theory is that investors all care only about the risk (variance or volatility) in their *overall* wealth. The variance of any individual component of that wealth does not matter per se. Since, by our reasoning in steps 1 and 2, all investors hold the same portfolio (the market portfolio), the only risk that matters to investors in any given asset is how that asset affects the risk in the market portfolio. But it is a fact of basic statistics that the marginal contribution of each asset to the variance of a portfolio is directly proportional to the covariance of the asset's periodic returns with the portfolio's periodic returns.[6] Thus, the only risk that matters to investors in an asset can be quantified by that asset's covariance with the market portfolio.

Step 4: Asset Pricing and Expected Returns. As all investors hold their entire wealth in the market portfolio, the variance in this portfolio quantifies the risk that all investors are exposed to. Therefore, the risk premium in the expected return to the market portfolio, divided by the variance in the return to the market portfolio, quantifies the "price of risk," that is, the market's required expected return risk premium *per unit of risk* (variance). Multiplying this price of risk by the amount of risk in each asset (that is, the risk that matters to investors, the asset's covariance with the market) gives the market's required risk premium in each asset's expected return:

$$E[r_i] = r_f + RP_i = r_f + COV_{iM}\left(\frac{E[r_M] - r_f}{S_M^2}\right) \tag{1a}$$

---

[6] To be more precise, the contribution of asset i in the variance of portfolio P, per unit of portfolio weight in asset i, is $2COV_{iP}$, for small relative weights (where COV_{iP} is the covariance between the asset's returns and the portfolio returns). This is seen as follows, using formula (A.6) for the variance of a portfolio, from the appendix to Chapter 21. Consider an original portfolio whose variance is S_P^2, and a new portfolio just like the old only with a slight incremental reallocation, adding a bit of asset i in the amount of weight w_i (a small fraction) by reducing the weight in the rest of the portfolio to $(1 - w_i)$. The variance of the new portfolio is $w_i^2 S_i^2 + (1 - w_i)^2 S_P^2 + 2w_i(1 - w_i)COV_{iP}$. However, as w_i is a small fraction, when we square this fraction, it becomes an order of magnitude smaller, so for practical purposes we can ignore the first term in the previous expression ($w_i^2 S_i^2 \approx 0$). By the same reasoning, we can treat $(1 - w_i)$ as effectively equal to unity ($1 - w_i \approx 1$). Thus, for practical purposes, the variance of the new portfolio is $S_P^2 + 2w_i COV_{iP}$. Thus, the *incremental* variance added by the reallocation to include asset i (as compared to the variance before the portfolio was adjusted) is *New variance − Old variance* $= (S_P^2 + 2w_i COV_{iP}) - S_P^2 = 2w_i COV_{iP}$. As we have added w_i share of asset i, this incremental addition to the portfolio variance, *per unit of asset* i *added*, is $(2w_i COV_{iP})/w_i = 2COV_{iP}$, which is what we set out to demonstrate.

where $E[r_i]$ is the market's equilibrium required expected return to asset i, $E[r_M]$ is the market's equilibrium required expected return to the market portfolio as a whole, r_f is the riskfree interest rate, COV_{iM} is the covariance between asset i and the market portfolio, and S_M^2 is the variance (volatility squared) of the market portfolio.

That does it: four steps. Formula (1a) is the Sharpe-Lintner CAPM. We have simplified a bit in order to present a less technical (hopefully more intuitive) derivation of this Nobel Prize–winning theory. But this is the complete model. It is important to understand where it comes from because such understanding can enable you to recognize both how it *can* be useful and circumstances in which it *cannot* be validly used.

The Sharpe-Lintner CAPM is usually expressed in a slightly different form than formula (1a). The more familiar formula uses a more intuitive measure of risk called **beta**. Beta simply normalizes the asset's covariance with the market as a fraction of the variance in the market as a whole. Beta is thus a relative measure of risk, quantifying the asset's risk as a fraction of the risk faced by investors in their overall wealth portfolios:

$$Beta_i = \frac{COV_{iM}}{S_M^2} \tag{2a}$$

Using beta, the CAPM as expressed in formula (1a) becomes

$$E[r_i] = r_f + RP_i = r_f + Beta_{iM}(E[r_M] - r_f) \tag{1b}$$

In words, the CAPM says that an asset's expected return risk premium is directly proportional to its beta. Any asset's risk premium equals its beta times the market price of risk, which is observable as the expected return on the market portfolio, that is, the expected return on investors' overall wealth.

As indicated in Exhibit 22-1, the CAPM provides financial economists and investment practitioners with a rigorous foundation for, and a way to more specifically quantify, the **security market line (SML)**. The SML is the famous graphical picture of the relationship between risk and return within the market for risky assets. This picture of the relationship between risk and return is so fundamental that way back in Chapter 9 we called it "financial economics in a nutshell."

It is interesting to note that a mathematically equivalent way to express beta is as the correlation between asset i and the market, multiplied by the ratio of asset i's volatility divided by the market portfolio's volatility:

$$Beta_i = \frac{S_i}{S_M} C_{iM} \tag{2b}$$

This makes it clear that the risk premium in an asset's required expected return is directly proportional not only to its risk as measured by the asset's own volatility (S_i), but also to its correlation with the market wealth portfolio (C_{iM}). An asset can be quite volatile, yet it still may not provide a high expected return if it is not highly correlated with the market portfolio. On the other hand, even an asset with relatively low volatility may command a relatively high risk premium if it is highly correlated with the market because in that case it does not provide investors with much diversification benefit in their wealth portfolios. Risk is defined by the *interaction* of the asset's own volatility and its correlation with the "market," that is, with investors' wealth portfolios.

Exhibit 22-1 The CAPM in Graphical Form (the security market line)

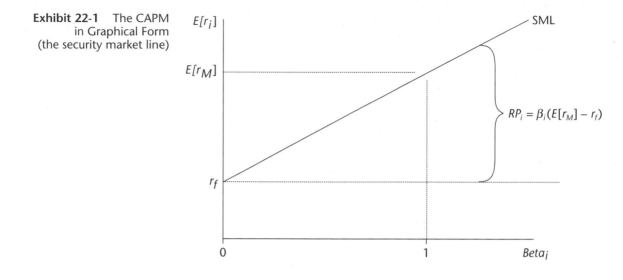

22.1.3 The Main Point in the Basic CAPM

The main investment insight provided by the CAPM is the *irrelevance of, and therefore lack of compensation for, diversifiable risk*. The CAPM suggests that, as covariance with the market portfolio is the only risk that matters to the capital market, it is therefore the only risk that will be priced in equilibrium. Risk that cannot be diversified away is referred to in asset pricing theory as **systematic risk**. Diversifiable risk, that is, the component of an asset's own total variance in excess of its covariance with the market, is referred to as the asset's **specific** (or **idiosyncratic**) **risk**.

$$S_i^2 = COV_{iM} + VAR\{\varepsilon_i\} \qquad (3)$$

where $VAR\{\varepsilon_i\}$ is the variance of asset i's idiosyncratic return component.[7] Since idiosyncratic risk can be diversified away, it does not matter to the investor.

Particularly after our discussion of portfolio theory in Chapter 21, you can probably see that this point about nonpricing of diversifiable risk is actually broader and deeper than the specific Sharpe-Lintner CAPM itself. No matter how the risk that matters to the capital market is defined, whether it is well measured by beta or not, it is only such risk that will be priced, by definition. Under the (rather reasonable) assumption that virtually all investors can diversify away risk that is very specific to any one asset or group of assets, it therefore follows that specific risk will not be priced.

An important investment strategy is implied by this result: investors should generally not hold undiversified portfolios. Since investors are not compensated by the market (in the form of expected return) for exposing themselves to specific risk, they should get rid of all such risk by diversifying their wealth portfolio. Indeed,

---

[7] By definition, idiosyncratic risk is the component of the asset's volatility that is not correlated with anything else. In a time-series statistical regression of asset i's periodic returns onto the market portfolio's periodic returns, $VAR\{\varepsilon_i\}$ would be the variance of the *residuals* from the regression (sometimes referred to as the errors because they are the difference between the returns predicted by the regression and the actual returns of asset i).

strictly speaking, the Sharpe-Lintner CAPM says that you should not hold any portfolio other than the "market" (scaled down to your wealth, of course, and levered up or down to conform to your risk preferences).

22.1.4 Isn't the CAPM Wrong?

At this point students often cry "foul." "The CAPM can't be right," they say, "it's based on false assumptions." Indeed it is. There is no such thing as a truly riskless asset. Markets are not perfectly efficient. All investors do not share the same expectations about the future. And we do not all hold the same portfolios (that is, relative weights in our wealth investments). Thus, *obviously*, the CAPM is "wrong" in the sense that it is not a *complete* description of reality of equilibrium asset pricing. Good empirical tests should be able to detect this fact, and indeed they do.[8]

In an important sense, however, this criticism misses the point, not only about the Sharpe-Lintner CAPM, but also about the fundamental nature and purpose of equilibrium asset price modeling in general, and indeed (if we may wax poetic), about the purpose of virtually all scientific theory. By this criterion of "wrongness," Newtonian physics is wrong, as it is built on simplified (false) assumptions that ignore the relativity of time and space. Yet who can deny that we learn a lot that is quite useful from the Newtonian model, both at a practical level and at a deeper, more fundamental level. Virtually all industrial and engineering advances up to at least the middle of the 20th century were based purely on Newtonian physics. Like Newtonian physics, the CAPM continues to be used widely in practice, not only by academics, but also by professionals in the investment industry.

What the CAPM loses as a result of its unrealistic assumptions, namely, the ability to model the world completely, is more than made up for by what the model gains by these assumptions, namely, the ability to simplify the world so that we can understand it better. The elegance in the basic CAPM enables us to obtain insights that we could not from a more complex model.

So, let's consider the value and usefulness, as well as the limits and shortcomings, of the CAPM from a more sophisticated perspective. In so doing, we can begin to see how it may be modified or extended particularly to improve its relevance for real estate.

22.1.5 Strengths and Weaknesses in the Basic CAPM

The CAPM, like any valuation model, can be viewed from either a normative or descriptive perspective. From the normative perspective, the model is addressing what *should* be, under the given assumptions. From this perspective we can gain what might be called wisdom, insight that improves our understanding. For example, the general point about the nonpricing of diversifiable risk is a key insight. The extreme suggestion that all investors should hold the same portfolio no doubt goes too far. But the suggestion that all investors should diversify their wealth is a good prescription and is seen to hold widely in reality.

---

[8] In a strict sense, the CAPM has been "flunking" empirical tests at least since the early 1970s, when famous studies by Black, Jensen, and Scholes (1972) and Fama and MacBeth (1973) were published. For some more recent discussion, see Fama and French (1992) and Black (1993).

From a descriptive perspective, the CAPM is addressing what *is*, out there in the real world. From this perspective, we hope to gain a practical tool to predict what will happen, a model of cause and effect in the real world. In this respect the CAPM, while not perfect, is useful in practice. Empirically, beta is not the whole story for explaining expected returns, but it is a big part of the story.

The CAPM is useful in practice presumably because the model's assumptions, while simplifications of reality, are not terribly far from the truth. Although asset markets are not perfectly efficient, they are reasonably efficient (especially securities markets such as the stock market). Although all investors do not hold the same expectations or the same portfolios, most investors hold fairly similar expectations and fairly similar portfolios (especially large institutional investors).[9] As a result, the CAPM works well enough to be useful, at least within the stock market, where the aggregate stock market (or a broad index such as the S&P 500) is used as an easily observable and measurable proxy for the theoretical market portfolio of the model. Indeed, beta has become virtually a household word on Wall Street and is regularly estimated and reported as a matter of course by stock analysts. It is especially widely used in the equity mutual fund business.

On the other hand, the hopes that were originally held for the basic Sharpe-Lintner CAPM have not been completely fulfilled. We now recognize that a substantial part of the cross-section of expected returns across assets within the stock market is not well explained by beta computed with respect to the stock market portfolio. Other risk factors, reflected in such indicators as the size of a firm and its book/market value ratio, have a strong influence on expected returns apart from a stock's beta with respect to the stock market.[10]

Nevertheless, it is important to keep in mind several caveats before excessively discounting the value of the basic CAPM. First, although beta (with respect to the stock market) is not the whole story about risk premiums within the stock market, it is an important part of the story. For example, once one controls for such other factors as firm size and book/market value ratio, beta describes a large portion of the remaining variation in average ex post returns to portfolios of stocks. Second, the additional risk factors that matter to the market apart from beta (e.g., the risk factors captured in such characteristics as firm size and current yield) do not *negate*, as much as they *refine*, the theoretical underpinnings of the basic CAPM.

For example, small firms and firms with high current yields or high book/market value ratios are often most susceptible to catastrophic failure in the event of macroeconomic downturns or capital market crises.[11] Exposure to this kind of risk

---

[9] The development and tremendous growth of passive "index funds" in the mutual fund industry was originally stimulated and largely motivated by the efficient market hypothesis and the type of reasoning that is reflected in the CAPM.

[10] One of the most influential studies in this regard is reported in Fama and French (1992).

[11] It is easier for a small firm to go completely out of business, in part because small firms may have less leverage with their creditors. Also, among the population of firms listed on the stock exchange, small firms and firms with relatively high book/market value ratios will tend more often than other types of firms to be, shall we say, distressed in some manner, or recovering from recent distress. This is because, in general, the stock exchange tends to attract firms that are relatively large and typically have a growth-oriented business strategy. The smaller-cap, lower-multiple stocks on the exchange therefore tend to include a larger proportion of "fallen angels." Such firms tend to be more vulnerable to crises or negative shocks in the real economy or the financial markets than are larger, more highly priced firms.

may not be well measured by firms' covariances with respect to the stock market.[12] Yet it is difficult for investors to diversify away such risk exposure because the downside outcomes are correlated with the overall economy and the capital market broadly defined. So investors demand an additional risk premium for this type of risk exposure, for fundamentally the same reason that they demand a risk premium for beta, namely, difficulty of diversifying away risk in their wealth or welfare. Thus, we see that in its more fundamental implications, such as the nonpricing of diversifiable risk, the basic CAPM remains largely intact.

22.2 APPLYING THE CAPM TO THE PRIVATE REAL ESTATE ASSET CLASS AS A WHOLE

The CAPM has relevant application to real estate investment in at least two different contexts or foci. The most obvious application is to REITs and other real estate firms within the stock market. This application will be discussed in Chapter 24 when we focus particularly on REITs. For now, it suffices to note that the CAPM is applied to REITs in virtually the same way, and as usefully, as it is applied to most other sectors of the stock market in general.

The more challenging and unique application of the CAPM to real estate, however, is to direct investment in the private property market. Even within this focus on privately traded real estate it is useful to distinguish two further levels at which one might try to apply the CAPM. At a more specific level, one could try to apply the CAPM *within* the private property market, for example, to quantify risk and expected return differences between different types of property in different locations. Application at this "sectoral" level will be the subject of the next section in this chapter. But at a more macrolevel, one could try to apply the CAPM broadly to the mixed-asset portfolio as a whole, encompassing private real estate as one of the major asset classes. It is to this macrolevel application that we turn our attention in the present section.

22.2.1 Brief History

By the 1970s and 1980s, the CAPM was so popular and widely used in the investment industry that many began to wonder why it was not being applied to real estate investment decision making. Inspired by MPT, institutional investors wanted to apply the same sophisticated investment analysis tools to private market real estate investment as to the rest of their mixed-asset portfolio, which consisted largely of stocks and bonds. In particular, as real estate was a "risky asset," a form of equity, it seemed that the CAPM should apply to real estate as well as it did to stocks.

---

[12]In part, this may be because such risk may not be "normal" (that is, represented by a Gaussian probability distribution) in a statistical sense, as it may be due to large, discrete events rather than continuous incremental change or news. In a sense, this type of risk may be more akin to event risk or default risk in corporate bonds or mortgages than to beta or covariance-based measures of risk. As we discussed in Chapters 18 and 19, default risk is typically measured by multiperiod average return measures such as yield degradation (either ex ante or ex post), rather than by periodic HPR-based risk measures such as beta. (The major source of beta in bond market HPRs is interest rate volatility, not changes in default risk.)

The problem was that when analysts calculated the beta for portfolios of commercial properties, they typically came up with zero, or even a negative number. It seemed that, according to the CAPM, real estate required little or no risk premium in its expected return, perhaps even a negative risk premium. Yet, real estate was clearly perceived in the capital market as a risky asset and seemingly offered a considerable risk premium in its expected return, typically around half as high as the stock market's risk premium.[13]

Of course, some people jumped on this discovery as an indication that real estate was a bargain, providing supernormal expected returns after adjusting for risk.[14] Others, viewing the glass as half empty, warned that this was evidence that the CAPM was fundamentally flawed as a model because it did not work for a major risky asset class such as real estate. Perhaps the simplifying assumptions in the CAPM made it too incomplete as an equilibrium model in the broader context of different asset classes.[15] Or perhaps capital markets were highly *segmented*, with the real estate asset market operating virtually isolated from the stock and bond markets, with different types of investors holding different types of wealth portfolios.[16]

There was probably some merit to both sides of the 1980s debate about the CAPM's applicability to private real estate. In any case, history would soon silence the debate through the painful lesson of the "Great Crash" in commercial property prices at the end of the decade. By the early 1990s it seemed far-fetched to argue either that real estate presented little risk or that its returns evidenced an excessive risk premium, at least ex post.[17]

[13] See the previous discussions of real estate ex post and ex ante returns in Chapters 7, 11, and 19.

[14] Of course, those who adopted this response often stood to gain from selling real estate, or from the expansion of the role of real estate in institutional investment portfolios. However, claiming that real estate had negative risk and presented a return/risk bargain did not necessarily help to overcome skepticism within the target investment community. Many Wall Street oriented investment decision makers were shy of real estate, in part because of a traditional image of Main Street as an unsophisticated arena where hucksters and snake-oil salesmen pushed property deals onto gullible investors in an inefficient asset market. Negative risk? Come on . . .

[15] An example of a well-thought-out presentation of this perspective was the New Equilibrium Theory (NET) put forth by Ibbotson, Diermier, and Siegel (1984). The idea was that investors had other concerns besides just risk defined as the volatility of their wealth. (Recall our discussion of investor concerns at the outset of Chapter 7.) In particular, investors no doubt dislike illiquidity, and so in equilibrium, assets with less liquidity than securities could command an expected return premium (e.g., an illiquidity premium) higher than that of more liquid securities of similar risk. The total expected return premium over T-bills would be built up of several layers corresponding to various types of "disutility" investors perceived in different types of assets. Although not as formally developed as the CAPM, this type of approach reflects long-held investor perceptions in the capital markets. (See also our discussion in Chapter 19 about bond yields.)

[16] In the extreme, this could imply that real estate might have its own market portfolio, and that a real estate CAPM might apply within the real estate market, with beta calculated with respect to this different market portfolio. But such extreme segmentation seems to fly in the face of modern capital market technology and practice, as well as the ERISA-based movement of institutional portfolios to include real estate. What would prevent large capital flows from one market segment to the other if risk-adjusted return expectations diverged significantly between the two market segments? Furthermore, there is no evidence that average ex post returns across portfolios of properties are explained (or even correlated) with such broad measures of the real estate market as the NCREIF index.

[17] Ironically, this "crash" turned out to have presented investors at the bottom of the property market in the early 1990s with, indeed, a return/risk bargain (for buyers going forward from the trough).

22.2.2 Broadening the Market Portfolio and Correcting for Smoothing

In fact, with the advantage of another decade of investment performance data (and a full market cycle behind us), it now appears that it may be possible to apply the basic Sharpe-Lintner CAPM to private real estate after all, at least at a broad-brush level across asset classes. The most elegant solution to the problem of applying the CAPM in this way is simply to be more careful in how one approximates the market portfolio in practice, and how one computes real estate periodic return statistics. Consider the market portfolio first.

According to the CAPM theory, as we described its derivation in section 22.1.2, the market portfolio should represent *all* the wealth of *all* investors, in other words, the aggregate wealth in the economy as a whole. Yet the CAPM is traditionally applied using the stock market alone as the "proxy" for this overall wealth portfolio or risk benchmark. Such a proxy works well enough as an approximation within the asset class of stocks. But when we move to a broader, mixed-asset level, to consider other asset classes such as private real estate, the stock market by itself is no longer a useful risk benchmark.

The other problem with early attempts to apply the CAPM to real estate had to do with the type of data that was being used to calculate the real estate beta. As noted in Chapter 9, periodic returns time-series data are necessary to calculate comovement statistics such as correlations and beta. Such data is readily available for individual stocks and for the stock market as a whole, based on highly liquid market values reflected in, for example, daily closing prices of stocks. In the case of privately traded real estate, however, periodic returns data is generally based on appraised values of properties.

Appraisals are estimates of property values typically derived by appraisers who are trained to "look backwards" in time to find prices of "comparable properties" that were sold in the past. Furthermore, indices or portfolios aggregating the appraised values of many individual properties usually include properties that are not reappraised every period. Thus, many valuations in the index or portfolio are "stale".

The result is that, compared with a more liquid contemporaneous market value index such as the stock market, real estate periodic return indices tend to be *lagged* and *smoothed* across time. This results in a tendency to underestimate the covariance between real estate and indices such as the stock market.[18]

Suppose we correct both of these problems, that is, the data problem and the market portfolio definition problem, and then apply the basic Sharpe-Lintner CAPM at the broad level of the three major risky asset classes that we considered in Chapter 21: stocks, bonds, and real estate. In particular, let's suppose that an overall national wealth portfolio consisting of equal one-third shares of stocks, bonds, and real estate would well approximate the theoretical market portfolio that the CAPM requires in principle.[19]

---

[18] Smoothing and other real estate periodic returns data issues will be discussed in more depth in Chapter 25.

[19] As described in Chapter 7 (Exhibit 7-4), the complete "pie" of the investible wealth in the United States is probably characterized by weights not too different from this assumption. The exact weights in Exhibit 7-4, aggregated within the three risky asset classes only, are 35% stocks, 39% bonds, and 26% real estate.

Exhibit 22-2a Typical Risk and Return Expectations

	Stocks	Bonds	Real Estate
Expected Return ($E[r]$)	12.00%	8.00%	9.00%
Volatility	15.00%	8.00%	10.00%
Correlation with:			
Stocks	100.00%	50.00%	25.00%
Bonds		100.00%	0.00%
Real Estate			100.00%

Now to compute our asset class risk and return measures according to the CAPM, let's use the example risk and return expectations we employed in Chapter 21. These expectations are repeated in Exhibit 22-2a.

In Chapter 21 we attributed these expectations to our investment hero, Bob. Although they are only example numbers, recall that they were developed with some care to be broadly reasonable and representative of typical expectations as of the late 1990s, with an assumed riskfree interest rate of 6%. Furthermore, the real estate second moments in these expectations (real estate's volatility and its correlations with the other asset classes) attempt to take account of, and correct for, the type of data-smoothing problems we described before.[20]

We can use the expectations in Exhibit 22-2a to compute the covariances between each asset class and the equally weighted overall mixed-asset wealth portfolio that we are using as the CAPM market portfolio. For example, the covariance between real estate and this market portfolio is 0.004583, computed as follows:[21]

$$COV[r_{RE}, r_M] = COV\left[r_{RE}, \frac{1}{3}r_{ST} + \frac{1}{3}r_{BN} + \frac{1}{3}r_{RE}\right]$$

$$= \frac{1}{3}COV[r_{RE}, r_{ST}] + \frac{1}{3}COV[r_{RE}, r_{BN}] + \frac{1}{3}COV[r_{RE}, r_{RE}]$$

$$= \frac{1}{3}S_{RE}S_{ST}C_{RE,ST} + \frac{1}{3}S_{RE}S_{BN}C_{RE,BN} + \frac{1}{3}S_{RE}^2$$

$$= \frac{1}{3}(0.10)(0.15)(0.25) + \frac{1}{3}(0.10)(0.08)(0) + \frac{1}{3}(0.10)^2$$

$$= 0.004583$$

[20] In addition to the smoothing issue per se, these expectations probably also reflect a somewhat longer-term perspective than one might get just by looking at annual frequency historical periodic returns data. Historical evidence suggests that over short intervals (such as quarters or years) there is less positive correlation (and perhaps more negative correlation) than what is presented here between real estate and the other asset classes. Considering the "long-interval expectations" problem noted in section 21.4.2, it makes sense to base strategic investment decisions on long-horizon performance expectations.

[21] Some basic algebraic properties of the covariance statistic are useful to keep in mind: $COV[aX, bY] = abCOV[X, Y]$, and $COV[X, (Y + Z)] = COV[X, Y] + COV[X, Z]$, where a and b are constants and X, Y, and Z are random variables.

Similarly, the covariances with the market portfolio are 0.010750 and 0.004133 for stocks and bonds, respectively. The variance of our equally weighted market portfolio is $S_M^2 = 0.006500$.[22] Thus, we can compute the beta of each of our three asset classes with respect to the overall mixed-asset market portfolio as follows:

$$Beta_{ST} = 0.010750/0.006500 = 1.66$$
$$Beta_{BN} = 0.004133/0.006500 = 0.64$$
$$Beta_{RE} = 0.004583/0.006500 = 0.71$$

Now suppose we normalize these betas with respect to the stock asset class. That is, suppose we express all of these betas as a fraction of the stock market beta. This will put these betas in the familiar frame of reference in which the stock market has a beta of unity, and the "market price of risk" is measured by the stock market's risk premium. With such a normalization, our mixed-asset betas become

$$Beta_{ST} = 1.66/1.66 = 1.00$$
$$Beta_{BN} = 0.64/1.66 = 0.38$$
$$Beta_{RE} = 0.71/1.66 = 0.43$$

Now we see that the real estate beta appears to be rather reasonable. With a beta of +0.43, real estate has just less than half the risk of the stock market, according to the CAPM, and long-term bonds have just a little bit less risk than real estate. These betas are pretty much in line with the return expectations shown in Exhibit 22-2a, which are broadly consistent with typical expectations in the real world.

To clarify this point, note that, by the expectations in Exhibit 22-2a, the market portfolio has an expected return of 9.67%.[23] Now recall that these return expectations are based on an assumed riskfree rate of 6%. Plugging the betas into the basic CAPM gives the following expected returns for each of the three major asset classes:[24]

Stocks: 6.00% + 1.66(9.67% − 6.00%) = 12.09%
Bonds: 6.00% + 0.64(9.67% − 6.00%) = 8.34%
Real Estate: 6.00% + 0.71(9.67% − 6.00%) = 8.59%

As seen graphically in Exhibit 22-2b, the basic theoretical CAPM fits pretty well these risk and return expectations.[25] The real estate expected return of 9% is just

---

[22] Computed using formula (A.6) from the Chapter 21 appendix: $(1/9)[0.0225 + 0.0064 + 0.01 + 2(0.006 + 0.00375 + 0)] = 0.006489$.

[23] This is computed as $(1/3)12\% + (1/3)8\% + (1/3)9\% = 9.67\%$.

[24] Expressed relative to the stock market risk premium, we get a similar result:

Stocks: 6.00% + 1.00(12.00% − 6.00%) = 12.00%
Bonds: 6.00% + 0.38(12.00% − 6.00%) = 8.31%
Real Estate: 6.00% + 0.43(12.00% − 6.00%) = 8.56%

[25] In fact, the mathematics of the CAPM make this type of result a forgone conclusion, in the following sense. We saw in Chapter 21 that Bob's risk and return expectations led to an optimal risky asset allocation of 28% stocks, 19% bonds, and 32% real estate, with a wealth return target of 9% and assuming the existence of a riskless asset yielding 6%. This implies that the optimal pure risky asset portfolio under Bob's expectations (and with a riskless asset yielding 6%) is 35% stocks, 24% long-term bonds, and 41% real estate. Under the CAPM assumptions, everyone would share Bob's risk and return expectations, so this would be the market portfolio. As it is the optimal portfolio under Bob's (and everybody else's)

Exhibit 22-2b Bob's Expectations and the CAPM Prediction

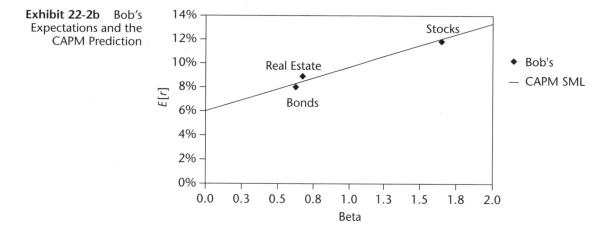

slightly above the CAPM security market line prediction of 8.6% (perhaps reflecting the need for an extra illiquidity premium compared with securities). The bond expected return of 8% is just slightly below the CAPM prediction of 8.3% (perhaps reflecting the fact that bonds have a special usefulness, and very little risk, for investors who can buy and hold them to maturity).[26] The stock market expected return of 12% is practically right on the predicted SML. While the expectations we are using here are just example numbers (Bob's estimates), they are broadly reasonable and in line with typical real world perceptions in the late 1990s (relative to a riskfree rate of 6%).[27]

expectations, so it is the market portfolio for which those expectations will lie directly on the capital market line (CML) connecting the riskfree asset's return to the market portfolio return and risk (volatility). If we used these 35/24/41 weights in the risk benchmark portfolio with respect to which we computed the asset class betas, then each asset class would lie directly on the security market line (SML) implied by such betas, and the market portfolio would have an expected return of 9.81% with volatility of 8.3%. We have not used this exact mathematically optimal portfolio as the risk benchmark for computing beta, but we have used a stylized market portfolio that is very similar. Our assumption of equal one-third weights in each asset class in our risk benchmark portfolio is similar to the 35/24/41 weights that would place our asset class risk and return expectations exactly on the SML. Thus, it is not surprising that our asset class risk and return expectations lie close to the SML implied by our equal-weighted three-asset-class market portfolio.

[26] It is interesting to note the similarity in risk and return between bonds and commercial property. This similarity was also touched on in our discussion in Chapters 13 and 19 regarding commercial mortgage returns and the question of positive leverage in commercial property investment. In Chapter 19, in particular, we noted some reasons mortgages and other long-term debt instruments might be viewed by the capital market as having nearly as much risk as (or conceivably even more risk than) underlying commercial property assets, where risk is defined "as it matters" to the capital market.

[27] If we define the risk benchmark portfolio using the exact risk asset class relative weights depicted in Exhibit 7-4 (35% stocks, 39% bonds, 26% real estate), then we get betas normalized on the stock market of 1.00 for stocks (by construction), 0.41 for bonds, and 0.35 for real estate. With a riskfree rate of 6%, this results in CAPM predicted return expectations of 12.1% for stocks, 8.5% for bonds, and 8.1% for real estate. Keep in mind, though, that the asset class shares in Exhibit 7-4, like Bob's risk and return expectations, are soft estimates. It would not be wise to attempt to infer very precise implications from these numbers (or anyone else's numbers, for that matter). We are dealing here at a broad-brush level of implications.

In summary, the basic Sharpe-Lintner CAPM does work, in essence, for real estate after all, at least at a broad-brush level *across* the asset classes.[28] This is a level that is useful for broad strategic and tactical investment policy making for managers responsible for mixed-asset portfolios, that is, portfolios that potentially include all the major asset classes. It also is a level that is relevant for adjusting the investment performance of managers or portfolios that encompass more than one broad asset class, for example, a real estate investment manager whose job includes allocation between direct private market investment and REIT equity investment.[29]

22.2.3 A Caveat: Capital Market Imperfections

It's time to backtrack a bit. We have not done full justice to the initial responses and criticisms that were made when people first tried to apply the CAPM to real estate using the model's simplistic stock-market-based form. Although the basic CAPM may work pretty well at the broad-brush level, in fact there is some merit both in the "real estate is a bargain" response, and in the "segmented markets" critique of the basic CAPM.

Consider first the notion that a bargain may exist in the relative prices of stocks and private real estate. This argument implicitly supposes either that the capital market is (perhaps temporarily?) out of equilibrium, or that the real estate and stock markets are not fully integrated within the broader capital market as a whole.[30] Thus, the "bargain" response and the "segmented markets" critique of the CAPM are based on the notion of market imperfections and should be considered together.

As we noted at the outset of section 22.1, the identification of this type of relative mispricing is exactly the kind of thing equilibrium asset pricing models can and should be used for. However, the idea that mispricing could exist at such a broad scale, that of entire asset classes, is what makes this argument so hard to swallow for many academic real estate economists, considering the possibilities of modern technology and the entrepreneurship evident in the U.S. investment industry. Surely, it seems, the means would be found to exploit differences in the price of risk across different asset

---

[28] From a historical perspective, it should be noted that the approach to applying the basic CAPM to private real estate described in this section (essentially, expanding the perception of the market portfolio and correcting for smoothing in the real estate periodic returns data) was developed from two different perspectives in dissertations completed around the end of the 1980s (see Geltner [1989] and Liu et al. [1990]). It should also be noted that the plausibility of the argument presented here is supported by the fact that the basic CAPM, even in its traditional stock-market-only form, works about as well for REITs as it does for other types of stocks. However, REITs are relatively low-beta, high-yield stocks. The basic CAPM typically underpredicts the average returns to such stocks, whether they are REITs or not. Such underprediction is consistent with multifactor or consumption-based models of risk, as will be discussed in the next section.

[29] Specific quantitative methods for using the CAPM to adjust portfolio returns for risk are presented in all major graduate-level investments textbooks. See, for example, Bodie, Kane, and Marcus (1999), Chapter 24. A single-index model like the basic CAPM allows a Treynor-type measure to be employed for risk adjustment.

[30] Asset markets are integrated, or not segmented, when capital can flow freely between them and investors of all types can participate in them. In such circumstances, one would expect that the market price of risk (the expected return risk premium per unit of risk) would be the same for all assets, no matter which submarket they trade in.

classes, and capital would flow accordingly across market segments until price discrepancies were corrected.[31]

Nevertheless, such mispricing is not completely implausible, at least for limited periods of time, and to some extent perhaps even permanently when one considers the nature of the differences between private markets for whole assets, such as the real estate market, and public markets for securities, such as the stock market. We have described these differences extensively in previous chapters, especially Chapters 7 and 12. In particular, in our discussion of the "dualing asset markets" (private real estate versus REITs) in Chapter 12, we noted that the stock market and the private real estate market are probably not perfectly integrated. Frictions, such as constraints and expenses associated with moving real property assets between private and public ownership, are nontrivial, though generally declining over historical time. This means that the same price of risk need not necessarily exist in both markets, especially in the past.[32]

We also noted in Chapter 21 that it is a bit difficult to square modern portfolio theory with the small share institutional investors allocate to real estate in their overall mixed-asset portfolios. In a sense, this is another way of saying that there is some evidence of a type of (untapped) risk/return bargain in real estate, at least from the perspective of MPT and institutional investors.

22.3 ATTEMPTING TO QUANTIFY SECTORAL RISK AND RETURN WITHIN THE PRIVATE REAL ESTATE ASSET CLASS: THE CUTTING EDGE

With our caveats noted, it is nevertheless probably safe to say that the basic CAPM does work pretty well at the broad-brush level of the overall mixed-asset portfolio, for comparisons across asset classes. In fact, arguably, the CAPM works better at this broad level than it does within the stock market, where it is most often employed in current practice. But what about the next level down? Can we apply the CAPM to quantify risk and model the market's ex ante risk premiums within the private property market, for example, to quantify the risk and return expectations for different types of property in different geographic locations? In short, can the CAPM explain the cross-section of the property market's expected returns across sectors within the overall private real estate asset class?[33]

---

[31] We are reminded of the old economist joke about market efficiency. Two economists were walking down a crowded sidewalk when they noticed a $20 bill lying on the path. They both started to stoop over to pick it up when they glanced at each other, caught themselves, and agreed it was not worth the effort. Surely the bill must be counterfeit, they agreed. If it were real, it would certainly have already been picked up by someone else on such a crowded sidewalk.

[32] See section 12.3.3 and footnote 32. We noted there a study by Ling and Naranjo (1999) that reports evidence of a lack of complete integration of the stock and private real estate markets during the 1978–94 period, based on a multifactor model of risk. An earlier study by Liu, Grissom, and Hartzell (1990) developed a formal expansion of the CAPM to recognize certain types of capital market segmentation and frictions, such as illiquidity in real estate.

[33] A note on terminology: The word *sector* in the present context originates in the stock market investment community. In the private real estate asset class, the word *segment* is often used rather than the word *sector*, to describe divisions in the overall asset class or groups of similar assets. To some extent, this difference in terminology reflects a real difference in the degree of integration within the two asset classes

22.3.1 Can the Basic CAPM Be Applied within the Private Real Estate Asset Class?

The short answer to this question is, alas, no. The basic CAPM, with a single risk factor based on asset periodic returns volatility or covariance with a single risk benchmark, does not seem to work very well. A picture of this problem can be seen in Exhibit 22-3, which shows a scatter-plot of ex post average excess returns (over T-bills) to a number of institutional quality commercial property portfolios, plotted across their betas computed with respect to the national wealth portfolio. Both the ex post returns and the betas are estimated using quarterly historical periodic returns data over the 1981–98 period. In Exhibit 22-3, the portfolios are the property type and geographical segments of the institutional property market as represented by the division subindices of the NCREIF Index. The risk benchmark for computing the measure of beta is a proxy for the national wealth portfolio consisting of equal one-third shares of stocks, bonds, and real estate.[34] The betas have been estimated correcting for "smoothing bias."[35] Each point in the graph represents one NCREIF subindex excess return and beta. Thus, each dot corresponds to one type of property (office, retail, or industrial) in one geographic division.[36]

If the basic CAPM worked well, then we would expect a scatter-plot such as that in Exhibit 22-3 to show a pretty clear relationship between the excess return (vertical axis) and the beta (horizontal axis). In particular, we would expect to see an indication of a positive linear relationship between risk (beta) and return. The dots in the graph should plot roughly along a positively sloped security market line intersecting the two axes near zero.

In fact, no such relationship is apparent in Exhibit 22-3. This is in spite of the fact that we have a rather broad spread in the explanatory variable (beta) and in the dependent variable (the ex post excess returns). Furthermore, the NCREIF subindices we are examining in this exhibit contain a large number of properties (sufficient to diversify away most idiosyncratic risk and random noise at the individual property level), and we have included a large number of periodic returns in the estimation (72 quarters' worth

(stocks versus private real estate). A sector is considered part of a well-integrated market, while a segment implies some possible lack of integration. However, the real estate terminology also reflects the close relation between the asset market and the space market in real estate. Even if the real estate asset market is much more integrated than the real estate space markets, sectors in the asset market are often based on segments in the space market. Sometimes the word *sector* in private real estate refers only to divisions in property usage type (e.g., office, retail, industrial, residential), while segments are defined also by geographical location. In any case, from a broader investment industry perspective, the term *sector* is more widely used and is employed throughout this chapter for the sake of consistency. However, in Chapter 27, where we will be dealing purely with private real estate, we will switch to the term *segment*.

[34] To be more precise, the national wealth portfolio in this case has been approximated as follows. The one-third stock market component consists of 90% S&P 500 and 10% small stocks (as reported in Ibbotson Associates' *SBBI Yearbook*). The long-term bond portion of the national wealth portfolio consists of 90% long-term Treasury Bonds (from the *SBBI*) and 10% commercial mortgages (from the GLCMPI). The real estate component consists of one-third aggregate (all-property) NCREIF index (NPI) and two-thirds single-family houses, as represented by the FNMA/FHLMC repeat-sale transaction-based price index (plus 6% per year to reflect imputed rent). The NPI has been unsmoothed (or delagged) in the national wealth portfolio.

[35] The technique described in Geltner (1991) was used to correct the beta estimates. This will be described further in Chapter 25, section 25.1.2.

[36] There are eight NCREIF geographic divisions: Northeast, Mid-East, Southeast, South-West, East-North-Central, West-North-Central, Mountain, and Pacific.

Exhibit 22-3 Single-Index Risk and Return within the Private Real Estate Market (NCREIF subindices), 1981–98

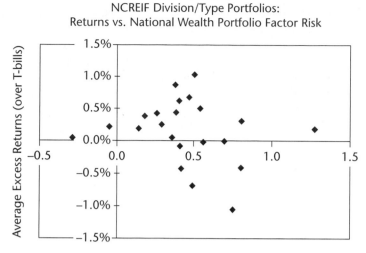

NCREIF Division/Type Portfolios: Returns vs. National Wealth Portfolio Factor Risk

Beta with respect to the National Wealth Portfolio, defined as equal one-third shares of stocks, bonds, and real estate.

of history). Furthermore, although not shown in Exhibit 22-3, similar results are observed from a wide variety of ways of defining and measuring beta.[37]

How can the CAPM work at the broad level, across asset classes (including the private real estate asset class), and not at this more specific level within the private real estate asset class? If beta with respect to the national wealth portfolio measures the risk that matters to the capital market at the broad level, why doesn't it capture the risk that matters within the property market?

One plausible answer to this question is that the property market cannot distinguish, ex ante, between the *relative* amount of risk in one property type or location and that in another. This may be because data is bad or information is poor, but it could also be because betas truly are not stable, relatively speaking, across property types and regions. Recall our discussion in Part II about the system of cities, location value within cities, and the economic bases of metropolitan areas. It may be that all these variables change over time and interact with investor preferences in ways that do not produce a stable structure of relative volatility and correlation across property types and locations.

Investors may feel pretty confident about the relative amount of risk in the real estate asset class as a whole, relative to stocks and bonds. They may feel that this relative amount of risk is fairly constant over long periods of time. Yet it might be quite logical for these same investors to lack confidence that they can fine-tune their perceptions of relative risk to the level of specific property types and geographic regions in any sort of way that is reliable or stable over time.

For example, suppose that over the past five or ten years, warehouses in Kansas City had twice as much volatility as retail malls in Denver. Does this imply that Kansas City warehouses will again be twice as volatile as Denver malls during the next

---

[37] For example, no ex post relationship is apparent between risk and return among institutional property market segments when beta is defined with respect to the stock market, to the aggregate NCREIF Index, or to national consumption.

five or ten years? Answer: no one knows. Not enough is known about location values, space markets, the property asset market, and the interaction among these determinants of value and future returns. Regional economic base analysis and forecasting is an inexact science dealing with an ever-shifting world. In some respects, properties' geographical immobility and functional inflexibility makes their futures more difficult to predict than those of the typical industrial or service corporation whose shares trade in the stock market. For example, Texas real estate moved countercyclical to the rest of the national economy during the high-oil-price days of the 1970s and early 1980s, but subsequently was more in sync with the national economy and national wealth.

If the property market cannot reliably perceive differences in risk at the level of individual property types and regions within the core institutional property asset class, then it will not require significantly or persistently different ex ante returns (going-in IRRs) across different property types and locations. Indeed, recall from our discussion at the end of Chapter 11 that little apparent difference exists among ex ante IRRs across property types within the institutional quality commercial property asset class. The result of such ex ante perceptions, if they are rational expectations, would be that ex post returns and betas would be spread out like a shotgun blast across the risk/return diagram, and no security market line would be apparent ex post *within* the institutional quality real estate asset class. This is apparently what we see in Exhibit 22-3.

22.3.2 Implications for Macrolevel Tactical Investment Analysis within the Private Real Estate Class

To the extent that the property market cannot fine-tune its perception of relative risk differences across property types and locations, the cross-section of ex ante market risk premiums will be flat. In other words, the opportunity cost of capital, used as the discount rate to value properties using the DCF procedure, will tend to be very similar for different types of properties in different locations. It seems from our discussion both here and in Chapter 11 that this is essentially the case within the institutional quality commercial property asset class in the United States.

This has an important implication for tactical investment analysis. Suppose, for example, that you conduct a market analysis of the space markets in a number of cities. From this study you believe that net rents will grow considerably faster over the next five years in certain sectors, say, for example, apartments in San Francisco and warehouses in Chicago. Now you plug your rent growth projections into a DCF analysis of typical current asset prices in those sectors (e.g., based on prevailing cap rates in each market) to compute the implied going-in IRRs in each sector. You might find, say, in San Francisco, that your above-average rental growth projection does not provide an above-average expected return. Asset market prices there must already be reflecting your rental growth expectation.

But you might find in other sectors, say, Chicago warehouses, that your rent growth expectations suggest that current asset prices provide an implied expected IRR above the current average IRR in the institutional property asset class as a whole. Now, if the property market could distinguish risk differences among sectors, then this above-average IRR might simply reflect above-average risk. But if the property market cannot distinguish risk differences, then you can immediately conclude directly from your computation of return expectations that Chicago warehouses are a "buy" sector. In other words, Chicago warehouses is a sector that presents the investor with above-normal expected returns. Of course this is only true to the extent

Is It Risk, or Is It Expected Return?
A Question of Terminology and Investment Culture

In the practice of the type of macrolevel real estate tactical investment analysis described in section 22.3.2, the terminology can often be a bit confusing. In part, this confusion reflects real estate's unique investment "culture," as compared to traditional securities market investment practice. In particular, real estate investment analysts will often refer to differences in risk across sectors. For example, they may make statements such as: "The Atlanta apartment market seems particular risky at present due to a current oversupply of new construction." It is important to distinguish risk as used in this context, from the concept of risk viewed from the perspective of mean-variance investment performance, the perspective that prevails in the stock market.

The former use of the word *risk*, deriving from a space market analysis (e.g., the apartment market in Atlanta), actually means that the expected rent and occupancy in the relevant space market over the coming months or years is below "normal" in some sense (e.g., below the long-run equilibrium level). If (and it is a big if), property asset market prices in the subject sector have not responded to reflect this below-normal expectation in rent levels or rent growth (and assuming the expectation is valid given all the currently available information), then expected returns in the asset market sector will also be below normal.

But this does not necessarily imply anything about the risk in the future investment performance of the subject asset market sector, if we define risk from a mean-variance perspective, the way it is usually conceived in the capital market. From this latter perspective, risk refers to periodic return volatility (or derivatives of this volatility, such as beta, the risk that matters from an asset pricing perspective in terms of the investment market's required ex ante return risk premium). For example, Atlanta apartment buildings may have a relatively safe return in the sense that it may be almost a sure bet that their returns will be below normal (or normal, if apartment property prices already reflect the bad news about future rental growth). From the perspective

of capital market and investments terminology, Atlanta apartments may or may not be overpriced, but this is a question largely of their expected return, not of their risk (volatility or beta).*

In a sense, you can think of risk as defined in the former (space market) usage as being more akin to the capital market concept of default risk as it applies in the corporate bond or mortgage market. Risk in this context refers to an expected gap (in an ex ante probabilistic sense) between the normal cash flow (akin to the contractual cash flow in a bond or mortgage) and the realized cash flow ex post. If the asset price does not reflect this probabilistic expectation (as in the par value of the bond or the contractual principal of the mortgage), then the probabilistic expected rate of return on the investment is less than its normal rate (e.g., the stated yield or contractual yield in the case of the bond or mortgage). Thus, application of the space-market-based concept of risk in a real estate tactical investment context suggests that such investment is viewed largely from an underwriting perspective like that which typifies the primary (new issuance) market for bonds or mortgages. This underwriting culture contrasts with the more trading-oriented perspective that prevails in the stock market and the secondary market for bonds. This is another example of how real estate investments (in particular, direct investment in the private property market) falls into a unique category different from traditional mainstream securities investments, often blending characteristics of both stock and bond investments at both the primary and secondary market levels.

---

*Of course, the volatility or uncertainty surrounding the future values of Atlanta apartments could conceivably be above normal (meaning, above its typical or historical level). But recall from section 22.3.1 that it is difficult to quantify property market sector volatility precisely and reliably over time. It is unlikely that the property market holds a very precise or stable idea about the volatility of Atlanta apartments in this regard, at least within the private (direct) property asset market.

that your space market forecast is correct (in an *ex ante* sense; that is, it is unbiased and based on complete information as it is available today).

In other words, a generally flat ex ante return cross-section within the private property market implies that any differences in expected returns that an investor can distinguish across sectors translate into apparent mispricing rather more directly than in the securities markets. Such mispricing presents tactical investment opportunities that may exist on either the buy or sell side of the property market, although the difficulty of constructing short-sales in direct real estate investment limits the ability to take advantage of asset overpricing unless the investor already owns properties in the overpriced sector.

One result of the difficulty of distinguishing risk differences across sectors within the private property market is the focus of macrolevel tactical investment analysis almost uniquely on the numerators in the asset valuation equation, that is, the future operating cash flow potential in different sectors. This is in some contrast to the stock market, for example, where more analytical attention is given to estimating risk differences across sectors. The focus on numerators (operating cash flows) in private real estate requires broad analysis of the space markets. In essence, investment analysts look for property types and locations that will provide higher than average rental growth. This type of space market analysis was discussed in Part II of this book. As noted there, both the supply side and the demand side of space markets must be considered in predicting rental growth. In short, identification of tactical investment opportunities in the private real estate asset class requires the application of urban economics and real estate market analysis. Accordingly, many institutional real estate investors devote considerable resources to this type of research. However, as noted, investors must also integrate the space market forecast with an analysis of current asset market prices in each sector to see where going-in IRRs look higher than normal.[38]

*22.3.3 A More Sophisticated Model of Equilibrium Asset Prices: Multifactor Risk Models

We noted back in section 22.1 that the basic CAPM omits some important parts of reality.[39] As a result, there have been major efforts to improve on the basic model, especially for applications to the stock market. Refinements and extensions in general equilibrium asset price modeling, developed during the last three decades of the 20th century (after the basic CAPM, and building from it), have in fact considerably improved our ability to understand and predict expected returns, at least within the stock market. Some of these developments have begun to be applied within the private property market, although such application was clearly in its infancy in the late 1990s. In this section we will attempt to take you to part of the "cutting edge" of current real estate research.

---

[38] The relationship among cap rates (current yields), growth rates, and total return expectations suggested by the constant-growth perpetuity model (equivalent to the Gordon growth model in stock market analysis) is often a useful tool in this regard. Recall from Part IV that $r = y + g$ in periodic simple HPRs, and this relationship also often holds approximately for multiperiod IRRs. Thus, if a macrolevel space market analysis reveals sectors with a high expected g component, and this is not offset by a low current yield (a low y, that is, a high price/earning multiple within the property market sector), then the expected total return (r) is relatively high in that sector.

[39] As noted, this is done on purpose, and it is both a strength and a weakness of the basic CAPM.

At a fundamental level, the more recent developments in equilibrium asset pricing models have done two things: (1) they have highlighted the importance of a consumption-based (rather than a wealth-based) conception of risk and reward; and (2) they have built on the CAPM notion of diversifiability of specific risk to allow a more robust model of price formation in asset markets known as the arbitrage model. The practical result of both of these developments has been to move asset price modeling in the direction of **multifactor** (or **multibeta**) **models** of investment risk. That is, they define the risk that matters to investors in *multiple dimensions*. Instead of considering only the covariance between each asset and a single risk factor (such as the national wealth portfolio), these models consider the covariance between each asset and several risk factors. Multifactor models have one major empirical advantage and one major theoretical advantage.

The empirical advantage is that multifactor models can be much more general statistically. In other words, any single-factor model (including the traditional CAPM) can be viewed as a special case of the multifactor model. From a statistical perspective, the more explanatory variables you have in the right-hand side of a regression of asset returns onto risk factors, the more variability in asset returns you can explain with the regression.[40] If any variables (i.e., factors) are not statistically significant in such empirical analysis, they can simply be dropped from the model.[41] Furthermore, multifactor models can be based on a much simpler characterization of asset market equilibrium, one in which we do not have to presume that we know anything about investors' portfolio allocations or risk and return expectations. In particular, multifactor models can rest on a so-called no-arbitrage characterization of asset market equilibrium prices. This is known as the arbitrage pricing theory, or APT for short.[42] In combination with their greater statistical flexibility, this theoretical advantage makes multifactor models more robust and powerful than the traditional single-beta CAPM.[43]

Through the 1990s, attempts to apply multifactor risk pricing models to real estate were confined largely to academic research and to the REIT sector of the stock market. In general, these studies found that multifactor models work about as well for REITs as they do for other sectors of the stock market, and that REITs have unique risk factors or factor "loadings."[44] (The term *loading* in this context refers to the sensitivity of the asset to the risk factor, comparable to the beta measure of the traditional CAPM.)

Applications of the multifactor model to privately traded commercial real estate equity is much more challenging, in part because of the problems described earlier regarding periodic returns data.[45] More fundamentally, recall from section 22.3.1 that

[40] This is true both longitudinally (across time) and cross-sectionally (across assets).

[41] However, it is important to keep in mind that if we are to really gain useful insights and tools from asset price modeling, our models must derive from more than just a statistical "data-mining" exercise. Coming up with models that explain a lot of variation is not the entire name of the game. We need a good dose of economic theory to let us know that what we are doing statistically makes sense at a more fundamental level.

[42] The APT was first developed by Stephen Ross in an article that is perhaps as famous as the Nobel Prize–winning studies that first developed the CAPM. (See Ross [1976].)

[43] See the appendix to this chapter for a more detailed explanation of multifactor models and the APT.

[44] Some of the major articles applying multifactor models to securitized real estate equity in the United States include Titman and Warga (1986); Chan, Hendershott, and Sanders (1990); Mei and Lee (1994); and Karolyi and Sanders (1998); among others.

[45] These include problems such as smoothing and ex post return measurement error, as well as shorter historical returns time-series, with lower-frequency HPRs.

it is very difficult to distinguish differences among risk and ex ante returns across assets or sectors within the private real estate asset class. This makes it difficult, even for elaborate and sophisticated multifactor models, to achieve significant results. Nevertheless, it is at this level of application that multifactor risk models may be able to add most to our understanding of risk and risk pricing in private real estate.

Through the end of the 1990s, one of the most interesting studies that attempted to apply multifactor risk modeling to private real estate was by Professors Ling and Naranjo at the University of Florida.[46] This study examined quarterly returns from 1978 through 1994 on portfolios of private commercial real estate (as well as REITs) defined in various ways (generally based on the NCREIF index, but corrected for appraisal smoothing). The Ling-Naranjo study was able to identify several risk factors that appeared to be statistically significant in the pricing of private real estate portfolios within the private real estate asset class. In other words, in contrast to the result described for a simple single-factor pricing model such as the traditional CAPM, it appears that the Ling-Naranjo risk factors enable a distinction in the ex ante risk premiums across different sectors within the private property market. Although multifactor risk models have yet to be applied in practice at this level, there may be some scope for such practical application. In any case, multifactor risk models such as the Ling-Naranjo model expand our understanding of risk and return in private real estate asset markets.

Some of the findings from the Ling-Naranjo study are summarized in Exhibit 22-4. This table shows the results of a cross-sectional regression of the ex post returns of real estate portfolios onto various risk factors. The real estate portfolios are of two types: REIT stock portfolios and private institutional quality commercial property portfolios based on the subindices of the NCREIF index (similar to the portfolios examined in Exhibit 22-3).

Ling and Naranjo identified five statistically significant risk factors: the stock market (as in the traditional application of the CAPM), national consumption, inflation risk, and two variables having to do with interest rates in the bond market. In addition, they employed three "conditioning variables." These are prior characteristics of the assets that help to predict average ex post returns.[47]

Under each type of portfolio, the table presents three rows of findings. The first row refers to the beta, or "loading," that is, the nature and degree of sensitivity of the portfolios to the various risk factors. The second row indicates the market price of risk for each factor, that is, the expected return risk premium per unit of risk for each factor. The third row multiplies the first two rows together to reveal the average magnitude (and sign) of the component of ex ante return risk premium associated with each risk factor.

Some of the factor loadings on these variables imply that the ex ante return risk premium component associated with that factor is negative. In other words, the asset's covariance with that factor produces a favorable effect for investors. An example of this is the real interest rate risk factor. If real interest rates turn out to be higher than previously expected, real estate returns generally turn out to be lower than previously expected, resulting in a negative beta of about 0.5 for this factor. The market

---

[46] The results of the Ling-Naranjo study were reported and summarized in two articles. A more practitioner-oriented explication of the study is contained in Ling and Naranjo (1998). A more in-depth academic description is contained in Ling and Naranjo (1997).

[47] These conditioning variables are not risk factors per se, but they may reflect types of risk that are not well quantified by statistical analysis. We will have more to say about them shortly.

Portfolio Group	Risk Factors[1]					Conditioning Variables[2]		
	GCONSUM	RLTBL	TERM	UI	MKT	NYLD	DIVP	SIZE
Portfolios of REIT Stocks:								
Average Beta*	0.838	−0.463	−0.312	−0.614	1.166	0.363	0.213	−0.026
Factor Price of Risk**	1.19%	2.48%	3.42%	1.02%	8.56%			
Risk Premium Component***	1.00%	−1.15%	−1.07%	−0.63%	9.98%	2.74%	3.09%	−2.24%
Portfolios Consisting of NCREIF Property Types by Region:								
Average Beta*	0.441	−0.487	−0.529	−0.151	0.061	0.742	0.360	−0.027
Factor Price of Risk**	1.62%	2.29%	1.37%	3.25%	8.56%			
Risk Premium Component***	0.71%	−1.12%	−0.73%	−0.49%	0.52%	5.60%	5.22%	−2.32%

[1] GCONSUM = Change in real national consumption; RLTBL = Real (net of inflation) Treasury Bill yield; TERM = Difference between long-maturity and short-maturity U.S. Treasury Bond yields; UI = Unexpected inflation (i.e., residuals from a time-series model of inflation); MKT = Return on the stock market.

[2] NYLD = NCREIF index current yield in the previous quarter; DIVP = Current yield on the S&P 500 in the previous quarter; SIZE = log of the market value of the market portfolio in the previous quarter.

* The average beta is defined as the average loading of each respective risk factor across the individual portfolios, within each portfolio group.

**Annualized.

***The risk magnitude is the product of the average beta and the corresponding factor price of risk. For the conditioning variables (NYLD, DIVP, and SIZE), the risk magnitude is defined as the product of the average beta and the annualized historical mean of the corresponding conditioning variable.

Source: Ling and Naranjo (1998).

Exhibit 22-4   Components of Ex Ante Risk Premiums within the Private Property Market (1978–94)

requires a positive component in the expected return risk premium of something over 2% (per annum), per unit of real interest rate risk. This means that real estate expected returns are actually less, by a little over 1%, as a result of this risk factor.

How can this be? Isn't risk a "bad" thing that investors must be compensated for by receiving a higher expected return? In fact, the sign of a risk factor component depends on the risk preferences in the capital market. Some risk factors are favorable in that they help investors to "hedge" their overall wealth or welfare, acting like diversifiers within investors' portfolios or like shock absorbers for changes in investors' consumption or welfare over time.

Consider the real interest rate risk factor, for example. Real short-term interest rates tend to rise when demand for capital is great, which tends to be when the economy and stock market are booming. The fact that real estate returns tend to be lower than average in such times is of less concern to investors because they are likely to be better off due to other components of their wealth or income. Real short-term interest rates tend to fall when the macroeconomy or the capital markets hit a downturn or crisis. In such times investors most value good performance from their investments, as they are most likely to be suffering reverses in either income or overall wealth. Real estate's negative beta with respect to real interest rates indicates that it is at precisely such times that, other things being equal, real estate will tend to perform better than average. Thus, the real interest rate risk factor (by itself) causes real estate ex ante risk premiums to be generally lower than they otherwise would be.

The Ling-Naranjo findings have several interesting implications. One is that the factor betas and the market prices of risk are rather different between the publicly traded REIT portfolios and the privately traded NCREIF-based portfolios. Differences in the betas suggests that REITs and private property behave rather differently in terms of covariance with some of the risk factors. However, the betas are generally of the same sign between REITs and private property, except that REITs tend to be more sensitive to the risk factors, especially to the stock market factor. This suggests that the major risk difference between REITs and private property is that REITs tend to be more volatile and more influenced by the stock market, at least at the quarterly frequency studied by Ling and Naranjo. However, differences in the market price of risk between the REITs and the private portfolios suggests that these two segments of the capital markets may not be well integrated, at least in terms of the short-run performance reflected in quarterly returns.[48]

Another interesting finding in the Ling-Naranjo study is the large relative importance of their so-called conditioning variables in determining the overall ex ante risk premiums. This is seen in the large positive risk premium components attributable to the current yield characteristics of the markets in which the real estate assets trade (the *NYLD* and *DIVP* variables). In general, higher yields imply higher ex ante expected returns. The effect of the conditioning variables actually swamps the risk factor effects in the case of private real estate. Most of the ex ante risk premium in private real estate appears to be determined by the yield in the property market and the stock market. One interpretation of this finding could be that the conditioning variables may be reflecting inertia (that is, short-term predictability of returns) in the private real estate market due to relatively less informational efficiency in that market.

Yet another interesting finding in the Ling-Naranjo study is the importance of consumption risk and other components of macroeconomic risk, such as interest rates and inflation. We noted previously that small firm size and high current yield tends to be associated with high ex ante returns in the stock market, perhaps reflecting investors' concerns about susceptibility to macroeconomic or capital market shocks. It may be that the consumption and macroeconomic factors in the Ling-Naranjo model are capturing some of this same phenomenon.

This hypothesis is suggested in part by the difference between so-called institutional quality commercial property and noninstitutional property. As noted in Chapter 11, noninstitutional property is generally smaller, of lower quality (which often means lower occupancy), and often in need of (or in the process of obtaining) physical development or rehabilitation of some sort. The Ling-Naranjo study necessarily included only institutional quality property.[49] However, recall from our discussion of private real estate expected returns back in Chapter 11 that the greatest difference in ex ante risk premiums in commercial real estate appears to be not across property types or locations among institutional quality properties, but rather between institutional and noninstitutional property.[50]

---

[48] This aspect of the study findings is pursued further by Ling and Naranjo in a follow-up article. See Ling and Naranjo (1999). Also see the text box at the end of this section.

[49] Data is generally unavailable for time-series of periodic returns to noninstitutional quality commercial property in the United States.

[50] An alternative explanation for the difference between institutional and noninstitutional yields was put forth by Williams (1999), who suggested that information asymmetry, agency costs, and market power on the part of noninstitutional investors allow an equilibrium in which noninstitutional quality property can earn supernormal returns for noninstitutional investors with local expertise.

The Question of Segmented Capital Markets: REITs versus Private Property

One of the most fundamental points raised in studies of REIT and private property market asset pricing and ex ante returns is the degree to which these two segments of the capital markets may not be fully integrated. Such lack of integration may be evidenced by persistent differences in the priced risk factors or in the market prices of risk for the same risk factors. We noted that the Ling-Naranjo study found evidence of such differences, as have other previous studies.* We also discussed the relationship between the REIT and private property markets previously, notably in Chapter 12, where we focused on microlevel valuation differences (see section 12.3, "Dualing Asset Markets"). Although we will touch on this topic still again in the next chapters, it is probably worthwhile at this point to summarize what we think about this controversial issue.

1. First, common sense and casual empiricism strongly suggest that the REIT market and the private commercial property market are not perfectly or completely integrated. Some persistent risk pricing differences probably exist.

2. Second, the jury is definitely still out on the exact nature, degree, and significance of the lack of integration and the pricing differences. Furthermore, researchers analyzing this question may well be (if we may be permitted to mix metaphors) shooting at a moving target. The capital markets are constantly evolving and developing. Clearly we can rule out the existence of extreme lack of integration between the two types of markets. We know that capital can flow massively between the two market segments over the long run or if pricing discrepancies become too large. There is also blatant empirical evidence against extreme segmentation. For example, if the private property market was completely isolated from the rest of the capital market, it would have its own CAPM with empirical evidence of its own security (i.e., property) market line based on a purely private real estate risk benchmark. We saw in section 22.3.1 (and Exhibit 22-3) that no such empirical evidence exists within the institutional property market. On the other hand, nontrivial "frictions," such as transaction costs and regulatory constraints, are involved in movement of assets (or capital) between the two market segments. Conceivably, such frictions can allow persistent pricing differences to some extent.

3. Third, the question of differential informational efficiency between the REIT and private property markets complicates the integration question both conceptually and empirically. REIT prices seem likely to respond more quickly to relevant news, but they may also display transient excess volatility and corrections. Over longer investment horizons, the two market segments are likely more integrated than they are in the short run.

In summary, the question of the relationship between REIT and private property markets will likely continue to be a focus of active research for some time in the academic real estate community, and no doubt a source of potential profit (as well as frustration) in the investment practitioner community.

*See, for example, Liu, Grissom, and Hartzell (1990); Mei and Lee (1994); Giliberto and Mengden (1996); and Karolyi and Sanders (1998).

22.4 CHAPTER SUMMARY

This chapter built on the foundation of portfolio theory to introduce you to equilibrium asset pricing models, a key tool used in both strategic and tactical investment decision making at the macrolevel. We attempted not only to review, at an introductory level, the use of such models in the stock market (which includes REIT applications), but also to go into more depth regarding applications of macrolevel asset pricing theory to privately traded real estate assets in the property market.

Asset pricing theory faces some of its most intellectually exciting challenges, and potential rewards, in the application to privately held property. In this regard, we pointed out the importance of distinguishing two levels of application. The broad, mixed-asset level deals with pricing *across* asset classes or types of investment products and arenas. At this level, an elegant single-index CAPM-type model probably works pretty well. The more specific sector level deals with pricing *within* the private property market. At this level, the difference between institutional quality and non-institutional properties looms large, and the simple single-index model fails to model priced risk differences, at least in practice if not in theory. Finally, we took you to the cutting edge of current research to show you how more sophisticated multifactor models may offer some promise at this level.

APPENDIX 22: ARBITRAGE PRICING THEORY AND THE MULTIFACTOR MODEL OF EQUILIBRIUM EX ANTE RISK PREMIUMS IN THE CAPITAL MARKET

As noted in the text of this chapter, the main thrust of equilibrium asset pricing theory since the 1980s has been in the development of multifactor risk models. Such models can be (although they are not all necessarily) based on the so-called **arbitrage pricing theory (APT)** of equilibrium asset price formation. This appendix will introduce you to the basics of this approach to asset price modeling.

We begin by supposing that the periodic returns to each asset i are generated by the following process.

$$r_{i,t} = E[r_i] + \beta_{i1}F_{1,t} + \beta_{i2}F_{2,t} + \varepsilon_{i,t} \tag{A.1}$$

In this process, $r_{i,t}$ is the return to asset i in period t. Part of this return simply consists of the prior expectation of what that return would be, $E[r_i]$, which is viewed here as constant over time. And part of asset i's return is purely random and idiosyncratic to i alone. This is the $\varepsilon_{i,t}$ term. The component of the risk (or variability over time) in asset i's return that is attributable to $\varepsilon_{i,t}$ can be diversified away because $\varepsilon_{i,t}$ is not correlated with any other asset's return. Furthermore, $\varepsilon_{i,t}$ is measured in such a way that the prior expectation of its value, labeled $E[\varepsilon_i]$, is zero.[51]

---

[51] This can be done simply by subtracting the mean value of the idiosyncratic return from its realization each period. If this mean value were important in forming the expected return to asset i, then it would appear as part of the constant $E[r_i]$ term in equation (A.1). However, as we know from discussion in both Chapters 21 and 22, most investors do not care about diversifiable risk, and so such risk does not affect the value of assets in equilibrium. Hence, there should be no affect of $\varepsilon_{i,t}$ on $E[r_i]$, which implies that, according to theory, $E[\varepsilon_i] = 0$.

On the other hand, the risk in asset i's return caused by the remaining two terms on the right-hand side of equation (A.1) cannot be diversified away. This *systematic risk* in asset i's return is caused by two factors, labeled F_1 and F_2. These factors represent the realizations of events or the arrival of new information that matters not only to the value of asset i but also to other assets as well. Therefore, it is impossible to diversify away exposure to these two factors completely, even in a large portfolio. In equation (A.1) these systematic risk factors are measured as deviations from the previously expected values of each factor. Thus, $E[F_1] = 0 = E[F_2]$.[52]

From the perspective of APT, the key point about F_1 and F_2 is that these factors are the *only* sources of randomness over time in asset i's return (other than the idiosyncratic component that can be diversified away). To apply the APT concept we do not have to know the risk factors (or even how many risk factors investors care about), *a priori* or from a theoretical basis. This is the beauty of the APT compared to other theories of asset equilibrium, such as the Sharpe-Lintner CAPM.[53] Empirical analysis will show us what the important factors are. In principle, they can be anything that is correlated with something investors care about (either positively or negatively), and that cannot be diversified away. In the real world they typically include things such as the stock market return, changes in interest rates, and changes in the national economy (such as GDP or national consumption).[54]

If we can observe the periodic returns of assets across time, and the periodic realizations of the nondiversifiable factors, then we can perform time-series regressions of formula (A.1), regressing $r_{i,t}$ onto $F_{1,t}$ and $F_{2,t}$ across time, thereby estimating the values of the risk sensitivities or factor loadings, β_{i1} and β_{i2}.[55] With these estimates, we can then perform a cross-sectional analysis, regressing long-run average returns, $E[r_i]$, onto the factor loadings across a number of different assets or asset classes to estimate the market price of risk associated with each factor. The result is an equilibrium model of expected returns with the following form:[56]

$$E[r_i] = r_f + \beta_{i1}P_1 + \beta_{i2}P_2 \tag{A.2}$$

A key point is that a model of expected returns such as (A.2) is in fact implied by our asset pricing assumption (A.1) together with the assumption that asset prices in the capital market cannot allow "arbitrage" profits to be earned. Arbitrage profit is

[52]Once again, this can easily be done simply by subtracting the mean value of each factor from its realization each period. The way in which the prior expected values of the systematic risk factors enter into asset i's expected return will be incorporated in the $E[r_i]$ term in equation (A.1).

[53]It would be a truly chaotic world indeed if *the common (i.e. nondiversifiable) component* of asset returns were not governed by a few underlying broad economic indicators. So the APT model makes sense in this regard.

[54]As suggested in the text of Chapter 22, certain factors may be better represented mathematically or statistically as conditioning variables, such as the size of the asset or its current dividend yield.

[55]A separate time-series regression must be done for each asset or asset class i. Factor loadings are measures of sensitivity of the asset to the risk factor, comparable to the beta in the traditional CAPM.

[56]Keep in mind that in this second-stage cross-sectional regression, the loadings (or betas) are the explanatory variables, and the factor risk prices, the Ps, are the parameters being estimated in the regression. We know which risk factor each price of risk corresponds to because we know which risk factor the corresponding beta was estimated from in the first-stage (time-series) regressions. Both the first- and second-stage regressions have a number of explanatory variables equal to the number of risk factors. The identification and discovery of the systematic risk factors can, in principle, be a purely empirical statistical process, although in practice some theoretical guidance is very useful.

defined as profit obtained without any risk or any investment outlay. It seems reasonable to suppose that most asset markets would be efficient enough so that if *arbitrage* opportunities existed, they would be quickly eliminated by a rush by investors to buy (or sell) any assets whose under- (or over-) pricing permitted such opportunities. Hence, we would expect that, at any given point in time, the prices of very few assets would violate a no-arbitrage restriction, and that no asset's price could violate such a restriction for any extended period of time.

To see how (A.2) is implied by (A.1) and the no-arbitrage assumption, suppose that the price of a diversified portfolio of individual assets violates formula (A.2). For example, suppose that according to formula (A.2) portfolio A should have an expected return of 10%. Yet you observe portfolio A selling for $90 per share when its expected payoff next year is $110 per share.[57] If most other assets conform to formula (A.2), then you could easily find a diversified portfolio of assets selling for $90 per share with expected payoff next year of $99. Let's call such a portfolio of other assets that conform to formula (A.2) portfolio B.[58] Now you could short-sell $90 worth of portfolio B and use the proceeds of that sale to purchase a share of portfolio A. Thus, you have made no net investment, yet you have the expectation of making $110 − $99 = $11 next year.[59]

Now, even if your $11 profit expectation is not without risk, it represents an *infinite* expected return on your investment (since your investment is zero). But in fact, if equations (A.1) and (A.2) completely describe reality, then there is not even any risk in your $11 profit. To see rigorously why this is the case involves more math than we (or you, probably) care to get into at this point. But you can see the basic intuition if we suppose that portfolio B not only has the 10% expected return implied by formula (A.2), but also has the same factor loadings as portfolio A. In other words, $\beta_{A1} = \beta_{B1}$, and $\beta_{A2} = \beta_{B2}$.

First, note that since both portfolio A and portfolio B are well diversified, there will be no idiosyncratic component of the return to either portfolio. The idiosyncratic components of the returns to individual assets in both portfolios will almost certainly cancel out across the large number of individual assets in each portfolio.[60] Furthermore, if equation (A.1) completely describes reality, then there is no source of risk or randomness in either portfolio's return other than the two systematic risk factors identified in that equation. In other words, there is nothing that could cause either portfolio's return next year to deviate from our prior expectation *except* the realizations of the two factors, $F_{1,t}$ and $F_{2,t}$. Therefore, portfolio A's return will be

$$r_{A,t} = E[r_A] + \beta_{A1}F_{1,t} + \beta_{A2}F_{2,t}$$
$$= 22.22\% + \beta_{A1}F_{1,t} + \beta_{A2}F_{2,t}$$

and portfolio B's return will be

[57] This means A has an expected return of 22.22%, equal to ($110 − $90)/$90.

[58] In other words, $r_f + \beta_{i1}P_1 + \beta_{i2}P_2 = 10\%$, for both $i = A$ and $i = B$. However, $E[r_A] = 22.22\%$ while $E[r_B] = 10\%$.

[59] As portfolio B has an expected return of 10%, $90 worth of B this year is expected to be worth $99 next year. To close out your short position next year, you will have to buy that much of portfolio B at that time. However, you will be able to sell your investment in A, which is expected to be worth $110 at that time.

[60] In other words, we will have $\varepsilon_{A,t} = 0 = \varepsilon_{B,t}$.

$$r_{B,t} = E[r_B] + \beta_{B1}F_{1,t} + \beta_{B2}F_{2,t}$$
$$= 10\% + \beta_{B1}F_{1,t} + \beta_{B2}F_{2,t}$$

This implies that *for certain* the profit on our investment position which is long $90 in A and short $90 in B will be

$$\$90[1 + (22.22\% + \beta_{A1}F_{1,t} + \beta_{A2}F_{2,t})] - \$90[1 + (10\% + \beta_{B1}F_{1,t} + \beta_{B2}F_{2,t})]$$

This simplifies to

$$\$90[(122.22\% - 110\%) + (\beta_{A1}F_{1,t} + \beta_{A2}F_{2,t}) - (\beta_{B1}F_{1,t} + \beta_{B2}F_{2,t})]$$

As $\beta_{A1} = \beta_{B1}$, and $\beta_{A2} = \beta_{B2}$, we can further simplify our certain return to

$$\$90[(122.22\% - 110\%) + (\beta_{A1}F_{1,t} + \beta_{A2}F_{2,t}) - (\beta_{A1}F_{1,t} + \beta_{A2}F_{2,t})]$$
$$= \$90[(122.22\% - 110\%) + \beta_{A1}(F_{1,t} - F_{1,t}) + \beta_{A2}(F_{2,t} - F_{2,t})]$$
$$= \$90[(122.22\% - 110\%) + \beta_{A1}(0) + \beta_{A2}(0)]$$
$$= \$90[(122.22\% - 110\%)] = \$90(12.22\%) = \$11$$

Thus, if we *really* know what determines the random systematic components of asset return realizations (i.e., if we have correctly estimated both equations [A.1] and [A.2]), then the APT shows how to make riskless profits for any portfolios whose expected returns do not conform to the model.[61]

Of course, short-sales of private real estate assets are generally not possible (and there are restrictions and expenses associated with short-sales even within public securities markets). But the inability to short-sell does not eliminate the profit incentive from trading on formula (A.2); it merely reduces the magnitude of such profits and the frequency of profit opportunity for the typical investor. For example, to profit from the underpricing of portfolio A in the previous example, the investor would have to find another source of cash besides the short-sale of portfolio B. If portfolio A were overpriced instead of underpriced, the investor could only profit if she already owned A (and so could sell A and buy B).

It also must be remembered that in the real world, we will never know the "true" formula (A.2) for certain. We can only estimate the true equilibrium pricing relationship among assets using empirical and theoretical analysis as we described in Chapter 22. Of course, this imperfection of our knowledge adds to the risk of trading across assets.[62]

---

[61] Suppose the mispricing was the other way around, with portfolio A selling above what formula (A.2) would predict, say, for $105. Then you would short-sell A and use $100 of the proceeds to buy B, keeping $5 as up-front profit, with a future cash flow expectation of zero. This expectation would be riskless if the "true" formula (A.2) is known completely.

[62] As noted, a particular problem may be that the "true" formula (A.2) is not stable over time. Risk factors and factor loadings may change over time, and in different ways for different assets or sectors.

In spite of these problems, multifactor equilibrium asset pricing models are fundamental tools for guiding rational tactical investment policy, both in principle and in practice. In the stock market such models are sometimes used at a very specific level to help with individual "asset picking." However, an important theoretical insight from APT is that *any one* asset can violate the no-arbitrage pricing restriction at any given point in time. Indeed, any one (or a few) individual assets can conceivably violate the no-arbitrage restriction for an extended period of time. Also, it is more difficult to estimate accurately the factor loadings (betas) for a single asset than for a group of assets. This causes equilibrium pricing models to be more accurate, in theory, when they are used to help guide tactical policy at a rather broad level, such as that of industry sectors or asset classes. On the other hand, for the same reason that the model is more accurate at this level, it is also usually more difficult to find apparent mispricing at the broader level. This is the challenge of tactical investment in efficient markets.

KEY TERMS

strategic investment decisions
tactical investment decisions
capital asset pricing model
  (CAPM)
market price of risk
market portfolio

beta
security market line (SML)
systematic (nondiversifiable) risk
specific (idiosyncratic) risk
market imperfections
segmented markets

integrated markets
risk factors
institutional quality real estate
multifactor (multibeta) model of
  risk
arbitrage pricing theory (APT)

STUDY QUESTIONS

22.1. What are equilibrium asset pricing models? Describe three practical uses for such models.

22.2. Which was developed first, the MPT or the CAPM? Why did the development occur in that order?

22.3. Why is beta referred to as a normalized measure of risk? In this normalization process, what (by definition) has a beta equal to unity?

22.4. In a nutshell, what is the main point of the CAPM? What is an important practical investment strategy implication of this point?

22.5. Describe two different levels, or foci, at which we might hope to apply the CAPM to real estate.

22.6. The CAPM was originally (and is still primarily only) applied within the stock market. Nevertheless, describe the two types of corrections or customizations to this narrow stock market application that allow the classical single-factor CAPM to be applied most elegantly to real estate at the broad-brush (mixed-asset) level. [Hint: The failure to consider these two points frustrated early attempts to apply the CAPM to real estate in the 1980s.]

22.7. Describe some capital market imperfections that render the CAPM a less than complete model of reality, especially for application to real estate.

22.8. How well does the single-factor CAPM seem to work within the institutional quality commercial property asset class? Discuss some possible reasons for your answer.

*22.9. Consider a simple multifactor asset pricing model with only two factors, the market portfolio and unexpected inflation. What would you expect to be the *sign* of the price of risk of each of these factors (+ or −)? [Hint: Other things being equal, would you expect investors to prefer an asset that is positively correlated with unexpected inflation?]

22.10. If the riskfree interest rate is 5%, the market price of risk is 6%, and the beta is 0.5, then, according to the classical single-factor CAPM, what is the equilibrium expected total return for investment in the asset in question?

*22-11. Fill in the first row of the following table (the expected returns) based on the single-factor CAPM, assuming that the market portfolio has an expected return of 10% and consists of equal one-third shares of stocks, bonds, and real estate, and assuming that the riskfree interest rate is 5%.

CAPM-Based Risk and Return Expectations

	Stocks	Bonds	Real Estate
Expected Return ($E[r]$)			
Volatility	20.00%	10.00%	8.00%
Correlation with:			
Stocks	100.00%	60.00%	30.00%
Bonds		100.00%	−10.00%
Real Estate			100.00%

23 Macrolevel Valuation I: Static Property Portfolios

Chapter Outline

Learning Objectives

After reading this chapter, you should understand:

◆ What is meant by the static portfolio concept, and the definition of macrolevel valuation for private real estate.

◆ What is meant by valuation measurement errors at the micro- and macrolevels and the fundamental causes of such errors.

◆ The two major types of valuation errors (noise and temporal lag), the nature of the practical trade-off between these two types of errors, and the difference in the optimal balance in this trade-off between the micro- and macrolevels of valuation.

◆ How and why macrolevel valuation of static portfolios based on microlevel appraisals tends to suffer from a temporal lag bias.

◆ Mass appraisal and how regression-based valuation techniques can improve macrolevel valuation in some circumstances.

The term *valuation* refers to the process of estimating or determining the value of assets. Nothing is more basic than this for the rational analysis of investment decisions. If you don't know how much an asset or portfolio is worth, how can you know how much you should pay for it or sell it for? Moreover, the more you know about how asset market values are determined, the more wisely you can make investment decisions. In Part IV of this book we introduced you to the basics of commercial property valuation from an investment perspective at the microlevel, that is, the valuation of individual properties. In Chapter 22 we introduced you to a fundamental part of the macrolevel valuation problem, namely, the valuation of investment risk. In this chapter and the next, we want to continue our treatment of macrolevel real estate valuation in two important directions: (1) **macrolevel property valuation**, that is, the valuation of passive or static portfolios of properties in the private market; and (2) valuation of actively managed funds or firms that deal in the trading, development, ownership, and operation of dynamic portfolios of properties, as exemplified by the valuation of REITs in the public stock market. The first of these considerations is the focus of the present chapter. REITs will be addressed in Chapter 24.

Before beginning this chapter, we should say a word about the nature of the material it contains. The valuation concepts addressed here are rather deep and subtle, including some fairly technical points. You may find this chapter a bit challenging. We urge you to give it a try anyway because of the fundamental importance of the topic for real estate. But don't get bogged down. While this chapter contains material that is important in its own right, in the big picture the primary role of this chapter in macrolevel real estate investment analysis is to lay the groundwork for Chapter 25. We designed Chapter 25 to be useful without a detailed understanding of all of the points in this chapter.

23.1 MACROLEVEL PROPERTY VALUATION: THE BASIC IDEA

Perhaps the most basic real estate valuation problem at the macrolevel is the valuation of a **static portfolio** of properties. This is sometimes also referred to as a standing portfolio.[1] It is defined as a portfolio consisting of a fixed set of individual properties, in which valuation is based on the private property asset market value. Of course, in this market, individual properties are traded, not whole portfolios at once, so we cannot directly observe the prices of whole portfolios. Conceptually, however, the value of a static portfolio is defined from this perspective simply as *the sum of the values of the individual properties comprising the portfolio*.[2] At a basic level, therefore, we have already covered this topic, in Chapters 10–12, in which we addressed microlevel

---

[1] A little more terminology may be helpful. More informally, what we are focusing on in this section is also sometimes referred to as the bricks and mortar value, or the property (or property-level) value, to distinguish this level of valuation from fund-level valuation or firm-level valuation (e.g., in the case of REITs, in particular). In Chapter 27 we refer to the static portfolio level as the macroproperty level to distinguish it from both the individual (micro) property level and the actively managed dynamic fund level or investment manager level. In England, the IPD refers to this level of valuation as market value, referring, of course, to the private property market. IPD refers to the fund level as the portfolio level (but not meaning a static portfolio), or the investment level.

[2] Note in particular that the static portfolio value is explicitly *not* defined as the price at which we could expect to sell the entire portfolio at once, en masse.

property valuation. However, some additional considerations become important at the macrolevel.

At this level, the focus is on the value of the portfolio as whole, that is, the *cross-sectional sum* of the constituent individual property values, rather than the value of any individual property in the portfolio. The general nature of this problem is therefore that of value *measurement* as distinguished from value *determination* in a causal sense, as the latter is done by the property market at the microlevel.[3] To state our portfolio valuation problem more precisely from a statistical perspective, it is a problem of value *estimation*. That is, the problem is how best to estimate the sum of the current values of a specified set of properties. Alas, depending on how the microlevel valuations are done, this whole will typically not simply equal the sum of the parts, as we will see in the remainder of this chapter.

Unfortunately, we must admit that the concepts and material in this chapter are often rather subtle and technical. We sympathize that they will not be everyone's cup of tea. But if you really want to understand macrolevel real estate valuation, it will be worth your effort to plow ahead and take it one step at a time. We cannot emphasize enough how fundamental this chapter is to building your real estate investment expertise at the macrolevel. Static portfolio valuation is not just an "ivory tower" theoretical concept. It underlies the computation of holding period returns (HPRs) in the private property market and is therefore basic to the quantification of investment performance. Periodic returns are defined as the return within each period of time on a static portfolio. Static portfolios are also necessary, at least in principle, for conducting macro property level performance attribution, a fundamental tool of investment management diagnosis and evaluation. Thus, the concepts presented in this chapter are fundamental to understanding subsequent topics, especially those treated in Chapters 25 and 27.

23.2 MACROLEVEL VALUATION BASED ON OPTIMAL MICROLEVEL VALUATIONS

As of the turn of the century, most commercial real estate valuations are optimized at the microlevel of individual property valuations. Macrolevel portfolio values are thus still largely determined in practice by simply adding individual property valuations that are not optimized for use at the macrolevel. For this reason, we must understand the implications this has for macrolevel valuation.

23.2.1 Some Microlevel Valuation Issues

Understanding macrolevel valuation requires that we first step back and reconsider in a bit more depth some aspects of microlevel valuation that we introduced only briefly in Part IV.[4] Recall in particular four characteristics of private property markets that distinguished them from public securities markets:

---

[3] Thus, value determination in the more fundamental causal sense was addressed primarily in Part IV (building on the earlier Parts I–III), as well as in Chapter 22 (and it will be considered again for REITs in Chapter 24).

[4] In Chapter 12 we delved most deeply into microlevel valuation. A brief review of that chapter, in particular section 12.2.1 and the Chapter 12 appendix, might be useful at this point if your memory of those sections is a bit rusty.

- The market is characterized by the trading of *whole assets* (that is, whole individual properties rather than securities or shares).

- Each individual property (i.e., traded asset) is *unique* at least to some extent (e.g., no two locations are exactly identical, not to mention structures, leases, and other features important in determining commercial property value).

- Each asset is typically traded only *infrequently* and at *irregular* intervals.

- Each trade is negotiated privately between only *one seller* and only *one buyer*.

These four characteristics make it difficult to obtain a clear and precise indication of what the current market value is for any given property at any given time. When trying to estimate the current market value of a subject property, you can observe the prices (or yields, or cap rates) at which similar properties traded in the past. But the traded properties are not identical to the subject property, and, of course, the past is not the same as the present. Because of this, the buyer and seller in any transaction go into their price negotiations with imperfect information about the current market value of the subject property. The result is that the transaction price they agree to generally will contain some unobservable random **noise** component that causes their price to differ from the conceptual definition of the current "market value" for the subject property.[5] This is also true for appraised values. Appraisers, like market participants, can only estimate market values imperfectly based on incomplete information. So appraised values also will tend to be dispersed randomly around the underlying "true" market value for a given property as of a given time.[6]

The chart in Exhibit 23-1 portrays this point graphically. The horizontal axis measures empirically observable value indications relevant to a given property (or type of property) as of a given time. These could be either transaction prices or (independent) appraised values, in principle all occurring at the same time. The vertical axis represents the theoretical (or ex ante) frequency with which we would expect to observe such value indications.[7] The mean of this theoretical frequency distribution is the true market

[5] Recall from Chapter 12 that the definition of market value is the price at which the subject property would be *expected* to sell in the current market. In more formal statistical terms, this is the *mean* of the contemporaneous cross-sectional transaction price distribution, that is, the *ex ante* expectation of the sale price of the subject property as of a given point in time. (See the Chapter 12 appendix for a more in-depth discussion.)

[6] Consider the following experiment. Hire two appraisers to appraise the same property as of the same point in time. Make sure the two appraisers cannot communicate, so their appraisals are made independently of one another. Do you think the two appraisers will come up with the same estimate of value? Not likely. Therefore, one, or both, of the appraisers *must* be wrong because conceptually there can be only one true market value of a given property as of a given point in time. Of course, this type of random dispersion in contemporaneous appraised values does not imply that either one of the appraisers has actually done anything wrong, or that one is better than the other. In fact, academic researchers are beginning to study appraiser behavior more scientifically, including the valuation dispersion phenomenon. We noted in a box in Chapter 12 that experiments and statistical analysis of appraisals have begun to give some indication of the magnitude of this type of cross-sectional dispersion. We suggested there that preliminary indications are that the typical standard deviation of random valuation dispersion is probably in the range of 5% to 10% of property value for typical commercial property appraisals in the United States, although some claim the random error is lower in indices such as the NPI. (This is suggested by the relatively smooth appearance of the NPI even for small subindices containing only a few dozen properties.) From the limited evidence currently available, it is difficult to say whether significantly more cross-sectional dispersion exists in transaction prices or in appraised values.

[7] The frequency distribution shown in Exhibit 23-1 is not referred to as an ex ante distribution because it is perceived prior to its realization in time. After all, Exhibit 23-1 depicts a "snapshot," only one point

Exhibit 23-1 Theoretical Cross-Sectional Dispersion in Observable Value Indications

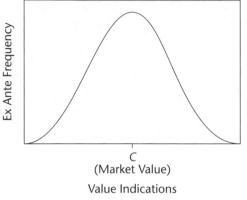

value of the subject property (or type of property) as of the given time. This is the point indicated in the middle of the horizontal axis, labeled C for consistency with the nomenclature used in the Chapter 12 appendix.

In reality we cannot observe the theoretical frequency distribution shown in Exhibit 23-1. We can only observe an empirical sample of value indications, the transactions or appraisals that happen to actually occur and get recorded, that are relevant to the subject property. Suppose, for now, that all of the observations in this empirical sample depict value indications as of the same time and are drawn randomly or representatively from the same type of property, namely, the subject type of property. Then the arithmetic mean of such a cross-sectional sample of value indication observations will be an unbiased estimator of the market value C as of the given time.

For example, suppose that the true market value is \$1,000,000, that is, $C =$ \$1,000,000. Of course, this underlying theoretical value is not empirically observable (by definition, as noted above). Suppose further that our only empirical data consists of three transaction price observations, which we will label V_1, V_2, and V_3. In other words, the size of our empirical sample, labeled n, is three: $n = 3$. In the appraisal profession, the transaction prices of properties similar to the subject property would be referred to as **comps** in the present context, short for "comparable properties." In particular, suppose that our three comps happen to be $V_1 =$ \$900,000, $V_2 =$ \$950,000, and $V_3 =$ \$1,100,000. The average value indication from the empirically available information is therefore \$983,333, computed as the cross-sectional sample arithmetic mean, as indicated in equation (1) by the "estimator" labeled $\overline{V}$:[8]

$$\overline{V} = \left(\frac{1}{n}\right)\sum_{i=1}^{n} V_i = \left(\frac{1}{3}\right)(900,000 + 950,000 + 1,100,000) = \$983,333 \qquad (1)$$

in time, so it says nothing about what happens before or after that point. Rather, the distribution is referred to as ex ante because it exists conceptually or theoretically in the entire relevant statistical "population," which in this case is a conceptual construct referring to all of the *potential* value indications that one could conceivably observe across an infinite number of independent appraisals or independent transactions of the subject property (or subject *type* of property) as of the same. This is, effectively speaking from the perspective of the statistical construct, an *infinite* population, and the frequency distribution is a marginal probability (or probability "density") distribution.

[8]Assume either that all four properties (including the subject property) are identical, or else that cross-sectional differences among the properties (such as size and age) have been somehow adjusted for, so that the value indications we have are for equivalent properties.

This cross-sectional average value of $\overline{V}$ = \$983,333 is therefore our best estimate for the (unobservable) true market value, C. However, unlike in the real world, we can "cheat" in this pedagogical example, so we know that the C in this case actually equals \$1,000,000, not \$983,333. The "error" in our estimate is therefore −\$16,667 in this case, or approximately 1.7% below the true value. Of course, this error does not necessarily imply that any of the parties to any of the three observable transactions did anything wrong, or that we did anything wrong by taking the average of the three prices as our best estimate for the true market value. It simply reflects the random noise that exists in empirical indications of real estate values. In this case, the error happened to be −1.7%. In another case it might be +1.7%, or +5%, or whatever.

It is important to reiterate that in the real world the \$1,000,000 true market value in this example would be unobservable and unknown. No one could know it, and therefore no one could compute the error as we just did. But this does not mean that the true market value does not exist in a conceptual sense, or that it is not important in practical reality. Indeed, C is more important than $\overline{V}$ in a sense, because if you own a property like our subject property, then C, not $\overline{V}$, is the most likely price at which you would be able to sell your property.[9] The true market value is the opportunity cost of holding your property as of the given time. In fact, $\overline{V}$ is not even equal to the actual price at which any one of the three comparable transactions took place, as you can see. In the end, the best we can say about $\overline{V}$ is only that it is the best estimate we can make for C, the number we really would like to know, as of this time.

For this reason, the "error" in $\overline{V}$, that is, the unobservable difference between $\overline{V}$ and C, is important not only conceptually but also in practice. Indeed, from a very practical perspective, we would like to minimize the expected magnitude of this error (other things being equal, anyway).

The science of statistics can begin to help us out a bit here. A very basic statistical fact states that the average (or ex ante) magnitude of the error we are concerned about here can be reduced if we can get a larger empirical sample. In other words, $\overline{V}$ will tend to be a more precise estimator of C if we can get more value indication observations, more comps, at least provided that all the observations are independent and drawn from the same underlying population (that is, representing the same type of property as of the same time).

The basic statistical principle we are using here is often called the Law of Large Numbers, or more precisely, the **Square Root of n Rule**. This latter name derives from the fact that the standard deviation of the theoretical dispersion of the mean of a sample around the mean of the underlying population from which the sample is drawn is *inversely* proportional to the square root of the size of the sample, n. Thus, for example, a sample of size n = 12 would tend to have only half as much typical magnitude of error as a sample of size n = 3 (because: 12 = 4 × 3, and $\sqrt{4}$ = 2).[10]

[9] Similarly, if you do not own a property like our subject property but you are in the market to buy such a property, C and not $\overline{V}$ is the most likely price you will have to pay.

[10] In fact, another statistical fact about the sample mean is that it not only has a standard deviation inversely proportional to $\sqrt{n}$, but it tends to have a particular probability distribution, namely, the bell-shaped "normal" (or "Gaussian") distribution, regardless of the frequency distribution of the value statistic in the underlying population. (This is the famous central limit theorem, or CLT, which statistics professors find very exciting.)

This has an obvious practical implication for estimating property market values at the microlevel. More accurate value estimation requires larger samples of empirical evidence. Thus, from an appraiser's perspective, using more comps is beneficial.[11]

Furthermore, the Square Root of n Rule has a corollary implication at the macrolevel. The sample size n that is relevant for portfolio valuation is not the average sample size used at the microlevel in the valuations of the individual properties that make up the portfolio. Rather, it is the total number of (independent) value indication observations used across all of the properties in the portfolio that matters at the macrolevel. For example, if a portfolio has 10 properties, and each property was evaluated independently using 3 comps (without overlap), then the sample size that is relevant at the macrolevel of the portfolio as a whole is 30, not 3. Thus, *the Square Root of* n *Rule is more effective at the macrolevel than at the microlevel.* But alas, things begin to get a bit more complicated in the real world.

*23.2.2 The Real World, the Time Dimension, and the Difference between Micro- and Macrolevel Valuation Errors

The real world of property valuation complicates the picture described previously. First, consider the fact that no two properties are identical. For this reason, when appraisers (or anyone else for that matter) use transaction price information from comps, they have to try to adjust the observable transaction prices to reflect cross-sectional idiosyncratic differences between the comps and the subject property.[12] Second (and even more important at the macrolevel), in the real world there is a fourth dimension: time. In the simple world depicted in the previous section we assumed only one point in time and that all the empirical value indications occurred at this one point in time. With only one point in time, the true market value of any given property (and hence the value of a static portfolio of properties) is unique and unambiguous. But in the real world, the true market value of any given property or portfolio changes over time, and the relevant transaction prices or appraised values are observed at different points in time, thereby providing value indications as of different points in time.

The effect of time is depicted in Exhibit 23-2, which shows time on the horizontal axis, property value on the vertical axis, and probability (or empirical observation frequency) in a third dimension figuratively coming up out of the page. The solid line between the Cs traces changes in the market value over time, indicated by the different value levels of C at the ends of consecutive calendar quarters. Such changes that purely reflect the time dimension are often referred to as **longitudinal** variation.

[11]However, this benefit is declining on the margin because accuracy only increases with the *square root* of n, not directly proportional to n. You gain less additional accuracy from one more comp than you did from the previous comp. Of course, the cost of finding and verifying additional comps (in terms of the appraiser's time and expense) may not be declining on the margin, at least after some number of comps is found. In practice, appraisals of commercial property are typically based explicitly on only a few sales comps, with three to five being perhaps the most common sample size.

[12]In performing this exercise manually, you always adjust each comp's value indication *toward the subject property*. For example, if the comp is better than the subject property, say, by 10%, then you would divide the comp's transaction price by 1.10 to arrive at an adjusted value indication for the comp. This way, when all of the comps' prices have been adjusted for differences between themselves and the subject property, the adjusted value indications can be viewed as a cross-sectional sample of value indications directly relevant to the subject property, the type of sample that can be averaged as in equation (1) to produce a value estimate for the subject property.

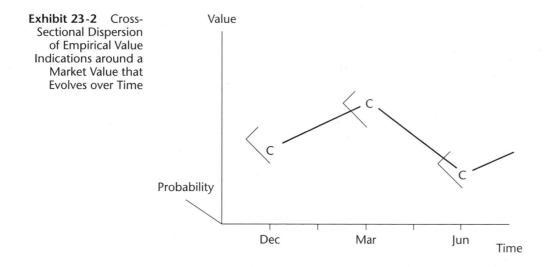

The empirical frequency distributions around each quarterly value of *C* (figuratively coming up out of the page on vertical lines corresponding to the ends of each quarter) indicate the cross-sectional dispersion in empirical value indications within each period of time. Differences across observations within a given point in time are referred to as **cross-sectional variation**.

Exhibit 23-2 would apply even if there were very little substantive differences between individual properties. As we noted in section 23.2.1, transaction prices or appraised values will exhibit random noise even for virtually identical properties simply due to the "thin" and private nature of the real estate market. But cross-sectional heterogeneity in properties exacerbates this problem. The more different properties are, the more difficult it is to use the transaction price of one property to make inferences about the market value of another property.

With this in mind, we should distinguish between two sorts of differences between any given subject property and its relevant comps, differences that appraisers must consider and try to adjust for in the real world: cross-sectional differences and temporal differences. The former are differences in the characteristics of the properties themselves, including physical qualities and size, location, the nature of leases and tenants, and so forth. In contrast, temporal differences refers to the fact that the comps will all have sold in the past, prior to the time at which the subject property is to be appraised. The true market value of the subject property will normally have changed over the relevant time span.

Appraisers adjust for both of these differences, but their adjustments are not perfect. In principle, the adjustment process reduces the typical overall magnitude of error in the appraisal estimation, but even in so doing the adjustment process becomes itself another source of error, in addition to the underlying random noise that exists in the raw transaction prices.

Whatever the source of appraisal error, let us now consider the nature of such error a bit more carefully. Recall, first, that the error we are referring to does not necessarily imply that appraisers are doing anything wrong. **Error**, in this sense, simply reflects the difference between the appraised value and the (unobservable) true market value.

In general, from a statistical perspective, it is useful to distinguish two potential types or components of appraisal error:

1. Purely random errors (aka "noise")
2. **Bias**, a systematic component of error that is common across all appraisals

Distinguishing these two types of errors is important because *only the purely random type of error is subject to the Square Root of n Rule.* Purely random errors become less and less important the larger the empirical observation sample. As noted, this effect can occur at either (or both) the micro- and macrolevel, either in the sample used to value each property or in the total sample represented by all of the properties in a portfolio being evaluated at the macrolevel. We noted that for this reason the Square Root of n Rule is more powerful in portfolio valuation. As a result, purely random error is less important at the macrolevel than it is at the microlevel.

In contrast, bias is not diminished by the sample size at either the micro- or macrolevel. For example, bias would occur if the estimated property value displayed a systematic tendency to be too high, or, alternatively, if it tended to be too low. Another example of bias would be if appraised values tended to lag in time behind true changes in market value.[13] The existence of bias implies that no matter how many empirical value indications we have to work with, our estimate of value will tend to be wrong as of the current point in time.

We can summarize the previous points in an important principle regarding the difference between micro- and macrolevel valuation:

Purely random error ("noise") is relatively more important at the microlevel (the "disaggregate" or individual property level), while systematic error ("bias") is relatively more important at the macrolevel (the "aggregate" or portfolio level).

*23.2.3 Optimal Valuation at the Micro- versus Macrolevel: The Problem of Temporal Aggregation

This principle has an important practical implication. It means that the value estimation procedure that is optimal at the microlevel of individual property appraisal may not be optimal at the macrolevel for estimating the value of an entire portfolio of many properties. If a trade-off exists between reducing random error and reducing bias, the optimal balance in such a trade-off will be different between the micro- and macrolevels.

In fact, such a trade-off does exist. To see what this is, we need to understand more about the nature of value estimation bias in real estate. To begin with, note that as there are two major types of differences between comps and the subject property that appraisers must adjust for, so there are two major sources of bias: cross-sectional and temporal. Let's consider each of these in turn.

The major culprit in the cross-sectional source of bias is what is often called sample-selection bias. This occurs if the comps tend to be drawn from a population

---

[13] In this case, appraised values would not be biased in a very long-term average, for example, over an entire cycle of property market values. (In a formal statistical sense, appraisals would be "asymptotically" or "unconditionally" unbiased.) However, appraisals would be biased at any given time (that is, they would be "conditionally biased," or in general biased in "finite samples" of time).

of properties that is cross-sectionally different in a systematic way from the subject property. To take a simple example, if we were trying to estimate the value of a subject property in Dallas, and all of our comps were in Houston, we would likely be susceptible to sample-selection bias. No doubt the appraiser would try to adjust for the difference between the Houston and Dallas property markets as best he could, but this adjustment would probably be imperfect, especially as the appraiser has no comps in Dallas to compare with the Houston comps. In this case, the appraiser might tend to underadjust for the difference between Dallas and Houston. His estimate of the value of the Dallas property would probably tend to lie somewhere between the actual Dallas market value and the actual Houston market value. Such a result can also be expressed as a weighted average between the true Dallas market value and the *appraised* value the appraiser would have estimated for the same property in Houston.

The temporal source of bias is often referred to as **temporal aggregation bias**.[14] To take a simple example, suppose the property market has recently turned around. In particular, suppose asset market prices had been rising or holding steady for a couple of years, and then suddenly the market turned sharply down within the past couple of months. The appraiser will no doubt be aware of this change. The trade press will be full of reports of deals falling apart and capital flowing out of commercial real estate. But the appraiser will have few, if any, actual transaction comps from the past couple of months to work with, and she will be unsure about how much values have fallen in general, or how relevant the general market downturn is for her unique subject property in particular.[15] Almost all of the empirical value indications available to the appraiser will be from the period of high prices earlier than two months ago. The appraiser will no doubt try to adjust her value estimate to reflect the new market, but her adjustment will tend to be imperfect, probably tending to underadjust. Her value estimate will probably end up falling somewhere between the actual current market value and the market value at a previous point in time. Such a result can also be expressed as a weighted average between the true current market value and a prior *appraised* value the same appraiser might have estimated for the same property at a time not too far in the past.

Now notice that in our description of the two sources of valuation bias in the preceding paragraphs there was a common element. In both cases we suggested that the appraiser was likely to underadjust for the true market value difference. Conceptually, however, bias need not necessarily involve underadjustment. By definition, bias is systematic error, so it must involve either a tendency to underadjust or a tendency to overadjust. (No tendency in either direction implies no bias, only purely random error.) But in fact, underadjustment is "rational," while overadjustment is irrational, and this distinction is stronger from a microlevel valuation perspective than from a macrolevel perspective.

To begin to see this point, let us consider a simple example of temporal bias. Suppose an appraiser can observe four comps transactions, two occurring in the current

[14] At the microlevel of individual property appraisals, temporal aggregation bias is often referred to as disaggregate-level appraisal smoothing. At the macrolevel of portfolio or index valuation, temporal aggregation bias is often referred to as the stale appraisal effect. Both of these concepts will be treated in more depth in Chapter 25.

[15] Note the treacherous interaction of the two sources of error: cross-sectional differences between properties and temporal changes in the market. The more unique the subject property is, the more difficult it is to make precise inferences about the subject property based on general market trends evident for other properties.

Nomenclature and Labeling Convention for Valuation Error Terms in Chapters 23 and 25

ε = (Observed Value) − (True Value) = "Theoretical Error"

Examples: $\varepsilon_{i,t} = V_{i,t} - C_{i,t}$, $\varepsilon_t = \overline{V}_t - C_t$

e = (Observed Value) − (Estimated Value) = "Residual"

Examples: $e_{i,t} = V_{i,t} - \hat{V}_{i,t}$, $e_{i,t} = V_{i,t} - V^*_{i,t}$

u = (Estimated Value) − (True Value) = "Estimation Error"

Examples: $u_{i,t} = \hat{V}_{i,t} - C_{i,t}$, $u_{i,t} = V^*_{i,t} - C_{i,t}$, sometimes $u_{i,t} = \overline{V}_{i,t} - C_{i,t}$

$\eta_t = \varepsilon_t - \varepsilon_{t-1}$ = First difference in errors (across time)

where

$C_{i,t}$ = Theoretical "true" value of "Asset i" as of time "t" (unobservable, by definition).

$V_{i,t}$ = Empirically observed value of "Asset i" as of time "t".

$\overline{V}_t$ = Average of observed values (across assets) as of t (equals observed value of the average, or may serve as estimate of individual true value $C_{i,t}$).

$\hat{V}_{i,t}$ = Statistical regression-based estimate of $C_{i,t}$.

$V^*_{i,t}$ = Appraisal-based estimate of $C_{i,t}$.

---

period and two occurring in the previous period. To simplify this example we will further suppose that the appraiser can adjust perfectly for cross-sectional differences between the properties, but he cannot adjust at all for temporal differences in the market. In other words, we can think of all four properties as being, for practical purposes, identical. However, random transaction noise is still a factor, and a real change in the market value of the subject property has occurred between the last period and the current period. In this simplified world, consider the optimal value estimate for the subject property from a microlevel perspective and from a macrolevel perspective. In particular, let's focus on the question of whether the appraiser should use all four available comps, or only the two from the current period.

To develop this example formally, we need to introduce some notation. Let $V_{i,s}$ be the empirically observed transaction price of comp i (where i = 1,2), which transacted in period s (where $s = t$ or $t - 1$, where t is the current period). Let C_t be the (unobservable) true market value (of both the subject property and the comps) as of the current period, and let $C_{t-1} = C_t - g_t$ be the similarly defined market value as of the previous period (where g_t is the market value appreciation during period t). Finally, let $\varepsilon_{i,s}$ be the purely random transaction price noise in comp i transacting in period s, defined as $\varepsilon_{i,s} = V_{i,s} - C_s$, for i = 1,2, and $s = t, t - 1$.

Now suppose the appraiser uses only the two comps transacting in the current period. His sample size will be n = 2, and his value estimation for the subject property as of the current period t, labeled V^*_t, will be as follows:

$$V_t^* = \left(\frac{1}{2}\right)(V_{1,t} + V_{2,t})$$

$$= \left(\frac{1}{2}\right)[(C_t + \varepsilon_{1,t}) + (C_t + \varepsilon_{2,t})]$$

$$= \left(\frac{1}{2}\right)(C_t + C_t) + \left(\frac{1}{2}\right)(\varepsilon_{1,t} + \varepsilon_{2,t}) \tag{2}$$

$$= C_t + \left(\frac{1}{2}\right)(\varepsilon_{1,t} + \varepsilon_{2,t})$$

Notice that the appraised value equals the current true market value plus a random error term that consists purely of transaction noise, with $n = 2$. Thus, the appraisal is an unbiased estimate of the current true market value. Since the expected value of random noise is always zero ($E[\varepsilon_{i,s}] = 0$), this lack of bias can be seen by taking expectations of both sides of (2):

$$E[V_t^*] = E[C_t + \left(\frac{1}{2}\right)(\varepsilon_{1,t} + \varepsilon_{2,t})]$$

$$= E[C_t] + \left(\frac{1}{2}\right)[E(\varepsilon_{1,t}) + E(\varepsilon_{2,t})] \tag{2a}$$

$$= E[C_t] + \left(\frac{1}{2}\right)(0 + 0)$$

$$= E[C_t]$$

Next suppose the appraiser uses all four comps, equally weighted, as follows:

$$V_t^* = \left(\frac{1}{4}\right)(V_{1,t} + V_{2,t} + V_{1,t-1} + V_{2,t-1})$$

$$= \left(\frac{1}{4}\right)[(C_t + \varepsilon_{1,t}) + (C_t + \varepsilon_{2,t}) + (C_{t-1} + \varepsilon_{1,t-1}) + (C_{t-1} + \varepsilon_{2,t-1})] \tag{3}$$

$$= \left(\frac{1}{4}\right)(C_t + C_t + C_{t-1} + C_{t-1}) + \left(\frac{1}{4}\right)(\varepsilon_{1,t} + \varepsilon_{2,t} + \varepsilon_{1,t-1} + \varepsilon_{2,t-1})$$

$$= \left(\frac{1}{2}\right)C_t + \left(\frac{1}{2}\right)C_{t-1} + \left(\frac{1}{4}\right)(\varepsilon_{1,t} + \varepsilon_{2,t} + \varepsilon_{1,t-1} + \varepsilon_{2,t-1})$$

Now compare equations (2) and (3). When the appraiser uses all four comps, he has $n = 4$ for the random noise component of his value estimation. This is twice as large a sample, so the accuracy of the appraisal is improved by a factor of the square root of two as compared to equation (2), as far as purely random error is concerned.

But the appraiser's estimate using all four comps is no longer unbiased. The appraisal estimate now suffers from temporal aggregation bias because the systematic component of the appraisal consists of a one-half weight on the current true market value plus a one-half weight on the previous period's true market value. The appraised value will tend to fall between the current period's true market value and the previous true market value. In other words, the appraised value will be biased by a tendency to lag behind the true market value in time. This is seen here:

$$E[V_t^*] = E\left[\left(\frac{1}{2}\right)C_t + \left(\frac{1}{2}\right)C_{t-1} + \left(\frac{1}{4}\right)(\varepsilon_{1,t} + \varepsilon_{2,t} + \varepsilon_{1,t-1} + \varepsilon_{2,t-1})\right]$$

$$= \left(\frac{1}{2}\right)E[C_t] + \left(\frac{1}{2}\right)E[C_{t-1}] + \left(\frac{1}{4}\right)(E[\varepsilon_{1,t}] + E[\varepsilon_{2,t}] + E[\varepsilon_{1,t-1}] + E[\varepsilon_{2,t-1}])$$

$$= \left(\frac{1}{2}\right)E[C_t] + \left(\frac{1}{2}\right)E[C_{t-1}] + \left(\frac{1}{4}\right)(0 + 0 + 0 + 0)$$

$$= \left(\frac{1}{2}\right)E[C_t] + \left(\frac{1}{2}\right)E[C_{t-1}] \tag{3a}$$

Defining the valuation error as: u_t, and bias as the expectation of this error, we see from equation (3a) that the bias when all four comps are used is

$$E[u_t] = E[V_t^* - C_t] = E[V_t^*] - E[C_t]$$

$$= \left(\frac{1}{2}\right)E[C_t] + \left(\frac{1}{2}\right)E[C_{t-1}] - E[C_t]$$

$$= \left(\frac{1}{2}\right)E[C_{t-1}] - \left(\frac{1}{2}\right)E[C_t]$$

Only if the property market value is constant through time ($E[C_t] = E[C_{t-1}]$, or more generally; $E[C_t] = E[C_s]$, for all $s \neq t$), will the four-comps procedure of (3a) produce an unbiased estimate of the current market value.

Thus, *at the microlevel of individual property appraisal, there is a trade-off between minimizing purely random error and minimizing bias.* The larger is the number of comps the appraiser uses (the larger the sample size n), the smaller will be the purely random error component in the appraisal. But, other things being equal, in order to use more comps, the appraiser must reach farther back in time, and/or go farther afield in space, in order to find the additional comps. This increases the bias component in the appraisal. The optimal appraisal procedure strikes a balance between these two error components.

The optimal balance is different between the micro and macro valuation levels because, as noted previously, the relative importance of the two error components is different at the micro- and macrolevels. Consider our previous simple example again. Suppose the appraiser uses the estimation procedure represented by equation (2) instead of that represented by equation (3). In other words, suppose the appraiser deliberately avoids using some available comps that are "old" and instead uses a smaller sample of comps that are entirely current. His valuation will contain more purely random noise, but no temporal aggregation bias. But the purely random noise will tend to diversify out of the aggregate valuation of a large portfolio containing many individual properties that have been appraised independently. So, while the larger-sample method represented by equation (3) may be preferable to the smaller-sample method represented by equation (2) for the purpose of individual property valuation (due to the need to minimize random error), equation (2) will definitely be preferable to equation (3) for the purpose of using such an appraisal as a component in an aggregate valuation of a sufficiently large portfolio.[16]

The previous example focuses on temporal bias. What about cross-sectional bias? In principle, cross-sectional bias is analogous to the temporal example we just described. But in practice, cross-sectional bias is often considered to be less of a problem in terms of the difference between optimal micro- and macrolevel valuation. Fundamentally, this is because we can move in all directions in three-dimensional space, whereas we can only move in one direction in one-dimensional time.

To see this point, let's go back to our example in which the appraiser does not have enough comps in Dallas so he includes evidence from some Houston transactions to improve (i.e., reduce the random noise component in) his valuation of Dallas properties. But in fact, if Dallas does not have enough comps, the appraiser is not restricted only to looking in Houston to expand his sample of comps. If he thinks values in Houston are lower than values in Dallas, then he can probably find another city, say, Chicago, in which values are higher than in Dallas. Then the appraiser can expand his sample in *both directions*, including both Houston and Chicago, thereby mitigating the cross-sectional bias. Thus, cross-sectional bias is not an inevitable result of the need to reduce microlevel valuation noise by the expansion of the comps sample.

If the appraiser fails to include Chicago, however, not only are his Dallas valuations biased, but also the resulting noise reduction in his Dallas valuations (the reason for his causing the bias) is no greater in a macrolevel portfolio of many Dallas properties than it is at the microlevel of an individual Dallas property valuation. If, say, the appraiser adds five comps in Houston to the sample of Dallas comps, then those *same* five comps are added to *every* Dallas property that is valued. Thus, no matter how many properties are in the Dallas portfolio, the sample size (n) is expanded by no more at the macrolevel than it is at the microlevel for any individual property valuation. For example, suppose there are 50 properties in our Dallas portfolio and there are two Dallas sales comps. Then the comps sample size for each individual

---

[16] For this conclusion to be definite, we have to assume that a sufficient number of properties (and cross-sectionally independent appraisals) in the portfolio ensure that at the macrolevel n is effectively large enough to eliminate any need to worry about random noise for practical purposes. In practice, this will often be the case, typically once the portfolio contains several dozen properties. At the microlevel the choice between the valuation approach represented by equation (2) versus (3) can be formalized by defining an objective function, such as the minimization of the ex ante mean squared error of the individual property appraisal. Then the preference for (2) versus (3) at the microlevel will depend on the relative magnitude of the cross-sectional dispersion in the purely random error component (the ε_i terms), as compared to the magnitude of the longitudinal dispersion (i.e., the appreciation volatility) in the true market value (the g_s terms). The relative preference for (2) versus (3) may also depend on the purpose and function of the appraisal estimate. For example, the appraiser's client may be more interested in an extensive documentation of the average market value across time (the larger the n, the better the documentation), rather than in a more up-to-date but less well-documented (and more error-prone) estimate that would result from a smaller sample of comps as in equation (2).

property valuation is $n = 2 + 5 = 7$. These same seven comps also represent the total comps sample for the entire 50-property portfolio. Suppose the cross-sectional dispersion in transaction prices has a standard deviation of $\pm 10\%$. Then the addition of the bias-inducing extra comps reduces the standard error in the valuation from $\pm 10\%/\sqrt{2} = \pm 7.1\%$, to $\pm 10\%/\sqrt{7} = \pm 3.8\%$, a reduction of $\pm 3.3\%$ in random error, the *same reduction at both the micro- and macrolevels*.[17]

Now contrast this situation with that of temporal bias. Substitute the word *past* for the word *Houston*, the word *present* for the word *Dallas*, and the word *future* for the word *Chicago*. The appraiser doesn't have enough comps in the present, so, in order to reduce noise in his present valuation estimates, he goes to the past for more comps. But note now that this is the *only* direction in which he can go in order to expand his observation sample, *backwards* in time, into the past. Since he cannot get any comps from the future, temporal bias is inevitable.

But what about the noise reduction benefit? When the appraiser decided he lacked sufficient comps in the present and so had to go back in time for more, this decision was made from a microlevel perspective. Suppose there are only two current comps for each property in the portfolio. These two comps are likely to be different for each different type and location of property. The more cross-sectional heterogeneity there is among the individual properties that are being appraised (and the greater the number of appraisers involved), the less overlap there will be among the current comps. Yet this type of cross-sectional diversity is inherent in the nature of a portfolio. *Portfolios are cross-sectional aggregations, not temporal aggregations*. As a result, when the individual property appraisals are aggregated together at the portfolio level, the overall macrolevel sample size is probably large enough so that it benefits very little in terms of noise reduction as a result of adding comps from the past.

To make this point more concrete, suppose, as before, that the portfolio contains 50 properties, and each property's appraisal is based on two current comps plus five past comps. And suppose (to take an admittedly extreme case) there is no cross-sectional overlap in comps. Then, as we saw before, the microlevel noise reduction is from a standard error of 7.1% to a standard error of 3.8%, a noise reduction of 330 basis points. At the macrolevel, however, the sample expansion is from $n = 50 \times 2 = 100$, to $n = 50 \times 7 = 350$, so the noise reduction is from $\pm 10\%/\sqrt{100} = \pm 1.0\%$, to $\pm 10\%/\sqrt{350} = \pm 0.5\%$, a noise reduction of only 50 basis points. It may have been worth it to take on the temporal bias at the microlevel to eliminate 330 basis points of standard error. But the temporal bias is just as great at the macrolevel in the portfolio valuation as it is at the microlevel in the individual property appraisals, while the noise reduction benefit is much less. It may not be worth the bias to eliminate only 50 basis points of noise, especially when the standard error without any bias is only $\pm 1\%$.[18]

---

[17]Other Dallas appraisers might go to other cities besides Houston to expand their comps samples so that the total comps sample size in the aggregate Dallas portfolio might expand by more than five. But if this were the case, then, unless Dallas is uniquely the *most* valuable city in the country, there will also tend to be no bias at the macrolevel. In such a circumstance we actually have only cross-sectional noise and no cross-sectional systematic error or bias, so it is meaningless to speak in terms of a noise-versus-bias trade-off. Obviously, if there is no trade-off, it makes sense to minimize noise. (And of course Dallas, or any one city, is unlikely to be *the* most valuable city in the country.)

[18]While this numerical example is greatly simplified, the numbers used here are in the ballpark of what is typical in the real world, except that there would be, of course, some overlap in the comps relevant to the valuation of the individual properties in a portfolio.

This fundamental difference between temporal and cross-sectional sources of bias tends to make temporal bias the major concern in the macrolevel valuation of static portfolios based on microlevel appraisals, in which the portfolio is viewed as the entire population of interest.[19]

This result, and the discussion in this and the preceding section, is summarized visually in Exhibit 23-3. The two boxes at the top of the exhibit represent the two types of considerations appraisers must address as potential sources of error: cross-sectional differences among properties and among transactions, and temporal differences (changes) in the relevant property market as a whole. The two boxes at the bottom of the exhibit represent the two types or components of valuation errors that result at the individual property level: noise and bias. The solid arrows on the right-hand side indicate that market changes and the resulting temporal bias are relatively more important in macrolevel valuation, whereas cross-sectional differences and random error tend to be more important at the microlevel.

The result is that optimal valuation procedures are different, in principle, between micro- and macrolevel valuation, at least regarding the trade-off between random error and temporal bias. However, appraisers are not hired to appraise entire portfolios. They are hired to value individual properties, *even when those properties are held as part of*

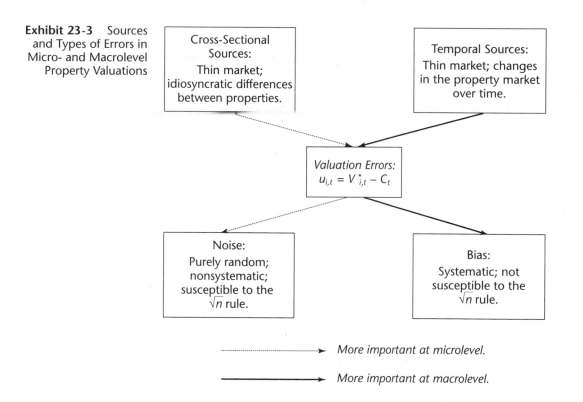

Exhibit 23-3 Sources and Types of Errors in Micro- and Macrolevel Property Valuations

Cross-Sectional Sources:
Thin market; idiosyncratic differences between properties.

Temporal Sources:
Thin market; changes in the property market over time.

Valuation Errors:
$u_{i,t} = V^*_{i,t} - C_t$

Noise:
Purely random; nonsystematic; susceptible to the $\sqrt{n}$ rule.

Bias:
Systematic; not susceptible to the $\sqrt{n}$ rule.

········► *More important at microlevel.*

———► *More important at macrolevel.*

[19] Cross-sectional bias is indeed a major concern in direct macrolevel valuation based on regression analysis, in which selection bias in the transaction price sample on which the regression is estimated may be a major concern. This issue will be addressed later. For now, we can focus on temporal bias as the major type of bias that is of concern in static portfolio valuations built up from microlevel appraisals of all of the constituent properties in the portfolio.

a portfolio or fund. As a result, property funds and entities producing commercial property indices must use individual appraisals to construct portfolio values. Thus, macrolevel valuation typically uses microlevel raw material that is not optimized for the macrolevel. In principle, adjustments at the macrolevel could improve the accuracy at that level, in general, to render the portfolio valuations more up-to-date. To understand this adjustment process, and how valuation procedures that are more optimal at the macrolevel can be developed, we must consider the nature of the microlevel appraisal process in more depth. In so doing, we will return to the point we raised earlier, that underadjustment is optimal behavior for microlevel valuation.

*23.2.4 Relationship between Appraised Values and Transaction Prices: Rational Behavior

As noted previously, the trade-off between purely random error and temporal aggregation bias at the microlevel involves finding an optimal balance between these two error components. In principle, this problem can be solved rationally. Here the term *rational* refers to optimal estimation in the sense of minimizing the ex ante mean squared error in the estimate. The trade-off we have described can be viewed as an exercise in optimal estimation in the presence of uncertainty and new information. This is the type of problem that a branch of statistics known as Bayesian statistics is designed to address. In this case, Bayesian statistics tells us how to optimally balance the new information provided by current comps and the old information represented by previous comps, given that noise (or uncertainty) surrounds both sources of information.

In a couple of famous articles, Professors Dan Quan and John Quigley applied Bayesian statistics to demonstrate that underadjustment represents rational behavior on the part of appraisers, at least as far as temporal aggregation is concerned.[20] In particular, under some simplifying assumptions, they showed that the following **partial adjustment model** is optimal for real estate value estimation:

$$V_t^* = \alpha \overline{V}_t + (1 - \alpha)V_{t-1}^* \tag{4a}$$

where V_t^* is the optimal appraisal for a given property as of period t, $\overline{V}_t$ is the current period's empirical value indication (e.g., from the transaction prices of current comps only), and α is a parameter whose value ranges between 0 (zero) and 1. In the **Quan-Quigley model** (which we will label **Q2** for short), the value of α depends on the ratio of the longitudinal variance in market value divided by the sum of the that variance plus the cross-sectional variance in the transaction price dispersion:

$$\alpha = \frac{VAR[g_s]}{VAR[g_s] + VAR[\varepsilon_i]} \tag{4b}$$

When you recognize that the previous appraised value is itself a function of older comp prices, it becomes clear that the Q2 model suggests that optimal appraisal is a **moving average** of transaction prices. Indeed, equation (4a) is called a first-order

---

[20] See Quan and Quigley (1989, 1991). A similar result was obtained in a slightly different theoretical model by Childs, Ott and Riddiough (2000).

autoregressive model because the current appraised value is a function of the previous period's appraised value. Expanding equation (4a), we see that it is equivalent to the following exponentially declining infinite moving average of current and past transaction prices of comps:

$$V_t^* = \alpha \overline{V}_t + \alpha(1 - \alpha)\overline{V}_{t-1} + \alpha(1 - \alpha)^2 \overline{V}_{t-2} + \alpha(1 - \alpha)^3 \overline{V}_{t-3} + \cdots \qquad (4c)$$

In this form, the Q2 model can be seen to be equivalent to a **simple exponential smoothing** model of the periodic transaction price value indications.[21]

The key parameter in the Q2 model is the adjustment parameter, here labeled α. The larger is α (closer to 1), the less lagged and smoothed will be the appraisal. This is most apparent by examination of equation (4a). Note that if $\alpha = 1$, then $V_t^* = \overline{V}_t$, and the appraised value is based purely on contemporaneous transaction price information.

With this in mind, the intuition in the **ratio of variances** formulation for α, expressed in equation (4b), is easy to see. If (or when) the real estate market has more asset price volatility (larger $VAR\{g_t\}$), then current market values will be more likely to differ from previous values. For this reason the appraiser should pay more attention to whatever current empirical market information is available (namely, the $\overline{V}_t$ value). If (or when) the current empirical value indications from the market are noisier (larger cross-sectional price dispersion, implying a larger typical magnitude of empirical observation "error," $VAR\{\varepsilon_i\}$), then current prices provide less information about the market. For this reason the appraiser should pay less attention to the current empirical information ($\overline{V}_t$) and more attention to the previous indications of market value as summarized in the previous appraised value of the property, V_{t-1}^*. The larger is α, the more weight current transaction prices, including any noise in those prices, will have in the appraisal. The smaller is α, the more weight previous market values will have in the current appraisal.

At first it might appear that the Q2 model applies as much to investors as it does to appraisers. If it is rational for appraisers to underadjust for new information, then isn't it also rational for market participants to similarly underadjust for new information when they decide the prices at which they are willing to transact? If so, then both appraisers and market participants might exhibit the same valuation behavior, in particular, that which is represented by the Q2 model, equation (4). This seems to imply that appraised values and transaction prices would both tend to be dispersed in the same way around the same underlying true value each period, and that there would be no resulting temporal bias in the appraised value as compared to transaction prices.

Yet many market participants believe that appraisals tend to lag behind market values in commercial property markets in the United States. From the rational Bayesian perspective of the Q2 model, this may be explained in terms of the difference we previously noted between the relative importance of random noise versus bias at the micro- and macrolevels. Real estate investors generally hold large portfolios of many individual properties. In negotiating transaction prices, their perspective therefore

---

[21] In general, moving averages present temporally smoothed representations of their underlying value series. Based on the Q2 model, in a graph of V_t^* and $\overline{V}_t$ across time (t), the former would appear to be a smoothed and lagged version of the latter. So-called simple exponential smoothing, as represented by equation (4c), is a classical mathematical technique to smooth out transient "noise" in a time-series, recognizing that when applied in this way it induces a lag in the series.

tends to be from the macrolevel, in terms of concern about the accuracy of property value estimation. At this level, purely random error in individual valuations matters relatively little. To put this in terms of the Q2 model, from the perspective of many market participants, $VAR[\varepsilon_i]$ may approximately equal zero in equation (4b), as far as they are concerned. This would make the optimal (rational) value of α near unity for market participants, based on equation (4b).

In contrast, as noted, appraisers are rarely hired to appraise an entire portfolio of properties all at once. Appraisers are generally hired to appraise individual properties and to maximize the accuracy of their appraisals of individual properties. Therefore, for appraisers the relevant $VAR[\varepsilon_i]$ is based on the microlevel perspective and is therefore larger than that for the typical investor. Thus, equation (4b) would imply a smaller optimal value of α for appraisers as compared to market participants, and this difference would result in (optimal) appraised values lagging behind (optimal) market values in time.[22]

23.2.5 Market Values and Appraiser Behavior: Broader Considerations and Empirical Evidence

The difference between appraisal-based valuations and transaction prices (and hence market values) may be reinforced or exaggerated if we bring in broader practical considerations, such as agency relationships and a more **behavioral** (less narrowly rationalistic) **model** of appraiser and investor behavior. For this purpose it is important to recognize that only the equation (4b) component of the Q2 model of appraiser behavior, the variance ratio formulation for the adjustment parameter α, is based on rational appraiser behavior and Bayesian statistics.[23] The general first-order autoregressive (or simple exponential smoothing) framework represented by equations (4a) or (4c) can accommodate more general models of appraiser behavior, models that would be reflected in different determinations of the confidence parameter, α.

For example, at a more intuitive level, the adjustment parameter α in equation (4a) is often referred to as the appraiser's **confidence factor**. In realistic appraisal situations, appraisers will presumably rely more heavily on recent transaction price information (employ a larger value of α) when they have more confidence in that information, or when such contemporaneous information is of sufficient quantity and quality to instill confidence in the appraisers that they "know where the current market is."

A broader model of appraiser behavior would consider the differences between appraisers' incentives and those of market participants. Real estate investors are often motivated by an "early bird gets the worm" philosophy, figuring that their best chance to make supernormal returns (or avoid subnormal returns) is to be quick on their feet, that is, to understand very well where the market is currently and where it is heading in the future. Indeed, almost by definition, successful investors have this ability, and unsuccessful investors tend to get weeded out in the competitive marketplace. In the high-pressure world of the real estate investor, past transaction prices are only useful or relevant to the extent they can help predict where market values are going in the

---

[22] Formally, this is saying that, while appraisers may seek to minimize the mean squared error in their value estimation at the individual property level (minimize $E[u_t^2]$), market participants might be more concerned to minimize the bias (minimize $E[u_t]$), where $u_t = V_t^* - C_t$.

[23] In fact, the Q2 equation (4b) is also based on other simplifying assumptions, such as that the true real estate market values follow a "random walk" over time.

future. In the United States, commercial property investors rarely hire appraisers to find out where the current asset market is or where it is headed.[24]

In contrast, appraisers in the United States often do not face the same type of incentive or motivation as market participants. Appraisers are trained to provide, and are often hired to provide, estimates of market value that are *well documented* as much as they are accurate (in the sense of being up-to-date). In some cases, the appraiser's client hires the appraiser more for the purpose of providing objective documentation about approximate property value than for the purpose of obtaining a highly up-to-date estimate of the value of the property. Even if this documentation role is not made explicit to the appraiser, it is often both easier and safer (in terms of the appraiser's possible liability for negligence) for the appraiser to err on the side of conservatism and not depart too far from the bulk of the objective evidence available at the time of the appraisal. And of course, objective evidence is by nature historical evidence, which means value indications from the past.[25]

Considering such differences in incentives and motivations, we can reasonably expect that, in terms of equation (4a), market participants might often tend to employ a greater α value (closer to unity) than appraisers would, effectively resulting in appraisals lagging behind transaction prices in time.

In fact, there is some clinical and empirical evidence to support this hypothesis. Because of its theoretical behavioral flexibility and its mathematical tractability, equation (4a) has been applied in several academic studies of appraiser behavior. Although the scientific study of appraiser and investor behavior is still in its infancy, two studies, one clinical and the other empirical, may shed light on where such analysis will lead.

The clinical study was the Diaz-Wolverton experiment, which examined the behavioral phenomenon referred to as **anchoring** by psychologists and behavioral economists. In the presence of uncertainty, people tend to "anchor" their value judgments on a readily observable or relatively certain value. This means that their estimate of an unobservable true value is overly influenced by a related (or even unrelated) observable

---

[24] This statement is probably less true in some other countries, notably the U.K. Although quantitative evidence is not definitive, there is some reason to believe that market participants may take appraisers more seriously in England than in America. Partly as a result of this (and partly as a cause of it), appraisers may tend to be more up-to-date in England. But this difference between England and the United States is facilitated by geographical and cultural differences between the two countries. For example, the commercial real estate market in England is geographically much simpler than that in the United States. Among other things, this makes it easier for appraisers (as well as market participants) in England to infer information relevant to the property market from observation of publicly traded property companies' share prices in the London Stock Exchange, a more informationally efficient asset market than the private property market. (See Barkham and Geltner [1995], for some evidence in this regard.)

[25] Another way of explaining the difference between the orientation of appraisers and that of market participants is as a result of career selection bias in the real estate industry. Suppose individuals have varying abilities to predict the future. Those with better ability can make more money as real estate investors than as appraisers, while those with less prediction abilities can make more money as appraisers than as investors. In an efficient career market, investors (i.e., market participants, those who set market prices) will, on average, tend to be more forward looking (i.e., less backward looking) than appraisers. (We first heard this point made by Joe Williams at a session of the Homer Hoyt Advanced Studies Institute.) Yet another point that is often made is that appraisals could be biased by an agency problem if clients systematically stand to gain or lose from appraisals coming out in a certain way. For example, evidence suggests that appraisals used in the residential mortgage approval process tend to be biased on the high side so as to support mortgage approval. (See, e.g., Chinloy, Cho, and Megbolugbe [1997].) Such an agency effect could also cause appraisals to lag behind transaction prices, at least at certain points in the property market cycle (e.g., just after a market downturn, when appraisers would be hesitant to show the full value loss).

value. Diaz and Wolverton used the autoregressive formulation in equation (4a) to examine whether appraisers who conduct repeated valuations of the same properties over time tend to anchor onto their previous appraisals.

In the Diaz-Wolverton experiment, a subject group of appraisers was asked to appraise a property in a city they were unfamiliar with. Several months later the subject group was asked to reappraise the same property based on updated information. A control group of appraisers was also asked to appraise the same property for the first time, using the updated information. The subject appraisers' average valuation lay between their earlier valuation and the control group's average valuation, and the difference between the two groups was statistically significant. In effect, the subject group was anchoring their new appraisals onto their previous appraisals.[26]

Of course, the Diaz-Wolverton results must be treated carefully. They need to be replicated, and even if their findings hold up, they do not necessarily imply that appraisers exhibit a greater degree of anchoring than do market participants. Nor do the results necessarily suggest that appraisers would anchor on a previous appraisal if faced with less uncertainty about the market for the subject property.[27] The Diaz-Wolverton results do suggest, however, that when appraisers are in a situation in which they repeatedly reappraise the same properties, they may tend to anchor onto their past appraisals. This situation is common among appraisers that are hired to appraise properties held in institutional portfolios, such as those that are used in the NCREIF index, and therefore is particularly important at the macrolevel. Also, if market participants rarely consider purchasing the same property twice, then transaction prices would not tend to exhibit this type of anchoring. Furthermore, if we assume that the appraisers in the Diaz-Wolverton control group were applying rational Q2-type valuation procedures (e.g., with α based on optimal microlevel calibration of equation [4b]), then the experiment suggests that appraisers involved in repeat valuations of the same properties may tend to employ additional behavioral lagging beyond what is implied by the "purely rational" Q2 model.

Whatever the reason for appraiser behavior, by the turn of the century some empirical evidence suggested that, in fact, appraisals tend to exhibit partial adjustment at the microlevel as compared to transaction prices, at least in the repeat valuation context. A notable study in this line was by Professors Hamilton and Clayton, who examined appraisals in the Canadian equivalent of the NCREIF index. They empirically estimated the α parameter of equation (4a) based on data consisting of the appraisals, the previous appraisals of the same properties, and the new comps available to the appraisers, that is, the relevant transactions that had taken place subsequent to the previous appraisals. In effect, Hamilton and Clayton were able to come close to estimating equation (4a) directly based on their empirical appraisal and comps data.[28] Their estimate of α was 0.2.[29] With $\alpha = 0.2$, the first-order autoregressive form of equation

---

[26] See Diaz and Wolverton (1998).

[27] It may be significant that the city in which the subject property was located was unfamiliar to the appraisers. Other experiments by Diaz and others suggest that anchoring may not occur when appraisers are more confident about their own knowledge of the market. (See, e.g., Diaz [1997].)

[28] To be more precise, Hamilton and Clayton (1999) had to work with cap rates rather than price levels. However, the cap rate is simply the inverse of the price per dollar of current income of the property, a way of scaling or normalizing the price.

[29] The statistical estimation standard error in their regression parameter estimate for α was only about ± 0.06. Thus, their estimate of α was some 13 standard errors below the no-lag value of $\alpha = 1$.

(4a) was able to explain about 49% of the variation in the Canadian data, a reasonably good fit for empirical studies of disaggregate appraised values.

It is worthwhile emphasizing that the Hamilton-Clayton study was a purely empirical study that did not assume anything in particular about what appraisers *should* do from a normative perspective, or about the informational efficiency or volatility of the property market. Once again, however, the Hamilton-Clayton study applied to a situation of repeat appraisals of properties held in institutional portfolios, with a typical reappraisal frequency of one year. Similar studies have not yet been made of first-time appraisals or those with longer intervals between the reappraisals.

23.2.6 Simple Macrolevel Delagging Procedure

Suppose that microlevel appraisals are indeed described by a first-order autoregressive process such as equation (4a), and that we can somehow estimate the value of α. Then equation (4a) can be inverted to solve for the purely contemporaneous transaction price indication of value, as follows:

$$\overline{V}_t = [V_t^* - (1 - \alpha)V_{t-1}^*]/\alpha \tag{4d}$$

Equation (4d) suggests a simple method to unsmooth or delag a time-series of macrolevel property valuations that are based on microlevel appraisals.

For example, suppose a static portfolio is evaluated at $100 million as of the end of 2001, based on a simple sum of microlevel appraisals all made as of the end of 2001. Suppose that the same portfolio was evaluated previously in the same manner at $95 million as of the end of 2000. And suppose that $\alpha = 0.2$. Then a simple way to update the year 2001 valuation to get rid of microlevel appraisal lag is as follows: The updated 2001 value estimate is

$$[\$100 \text{ million} - (0.8)\$95 \text{ million}]/0.2 = \$120 \text{ million}$$

While this approach is simple, a couple of caveats should be kept in mind. First, the result depends sensitively on the correct value of α. Second, like any valuation technique, it cannot escape the noise-versus-lag trade-off. Although the value estimate of $120 million may be more up-to-date than the $100 million estimate, the $120 million figure is also subject to more purely random error.[30]

23.2.7 Summarizing Up to Here

Section 23.2 introduced you to the basic nature of macrolevel property valuation based on appraisals or value estimations that are optimized at the microlevel. As we have covered a lot of ground here, let us summarize this section by noting three major points.

---

[30] Even though the value estimation of a large portfolio will tend to have less random noise than individual property valuation (due to the Square Root of n Rule), there will still be some noise in the portfolio valuation. Any noise that exists in the appraisal-based portfolio valuation will be magnified by the delagging formula (4d), negating, at least to a degree, the benefit of the Square Root of n Rule. Note also that the revised delagged estimate of $120 million for the example 2001 portfolio valuation does not imply that the portfolio value increased from $95 million to $120 million in the preceding year, as the $95 million 2000 valuation would also have been lagged.

1. **The Noise versus Lag Trade-Off Principle.** Perhaps the most fundamental point we raised in this section is that there is a trade-off in real estate valuation between minimizing purely random noise and minimizing temporal lag bias. As a general rule, it is not possible to optimize simultaneously within both of these dimensions. *This principle holds at both the micro- and macrolevels.*

2. **The Difference between the Micro- and Macrolevels.** While the noise-versus-lag trade-off applies at both levels, the optimal balance in that trade-off will generally be different between the two levels because noise is relatively less important at the macrolevel (thanks to the Square Root of *n* Rule), while temporal lags are relatively more important at the macrolevel.

3. **The Need to Adjust Macrovalues.** This third point follows from the second. Macrolevel valuations based on procedures that are optimized for the microlevel will often, though not always, need to be adjusted for use at the macrolevel, at least in principle. The reason macrovalues will not always need to be adjusted follows from the trade-off principle, and from the fact that adjustment may be costly. Adjusting macrolevel valuations to address the temporal lag problem will typically increase the random error problem. Thus, such adjustment will be most important when temporally lagged valuation could harm the usefulness or effectiveness of the macrolevel valuation. It will be less important or less desirable when the usefulness of the macrovaluation is very sensitive to purely random error.

23.3 MASS APPRAISAL: THE USE OF MODERN REGRESSION ANALYSIS IN MACROLEVEL VALUATION

The preceding section described the difference between optimal micro- and macrolevel property valuation, ending with the suggestion in equation (4d) for updating macrolevel valuations that are based on microlevel appraisals. However, this correction procedure requires a time-series of repeat valuations of the property portfolio and, as noted, it will tend to result in a rather noisy estimate of macrolevel value. So, we are left less than satisfied, asking whether other approaches exist.

In this section we will approach the problem of macrolevel valuation from a different direction. Instead of building up the macrolevel portfolio value as the sum of individual property appraisals that are optimized for microlevel valuation, we will consider a technique to appraise optimally the entire portfolio at once. In keeping with the definition of macrolevel property valuation, we will still define the valuation problem as a sum of individual property values, but we will estimate those values in a manner that can be optimized for the macrolevel. While several general approaches could be considered in this regard, the approach we want to introduce to you here is what is called **mass appraisal**.

As of the turn of the 21st century, mass appraisal was primarily used only for residential property valuation by local government property tax assessment authorities and residential mortgage lenders. But mass appraisal techniques will likely be employed increasingly in commercial property appraisal, not only by local governments and commercial mortgage lenders (and/or by CMBS rating agencies), but also by institutional investors managing large portfolios of commercial properties.[31] An extension of mass appraisal is also beginning to be used in the construction of periodic return indices of commercial property investment performance, in the form of repeated-measures regression-based indices, as will be discussed in Chapter 25 and in the appendix at the end of this book. So it is important that you understand at least the basics of this procedure.

23.3.1 The Basic Idea: The Hedonic Value Model

To begin, recall that the problem with traditional microlevel valuation is that appraisers are unable to observe a sufficient number of contemporaneous transaction prices of properties that are sufficiently similar to the subject property. So they go back in time to get more comps that are similar to the subject property, but then they fail to adjust sufficiently for temporal changes in the market, at least from a macrolevel perspective. In other words, in order to deal with the problem of cross-sectional *heterogeneity* in properties, temporal bias is introduced.

This problem can be mitigated by making more efficient use of transaction price data. In particular, if we can effectively model the relationship between heterogeneous property characteristics and the market values of individual properties, then we can better control for these differences, enabling us to go farther afield to obtain larger sample sizes. A more sophisticated model of the value effects of cross-sectional heterogeneity might also enable us to control for these effects across time, which would then enable us to expand the usable sample of comps by extending the database back across time, without inducing a temporal lag. Effectively, the Square Root of *n* Rule would be employed to maximum efficiency.

The basic economic theoretical device to enable this type of development is called the **hedonic value model (HVM)**. The HVM views a property as a "bundle" of useful characteristics, such as location, size, age, property amenities, and so forth. The value of the property simply equals the sum of the values of each component in this bundle.[32] For example, a single-family home consists of empirically observable, quantifiable characteristics, such as its size and age. To take a very simplistic example for illustrative purposes, suppose that the only thing home buyers cared about was the number of bedrooms, the age of the house, and which "side of the tracks" it was on. The following equation might then represent a hedonic model of the value of a house as of year t:

$$House\ Value_t = (\$50,000)(Bedrooms_t) + (\$75,000)(Goodside_t) - (\$2,000)(Age_t)$$

---

[31] The rise of "e-commerce" on the Internet may increase the opportunities in this regard if information about the trading of commercial properties becomes more centralized and easily available in electronic form.

[32] The word *hedonic* is rooted in the notion that goods derive their value from their ability to provide pleasure for their owners or users. This derivation is more directly relevant to owner-occupied houses, which are consumption goods at least as much as they are investment goods. However, the term *hedonic model* has come to represent a more general concept in which value is decomposable into a bundle of empirically observable qualitative and quantitative characteristics, whether or not such characteristics produce pleasure for the owner or user of the good. Commercial property is, of course, a production good rather than a consumption good, so presumably pleasure is not the purpose (or is it?)

Thus, a 10-year-old, 4-bedroom house on the "good" side of the tracks would be worth \$255,000.[33] Similarly, a 30-year-old, 3-bedroom house on the "wrong" side of the tracks would be worth \$90,000.

The point is that the HVM allows us to quantify the value effect of the cross-sectional heterogeneity in the property population. A single valuation model applies, in theory, to all of the individual properties in the population, as of a given time.

The three variables in the preceding example, *Bedrooms*, *Goodside*, and *Age*, are called **hedonic variables**. They measure cross-sectional differences in properties, differences that matter in the relevant property asset market. The value impact of each hedonic variable is determined by a value parameter, or coefficient, that gives the effect on market value per unit of the hedonic variable. Value coefficients are sometimes referred to as the characteristic prices of the hedonic characteristics. For example, in the previous HVM, each bedroom is worth \$50,000, so this is the value parameter for bedrooms. Once we know the value parameters, we can apply the hedonic value model to each property in a portfolio to, in effect, evaluate all the properties at once, en masse (hence the term *mass appraisal*).[34] Mass appraisal is in fact a form of mass production, such as the manufacturing of cars, only we are valuing properties instead.

*23.3.2 The Statistical Tool: Hedonic Regression

If you know anything about the statistical procedure known as regression analysis, then it is no doubt obvious to you that this is the basic analytical tool that is employed to apply the HVM and implement mass appraisal in practice. In particular, a regression analysis that is used to empirically quantify (or "calibrate") an HVM is referred to as a **hedonic regression**.[35] A general specification of a typical HVM might look something like the following, as a regression model:

$$f(V_{i,t}) = \beta_{0,t} + \beta_{1,t} H_{1,i,t} + \beta_{2,t} H_{2,i,t} + \cdots + \varepsilon_{i,t} \tag{5}$$

Here, $f(V_{i,t})$ is some function of the observable transaction price of property i in period t. For example, $f(V_{i,t})$ is often defined as the natural log of $V_{i,t}$.[36] $\beta_{0,t}$ is a constant term (or "intercept"). The $H_{k,i,t}$ are the hedonic variable values for property i as of time t. For example, in our simple house model, H_1 is the number of bedrooms;

[33] The characteristic labeled here as "Goodside" is what is called in statistics a "dummy variable," meaning that it is like a switch, taking on different discrete values depending on a given condition for the given observation. In the present example, "Goodside" equals 1 if the house is located on the "good" side of the tracks, and 0 if it is not. The \$255,000 valuation is computed as $50,000 \times 4 + 75,000 \times 1 - 2,000 \times 10 = \$200,000 + \$75,000 - \$20,000$.

[34] Of course, we have to know the current values of all the hedonic variables for each property in the portfolio. In this example we would have to know the number of bedrooms, the age, and the location of each house in the subject portfolio.

[35] Appendix A in Chapter 25 presents a basic introduction to statistical regression, in case you have no idea what we are talking about here or your statistics textbook is not handy. Fear not, however, for it is not the purpose of this chapter to delve deeply into the statistical nuts and bolts of regression analysis. We will highlight only a few points that are of particular relevance to our problem at hand, macrolevel valuation. Regarding terminology, we should note that in practice, the term *hedonic regression*, or *hedonic regression model*, is often used interchangeably with the term *mass appraisal*. This makes sense, as hedonic regression is the primary practical methodology used to implement mass appraisal.

[36] Logs are often used because they are convenient mathematically, and the estimated models often fit the data better that way.

H_2 is the location dummy variable, *Goodside*, and H_3 is the house age in years.[37] The $\beta_{k,t}$ parameters (other than the intercept) are the value parameters or characteristic prices, relating the hedonic variables to the value function. $\varepsilon_{i,t}$ is the random transaction price noise associated with observation i.[38]

The specific variables and functional form of the hedonic regression model is referred to as the model **specification**. The specified model would be estimated or calibrated (that is, the parameter values, the βs, would be quantified) based on a database of transaction price observations (tagged by the i subscript: $i = 1,2,\ldots,n$), together with data about the hedonic characteristics of the properties. For purposes of macrolevel valuation, the estimated HVM is applied to each property in the portfolio to be evaluated. This is done by substituting into equation (5), for each property in the subject portfolio, the property's current values of the $H_{i,t}$ variables.[39]

Of course, practical hedonic models of real estate value are much more complicated than the simple example we described previously. They contain many more hedonic variables and different mathematical functional forms. They often contain numerous **dummy variables** to represent different neighborhoods and qualitative characteristics, and they may use sophisticated statistical techniques such as nonparametric estimation and spatially autocorrelated error correction to allow for flexible functional forms and make the most efficient use of the available transaction price data.[40] But the basic idea is represented by equation (5), as illustrated in our simplistic house example.

23.3.3 Application to Commercial Property

In real estate, hedonic value models were first applied to houses. Application to commercial property began only recently and is still in its infancy.[41] At the conceptual level, commercial properties have one obvious advantage and one obvious disadvantage over houses, as far as the HVM is concerned.

The advantage is that much of the cross-sectional value difference that the HVM must try to capture is already encompassed in the annual rent or income earned by each property. Larger and better properties will earn more rent or net income than smaller

---

[37] In equation (5) we have put time subscripts on the hedonic variables. This is the most general (and data-hungry) assumption. In practice, some hedonic variables might not be time-subscripted, depending on the HVM specification and the estimation procedure being employed (more on this later).

[38] If it were not for the existence of $\varepsilon_{i,t}$, we would observe the true market value, $C_{i,t}$, in each transaction, rather than a noisy indication of market value. (This distinction was explained in section 23.2.1.)

[39] There is interesting flexibility in the way HVMs can be applied. For example, apart from valuing a defined static portfolio, the HVM can be used to value any arbitrarily defined hypothetical property simply by defining the hedonic variable values of the property. Thus, a representative property of a certain type may be defined and valued using the HVM. (See the appendix at the end of this book for additional discussion in the context of applying HVMs to the development of transaction-based commercial property return indices.)

[40] For example, see Pace, Barry, Clapp, and Rodriquez (1998), and Basu and Thibodeau (1998). Also, an interesting shortcut that can make more efficient use of data in hedonic price modeling was discovered by Professors Clapp and Giacotto. They showed that one can often collapse many hedonic variables into a single publicly available variable, namely, the property tax assessed valuation of the property. Assessed valuations will generally not be extremely up-to-date, but as they are often based on mass appraisal techniques, it is not surprising that they capture much of the value effects of cross-sectional heterogeneity in properties. (See Clapp and Giacotto [1992, 1998].)

[41] For a simple, highly readable example of an application to apartment properties in Dallas, see Crosson, Dannis, and Thibodeau (1996). Another easily readable article, applying hedonic valuation to office buildings in Phoenix, is in Downs and Slade (1999).

or lower-quality properties. Yet rent or net income can often be empirically observed for commercial properties along with their transaction prices. By employing the rent or income as a hedonic variable, commercial property HVMs have an advantage over the valuation of non-income-producing real estate.

Nevertheless, even after controlling for property rent or NOI, commercial property values show important cross-sectional differences. Some of the hedonic variables, apart from rent or NOI, that one would expect to be important in capturing such heterogeneity include the following:[42]

- Property usage type
- Building size
- Building age
- Current building occupancy or vacancy rate
- Local space market average occupancy or vacancy rate
- Location ("and location and location," that is, MSA, type of location within the MSA such as CBD or suburban, and specific neighborhood)
- Quality and physical condition or class (such as institutional or noninstitutional, class A or class B)
- Single versus multitenant
- Average lease expiration

This brings us to the disadvantage commercial properties face over houses in HVM development. Commercial property HVMs are not simple. They require numerous hedonic, location, and time dummy variables. The development of such regression models is a data-hungry business. Yet commercial property value modeling faces a relative scarcity of data. Commercial properties are much less numerous than houses in the United States, and so far fewer transaction price observations are available to work with. This is no doubt one reason hedonic value modeling is less advanced in commercial property applications than in housing applications.[43]

[42] The Crosson-Dannis-Thibodeau (1996) analysis of apartment portfolios in Dallas used the value level (per property or per apartment unit) as the dependent variable, and the following variables on the right-hand side: NOI, age, number of units, average size of units, and market vacancy rate, as well as dummy variables for neighborhood and year of sale. If rent or NOI differences were sufficient to explain cross-sectional variation in Dallas apartment prices (i.e., if cap rates showed no systematic cross-sectional variation), then only the NOI variable would have been statistically significant. Instead, the Crosson et al. study found statistical significance in 4 other hedonic variables as well as 7 of their 11 neighborhood location dummy variables. The Downs-Slade (1999) study of Phoenix office buildings also found a number of statistically significant hedonic variables (although they apparently did not have information on property NOI, so it is difficult to say how much some of their hedonic variables might be theoretically "collapsible" into an NOI or rent variable).

[43] There are probably institutional reasons as well. Commercial real estate lacks a large, central repository of transaction price information comparable to FNMA/FHLMC in the housing industry. Also, urban economics as an academic discipline has traditionally been more focused on housing prices than on commercial property prices, and most of the development of HVMs has been spearheaded by urban economists.

23.3.4 Why Mass Appraisal?

If data scarcity makes mass appraisal more difficult for commercial property, then what makes us think it will become more widely used? More specifically, how can we claim that regression-based valuation would be more efficient or effective than traditional micro-optimal appraisal for portfolio valuation? Well, to be honest, it may not be. And we would not want to leave you with the impression that there are not potential statistical pitfalls and problems in the application of HVM to commercial portfolio valuation. Indeed, we should highlight some of these problems.

But let's begin by stating the basic case in favor of regression-based valuation of portfolios. The basic statistical argument is rather simple. Suppose we know the "true" (or "correct") specification of equation (5) that really captures the way property market values are determined, and we can get the data necessary to apply this model. Then regression-based mass appraisal makes the most efficient use of transaction price data, not only for macrolevel portfolio valuation but also for microlevel valuation. This is simply because regression procedures are designed for precisely this purpose, to make the most efficient use of data to estimate quantitative relationships among variables in the population from which the data is drawn.[44]

Now this puts the traditionalists on the defensive. In order to argue that mass appraisal is *not* the most efficient way to go, they can make either of two points. The first point is that it is expensive to gather sufficient data and spend the time necessary to specify and estimate a mass appraisal model. This is true. But this argument carries much more weight at the microlevel, where individual properties are being appraised. If one has to appraise an entire portfolio of properties as of the same time, then one already has to spend a lot of time and effort gathering data and performing valuation analyses. There are economies of scale to such data gathering and analysis, and regression-based valuation techniques are a good way to take advantage of such economies.

The second argument against mass appraisal is more fundamental. The criticism is that no one can really know the true HVM. No practical specification of equation (5) is going to be exactly correct. That being the case, we cannot say, from a rigorous or "scientific" perspective, that regression analysis is more effective or efficient than traditional custom-tailored microlevel appraisal. However, even traditional microlevel appraisal involves an implicit, if not explicit, assumption of a valuation "model." On what basis should we assume that the (usually more implicit and subjective) custom-tailored microlevel model is superior to the (more explicit and objective) mass valuation model? From our discussion in section 23.2 of this chapter, it seems likely that any superiority of microlevel appraisal is based on a microlevel perspective, in terms of microlevel optimization of the valuation procedure. This brings us back to the point that motivated this section of this chapter. Optimal microlevel valuation is not the same as optimal macrolevel valuation. In particular, optimal microlevel valuation tends to place too much importance on the elimination of noise, from the macroperspective, and in so doing tends to result in appraisals that have excessive temporal lag, again from the macroperspective.

So we have come full circle, needing to explain one last point. How is it that mass appraisal can avoid temporal lags better than traditional microlevel appraisal?

---

[44]At the most basic level, this objective of regression analysis is represented by the Gauss-Markov theorem. Check out the basic introduction to regression analysis in any introductory statistics text for an explanation of this point. (For example, see Chapter 3, Pindyck and Rubinfeld [1991].)

What about the Income Method of Appraisal?

Perhaps the most important thing that microlevel valuation can do for commercial properties that, as far as we know, has yet to be attempted in a regression-based procedure at the mass level, is what professional appraisers call the income method of valuation. In particular, at the microlevel the specific leases, rents, operating expenses, and capital expenditures of individual properties can be projected for each year in the future, and multiyear DCF analysis can be conducted, as we described in Part IV. Thus, the value estimation procedure can be modeled more directly on the way value is determined by investors in the property market. However, as we pointed out in Part IV, a number of assumptions must be made in income-based valuation, such as assumptions about the market's expectations about future rental growth rates, required returns (discount rates), current and future cap rates, and so forth. Income-based valuation depends heavily on these assumptions, and appraisers look to the market, as indicated by actual transaction prices, to help them make these assumptions. This makes the income method effectively not that different from the pure market method (that is, based on the observation of the transaction prices of comparable properties). The trade-off between noise and temporal lag still exists and is resolved at the microlevel in a manner that is optimal at that level.

Furthermore, since multiyear DCF valuation is useful at the microlevel, it might be just as useful at the macrolevel. In principle, nothing prevents HVMs for commercial properties from being specified with each year's future projected cash flow as a "hedonic" variable on the right-hand side of equation (5). Thus, there is no reason in principle why the income method cannot be applied through regression analysis at the mass level.*

Alternatively, a different approach to applying the income method at the macrolevel would be to redefine static portfolio valuation based on application of the income method directly at the macrolevel, that is, by projecting and discounting the aggregated cash flows of the portfolio as a whole without using regression analysis to infer valuation implications from transaction price evidence. Indeed, this is the way a portfolio of properties would probably be valued in the market if it were to be sold all at once as a single asset, and this is largely the way multiproperty real estate firms such as REITs are evaluated in the stock market, as we will see in Chapter 24.

---

*For example, using the nomenclature of equation (5), the dependent variable could be defined simply as the transaction price level, $V_{i,t}$, the intercept could be dropped, H_1 could be the property's first year projected net cash flow (year $t + 1$), H_2 could be the property's second year projected net cash flow (CF_{t+2}), and so on, through to a uniform terminal year, say, H_{10}, which would include the reversion cash flow. The estimated β_k coefficients would then represent estimates of the discount factors corresponding to each future year's cash flow expectation. (Thus, the coefficients would be the inverse of the compounded expected total returns up through the time corresponding to each future year.) This is a special case of essentially the same regression specification as the value-weighted arithmetic average repeated-measures regression (RMR) method for estimating a real estate periodic total return index, described in Appendix B of Chapter 25. The difference is that here the empirical valuation observations (in this case transaction prices instead of appraised values) are all in the present period, and the estimated index (or portfolio) returns are expectations for the future (ex ante returns rather than ex post). If the estimation database includes longitudinal as well as cross-sectional variation (the dependent variable includes prices from times prior to t), then both past and future ex ante returns will be estimated, and the specification would be as described in Appendix B of Chapter 25 (e.g., regarding time periods prior or subsequent to the 10-year cash flow projection in a given valuation observation).

The answer to this question is, first, that mass appraisal does not necessarily or automatically avoid the temporal lag problem. Hedonic regressions are typically estimated on **pooled databases**, that is, samples of transaction prices that span not only different properties (cross-sectional variation) but also multiple periods of past time (longitudinal variation). If the effect of time on market value is not carefully represented and controlled for in the specification of the HVM, then mass appraisals will be as temporally lagged as traditional appraisals (or even more so).

But the explicit HVM enables the analyst to see exactly how time is (or is not) being incorporated into the valuation model, and to specify a model that adequately captures the effect of time.

For example, at one extreme, all of the hedonic variables can be time-subscripted (as in equation [5]) or, what is essentially equivalent, the hedonic regression can be reestimated in each period on purely contemporaneous cross-sectional transaction price data. This option is usually not practical for commercial property appraisal, however, for the same reason it is not used in microlevel appraisal, namely, insufficient data. An alternative approach that allows pooled databases to be used is to employ dummy variables for each time period, constraining the strictly cross-sectional hedonic variables (such as building size or location) to have value coefficients that are constant across time.[45]

23.3.5 A Final Statistical Consideration: The Trade-Off Is Still with Us

Using techniques such as time dummy variables, mass appraisal can avoid the temporal lag bias problem, at least in principle. And by making efficient use of much larger transaction sample sizes than are used in traditional microlevel appraisals, mass appraisal can help with random noise as well. Nevertheless, before closing this section, we must come back to the fundamental principle we noted in section 23.2, the trade-off between random noise minimization and temporal lag minimization. Mass appraisal does not abolish this trade-off; it only allows the trade-off to be addressed more explicitly and optimally from a macrolevel valuation perspective.[46] A theoretically perfect HVM (including all of the variables and the "true" mathematical form of the valuation model) would still be subject to empirical **estimation error** in the real world, due simply to random noise in transaction prices, that is, the dispersion of transaction prices around the relevant true market values. Such a perfect specification would exhibit only purely random error. But the reality is that the specification of a practical HVM always involves the noise-versus-lag trade-off due to limited empirical data availability.[47]

---

[45] In effect, the time dummies represent separate intercepts for each period of time. For example, the time dummy variable for period t takes the value of unity if transaction observation i occurred in period t, and the value of zero if the i transaction did not occur in t. This is essentially the same as the Court-Griliches procedure described in the appendix at the end of this book, in connection with the construction of transaction-based periodic appreciation return indices. (See, e.g., Fisher, Geltner, and Webb [1994].)

[46] Keep in mind that least-squares estimation of a regression model simply minimizes the dispersion in the squared residuals (the differences between the regression model value predictions and the corresponding empirically observed transaction prices) within the estimation database. If this database is pooled (including temporal as well as cross-sectional variation), then the least-squares minimization does not necessarily imply the minimization of either the purely cross-sectional residuals or the purely longitudinal residuals (which may be unobservable as such, empirically), but rather only the minimization of the combined-source residuals (that is, the pooled residuals). There is thus no guarantee that the implied balance between the two types of error is optimal from an investment analysis perspective.

[47] We should note that the trade-off is not ironclad. There are statistical noise "filtering" techniques that do not necessarily induce a lag, such as the ridge regression suggested by Goetzmann (1992). But such techniques have limitations, and, relevant to our present point, they typically must be applied at the mass appraisal level based on regression-type procedures in the context of frequent periodic revaluations of the portfolio. They can mitigate the noise-versus-lag trade-off, but not abolish it.

More generally, there are two sources of potential bias in mass appraisal:

- **Sample selection** occurs when the estimation database is not drawn randomly or representatively from the underlying population of properties represented by the portfolio to be evaluated.
- **Specification error** occurs when the wrong HVM is used in the regression analysis, that is, the HVM is not the true market value model, either because some relevant explanatory variables are left out or the functional form of the model is not correct.

Either or both of these problems can cause serious bias in macrolevel valuation, even in large portfolios, because, like all sources of bias, they are not susceptible to mitigation by the Square Root of n Rule. Furthermore, the magnitude and direction of such bias is often difficult to determine unless we know more about the specific nature of the sample selection or the specification error. The complexity of hedonic valuation makes it difficult to avoid these sources of bias completely. However, it should be remembered that traditional microlevel appraisal can also be subject to both of these same sources of bias.[48]

23.4 CHAPTER SUMMARY

Well, we told you this would be a rather difficult chapter.[49] We suspect that if you were able to read this whole chapter without falling asleep more than once, then you are at least two standard deviations from the norm of human personalities and will probably be happier having a career in the research department than in the sales department.[50] But even if you only skimmed through the major points in this chapter and puzzled over the exhibits, you should agree that this is basic stuff. It doesn't get any more basic than understanding how to measure or estimate the value of a static portfolio of properties. The technical points we covered here, the meaning, nature, and typical magnitude of noise, and bias, and especially the nature of the trade-off between noise and temporal lagging, are clearly very relevant and important in such valuation. Yet this is an aspect in which real estate is somewhat unique. These measurement issues are much more prominent and important in private real estate investment than they are in publicly traded securities investment. You haven't really become a real estate investment analyst (as opposed to a more generic type) until you have mastered the concepts in this chapter (and/or Chapter 25), at least at some level.

---

[48] Temporal lag bias typically enters the hedonic regression through a combination of the sample selection and specification error sources of bias. For example, if the transaction price sample in which the model is estimated goes back beyond the current period, then it is drawn at least partly from a stale population that will bias the estimated value toward the past. This problem can be mitigated by including time dummy variables in the regression, but only by dealing with the noise-versus-lag error magnitude trade-off.

[49] Too nerdy even for Bob to make an appearance!

[50] You may be almost as nerdy as we are!

KEY TERMS

macrolevel property valuation
static (standing) portfolio
noise
market value
comps
Square Root of *n* Rule
longitudinal variation
cross-sectional variation
errors
bias
noise-versus-lag trade-off
temporal aggregation bias

partial adjustment model of appraisal
Quan-Quigley model (Q2)
moving average
autoregression
simple exponential smoothing
ratio of variances
behavioral model of appraisal
confidence factor (in appraisal)
anchoring behavior
delagging (appraised values)
mass appraisal

hedonic value model (HVM)
hedonic variables
hedonic regression
specification (of regression model)
estimation (of regression model)
dummy variables (and time dummy variables)
pooled database
income method (of appraisal)
estimation error
sample selection
specification error

STUDY QUESTIONS

23.1. Briefly describe four characteristics of private property markets that distinguish these asset markets from pubic securities markets such as the stock exchange. What are the implications of these differences regarding the nature of the asset transaction prices that are observed in the asset market?

23.2. Three nearly identical properties are all sold as of the same date, for prices of $2,650,000, $2,450,000, and $2,400,000.

a. What is your best estimate of the market values of each of two other properties that are virtually identical to the first three, as of that same date?

b. If one of those additional properties actually did sell for a price of $2,550,000, what is your estimate of the market value of the fifth property as of that same date?

c. What is the market value of the fourth property?

d. What is your best estimate of the error or noise (defined as the difference between the transaction price and the market value) in the observed transaction prices of all four properties?

23.3. In question 23.2, how much did the accuracy of your estimate of market value improve as a result of the addition of the fourth empirical valuation observation (i.e., what is your estimation error with the fourth transaction, and what is it with only the first three)?

23.4. What is the difference between purely random error (noise) and systematic error (bias), and how is this difference related to the Square Root of *n* Rule? Which of these two types of error is relatively more important at the microlevel of individual property value estimation, as compared to the macrolevel of static portfolio value estimation?

23.5. What is the noise-versus-lag trade-off in individual property appraisal?

23.6. Suppose the longitudinal variance in property value appreciation (volatility) is 5% per calendar quarter. And suppose the standard deviation of the cross-sectional dispersion in observable transaction prices at any given time is 10% of the property value. According to the Quan-Quigley (Q2) Model, what is the partial adjustment factor (appraisal confidence factor, α)? What is then the Q2 partial adjustment model of appraisals as a function of current average transaction prices and previous quarter's appraised value?

23.7. Write out the first four terms on the right-hand side of the exponential moving-average (simple exponential smoothing) model that equates to the $V_t^* = 0.2\overline{V}_t + 0.8V_{t-1}^*$ autoregressive model of appraisal as a function of average transaction prices.

23.8. What is anchoring behavior, and what is the significance of the Diaz-Wolverton experiment that found some evidence of anchoring behavior on the part of appraisers' repeat valuations in conditions of uncertainty?

23.9. Suppose the following is the hedonic value model (HVM) of office buildings in a certain portfolio.

$$Bldg.\,Value_t = (\$100)(SF\;Area_t) + (\$5,000,000)(CBD\;location_t) - (\$2,000,000)(Age_t)$$

Use mass appraisal based on this HVM to value a static portfolio as of time t, consisting of three buildings as described in the following table:

Building	SF Area	CBD Location*	Age
1	500,000	0	5
2	1,000,000	1	10
3	750,000	0	7

*Note: This is a dummy variable: 1 = Located in CBD, 0 = Located in suburbs.

23.10. Name at least five hedonic variables that you would expect to be important in real world HVMs of apartment properties. Would any of these be different for office properties?

23.11. Briefly discuss the potential advantages of mass appraisal as compared to traditional microlevel appraisal for purposes of valuing a static portfolio consisting of numerous individual properties.

24 Macrolevel Valuation II: REITs

Chapter Outline

Learning Objectives

After reading this chapter, you should understand:

◆ The basic process of macrolevel valuation at the investment entity level as exemplified in the valuation of REITs by the stock market.

◆ The difference between growth and income stocks and the nature of REITs in this regard.

◆ The basic regulatory constraints faced by REITs, and some of the unique accounting terminology and conventions used in the analysis of REIT stocks.

◆ Some of the major considerations and objectives in REIT management strategy

◆ The two major models that describe the fundamental nature of REITs, and the implications these two models have for REIT valuation.

$\mathbf{C}$hapter 23 introduced you to macrolevel valuation at one end of the spectrum. In this chapter we are going to leap to the other end, by focusing on the valuation of REITs in the stock market. To see what we mean, recall the basic concept of the macrolevel in real estate investment. This level refers to portfolios or collections of many properties, and to the investment analysis and decision making that relate directly to such collections.

In Chapter 23 we focused in depth on the valuation of the static portfolio of properties, the macrolevel bricks and mortar. Valuation there was simply the cross-sectional sum of the values of the individual properties as they are each valued in the private property market. We ignored any **investment entity** that owned or controlled the properties and could be invested in and traded as such. Another way of describing this is to say that in Chapter 23 the entity level, if there was any at all, was assumed to be completely passive, costless, and transparent.

At the other extreme, a macrolevel investment entity not only exists, but it is very active and can be invested in and traded as such. This is what REITs are. They own portfolios or collections of properties, but the portfolios are not static. Rather, they are dynamic, constantly changing, not only as the REIT buys and sells individual properties, but often as the REIT engages in construction and development activity as well. Indeed, the REIT industry evolved in the early 1990s, so that the major REITs today are very active operating firms, a far cry from passive portfolios of properties. A typical large REIT at the turn of the 21st century viewed itself as providing vertically integrated commercial real estate goods and services to customers (in the form of tenants and, indirectly, other users of the built space, such as shoppers using a mall). The vertical articulation in a single firm may span from raw land acquisition and development, through portfolio management (also known as **asset management**), to operational-level property management.

Equity shares of the major REITs are publicly traded in the stock exchange. Viewed by Wall Street as operational firms, that is, actively managed corporations, they are valued as such (i.e., not as passive portfolios of properties). Thus, REITs are valued in essentially the same way other publicly traded firms are valued, as discounted projected future cash flow streams, in which the cash flows are aggregated across all of their real estate holdings and dealings, including expectations of future cash flows from assets that do not even yet exist or that the REIT does not currently own. Nevertheless, although REITs are valued in the stock market essentially like any other firm, REITs are *real estate* firms, **pure plays** in the sense that their assets and activities are largely restricted to real estate because of their claim to REIT tax-exempt status. Consequently, it is appropriate to view REITs as macrolevel real estate investment entities.

Between these two extremes, the static portfolio of Chapter 23 and the actively managed REIT firms of this chapter, are a host of real estate investment entities, products, and vehicles that are less passive and transparent than the static portfolio but less active and closed than REITs. These include vehicles such as limited partnerships, commingled funds, and even some smaller REITs that are passively managed or finite-lived. We won't focus in depth on these intermediate vehicles, although they are important.[1] Our excuse is that, by exploring the two extremes of this spectrum in some depth, we figure you can interpolate on your own, to gain insight regarding the intermediate vehicles.

With this in mind, the purpose of the present chapter is to introduce you to the modern REIT industry in more depth than we have already covered it (in Chapter 7), and from a macro- rather than microlevel perspective (as the latter was already covered in Chapter 12). Our particular concern at this level is with the process and nature of REIT valuation in the stock market. In this focus there is an important conceptual distinction from Chapter 23. Here we are considering value *determination* by the market, in a *causal* sense, whereas in Chapter 23 we addressed value *estimation* or *measurement*, in an *observational* sense. In addition to valuation, we also want to touch in this chapter on some practical and strategic issues regarding the REIT industry.

With this in mind, Chapter 24 is organized into four sections. The first covers the basics of firm valuation in the stock market as this applies specifically to REITs. The second section covers some of the nuts and bolts of REIT analysis, including some terminology and accounting issues that are unique to REITs. The third section provides

---

[1] They were discussed in Chapter 7, and will be again in Chapter 26.

a brief strategic review of the industry at the turn of the century, including consideration of issues such as economies of scale, financing, agency costs, and management specialization. A fourth section in this chapter returns to the question of REIT valuation, to consider some deeper issues unique to real estate and the REIT industry.

24.1 REIT VALUATION IN THE STOCK MARKET

REIT equity is securitized, and it trades in the public stock exchanges, at least as regards our focus in this chapter.[2] Therefore, it should come as no surprise that REITs are valued essentially the same way other stocks are valued. The U.S. stock market is one of the most efficient branches of the capital market in the world, so it would be surprising indeed to find REITs segmented off in their own corner of a market that is otherwise highly integrated. In this section we will introduce you to the basics of how the stock market determines equity share values, and we will mention some aspects of this equation that are unique for REITs.

24.1.1 The Gordon Model

The value of a REIT's equity in the stock market derives fundamentally from an infinite-horizon DCF valuation similar to that introduced in Chapter 10 at the microlevel of individual property valuation. Now, however, the net cash flows that matter are the dividends paid out by the REIT to its stockholders. Letting E represent the value of the firm's equity as of the end of year 0 (the present), we have

$$E = \frac{DIV_1}{1+r} + \frac{DIV_2}{(1+r)^2} + \frac{DIV_3}{(1+r)^3} + \cdots \tag{1}$$

where DIV_t refers to the annual dividends expected to be distributed by the REIT in year t, and r refers to the stock market's required long-run total return expectation for investments in the REIT's shares.[3]

---

[2] REITs are not required to list their shares in public exchanges, and a number of "private REITs" do exist. However, our focus in this chapter is on the large to medium-size "mainstream" REITs that make up the bulk of the industry capitalization.

[3] The discount rate, r, is the REIT's average equity cost of capital, expressed in the form of a single (blended) long-run multiperiod required expected return (like a going-in IRR, but at the level of the firm's equity). In previous chapters we often labeled this long-run required return expectation $E[r_E]$ to emphasize that it is an *ex ante* expectation of the return to levered equity. Similarly, the DIV_t amounts are expectations. Here we suppress the equity subscript and the $E[\ ]$ part of the label for simplicity of illustration only. Note that the numerators and denominators on the right-hand side of the valuation equation are measured at the before-tax level from the perspective of the REIT investors. This is convenient, as E refers to the firm's equity market value, so DIV_t and r can be related directly to empirically observable public information on the REIT share price and dividends. However, recall from Chapter 12 that market value is determined more fundamentally as the investment value to the marginal investors. In the case of REITs, these marginal investors will generally be taxed individuals. Thus, the more fundamental equity valuation equation is

$$E = \frac{(1-\tau)DIV_1}{1+atr} + \frac{(1-\tau)DIV_2}{(1+atr)^2} + \frac{(1-\tau)DIV_3}{(1+atr)^3} + \cdots$$

where τ and atr are, respectively, the relevant personal income tax rate and the equity-after-tax opportunity cost of capital (expressed as a dollar-weighted, blended going-in IRR rate) for the marginal shareholders of the REIT.

While formula (1) is the fundamental valuation model, a shortcut, known as the **Gordon growth model (GGM)** is more famous and more widely used.[4] This is probably the simplest, oldest, and still most widely used model of stock market valuation of a firm's equity. It follows directly from formula (1) and the constant-growth perpetuity formula introduced in Chapter 8.[5] The GGM value of a REIT's equity, is given in formula (2):

$$E = \frac{DIV_1}{r - g} \qquad\qquad (2)$$

Formula (2) is obviously a shortcut compared to formula (1) because the analyst does not have to forecast each future year's dividend explicitly. Instead, in the Gordon model the analyst only has to estimate the market's expected long-term average growth rate in the firm's future dividends, g. By assuming that this growth rate is expected to hold every year (i.e., constant growth) and to be maintained ad infinitum, the long valuation formula in (1) collapses into the simpler formula (2).

Thus, REIT valuation in the stock market typically revolves around estimates of three variables: DIV_1 and g have to do with the firm's future cash flows and dividend distributions, while r has to do with the firm's equity risk as perceived by the stock market, and the stock market's preferences for such risk. As the GGM assumes a constant growth rate in dividends over the long run, it is only an approximation of reality. In order to make the model work as well as possible, the variables employed in it should reflect long-run average stabilized or maintainable levels for each variable, the annual dividend, the growth rate in those dividends, and the market's expected return on investments in the firm's stock. Temporary aberrations or transient effects in any of these variables can distort the empirical application of the GGM to any given firm. With this in mind, let us briefly consider each of the three variables in the Gordon growth model.

The dividends paid out by the REIT, DIV_1, must be taken from the net equity cash flow earned by the REIT from its property holdings and sales. Thus, stock market analysts and investors must study the nature of the firm's current property holdings and operations, as well as its debt obligations, as these will largely determine the firm's ability to pay dividends in the short run, at least in terms of the stabilized or maintainable rate for such cash payouts.[6]

The long-run average growth rate expected for the firm's dividend growth, g, will typically reflect two major considerations. The most basic is sometimes referred to as **existing property cash flow growth**, or **same-store growth** (in the case of REITs specializing in retail properties). This refers essentially to growth in what we labeled in Chapter 14 the **equity-before-tax cash flow (EBTCF)** of the static portfolio of properties consisting of the stabilized operating properties the REIT already owns, net of existing debt service obligations.[7] This, in turn, reflects the growth in the firm's

---

[4]Although the GGM was not originally invented by Gordon, its modern usage is most often attributed to Gordon and Shapiro (1956).

[5]See formula (10) in section 8.2.5 of Chapter 8.

[6]For example, a firm can temporarily pay out more cash than it earns from operations by selling its assets or using financing techniques. But the long-run maintainable level of dividends will generally have to come largely from property operational earnings. This is particularly true because the REIT tax status requires that most properties be held at least four years, which precludes widespread use of "merchant building" or short-term development and trading strategies.

[7]See Exhibit 14-2 and the discussion in section 14.2.3 in Chapter 14. This is based even more fundamentally on the property-level operating cash flows described in depth in section 11.1 of Chapter 11.

underlying property (static portfolio) net operating cash flow (PBTCF), as levered by the firm's existing debt.

The second consideration that can affect the market's perception of the firm's ability to grow dividends in the long run has to do with the ability of the REIT's management to obtain and effectively implement **growth opportunities**. This refers to the ability of the firm to find and execute deals or projects that have a *positive NPV* in terms of the market value of the firm's stock, as determined in the stock market. While growth opportunities that are maintainable over the long run exist most fundamentally at the microlevel (e.g., in the firm's management's ability to execute astute "buy low" and "sell high" deals, or to entrepreneurially develop unique new properties, or to creatively manage the operations of properties they acquire), there may also be macrolevel or firm-level growth opportunities, such as taking advantage of economies of scale, building franchise value, and so forth. Thus, the market's perception of the firm's management's long-run abilities has a large impact on the market's estimation of the growth variable, g, in the Gordon growth model.

Holding the other two variables constant, even relatively small variations in the market's perception of the REIT's long-run growth rate can have a large impact on REIT value. For example, if, in the context of the GGM, g increases from 2% to 3% while the REIT's cost of capital remains at 12%, the REIT price as a multiple of its current annual dividend will increase from 10 to 11.1, a jump of 11% in share value.[8] A similar fall in share price would occur with a 100-basis-point reduction in long-run growth expectations. Much of the fundamental volatility in a REIT's share price probably derives from these types of fluctuations in the market's long-run growth expectations for the REIT.

The market's perception of the REIT's management's long-run abilities also has a large impact on the third variable in the GGM, the market's required expected long run total return, r, which is the REIT's **average equity cost of capital**. As always, $r = r_f + RP$, so the market's required total return expectation equals the current risk-free interest rate (as approximated by the T-bill yield) plus the market's required risk premium for the given firm. Thus, the market's perception of the amount and nature of risk in the firm's future dividends and share value is crucial in determining r. The risk in the firm consists of some combination of the risk in the static portfolio of the firm's existing stabilized operating properties plus the risk in the firm's micro- and macrolevel growth opportunities as determined by the firm's current position and the ability of the firm's management to continue to find and execute such growth opportunities. This underlying firm risk is then further affected in its equity risk by management's use of financial leverage. In other words, much of the firm's fundamental equity risk is attributable to the market's perception of the risk in the firm's management ability. In principle, equilibrium asset pricing models such as the CAPM and other approaches discussed in Chapter 22 can be used to help estimate the market's required expected risk premium, RP, as this is applicable to a given firm or, more realistically, to a class of similar types of firms.[9]

---

[8] The firm value goes from $E = DIV_1/(0.12 - 0.02) = DIV_1/(0.10) = 10\ DIV_1$ to $E = DIV_1/(0.12 - 0.03) = DIV_1/(0.09) = 11.1\ DIV_1$.

[9] Empirical estimation of beta for a given firm is difficult to do in a very precise or reliable manner, in part because firms change over time and often provide short historical time-series of returns data, and also because the idiosyncratic risk at the individual firm level reduces the precision at which beta can be estimated from a time-series regression of the firm's returns onto the stock market returns. Also, it is important to be careful in practice about using the simple GGM and CAPM-based estimates of the market's required r to find "underpriced" REITs. While this is not impossible theoretically, in practice it is

Now recall from Chapter 9 that the total return, r, can be broken out into components in two different ways. We can view r as the riskfree rate plus the risk premium as described earlier, or we can also view r as the current dividend yield rate plus the expected growth rate in the share value and/or future dividend levels: $r = y + g$. This provides another way to help estimate the long-run total return requirement for a given REIT, or (once again, more realistically in empirical applications) for a class or type of stocks (such as large-cap retail REITs, mid-cap apartment REITs, etc.). The historical track record of the firm in providing growth in its dividends can be used to at least provide an empirical starting point for estimating g, and this can be added to the firm's current (or recent past average) dividend yield rate, y, to arrive at an estimate of the market's required total return, r. Of course, this is just turning the Gordon growth model around, solving equation (2) for r instead of for E:

$$r = \frac{DIV_1}{E} + g \qquad (2a)$$

Nevertheless, this exercise often provides an interesting empirical perspective.[10]

Of course, both risk and growth expectations can be affected by the finance policy determined by the firm's management, such as the use of various degrees of financial leverage.[11] But in many cases the effect of leverage will impact the market's perception of DIV_1, r, and g in offsetting ways, leaving the firm's equity value per share largely unchanged.[12] Similarly, merely engaging in the mechanical trade-off between current dividend yield and long-run growth, that is, converting between the y and g components of the total expected return by paying out as dividends greater or smaller proportions of the firm's net cash flow, does not generally affect the value of the firm's equity shares (that is, holding constant the firm's equity cost of capital and the expected fundamental growth opportunities possessed by the firm).[13]

---

much more likely that your estimates of r or g are wrong, or that the GGM is too simplistic a valuation model for the REIT in question. Remember, the stock market is pretty efficient, which means that easy ways of finding undervalued stocks do not exist.

[10] Obviously, as a purely mechanical mathematical tool, the GGM (or constant-growth perpetuity model) can be used to solve for any one of its three constituent variables as a function of the other two. This allows for interesting empirical analysis and speculation, especially if combined also with the $r_f + RP$ model of r based on an equilibrium asset pricing model.

[11] Such leverage is affected not only by the overall amount of debt, but also by the type of debt in terms of short-term versus long-term, and fixed rate versus floating or adjustable interest rate debt. In general, shorter-term and adjustable or floating rate debt will increase financial leverage (and equity risk) more than longer-term or fixed rate debt. Note, however, that REITs may be less sensitive to risk magnification in the use of adjustable rate debt than some other types of firms because of real estate's propensity to act as an inflation hedge, with underlying asset returns tending to be positively correlated with unexpected changes in inflation. (See Chapters 15 and 19 for further discussion.)

[12] Our discussion in Part V about optimal capital structure and the effect of debt financing on the value of the levered equity is relevant at the firm level.

[13] This can be seen as follows (using the GGM assumption of constant growth). The numerator of the GGM in equation (2), DIV_1, equals the firm's current level of earnings times one minus the "plowback ratio" (p), the proportion of earnings retained for future investment: $DIV_1 = (1 - p)EPS_1$, where EPS_1 is the firm's earnings per share in year 1. Now define y_E as the equity income yield from the firm's underlying asset equity, and V_0 as the firm's underlying asset equity value per share at the beginning of year 1, and g_E as the annual growth rate in the firm's underlying asset equity value. Then we have $DIV_1 = (1 - p)y_E V_0$ and $DIV_2 = (1 - p)y_E[(1 + g_E)V_0 + py_E V_0] = (1 - p)y_E(1 + g_E + py_E)V_0 = (1 + g_E + py_E)DIV_1$. In other words, the growth rate in dividends (g in the GGM) equals the growth rate in the underlying

24.1.2 Fundamental Growth Opportunities

Investors often think of stocks as either **growth stocks** or **income investments**. The former are purchased with the expectation that most of the total return will come in the form of capital gains and that dividends will tend to grow over time faster than inflation. The latter are purchased largely for their current dividend yield rate and perhaps the expectation that the share price (and dividend level) will probably not increase much more than the general inflation rate.

From the discussion in the preceding section, you can see that, at least to some extent, a firm can control its placement in the growth-versus-income spectrum by its dividend policy, that is, by regulating its plowback ratio, the proportion of its cash earnings it retains and invests as opposed to those it pays out as current dividends. But this ability is actually limited by the firm's capacity to invest its retained earnings in investments that have at least nonnegative NPVs in the eyes of the stock market investors in its shares. If investors perceive that a firm is retaining earnings only to invest in negative-NPV projects, they will soon sell the stock, driving down its share price until the firm's management wises up (or the firm gets bought out and has its management replaced). For this reason, firms that are true long-run growth stocks must generally be characterized as having substantial and persistent fundamental growth opportunities, defined as positive-NPV investment opportunities.

asset equity value (g_E) plus the plowback ratio times the underlying asset equity yield (py_E): $g = g_E + py_E$. Thus, by the GGM, the value of the firm's equity equals

$$E = \frac{DIV_1}{r - g} = \frac{(1 - p)y_E V_0}{r - g_E - py_E}$$

But altering the firm's plowback ratio, p, does not in itself change the risk of the firm (holding real growth opportunities constant), so $r_E = r$, and therefore, $y_E = r_E - g_E = r - g_E$. Substituting this equality into the previous equation, we obtain

$$E = \frac{(1 - p)y_E V_0}{r - g_E - py_E} = \frac{(1 - p)y_E V_0}{r - g_E - p(r - g_E)} = \frac{(1 - p)y_E V_0}{(1 - p)(r - g_E)} = \frac{y_E V_0}{r - g_E} = \frac{EPS_1}{r - g_E}$$

In other words, the value of the firm's equity is independent of the plowback ratio, p, and therefore not affected by mere shifting from g_E to $g = g_E + py_E$ as a result of altering the plowback ratio, holding constant the firm's risk and the firm's fundamental growth opportunities (i.e., its positive-NPV opportunities). Note that in these circumstances the firm's equity may be valued either as the firm's current earnings per share divided by $r - g_E$, or its current dividends per share divided by $r - g$:

$$E = \frac{EPS_1}{r - g_E} = \frac{DIV_1}{r - g}$$

Another way of understanding this result is to note the mathematical equivalence between the assumption that the stock market correctly values the firm's equity and the assumption that the firm does not change its risk (hence, does not change its average equity cost of capital) merely by changing its plowback ratio, holding constant its real growth opportunities and business risk. That is,

$$(E = V_0) \Leftrightarrow (r = r_E)$$

This equivalence is demonstrated in the previous equations, recognizing that $r_E = y_E + g_E$. In other words, if the stock market is informationally efficient, merely altering the firm's plowback ratio without a substantive reason to do so will not affect the firm's equity share price.

This point can be conceptualized by considering two hypothetical REITs, Beneficial of Boston (BOB) and Sioux Realty (Sioux). BOB is a perpetual, but completely passive owner of a portfolio of fully operational, income-generating commercial properties in the Northeast. These properties are expected to generate $100 million per year in perpetuity, and BOB has no debt. The stock market requires an expected total return of 10% for investment in BOB, giving BOB a firm value of

$$E_{BOB} = \frac{\$100 \; million}{0.10 - 0.0} = \frac{\$100 \; million}{0.10} = \$1,000 \; million$$

based on the GGM.

Like BOB, Sioux has no debt. Sioux's assets consist of stabilized properties very much like BOB's, only producing $50 million earnings per year instead of $100 million, plus Sioux owns the development rights to a land parcel. The construction project required to develop this land is expected to take one year and to require $2,400 million in construction cost including interest on the construction loan, which will cover all construction costs and be payable on project completion in one year. It is expected that the completed project will have a value in one year of $3,000 million, and Sioux will own this property free and clear once the construction loan is paid off.[14] Thus, the expected NPV of the construction project that Sioux owns the rights to is $600 million ($3,000 million − $2,400 million) one year from now. This is a rather risky expected value, however, because it is inherently levered, and it depends on the value of a building that does not yet exist.[15] Therefore, the stock market requires a 20% expected total return on this component of Sioux's assets, while requiring only a 10% return on Sioux's existing operational properties (of course). The value of Sioux is thus

$$E_{SIOUX} = PV(Existing) + PV(Growth)$$

$$= \frac{\$50 \; million}{0.10 - 0.0} + \frac{\$600 \; million}{1 + 0.20}$$

$$= (\$500 + \$500) \; million$$

$$= \$1,000 \; million$$

Thus, the two REITs have the same market value, but the value of one derives purely from existing operational assets, whereas half of the other's current market value is due to a growth opportunity. This causes BOB and Sioux to have very different current price/earnings ratios. BOB's *P/Earn* is

$$P/Earn_{BOB} = \frac{\$1,000 \; million}{\$100 \; million} = 10$$

while Sioux's is

$$P/Earn_{SIOUX} = \frac{\$1,000 \; million}{\$50 \; million} = 20$$

[14] How the loan will be paid off does not matter at this point. Sioux might take out a long-term mortgage, issue long-term bonds, or sell additional equity shares in the stock market.

[15] Real estate development is characterized by operational leverage, whether or not financial leverage is employed, because the construction costs are relatively fixed and certain, while the value of the asset to be built is more volatile and less certain. (See Chapters 28 and 29 for a treatment of real estate development as an investment.)

Furthermore, assuming that both of these REITs pay out all of their current earnings as dividends, this implies that BOB has a dividend yield of 10%, while Sioux has a dividend yield of 5%. But this does not imply that BOB's cost of equity capital is higher than Sioux's. In fact, at the firm level, Sioux's cost of capital is greater than BOB's. BOB's cost of capital (*r*) is 10%, while Sioux's is 10% for the 50% of its current firm value that is based on the existing operational assets, but it is 20% for the other 50% of Sioux's asset value. Thus, Sioux's firm-level cost of capital is 15%.[16]

Now it is important to recognize why Sioux's value is due partly to growth opportunities, and therefore why Sioux has a higher price/earnings multiple than BOB. It is because Sioux has positive-NPV investment opportunities. But why (or how) does Sioux have such positive investment opportunity? It is because Sioux *already owns* the land (or at least the development rights to the land) necessary for the development project. If Sioux did not already own this land, it would have to buy it in order to undertake the project and subsequently own the completed building free and clear. In such a circumstance, Sioux might very well not have a positive-NPV opportunity because the price of the land might be $500 million. Recall from our discussion in Chapters 10 and 12 that positive-NPV investment opportunities are rare and usually require the possessor to have some unique ability or circumstance. In Sioux's case its unique circumstance is that it already owns the land, and developable land is one type of real estate asset that provides growth-oriented investment.[17]

24.1.3 Are REITs Growth Stocks or Income Stocks?

With this understanding of the fundamental difference between growth stocks and income stocks (and between land and operational real estate assets), you can now probably see that most REITs are income stocks, not growth stocks, at least in the long run, for two fundamental reasons. First, in order to maintain their tax-exempt status, REITs are required to pay out 90% of their annual book earnings as dividends. This restricts to some degree the ability of some REITs to retain earnings for reinvestment. More important, however, the fundamental nature of real estate as an underlying asset dictates the income-oriented nature of most REITs, at least those that do not own much raw land or development rights. Stabilized operational commercial properties are, by their very nature, income-oriented assets, not growth-oriented assets. In general, the only major type of real estate asset that offers long-run maintainable growth stock characteristics is raw land or other such development rights.[18]

[16] Recall that a firm's *average* cost of capital does not necessarily equate to its *marginal* cost of capital for incremental asset purchases or investments. Thus, this difference in firm-level cost of capital between BOB and Sioux does not generally imply that either REIT can afford to pay more (or less) for any given property. (See section 12.3.5 in Chapter 12.)

[17] See Chapters 28 and 29 for an in-depth discussion of the investment characteristics of land and real estate development.

[18] As noted, the REIT tax status restrictions discourage concentration on pure "merchant building," that is, development not followed by a subsequent fairly long-term holding of the stabilized operating property, as most REIT assets must be held at least four years. For this reason, many companies that specialize in construction for sale do not elect REIT tax status. Such firms are sometimes referred to as real estate operating companies (REOCs).

While REITs in general, and over the long run, tend to be income stocks rather than growth stocks, a paraphrase of Abraham Lincoln is in order here:

Most REITs are not growth stocks most of the time,
but some REITs are growth stocks most of the time,
and most REITs are growth stocks some of the time.

Individual REITs may experience extended periods of substantial growth in share price for a variety of reasons, in addition to successful investment in raw land and heavy involvement in development activity. If the firm has unique entrepreneurial abilities in property transactions and/or operating management, or if it is able to tap into economies of scale, or to develop franchise value or economies of scope, it may engage in substantial positive-NPV investments for an extended period of time. Such results may be viewed as idiosyncratic, characteristic of specific firms but not a widespread characteristic of the REIT industry as a whole over the long run.

24.1.4 A Unique Environment: Parallel Asset Markets

Most of what we have said so far about REIT valuation could also be said about many other types of stocks. But there is one aspect related to the growth versus income question in which the REIT industry is rather unique. Apart from idiosyncratic growth specific to individual firms, all (or most) REITs in general will occasionally face periods of growth opportunity because of a unique feature of real estate that distinguishes REITs from most other non-real-estate firms that trade in the stock market. This is real estate's unique **dual asset market** situation, in which two parallel markets exist for trading real estate assets: the private property market (for trading individual whole properties directly) and the stock market (for trading REIT shares that provide equity ownership of underlying properties indirectly).

This unique circumstance was discussed extensively in Chapter 12 from a micro-level perspective.[19] The key point to reiterate here is that the stock market valuation of property (indirectly, in REITs) and the private property market valuation of property (directly) are not always consistent. The stock market sometimes values properties more highly than the property market does, and other times the reverse is true. In the long run, the two markets tend to agree. *The ability of capital to flow from one market to the other ensures that such agreement will tend to occur on average over the long run.* But in the short run, often, in historical experience, for periods lasting up to several years, the two markets may disagree about value. This disagreement can occur in either direction, but in general, when it occurs, the REIT market tends to be ahead of the private property market in time. In other words, after a period typically ranging from one to three years in historical experience, the property market often follows in the direction in which the REIT market previously led.

When the stock and property markets disagree about property value, REITs face either positive- or negative-NPV opportunities from buying properties at market value in the property market. Another way of putting this is to say that there have been prolonged periods in which REITs could implement positive-NPV investment strategies either by buying or selling in the private property market. When the stock market values property more highly than the private property market does, REITs can

---

[19] See section 12.3 in Chapter 12.

grow merely by buying properties, and this can turn most REITs temporarily into growth stocks. When the property market values properties more highly than the stock market does, REITs can earn positive-NPV profits for their shareholders by selling properties into the property market. In such periods REITs need to become "shrinking stocks," for the benefit of their stockholders, although they need not necessarily get out of the real estate *operating* business.[20] There may also be extended periods of time in which REIT values and property market values are more or less in agreement.[21]

As a result of the shifting relative valuations of property by the stock market and the private property market, REIT investors have to cope with the fact that many REITs can change their stripes, so to speak, from being growth stocks with high price/earnings multiples, to being income stocks with low price/earnings multiples, to occasionally being shrinking stocks with very low price/earnings multiples. Predicting these turning points in REIT valuation is difficult to do very precisely, which is a source of risk in REIT investment and a source of frustration among some REIT investors. However, the private property market is relatively predictable, and this helps to make possible the profitable redeployment of capital between the two types of markets, for some investors.

The stock market's perception and valuation of REIT growth opportunities, and the relative valuation differential between the stock and property asset markets, can be quantified to some extent by the comparison of REIT share prices with their **net asset values (NAVs)**. To understand this term, you must first realize that REITs are not required to **mark-to-market** their property asset holdings in their official balance sheets. That is, REITs are not required to appraise their property holdings at their current market values in the private property market. Properties are typically carried on REIT books at their historical purchase prices or investment costs, less accumulated depreciation. Thus, a simple comparison of the book value versus market value of a REIT's equity shares will not generally tell you whether the stock market perceives positive, negative, or neutral fundamental growth opportunities for the REIT. The accounting-based **book/market value ratios** that stock analysts regularly tabulate for other types of stocks are not very meaningful in the case of REITs.

With this in mind, stock analysts specializing in REIT stocks often attempt to estimate the current private property market valuations of a given REIT's property holdings. In effect, they perform something akin to a mass appraisal of the REIT's properties, although they typically use shortcut procedures rather than regression-based analysis such as we described in Chapter 23.[22] After subtracting the value of the REIT's debt liabilities, we arrive at the REIT's NAV per share.

The REIT's NAV per share is then compared to the REIT's equity share price. The difference reflects the stock market's current perception regarding the REIT's fundamental growth opportunities. If the REIT's share price exceeds its NAV, the stock market apparently perceives positive growth opportunities for the REIT. Implicitly,

[20] See the accompanying text box.

[21] However, see the discussion in section 24.4.

[22] For example, the analyst might estimate an approximate, typical prevailing cap rate reflective of the current private property asset market relevant for the REIT's property holdings and apply this cap rate to the REIT's current net operating income from their property holdings. Some specific adjustments might be made for special cases, such as newly developed properties that are still in a lease-up phase. Non-asset-based earnings, such as from property management, must also be evaluated and included, usually by use of a price/earnings multiple.

REIT Prices Have Hit the Lower Band
by Mike Miles, Editor

The following editorial appeared in the fall 1999 issue of Real Estate Finance; *it was written by the journal's editor, Mike Miles. Read this editorial and then think about the* Discussion Questions *at the end of the box.*

There is a strong intuitive argument for REITs trading within a "banded range" around private real estate prices. Beyond the logic, recent history seems to prove the case.

The logic: The pricing story is most easily told from the REIT CFO perspective. In the mid-1990s, REITs were trading at well above net asset value (NAV). The astute CFO realized that earnings could be increased by issuing new shares and buying properties. Such equity offerings, followed by property purchases, constituted "accretive acquisitions." Growing earnings through financial transactions is what CFOs like to do, and, in fact, REIT capitalization grew dramatically during this period.

After the drop in prices in 1998, the reverse situation held: REITs were trading at less than NAV. In this situation, the CFO can improve FFO per share by selling property. While this doesn't at first seem to be a "growth strategy," it needn't necessitate a shrinking of the company. Over the last year, we have seen sales of property from REITs to private limited partnerships. The limited partnership is typically made up of 75% new money (often pension funds) and 25% the REIT itself. The REIT continues to manage the properties and thus enjoys all the economics of scale that come with size while protecting its key employees during a period of low stock prices. From the pension fund's perspective, the situation works well, since acquisitions are relatively easy. The co-investor is already managing the property and has his money on the table in exactly the same position as the pension fund's money.

Selling properties into a limited partnership, like selling shares and buying properties, is not a costless transaction. In a price-inefficient market, the REITs have to pay up a bit during an acquisition phase and be a bit flexible in the sales phase. The pricing bias plus the legal and brokerage costs of the transaction could be in the 5% to 10% range. This suggests that REIT prices should trade around private prices, with the band being somewhere between 10% and 15%.

During the REIT boom days of the mid-1990s, REIT acquisitions clearly drove private market pricing, so that many market participants thought it was the REITs in the "driver's seat." However, REITs constitute only about 5% of the commercial real estate universe. Consequently, they are big enough to have a material impact on pricing when their shares are trading above NAV, but they do not constitute the biggest share of the market. Hence it is perfectly logical for this smaller (though still substantial) segment to trade around pricing in the overall market.

What drives REIT NAV to be above or below the private market price? Clearly, many REIT investors are not strictly real estate investors. Consequently, they drive REIT pricing up or down depending on real estate's relative attractiveness to other investment opportunities. When real estate was coming out of a severe depression and rents were expected to rise rapidly, real estate was favored. The accretive acquisitions game added to same property rent growth to produce what looked like a legitimate growth story. Longer-term REITs are not growth vehicles, they are value stocks. Today, value is out of favor, as are small- and medium-cap stocks. When the market turns, and mixed-asset investors again see real estate as a preferred alternative, one can expect REIT share pricing in excess of NAV. This is simply because the REITs are the way such investors can execute a real estate strategy quickly and with some degree of liquidity.

The more interesting question is "when will this all happen?" My friend Barry Greenfield is fond of saying, "REITs will rally when it is time to sell Microsoft," and that is really "the story." Today, private real estate pricing is quite attractive on a yield basis relative to both its history and to yields in the stock and bond markets. However, while this may be a plus for strictly real estate investors, the fact remains that mixed-asset investors have suffered dramatically if they failed to be in the larger global stocks and/or technology issues over the last few years. Mixed-asset investors who chose to invest in real estate because of "excessive stock prices" or the "better relative value in real estate" have been slaughtered.

REIT prices are banded around private prices. They trade above private prices when real estate looks good relative to stocks and bonds. Today, real estate, in general, is cheap compared to stocks and bonds, and REITs are trading well below NAV. Going forward from such a position, the only things that could hurt securitized real estate are a large drop in rents that would drop private pricing or a drop in the stock market, which would hurt real estate's relative attractiveness. Basically, securitization trades one risk factor for another: less illiquidity risk for more overall market risk. Bottom line, REITs look like a great "cash substitute" if you are a little bearish.

Discussion Questions

1. What does the author mean by the "lower band" he refers to in the title of the editorial? How has he estimated what this lower band is? What is the implication about the author's perception of stock market valuation of property (REIT equity prices) as a ratio of private property market valuation (REIT NAV) as of the fall of 1999?

2. Can you imagine an editorial like this being written about any other sector of the stock market, say, airline stocks, automotive stocks, high technology stocks, or public utilities? Why or why not?

3. Describe the general mechanism this article mentions for how REITs can continue to operate and even prosper during a period when the stock market valuation of property is lower than the property market's valuation (i.e., REIT NAV is greater than REIT stock market capitalization).

Source: *Real Estate Finance* 16(3): 1–2, Fall 1999. © 1999 Institutional Investor, Inc., Reproduced by permission. All rights reserved.

---

the NPV of those growth opportunities equals the difference between the REIT's share price and its NAV based on the REIT's current stabilized operating properties.[23] If the NAV is greater than the REIT's share price, this difference reflects negative growth opportunities, or the stock market's perception of less value in property holdings than is reflected in current private property market valuations.

24.2 REIT ANALYSIS, TERMINOLOGY, AND ISSUES

Apart from the dual asset market environment discussed in the preceding section, REITs are unique in other respects, compared to most other types of stocks. In this section we will introduce some of the unique features and terminology associated with the analysis and evaluation of REIT stocks.

24.2.1 Tax and Regulatory Constraints

Perhaps the most notable feature of REITs as compared to most other types of stocks is that REITs are exempt from corporate income tax. The rationale for this exemption is that REITs are viewed as investment vehicles, similar to mutual funds. Exemption from corporate-level taxation enables REIT shareholders to avoid the double taxation of corporate income that characterizes most stocks. In effect, REITs have tax advantages similar (though not identical) to pass-through entities such as partnerships, while retaining the limited liability afforded by the corporate ownership form. Of course, when the IRS giveth, it usually also taketh. In order to maintain this favorable tax treatment, REITs are subject to some unique restrictions on their operations

---

[23]As noted, developable land parcels owned by the REIT, and development projects in the construction or lease-up phase, may be considered growth opportunities or growth-oriented assets even though they are included in the REIT's NAV. To this extent, the share price minus NAV difference may understate the REIT's growth opportunities or its growth-oriented nature as a firm.

and activities. These restrictions are designed essentially to maintain REITs as a somewhat passive investment vehicle, not too far removed from the original "mutual fund for real estate" idea. The regulations are also designed to ensure that REIT investment is accessible to small individual investors, the original intent of the 1960 REIT-enabling legislation. The following major restrictions faced REITs as of the end of the 1990s:

1. A REIT cannot be a closely held corporation in the sense that five or fewer individuals (and certain trusts) may not own more than 50% of the REIT's stock, and there must be at least 100 different shareholders. This is known as the **five-or-fewer rule**.[24]

2. Seventy-five percent or more of the REIT's total assets must be real estate, mortgages, cash, or federal government securities, and 75% or more of the REIT's yearly gross income must be derived directly or indirectly from real property ownership (including mortgages, partnerships, and other REITs).

3. Ninety percent or more of the REIT's annual taxable income must be distributed to shareholders as dividends each year.[25]

4. REITs must derive their income from primarily passive sources such as rents and mortgage interest, as distinct from short-term trading or sale of property assets. They cannot use their tax status to shield non-real-estate income from corporate taxation. A REIT is subject to a tax of 100% on net income from "prohibited transactions," such as the sale or other disposition of property held primarily for sale in the ordinary course of its trade or business. However, if the REIT sells property it has held for at least four years and the aggregate adjusted basis of the property sold does not exceed 10% of the aggregate basis of all assets of the REIT as of the beginning of the year, no prohibited transaction is deemed to have occurred.

Obviously one of the results of these restrictions is that REITs are less able than other firms to retain earnings for investment purposes, as 90% of their annual earnings must be paid out as dividends. This means that REITs must go outside the firm to the capital market more frequently than would otherwise be the case to obtain either debt or equity capital in order to make new investments. In fact, however, many REITs actually distribute more than the minimum 90% of taxable earnings in dividends, suggesting that this distribution constraint is not binding. One reason is that REITs are able to depreciate their property holdings. Depreciation expenses shield considerable amounts of REIT cash flow from being reflected in taxable earnings.[26] In the 1990s the 90% of earnings distribution requirement typically equated to about 60% of operational cash flow, while the typical REIT actually distributed 65% to 85% of its cash flow during that period.

---

[24] Since 1993, pension funds are considered for the purpose of this rule to represent as many owners as there are members of the pension plan. Thus, in effect, institutional investors are not limited by the five-or-fewer rule.

[25] Prior to the REIT Modernization Act of 1999, REITs had to pay out 95% of their annual taxable income in dividends. (The act took effect on January 1, 2001.)

[26] Some REIT dividends are often considered to be distributions of invested capital and are not subject to income taxes even at the personal shareholder level.

24.2.2 REIT Earnings Measures

Depreciation expenses are a particularly large portion of REIT expenses because REITs are very capital-intensive firms, compared to most other types of stocks. As we pointed out in Chapter 14, depreciation expenses are not like most other types of expenses in that they are not a cash outflow, but represent a purely accrual item. Furthermore, in the case of real property, the depreciation is often not matched by an actual loss in nominal value of the property over time, as inflation may match or exceed the rate of real depreciation in the property. For these reasons, REIT taxable earnings, essentially the "official" (i.e., GAAP) accounting-based **net income** of the firm, are widely viewed as not comparable to the earnings reported for most other types of stocks. As a result, other measures are widely used to track REIT earnings for purposes of analyzing REIT stock values. The two most widely used such measures are referred to as FFO and FAD.

FFO stands for "**funds from operations.**" It is defined as follows. Start with the firm's GAAP net income. Then,

> Add back: *Real property depreciation expense.*
> Add back: *Preferred stock dividends and distributions to OP unit-holders.*[27]
> Deduct: *Net gains from property sales and extraordinary items.*

The result is FFO. As you can see, this is essentially the income from the firm's ongoing operations. FFO in REITs is often equated loosely to net operating income (NOI) in direct property holdings, but an important distinction must be made between these two measures. NOI is a *property-level* measure that does not include the effect of debt service or financial leverage. FFO is a *firm-level* measure. As most REITs employ debt financing, the typical REIT FFO represents levered equity operating income.

FAD stands for "**funds available for distribution.**"[28] It is defined as follows. Start with the firm's FFO as defined earlier. Then,

> Deduct: *Capital improvement expenditures (CI).*[29]
> Deduct: *Amortization of debt principle (AMORT).*
> Adjust for: *Straight-line rents.*[30]

The result is FAD. As the name implies, FAD is considered to be a better representation than FFO of the actual cash flow received by the firm available for distribution to shareholders in a given year. FAD is most directly comparable to the equity-before-tax

---

[27] OP unit holders are investors in the REIT's "umbrella partnership," if the REIT is an UPREIT. (See section 24.2.3.)

[28] FAD is also sometimes referred to as "adjusted funds from operations" (AFFO) or "cash available for distribution" (CAD).

[29] This refers to expenditures to maintain the revenue-earning potential of existing properties, not expenditures for expansion or development of new properties.

[30] Accounting rules allow rent concessions and other variations over time in the rent levels specified in long-term leases to be "straight-lined." This means that the average rent over the entire lease contract is reported each year. This results in the firm's reported rental income exceeding actual rent cash flow received during the early years of the lease, and falling short during later years. FAD adjusts for this effect to report the actual rental cash flow each year.

cash flow (EBTCF) line item described at the property level in Chapter 14.[31] In the late 1990s the typical REIT's FAD was about 1.6 times its GAAP net income.

Price/earnings ratios (P/Es) are often reported and examined in the stock market, and when such measures are computed for REITs, they are typically based on either FFO or FAD as the earnings measure. The typical REIT P/E ratio based on FAD was around 10 at the turn of the 21st century, much lower than the typical P/E ratio for other types of stocks at that time. However, while FFO and FAD may indeed be more meaningful measures of REIT earnings than GAAP net income, it must nevertheless be remembered that most other firms' P/Es are typically reported based on the GAAP income measure. Exact apples-to-apples comparisons across stock market sectors, and even across individual firms within sectors, are difficult to make.

24.2.3 Agency Costs: Conflicts of Interest

Any large firm involves various interest groups or **stakeholders**, for example, stockholders, bondholders, other creditors, managers, employees, and customers. While all of these groups share common interests in the firm, inevitably **conflicts of interest** arise. The structure and governance of the firm, as well as its operating procedures, generally attempt to minimize the conflicts and promote the common interests and synergy. But no complex human organization is perfect, and remaining conflicts of interest can potentially reduce the value of the firm as measured by its equity share price, the stockholders' interest. The general economic term for such reduction in firm value is **agency cost**, referring to the potential conflict of interest between the principal party, the stockholders (that is, the owners of the firm), and their agent, the firm's professional management.[32] REITs are not immune to the general types of conflict of interest and agency cost that can plague any firm. But REITs also have some unique issues in this regard.

In the old days of the REIT industry, that is, prior to the 1990s, REITs were always very small firms (by stock market standards), usually very passive in their investment styles, and virtually always run by external managers. In fact, until 1986 REITs were required to hire external advisors to manage their assets. The external manager did not have any ownership share in the REIT. In this structure the REIT owners (that is, the stockholders as represented by the REIT board of directors) could only hire or fire the advisor. They could not hire or fire the individual employees who actually ran the REIT but worked directly for the advisor, not for the REIT. This blunted the line of authority from ownership to management and made active, vertically integrated management almost impossible. It also allowed a number of unique conflicts of interest to occur. For example, the external advisor who actually ran the REIT operations was often paid a fee that was determined solely by the value of the assets under management. As a result, there was a built-in conflict of interest regarding property acquisitions and dispositions. It would rarely ever be in the advisor's interest to sell properties, even if such sales were highly profitable. With REITs being so small, and comprising such a small share of the stock market, very few Wall Street stock analysts specialized in REITs, and most major institutional investors could not

[31] See section 14.2.3, Exhibit 14-2.

[32] Other types of conflict of interest resulting in agency cost are also possible. For example, we noted in Chapter 15 the possibility of conflict of interest between different classes of investors, such as stockholders and bondholders. (See section 15.3.3 in Chapter 15.)

invest in most REITs because of the five-or-fewer rule described in section 24.2.1. As a result, there was little effective scrutiny and oversight of REITs in the marketplace, and REITs developed a reputation for having major agency cost problems.

The so-called "modern REIT" is a very different animal. Internally managed like most industrial and service corporations in other sectors of the stock market, it is typically a large- to medium-size firm tracked by a number of Wall Street analysts that specialize in REITs. It has a number of large, institutional investors, as well as substantial stock ownership on the part of top managers. Its governing board of directors includes both external members and top management. Operations in modern REITs typically encompass the provision of specialized, vertically integrated commercial real estate services at both the portfolio and property levels, and potentially range from raw land acquisition through development, ownership, management, and leasing. This new structure has mitigated many of the old conflicts and agency costs, but some unique problems remain, and some additional problems have arisen in the new system. Here we will note only a few of the most commonly mentioned, to give you an idea of the types of conflicts of interest that can cause suboptimal performance in REITs.[33]

1. **Transaction bias in UPREITs.** As noted in Chapter 7, many of the modern REITs since the 1990s were organized as umbrella partnership REITs.[34] That is, they do not own real estate directly. Instead, they own units in an **umbrella partnership**, also known as an **operating partnership (OP)**, which directly owns and operates the REIT's properties. This structure enables the REIT to acquire properties from taxable individuals while allowing those individuals to defer realizing a capital gain taxable event. But the resulting structure is very complex, and sets up some potential conflicts of interest. One of the most noteworthy is the fact that the REIT may share with outside OP unit holders the control of the timing of sales of properties from the OP. These outside unit holders will typically have a greater capital gains tax liability than the REIT shareholders will have in the event of a sale of property. A tax-based conflict of interest is thereby set up between the REIT shareholders and the outside OP unit holders regarding the timing or desirability of the sale of certain properties.

2. **Real estate interests outside the REIT.** It is not uncommon for a REIT to be originally sponsored by, and to remain effectively controlled by, an individual or group of individuals who are successful private real estate entrepreneurs and managers. Of course, this in itself makes eminent sense. However, for a variety of reasons, the sponsoring individual or group may not place all of their real estate interests within the REIT.[35] For example, some properties may remain outside the REIT, or a property management or leasing business may remain outside the REIT, yet still be owned by the group that effectively controls the REIT. This can cause a potential for two types of conflicts of interest as identified by Sagalyn (1996), **resource allocation**, and **competitive affiliates**. The former refers to the fact that the top managers of the

---

[33] For a more detailed and comprehensive, yet quite readable summary of conflicts of interest in the modern REIT, see Sagalyn (1996). Much of the remainder of this section is based on Sagalyn's article.

[34] See section 7.1.3 in Chapter 7.

[35] Some of these reasons could make good management sense. For example, it may be desirable to focus the REIT on only one aspect of the sponsoring group's real estate interests, so as to enable the REIT to benefit from specialized management expertise.

REIT may have other demands on their time and interest besides the REIT and may therefore neglect some duties at the REIT in order to serve their interests outside the REIT. The competitive affiliates conflict of interest refers to the fact that the REIT managers may have outside interests that actually compete with the REIT. For example, a REIT manager may own properties that compete with the REIT's properties, or may operate a leasing brokerage business that would benefit from leasing space to buildings that compete with the REIT's buildings.[36]

3. **Potential for self-dealing.** Another type of conflict of interest that may be set up when REIT managers or sponsoring shareholders have outside interests is what Sagalyn termed **self-dealing.** This refers to the REIT dealing with affiliated entities in less-than-arms-length transactions. For example, the REIT might hire a firm that is affiliated with its managers or sponsoring shareholders to provide property management or leasing services. If the arrangement involves so-called "sweetheart" terms, providing the outside entity with a better than normal arrangement, then this obviously harms the REIT's other shareholders.

In spite of potential problems such as these, it seems likely that the governance structure and highly competitive stock market environment in which REITs trade are generally able to combine to keep agency costs down to a level that is not much worse in the modern REIT industry than it is in other sectors of the stock market. It is nevertheless important for investors and analysts to be aware of the potential dangers.

24.3 SOME CONSIDERATIONS OF REIT MANAGEMENT STRATEGY

Back in Part II of this book, when we were describing the urban economic principles that underlie real estate phenomena, we noted the traditional real estate cliché that only three things matter in real estate: location, location, and location. In the 1990s, at the outset of the development of the modern REIT industry characterized by internally managed, vertically integrated corporations, REIT promoters and analysts were fond of paraphrasing that traditional cliché with a new one, claiming that three things mattered in the successful REIT: management, management, and management. Like most clichés, what makes this one amusing is that it contains an important grain of truth. In this section we aim to note briefly several REIT strategic management considerations or goals that are often important.

Financial Strategy. Financial strategy is a classical component of overall firm-level business strategy. This is particularly true in the case of a capital-intensive industry such as real estate. While the overview of capital structure presented in Chapter 15 is relevant to REITs, we will point out here some considerations that are particularly noticeable in the financial behavior of REITs.

[36] An important feature of agency cost is the fact that this type of cost may be incurred by shareholders (in the form of diminished share value) even if the conflict of interest has not yet actually materialized, in the sense that no behavior actually contrary to the interest of the REIT shareholders has actually yet occurred. The mere presence of the conflict of interest, the setting up of some positive probability that management behavior contrary to shareholder interest might occur, can cause a diminution in shareholder value.

The first point to note is that REITs' 90% earnings distribution requirement may tend to put some REITs under some added financial stress. The distribution requirement means that, in order to grow, REITs must go to external sources of capital more frequently.

This situation is perhaps made more acute by the stock market environment in which REIT shares trade. Although it need not be so, the stock market tends to be "the land of growth," that is, the stock market tends to like growth and to reward firms that it perceives as able to grow over the long run. As described in section 24.1, the stock market rewards growth firms with higher price/earnings multiples in their share prices, which redounds to the benefit of the original shareholders in those firms.[37] So it is natural for REITs to want to try to grow, and this requires infusions of external capital into the firm. Such capital comes generally in the form of either debt or equity.[38] Equity generally comes with less risk (to the preexisting shareholders) and fewer strings attached than does debt (although it may risk diluting the existing directors' control of the firm in the long run). In addition, REITs do not have the need for corporate income tax shields that most profitable corporations have, which causes those corporations to prefer debt over equity.[39] For these reasons, we might expect that REITs would tend to prefer equity over debt financing.

Yet this natural preference for equity is mitigated to some extent by the growth imperative. As noted previously, real estate underlying assets are generally not growth oriented. It is difficult to generate long-term growth opportunities in the real estate field, particularly if the mainstay of your business is income property investment and operation rather than raw land investment or development. We noted in Chapter 13, however, that financial leverage can often be employed to convert income-oriented, low-growth underlying assets into higher-growth (lower-yield) equity investments.[40] If a REIT can borrow at interest rates lower than its properties' total returns, then positive leverage will exist in the REIT's equity.[41] Indeed, if the REIT can borrow at debt constants (including amortization as well as interest) lower than its properties' current income yields, then it will be able to shift its equity total return relatively toward the capital gain component without sacrificing current yield.[42] These financial leverage considerations give debt financing considerable appeal to REITs, even though REITs lack the tax-driven appetite most corporations have for debt financing.[43]

But let's continue on in this point/counterpoint vein. If REITs have a desire for financial leverage, this desire tends to be kept in check by the stock market's squeamishness about REIT debt. The stock market is famously "once bitten, twice shy." REITs have gotten into trouble in the past as a result of being too highly leveraged,

---

[37] Note, however, that only a favorable change in the REIT's price/earnings multiple causes a capital gain "pop" in preexisting shareholders' value, a supernormal return realization (ex post).

[38] Preferred stock is a middle ground that has some popularity among REITs.

[39] Recall our discussion of double taxation in Chapter 15. This also has implications for "signaling" or "pecking-order" theories of preference for debt over equity.

[40] This is different from simply converting current income (y) to capital gain (g) by increasing the plowback ratio. Financial leverage alters the nature of the equity total return, including its risk.

[41] Note that such an increase in the REIT's equity total return expectation does not necessarily (or generally) imply an increase in the REIT's overall firm-level cost of capital, which is measured by its weighted average cost of capital (WACC), including the cost of the debt capital. (See section 13.3 in Chapter 13, and section 15.3 in Chapter 15.)

[42] See sections 13.4 and 13.5 in Chapter 13.

[43] In addition, there are other arguments both for and against debt financing, as discussed in Chapter 15.

most famously in the "REIT debacle" of the early 1970s. Excessive leverage played a prominent role in the widespread commercial property financial problems at the end of the 1980s as well.[44] As a result of these memories, perhaps, the stock market has the reputation for severely penalizing REITs that find themselves with large amounts of debt relative to the stock market's valuation of their equity. For the most part, therefore, REITs try to remain with debt amounts no more than about 40% of their total asset value. This is probably a bit less debt than is typically employed by taxable privately held real estate firms.

This relatively conservative debt position, combined with the pressure for growth, makes it easy for REITs to be tempted by a strategy of using low-interest debt to maximize the degree of positive leverage. This typically implies a temptation to borrow using short-term and floating or adjustable rate debt. Of course, there is no free lunch. This type of debt magnifies the REIT's equity risk and can result in a an asset/liability maturity gap or maturity "mismatch" problem.[45] Since this is an obvious danger, the type of problem that caused the REIT debacle of the early 1970s, REIT analysts in the stock market tend to be on the lookout for it, and responsible REIT managers are pretty good at resisting the temptation. In short, REIT financial strategy is often a balancing act, a tension between opposing objectives and constraints.[46]

Management Specialization. A prominent characteristic of REIT management strategy during the 1990s, one that distinguished the new REITs of that decade from the older ones, was the tendency of REITs to specialize or focus on one type of property, or sometimes two closely related types, such as industrial and office properties.[47] Earlier REITs had often been diversified by property type. The idea was that the REIT's investors would want a diversified portfolio of properties. This may have made some sense when REITs were viewed as passive investment vehicles, but in fact, REIT investors can diversify on their own by buying different types of REIT stocks, and the more sophisticated institutional investors of the 1990s preferred to make these types of diversification decisions themselves. Furthermore, once REITs became more actively managed entities, it became clear that management expertise could usually be more effective when it was specialized by property type. Also, perhaps more important, the stock market can more easily understand and analyze a REIT that is specialized into one of a few somewhat standard space market segments.[48] Led by health-care REITs in the late 1980s, REITs in the 1990s tended to specialize in fields such as apartments, shopping malls, smaller retail centers, hotels, and office and industrial properties (or the combination of these two). Smaller, more unique niches have also been developed, such as self-storage, manufactured housing, golf courses, and others.

[44] See Chapter 7, section 7.2.3.

[45] See Chapter 19, section 19.1.4.

[46] Empirical evidence on REIT capital preferences during the 1990s is provided in Ghosh, Nag, and Sirmans (1997). Their study documents a slight tendency to favor equity over debt financing, particularly during periods of favorable stock market valuation of REITs.

[47] Industrial and office properties have similar leasing characteristics and often involve the same firms, or same types of firms, as tenants. Some properties are even hybrids or mixtures of office and warehouse uses.

[48] A recent study by Dennis Capozza and Paul Seguin provides evidence that the primary value of specialization is not added value in the firm's operating profitability, but rather in the stock market valuation of the firm. See Capozza and Seguin (1999).

Franchise Value. Another strategy that some major REITs began to pursue seriously in the 1990s was to add value by building **brand name recognition** and reputation among their ultimate customers, the users of their spaces. This strategy has worked successfully for some firms in other branches of the service sector, such as retail and restaurant chains. Among the most notable attempts to build brand image was that of Simon, a shopping mall REIT. The Simon brand was displayed prominently in all of its malls and promoted through both hard-copy media and the Web. The idea was that if Simon malls were consistent enough in quality and service, then perhaps consumers would attach some value to the brand and choose Simon malls over other more convenient malls when traveling. Moreover, brand recognition may work synergistically with geographical scope to build franchise value. For example, a tenant in a Post Property apartment decides to move to another city and needs to break her lease. Rather than charging the tenant a deposit penalty, the property manager allows the tenant to break the lease provided she moves into another Post property in her new city. High-quality service and consistent amenities may help such a REIT keep tenants longer and experience lower-than-average vacancy rates in its overall portfolio of properties. So while the strategy of building franchise value remains somewhat unproven in the REIT industry, there is some logic to support the idea of trying to build franchise value when combined with economies of scale and geographic scope.

Vertical Integration. Vertical integration refers to the concept of a single firm controlling several linked stages in the production process, for example, from iron ore to steel to cars in the classical example of the Ford Motor Company early in the 20th century. The old REITs before the 1990s were confined largely to one phase of the process of the production of commercial property goods and services, namely, the role of capital provision (investment) and ownership of existing income-producing properties, which sometimes included some aspects of the role of portfolio or asset management. Vertical integration involves going "upstream" in the production process to the construction and development of new buildings, and even the acquisition of land sites for future construction. It also involves going "downstream" in the production and delivery process to include property management, leasing, and other related services. A key advantage of vertical integration is that it gives a REIT flexibility to survive, and even profit from, the changes in the relative valuations between the stock and property markets, as described in section 24.1.4. For example, vertical integration allows REITs to profit by selling properties when their NAV exceeds their stock market valuations, while retaining operating scale and geographical scope by continuing to control the operational management of the properties they sell.[49] Most modern REITs exhibit at least some degree of vertical integration, and this has become a hallmark of modern REIT management strategy.

Economies of Scale. The concept of scale economies refers to the phenomenon in which the average cost of production declines with an increasing rate of production. Most capital-intensive industries in the United States exhibit scale economies, at least up to a point. Several leaders of the REIT industry in the 1990s argued forcefully that REITs are subject to this same phenomenon, that larger REITs would experience

---

[49] See the editorial by Mike Miles in the text box at the end of section 24.1.4.

lower average costs than smaller REITs.[50] The implication is that the big REITs will tend to get bigger (presumably by some combination of buying or merging with other REITs, buying properties in the private property market, and/or building new properties themselves), until the scale economies are exhausted. This suggests that the industry will tend to consolidate, as happened in the 20th century, for example, in such industries as automobile and aircraft manufacturing.[51] If this is true, then REITs can "grow by growing," in a sense. In other words, REITs may face positive-NPV opportunities from routine expansion (i.e., even when there is no positive NPV from the investment at the *microlevel*) simply because the increased scale will allow their average total costs to decline. This has obviously important strategic implications, not only for individual REITs, but also for investors interested in the industry as a whole.

But is it true? Do REITs really face economies of scale, and if they do, are the scale economies very significant, and at what size of firm do they play out and get essentially exhausted? These are questions that have yet to be answered definitively, although some serious academic research was beginning to be focused on this question around the turn of the 21st century. Early empirical studies sponsored by the Real Estate Research Institute (RERI), and carried out by Martina Bers and Thomas Springer found evidence of scale economies in REIT administrative and management expenses, although the cost advantages appeared to be relatively minor and largely exhausted at fairly small scales. But the largest component of REIT total costs is the cost of capital. In a more recent RERI-sponsored study, Brent Ambrose and Anthony Pennington-Cross examined 126 equity REITs during the late 1990s, relating their capital cost to their size using a classical economic production function. Their study found evidence of substantial scale economies in capital cost, probably driven largely by the increased liquidity of larger-capitalization stocks, and the need of large institutional investors to place capital into more liquid stocks. In other words, controlling for risk, REIT firm-level average capital cost (as measured by the firm-level WACC) appeared to decline significantly with firm size. Furthermore, this cost advantage seemed not to be exhausted even within the largest quartile of REITs (measured by market capitalization).[52]

Yet if these findings hold up, this is a rather different type of scale economy than the classical concept exhibited in manufacturing industries. Can true scale economy really be based largely on financial capital costs rather than on production technology in the underlying physical capital? If such financial-based economies are really important, one wonders whether the financial services and investment industries will be able to come up with methods and vehicles to pool REIT shares or otherwise enable smaller REITs to tap into some of the liquidity-oriented capital cost reductions enjoyed by larger REITs. In a response to the Linneman thesis of scale economy, John Vogel advanced the notion that firms need not own real estate in order to reap scale economy benefits of property management.[53] In short, the jury is still out, although considerable evidence does seem to suggest that significant scale economies were at work in the REIT industry during the 1990s.

---

[50] Average cost refers to cost per unit of output. In the case of REITs, average cost might be measured as the total cost (including not only the operating costs but also the required return on capital) per year, per square foot of space offered to tenants.

[51] Peter Linneman (1997) presented these arguments eloquently.

[52] See Bers and Springer (1998), and Ambrose and Pennington-Cross (2000).

[53] See Vogel (1997).

Power in the Space Market. The last major REIT management strategy consideration we will note here is the idea of a REIT using its size and access to capital to corner the market by concentrating its space ownership within a few geographically confined space markets. Rental markets are often sufficiently segmented so as to enable such concentrated ownership to impart some **market power** (i.e., ability to influence rents) to the dominant space owner, at least in the short run. Yet they are not so segmented as to make such a strategy run afoul of antitrust laws (presumably). Nevertheless, while some REITs did develop semidominant ownership positions in a few markets during the 1990s, it is not clear that this strategy was driven so much by a pursuit of market power as simply by geographical specialization and concentration of local expertise. In fact, it is rare to find geographically constrained space markets that are so unique that they cannot face substantial competition from substitute locations, at least over the medium-term horizon in which new construction can occur. Nevertheless, large REITs do have some ability to pursue a market power strategy, and such a strategy probably does offer some potential profit in many cases.

24.4 FUNDAMENTAL NATURE AND VALUE OF REITS: TWO MODELS

We discussed extensively in previous sections of this chapter, and in Chapter 12, the unique implications for REITs of the existence of two parallel asset markets, the stock market in which REITs' equity shares trade and the private property market in which REITs' underlying physical assets trade. We made the point that these two asset markets' valuations may be inconsistent for extended periods of time. Such inconsistency is fascinating from an intellectual perspective for anyone interested in financial economics and the functioning of capital asset markets. It is also of great practical import, with huge implications for the nature of investment risk and return for both direct private property investment and REIT investment. Because of this importance, we think it is worthwhile to add in this section another perspective on differential valuation between the stock and property markets.

Our previous treatment of this issue was largely from a microlevel perspective, suggesting that the stock and property markets sometimes have different valuations of the same underlying physical properties. From that perspective, we argued that the two markets would tend to agree about value in the long run.[54] We suggested that disagreements at this level might tend to largely reflect differences in the informational efficiency between the two markets, with the stock market's valuation evident in REIT share prices tending to lead in time the private property market's valuation evident in property market values. We suggested that such a lead/lag relationship, although certainly not lockstep or deterministic, has been fairly pronounced in the historical evidence and has tended to range from one to three years in length (i.e., that has been the typical time lag between major turning points in market value trends).[55]

---

[54] While this seems likely, it is not necessarily the case, as the two asset markets could have different investor clientele on the margin, with different perceptions of, and preferences for, underlying property risk.

[55] See, for example, Gyourko and Keim (1992), Barkham and Geltner (1995), and Geltner and Goetzmann (2000).

While this microlevel perspective is no doubt an important part of the reality explaining differential valuations between the two markets, there is another, more purely macrolevel perspective on differential valuation.

The macrolevel explanation of differential valuation is based on two very different models of what REITs are. One model says that REITs essentially are largely passive investment vehicles, like **closed-end mutual funds**, only they hold real estate assets instead of stocks.[56] The other model says that REITs are **operating corporations**, actively providing income property goods and services to tenants and other users. To the extent that differential valuation between the stock and property markets is due to either one of these two macrolevel models of what REITs are, such differential valuation can endure indefinitely, in principle, at least within a certain band-width of relative value reflecting the transaction costs of converting assets from one ownership structure to another.[57] In particular, the closed-end mutual fund model suggests that REIT shares will generally tend to trade at values *below* their NAVs. The operating corporation model suggests that REIT shares will generally tend to trade at values *above* their NAVs. The reason for this difference is explained here.

First consider the closed-end mutual fund model of REITs. In this model REITs add value largely as pass-through securities, mechanisms to enable small investors to invest in diversified portfolios of income property equity while retaining liquidity and avoiding the need to become active in the operational management of real estate. Such REITs may also try to add value through successful active portfolio management, that is, trading of properties, but the high search and transaction costs of trading directly in the private property market, combined with the REIT tax-status restrictions against active trading of properties, severely limits the degree to which REITs-as-mutual-funds can add value by active trading.

Offsetting any such additions to value, REITs-as-mutual-funds introduce additional costs and sources of risk. One type of additional cost is simply the additional layer of management and administration, the cost of asset or portfolio management. (This cost will tend to be greater the more actively the REIT is managed.) Of course, one way or another, investors would have to absorb much of this extra layer of costs themselves anyway if they chose to invest directly in property.[58] A more important type of cost added by REITs-as-mutual-funds is agency cost. This type of cost was described in section 24.2.3. Yet another type of cost added at the macrolevel is attributable to the fact that the stock market may understand less well how to evaluate portfolios of properties than the property market does. The stock market is very informationally efficient in some respects, but real property valuation is a somewhat specialized field that the typical stock market investor or analyst probably understands less well than the typical private property market investor or appraiser. When

---

[56] Closed-end mutual funds issue equity shares and invest the proceeds in a portfolio of securities, which the fund managers typically trade actively, buying and selling securities in an attempt to add value to the portfolio. Unlike open-end funds, closed-end fund shares do not trade at the current market-value-based NAV of their portfolio. As the fund shares trade directly in the stock market, nothing requires that their market prices must exactly equal the contemporaneous market-value-based NAV per share of the fund. In fact, closed-end fund shares typically trade at values different from their NAVs.

[57] The Mike Miles editorial reprinted earlier suggests that the band value bound for long-run sustainable valuation difference is in the neighborhood of 10% to 15%, but this is only a crude estimate of a limit that may change over time.

[58] For example, just because an investor finds properties to invest in herself, does not mean that this search and acquisition process is costless.

investors do not understand something, they regard it as being risky (perhaps right-fully so from their perspective), and they discount its value accordingly. Thus, per-haps somewhat ironically, the REIT-as-mutual-fund may lose some value due to this loss of transparency and understandability.

Apart from the previous considerations that are somewhat peculiar to REITs, it should be recognized that closed-end mutual funds tend to trade at a discount to NAV even when their investment portfolios consist only of publicly traded securi-ties. The reason is that the additional layer of management and control inserted between the investor and the underlying assets adds a layer of risk, even when the assets held by the fund are readily understood by investors, such as ordinary common stocks. The mutual fund managers may be as likely to beat the market as fall short of the market (or even more likely to beat the market), but their asset-management-level decision making adds a layer of risk.[59] In equilibrium, investors must be com-pensated, in the form of higher expected returns, for bearing this extra layer of risk. The only way to obtain higher average returns is for the closed-end fund shares to trade at a price below their NAV, on average. This is known as the **closed-end mutual fund discount**. This discount is well documented empirically among stock market closed-end mutual funds, and there is no reason to assume that REITs-as-mutual-funds would be able to avoid it.

Now consider the other model of REITs, that they are operating corporations. In this model REITs are not passive pass-through vehicles at all. They are entrepreneurial providers of goods and services in a capital-intensive industry that is probably charac-terized by at least some degree of scale economy. Even in the absence of favorable asset valuation in the private property market, some REITS may have substantial idiosyn-cratic growth opportunities, based on either microlevel or macrolevel strategies.[60] Suc-cessful REITS will develop and nourish the ability to add value creatively in order to find and take advantage of such growth opportunities. Such REITs will generally not be high-flying growth stocks such as the typical technology or e-commerce start-ups that operate in industries in the midst of rapid expansion based on cutting-edge technolog-ical breakthroughs. But they will be able to put together sustained track records of mod-est growth along with solid provision of ongoing income in the form of dividends. Such firms will expand over the long run. REITs that have less effective and less capable man-agement will not grow and will probably tend to shrink or be taken over by more suc-cessful REITs, according to the stock market's iron "law of the jungle." Over time, competition in the capital market will tend to weed out the less efficient and less entre-preneurial REITs, leaving only the most capable operating corporations.

This model sees REITs as essentially very much like the typical industrial and service corporations that characterize most sectors of the stock market. In this model, the REIT sector will ultimately probably be dominated by relatively few, relatively large firms. Most successful firms in the stock market trade at market values in excess of their book values (and less successful firms tend to die out). In REIT terms, this would translate into a tendency for the surviving firms to trade at prices above their NAVs, on average over time, reflecting the growth opportunities the successful firms are able generate on a sustained basis.

[59]Note that a subtle distinction exists between adding a layer of *cost* (as we discussed in the preceding para-graph) and adding a layer of *risk* (as we are suggesting here). Adding a layer of cost reduces the expected value (ex ante mean) of the investment's future value, while adding a layer of risk increases the uncertainty surrounding the investment's future value (without necessarily changing its expected value).

[60]Some such types of strategies were discussed in previous sections.

Either one of these two models of what REITs are can exist on a sustained basis indefinitely. One model would have REITs tending to trade at a discount to their NAV, while the other would produce the opposite result. Of course, it is possible for both of these models to be true simultaneously, in the sense that REITs are heterogeneous. The mutual fund model may fit some REITs better, while the operating corporation model may fit other REITs better. But there may also be a tendency for the stock market to stereotype sectors of the market or types of stocks. Robert Shiller characterized this type of investor behavior as **mental compartmentalizing**.[61] Such behavior could result in all REITs tending to get painted with the same brush to a greater degree than is rationally warranted. The stock market may tend to paint all (or most) REITs with either a "mutual fund brush" or an "operating corporation brush."

Which brush the stock market uses to paint REITs may change over time. These changes may be led in part by real changes in the nature of the typical REIT and in the environment in which REITs must operate. In this respect there may be an important interaction between microlevel and macrolevel differential valuation between the stock and property markets. When asset values are very high in the private property market, it is very difficult even for highly capable, entrepreneurial REITs to find growth opportunities. In such times all or most REITs necessarily become relatively passive. In such a circumstance it is relatively difficult for REITs to act very differently from the behavior implied by the mutual fund model, and it is relatively easy for the stock market to paint REITs with the mutual fund brush. Exactly the opposite is the case when asset values in the private property market are abnormally depressed. Then it is easy for REITs to find growth opportunities and for the stock market to take out its operating corporation brush. Of course, the irony is that, to no small degree, the stock market's perception of what REITs are can become a self-fulfilling prophecy. If the stock market perceives REITs as mutual funds and accordingly discounts their values below their NAVs, then this makes it relatively difficult for REITs to act like entrepreneurial, growing corporations because the most natural source of capital to finance such growth, the issuance of stocks and bonds in the public capital market, is rendered difficult and costly.[62] The perception creates the reality, to some extent.[63]

During much (but not all) of the 1970s and 1980s, REITs were perceived largely in the mutual fund model, and they tended to trade at a discount to their NAV. During most (but not all) of the 1990s, REITs were perceived largely in the operating corporation model. This difference was not merely perception, however. In fact, substantive changes occurred in the industry, beginning with the 1986 tax reform act that facilitated internal management by REITs. The huge inflow of capital to REITs via the stock market during the 1990s largely financed firms that were set up in the

---

[61] See Shiller (1998).

[62] Such a stereotype-based discounting of REIT value below NAV would tend to drive up REITs' stock-market-based cost of capital.

[63] We should be careful not to overstate this point. If a negative perception by the stock market is not supported to a considerable extent by the relevant reality within the property and space markets, then REITs will be able to avail themselves of alternative sources of finance, such as the private capital sources that traditionally supply the private property market (e.g., commercial mortgage debt and private equity from individuals and institutions). Nothing prohibits REITs from engaging in various lending, partnership, or joint-venture arrangements, including creative deal structures that allow flexibility in refinancing should the relative market valuations turn around in the future.

operating corporation model.[64] Exactly where the industry will head in the early part of the 21st century is difficult to predict, but we're betting on the operating corporation model, probably mixed to varying degrees at different times with the mutual fund model.

24.5 CHAPTER SUMMARY: SOME REIT INVESTOR CONSIDERATIONS

This chapter provided an introduction to a fascinating and evolving group of firms that cut across, and link, the stock market and the private property market. REITs are unique whether your perspective is that of a stock market investor or a private property market investor. While unique investments are challenging to understand and deal with, they can provide unique opportunities. In this chapter we sought to present only the most fundamental and abiding concepts and principles relevant to understanding REIT valuation and REIT investment. Although we also presented some of the nuts and bolts of REIT analysis and terminology, our presentation of strategic considerations was largely from the perspective of REIT managers. In closing this chapter, therefore, we will mention briefly a couple of strategic and tactical concerns and issues from the perspective of REIT investors.

1. **Choosing between public and private real estate investment.** An important threshold question all real estate investors face is how to place their real estate investment capital: in the public equity market via REITs, or in the private property market (directly or indirectly) via private market vehicles. While there are a variety of considerations in addressing this choice, the major trade-offs were touched on in Chapter 7, and you can now understand them in more depth based on our presentation of portfolio theory in Chapter 21. REITs provide more liquidity than private market investment for the average investor, but they also provide less diversification of a wealth portfolio that is dominated by stocks and bonds. This is because REIT returns tend to be more highly positively correlated with stock and bond returns than are private property market returns. The efficiency of the stock market can tend to give REIT investors more protection against making foolish mistakes, and therefore may require less intensive or less sophisticated and specialized due diligence, assuming investors use common sense and basic investment prudence. Thus, REITs are probably the preferred route for small, nonspecialized investors who want some real estate in their portfolio. Larger, more sophisticated investors will typically have the ability, and gain some benefit, from using both REIT and private market investment vehicles simultaneously in various mixes depending on their objectives and where they perceive the market to be in terms of the real estate asset market cycle.

2. **REIT behavior in up and down stock markets.** Most REIT investors, whether large or small, combine their REIT investments with relatively large holdings in the other sectors of the stock market. It is therefore of particular interest how

---

[64]Interesting evidence on the shift in perceived models between the 1980s and 1990s is provided by differences in IPO behavior between the two periods. See Ling and Ryngaert (1997) for an analysis of this evidence. We should also note that individual REITs can always be exceptions to the prevailing view. For example, the Washington REIT put together a track record of sustained growth during the 1970s and 1980s, specializing in operating a diversified mix of properties in the Washington D.C. area.

REITs tend to perform relative to the stock market, including how this performance may tend to differ between "up" and "down" stock markets. While past behavior in this regard is not necessarily a foolproof guide to future behavior, some pretty strong empirical evidence has been compiled regarding REIT behavior relative to the stock market. Much of this evidence seems to present a fairly consistent picture between the "old REITs" of the pre-1992 world and the "new REITs" of the 1990s. In general, REITs are low-beta stocks, but they are certainly not zero-beta assets. Defining beta with respect to the stock market as a whole, REIT betas have remained consistently near 0.5 over the long run.[65] Although REIT betas declined slightly during the 1990s, the difference was small. REITs have consistently shown higher betas with respect to small stocks than with respect to large stocks, and higher betas in declining stock markets than in advancing stock markets.[66] This suggests that REITs may be of greater diversification benefit to investors whose stock holdings are dominated by large-cap stocks, and that REITs are not particularly good vehicles for investors who feel they can time the stock market by buying just before upswings and selling just before downswings.

KEY TERMS

investment entity
asset management
pure plays
Gordon growth model (GGM)
existing property cash flow growth
same-store growth
equity-before-tax cash flow
  (EBTCF)
growth opportunities
average equity cost of capital
growth stocks
income investments
dual asset markets
net asset value (NAV)

mark-to-market
book/market value ratio
five-or-fewer rule
GAAP net income
funds from operations (FFO)
funds available for distribution
  (FAD)
straight-line rents
stakeholders
conflicts of interest
agency costs
umbrella partnership (operating
  partnership [OP])
resource allocation

competitive affiliates
self-dealing
franchise value
brand name recognition
vertical integration
economies of scale
market power (in the space market)
closed-end mutual fund (model of
  REITs)
operating corporation (model of
  REITs)
closed-end mutual fund discount
mental compartmentalizing

[65] REIT volatility has averaged slightly greater than that of the S&P 500. From 1975 through 1998 REIT annual volatility was around 17% (based on the NAREIT index), during which time the S&P 500 annual volatility was just under 14%.

[66] These results are developed and clearly presented in a very readable article by Michael Goldstein and Edward Nelling (1999).

STUDY QUESTIONS

24.1. Explain the Gordon growth model (GGM) of stock market equity valuation. What are the major mathematical simplifying assumptions in this model? What are the implications of these simplifying assumptions for application of the model to REIT valuation?

24.2. On January 31, 2000, General Growth Properties, a major shopping mall REIT, was trading at a share price of $28.50, at which price its then-current (year-2000) annual dividend of $2.04/share provided a yield of 7.2%. At that time, several analysts who followed General Growth closely were predicting future growth in earnings at a rate of nearly 10% per year for the subsequent five years, although same-store rental growth during the preceding year had been only 5.3%.

   a. If the analysts' earnings growth rate expectations accurately reflected the stock market's long-run average growth expectations for General Growth's dividends as of January 31, 2000, then, based on the GGM, what was the stock market's implied long-run average required expected rate of total return for investment in General Growth equity?

   b. If the market's long-run growth expectations were better reflected by the previous year's same-store rental growth rate, what was the market's required total expected return?

   c. With the 5.3% growth expectation assumption of question (b), what is the market's implied required ex ante risk premium for General Growth equity, given that T-bills were yielding about 5.5% at that time?

   d. If the required total return expectation you calculated in question (b) was indeed the market's required return for General Growth, but the most accurate long-term dividend growth rate expectation for General Growth was actually halfway between the 5.3% same-store rental growth rate and the analysts' 10% earnings growth rate prediction, then what was the extent of the market's "underpricing" of General Growth stock on January 31, 2000?

24.3. The Donald Grump Corporation, a publicly traded REIT, has expected total return to equity of 13%, average interest rate on their debt of 7.5%, and a debt/total asset value ratio of 40%.

   a. What is Grump's equity average cost of capital?

   b. What is Grump's firm-level overall average cost of capital [Hint: Use the WACC formula (1) from section 13.3 of Chapter 13.]

24.4. Bob & Sue Realty (BSR) is a publicly traded REIT that has no debt and a current dividend yield of 8%, with a current share price/earnings multiple of 12.5. The current consensus expectation among stock analysts who follow BSR is that BSR can provide a long-term average growth rate in its dividends per share of 5% per year.

   a. What is BSR's plowback ratio (i.e., what proportion of its earnings does it retain and not pay as dividends)?

   b. Assuming the stock market agrees with these analysts expectations, what is BSR's firm-level average cost of capital? [Hint: As BSR has no debt, you can use the GGM directly to answer this question.]

24.5. The Rentleg Distribution Center is a warehouse complex near the Cincinnati Airport in Northern Kentucky, in a market where such buildings currently sell at 10% cap rates (net cash flow/property value), with 1.0% expected long-run average annual growth (in both value and cash flow). This property has initial net cash flow of $2,500,000 per year. Both the Grump REIT and BSR (from the questions 24.3 and 24.5) are considering bidding to buy the Rentleg Center.

    a. Ignoring possible differential valuation between the stock and property markets, what is the (marginal) opportunity cost of capital for acquisition of the Rentleg Center by either REIT (i.e., what is the *discount rate* relevant for a DCF valuation of the Rentleg Center on the part of either one of the two REITs)?

    b. What is the maximum price Grump can offer for the Rentleg Center without its share price being diluted?

    c. What is the maximum price BSR can offer for the Rentleg Center without its share price being diluted?

    d. If BSR is able to purchase the Rentleg Center for $24,000,000, what will be the change in the (aggregate) value of BSR's equity as a result of this transaction (assuming the stock market had not already factored such expected purchase into its valuation of BSR's shares)?

24.6. What are the restrictions on REIT annual gross revenue sources and taxable income distributions necessary for a REIT to maintain its exemption from corporate income tax?

24.7. Define funds from operations (FFO) and funds available for distribution (FAD), and explain why these measures are used instead of GAAP net income to quantify REIT earnings.

24.8. In 1999 General Growth Properties (the shopping mall REIT that was the subject of question 24.2) reported GAAP net income of $78,806,000. It also reported the following income statement items:

Real estate depreciation:	$147,746,000
Preferred stock dividends:	$ 24,468,000
Allocations to OP unit holders:	$ 26,983,000
Net gains from sale of real estate assets:	$ 2,058,000
Net loss from extraordinary items:	$ 13,786,000

    a. What was General Growth's funds from operations (FFO) for 1999?

    b. Given that General Growth reported a 1999 net straight-line rental adjustment loss of $14,619,000 and capital expenditures of $27,500,000, what was General Growth's 1999 funds available for distribution (FAD)?

    c. What was General Growth's 1999 FAD/GAAP net income ratio?

    d. Given that General Growth paid out $143,826,000 in common stock dividends in 1999, what was its dividend/FFO ratio?

    e. What was General Growth's plowback ratio based on its FAD (and deducting distributions to preferred shareholders and OP unit holders as well as common dividends)?

    f. By how much of a percentage did General Growth exceed the 90% minimum earnings payout requirement (based on GAAP net income)?

24.9. What are agency costs as they apply to REITs? Describe some conflicts of interest and agency cost issues that are unique to the REIT industry.

24.10. What are the major competing considerations that pull REITs toward the use of either debt or equity sources of external capital?

24.11. Describe three of the five major strategic considerations or objectives (other than financing strategy) that were prominent in the REIT industry during the 1990s, as suggested in section 24.3 of this chapter.

24.12. What are the two major competing models of the fundamental nature of REITs, and what are the typical value implications of each model in terms of the stock market's valuation of REIT equity as compared to NAV?

25 Data Challenges in Measuring Real Estate Periodic Returns

Learning Objectives

After reading this chapter, you should understand:

◆ The major types of errors that tend to be present in empirical real estate periodic return data.

◆ The characteristic signs of the presence of such errors, and the effects such errors have on analysis relevant to macrolevel investment decision making.

◆ The different ways in which it is conceptually possible to define "true" real estate returns, the temporal relationship among these different definitions of true returns, and the relevance of different definitions for various types of practical decision problems.

◆ Several approaches for adjusting, correcting, or improving appraisal-based real estate returns series for some purposes, in relation to the NCREIF Index, and when it is and is not necessary to make such adjustments.

In Chapter 9 we introduced and defined the concept of periodic returns, or time-series of holding period returns (HPRs). At frequent and crucial points throughout this book we have used such returns, for real estate and other asset classes, in a variety of ways. For example, in Chapter 7 we compared the investment performance of the various asset classes, considering both risk and return, and to make such comparisons we used HPR series. In Chapter 11, real estate periodic returns were important in our analysis of real estate cost of capital. They were also important in our discussion of leverage in Chapter 13, and our discussion of the investment performance of commercial mortgages and their role in the overall investment portfolio in Chapter 19. In Chapters 21 and 22, periodic returns were the raw material for computing or estimating the expected returns, volatilities, and correlations that are necessary to apply modern portfolio theory and develop measures of risk and models of risk valuation and equilibrium asset pricing. Moreover, we will see in Chapter 27 that HPRs are fundamental to measuring and analyzing investment manager performance. In short, particularly (but not uniquely) at the macrolevel, modern investment theory and practice absolutely *depends* on the basic data raw material represented by time-series of periodic returns.

The existence, reliability, and meaningfulness of such returns data is taken for granted in the securities industry. For stocks and bonds the history of such data goes back to the early decades of the 20th century. The nature of public exchange trading of securities makes it easy to observe and measure periodic returns reliably and precisely, even at frequencies as high as daily for many securities. The existence of such vast quantities of high-quality data is a gold mine for the science of financial economics the likes of which is the envy of all branches of social science.

In the 1970s, real estate investment industry leaders realized that in order for the investment establishment to perceive private real estate with a degree of credibility and legitimacy approaching that of stocks and bonds, it was necessary to compute, compile, and disseminate series of real estate periodic returns. So, beginning in the 1970s, commercial property periodic returns have been reported and used in the investment industry. The "flagship" **NCREIF Property Index (NPI)** dates from the beginning of 1978, reporting quarterly total returns as well as income and appreciation components ever since, a history that is now over two decades long.

At first the real estate returns series were viewed skeptically by both academics and industry traditionalists, and their use was not widespread. Over time they have gradually become better constructed, more useful, better understood, and more widely accepted and used. There was good reason for the initial skepticism, however, and unique problems with real estate periodic returns remain. The most fundamental reasons for these problems were introduced in Chapter 23, but additional problems exist in the construction of real estate periodic return indices. While there is hope for improvement, some problems are inherent and will remain. The purpose of this chapter is to acquaint you with these problems and their implications.

It is very important to recognize at the outset that the unique problems with private real estate returns data do not imply that this data is not useful. Indeed, this data is very useful, even vital, as you can tell by how much we have used it in this book, for example. But the unique problems with real estate returns data do imply that the use of this data is trickier than that of securities returns data. If you are not careful, you can be misled. The unique real estate problems also mean that there is a danger in the long run of a loss of credibility and legitimacy for the real estate asset class within the broader investment community. If users of real estate returns data do not understand the unique problems, how to address them, and how one can and cannot use this data, then they (and their clients) will tend to be disappointed in the long run. As a result, investors may lose faith in the ability of real estate returns data to provide useful information, and therefore be unable to invest in private real estate with a degree of knowledge and diligence comparable to that in stocks and bonds. Therefore, understanding the unique issues and problems associated with private real estate returns data is very important, not only for you personally in your own macro-level professional work, but as a type of public duty, for the long-term health of the commercial real estate investment industry.

With this motivation in mind, we urge you to fasten your seatbelts and have a go at this chapter. It is a lineal descendant of Chapter 23, and therefore, like that chapter, is rather more technical than most in this book. But like Chapter 23, the material in this chapter is very basic, and very important. It is part of the basic toolset of the modern, sophisticated real estate investment analyst.

25.1 FROM VALUE LEVELS TO RETURNS: THE GENERAL NATURE OF PERFORMANCE MEASUREMENT ERRORS

As noted, this chapter picks up where Chapter 23 left off. Chapter 23 addressed problems measuring real estate *value levels*. The present chapter addresses problems measuring and using real estate *returns*, which are essentially changes over time in value levels of static portfolios.[1] Thus, the problems in the levels bring related problems in the returns. Understanding these problems will give you a good basis for knowing how to be an educated user of real estate periodic returns data.

To begin, recall from Chapter 23 that private real estate valuations typically have two types of **errors**, that is, differences between the empirically observable valuations and the unobservable true contemporaneous market values. One type of error is purely **random noise**. The other type of error is **temporal lag**. Transaction prices have only the first type of error, random noise, which is subject to the Square Root of n Rule. Appraised values typically have both sorts of errors. At the macrolevel of portfolio valuation, however, the Square Root of n Rule is most effective, so random noise may be a minor factor, especially in very large portfolios or indices composed of many properties. But the temporal lag is not reduced by the size of the portfolio or index. What we want to understand now is how these two types of errors in the value levels affect the returns that are derived from the value levels.

25.1.1 The Pure Effect of Random Noise

Consider a static portfolio, that is, a fixed set of properties. Now let's make an unrealistic assumption in order to illustrate a basic point. Suppose all of the properties in the portfolio always are sold at the same time each period, say, at the end of each calendar year. The properties are all the same, and the transactions are all synchronous.

---

[1] Perhaps we should explain why we interposed Chapter 24 between Chapter 23 and this chapter. In fact, as you will see, REIT returns data is relevant and useful for understanding and addressing some aspects of the data problems in private real estate returns. So we thought it would make sense to describe the nature of REIT values in some depth before we continued addressing private real estate data problems in this chapter.

How will the empirically observable transaction-price-based annual appreciation returns to this portfolio differ from the unobservable appreciation returns to the same portfolio based on the true market value of the portfolio? The answer is that the empirical appreciation returns will differ from the true returns due purely to the effect of random noise, because that is the only type of error present in transaction prices (this is by our definition of market value), and because all of the properties in this portfolio transact at the end of each period. More specifically, what does this effect of random noise look like?

To answer this question, let us set up this problem formally. Let $\overline{V}_t$ be the natural log of the empirically observable value of the portfolio as of the end of year t, where this value is computed as the cross-sectional sum of the year-t transaction prices of all the constituent properties. We are taking the log of the value here only to simplify the math.[2] Let C_t be the natural log of the corresponding unobservable true market value of the same portfolio as of the end of year t. The unobservable difference between these two log values is a purely random cross-sectional noise term labeled ε_t:

$$\varepsilon_t = \overline{V}_t - C_t \tag{1}$$

Now, since we are working in log levels, the returns (continuously compounded) are simply the arithmetic differences in the levels across time. Thus, the empirically observable appreciation return in year t is $\bar{r}_t$, defined as follows:

$$\bar{r}_t = \overline{V}_t - \overline{V}_{t-1} \tag{2a}$$

and the unobservable true return to the portfolio during year t is r_t, defined as

$$r_t = C_t - C_{t-1} \tag{2b}$$

Now substituting equations (1) and (2b) into (2a), we can see the empirically observable periodic return expressed in terms of the unobservable true return and the random noise:

$$\bar{r}_t = (C_t + \varepsilon_t) - (C_{t-1} + \varepsilon_{t-1}) = (C_t - C_{t-1}) + (\varepsilon_t - \varepsilon_{t-1}) = r_t + (\varepsilon_t - \varepsilon_{t-1}) \tag{3a}$$

Thus, the observable return equals the true return plus an error term that is the longitudinal difference in the cross-sectional noise realizations. Let's label this return noise using the Greek letter *eta*: $\eta_t = (\varepsilon_t - \varepsilon_{t-1})$:

$$\bar{r}_t = r_t + \eta_t \tag{3b}$$

What is the effect of this type of return noise? How does it change the observable returns from the true returns? Well, it does not change the expected value of the periodic return because the expected value of both ε_t and ε_{t-1}, and therefore of η_t, is zero. But it does change the volatility, that is, the standard deviation of the periodic returns across time. In particular, it increases the volatility, adding spurious "extra" volatility to the returns over time. Noise also affects the autocorrelation in the returns time-series, that is, the way the periodic returns are correlated with each other across time.

---

[2] This is a device to change awkward multiplicative expressions into simpler additive ones that are easier to deal with. Our use of logs in this way has no substantive bearing on the problem or the results.

In particular, it reduces any positive first-order autocorrelation (that is, correlation between consecutive returns) that might exist in the true returns, and may make uncorrelated true returns appear to have negative autocorrelation.[3] Noise does not affect the theoretical covariance between the returns and any exogenous series because, by definition, a purely random variable has no covariance with any other series. Therefore noise does not affect the theoretical beta (or systematic risk) as we defined it in Chapter 22.[4] Finally, combining these **volatility** and **covariance effects**, noise reduces the apparent cross-correlation between the noisy series and any other series.[5] Thus, noise can make it appear as if two real estate market segments are less correlated than they actually are.

Exhibit 25-1a shows an example of the effect of noise on returns, based on a simulation of hypothetical data. Time is on the horizontal axis, with the periodic returns indicated on the vertical axis. The solid line in the chart is the true return realization over time. The dotted line is the empirically observable return realization.[6] Notice that the empirical return is more volatile. It is also spikier or more sawtoothed in appearance, with large returns tending to be followed by opposite-signed returns. This is typical of excess volatility that leads to overshooting in the observed value levels that are subsequently corrected in later observations. This is seen more directly in Exhibit 25-1b, which shows the same simulated history, only in the value levels rather than the returns. For example, the empirical valuation in one period might happen to have a positive error, while the valuation in the next period might happen to have a negative error. The result would be a large apparent negative return, due purely to the difference in errors, when the true return was near zero. In general, note that random noise causes the observed value level series to sort of dance around the unobservable true value level series.

[3] Note that while the observation errors in levels, the ε_t, are uncorrelated across time, the return noise that results from these errors, the η_t, have negative first-order autocorrelation. Using the terminology and definitions presented in the appendix to Chapter 21, we can see the following. Regarding volatility, considering that random noise (ε_t) is uncorrelated with anything, neither with true returns nor with itself across time, we see that

$$VAR[\tilde{r}_t] = VAR[r_t + \varepsilon_t - \varepsilon_{t-1}] = VAR[r_t] + VAR[\varepsilon_t - \varepsilon_{t-1}] = VAR[r_t] + 2VAR[\varepsilon_t]$$

(Note that moments in r_t are longitudinal while moments in ε_t are cross-sectional.) Regarding the first-order autocorrelation, this will equal the autocovariance divided by the variance we just computed. The autocovariance is

$$COV[\tilde{r}_t, \tilde{r}_{t-1}] = COV[r_t + \varepsilon_t - \varepsilon_{t-1}, r_{t-1} + \varepsilon_{t-1} - \varepsilon_{t-2}]$$
$$= COV[r_t, r_{t-1}] - COV[\varepsilon_{t-1}, \varepsilon_{t-1}]$$
$$= COV[r_t, r_{t-1}] - VAR[\varepsilon_t]$$

Thus, the first-order autocorrelation in the noisy series is arithmetically less than that in the true series.

[4] However, noise does make it more difficult to precisely estimate the true beta using empirical returns data. In other words, it does not affect the expected value of the beta coefficient estimate in a regression, but it does increase the standard error in that estimate.

[5] The cross-correlation coefficient between two series equals the covariance divided by the product of the volatilities of the two series.

[6] In the simulation, the true returns were generated randomly from a process that was normally distributed with 5% volatility per period, and the random value level observation error was generated from a process that was normally distributed with a cross-sectional standard deviation of 10%.

Exhibit 25-1a   The Pure
Effect of Noise in
Periodic Returns

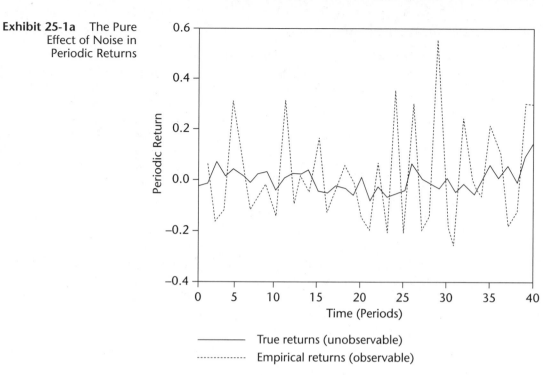

True returns (unobservable)

Empirical returns (observable)

Exhibit 25-1b   The Pure
Effect of Noise in
Periodic Value Levels

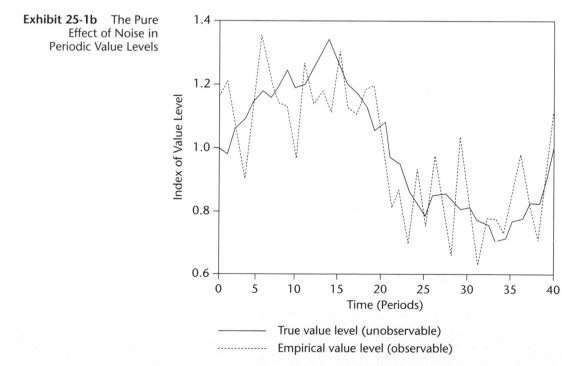

True value level (unobservable)

Empirical value level (observable)

25.1.2 The Pure Effect of Temporal Lag

Now let's look at the impact on periodic returns of the other type of error common in real estate valuations, temporal lag. To illustrate the pure effect of this type of error, we will consider another unrealistic hypothetical situation. Again we have a static portfolio, but now we will assume that there are an infinite number of properties in the portfolio so that the effect of random noise completely washes away. However, instead of all the properties transacting at the same time at the end of every year, now we will suppose that half the properties transact at the end of each year, and half the properties transact at the beginning of each year. We may assume that the beginning of the year is only one day after the end of the previous year so that, in effect, in each year t, half of the portfolio valuation is derived from transaction prices occurring at the end of year t and half of the portfolio valuation is derived from transaction prices that occurred, in effect, one year ago, at the end of year $t-1$.

Alternatively, and equivalently, we may assume that the entire portfolio valuation each year is based on appraisals rather than transaction prices. The appraisals all occur at the end of the calendar year, but they display a temporal lag bias in which the appraised value for each property as of the end of year t consists of a one-half weight on the true value as of that time, plus a one-half weight on the true value as of the end of the previous year.

In other words, whether it is due to transaction price observations that are staggered in time, or due to appraisals that are all synchronous at the end of the year but that have a temporal lag bias, the result is that the empirically observed value of the portfolio as of the end of year t, labeled V_t^*, is given by the following formula (once again, we are working in log levels rather than straight levels):[7]

$$V_t^* = \left(\frac{1}{2}\right)C_t + \left(\frac{1}{2}\right)C_{t-1} \tag{4}$$

Since we are working in log levels, once again we can simply take the arithmetic difference across time to compute the empirically observable periodic appreciation return implied by equation (4), which we will label r_t^*. The empirical return thus is given by

$$
\begin{aligned}
r_t^* = V_t^* - V_{t-1}^* &= \left[\left(\frac{1}{2}\right)C_t + \left(\frac{1}{2}\right)C_{t-1}\right] - \left[\left(\frac{1}{2}\right)C_{t-1} + \left(\frac{1}{2}\right)C_{t-2}\right] \\
&= \left[\left(\frac{1}{2}\right)C_t - \left(\frac{1}{2}\right)C_{t-1}\right] + \left[\left(\frac{1}{2}\right)C_{t-1} - \left(\frac{1}{2}\right)C_{t-2}\right] \\
&= \left(\frac{1}{2}\right)(C_t - C_{t-1}) + \left(\frac{1}{2}\right)(C_{t-1} - C_{t-2}) \\
&= \left(\frac{1}{2}\right)r_t + \left(\frac{1}{2}\right)r_{t-1}
\end{aligned}
\tag{5}
$$

[7] Just to reiterate, there are no random noise terms in equation (4) only because we have "assumed them away," by the device of our hypothetical assumption of an infinite property population in the portfolio. This unrealistic assumption is made to illustrate the pure effect of temporal lag.

Thus, the empirically observable return consists of one-half weight on the true current return, plus one-half weight on the previous period's true return. The empirical return is called a **moving average** of the true returns across time.

The effect of return lagging like this is pretty obvious, and it is depicted visually in Exhibits 25-2a and 25-2b, which may be compared to their counterparts in Exhibit 25-1a and b.[8] The empirical returns in Exhibit 25-2a appear "smoothed" and lagged in time behind the unobservable true returns. The same is true of the value levels depicted in Exhibit 25-2b. Note in particular that the observable value level series tends to be shifted to the right in the graph, with turning points tending to occur later in time, as compared to the unobservable true value level series.

In terms of the effect of temporal lag bias on the periodic returns time-series statistics, first consider the average return across time. Temporal lagging does not change the long-run (or "unconditional") expected value of the periodic return. However, in any finite sample of time, temporally lagged returns will be "conditionally" biased. That is, the direction of the bias depends on the direction in which the true returns have been trending, if any. For example, if true returns have been increasing over the relevant history, then temporally lagged returns will be biased low, with the average empirical return tending to be lower than the average true return during the history.

Turning to the second moment statistics, the pure effect of lagging in the form of a moving average of the true returns is to reduce the apparent volatility (total risk) of the observable real estate returns. The more important second moment effect of lagging, however, is that it reduces the apparent beta (systematic risk) of the real estate returns measured with respect to a nonlagged risk benchmark.[9] For this reason, the effect of temporal lagging on periodic returns series is often referred to as **smoothing**, or **appraisal smoothing**, as such lagging in appraisal-based indices is often attributed at least in part to the macrolevel valuation impact of the microlevel appraiser behavior described in Chapter 23.

What about the cross-correlation and beta of a lagged real estate series with respect to another similarly lagged series? These effects are complicated considering that the underlying true returns are likely to be autocorrelated and contain lagged cross-correlation terms. It is likely, however, that the pure effect of temporal lag bias will in most cases cause only very slight bias, if any, in the cross-correlation and beta

---

[8] All of these exhibits were generated from the same simulated hypothetical historical sample of true returns.

[9] More precisely, the apparent beta is biased toward zero, as beta can have either a positive or negative sign in theory. Actually, however, it is only the *contemporaneous* beta that is reduced with respect to a non-lagged risk benchmark such as the stock market (or the REIT market, for example). It is possible to correct such bias by adding the contemporaneous and lagged betas. This can be seen as follows using our two-period moving-average lag, defining x_t as a non-lagged (i.e., unpredictable) series, and remembering that $BETA[r_t^*, x_t]$ is defined as $COV[r_t^*, x_t]/VAR[x_t]$:

$$COV[r_t^*, x_t] = COV[(1/2)r_t + (1/2)r_{t-1}, x_t] = (1/2)COV[r_t, x_t] + (1/2)COV[r_{t-1}, x_t]$$

$$= (1/2)COV[r_t, x_t]$$

because x_t is not predictable (as in the case of stock market returns, for example). Therefore, $COV[r_{t-1}, x_t] = 0$. Of course, these are all theoretical (or "long-history") relationships relating to bias (or the central tendency) in the real estate statistics. Actual results in any finite empirical sample can differ. If the true real estate returns are predictable by the exogenous variable, then the sum of the contemporaneous and lagged betas might overcorrect the smoothing bias. (See Geltner (1991) and Study Question 15-3 at the end of this chapter.)

Exhibit 25-2a   The Pure Effect of Temporal Lag in Periodic Returns

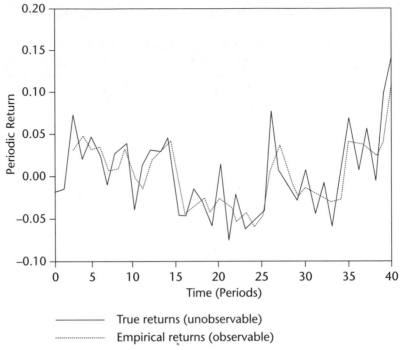

————— True returns (unobservable)

·············· Empirical returns (observable)

Exhibit 25-2b   The Pure Effect of Temporal Lag in Periodic Value Levels

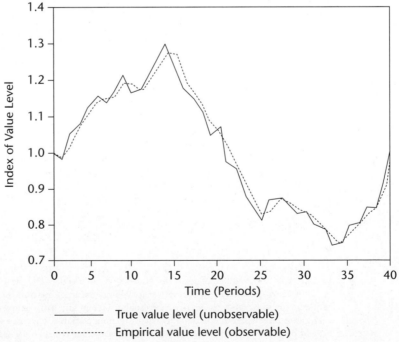

————— True value level (unobservable)

·············· Empirical value level (observable)

statistics between two similarly lagged real estate series.[10] Thus, for example, the beta of a component of the NPI with respect to the total NPI will probably not be seriously biased, as both series have similar lags. Any bias that might be present, is likely to be slightly on the low side, that is, with the apparent cross-correlation or beta tending to be lower in absolute value than the true cross-correlation or beta.[11]

Regarding cross-temporal statistics, the pure effect of temporal lag bias in the returns series is usually to impart apparent positive autocorrelation into the empirical returns series, more so than is present in the unobservable true returns.[12] This tends to exaggerate the effect, noted in the appendix to Chapter 21, that long-interval (lower-frequency) periodic returns become relatively more volatile, compared to non-lagged series, than short-interval (high-frequency) returns.[13] This causes the apparent long-interval betas of lagged series with respect to nonlagged series to be greater than short-interval betas, and this effect tends to be magnified in the apparent beta

---

[10] Based on our two-period moving average lag model from equation (5), the contemporaneous beta between two similarly lagged series, r_t^* and x_t^*, expressed in terms of the underlying true returns, is

$$\frac{\left(\frac{1}{2}\right) COV[r_t, x_t] + \left(\frac{1}{4}\right)[COV(r_t, x_{t-1}) + COV(x_t, r_{t-1})]}{\left(\frac{1}{2}\right)[VAR(x_t) + COV(x_t, x_{t-1})]}$$

Thus, if there were no cross-temporal effects in the true returns, the beta between the lagged series would be unbiased. Of course, inefficiency in the property market can cause true private real estate returns to have cross-temporal effects. However, these effects may approximately offset each other in the numerator and denominator in the previous expression.

[11] Examining the ratio in the previous footnote, note that if lagged cross-covariance tends to be a bit less than autocovariance, then the beta (and similarly the cross-correlation coefficient) will be biased slightly toward the low side (toward zero).

[12] To see this, consider the first-order autocovariance using our previous example of the two-period moving average:

$$COV(r_t^*, r_{t-1}^*) = COV[(1/2)r_t + (1/2)r_{t-1}, (1/2)r_{t-1} + (1/2)r_{t-2}]$$

$$= (1/4)[COV(r_t, r_{t-1}) + COV(r_{t-1}, r_{t-2}) + COV(r_{t-1}, r_{t-1}) + COV(r_t, r_{t-2})]$$

$$= (1/2)COV(r_t, r_{t-1}) + (1/4)VAR(r_t) + (1/4)COV(r_t, r_{t-2})$$

The autocorrelation coefficient is just the autocovariance divided by the series variance. As we noted earlier, the pure effect of moving-average-based lagging is to reduce the apparent volatility in the series ($VAR[r_t^*] < VAR[r_t]$). Thus, at least in the absence of random noise, temporal lag bias will usually increase the autocorrelation in the observable series as compared to the true series, just the opposite of the effect of random noise (regarding the first-order autocorrelation).

[13] Both the variance and the covariance with nonlagged series are more than proportional to the length of the return periods in the case of positively autocorrelated periodic returns. For example, annual returns have more than four times the covariance and variance (more than twice the volatility) of quarterly returns, and this effect is magnified the greater is the positive autocorrelation.

of a moving-average lagged series.[14] Not surprisingly, moving average lagged returns are more predictable in advance than true underlying returns.

25.1.3 Putting the Two Effects Together

In the real world, most practical empirical real estate periodic returns series will contain at least a little bit of both of the "pure" types of errors described in the two preceding sections. The fundamental trade-off between these two sources of error noted in Chapter 23 makes it impossible to avoid both error sources simultaneously.

The noise component, η_t, will be more important in smaller portfolios and may well dominate in individual property returns.[15] Because of the Square Root of n Rule, noise will be less important in returns to large portfolios or indices, although it will never disappear completely. Even though statistical regression is a very efficient tool for handling large amounts of data, noise will still be present in regression-based price indices. Referred to in statistical terms as estimation error, random noise may often be the more important of the two error components in regression-based indices derived from transaction prices, at least provided that the regression is specified and estimated so as to avoid most temporal lag bias.

In contrast, the temporal lag effect will typically dominate in large portfolios or indices that are based on appraised values. Temporal lag effects can also be important in regression-based indices if the regression is estimated based on **pooled transaction price data** (that is, data in which the observations are drawn from multiple periods of time), unless care is taken to control properly for time effects in the regression specification and estimation process. Only an index based purely on fully contemporaneous transaction prices would avoid the lag effect altogether.

It is important to note that, in some respects, the two types of error effects will tend to mask each other in the empirical returns. In reality, it is not possible to separate out the pure effects as we have done in the preceding two sections. For example, the volatility-magnifying effect of return noise will tend to offset, to some degree at least, the volatility-dampening effect of the moving-average temporal lag. Similarly, the negative autocorrelation component imparted by the random noise will tend to offset the positive autocorrelation effect of the temporal lag.[16] This type of masking can make it difficult to correct the effect of error on the volatility of the empirical return series. On the other hand, systematic risk (or beta) is more amenable to correction because noise does not affect the theoretical beta, while we know that temporal bias dampens the observable beta toward zero, the more so the greater the lag.

Exhibit 25-3 presents a visual example of the mixed-errors situation, based on the same underlying simulated true returns as those in the previous exhibits. The true returns and market value levels are indicated, in Exhibits 25-3a and 3b respectively,

---

[14] This point was noted in Chapter 21 regarding true real estate returns, as a partial explanation for the apparent low allocation to real estate in institutional portfolios, as long-horizon investors should care more about long-interval returns.

[15] Periodic returns series of individual property returns are rarely used as such. In the first place, individual properties are typically rather small assets that have relatively little economic or statistical significance by themselves. Furthermore, in addition to the noise and lag effects described earlier, observable individual property value levels are flat (zero appreciation) between appraisals or transaction observations. This gives individual property returns a very spiky appearance and their value level series a very artificial-looking steplike or sticky appearance. For these reasons (among others), the major return measure used at the individual property level is the multiperiod IRR, rather than periodic HPRs. (See Chapters 9 and 27 for additional discussion relevant to this point.)

[16] This is in the first-order statistic only.

Exhibit 25-3a Periodic Appreciation Returns Based on Market Values, Transaction Prices, and Appraised Values (simulated data)

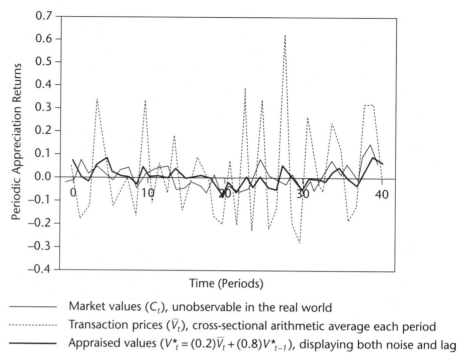

——— Market values (C_t), unobservable in the real world

------------ Transaction prices ($\bar{V}_t$), cross-sectional arithmetic average each period

━━━ Appraised values ($V^*_t = (0.2)\bar{V}_t + (0.8)V^*_{t-1}$), displaying both noise and lag

Exhibit 25-3b Market Values, Transaction Prices, and Appraised Values (simulated data)

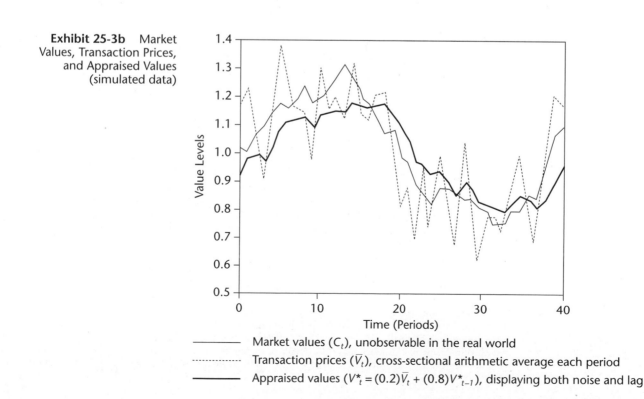

——— Market values (C_t), unobservable in the real world

------------ Transaction prices ($\bar{V}_t$), cross-sectional arithmetic average each period

━━━ Appraised values ($V^*_t = (0.2)\bar{V}_t + (0.8)V^*_{t-1}$), displaying both noise and lag by the thin solid line. The dotted line reflects the effect of random noise only. In the real world we might observe the dotted line in Exhibit 25-3b as the average transaction price in each period among the properties in the subject population that happened to transact during that period.[17] The dotted line in the returns chart in Exhibit 25-3a is simply the percentage difference in these average prices each period, identical to the returns shown in Exhibit 25-1a.

Now suppose that all the properties in the subject population are appraised at the end of each period, based on appraisers' observations of the transaction prices in the current and past periods. In particular, suppose that appraisers apply the following first-order autoregressive (simple exponential smoothing) valuation equation, which was discussed extensively in Chapter 23:[18]

$$V_t^* = \alpha\overline{V}_t + (1 - \alpha)V_{t-1}^* \qquad\qquad (6)$$

In particular, suppose that the partial adjustment factor, α, is 0.2.[19]

Under this assumed appraiser behavior, the thick line in Exhibit 25-3 traces out the appraisal-based index appreciation returns and value levels for our simulated population of properties. Note that the appraisal-based returns and values include both random noise and temporal lag effects, and that to some extent these effects mask each other. For example, the volatility apparent in the appraisal-based return in Exhibit 25-3a looks to be about the same as the true return volatility. The effect of the noise largely cancels out the effect of the moving-average lag such that, in this example, the appraisals end up with about the same volatility as the true returns. But this is really a coincidence. The observable appraisal-based volatility might be either greater or less than the unobservable true volatility.[20] In practice, it could be difficult to say, rigorously speaking, in which direction the appraisal volatility bias might lie.[21] What is more certain, however, is that much of the volatility that is empirically

---

[17] This would certainly be a finite, and probably even rather small, sample. Therefore, it could not eliminate the noise as we assumed in the preceding section when we assumed an infinite population.

[18] See in particular equation (4a) in section 23.2.4.

[19] Recall that this is the empirical estimate in the Russell Canadian Property Index data examined by Hamilton and Clayton (1999).

[20] In fact, although it is difficult to detect visually in Exhibit 25-3, the appraisal-based return volatility in this simulation example is actually less than the true return volatility. The former is 3.5% and the latter is 5%. Furthermore, in order to illustrate the point about random noise, we have probably exaggerated the amount of noise in our simulation example. In the exhibits in this section we have assumed a 10% cross-sectional standard deviation in the simulated transaction prices, the $\overline{V}_t$. In reality, if the standard deviation in any one transaction price observation ($V_{i,t}$) is on the order of 5% to 10%, then the standard deviation in the cross-sectional average price ($\overline{V}_t$) is that amount divided by the square root of n_t, where n_t is the number of comparable property transaction observations in period t. It is of course the sample mean $\overline{V}_t$ standard deviation that is relevant in equation (6). (See Chapter 23 for further discussion of the effect of the Square Root of n Rule in macrolevel valuation.)

[21] Much of the academic and professional literature relating to the NCREIF Property Index (NPI) has been motivated by the suspicion that in that appraisal-based index the quarterly volatility is lower than the true quarterly volatility, at least if one removes the effect of the annual fourth-quarter spikes. The smooth appearance of the NPI, along with its strong positive autocorrelation, suggests that this index has very little random noise. There are also reasons based in economic theory and casual empirical observation of the United States commercial property market that suggest a bias toward dampened volatility in the NPI. For example, it is often thought that modern portfolio theory and equilibrium asset pricing theory as described in Chapters 21 and 22 make it difficult to explain observed allocations to (and valuations of) real estate unless true volatility is greater than that indicated by the NPI. However, as we suggested in

observable in the appraisal-based index is spurious—not real changes in market value, but merely the reflection of random noise.

Unlike random noise, the lag of the empirically observable appraised values behind the market values does not tend to get washed out, and it is clearly evidenced in Exhibit 25-3b by the horizontal gap between the thick and thin lines in the chart. On average, this gap is about four periods long in our example simulation and can be seen most prominently in the lagged turning points in the market value cycle. The appraisal-based index does not register the turning points until, typically, about four periods after the true turning point. Of course, this lag would not be directly observable in the real world because the true market returns and values would be unobservable. The same lag also exists between the appraisal-based index and the average transaction prices, which would be empirically observable. However, the noisiness of the transaction price series obfuscates the picture, making it difficult to see clearly the lag in the appraised values relative to the transaction prices.

25.1.4 What about the *Total Return?*

The preceding three sections introduced you to the major types of measurement errors that are unique to private real estate regarding empirical periodic returns series. The discussion and examples so far considered only the appreciation component of the total HPR. However, most of the volatility in periodic returns series derives from the appreciation return component, so the points made previously about appreciation returns generally carry through to the total returns as well.[22]

25.2 WHAT IS TRUTH? LAGS AND THE TIME LINE OF PRICE DISCOVERY IN REAL ESTATE

The previous section made clear that one of the major types of errors in private real estate periodic returns data is temporal lag bias. This type of error is particularly prominent and important in macrolevel appraisal-based returns, such as those tracked for large portfolios and benchmark indices such as the NPI. With this in mind, we need now to step back and consider a broader and deeper question.

"What is truth?" Pontius Pilate asked in a famous Biblical passage. We won't get quite that heavy here, but it is certainly relevant for us to ask this question in the context of real estate return measurement errors. After all, it is impossible to define *error* without defining *truth*. As a result, it is impossible to appreciate the nature and magnitude of the temporal lag bias problem in real estate without such a definition.

Up to now, we have been defining true returns as those based on market value as this term has been previously defined in this book regarding the private real estate asset market, namely, the *expected* (or *ex ante*) sale price in the current relevant market for the subject asset. But the problem of temporal lag bias often arises in contexts that

Chapter 21, there may be other explanations for the low real estate allocation. Strictly speaking, the point raised by Lai and Wang (1998), that the direction of volatility bias in the NPI has not been rigorously proven, remains valid. (See also Chinloy, Cho, and Megbolugbe [1997], and Gatzlaff and Geltner [1998].)

[22]Remember that the denominator in the formula for the periodic income return component is the beginning period asset valuation. Thus, income return components are also affected directly by valuation errors. For example, assuming contemporaneous income is accurately observed, the income return component will be biased low when the asset valuation is biased high, and vice versa.

are different from or broader than what is implied by this definition of truth. For example, consider the following practical decision problems, all of which involve, directly or indirectly, the use of appraisal-based periodic returns data for private real estate:

1. A private market real estate investment manager using a timing-based tactical investment policy wants to know if the institutional office property market "turned around" last quarter, or was it the previous quarter, or two quarters ago, or has it not yet turned?

2. A consultant considering portfolio allocation strategies wants to know the long-run beta (or long-run relative volatility and correlation coefficient) between real estate and the stock market.

3. An advisor to a wealthy individual trying to decide between private direct investment and REIT shares for the real estate component of her wealth portfolio wants to know the beta of private real estate compared to that of REITs, in both up and down stock markets.

4. An acquisition officer involved in a protracted negotiation for a major property wants to know how far property market values have fallen, in general, during the past calendar quarter.

5. A manager of a large portfolio whose annual incentive fee is pegged to the NPI is wondering why his recently appraised portfolio didn't beat the NPI last year even though he believes his appraisers are competent and he's sure he did better than most of his competitors last year.

6. An appraiser wants to know the approximate ex post time-weighted mean total return risk premium of institutional quality real estate over T-bills during the past quarter century, to help her estimate the appropriate cost of capital to use in a DCF valuation.

For the manager in problem 1, a definition of true market value based on contemporaneous empirically observable transaction prices in the private market may be sufficient. The consultant in problem 2 might find something closer to a REIT market based definition of truth more relevant for defining or measuring the temporal lag that is (or should be) of most concern in her problem of measuring long-run beta, at least from some perspectives. The advisor and the acquisition officer in problems 3 and 4 might prefer a constant-liquidity definition of private market value, rather than one based only on consummated transaction price evidence. The relevant truth for the manager in problem 5 might simply be a fully contemporaneous appraisal-based valuation of his benchmark. Finally, an appraisal-based index that is not completely contemporaneous, like the NCREIF index, might be quite adequate for the problem faced by the appraiser in problem 6.

If you do not have a clear conception of what is the relevant truth for the type of problem you are trying to address, then you can get very confused in your attempts to analyze the problem. Yet this question of truth is so basic and underlying in nature that analysts and decision makers often do not even explicitly consider it. The result is practical decision situations in which the analysts are confused without even knowing they are confused, a potentially dangerous situation! To avoid this situation yourself, we think it is helpful to consider a time line of price discovery as it relates to different types of empirical and conceptual real estate periodic returns series.

25.2.1 What Is Price Discovery?

The term **price discovery** is borrowed from the literature on asset market microstructure. It refers to the process by which asset market prices are formed through the discovery and incorporation by market participants of information relevant to the values of the assets. Some asset markets are more informationally efficient than others, leading to different speed of price discovery, and a resulting temporal lead/lag relationship in the market prices of related assets that trade in different types of markets. For example, as we have noted repeatedly in this book, the stock market is more informationally efficient than the private property market, resulting in REIT share prices tending to lead property market values in time.

25.2.2 Multistep Real Estate Time Line of Information Incorporation into Observable Value

To build your intuition regarding different relevant "true values" in real estate, consider the following simple situation. Suppose that for a long time no new information has arrived relevant to the value of real estate assets. Prices of REIT shares, as well as prices of privately traded property, not to mention appraised values, are all stable and steady. The time is now $t-1$, and all real estate price indices are at a level we can set at 100.

Now into this very dull world a piece of news, that is, *new* information, arrives suddenly, unpredicted (of course, or it wouldn't be news). The information arrives precisely at time t, and it is relevant to the value of all real estate assets. In fact, for illustrative purposes suppose that this information is relevant to all real estate assets in the same direction and same magnitude (although this will not become fully apparent empirically for some time). In particular, as a result of this new information the value of all real estate assets has just decreased by 10%. Then, immediately after the arrival of this one piece of news, the world becomes very boring again and no new information relevant to real estate values arrives anymore for a long time.

OK, it's a strange and very unrealistic situation we have just depicted, but it serves to illustrate the time line we want you to become familiar with. Let's think about how different types of real estate price or value indices might respond to the news that arrived at time t. In particular, we will identify and define five different such indices, at a conceptual level: (1) A REIT share price index, (2) a constant-liquidity private market value index, (3) a contemporaneous transaction-price-based private market value index, (4) a contemporaneous appraised value index, and (5) an appraisal-based index with staggered appraisals such as the NPI. We will consider each of these in turn, as we walk through the index response pattern illustrated in Exhibit 25-4.

Index 1: REIT Share Price Index. This index is based on the market prices of publicly traded REIT shares traded in the stock exchange. This is the densest, most liquid market relevant to the trading of real estate equity assets, and so it has the most informationally efficient price discovery. This index moves first and fastest. However, it may be subject to some excess volatility. This is indicated by the fact that the REIT index overshoots the mark at index level 90, falling to a level slightly below that, before it corrects itself.[23] Line 1 in Exhibit 25-4 traces the path of the REIT index

---

[23] The existence of this type of excess volatility in the stock market is somewhat controversial, although some tendency in this regard seems to be fairly widely accepted now among financial economists, and there are several theories to explain it (e.g., irrational investor behavior models, noise trader models, and so forth). Excess volatility of this nature has much in common with the random noise described in

Exhibit 25-4 News-Response Time Line for Various Stylized Real Estate Indices

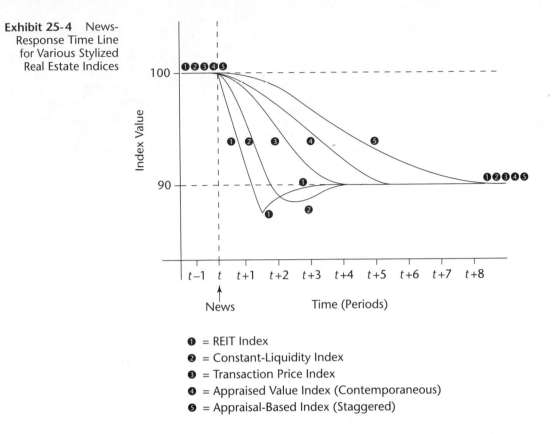

● = REIT Index
❷ = Constant-Liquidity Index
❸ = Transaction Price Index
❹ = Appraised Value Index (Contemporaneous)
❺ = Appraisal-Based Index (Staggered)

over time from just prior to the arrival of the news to past the time when all indices have fully reflected the news. In practice, REIT indices show very little autocorrelation or inertia over time at quarterly or lower frequencies, although there may be some tendency for slight negative autocorrelation at some frequencies (presumably reflecting the excess volatility noted previously).

Index 2: Constant-Liquidity Private Market Value Index. This is an index of market values in the private property market. However, this index is meant to represent the asset values that would equilibrate the market with a constant amount of liquidity through time. When bad news arrives, news that suggests market values should fall, many real estate investors who were previously planning to buy become unsure of how much they should reduce the "reservation prices" they had previously been willing to pay.[24] They tend to hold back, waiting to see if they can find out more about the new values. This tends to cause a reduction in liquidity, making it take

---

section 25.1.1 regarding private real estate indices, as far as some of the statistical effects are concerned. However, stock market excess volatility is different in its basic nature and source from the type of noise we considered previously, as it does not generally imply the existence of any measurement error in the market values or returns that are quantified in the index.

[24]As discussed in the appendix to Chapter 12, the buyer's reservation price is the price at which he will stop searching or negotiating (for a lower price) and commit to a deal. This same type of uncertainty happens in the REIT market, but it gets resolved much more quickly there due to the much denser market, with active multiple buyers and sellers publicly trading homogeneous shares.

longer to sell properties. In order to maintain constant liquidity, in other words, to be able to expect to sell a property as quickly right after the arrival of the bad news, sellers would have to mark their reservation prices down farther than the ultimate typical transaction price for similar properties. Although this effect is temporary, such an index would tend to reflect greater volatility than an index based on consummated transaction prices. The price path of Index 2 is indicated by line 2 in Exhibit 25-4. In effect, the constant-liquidity index must reflect "bid prices" (from buyers) during a down market, and "ask prices" (seller offers) during an up market.

In fact, actual real estate markets tend not to maintain constant liquidity through time. Therefore, it is not possible to estimate empirically a constant-liquidity private market index based purely on empirical price observations in the private market. But nor is such an index represented by REIT prices because the private market is not as dense and liquid as the REIT market.[25]

At first, it might seem that a constant-liquidity private market value index would represent market values that reflect nearly "full information," which would suggest relatively little inertia and therefore relatively little autocorrelation in returns. But in fact, this is probably not the case. The assumption of constant liquidity across time does not generally imply complete informational efficiency of the type that would eliminate virtually all inertia in returns. For example, search and transaction costs, and the thinness of the real estate market, are not assumed away in Index 2. A constant-liquidity private market is still a *private* market, in which unique whole assets are infrequently traded at irregular intervals. The conceptual definition of constant liquidity does not imply that the long-run average amount of liquidity (as represented by the time it takes to sell an asset) is changed from that which prevails in the actual private market. Because of this, it seems likely that the market returns implied by Index 2 would contain some positive autocorrelation, especially at the quarterly frequency and to a lesser extent at the annual frequency as well.

Index 3: Contemporaneous Transaction-Price-Based Index of Private Market Values. This would be an index reflecting the expected sales price within each period of time (i.e., the cross-sectional mean). Like Index 1, but unlike Index 2, this type of index could conceivably be estimated using empirically observable data, namely, transaction prices.[26] Of course, any empirically based transaction price index would in practice tend to exhibit estimation error or measurement noise of the type described in section 25.1.1.[27] It is also important to recall from our prior discussion that the prices observed in consummated transactions do not generally reflect constant liquidity across time. Indeed, liquidity can vary widely in the private real estate market, and this must be kept in mind in making use of any index based on transaction prices. Liquidity variation is one reason we would expect consummated transaction prices in the private property market to move slightly more sluggishly than the constant-liquidity

---

[25] Other differences between REIT returns and property-level (static portfolio) returns, as described in Chapter 24, are ignored in this simple example, but in reality they would of course be important.

[26] As is discussed in more depth in the appendix at the end of this book (and as we touched on in Chapter 23), some sort of regression-based procedure would normally be used to construct such an index.

[27] In reality, transaction-price-based indices are also potentially susceptible to temporal lag bias. This point was noted in Chapter 23. See Geltner (1993a) for additional discussion. However, in the present context, we are defining our conceptual transaction-based index to be contemporaneous, that is, completely free of temporal lag bias, and also free of noise (reflecting the theoretical *ex ante* mean transaction price each period, not any finite-sample empirical average).

values tracked by Index 2. Moreover, we would not expect transaction prices to overshoot the new full-information value the way the two previous indices did. Thus, at least at the conceptual level (in the absence of empirical estimation error) transaction price indices should be a bit less volatile and slightly more lagged in time, displaying more positive autocorrelation in quarterly or annual periodic returns, as compared to the two previously defined indices. The transaction price index is represented in Exhibit 25-4 in its conceptual definition, without any estimation error, by line 3.

Index 4: Contemporaneous Appraised Value Index. This is an index based on microlevel appraised values, that is, the cross-sectional aggregation of individual property appraisals, but with all of the properties being appraised as of the current point in time. Thus, conceptually, the only difference between this index and the transaction-price-based index is the temporal lag present in optimal microlevel appraisal, as described in Chapter 23.[28] This index will thus be a bit smoothed and lagged in time behind the transaction price index, as appraisers wait to compile evidence from transaction prices before they finalize their own opinions of how the news that arrived at time t changed the value of real estate. This index is indicated in Exhibit 25-4 by line 4.

Index 5: Appraisal-Based Index with Staggered Appraisals. This index is based on the same type of valuation observations as those in the previous index, only in this index not all properties are reappraised as of the same point in time. Properties that are not reappraised contemporaneously enter the index at their last appraised value, which would have been made as of a previous point in time. Thus, this index suffers from a stale appraisal problem. For example, all of the properties composing the index might be reappraised annually, but staggered evenly through time, so that one-fourth of the properties are reappraised every calendar quarter. Obviously, this would make this index a lagged moving average of the contemporaneous appraisal-based index. This would make this index a smoothed and temporally lagged version of the previous index, as depicted in line 5 in Exhibit 25-4.

Let us now summarize the time line we have just described, as illustrated in Exhibit 25-4. The effect of the news arriving at time t is incorporated at varying rates into the real estate prices or values defined and measured in the five different ways described by these five conceptual indices. The index value levels traced through time from the left-hand edge of Exhibit 25-4 at the old value level of 100 are splayed out and arrive at the new ultimate value level of 90 spread across time. The REIT index, constant-liquidity index, and contemporaneous transaction price index arrive at the new valuation first.[29] They are followed by the contemporaneous appraised values. Then the appraisal-based index with the staggered (stale) appraisals pulls up the rear, arriving last at the 90 mark.[30]

---

[28]Again, in empirical reality, both this index and the previous could contain random noise. This possibility is ignored here at the conceptual level.

[29]Probably in that order, that is, the REIT index first, then the constant-liquidity index, then the transaction index. But this order is not definite at the conceptual level, particularly given the excess volatility (in some sense) in the first two indices, and the asymmetrical response of the constant-liquidity index to good versus bad news (e.g., real estate market liquidity is typically increased by good news, but decreased by bad news). Transacton prices reflect "bid" prices in "up" markets, "ask" prices in "down" markets.

[30]How long is the total lag, between when the REIT index first hits 90 and when the stale appraisal-based index finally settles down there? No one knows. Also, the length certainly varies over time, and for different types of news (and different types of property). Our guess is that three years was a rough average in the United States during the latter part of the 20th century.

Obviously, the temporal lag bias in real estate values depends on which of these five indices one is using, and which one is taken as the truth against which the bias is defined and measured. Each of the five indices represents a different way of measuring real estate value, and therefore, in a sense, a different *definition* of value. If we are using a staggered appraisal-based index such as Index 5 (e.g., an index not unlike the NCREIF index), then the bias is relatively small if the relevant true value is defined by a contemporaneous appraisal-based index such as Index 4. But the temporal lag is much longer, and the smoothing is much greater, when measured or compared against a REIT-based index such as Index 1.

25.2.3 So Where Is the "Truth"?

This brings us back to the question that motivates this section. Will the *real* "true" real estate value definition please stand up? Well, actually, "no", it won't, because there is not one, single definition of "true" real estate value that is most useful or relevant for all decision and analysis situations. The definition of true private market real estate value that we have been using in this book is generally well represented by either Index 2 or 3 in the stylized response time line in the previous section, either the constant liquidity or the contemporaneous transaction-price-based conceptions of value. We have not always made it clear whether the market value concept we have been using required a constant-liquidity constraint (which would suggest Index 2 is more appropriate), or whether it required an empirical observability constraint (which would suggest Index 3).

In any case, the point of this section is that you need to be aware of the different conceptual possibilities, both regarding what you would *like* to know, and what data you actually have to work with. To make this point more concrete, let's return briefly to some of the decision problems we posed at the outset of this section.

Let's begin by recalling the investment manager in problem 1. Actually, this guy is our famous real estate investor from previous chapters, Bob. In this case Bob wants to know if the market for office property has already turned around. The market in question is the private property market because that is where Bob must buy or sell real estate. This suggests that either Index 2 or Index 3 is the relevant truth for Bob, for these are the two definitions of private market value. Of these two definitions, the contemporaneous transaction price based definition, 3, is potentially more empirically observable and also conceptually more relevant if Bob has the flexibility to absorb some variation in liquidity (i.e., time in the market). Alas, the data Bob has to work with actually comes from indices more like 1 and 5. REIT indices such as Index 1 are readily available, and the NPI is essentially a staggered appraisal-based index like Index 5. What should Bob do?

We will address this question in more depth in the next section, but for starters Bob needs to at least recognize the difference between the information he has and the information he wants, at least at a general and qualitative level. In particular, Bob needs to recognize that the NPI returns are smoothed and lagged representations of what he is interested in, and that the REIT returns are leading and possibly noisy indicators of what he is interested in. Just recognizing this may help Bob out. Suppose a relevant (office-oriented) REIT index turned sharply up a couple of years ago and remained strongly and consistently positive since then. And suppose the NCREIF Office Index had been falling steeply but now has almost flattened out (though not yet bottomed). In this case, it is a good bet that the office property market has already turned around and is headed up.

Now consider the acquisition officer in problem 4. In fact (you guessed it), this is Sue. She is probably thinking in terms of a constant-liquidity value index when she is wondering how far values have fallen. After all, she is in the midst of negotiating a deal to buy. The fact that values have suddenly fallen gives her more cards to play. If the seller really wants to sell the property now, then he will have to be willing to accept a price that can move the property in the face of the market downturn. Of course, the seller may not be that interested in closing the deal, but it would be unwise of Sue to assume, without even trying, that she could not get the property for a price as low as the constant-liquidity value. In order to make that effort, however, Sue would obviously like to find out how far (in percentage terms) the constant-liquidity value has fallen.

Finally, what about the portfolio manager in problem 5? His name is Pete. Alas, poor Pete. He has gone to the trouble of having all of his properties currently appraised so he can show as much growth in value as possible for his client in a period when he feels he has done relatively well. Imagine his frustration when he finds that he has been beaten by the NCREIF Index, an index that supposedly includes all of his peers, the competing managers he thinks he has beaten. The problem, however, is that the NPI is not current. It is like Index 5 in our time line, with staggered re-appraisals. If the growth in market value in general has been slowing down, then the lag in the NPI relative to Pete's current reappraisals can cause the NPI to beat Pete's return performance even if Pete really did beat his peers during the relevant historical period. What Pete needs is a benchmark like Index 4, a contemporaneous appraisal-based index. Then he could have an up-to-date apples-to-apples comparison between his current performance and his benchmark's current performance, as measured by appraisals.

25.3 WHAT IS TO BE DONE?: DEALING WITH TEMPORAL LAG BIAS IN APPRAISAL-BASED RETURNS

If you have made it through the two preceding sections, then you should congratulate yourself.[31] Section 25.1 acquainted you with the nitty-gritty statistical "trees" of the problem of errors in real estate returns. Section 25.2 took you back to view the forest as a whole, the big picture, from a rather deep and subtle conceptual perspective. Neither of these sections was easy reading, we know. But together they give you a pretty good idea about the nature of the real estate periodic returns data problem. But where does this leave us? We seem to have a complicated problem but no solutions.

This brings us to the title question of this section: *What is to be done?*[32] We won't try to answer this question for all of the data problems we raised, or definitively for any of the problems. Nevertheless, the last decade of the 20th century saw considerable advancement of understanding regarding the problem of temporal lag bias in appraisal-based indices, including some suggestions for how to deal with this problem, at least in some circumstances.

To put this issue in the context of the response time line we introduced in the previous section, it is important to recognize that, currently, virtually all of the publicly available and widely used periodic returns indices for commercial property in

---

[31] We suggest that you celebrate by getting yourself a coffee and donut before continuing on into this section.

[32] Of course we hate to plagiarize Comrade Lenin, but we must ask the same question he did in his famous (or infamous) 1902 pamphlet.

the United States come from the two extremes of this time line. Practically all of our commercial real estate returns series are either from REIT-based indices such as Index 1, or appraisal-based indices that have some stale appraisals like Index 5. Yet, as you have gathered from our previous discussion, what analysts and the decision makers they are assisting typically really need is something more like Indices 2, 3, or 4, that is, the value (and return) definitions between the two extremes, in terms of the smoothing and the temporal lag.

One way of looking at this problem is to approach it from the perspective of the publicly available appraisal-based index at the right-hand extreme, namely, the NCREIF Property Index (NPI). This index suffers from rather serious temporal lag bias with respect to private real estate market value (defining market value by either the timeline Index 2 or Index 3). The NPI is even lagged with respect to a contemporaneous appraisal-based index (like Index 4). So, we can pose our question in the following more specific terms: What can be done about temporal lag bias in the NPI?

25.3.1 The First Step: Getting Rid of Stale Appraisals

The first step in addressing this problem is to go from an index like 5 to an index like 4, in other words, to get rid of the **stale appraisal effect** in the NPI. This turns out to be a rather easy step, at least conceptually.

Essentially, the stale appraisal problem can be viewed as a **missing valuation observation problem**. Instead of a complete set of reappraisal observations for all properties in the index portfolio every period, we have, in each period, some properties (actually most of them) for which we cannot observe an updated appraisal. These are the missing observations.

The missing valuation observation problem is the same problem that faces people trying to construct transaction-price-based indices of real estate using data on the changes in value evident between consecutive sales of the same properties. This problem was first addressed nearly 40 years ago by academic statisticians interested in housing price changes. They developed a very clever regression model specification, typically referred to in the housing literature as the repeat-sales regression (RSR). More generally, this may be referred to as a **repeated-measures regression (RMR)**, as the valuation observations need not be transaction prices, but can be appraisals just as well. Bailey, Muth, and Nourse developed the RSR in 1963.[33] Appendix B, at the end of this chapter, walks through a simple numerical example of how the RMR procedure works.[34]

At the turn of the century, NCREIF was planning the imminent commencement of regular publication of an RMR-based version of the quarterly NCREIF Index.[35] Such a version of the NCREIF Index would largely eliminate the stale appraisal problem in the index, making it a true quarterly index, rather than, like the NPI, an annual index partially updated each quarter but never fully up-to-date. In effect,

---

[33] This methodology has since been further developed and extended. Examples of some important extensions include those described in Bryan and Colwell (1982), Case and Shiller (1987), Shiller (1991), Goetzmann (1992), Clapp and Giacotto (1998), and Geltner and Goetzmann (2000). Geltner and Goetzmann applied the methodology specifically to the NCREIF Index.

[34] If you are rusty on what regression analysis is and how it works, Appendix A of this chapter, introduces the basics of how regression analysis works, providing a foundation for Appendix B.

[35] At press time, plans were to call this version the **Current Value Index (CVI)**.

Exhibit 25-5 RMR-Based Version of the NCREIF Index (CVI), Compared to the Official NPI, Quarterly Appreciation Value Levels, 1978–99

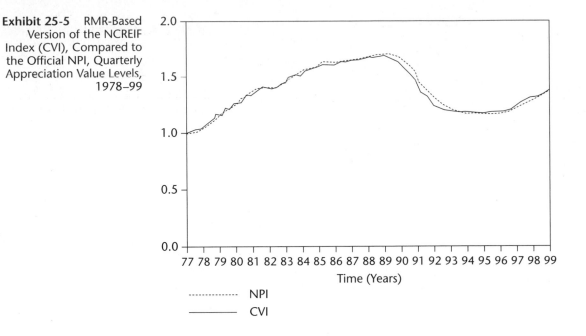

an RMR-based version of the NPI would be a contemporaneous appraisal-based index, like Index 4 in our response time line, thus moving us one step closer to a true market value index.[36]

Exhibit 25-5 compares the RMR-based version of the NPI to the official NPI, as of late 1999. The exhibit depicts the accumulated appreciation returns or implied capital value levels. Note that the RMR leads the NPI slightly in time.[37] Also, although not apparent in the chart, the RMR eliminates most of the **seasonality** in the NPI.[38]

25.3.2 Can We Take a Second Step?

Wouldn't it be nice if we could take the next step and go from an index like 4 in our timeline, to an index like 3 or 2, a true market-value-based index for the private real estate market? Ideally, we would like to have an index of private market real estate returns that is as precise and reliable an indicator of true contemporaneous market returns as the data we have for publicly traded securities such as REITs.

---

[36]Using the RMR procedure, properties included in the index need not necessarily be reappraised annually, or at any regular frequency, as long as some properties are appraised within each quarter. Thus, the RMR procedure offers the technical possibility of expansion of the population of properties in the index to include types of properties that are not annually reappraised, for example, properties that are on the minimum three-year reappraisal cycle mandated by ERISA.

[37]From a statistical perspective, the RMR "Granger causes" the NPI with a four-quarter lag. This means that a significant positive cross-correlation exists between the RMR returns and the NPI returns four quarters later, but no such significant cross-correlation exists in the other direction (that is, between the NPI and the RMR four quarters later).

[38]The NPI has been susceptible to spikes in the fourth calendar quarters due to the fact that more properties are reappraised in the fourth quarter than in other quarters. This makes the NPI more up-to-date at the end of the calendar year than in previous quarters. The seasonal bunching of reappraisals has been gradually diminishing in the index database since the 1980s.

Alas, the practical truth is that this will probably never be possible in a complete sense. The fundamental reason is twofold. First, while purely random noise can be minimized in the process of developing macrolevel returns series, from a practical perspective noise can probably never be completely eliminated, at least not without throwing some of the baby out with the bathwater. Second, as long as there is some noise in our returns data, we cannot get around the noise-versus-lag trade-off described in Chapter 23. As a result, we can only reduce the lag in empirical private market returns series at the expense of magnifying the noise in the resulting delagged or unsmoothed series. What these two problems mean is that the truth we are aiming at, whether defined by our time line Index 2 or Index 3, is inherently unobservable in any finite sample of properties. Therefore, it will always be impossible to know the exact relationship between estimated value series such as appraisal-based or regression-based indices (which ultimately must be empirically based) and the underlying truth we are interested in.[39]

To make this problem more concrete, let's go back to the simulated real estate return data we were using for an illustrative example in section 25.1. Exhibit 25-3b has been reproduced here as Exhibit 25-6, with some relabeling of the variables. Suppose the empirical data available to us is a fully contemporaneous appraisal-based index like our time line Index 4 (or the RMR-based version of the NPI). This is represented by the thick line in Exhibit 25-6. Now suppose that we could somehow know the actual valuation model appraisers used to relate transaction price information to appraised values in the population of properties and the history represented in Exhibit 25-6. In particular, suppose we knew that appraisers used the valuation model specified in equation (6) with $\alpha = 0.2$, repeated here as equation (7):

$$V_t^* = (0.2)\overline{V}_t + (0.8)V_{t-1}^* \tag{7}$$

where V_t^* is the appraised values and $\overline{V}_t$ is the actual average transaction price, in period t.

Then, as we suggested in Chapter 23, we could invert equation (7) to solve for the periodic average transaction price levels, $\overline{V}_t$ as a function of the observable appraisal-based series, V_t^*:

$$\overline{V}_t = (V_t^* - (0.8)V_{t-1}^*)/(0.2) \tag{7a}$$

But when we do this, the value series we recover would not be the true market value series indicated by the thin line in Exhibit 25-6. Instead, we recover the noisy series indicated by the dotted line. And yet, you might think that this is the best we could hope to do because here we have assumed that we knew the exact valuation model used by the appraisers represented in the appraisal-based index.

Actually, we can do a bit better than this because there are statistical techniques to filter out noise. Furthermore, in large appraisal-based portfolios or indices, noise is usually not as big a problem as it appears to be in Exhibit 25-6, where we have exaggerated it a bit to illustrate our point. Nevertheless, the basic point we want you to realize here is that you must consider the trade-off between temporal lag and random noise carefully when you attempt to eliminate temporal lag from appraisal-based indices.

---

[39] Of course, at some level we could make this same statement about periodic returns data for publicly traded securities as well.

Exhibit 25-6
Contemporaneous
Appraised Values,
Unsmoothed Values, and
True Market Values
(simulated data)

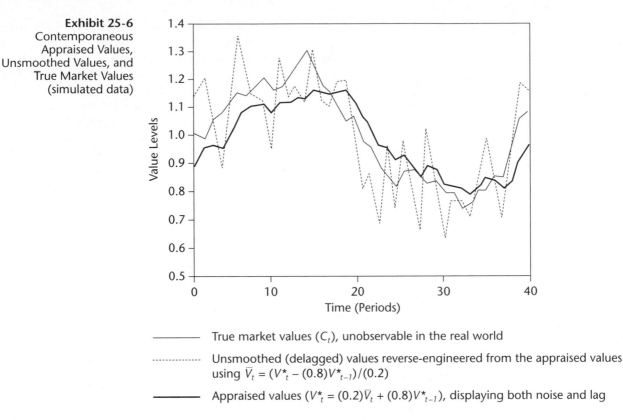

——————— True market values (C_t), unobservable in the real world

··············· Unsmoothed (delagged) values reverse-engineered from the appraised values using $\bar{V}_t = (V^*_t - (0.8)V^*_{t-1})/(0.2)$

——————— Appraised values ($V^*_t = (0.2)\bar{V}_t + (0.8)V^*_{t-1}$), displaying both noise and lag

25.3.3 Some Practical Approaches for Delagging Appraisal-Based Returns

With the previous considerations in mind as important background information, you are ready to learn about some techniques that have been developed to deal with the temporal lag problem in appraisal-based returns series. Beginning in the late 1980s and continuing throughout the 1990s, several techniques were developed to address the need to go from indices like our time line Index 4 or Index 5, and indeed even from REIT-based indices like the time line Index 1, to indices like 2 or 3. These techniques have found some use both in academic studies (where some of them are rather widely employed) and in professional practice (where they are sometimes used, and we suspect their use will become more widespread in the coming years, at least for some purposes). In the following sections we will describe briefly three different types of delagging approaches, also known as unsmoothing (or desmoothing) procedures.

1. Get Rid of the Autocorrelation. This is the oldest unsmoothing technique, and during the 1990s was the most widely employed in academic studies.[40] The idea is that returns with no lag should have no autocorrelation, or at least very little autocorrelation.

[40]As far as we know, this technique was first employed to derive a simulated delagged returns series from the NPI in a study by Fisher, Geltner, and Webb (1994). This general approach is also widely employed in Great Britain, where it has been developed to greater statistical sophistication (such as the use of Kalman filters to allow time-varying delagging), for the purpose of delagging the IPD index. (See Brown and Matysiak [2000].)

This idea is based on the classical financial economic concept known as **weak-form market efficiency (WFME)**. According to the WFME hypothesis, asset market returns series should not be able to predict themselves.

Statistically, we can eliminate autocorrelation from the NPI returns by taking the residuals from a univariate time-series model of the NPI. For example, a simple first- and fourth-order autoregression works quite well on the NPI. That is, you regress the NPI quarterly returns onto themselves lagged one and four quarters:

$$r_t^* = \hat{a}_1 r_{t-1}^* + \hat{a}_4 r_{t-4}^* + e_t \tag{8}$$

The residuals from this regression, the e_t, should contain very little autocorrelation or predictability. They are therefore presumed to reflect the timing and value-directional implications (e.g., favorable or unfavorable implications) of news that arrived in each period, relevant to the value of the properties in the NPI. If e_t was positive, then the net effect of news arriving in period t was favorable for the NPI properties. If e_t was negative, then the reverse is true.[41] If real estate market prices fully reflected this news immediately, then real estate returns would be perfectly correlated with these residuals. Thus, we can model the delagged real estate returns as a simple affine linear function of the residuals:

$$\hat{r}_t = \mu + \lambda e_t \tag{8a}$$

where $\hat{r}_t$ are the estimated (simulated) delagged returns, and μ and λ are parameters chosen by the analyst to give the simulated returns series a mean and volatility that seem reasonable.[42]

A good name for this procedure is **zero-autocorrelation delagging** and, as noted, it was widely used in academic studies during the 1990s. This is probably at least partly because it can be applied simply, using standard statistics packages and the publicly available NCREIF Index returns. Also, the WFME hypothesis is widely employed in mainstream academic financial economics literature, so academics that come from a financial economics background are in the habit of using it. But the WFME hypothesis is also a major weakness of this procedure. It seems unlikely that true private market real estate returns really lack autocorrelation at the quarterly or even annual frequency (whether we define the true returns either by Index 2 or by Index 3). Another important problem with this procedure is that it falls victim to the noise-versus-lag trade-off

---

[41] Such residuals from a time-series regression are sometimes referred to as innovations.

[42] This procedure is described in more depth in Appendix C at the end of this chapter. Note that, by construction, the residuals from a statistical regression have a zero mean. So a positive value of μ is necessary to give the simulated real estate returns a positive mean. Similarly, the nature of the autoregression in equation (8) is that the residuals will have less volatility than the appraisal-based returns we started with, the r_t^* series. Normally, we assume that "true" real estate market returns have at least as much quarterly volatility as is apparent in the NPI. Thus, most analysts employing this procedure would like to use a λ value at least as great as the ratio of the NPI volatility divided by the e_t volatility. Various methods are used to estimate the "true volatility." One approach is simply to assume that the true return series mean equals that observed in the NPI. Application of this "mean equality constraint" allows the implied "true volatility" to be backed out, derived endogenously in the delagging procedure. (See Appendix C for details.) However, it should be noted that in practice the mean-equality approach often results in volatility that seems to be implausibly large for quarterly-frequency returns based on the NPI.

we described previously. While the simulated delagged returns may do a reasonably good job of eliminating the temporal lag bias in the NPI returns, they probably magnify any random noise present in the index.

Both of these problems may be apparent in the example application of the zero-autocorrelation delagging technique shown in Exhibit 25-7. The chart shows the traditional quarterly NPI appreciation value level (dashed line), and a delagged version of that index based on the zero-autocorrelation technique described here (solid line).[43] The chart covers the period from the end of 1983 through the third quarter of 1999, with the indices both arbitrarily set equal to unity at the beginning. This time period depicts the peak, fall, and subsequent recovery in the institutional property market in the 1990s. While the zero-autocorrelation index shows an earlier and steeper fall at the end of the 1980s (a feature that most real estate market participants would probably agree with), it also shows some evidence of random noise, and perhaps excessive delagging.

Considering these features, the major usefulness of the zero-autocorrelation delagging approach, and the way it is often used in academic studies, is in combination with the NPI. This way the zero-autocorrelation series serves as one side of a "bracket" around true private market returns like the time line Index 2 or Index 3. Since, if anything, the zero-autocorrelation procedure overshoots the mark, providing perhaps a bit too much delagging of the NPI, the use of the two indices together can provide a type of sensitivity analysis. If a finding or result of an analysis holds under both the NPI and zero-autocorrelation measures of real estate returns, then it is probably a finding or result that applies to private property market returns.

Exhibit 25-7 NPI versus Zero-Autocorrelation Delagged Index Appreciation Value Level, 1984–99

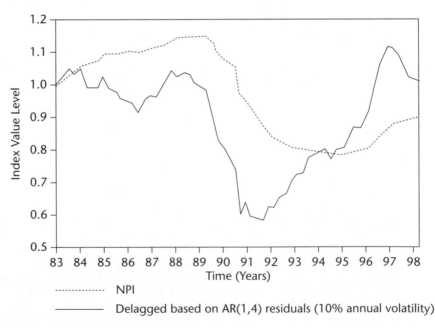

-------------- NPI

———— Delagged based on AR(1,4) residuals (10% annual volatility)

[43] In this example, we have exogenously fixed the delagged volatility at 10% per year. If we used the mean-equality constraint to allow endogenous volatility, the resulting delagged index would have considerably more volatility, over 15% per year.

2. Blend REIT and NCREIF Returns. Now take a look back at our response time line in Exhibit 25-4. In the real world, the empirical data we have is from the two extreme ends of the temporal lag spectrum. REIT-based indices such as the NAREIT Index are like the response time line Index 1. Staggered appraisal-based indices such as the NPI are like Index 5. In the typical situation in which we are concerned about appraisal lag, we ideally want an index like 2 or 3, which is between these two extremes. It therefore seems intuitive that we should be able to get approximately to where we want to go by taking some sort of blend of REIT-based and appraisal-based indices. Exhibit 25-8 depicts a simple version of this approach, the appreciation value levels implied by a 50/50 blend of NAREIT and NCREIF quarterly appreciation returns.

The simple blend shown in Exhibit 25-8 seems to have some of the same strengths and weaknesses as the zero-autocorrelation approach. After all, REITs as actively managed and levered firms are different in a number of ways from relatively passive, unlevered property portfolios. It is a bit naive to assume true real estate market returns would be an exact and constant 50/50 split. However, more sophisticated statistical procedures can be employed to possibly refine this general approach of blending different indicators of property returns. Professors Ling, Naranjo, and Nimalendran explored the use of a technique known as latent variables regression, in a 1998 study for the Real Estate Research Institute.[44] They used more sources of real estate return indicators beyond just the NAREIT and NCREIF Indices. While this technique was only just beginning to be developed at a practical level by the end of the 1990s, it may offer promise in the future.

Exhibit 25-8 NPI versus 50/50 NAREIT/NPI Blend Index Appreciation Value Level, 1984–99

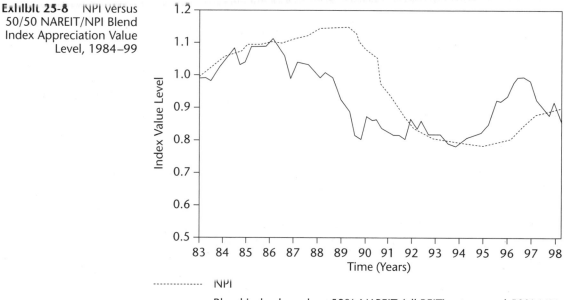

---------- NPI

———— Blend index based on 50% NAREIT (all REIT) return and 50% NPI return

---

[44] See Ling, Naranjo, and Nimalendran (1998).

3. Reverse Engineering of Appraiser Behavior. A final approach that saw some practical use during the 1990s and we believe shows additional promise for the future is what might be termed **reverse engineering** of appraisal-based returns. This approach is, in essence, what we did in the example we described in section 25.3.2 and depicted in Exhibit 25-6 based on simulated data, except that one attempts to deal with the noise-magnification problem if it appears to be serious. The basic idea is to define and calibrate a model of microlevel appraiser behavior that allows one to recover the underlying contemporaneous transaction-price-based returns from observable appraisal-based returns, as in equation (7a). What we are doing here is working from the assumption that appraised values are based on observations of contemporaneous and lagged transaction prices (comps, as these were called in Chapter 23). In this case, it is theoretically possible to "reverse-engineer" the appraisal-based returns to recover the transaction-price-based returns on which the appraisals were based, at least approximately.

The first-order autoregressive model (which is equivalent to a simple exponential smoothing moving-average model of transaction price levels) seems to present a reasonable general starting point for a depiction of the relationship between transaction prices and appraised values, as discussed in Chapter 23. The more difficult part of the problem is quantifying (or "calibrating") this **appraiser behavior model**. For example, in the first-order autoregression model (equation [6]), we need to estimate the proper value to use for the α parameter.

This calibration cannot be done simply by estimating a statistical autoregression model of the appraisal-based returns series. The statistical nature of such a procedure is that it would estimate α so as to produce regression residuals that had no autocorrelation. But we do not know that the "true" real estate returns we are aiming at have no autocorrelation.[45] In fact, we suspect that they probably have some positive autocorrelation, but we do not know how much.

In some cases empirical data on microlevel appraisal procedures may allow estimation of the appraiser behavior model, as in the case of the 1999 Hamilton-Clayton Canadian study cited in Chapter 23. Such data may become more widely available in the future.[46]

Another approach is to compare transaction prices to contemporaneous appraised values of the same properties, if one can get such data. For example, the transaction prices of properties sold from the NCREIF Index can be compared with their recent prior appraisals (updating the prior appraisals to make them contemporaneous to the transactions, using the appraisal-based index to update the prior appraisals). Then, by comparing the percentage differences between the transaction prices and the appraised values, with the contemporaneous percentage rate of appreciation in the appraisal index, one can obtain an approximate, but rather direct, empirical indication of the length of the temporal lag in the microlevel appraisals.[47]

Once you are satisfied that you have a plausible model of microlevel appraiser valuation behavior, the next step is to apply the model to a fully contemporaneous

---

[45] Recall that this was one of our criticisms of the zero-autocorrelation delagging procedure we discussed previously.

[46] For example, index producers like NCREIF could require that data contributors report information about the sales comps used in the periodic property valuations reported into the index. This is already done in England, where the IPD collects not just the appraised values but also key information used by the appraisers in each valuation, for all valuation reports used to construct the IPD Index.

[47] Preliminary work of this nature, by one of the authors and Professor Jeff Fisher at Indiana University, suggests that the typical lag in microlevel appraisals in the NCREIF index may be in the range of two to four calendar quarters. A lag of three quarters implies that the quarterly autoregressive appraiser behavior model would have an α parameter value of 0.25.

appraisal-based index, such as the RMR-based version of the NCREIF Index (the CVI), so as to reverse-engineer the appraisal-based returns (as in equation {7a}), thereby recovering an estimate of the underlying transaction-price-based returns. However, unless the appraisal-based index is first cleansed of even minute amounts of random noise, the noise-magnification effect of the delagging model will result in a noisy transaction price index, as occurred in our simulated example with equation (7a) in Exhibit 25-6. It will therefore often be necessary to filter out virtually all noise from the appraisal-based index used in this procedure. One approach that can be used to do this is a statistical procedure known as **ridge regression**, which can be applied when estimating the RMR-based appraisal index.[48]

Of course reverse engineering, like all attempts to recover true private market returns, will never be perfect. The appraiser behavior model will never be exactly correct, and it will never be objectively possible to remove all noise, and *only* noise, from the appraisal-based index that serves as the input to the reverse-engineering process. Another limitation is that, unlike the two previously described approaches, the reverse-engineering procedure can only be used to estimate appreciation returns, not total returns. However, as noted, most of the interesting periodic changes are in the appreciation component, and this is the component people are typically most concerned about when addressing the problem of temporal lag bias in appraisal-based returns.[49]

With these caveats in mind, the reverse-engineering approach seems to hold some promise, at least for the NCREIF Index. Exhibit 25-9 depicts an example of this

Exhibit 25-9 NPI versus REI Appreciation Value Level Index (TVI), 1984–99

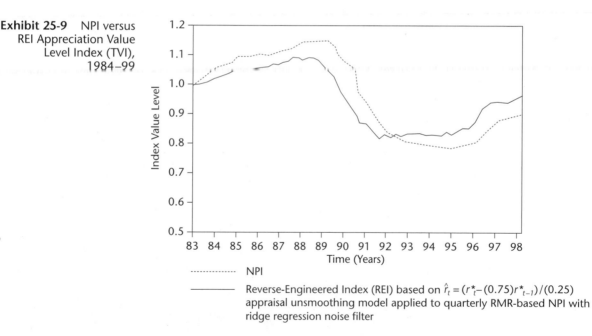

- - - - - - - - NPI

———— Reverse-Engineered Index (REI) based on $\hat{r}_t = (r^*_t - (0.75)r^*_{t-1})/(0.25)$ appraisal unsmoothing model applied to quarterly RMR-based NPI with ridge regression noise filter

[48] The ridge regression was first proposed as a noise filter for regression-based real estate price indices by Professor William Goetzmann. (See Goetzmann [1992].) Use of the ridge in this context is essentially a Bayesian statistical approach. That is, the analyst must have some *a priori* criteria regarding reasonable behavior of the final estimated true returns series. The ridge regression is applied so as to achieve those criteria. The advantage of the ridge procedure in this context is that it filters out random noise *without inducing a temporal lag bias*, a rare and valuable trait.

[49] In effect, the reverse-engineered index is most useful as an indicator of market trends and second moment returns statistics characteristics. For these purposes limitation to the appreciation component only of the total return is not much of a handicap.

A Simple One-Step Version the NPI Reverse-Engineering Model

An earlier reverse-engineering model for the NPI was developed by Geltner (1993b) based on the Quan-Quigley model of rational appraiser behavior described in Chapter 23. The 1993 model simultaneously deals with the stale appraisal problem and the microlevel appraisal lag, working directly on the traditional NPI, rather than the RMR-based version of the NPI. It thus goes in a single step from an Index 5 type of return to an Index 2 or 3 type of return. However, this model can only be applied at the annual frequency to calendar year appreciation returns. At that frequency, noise does not appear to be a problem in the application of this model. The one-step model is sometimes referred to as an unsmoothing model or reverse filter. It has the same first-order autoregressive form as equation (6), with $\alpha = 0.4$, and it is applied to the traditional NPI (which includes stale appraisals) rather than to the RMR-based (CVI) version of the NCREIF Index (which eliminates the stale appraisals). In other words, the reverse-engineered calendar year t appreciation return equals 2.5 times the difference between the NPI return for that year minus 60% of the previous year's NPI return:

$$\hat{g}_t = (gNPI_t - (0.6)gNPI_{t-1})/(0.4)$$

Because the one-step model is so simple, it has been used in some academic and industry studies, and we have used it in most of the annual NCREIF statistics we have shown in this book. But how does it compare to the quarterly reverse-engineered index example we have shown in this chapter based on the CVI and $\alpha = 0.25$? Keep in mind that the one-step model is an annual model, so its α value applies at the annual frequency. In general, of course, the same chronological temporal lag is measured by a smaller value in lower frequency returns because the length of the lag is measured in number (or fraction) of return periods (e.g., a lag of one-half year is 0.5 years but 2 quarters). In the simple exponential smoothing model, α equals the inverse of the quantity one plus the average lag measured in number of periods. An annual α value of 0.4 would therefore equate to a quarterly α value of 0.14. (The annual α of 0.4 implies an annual lag of $1/\alpha - 1$, or 1.5 years, implying a quarterly α of $1/[1+6]$, or 1/7.) However, the one-step model cannot be employed at the quarterly frequency because of the seasonality problem in the NPI. In fact, because of the additional lag caused by the stale appraisal effect, an annual smoothing parameter of $\alpha = 0.40$ applied to the NPI is probably roughly consistent with a quarterly smoothing parameter in the neighborhood of $\alpha = 0.25$ applied to the CVI.

type of estimation of true quarterly private market appreciation returns, based on the NPI. Notice in Exhibit 25-9 that the reverse-engineered index corrects at least part of the appraisal lag in the NPI, typically leading the NPI by about a year. Yet it seems to avoid the excessive noise problem that plagued the other delagging examples we looked at previously.[50]

Before leaving our discussion of appraisal-based indices, let's look briefly at Exhibit 25-10. This exhibit depicts, within the same chart, all three of the lag-adjustment pro-

[50] The reverse-engineered appreciation index depicted in Exhibit 25-9 is based on a quarterly first-order autoregressive model of microlevel appraiser behavior with $\alpha = 0.25$, applied to a ridge-regression-based RMR with the criterion that the resulting reverse-engineered returns series should have positive first-order autocorrelation and volatility similar to that of an RMR estimated without the ridge (classical non-Bayesian estimation). The resulting autocorrelation and volatility of the reverse-engineered returns are characteristic of a series that is largely free of random noise. In Appendix D at the end of this chapter this reverse-engineered index is compared with a pure transaction-price-based version of the NCREIF index based only on properties sold from the NCREIF index, using the RMR type procedure described earlier. As is apparent in Appendix D, the reverse-engineered index shows major turning points in property market value at almost exactly the same time as the pure transaction-price-based index, after the latter is corrected for excessive noise using the ridge regression technique.

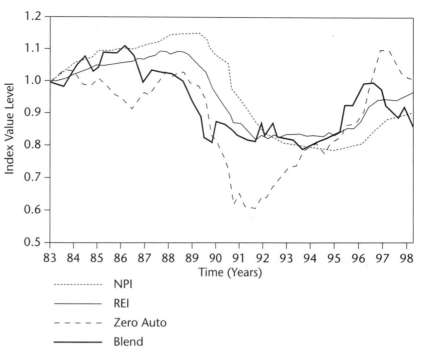

Exhibit 25-10
Comparison of Various
Delagged Value Series
and NPI

cedures we have described here, along with the NPI, as represented by their accumulated quarterly appreciation value levels, all indexed to unity as of the end of 1983. Presented together, we can see the similarities and differences across these procedures. The volatility of the zero-autocorrelation index stands out, as does the smoothness of the reverse-engineered index.[51] It is interesting that all three of the adjusted indices began a major drop at the end of 1989, but the NPI did not really begin to fall until a year later. Also, all three of the adjusted indices showed some sort of sharp, favorable turn at the end of 1992, at least temporarily, while the NPI only gradually bottomed out in early 1996.[52] At the end of the 1990s, both the zero-autocorrelation and blend indices were headed decidedly down, while both the reverse-engineered index and the NPI were headed up, with the reverse-engineered index only registering a slight "hiccup" in the third quarter of 1998.[53] Finally, the overall impression is that the line tracing the NPI lies generally to the right of the other three, with the horizontal distance between the NPI and the other indices (i.e., the temporal lag) being about one year in the case of the reverse-engineered index, and more like two years in the case of the other two indices.[54]

[51] The quarterly volatilities over the sample shown here are 5% for the zero-autocorrelation index (by construction), just over 3% for the blend index, and about 1.5% for both the reverse-engineered index and the NPI.

[52] At the end of 1992 the zero-autocorrelation index turns from negative to positive, the reverse-engineered index turns from negative to a choppy sideways trend, and the blend index turns from flat to temporarily up.

[53] During this period, the reverse-engineered index was the only one of the four indices whose behavior seemed to match what the trade press was saying at the time about what was going on in the institutional property market. (See, for example, contemporary editions of *The Investment Property & Real Estate Capital Markets Report*, or *The Korpacz Real Estate Investor Survey*.)

[54] While these horizontal distances seem plausible based on the nature of the delagging involved, they are a function of the arbitrary equation of all three value level indices as of the end of 1983.

Is It Always Necessary to Delag Appraisal-Based Returns Data?

We have put a great deal of effort in this book, not only in this chapter but starting in Chapter 23, into educating you about the nature of the errors in appraisal-based returns series. Now we have sketched three general approaches for adjusting such returns series to deal with the temporal lag bias problem. You might get the impression from all this bother that we think appraisal-based returns are nearly meaningless, or that in any case one should never use them without some sort of adjustment such as we have described here.

But this is not true. In part, we have had to err on the side of risking giving you this impression because so many people in the real world, mostly in professional practice but to some extent even in academia, are unaware of the problems and issues we have raised here. The bias in current practice is to pay *too little* attention and heed to these problems. This is an understandable bias because, admittedly, recognizing these problems makes life more complicated. It muddies the waters, makes analysis and definitive conclusions more difficult, and potentially risks confusing clients and damaging the credibility of the real estate asset class among investors. But the data problems we have described are real, and in the long run the truth comes out. Therefore, the greater long-run threat to the credibility of real estate is to ignore these problems or to downplay their significance. That is why we are trying to correct the bias we perceive in real world perception and practice by placing so much emphasis on private real estate data problems.

Nevertheless, having said that, let's try to balance the impression we leave, at least a little bit. First of all, let us state clearly for the record that (1) *appraisal-based returns are meaningful* (even when they have some staleness, as in the NPI), and (2) *you do not ALWAYS have to adjust appraisal-based returns in order to use them properly.* Regarding the first point, if appraisal-based returns were meaningless, then we could not even adjust them to get closer to the truth. But we have just shown you three ways, *all based on appraisal returns*, to do just that. As for when you do and when you don't need to adjust appraisal-based returns, the general answer to this question is that you *only* need to adjust them when failure to adjust them could give results or impressions that are misleading in some important way. This is not always.

Here are four typical situations or circumstances in which you don't need to adjust appraisal-based returns data:

1. **Apples-to-apples comparisons.** Suppose you are comparing the time-weighted average return achieved over some historical period by two managers, or two indices, or two types of property, and so forth. The mean return is conditionally biased due to the temporal lag, but if the amount of lagging is about the same between the two subjects being compared, then this bias cancels out in the comparison. You can use the appraisal-based returns without adjustment, keeping in mind that the historical time period actually being covered is a little behind what it nominally appears to be.

2. **When the statistic of interest is unaffected by appraisal return error**. As we pointed out in section 25.1, not all statistics are greatly affected by appraisal return error. Most notably, the long-run geometric mean return is pretty robust, measured over a complete cycle in the relevant property market. Thus, long-run investment performance is well depicted by appraisal-based returns. Also, contemporaneous cross-correlation or beta statistics (regression coefficients) between two returns series that are similarly lagged are not greatly affected by appraisal return errors, provided they don't have much noise (i.e., provided the subject portfolios or indices are rather large, containing numerous individual properties).

3. **You just want to know the long-run beta.** Suppose you want to know the beta of real estate with respect to the stock market, over the long run, or any long-run systematic relationship between private real estate returns and some unpredictable series (i.e., the regression coefficient between real estate and a nonlagged asset market return series). The apparent contemporaneous beta statistic is biased toward zero, but we can correct this bias without deriving an adjusted returns series, simply by adding the contemporaneous and lagged betas, as described in section 25.1.

4. **Use as a bracket.** Unadjusted appraisal-based returns are useful as one end of a bracket, for example, as we described regarding use of the zero-autocorrelation-based adjustment. Similarly, since the NPI and REIT

continues

indices bracket the two extreme ends of the price discovery time line we described in section 25.2, it is possible to use the NPI together with a pure REIT-based index to put a sensitivity range or confidence boundary around analytical results relating to "true" private property market returns. In other words, we don't have the "point estimate" for the finding we are after, but we have a "confidence range" around this finding. If a finding holds in both extremes, in many cases it will be logical to presume it would hold in the center.

With these considerations in mind, we say: Go forth! Use appraisal-based returns data as you see fit. Handle them with care, of course. Be aware that sometimes a little knowledge is worse than no knowledge. But, if you keep in mind the caveats and adjustment tools we presented in this chapter, we feel sure that you should be able to make good use of appraisal-based returns data. Such data are a unique, rich, vital, and irreplaceable source of information about commercial property investment portfolio performance.

25.4 CHAPTER SUMMARY

In this chapter we gave you an in-depth education about the nature of private market real estate periodic returns data, the raw material on which virtually all quantitative macrolevel real estate investment analysis is based, either directly or indirectly. To put it metaphorically, this chapter has, together with Chapter 23, taken you to the sausage factory, and dared to show you how the sausage was made.[55] We hope that not too many of you have swooned at the sight (either metaphorically or otherwise). If your reaction after a first reading of this chapter is something akin to "Yuk!, Gross!," you are in good company. Nevertheless, we hope that you will come back to the factory again, and perhaps again, until you get used to it. Once you get over the initial reaction, you will notice that a lot of the ingredients that go into the sausages are quite wholesome and healthy, although others, admittedly, are not. Still, in the long run you are better off knowing what goes in. After all, you are what you eat, and the sausages themselves are quite tasty.[56]

In the remainder of Part VII we will relieve you of having to deal at such a technical level and address some subjects that practitioners in the real world of macrolevel real estate investment deal with on a daily basis. You will see how the data issues described in this chapter are relevant.[57]

---

[55] What is it with us and sausages?

[56] Of course we apologize for carrying this metaphor so far, but it really does seem to work, and you have to allow a couple of nerdy professors the right to be a bit punchy now and then.

[57] For those of you with a more technical bent, we should also mention that there is a technical appendix at the very end of this book that touches on a subject that is a logical extension of the data issues explored in this chapter, namely, the use of regression models to develop real estate periodic return indices based directly on transaction price data.

APPENDIX 25A: INTRODUCTION TO REGRESSION ANALYSIS AS A SOLUTION OF SIMULTANEOUS EQUATIONS

You have no doubt already been introduced, probably in a basic statistics course, to the ubiquitous statistical tool known as regression analysis. You know that regression is a way to quantify the relationship between one variable and one or more others. The purpose of this appendix is to show how regression analysis can be viewed as a solution to a system of simultaneous equations. This perspective of regression can shed new light on the usefulness of this tool for constructing indices of real estate periodic returns. Such a use of regression analysis is demonstrated in Appendix B. The present appendix simply lays the foundation for Appendix B by introducing regression analysis with a very simple numerical example.

A25.1 The Basic Idea

Suppose a certain population is characterized by two variables that we think are related in a linear way within that population. To be more concrete, let's say it is the height and weight of adult males in the U.S. population. We theorize that the average relationship between height and weight within this population is given by the following relationship:

$$W = \alpha + \beta H \tag{A1a}$$

where W is a person's weight in pounds and H is his height in inches. In this theory, or model, there are two variables, W and H, and two coefficients, α and β. The coefficient α is a constant term or intercept.[58] The second coefficient, β, is a "slope" coefficient, indicating the average number of incremental pounds (over the α amount) associated with each inch of height. The general form of this theoretical model is shown graphically in Exhibit A25-1.

Now let's suppose that the theoretical relationship depicted in equation (A1a) and Exhibit A25-1 is actually true. That is, the average relationship between height and weight in the population is indeed described by this type of affine linear relationship.[59] Let us further suppose that the true values of α and β happen to be: α = 100 pounds, and β = 1.0 pounds/inch. Thus, the true average relationship between height and weight in the population is described by equation (A1b):

$$W = 100 + H \tag{A1b}$$

However, this underlying "truth" is not empirically observable. No one can know for certain the true average relationship indicated in equation (A1b). People can only estimate the true relationship.

In order to see how such estimation is done with regression analysis, let's back up a minute and consider equation (A1a) again. If equation (A1a) is our general

[58]In a formal mathematical sense α represents the weight that a person of zero height would have (on average in the population). In reality, of course, there are no zero-height individuals in the population (or even anything close to it), so α in this model is simply serving as a calibration device.

[59]A pure linear relationship is one of direct proportionality. An affine relationship includes a constant (or nonzero intercept), as in our model here.

Exhibit A25-1 Simple Bivariate Linear Model

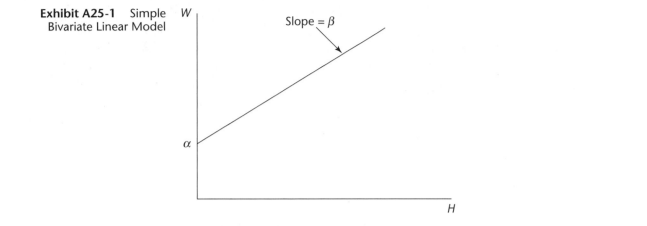

theoretical model of the average relationship between height and weight in the population, then what we are saying at the "microlevel" about the height and weight of *individual* people is represented in equation (A1c):

$$W_i = \alpha + \beta H_i + \varepsilon_i \tag{A1c}$$

Here, W_i is person i's weight and H_i is his height. The ε_i is an "error" term associated with individual i, though of course it does not imply that individual i has done anything wrong. ε_i is simply the difference between individual i's height/weight relationship and the average height/weight relationship in the population. We are only trying to capture the average relationship in our theory in equation (A1a).

Equation (A1c) is amenable to statistical analysis and empirical estimation. The statistical problem is that we want to estimate the numerical values of the two coefficients, α and β. Suppose we have a sample of three individuals drawn randomly from the population: Joe (labeled as individual i = 1), Pete (i = 2), and (of course) Bob (i = 3). We thus have a sample (or estimation database) of size n = 3. Suppose that the heights we observe for these three individuals are: H_1 = 74 inches (Joe's height), H_2 = 70 inches (Pete's height), and H_3 = 72 inches (Bob's height). Now, because this is a made-up numerical example, we can know from equation (A1b) that if these individuals all displayed the true average relationship between height and weight in the population, then their weights would be 174, 170, and 172 pounds, respectively for Joe, Pete, and Bob. But if this were the real world, we would not know the true values of α and β. We would only have our empirical sample of three observations from which to try to infer the true values of α and β.

Now suppose, very typically, that none of our three individuals happens to display exactly the true (unknown) average height/weight relationship of the population. Joe, Pete, and Bob each has his own idiosyncratic body shape. The actual height and weight observations in our sample of three are indicated in the following table:

Observation # (i)	Name	Weight (W_i)	Height (H_i)
1	Joe	168	74
2	Pete	166	70
3	Bob	183	72

How are we to use this empirical data to estimate the true values of α and β? The classical (and by far most common) approach is to plug the height and weight from each observation into our empirical equation (A1c) and then solve the resulting system of simultaneous linear equations. Since we have three observations (three data points), we will have three equations. Each of the following equations is one indication of the true average height/weight relationship:

$$
\begin{aligned}
Joe : & \quad 168 = \hat{\alpha} + 74\hat{\beta} + e_1 \\
Pete : & \quad 166 = \hat{\alpha} + 70\hat{\beta} + e_2 \\
Bob : & \quad 183 = \hat{\alpha} + 72\hat{\beta} + e_3
\end{aligned}
\qquad \text{(A2)}
$$

Notice that each equation in the (A2) system is formed by substituting a given observation's data into equation (A1c), with only two minor modifications. We changed the coefficient labels from α and β to $\hat{\alpha}$ and $\hat{\beta}$, because when we solve this system of equations for $\hat{\alpha}$ and $\hat{\beta}$ we will have only estimates of the true α and β. These estimates will almost certainly not equal the true values of α and β (which are unknowable anyway). We also changed the ε_i terms in equation (A1c) to e_i terms, to indicate that these are not deviations of our observations from the true average population height/weight relationship, but rather only from our *estimate* of that relationship. As such the e_i terms in the (A2) system are often called residuals, to distinguish them from the (unobservable) true "error" values in (A1c).

Now note that in the system of equations (A2) we have more equations (observations) than we have unknowns (coefficients), not counting the residual terms. In particular, we have three equations (Joe, Pete, and Bob), and two unknowns ($\hat{\alpha}$ and $\hat{\beta}$). It is a fact from basic algebra that such a system will not generally have only one solution (that is, one pair of values for $\hat{\alpha}$ and $\hat{\beta}$) that will solve all of the equations simultaneously. The classical (and most common) way to deal with this problem is to find the solution that minimizes the sum of the squared values of the residuals, the e_i terms. That is, we find the values of $\hat{\alpha}$ and $\hat{\beta}$ that minimize $\sum_{i=1}^{n} e_i^2$. This is called "ordinary least squares" (OLS) estimation. This method of estimating the true values of α and β from a sample of data has several appealing properties from a statistical perspective.[60] (It is provided in all modern computer spreadsheet software.)

Suppose we apply this OLS method to the data we have on Joe, Pete, and Bob. We will get the values of: $\hat{\alpha}$ = 136 pounds, and $\hat{\beta}$ = 0.5 pounds/inch. Alas, these estimates are not very close to the true values of 100 and 1.0. But we only have a sample of three (and we are thrown off to some extent by the fact that Bob is a bit, well, in his own words, "pleasantly and pleasingly overweight"). This numerical example is summarized in Exhibit A25-2.

---

[60]Under some typical assumptions, OLS is unbiased (the expected values of the coefficient estimates are the true values of the coefficients), consistent (as the sample size gets larger, that is, as $n \rightarrow \infty$, the coefficient estimates will approach the true coefficient values), and efficient (there is no other way to estimate the coefficients that will have less average error). Dust off your basic statistics textbook if you want to know more.

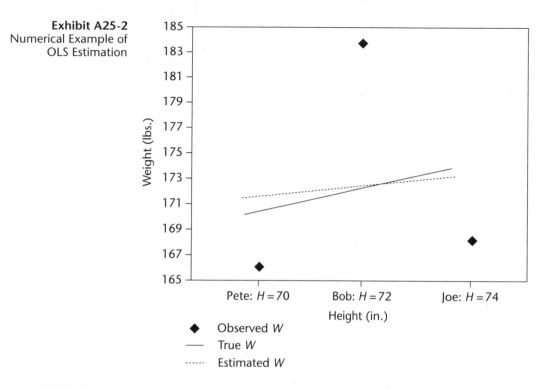

Exhibit A25-2
Numerical Example of
OLS Estimation

Legend:
◆ Observed W
—— True W
------ Estimated W

A25.2 Hedonic Models of Real Estate Value

The problem of trying to estimate the market values of thinly traded assets, such as commercial properties, is very analogous to the example we just examined and is therefore quite amenable to a solution based on statistical regression. In each period of time, say a quarter or a year, we can obtain valuation observations of a number of individual properties, either as transaction prices or appraisals. These valuation observations are dispersed cross-sectionally around the average valuation within each period of time, in the same way that the weights of Joe, Pete, and Bob were dispersed around their average weight.

Of course, real estate values are more complex than the simple height/weight relationship considered earlier. A number of variables influence property value at any given time, even if we "normalize" that value by measuring it as a multiple of the property's current income. Chapter 23 noted a number of variables such as location, building age, size and quality, vacancy rate, lease expiration, and so on. These were called hedonic variables because they reflect the quality of the property. Hedonic valuation models are multivariable regressions rather than simple bivariate models like the one in the previous section. But the principle is the same.

APPENDIX 25B: REPEATED-MEASURES REGRESSION (RMR) PROCEDURE FOR REAL ESTATE RETURN INDEX ESTIMATION

The estimation of the periodic percentage changes across time in the market value of a population (or portfolio) of properties is a slightly different problem than that of estimating the value of the population as of a single point in time, although these problems are related. The main additional problem is the need to control for quality differences in the properties whose valuations are observed in different periods of time. This problem can be viewed as a "missing observation" problem. One of the major methods for dealing with this type of problem is the repeated-measures regression (RMR). In this appendix we will present a simple numerical example of one variant of this method. In particular, we will examine the value-weighted arithmetic average price index first developed by Robert Shiller (for price indices) and Geltner and Goetzmann (for total return indices).[61]

B25.1 Simple Numerical Example of How the RMR Works

To see how we can deal with the missing observation problem using regression analysis, consider a very simple numerical example. Suppose we are trying to estimate the periodic appreciation returns over a history spanning two periods of time (from the end of a base period through two subsequent consecutive periods) for a portfolio (or population) consisting of two properties. Suppose further that we have no valuation observation for one of the properties in the first period. Thus, we have, in its simplest form, the missing valuation observation problem described in the preceding paragraph.

In this example we will assume that the valuation observations of the two properties are appraised values, but as far as the statistical index estimation methodology is concerned the valuations could as well be transaction price observations. Furthermore, to simplify the present illustration, we will assume that the two properties are identical and that no cross-sectional dispersion in the periodic appreciation returns exists between the two properties.[62] (However, we assume that we do not know that the two

---

[61]The term *arithmetic average price index* refers to the fact that the price index level within each period is an arithmetic *cross-sectional* average of the values of the constituent properties. (The *longitudinal* average return in the resulting index, computed across time, can, of course, be computed on either an arithmetic or geometric basis.) The term *value-weighted* refers to the fact that, in computing the cross-sectional average values, individual property valuations are weighted in proportion to the value of the property. The result is an index of aggregate portfolio value, treating the constituent properties as a "population" in the statistical sense. (See further discussion relevant to this point in Chapter 27, regarding the use of real estate return indices as benchmarks for performance evaluation.) Shiller (1991) first described the technique explained in this appendix. Geltner and Goetzmann (2000) later extended the technique to total returns.

[62]In reality, such dispersion would of course exist, due both to genuine indiosyncratic differences in individual property returns, and to random individual valuation observation errors (or noise, as described in Chapter 23). At a basic level, such cross-sectional dispersion in returns is dealt with in the regression procedure in the same way that the variation among Joe, Pete, and Bob was dealt with in the previous illustration in Appendix A: the OLS estimation procedure minimizes the sum of the squared residuals in the estimation database. This is essentially an averaging process, relying on the Law of Large Numbers (aka, the Square Root of n Rule). However, in practice noise and the resulting estimation error is a major concern, and more sophisticated techniques have been developed to filter noise from estimated periodic returns indices. One approach that seems to work quite well is the Bayesian use of the ridge estimator

properties are identical; hence, we must try to estimate the return that is missing from the empirical database.)

As in the example in the first part of this appendix, let's suppose that we know something that will never actually be known in the real world, namely, the true appreciation return to each property (and therefore to the portfolio) each period. In particular, suppose that the true property market values each period are as indicated in Table 1:

Table 1 True Value Information (unobservable and unknown)

Property	Period t Value	Period $t + 1$ Value	Period $t + 2$ Value
Property 1	$1,000	$1,100	$1,100
Property 2	$1,000	$1,100	$1,100

It is obvious from this information that the true appreciation returns to the portfolio are 10% in period $t + 1$ and 0% in period $t + 2$.

However, the information in Table 1 is unobservable and unknown. The observable data is indicated in Table 2:

Table 2 Empirically Observable Information

Property	Period t Appraisal	Period $t + 1$ Appraisal	Period $t + 2$ Appraisal
Property 1	$1,000	$1,100	$1,100
Property 2	$1,000	NA	$1,100

The missing valuation observation is on property 2 during period $t + 1$.

We address this problem using Shiller's arithmetic average repeated-measures regression (RMR), which we can set up as a system of simultaneous linear equations, just as we did in Appendix A of this chapter. The RMR uses dummy variables on both the left-hand sides (LHS) and right-hand sides (RHS) of the equations. Each equation corresponds to a repeat-appraisal pair observation, that is, two sequential appraisals of the same property. In this example we have three observations in the database. The first observation corresponds to property 1's appraisals in periods t and $t + 1$. The second observation corresponds to property 1's appraisals in periods $t + 1$ and $t + 2$. The third observation corresponds to property 2's appraisals in periods t and $t + 2$.

The variables in the RMR are defined as follows. The LHS (dependent variable) is zero unless the first of the two appraisals occurred in the base period (in this case,

---

described by Goetzmann (1992), for example, as implemented in the manner described in Geltner and Goetzmann (2000). Other statistical approaches also exist for filtering noise without inducing a lag. For example, McMillen & Dombrow (2000) propose a flexible fourier parametrization of time. Another approach that has been tried with some success in transaction-price-based housing indices is the use of minimum mean absolute difference (MAD) estimation instead of OLS. MAD estimation fits the regression to minimize the sum of the absolute values of the residuals rather than the squared residuals as in OLS. As a result, MAD estimation is less influenced by "outliers," observations that are far from the mean (and thus may reflect faulty data or particularly noisy transactions). Also, to help deal with statistical problems caused by the true idiosyncratic return source of noise, a three-stage weighted least squares (WLS) procedure pioneered by Case and Shiller (1987) is typically used in transaction-price-based indices, in which the empirical valuation observations in the database occur at long and highly variable intervals.

period t), in which case the LHS takes on the value of this first appraisal. The RHS consists purely of dummy variables corresponding to the periods for which returns are to be estimated. Thus, in our example there are two variables on the RHS of the regression equations, one for period $t + 1$, and the other for period $t + 2$. Each dummy variable assumes a value of zero if its time period is either before the first appraisal or after the second appraisal in the observation, or if its time period lies between the times of the two appraisals. If the first valuation in the observation occurred during the time period the dummy variable represents, then that variable takes the value of the *negative* of that first valuation for the observation. If the second valuation in the observation occurred in the period the dummy variable represents, then the dummy variable takes the *positive* value of that second valuation.[63]

The RMR empirical model (corresponding conceptually to equation [A1c] of Appendix A of this chapter) is thus, for our current three-period example,

$$V_{t,i} = \beta_{t+1} D_{t+1,i} + \beta_{t+2} D_{t+2,i} + \varepsilon_i \tag{B1}$$

where $V_{t,i}$ is the LHS dummy variable (for observation $i = 1, 2, \ldots, n$); the $D_{t+1,i}$ and $D_{t+2,i}$ variables are the RHS dummy variables for return estimation periods $t + 1$ and $t + 2$; the β_{t+1} and β_{t+2} coefficients are the two coefficients to be estimated corresponding to the two return periods ($t + 1$ and $t + 2$ respectively); and the ε_i term is as defined previously, the theoretical model's "error" associated with observation i.[64]

The observations and variable values for the RMR in our present example are summarized in Table 3:

Table 3 Data for Estimating the RMR on the Example Database from Table 2

Observation # (i)	LHS (Base Period) Value ($V_{t,i}$)	RHS $t + 1$ Variable Value ($D_{t+1,i}$)	RHS $t + 2$ Variable Value ($D_{t+2,i}$)
1 (Prop. 1, $V_{t,1}$ & $V_{t+1,1}$)	$1,000	$1,100	0
2 (Prop. 1, $V_{t+1,2}$ & $V_{t+2,2}$)	0	−$1,100	$1,100
3 (Prop. 2, $V_{t,3}$ & $V_{t+2,3}$)	$1,000	0	$1,100

The coefficient values in the regression model equation (B1) are estimated as in our example from Appendix A of this chapter, by solving the system of simultaneous

---

[63]To estimate a periodic *total* return index instead of just appreciation returns, add also the net cash flow from the property to its owner each period to the previously described dummy variables corresponding to each period *between* the two valuations (that is, to the dummy variables subsequent to the first valuation, up to and including the dummy variable corresponding to the period of the second valuation). In other words, in a total return index the dummy variables during the periods of and between the two valuation observations register the net cash flows one would use in a DCF or IRR analysis of the property between those two valuations. Prior to and subsequent to the two valuations in each observation, the dummy variables take the value of zero for the given observation.

[64]These "errors" are due to cross-sectional dispersion in the data, as described previously.

equations so as to minimize the sum of the squared residuals. Specifically, the system to solve (corresponding conceptually to the [A2] system of Appendix A) is

$$Obs.1: \quad 1000 = \hat{\beta}_{t+1}(1100) + \hat{\beta}_{t+2}(0) + e_1$$

$$Obs.2: \quad 0 = \hat{\beta}_{t+1}(-1100) + \hat{\beta}_{t+2}(1100) + e_2 \qquad \text{(B2)}$$

$$Obs.3: \quad 1000 = \hat{\beta}_{t+1}(0) + \hat{\beta}_{t+2}(1100) + e_3$$

Thus, once again, we have three linear equations with two unknowns (not including the residuals). In general, we would once again estimate the $\hat{\beta}_{t+s}$ coefficient values as those that minimize the sum of the squared residual values across the three equations (OLS regression).[65] However, in the present example there is no cross-sectional dispersion (no noise) in our data, so there will indeed be a single consistent solution that exactly and simultaneously solves all three equations. (In other words, we can minimize the $\sum_{i=1}^{n} e_i^2$. term at zero, with $e_i = 0$ for all $i = 1,2,3$.) The solution to the system (B2) is $\hat{\beta}_{t+1} = 0.90909$, $\hat{\beta}_{t+2} = 0.90909$.[66]

These coefficient values are the inverses of the periodic values of an index of the accumulated compound value levels of the portfolio properties, where the index starts out at a value of unity in the base period. In particular

$$1/\hat{\beta}_{t+1} = 1/0.90909 = 1.10$$

$$1/\hat{\beta}_{t+2} = 1/0.90909 = 1.10$$

Thus, the implied appreciation returns for the portfolio are

$$\hat{g}_{t+1} = (\hat{V}_{t+1}/\hat{V}_t) - 1 = (1.10/1) - 1 = 10\%$$

$$\hat{g}_{t+2} = (\hat{V}_{t+2}/\hat{V}_{t+1}) - 1 = (1.10/1.10) - 1 = 0\%$$

These are, of course, the exact true periodic appreciation returns to the portfolio, as we know from Table 1 but which are not directly observable (given the data in Table 2), due to the missing valuation observation problem.

[65]In real world practice, the valuations, the $V_{t+s,i}$ values, are observed with "error" (this is true whether they are appraised values or transaction prices because of the cross-sectional noise or dispersion in such values around the true market value for any given property at any given time). Therefore, an instrumental variable estimation must be employed to address this "errors in variables" problem, as described in Shiller (1991).

[66]To check that this is indeed the solution, plug these values back into the system:

$$Obs.1: \quad 1000 = 0.90909(1100) + 0.90909(0) = 1000 + 0 = 1000$$

$$Obs.2: \quad 0 = 0.90909(-1100) + 0.90909(1100) = -1000 + 1000 = 0$$

$$Obs.3: \quad 1000 = 0.90909(0) + 0.90909(1100) = 0 + 1000 = 1000$$

B25.2 General RMR Value-Weighted Arithmetic Periodic Total Return Specification

The preceding numerical example demonstrates that the RMR procedure can solve the missing valuation observation problem for private market real estate portfolios.[67] The reason this procedure works in general can be seen as follows. Start with the definition of the HPR formula from Chapter 9:

$$1 + r_{t+1} = \frac{CF_{t+1} + V_{t+1}}{V_t} \tag{B3}$$

where r_t is the total return in period t, V_t is the asset value at the end of period t, and CF_t is the net cash flow generated by the asset during period t (with cash flow to the investor signed positively and cash flow from the investor signed negatively).[68] An algebraic expansion of equation (B3) to encompass more time periods shows the relation between the periodic total returns and the observations of terminal asset valuations and intermediate cash flows, as seen in equation (B4).

$$0 = -V_t + \left(\frac{1}{1 + r_{t+1}}\right)(CF_{t+1}) + \left(\frac{1}{1 + r_{t+1}}\right)\left(\frac{1}{1 + r_{t+2}}\right)(CF_{t+2}) + \cdots$$
$$+ \left(\frac{1}{1 + r_{t+1}}\right) \cdots \left(\frac{1}{1 + r_{t+T}}\right)(CF_{t+T} + V_{t+T}) \tag{B4}$$

Note that in equation (B4) we have only two observations of the asset value, and these are not in adjacent periods of time, one at the end of period t and the next at the end of period $t + T$. Between, we observe only the cash flows generated each period by the asset. These are essentially the characteristics of the property-level historical data available in the typical private real estate portfolio information database. Notice further that equation (B4) is linear in the inverse of the accumulated value level of the compounded returns. Thus, we can use linear regression to filter out noise and idiosyncratic effects to estimate a total return index level for a given population of properties. The dummy variable regression specification described in the previous section accomplishes this result. The β_{t+s} coefficients equate to the products (discount factors) multiplying the cash flow (and valuation) terms on the RHS of equation (B4).

[67]Even if the individual assets are modified between successive valuation observations, as by the addition of capital improvements or expansions, a true periodic total return index can still be estimated using this technique provided one has data on the periodic capital expenditures, and these expenditures are subtracted out of the net cash flows each period, in the same manner as would be appropriate for a DCF valuation or IRR analysis of the property, as described in an earlier footnote.

[68]Note that this formula applies at the microlevel for any given property i. Here we suppress the i subscript for simplicity of illustration. Typically, of course $CF_t = NOI_t + PS_t - CI_t$, where NOI_t is the net operating income generated by the property during period t, PS_t is the partial sales receipts (received from sale of part of the property), and CI_t is the capital improvement expenditures disbursed on the property during period t.

APPENDIX 25C: ZERO AUTOCORRELATION DELAGGING PROCEDURE: A TYPICAL APPLICATION

This appendix presents a detailed example of the application of the zero-autocorrelation-based procedure for delagging appraisal-based returns indices, as described in section 25.3 of this chapter. In particular, the procedure described here is the way this procedure is typically applied to the *quarterly* NCREIF Property Index (NPI).[69]

The procedure begins with a first- and fourth-order autoregressive model of the NPI returns:[70]

$$r_t^* = a_1 r_{t-1}^* + a_4 r_{t-4}^* + (wr_t - w\mu) \tag{C1}$$

where

r_t^* = NPI return in quarter t

r_t = unsmoothed (liquid, or full information) return (characterized by lack of autocorrelation)

a_1, a_4 = factors reflecting autocorrelation (including seasonality: the fourth-order lag), to be estimated in the autoregression model

w, μ = a weight and a constant chosen to give the unsmoothed returns the desired mean and volatility ($w = 1/\lambda$ determines volatility, μ is the mean).

$(wr_t - w\mu)$ = the "residuals" from the autoregression (zero mean, zero autocorrelation) = e_t.

As $(a_1 r_{t-1}^* + a_4 r_{t-4}^*)$ is the predictable part of r_t^*, so the regression residuals, e_t, are the unpredictable "news" in the NPI returns. The w and μ are devices to blow up these residuals into simulated returns. Thus, we have the unsmoothed return:[71]

$$r_t = \mu + (1/w)e_t \tag{C2}$$

where e_t is the autoregression residual and μ is the mean of the unsmoothed return.

The analyst may set values for w and μ on the basis of *a priori* opinion about the true mean and volatility. Alternatively, one can apply a mean-equality constraint to set μ equal to the NPI mean return, on the assumption that temporal lag does not bias the unconditional (long-run) mean return. This results in a specification for w as $w = (1 - a_1 - a_4)$. This allows the analyst to avoid making an *a priori* assumption about the true volatility.

[69]The approach described here was first applied in Fisher, Geltner, and Webb (1994).

[70]Note that, in principle, if the AR(1,4) specification is a good model for the NPI quarterly returns, then there should be no constant (or intercept) term in equation (C1). A more general ARMA specification would allow a better fit and residuals that are more completely white noise. But the AR(1,4) specification is intuitive, easy to remember, and generally good enough. Its use saves the time of having to decide on an optimal specification. Note that the AR(1,4) model is meant to be applied to the traditional NPI, whose seasonality is the reason for the fourth-order term.

[71]Note that equation (C2) here equates to equation (8a), and that w is the inverse of λ, as presented in the main body of the chapter.

The mean-equality constraint, $E[r_t^*] = E[r_t]$, works as follows:[72]

$$\begin{aligned}
E[r_t^*] &= E[a_1 r_{t-1}^* + a_4 r_{t-4}^* + e_t] \\
&= E[a_1 r_{t-1}^* + a_4 r_{t-4}^* + (wr_t - w\mu)] \\
&= a_1 E[r_{t-1}^*] + a_4 E[r_{t-4}^*] + wE[r_t] - w\mu
\end{aligned}$$

Assuming stationarity:

$$\begin{aligned}
&= a_1 E[r_t^*] + a_4 E[r_t^*] + wE[r_t] - w\mu \\
&= (a_1 + a_4)\, E[r_t^*] + wE[r_t] - w\mu
\end{aligned}$$

and now equate means:

$$\begin{aligned}
&= (a_1 + a_4)\, E[r_t] + wE[r_t] - w\mu = E[r_t] = E[\mu + e_t/w] = \mu \\
&= (a_1 + a_4 + w)\mu = \mu
\end{aligned}$$

$$\Rightarrow w = 1 - a_1 - a_4$$

Thus, in terms of equation (8a):

$$\lambda = 1/(1 - a_1 - a_4)$$

As a caveat, it should be recognized that there are several unrealistic assumptions in this procedure. For one thing, the model is noiseless, ignoring the existence and effect of purely random error in the NPI. Another simplification is that this model assumes "stationarity," that is, it assumes that the same model applies all the time. In reality, in the case of the NPI, a somewhat different model would likely apply in different calendar quarters. For example, the contemporaneous moving-average parameter w would likely be larger, and the other lagged parameters (w_1, w_2, . . .) would likely be smaller, for modeling fourth-quarter returns than for modeling quarterly returns during the other calendar quarters. (This is because more properties in the NPI tend to be reappraised during the fourth calendar quarters. Properties that are not reappraised in a quarter go into the NPI with an effective value of zero for w, dampening toward zero the aggregate value of w that applies to the NPI as a whole.) Of course, as noted in the main body of the chapter, the biggest problematical assumption in this procedure is that it assumes that the true private market real estate returns lack autocorrelation, as if the real estate market were as liquid and informationally efficient as the stock market.

---

[72]It should be noted that, as this model is using continuously compounded returns (log differences), in equating means it is like equating geometric means or the beginning and ending value levels (at least relatively). This is not such a bad assumption in the middle of the cycle, but is more problematic just after turning points.

APPENDIX 25D: COMPARING REVERSE-ENGINEERED AND PURE TRANSACTION-PRICE-BASED VERSIONS OF THE NCREIF APPRECIATION INDEX

Section 25.3.3 presented a reverse-engineered version of the NCREIF index appreciation returns (REI). This index was designed to recover something like a contemporaneous transaction-price-based version of the NCREIF appreciation, along the lines of index 3 in the conceptual price discovery time line in Exhibit 25-4. Section 25.3.1 and Appendix B of this chapter also presented a repeated-measures regression (RMR) procedure for estimating quarterly returns when empirical valuation observations are not available for every property in every quarter.

In section 25.3.1 the application of this RMR methodology was to appraised valuation, but we noted in Appendix B that this methodology can also be applied to a database consisting purely of transaction price observations, provided one has at least two "repeat sales" of each property. Thus, a repeat-sales version of the NCREIF index can be estimated based purely on transaction prices, using only the properties that have been sold out of the NCREIF index. The first sale price in each observation is the value at which the property originally entered the NCREIF index database.[73] The second sale price is the price at which the property was sold (and exited the NCREIF index database). We will label this the RSI.[74]

Exhibit D25-1 presents the REI and the RSI appreciation value levels from 1988

Exhibit D25-1 Reverse-Engineered versus Repeat-Sales Versions of the NCREIF Index Appreciation Levels (1988Q1=1)

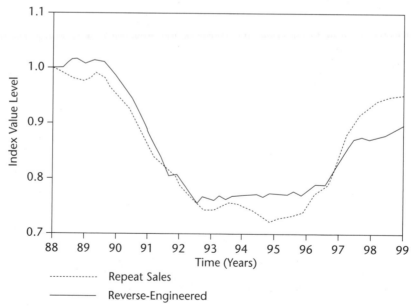

------- Repeat Sales

———— Reverse-Engineered

[73]In some cases, this may not be a transaction price. For example, the property might not have been just purchased, but rather the investment manager owning the property might have just joined NCREIF. Nevertheless, in most cases the valuation at which a property enters the NCREIF database is usually a transaction price, or else an appraisal conducted shortly subsequent to the property's purchase.

[74]Note that in the case of a transaction price based index the value observations should normally be equally weighted in estimating the RMR, rather than value-weighted as we described in Appendix B, because the properties that transact are usually a sample rather than an entire population. The RMR can be equal-weighted simply by normalizing each observation based on its first evaluation.

through the third quarter of 1999.[75] It is interesting to note that both indices trace a broadly consistent pattern, with approximately equal magnitude of fall and rise, and very nearly identical timing of the major turning points. This suggests that the REI is well calibrated with $\alpha = 0.25$ in equation (6) in Chapter 25, correctly capturing the average length of the appraisal lag. The conceptual advantage of the REI over the RSI as estimated here is that the REI is based on more data, including not only the transaction prices of the sold properties but also the serious reappraisals of the properties that remain in the NCREIF index. This may be why the REI picked up the downtick in the institutional property market in the third quarter of 1998, whereas the RSI did not reveal this real event.[76] However, as noted in Appendix B, the RMR procedure on which the RSI is based allows for the production of a total return index, whereas the reverse-engineering methodology on which the REI is based only permits an appreciation return index to be constructed.

[75]The RSI depicted here was estimated based on approximately 2,700 repeat-sale observations, all the properties sold from the NCREIF index between 1988 and 1999, or an average of about 60 repeat-sale observations per quarter. With this number of observations the RSI would be very noisy but for the use of the ridge regression noise filter as described in Goetzmann (1992) and Geltner and Goetzmann (2000).

[76]In response to the sudden market drop in the third quarter of 1998, a number of pending sales transactions among NCREIF properties were simply canceled or postponed, not showing up in that quarter in the database from which the RSI was estimated. The remaining sales that did close in the third quarter of 1998 did not reflect the market downtick (not surprisingly, but also not characteristic of the market as a whole in that quarter). In effect, the RSI suffers from sample selection bias. The properties that happen to be sold from the NCREIF database in any given quarter are not necessarily representative (in terms of their transaction prices) of the entire population of NCREIF properties (in terms of their current market values).

KEY TERMS

NCREIF Property Index (NPI)
return errors
random noise
temporal lag
longitudinal (temporal) variation
cross-sectional (nontemporal) variation
volatility effects (of return errors)
covariance effects
moving average
smoothing (or appraisal smoothing)
conditional and unconditional mean return effects (of return errors)
beta effects
cross-correlation effects

autocorrelation effects
pooled transaction price data
price discovery
Index 1 (REIT-based returns)
Index 2 (constant-liquidity private market returns)
Index 3 (observable contemporaneous transaction price returns)
Index 4 (contemporaneous appraisal-based returns)
Index 5 (staggered appraisal-based index returns)
stale appraisal effect
missing value observation problem
repeated-measures regression (RMR)

current value index (CVI)
seasonality (in NPI)
unsmoothed (delagged) returns
noise-versus-lag trade-off
weak-form market efficiency (WFME)
zero-autocorrelation delagging
REIT/appraisal blend delagging
reverse engineering (of appraisal-based returns)
appraiser behavior model
ridge regression (Bayesian noise filter)
one-step reverse-engineering model

STUDY QUESTIONS

25.1. Describe and contrast the pure effect of random noise and the pure effect of temporal lagging in terms of how an empirical appraisal-based periodic return index would differ from the unobservable underlying true returns. When is the noise effect relatively more important? When is the temporal lag effect typically more important?

25.2. In what sense can random noise and temporal lag bias mask each other in typical real world appraisal-based indices? When is such masking likely to be most important?

25.3. Suppose you regress a time-series of appraisal-based index periodic returns onto both contemporaneous and lagged securities market returns that do not suffer from lagging or measurement errors. That is, you perform the following regression, where $r_{M,t}$ is the accurate market return in period t and r_t^* is the appraisal-based real estate return in period t:

$$r_t^* = \alpha + \beta_0 r_{M,t} + \beta_1 r_{M,t-1} + \beta_2 r_{M,t-2} + \beta_3 r_{M,t-3} + \varepsilon_t$$

The resulting contemporaneous and lagged beta values are

$\hat{\beta}_0 = 0.05$

$\hat{\beta}_1 = 0.15$

$\hat{\beta}_2 = 0.10$

$\hat{\beta}_3 = 0.00$

What is your best estimate of the true long-run beta between real estate and the securities market index?

25.4. Describe five different conceptual or observable definitions of commercial property value levels (or periodic appreciation returns). Describe the dynamic behavior of each definition in response to the arrival of news.

25.5. What is the conceptual rationale for the zero-autocorrelation delagging procedure? What is the major conceptual weakness in this approach for application to commercial property returns? How is this approach useful?

25.6. What is the conceptual rationale for the REIT/appraisal blend approach to delagging appraisal-based returns?

*25.7. Suppose you have reason to believe that appraisal behavior is well characterized by the following autoregression model relating quarterly appraised values to average transaction prices:

$$V_t^* = 0.3\overline{V}_t + 0.7V_{t-1}^*$$

where the V values are in log levels. Now suppose that a quarterly appraisal-based index (based on fully contemporaneous appraisals, that is, without stale appraisals) indicates an appreciation return of 1% in the current quarter (t), and 1.5% in the previous quarter ($t-1$). Assuming that the appraisal-based index has been cleansed of random noise, what is the implied current period contemporaneous transaction-price-based appreciation return (like Index 3) suggested by a reverse engineering of the appraisal behavior?

25.8. The official NCREIF Property Index appreciation return for calendar year 1996 was 1.34%, for 1997 it was 4.54%, and for 1998 it was 7.01%. Use the simple one-step reverse-engineering formula described in the box in section 25.3.3 to estimate what the true annual contemporaneous transaction-price-based appreciation returns were in 1997 and 1998 for the NCREIF index.

26 Real Estate Investment Management, Part I: The Institutional Landscape

Learning Objectives

After reading this chapter, you should understand:

◆ The essential characteristics of the real estate investment management industry for direct investment in the private real estate market in the United States.

◆ The major responsibilities and functions of the real estate investment manager, and how these relate to the firm's strategic environment.

◆ The major investment products in the private real estate investment industry, and the major role or type of investor each is designed to serve.

$\mathbf{A}$t the outset of Part VII we said that we would address three major macrolevel real estate investment decision arenas: broad strategy, tactical investment, and implementation of investment policy. So far, most of the material we have covered in Part VII has focused primarily on strategic and tactical investment decision making, and on fundamental valuation, performance measurement, and data issues that relate to all decision arenas. In this chapter and the next, we will focus more specifically on the implementation question and related issues concerning the "institutional landscape" in which macrolevel real estate investment activity takes place. In particular, this chapter will focus on the professional real estate investment management industry and its interaction with the investor community, particularly institutional investors. It is important to understand this industry because it plays a central role in commercial property investment in the United States. If you work with large-scale commercial property investment in the United States and you don't work directly for a real estate investment manager, then you may very well be either a client of such firms, a consultant analyzing such firms, or a broker trying to sell to or buy from such firms.

This chapter will begin with an introduction and overview of the real estate investment management industry in the United States and the major types of investment products that have traditionally been most popular.

26.1 REAL ESTATE INVESTMENT MANAGEMENT

In Chapter 7 we presented an overview of the investment industry in the United States. There we noted the heterogeneity of investors, including differences along such dimensions as the amount of capital they have available, the nature of resources and expertise they possess relevant to managing investments, and the nature of the legal and regulatory constraints under which they operate. As a result, many investors either cannot, or prefer not to, manage directly all of their investments themselves. The result has been the development of a major branch of the investment industry consisting of **professional investment management advisory firms**. Such firms help a variety of investors place and manage capital in many types of investment products and asset classes. The common characteristic is that they operate in a "fiduciary" capacity on behalf of their clients.[1]

Most investment management firms concentrate primarily in investments in publicly traded securities (stocks and bonds), but some firms offer services for direct investment in the private property market. Real estate investment management firms come in a variety of shapes and sizes. Some are independent firms specializing purely in the private property market; indeed, some are very small "boutique" firms specializing in one particular type of property. Others are branches or departments of broader investment or financial firms that offer private property investment management as one of a broad range of investment and financial services. While some firms work primarily for wealthy private individuals, the most prominent branch of the real estate investment management industry at the macrolevel in the United States during recent decades has been oriented toward working primarily for pension funds and other tax-exempt institutions (such as endowment funds). Some real estate investment management firms will manage client investments in publicly traded REITs as well as (or instead of) direct investment in the private property market, and some firms include investment in commercial property debt products as well as equity products (e.g., either CMBS or whole loan commercial mortgages).

As noted, one of the largest segments of the professional real estate investment management industry in the United States during the 1990s focused on the management of pension fund and other tax-exempt institutions' real estate investments. This branch of the industry has been a leader in developing sophisticated professional management techniques at the macrolevel, and it will be our primary focus in this chapter and in Chapter 27.[2] The pension fund real estate advisory business has its historical origins in the passage of the **Employee Retirement Income Security Act (ERISA)** by Congress in 1974. As we described in Chapter 7, this law encouraged large to medium-size pension funds to consider real estate investment as a diversifier

---

[1] A **fiduciary relationship** legally binds the agent in a role of "trust" for the principal party, resulting in certain legal standards and responsibilities governing the agent's behavior. For example, a fiduciary must adhere to strict reporting requirements, and investment decisions must be guided by the so-called "prudent investor" rule. This prohibits inappropriate or irresponsible management of the client's capital and often dictates a somewhat conservative approach. While not all investment manager/client relationships are fiduciary relationships in the strict legal sense, many are, and something of this spirit permeates most of the others.

[2] Of course, the more basic points and principles raised in Chapters 26 and 27 are generally applicable to other branches of the industry as well. Depending on how one defines the real estate investment management industry, the other major branches might include bank trust departments that work primarily for wealthy individuals, insurance companies that work for their own accounts, and corporate real estate departments.

of their traditional stock and bond portfolios and led to a large demand for specialized real estate investment management.

Most real estate investment management firms evolved from one of two sources. Many of the largest real estate investment management firms grew out of (and often remain part of) life insurance companies and other financial service firms, such as investment banks and commercial banks. Historically, many such firms developed expertise in the management of commercial property investments through the experience gained managing their own property investments for their own account.[3] These firms are often focused primarily on traditional **institutional quality commercial property**, the core of the typical pension fund real estate portfolio.

Real estate investment management firms also evolved out of successful private real estate development and/or investment firms. Many of these firms are smaller and specialize in certain types of properties or locations. Sometimes these may include investments that are beyond the traditional conception of institutional quality property, such as specialized property types, "turnaround investments," development projects, and land investments.[4] These types of investments are often regarded as **opportunistic investments** in the institutional portfolio, a relatively small portion of the overall portfolio with the objective of seeking higher returns even though this implies taking on more risk.

Of course, there are also other sources and types of real estate investment management firms. Equity mutual funds are involved in some aspects of the business, especially for investments in REIT shares. Also, a few large pension funds directly manage much of their real estate investments themselves.

26.2 SALIENT FEATURES OF REAL ESTATE INVESTMENT MANAGEMENT

In Parts I and II of this book we noted that real estate space markets are highly segmented (both geographically and functionally, that is, for different types of property). We also noted in Chapter 7 that direct investment in real property involves **operational management responsibility** for the investment assets. In Chapter 12 we described how the private trading of whole, unique assets tends to make the property market less informationally efficient than securities market. We noted that this brings both dangers and opportunities at the microlevel, such as the possibility of doing deals that have nonzero NPV, even when evaluated from a market value perspective.[5] Because of these characteristics of direct investment in private real estate, specialized expertise is required. Real estate investment management firms provide this expertise. In particular, such firms provide expertise both in commercial property markets and in property asset operational management.

---

[3]In the life insurance industry this is referred to as the company's "general account," as distinct from third-party management business, which typically involves the use of "separate accounts."

[4]Some specialized property types include, for example, agricultural and timber lands, golf courses, parking lots, hotels and restaurants, and speculative land. The term *turnaround investments* refers to properties that are currently underperforming and typically in need of substantial capital investments to turn them around in the space market.

[5]See section 12.2 in Chapter 12.

This expertise distinguishes real estate investment management firms from investment firms that deal strictly in the securities markets. Securities investment managers do not have to go out and *find* specific assets to invest in. The available securities are publicly listed. Nor do securities managers have to *negotiate* purchase and sale terms for the assets they invest in. Securities are purchased at market value (or via limit orders) in the public exchanges. Finally, securities managers are not responsible for the operational management of the assets they own or manage for their clients, as investors in stocks typically own only a small fraction of the controlling interest in the listed firms. For all of these reasons, real estate investment management services are typically quite a bit more expensive per dollar of assets under management than are securities investment management services.[6]

In fact, asset operational management responsibility is particularly important in real estate investment. Because transaction costs for buying and selling real property are relatively high (as a proportion of asset value), real estate assets must generally be held for long periods of time in order to mitigate the impact of transaction costs in the multiperiod average return obtained by the investor. Furthermore, as noted in Chapter 7, most types of commercial property provide investment returns primarily from the generation of operating income, rather than capital gain. For both of these reasons (long holding periods and income-based returns), much of the total return ultimately earned by the investor derives from how well the asset management function is carried out by the investment manager.

26.3 RESPONSIBILITIES AND FUNCTIONS OF THE INVESTMENT MANAGER

Professional real estate investment management involves a number of tasks or functions, are listed here.

1. Investment Advisory Services. Broadly, *investment advisory services* refers to advice regarding macrolevel real estate investment decisions, potentially including both strategic and tactical policy. For example, many management firms offer advice concerning the allocation of all or part of the client's real estate investments.[7] Should the client include apartment properties in her portfolio? If so, what percentage of her overall real estate investment should be allocated to apartments, and what geographical distribution should be targeted? What size, quality level, and type of properties should be targeted at the present time? These are the types of allocation and tactical questions, starting from the broad and moving toward the more specific, for which real estate investors need expert answers. Although less common, investment managers also offer

---

[6]During the 1990s, typical real estate investment management fees for large institutional investors were in the neighborhood of 100 basis points per year, as a fraction of the value of the assets under management. Apart from pecuniary considerations, we hasten to add that, if you are fascinated by cities and land and geography and economics and finance (in short, if you've got real estate "in your blood"), then the fact that real estate investment management has this unique characteristic of encompassing and integrating investment management *per se* with financial and operational management of real assets, makes it an exciting and appealing career consideration.

[7]In some cases allocation advice or analysis may extend beyond the real estate asset class, or beyond the private property market, to the mixed-asset or "multiquadrant" level.

advice on the timing of the client's real estate investments, at least within the real estate asset class.[8]

2. Asset Selection and Transaction Execution. The one function that virtually all real estate investment managers perform is to find, buy, and sell properties on behalf of their clients (or for property "funds" that they operate for investors). As distinct from the advisory function described previously (with which it should be integrated), asset selection and transaction is essentially a microlevel function. It requires familiarity with the local space and asset markets in which the firm operates. It is a transaction-oriented function that encompasses both acquisition and disposition of properties. A big part of the daily activity in carrying out this function is *searching*, either for properties to acquire or for buyers who will purchase properties the manager wants to sell.[9] This function also includes *deal structuring* and *negotiation*.[10] Investor clients rely on managers to help them avoid the negative-NPV danger posed by the inefficiency of the private real estate market.

Sometimes managers go beyond dealing only with existing fully operational properties to pursue acquisitions that include a considerable construction component, either new development or rehabilitation of existing buildings. Most commonly, real estate investment managers undertake such projects in a team with a firm that specializes in real estate development and construction. The developer partner might often be a REIT or a private development firm with the necessary local expertise and development experience. Investment in development projects is generally more risky than investment in existing fully operational buildings. If the manager's investor clients are rather conservative (that is, relatively risk averse, as is often the case, for example, with many pension funds), then the deal may be structured so the manager has a lower-risk preferred or senior position, perhaps involving a debt instrument.

3. Investment Product Development. Many real estate investment managers offer somewhat standardized "products" or "vehicles" designed to enable a relatively large number of smaller investors to place capital into the private real estate asset class. At one extreme, these products may be structured as securities, with relatively small, homogeneous "units" offered for sale to the general public. This type of operation comes under the regulation of the Securities and Exchange Commission (SEC), whether or not the securities will be listed and traded in a public stock exchange. This type of product is relatively rare in the United States. More common are private offerings designed specifically for tax-exempt institutions or wealthy private investors. In any case, there is considerable work, as well as scope for entrepreneurial creativity, in the design and development of vehicles that pass the investment performance

---

[8]Obviously, a manager specializing in one type of investment product or asset may not be the most unbiased source of advice about the timing of placing capital into, or out of, that particular type of investment product or asset. At least as a general characterization, investment managers, as such, make their living largely by procuring and managing investment capital for their specialty of investment. For broader and more objective advice about investment strategy and timing, investors often hire consulting firms, some of which specialize in the area of real estate investor "client-consultant" services. In principle, such firms do not manage capital, and they do not work for investment managers. Indeed, one of their functions is often to help the investor client evaluate and/or select an investment manager.

[9]Professional commercial property brokers assist investment managers in the search function.

[10]Brokerage firms may also help in these functions, and investment managers often hire legal firms or specialized consulting firms to assist in various ways. However, the investment manager will typically be the only party that is in a formal fiduciary relationship with the ultimate investor client.

characteristics of private property ("bundled" or "unbundled" in various ways) from the property level to ultimate investors. As noted in Chapter 7, this is a classical role of the investment industry, enabling underlying physical assets to serve the variety of investment needs and objectives of a heterogeneous population of investors.

4. Asset Management. We already mentioned that one of the salient features of direct investment in private property assets, as compared to securities investments, is the responsibility for operational management of the assets that are held. This is because *whole assets* are typically traded in the private property market, so equity investors generally have controlling ownership shares (sometimes with one or a small number of joint venture partners). As noted, the long holding periods typical of private property investment mean that asset management is often a major profit center for the management firm and/or its investor clients (as a major source of investment returns).

The typical large-scale real estate investment management firm is organized into departments, one of which will typically be **asset management**, while another will often be called something like **acquisition and disposition**. The latter is populated by transactions specialists, the "deal-doers," whose workload is directly and immediately impacted by the volume of capital flow into or out of the firm's management. The asset management department, on the other hand, has an ongoing function, with a workload more proportional to the *stock* of assets under management than to the *flow* of capital.

Asset managers are responsible not only for overseeing property-level operational management, but also for the longer-run strategic management and development of the property portfolio. Thus, like the deal-doers, asset managers also need to be expert in both real estate space and asset markets, and intimately familiar with the local markets in which they operate. It is not uncommon for individuals to rotate between asset management and acquisition/disposition either within or between management firms. It is important for the asset management function to be integrated rationally with the acquisition/disposition function, for one of the strategic jobs at the intersection of these two functions is the decision of when (and how) to sell assets currently held by the manager, and what sort of new acquisitions to target for the portfolio.

In commercial property investment, the management function is typically divided into two levels. At the more "macro" level is the function referred to as asset management per se, which involves the oversight of an entire portfolio of properties. This function is almost always carried out directly by the investment management firm "in house." At the "micro" or property level, operational management is referred to as **property management**. This includes such activities as physical facilities management, leasing, tenant servicing, property cash flow budgeting, collection and management, and capital improvement planning and budgeting. While property management is sometimes performed directly by the investment manager, it is often contracted out to specialized property management firms. In any case, it is in the purview of the management firm's asset managers and should be integrated with the overall asset management strategy of the portfolio.[11]

---

[11] For example, leasing strategy and the marketing or positioning of properties within their space markets needs to be rationalized between the "macro" asset management level and the "micro" property management level. Property managers typically work with leasing brokers to help with the leasing function. Leasing will be discussed in more depth in Part VIII.

5. Support Functions: Communication and Research. The four previously described functions represent service "products" the real estate investment management firm sells to its clients. In order to effectively "produce" or deliver these services for their clients, and in order to build and operate the investment management business, the management firm must also provide or acquire several other support functions or services.[12] For example, communication with clients is extremely important in a fiduciary business in which one is managing the clients' money. A key part of this is the compiling, analysis, and reporting of investment performance information. This analysis function can also provide a useful diagnostic and decision-support function within the investment management firm.[13]

Related to this latter function, another very important support activity for the investment management firm is **investment research**. In fact, the real estate investment management firm's research department can focus quite broadly, providing valuable insight and information for any and all of the four products described previously, as well as useful internal analytical and diagnostic information. The research department should be the long-range eyes and ears of the investment management firm, as well as its repository of wisdom. The research department needs to develop and organize decision-relevant information and knowledge concerning both the space markets and the property asset markets, as well as the broader capital market. To do this, the research department will often work with specialized consultants and data vendors dealing with both the space and asset markets, as well as the general economy and capital markets as a whole.

While a few of the largest real estate investment management firms have always had research departments, the property market downturn and financial crisis of the early 1990s led to a substantial expansion of the role of research in the industry. In some management firms, the director of the research department sits as an *ex officio* voting member on the firm's **investment committee**, a high-level interdepartmental committee that typically has the final review and approval authority over all of the firm's acquisition and disposition decisions. Many investment management research departments include "quant" types with PhD or technical graduate degrees. However, industry research must always provide information that is directly useful to decision making, and research departments are also typically expected to be able to help with the firm's marketing efforts and to communicate effectively with clients who may lack specialized expertise.

Not all investment management firms undertake to provide or offer all of the products or services described here. Some provide only one or two of these functions in house. They may contract out for some functions, or work in tandem with other

---

[12] In addition to the communication and research functions described here, other functions and departments in a typical large investment management firm might include risk management (e.g., hazard insurance), engineering, information technology, and, of course, accounting.

[13] Specialized consulting firms also help to provide analysis and diagnostic services to investment management firms. For example, in Britain most investment managers (and other major commercial property owners) contribute standardized property-level and fund-level investment performance data to a private firm (the Investment Property Databank—IPD) that is then able to compare each owner's performance (on a proprietary basis) with the average performance of similar properties held by other owners in a "peer group" of similar owners. This type of service is expanding in a number of countries, although as of the end of the 1990s this type of service was not exactly available in the United States. In the United States, a variety of consulting services and information vendors, as well as the National Council of Real Estate Investment Fiduciaries (NCREIF) provide investment managers with information relevant to the commercial property asset and space markets.

Industry Associations and Real Estate Information Standards

Our description of the private real estate investment management industry in this chapter focuses on private firms and investment products. But private firms alone are not sufficient to establish and maintain a well-functioning investment industry. Industry associations, nonprofit organizations of the major interest groups, and "players" in the industry serve several vital functions. Some of the major industry associations as of the turn of the century included the following:

- **National Council of Real Estate Investment Fiduciaries (NCREIF).** Formed in 1982, NCREIF's mission is to promote private real estate as a credible asset class for institutional equity investment by collecting and disseminating information. NCREIF is most famous for the NCREIF Property Index (NPI) that it produces and publishes quarterly. NCREIF also plays a leading role in developing, updating, and implementing the Real Estate Information Standards (discussed later in this box).

- **Pension Real Estate Association (PREA).** This is the major forum of the major group of institutional investors in private real estate, the pension plan sponsors. The major investment management firms are also members of PREA, and PREA meetings are important forums for managers and investors to get together at the executive level. (In contrast, NCREIF tends to focus more on the technical or research level, although NCREIF also encompasses both plan sponsors and managers.) PREA's mission emphasizes promotion of the private real estate asset class through research and education.

- **National Association of Real Estate Investment Managers (NAREIM).** This association is specifically for the private real estate investment management firms, and it serves as the major forum for the executives of such firms to exchange ideas and concerns. Along with PREA and NCREIF, NAREIM is responsible for promulgating and updating the Real Estate Information Standards.

One of the most important functions of industry associations such as these is to improve the efficiency

and credibility of the private real estate asset class through the development and promulgation of common information standards regarding the measurement and reporting of investment performance. A major advance was made in this regard in 1997, with the formal adoption by all three of the previously described associations of the official **Real Estate Information Standards (REIS)**. The REIS serve a role in the private real estate investment industry much like that served by the investment performance reporting standards promulgated by the **Association for Investment Management and Research (AIMR)** in the securities industry. Indeed, the REIS are based on, and consistent with, AIMR standards wherever possible, but go beyond AIMR guidelines in areas peculiar to private real estate.

Information standards such as the REIS enable more meaningful apples-to-apples comparisons to be made across investment managers and private real estate funds. They help to standardize, clarify, and make "transparent" the accounting, appraisal, and performance measurement definitions and procedures that underlie the quantitative reporting of investment performance, building on other industry standards, such as those promulgated by the accounting industry (GAAP) and the appraisal industry (the Appraisal Institute). For example, the REIS address the nuts and bolts of procedures for calculating holding period and multiperiod returns and return components (e.g., what expenditures should be capitalized as opposed to expensed). They also help to standardize useful definitions, such as property type classifications (e.g., what is the definition of an office building, or how should rentable square feet be measured).

The development of the REIS in the late 1990s, and their annual review and updating by the three associations noted earlier, represents an unglamorous, nonheadline activity that nevertheless contributes greatly to the long-run efficiency and credibility of private property investment.*

---

*For more information about the REIS, contact any one of the organizations noted. A general introduction to the REIS is presented by Greig (1997).

firms. As a general rule, at least two or three of the previously described products and services are bundled together, not sold separately by investment management firms.[14] In some cases, the investor clients provide some of the functions for themselves on their own, or contract directly for some functions with other specialized firms. However, it should be clear that the overall process of investment management typically should encompass all of the functions noted, in whatever manner they are organized and structured (not necessarily in a single firm).

26.4 PRIVATE REAL ESTATE INVESTMENT PRODUCTS

The major traditional types of investment products and vehicles offered by real estate investment management firms span a range designed to accommodate investors of different sizes and types. Some of the most common types of products are described briefly here:

- **Open-end commingled funds (CREFs) or property unit trusts (PUTs).** With this type of product, an ongoing portfolio of properties is offered to many investors, with investors allowed (in principle) to cash in and out at stated (fairly frequent) intervals (e.g., quarterly), based on appraised values of the properties in the fund or trust.[15] In the United States, this type of product is typically aimed largely at institutional investors (defined-benefit pension plan sponsors), with fund units typically selling for a few hundred thousand dollars, which aims this type of product at investors wishing to put less than $50 million into real estate. However, it is possible in principle to offer smaller-denominated units, and at least one pension plan sponsor in the United States has set up a vehicle like this to enable individual defined-contribution plan members to invest directly in private real estate at their own discretion. In some countries, vehicles like this are fairly actively traded in secondary markets, where their unit prices are quoted. Some secondary market trading also occurs in the United States, though a mechanism to facilitate such trading, called the Institutional Real Estate Clearinghouse, failed in the 1990s.

- **Closed-end funds or unit trusts and RELPs.** This is similar to the open-end product just described, only the investors cannot cash in and out at will; the fund is closed to new investors once it is capitalized, and it faces a finite lifetime at which point it will be liquidated. Units in such funds for institutional investors are typically purchased for a few hundred thousand dollars, and the product is typically designed for institutional investors wishing to put $50 to $100 million in real estate. This type of product was marketed widely to individual investors, with much smaller unit sizes, as **real estate limited partnerships (RELPs)** in the 1970s and 1980s. At that time RELPs were oriented primarily toward tax shelter, as the partnership structure allowed the liberal tax allowances that were available on private real estate in those days to be passed directly through to the individual

---

[14] For example, it is rare for investment management firms to sell advisory services separately. Such services are provided as part of the capital placement and management service, or are provided separately by consulting firms as opposed to management firms.

[15] To be more precise, CREF unit values are based on the fund net asset value (NAV), which typically includes some small non-real-estate holdings (primarily cash). The real estate assets are valued based on appraisals.

taxed investors. Whenever products such as this are offered to individual investors or the public at large, they come under regulation by the Securities and Exchange Commission (SEC).

- **Private REITs.** In the 1990s, funds of the type just described were sometimes structured as private REITs, a structure that facilitated co-investment and active management by the investment manager, and which made it easier to transfer ownership shares among a broader potential clientele of different types of investors. (As noted in Chapter 24, REITs must have at least 100 shareholders, no five or fewer of which can own more than 50% of the outstanding shares, but they need not be publicly listed.) Private REITs are often viewed as vehicles to develop an investment performance track record, which might enable the REIT to be taken public in the future when the stock market is favorable (so-called "incubator REITs").

- **Discretionary separate accounts.** With this type of service, the investor hires the manager to buy and manage properties on the investor's behalf, with the manager having the discretion as to which properties to buy and sell. Each separate account is managed on behalf of a single investor, allowing a more custom-tailored service for larger investors. Separate accounts typically require a minimum investment of several dozens of millions of dollars. They are aimed at investors wishing to put a total of several hundred million dollars into real estate altogether (typically using several managers).

- **Nondiscretionary separate accounts.** These are the same as discretionary separate accounts, only the manager cannot make final property-level purchase and sale decisions without approval by the client.[16] This vehicle requires more client expertise and involvement and is most appropriate for investors whose total private real estate investments are on the order of $1 billion or more, giving them the scale to be able to afford some specialized real estate investment staff of their own. Many of the largest pension funds fall into this category.

The types of products described here are the major categories for investors interested in the private property market in the United States in the 1990s. As noted in previous chapters, an alternative approach to real estate equity investment via the public stock exchange is to invest in REIT stocks, either directly or through specialized equity mutual funds or separate accounts. Most REIT mutual funds in the 1990s were "actively managed," with the investment managers attempting to select REIT stocks that they thought would outperform the average. But at least one major mutual fund offered a "passively managed" REIT index fund.[17] The 1990s also saw the advent of "hybrid" or "multiquadrant" investment vehicles that would place capital into both private property holdings directly, and/or into REIT shares (or CMBS investments).[18]

---

[16] In practice, the distinction between discretionary and nondiscretionary accounts is a relative one, and rather fuzzy at that. Even so-called discretionary accounts often subject the manager to some constraints and a formal approval process.

[17] Passive funds do not try to "beat the market." They maintain low turnover and low management expenses by pegging their allocations across individual stocks to the asset weights in a market-value-based index. The most widely used REIT indices in the 1990s were the NAREIT, Morgan-Stanley, and Wilshire indices.

[18] The term *quadrant* in this usage refers to a division into public and private asset markets, and into equity and debt types of investment products, a classification similar to what we used to classify asset markets in Exhibit 1-5 in Chapter 1.

These were offered to institutional investors by some mutual funds as well as some traditional real estate investment managers and specialized firms, either as funds or separate accounts.

26.5 REAL ESTATE INVESTMENT MANAGEMENT FIRMS: OBJECTIVES AND STRATEGIC CONSIDERATIONS

Exhibit 26-1 schematically depicts the ends, means, and major causal relationships acting strategically on the typical real estate investment management firm. At the top of the diagram is the major overall long-run consideration for the owners and managers of the firm, namely, the value of the firm. This value is shared by the partners and/or shareholders of the firm, and its maximization may be considered to be the primary goal of the firm's management. At the bottom of the diagram are four broad causal factors that underlie the firm's results. These include the overall capital market, the real estate asset and space markets, client preferences, and actions taken by the real estate investment management firm itself.

The underlying causal factors interact with each other to determine the flow of investment capital into or out of the management firm. The only one of the four causal factors directly under the control of the investment management firm is the firm's own actions, indicated in the box at the bottom right. The manager's actions are of course reactions to past, present, and perceived future trends, events, and opportunities (or dangers) in the commercial property space and asset markets (which in turn are affected by the capital market and the real economy, broadly defined). The manager's actions include real estate asset management and investment decisions (such as acquisition, disposition, and leasing or capital improvement investment decisions) that, interacting with the space and asset markets, result over time in a certain investment performance outcome for the client (indicated in the box to the right at the next level up in the flow of causality).

The manager's actions are also influenced by client needs and preferences, and the manager can itself take actions to directly influence client attitudes, perceptions, and preferences regarding real estate in general, and the manager in particular. This would include actions such as client communication and advisory services. Thus, the direct flow of causality between manager actions and client preferences is two-directional. The client is also influenced directly by the capital market (and the general economic environment, as well as the client's own particular needs and circumstances), and by the client's own direct perception of the real estate space and asset markets.

Note that there is an important long-run feedback loop of causality (or it might be called a reputation or trust loop) running from the manager's performance outcome for the client back to the client's preferences (and perceptions) regarding the manager. Obviously, the better the investment performance outcome the manager achieves for clients, other things being equal, the more favorably clients will be disposed toward the manager as the relationship develops over time. Client attitudes and preferences relevant to the manager will interact with client perceptions of the manager's performance results to determine the amount of capital flowing to (or from) the manager (represented by the left-hand box in the second level of causal flow in the exhibit).

Client capital flow to (or from) the manager is the major long-run determinant of how much capital the manager has under management. However, assets under management are **marked to market**, that is, regularly appraised on the basis of their market value in the current property market. Thus, the total value of the manager's

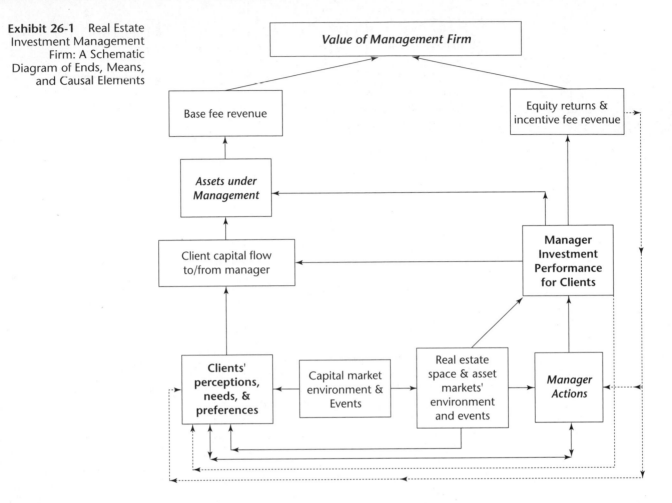

assets under management (AUM) is also influenced by movements in the real estate asset market and the manager's investment performance therein. The magnitude of the AUM is typically an important determinant of the profitability of the management firm, especially for the more traditional "core" real estate investment managers. A large proportion of managers' revenues consist of **base fee revenue,** which is determined as a constant percentage (per year) of the total value of the AUM.[19] Thus, the manager's base fee revenue is directly proportional to the magnitude of the AUM.[20]

---

[19] This may raise a potential for conflict of interest between the client and the manager regarding the appraisal of the properties under management. The manager stands to lose revenue if the properties are appraised at a lower value. The contractual arrangement between the client and manager (or the governance procedures of the fund) will often address this problem by providing for the use of independent fee appraisers (at some minimum interval for each property) and/or for the investors/clients to have some voice in the hiring or review of the appraisers.

[20] Some revenue is also often obtained as lump sums either going in (aka front-end fees) and/or going out (aka back-end fees), that is, when the capital flows into or out of the manager's management. However, much of this revenue may be in the form of acquisition fees or disposition fees, much of which must be used to cover expenses associated with the search and transaction costs of real estate purchase and sales.

Another source of manager revenue and/or long-run profitability and firm value growth derives directly from the manager's investment performance. Real estate investment management firms sometimes take equity positions of various types in the investments they manage for their clients. For example, the manager may be an equity **co-investment** or joint venture partner with its clients, or it may have residual general partnership interests (for example, in a RELP), or the manager may simply have levered equity positions in assets in which clients have debt or preferred equity positions. Even in the absence of equity participation, the manager's compensation package from the client may include performance incentive fee components. For example, the manager may get a bonus if the client achieves a higher return (perhaps relative to some benchmark indicator of relevant investment performance) over a specified time period.[21]

Smaller, more entrepreneurial investment management firms, often (but not always) specializing in "opportunistic" properties, have traditionally relied more heavily on equity and incentive fee components than do the large "institutional core" investment managers.[22] However, the 1990s saw an expansion in the use of such arrangements even among the traditional core managers. If equity and incentive fee arrangements are well structured, they can help to align the interests of managers and their clients. If they are poorly structured, they may exacerbate agency costs and cause ill feeling on the part of the client, the manager, or both.[23] Thus, there is a potential long-run feedback loop from the equity or incentive fee arrangements to both manager actions and client perceptions. Ultimately, the total profits of the investment management firm (both present and future, and therefore, the value of the firm for its partners and shareholders) derive from the combination of the AUM-based and the performance-based revenues and profits.

---

[21] One form of incentive fee arrangement pays the manager a bonus regularly, for example, at the end of every year based on performance during the preceding year (often based on appraised values of the properties held for the client, as well as net operating income). Another form of incentive fee is strictly "back end," based on the realized IRR and paid only after liquidation of the investment, or after a multiyear holding period or management contract period (based on appraised value at the end of the period).

[22] Some legal restrictions, for example in the ERISA, place limits on the use of incentive management fees by certain types of investors. In the extreme, if the manager does not provide investment advice or take fees for AUM, then the manager is no longer a manager as such (a fiduciary), but rather a pure joint venture partner (or debtor) of the investor.

[23] The different ways in which the manager's equity and/or incentive fee interests can be structured can have important implications for the degree to which the client and manager share common interests or face conflicting pecuniary incentives, under different circumstances. To take a simple example, suppose the manager's bonus incentive fee (or subordinated equity position) pays off significantly for the manager only if the investment yields a very high return (e.g., there is a "hurdle" or client-preferred return component). Then, other things being the same, the manager has a greater incentive than the investor client to invest in assets that have a lot of specific risk and volatility, as the manager loses less from the downside of such risk and gains more from the upside. Another problem to consider is how manager equity involvement may constrain investors' flexibility to change managers or decide on their own when and how to sell assets. Real estate deal structures and investment management relationships can be quite complicated and require careful attention by all parties so as to minimize potential conflicts of interest and resulting agency costs. The art of successful relationship design is based on good communication and a recognition of the strengths and weaknesses, the objectives and constraints, of all parties to the arrangement.

26.6 CHAPTER SUMMARY

This chapter introduced some of the major features of the "institutional landscape" of commercial property private equity investment in the United States at the turn of the century. Real estate investment management plays a pivotal and important role in the overall real commercial property investment industry. It is a dynamic, ever-changing business in a rapidly evolving investment industry. Technological development, regulatory reforms, and the constant working of entrepreneurial innovation will carry the real estate investment industry forward into the 21st century. Perhaps you will be a part of this progress!

KEY TERMS

Professional investment
    management advisory firms
fiduciary relationship
Employee Retirement Income
    Security Act (ERISA)
institutional quality real estate
institutional real estate core
    portfolio
opportunistic investments
operational management
    responsibility
nonzero NPV deals
investment advisory services
asset selection
transaction execution
investment product development
asset management

acquisition and disposition
property management
investment research
investment committee
National Council of Real Estate
    Investment Fiduciaries
    (NCREIF)
Pension Real Estate Association
    (PREA)
National Association of Real Estate
    Investment Managers
    (NAREIM)
Real Estate Information Standards
    (REIS)
Association for Investment
    Management and Research
    (AIMR)

commingled real estate fund
    (CREF)
property unit trust (PUT)
open-end fund
closed-end fund
real estate limited partnership
    (RELP)
private REIT
separate accounts
discretionary accounts
nondiscretionary accounts
marked-to-market
assets under management (AUM)
base fee revenue
performance incentives
co-investment

STUDY QUESTIONS

26.1. What does a professional real estate investment advisory firm do, in essence, and why is there a need for such firms?

26.2. What is the difference between the "institutional core" real estate portfolio and "opportunistic" real estate investments?

26.3. Describe the major responsibilities and functions of the typical real estate investment management firm in the United States.

26.4. What were the three major trade associations involved in the U.S. pension-fund-oriented real estate investment advisory industry as of the turn of the 21st century? What are the Real Estate Information Standards?

26.5. Describe five general types of private market real estate investment products and the general role of or target investor for each product.

26.6. Briefly describe in general the major objectives, sources of profit, and strategic considerations of the typical pension-fund-oriented real estate investment management firm.

Real Estate Investment Management, Part II: Performance Attribution and Evaluation

27

Chapter Outline

Learning Objectives

After reading this chapter, you should understand:

◆ What is meant by investment performance attribution at both the macro property level and the portfolio level.

◆ How to quantify segment allocation versus asset selection effects in a portfolio's differential performance relative to an appropriate benchmark.

◆ What is meant by formal, quantitative investment performance evaluation, and the role of this function in the relationship between investment managers and their investor clients.

◆ The nature of manager "custom benchmarking" in the private real estate asset class, and how this differs from corresponding practices in the public securities investment industry.

This chapter will begin with macrolevel investment performance attribution and manager evaluation, before going into more depth to examine some nuts and bolts of the investment management business with a consideration of benchmarking and incentive contracting. Our focus in Chapter 27 will be on direct investment in the private property market, where assets are privately held and privately traded, as opposed to investment in publicly traded commercial real estate securities such as REITs and CMBS. It is at the direct investment level that real estate investment management is most specialized and distinct from "mainstream" securities investment management.

However, as always, we are dealing with fundamental principles in this chapter, and such principles tend to apply broadly for many types of investments.

27.1 MACROLEVEL INVESTMENT PERFORMANCE ATTRIBUTION

An important tool that is often useful in real estate investment management is investment **performance attribution**. The idea is to break down into components the ex post total return of a given portfolio or manager in order to learn something about the nature and source of the total return. Performance attribution is useful for two broad purposes: diagnosis and evaluation. The former purpose is primarily of interest to managers, to help them understand the sources and causes of their realized performance. The use of performance attribution in manager evaluation is of interest both to managers and investor clients, as it can help investors to judge and compare the performance results of competing managers.

In both its evaluation and diagnostic function, performance attribution analysis is often combined with **benchmarking**, the comparison of a given manager's performance results with the average results of some suitably defined index or peer group of similar properties or managers. Performance evaluation and benchmarking will be discussed later in this chapter. For now, let's look at how performance attribution is done at the macrolevel.

27.1.1 Macro Property Level Performance Attribution

In an appendix to Chapter 10 we described *microlevel* performance attribution, an approach to "parsing" (or breaking down into its components) the IRR at the level of the individual property investment so as to provide some insight regarding the sources of the overall multiperiod return on the investment. At what might be termed the **macro property level**, performance attribution can also apply the same IRR parsing as was described in the Chapter 10 appendix, only aggregated across an entire portfolio of properties. At this level, the objective is to attribute property-level multiperiod returns to: (1) the initial cash yield (going-in cap rate), (2) the growth in net cash flow during the holding period (which may be further broken down into rental growth and/or expense reduction components), and (3) the effects of change in the cash yield (cap rate) between the initial purchase and the terminal (resale, or current appraisal) point in time.[1]

This level of performance attribution normally requires a constant sample of properties, that is, what we referred to in Chapters 23 and 25 as a static portfolio. Macro property level performance attribution is most useful to the investment manager for diagnostic purposes, to help the manager understand the sources of his performance results, especially at the level of property operational management, and particularly if

---

[1] See the Chapter 10 appendix for further details and a numerical example. Note also that macro property performance attribution is often "layered" so as to identify only two components at each level. For example, total return may be broken down in a first layer into income and appreciation components. Then, at a second layer the income return component may be broken down into revenue and expense components, while the appreciation return component is further broken down into net cash flow change and current yield change components. While this process can be informative, keep in mind that the identification and ordering of the layers and components is somewhat arbitrary.

the manager's results are compared with an appropriate benchmark of other similar properties.[2] Remember, however, that property performance is somewhat random over time. As a result, the use of ex post performance information for diagnostic purposes is essentially an exercise in **statistical inference**.

This raises issues regarding the best methods for making quantitative performance measurements for this purpose. For example, the IRR of a portfolio of properties (and hence the parsing of that IRR) can be calculated in various ways. One way is to aggregate the cash flows across all the properties in the static portfolio, and then compute the aggregate portfolio IRR. This will effectively value-weight the performance of individual properties within the portfolio (e.g., larger properties will "count more" in the portfolio IRR). An alternative approach would be to compute the IRR for each property individually (over the same common time interval) and take the cross-sectional arithmetic average across these individual property IRRs. If each property is viewed as an equally representative example of the manager's performance, then this latter approach (which weights equally the results for small and large properties) is more correct from a statistical perspective. The equally weighted average is, in principle, the best estimator of the manager's underlying performance tendency for the type of property in question (over the time sample covered, assuming all properties are equally representative).[3]

Another, more conceptual, question is what type of return measure to use, the IRR or the time-weighted geometric average return over the relevant span of time.[4] Recall from Chapter 9 that the IRR is "dollar-weighted," so that it reflects the effect of the timing of capital flow into or out of the investment. At the *property level* (that is, assuming we are measuring a constant set of properties over a common sample of time), the investment manager normally does indeed control the timing of capital flow into and out of the properties. For example, the investment manager (or a property manager for whom the investment manager is responsible) usually decides when to lease vacant space, how much and when to spend on capital improvements, and so forth. In general, net cash flow at the property level is assumed to flow from (or to) the property each period (e.g., each month or quarter) in response to the investment manager's own actions (or actions for which the manager is responsible). Thus, in most circumstances, the IRR is probably the best measure of return to use for macro property level performance attribution.[5]

[2]Note that in principle the benchmark also should be a static portfolio or fixed sample of properties.

[3]However, the cross-sectional arithmetic average IRR is sensitive to individual property "outliers," which can be a problem due to the mathematical nature of the IRR. One or a few properties in the portfolio may have extreme, ambiguous, or mathematically nonexistent IRRs over the given time period. In such circumstances the analyst faces three options: (1) drop the outliers from the analysis; (2) use the portfolio aggregate cash flows to compute the portfolio IRR on a value-weighted basis as noted previously; or (3) use a modified version of the IRR at the individual property level, such as the Financial Management Rate of Return—FMRR (as described in traditional investments texts). None of these three options is without potential ambiguity or bias from a statistical perspective. Statistical issues in manager performance evaluation will also be discussed in section 27.2.

[4]A third possibility, the time-weighted arithmetic average, can be used to aggregate performance attribution components across time, but is not widely employed in practice because it is sensitive to the periodic return volatility and does not incorporate the effect of return compounding over time. (See Chapter 9 for further discussion.) Furthermore, at the property level, the meaning and performance implications of the return components may change in the process of computing the multiperiod average. For example, the average income yield across annual returns does not necessarily reflect the initial income yield at the time when the property was acquired.

[5]The IRR also has the practical advantage, noted in Chapter 9, of not needing intermediate valuations of the properties in order to be computed. Thus, IRR-based macro property performance attribution can

Finally, it is well to recall our caveat in the Chapter 10 appendix that return parsing is not an exact science, and that it is sensitive to the length of time over which the return is measured. It is also important to carefully consider the meaning of property level performance attribution measures. For example, if the initial yield component of the return does not correspond to the yield at the time when the property was acquired, then it is not clear what implication this component of the return can logically hold regarding the investment manager's performance, even in comparison with a benchmark. Similar questions about meaning may be raised about other components of property-level performance attribution.

27.1.2 Portfolio-Level Performance Attribution

At the **portfolio level**, the key components of investment performance attribution are traditionally defined as **allocation** and **selection**. These are the two major "jobs" that an active portfolio manager may potentially perform. Such a manager may decide how to allocate the total investment capital across a range of exhaustive and mutually exclusive **segments**, that is, classes or types of assets within her purview, and/or she may decide which particular individual assets to buy (and sell) within each segment. The terms *allocation* and *selection*, like the basic idea of performance attribution at the portfolio level, have their origins in the stock-market-based component of the investment industry.[6] We need to see how this tool translates into application to private real estate investment. Let's begin with a consideration of the two basic attributes: allocation and selection.

As noted, allocation refers to the chosen segment weights in the portfolio. As an attribute of investment manager performance, allocation is a very similar concept in real estate and in the stock market. In the stock market, segments may refer to industry groupings or to attributes of the stock, such as market capitalization or current yield. In the private real estate asset market, segments are typically based on the space market to some extent and are usually defined by building usage type and the geographical location of properties. For example, an allocation decision would be to invest 60% in warehouses and only 40% in office buildings.[7] The basic idea is the same as in the stock market. Segment allocation is a broader-level, more "macro" decision than selection.

Selection, on the other hand, refers to the more microlevel decision of which particular individual assets are picked by the manager to include in the portfolio. In the stock market this is a clear and meaningful concept. Within a given segment any manager can invest any amount in any individual asset (that is, any individual firm's stock). Similarly, in real estate an investment manager can decide which individual

be conducted on portfolios that are not regularly reappraised, as long as beginning and ending point valuations are available.

[6] Beware of the terminology difference between the stock market and real estate market communities. As noted in Chapter 22, the term *segment*, as it is used here often corresponds to the term *sector* as it is used in the stock market. Our adoption of the real estate *segment* terminology in this chapter should not be taken to imply that the real estate asset market is actually segmented, in the economic sense of lacking integration or a common equilibrium across the various property types and locations. As noted in Chapter 1, information and capital flow freely across the entire real estate asset market. While the private real estate asset market may not be as integrated as the stock market (in an economic sense), it is certainly much more integrated than the real estate space market.

[7] Or to invest 60% east of the Mississippi and only 40% west of the Mississippi. Or to invest 36% in warehouses east of the Mississippi, 24% each in offices east and warehouses west, and 16% in offices west of the Mississippi. You get the idea. (Actually, as we noted in Part II, metropolitan areas usually make more sense as geographical units, rather than broad, multistate regions.)

properties to buy or sell. However, real estate require some additional considerations. First, only assets that are for sale can be bought, so the manager cannot choose from among the entire potential universe of individual assets. Second, only whole assets are traded, so in general more than one manager cannot invest in the same asset at the same time. Third, to invest in a given asset, the entire amount of its value must be invested.[8] Fourth, transaction costs are high, mandating long holding periods. Fifth (and above all), the investment manager is responsible for the operational management of the assets he selects. Indeed, as noted in Chapter 26, a large part of the total investment performance may be attributable to operational management.

For all of these reasons (but especially the last), the asset selection function in private real estate is more complicated than it is in stock market investment management. At the portfolio level it is really not possible to distinguish the component of overall performance due to asset selection *per se* (as understood in the stock market) from the performance component due to operational management of the assets.[9] Nevertheless, there is still some interest and potential usefulness in quantitatively attributing performance at the portfolio level to allocation and selection.

To see how this is done, let's consider a simplified example. Suppose Bob and Sue were each hired at the same time to place $100 million worth of capital into private real estate investments in the industrial and office property segments (and then to manage those investments). Their clients gave them discretion over how much to allocate to each of the two segments. Bob immediately went out and bought $90 million worth of industrial buildings and $10 million worth of offices. Sue did just the opposite, buying $10 million of industrial and $90 million of offices. A few years later, these two intrepid investment managers got to talking at a cocktail reception at a meeting of the Pension Real Estate Association. Realizing the amazing coincidence of both being hired at the same time for the same type of investment management job, and noting that they had both placed rather strong, and opposite, segment bets, they decided to compare their performances.

The table in Exhibit 27-1 shows the returns both managers earned for their clients, both in total and broken down by segment. Much to his chagrin, Bob had to admit that Sue had beaten him. Over the three years, her annual average return was 9.70%, versus Bob's 9.20%, a differential of 50 basis points. However, a more careful examination of the returns each manager earned by segment reveals differing sources for their relative performances. Bob clearly beat Sue in property selection performance because *within* each segment Bob's properties earned higher returns than Sue's. His industrial properties returned 9% to her 7%, while his office properties returned 11% to her 10%. But Sue beat Bob in allocation performance. Her decision to allocate a greater share of her capital to office than industrial properties turned out to have been advantageous because of the generally better performance of office properties as compared to industrial properties. In this case, Sue's superior segment bet dominated over Bob's superior selection performance to give Sue the overall advantage.

The idea in portfolio-level performance attribution is to break down the total return differential between two managers' performances (or, more often between a manager and a relevant benchmark) into two components, one based on allocation and

---

[8] Unless a joint venture equity deal can be put together, or debt can be employed (with resulting implications on risk and return).

[9] Performance attribution at the macro property level, as described in the preceding section, may shed some light on the role of property-level operational management, but with the caveats noted there (and in the Chapter 10 appendix).

Exhibit 27-1 Bob's and Sue's Returns Realized for Clients

Weights	Bob	Sue
Industrial	90%	10%
Office	10%	90%

Returns	Bob	Sue
Total portfolio	9.20%	9.70%
Industrial properties	9.00%	7.00%
Office Properties	11.00%	10.00%

the other on selection. However, the overall performance differential is a nonlinear function of the pure allocation and pure selection performance differentials, so there is no unambiguous way to attribute the total differential completely and exactly to these two sources. Nevertheless, some reasonable quantification can be attempted. To see how, let's carry on with our Sue-versus-Bob comparison.

Consider allocation performance first. Suppose we want to quantify how much of Sue's overall 50-basis-point differential over Bob is attributable to her allocation difference with respect to Bob. One way to do this would be to multiply Sue's return performance within each segment by the difference between her allocation and Bob's allocation, and add these products across all the segments. This is demonstrated, in formula (1a):

$$A_S - A_B = r_{SI}(w_{SI} - w_{BI}) + r_{SO}(w_{SO} - w_{BO})$$
$$= 7\%(0.1 - 0.9) + 10\%(0.9 - 0.1) \tag{1a}$$
$$= -5.6\% + 8\% = +2.4\%$$

The implication is that Sue outperformed Bob by 240 basis points on the basis of her superior allocation.

The fact that Sue's overall performance differential was less than this, only 50 basis points, reflects the fact that she lost ground relative to Bob in the other attribute of performance, namely, selection. In fact, the simplistic implication is that she lost 190 basis points compared to Bob as a result of her relatively inferior selection: $+2.4\% - 1.9\% = +0.5\%$.

Now suppose we apply the same reasoning to quantify Sue's selection performance differential directly. That is, we multiply the difference between her return and Bob's return within each segment by Sue's allocation weights and sum these products across the segments, as here:

$$S_S - S_B = w_{SI}(r_{SI} - r_{BI}) + w_{SO}(r_{SO} - r_{BO})$$
$$= 0.1(7\% - 9\%) + 0.9(10\% - 11\%) \tag{1b}$$
$$= -0.2\% - 0.9\% = -1.1\%$$

By this way of figuring, Sue's inferior selection performance cost her only 110 basis points relative to Bob, instead of the 190-basis-point loss we previously computed as a result of formula (1a). If selection's effect in the differential is only 110 basis points, then allocation's contribution is not 240 basis points, but only 160 basis points, as $1.60\% - 1.1\% = +0.5\%$.

We used a consistent approach across both (1a) and (1b), basing our computation in both cases on Sue's results in the *other* attribute.[10] The only difference in arriving at our two conflicting answers for the performance attribution is the order in which we did the computations. If we compute the allocation effect first, we get an implied attribution of +2.4% to allocation and −1.9% to selection. If we compute the selection effect first, we get an implied attribution of +1.6% to allocation and −1.1% to selection. Which is the real answer?

Well, how about neither. When we use either of these two approaches, we are contaminating the "pure" allocation or selection effects by arbitrarily including the effect of interaction between the two effects with one or the other. For example, in computing Sue's −110-basis-point selection differential in formula (1b), we used Sue's allocation weights. Suppose we had used Bob's allocation weights instead. Then we would have gotten the −190-basis-point effect we computed from (1a):

$$S_S - S_B = w_{BI}(r_{SI} - r_{BI}) + w_{BO}(r_{SO} - r_{BO})$$

$$= 0.9(7\% - 9\%) + 0.1(10\% - 11\%)$$

$$= -1.8\% - 0.1\% = -1.9\%$$

But why should either Sue's or Bob's allocation weights be "correct" for quantifying Sue's selection effect? Sue's weights are faulty because their use combines the effect of her allocation decision with that of her property selection performance, destroying the "purity" of the measurement of her selection performance. Bob's allocation weights are similarly faulty in this context because there is no logical reason to use Bob's allocation weights to quantify Sue's selection performance. What are we to do?

27.1.3 Use of a Benchmark in Performance Attribution

The only way out of our dilemma is to try to identify a reasonable **benchmark**, that is, a reference point that makes sense as a basis on which to quantify a manager's performance. We will discuss the question of an appropriate definition of benchmarks for private real estate performance in the next section. For now, let's suppose that Bob is a good benchmark for quantifying Sue's performance. This might be the case, for example, if Bob's allocation weights across segments and his return performance within each segment were typical of the investment managers in Sue's peer group of investment managers with similar specialties, foci, and objectives to Sue's. Or it might be the case if Bob's segment weights and in-segment returns were broadly representative of the entire market of all the industrial and office properties in the country. In any case, let's assume that Bob's performance is a good benchmark for Sue's performance.

In this case, it makes sense to quantify the pure effect of Sue's allocation performance by computing the effect of the difference between her and her benchmark's segment weights measured *conditional on the benchmark's in-segment return performance*. Similarly, it makes sense to quantify the pure effect of Sue's selection performance by computing the effect of the difference between her and Bob's returns within each segment, *conditional*

---

[10] That is to say, to quantify the effect of the allocation difference, we used Sue's selection performance, and to quantify the effect of the selection difference, we used Sue's allocation.

on the benchmark's segment allocation weights. Using Bob's results as the benchmark, this perspective reveals that Sue's pure allocation performance effect is +160 basis points, and her pure selection performance effect is −190 basis points:

$$A_S - A_B = r_{BI}(w_{SI} - w_{BI}) + r_{BO}(w_{SO} - w_{BO})$$

$$= 9\%(0.1 - 0.9) + 11\%(0.9 - 0.1) \tag{2a}$$

$$= -7.2\% + 8.8\% = +1.6\%$$

$$S_S - S_B = w_{BI}(r_{SI} - r_{BI}) + w_{BO}(r_{SO} - r_{BO})$$

$$= 0.9(7\% - 9\%) + 0.1(10\% - 11\%) \tag{2b}$$

$$= -1.8\% - 0.1\% = -1.9\%$$

Alas, these two pure effects do not add up to the total performance differential between Sue and her benchmark: +1.6% − 1.9% = −0.3% ≠ +0.5% = 9.70% − 9.20%. This is a consequence of the nonlinearity of the total return performance differential as a function of the allocation and selection effects.[11] As a result, the total differential between Sue's performance and her benchmark consists not only of the two "pure" effects of allocation and selection, but also of an **interaction effect** that combines these two. In fact, at a fundamental conceptual level, we cannot really account for the interaction effect in a way that is not arbitrary in terms of attributing this effect either to allocation or selection. The most logically sound approach is to leave the interaction effect separate, as a third attribute of the overall performance differential.[12] In our present example, the interaction effect in the differential of Sue's return over her benchmark is +80 basis points, as +1.6% − 1.9% + 0.8% = +0.5%.

The performance attributions that result from all three of the approaches we have described are summarized in Exhibit 27-2 for the numerical example we have been working with here. The first two columns in the table depict the approach based on formulas (1a) and (1b), respectively, in which results are conditional on the order in which the effects are computed. The third column depicts the approach represented by formula (2), which is independent of order of computation and provides a logical quantification of the "pure" functional effects, with the interaction effect quantified

---

[11]
$$r_S - r_B = (w_{SI}r_{SI} + w_{SO}r_{SO}) - (w_{BI}r_{BI} + w_{BO}r_{BO})$$

$$= (w_{SI} - w_{BI})r_{BI} + (w_{SO} - w_{BO})r_{BO} = \text{Pure allocation}$$

$$+ w_{BI}(r_{SI} - r_{BI}) + w_{BO}(r_{SO} - r_{BO}) = \text{Pure selection}$$

$$+ [(w_{BI}r_{BI} + w_{BO}r_{BO}) + (w_{SI}r_{SI} + w_{SO}r_{SO})$$

$$- (w_{BI}r_{SI} + w_{BO}r_{SO} + w_{SI}r_{BI} + w_{SO}r_{BO})] = \text{Interaction effects}$$

[12] The interaction effect is sometimes referred to as the cross-product, as that is what it is from a mathematical perspective. Some analysts suggest that the interaction effect itself is indicative of a specific ability on the part of the manager, namely, the manager's success in specialization that leads the manager to overweight segments within which the manager has relatively superior selection skills (even though such segments might not be strategically superior from an overall allocation perspective). But perhaps this is trying to read too much from the "entrails." When all is said and done, the interaction effect is just that, the combined (multiplicative) effect of both allocation and selection.

Exhibit 27-2 Sue-Bob
Attributes

Attribute	Conditional on Order of Computation		Unconditional
	Allocation 1st	Selection 1st	
Allocation	2.40%	1.60%	1.60%
Selection	−1.90%	−1.10%	−1.90%
Interaction			0.80%
Total differential	0.50%	0.50%	0.50%

separately.[13] In the late 1990s, this latter approach, in which the interaction effect is quantified explicitly and not lumped together with either pure performance attribute, was formally adopted as a recommended industry standard in Australia.[14]

27.1.4 The Case for Using Manager Allocation Weights in the Benchmark

Let's return for a moment to the approach represented by formula (1b) in which the manager's allocation weights are applied to the benchmark's selection performance in order to quantify the manager's selection performance differential with respect to the benchmark. This approach is in fact employed widely in practice to quantify the manager's selection performance effect.

The intuitive appeal of this approach is that it seems only fair to give credit to managers for their own allocation weights when quantifying the effect of their differential return performances within segments. But it is obvious that in so doing, one

---

[13] It should be noted that the portfolio-level attribution measures described here are essentially single-period measures. In applying such attribution analysis to multiperiod spans of time, a certain amount of arbitrariness or obfuscation tends to occur because in reality segment weights will tend to change gradually over time, both in the manager's and the benchmark portfolio. In practice, alternative approaches to quantifying the attribution measures over multiperiod spans of time include (1) using the initial, terminal, or average (across the overall time span) allocation weights applied to the time-weighted average multiperiod returns within each segment; and (2) computing the single-period attribution measures within each period, and then taking the arithmetic average of the attribution measures across the overall time span. The former approach is somewhat arbitrary and inaccurate in the segment weightings. The latter approach relates to the arithmetic mean time-weighted return, not the geometric mean that is typically used for the overall return measure in performance evaluation. However, the latter approach has a better statistical justification, as it does not violate the single-period nature of the attribution measures, but simply views each periodic return as an equally representative sample of time for indicating the manager's performance attribution. The arithmetic time-weighted mean also has the advantage of being completely decomposable into the sum of the arithmetic time-weighted average income return component plus the arithmetic time-weighted average appreciation return component.

[14] Relative to its economic size, Australia has a very large and advanced commercial property investment industry, including both publicly and privately traded assets and investment vehicles. However, the country came rather late to formal organization and institutionalization of investment performance data compilation, a decade or more after NCREIF in the United States and IPD in Britain. As a result, the Property Council of Australia (PCA) sought to learn from the experiences of other nations in this regard when it first published its Performance Measurement & Presentation Standards in 1998. In North America, the approach described here is also used by many analysts and has been described in several publications. (See, for example, Hamilton and Heinkel, [1995], and Lieblich [1995].)

is mixing the effects of two performance functions, allocation and selection. By the same reasoning, it would be only fair to apply the formula (1a) approach to quantifying the allocation effect (using managers' own within-segment returns to quantify the impact of their segment weight differences versus the benchmark). Of course, formulas (1a) and (1b) do not add up to the total return differential: 2.4% − 1.1% = 1.3% ≠ 0.5%.

In some circumstances, however, the argument for the use of formula (1b) to quantify the selection effect makes sense. Suppose the manager does not have control over her own allocation (e.g., the client did not give the manager discretion over the segment weights). Or suppose the manager's benchmark is considered appropriate as a benchmark for within-segment returns but not for segment allocation. In such circumstances, it makes sense to "customize" the manager's benchmark by recasting the benchmark segment weights to equal the manager's segment weights. In other words, the manager's benchmark should be computed with the benchmark in-segment returns but the manager's segment weights. In this case, a direct comparison of the manager's return with such a customized benchmark return will be equivalent to formula (1b), and the entire overall performance return differential between the manager and the benchmark will consist purely of the selection effect (the pure allocation and interaction effects will be zero, by construction).

27.2 INVESTMENT PERFORMANCE EVALUATION AND BENCHMARKING

Our discussion of manager benchmarks in the previous section is a good stepping-stone to our next topic, performance evaluation. Performance evaluation is one of the most basic and important tasks in the investment industry. In the context of investment management, performance evaluation refers to the need to arrive at some sort of judgment about how well a given manager has performed, either in absolute or in relative terms.[15] While performance evaluation broadly involves considerations that cannot be well quantified, some aspects of the job can be quantified, and it is to quantitative evaluation that we turn our attention now.

27.2.1 The Basic Idea

A typical performance evaluation of an investment manager or an investment fund is presented in Exhibit 27-3, which depicts the evaluation of two managers, A and B. After a period of time, typically three to five years, the average return achieved over that period is computed for each manager.[16] The returns achieved over that same

---

[15] This need exists for all parties, both the managers and the investors.

[16] Normally, the time-weighted average return is used (in particular, the geometric average) because at the portfolio or fund level (as distinct from the property level), the investment manager does not usually have much control over the timing of capital flow. As noted in Chapter 9, time-weighted average returns are neutral with respect to capital flow timing, while dollar-weighted returns reflect the effect of such timing. If the manager does substantially control the timing of capital flow, then the IRR might be a more appropriate measure of the manager's performance. However, benchmark performance should always be measured by a time-weighted return. The benchmark is meant to be neutral with regard to performance actions. In the case of capital flow timing, such neutrality is represented by the time-weighted average return. The geometric mean is typically used rather than the arithmetic mean because

Exhibit 27-3 Graphical Depiction of Typical Investment Manager Performance Evaluation

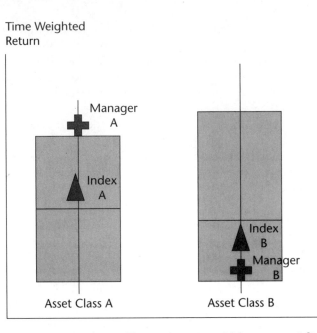

Assett Class or Investment Management Style

period of time are also computed for each other manager in a **peer universe** of all the competing managers (or funds) who also specialize in the same type of investments. In Exhibit 27-3 the manager's performance is indicated by the cross. The vertical line indicates the 5th and 95th percentile range of the manager's peer universe. The box indicates the middle two quartiles, and the horizontal line inside the box indicates the median manager's performance within the peer universe. The triangle indicates the return recorded by a passive index that is broadly representative of the type of assets the manager specializes in. (**A passive index** is one whose allocations across assets remain relatively constant.)

In the example shown in Exhibit 27-3, manager A did quite well, performing in the upper quartile of her peer universe and substantially beating the relevant passive index. She will likely be rehired and may have earned an incentive fee. It doesn't look so good for manager B. The investor likely will fire manager B or reduce his allocation in the future, probably hiring one of his competitors instead. (Note that manager A

performance evaluation is a backward look at history (rather than a forecasting exercise in which the statistical properties of the arithmetic mean would be useful), and because the geometric mean is not sensitive to the volatility in the periodic returns. (The arithmetic mean is greater the more volatile the returns.) It should also be noted that at the portfolio or fund level being addressed here (as distinct from the property level considered in section 27.1.1), the periodic HPRs are normally computed as *value-weighted* (cross-sectional average) returns *within* each period. That is, within each period, the return to each property is not weighted equally but by the relative value of the property within the portfolio. This type of value-weighting is necessary to enable the HPR each period to reflect the actual return to the portfolio within that period. The focus here (and in the portfolio-level attribution analysis described in sections 27.1.2–4) is on portfolio-level returns, rather than viewing each property as a sample of the manager's performance.

probably is not a competitor to manager B, as they are in two different asset classes or management styles.[17])

27.2.2 Benchmarks in the Private Real Estate Asset Class

In Exhibit 27-3 the manager's performance is compared both with respect to the median of her peer universe and with respect to a passive index broadly representative of her asset class. For example, in the public equity investment business, if the manager specializes in large-capitalization stocks, then the peer universe would consist of all the major mutual funds with a similar specialty. The most widely used passive index to benchmark large-stock performance is the Standard & Poors Composite 500 Index (the S&P 500).

In the example shown in Exhibit 27-3, manager A has beaten both the benchmark index and her average competitor. Manager B has been beaten by both of these reference points. More generally, however, there is potential ambiguity in this process. A manager might, for example, beat the average competitor but fall short of the relevant passive index, or vice versa.

So, which type of reference point is better as a benchmark for judging manager performance? Should it be some central tendency of the manager's peer universe (say, the mean or median), or should it be a passive index? In the securities investment industry, both types of benchmarks are used, but there is a general conception that passive indices are a bit better, in principle. This is primarily for two related reasons:

- In the public securities markets, passive indices are essentially replicable by both the manager and the client.

- Therefore, the client can presumably invest in the passive index as an alternative to hiring an active manager.

In contrast to the stock market, private real estate does not really have a truly passive index and indeed, a passive index is not possible. Fundamentally, this is because private real estate investment managers have to be responsible for the operational management of the properties they own on behalf of their clients, as described in Chapter 26. Furthermore, as noted, private real estate investment necessarily involves long holding periods because transaction costs are high. Therefore, as we pointed out in Chapter 26, much of the overall investment performance is attributable to how well properties are managed while they are held. This is **active management**, of necessity.[18]

---

[17] The placement of manager A's and manager B's performance evaluations together in Exhibit 27-3 is done merely for illustrative purposes. It is not meant to imply that there should be a head-to-head competition between these two managers. Such direct comparisons would normally only take place between managers within the same asset class or segment (or "style") of investments, to avoid an apples-to-oranges comparison.

[18] The term *active management* in the investment management industry has traditionally been defined from a public securities market perspective. In that context, of course, active management does not imply operational management of the investment assets, as this is not possible for investment managers in the securities industry. But in a broader sense, active management refers to the attempt to beat the market, or to outperform the average or typical portfolio of assets, by whatever means are at the disposal of the

Is It a Sample or Is It a Population: The Statistical Nature of Benchmark Indices

Benchmark property-level real estate investment performance indices such as the NCREIF index are often spoken of in common parlance as being a **sample** of a larger underlying population of all the commercial properties of a certain class or type. Indeed, much basic research conducted using such indices effectively treats property indices this way, as they are taken, for example, to represent the performance of an entire asset class (which is generally somewhat vaguely defined). However, it is important to realize that, in the context of performance evaluation of investment managers, benchmark indices such as the NCREIF index are not playing the role of statistical samples of some larger underlying population of properties. Rather, such indices in this context are themselves meant to define an entire **population**, namely, the population of all properties held by the relevant peer group of managers.

In the field of statistical inference, there is a large conceptual difference between a population and a sample of a population. One implication of this difference is that, if the index is viewed as a sample of a larger population, then, at least ideally, it should not be a value-weighted index, that is, an index constructed as the cross-sectional average of the individual property returns each period weighted by the relative magnitude of the property value within the overall population. Instead, the ideal index from a statistical sampling perspective would be equally weighted across properties within each period. However, the NCREIF index is, quite intentionally, a value-weighted index. This suggests that the designers of that index intended that it be viewed as a population rather than as a sample.*

*As of the late 1990s, NCREIF was developing a web site that would give its members the ability to construct equal-weighted custom indices using the NCREIF database of property level returns.

Not only is it effectively impossible to have a passive index in the private real estate asset class, but the major reasons such indices make better benchmarks do not apply within this asset class. First, because of the long holding periods, the segment weights in the relevant private real estate peer universe are likely to be much more stable over time than those of the typical actively managed portfolio in the securities markets. This makes the peer universe at least somewhat replicable, in terms of segment allocation. Second, even if we had a static portfolio index with constant segment weightings in private real estate, such an index would not present an alternative to active management for the investor. For one thing, in the private property markets whole assets are traded. Any specific assets in a static portfolio index would already be owned by someone else. For another thing, passive investors cannot generally invest directly, by themselves, in a portfolio of properties as an alternative to hiring an active manager because of the specialized expertise that is required for direct investment in the private property market (including the need for operational management expertise).

manager. In the case of securities investment managers, this is limited to the use of investment research and the employment of active trading strategies or target allocations. Private real estate investment managers may employ these types of activities, broadly defined, although in a more sluggish asset market, dealing with assets that are primarily income generators rather than growth plays, and in an environment of high transaction costs. But in addition to these traditional active management tools, private real estate investors can, indeed must, use their control over property-level operational management of the assets to try to improve their investment performance.

Instead of passive indices such as the S&P 500, the only type of periodic return indices available to serve as benchmarks in the private real estate asset class are peer group indices. These are indices, like the NCREIF index in the United States and the IPD index in Great Britain, that essentially reflect the property-level performance of all (or most) of the private real estate investment managers in the country.[19] As such, they correspond conceptually to the central tendency of a given manager's relevant peer group.[20]

27.2.3 Matching Evaluation, Responsibility, and Authority

In selecting (or constructing) a benchmark for use in manager performance evaluation, it is important to adhere to the basic management principle of equating responsibility with authority. In general, an investment manager should not be held responsible for, or evaluated on the basis of, factors that are beyond his decision authority or control, especially if the client has explicitly denied the manager discretion over such factors.

This issue commonly arises in the area of segment allocation. Asset market segments in private real estate typically correspond to space market segments characterized by property type and geographic location. Due to the need for local expertise, it is not uncommon for real estate investment managers to be specialized within one or a few market segments. For example, a manager may be hired by a client for the specific purpose of placing capital into the apartment property segment, perhaps within a proscribed geographic region. It would generally be unfair or misleading to benchmark such a manager's performance to an index that included other types of property besides apartments, and/or other geographic regions beyond the manager's purview.

On the other hand, if a manager is given discretion to choose allocational weights across more than one property market segment, then his benchmark should include all of the segments in the manager's potential choice set. In this case, the question arises as to what segment weightings to use in the manager's benchmark. A numerical example of this issue can be seen in our previous story of Bob and Sue.[21] Recall that both Bob and Sue had discretion to allocate within the industrial and office segments. Bob chose a 90%/10% allocation, while Sue chose a 10%/90% allocation.

---

[19] While a peer universe contains, in principle, all of the managers of a certain type that are currently active, a potential "survivorship bias" problem is often raised concerning the appropriateness of peer universes as compared to passive indices for performance benchmarks in the securities industry. Survivorship bias occurs when funds or managers who have failed or been taken off the market disappear from the peer universe. However, there is some reason to believe that, at least through the 1990s, survivorship bias was not a serious problem in the NCREIF index. For one thing, the NCREIF index is a *property-level*, as opposed to *fund-level*, index. Also, real estate managers and funds tend to be more stable than stock market funds. Indeed, the number of investment managers and properties covered by the NCREIF index remained fairly stable even through the major real estate downturn of the early 1990s. One reason is that real estate funds and managers often do not fail outright, but are acquired by other funds or managers, typically resulting in the properties remaining in the index, or exiting on the basis of transaction prices or updated appraised values that largely reflect recent value losses.

[20] Note, however, that property-level performance is "gross" of management fees and other fund-level or manager-level impacts on the net returns actually received by the investor client. This is true also for passive index benchmarks in the securities industry, such as the S&P 500. Of course, what really matter to the investor are the net returns received at the investor level. Indeed, for taxed investors, the after-tax returns are most relevant.

[21] See sections 27.1.2 through 27.1.4.

What should be the segment weightings in an appropriate benchmark index for evaluating their performances?

In the private real estate asset class, there is probably no good general answer to this question. The appropriate benchmark will depend on the client's overall investment strategy and the client's particular objectives for the given manager. However, a couple of general principles can be enumerated:

- The segment weights in the manager's benchmark should be mutually agreed upon by the client and the manager in advance, that is, at the outset of the management contract period. (Midcourse changes should be made only with the consent of both parties.)
- It should be possible for the manager to at least approximately replicate his benchmark's segment allocation weights, if he wants to.[22]

Both of these principles generally require that the benchmark segment weights be constant over the period of the manager's contract. Unfortunately, the segment weights in a peer-universe-based index such as the NCREIF index are not constant over time. However, for the reasons previously noted, segment allocations change only gradually in the typical private property return index. Furthermore, a manager's custom benchmark can be defined using property-level (i.e., within-segment) returns from the peer universe index, rebalanced to reflect constant segment weights agreed upon by the manager and client.

In the absence of a compelling reason otherwise, the simplest segment weights to use in the manager's custom benchmark would be equal weights across all the segments within the manager's purview. Alternatively, in the stock market, the capital asset pricing model (CAPM) is often invoked as a basis to suggest that the segment weights in a manager's benchmark index should reflect the **market portfolio**. In real estate, this would reflect the market-value-based segment weights of all commercial property in the country (or at least of all institutional quality commercial properties, for an institutional core manager, for example). However, as we saw in Chapter 22, the CAPM does not work very well as a descriptor of reality *within* the private real estate asset class. There may therefore be less theoretical rationale for the use of market-based weights in a manager's benchmark in private real estate investment, as compared to stock market investments.[23]

On the other hand, a client and/or manager may feel that market weights make at least as good a benchmark as any other. In particular, market weights approximately reflect the relative abilities of different segments to absorb new investment without price distortion. Market weights may also approximate the relative ease for the manager in finding assets for sale in the different segments. In this sense, market weights may approximate something like passive index segment weightings.[24]

---

[22] In other words, if the manager does not wish to place a bet against the segment allocation in his benchmark, he should not have to.

[23] In other words, there is perhaps less theoretical reason within the private real estate asset class as compared to the stock market, to view the market portfolio as reflecting an optimal segment weighting in a normative sense. Furthermore, from a practical perspective, it is difficult to estimate precisely market portfolio weights within the commercial property asset class. For an example of an attempt to quantify the geographic allocation across regions in the United States, see Mahoney, Malpezzi, and Shilling (2000).

[24] Recall, however, that specialized local expertise is necessary to enter into specific real estate market segments. One should be wary of defining a benchmark that encourages a manager to go into territories she is not familiar with. If market weightings are to be used, they should be applied only across the segments in which the manager has sufficient expertise and resources to operate effectively.

27.2.4 The Problem of Statistical Significance

When people seek to evaluate investment manager performance quantitatively as compared to a benchmark, the underlying purpose of such evaluation is usually perceived to be the identification of managers with superior versus inferior investment abilities. Investors want to place their capital with superior managers and avoid using inferior managers. Rigorously speaking, **superior investment ability** is the ability to *consistently* beat an appropriate benchmark, as opposed to a random outcome in which a manager happened to beat the benchmark over a given period of historical time. Similarly, inferior ability is the opposite, the tendency to get consistently beaten by the appropriate benchmark, as distinguished from a random streak of bad luck.

This perception of the purpose of performance evaluation raises a fundamental conceptual problem in practice. This problem exists whether evaluation is being done in the context of the public securities market or the private real estate market. The problem is a lack of **statistical significance** in ex post performance differentials. What does this mean?

A basic characteristic of risky assets is that their realized returns vary randomly around their rational ex ante expectations. This **randomness in ex post returns** is simply a reflection of the risk in the assets from an investment perspective. Performance evaluation must be based on ex post returns, the only kind of returns that can be quantified objectively and that reflect the actual realized performance of the manager. The existence of randomness in these returns means that performance evaluation is an exercise in statistical inference. Based on a sample of time (the history over which the performance evaluation is being conducted), we are trying to infer what is the central tendency of the manager's differential performance relative to the benchmark over all (or any given interval of) time.[25] The greater the randomness in ex post returns, and the shorter the historical time sample for which we have differential performance data, the less accurately we can infer the central tendency from the available empirical evidence.

Consider a simple numerical example. Suppose a manager's quarterly holding period returns are compared against those of an appropriate benchmark over a three-year period. That is, we have 12 observations (or sample drawings) about the underlying "true" (or population) difference between manager i's quarterly return and the benchmark's quarterly return. (Label this true difference $E[r_i - r_B]$.) Suppose we have very favorable circumstances for inferring this difference. In particular, suppose the true difference is constant over time, and we observe the realized returns to both the manager and the benchmark without error. Suppose also that the true quarterly volatility is only 5% in both r_i and r_B, and the correlation between the manager's returns and the benchmark returns is 90%.[26] Then manager i's average quarterly return would have to

[25] Another way of putting this is as follows. Suppose a manager beat his benchmark by 50 basis points over the past three years. What does that imply about how we can rationally expect this same manager to perform relative to the same benchmark over the *next* three years?

[26] The longer the observation sample, the lower the volatility, and the higher the correlation, the easier it is to accurately infer the true difference from the sample drawings. During the 1980s and 1990s, the quarterly volatility of the S&P 500 was about 8%, that of long-term government bonds was about 6%, while the volatility of the NCREIF Property Index (NPI) was only about 2%. However, as described in Chapter 25, the NPI is smoothed due to the effects of appraisal valuations and temporal aggregation. This means that quarterly NPI returns are highly positively autocorrelated. As a result, in a time sample of, say, 12 quarters, the NPI does not really provide 12 *independent* observations of the return, in contrast to an index such as the S&P 500, for example. As we suggested in Chapter 25, if we delagged the NPI so that its quarterly periodic returns were like independent observations (i.e., if we applied

exceed the average benchmark return by over 130 basis points (an annualized return difference of over 5%) before we could conclude with statistical significance that the central tendency of the manager's return exceeds that of the benchmark's return, in other words, that the manager can beat the benchmark as a result of skill rather than a random outcome.[27] But it is very rare to find a manager's return beating the benchmark by this much.[28]

As a result of considerations such as these, at least one major national real estate investment industry association, that of Australia, formally recommended that a **health warning** should accompany the presentation of real estate investment performance results. The suggested wording as of 1998 was:[29]

> *Past investment performance is not an adequate test of comparative performance, nor a reliable indicator of the expected absolute level of returns in the future.*

the zero-autocorrelation adjustment described in Chapter 25, so as to make real estate returns more closely resemble stock market returns statistically), then the volatility of the NPI would easily exceed 5% per quarter. Furthermore, 90% is much greater correlation than one can usually obtain between a manager's portfolio and an appropriate benchmark. For example, Myer and Webb (1993) regressed the quarterly HPRs of professionally managed private real estate portfolios onto the NPI over 29 quarters. The average R^2 of these regressions across the 47 portfolios they examined was 0.25. This implies an average correlation of SQRT(0.25), or 50%.

[27] Note that for this type of inference we use the arithmetic average return rather than the geometric average. The computations behind this conclusion are as follows. If σ_i is the manager's volatility, σ_B is the benchmark's volatility, and C is the correlation between the two, then the following formula gives the standard deviation of the difference between the manager's return and the benchmark's return, $r_{i,t} - r_{B,t}$:

$$\sigma_{i-B} = (\sigma_i^2 + \sigma_B^2 - 2C\sigma_i\sigma_B)^{(1/2)} = [0.05^2 + 0.05^2 - 2(0.9)(0.05)(0.05)]^{(1/2)} = 2.24\%$$

Dividing this by the square root of $N - 1$, where N is the number of observations, gives the standard error of the observed average difference:

Standard Error $= \sigma_{i-B}/[(N - 1)^{(1/2)}] = 2.24\%/3.32 = 0.675\%$

Two standard errors are required for statistical significance (95% confidence), which would be $2 \times 0.675\%$, or 1.35% per quarter. This equates to about 5.5% annualized. Note also that, although the arithmetic average return is, in principle, more appropriate for this type of statistical comparison, it is still necessary to consider the effect of volatility on the arithmetic average return, if the two performance series being compared display different volatility (which is not the case in the present numerical example). One (somewhat crude or informal) way to adjust for the effect of volatility on arithmetic mean returns is to simply use the geometric mean returns of the two series being compared, even though the confidence limits are computed as above, based on arithmetic means.

[28] In the 47 portfolios they examined, Myer and Webb (op. cit.) found only 16 whose returns exceeded the NPI with statistical significance. (A more recent study, reported in Myer and Webb [1997], found similar results in this regard.) Furthermore, as noted, such indications of statistical significance assume that the underlying relationship between the manager and the benchmark is constant over time, and that the realized holding period returns to both the manager and the benchmark can be observed without error each period. In reality, these assumptions are not true even in public securities markets, but especially in the private real estate market. Return measurement errors such as those described in Chapter 25 muddy the waters and may require even larger spreads before one can conclude with confidence that a manager actually beat her benchmark by a sufficient margin to rule out luck as the cause.

[29] The warning label presented here is taken from the First Edition (1998) of the *Australian Investment Performance Measurement & Presentation Standards*, published by the Property Council of Australia.

27.2.5 Implications of the Lack of Statistical Significance: Will the *Real* Purpose of Performance Evaluation Please Stand Up

At first glance, it would seem that the difficulty of making rigorous inferences about managers' investment abilities on the basis of the evidence in their realized performances would render quantitative performance evaluation pointless. Could a simple statistical point really undercut an endeavor that so many people spend so much effort on in the real world? Probably not, for at least a couple of reasons, described here.

Including Nonquantitative Considerations. Investors rarely base their judgments about manager performance solely on the basis of quantitative analysis. Managers generally explain and describe their investment and management philosophy, their strategy, tactics, and management procedures, in some detail for their clients or potential clients. Investors make judgments in part based on these **manager stories**. If the story makes sense, the investor will factor this nonquantitative information in with the quantitative evidence. The two types of information together may allow a substantially more accurate judgment to be made about a given manager's ability, at least relative to his competitors.

Ex Ante Role of Performance Evaluation. The critique of performance evaluation from a statistical significance perspective in section 27.2.4 viewed the purpose of such evaluation from a rather narrow, *ex post* perspective. It suggested that, if performance evaluation is for the purpose of inferring, ex post, which managers are truly superior and which are truly inferior (based on skill), then it will often be very difficult to achieve this purpose. But this is certainly not the only, and perhaps not even the primary, purpose of investment manager performance evaluation (even though many practitioners may consciously perceived it as such). In fact, performance evaluation serves an *ex ante* purpose that may be more important than its *ex post* purpose. To see this, consider the following characterization of the relationship between investors and managers.

Suppose the typical investor hires the typical manager in a three-year contract at the end of which the manager's performance will be formally evaluated. An incentive fee or bonus based on this retrospective evaluation may (although need not necessarily) be included in the management contract. The performance evaluation that occurs at the end of the contract formally (and empirically) applies to the preceding three years, the years during which the manager worked for the client. In this formal *ex post* usage, the evaluation probably will lack statistical significance. But the mere prospect that the evaluation *will be performed* has an impact on the manager's incentives and behavior *ex ante*, that is, *prior to* the expiration of the contract. By working harder (or "smarter") for the client, the manager increases the likelihood (ex ante) of beating her benchmark.[30] This increases the likelihood that the manager will be rehired for a subsequent multiyear period (and it increases the manager's expected earnings from any incentive fee component of the contract based on the formal evaluation). Thus, on an ex ante basis, the use of formal performance evaluation helps to set up an **interest**

---

[30] Incidentally, since this is as true for a peer universe benchmark as it is for a passive index, from this ex ante incentive perspective, peer-universe-based benchmarks are generally as functional as passive indices.

alignment between the manager and the investor, thereby reducing agency costs in the investment industry.

Ex post, water is over the dam, and often little can be concluded, rigorously speaking. The real purpose (or more important role) of formal, quantitative investment performance evaluation probably lies in the ex ante role just described, particularly in combination with the (often nonquantitative) plausibility of the managers' stories. This is true both in real estate and securities investment management.

The importance of the ex ante role of performance evaluation does not mean that the statistical problems with ex post inference can be ignored, however. The role of randomness in ex post returns, and also of ex post return measurement difficulties especially in the private real estate asset class, should be carefully considered.[31] This is particularly important in constructing investment management contracts that have **incentive fee** provisions based on performance evaluation (e.g., the use of performance **bogeys**). Too much randomness and lack of precision in the relationship between the ex post performance measure and the actual investment skill and diligence applied ex ante by the manager will act to demoralize or discourage good managers. The results could be perverse from the perspective of aligning the interests of the investor and manager. For example, if too large a portion of the manager's overall fee is based on ex post performance relative to a bogey, then the best managers may shun investors who demand such contracts, or both sides may end up just "gaming" the incentive.[32]

The importance of minimizing randomness in the ex post return differential between the manager and an incentive contract bogey highlights the importance of selecting an appropriate benchmark for the manager's performance evaluation. Our previous point about matching responsibility with authority is obviously important in this regard.

27.2.6 Adjusting for Risk

Risk and return go hand in hand in the capital markets. The market naturally provides investors with greater average returns, over the long run, for more risky investments. This means that, on average or from an ex ante perspective, managers can increase their returns (and increase their probability of beating any given reference point) by taking on more risk. But obviously, this is not what investors have in mind when they aim at rewarding managers for beating reference points or providing managers with incentives to work more diligently. Superior (or even just diligent) investment management does not consist simply of using the capital market's return/risk

---

[31] As noted in Chapter 25, temporal lag bias in real estate returns may not be a prohibitive problem in performance evaluation, as such bias may largely cancel out in the performance differential between the manager and his benchmark. It is important, however, to ascertain whether the degree of lagging is similar in the manager's reported returns and those of the benchmark. If the lag is similar, then smoothing or lagging will probably not much affect the performance evaluation. However, random noise (purely random return measurement error as distinct from temporal lag bias) may still pose a serious measurement problem in the performance differential. Such measurement error is an additional source of randomness beyond the underlying volatility in the true returns across time. Noise will be a particular problem if either the manager's portfolio or the benchmark contains a relatively small number of individual properties or appraisers.

[32] In the extreme, if too much random measurement error exists in quantifying the performance differential between the manager and the benchmark, then poor managers will have almost as good a chance of earning an incentive fee as superior managers.

trade-off to provide higher average returns for the investor. Therefore, it is essential to control for risk in investment performance evaluation.

Broadly speaking, this can be done in either of two ways, either by adjusting the performance measure, or by restraining the manager's leeway to modify the risk in her portfolio away from the risk in her benchmark. Let's briefly consider each of these approaches in the context of the private real estate asset class.

In the first approach the manager's ex post return and that of her benchmark are quantitatively adjusted for risk. The performance evaluation is made using **risk-adjusted returns** rather than unadjusted raw return results. This approach is treated extensively in mainstream investments textbooks, and has found some application in real world practice in the stock market. It includes measures such as the Sharpe ratio, the Jensen alpha, the Treynor ratio, and various others.[33] The advantage of this approach is that, if it can be done well enough, it reduces the need for the manager's benchmark to have the same risk as that of the manager's portfolio.

Unfortunately, there are some problems with quantitative risk adjustment for manager performance evaluation. In principle, the key to this technique is that the measure of risk in the manager's and benchmark portfolios (for example, the beta, if a CAPM definition of risk is being used) should reflect the amount of risk *as it matters to the capital market*. In theory, this is the only way the risk adjustment can reflect the **market price of risk**, that is, the way the market would adjust the expected return risk premium, to reflect the amount of risk in the portfolio. But practical problems in risk measurement, as well the fundamental theoretical state of the art in equilibrium asset price modeling (as described in Chapter 22), make this type of risk adjustment an inexact science. This problem, combined with the previously described difficulties with statistical precision in the estimation of performance differentials even without adjusting for risk, takes the wind out of the sails of formal, quantitative risk adjustment in investment performance evaluation. This is probably the main reason this approach is not very widely used in real world practice even in the stock market.

There are even greater difficulties, both theoretical and practical, in applying formal quantitative risk adjustment to investment in the private real estate market. These include the data problems described in Chapter 25, as well as the theoretical problems described in Chapter 22. In particular, recall that a single-index CAPM-type model does not work well within the private real estate asset class. We do not know how to distinguish the beta of one type of property from that of another, and there seems to be little clear or stable differences in expected returns across different property segments (within the core institutional quality property market). More sophisticated multifactor risk models may improve this situation, but the practical development of such models is still in a very embryonic stage. Furthermore, multifactor risk models do not provide a one-dimensional measure of risk that can be used to develop a single, unambiguous measure of a portfolio's risk-adjusted return.[34]

---

[33] For a good presentation of these measures and their strengths and weaknesses, see for example, Brodie, Kane, and Marcus (1999). These types of measures are not widely employed in private real estate investment performance evaluation, although Sharpe ratios are often reported (see text box).

[34] A Jensen Alpha measure can be calculated for a portfolio using a multifactor risk model, but such a measure only identifies the sign of the portfolio's risk-adjusted return (i.e., it tells whether the return is above or below the Security Market Hyperplane). It does not generally allow a rank-ordering of the risk-adjusted return performance of two portfolios that have the same signed alpha but different amounts of risk.

What about the Sharpe Ratio?

The Sharpe ratio, which we defined in Chapter 21 is one quantitative risk-adjusted return measure that is rather widely reported in private real estate investment. It is computed as the risk premium per unit of risk, where *risk* is defined as the volatility of the subject manager or portfolio. While this measure is of some general interest, to our knowledge it has not been widely used in formal performance evaluation in the private real estate asset class. This is probably for the best, as there are several theoretical and practical problems with the Sharpe ratio for use in the typical real estate management situation.

The most serious theoretical problem with the Sharpe ratio is that the volatility of the manager's portfolio is generally not the measure of risk in that portfolio that matters to the capital market. Therefore, it is not the measure of risk that will be priced. As a result, the Sharpe ratio is likely to be misleading as an adjustment for a portfolio's return to account for its risk. Related to this is the fact that any one real estate manager or portfolio will typically be responsible for only a small fraction of an investor client's total wealth portfolio. In this case, the denominator in the Sharpe ratio does not measure the contribution of the subject portfolio to the risk that matters to the investor, which is the volatility in the investor's total wealth portfolio (see Chapters 21 and 22).*

In addition to this theoretical problem, the Sharpe ratio faces another, more practical problem particularly within the private real estate equity quadrant. As we described in Chapter 25, private real estate returns must be based on appraisals or whole asset transaction prices that are "noisy." We noted there that noise affects the volatility of asset returns. The greater the noise in the valuations, the greater the volatility in the return time-series derived from those valuations. But the greater the number of properties in the portfolio, the less the effect of noise. (Remember the Square Root of *n* Rule.) So the effect of random error on the volatility of a portfolio or index will vary, depending on how many individual properties are in it. Of course, different managers will typically hold different numbers of properties. And any given manager will typically hold a different number of properties (usually fewer) than what is in her benchmark. Thus, noise will differentially affect managers, and their benchmarks, and this will bias any performance comparison or evaluation based on the Sharpe ratio.

---

*A point raised in defense of the Sharpe ratio in this regard is that the risk that actually matters to the capital market may be *proportional to* an asset's volatility, if all the relevant assets (in the manager's choice set) have the same correlation with the market risk benchmark. In the case of private real estate assets, no one is really sure what this benchmark is, or what the "true" correlation between real estate and such a risk benchmark would be anyway, so the assumption of equal correlation is implicitly applied, allowing the use of the Sharpe ratio (as a kind of "better than nothing" fallback). The weakness in this argument is apparent.

This does not mean that one can ignore the issue of portfolio risk in real estate performance evaluation. What it means is that one must fall back onto the second general approach for controlling for risk. For want of a better label, we will call this the **nonquantitative risk control**, to distinguish it from the previous technique. The basic idea in this approach is to constrain the manager to investing only in assets that are of essentially equal risk, which is also the risk of the manager's benchmark. Then we do not need to adjust for risk quantitatively. We can compare directly the unadjusted returns.[35]

---

[35] In the stock market, nonquantitative risk control requires much more narrow constraints on the manager's investment choice set than it does in private real estate because of the real estate market's difficulty in distinguishing risk differences across institutional property market segments (see section 22.3 in Chapter 22). For example, even if a stock market investment manager was limited to investing only

In private real estate, the implementation of this approach typically requires restricting the manager regarding the use of leverage and regarding investments in **noninstitutional (noncore) properties.** For example, development projects or properties in need of rehabilitation are generally perceived to contain more risk than high-quality, fully operational properties. Properties that are smaller or of lower quality than traditional institutional core real estate assets may contain more risk.[36] Of course, the manager's benchmark must conform to the same constraints in this regard. Effectively, this confines the ability to rigorously control for risk to the institutional core of the private property market because benchmark indices of periodic returns do not exist as yet for noninstitutional commercial property in the United States.[37]

27.3 CHAPTER SUMMARY

With this chapter, we conclude Part VII, our coverage of the macrolevel of real estate investment. This chapter extended our broader, institutional focus on the real estate investment industry of the previous chapter by focusing on some of the basic principles, tools, and procedures used in the investment management industry, with particular reference to their use in the private property asset class. We described in some detail the techniques of investment performance attribution at both the macro property level and the portfolio level. We pointed out the importance of formal, quantitative investment performance evaluation in real estate. We also described the nature and role of such evaluation, including some subtleties and unique features that distinguish the private real estate equity asset class in this regard.

in aerospace stocks, or only in "value stocks," the individual assets (stocks) in such a choice set would exhibit a wide range of perceived risk (and hence expected return). Nevertheless, even in the stock market, nonquantitative risk control is probably the major approach actually used in the real world practice of investment performance evaluation (if not in the academic textbooks).

[36] See our discussion in section 22.3 in Chapter 22 regarding the nature of risk in real estate, as it matters to the asset market.

[37] FNMA and FHLMC produce transaction-price-based indices for housing in the United States (based on the repeat-sales regression technique), and these indices do include some small-scale apartment properties. It is conceivable that in the future such indices could be developed for commercial property. However, repeat-sale indices only track the capital gain component of the total investment return, and they may not adequately include the effect of capital improvement expenditures on the properties. There may also be problems of sample-selection bias if the properties that happen to transact most frequently differ in investment performance from that of the types of properties in the manager's choice set.

KEY TERMS

performance attribution
benchmarking
macro property level (performance
    attribution)
statistical inference
portfolio level (performance
    attribution)
allocation
selection
segments (in the asset market)
benchmark
interaction effect

performance evaluation
peer universe
passive index
active management
population (versus sample)
responsibility and authority
    matching
market portfolio
superior investment ability
statistical significance
randomness in ex post returns
health warning

manager stories
ex ante role (of performance
    evaluation)
interest alignment
incentive fees
bogeys
risk-adjusted returns
market price of risk
Sharpe ratio
nonquantitative risk control
noninstitutional (noncore)
    properties

STUDY QUESTIONS

27.1. What is performance attribution? How is it used? Describe the three major performance attributes that are typically identified and quantified at the macro property level.

27.2. Why is property-level performance attribution usually best done based on the cross-sectional average IRR? What is the statistical-inference-based argument for equally weighting the IRRs across properties, for purposes of performance attribution.

27.3. What are the two major performance attributes typically identified at the portfolio management level?

27.4. What is meant by the term *interaction effect* in portfolio-level performance attribution. Why can't this effect be lumped together with either allocation or selection?

27.5. Piet and Tony are two apartment property investment managers hired one year ago by two different investors. In both cases the managers were free to use their own judgment regarding geographical allocation between properties in the East versus West of the country. Piet allocated his capital equally between the two regions, while Tony placed three-quarters of his capital in the Western region. After one year their respective total returns were as depicted in the following table. As you can see, Piet beat Tony by 100 basis points in his total portfolio performance for the year.

Tony's and Piet's Returns Realized for Clients

Weights	Tony	Piet
East	25%	50%
West	75%	50%

Returns	Tony	Piet
Total portfolio	9.50%	10.50%
East	8.00%	9.00%
West	10.00%	12.00%

a. How would you attribute this 100-basis-point differential between allocation and selection performance if you wanted to condition your attribution on computing the allocation performance component first?

b. How would you attribute this 100-basis-point differential between allocation and selection performance if you wanted to condition your attribution on computing the selection performance component first?

c. How would you attribute this 100-basis-point differential among pure allocation performance, pure selection performance, and a combined interaction effect, if you wanted to compute an *unconditional* performance attribution that was independent of the order of computation?

27.6. In question 27.5, suppose that Piet did not have discretion to choose his allocation weights between the East and West regions, but was specifically requested by his client to place capital equally between the two regions (as he did). Suppose further that the within-region performance achieved by Tony represents an appropriate benchmark for property-level performance within each region. Then what is an appropriate benchmark for evaluating Piet's performance, and what is Piet's performance differential with respect to that benchmark?

27.7. What is the difference between a peer universe and a passive index, as a benchmark for evaluating investment manager performance? Why are passive indices often preferred in this role in the evaluation of stock market investment managers? Why don't passive indices exist in the private real estate market? Why are the arguments against peer universe benchmarks less persuasive in the private real estate market than in the stock market?

27.8. In what sense (or in what role or uses) is the NCREIF index best viewed as a population (in the statistical sense)? In what sense (or in what role or uses) is the NCREIF index best viewed as a sample?

27.9. Why is it important to try to match responsibility with authority in investment management, and to evaluate the manager's investment performance on the basis of the authority the manager is given by the client (as aligned with his responsibility, hopefully)? Describe two general principles for achieving this type of balanced and fair performance evaluation. Describe some additional considerations in attempting to implement these principles in private real estate management.

27.10. Briefly discuss some pros and cons in the use of market weights to define a real estate investment manager's benchmark used in performance evaluation.

27.11. What is the problem of statistical significance in investment manager performance evaluation? Why is this problem even more severe in the private real estate market than in the stock market?

*27.12. Suppose we can observe and measure with perfect accuracy the quarterly total returns obtained by both a manager and her appropriately defined benchmark. Suppose further that these returns are independent across time in both cases (that is, they lack serial correlation, like stock market returns). Suppose both the manager and the benchmark have quarterly return volatility (standard deviation across time) equal to 3%. And suppose the correlation between the manager and benchmark returns is +75%. By how much must the manager's five-year average quarterly return exceed that of her benchmark in order to be able to conclude with usual statistical significance that the manager's performance differential was not just a random outcome?

27.13. Discuss the implications of the difficulty of rigorously identifying superior investment manager performance (in the sense of identifying a replicable performance outcome based on skill rather than luck). What is the *ex ante* role of quantitative performance evaluation?

27.14. What are the dangers of excessive randomness or arbitrariness in the use of investment management performance incentive fees?

27.15. Describe the difference between the quantitative (risk-adjusted-return based) and nonquantitative methods for controlling for risk in investment manager performance evaluation. Why is it even more difficult to apply the quantitative approach in the private real estate sector than in the stock market sector?

27.16. Define the Sharpe ratio. What are the problems with the Sharpe ratio as a quantitative measure of risk-adjusted return for use in performance evaluation in the private real estate sector?

PART VII

References and Additional Reading

References are grouped by chapter topic. However, some references are relevant to more than one topic area (and may be cited in more than one chapter), but are listed here only once in this bibliography.

Chapters 21 and 22: Portfolio & Asset Pricing Theory

Arrow, K., "A Difficult in the Concept of Social Welfare," *Journal of Political Economy* 58: 328, 1950.

Bajtelsmit, V. and E. Worzala. "Real Estate Allocation in Pension Fund Portfolios." *The Journal of Real Estate Portfolio Management* 1(1):25–38, 1995.

Black, F. "Beta and Return." *Journal of Portfolio Management* 20:8–18, Fall 1993.

Black, F., M. Jensen, and M. Scholes. "The Capital Asset Pricing Model: Some Empirical Tests." in M. Jensen (ed.), *Studies in the Theory of Capital Markets*, New York; Praeger, 1972.

Breeden, D. "An Intertemporal Asset Pricing Model with Stochastic Consumption and Investment Opportunities." *Journal of Financial Economics* 7: 265–296, 1979.

Chan, K., P. Hendershott, and A. Sanders. "Risk and Return on Real Estate: Evidence from Equity REITs." *AREUEA Journal* 18(1): 431–452, spring 1990.

Ciochetti, B., J. Sa-Aadu, and J. Shilling "Determinants of Real Estate Asset Allocations in Private and Public Pension Plans." *Journal of Real Estate Finance & Economics* 19(3):193–210, November 1999.

Ciochetti, B. and J. Shilling. "Pension Plan Real Estate Investment in an Asset/Liability Framework." University of North Carolina Working Paper, 1999.

Eichholtz, P. "Does International Diversification Work Better for Real Estate than for Stocks and Bonds?" *Financial Analysts Journal* 52(1): 56–62, Jan./Feb. 1996.

Fama, E. and K. French. "The Cross-Section of Expected Stock Returns." *Journal of Finance* 47(2): 427–465, June 1992.

Fama, E. and J. MacBeth. "Risk, Return, and Equilibrium: Empirical Tests." *Journal of Political Economy* 81: 607–636, May 1973.

Fama, E. and W. Schwert. "Human Capital and Capital Market Equilibrium." *Journal of Financial Economics* 4(1): 95–125, 1977.

Firstenburg, P., S. Ross, and R. Zisler. "Real Estate: The Whole Story" *Journal of Portfolio Management* 1988.

Gatzlaff, D. "Pension Fund Investment: Further Analysis of Fund Allocations to Real Estate." Real Estate Research Institute (RERI) Working Paper W-32, 1995.

Geltner, D. "Estimating Real Estate's Systematic Risk from Aggregate Level Appraisal-Based Returns." *AREUEA Journal* 17(4): 463–481, winter 1989.

Geltner, D., N. Miller, and J. Snavely. "We Need a Fourth Asset Class: HEITs." *Real Estate Finance* 12(2): 71–81, summer 1995.

Geltner, D., J. Rodriguez, and D. O'Connor. "The Similar Genetics of Public and Private Real Estate and the Optimal Long-Horizon Portfolio Mix." *Real Estate Finance* 12(3): 13–25, fall 1995.

Giliberto, S. M. "The Allocation of Real Estate to Future Mixed-Asset Institutional Portfolios." *Journal of Real Estate Research* 7(4): 423–432, fall 1992.

Giliberto, S. M. and A. Mengden. "REITs and Real Estate: Two Markets Reexamined." *Real Estate Finance* 13(1): 56–60, spring 1996.

Graff, R. and M. Young, "Real Estate Return Correlations: Real-World Limitations on Relationships Inferred from NCREIF Data." *Journal of Real Estate Finance & Economics* 13(2): 121–142, September 1996.

Hartzell, D., J. Heckman, and M. Miles. "Diversification Categories in Investment Real Estate." *AREUEA Journal*, 14(2): 230–254, summer 1986.

Ibbotson, R., J. Diermier, and L. Siegel. "The Demand for Capital Market Returns: A New Equilibrium Theory." *Financial Analysis Journal*, 40(1), January 1984.

Ibbotson, R. and L. Siegel. "Real Estate Returns: A Comparison with Other Investments." *AREUEA Journal* 12(3): 219–242, fall 1984.

Kallberg, J., C. Liu, and D. Greig. "The Role of Real Estate in the Portfolio Allocation Process." *Real Estate Economics* 24(3): 359–377, fall 1996.

Karolyi, G. A. and A. Sanders. "The Variation of Economic Risk Premiums in Real Estate Returns." *Journal of Real Estate Economics & Finance*, 17(3): 245–262, November 1998.

Liang, Y., F. C. N. Myer, and J. Webb, "The Bootstrap Efficient Frontier for Mixed-Asset Portfolios." *Real Estate Economics* 24(2): 247–256, summer 1996.

Ling, D. and A. Naranjo. "Economic Risk Factors and Commercial Real Estate Returns." *Journal of Real Estate Finance & Economics* 14(3): 283–307, May 1997.

Ling, D. and A. Naranjo. "The Fundamental Determinants of Commercial Real Estate Returns." *Real Estate Finance* 14(4): 13–24, winter 1998.

Ling, D. and A. Naranjo. "The Integration of Commercial Real Estate Markets and Stock Markets." *Real Estate Economics* 27(3): 483–516, fall 1999.

Lintner, J. "The Valuation of Risk Assets and the Selection of Risky Investments in Stock Portfolios and Capital Budgets." *Review of Economics and Statistics* 47: 13–37, February 1965.

Liu, C., T. Grissom, and D. Hartzell. "The Impact of Market Imperfections on Real Estate Returns and Optimal Investment Portfolios." *AREUEA Journal* 18(4): 453–478, winter 1990.

Liu, C., D. Hartzell, T. Grissom, and W. Grieg. "The Composition of the Market Portfolio and Real Estate Investment Performance." *AREUEA Journal* 18(1): 49–75, spring 1990.

Liu, C., D. Hartzell, and T. Grissom. "The Role of Co-Skewness in the Pricing of Real Estate." *Journal of Real Estate Finance & Economics* 5(3): 299–319, September 1992.

Liu, C., D. Hartzell, and M. Hoesli. "International Evidence on Real Estate Securities as an Inflation Hedge." *Real Estate Economics* 25(2): 193–221, summer 1997.

Markowitz, H. "Portfolio Selection." *Journal of Finance* 7: 77–91, March 1952.

Mei, J. and A. Lee. "Is There a Real Estate Factor Premium." *Journal of Real Estate Finance & Economics* 9(2): 113–126, September 1994.

Miles, M. and T. McCue. "Diversification in the Real Estate Portfolio." *Journal of Real Estate Research* 7: 17–28, 1984.

Myer, F. and J. Webb. "Return Properties of Equity REITs, Common Stocks, and Commercial Real Estate: A Comparison." *Journal of Real Estate Research* 8(1): 87–106, winter 1993.

Ross, S. "The Arbitrage Theory of Capital Asset Pricing." *Journal of Economic Theory* 13: 341–360, 1976.

Ross, S. and R. Zisler. "Risk and Return in Real Estate." *Journal of Real Estate Finance & Economics* 4(2): 175–190, June 1991.

Sharpe, W. "Capital Asset Prices: A Theory of Market Equilibrium Under Conditions of Risk." *Journal of Finance* 19: 425–442, September 1964.

Titman, S. and A. Warga. "Risk and Performance of Real Estate Investment Trusts: A Multiple Index Approach." *Real Estate Economics* 14: 414–431, 1986.

Webb, J. and J. Rueben. "How Much in Real Estate: A Surprising Answer." *Journal of Portfolio Management* 13: 10–14, 1987.

Williams, J. "Agency, Ownership, and Returns on Real Assets." Real Estate Research Institute (RERI) Working Paper, 1999.

Young, M. and R. Graff. "Real-Estate is Not Normal—A Fresh Look at Real-Estate Return Distributions." *Journal of Real Estate Finance and Economics* 10(3): 225–259, May 1995.

Ziobrowski, B. A. "Exchange Rate Risk and Internationally Diversified Portfolios." *Journal of International Money & Finance* 14(1): 65–81, February 1995.

Chapters 23 and 25: Appraisal Behavior & Return Statistics

Bailey, M., R. Muth, and H. Nourse. "A Regression Method for Real Estate Price Index Construction" *Journal of the American Statistical Association* 58: 933–942, 1963.

Basu, S. and T. G. Thibodeau. "Analysis of Spatial Autocorrelation in House Prices." *Journal of Real Estate Finance and Economics* 17(1): 61–85, July 1998.

Blundell, G. and C. Ward. "Property Portfolio Allocation: A Multi-Factor Model." *Land Development Studies* 4: 145–156, 1987.

Brown, G. "The Information Content of Property Valuations." *Journal of Valuation* 3: 350–357, 1985.

Brown, G. and G. Matysiak. *Real Estate Investment: A Capital Market Approach*. London: Pearson Education, 2000.

Bryan, T. and P. Colwell. "Housing Price Indices." In C. F. Sirmans (ed.), *Research in Real Estate*, vol. 2. Greenwich, CT: JAI Press, 1982.

Case, B. and J. Quigley. "Dynamics of Real-Estate Prices." *Review of Economics and Statistics* 73(1): 50–58 February 1991.

Case, K. and R. Shiller. "Prices of Single Family Homes Since 1970: New Indexes for Four Cities." *New England Economic Review*: 45–56, Sept./Oct. 1987.

Case, K. and R. Shiller. "Forecasting Prices and Excess Returns in the Housing Market." *AREUEA Journal* 18(3): 253–273, fall 1990.

Childs, P., S. Ott ,and T. Riddiough. "Noise, Real Estate Markets, and Options on Real Assets." MIT Center for Real Estate Working Paper, 2000.

Chinloy, P., M. Cho, and I. Megbolugbe. "Appraisals, Transaction Incentives, and Smoothing." *Journal of Real Estate Finance & Economics* 14(1/2): 89–112, January/March 1997.

Clapp, J. and C. Giacotto. "Estimating Price Indices for Residential Property: A Comparison of Repeat Sales and Assessed Value Methods." *Journal of the American Statistical Association* 87: 300–306, June 1992.

Clapp, J. and C. Giacotto. "Price Indices Based on the Hedonic Repeat-Sales Method: Application to the Housing Market." *Journal of Real Estate Finance & Economics* 16(1): 5–26, January 1998.

Crosson, S., C. Dannis, and T. Thibodeau. "Cutting-Edge, Cost-Effective Valuation for Accurate Portfolio Level Appraisal." *Real Estate Finance* 12(4): 20–28, winter 1996.

Diaz, J. "An Investigation into the Impact of Previous Expert Value Estimates on Appraisal Judgment." *Journal of Real Estate Research* 13(1): 49–58, 1997.

Diaz, J. and M. Wolverton. "A Longitudinal Examination of the Appraisal Smoothing Hypothesis." *Real Estate Economics* 26(2): 349–358, summer 1998.

Downs, D. and B. Slade. "Characteristics of a Full-Disclosure Transaction-Based Index of Commercial Real Estate." *Journal of Real Estate Portfolio Management* 5(1): 94–104, 1999.

Fisher, J, D. Geltner, and R. B. Webb. "Value Indices of Commercial Real Estate: A Comparison of Index Construction Methods." *Journal of Real Estate Finance & Economics* 9(2): 137–164, 1994.

Fisher, J., M. Miles, and R. B. Webb. "How Reliable Are Commercial Appraisals: Another Look." *Real Estate Finance* 16(3), fall 1999.

Gatzlaff, D. and D. Geltner. "A Transaction-Based Index of Commercial Property and Its Comparison to the NCREIF Index." *Real Estate Finance* 15(1): 7–22, spring 1998.

Gatzlaff, D. and D. Haurin. "Sample Selection Bias and Repeat-Sales Index Estimates." *Journal of Real Estate Finance and Economics* 14, 33–50, 1996.

Geltner, D. "Estimating Real Estate's Systematic Risk from Aggregate Level Appraisal-Based Returns." *AREUEA Journal* 17(4): 463–481, winter 1989.

Geltner, D. "Smoothing in Appraisal-Based Returns." *Journal of Real Estate Finance & Economics* 4(3): 327–345, September 1991.

Geltner, D. "Temporal Aggregation in Real Estate Return Indices." *AREUEA Journal* 21(2): 141–166, 1993a.

Geltner, D., "Estimating Market Values from Appraised Values Without Assuming an Efficient Market." *Journal of Real Estate Research* 8(3): 325–346, 1993b.

Geltner, D. "Using the NCREIF Index to Shed Light on What Really Happened to Asset Market Values in 1998: An Unsmoother's View of the Statistics." *Real Estate Finance* 16(1): 69–80, spring 1999.

Geltner, D. and W. Goetzmann. "Two Decades of Commercial Property Returns: A Repeated-Measures Regression-Based Version of the NCREIF Index." *Journal of Real Estate Finance & Economics,* forthcoming, 2000.

Giacotto, C. and J. Clapp. "Appraisal-Based Real Estate Returns under Alternative Market Regimes" *AREUEA Journal* 20(1): 1–24, 1992.

Giliberto, S. M. "Equity Real Estate Investment Trusts and Real Estate Returns." *Journal of Real Estate Research* 5(2): 259–264, summer 1990.

Goetzmann, W. "The Accuracy of Real Estate Indices: Repeat Sale Estimators." *Journal of Real Estate Finance & Economics* 5(1): 5–54, March 1992.

Goetzmann, W. "The Single Family Home in the Investment Portfolio." *Journal of Real Estate Finance & Economics* 6(3): 201–222, May 1993.

Graff, R. and M. Young. "Real Estate Return Correlations: Real-World Limitations on Relationships Inferred from NCREIF Data." *Journal of Real Estate Finance & Economics* 13(2): 121–142, September 1996.

Hamilton, S. and J. Clayton. "Smoothing in Commercial Property Valuations: Evidence from the Trenches." *Real Estate Finance* 16(3), fall 1999.

Lai, T. and K. Wang. "Appraisal Smoothing: The Other Side of the Story." *Real Estate Economics* 26(3): 511–536, fall 1998.

Ling, D., A. Naranjo, and M. Nimalendran. "Estimating Returns on Commercial Real Estate: A New Methodology Using Latent Variable Regression." Real Estate Research Institute (RERI) Working Paper, January 1999.

McMillen, D. and J. Dombrow. "Estimating Price Indexes in Metropolitan Submarkets: A Flexible Fourier Repeat Sales Approach." University of Chicago Working Paper, February 2000.

Pace, R. K., R. Barry, J. M. Clapp, and M. Rodriquez. "Spatiotemporal Autoregressive Models of Neighborhood Effects." *Journal of Real Estate Finance and Economics* 17(1): 15–33, July 1998.

Pindyck, R. and D. Rubinfeld. *Economic Models and Economic Forecasts.* New York: McGraw-Hill, 1991, Chapter 3.

Quan, D. and J. Quigley. "Inferring an Investment Return Series for Real Estate from Observations on Sales." *AREUEA Journal* 17(2): 218–230, summer 1989.

Quan, D. and J. Quigley. "Price Formation and the Appraisal Function in Real Estate Markets." *Journal of Real Estate Finance & Economics* 4(2): 127–146, 1991.

Shiller, R. "Arithmetic Repeat Sales Price Estimators." *Journal of Housing Economics* 1(1): 110–126, March 1991.

Williams, J. "Pricing Real Assets Under Rational Expectations." Working Paper, 2000.

Chapter 24: REIT Valuation

Ambrose, B. and A. Pennington-Cross. "Economies of Scale in Multi-Product Firms: The Case of REITs." Real Estate Research Institute (RERI) Working Paper, 2000.

Barkham, R. and D. Geltner. "Price Discovery in American and British Property Markets." *Real Estate Economics (formerly AREUEA Journal)* 23(1): 21–44, Spring 1995

Bers, M. and T. Springer. "Sources of Scale Economies for REITs." *Real Estate Finance* 14(4): 47–56, winter 1998.

Capozza, D. and P. Seguin. "Managerial Style and Firm Value." *Real Estate Economics* 26 (1): 131–150, 1998.

Capozza, D. and P. Seguin. "Focus, Transparency and Value: The REIT Evidence." *Real Estate Economics* 27(4): 587–620, 1999.

Garrigan, R. and J. Parsons (eds.). *Real Estate Investment Trusts: Structure, Analysis, and Strategy.* New York: McGraw-Hill, 1997.

Ghosh, C., R. Nag, and C. F. Sirmans. "Financing Choice by Equity REITs in the 1990s." *Real Estate Finance* 14(3): 41–50, fall 1997.

Giliberto, S. M. and A. Mengden. "REITs and Real Estate. Two Markets Reexamined." *Real Estate Finance* 13(1): 56–60, spring 1996.

Goldstein, M. and E. Nelling. "REIT Return Behavior in Advancing and Declining Stock Markets." *Real Estate Finance* 15(4): 68–77, winter 1999.

Gordon, J. and E. Shapiro. "Capital Equipment Analysis: The Required Rate of Profit." *Management Science* 3: 102–110, October 1956.

Gyourko, J. and D. Keim. "What Does the Stock Market Tell Us About Real Estate Returns?" *Real Estate Economics* 20(3): 457–486, fall 1992.

Ling, D. and M. Ryngaert. "Valuation Uncertainty, Institutional Involvement, and the Underpricing of IPOs: The Case of REITs." *Journal of Financial Economics* 43(3): 433–456, March 1997.

Ling, D. and A. Naranjo. "The Integration of Commercial Real Estate Markets and Stock Markets." *Real Estate Economics* 27(3): 483–516, fall 1999.

Linneman, P. "Forces Changing the Real Estate Industry Forever." *Wharton Real Estate Review*, spring 1997.

Naranjo, A. and M. Ryngaert. "The Predictability of Equity REIT Returns." Real Estate Research Institute (RERI) Working Paper, 1998.

Sagalyn, L. "Conflicts of Interest in the Structure of REITs." *Real Estate Finance* 13(2): 34–51, Summer 1996.

Shiller, R. "Human Behavior and the Efficiency of the Financial System." National Bureau of Economic Research Working Paper #6375, 1998.

Taylor, L. "Financial Analysis of REIT Securities." R. Garrigan and J. Parsons, (eds.), *Real Estate Investment Trusts.* New York: McGraw-Hill, 1998.

Vogel, J. "Why the Conventional Wisdom about REITs Is Wrong." *Real Estate Finance* 14(2): 7–12, summer 1997.

Chapters 26 and 27: Real Estate Investment Management

Brodie, Z., A. Kane, and A. Marcus. *Investments*, 4th ed. Boston: Irwin, McGraw-Hill, 1999, Chapter 24.

Greig, W. "Standardizing Information on Privately Held Real Estate Investments." *Real Estate Finance* 13(4): 59–62, winter 1997.

Hamilton, S. and R. Heinkel. "Sources of Value-Added in Canadian Real Estate Investment Management." *Real Estate Finance* 12(2): 57–70, summer 1995.

Lieblich, F. "The Real Estate Portfolio Management Process." In J. Pagliari (ed.), *The Handbook of Real Estate Portfolio Management*, Irwin, Chicago: 1995.

Mahoney, J., S. Malpezzi, and J. Shilling. "Implications of Income Property Stock Data for Real Estate Investment Portfolio Location." *Real Estate Finance* 16(4), winter 2000.

Mei, J. "Assessing the 'Santa Claus' Approach to Asset Allocation." *Real Estate Finance* 13(2): 65–70, Summer 1996.

Myer, F. C. N. and J. Webb. "The Effect of Benchmark Choice on Risk-Adjusted Performance Measures for Commingled Real Estate Funds." *Journal of Real Estate Research* 8(2): 189–203, 1993.

Myer, F. C. N., J. Webb, and L. T. He. "Issues in Measuring Performance of Commingled Real Estate Funds." *Journal of Real Estate Research* 3(2): 79–86, 1997.

Property Council of Australia, *Australian Investment Performance Measurement & Presentation Standards*, Property Council of Australia, Sydney, 1998.

Real Estate Development and Other Selected Topics

The preceding 7 parts and 27 chapters have taken you through quite a tour. You have seen the microlevel of real estate transactions and deals, and the macrolevel of portfolio strategy, tactics, and investment management. You have seen the urban economic foundation of real estate investment in the space market, as well as the financial economics perspective on both equity and debt investment. But there are still a few particular topics that we have not covered in depth or as a particular focus in any of the previous parts. This last part is therefore a bit of a grab bag, a mixture of topics that we think are important, but that are distinct enough to have been left out of the flow of the previous parts. If there is a common theme in Part VIII, it is to bring you back to the link between the asset and space markets we first described in Parts I and II of this book, but now with a more specific microlevel focus on some topics that are particularly important in commercial property investment.

In particular, Part VIII will focus major attention on the financial analysis of real estate development, beginning with the closely related but more fundamental topic of land valuation, including the so-called real options model. This will occupy Chapters 28 and 29. A second major topic is that of leases and leasing strategy, which will be covered in Chapter 30. Finally, we have added an appendix that deals with the rather technical topic of the use of statistical regression procedures to develop transaction-price-based indices of commercial property price appreciation.

28 Real Options and Land Value

Learning Objectives

After reading this chapter, you should understand:

◆ The call option and how this concept can be used
to understand the value of land.

◆ Some of the insights option valuation theory
provides for understanding real estate development
behavior, including how overdevelopment can be
rational in some circumstances.

◆ The Samuelson-McKean formula, and how it can
be used to shed light on land value, development
timing, and the opportunity cost of capital for
investment in land speculation.

$\mathbf{L}$and value is probably the most fundamental topic in all of real estate. We saw in
our discussion of the real estate system in Part I the pivotal role land value plays as
the key link between the asset and space markets in the real estate development
process. In addition, we saw the crucial role of land value in urban economic analysis
and in the shape and dynamics of real world urban development. Indeed, land is the
fundamental defining characteristic of real estate, and the nature of land valuation
helps to define the investment characteristics of most major real estate assets. In this
chapter we will introduce you to a very useful (and Nobel Prize–winning) tool that
was developed during the last couple of decades of the 20th century for the purpose
of helping to understand, analyze, and evaluate land and the real estate development
process. This tool is financial **option valuation theory (OVT)**, and especially the
branch of that theory known as **real options**.

28.1 CALL OPTIONS: SOME BASIC BACKGROUND AND DEFINITIONS

In finance, an **option** is defined as follows:

> *An option is the right* **without obligation** *to obtain something of value upon the payment or giving up of something else of value.*

The person having such a right is referred to as the owner or holder of the option. The asset obtained by the **exercise** of the option is often referred to as the **underlying asset**, while that which is given up is referred to as the **exercise price** of the option. The option holder has the right to decide whether or not to exercise the option. If the option can be exercised at any time (prior to an expiration date, or maturity, if the option has such), then the option is said to be an **American option**. If the option can only be exercised on its expiration date (not before), then the option is said to be a **European option**. In any case, option exercise is irreversible because, in the act of exercising the option, the option itself is thereby given up, that is, an option can only be exercised once.

OVT consists of a body of theory and methodology for quantitatively evaluating options. Included as an integral part of such valuation is the problem of specifying the conditions when it is optimal to exercise the option, if it is an American option. The classical types of options in financial economics for which OVT was first developed are the stock options and warrants that are traded in several public exchanges and widely issued to corporate executives as an incentive component of their compensation. For example, the classical common stock **call option** gives the holder the right, without obligation, to purchase at a stated price per share a specified number of shares of the common stock of a specified company on or before a certain date.

28.1.1 Simple Real World Example: Time, Uncertainty, and a Microsoft Call Option

To gain an understanding of the essential nature of call options, let's consider a simple concrete example from the real world. Call options on Microsoft stock are sold regularly on several exchanges, including the Chicago Board of Trade. On February 18, 1997, you could have bought on that exchange a call option on Microsoft stock with a strike price of $100 per share expiring on April 18, 1997. On the options exchange the market price of this call option at that time, two months prior to its expiration, was $5 per share of the underlying stock. On that same day Microsoft stock was trading at $97.375 per share on the NASDAQ stock exchange. In other words, as of February 18, the value of the option to purchase Microsoft for $100 per share at any time between then and April 18 was $5 per share, even though Microsoft's price as of February 18 was actually less than $100. Why would investors have been willing to pay good money for the right to purchase Microsoft at a price higher than what they could purchase it for directly?

The answer, of course, is very simple. Investors were willing to pay a positive price for this "out-of-the-money" Microsoft option because there was some probability that

Microsoft's share price would rise to a level above $100 at some time between February 18 and April 18.[1] Indeed, if the market price of the option with a $100 strike price was $5, then the market must have perceived considerable probability that Microsoft shares would rise not just above $100 but above $105 at some time between February and April. For example, if Microsoft rose to $106, you could exercise the option to purchase the stock at $100 and then immediately sell the stock at $106. The $6 difference would more than compensate for the $5 price you had to pay for the option on February 18.

As you can see, options play on two key factors: time and uncertainty, and these factors are brought to bear in a particularly intense and interesting way. This is because options present their owners with what is called a **contingent claim**, that is, a claim that will have some value under some future scenarios but no value at all under other future scenarios. For example, if Microsoft stock never rose above $100 between February 18 and April 18, then the call option with the $100 strike price that was selling for $5 on February 18 would never have any exercise value, and it would expire worthless on April 18. The option has value ultimately only under some contingencies, namely, when and if Microsoft's share price rises above the $100 strike price prior to the option expiration.

28.1.2 Option Premium

Another key feature of option valuation is the fact that options can (and normally do) have value over and above their current exercise value. For example, the Microsoft call option with the $100 strike price had no current exercise value as of February 18 because the option's exercise price ($100) was then above the market price at which the stock could be purchased directly without the option ($97.375). You gain no positive value in exercising an option that requires you to pay $100 for an asset that is only worth $97.375. Indeed, you would lose $2.625 by exercising the option at that time. The difference between the option value and its current exercise value is called the **option premium**. The option premium in the Microsoft example is $7.625, as $5.00 − ($97.375 − $100.00) = $5.00 − (−$2.625) = $7.625. On the same day an otherwise identical call option on Microsoft, but with a strike price of $85 instead of $100, was selling for $14.375. This second option was more valuable because it had a lower strike price. But it had a smaller option premium, only $2.00, as $14.375 − ($97.375 − $85.00) = $14.375 − $12.375 = $2.00.

Option values will always have a positive (or at least nonnegative) premium above their current exercise value for two reasons: (1) the option holder is never obligated to exercise the option, and (2) uncertainty as well as predictable trends in the future value of the underlying asset cause there to be at least some chance that the underlying asset will be worth more in the future (prior to the option expiration) than it is today. The first reason, the lack of any exercise obligation, gives the option holder the flexibility to avoid unfavorable exercise. The second reason, the possibility of superior underlying asset value in the future, provides the potential upside opportunity that allows the option holder to use this flexibility not only to avoid a negative outcome but also to achieve a positive advantage via favorable exercise of the option. In other words, a big part of the art of successful investment in options is effective timing of the exercise of

---

[1]An option is said to be "out of the money" if its current exercise value is negative, that is, if the current value of its underlying asset is less than the current value of its exercise price. The option is "in the money" if its current exercise value is positive.

the option. Consideration of such timing is therefore part of what determines the value of the option.

From the previous considerations, it should also be intuitive that the option premium will tend to be more valuable (holding other things equal)

(1) the longer the maturity of the option (that is, the longer until the option expires), and

(2) the more uncertainty there is in the future value of the underlying asset, that is, the more volatile *(or variable) is the value of the underlying asset over time.*

28.2 REAL OPTIONS: THE CALL OPTION MODEL OF LAND VALUE

Although the preceding basic principles of option valuation were long understood qualitatively, developing a rigorous model to value options quantitatively and specify their optimal exercise timing was a considerable technical challenge. The key break-throughs occurred in the late 1960s and early 1970s. The names most associated with early option pricing model development include the economist Paul Samuelson and his mathematician partner Henry McKean, Robert C. Merton (a student of Samuelson's who became a leading financial economist), and the famous pair of, Fischer Black, a physicist-turned-economist, and Myron Scholes. The so-called Black-Scholes model of option valuation (sometimes referred to as the Black-Scholes-Merton, or BSM, model) was the most famous single development, published in 1973. The Black-Scholes model is now a standard tool of option traders and is even "hard-wired" into some business calculators.[2]

Since the early 1970s OVT has seen a tremendous flowering and has resulted in a virtual revolution in both the theory and practice of the investment and corporate finance industries. This is because it was quickly realized that, in a sense, *options are everywhere*, not just in the common stock options traded on the option exchanges. For example, we noted in Chapter 16 how the prepayment clause in a mortgage gives the borrower the right without obligation to pay off the mortgage before its maturity. The prepayment clause in the mortgage is thus an option.[3] We also saw there how the ability of the borrower of a nonrecourse mortgage to default on the debt may be viewed as a type of option (in this case a put option, wherein the borrower gives up to the lender the remaining value of the collateral property firm and thereby obtains release from the original debt obligation to the lender). There are many other examples of how common financial assets, claims, and arrangements can be viewed as options or as containing important option components. Some of these examples and applications are in real estate. Perhaps the most fundamental application of OVT to real estate is the application of what is known as real options to land valuation and the behavior of real estate developers.

In general, *real options* refers to the study of options whose underlying assets (that is, either what is obtained or what is given up on the exercise of the option) are real

---

[2]Myron Scholes and Robert Merton shared the Nobel Prize in Economics in 1997 for their development of OVT. (Black would certainly have also been included except that the Nobel Prize is not awarded posthumously.)

[3]In this case it is a call option on the mortgage itself.

assets (i.e., physical capital) as opposed to purely financial assets. For example, a building or a factory is a real asset, whereas shares of common stock or a release from a mortgage debt obligation are financial assets. The default option in mortgage debt that we noted in Chapter 16 (the mortgagor's put option) is an example of a real option because the borrower is giving up real property. But a deeper or more fundamental level of application of real option theory to real estate is to apply the option model to the land itself, the asset that is characteristic of all real estate. When we do this, we go to the very heart of the real estate system because OVT can now shed light directly on the relation between land value and the timing and nature of the development of buildings on the land.

This application of real options theory to real estate is what may be termed the **call option model of land value.** In this model land is viewed as obtaining its value through the option it gives its owner to develop a structure on the land. More broadly, the landowner's option includes also the option to demolish and/or redevelop any existing structures on the land. However, unless the existing building is quite old or small, or the development of the city and neighborhood has rendered the existing structure inappropriate for the best use of the location, the cost of demolishing the existing building (in particular, the *opportunity cost* of the forgone revenues that building could earn) will normally be so great as to minimize the redevelopment option value. Thus, the option model of land value is most applicable either to vacant (or nearly vacant) land, or else to land in transition zones where the highest and best urban use of the land is changing.[4] In any case, it is important to keep in mind that the real option that is viewed as giving land its value is, essentially, the *land development option.*

The study of real options arose from two major strands in the academic literature. One strand came from the branch of financial economics known as capital budgeting, the study of how to make good decisions regarding the purchase and use of physical plant and equipment. The other strand came from urban economics with its focus on the value of land and the relation between location value and urban spatial form. By the late 1980s researchers realized that these two strands of inquiry were really studying essentially the same thing and using essentially same OVT models![5]

It is easy to see that real estate development is essentially the same type of activity as what industrial corporations attempt to manage through their capital budgeting process. Real estate development consists of the allocation of scarce financial capital to the construction of physical assets (in this case, buildings) that will remain in place for a long time earning cash flow (in this case, net rents) by their operation. The construction process is essentially *irreversible*: once the buildings are in place, it is usually too expensive to seriously consider tearing them down and starting again from scratch (at least not for a number of years). Thus, the option is given up by its exercise, just as is the case with financial options. The call option characteristic of the physical investment decision (whether it be a real estate development project or the construction of a new microprocessor factory) consists in the fact that the option

[4]Recall our discussion of neighborhood and property life cycles in sections 5.3 and 5.4 of Chapter 5.

[5]Some of the pioneers in developing this literature in the 1980s included Sheridan Titman, Joseph Williams, and Dennis Capozza from the real estate side, and Robert McDonald, Daniel Siegel, and Stewart Myers from the capital budgeting side. However, the mathematical formula that they were all dealing with (more or less), at least in its simplest form, had been developed by Paul Samuelson and Henry McKean back in 1965, as a model of "perpetual American warrants." This formula will be presented in the last section of this chapter.

holder (the industrial corporation or the developer/landowner) has the right without obligation to undertake the construction project (i.e., to exercise the option by paying the exercise price, in this case, the construction cost), and upon completion of the construction project the (now former) option holder has obtained a valuable asset (the underlying asset in this case is the built property or the factory).

The reason the call option model of land value can have such a fundamental and central place in furthering our understanding of real estate is that it relates directly to some crucial links in the big picture of the real estate system as we defined this system way back in Chapter 2. Land is the characteristic component that distinguishes real estate from other types of capital assets. The call option model allows us to better understand and quantify land value. Real option theory sheds light on the important link between land value and real estate development. If you recall from Chapter 2 our depiction of the big picture of the real estate system in Exhibit 2-2 and 2-3, you will remember the crucial role that the development industry plays in providing the long-run link between the real estate asset market and the real estate space usage market. From Chapters 4 and 5 you will also recall the crucial role that the land market plays in determining urban spatial form. All of these issues can be addressed in a more rigorous and quantitative way, and can be integrated as never before, using real option theory and the call option model of land value.

28.2.1 New Insight into the NPV Rule

One of the first points that is often highlighted from real options theory is its implications regarding the basic NPV rule we introduced in Chapter 10. It is often said in the corporate capital budgeting literature that option theory shows that the classical NPV rule of investment is too simple. Option theory suggests that it will usually not make sense to invest in a project that has a small positive net present value (NPV) as this is quantified in the typical corporate capital budgeting application. Instead, it will usually make more sense in the corporate context to wait until the NPV is substantially positive before investing.

This point holds for the same reason that one would typically not exercise the $100 option on Microsoft stock as soon as Microsoft's share price reaches $101, at least not unless the option is about to expire or Microsoft is about to issue a dividend to current stockholders. If Microsoft is trading at $101 and the option still has time before it expires, then there is a good chance Microsoft will go above $101 before the option expires, allowing the option holder to make even more money from later exercise. It will generally be worth waiting for such a possibility, which is why there will be an option premium in the option price. Even if the option holder does not want to wait, it would make more sense to sell the option than to exercise it and sacrifice the option premium.

However, a careful reading of the NPV investment rule suggests that option theory does not really negate or modify the old rule. We simply have to be careful about how we apply the rule. Recall from Chapter 10 that the NPV rule is to invest so as to *maximize* your NPV. We don't just invest in any and all positive-NPV projects when there are mutually exclusive alternatives. Instead, we pick the alternative that has the maximum NPV. The irreversibility of construction projects means that to invest today excludes the possibility of investing later (e.g., in the same or another construction project on the same land). Building today versus building next year are mutually exclusive alternatives on a given site. Maximizing the NPV would require selecting the construction timing that has the highest NPV, discounted to today. Applied this way, the NPV rule should still hold.

Another way of seeing this point that is more relevant for real estate applications is to include the current value of the option premium as part of the cost one is incurring by exercising the development option. Whenever one considers the costs and benefits of an investment, one must be careful to include *all* costs and benefits. For an irreversible project, the costs include the option premium that is given up by undertaking the project. The value of this option premium may often be hard to see and to quantify in the case of industrial corporate capital projects, in which highly unique and proprietary types of equipment or physical assets are to be built, perhaps within existing plants and facilities already owned by the corporation. But in the case of the typical real estate development project, the option premium should be more readily observable (albeit still not perfectly so) in the current market value of the land. In a well-functioning land market the development option premium should normally be included in the current market value of the land. This land value is always an *opportunity cost* of the development project (even if the developer already owns the land).[6]

28.2.2 Land Development Option Contrasted with Financial Options: Some Implications for Overbuilding

The development option inherent in land ownership has some particular characteristics that distinguish it from most financial options. For one thing, the landowner's development option is normally a **perpetual option**. Unlike most financial options, there is no expiration date or maturity, no time after which the landowner will have lost his or her option to build on the land. Other things being equal, option values are greater the longer the time until they expire, so perpetual options tend to be more valuable. Also, optimal exercise of a perpetual option will be based entirely on the cash payout from the underlying asset, which the option holder obtains by exercising the option. That is, development occurs fundamentally, in principle, to generate positive net operating cash flow from the developed property.

A second unique feature of the land development option is that exercise is not immediate. It takes **time to build**. Between the time the decision to build is made and the time the project is completed, the market may change, and there is uncertainty in this change.

In the 1990s a professor at Stanford University Business School, Steven Grenadier, developed an OVT model that shows how the time-to-build phenomenon can help to explain a type of overbuilding that seems to occur more frequently in real estate space markets characterized by large buildings that take longer to build.[7] We noted in Chapter 2

---

[6] There may be special circumstances in which the developer's opportunity cost does not exactly reflect the current market value of the land, such as, for example, when the developer does not own the land outright but has only a finite-lived "use-it-or-lose-it" option to develop on the land. However, even in such cases the current market value of the land would normally represent an opportunity cost from the perspective of society (as distinct from the private perspective of the developer with the option). Note also that the value of the newly built property on completion of the development will include the (remaining) value of the land. This land value will now be minus its initial development option value (which has been exercised), but will now include the redevelopment (or abandonment) option value. Normally, this redevelopment option value will be quite small in a newly developed property, as pointed out in our discussion of property life cycles in section 5.4 of Chapter 5.

[7] See Grenadier (1995a, 1995b).

the tendency of real estate space markets to become overbuilt from time to time. In this context, **overbuilding** may be defined as the production of more space than there is usage demand for at the time the construction is completed. In our presentation of the DiPasquale-Wheaton four-quadrant diagram in Chapter 2 we showed how myopic behavior on the part of investors and developers could explain such overbuilding.[8] But the Grenadier model offers a more rational explanation, that is, an explanation that is consistent with rational expectations and forward-looking land-value-maximizing behavior on the part of developers and investors.

Grenadier noticed that overbuilding seems to be more severe in space markets characterized by large buildings and widespread use of long-term leases, such as CBD office markets. The Grenadier model suggests that overbuilding in such markets may be a rational response to the **leasing option** held by the developer/owner of the building being constructed. As with all options, the leasing option presents its holder with flexibility, which can be used to the benefit of the option holder. The magnitude of this potential option benefit may be greater the longer the time to build because longer construction time allows a greater range of extreme outcomes in the space market demand. In effect, the lease option is given a longer maturity the longer the time to build. If demand turns out to be above expectations, the landlord/developer can benefit by locking in high-rent, long-term leases. If the space market turns out to be worse than expected, the landlord does not have to sign long-term leases. The developer can wait for the market to turn around (at least, if he is not too highly levered so that he can maintain control of the project). The asymmetry in this effect of "good" and "bad" leasing outcomes for the landlord can, in some cases, make it worthwhile to commence construction even when there is a substantial chance that usage demand may not be sufficient to fill the building at the time the project is completed.[9]

A third important difference between land and the typical financial option is that in the case of land it may not be possible to observe with perfect accuracy the current value of the underlying asset. While uncertainty in the future value of the underlying asset is an inherent characteristic of all options, in the case of financial options one can usually observe rather precisely the current market value of the underlying asset (as, for example, the shares of Microsoft stock that were trading for $97.375 in our earlier example). For reasons we described in Chapters 12 and 23, real estate is a bit different in this regard. Due to the "thinness" of the property market, asset values can only be observed *approximately*, or with random noise. This can affect the timing of option exercise and may have implications for the overbuilding phenomenon.

When the current value of the underlying asset is not perfectly observable, there may be heterogeneous information about the true value of the underlying asset (the built property, if it were existing today). In particular, different landowner/developers may have different amounts or quality of information and expertise concerning such value.

---

[8] See also section 6.2 in Chapter 6 for a more detailed development of the dynamics of myopic behavior, with implications for cyclicality and overbuilding.

[9] Of course, having a completed (but empty) building does not force the landlord to lease out all the space immediately. The point of the Grenadier model is *not* that longer construction time is better than shorter construction time, ceteris paribus. Rather, the point is that *some* of the additional cost of long construction times is mitigated by the value of the leasing option, and this additional value can make it worthwhile to commence construction when the project might not otherwise make sense from a rational (e.g., NPV-rule) perspective. This effect is greater in markets where, due to the needs of tenants, long-term leases are the norm. (See Chapter 30 for further discussion of leasing strategy.)

Recent research has shown how such current value uncertainty and information asymmetry can lead to rational herd behavior or follow-the-leader type **cascades** in which periods of very little development are followed by periods of frenzied development.[10]

This relates to a fourth important difference between real and financial options. Typically, the exercise of real options will produce unique, whole assets that will add to the supply side of the market for the use of such assets. In other words, the exercise of real options converts financial into physical capital and thereby impacts on supply and demand in a real market. This is not generally the case for financial options. For example, when we exercise our call option on Microsoft stock at the $100 strike price, someone else who sold the option in the first place must give us his Microsoft shares at the $100 price. No new shares of Microsoft are created or issued, and no additional capital flows to Microsoft.

In contrast, suppose in a certain office market there is usage demand for an additional one million square feet of office space. If one landowner/developer decides to build a million-square-foot office building on her land, then her decision to exercise her option causes a flow of financial capital that results in the construction of one million square feet of physical capital (in the form of the office building) in that office market. That one option exercise decision by that one landowner/developer has, in this example, all by itself exhausted the demand for new office space in the relevant market. This, in turn, severely negatively affects the option value of other land parcels that might have served as the sites for new office buildings. This "lumpiness" of real estate supply adds a gaming dimension to the **development timing** decision, in which developers strive to beat each other to the punch, possibly resulting in overbuilding or redundant construction.[11]

28.2.3 Using Option Theory to Understand Overbuilding

You can see from the preceding discussion that OVT provides a simple way of understanding at least some real estate overbuilding phenomena on the basis of rational behavior. Considering the importance of overbuilding both from a social perspective and for its effects on individual real estate developers and investors, let us pursue in greater depth a simplified description of one of the key insights to which OVT leads us in this regard.[12]

Imagine that as a landowner your development option is perhaps not perpetual after all, but may in fact expire at some point in time. In particular, your development option will expire when the other landowner/developers in the area exercise their development options sufficiently to exhaust the usage demand for new built space in the area. The exact expiration date on your option is therefore unknown and uncertain,

---

[10] See Grenadier (1996). Noise may also cause the first or lead developer to wait longer than she otherwise would. See Childs, Ott, and Riddiough (2000).

[11] See Grenadier (1996) and Williams (1993). We should also note that there is a fifth difference between real options and financial options that can be important from a technical perspective. This is that the underlying assets in real options often either do not trade in a well-functioning market at all, or (as in the case of real estate) they trade in a market that is less informationally efficient than financial asset markets (hence, the underlying asset prices are more sluggish and contain inertia in their returns).

[12] The following is a simplification of the theories of Grenadier (1996); Childs, Ott, and Riddiough (2000); and Williams (1993).

as it depends on these other developers' decisions (as well as on the magnitude of usage demand for built space in the area, a quantity that may also be difficult to estimate exactly).

Now it is a basic (and rather intuitive) principle of OVT that the shorter is the time until expiration of an option, the smaller is the option premium, and the lower are the requirements for immediate exercise of the option to be optimal (that is, profit-maximizing, or rational). In the extreme, it is never optimal to allow an in-the-money option to expire unexercised. Therefore, in the presence of competing developers and a finite usage market demand, there will be strong pressure on you to build immediately as soon as it appears that the market value the newly developed property would have is greater than your construction cost exclusive of your land value (that is, treating your land cost as "sunk"). In effect, the competition pressures you to ignore any option premium in your land value, as the competition's actions can cause your option to "expire," losing not only its premium but indeed its entire value.[13] Your fellow landowner/developers are in the same position as you are. Everyone is under pressure to develop as soon as their development option is in the money. If they all act accordingly (in effect, each one trying to beat the other to fulfill the finite usage demand), they will tend in the aggregate to build too much space too soon. Thus, overbuilding will tend to occur in the space market.

It is important to note that this type of overbuilding occurs even though each individual is acting rationally in his or her own best interest given the available information. OVT thus allows us to see how real estate's famous overbuilding and boom and bust cycles may result from rational individual behavior, rather than "crazy developers" with "edifice complexes," or from myopic or backward-looking expectations about the future.

This rational behavior at the individual level does not imply, however, that the result is rational for society as a whole. Contrast the previous case with a (hypothetical) case in which all the land is held by one rational (i.e., land-value-maximizing) monopoly owner. With one owner it is clear that the development option never expires (after all, the land never physically goes away). With the perpetual option it would normally be optimal to wait and not develop until the option was more deeply in the money, that is, until the usage demand bids up the value of the built property to a price well above the level of just the construction cost exclusive of land value. Such waiting would maximize the land value, and therefore the landowner/developer's profits, and avoid overbuilding. Society as a whole would be better off, in that land and building capital would be more efficiently allocated. Physically, the result would be new space built in smaller quantity and/or later in time (after more usage demand had built up). Note also that, as we have previously seen that options tend to be more valuable the more uncertainty or volatility exists in their underlying asset values, the theory therefore suggests that the overbuilding problem will tend to be worse in markets in which real estate values are fundamentally more volatile, such as in places where the economic base tends to grow unevenly, in fits and starts over time, for example.

[13] Remember that the land value is just the development option value; if that option expires unexercised, the land will be worthless, at least in the somewhat simplified circumstances described in this example (in which the usage demand is permanently exhausted by the competing developments).

28.3 SIMPLE NUMERICAL EXAMPLE OF OVT APPLIED TO LAND VALUATION AND THE DEVELOPMENT TIMING DECISION

To gain a more concrete understanding of OVT in its fundamental application to real estate, let's walk through a very simple example of how the development option affects land value and the development timing decision. Consider a vacant land parcel and its potential development as summarized in Exhibit 28-1. Suppose the best project that could currently be built on the site is an apartment building that would be worth $1 million under present market conditions. (In other words, the property with a new such building on it could be sold for $1 million today, and this of course includes the value of the land beneath the apartment building.) Suppose the construction and development cost (including developer profit but exclusive of land cost) would currently be $800,000 to build this project. The classical residual method of land valuation would quantify the land value at $200,000, the difference between the current built property value and the current development cost, that is, the current exercise value of the development option.[14]

This $200,000 value is the net present value (NPV) of the development project, exclusive of land cost, if the development were undertaken today. Note that, as this NPV is positive, it would make sense to undertake the development today *if this was our last opportunity to do so* (i.e., if the development option expired after today).

Now suppose that the development option does not expire today, but rather will exist another year at least. Further suppose that it is reasonable to expect that, given trends in the real estate market, if we waited a year, a more favorable development circumstance would present itself. Suppose we expect that a similar apartment building built a year from now instead of today would be worth, say, 10% more, or $1,100,000.[15] Suppose it is also reasonable to expect that construction and development costs will also have risen, but not as much, say 5%. So projected construction costs if we delay one year are $840,000, instead of the $800,000 if we build today.

Now consider the expected NPV of the development project as of the time of development under these two mutually exclusive alternatives: building today or waiting and building in one year. The NPV in the first case is the $200,000 that we noted earlier. The NPV in the second case would be $260,000, calculated as the difference between the $1,100,000 expected property value and its $840,000 expected construction cost.

But this second NPV is as of a time one year in the future. Furthermore, it is an *expected* NPV, based on our expectations as of today about the situation one year in the future. As there is some uncertainty about what the future will bring, this future NPV is risky, much more risky than the first NPV associated with building the project today. To compare these two alternatives we therefore need to account for the time and risk differences between the two NPVs. This is traditionally done by applying a risk-adjusted discount rate to the second NPV in order to discount it back to a present certainty-equivalent value comparable to the first NPV. The appropriate discount

[14] In a competitive land market, the price of the land would presumably be bid up to $200,000, as ownership of the land gives the right to undertake the development project.

[15] In this example we are ignoring the time that it takes to complete construction, assuming, in effect, that development is instantaneous. This simplifies the illustration without changing the essential point.

Exhibit 28-1 Example of Option Premium in Land Value and Value of Waiting to Build

	Today (Known)	Next Year (Expected)
	(Values in Thousands)	
Valuation of built property	$1000	$1100
Construction and development cost (excludes land)	800	840
NPV (immediate construction)	$ 200	$ 260

NPV today of construction next year, @ 20% discount rate: 260/1.2 = $217

- Land is worth $217;
- Current HBU = Hold undeveloped;
- Option Premium = 217 − 200 = 17.

$17 = Value of option to choose optimal timing of development

rate to use is the expected total return to the speculative land investment. As such land investment is considered to be quite risky, investors would probably require a rather high expected return, say, 20% per annum. This gives us a present value of $217,000 for the second NPV, calculated as $260,000/1.20.

Thus, on a present certainty-equivalent basis, the NPV of the first alternative (to build today) is $200,000, while the NPV of the second alternative (to wait and build one year from today) is $217,000. As these two values are now directly comparable, and mutually exclusive, the value-maximizing decision is clearly to wait and develop next year. As the landowner has the right to make this decision, this implies that the land value today must be $217,000, not the $200,000 current exercise value.[16] The difference, $17,000, is the option premium, which clearly derives from the option value of the land, the flexibility provided by land ownership to the owner to develop the land at whatever time he chooses.

Note that if the land is worth $217,000, then the NPV of the best current development project, *including the opportunity cost of the land*, is negative (equal to −$17,000, which is the $1,000,000 current newly built property value less the $800,000 construction and development cost, less the $217,000 land value). Thus, based on the NPV criterion including the opportunity cost of the land, development would not currently be optimal, and the highest and best use (HBU) of the land would at this point be to hold the land vacant. Notice that this result is due completely to the option premium of $17,000 in the land value. Our analysis shows the source of the value of the land and reveals how much of this is due to the option premium.

In the previous example uncertainty in the future was not explicitly considered, although it was the reason we used the high (20%) discount rate to obtain the certainty-equivalent NPV of the wait-to-build alternative. If there had been no uncertainty at all, that is, if the future expected values for next year in Exhibit 28-1 were certain, then we would have used a lower discount rate, and we would still have gotten the same result that we should wait to build. In such a case, what we

---

[16] In a competitive land market the price of the land would presumably be bid up to $217,000, as any landowner would have the right to postpone development one year.

have been calling the option premium would be even larger, and it would purely reflect the growth trends in the value of the developed property and in construction costs. To the extent that the option premium derives from the growth trend rather than from uncertainty, the option premium is sometimes referred to as a **growth premium**, as we described in section 5.1 of Chapter 5. But it is important to realize that the option premium, and the result that it is optimal to wait to build, can result purely from *uncertainty* in the future value, even without a growth trend.

To see this, consider the example shown in Exhibit 28-2. The situation at the present time is as before: a building worth $1 million can be developed on the land at a construction cost of $800,000, for an immediate exercise value of $200,000. If we wait until next year, there is considerable uncertainty. The building might then be worth only $600,000 (due, perhaps, to the likelihood of excessive overbuilding in the market). There is a 60% chance that this will indeed be the case. On the other hand, there is a 40% chance that by next year the building will be worth $1,600,000 (due, perhaps, to the possibility that a major shopping mall or sports franchise will decide to locate nearby, and/or the entire region will be declared a "historical zone" in which future development after next year is prohibited, for example). The possible future contingencies and their probabilities are shown in a simple binomial branch diagram in Exhibit 28-3. With this future scenario the *expected value* (as of today) of the developed property next year is *the same as it is today*: $1,000,000 (calculated as 60% × $600,000 + 40% × 1,600,000, or $360,000 + $640,000 = $1,000,000). Thus, in this example there is no positive trend or expected growth in the underlying built property market. Furthermore, there is certain inflation in the construction costs, from $800,000 today to $900,000 next year.

Now we can see how the flexibility allowed by the lack of obligatory exercise of the development option enables the landowner to take advantage of the future possibilities. The landowner can simply choose not to develop if the downside $600,000 value outcome occurs next year. (The NPV of development at that point would be −$300,000 = $600,000 − $900,000, while the NPV of doing nothing would be zero.) Yet the possibility of developing under the upside $1,600,000 contingency gives an expected value for the development option next year equal to $280,000, even though there is only a 40% chance that the favorable scenario will occur, and construction costs

Exhibit 28-2 Numerical Example of Option Premium Value Due to Future Uncertainty in Built Property Value

	Today	Next Year	
Probability	100%	60%	40%
Value of developed property	$1,000	$600	$1,600
Development cost (excluding land)	$800	$900	$900
NPV of exercise	$200	−$300	$700
Future values (actions)		0	$700
		(Don't build)	(Build)
Expected values (Probability × outcome)	$200 (1.0 × 200)	$280 (0.6 × 0 + 0.4 × 700)	
PV (today) of alternatives @ 20% discount rate	$200	$233	

Land value today = MAX(200, 233) = $233

Exhibit 28-3 Branch Diagram of Future Scenarios' Values and Probabilities

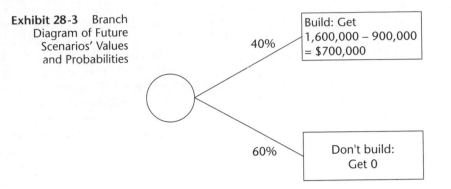

40% → Build: Get 1,600,000 − 900,000 = $700,000

60% → Don't build: Get 0

are projected to increase to $900,000 ($280,000 = [0.4][$1,600,000 − $900,000] + [0.6][0].) Even with the 20% discount rate, this results in the wait-to-build alternative having a present value today of $233,000 (as $280,000/1.20 = $233,000).[17]

This $233,000 land value includes an option premium of $33,000 and suggests that the optimal decision is not to build today, but rather to wait and hold the development option open, even though this implies a 60% chance that the option will expire unexercised (in this simple two-period world). In this example, the $33,000 option premium is not due to expected growth in the built property values but rather is due purely to the uncertainty in future property values, and the irreversibility of the construction decision, that is, the loss of the development option once it is exercised. This is therefore an example of the **irreversibility premium** described in section 5.2 of Chapter 5.

To conclude this demonstration, we should note that the scenario considered here was greatly simplified from typical reality. The procedure used here is essentially what is known as **decision tree analysis**, which is sufficient to handle simple discrete characterizations of the number and timing of the decision alternatives faced by the landholder. More complete representations of the property valuation possibilities in continuous time requires much more technical mathematical procedures.[18] However, there is one complete option valuation formula that is relatively easy to understand and apply, and that is quite relevant to at least the simple land valuation problem. This formula, originally developed by Paul Samuelson and Henry McKean, will be presented in the next section.

*28.4 SAMUELSON-MCKEAN FORMULA APPLIED TO LAND VALUE AS A DEVELOPMENT OPTION

The quantitative application of OVT is in general a very technical subject, often requiring specialized mathematical and programming knowledge. However, some simplified approaches exist for quantifying some basic problems. One of the simplest

---

[17]Once again, a competitive land market would bid up the price of the land today to $233,000, as this value would provide the market's required expected return of 20%.

[18]One approach that is widely taught in corporate finance is to extend the tree structure shown in Exhibit 28-3. Each possible contingency in each succeeding period of time can be represented as a valuation node relating to possible future valuation nodes in the succeeding period. Under certain assumptions about how the value of the underlying asset and exercise price evolve over time, this can result in a simple and intuitive option valuation framework. However, this "binomial model" requires a finite expiration date for the option and is therefore less relevant for land valuation.

option valuation formulas relevant for real estate is also one of the first such formulas to be developed in the economics literature. This formula, developed by the Nobel Prize–winning economist Paul Samuelson and his mathematician partner Henry McKean, was first published in 1965 as a formula for pricing "perpetual American warrants" (that is, a perpetual call option that can be exercised at any time on a dividend-paying underlying asset). This **Samuelson-McKean formula** turned out to be very similar to real option models subsequently developed for capital budgeting decisions by Robert McDonald and Daniel Seigel, and for urban land valuation by Joseph Williams, Dennis Capozza, and others.[19]

Although it should be treated as a simplification of the complete land valuation and optimal development problem, the Samuelson-McKean formula can nevertheless be of practical value in quantifying vacant land value, shedding light on expected returns to land investment, and providing some insight into the optimal timing of development. Furthermore, unlike much quantitative option methodology, the Samuelson-McKean formula can be understood easily without specialized mathematical knowledge, and can be applied easily with no more sophisticated tools than a personal computer spreadsheet. In spite of this simplicity, it is a conceptually consistent valuation and optimal development model, allowing for continuous time and an infinite time horizon. For these reasons, we present the Samuelson-McKean formula in this section.[20]

The Samuelson-McKean formula requires as inputs three parameter values, which describe the underlying real estate and capital markets: the riskfree interest rate, the built property current cash yield rate, and the volatility in the built property value. Let r_f be the riskfree interest rate, and y be the built property's current cash yield rate (i.e., the net operating rent as a fraction of the property value, in effect, the cap rate of the property).[21] The riskfree rate can be measured by the yield to Treasury Bills, and so is typically 4% to 6% per annum, while property yields are typically in the 7% to 10% range for commercial properties in the United States (as described in Chapter 11). Let S be the volatility in the built property market value, measured by the standard deviation of individual property total returns across time. The relevant volatility here is that of properties that are already developed and in operation, not vacant land parcels, and it is the volatility of an *individual* property as distinct from that of a diversified portfolio of properties.[22] Typical values for this volatility measure would be 10% to 25% per year, for commercial properties in the United States. Given values for these three parameters, we can define the **option elasticity** measure, η, by the following formula:[23]

$$\eta = \{y - r_f + S^2/2 + [(r_f - y - S^2/2)^2 + 2r_f S^2]^{1/2}\}/S^2 \tag{1a}$$

[19]Some of the urban economic applications extended (and thereby complicated) the basic model in order to consider optimal density, as well as optimal timing, of the real estate development.

[20]In some sense, the Samuelson-McKean formula is for real estate what the Black-Scholes formula is for corporate finance, a simplistic but useful tool.

[21]The cap rate in this usage should be defined net of a reserve for capital expenditures, so as to reflect a long-run "stabilized" yield rate for the built property.

[22]Thus, this volatility includes idiosyncratic risk components that would diversify out of a large portfolio.

[23]The measure η is referred to as the option elasticity, because when the option is alive (not yet exercised, e.g., the land not yet developed), η gives the percentage change in value of the option (e.g., the raw land) associated with a 1% change in the value of the underlying asset (e.g., built property).

For example, if $r_f = 5\%$, $y = 9.75\%$, and $S = 20\%$, then $\eta = 4.00$.

Apart from the option elasticity, the other values that enter into the value of a given land parcel are the built value and construction cost of the best project that could be built on the site. Define V to be the value of the newly developed property. Label as K the construction and development cost (including developer fees for service but excluding land cost). Then, under the assumptions of the Samuelson-McKean formula, the vacant land value, here labeled *LAND*, is given by[24]

$$LAND = (V^* - K)\left(\frac{V}{V^*}\right)^{\eta} \tag{1b}$$

In this formula V^* is the **hurdle value** (sometimes referred to as the **critical value**) of the developed property below which the land should be held undeveloped for the time being and above which it is optimal to develop the land immediately. In other words, V^* is the value of the completed project that signals that immediate development of the land is now optimal. This hurdle value is a simple function of the development cost and the option elasticity defined earlier:

$$V^* = K\eta/(\eta - 1) \tag{1c}$$

Thus, $\eta/(\eta - 1)$ is the **hurdle benefit/cost ratio**, that is, the ratio of built property value divided by construction cost exclusive of land cost, which triggers immediate optimal development. This hurdle ratio is purely a function of the option elasticity, which in turn is a function of the three parameters characterizing the relevant asset markets: the riskfree interest rate, the built property current cash yield, and the volatility of the built property asset value. Thus, in the Samuelson-McKean formula the hurdle benefit/cost ratio is independent of the scale of the project (i.e., the size of the land parcel).

While the Samuelson-McKean formula may seem a bit daunting at first, it should be clear that anyone with basic spreadsheet skills could easily copy this formula into the cells of a spreadsheet and thereby harness the power of a very sophisticated economic theory to obtain some useful insights not only about the value of a given land parcel but also about the optimal timing of its development.[25] In particular, we see that the Samuelson-McKean formula not only gives the value of the land, but also characterizes the construction benefit/cost ratio (exclusive of land cost) that is necessary for

---

[24] Here we are ignoring considerations of time to build, the time required for the construction project to be completed. In effect, all three values in formula (1b) are valued as of the same point in time. Treatment of construction project duration will be considered in Chapter 29.

[25] The major technical assumptions used in the technical derivation of the Samuelson-McKean formula are the following: (1) underlying asset values (in this case built property values) follow a random walk (with drift) in continuous time; (2) instantaneous returns to underlying assets are normally distributed; (3) the parameters in the model (riskfree rate, volatility and current yield of the underlying asset, and exercise price) are all known and constant; and (4) it is possible to construct riskless arbitrages between the underlying asset, the riskfree asset, and the call option (in this case, land). Obviously, these assumptions are violated in the real world, not only in the case of real estate but also in other applications of real options theory. Some, but not all, of the unrealistic assumptions can be relaxed with more sophisticated models. In any case, the Samuelson-McKean formula seems to work pretty well in the sense that it gives results that are plausible and seem to agree broadly with typical empirical reality.

immediate development to be optimal (formula [1c]). This in itself is useful and interesting information.

Similarly, the option elasticity measure η, as given in (1a), is not only useful as a stepping-stone to derive the development hurdle ratio and land value, but also contains useful information in its own right. This elasticity is the percentage change in vacant land value associated with a 1% change in the values of built properties in the underlying real estate market. In principle, the risk premium in the expected return required by investors holding speculative land should be proportional to this elasticity, according to the following formula:

$$RP_{LAND} = \eta RP_P \tag{2}$$

where RP_{LAND} is the risk premium (i.e., return over and above the riskfree interest rate) in the vacant land holding, and RP_P is the risk premium for built properties in the underlying real estate asset market.[26] For example, if the risk premium for unlevered investment in built property is 350 basis points, and the option elasticity in the vacant land value is $\eta = 4$, then the risk premium in the vacant land expected return would be 14% ($4 \times 3.5\%$). If the riskfree interest rate were 5%, then the total expected return requirement for investors would be 8.5% for built property and 19% for vacant land.[27]

The relationship among built property volatility and current cash yield, land value, and the hurdle benefit/cost ratio, as implied by the Samuelson-McKean formula, are displayed graphically in Exhibits 28-4 and 28-5. In these exhibits the construction and development cost (K) is assumed to equal unity, so the land values and built property values on the vertical and horizontal axes respectively should be considered to be measured *per dollar of construction cost* (i.e., per dollar of K). Thus, the values on the horizontal axis may be interpreted as development project benefit/cost ratio values (where costs are exclusive of land value).

Exhibit 28-4 shows the Samuelson-McKean formula for values that were typical of the commercial property market in the late 1990s: $S = 15\%$, $y = 8\%$, and $r_f = 5\%$ (all rates per annum). The straight diagonal line represents the NPV (exclusive of land cost) of immediate development of the land (i.e., the exercise value of the development option).[28] The curved line is the land value based on the Samuelson-McKean formula, as a function of the built property value. The point at which these two lines meet is the point at which immediate development is optimal, when the built property would

---

[26] The fundamental reason for this result is that options are, formally, derivative assets based on their underlying assets. Thus, the return to the land is in principle perfectly correlated with the return to the built property market, only with a volatility equal to η times the built property volatility. Thus, regardless of the "risk benchmark" on which the capital market bases its pricing of the risk in the built property (i.e., regardless of the basis for the built property's expected return risk premium, such as beta for example, as discussed in Chapter 22), the land will have η times that much risk.

[27] Recall that in our discussion of the opportunity cost of capital for real estate in Chapter 11 we suggested that typical return requirements for vacant land were in the range of 15% to 30% per annum, as of the late 1990s.

[28] Negative values of the immediate development NPV exclusive of land value are not shown, but can be inferred as the straight, diagonal line extension below the horizontal axis. Built property values of less than $1 per dollar of construction cost naturally result in negative NPV of immediate development even without considering the opportunity cost of the land. On the other hand, the land itself would never be worth less than zero, as the landowner is not obligated to exercise his option.

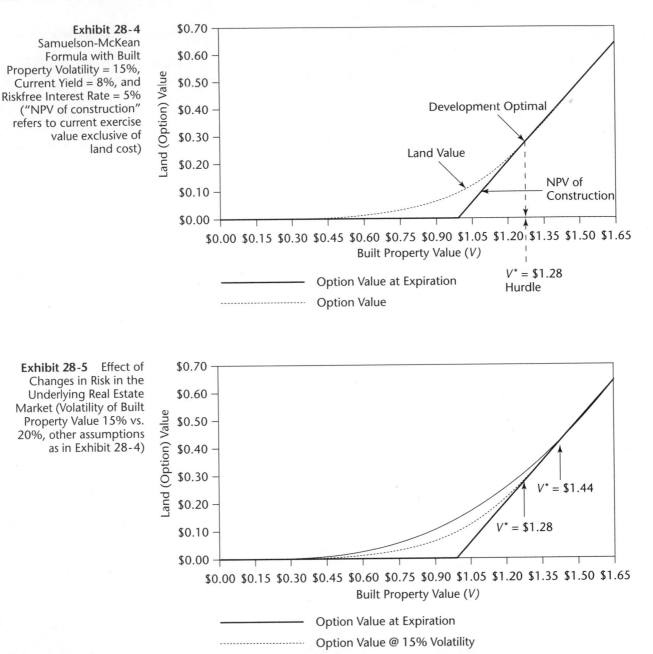

Exhibit 28-4 Samuelson-McKean Formula with Built Property Volatility = 15%, Current Yield = 8%, and Riskfree Interest Rate = 5% ("NPV of construction" refers to current exercise value exclusive of land cost)

Exhibit 28-5 Effect of Changes in Risk in the Underlying Real Estate Market (Volatility of Built Property Value 15% vs. 20%, other assumptions as in Exhibit 28-4)

have value V^*. This is the first point (i.e., lowest value of V) at which the development project would have a nonnegative NPV when the opportunity cost of the land (including its option premium value) is included in the NPV calculus.

As an example of how we would apply the Samuelson-McKean formula, let's return to the numerical example in section 28.3. There we had a land parcel that could be developed today to obtain an apartment building worth $1 million, with a construction and development cost exclusive of land totaling $800,000. Let's further suppose that the apartment and capital market environment is well described by the parameters underlying Exhibit 28-4, that is, a riskfree interest rate of 5%, a current net cash yield on the built property of 8%, and volatility in the built property value of 15% per year.[29] With the current built property value at $1,000,000 and construction cost at $800,000, we see that the current benefit cost ratio is 1,000,000/800,000, or 1.25. Looking at the $1.25 point on the horizontal axis in Exhibit 28-4, or plugging the previous numbers into the Samuelson-McKean formula (1b), we get an implied land value of $0.2509 per dollar of construction cost, or $200,738.[30] This includes $738 of option premium value in excess of the $200,000 valuation under the immediate development assumption. This implies that immediate development of the apartment building would have a negative NPV of $738, including consideration of the opportunity cost of the land. (This is found as the $1,000,000 benefit value of the completed built property, minus the $800,000 construction cost, minus the $200,738 value of the land.)

In this example the hurdle value of the built property at and above which it is optimal to develop the land immediately is $1,020,557, equal to the hurdle benefit/cost ratio of 1.2757 times the $800,000 construction cost.[31] Not unless and until we could sell the completed developed property for at least $1,020,557 should we develop the land.[32]

For built property values in excess of the V^* threshold, if the land has still not been developed, then there is no more option premium and the value of the land simply equals the NPV of immediate development exclusive of land cost. However, under the assumptions of the Samuelson-McKean model, allowing the potential built property value to rise above the V^* without developing the property is suboptimal, and the land should be developed immediately.

---

[29] Note that there are implications here about the dynamics of the market for the apartment building. Suppose the expected total return on the built property is 10% per year. Then the 8% current yield implies expected growth of 2%, so the expected value of the property one year from now would be $1,020,000. On the other hand, if the expected return on apartment buildings is only 8.5%, then the expected growth is only 0.5%. Recall the basic relationship among periodic return components from Chapter 9: $r = y + g$.

[30] Applying formula (1a) we obtain the following value for the option elasticity:

$$\eta = \{8\% - 5\% + (15\%)^2/2 + [(5\% - 8\% - (15\%)^2/2)^2 + 2(5\%)(15\%)^2]^{1/2}\}/(15\%)^2 = 4.63$$

Applying this elasticity value in formula (1c) we obtain a hurdle value of

$$V^* = \$800,000[4.63/(4.63 - 1)] = \$1,020,557$$

Applying this hurdle value in formula (1b) we obtain a land value of

$$LAND = (\$1,020,557 - \$800,000)(\$1,000,000/\$1,020,557)^{4.63}$$
$$= \$200,738$$

when the current value of the built property is $1,000,000 ($V$).

[31] $\$1,020,557/\$800,000 = 1.2757$

[32] The option elasticity value of 4.63 has implications for the market's required return (opportunity cost of capital) for holding the land undeveloped. If fully operational apartment properties are commanding a 10% expected total return, then the 5% riskfree interest rate implies that apartments (with 15% volatility) require a 5% risk premium. This would imply that the land requires a $4.63 \times 5\% \approx 23\%$ risk premium, or $5\% + 23\% = 28\%$ expected return. If, on the other hand for example, apartment properties are only commanding an 8.5% expected return, then this implies a 3.5% risk premium in the underlying asset, hence a $4.63 \times 3.5\% \approx 16\%$ risk premium, or $5\% + 16\% = 21\%$ expected return required for the speculative land investment.

Exhibit 28-5 shows how land value and the hurdle built property value V^* both increase with the volatility in built property values. This reveals how greater risk in the underlying real estate market results in greater land value (other things being equal), but more tendency to delay development, as projects must pass a higher benefit/cost hurdle to make immediate development optimal.[33] This is what underlies the urban form result noted in Chapter 5 that cities with more volatile economic bases will tend to have smaller, denser spatial configurations. (See section 5.2 in Chapter 5.)

28.5 CHAPTER SUMMARY

This chapter introduced you to option value theory, to the concept of real options, and to the call option model of land value and optimal development. We also presented a simple option valuation formula, the Samuelson-McKean formula, which is useful for analyzing and gaining insight regarding land value, development timing, and the opportunity cost of capital for speculative land investments. The perspective and tools presented here are useful for dealing with one of the most fundamental and important issues in all of real estate, whether viewed from an urban economics/space market perspective or a financial economics/asset market perspective. Land valuation and development lies at the nexus of these perspectives, at a central point in the real estate system we described way back in Chapter 2. The next chapter will extend our treatment of this important topic, taking it to a more practical level.

KEY TERMS

option valuation theory (OVT)
real options
option
exercise of options
underlying asset
exercise price
American option
European option
call option

contingent claim
option premium
call option model of land value
perpetual option
time to build
overbuilding
leasing option
cascades (of development)
development timing

growth premium
irreversibility premium
decision tree analysis
Samuelson-McKean formula
option elasticity
hurdle value (critical value)
hurdle benefit/cost ratio

[33] Of course, increasing built property risk could also reduce the value of built properties, and this effect would reduce the value of land.

STUDY QUESTIONS

28.1. Define what is meant in financial economics by the concept of a call option.

28.2. What is the option premium? Describe the two sources of the positive value of this premium.

28.3. What is the general relationship between option value and the maturity or time left until expiration of the option?

28.4. Describe the call option model of land value. What is the underlying asset in this model? What is the exercise price? What is the typical maturity of the land development option?

28.5. What do people mean when they say that option theory is an exception to the NPV rule? Do you agree that this is truly a valid exception to the NPV rule? Illustrate your answer with a simple example from real estate.

28.6. On a certain parcel of land you could build a project worth $2 million today, for a construction cost of $1.8 million. If you wait and do not build the project until next year, the project would most likely then be worth $2.2 million, and the construction cost would be $1.9 million. If investors require a 25% expected return for holding land, what is the value of the land today? Should you build the project today or wait until next year?

28.7. In question 28.6, suppose there is a 50% chance that the project next year will be worth $2.6 million, and a 50% chance that it will be worth only $1.8 million, with the construction cost still $1.9 million in both cases. The project today would certainly be worth $2 million and cost $1.8 million, as before. Under these circumstances (and still assuming a 25% required return on land), how much is the land worth today? Explain why the land is worth more in this problem than in the previous problem. Also, explain why it is better not to build the project today even though there is a 50% chance the project will be unprofitable next year.

*28.8. Suppose the riskfree (i.e., government bond) interest rate is 6%, the current cash yield payout rate on newly built property is 9%, and the annual volatility of individual property total returns is 20% for built properties that are leased up and operational. Use the Samuelson-McKean formula to answer the following questions concerning a vacant but developable land parcel.

a. If built property has a 5% risk premium in its expected total return (11% total return), what is the risk premium and expected total return for the land parcel? [Hint: Use the elasticity formula (8.11a) and the risk premium formula (8.11c).]

b. What is the value of the land parcel if a building currently worth $1,000,000 new could be built on the land for a construction cost of $800,000?

c. What is the hurdle benefit/cost ratio above which the land should be developed immediately?

d. What value of newly built property does this suggest is required before the land should be developed?

e. Under these conditions should the land be developed immediately or is it better to wait?

*28.9. Suppose the riskfree (i.e., government bond) interest rate is 5%, the current cash yield payout rate on newly built property is 7.5%, and the annual volatility of individual property total returns is 25% for built properties that are leased up and operational. Use the Samuelson-McKean formula to answer the following questions concerning a vacant but developable land parcel.

a. If built property has a 4% risk premium in its expected total return (9% total return), what is the risk premium and expected total return for the land parcel? [Hint: use the elasticity formula 8.11a and the risk premium formula (8.11c).]

b. What is the value of the land parcel if a building currently worth $2,500,000 new could be built on the land for a construction cost of $2,200,000?

c. What is the hurdle benefit/cost ratio above which the land should be developed immediately?

d. What value of newly built property does this suggest is required before the land should be developed?

e. Under these conditions should the land be developed immediately or is it better to wait?

29 Financial Analysis of Real Estate Development Projects

Chapter Outline

Learning Objectives

After reading this chapter, you should understand:

◆ The typical real estate development project decision process, at a broad-brush level

◆ The role of financial analysis in development project decision making, and the mortgage-based simplified techniques that are widely employed in this role in current practice, including their strengths and weaknesses

◆ The more rigorously correct NPV-based approach to financial evaluation of development projects

◆ The basics of construction loan mechanics.

We cannot overemphasize the importance of real estate development. The construction and major rehabilitation of commercial buildings not only is often a make-or-break activity for individual real estate entrepreneurs and firms, but it also has tremendous social and public consequences in the shaping of the future urban environment. Financial analysis is a crucial component of the process of real estate development decision making. Projects that pass the financial screen get funding and get built. Projects that don't pass remain pipe dreams.

In the previous chapter we noted that the financial analysis of real estate development projects is an exercise in capital budgeting, a term borrowed from the corporate finance literature. Capital budgeting is the field from which the NPV rule arose. It is a microlevel investment decision arena whose basic concepts and principles were treated in Part IV of this book, particularly in Chapters 10 and 12. On top of that,

Chapter 28 presented some important fundamental economic principles that relate particularly to real estate development project evaluation and decision making.

What remains for us to do in the present chapter is to extend our treatment of this topic to a more practical level. In particular, we will take a look at how development project financial feasibility is typically quantified in the real world, and we will examine the nuts and bolts of the application of the NPV investment decision procedure to the typical commercial property development project. Our practical examination of this topic will also include a brief introduction to the mechanics of construction loans.[1] Throughout this chapter, our perspective will be primarily that of the private sector real estate developer.

29.1 OVERVIEW OF THE DEVELOPMENT DECISION-MAKING PROCESS

From an economic perspective, development projects are crucial points in space and time where financial capital becomes fixed as physical capital. More broadly, they are where ideas become reality. In the preface of this book we pointed out that real estate is a multidisciplinary field. In no aspect of real estate is this more apparent and important than in the development process. In fact, development decision making can be represented as a process that moves iteratively from one disciplinary perspective to another.

Such a model of development was perhaps first articulated by James Graaskamp, a famous real estate professor and the director of the Real Estate Center at the University of Wisconsin from 1964 until his death in 1988. Graaskamp suggested that development decision making in the private sector could typically be described by one of two situations: a *site looking for a use, or a use looking for a site*. In the former case, the site is already under the control of the developer, and the analyst undertakes what is, in effect, a highest and best use (HBU) study. It is not uncommon for developers to "inventory" land, that is, to buy and hold land when it is cheaper and not yet ready for development. This results in the **site-looking-for-a-use** type decision making, the type local public sector authorities are often involved in.

On the other hand, in the case of a use looking for a site, the decision maker already knows the type of development it wishes to pursue. The question is where to best pursue such a project: what will be the level of usage demand and competition at any given location? In a large development firm, the early stages of most development studies are of this **use-looking-for-a-site** type, with the developer having a particular expertise in a certain type of product, such as warehouse, office-warehouse, senior-oriented housing, and so on. The use-looking-for-a-site activity is also a crucial part of the business of retail firms, many of which work with real estate development firms specializing in retail development.

The process of development analysis, design, and decision making is highly iterative, as depicted in Exhibit 29-1, which is based on Graaskamp's teaching. A given development concept will cycle through analysis from at least four different disciplinary perspectives: urban economics (the real estate space market), architectural/engineering disciplines (physical analysis), legal/political analysis, and financial

[1] The distinction between construction loans and permanent loans, and the basic method of operation of the construction loan industry, was described in section 16.1 of Chapter 16.

Exhibit 29-1   Iterative, Multidisciplinary Process of Real Estate Development Decision Making (the Graaskamp Model)

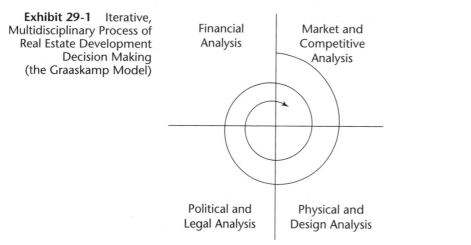

economics (the capital market and real estate asset market), not necessarily in that order (or indeed in any fixed order). Expertise is needed in all of these disciplines and perspectives (and sometimes others as well), and just as important, entrepreneurial creativity is needed to integrate and pull together the various perspectives, to synthesize analysis from various fields into a feasible project. With each iteration, the project design and the decision become more detailed and closer to fruition. This is indicated in the figure by the arrow spiraling toward the center, the point of synthesis and action.[2] While all of the four disciplines and perspectives portrayed in Exhibit 29-1 are important, our focus in this chapter is on the top left quadrant of the picture, the financial analysis of the project.

29.2 BASIC INFORMATION: ENUMERATING PROJECT COSTS AND BENEFITS

In the iterative process depicted in Exhibit 29-1, one of the information products that needs to be refined progressively is a realistic budget for the project. In fact, two types of budget are important in development projects, each focusing on a different time period or phase of the project. The first is called the **construction and absorption budget**. It covers the period from the beginning of construction until the building is fully leased and operational. It relates to the investment *cost* side of the NPV equation and includes the cost of land acquisition (or opportunity cost of land development), site preparation, hard and soft construction and design costs, and lease-up costs including the need for working capital until the building breaks even. The second type of budget is known as the **operating budget**. It covers the period beyond the end of the absorption or lease-up of the new structure. The projected operating budget underlies the *benefit* side of the NPV equation, namely, the value of the newly completed built property. This value, as we know from Part IV of this book, is based on the projected net cash flows the completed building is expected to generate.

---

[2]Hopefully, the diagram in Exhibit 29-1 does not imply a process spiraling out of control!

In analyzing development projects, the operating budget and the resulting estimate of completed project value are often focused on a single so-called **stabilized** year, with valuation based on direct capitalization of that year's NOI rather than on a multiyear DCF analysis. Such a budget is referred to as a *stabilized annual operating budget*, as it applies to a point at which the building's cash flow has become more or less stable, reflecting the building's long-run ongoing operating characteristics.[3] As such, the operating budget is typically characterized by items you became familiar with in Chapter 11:

Potential gross income (PGI)
- Vacancy allowance
= Effective gross income (EGI)
- Operating expenses (and capital reserve)
= Net operating income (NOI)

The development of the operating budget is derived from analysis of the relevant space market, the upper-right quadrant in Exhibit 29-1, based fundamentally on the principles of urban economics and the methods of market analysis.[4]

The other side of the NPV equation, the cost side dealt with in the construction and absorption budget, is a very different animal. It arises from the lower-right-hand quadrant in Exhibit 29-1, based fundamentally on the engineering and architectural disciplines. The major component of the construction and absorption budget typically concerns the construction phase. Costs associated with this phase are traditionally divided into two major categories: **hard costs** and **soft costs**. The former includes the direct cost of the physical components of the construction project: building materials and labor. Soft costs typically include just about everything else in the construction phase, such as design, legal, and financing costs. (The latter includes the interest on the construction loan.) Land acquisition or opportunity cost is sometimes classified as a soft cost, although it is more commonly treated as a hard cost, or as a separate item altogether. Typical hard and soft cost items are shown here:

Hard Costs
- Land cost
- Site preparation costs (e.g., excavation, utilities installation)
- Shell costs of existing structure in rehab projects

[3] Recall from our discussion of direct capitalization versus multiyear DCF valuation in Chapter 10 that the latter is most valuable when there is a need to account for existing ("vintage") long-term leases in the property, leases that may have been signed prior to the current conditions in the rental market, or when there is a lease expiration pattern that is not typical for the type of property in question. Of course, development projects usually do not have vintage leases, and it normally does not make sense to expect that they will have atypical lease expiration patterns. Thus, it is usually a reasonable shortcut in analyzing development projects to use the simpler direct-capitalization evaluation procedure for the (projected) completed building, rather than a full-blown multiyear DCF procedure.

[4] A detailed exposition of this quadrant is beyond the scope of this book, although a basic introduction to space market analysis was provided in Chapter 6.

- Permits
- Contractor fees
- Construction management and overhead costs
- Materials
- Labor
- Equipment rental
- Tenant finish
- Developer fees

Soft Costs
- Loan fees
- Construction interest
- Legal fees
- Soil testing
- Environmental studies
- Land planner fees
- Architectural fees
- Engineering fees
- Marketing costs including advertisements
- Leasing or sales commissions

In addition to the construction phase, many development projects will also require the developer to budget for an **absorption** or **lease-up phase**, as indicated by the last items in the previous list. An absorption budget will be necessary when the project is being built at least partially "**on spec**" (short for "on speculation"); in other words, at least some of the space in the project is not preleased at the time the development decision is being made. The developer must line up in advance the financial resources necessary to carry the project through to the break-even point. In addition to working capital necessary to operate a less-than-full building, the absorption phase budget often requires particular expenditures for marketing the new building. The absorption phase may include major expenditures on leasing commissions and tenant improvements or **build-outs**.[5]

From a property-level cash flow perspective, the absorption phase may be considered to be over when the new building begins to break even on a current cash flow basis. However, from a financial perspective, the absorption phase continues until the building is stabilized (as this term was defined earlier, that is, until the building is at or near its expected long-term occupancy level). Not until the stabilization point is reached does the investment risk in the asset fall to that of a fully operational ongoing property, and only then is the permanent lender typically willing to provide a traditional long-term commercial mortgage.

---

[5] Build-outs (or tenant finish) are tenant improvements on unfinished space, for example, to finish and customize space for a specific long-term tenant.

29.3 CONSTRUCTION BUDGET MECHANICS

A key feature of development projects is the fact that construction takes place over a period of time, typically several months to over a year depending on the scale and complexity of the project. Both in theory and in practice, the effect of the temporal spread of construction costs is often dealt with through the device of a **construction loan**, which enables the developer to avoid most cash outflows until the project is completed, at which time the construction loan must be paid back including interest that has accrued on the funds drawn down during the construction project. We will review the basic mechanics of construction loans in this section.[6]

When a construction loan is initially signed, it normally provides for a specified maximum amount of cash for the developer, in the form of **future advances**, based on the projected construction budget and schedule. Funds are **drawn down** out of this commitment as they are needed to pay for construction put in place. The lender verifies the physical construction before disbursing each **draw**. The developer/borrower typically pays no cash back to the bank until the project is completed. At that point the developer may take out a **permanent loan** secured by the built property and use the proceeds from this loan to pay back the construction lender. Of course, this is not the only way to pay off the construction loan, as the developer may invest his own equity at that point, or may obtain long-term equity partners, or may sell the property.

During the construction period the developer will draw down the construction loan based on a schedule agreed to at the outset. For smaller projects, invoices and receipts from subcontractors along with affidavits that all prior work has been completed and paid for will usually suffice for the lender, along with some site inspections, to be sure that the work and materials specified in the budget have actually been used. For large projects, cash might be drawn down from the loan commitment based on a completion schedule of construction phases, such as site preparation, foundation work, framing, and so on, with each component resulting in the draw for a certain percentage of the total loan. Even though the construction budget normally includes contingency amounts for unexpected costs, lenders often hold back a reserve in the range of 10% of the total construction budget. This reserve will only be paid out when the project is completed, as evidenced by a **certification of occupancy** from the local building inspection authority.

At the time the construction loan is being negotiated, the lender will often require an engineering review of the proposed construction budget. At that time the construction lender will also typically consider the projected lease-up phase and review the projected stabilized operating budget of the completed building from the perspective of permanent loan underwriting criteria, as described in Chapter 18. The construction lender needs to feel confident that the completed project will support a permanent loan sufficient to pay off the construction loan.[7] A permanent loan that is used to pay off a construction loan is often referred to as a **take-out loan**. Indeed, the

---

[6] See section 16.1 in Chapter 16 for a an overview of the commercial mortgage industry and the role of construction loans in that industry.

[7] Note that, as the permanent loan will typically not be made for more than a 75% LTV ratio, this implies that the construction costs must generally be less than the total value of the completed project. The difference represents the developer's equity in the project, which often equates more or less to the cost of the land.

classical method of construction lending is for the institution making the construction loan to require that the developer obtain a commitment in advance by a permanent lender, sufficient to cover the projected construction loan balance due. The permanent lender considers the projected loan/value (LTV) ratio and debt service coverage ratio (DCR) forecasted for the completed project before committing to the permanent loan.[8] The permanent loan commitment is often contingent on the building achieving a certain occupancy or rent level by a certain time.[9]

In order to develop the construction budget and estimate the amount of cash the developer will have to come up with at the time of project completion (or the amount he must borrow in the take-out loan), a key calculation is the **accrued interest** that will be due when the construction loan is paid off. For example, for a construction loan with an 8% interest rate (per annum, monthly compounding), the accrual of interest in the loan balance is illustrated in the following table for the first three months of a construction project, in which a total of $2,750,000 of direct construction cost has been expended and financed by the loan. Note that the loan balance exceeds this direct cost amount ($2,780,100 is greater than $2,750,000). This is the effect of the time value of money (including a risk premium for the construction lender), as accrued interest is compounded forward across time.[10]

Month	New Draw	Current Interest	New Loan Balance
1	$ 500,000	$ 3,333.33	$ 503,333.33
2	$ 750,000	$ 8,355.55	$1,261,688.88
3	$1,500,000	$18,411.26	$2,780,100.14
4	and so on		

In the example in the table, the interest at the end of the first month is computed as $3,333.33 = $500,000(0.08/12). This accrued interest then becomes part of the loan balance on which further interest will accrue. The interest computation in the second month is thus $8,355.55 = ($503,333.33 + $750,000)(0.08/12). The balance at the end of the second month is computed as $1,261,688.88 = $503,333.33 + $750,000 + $8,355.55. This type of accrual and compounding of interest continues until the construction project is complete. The total balance due on the loan then includes both the direct construction costs and the **financing cost**, or cost of construction capital, namely, the interest on the funds borrowed for construction. In the typical construction budget this interest cost is listed as a separate item.

---

[8] See Chapter 18, section 18.2.1, for an explanation of these and other commercial mortgage underwriting criteria.

[9] Sometimes the lease-up phase is covered in the construction loan (a "mini-perm" loan), and sometimes it is covered in a separate "bridge loan."

[10] In the example in the table it is assumed that the draws are made at the *beginning* of each month, and the loan balance refers to the balance at the *end* of the month. This is the most common approach for budgeting, although end-of-month draws or beginning-of-month balances are sometimes used. For budgeting purposes it does not matter which assumption is made, as long as the requisite interest is accrued as soon as funds are disbursed from the bank. (This is an application of the "four rules" of loan payment and balance computation described in section 17.1.1 of Chapter 17.)

29.4 SIMPLE FINANCIAL FEASIBILITY ANALYSIS IN CURRENT PRACTICE

With the preceding information as background, let's turn to the typical current practice of financial analysis of development projects, focusing on the financial feasibility of the project. This is best done by considering some concrete examples. For this purpose we can call on Bob, (you may have guessed), who is a typical real estate developer on Main Street. Bob owns several strategically located, commercially zoned vacant land parcels in Midwest City, and he specializes in building small to medium-size office and retail buildings. Some of his projects can be characterized as a site looking for a use, while others are better described as a use looking for a site. His overall project design and decision-making process can be well described by the iterative approach depicted in Exhibit 29-1. To deal with the financial analysis aspect of this process (the upper-left-hand quadrant in Exhibit 29-1), Bob employs a simple, easy-to-understand methodology. We will call this methodology **simple financial feasibility analysis (SFFA)**, and we will describe it in this section.

29.4.1 Simple Feasibility Analysis Explained

The basic idea in SFFA is, well, *simple*. It is assumed that the developer will "borrow to the hilt," that is, he will take out the maximum permanent loan the completed project will support. (After all, this is what Bob usually does.) With this assumption, Bob does not need to know (or to assume) anything about the capital market except what he can easily observe in the commercial mortgage market. Through his contacts among local mortgage brokers and bankers, Bob can easily keep track of current mortgage interest rates and underwriting criteria such as the maximum allowable LTV ratio and DCR requirements. Combined with the borrow-to-the-hilt assumption, this information is sufficient to ascertain either what sort of rental market is required given a land and construction cost, or what sort of land and/or construction cost can be afforded given a rental market for a completed structure. In other words, Bob can apply SFFA to address the financial feasibility of both the site-looking-for-a-use and the use-looking-for-a-site types of projects.

Take the site looking for a use first. The procedure Bob uses in this case to analyze financial feasibility often starts with a presumed land and construction cost and ends with the required minimum rent per square foot of built structure that will be necessary to make the project financially feasible.[11] The specific steps in this procedure are shown in Exhibit 29-2.

A good example of this procedure in action was a rehab opportunity Bob considered recently. A certain class B office building in a fantastic location had been recently vacated by a major owner/occupant. The building was 30,000 gross square feet with

---

[11] When the developer already controls the site, he typically has a fairly firm idea of how much the land is worth. The land value, combined with legal/political and architectural/engineering considerations, typically then provides a general implication for the usage type and the scale or magnitude of project that probably makes sense. This, in turn, suggests the rough magnitude of construction cost that would make sense. (In principle, the hurdle benefit/cost ratio described in section 28.4 of Chapter 28 is relevant in this regard, suggesting the magnitude of construction that would make immediate development optimal.) In the iterative analysis, design, and decision-making process characteristic of development projects, this cost information then begs to be checked against what the demand in the space market will support.

Exhibit 29-2   SFFA Front-
Door Procedure

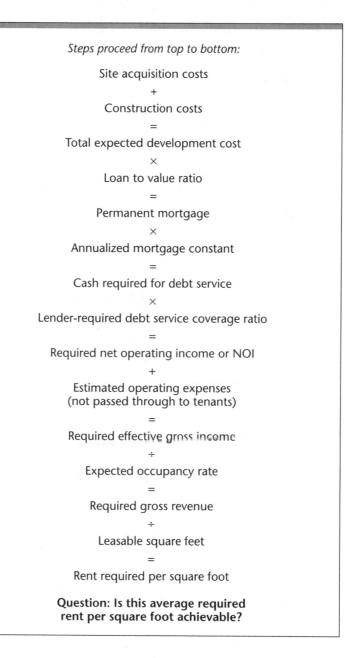

Steps proceed from top to bottom:

Site acquisition costs

+

Construction costs

=

Total expected development cost

×

Loan to value ratio

=

Permanent mortgage

×

Annualized mortgage constant

=

Cash required for debt service

×

Lender-required debt service coverage ratio

=

Required net operating income or NOI

+

Estimated operating expenses
(not passed through to tenants)

=

Required effective gross income

÷

Expected occupancy rate

=

Required gross revenue

÷

Leasable square feet

=

Rent required per square foot

**Question: Is this average required
rent per square foot achievable?**

27,200 square feet of leaseable area. Bob knew that rents for class C+ or B− space in that location were running around $10 per square foot per year with most operating expenses passed through to the tenants.[12] Bob was pretty sure he could buy the building for $660,000 and fix it up for about $400,000 in hard costs and $180,000 in soft costs including funds for a new marketing program, financing during rehab, and operating costs during the lease-up period which he estimated would take only a few months. A local lender indicated that they would provide an 80% LTV mortgage with

---

[12] Note the iterative nature, or circularity, of the development analysis procedure. Even though this is a site looking for a use, Bob already has a rough idea of the use, at least in terms of the typical market rents.

a 120% DCR if Bob personally signed on the note for 20% of the loan balance. The interest rate was 11.5% on a fixed rate 20-year-amortization monthly-payment mortgage. Bob's market research indicated that less than 5% vacancy was typical for well-located newly rehabbed projects. Given the superior location of this building, Bob figured a 95% stabilized occupancy rate was, if anything, conservative. Bob estimated stabilized operating expenses at $113,000 per year based on prior occupant figures. Even though some of this might be passed through to the tenants, Bob decided to assume initially that the landlord would bear all of these expenses, in order to be conservative, and because much of this expense figure was based on an old (but efficient) centralized heating system that made energy costs difficult to prorate to individual tenants. The question Bob wanted to get a quick take on was, What are the required rents for this project and, therefore, does it look feasible?

Applying the procedure in Exhibit 29-2, here is how Bob answered his question:

Site and shell costs:	$ 660,000
+ Rehab costs:	580,000
= Total costs (assumed equal to value):	$1,240,000
× Lender-required LTV	80%
= Permanent mortgage amount:	$ 992,000
× Annualized mortgage constant:[13]	0.127972
= Cash required for debt service:	$ 126,948
× Lender-required DCR:	1.20
= Required NOI:	$ 152,338
+ Estimated operating expenses (landlord):	113,000
= Required EGI:	$ 265,338
÷ Projected occupancy (1-vac):	0.95
= Required PGI:	$ 279,303
÷ Rentable area:	27,200 SF
= Required rent/SF:	$ 10.27/SF

Financial feasibility appears to require a gross rent of a little over $10/SF. As Bob's assumptions in applying the previous procedure were (he believed) a bit on the conservative side, and market rents did indeed appear to be around $10/SF, the project looked feasible to Bob.[14]

---

[13] From Chapters 8 and 17 we have the monthly mortgage constant:

$$(0.115/12)/[1 - 1/(1 + 0.115/12)^{240}] = 0.010664.$$

This figure times twelve is the annual constant: $0.010664 \times 12 = 0.127972$.

[14] Note that to apply this procedure Bob had to assume that the value of the completed project as it would be judged or appraised by the lender would be at least equal to his total projected construction cost of $1,240,000. His familiarity with the local property asset market suggested that typical cap rates for similar buildings once fully rented seemed to be around 10.5%. Applying this to the projected NOI of $152,338 implied a projected property value of $1,451,000, well over the $1,240,000 construction cost, so Bob felt he was safe in this regard.

Exhibit 29-3   SFFA Back-Door Procedure

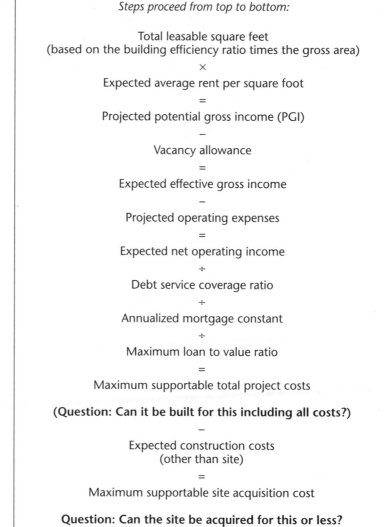

Steps proceed from top to bottom:

Total leasable square feet
(based on the building efficiency ratio times the gross area)

×

Expected average rent per square foot

=

Projected potential gross income (PGI)

−

Vacancy allowance

=

Expected effective gross income

−

Projected operating expenses

=

Expected net operating income

÷

Debt service coverage ratio

÷

Annualized mortgage constant

÷

Maximum loan to value ratio

=

Maximum supportable total project costs

(Question: Can it be built for this including all costs?)

−

Expected construction costs
(other than site)

=

Maximum supportable site acquisition cost

Question: Can the site be acquired for this or less?

The SFFA procedure applied in the previous manner is sometimes referred to as **front-door feasibility analysis**. A **back-door feasibility analysis** would go in the reverse order: starting from expected market rents and ending with the amount that can be afforded for site acquisition. Back-door analyses are more typical of use-looking-for-a-site type projects. The back-door version of the SFFA is presented in Exhibit 29-3.

An example application of the back-door version of SFFA was another recent project Bob considered. In this case the project was a new development, an office building with 35,000 SF of **gross leasable area (GLA)** and an 85% **efficiency ratio**, implying a **net rentable area (NRA)** of 29,750 SF.[15] The idea for this project came

[15] Gross leasable area (GLA) is the total interior space in the structure, including common areas such as lobbies and corridors. Net rentable area (NRA) is the space tenants directly pay for in their leases. Rents are typically quoted in the space market per NRA square foot.

from a former business partner of Bob's who was interested in leasing a major portion of such a building, and who believed that Bob was quite capable of delivering on such a development project in an efficient and effective manner.

Bob believed that, given the proposed design and tenant finishings, the achievable rent in this building would be about $12/SF in any of several suburban neighborhoods where office buildings of this type were in demand in Midwest City. Preliminary design work indicated that the hard and soft costs, excluding site acquisition, would be about $2,140,000. Vacancy rates in the types of space markets relevant for this building were running 8% on average. Based on past experience, Bob estimated that operating expenses not passed through to tenants would be $63,000 per year. For this project the permanent lender wanted a DCR of 120% and an LTV of no more than 75% of finished value, with 9.0% interest and 20-year amortization. Bob found a potential site for the project that looked quite promising. The owner of the site wanted $500,000. Bob needed to decide whether it was worth it. He answered this question according to the steps in Exhibit 29-3, as follows:

Potential gross revenue (29,750 × $12):	$ 357,000
− Vacancy at 8%:	$ 28,560
= Effective Gross Income:	$ 328,440
− Operating expenses not passed on:	$ 63,000
= Net operating income:	$ 265,000
÷ 1.20 (required debt coverage):	$ 221,200
÷ 12 (monthly debt service):	$ 18,433
⇒ Supportable mortgage amount:	$2,048,735
÷ 0.75 LTV (= minimum required value):	$2,731,647
− Construction cost:	$2,140,000
= Supportable site acquisition cost:	$ 591,647

As $591,647 is greater than the $500,000 price the seller was asking for the site, Bob concluded that this project was financially feasible.[16]

29.4.2 Problems with the Simple Approach

The SFFA procedures described earlier are widely used by developers in real world practice. They have the advantage of being simple and easy to understand without much financial economic expertise. In particular, they do not require any knowledge

---

[16] Note the sensitivity of this result to the loan interest rate. If the rate were 50 basis points higher, at 9.5%, the affordable loan would be only $1,977,511, resulting in maximum outlays at the 75% LTV of $2,636,682, and implied maximum feasible site acquisition costs of $496,682, less than the $500,000 price. Also note the assumptions that are imbedded in the back-door procedure. The 75% LTV ratio is applied to the estimated supportable loan to derive the minimum required finished building value from the lender's perspective. Yet the building might in fact be worth either more or less than this amount, depending on the prevailing cap rates in the property asset market. If the building would in fact be worth more than this amount, then Bob could actually afford to pay more than $591,647 for the site. If it would be worth less than the affordable loan divided by 0.75, then Bob could not afford to pay as much as $591,647.

or assumptions about the capital market beyond what can be observed easily in the commercial mortgage market. They are sound enough to have some practical utility as a "back of envelope" tool for preliminary analysis. But it is important to recognize that the SFFA procedures *do not provide a complete or correct financial evaluation of a development project.*

As we have noted before, the decision to undertake a real estate development project is a capital budgeting decision, in effect, a capital allocation decision at the microlevel, like any other microlevel investment decision in the private real estate asset market. The NPV decision rule that we introduced in Part IV of this book tells whether such decisions are in the interest of those investing their capital. To the extent that the developer is not just a fee-for-service provider, but is in fact a real estate investor as well (which is usually the case), the developer shares this capital budgeting perspective, and should consider **financial feasibility** from a broader and deeper perspective, that of **financial desirability**. The developer/investor is generally a landowner, either prior to the development or as a result of the development project. As such, the developer/investor wants to know whether it is *optimal* to proceed with the project, in the sense of the question: *Does undertaking the proposed development project now maximize the wealth of the landowner/developer?*

From this perspective it is easy to see why the developer usually is (or should be) governed by the NPV investment decision rule. Recall from Chapter 10 that this rule requires that undertaking the project must not involve a negative-NPV investment, and must maximize the ex ante NPV over all mutually exclusive feasible alternatives. The basis of the NPV rule in the wealth maximization principle implies that *if the NPV rule is being violated, then money is being left on the table,* that is, the developer is reducing her net worth (or shareholder value) as a result of undertaking the project, *compared to what she could have done instead.*

The SFFA procedures fail to account for the NPV rule because they do not quantify the value of the finished project, what we referred to in Chapter 28 as the underlying asset (V). Therefore, the SFFA procedures cannot possibly compute the NPV of the project, either explicitly or implicitly. As a corollary, they fail to provide or even allow for an estimation of the expected return (the going-in IRR) for the development phase of the project. In essence, they look only at how big a loan can be obtained and ignore the evaluation of the equity investment in the development. As a result of these shortcomings, the SFFA procedures make it difficult to relate development financial analysis and investment decision making to the mainstream of investment decision making in the broader capital market. To put it a bit simplistically, Wall Street wants to know the expected return to the development project equity so this can be compared to the relevant opportunity cost of capital (OCC).

Even for the purpose of estimating financial feasibility, the SFFA procedures are needlessly restrictive and complex as a result of their implicit assumption that the completed project will be financed to the maximum possible extent with debt. This may be a plausible enough assumption for small individual developers on Main Street, but it is hardly realistic for larger-scale developers, especially those who tap the public equity markets for capital.

Because the SFFA procedures do not provide a complete or correct investment evaluation criterion, when developers use nothing but such procedures, they are placing the entire burden of making correct capital allocation decisions onto the *external* capital providers, typically the construction and permanent lenders. Yet these providers of debt capital have no equity directly at risk, and they face little upside potential from a successful project. It is a fundamental fact that debt investors do not face the same incentives that providers of equity capital do for making optimal capital allocation decisions.[17]

There is thus a broader social reason, for the sake of the efficiency of capital allocation in the economy, why it is important especially for larger-scale, more sophisticated developers to use financial analysis methods that are more sound from a financial economic and broad capital market perspective. We therefore turn in the next section to a discussion of how to apply the NPV investment decision rule to development projects.

29.5 APPLYING THE NPV RULE TO DEVELOPMENT PROJECTS

The basic NPV rule was presented and discussed in Chapter 10. In Chapter 14 we extended the basic rule to encompass the use of debt financing, making use of the value additivity principle and the APV rule as a useful shortcut that can avoid unnecessary muddying of the waters when nonsubsidized (market rate) debt is employed. The principles and procedures introduced in those two chapters are completely applicable to the financial evaluation of development projects. In this section we are only going to get a bit more specific about this application. In particular, development projects are typically characterized by three somewhat unique features as compared to investments in existing fully operational properties:

1. **Time-to-build:** In development projects the investment cash outflow is spread out in time, instead of occurring all at once up front.
2. **Construction loans:** Use of debt financing is almost universal in the construction phase of the typical development project, and this debt typically covers all of the construction cost.
3. **Phased risk regimes:** The investment typically involves very different levels of investment risk between the construction (or development) phase, the absorption (or lease-up) phase, and the long-term (stabilized or permanent) phase when the completed project is fully operational.

The correct application of the NPV rule to development projects requires a consideration of these three unique features.

29.5.1 Recommended General Procedure

To begin this consideration, recall that in Chapter 10 we defined the NPV of the investment from the buyer's perspective as being equal to the difference between the value of the property being obtained and the cost of obtaining it, which we labeled as

$$NPV = V - P \tag{1}$$

---

[17]As an aside, one could make a strong argument that one of the key ingredients in the success of American capitalism in general has been its ability to maintain an efficient balance between the use of debt and equity capital.

In the application to investment in existing properties, V is the value of the operating property being obtained, and P is the price of obtaining the property. More generally, the NPV can be thought of as the benefit minus the cost of the investment:

$$NPV = B - C \tag{1a}$$

In order for the NPV rule to make sense, both the benefit and the cost must be measured in present, certainty-equivalent dollars, that is, in dollars adjusted for risk as of the time the investment decision is being made. Otherwise we would be comparing apples to oranges. Labeling the present (decision time) as time zero, we can clarify the NPV evaluation by subscripting the benefit and cost measures to indicate the point when they are measured, as follows:

$$NPV_0 = B_0 - C_0 \tag{1b}$$

In the case of investments in fully operational properties, it is relatively easy to estimate both the benefit and cost as of time zero and thereby to quantify equation (1b) directly. In the case of development projects the quantification of (1b) is a bit more complicated because of the three features noted earlier. As a general rule, the most useful and convenient way to apply the NPV rule to development projects is to work with two points in time:

- The present (time zero) is conceptually the time when the decision to proceed with the development project is made and the opportunity cost of the land is incurred.

- The time of project completion (time T) is when the structure is physically completed.

In practice, this second point in time is a bit vague and may be defined a bit flexibly. It may be viewed as the end of the construction phase, the end of the absorption phase, or some intermediate point between these two (i.e., during the absorption phase). The practical issue in this definition is what point in time the investment risk shifts from being essentially that of a development project to being essentially that of an operational asset. In reality, of course, this shift in risk is somewhat gradual and continuous in time, so any single breakpoint into two discrete phases will be somewhat arbitrary. Nevertheless, in the typical commercial property development it usually makes sense to define a single point in time that demarcates the end of the development phase. However, if the lease-up phase is expected to be significant, then it may make sense also to treat this phase separately from both the development phase and the permanent phase of stabilized operation.

No matter how the lease-up phase is treated, the basic idea in development project evaluation is to evaluate the first phase, that is, the development phase, as such. The decision at time zero is whether to undertake the development project at that point in time.[18] Once you have decided to build, that is, to begin construction, it rarely makes sense to stop before you have a physically complete structure; and once

---

[18] More precisely, at time zero the developer faces three mutually exclusive and exhaustive decision alternatives. If the developer owns the land, the alternatives are to (1) build now, (2) wait and hold the land undeveloped for now and do something else with the developer's human resources, or (3) sell the land now and do something else with the financial capital proceeds from the land sale and also do something else for now with the developer's human resources. If the developer does not own the land, then the alternatives are essentially the same from an economic perspective: (1) buy the land now and build

you have a physically complete structure, there is really not much of a decision left to be made: it is then obvious that you have to lease the building if it is not already leased. This is why it usually makes most sense to define the second point in time useful in evaluating development projects as the end of the construction phase (as typically evidenced by the certification of occupancy), the beginning of the absorption phase.

From a practical perspective, the end of the construction phase is typically a useful point to work with for another reason: it is usually when the construction loan comes due. It is therefore relatively easy to pin down the value of the expected cash outflow from the developer at that point, because a construction loan budget is nearly always prepared in the planning stages of a development project. If the construction loan covers all of the development costs other than the land and some other relatively minor up-front costs, then the development phase essentially consists of cash flows faced by the developer at two and only two points in time: time zero and time T, the end of the construction phase.

Thus, to summarize up to here, we will work with two points in time to quantify the NPV of the development project. The first point, time zero, is the present, when the development decision must be made. The second point is when the certificate of occupancy is obtained and/or the construction loan comes due.

Focusing on these two points, we can calculate the NPV of the development project in three steps:

Step 1: Compute the time-zero investment. This consists of the land opportunity cost as of time zero (usually the current market value of the site), plus any other up-front costs or fees that must be paid at that point, such as design costs, some developer fees (to cover developer overhead, for example), and construction loan origination fees.[19] We will label this time-zero investment C_0, where $C_0 = LAND + FEES$.[20]

---

immediately, (2) buy the land now but hold it for future building, and (3) do not buy the land now (possibly losing the opportunity to buy it later) and do something else with the developer's available capital and human resources. In some cases a fourth alternative can be worked out in the form of the purchase of a finite-lived option to buy the land (or just the development rights on the land). In that case the development decision is postponed to a later point when the choice will be whether to exercise this option or allow it to expire unused. In all cases, the opportunity cost facing the developer, associated with a decision to proceed with development as of time zero, equals the maximum of the time-zero values (to the developer) of the other mutually exclusive decision alternatives forgone by the development. For example, if the developer owns the land free and clear, the opportunity cost of development at time zero is the maximum of either the current market value of the land or the present value of waiting and holding the land for future development. (The value of holding the land undeveloped for the time being could exceed the market value of the land if the developer/landowner has a unique ability to use the site, allowing the developer's investment value for the site to exceed the market value of the land. See Chapter 28, section 28.3, and Chapter 12, section 12.1.2.)

[19] As noted previously, the option to sell the land (or development rights as such) is forgone when the development project is undertaken, making the land market value an opportunity cost of the development project. However, the market for raw land is typically rather thin, even by real estate standards. This often makes it difficult to estimate the market value of the land accurately. As we noted in Chapter 12, the market value (MV) of developable land is often conceptualized, in principle, as being equal to the investment value (IV) the land would have for the *second-best* developer. The idea in this conception is that the difference between the value the *first-best* developer can achieve and what the second-best developer can achieve is MV-based positive NPV for the first-best developer attributable to his unique position and/or entrepreneurial creativity. If the first-best developer already owns the land, there is therefore the possibility, based on his IV, that waiting to develop later has a higher value than the current MV of the land. In this case, the opportunity cost of developing at time zero is the *higher* of these two values: the current MV of the land and the current IV-based value of waiting to possibly build later instead of today. (See Chapter 28.)

[20] The variable we are here labeling *LAND* is essentially the same as the variable with that same label in Chapter 28.

Step 2: Compute the NPV of project construction as of the time of completion, exclusive of the time-zero costs quantified in step 1. We will label this second component $NPV(cons)_T$, where $NPV(cons)_T = V_T - L_T$, with V_T being the value of the physically complete project at time T, and L_T being the value of the construction cost owed by the developer as of the time of completion (typically the balance due on the construction loan).[21]

Step 3: Discount the $NPV(cons)_T$ amount to time zero at a discount rate reflecting the opportunity cost of capital for the development phase, and compare this present certainty-equivalent value to the C_0 time-zero investment. This comparison gives the NPV of the development project as of time zero—the present, certainty-equivalent NPV:

$$
\begin{aligned}
NPV_0 &= B_0 - C_0 \\[6pt]
&= \frac{NPV(cons)_T}{(1 + E[r_C])^T} - C_0 \\[6pt]
&= \frac{V_T - L_T}{(1 + E[r_C])^T} - (LAND + FEES)
\end{aligned}
\tag{2}
$$

where $E[r_C]$ is the capital market's required expected return to investments with risk comparable to that of the construction phase of the development project.

29.5.2 Estimating the OCC for the Development and Lease-Up Phases

One of the most difficult steps in applying the NPV approach to development project evaluation is estimating the appropriate opportunity cost of capital for the development and lease-up phases of the project. Yet to try to avoid this step is merely to sweep the monkey underneath the rug (he will come out again!). There is no way to do correct development project financial decision making without coming to grips with the

---

[21] L_T is similar to the construction cost exclusive of land labeled K in the Samuelson-McKean formula described in section 28.4 of Chapter 28. However, there are two differences between L_T as defined here and K as defined in the previous chapter. One is that L_T is measured as of a future point in time, T, whereas K was measured as of the investment decision time zero. Another difference is that L_T does not include development fees that must be paid at time zero (what we are here labeling $FEES$). As you may recall from Chapter 28, the Samuelson-McKean formula does not explicitly consider the time-to-build, the fact that construction is not instantaneous, and K is defined to include all development costs other than the land. Conceptually, it is possible to convert the variables being defined in this chapter to those in the Samuelson-McKean formula as follows: $K = FEES + PV(L_T)$, and $V = PV(V_T)$. The OCC appropriate here as the discount rate in the present value operator on L_T would normally be well represented by the construction loan interest rate (assuming L_T is measured by the projected construction loan balance at project completion). However, the OCC appropriate in the present value operator on V_T is more difficult to define or observe directly. In the case of a fully preleased development project, the OCC relevant to discounting V_T would equal the unlevered OCC of fully operational built property of the type being developed. However, in speculative commercial property development, the appropriate OCC for discounting V_T would normally be a bit higher than this. The difficulty of knowing what discount rate is appropriate for V_T before the built property even exists is one reason we suggest not attempting to bring V_T back to time zero separately, but only within $NPV(cons)_T$, where the OCC for the development phase is appropriate and can be estimated directly as such (see section 29.5.2). This implies that one must grow the construction cost cash flows forward to the time of completion even if no construction loan is actually being used in the project.

question of whether the project can cover its cost of capital. The fact that we cannot be certain that we have estimated the exactly correct OCC is not an excuse for ignoring the problem. Here are some tips for how to think about the OCC of the development and lease-up phases.

First, consider the development phase OCC, what was labeled $E(r_C)$ in formula (2). This is usually more important than the lease-up phase OCC, and fortunately it is easier to estimate in some respects because more empirical evidence can be observed. Everyone agrees that development is risky, and therefore that the OCC for investment in development projects should be relatively high, reflecting a large risk premium in the expected return. But how high is high enough? To answer this question, keep in mind that, fundamentally, development is risky for two reasons.

1. **Development has operational leverage.** The most ubiquitous reason development projects are highly risky is that development projects are inherently levered, and usually rather substantially so, at the *operational* level, whether or not any construction loan is used to finance the project.[22] This is because development value is the *difference* between the value of the completed building and the cost of constructing it. You can think of development value as a net value consisting of the value of an asset minus a liability. The asset is the completed building; the liability is the construction cost. The asset has a very long duration and considerable volatility in its value over time. The liability has a relatively short duration, and its costs are relatively fixed and known for certain in advance. As a result, the risk in the development phase is the risk in the completed built property magnified by the effect of this operational leverage.[23] This source of development phase risk is present even in projects that are entirely preleased.[24]

2. **Uncertainty is resolved gradually.** The second source of development phase risk is uncertainty about the exact nature of the rental market for the building being constructed. This uncertainty may be greater than exists for existing fully operational buildings because the building being built does not yet exist. It has no existing tenants and no existing track record or experience in the rental market. This source of risk is resolved gradually during the development and lease-up phases and is only present in speculative development projects, that is, those that are not preleased. This source of risk may also be negligible where a sufficiently dense rental market exists for the type of building being built, so that the nature of the relevant rental market is pretty

---

[22] The use of a construction loan does increase the degree of leverage by pushing back the timing of the equity investor's payment for the construction. To see this, imagine the extreme opposite: a construction bond, in which the investor pays for the construction in advance, at time zero. Then the development project is like an unlevered forward purchase of the completed property. All-equity payment of construction costs as they occur is an intermediate case between such a bond and the more normal use of a construction loan. Note, however, that leverage does not change the NPV of the development project. The methodology described in this section (which calls for growing all construction costs forward to time T) will give the correct NPV, whether or not a construction loan is used.

[23] It may be helpful at this point to look back at our simple discussion of the effect of leverage on risk presented in Chapter 13, in section 13.2.2 and Exhibit 13-3. Replace the words *property value* with the words *built property value*, the words *levered equity value* with the words *development project value*, and the words *debt value* with the words *construction cost*.

[24] The operational leverage inherent in development projects is analogous to the fact that a financial call option can be evaluated as a levered long position in its underlying asset, and is why land can be valued as a call option, as described in Chapter 28.

obvious from the outset of the project, provided also that there is relatively little use of long-term leases with contractually fixed rents in the relevant space market.

With these fundamental conceptual points in mind, several approaches exist for quantifying an estimate of the appropriate OCC for the development phase. Three of the most useful are noted here.

1. **Lever up the built property risk premium using the WACC formula.** The operational leverage source of development phase risk can be accounted for, at least as a rough approximation, using the WACC formula introduced in Chapter 13. For example, in formula (2) of section 13.3.2, you can interpret the levered equity return (r_E) as the OCC for the development phase, the underlying property return (r_P) as the OCC for the fully operational built property, and the debt return (r_D) as the OCC for the construction project cash flows (or the expected return in a hypothetical construction loan). The LTV ratio in the Chapter 13 WACC Formula can be reinterpreted in the present context as the ratio of construction cost (exclusive of land value) divided by the expected completed built property value (unlevered), both as of the time of completion: L_T/V_T. This results in the following formula for the OCC of the development phase as a function of the OCC of the built property and the construction loan:[25]

$$\text{OCC} = E(r_C) = [r_P - (L_T/V_T)r_D] / [1 - (L_T/V_T)] \qquad (3)$$

For example, suppose the OCC of fully operational built property of the type being constructed commands a 400-basis-point risk premium (unlevered), the construction loan would typically command a 100-basis-point risk premium (over T-bills in its expected return), and the construction cost is expected to be 80% of the completed built property value as of the time of completion (land is 20%). Then by formula (3) the OCC of the development phase would require an expected return risk premium of 1600 basis points:

$$1600 = [400 - (0.8)100] / (1 - 0.8)$$

Thus, if T-bills were yielding 5%, then the development phase OCC would be 21%.[26]

---

[25] Note that L_T should reflect the value of all of the construction costs, regardless of whether a construction loan is actually used for either all or part of those costs. In other words, L_T is the time-T equivalent of the construction cost cash outflows.

[26] The same result is obtained working with expected returns (OCC) rather than risk premiums. With the 5% T-bill yield the OCC (or going-in IRR) for the built property is 9%, and the construction loan expected return is 6%:

$$21\% = [9\% - (0.8)6\%]/(1 - 0.8)$$

Note that in applying this procedure, in principle, the *expected return* to the construction loan lender (that is, the loan's unconditional expected return reflecting the expected probability and loss in the event of default on the construction loan), not the loan's stated yield as reflected in its contractual interest rate, should be employed as the r_D or construction cost OCC variable in formula (3). As construction loans typically contain very little interest rate risk, almost all of their stated yield risk premium consists of

2. Apply the OCC of speculative land investment. Another way to get an idea of the appropriate OCC for the development phase is to use the expected return to the land, that is, to the development rights. The rationale for this is that the primary investment during the development phase is, in effect, the land. Therefore, land investment risk is probably similar to development risk in most cases. A method for obtaining some quantitative insight into the OCC for land investment was discussed in Chapter 28, section 28.4, using the Samuelson-McKean formula for the "real option" value of land.[27] As a general ball-park range, we noted in Chapter 11 that the typical expected return on raw land speculation was considered to be in the 15% to 30% per annum range during the 1990s, when general inflation was averaging around 3%.[28]

3. Evidence from the stock market. Another approach to gaining insight about the development phase OCC would be to examine the long-run average total return risk premium earned by publicly traded firms engaged purely (or largely) in real estate development activity. Such **pure play stocks** would consist mostly of **merchant builder firms**, that is, firms that build buildings that are then sold pretty much as soon as they are physically completed. This would largely include housing developers, such as some real estate operating companies (REOCs) that are included in some specialized stock indices.[29] These firms typically have relatively high betas and therefore command risk premiums (over T-bill yields) typically well in excess of that of the stock market as a whole, that is, well in excess of 6% or more.[30]

With this information about the appropriate OCC estimate for the development phase in mind, what can we say about the OCC for the lease-up phase? In fact, it is even more difficult to observe empirically the market's OCC for the lease-up phase than it is that of the development phase. Conceptually, however, we have a sense that the lease-up phase is less risky than the development phase, but more risky than the stabilized operational phase, and therefore faces an OCC between those of the two other phases. Furthermore, the lease-up phase is often rather short and less important in the overall project evaluation than either of the other two phases. (This provides some comfort in that if we err in our estimate of the lease-up phase OCC, we probably do less damage to the overall project assessment.) Indeed, in the case of preleased development projects, there is no lease-up phase at all, so we need not worry about its OCC.

default risk premium, of which the ex ante yield degradation component is not included in the unconditional expected return on the loan. (See Chapter 19, section 19.2.1.) Similarly (ignoring the construction loan), the direct construction cost cash flows probably contain very little systematic risk (e.g., beta near zero), suggesting an OCC (r_D) rate typically only slightly above the T-bill rate.

[27] Recall, conveniently, that in the Samuelson-McKean formula the option elasticity is independent of the scale or current benefit/cost ratio of the development project, and the land risk premium is related to the built property risk premium purely as a function of the option elasticity. (See formulas [1a] and [2] in Chapter 28.)

[28] This figure is based on investor surveys such as *The Korpacz Report*.

[29] For example, the Wilshire Real Estate Index includes REOCs as well as REITs.

[30] In applying this procedure it is probably not necessary to delever these firms' betas, in principle, unless the financial leverage used by such firms goes beyond the operational leverage inherent in the development process based on the land value as the equity contribution. In other words, if the debt used by the merchant builder firm essentially equates to construction loans covering only construction costs and no land acquisition costs, then the firm's financial leverage merely reflects the operational leverage inherent in the development process, and the firm beta directly reflects the underlying risk of development operations as such.

In speculative development projects, as with the OCC of the development phase, there are conceptually two potential sources of "extra" risk in the lease-up phase as compared to the risk in the stabilized building. One source is the same as the second source we mentioned for development phase risk, namely, the resolution of rental market uncertainty. While the building does physically exist at the outset of the lease-up phase, it still has no track record or history in the rental market. As tenants are found for the building, the uncertainty surrounding exactly how it will fit in the rental market gets gradually resolved, but until then, this type of uncertainty may add somewhat to the lease-up phase risk as compared to that of the stabilized building. This source of risk may be negligible in the case of very standard buildings in dense rental markets.

The second source of extra risk in the lease-up phase simply reflects the difference between interlease and intralease risk and discounting, as we introduced this concept in Chapter 10.[31] The OCC for the stabilized building is really a *blended* rate, consisting of an average between a relatively low intralease OCC that reflects the contractually fixed cash flows in signed leases, and a relatively higher interlease OCC that reflects the residual risk inherent in the rental market for the building (even if this market is well known and understood). In a stabilized building more of the cash flows and more of the present value are attributable to the existing leases in the structure, resulting in a blended IRR that is closer to the intralease discount rate than is the case in a building that is just being leased up. In other words, even if the first source of extra risk in the lease-up phase does not exist (i.e., the nature of the tenant market for the building is fully resolved and understood), the lease-up phase OCC lies between that appropriate for pure interlease or residual risk (i.e., rental market risk) and that of the fully leased up building (which includes a lot of contractually fixed cash flows). This would typically result in the lease-up phase OCC being only modestly higher than the stabilized building OCC, perhaps 100 to 300 basis points extra risk premium.

To summarize with an example, if the stabilized building realistically presents a going-in IRR of 9%, then the lease-up phase OCC might be in the neighborhood of 10% to 12%, unless there is still substantial uncertainty to be resolved about the nature of the rental market the building will fit into, in which case a somewhat higher discount rate might be appropriate. This is far lower than the appropriate OCC for the development phase, which might be in the neighborhood of at least 15% to 20% for the same building.

29.5.3 Simple Numerical Example

The best way to convey a concrete understanding of the procedure suggested by equation (2) is to examine a stylized numerical example. Consider a simple speculative development project with the following characteristics:

- The current (time-zero) market value of the land is $2,000,000. In addition, there are $200,000 in up-front design fees and developer costs attributable to time zero.

- The construction phase of the project is expected to take three years. The construction contractor must be paid in three annual payments at the ends of years 1 through 3 (that is, payments at one, two, and three years in the future from time

[31] See section 10.2 in Chapter 10, and the answer to study question 10.23 at the back of the book.

zero). Each of these payments is contracted to be $1,500,000. While the exact amounts may vary ex post due to change-orders, these costs are largely fixed by the preexisting physical design of the structure. In our example, we will assume that a construction loan will be obtained at a projected interest rate of 7.5% plus a $20,000 up-front origination fee. The construction loan will cover all of the projected $4,500,000 direct construction cost, and the loan will be due in its entirety at the end of year 3.

- The opportunity cost of capital invested in the development phase (the discount rate appropriate for the expected $NPV(cons)_3$ amount) is assumed to be 20% per annum.

- In our example project the construction phase is expected to be followed by two years of absorption, with two annual net cash flows during this phase, at the ends of years 4 and 5. The expected net cash flow during year 4 is −$100,000, as the building is expected still to be largely empty and to be incurring substantial tenant build-out and leasing expenses during that year. The expected cash flow in year 5 is +$400,000, reflecting more rental revenue and fewer leasing expenses as the building fills up that year. This lease-up phase is less risky than the development phase, but more risky than the stabilized operating phase. Let's say in this example that the OCC for the absorption phase is 300 basis points higher than that for the fully operational property.

- The lease-up phase is followed by the long-term fully operational phase of the completed project, starting from year 6 and extending indefinitely into the future. In our simple stylized project the net cash flows from this phase are expected to start out at $800,000 per year and grow annually each year thereafter at a rate of 1% per year. From the perspective of the beginning of year 6 when the building has first become stabilized, these expected future cash flows have the risk of an unlevered investment in a fully operational property. Let's say that this is an amount of risk that warrants a 9% discount rate (going-in IRR from that time forward).

Given this information, we can calculate the NPV of the development project as follows. We will start with the value of the stabilized property as of the end of year 5 (beginning of year 6). This value is projected to be $10,000,000, as estimated in the following equation (using the constant-growth perpetuity formula described in Chapter 8):[32]

$$V_5 = \$10,000,000 = \frac{\$800,000}{1.09} + \frac{(1.01)\,\$800,000}{1.09^2} + \frac{(1.01)^2\,\$800,000}{1.09^2} + \cdots$$

$$= \frac{\$800,000}{0.09 - 0.01}$$

$$= \frac{\$800,000}{0.08}$$

---

[32] Note that this valuation is equivalent to simply applying a projected direct capitalization rate of 8% to the projected stabilized year-6 property net income of $800,000. As noted in section 29.2, this direct capitalization shortcut is typically used in practice in evaluating development projects. Here we depict the full multiyear DCF valuation in order to illustrate the different cost of capital employed in the various project phases. Note that within our stabilized operational phase a 9% cost of capital is being

The next step is to account for the projected two-year lease-up phase of the project. This phase has projected cash flows of –$100,000 and +$400,000, at the ends of years 4 and 5, respectively, with the expected stabilized property value of $10,000,000 also realized at the end of year 5. These lease-up phase net cash flows must be discounted back to arrive at a projected value as of the end of year 3, our project completion year. We apply the lease-up phase opportunity cost of capital in this process, which in this case requires a risk premium 300 basis points higher than the OCC we used in the previous step for the stabilized property. Thus, the discount rate for the lease-up phase is 12%. This gives a projected asset value as of the end of year 3 of $8,201,531, computed as follows:

$$V_3 = \$8,201,531 = \frac{-\$100,000}{1.12} + \frac{\$400,000 + \$10,000,000}{1.12^2}$$

It is important to note that the lease-up phase opportunity cost of capital must be applied as the discount rate even to the $10,000,000 projected value of the stabilized property. This is because, as of the end of year 3, the lease-up phase has yet to be completed, and we have the risk of that phase to go through before we obtain the expected $10,000,000 value. The 9% OCC we employed to derive the $10,000,000 valuation in the previous step was only appropriate in the stabilized fully operational phase, by which time there will be less uncertainty about the rental market for the building, and much of the building's present value will be attributable to future cash flows that are already contractually fixed in existing leases. As of the end of year 3 there is more uncertainty surrounding what type of tenants we can market the building to, and what sort of rents we can obtain in the relevant space market.[33] This uncertainty as of year 3 does not change our *expectation* of the $10,000,000 value, but it does affect the *risk* surrounding that expectation prior to its realization.

The $8,201,531 value we just computed is our expected value of the benefit of the development phase of the project, the value of the physically complete asset as of the time of completion of construction, the value we labeled V_T (or in this case, V_3) in equation (2) in section 29.5.1. This value can be compared directly with the construction costs the developer will have to pay at that time in the form of the construction loan, which comes due then. Recall that the construction loan is expected to have an interest rate of 7.5%. Therefore, the developer will owe the lender $4,845,938 at the end of year 3, computed as follows:[34]

employed as our discount rate. Note also that there is no need to muddy the waters by bringing into consideration the permanent loan that may be used to finance continued ownership of the stabilized property by the developer. In fact, the method of financing the completed project is, in principle, a separate decision from the decision of whether to develop the building in the first place. Our discussion in Chapter 14 regarding the use of the APV procedure is relevant in this regard. Unless the permanent loan is subsidized, the borrowing transaction is essentially zero NPV and will not change the evaluation of the development project. (See section 14.4 in Chapter 14.)

[33] As noted in the previous section, this lease-up phase discounting is comparable to the concept of intralease and interlease discount rates discussed in Chapters 8 and 10. (See in particular section 8.2.7 in Chapter 8 and section 10.2.2 in Chapter 10.)

[34] Note that here we have assumed that the construction payments are due to the contractor at the ends of the years. Thus, the first payment (and draw on the construction loan) is projected to occur at the end of year 1, and so must be grown forward in time and compounded two years (to the end of year 3) at the interest rate of 7.5%. The second payment is grown for one year, and the third is contemporaneous with the loan due date.

$$L_T = \$4,845,938 = \$1,500,000(1.075)^2 + \$1,500,000(1.075) + 1,500,000$$

As the construction loan covers all of the construction costs, the $4,845,938 payment is the developer's only projected cash outflow after time zero, the value we labeled L_T in equation (2).[35] As the $4,845,938 cost projection and the $8,201,531 value projection are both risk-adjusted values as of the same time (the end of year 3), these values are directly comparable. This enables us to compute the projected net present value of the construction phase of the project as of the time of its completion, what we labeled $NPV(cons)_T$ in equation (2). This is seen to be:

$$NPV(cons)_3 = V_3 - L_3 = \$8,201,531 - \$4,845,938 = \$3,355,593$$

The risk of this projected difference between the construction benefit and cost is the risk of the development phase of the project. Therefore, the 20% development phase OCC must be applied to discount this year-3 value back to time zero. Thus, the time-zero value of the development project benefit is $1,941,894, computed as

$$B_0 = \$1,941,894 = \frac{\$3,355,593}{1.20^3}$$

This is the value labeled B_0 in equation (2). The time-zero cost of the development project consists of the $2,000,000 opportunity value of the land plus the up-front fees, including the $200,000 developer and design fees and the $20,000 loan origination fee. Thus, the total time-zero cost of the development project is $2,220,000. This is the value labeled C_0 in equation (2). Thus, the NPV of the development project as of time zero is −$278,106, computed as:

$$NPV_0 = B_0 - C_0 = \$1,941,894 - \$2,220,000 = -\$278,106$$

[35] Note that we are here using the value additivity principle in what might be called a reverse manner to the way we used it previously to allow us to ignore the permanent loan in the valuation of the completed building. Because of the ubiquity of construction loans and their tendency to cover all construction costs, it is convenient to use the loan cash flow at this point (the construction loan balance due) instead of the all-equity cash flow (as if there were no construction loan). As before, we can invoke the value additivity principle to infer that, unless the construction loan is subsidized, the year 3 certainty-equivalent value of the all-equity construction cost cash outflows would be the same as the projected construction loan balance due at that time (i.e., the construction loan is itself a zero-NPV transaction). However, we are cheating a bit in this regard. As noted previously, it would be more correct to grow the projected construction cost draws at a rate equal to the *unconditional expected return* on the construction loan rather than at the contractual interest rate on that loan. The expected return is less than the contractual interest rate because of the ex ante yield degradation due to the default risk borne by the construction lender. The effect of our shortcut in this example is small, however, and biases the resulting NPV calculation on the conservative side, that is, toward finding a lower NPV than really exists. We will therefore ignore this effect in the present example to simplify the illustration (in effect assuming that the developer would never default on the construction loan). If you want to be more strictly correct and include the construction loan default risk effect in practice, you could recompute the projected construction loan balance using an interest rate typically 100 to 200 basis points lower than the projected actual construction loan interest rate, or a rate slightly above the currently prevailing rate on government bonds of duration equal to the projected construction period. All other steps in the NPV computation would remain as described in this example.

As this value is negative, it does not make sense to proceed with this development project at this time.[36] Perhaps a better project can be designed for this site than the one considered here. But if this is the best project this developer can come up with, then she faces two choices. If she already owns the land, she could continue to hold it undeveloped for the time being, for possible future development. Perhaps the highest and best use (HBU) of the site will change to allow a more lucrative type of development project.[37] If this does not seem to be a good prospect, then there is no point in holding the land. This developer should sell it, for the expected price of $2,000,000. If the developer does not own the land, then she should not buy it (at the presumed price of $2,000,000). If the land can be bought for less than $2,000,000 − 278,106 = $1,721,894 (or, if the developer already owns the land and cannot sell it for more than that amount), then the development project will be financially desirable after all.

29.5.4 Summarizing the Advantages of the Recommended Procedure

The NPV-based procedure described in this section has a number of advantages for the evaluation of development projects and the financial analysis of the development decision. We will list several of the most important advantages.

1. **Consistent with underlying theory.** The procedure described here is consistent with the NPV rule we presented in Part IV of this book. As noted, this decision rule is based on the wealth maximization principle and is therefore consistent with widely accepted fundamental economic theory.[38]

2. **Simplicity.** The NPV-based procedure avoids the need to make assumptions about the permanent loan that may (but need not necessarily) be used to finance long-term ownership of the built property. This makes this procedure particularly appropriate for development and investment entities that might not "borrow to the hilt" in their capital structure, such as REITs or pension funds. The procedure described here also permits the use of simple direct capitalization to value the stabilized built property, and so is as simple in this regard as conventional procedures such as the SFFA procedure described in section 29.4.

[36] This result is perhaps not surprising. A project that takes three years to build and then another two years to lease up would not usually make financial sense, unless the land was very cheap and/or the built property value/income multiple was abnormally high, neither of which is true in this case. Even if we didn't employ the shortcut of using the projected construction loan balance as the construction cost, this project would still not work. For example, if we grew the expected $4,500,000 construction draws at a 6% rate instead of the 7.5% construction loan interest rate, we would get a projected L_3 value of $4,775,400, which would result in $NPV(cons)_3 = \$3,426,131$, giving $B_0 = \$1,982,715$, which is only 2% more than the $1,941,894 figure in our shortcut, and still results in a negative NPV of −$237,285.

[37] This requires a realistic expected return on the $2,000,000 land investment of at least 20% per year.

[38] The procedure described here is also consistent with real options valuation theory as described in Chapter 28, provided that the opportunity value of the land incorporates the development option value. As noted, this will normally be the case as far as market value is concerned, the so-called second-best developer valuation of the land. Depending on the degree of uniqueness in a developer's ability to use a given land parcel, it may be necessary for the first-best developer to explicitly consider the value of waiting to build. In other words, a first-best developer who obtains an apparent positive NPV from development at time zero using the procedure described in this section based on the market value of the land should also consider the NPV of the mutually exclusive alternative of waiting to build the same (or better) project at a future time. (See sections 28.2 and 28.3 in Chapter 28.)

3. **Explicit identification of the relevant OCC.** The key innovation in the recommended procedure as compared to the more conventional approaches is that the NPV-based procedure explicitly identifies multiple risk regimes, focusing on at least two points in time and at least two opportunity costs of capital (three if the absorption phase is treated separately as in our numerical example). We argue that multiple risk regimes and valuation time focal points are important and irreducible elements of the development decision that cannot be ignored in a correct evaluation procedure. They therefore are included implicitly if not explicitly in any development project valuation procedure. Making the relevant assumptions about the time-to-build and the OCC explicit can only serve to enlighten and improve the decision process. In addition, the identification of explicit cost of capital estimates (e.g., the 9%, 12%, and 20% rates we used for the three phases in our numerical example) makes development project evaluation and decision making more directly comparable to mainstream corporate finance and the equity valuation procedures used in the stock market. This can help to link Wall Street and Main Street. Such linkage facilitates value-maximizing investment decision making, particularly in publicly traded firms, or firms that tap the public capital market for equity capital even if it is "outside" capital.[39]

4. **Explicit identification of land value.** The NPV-based procedure makes explicit the land value that would be necessary to make a project financially worthwhile as of time zero. If the recommended procedure results in a negative NPV, it becomes clear that if the land could be acquired for an amount equal to the negative NPV less than the land value used in the analysis, then the project is feasible.[40] If the above procedure results in a positive NPV, then we see the amount the land could conceivably be worth by adding the positive NPV to the land value used in the analysis. This information can be useful in negotiating land deals, and in rank-ordering the financial desirability of alternative development projects.

5. **Front-door or back-door possible.** The NPV-based procedure described here can be applied in either the front-door or back-door direction. The numerical example illustrated earlier was the latter, ending up effectively with the implied supportable land acquisition cost at time zero. To apply the procedure in the front-door direction, starting with a known land value and ending with an implied required rent, simply reverse the procedure.[41] In fact, you can "back into"

---

[39] By quantifying the developer's total return, we are developing a measure that can be compared easily with the returns one can expect to earn in other risky ventures, such as investment in small growth stocks or venture capital funds. Returns in the 15% to 30% range are not uncommon for such risky investments. Viewed from a macrolevel investment allocation perspective, real estate development should provide expected returns that are comparable on an apples-to-apples basis with the expected returns provided by other high-risk alternative allocations of capital.

[40] For example, we saw in the numerical example that if the land could be purchased for as little as (or not sold for more than) $1,721,894, then the project would work.

[41] Grow the C_0 amount forward compounded at the development phase cost of capital for the construction period. Add the projected cost of construction (loan balance) as of that time. Grow this combined amount forward at the lease-up phase cost of capital for the length of the lease-up phase (along with the projected lease-up phase net cash flows) to the point of stabilization. (This step may be skipped, effectively combining lease-up into construction, if lease-up is projected to be a short period.) Then multiply the resulting projected stabilized built property value by the projected cap rate at that time to derive the required NOI. Add projected stabilized operating expenses (to be paid by the landlord), divide by the projected stabilized occupancy rate in the building, and then divide by the number of leasable square feet to arrive at the required rent that implies a zero NPV for the development project as of time zero.

Do Developers and Lenders Really Use NPV?

You don't have to be a genius to see that some pretty bad real estate development decisions get made in the real world. (Of course, hindsight helps, but some projects had to have been turkeys even when the decisions were made.) Nevertheless, we suspect that most real estate development decisions are in fact at least approximately consistent with the correct application of the NPV rule (ex ante), even though the developers and lenders may not be explicitly or consciously thinking of their decision process along the lines of the NPV rule. Why do we say this?

Astute developers do not make crucial decisions just on the basis of whether a project looks feasible according to incorrect procedures such as the mortgage-based SFFA described in section 29.4. The other, broader part of their decision reasoning is often, however, intuitive and qualitative rather than explicit and quantitative. For example, developers usually add a required "developer's fee" or "developer's profit" to the construction cost (sometimes a part of this fee is hidden in other cost items). While this fee does not explicitly quantify the developer's cost of capital in the form of a required total return (including an explicit risk premium), it may have the same effect as the application of an appropriate equity cost of capital in an explicit NPV analysis. Second, developers usually face a capital or resource constraint in practice, or believe they do. That is, they can only do so many projects at once. This means they cannot do all the projects that appear to be financially feasible (and that they might think they

would like to do, if they could). As a result, developers are forced, in effect, to rank-order projects and consider feasible combinations of projects. It seems likely that a big part of what makes developers successful is their ability to do this rank-ordering rationally, that is, to choose among mutually exclusive alternatives to pursue those that look best on the basis of the magnitude of the perceived profit or surplus.

In other words, virtually by definition, successful developers are those who maximize their wealth. And that is what the correct application of the NPV procedure does: by definition and construction, the NPV decision rule maximizes wealth. Thus, successful developers are doing the same thing that the NPV decision rule does. So, implicitly if not explicitly, they must be applying the NPV rule. Another way of saying this is to say that application of the NPV rule ensures that developers cover their cost of capital. Less successful developers may not be applying the NPV rule, but they tend to fall by the wayside over time, as any firm that does not cover its cost of capital eventually shrinks or dies.

What we would like to suggest is that even successful developers may find it useful to make more explicit and quantitative that which they have been doing all along implicitly, and less successful developers may be able to improve their performance significantly by the use of the NPV rule.

---

any one unknown variable in the preceding procedures. For example, if you know the land value and the likely rents, you can back into the required construction cost. If you know (or posit) all of the costs and values, then you can back into the expected return on the developer's equity contribution for the development phase.[42]

In summary, in our experience, following the NPV-based procedure described in this section can avoid a lot of muddled thinking in the financial evaluation of development projects. In current practice, when procedures more sophisticated than the

[42] This would be an IRR-oriented approach rather than an NPV-oriented approach, but it would be consistent with NPV as long as you watch out for mutually exclusive alternatives of different scale. (See section 10.6.2 in Chapter 10.) The hurdle IRR is the OCC for the development phase.

SFFA described in section 29.4 are employed in development analysis, the focus is often on an attempt to quantify a levered equity IRR that may mix different risk regimes (e.g., development and long-run investment) and make it difficult to compare projects of different scales.[43] It is also difficult to know the appropriate levered equity OCC for determining the hurdle IRR when the analysis is applied to long-run levered equity with an assumed permanent mortgage.[44]

29.6 CHAPTER SUMMARY

This chapter built on the theoretical treatment of land value and development timing presented in Chapter 28 to present an overview of the development decision-making process and a practical methodology for the financial analysis and evaluation of development projects. We introduced the basic mechanics of construction loan budgeting and presented an example of the simplified financial feasibility analysis procedures widely used in practice. The main point of this chapter, however, was to present and advocate the use of an NPV-based financial evaluation procedure for real estate development projects. The recommended procedure is consistent with modern corporate capital budgeting and securities investment theory, as well as with the valuation methodology presented in Parts IV and V of this book.

KEY TERMS

site looking for a use
use looking for a site
construction and absorption budget
operating budget
stabilized (year or cash flows)
hard costs
soft costs
absorption or lease-up phase
speculative (or "spec") development
tenant build-outs
construction loan

future advances
draw-down (of loan commitment)
permanent loan
certification of occupancy
take-out loan
accrued interest
financing costs (construction loan
    interest)
simple financial feasibility analysis
    (SFFA)
front-door feasibility analysis

back-door feasibility analysis
gross leasable area (GLA)
efficiency ratio
net rentable area (NRA)
financial feasibility
financial desirability
time-to-build
phased risk regimes
pure-play stocks
merchant builder firms

---

[43] Incidentally, development projects are one area in which a technical problem may crop up in computing the IRR. Recall from Chapter 9 that it may be impossible to compute an unambiguous IRR when the direction of cash flow alternates over time. This does not normally happen with investment in stabilized properties, but it is not uncommon in development and redevelopment projects, in which net cash outflows may follow net cash inflows. Of course, it is always possible to compute the NPV, even when an unambiguous IRR cannot be computed.

[44] See section 14.4 in Chapter 14, and the appendix to Part V at the end of Chapter 15.

STUDY QUESTIONS

29.1. Describe the four disciplines or professional perspectives that are involved in the design, analysis, and decision making of the typical real estate development project in the private sector.

29.2. Describe the two types of budget that are necessary in the real estate development decision making process.

29.3. You wish to build an office/warehouse project, also known as R&D space or flex space, because that's what you're good at. Market rents seem to be around $15 per square foot per year with a 5% vacancy rate in the local area. All expenses are passed through to tenants except property taxes, insurance, and management, which you estimate at $5 per square foot per year. Mortgage rates are 11% for a 20-year loan with a 5-year balloon. Construction costs for your planned 20,000-gross-leaseable-square-foot project are estimated at $1,030,075 in total. All 20,000 SF are rentable. The debt service coverage ratio required is 120% and the maximum LTV ratio is 75%. Use the SFFA back-door procedure to determine what you could pay for the land.

29.4. In question 29.3, use the front-door SFFA procedure to determine what the required rents would be per square foot if the total of your construction and site acquisition costs were $1,300,000?

29.5. Describe the three features that characterize real estate development projects and distinguish them from investments in fully operational properties. What two points in time are useful to define for the purpose of applying the NPV investment rule to development projects?

29.6. In question 29.3, suppose the $1,030,075 construction cost is a projected construction loan balance covering all construction costs (including interest) as of one year after start of construction. Suppose that lease-up will be instantaneous and the projected cap rate on the completed property will be 10%. Apply a back-door version of the NPV-based financial evaluation procedure recommended in section 29.5 to estimate the land acquisition costs that can be supported by this project if the development phase OCC is 15%. (Ignore any other up-front development costs or fees other than land acquisition.)

29.7. Using the assumptions in questions 29.6 and 29.4, apply a front-door version of the recommended NPV-based procedure to derive the required rents if the up-front land acquisition cost (inclusive of any other up-front development fees) is $700,000.

29.8. The following table shows the projected draws to pay the construction costs of a project that is expected to take four months to complete. The draws are projected to occur at the beginning of each month. What is the projected balance due on a construction loan at the end of the fourth month if the interest rate is 10% per annum with monthly compounding?

Month	Draw
1	$1,000,000
2	$2,000,000
3	$1,500,000
4	$2,500,000

*29.9. Consider the following development project to build a 100% preleased office building. The time zero opportunity cost of the land is $15,000,000. Construction cost draws are projected to be $40,000,000 occurring as follows: $10,000,000 at time zero, $20,000,000 one year later at the end of year 1, and a final $10,000,000 cost at the time of project completion at the end of year 2. The value of the completed stabilized property at the end of year 2 (V_T) is projected to be $65,000,000. T-bills are currently yielding 5.5%. Although a construction loan for this project would carry an interest rate of 8%, 200 basis points of this interest rate is to cover ex ante yield degradation (as described in section 18.1 of Chapter 18 and section 19.2.1 of Chapter 19). The OCC of the construction costs (and the unconditional expected return on the construction loan) contains only a 50-basis-point risk premium over T-bills, that is, a 6% OCC. With this information in mind, answer the following questions about this development project.

a. Use the unconditional expected return on the construction loan to determine the expected construction cost for this project (exclusive of land value), evaluated as of the time of completion at the end of year 2 (L_T), and the projected construction project NPV as of that time, $NPV(cons)_2$.

b. Assuming that the stabilized property would command an investment risk premium of 300 basis points over T-bills in its going-in IRR, use the WACC formula and the projected operational leverage in the completed project (i.e., as reflected in L_T/V_T) to estimate the OCC relevant for the development phase investment in this project, $E(r_C)$. [Hint: Use formula (3) from section 29.5.2.]

c. Use this WACC-based estimate of the development phase OCC you just estimated to compute the NPV of this development project as of time zero, ignoring any up-front time-zero costs other than the land.

d. If there would also be $1,000,000 of additional up-front fees and costs (besides the land), then, based on your answer in (c), what is the implied maximum price the developer could pay for the land such that this development project would still be desirable at the present time?

e. Assuming that $15,000,000 is the true current market value of the land (and that other up-front development fees would be no more than the $1,000,000 noted in [d]), and assuming that the $40,000,000 cost and $65,000,000 value projections are realistic, what does your analysis in (d) tell you about the relative ability of this developer to use this land parcel as compared to other developers? [Hint: See footnote 19 in this chapter.]

f. If the subject developer is the first-best developer of this site, then is it possible that immediate initiation of the $40,000,000 construction project might not be optimal for this developer? Explain. [Hint: See Chapter 28, section 28.3, and footnote 19 in this chapter.]

30 Leases and Leasing Strategy

Chapter Outline

Learning Objectives

After reading this chapter, you should understand:

◆ The major characteristics and descriptive
terminology used in commercial property leases
in the United States.

◆ What is meant by "effective rent," and how to
calculate it.

◆ The major factors determining lease value to the
landlord that are left out of the effective rent
calculation.

◆ The major leasing strategy issues and trade-offs
facing landlords and tenants.

The operating cash flow on which the value of commercial properties is fundamentally based is usually governed largely by leases, at least on the revenue side. In residential properties leases are short term, typically yearly or month-to-month. In lodging properties there are generally no leases at all. But in most other types of commercial property long-term leases of various types are the norm. In all cases, the nature of leases, and the major considerations in leasing strategy, are key elements in the operational management of commercial properties and important fundamental determinants of the investment performance and value of such assets. In this last chapter we will introduce some of the basic terminology, analytical tools, and strategic considerations regarding commercial property leases and leasing.

30.1 COMMERCIAL PROPERTY LEASE TERMINOLOGY AND TYPOLOGY

A **lease** is a contract between a holder of property rights and a consumer or user of at least some of those rights, covering a specified period of time. The property owner or landlord is referred to as the **lessor**.[1] The tenant is referred to as the **lessee**. Normally, the lease gives possession and usage rights, but not development or redevelopment rights. An exception to this is the case of very long-term leases of land, often referred to as **ground leases**. Legally, a lease is a contract and therefore an exchange, in this case, of rights for money. The money, or price of the lease, is normally called **rent** and is typically paid periodically, although up-front payments may also be included. In addition to possessory rights, the lease contract normally specifies other rights and duties on the part of the tenant as well as the landlord, and statutory (or common) law also dictates certain requirements, especially for residential properties. For example, the landlord may be required to provide a certain type of parking or signage. Lease law is an extensive branch of the law, and commercial lease contracts are usually very complex legal documents.[2]

30.1.1 Basic Lease Typology: The Responsibility for Expenses

Commercial property leases vary in how the operating expenses of the building are treated. Some leases require the landlord to pay these expenses, some leases require the tenant to pay them, and others provide for various forms of sharing of the operating expenses. By shifting some or all of the operating expense burden to the tenant, the landlord gains the obvious advantage of some protection against inflation in operating costs. The reduction in inflation risk to the landlord is offset by an increase in this risk to the tenant. Broadly, the different ways of handling operating expenses are represented in three types of leases: gross, net, and hybrid leases.

1. **Gross lease.** In a gross lease the landlord pays the operating expenses. This is also called a full service lease because the landlord provides such services as electricity, heat, water, cleaning, maintenance, security, and so on, at no expense to the tenant. Generally, telecommunications services are not included even in a full service lease.
2. **Net lease.** In a net lease the tenant is responsible for paying the operating expenses of the building. In a pure net lease (sometimes referred to as **triple net** or **NNN**), all or almost all of the operating expenses of the building are charged to the tenant, including even expenses that are fixed, that is, not sensitive to the level of occupancy in the building, such as property taxes and insurance costs. However, even

---

[1] The lessor is not necessarily the underlying property owner. He may be a leasehold owner, for example, the master tenant subleasing space to a subtenant.

[2] Lease law is beyond the scope of this text. For a treatment of this subject, the reader is referred to the voluminous literature on real estate law and lease law. A very readable introductory example is Jennings (1995).

with a pure net lease the landlord may cover some expenses, such as the property manager's fees and costs specifically associated with leasing activities. In multitenant buildings, net leases usually provide for all of the building's expenses (even those associated with running the common areas, such as elevators, security, and lighting of lobbies) to be charged to individual tenants on a pro rata basis, determined by the fraction of the total rentable floor area occupied by each tenant. Typically, an estimate of building operating expenses are derived for the current year based on the past year's actual expense record, and monthly expense reimbursements will be paid by the tenants based on this estimate. Periodically (typically at the end of the year) the accounts are squared on the basis of the operating expenses actually incurred as evidenced in an auditable record. The total payments from the tenants to the landlord thus consist of two components: the net rent payment and the expense reimbursement.

3. Hybrid lease. A hybrid lease involves some aspects of both gross and net leases. In other words, the tenant and landlord share the payment of building operating expenses. This may be done in various ways. One common approach is for certain specific expenses to be designated as the tenants' responsibility while other expenses are the landlord's responsibility. For example, the landlord might pay the fixed costs of property taxes and insurance, as well as utilities and services that cannot be metered separately for each tenant, such as water, building security, and common area costs, while the tenants are responsible for other utility and maintenance costs that can be attributed to each tenant.

A different approach to sharing expenses is known as **expense stops,** in which the tenant agrees to pay all operating expenses above a specified annual level known as the "stop." In effect, the expenses for the landlord stop growing at the specified stop level. This technique for sharing expenses is obviously designed to protect the landlord against inflation in operating expenses, as well as to provide the tenant with an incentive to keep operating costs down, while still providing the tenant with something pretty close to a full service lease. The expense stop is usually set at or near the level of operating expenses at the time the lease is signed, thereby guaranteeing the landlord against any effective increase in operating expenses she will have to pay during the life of the lease.

In multitenant buildings the expense stops are typically negotiated separately for each lease, resulting in each lease possibly having a different stop amount. The expense stop provision causes tenants to be responsible for making expense reimbursement payments to the landlord based on their individual expense stop levels and a pro rata assignment of expense responsibility determined by the fraction of the building's rentable space each tenant occupies. For example, suppose a 100,000-SF building has two tenants, tenant A occupying 60,000 SF and tenant B 40,000 SF. Suppose the total operating expenses of the building are $500,000, (i.e., $5.00/SF) and tenant A has an expense stop of $4.00/SF while tenant B has an expense stop of $4.50/SF. Then, in addition to their rent, tenant A would owe the landlord $60,000 ([$5.00 − $4.00] × 60,000 SF) and tenant B, $20,000 ([$4.50 − $4.00] × 40,000 SF) in expense reimbursements.

30.1.2 Types of Rent Changes in Leases

One of the most important characteristics of long-term commercial property leases that is of interest to investors is the way the rent is specified to change over time during the term of the lease contract. Rent changes serve several purposes. The most basic purpose is to reflect changes in the relevant space market that cause the equilibrium rent to change for new leases being signed in that market. Another purpose in the case of gross leases is to help protect the landlord from inflation in the operating expenses of running the building. A third purpose, which is important in retail leases, is to allow the landlord to share in the tenant's operating profits, as these profits are typically attributable in part to the store location. The five most common types of rent change provisions in long-term leases in the United States are described here.

1. **Flat rent.** The simplest type of lease rental agreement provides for a fixed, constant rent level throughout the term of the lease. Virtually all short-term leases have flat rent, and flat rent is not uncommon in longer-term leases as well, particularly during times of low general inflation.

2. **Graduated rent.** The simplest type of lease that provides for a changing rent is called a graduated lease. Such a lease includes specified **step-ups** (or steps) in the rent. In this structure, both the timing and the amount of the rent changes are specified up front in the lease contract. For example, a 10-year graduated lease might start at $15 per square foot with a provision that at the end of every two years (i.e., after years 2, 4, 6, and 8), the rent will increase by $1 per SF.

3. **Revaluated rent.** A revaluation lease also specifies in the lease contract the *times* when the rental payments may change, but it does not specify in advance the exact dollar *amounts* of the rent changes. Instead, the lease specifies that the property (or the particular rental space and rental market) will be appraised by a professional real estate appraiser, and the rent will be adjusted accordingly. Sometimes, such revaluations call for upward-only adjustments in rent, while other leases allow the adjustment to be in either direction. In the latter case, this becomes a mechanism to keep the rent current with the changes in the local rental market. For example, a 20-year revaluation lease might specify that after every fifth year the property will be appraised by a certified appraiser and the rent set at one-tenth the property value, per year. Or the lease might call for an analysis of rents on new leases signed on comparable spaces in the local rental market and require the subject rent to be adjusted to the estimated fair market rental rate. Revaluation leases are particularly appropriate for very long-term leases.

4. **Indexed rent.** Indexed leases call for the rent to be adjusted according to some publicly observable and regularly reported index, such as the consumer price index (CPI) or the producer price index (PPI). A typical indexed lease might require rents to be adjusted annually at some percentage of the CPI. For example, a 50% CPI adjustment would require the rent to be increased by 2.5% if inflation had been 5% (i.e., if the CPI had increased by 5%) during the preceding year. "Full" (i.e., 100%) CPI adjusted leases are not uncommon, but often the adjustment is less than full (50% being a typical level) because it may be perceived that building operating expenses typically do not grow as fast as inflation, or that the market rents that the building could charge would not grow as fast as inflation.

As a numerical example of how CPI-adjusted rent works, consider a lease that calls for an annual 75% CPI adjustment in the rent on the lease anniversary every July, based on the change in the CPI between the previous May and the May prior to that. Suppose the CPI in May of the prior year was 240 and the CPI in May of the current year was 250. Then there was $(250/240) - 1 = 4.17\%$ inflation. Seventy-five percent of 4.17% is 3.13%. So if the rent had been $12/SF per year (paid as $1/SF each month), then the new rent as of July would rise to $12.38/SF per year ($1.0313/SF paid each month), based on $1.0313 \times 12 = \$12.38$.

5. Percentage rent. Percentage leases also involve changes in rent over time. In this case, however, the motivation and nature of the change is rather different from the foregoing examples, and the application of percentage rent is limited to retail property space. In a percentage lease the rent is a specified percentage of the sales revenue or net income earned by the tenant in the rented space. Often the rent will include both a fixed component referred to as the **base rent** (which may or may not have any of the previously described change provisions) plus a percentage component. Sometimes the percentage component only applies to revenue or profits above a specified threshold amount. Percentage rents are especially common in class A multitenant retail space, such as shopping malls. For example, the rent for a boutique space in a shopping mall might be defined as $10/SF per year plus 5% of the gross sales receipts of the store during the preceding year, prorated monthly. Obviously, such a lease would require a provision in the contract enabling the mall owner to audit the books of the shop.

30.2 LEASE CHARACTERISTICS AFFECTING VALUE OR RENT

A number of characteristics go into the determination of the rent that the parties agree to in a lease, and also into the value the lease then has to the landlord once it is signed. Later in this chapter we will discuss leasing strategy considerations more broadly from both the landlord and tenant perspectives. At this point, however, it may be useful by way of background to call your attention to several characteristics of the space, the tenant, and the lease itself that help to determine either the rent or the lease value (or both).

1. Space. The most basic and obvious determinant of the rent the landlord can charge is the nature of the product the tenant is getting in return for the rent, namely, the space itself. Obviously, location is an important characteristic of the space. As noted in the early parts of this book, location is important at several levels, ranging from the metropolitan area to the neighborhood to the specific site and even the location of the space within a multitenant building. For example, higher floors may command higher rents if views are valued or prestige is associated with high locations in the building. Rent and rentability are also strongly influenced by the physical and architectural qualities of the building and of the specific space being leased. In addition, the size, shape, and configuration of the space is also often of great importance in determining its usefulness to the tenant, and therefore the rent that can be charged. Two spaces in nearly identical locations may command very different rents because they are of different sizes or shapes. In general, rent per square foot tends to decrease with the size of the space, and occupancy of an entire floor can bring certain efficiencies or benefits to both the landlord and the tenant.[3]

2. Tenant. Who the lessee is can also be important to the landlord. Some tenants are inevitably more desirable than others due to credit quality, prestige, or synergy with other tenants. The orchestration of positive externalities among tenants is a key part of the job of shopping mall managers, for example, as certain combinations and spatial positioning of types of shops will lead to greater sales volumes for all. Tenants that rent

---

[3] For example, there may then be no need for a common area on the floor.

large blocks of space early in the development of a new building provide a particular benefit for the landlord/developer. High-profile, prestige tenants whose names may appear on the outside of the structure also bring a particular benefit to the landlord. Two tenants in nearly identical spaces may not pay the same rent for reasons such as these.

3. Date and term of the lease. The length of time covered by the lease (the **lease term**), as well as the time the lease is signed and when it expires, can have value implications for the landlord. Other things being equal, landlords would typically prefer longer-term leases or leases that do not expire when a large number of other leases in the same building are scheduled to expire.

4. Rent. Obviously, the level of the rent, and the provisions for rent changes during the term of the lease, are fundamental and direct determinants of the value of the lease to the landlord. Indeed, this characteristic of lease value is so basic that we only mention it here to make the point that rent is not the *only* determinant of lease value. Other characteristics and considerations in this list interact with the rent in the overall determination of lease value for the landlord.

5. Concessions. Landlords often provide tenants with various forms of concessions, such as rent abatements and tenant improvement allowances, moving expense allowances, and so forth.[4] In general, concessions reduce the net cash flow the landlord receives from the lease, particularly at the outset or during the early stages of the lease. Landlords provide concessions to tenants as "sweeteners" to get them to sign leases that they otherwise would not agree to, with provisions that are beneficial to the landlord, or at a time when the rental market is unfavorable for the landlord.

6. Lease covenants. The value of a lease to a landlord can be influenced by the specific covenants or provisions that are in the lease contract. In general, such provisions may limit or expand the landlord's and the tenant's rights and duties in ways that affect value. For example, tenants have the right to **sublet** (or assign the use of) their space unless this right is explicitly negated or limited in the lease contract. The ability to sublet the space gives the tenant flexibility and potential value. On the other hand, the landlord may want to control the type of tenant that moves in, or to share in any increase in rent.

7. Lease options. Leases often provide explicit options to either the tenant or the landlord. Some such options can importantly influence value. As noted in Chapter 28, in general an option refers to a right without obligation to obtain some benefit, perhaps requiring the payment of some additional sum to exercise the option. Options provide valuable flexibility to the option holder, but they may restrict the rights of the opposite party (the option grantor, either the landlord or tenant), thereby reducing value to that party (ceteris paribus). The most common lease options that benefit tenants include the following:

- **Renewal option:** Entitles tenant to renew the space at the end of the lease, either at a specified rent, or at prevailing market rents. If it is the latter, this option is similar to a right of first refusal.
- **Cancellation option:** May be written either for the landlord or tenant, entitling the option holder to cancel the lease prior to the end of the lease term (with specified notice).

---

[4] While some level of tenant improvement may be considered to be normally provided by the landlord (especially in a new or reconstructed building where the space has not been completely finished out), the provision of extra large tenant allowances for either tenant improvements or moving may be viewed as a concessions.

- **Expansion option:** This may be in the form of a **right of first refusal** to the tenant for space adjacent to the leased space, or it may be a true lease option specifying a rent at which the tenant has the right but not obligation to take specified space during some specified window of time.

30.3 EFFECTIVE RENT

Effective rent is a level annuity that has the same present value as that of the expected lease cash flows. Effective rent can be computed from either the landlord's or tenant's perspective. When dealing with long-term leases, the effective rent construct can aid in the comparison across alternative lease structures and lease terms, although one must be careful in making such comparisons. The effective rent typically does not satisfactorily quantify all of the relevant issues to either side.[5]

Effective rent is computed in two steps. First, you calculate the present value of the expected cash flow under the lease. We will label this value LPV:

$$LPV = CF_1 + \frac{CF_2}{1 + k} + \frac{CF_3}{(1 + k)^2} + \cdots + \frac{CF_T}{(1 + k)^{(T-1)}} \qquad (1a)$$

where T is the lease term, CF_t is the net cash flow to the landlord in year t, and k is the discount rate.[6] To compute effective rent from the tenant's perspective, the CF_t amounts should represent the tenant's gross cash outflows due to all space occupancy costs, including payment of whatever building operating expenses are not covered by the landlord (e.g., in a net lease). In the second step of the effective rent calculation, you determine the annualized value (or equivalent level annuity payment) of the LTV:[7]

$$Effective\ rent = \frac{(LPV)k}{(1 + k)[1 - 1/(1 + k)^T]} \qquad (1b)$$

where k is the same discount rate as previously, and T is again the term of the lease.[8]

---

[5] In common practice, effective rent is often defined ignoring present value discounting, simply as the sum of all lease cash flows divided by the lease term. However, this is obviously incorrect and can give misleading comparisons.

[6] Here we are depicting annual cash flows for simplicity of illustration, but a more precise calculation would use monthly cash flows for monthly rent, although the effective rent is then often quoted in nominal annual terms as 12 times the monthly rent. Also, note that in leases (unlike mortgages and most other financial calculations) payments are usually *in advance* (that is, at the beginnings of the periods, rather than *in arrears*). Thus, the first cash flow is usually at time zero and therefore undiscounted (already in present value). However, with concessions, this first cash flow may be zero or even negative, for example, if the landlord must pay the tenant's moving costs.

[7] See equation (8a), in section 8.2.3 in Chapter 8.

[8] Note that in real world practice the annuity in arrears formula is often used, technically incorrectly, although usually it makes no difference.

30.3.1 Discount Rate in the Effective Rent

In the computation of effective rent, it is common practice for the discount rate (k) to be approximated rather casually for the typical tenant, using some conventional rule of thumb. For example, in the 1990s 10% per year (or 0.833% per month) was widely used. When such "blanket" rule-of-thumb discounting is used, with the same rate applied to all leases and all tenants and without regard to the current yields and term structure of interest rates in the bond market, the effective rent calculation is in theory little more than a type of shorthand way of quoting rents to account for concessions and landlord capital expenditures (such as tenant improvement expenditures, TIs). Effective rent used in this way does not measure very precisely the impact of the lease on the market value of the lessor's property rights. While effective rent defined in this simplified way does have some practical usefulness, in the present chapter we will suggest a slightly more correct and sophisticated approach that is still intuitive and easy to apply.

Suppose we are interested in defining the effective rent so that it reflects the market value that the lease would have, say, in a lease-obligation-backed security (LOBS) traded in the bond market.[9] Then the discount rate used in the effective rent calculation should reflect the credit rating of the tenant as well as the current yield curve in the bond market. In other words, k should equate to the rate at which the tenant could borrow money in an unsecured loan with duration equal to the duration of the lease cash flows.[10] After all, the lease cash flows are contractual cash flows backed by the credit of the tenant, similar to loan cash flows pledged to a lender when the tenant borrows money.[11] In fact, the tenant's borrowing rate is a good rate to use to compute the effective rent from the tenant's perspective, at least for a typical fixed-rent lease.[12]

The computation of effective rent from the landlord's perspective may be viewed a little differently. The landlord is typically interested in using the effective rent to measure the impact of the lease on the market value of his property rights. For this purpose, it makes more sense to define the effective rent based on the present value attributable to the leased space over the period of time covered by the lease. This present value consists of two components. The first is the value of the lease itself, for example, as it would be valued as a component in a LOBS traded in the bond market, as we just described. To evaluate this component of the landlord's value, the tenant's borrowing rate on an unsecured loan would indeed be the correct discount rate, as we described earlier. But another component to the landlord's value is usually associated with the leased space. If there is a positive probability that the tenant will default on her lease, then discounting the lease cash flows at the tenant's unsecured borrowing rate will reflect the effect of this default probability on the present value of the lease. In other words, the lease present value will be reduced by the probability that some components

---

[9] LOBS were defined in Chapter 20, and discussed briefly also in section 10.2.4 in Chapter 10.

[10] Duration was defined in Chapter 19, section 19.1.1.

[11] If the lease includes revaluation, indexing (such as CPI adjustments), or percentage of sales components, then the lease cash flows will not be exactly like those of fixed interest rate bonds, as they will have some contractual volatility. Such differences could affect the appropriate discount rate in either direction. For example, a CPI-adjusted lease results in the lease being a partial hedge against inflation risk (better than bonds), and therefore should probably be discounted at a lower OCC than the tenant's borrowing rate.

[12] Note that the default risk is based on the probability that the tenant will become insolvent or declare bankruptcy. Thus, for example, if the U.S. government is the tenant, then the yield on the appropriate duration Treasury Bond would be the correct discount rate for computing the effective rent.

of the contractual lease cash flow might never be paid by the tenant.[13] These unpaid rents would indeed be losses to the bondholders of a LOBS backed by the lease.[14] But the landlord probably would not face that much loss in cash flow from the leased space in the event of tenant default during the lease term. In a long-term lease, it is likely that the landlord would be able to evict the defaulted tenant and rent the space to a new tenant before the end of the original lease term. For this reason, a lower discount rate, better approximated by the rate at which the tenant could borrow on a *secured* loan, would typically be a more appropriate discount rate to use to compute the effective rent from the landlord's perspective.[15]

30.3.2 Effective Rent Numerical Examples

To illustrate the calculation and usage of the effective rent as defined, we will examine two hypothetical leases in this section, from both the landlord's and the tenant's perspectives. Both leases are net, that is, the tenant pays the operating expenses.

Lease A is characterized as follows:

- Term: 5 years
- Rent: $20/SF, net
- Concessions: 1 year free rent, up front
- Tenant still pays operating expenses during rent holiday

Assuming a discount rate of 7%, lease A's effective rent is seen to be $15.44/SF, computed as follows:[16]

$$LPV = \$0 + \frac{\$20}{1.07} + \frac{\$20}{(1.07)^2} + \frac{20}{(1.07)^3} + \frac{\$20}{(1.07)^4} = \$67.74$$

$$\textit{Effective rent}(A) = \$67.74(.07)/\{1.07[1 - 1/(1.07)^5]\} = \$15.44/SF$$

[13] Recall from Chapters 18 and 19 that the loan interest rate reflects the stated yield, which includes an ex ante yield degradation component so that the contractual cash flows (without provision for expected losses due to default) will discount at the stated yield rate to the present value of the loan. See, for example, section 19.2.1 in Chapter 19.

[14] Actual LOBS often have default protection provided or paid for by the landlord. For this reason the yield on LOBS may not be reflective of the appropriate unsecured tenant borrowing rate to use in computing the effective rent on a specific lease.

[15] Note that, in principle, the state variable that governs the tenant's lease default event is the net income or value of the tenant's firm, not the market rent or value in the real estate space or asset market in which the building is situated. In the absence of an explicit cancellation option written into the lease, only limited liability and bankruptcy law enables the tenant to have a put option on their leased space, that is, the ability to avoid payment of remaining rents under the lease. More sophisticated approaches to lease valuation based on real options valuation theory (as introduced in Chapter 28) can often allow a more rigorous valuation of leases, particularly complex leases involving options of various types written into the lease. For example, Steve Grenadier (1995b) developed a procedure that also incorporates the dynamics of the space rental market into the lease valuation procedure.

[16] Note that the effect of the concession of one year free rent causes the first year's cash flow to be zero. In the present example we have ignored leasing costs borne by the landlord, such as tenant improvement expenditures (TIs). In reality, such costs often cause the first year of the lease to have net negative cash flow for the landlord. In any case, it is important to include the effect of landlord leasing costs such as TIs in the computation of the effective rent from the landlord's perspective, for purposes of comparing the value of alternative lease proposals.

Lease B is characterized as follows:

- Term: 6 years
- Rent: $24/SF, net
- Concessions: 2 years free rent, up front
- Tenant still pays operating expenses during rent holiday

Again assuming a discount rate of 7%, lease B's effective rent is seen to be $14.90/SF, as computed here:

$$LPV = \$0 + \frac{\$0}{1.07} + \frac{\$24}{(1.07)^2} + \frac{\$24}{(1.07)^3} + \frac{\$24}{(1.07)^4} + \frac{\$24}{(1.07)^5} = \$75.97$$

Effective rent (B) = $75.97(.07)/\{1.07[1 - 1/(1.07)^6]\}$ = $14.90/SF

Other things being equal, the landlord would prefer lease A because $15.44 > $14.90. Now consider these same two leases from the perspective of the tenant. As these are net leases, the tenant must add the expected operating expenses he will have to pay in order to compute the total effective rent from his perspective.[17] This is necessary so that comparisons between alternative leases with different expense provisions can be made on an apples-to-apples basis. Supposing that operating expenses are initially $10/SF and are expected to grow at a rate of 2% per year, we have the following effective rent calculations from the tenant's perspective. Note that we will use a modestly higher discount rate of 8% instead of 7% to reflect the lack of residual value in the event of default.

Lease A (tenant's perspective):

$$LPV = \$10.00 + \frac{\$30.20}{1.08} + \frac{\$30.40}{(1.08)^2} + \frac{\$30.61}{(1.08)^3} + \frac{\$30.82}{(1.08)^4} = \$110.99$$

Tenant effective rent (A) = $110.99(.08)/\{1.08[1 - 1/(1.08)^5]\}$ = $25.74/SF

Lease B (tenant's perspective):

$$LPV = \$10.00 + \frac{\$10.20}{1.08} + \frac{\$34.40}{(1.08)^2} + \frac{\$34.61}{(1.08)^3} + \frac{\$34.82}{(1.08)^4} + \frac{\$35.04}{(1.08)^5} = \$125.86$$

Tenant effective rent (B) = $125.86(.08)/\{1.08[1 - 1/(1.08)^6]\}$ = $25.21/SF

---

[17] Landlord capital expenditures offered to the tenant as part of the lease package (TIs) need not generally be explicitly incorporated in the tenant's effective rent calculation. However, in comparing alternative lease proposals, the tenant needs to consider possible differences between the TIs being offered in the different proposals. Obviously, common sense must apply in evaluating an overall lease proposal package. It may make sense for a tenant to pay a higher effective rent if in return he receives a TI allowance or build-out from the landlord that makes the space sufficiently more attractive.

Thus, not surprisingly, the tenant has the opposite preferences to the landlord. *Other things being equal*, the tenant prefers lease B over lease A, because $25.21 < $25.74.[18]

The leases we have examined here are very simple, involving no renewal or cancellation options. Appendix A at the end of this chapter presents a simple way of approximately adjusting the effective rent calculation to incorporate a renewal option.

30.3.3 Summarizing Effective Rent

Although effective rent, when properly calculated based on a risk-adjusted discount rate, gives an important indication of the value of a given lease, neither the tenant nor the landlord should necessarily prefer the lease alternative with the best (i.e., lowest or highest, respectively) effective rent. The reason is that important strategic considerations are left out of the effective rent calculation. In the remainder of this chapter we turn our attention to these broader leasing strategy considerations.

30.4 BROADER LEASING STRATEGY CONSIDERATIONS: TERM LENGTH AND THE SPACE MARKET TERM STRUCTURE OF RENT

Among the most important leasing strategy considerations not present in the effective rent calculation is the length of the lease term. We will consider this issue in this section from both the landlord and tenant perspectives, including a consideration of implications for the resulting empirical **term structure of rents**, that is, the way rents vary in the space market at a given time as a function of the lease term. A good way to approach this question is to consider what is left out of the effective rent construct we described in the previous section. In other words, why would a landlord sometimes prefer a lease alternative with a lower effective rent, or a tenant prefer an alternative with a higher effective rent?

30.4.1 Interlease Risk

As noted in the previous section, the tenant's borrowing rate reflects the risk *within* each lease once it is signed, that is, the risk that needs to be considered in the **intralease discount rate**. This is the only risk relevant to determining the present value of the lease once it is signed, and hence the only risk that is incorporated in the effective rent measure (via the effective rent discount rate, k). But the intralease discount rate does not well reflect the risk *between* leases across time, the risk relevant for what we previously called the **interlease discount rate**.[19] The interlease discount rate is the rate applied to discount expected future cash flows from leases not yet signed, discounting across time periods between the successive lease signing dates. The interlease discount rate is typically higher than the intralease discount rate because the expected cash flows are not contractually fixed between leases: it is not known for certain at what rent level a future lease will be signed. Thus, the expected cash flows beyond an existing lease are more risky than those within an existing lease.

---

[18] To facilitate comparisons between alternative lease offers, effective rents should normally be based on net cash flows, that is, *net* rents from the landlord's perspective and *gross* rents from the tenant's perspective.

[19] Differential intra- and interlease discounting was introduced in Chapter 8 (section 8.2.7) and Chapter 10 (section 10.2.2).

There is an important implication from the fact that interlease risk is not reflected in the effective rent calculation: *longer-term leases reduce risk in a way that is not reflected in the effective rent calculation*. Longer-term leases reduce the uncertainty in the landlord's future cash flow expectations by contractually fixing more future years' worth of cash flow from the building. This makes the landlord's property rights more like a bond and less like property equity, in terms of investment performance. Other things being equal, this would typically be perceived as making the landlord prefer longer-term leases at the same effective rent, or be willing to accept lower effective rent for longer-term leases, relative to a projection of what the future short-term (or **spot**) rents will be. Appendix B at the end of this chapter presents a numerical example and quantitative discussion of this issue.

30.4.2 Releasing Costs

Another consideration that is important in leasing strategy, but that is left out of the effective rent calculation, is **releasing costs**. Typically both the landlord and the tenant face costs associated with releasing. Many of these costs are typically not included in the effective rent calculation. For example, landlords face expected vacancy and search costs to find a new tenant whenever a lease expires without being renewed. Tenants face moving costs, including disruption of operations. Because releasing presents potential deadweight costs to both sides in the lease agreement, releasing considerations generally affect both sides of the lease negotiation, landlord and tenant, in the same direction as far as preferred lease term is concerned. In particular, releasing costs make it advantageous for both sides to prefer longer-term leases, ceteris paribus. In this respect releasing costs are different from the interlease risk we considered in the previous section. Interlease risk causes landlords to prefer longer-term leases, while tenants prefer shorter-term leases, ceteris paribus. Thus, interlease risk has a clear implication for a downward-sloping term structure of rents as an equilibrium result in the space market (as shown in Appendix B), while releasing costs do not carry a general implication for the term structure of rents. Instead, the consideration of releasing costs suggests a general bias toward longer-term leases at whatever term structure of rents prevails in the market, so as to minimize releasing costs over the long run.

30.4.3 Flexibility (Option Value) in Leases

Certain characteristics of leases and leasing strategy can affect the future decision flexibility of either the tenant or the landlord, or both. Flexibility is valuable because it gives options to decision makers. Some considerations and factors that relate to the flexibility issue include expectations about the future rental market, tenant expectations about their future space requirements, and landlord concerns about building redevelopment rights. None of these considerations are reflected in the effective rent calculation per se.

1. **Expectations about the future rental market.** Expectations regarding the future trend in spot rents in the relevant space market make the opportunity cost of the lease a function of the lease term. For example, if spot rents are expected to rise, then longer-term leases must have higher effective rents than they otherwise would. This is required for both landlords and tenants to be indifferent between long-term and short-term leases. With rising spot rent expectations, the expected opportunity cost (to the landlord) or opportunity value (to the tenant) of forgoing a strategy of rolling

over short-term leases is greater for longer-term leases within the horizon of rising projected short-term rents. If, on the other hand, spot rents are expected to fall, then the opposite is the case and longer-term leases should have lower effective rents relative to shorter-term leases than would be the case otherwise. This expectation effect overlays the generally slightly downward-sloping equilibrium term structure of rents with constant spot rent expectations due to the interlease risk effect noted in section 30.4.1.[20]

If landlord and tenant expectations differ regarding the future trend in spot rents in the market, such differences might be either complementary or conflicting in terms of reaching a negotiated lease agreement. For example, if the tenant believes rents will rise and the landlord believes rents will fall, then expectations are **complementary** in the sense that it will be easier for the two sides to come to an agreement. If the landlord believes rents will rise and the tenant believes rents will fall, then expectations are **conflicting** in the sense that it will be more difficult for the two sides to agree to a rent level. In the event of conflicting expectations, if one side or the other (or both) can convince the other to change his or her space market rent expectations at least partially in the direction of the other's, then agreement will be facilitated. If space market expectations are conflicting and not reconcilable, then agreement will be facilitated by reducing the lease term length, thereby reducing the impact of future changes in market rents on the opportunity cost of the lease. In effect, *shorter lease term length increases option value* for both the landlord and the tenant by providing more flexibility to take advantage of favorable developments in the rental market.[21] Thus, rental market expectations will typically lead both landlords and tenants in the same general direction, namely, toward preferring shorter-term leases. In this respect, space market expectations do not carry an overall general implication for the equilibrium term structure of rents.

2. Tenant expectations about future space requirements. Expectations regarding tenant future space requirements influence the ideal lease term length from the tenant's perspective. For example, if the tenant knows she will need the space for exactly three years, then a three-year lease term would normally be best. If the tenant expects her business to grow steadily in size, then shorter-term leases may be preferred in expectation of a future need to expand. Lease options on adjacent space or other space in the same building can sometimes also help with such expectations. In general, the more uncertainty surrounding the tenant's future space needs, the greater the value to the tenant of retaining flexibility in her space commitments, and therefore the greater the option value to the tenant in signing shorter-term leases.[22]

[20] Note that, at least from the landlord's perspective, the spot rent expectations that matter are those relevant to a given (aging) building, not the average rent in the space market across all buildings currently in that market at each point in time. The age of the average building in the market may not increase with chronological time, as the building stock in the submarket may be renewed. But the opportunity cost of long-term leasing to the landlord is based on what the landlord could rent the space in the given building for in short-term leases rolled over at the prevailing short-term market rent. This is also the relevant opportunity value for the tenant, holding the level of service constant at that provided by the same building over time.

[21] In effect, the longer the lease term is, the longer will be the period of time over which the releasing option is given up. As noted in Chapter 28, options always have positive value.

[22] Note that it is not the lease itself, but rather the absence of a lease commitment that contains option value. The less space and time is encumbered under leases, the more option value remains.

3. Landlord's redevelopment option. On the landlord side, a lease encumbers the property owner's normal right to demolish or redevelop the leased building structure. A shorter-term lease reduces the length of time for which this right is relinquished, thereby preserving more flexibility for the landlord in this regard. Once again, the option value lies not in the lease, but in the lack of lease, temporally speaking.

To summarize, the three flexibility considerations and factors noted here, market rent expectations, tenant future space requirement expectations, and the value of the landlord's redevelopment option, all suggest a greater value for shorter-term leases, other things being equal. Thus, flexibility considerations work in the opposite direction to releasing cost considerations, presenting both parties with a similar trade-off decision. Cancellation options written into leases (on either or both sides) can preserve some or all of the flexibility option value for either (or both) the landlord and tenant, making such options potentially very valuable.

30.4.4 Staggered Lease Expirations and Releasing Risk

The considerations regarding optimal lease term consider each lease separately from the other leases in a building (or portfolio of buildings owned by the landlord). From the landlord's perspective it may not be desirable to have all (or most) leases expiring at (or near) the same future point in time. If a bunch of leases expire around the same time, the building will be heavily exposed to the vicissitudes of the rental market at a single point in time. The risk or volatility in the building's future cash flow can be reduced by staggering lease expiration dates more uniformly across time. Depending on what the future lease expiration pattern looks like in a given building, this may cause the landlord to prefer either a longer or shorter lease term length in a given deal than would otherwise be the case.

30.4.5 Summary: Rent Term Structure and Optimal Lease Term Length

In section 30.4 we raised four considerations of leasing strategy that are not included in the effective rent calculation: interlease rental market risk, releasing costs, flexibility considerations, and lease expiration timing considerations for the landlord. The first consideration, interlease rental market risk, implies that, other things being equal (such as the rent), landlords prefer longer-term leases and tenants prefer shorter-term leases. In equilibrium this likely results in longer-term leases tending to have lower rents than they otherwise would (relative to expectations about future spot rent levels), but given that, it implies that lessors and lessees will be *neutral with respect to lease term length*. The second consideration, releasing cost, implies that longer-term leases will be preferred by both lessors and lessees, and therefore carries no general implication for the equilibrium term structure of rents. The third consideration, flexibility, implies that shorter-term leases will be preferred by at least one party, probably by both parties in the lease, and therefore carries no general implication for the equilibrium term structure of rents. Finally, the fourth consideration, lease expiration timing, will have implications that could go either way regarding lease term length depending on the specifics of the situation, and therefore holds no general implication for the term structure of rents.

The overall result of all of these strategic leasing considerations can therefore be reduced to the following general principles:

1. The equilibrium term structure of rents will tend to be characterized by a slight downward slope over the lease term (i.e., lower rents in longer-term leases), relative to the general trend in spot market rents (i.e., if rent expectations are sufficiently rising, then the term structure of rents will be upward-sloping).

2. Optimal lease term length is largely a trade-off between releasing costs and the value of flexibility.

3. Based largely on (2), specific space submarkets or market sectors (property usage types) will typically have characteristic lease term lengths that largely prevail within each market.

As a result of point (3), here are some stereotypical characteristic lease terms that prevailed in various types of commercial property space markets during the latter part of the 20th century.[23]

Hotel:	1 day–1 week
Apartment:	1 year
Small retail:	2–5 years
Office:	3–10 years
Anchor retail:	5–15 years
Industrial:	5–20 years

In general, releasing costs are lowest in hotels, second lowest in apartments, and highest in anchor retail and industrial leases. The need for (and value placed on) flexibility of lease termination is greatest in hotels and apartments and lowest in anchor retail and industrial space. Small retail and typical office space fall midway between, in both the releasing cost and the value of flexibility dimensions.

30.5 OTHER LEASING AND RENT ISSUES

In addition to the optimal term length and term structure of rent considerations described in the preceding section, several other issues that are not internalized within the effective rent calculation are important in an overall consideration of leasing strategy and leasing behavior. We will briefly note a few of the most important in this section, including microspatial trade-offs and synergies, the use of percentage rents, the use of concessions, and the question of optimal search behavior on the part of landlords for tenants.

---

[23] These characteristic lease terms were fairly widespread and fairly stable over time. Additional factors are also involved in determining the characteristic lease terms, in addition to the releasing cost/flexibility trade-off described here. For example, see Grenadier (1995b, 1995c).

30.5.1 Microspatial Trade-Offs and Synergies

Microspatial considerations refer to issues regarding the design and management of space *within* a single property or project. This includes issues and decisions such as externalities, synergies, and trade-offs across tenants and across leasable spaces, some of the most interesting and important considerations in commercial property management. In many cases the value of a commercial property can be greatly affected by the use of clever mixing and matching of different types of tenants and different types of spaces. These types of considerations are often particularly important in retail, office, and mixed-use properties. Because they are not reflected in the effective rent calculation, they explain why a landlord might rationally offer a lease with a lower effective rent to one tenant, or why a tenant might knowingly choose a lease alternative with a higher effective rent. Some examples of microspatial considerations include the following.

1. **Optimal space size.** Larger spaces usually command less-than-proportionately higher rents (i.e., rent/SF tends to decline with the size of the leased space). However, smaller spaces (i.e., greater numbers of tenants) involve higher management costs (per SF) for the landlord, and often less efficient use of the building's gross space potentially available (due to the need for more common areas). Also, it is typically difficult to find tenants for particularly small or irregularly shaped spaces. Space size and configuration issues such as these are particularly important in the design phase of building development or redevelopment, but may also be important whenever long-term leases of large spaces expire, presenting possibilities for subdivision or consolidation and reconfiguration of leasable spaces.

2. **Tenant mix synergies.** Certain types of tenants generate positive externalities by enabling other nearby tenants to earn higher profits. The opposite may also be the case, as incompatible adjacent tenants generate negative externalities.[24] An extreme and important example of positive externalities is what is known as **anchor tenants**. Most prominent in retail development, the anchor in a shopping center draws customers who then shop at smaller tenants' stores. Anchor tenants in office buildings may add prestige to buildings, perhaps by having the building named after them. The landlord is normally able to capture a large portion of such positive externalities in the rents charged to the nonanchor tenants. Therefore, from the landlord's perspective (as well as that of the anchor tenant) it makes sense for the landlord to share such externality benefits with the anchor tenant, and to use such sharing to help lock the anchor tenant into a long-term commitment to the property. This is one reason anchor tenant leases are often for very long terms and at effective rents that are favorable to the tenant. In some cases the anchor tenant may obtain an equity or equity-like position in the property. In retail properties the landlord may also, in effect, have an equity-like position in the anchor tenant, as the rent may include a percentage component (this reflects the fact that landlord and anchor tenant are often, in effect, equity partners in the retail development). The art of tenant mixing extends not only to matching the right sort of anchors with the right sort of nonanchor tenants, but also includes optimal mixing, matching, and location of the nonanchor stores. Use of short lease terms and/or renewal and cancellation options on both sides is common in many retail centers to enable the tenant mix to be constantly optimized in the dynamic retail market where flexibility is particularly important.

[24]The concept of externalities was defined in Chapter 3, section 3.3.1.

30.5.2 Why Percentage Rents?
(Consideration of Optimal Rent Structure)

Percentage rents, in which the tenant pays to the landlord a proportion of the revenues earned in the rented space, are common in class A retail property, especially among small tenants in multitenant properties such as malls and shopping centers. This arrangement often makes sense for several reasons.

1. Incentive compatibility. Percentage rents give the landlord a direct incentive to help maximize store revenues. Landlords have some influence over store revenues because landlords control the tenant mix in the shopping center, and some mixes provide more synergy and positive externalities than others. Without sufficient incentive, landlords might not optimize the tenant mix.

2. Risk reduction. Many retail tenants are small businesses, and rent is typically a larger portion of the total operating expenses of small retail businesses than it is of other types of firms. This makes such firms more sensitive to the leveraging of their business operating risk caused by fixed rents. If rent is proportional to revenue, then this leveraging effect is reduced. This is depicted in Exhibit 30-1, which shows, in a stylized way, the difference in the net income volatility of the tenant's store with fixed versus percentage rent. The difference between the heavy solid gross operating margin line and the rent line (either fixed or percentage, the latter indicated by the dashed line) is the tenant's net revenue stream over time. Notice that with percentage rents the landlord is, to a degree, like an equity partner of the tenant, sharing in the tenant's operating risk and growth.

In fact, the use of fixed and percentage rent components can be varied so as to produce different effects depending on the nature of the tenant. By increasing the fixed base rent component and decreasing the variable percentage component, the resulting increased operating leverage places the retail tenant under more pressure and more incentive to maximize revenue. The landlord may want to place some tenants under

Exhibit 30-1 How Percentage Rent Reduces Operating Leverage

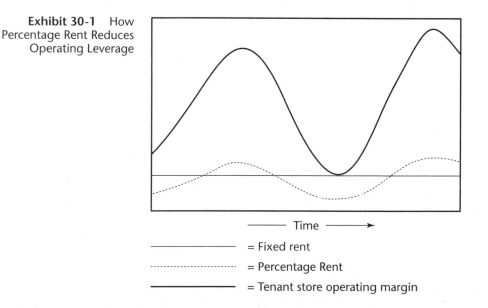

———— Time ————→

———————— = Fixed rent

· · · · · · · · · · · · · = Percentage Rent

———————— = Tenant store operating margin

such pressure and incentive, if the tenants are financially strong enough to handle the risk, and if by increasing their revenues the tenants will increase total shopper flow-through in the center, thereby bringing positive externalities to the other stores. This argument will tend to apply more to anchor tenants and tenants that are large national chains.

30.5.3 Why Concessions?

Why are quoted rents "stickier" than effective rents? Why do landlords often seem to prefer to give out free rent and generous TI and moving expense allowances up front instead of taking a lower regular rent? For example, in our numerical example in section 30.3.2, why does the $20/SF lease A not simply charge the tenant $15.44/SF every year for five years starting immediately, rather than take no cash flow at all for the first year? Several reasons are worth pointing out.

1. **To ease tenant moving or start-up expenses.** It is not uncommon for a new tenant to be under more financial or cash flow strain when they first move into a new space. They may be just starting up, or expanding, or incurring large moving expenses. Thus, up-front concessions often help to ease this burden, in effect, matching better the timing of rental expenses with revenue generation by the tenant. This argument particularly applies to concessions such as TIs and moving allowances.

2. **Strategic timing of cash flow receipts.** There may be some strategy in the timing of cash flow receipts. Higher future cash flows may make it easier to sell the building at a higher price or to refinance the loan on the building, if these events are more likely to occur in the future than in the near term. This might make sense if the landlord has more liquidity at present than she expects to have in the future. It might also make sense if the property asset market is not fully rational, susceptible to NOI illusions in which property buyers or lenders are ignorant of the typical use of concessions on the part of property owners and sellers. This does not sound very likely, but even if there is only a small chance of getting away with such an illusion, why throw away that chance?

3. **The value of private information in a thin market.** The **quoted rent** (aka **asking rent**, e.g., the $20/SF in lease A) is what gets reported to the public and to the other tenants. The concessions are usually much more a private matter between the lessor and lessee. Thus, concessions are a way of concealing from other existing or prospective tenants (and from competing landlords, or perhaps even potential investors) exactly how low a rent the tenant is paying and how soft is the demand for the building. In a thin market with imperfect information, keeping such information private may have some value in some circumstances.

30.5.4 Optimal Asking Rent and Optimal Vacancy

What is the optimal vacancy rate for an existing building? Why isn't the optimal rate zero? Of course, vacancy is not an objective or goal as such, so it may seem silly to think of an optimal vacancy rate. Nevertheless, if space is never vacant in a multi-tenant building, that is probably a sign that the landlord is not maximizing the long-run profit the building can earn. Simply put, if, on average, 10% higher rents could be charged if the landlord absorbed 5% average vacancy (by taking enough time to search for more eager or appropriate tenants when leases expire), then the result would be 5% higher profits for the building. The optimal vacancy rate results from value-maximizing management of the building. It will vary from building to building and can never be pinned down precisely, but we can say something about it by focusing the analysis on a question of more direct relevance to the landlord: what is the **optimal asking rent** as the landlord searches for tenants to fill vacant space?

Recall that in real estate we typically have **noisy price information**. This is typically true in the space market as much as it is in the asset market, and it lies at the root of the concept of **rational vacancy**, the idea that there is an optimal vacancy rate greater than zero for every building. The uniqueness of tenants and buildings and locations underlies the reason it makes sense for there to be some vacancy. Uniqueness of space and tenants makes the rental market **thin**, that is, there are not constantly a lot of very similar potential tenants doing deals for a lot of very similar spaces. Market thinness causes a lack of good information about the nature of the rental market, including the question of what effective rent would clear the market for any given building at any given time. In the absence of perfect information about the price at which a given space can rent, it makes sense to spend some time searching, probing the market. If you want to get a more concrete feeling for this point and see how the concept of optimal asking rent can be analyzed, check out Appendix C at the end of this chapter. There we present a simple quantitative model of optimal tenant search policy from the landlord's perspective.

30.6 CHAPTER SUMMARY

Commercial property leases and leasing strategy are among the most fundamental, important, and complex topics in real estate investment and property management. Understanding long-term leases and leasing strategy is also central to many types of professional real estate careers. This chapter only skimmed the surface, presenting an introduction and overview of the leasing topic. Nevertheless, we covered much of the basic terminology and basic analytical tools relevant to current professional practice for finance and investment-oriented users.

APPENDIX 30A: VALUING A LEASE RENEWAL OPTION

Leases often contain a variety of options written explicitly into the lease contract, modifying the rights and responsibilities that the landlord and tenant would otherwise face. Some options belong to the tenant, and some, to the landlord. In general, it is rather complicated to quantify fully and rigorously the effect such options have on the value of the lease to either party. The most sophisticated approach involves the use of financial option valuation theory (OVT), which you were introduced to in Chapter 28. Steve Grenadier and others have developed the application of OVT to lease valuation.[25] However, a less rigorous, more intuitive technique known as decision tree analysis (DTA) is sometimes used to quantify approximately option values in this context. In this appendix we will demonstrate this approach for a simple numerical example of a tenant's renewal option.

Consider again the example five-year lease A from section 30.3.2, with a nominal rent of $20/SF. Recall that we estimated the effective rent of this lease at $15.44 from

---

[25]See, in particular, Grenadier (1995b), for an elaboration of this approach, which is quite technical.

the landlord's perspective, using a discount rate of 7%. Now suppose that the lease also grants the tenant an option to renew after five years, for another five years, at $20/SF. The effect of this renewal on the effective rent from the landlord's perspective can be quantified in four computational steps.

Step 1. *Describe the subjective probability distribution of market rents at the time the option matures, based on current information.* In our example, suppose the landlord believes that at the end of five years (the lease first term expiration date), there is a 50% chance that rents in the relevant space market will be $22/SF, and a 50% chance that they will be $18/SF. This expectation is depicted in a binomial branch diagram in Exhibit A30-1a.[26]

Step 2. *Quantify the present value of the renewal option under each future scenario.* Assuming the discount rate is still 7%, if market rents are $22/SF, then the option to renew the lease for five years at $20/SF will be worth[27]

$$LPV_5 = (\$22 - \$20) + \frac{\$22 - \$20}{1.07} + \frac{\$22 - \$20}{1.07^2} + \frac{\$22 - \$20}{1.07^3} + \frac{\$22 - \$20}{1.07^4} = \$8.77$$

Note that the tenant is entitled to pay only the difference between the projected market rent ($22) and the rent if she exercises the option ($20) that is the benefit (to the tenant) or cost (to the landlord) of the renewal option exercise. Also note that as the rent is paid in advance (with no up-front concessions presumed for a new lease), the exercise of the renewal option has its initial $2 incremental impact at the end of year 5 (beginning of year 6), and so is not discounted in the computation of the year-5 present value.

On the other hand, if market rents are $18/SF as of the end of year 5, then the lease renewal option will be worth nothing, as there would be no point in the tenant renewing at $20 when she can get a lease for $18 in the then-prevailing market. So the option simply would not be exercised.

The decision tree representation of the conditional option value as of the end of year 5 is shown in Exhibit A30-1b.

Step 3. *Quantify the risk-adjusted present value today (time zero) of the future option value.* This is done in two steps that can usually be done in either order.[28]

Step 3a. *Discount each conditional future value back to the present.* Normally, a pretty high opportunity cost of capital (OCC) should be used in this discounting because

---

[26] In general, the trees in DTA can have more than two branches. Each node represents a decision or valuation point, and the branches going forward in time from each node specify mutually exclusive, exhaustive subsequent states conditional on the node from which they branch. Thus, the probabilities across all branches coming out of each node must sum to 100%, as these are probabilities conditional on the node having been arrived at.

[27] Some indication of the reasonable expectation of forward short-term interest rates can be obtained from examination of the yield curve in the bond market. (See the discussion of ARMs in section 17.1.2 of Chapter 17, and the discussion of the yield curve in section 19.1.3 of Chapter 19.)

[28] The order does not matter because of the distributive property of addition and multiplication: $[(0.5)x + (0.5)y]/(1 + r) = (0.5)x/(1 + r) + (0.5)y/(1 + r)$.

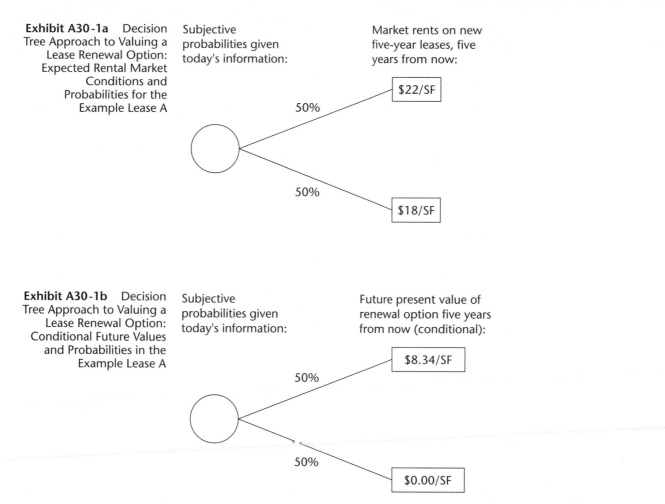

Exhibit A30-1a Decision Tree Approach to Valuing a Lease Renewal Option: Expected Rental Market Conditions and Probabilities for the Example Lease A

Subjective probabilities given today's information:

Market rents on new five-year leases, five years from now:

50% — $22/SF

50% — $18/SF

Exhibit A30-1b Decision Tree Approach to Valuing a Lease Renewal Option: Conditional Future Values and Probabilities in the Example Lease A

Subjective probabilities given today's information:

Future present value of renewal option five years from now (conditional):

50% — $8.34/SF

50% — $0.00/SF

options tend to be pretty risky, especially if they are not deeply "in the money" (i.e., almost certain to be exercised). For example, if existing lease payments are discounted at 7%, and unlevered property cash flows are generally at, say, 9%, then future option values might discount at, say, 15%:[29]

$$\text{PV}(\$8.77 \text{ in 5 yrs.}) = 8.77/(1.15)^5 = \$4.36$$
$$\text{PV}(\$0.0 \text{ in 5 yrs.}) = 0/(1.15)^5 = \$0$$

Step 3b. *Sum across the possible scenario present values, weighted by their present subjective probabilities of occurrence.* In this case,

$$(.50)4.36 + (.50)0 = \$2.18$$

---

[29] Note that the risk in the option will probably change over time as new information arrives relevant to the likelihood of option exercise. The difficulty of knowing the correct discount rate to employ in this step is a major weakness in the DTA approach (as compared, for example, to the more rigorous, but much more technical and complex, OVT-based approach).

Are Renewal Options "at Market Rent" Worthless?

Lease renewal options are often written giving the tenant the right to renew at the market rent prevailing at the time of lease expiration. There might be a provision for this market rent to be determined by an appraiser if the tenant and landlord cannot agree as to what the market rent is at that time. In a highly efficient ("information rich") rental market (i.e., one in which there is a lot of easily available information about the rents and other terms in the leases being signed, and where there is a lot of leasing activity employing relatively homogeneous leases on relatively homogeneous spaces), this option is effectively no more than a right of first refusal. Such rights have value to the tenant because they enable the tenant to be assured that he can avoid the cost of moving if he doesn't want to move. They may have some slight cost to the landlord because they remove some potential negotiating leverage the landlord could otherwise use to try to obtain a slightly above-market rental rate from the tenant (on the basis that the tenant would save moving expenses).* In a thin ("information poor") market like many real estate rental markets, the option to renew at market value has an additional value to the tenant (and cost to the landlord). In a thin rental market it is never obvious exactly what the market rent is for a given space at a given time (hence the possible need for an appraiser to arrive at a value estimation). In such circumstances, the landlord might be able to find a particularly eager tenant who was willing to pay, in effect, more than the going market rent (and more even than the existing tenant, who would face moving costs if he did not renew). While the chance of this happening might be small, nothing prevents the landlord from trying, unless the tenant has a renewal option.**

Thus, in real estate a renewal option may have some value to the tenant (and cost to the landlord) even if the option is only for renewal at prevailing market rates, and assuming the contract gives the tenant some power over the estimation of what that market rate is (e.g., by giving the tenant a say in the selection of the rent appraiser). To quantify the value of such a renewal option, one could use a decision tree framework similar to that described in this appendix. From the landlord's perspective the upside (opportunity cost) branch would be based on the difference between the expected market rent and the potential upside that the landlord might be able to get from an eager tenant willing to pay more than market rent (net of the landlord's expected search costs) or from the existing tenant who would avoid moving costs by renewing. From the tenant's perspective the upside branch would be based on the minimum of either the landlord's differential noted earlier, or the expected moving costs the tenant would face if required to move to another equivalent space at the market rent. In both cases the downside branch would have a zero value as in the previous example. The values would be discounted and multiplied by probabilities as in the previous example, with the upside probability reflecting the ex ante likelihood that the landlord could get the above-market lease from either a new tenant or the existing tenant.

*Note, however, that the tenant has a counterthreat in a thin leasing market: If the tenant leaves, the landlord will typically have to incur some search and transaction costs to find a new tenant, even without charging more than the "market rent."

**Note that optimal search behavior on the part of the landlord does not imply that the ex ante expectation is that the landlord will find an above-market tenant, but it may imply some possibility that the landlord will find such a tenant.

This gives the present value today of the lease renewal option. This is a negative value (or positive cost) to the landlord, who gives the option to the tenant.

Step 4. *Convert the renewal option present value to an impact on effective rent.* Using the annuity formula (for cash flows in advance), a PV of $2.18 equates to a five-year 7% annuity of $0.50 per year:

$$\$0.50 = (7\%)(\$2.18)/\{(1 + 7\%)[1 - 1/(1 + 7\%)^5]\}$$

So the impact of the renewal option is to reduce the effective rent of lease A from $15.44 to $14.94 for the landlord.

APPENDIX 30B: NUMERICAL EXAMPLE
OF LANDLORD LEASE TERM INDIFFERENCE RENT

We noted in section 30.4.1 that consideration of interlease risk typically makes the landlord prefer longer-term leases, other things being equal (such as the rent and the expected future market rent). The implication of this is that the landlord will be indifferent between longer-term leases with lower effective rents and shorter-term leases with higher effective rents. For the same underlying reason, tenants will typically have the opposite term preference based on interlease risk, preferring shorter-term leases, other things being equal. This results in tenants having the same general downward-sloping indifference rent. That is, tenants typically will be willing to pay higher rents for shorter-term leases, at least in the face of flat future market rent projections. This general relationship, and the typical magnitude of the implied indifference rent slope, will be demonstrated with a simple numerical example in this appendix.

Suppose that the rental market is characterized as follows:

- The intralease discount rate is 8% for both the landlord and the tenant.
- The interlease discount rate is 12% for both the landlord and the tenant.
- Spot rents (short-term leases) are expected to remain flat at $100/year, net.
- There are no releasing costs and there is no vacancy between leases.

Under these assumptions the building value to the landlord is a perpetuity of the expected future rental payments.

Now consider the building value assuming short-term rental, that is, with the building entirely exposed to spot rental market every year. In this case all expected cash flows are discounted at the interlease discount rate because there are no long-term leases locking in contractually fixed rents. Thus, the building value (V) is $833.33, calculated as follows:

$$V = \frac{\left[\frac{1.08}{0.08}\left(1-\left(\frac{1}{1.08}\right)^1\right)\$100\right]\Big/1.12}{1-\left(\frac{1}{1.12}\right)^1} = \frac{\$100}{0.12} = \$833.33 \tag{B.1}$$

In formula (B.1) we have expanded the simple perpetuity formula as an infinite series of one-period annuities to illustrate that we are evaluating the building as a series of short-term leases, within each of which the intralease discount rate of 8% may be applied.[30] Formula (B.1) assumes that rents are paid annually in advance, with the first rent payment to be received at the end of the first year when the first

---

[30] You should recognize the expression in the square brackets in the numerator of (B.1) as the present value of a level annuity with payments in advance ($n = 1$, $r = 8\%$). This value is received every $T = 1$ years in perpetuity, starting one year from the present. So the rest of formula (B.1) is the level infinite geometric series formula, discounted to time zero. The overall numerator is the value of the first term in the series (the value of the first lease, as of time zero). The denominator on the bottom is one minus the common factor discounting each subsequent lease: ($1/[1 + r]^T$), where r is the interlease discount rate, and T is the length of each lease term (in this case, 12% and 1, respectively).

lease will be signed (as if this is a new building with one year expected until the first rental payment).

Now consider the same building value assuming that the space will be perpetually released once every 10 years in successive 10-year long-term leases made at the spot market rate each time (of course, with the same assumptions as before regarding rent paid in advance and the first lease signed one year from present). In this case the value of the building would be $954.30, computed as in formula (B.2).[31]

$$V = \frac{\left[\frac{1.08}{0.08}\left(1 - \left(\frac{1}{1.08}\right)^{10}\right)\$100\right]\Big/1.12}{1 - \left(\frac{1}{1.12}\right)^{10}} = \$954.30 \tag{B.2}$$

Note that the expected effective rent in the 10-year leases in (B.2) is the same as that in the 1-year leases (spot rent) in (B.1), namely, $100.[32] Yet we have a higher building value in (B.2). It appears that the landlord can increase property value simply by signing longer-term leases, provided she can get the same rent per year. Mechanically, the increased use of the intralease discount rate in the building perpetuity valuation, reflecting the reduced cash flow uncertainty due to the use of long-term leases, allows a 14.52% increase in building value in this case, from $833.33 to $954.30.

Another way of putting this is to say that, all else being equal and assuming constant projected future spot rents, landlords should be indifferent between shorter-term leases at higher rents and longer-term leases at lower rents. In particular, in the previous example (with an 8% intralease discount rate and a 12% interlease discount rate), rents for 10-year leases could be 1/1.1452 = 87.32% of the short-term spot rental rate, and the landlord would then be indifferent between either a 1-year lease and a 10-year lease because either type of lease would give the same property value. If spot rents are $100, then this indifference on the part of landlords would occur if 10-year lease rents were $87.32 per year, as confirmed in formula (B.3):

$$V = \frac{\left[\frac{1.08}{0.08}\left(1 - \left(\frac{1}{1.08}\right)^{10}\right)\$87.32\right]\Big/1.12}{1 - \left(\frac{1}{1.12}\right)^{10}} = \$833.33 \tag{B.3}$$

Alternatively, if effective rents on 10-year leases were indeed $100, then the spot rent on short-term leases would be $114.52 for landlord indifference.

In general, if future spot rents are projected to remain constant at the current level, then the indifference rent will assume a downward-sloping curve as a function

---

[31] Mathematically, formula (B.2) is the same formula as formula (B.1), the level annuity formula imbedded in the level perpetuity formula, discounted one period to time zero. The only difference is that in (B.2) the lease term, T, is 10 years instead of 1 year. (See section 8.2.7 in Chapter 8.)

[32] This is consistent with the flat rent expectations in the space market.

Exhibit B30-1
Indifference Rent as a
Function of Lease Term
(due to interlease risk
impact only, assuming flat
spot rent expectations)

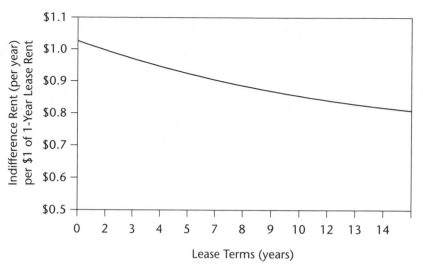

of the lease term, as indicated in the chart in Exhibit B30-1 (which assumes an intralease discount rate of 8% and an interlease discount rate of 12%).[33]

Now consider the tenant's perspective on this same issue. The key point is that, assuming the same intralease and interlease discount rates, the absolute present value of a perpetual stream of rent payments is the same to the tenant as it is to the landlord, only this cash flow stream is a cost to the tenant whereas it is a positive value to the landlord. In other words, the tenant cash flow stream is just the negative of the landlord's cash flow stream. Thus, tenants have the same downward-sloping lease term indifference rent curve as landlords do (with constant spot rents).

An example may clarify the intuition behind this result. Suppose the tenant produces widgets that are sold for $1 each with a variable production cost of $0.50 each. Expected production is 1,000 widgets per year in perpetuity. The opportunity cost of capital for widget production investment (apart from rent) is 10% per year. If the rent is $100/year then the value of the tenant firm is

$$V = PV(widget\ net\ income) - PV(rent)$$
$$= \$500/0.10 - PV(rent)$$
$$= \$5,000 - \$833 = \$4,167, \text{ if 1-year leases at } \$100/year$$
$$= \$5,000 - \$954 = \$4,046, \text{ if 10-year leases at } \$100/year$$

Thus, the tenant prefers short-term leases.

[33] Note that the intralease and interlease discount rates are not generally based on the same point in the bond market yield curve. In particular, the intralease discount rate is based on the yield of bonds with the same duration as the lease cash flows, while the interlease discount rate is based on the yield of bonds with duration equal to the lease term. As leases are characterized by level payments in advance, the lease duration is substantially shorter than the lease term. Thus, if the bond market yield curve has its typical upward-sloping shape, then this is another reason (in addition to space market risk) that the interlease discount rate is typically higher than the intralease discount rate.

As a result, the equilibrium rent term structure that would allow both landlords and tenants to be indifferent across leases of different term lengths is downward-sloping. Tenant firm value equals[34]

$$V = \$5,000 - \$833 = \$4,167, \text{ if 1-year leases at } \$100/\text{year}$$
$$= \$5,000 - \$833 = \$4,167, \text{ if 10-year leases at } \$87.32/\text{year}$$

[34]Again, this assumes constant future projected spot rents. If future spot rents are not constant, the declining indifference curve refers to rent *relative to* what it would otherwise be, reflecting the expected future spot rents as well as the impact of rental market risk.

APPENDIX 30C: SIMPLE MODEL OF OPTIMAL LANDLORD SEARCH FOR TENANTS

This appendix presents a simple numerical example of optimal landlord behavior searching for tenants, in the form of a model of optimal asking rent. The analysis here may also be of interest as an example of how modern business quantitative analysis techniques can be used to shed light on basic commercial property management and investment decision issues.

Consider the following simplified model of optimal asking rent for a landlord with an empty space. In particular, suppose the search problem is characterized by the following conditions:

1. Potential tenants "arrive" (or are found) randomly at an average rate of one per month. The expected wait time until the first potential tenant is found is one month, until the second is found is two months, etc.[35]

2. The ex ante probability distribution of the maximum rent each potential tenant will accept (the tenant's reservation rent) is a normal probability distribution with a mean of $10/SF/year and a standard deviation of ±$1/SF/year. All leases are for five-year lease terms, annual rent, payments at beginnings of years. The landlord only finds out what each tenant is willing to pay when that tenant "arrives."

3. If the tenant refuses the landlord's asking rent, the landlord has to wait until the next potential tenant arrives, and the space remains vacant during the wait time. When the space leases, it will always lease at the landlord's asking rent.[36]

4. When a lease expires, this process repeats (no renewals), in perpetuity.

5. The intralease discount rate is 8%; the interlease discount rate is 12%.

Given this situation, the question we want to answer is, What asking rent will maximize the present value of the building?

To answer this question we can specify the following analytical model. Let

$$A = \text{Asking rent}$$

$$N(A;10,1) = \text{Cumulative normal probability less than } A \text{ when mean is 10 and STD is 1}[37]$$

$$p = \text{Probability tenant refuses landlord's offer} = N(A;10,1)$$

$$w = \text{Expected wait time (in years) until space is leased (average length of vacancy period between leases)}$$

---

[35] This is what is known as a Poisson arrival process. It is characterized by being "memoryless," that is, one arrival is not influenced by another arrival. Obviously, this is a simplification of the real world process by which landlords and tenants search for each other, but it does capture much of the essence of the reality. Mathematically, the probability that the first potential tenant will be found t periods from now is $\lambda e^{-\lambda t}$, where e is the base of natural logs (approximately 2.7183) and λ is the average rate of arrival per period. In a Poisson process, the expected time until the first arrival is the inverse of the arrival rate, $1/\lambda$, and the expected time until the nth arrival is n/λ. Measuring time in years, condition (1) is postulating $\lambda = 12$ arrivals/year.

[36] Conditions (2) and (3) together represent the lease negotiation process. Once again, the model abstracts and simplifies from the real world, while still capturing much of the essence.

[37] For example, in Excel this quantity is given by the function NORMDIST(A,10,1,1).

L = PV of each lease at time of signing (intralease discounting)

V = PV of building (perpetuity)

vac = Expected vacancy rate for building

Now consider the expected wait time, w. As p is the probability any one potential tenant will refuse the landlord's offer, $(1 - p)$ is the probability any one tenant will accept the offer. The expected time until the first tenant arrives is $(1/12)$ years. Similarly $(n/12)$ is the expected time (in years) until the nth potential tenant arrives. But the second potential tenant will never arrive if the first one accepts the landlord's offer. And the third tenant will never arrive if the second one accepts the landlord's offer. Consider the expression:

$$(n/12)(p^{n-1})(1 - p) \tag{C1}$$

This expression is the product of three factors: $(n/12)$ is the expected time until the nth potential tenant arrives; p^{n-1} is the probability that all $n - 1$ previous arrivals have refused the landlord's offer (i.e., the probability that the landlord has to wait for the nth arrival); and $(1 - p)$ is then the probability that the nth arrival will accept the landlord's offer. The unconditional expected waiting time for the landlord, w, is thus a sum of expressions like (C1), summed across all of the possible number of potential tenant arrivals, which is, in principle, infinite ($n = 1, 2, \ldots, \infty$). Therefore, the landlord's expected waiting time until she finds a tenant for a given space is

$$w = \frac{1}{12}(1 - p) + \frac{2}{12}p(1 - p) + \frac{3}{12}p^2(1 - p) + \cdots \tag{C2}$$

Equation (C2) is an infinite series, but it has a simple finite value, namely,[38]

$$w = \frac{1}{(1 - p)12} \tag{C2a}$$

Lease value as a function of the asking rent, A, is given by the annuity formula (with payments in advance):

$$L = \frac{A(1.08)\,[1 - (1/1.08)^5]}{0.08} \tag{C3}$$

The property value, V, is then given by the formula for the sum of an infinite geometric series, as a perpetuity of leases, each expected to occur $5 + w$ years after the previous lease was signed, discounting at the interlease discount rate between leases. The first lease is expected to be signed w years from time zero:[39]

---

[38] There is some intuition in this result. A Poisson arrival process with arrival rate λ in which each arrival has an independent probability $(1 - p)$ of being a "hit" is equivalent to a Poisson arrival process of hits with arrival rate $\lambda(1 - p)$. In a Poisson process, the expected time until the first arrival is the inverse of the arrival rate. Thus, the expected time until the arrival of the first hit is $1/[\lambda(1 - p)]$, or in the present case, $1/[12(1 - p)]$.

[39] Recall that the formula for an infinite geometric series is the first term in the series divided by the quantity one minus the common ratio. (See sections 8.2.1 and 8.2.7 in Chapter 8.)

$$V = \frac{L/(1.12)^w}{1 - (1.12)^{(w+5)}} \tag{C4}$$

The average vacancy in the space is simply given by the expected time between leases divided by the lease term (five years):

$$vac = w/(w + 5) \tag{C5}$$

This model can be easily solved quantitatively in a computer spreadsheet. Try some values of the asking rent, A, until you find the one that maximizes the present value of the space, V. Here is the result of such an iterative search procedure, starting at the average potential tenant reservation rent of $10/SF, and working up from there.

A	V
$10.00	$95.48
$11.00	$96.04
$12.00	$54.64
$10.90	$96.87
$10.80	$97.40
$10.70	$97.68
$10.60	$97.75
$10.50	$97.65

Thus, the optimal asking rent in this case is $10.60/SF (to the nearest dime), which gives a building value of $97.75/SF. At this asking rent the expected waiting time to find a tenant that takes the rent (expected vacant period between leases) is $w = 0.304$ years, that is, between three and four months. This implies an optimal long-term average vacancy rate of $vac = .304/5.304 = 5.7\%$.[40]

Now repeat this example only suppose the landlord's ex ante uncertainty surrounding the rent the potential tenants will take is doubled. That is, assume everything is the same except the standard deviation of the normal probability distribution is $2/SF instead of $1/SF. Thus, $p = N(A;10,2)$. Now we find that the optimal rent is $11.80/SF, giving a building value of $104.87/SF with an average vacant period of 0.453 years (about five months) and an average vacancy rate of 8.3%.

Note that the optimal asking rent, the optimal average vacancy rate, and the building value all increase with the uncertainty or range in the maximum rent the potential tenants are willing to accept. This is a general result. The two cases examined here are shown in the graph in Exhibit C30-1. (The numbers on the left-hand vertical scale refer to $/SF for the top [solid] lines indicating property value, and this same

---

[40]At the $10.60 asking rent, the probability of potential tenant refusal is $p = N(10.60;10,1) = 72.6\%$, which gives an acceptance probability of $1 - 0.726 = 0.274$. This gives an expected wait between leases of $w = 1/[(0.274)12] = 1/3.288 = 0.304$ years.

Exhibit C30-1 Landlord Optimal Asking Rent and Vacancy Rate as a Function of Rental Market Uncertainty (Assumptions: Tenant maximum rent distribution normal with mean = $10/SF, lease term = five years, intralease discount rate = 8%, interlease discount rate = 12%.)

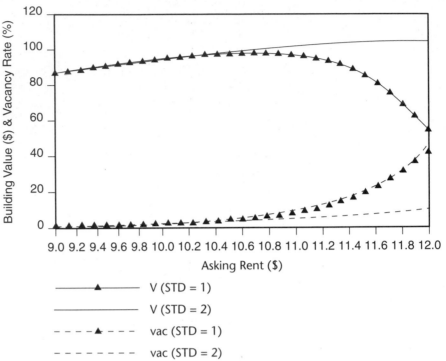

scale refers to average percent vacancy for the bottom {dashed} lines. The triangle markers indicate the case with the lower rent uncertainty.) The general shapes of the curves in this graph are also a general result for typical realistic numbers.

From the previous analysis we can derive several results about the optimal asking rent for the landlord in this simple model:

- Other things being equal, the optimal asking rent is higher the more uncertainty there is about the rental market.

- The greater is the rental market uncertainty, the more "forgiving" is the negative impact on property value due to an equal dollar magnitude error on the landlord's part in not selecting the optimal asking rent (i.e., the curve is "flatter" for higher variance in the rent distribution, at least on the upside).

- The effect on property value is relatively forgiving for erring on the side of asking too low a rent, while the negative value impact of asking too high a rent can be much more severe, especially when there is little uncertainty about the rental market.

- Other things being equal (such as the mean expected tenant reservation rent), and assuming optimal landlord behavior, the property is more valuable the greater is the uncertainty in the rental market, but this value effect is small even though our model ignores the effect of rent uncertainty on the interlease discount rate (which might dampen or reverse this result).

Although the model on which these conclusions are based is a simplification of reality, the first three conclusions are fairly robust if one interprets them broadly or "figuratively." For example, they can be paraphrased in the following two more general principles of optimal tenant search and leasing strategy for a landlord:

1. Be a bit daring and aggressive in pursuit of good leasing deals if you have a lot of uncertainty about the rental market. (This is a generalization of the first two preceding points.)

2. Be conservative and play it safe if the landlord is very risk averse or if the rental market is very obvious, with little uncertainty about market rents. (This is a generalization of the third previous point.)

KEY TERMS

lease	revaluated rent	interlease discount rate
lessor	indexed rent	spot rents
lessee	percentage rent	releasing costs
ground lease	base rent	complementary expectations
gross (full service) lease	lease term	conflicting expectations
net lease	concessions	microspacial considerations
rent	lease covenants	tenant mix synergies
triple net (NNN) lease	sublet	anchor tenants
hybrid lease	lease options	quoted (asking) rent
expense stops	right of first refusal	optimal asking rent
flat rent	effective rent	noisy price information
graduated rent	term structure of rents	rational vacancy
step-ups	intralease discount rate	thin markets

STUDY QUESTIONS

30.1. Describe the major ways in which commercial leases specify rent changes over time during the lease term.

30.2. Under what conditions are rent concessions typically offered?

30.3. Why do landlords usually offer rent concessions, such as free rent up front, when supply exceeds demand, rather than just reducing the rent?

30.4. Why might a landlord prefer a lease with a lower effective rent?

30.5. Calculate the effective rent of the following leases from the landlord's perspective, assuming the tenant faces a 10% borrowing rate:

a. 5-year net lease, $15/SF, 1 year free rent up front

b. 5-year net lease, starting at $10/SF, with step-ups of $1 each year

c. 5-year net lease, starting at $10/SF, CPI adjustments every year equal to 50% of the change in the CPI. CPI change (inflation) is expected to be 5% per year.

d. 5-year gross lease, $20/SF, expenses expected to be $8/SF initially, growing at 3% per year

e. 5-year gross lease, $20/SF, expense stop at $8/SF, expenses expected to grow at 3% per year

f. 6-year net lease, $15/SF, tenant improvements paid by landlord at beginning in the amount of $20/SF

*30.6. Use the methodology described in Appendix A of this chapter to quantify the impact on the effective rent of the lease in question 30.5(a), if the lease also includes a renewal option for the tenant, giving the tenant the right (but not obligation) to renew the lease after five years at $16/SF. Assume that the present subjective probability regarding the market effective rents for new five-year leases, five years from now, is that there is a 50% chance that the market rent will be $18/SF, and a 50% chance that it will be $14/SF. Discount existing lease cash flows at 10% for the purpose of determining effective rent or existing lease present value, and future option values at 20% per year for the purpose of determining risk-adjusted present value.

*30.7. You are representing a landlord in a lease negotiation with a prospective new tenant who would occupy a vacant space in a newly completed building. You have proposed a 10-year lease at an effective rent of $18/SF. The tenant is interested, but has indicated he might prefer a shorter-term lease. You believe the rental market is currently "in balance" and will remain so over the foreseeable future (i.e., future spot rents will remain about the same as they are today). Assuming a tenant borrowing rate of 8% and an interlease discount rate of 12%, what effective rent on a five-year lease would be equally desirable for your client as the $18/SF rent you proposed on the 10-year lease? [Hint: Use the procedure described in Appendix B of this chapter.]

*30.8. You are a leasing agent working for a landlord who has some vacant space to fill. You believe you can find potential tenants at an average rate of two per month. Typical leases in this market are for five years, with net effective rent around $15/SF per year (annual payments in advance, with 8% tenant borrowing rate and 12% landlord required return between leases). Based on your knowledge of the rental market, you feel that the typical potential tenant you would find for this space would have a normal probability distribution of acceptable rent ranging around the $15/SF figure with a standard deviation of ±$3/SF. What is the optimal asking rent so as to maximize the landlord's present value of her building, and what can you tell her about how long to expect until you get a tenant? [Hint: Use the model described in Appendix C of this chapter.]

30.9. Discuss why there is often a common prevailing lease term in a given rental market.

30.10. Explain how rental market risk would typically cause the landlord to prefer longer-term leases and the tenant to prefer shorter-term leases holding effective rent constant. [Hint: Consider interlease or rental market risk and how this affects building value from the landlord's perspective and how it affects the value of the tenant's firm.]

30.11. What factors would tend to make both landlords and tenants prefer shorter-term leases, ceteris paribus?

30.12. What factors would tend to make both landlords and tenants prefer longer-term leases, ceteris paribus?

30.13. Discuss the pros and cons of a simple definition of effective rent, such as the undiscounted sum of all the rental payments divided by the lease term, versus a DCF-defined effective rent based on the tenant's borrowing rate as the intralease discount rate.

PART VIII

References and Additional Reading

Black, F. and M. Scholes. "The Pricing of Options and Corporate Liabilities." *Journal of Political Economy* 81: 637–659, 1973.

Capozza, D. and R. Helsley. "The Fundamentals of Land Prices and Urban Growth." *Journal of Urban Economics* 26: 295–306, 1989.

Capozza, D. and Y. Li. "The Intensity and Timing of Investment: The Case of Land." *American Economic Review* 84(4): 889–904, September 1994.

Childs, P., S. Ott, and T. Riddiough. "The Value of Recourse and Cross-Default Clauses in Commercial Mortgage Contracting." *Journal of Banking and Finance*, April 1996.

Childs, P., S. Ott, and T. Riddiough. "The Pricing of Multi-Class Commercial Mortgage-Backed Securities." *Journal of Financial and Quantitative Analysis*, December 1996.

Childs, P., S. Ott, and T. Riddiough. "Noise, Real Estate Markets, and Options on Real Assets." MIT Center for Real Estate Working Paper, 2000.

Dunn, K. and C. Spatt. "An Analysis of Mortgage Contracting: Prepayment Penalties and the Due-on-Sale Clause." *Journal of Finance*, 1985.

Epperson, J., J. Kau, D. Keenan, and W. Muller. "Pricing Default Risk in Mortgages." *AREUEA Journal* (subsequently *Real Estate Economics*) 13(3), fall 1985.

Geltner, D. "On the Use of the Financial Option Price Model to Value and Explain Vacant Urban Land." *AREUEA Journal* 17(2): 142–159, summer 1989.

Geltner, D., T. Riddiough, and S. Stojanovic. "Insights on the Effect of Land Use Choice: The Perpetual Option on the Best of Two Underlying Assets." *Journal of Urban Economics* 39(1): 20–50, January 1996.

Graff, R. and M. Young. "Real Estate Return Correlations: Real-World Limitations on Relationships Inferred from NCREIF Data." *Journal of Real Estate Finance & Economics* 13(2): 121–142, September 1996.

Grenadier, S. "The Persistence of Real Estate Cycles." *Journal of Real Estate Finance and Economics* 10, 95–119, 1995a.

Grenadier, S. "Valuing Lease Contracts, A Real Options Approach." *Journal of Financial Economics* 38(3): 297–331, 1995b.

Grenadier, S. "Flexibility and Tenant Mix in Real Estate Projects." *Journal of Urban Economics* 38(3): 357–378, 1995c.

Grenadier, S. "The Strategic Exercise of Options: Development Cascades and Overbuilding in Real Estate Markets." *Journal of Finance* 51(5): 1653–1679, December 1996.

Jennings, M. *Real Estate Law*, 4th ed. Cincinnati: South-Western, 1995.

Kau, J., D. Keenan, W. Muller, and J. Epperson. "Pricing Commercial Mortgages and Their Mortgage-Backed Securities." *Journal of Real Estate Finance & Economics* 3(4): 333–356, December 1990.

McDonald, R. and D. Siegel. "The Value of Waiting to Invest." *Quarterly Journal of Economics* 101: 707–728, November 1986.

Merton, R. C. "The Theory of Rational Option Pricing." *Bell Journal of Economics and Management Science* 4: 141–183, spring 1973.

Quigg, L. "Empirical Testing of Real Option-Pricing Models." *Journal of Finance* 48: 621–639, June 1993.

Riddiough, T. and H. Thompson. "Commercial Mortgage Pricing with Unobservable Borrower Default Costs." *Real Estate Economics* (formerly *AREUEA Journal*) 21(3): 265–292, fall 1993.

Samuelson, P. "Rational Theory of Warrant Pricing." *Industrial Management Review* 6: 41–50, spring 1965.

Titman, S. "Urban Land Prices Under Uncertainty." *American Economic Review* 75(3): 505–514, June 1985.

Titman, S. and W. Torous. "Valuing Commercial Mortgages: An Empirical Investigation of the Contingent Claims Approach to Pricing Risky Debt." *Journal of Finance* 44: 345–373, 1989.

Williams, J. "Real Estate Development as an Option." *Journal of Real Estate Finance & Economics* 4(2): 191–209, June 1991.

Williams, J. "Equilibrium and Options on Real Assets." *Review of Financial Studies* 6: 825–850, 1993.

Appendix
Real Estate Transaction Price Indices
Based on Regression Analysis

At the turn of the 21st century no regularly published index of commercial property prices existed in the United States.[1] This is probably largely due to the lack of a central price data-collection agency, such as exists in the housing industry in the form of the major secondary mortgage market agencies. But there is reason to hope that the development of the Internet and e-commerce in the commercial property market will facilitate centralized price data collection and make it easier to produce transaction-based commercial indices in the future. This appendix presents some techniques and considerations relevant to the development and use of such indices in commercial property investment analysis.

1. HEDONIC AND REPEAT-SALES REGRESSION-BASED INDICES

Let's begin with the basics. For an index of property values, the appreciation return during a given period of time is based on the percentage change in the value of the population of properties the index is meant to represent between the beginning and end of the given period. This population can be thought of as a static portfolio consisting of the same properties at the end of the period as at the beginning of the period. In a periodic return index, the periods are regular and short, such as years or even calendar quarters. Thus, in principle, to compute a periodic return index we need valuations of each property at regular and frequent intervals. The problem is that individual properties do not transact at regular and frequent intervals. In order to help us solve this fundamental problem using regression-based statistical tools, we can conceptualize it in two ways: one way leads to what is called repeated-measures indices, and the other leads to hedonic indices.

The first way we can conceptualize the fundamental return estimation problem is to note that it is, in effect, a "missing observation" problem. This is the same type of problem as the stale appraisal problem in the NCREIF index that we described in Chapter 25.[2] To address this type of problem, we need to estimate the periodic values of the properties

---

[1] A small exception was the multifamily component of the FNMA/FHLMC repeat-sales housing price index.

[2] See section 25.3.1 in Chapter 25.

in the static portfolio when we have no empirical valuation observations for those properties. In the case of a transaction-based index, we want to base the value estimations directly on transaction price evidence.[3]

In fact, we even need to estimate the values of properties when we do have empirical valuation observations because the empirical valuation observations themselves are noisy indications of the "true" market values we are interested in. Thus, our macrolevel valuation procedure must address two problems simultaneously: filling in missing valuation observations and filtering out random noise.

The second way of looking at the fundamental periodic return estimation problem is as follows. All of the properties in our index portfolio do not transact every period. But within each period, some of the properties in our index portfolio (or, more broadly, some of the properties in the underlying population represented by our index) do transact. Thus, we have some transaction price observations for properties each period, just not the same properties. Now if we simply computed the percentage difference between the average prices of the properties that sold during period t and period $t-1$, we would be comparing apples and oranges. The properties that sold in the two periods would be, for the most part, different properties. As a result, there would generally be differences in the average "quality" of the properties selling in one period as compared to the previous period.

Thus, our problem can be viewed as a need to control for quality differences in the properties that happen to sell in consecutive periods of time. For example, suppose the properties that sold in period t happened to be, on average, rather low quality buildings, while those that sold in period $t+1$ happened to be, on average, rather high quality buildings. If we just took a simple average of the valuation observations within each period, we might be led to think that an increase in market value had occurred between period t and period $t+1$ when in fact no such increase had occurred at all. The difference, which appeared to be "longitudinal" (that is, *across time*) in nature, was in fact "cross-sectional" (that is, *across properties within a single period of time*) in nature. So we need to be able to distinguish price differences due to cross-sectional differences in properties (heterogeneity) from price differences due to changes in the property market over time (temporal effects).

As noted, the first of these two conceptualizations of the periodic return estimation problem in private real estate leads to the repeat-sales regression (RSR) procedure, or, more generally, to the repeated-measures regression (RMR) procedure (because the index can be based on appraised values as well as on transaction prices). This procedure was described in Appendix B at the end of Chapter 25. The second conceptualization leads to the use of a hedonic regression model (HRM) to produce the price index. This type of model was introduced in Chapter 23 in the context of macrolevel valuation.

2. HEDONIC REGRESSIONS AND INVESTMENT APPRECIATION RETURN INDICES

As we already described the RMR in some depth in Chapter 25, let's now examine the HRM approach to constructing price indices, and their use in investment appreciation return series. First, consider a simple hedonic regression model of property

---

[3]Appraisal-based indices are based indirectly on transaction price evidence, as appraisers consider such evidence in producing their estimations of value.

value, as we described in Chapter 23, and as depicted in slightly simplified form in equation (1):

$$V_{i,t} = \beta_{0,t} + \beta_t H_{i,t} + \varepsilon_{i,t} \tag{1}$$

In equation (1), $V_{i,t}$ represents the natural log of the price of property i that sold in period t, and we have simplified the hedonic value model for illustration purposes by representing it as having only one hedonic variable, labeled $H_{i,t}$. Thus, $\beta_{0,t}$ is the valuation intercept as of period t, and β_t is the value effect parameter of the hedonic variable (also known as the hedonic characteristic price) as of period t.[4] As usual, $\varepsilon_{i,t}$ represents the regression error due to random noise in the price of the transaction of property i in period t.

The simplest way to use this model to construct a transaction-based price index is to estimate the model each period based on purely cross-sectional price data that are current in that period. Now suppose the static portfolio defining the index consists of a set of n properties, the same properties in both periods t and $t - 1$. Using the estimated parameter values from the hedonic regression in each period, it is possible to compute the value of each property in each period:

$$\hat{V}_{i,t} = \hat{\beta}_{0,t} + \hat{\beta}_t H_{i,t}$$
$$\hat{V}_{i,t-1} = \hat{\beta}_{0,t-1} + \hat{\beta}_{t-1} H_{i,t-1} \tag{1a}$$

The static portfolio value in each period is then computed as the cross-sectional sum of the individual property estimated values:[5]

$$\hat{V}_t = \sum_{i-1}^{n} \hat{V}_{i,t}$$
$$\hat{V}_{t-1} = \sum_{i=1}^{n} \hat{V}_{i,t-1} \tag{2a}$$

Then the transaction-based appreciation return for the index in period t would equal the percentage change in the portfolio value across the two periods: $\hat{r}_t = (\hat{V}_t - \hat{V}_{t-1})/\hat{V}_{t-1}$.

An alternative procedure for using a hedonic regression model to compute a periodic appreciation return index is to define a single, hypothetical representative property. For example, if the index is meant to represent CBD office properties, then one might define the representative property as having hedonic variable values that are a weighted average of the hedonic variable values of all the CBD office properties in the

[4] For example, very simplistically, $H_{i,t}$ might be the size of property i when it sold in period t. More practically (if we really were to have only one hedonic variable on the right-hand side of the valuation equation), $H_{i,t}$ might be the assessed value of property i as of period t, as used by the local property tax authority. (See Clapp and Giacotto [1992].)

[5] To be more precise, we would take the antilog of each property's log-value estimation from equation (1a) before computing the cross-sectional summations in (2a).

country.[6] Then one computes the index value by applying the hedonic valuation model to the hypothetical representative property (h):

$$\hat{V}_t = \hat{\beta}_{0,t} + \hat{\beta}_t H_{h,t}$$

$$\hat{V}_{t-1} = \hat{\beta}_{0,t-1} + \beta_{t-1} H_{h,t-1}$$

(2b)

The appreciation return is then given as $\hat{r}_t = \hat{V}_t - \hat{V}_{t-1}$.[7]

No matter which of these methods is used to compute the index appreciation returns, there is a problem with the method of reestimating a new hedonic valuation regression each period. The problem is that hedonic valuation models tend to be rather complex. They require a lot of observations to be estimated with much accuracy. Especially in the case of commercial properties, it is difficult to obtain enough transaction price data to estimate a new hedonic model each period. This will make the hedonic valuation model too noisy.

A second approach that makes more efficient use of data for the purpose of periodic price-change estimation is what is known as the Court-Griliches procedure.[8] In this approach a single hedonic valuation model is estimated based on a pooled database.[9] This is more efficient because many of the hedonic variables remain essentially constant through time ($H_{i,t} = H_{i,s}$, for all $t \neq s$).[10] By constraining the hedonic price characteristics (the β_t value parameters) to be constant ($\beta_t = \beta_s$), the estimation database can be expanded across time without greatly expanding the number of parameters to be estimated. In order to do this without losing the ability to capture temporal valuation changes, the hedonic regression must allow for a separate intercept in each period. This is done through the use of time dummy variables, one dummy variable for each time period in the database.[11] Each dummy variable assumes a value of unity if the transaction observation occurred in the time period represented by the dummy, or zero if it occurred in another period. The resulting Court-Griliches hedonic regression specification is shown in equation (3):

---

[6] For example, if the hedonic model contains location dummy variables for each metropolitan area (MSA), then the representative property might be defined with fractional values for each location dummy variable equal to the proportion of the aggregate index value located in each MSA. Needless to say, the process of defining an appropriate representative property is complex and full of interesting issues. For example, should one use the mean or median value of the hedonic variables within the index population to define the hedonic variable values for the representative property?

[7] Note that in this case it is not necessary to take antilogs of the microlevel hedonic value estimates, as no cross-sectional aggregation is required. The return is the arithmetic difference because the hedonic value is in logs.

[8] This approach is named after two statisticians who developed the procedure to estimate constant-quality price indices for products that are subject to technological improvement, such as cars and computers. Court's work on cars dates from the 1930s. Griliches rediscovered Court's technique a couple of decades later. (The classical articles are Court (1939), and Griliches and Adelman (1960).

[9] A pooled database contains valuation observations not only from a number of different properties but also spanning the entire time over which one is trying to estimate the price index. Such a database thus includes both cross-sectional variation (across properties) and longitudinal variation (across time).

[10] For example, the property location remains constant, as does its size, typically.

[11] A dummy variable is rather like a switch, taking on a predetermined value according to whether a certain condition is satisfied by the observation.

$$V_{i,t} = \sum_{s=1}^{T} \beta_{0,s} D_{i,s} + \beta H_i + \varepsilon_{i,t} \qquad (3)$$

where the $D_{i,s}$ are the time dummy variables for the periods $s = 1, 2, \ldots, T$, the periods for which the appreciation return index is being estimated. For price observation i, $D_{it} = 1$, and $D_{i,s} = 0$ for all other periods $s \neq t$.

The basic idea in the Court-Griliches procedure is that the cross-sectional component of the model (the βH_i part of the right-hand side of equation [3]) captures the purely cross-sectional effects on property value, while the temporal component of the model (the time dummy variables) captures the purely temporal effects on value. In particular, the coefficients on the time dummy variables reflect the cumulative growth in log value above the base period, associated with each period (s) of time. Given that value is measured in log levels (that is, the natural log of the property value), the arithmetic differences between the adjacent time dummy variable coefficients will trace a history of the implied property market value percentage changes (measured as continuously compounded returns). Thus, we have

$$\hat{r}_t = \hat{\beta}_{0,t} - \hat{\beta}_{0,t-1} \qquad (3a)$$

Note that in the Court-Griliches specification, we lose the ability to see *why* the property index value changed from one period to the next. To what extent was the change in value due to a change in the hedonic characteristic price ($\beta_t \neq \beta_{t-1}$), as opposed to a change in the value of the hedonic variable ($H_{i,t} \neq H_{i,t-1}$)? We cannot tell. All sources of the value change across time will be combined in the time dummy variable coefficients.

This loss of underlying structural explanatory power in equation (3) as compared to equation (1) is a major problem for an urban economist trying to understand the fundamental determinants of property value. But it may be of less concern to an investment analyst more interested in the volatility and temporal comovement characteristics of property as compared to other investments.[12]

Nevertheless, even from a pure investment performance perspective, the loss of the ability to understand the source of value changes in the Court-Griliches procedure can be problematic. For example, some changes in some hedonic variables have cash flow impacts on the property owner. Most notable in this regard are improvements in existing properties that result from capital expenditures. To the extent that temporal value change in the index is due to hedonic changes that have cash flow impacts for owners, such temporal value change does not necessarily represent a net component of the total HPR earned by the index property owners.

A particular problem in the use of the Court-Griliches procedure to quantify investment appreciation returns has to do with the property age hedonic variable. It is impossible to define a well-specified hedonic value model without including age as

---

[12] At the risk of oversimplifying, it might be said that, among economists studying real estate, those with a more urban economics bent tend to be more interested in cross-sectional effects and temporal first moments, while those with a more financial economics bent look to transaction-based price indices primarily for information about temporal second moments (such as volatility, covariance, and autocorrelation). Information about real estate HPR first moments can often be obtained well enough from appraisal-based indices, as noted in Chapter 25 (see section 25.3).

one of the hedonic variables. Yet the Court-Griliches specification forces age to be a purely cross-sectional variable. In the Court-Griliches procedure the effect of age on property value is seen in the value parameter coefficient estimated for age (the $\hat{\beta}_{AGE}$ coefficient), not in the $\hat{\beta}_{0,t}$ time dummy variable coefficients from which the value index is derived. This age effect exacerbates the capital expenditure problem noted previously. It means that Court-Griliches value growth does not include the effect of the passage of real time on property value, that is, it ignores the effect of real depreciation.

For these reasons, it is more accurate to think of a Court-Griliches value index as an index of the average prices of properties sold each year in a *dynamic* population of properties, rather than as an appreciation return index for a *static* portfolio. The Court-Griliches index thus represents average prices in a market that includes new and refurbished buildings being added and old buildings being demolished and subtracted from the database over time. As a result, the average age of properties in the market will generally increase less than the passage of real chronological time (if it increases at all), and the quality level of the sold properties will reflect the effect of capital expenditures on the properties.

To convert a Court-Griliches index from an indicator of market price changes to an indicator of investment appreciation returns, one must account for the effect of both capital expenditures and real depreciation. The former requires that estimates of average capital expenditures per period (as a percent of property value) be subtracted from the index growth.[13] The latter requires that the effect of one period's worth of aging be subtracted from index growth in order to approximate periodic investment appreciation returns.[14]

3. RELATION BETWEEN THE COURT-GRILICHES MODEL AND THE REPEATED-MEASURES REGRESSION MODEL

As noted, the two most widely used procedures for constructing transaction-based price indices in the housing literature are the Court-Griliches hedonic regression model described in the preceding section and the repeated-measures regression (RMR) procedure described in Chapter 25. In fact, the RMR model can be derived directly from the Court-Griliches model. Understanding this relationship can improve your understanding of the strengths and weaknesses of each procedure, for the purpose of constructing transaction-based return indices.[15]

Begin with the basic Court-Griliches model, as presented in the previous section and reproduced here:

$$V_{i,t} = \sum_{s=1}^{T} \beta_{0,s} D_{i,s} + \beta H_i + \varepsilon_{i,t} \tag{3}$$

[13] Care should be taken not to either miss or double-count capital expenditures in computing the total return. If capital expenditures are subtracted from the appreciation return component, then they should not also be subtracted from the income return component. (See the discussion in section 9.2.3 of Chapter 9.)

[14] In other words, it is necessary to subtract real depreciation from the index value change. In principle, such depreciation can be estimated from the coefficient on the cross-sectional age variable. (Recall from Chapter 11 that typical real depreciation rates for commercial property in the United States are in the neighborhood of at least 1% to 2% per year.)

[15] This section is based on Clapp and Giacotto (1992).

where $V_{i,t}$ is the log price of property i sold in period t; H_i is the cross-sectional hedonic property descriptor, and $D_{i,s}$ are the time dummy variables.

Now consider a transaction price database of the type that is used to estimate an RMR-based index. The RMR model is estimated from a database consisting only of the longitudinal changes in value within the same properties across time. In such a database all the properties have been sold at least twice, so that it is possible to define each observation i based on a *pair* of consecutive price observations for the same property. To be more precise, we may specify an RMR model by defining the dependent variable observations as the log of the second sale price minus the log of the first sale price for a given property.[16] Thus, expressed in terms of the Court-Griliches model in equation (3), the RMR is shown in equation (4):

$$V_{i,s} - V_{i,f} = (\beta_{0,s} + \beta H_i + \varepsilon_{i,s}) - (\beta_{0,f} + \beta H_i + \varepsilon_{i,f})$$

$$= (\beta_{0,s} - \beta_{0,f}) + (\beta H_i - \beta H_i) + (\varepsilon_{i,s} - \varepsilon_{i,f}) \qquad (4)$$

$$= (\beta_{0,s} - \beta_{0,f}) + (\varepsilon_{i,s} - \varepsilon_{i,f})$$

Note that the hedonic variables cancel out because in the Court-Griliches model these are purely cross-sectional variables that remain constant across time within each property. Thus, the dependent variable is the cumulative percentage change in property i's price between its first and second sale. The right-hand side of the regression consists purely of time dummy variables that take on the values of positive one if the second sale occurred in the time period represented by the dummy variable; negative one if the first sale occurred in that time period; or zero otherwise. With this specification the coefficients on the RMR dummy variables represent the cumulative log value levels of the index. The price index in levels is the antilogs of these coefficients, and the continuously compounded periodic appreciation returns are the differences in the coefficients:

$$\hat{r}_t = \hat{\beta}_{0,t} - \hat{\beta}_{0,t-1} \qquad (4a)$$

This derivation of the RMR from the Court-Griliches model highlights two important points relevant to the use of RMR-based price indices to construct periodic investment appreciation return series. First, the RMR is seen to be based (implicitly) on the Court-Griliches assumption that property hedonic variables remain constant over time. To the extent that property hedonic characteristics actually change between sales, *and these changes impact the property owner's cash flows* (e.g., capital improvement expenditures), the RMR-based index will overstate the net impact of price appreciation on the typical investor's total HPR. Second, since each observation in the RMR estimation dataset is a *longitudinal* observation within itself (that is, each observation is a price change purely over time, not across properties), and property age is *not* included as a cross-sectional variable on the right-hand side of the RMR specification,

---

[16] This is a different RMR specification from the one demonstrated in Appendix 25B. The specification described here produces an equally weighted geometric (cross-sectional) mean index for appreciation returns only, whereas the specification in Appendix 25B produces a value-weighted arithmetic (cross-sectional) mean index for either appreciation returns or total returns (if the necessary cash flow data is available).

the RMR index *will* include the effect of property aging. Thus, unlike the Court-Griliches model, an RMR index need not be adjusted to reflect real depreciation. The RMR model therefore represents, in that sense, a more useful specification than does the Court-Griliches model for purposes of inferring a series of periodic investment appreciation returns.

REFERENCES AND ADDITIONAL READING

Clapp, J. and C. Giacotto. "Estimating Price Indices for Residential Property: A Comparison of Repeat Sales and Assessed Value Methods." *Journal of the American Statistical Association* 87: 300–306, 1992.

Court, A. "Hedonic Price Indices with Automotive Examples." *The Dynamics of Automobile Demand*, General Motors Corporation, 1939.

Gatzlaff, D. and D. Geltner. "A Transaction-Based Index of Commercial Property and Its Comparison to the NCREIF Index." *Real Estate Finance* 15(1): 7–22, 1998.

Geltner, D. "Temporal Aggregation in Real Estate Return Indices." *AREUEA Journal* 21(2): 141–166, 1993.

Griliches, Z. and I. Adelman. "On an Index of Quality Change." *Journal of the American Statistical Association* 56:535–548, 1961.

Answers to
Selected Study Questions

CHAPTER 1

1.2. Real rents will not necessarily rise just because demand for usage of space is rising. The reason is that supply will also tend to increase to keep pace with demand. Real rents will only increase with increasing demand if it costs more (in real terms, i.e., after general inflation is subtracted) to build new buildings than it did to build the already existing buildings (including the cost of the land). This will generally be the case only when constraints on the supply of available land cause a scarcity of easily buildable sites.

1.4. The curve is kinked because of the long life of structures. When demand for built space falls, the supply of buildings does not fall. As demand grows, new supply of built space can be added at the long-run marginal cost, which is the cost of developing property, including the land cost. This is usually not much more, or even less (in real terms), than it cost to build previous buildings, so the supply curve for additional space is approximately flat. Let Q^* be the existing stock of built space in the market, and R^* be the replacement cost rent, or long-run equilibrium rent in the market. Then the typical supply function looks something like this:

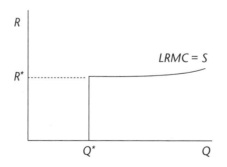

1.6. At first (late 1970s to early 1980s), usage demand growth apparently kept pace with supply growth, allowing real rents to remain constant. Then capital flow into the real estate asset market led developers to increase the supply of built space in the mid- to late 1980s (from Q[80] to Q[90]), but demand either did not increase or did not increase as much as supply during that period (represented by the D[80],D[90] demand function). So, by the early 1990s, there was excess supply, forcing real rents down below the level at which they had been in the early 1980s [R(90) < R(80)]. Thus, while rents kept pace with inflation in the late 1970s and early 1980s, they fell behind inflation during the late 1980s and early 1990s. By the late 1990s usage demand had grown sufficiently to absorb the excess supply of space (D[96]), bringing space markets back to long-run equilibrium levels and allowing rents again to grow at nearly the rate of inflation. The real level of rents was below what it had been when it had previously been in equilibrium in the 1980s, indicating a declining long-run marginal cost curve (downward-sloping long-run supply function, on average, for downtown office properties, perhaps due to a decline in the value of centrality of location).

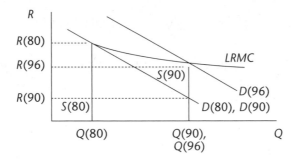

1.8. **a.** $10 million/9.60% = $104,166,667
     b. $3.5 million/8.88% = $39,414,414

CHAPTER 2

2.6. Exhibit 2-5 shows a widening gap with net rents falling farther and farther below the CPI (falling real rents) during the late 1980s and early 1990s. In looking for an explanation purely in the northwest quadrant of the 4Q model, that is, an explanation in the asset market, one would have to posit an increase in investor demand for real estate during the early-to-mid-1980s. This would have resulted in a repricing of real estate assets, reflected by a reduction in cap rates prevailing in the property market. This would have reflected a flow of financial capital into real estate, and the development industry would have converted that financial capital into physical capital in the form of additional stock of space supply, bringing down equilibrium rents in the long run. The picture would resemble that in Exhibit 2-4b.

CHAPTER 3

3.2. According to the simple version of the rank/size rule given in the text, Boston's population should have been 19,938,492/7 = 2,848,356. This is only about half of Boston's actual population of 5,563,475. This shows that the simple version of the rank/size rule given in the text does not quite fit the U.S. system of cities. In particular, the cities tend to be a bit larger than what is predicted by the simple rule. The more general statement of Zipf's Law is as follows:

$$N_j = \frac{K}{j^\beta}$$

where N_j is the population of the jth rank city, K is an unspecified constant, and the exponent β is a constant whose value is "near one." For the top 30 U.S. cities shown in Exhibit 3-1b, statistical regression analysis indicates that K is a bit larger than the population of New York (about 24 million instead of 20 million), and β is about 0.8.

3.3. The rank/size rule is most applicable within a system of cities, that is, the cities within a geographically integrated economy. Economic integration within Europe is a relatively recent development, and at the end of the 20th century Europe was still less economically integrated into a single economy than is the case for the United States.

A regression of the 11 European cities shown in Exhibit 3-6 indicates a β exponent of only 0.55 (Zipf's Law suggests this should be close to 1). The pattern seen in Exhibit 3-6 suggests that a British system has been superimposed onto a continental system in which Mediterranean cultures seem to have a greater preference for large cities than do Germanic cultures. As Europe becomes more integrated, the pattern of European city sizes should gradually conform more to Zipf's Law. This suggests that London may grow, and/or Paris may shrink, relative to the other cities. Prospects are also good for Berlin to grow in rank due to its central location and reestablishment as the capital of Europe's most populous country.

3.6.   The aircraft engine factory and the hotel serving out-of-town convention business are clearly part of the basic (export) sector of the local economy. The revenue obtained from these businesses comes primarily from sources outside of the local area. A grocery store is clearly not part of the basic sector, as it serves primarily only a local clientele. The motel serving traveling salesmen is probably also best classified as part of the nonbasic sector. Although its guests come from out of town, they are not part of a local production process that sells to out-of-town customers. Rather, the opposite is true; they are selling to the locals. (They are part of the import sector rather than the export sector.)

CHAPTER 4

4.4.   The land rent would be $50,000 per year, the residual after all the other factors have been paid: $600,000 - 450,000 - 100,000 = 50,000$.

4.7.   Other things being equal, denser land uses will have a higher land bid-rent at a central location because they make more intensive use of the land. If the residual value is $100 per year per widget made, then a site that makes 2,000 widgets per acre can pay $200,000 in land rent, while a site that makes only 1,000 widgets per acre can pay only $100,000 land rent. More intensive land use will also cause higher-density uses to have a steeper bid-rent function, as the bid-rent gradient for a given land use is directly proportional to the transport costs per acre of land, and more intensive uses tend to have greater transport costs per acre of land. Thus, lower-density uses will not be able to compete against the higher bid rents offered by higher-density uses near central points, while more intensive land uses will not be profitable at locations farther from central points, where transport costs would be higher.

4.10.   The location premium at the center equals the transport costs at the periphery. So the annual transport cost at the periphery is $6,000/acre, or $2,000 per capita (given the density of three persons per acre). If the annual commuting cost per mile of distance from the CBD is $200 per person, then the radius of the city is 10 miles (computed as $2,000 total cost divided by $200 cost per mile).

4.15.   About $\frac{1}{2}\%$ (see footnote 7).

CHAPTER 5

5.2.   Other things being equal, greater uncertainty about future land rents results in higher current land values and higher current land rents. Greater uncertainty means that rational or optimal development would await higher current land rents in order to justify conversion to urban usage (the irreversibility premium). Other things being equal, this would result in a smaller city size (greater density and/or less urbanization).

5.3.   Site 1 would sell for $150,000/(0.12 - 0.03) = 150,000/.09 = $1,667,000. Development of site 1 would cost $1 million for construction plus $1 million for the land (opportunity value), for a total of $2 million. Thus, current development of site 1 is not profitable: $1,667,000 - $2,000,000 = -$333,000, a negative net value proposition.

Site 2 would sell for $800,000/(0.12 - 0.01) = 8000,00/.11 = $7,273,000. Development of site 2 would cost $5 million for construction plus $2 million for the land (opportunity value), for a total of $7 million. Thus, current development of site 2 is profitable: $7,273,000 - $7,000,000 = $273,000, a positive net value proposition.

5.7. Neighborhood succession theory suggests that land rents will tend to remain nearly constant, in real terms, during long periods of stability in the life of a neighborhood. There may be occasional periods of rapid change in land rent and land value in the neighborhood, either positive or negative, as the neighborhood changes its optimal use and density (i.e., as the neighborhood HBU changes) due to evolution of the metropolitan area.

5.11. $0.3 = (1 + x)^{30} \rightarrow x = 0.3^{1/30} - 1 = -0.039 \rightarrow 3.9\%$ per year property value depreciation below the growth rate in location value. The growth in location value may be either positive, negative, or zero.

CHAPTER 6

6.11. $(1,000,000 + 2,000,000)/(1,500,000/12) = 24$ months' supply. This does not indicate an oversupply, as the months supply only exactly equals the typical development project duration. This market would seem to be in approximate balance. There is room to pursue new development projects, as without more development this market will have zero vacancy in two years, less than the natural vacancy rate in any market.

CHAPTER 7

7.5. The possibility of direct ownership of underlying physical assets that are not too large enables a well-functioning asset market to exist trading the underlying physical assets directly. This is the commercial property asset market. This differs from the typical mainstream industrial corporate situation, in which there is generally not a well-functioning asset market trading the underlying physical assets directly. If there were such, then the market values for the underlying assets, which one could observe in the market that directly trades those assets, would be important information to help the corporation know whether they should invest the necessary funds to expand by buying or building additional physical assets. For example, if it would cost the corporation $10 million to build a new blast furnace itself, but it were possible to buy a new blast furnace in the "blast furnace market" for $9 million, then it would not make sense for the corporation to build a new one themselves.

7.11. Using the ending values per dollar of starting value for both real estate and stocks, as well as the CPI (representing the effect of inflation on the number of dollars with equivalent purchasing power), we can examine Exhibits 7-7a and 7-7b to answer these questions as a problem in ratios.

    a. Ending R.E. value = $5,000,000 × (Ending R.E. value/Beginning R.E. value)
= $5,000,000 × (4.75/1.00) = $23,750,000

        Ending stock value = $5,000,000 × (Ending stock value/Beginning stock value)
= $5,000,000 × (3.31/1.00) = $16,550,000

    b. Ending real R.E. value = End Nominal/(Ending CPI/Beginning CPI)
$23,750,000/(2.69/1.00)
= $8,828,996

        Ending real stock value = $16,550,000/(2.69/1.00)
= $6,152,416

    c. Ending R.E. value = $5,000,000 × 2.97 = $14,850,000
Ending stock value = $5,000,000 × 11.83 = $59,150,000
Ending real R.E. value = $14,850,000/1.62 = $9,167,000
Ending real stock value = $59,150,000/1.62 = $36,512,000

7.13. There is no single correct answer to this question. Clearly unique factors and events served to push up commercial property prices during the 1980s. These included (perhaps among others) the inflationary environment of the 1970s and early 1980s, the tax incentives of the 1982 tax act as well as earlier tax codes, the deregulation of the savings and loan industry, and the growth of pension funds and their interest in real estate investment. Also, unique historical events undercut real estate values in the late 1980s and early 1990s. These included (among others) disinflation, the tax reform act of 1986, the savings and loan crisis. and FIRREA. These events will never repeat themselves exactly in the future, and they no doubt had a causal influence in the rise and fall of commercial property prices during the 1980s and early 1990s. On the other hand, there will always be unique historical events; only the specific events do not repeat. The future will never be perfectly predictable, and even rational and efficient capital markets will sometimes misallocate capital in retrospect, which could lead to overbuilding in the space markets. There may be inherent or fundamental characteristics of real estate markets or the real estate system that makes it prone to boom and bust cycles.

7.14. The major institutional sources of capital for commercial real estate in the late 1990s included commercial banks (especially for development capital in the form of construction loans), life insurance companies, pension funds, and public market vehicles including REITs and CMBS (some of whose investment comes from institutions such as mutual funds and pension funds). During the 1990s the public market vehicles greatly increased their relative importance.

CHAPTER 8

8.1. $15,000/1.12 = \$13,393$

8.3. $15,000/1.12^2 = \$11,958$

8.5. $20,000 \times 1.12^2 = \$25,088$

8.7. $15,000/\{[1 + (.12/12)]12\} = 15,000/1.01^{12} = 15,000/1.126825 = \$13,312$

8.9. $20,000 \times \{[1 + (.12/12)]^{(2\times12)}\} = \$25,395$

8.11. $[1 + (.08/12)]^{12} - 1 = .0830 = 8.30\%$

8.13. $[1 + (.08/2)]^2 - 1 = .0816 = 8.16\%$

8.15. $10\% \ BER \rightarrow [1 + (.10/2)]^2 - 1 = .1025 = 10.25\% \ EAR$
$10.25\% \ EAR \rightarrow [(1 + 0.1025)^{1/12} - 1] \times 12 = .0980 = 9.80\% \ MER$

8.17. $10\% \ MER \rightarrow [1 + (.10/12)]^{12} - 1 = .104713 = 10.4713\% \ EAR$
$10.4713\% \ EAR \rightarrow [(1 + 0.104713)^{1/2} - 1] \times 2 = .1021 = 10.21\% \ BER$

8.19. $\exp(.08) - 1 = 1.0833 - 1 = 8.33\%$

8.21. $(30,000/15,000)^{(1/5)} - 1 = 14.87\%$

8.23. $12 \times [(30,000/15,000)^{[1/(5\times12)]} - 1] = 13.94\%$

8.25. $LN(30,000/15,000)/5 = 13.86\%$

8.27. $LN(30,000/15,000)/LN(1 + .10)$
$= 0.69315/0.09531 = 7.27$ years

8.29. $[LN(30,000/15,000)/LN(1 + .10/12)]/12$
$= (0.69315/0.00830)/12 = 6.96$ years

8.31. $LN(30,000/15,000)/.10 = 6.93$ years

8.33. $15,000 \times [1 - (1/1.09)^{10}]/.09 = \$96,265$

8.35. $EAR = [1 + (.09/12)]^{12} - 1 = 9.38\%$
$15,000 \times [1 - (1/1.0938)^{10}]/.0938 = \$94,675$

8.37. $1,250 \times (1 - \{1/[1 + (.09/12)]\}^{(10\times12)})/(.09/12) = \$98,677$

8.39. $98,677$ (from previous question) $+ 50,000/[1 + (.09/12)]^{(10\times12)}$
$98,677 + 20,397 = \$119,074$

8.41. $80,000 \times (.10/12)/\{1 - 1/[1+(.10/12)]^{(25\times12)}\} = \$726.96$

8.43. $-LN[1 - (.10/12)(50,000/500)]/LN(1+.10/12)$
$= -LN(0.16667)/LN(1.00833) = -1.7918/.0083$
$= 215.9$ months

8.45. $1,000 \times [1 + .10/12) \times (1 - \{1/[1 + (.10/12)]\}^{(5 \times 12)})/(.10/12) = \$47,458$

*8.47. $\$1,000,000 \times (.06/12)/([1 - 1/(1 + .06/12)^{60}](1 + .06/12)^{60})$

$= \$14,332.80$. (This takes the formula for the PV as a function of PMT and FV, converts it to a formula for FV as a function of PMT by multiplying by $(1 + i/m)^N$, then inverts this to solve for PMT as a function of FV.

*8.49. Level annuity value is

$PV = \$30(1 - 1/1.08^{10})/0.08 = \$201.30/SF$

Plug this into growth-annuity formula and invert:

$CF_1 = 201.30(0.08 - 0.03)/[(1 - (1.03/1.08)^{10}] = \$26.66/SF$

8.51. $\$10/[0.10 - (-0.01)] = \$10/0.11 = \$90.91/SF$

8.53. (a) NPV at $\$180,000$ and 11% discount rate is $+\$4,394$:

$$4,394 = -180,000 + \left(\frac{15,000}{1 + 0.11}\right) + \left(\frac{16,000}{(1 + 0.11)^2}\right) + \left(\frac{20,000}{(1 + 0.11)^3}\right)$$
$$+ \left(\frac{22,000}{(1 + 0.11)^4}\right) + \left(\frac{(17,000 + 200,000)}{(1 + 0.11)^5}\right)$$

(b) IRR at $\$170,000$ is 13.15%:

$$0 = -170,000 + \left(\frac{15,000}{1 + 0.1315}\right) + \left(\frac{16,000}{(1 + 0.1315)^2}\right) + \left(\frac{20,000}{(1 + 0.1315)^3}\right)$$
$$+ \left(\frac{22,000}{(1 + 0.1315)^4}\right) + \left(\frac{(17,000 + 200,000)}{(1 + 0.1315)^5}\right)$$

*8.55. The rent in the initial lease will be $20 \times 100,000 = \$2,000,000$ per year. The first lease when it is signed will have a PV of $\$8,624,254$. This is a level annuity in advance: $2(1.08/0.08)[1 - (1/1.08)^5] = 8.624254$. The PV today of that first lease is $8,624,254/1.12 = \$7,700,227$. The rent on each subsequent lease will be 1.02^5 higher than the rent on the previous lease, but its PV will be discounted by five more years at 12%. This is a constant-growth perpetuity with a common ratio of $(1.02/1.12)^5$. Thus, apply the perpetuity formula of the geometric series: $PV = a/(1 - d) = 7,700,227/[1 - (1.02/1.12)^5] = 20,615,582$. The space is worth $\$20,615,582$ today.

CHAPTER 9

9.1.

V0	$11,250,000
V1	$12,500,000
CF	$950,000
Inflation	0.0350
T-bond	0.0500
a. Nominal income return	0.0844
b. Nominal appreciation return	0.1111
c. Nominal total return	0.1956
d. Risk premium	0.1456
e. Real appreciation return	0.0735
f. Continuously compounded total	0.1786
g. Continuously compounded appreciation	0.1054

9.2.

Excel set-up:	Values	Returns
V0	$4,200,000	
Low	$3,750,000	−0.1071
Medium	$4,200,000	0.0000
Medium	$4,200,000	0.0000
High	$5,000,000	0.1905
a. Mean	$4,287,500	0.0208
b. STDEVP	$450,521	0.1073

9.3.
    a. 0.0373 versus .0375 = 2 basis points per quarter or 8 basis points per year
    b. 0.0164 Income return versus .0189
        0.0211 Appreciation return vesus .0186
        Difference is 25 basis points/quarter =100 basis points/year

9.4.

	YYQ	BOS	SF
	961	0.0486	0.0242
	962	0.0303	0.0298
	963	0.0310	0.0323
	964	0.0236	0.0680
	971	0.0324	0.0291
	972	0.0329	0.0438
	973	0.0464	0.0371
	974	0.0429	0.1000
	981	0.0582	0.0730
	982	0.0375	0.0793
a. Arithmetic mean		0.0384	0.0517
b. Standard deviation		0.0105	0.0263
c. Geometric mean		0.0383	0.0514
f. Sharpe ratio		BOS: 2.2283	SF: 1.3842

9.5. Fund Data:

	Year				3-Year Total
	1995	1996	1997	1998	
Given Data:					
Unit value beginning of year		$100,000	$98,000	$112,000	
Unit value end of year		$98,000	$112,000	$118,000	
Income paid out per unit (end of year)		$5,000	$10,000	$7,000	
Calculated Data:					
Capital gain per unit		($2,000)	$14,000	$6,000	
Capital return		−2.00%	14.29%	5.36%	
Income return		5.00%	10.20%	6.25%	
a. Total period-by-period return (HPR)		3.00%	24.49%	11.61%	
1 + HPR		1.0300	1.2449	1.1161	
Compound ("chain-linked") value (beginning of year):		1.0000	1.0300	1.2822	
Compound ("chain-linked") value (end of year):		1.0300	1.2822	1.4311	
b. CREF time-weighted geometric mean return, 1996–1998:					12.69%
Investor's Actions and Cash Flow Results:					
Units of CREF held (beginning of year)		2.0	2.0	2.0	
Cash to investor from income distribution	$0	$10,000	$20,000	$14,000	
Units bought at end of year	2.0	0.0	0.0	0.0	
Cash from investor to purchase units	$200,000	$0	$0	$0	
Units sold at end of year		0.0	0.0	2.0	
Cash to investor from liquidation of units		$0	$0	$236,000	
Units held (end of year)	2.0	2.0	2.0	0.0	
Total net cash flow stream for Maxwell's IRR:	($200,000)	$10,000	$20,000	$250,000	
c. IRR for investor:					12.55%

d. The time-weighted geometric mean return.

9.6. Investor's Actions and Cash Flow Results:

	Year				3-Year Total
	1995	1996	1997	1998	
Units of CREF held (beginning of year)		1.0	2.0	1.0	
Cash to investor from income distribution	$0	$5,000	$20,000	$7,000	
Units bought at end of year	1.0	1.0	0.0	0.0	
Cash from investor to purchase units	$100,000	$98,000	$0	$0	
Units sold at end of year		0.0	1.0	1.0	
Cash to investor from liquidation of units		$0	$112,000	$118,000	
Units held (end of year)	1.0	2.0	1.0	0.0	
Total net cash flow stream for Maxwell's IRR:	($100,000)	($93,000)	$132,000	$125,000	
a. IRR for investor:					15.36%

b. Because of the timing of the capital flow into and out of the investment, which in this case was favorable for the investor (bought low and sold high).

c. Because the time-weighted return is independent of the timing of capital flow into or out of the fund, a factor that is not controlled by the fund managers, whereas the IRR does reflect the effect of this timing decision, which in this case is controlled by the investor.

d. The IRR would not be a fair measure of the investment decision maker's performance if that decision maker did not have control over the timing of the capital flow.

Fund Data (Same as Question 9.5):

	Year			3-Year Total
	1996	1997	1998	
Unit value beginning of year	$100,000	$98,000	$112,000	
Unit value end of year	$98,000	$112,000	$118,000	
Income paid out per unit (end of year)	$5,000	$10,000	$7,000	
Calculated Data:				
Capital gain per unit	($2,000)	$14,000	$6,000	
Capital return	−2.00%	14.29%	5.36%	
Income return	5.00%	10.20%	6.25%	
Total period-by-period return (HPR)	3.00%	24.49%	11.61%	
1 + HPR	1.0300	1.2449	1.1161	
Compound ("chain-linked") value (beginning of year):	1.0000	1.0300	1.2822	
Compound ("chain-linked") value (end of year):	1.0300	1.2822	1.4311	
CREF time-weighted geometric mean return, 1996–1998:				12.69%

CHAPTER 10

10.12. The most important problem with the hurdle rate rule is that it does not account for differences in scale among mutually exclusive projects. In selecting the project with the highest spread over its hurdle rate, the investor might not be maximizing the present value of his wealth. A second problem is technical: in some circumstances the project's IRR is mathematically indeterminate. Both of these problems can be dealt with by applying the NPV investment decision rule rather than the hurdle rate decision rule.

10.13.

$$V_0 = \sum_{t=1}^{5} 25,000\,/(1.12)^t + \sum_{t=6}^{10} 30,000\,/(1.12)^t + 300,000\,/(1.12)^{10}$$

$$= \$248,075$$

HP-IDB calculator steps:

$0 \rightarrow CF_0$

$25,000 \rightarrow CF_1,\ 5 \rightarrow N_1$

$30,000 \rightarrow CF_2,\ 4 \rightarrow N_2$

$330,000 \rightarrow CF_3$

$12 \rightarrow I/YR$

$NPV \rightarrow 248,075$

10.14. a. No: $NPV = \$248,075 - \$260,000 = -\$11,925 < 0$

    b. $11.24\% < 12.00\%$

$$-260,000 \rightarrow CF_0$$
$$25,000 \rightarrow CF_1, 5 \rightarrow N_1$$
$$30,000 \rightarrow CF_2, 4 \rightarrow N_2$$
$$330,000 \rightarrow CF_3$$
$$IRR \rightarrow 11.24\%$$

    c. By definition: IRR at $\$248,075$ is 12.00 percent. NPV at $\$248,075$ is 0.

10.15. $\$263,853$. (Same as 10.13, only $11 \rightarrow I/YR$.) This is a 6.36% increase in value $(263,853/248,075 = 1.0636)$ from a one-point change in discount rate.

10.16. $\$254,656$. This is a 2.65% increase in value $(254,656/248,075 = 1.0265)$ from a roughly one-point change in market rent growth rate, even with five years' fixed cash flows from vintage leases.

$$0 \rightarrow CF_0$$
$$25,000 \longrightarrow CF_1, 5 \rightarrow N_1$$
$$31,250 \rightarrow CF_2, 4 \rightarrow N_2$$
$$343,750 \rightarrow CF_3$$
$$12 \rightarrow I/YR$$
$$NPV \rightarrow 254,656$$

10.17. $+\$3,421,053$

10.18. 13.80%

10.19. a. 13%

    b. 11%

    c. 2% (200 basis points) likely disappointment

10.20. a. $\$8.66$ million, the PV of the operating CF stream discounted at 6%.

    b. The property can be bought for $\$12.14$ million, the PV of the projected CFs (including reversion) discounted at the 10.50% blended rate prevailing in the market. The projected reversion ($\$14$ million in 10 years) is worth $\$4.51$ million, discounting at 12%. So the sum of the lease value plus reversion value is $\$8.66 + \$4.51 = \$13.17$ million. Thus, the NPV to the buyer of the deal is $NPV = V - P = \$13.17 - \$12.14 = +\$1.03$ million. [Note: For this NPV to be immediately realizable as a liquid market-value-based NPV, it must be possible to actually sell the unbundled parts of the property at the noted prices.]

10.21. GIM $= \$10$ million$/\$2$ million $= 5$

    Cap rate $= \$1$ million$/\$10$ million $= 10\%$

10.22. a. Property A's $E[r] = 11\%$; property B's $E[r] = 9\%$.

    b. Property A must be more risky, as it has the higher expected total return, which must therefore reflect a higher expected risk premium: $E[r] = r_f + RP$.

    c. Property A's $E[g] = 1\%$; Property B's $E[g] = -1\%$.

    d. IRR equals cap rate plus growth. [Note: This relation is exact in this case, but more generally is approximate, as noted in Chapter 9.]

*10.23. The value of the initial lease as of time zero (the present) is $(1 - d^5)/(1 - d)$ per dollar of initial rent, where $d = 1.01/1.08$. (Recall the constant-growth annuity formula from Chapter 8.) This value is $(1 - 0.7153)/(1 - 0.9352) = 0.2847/0.0648 = \$4.39$ per dollar of initial rent. The expected value of the second lease is this amount times 1.01^5, as of the time of its expected signing in five years (because rents are expected to grow at 1% per year over the intervening five-year interval. The present value (as of time zero) of this second lease is thus $1.01^5/(1 + r)^5$ times the value of the first lease, where r is the interlease and reversion discount rate (i.e., the rate that applies to property cash flow that is not yet locked into lease contracts), as the second lease is not yet contracted as of time zero. Similarly, the present value of the third lease is $1.01^{10}/(1 + r)^{10}$. By inspection we can see that the value of the property can be represented by the following geometric-growth perpetuity, per dollar of initial rent:

$$V = (1 + d + d^2 + \ldots)4.39, d = [1.01/(1 + r)]^5$$

Thus, the value of the property is given by

$$V = \$4.39/(1 - d) = \$4.39/\{1 - [1.01/(1 + r)]^5\}$$

But we also know that the cap rate is 9%, so the value of the property equals 1/0.09 per dollar of initial rent. Thus, we have

$$\$1/0.09 = \$4.39/\{1 - [1.01/(1 + r)]^5\}$$

Solving this equation for the unknown reversion discount rate r, we get

$$(0.09)(4.39) = \{1 - [1.01/(1 + r)]^5\}$$
$$[1.01/(1 + r)]^5 = 1 - (0.09)(4.39) = 0.6049$$
$$1.01/(1 + r) = 0.6049^{(1/5)} = 0.90435$$
$$(1 + r)/1.01 = 1/0.90435 = 1.10577$$
$$1 + r = (1.01)(1.10577) = 1.1168$$
$$r = 0.1168$$

In other words, the implied discount rate for interlease and reversion cash flows is 11.68% when the observed cap rate is 9% and the tenant borrowing rate is 8%, with five year leases and an annual rent growth of 1%.

The general expression for the procedure we have used here is as follows:

$$r = (1 + g) \Bigg/ \left\{1 - k\left[\frac{1 - [(1 + g)/(1 + r_L)]^T}{1 - (1 + g)/(1 + r_L)}\right]\right\}^{(1/T)} - 1$$

where

r = The implied interlease (and reversion) discount rate

r_L = The intralease discount rate (observed as the tenant borrowing rate)

g = The annual growth rate in net rents (within and between leases)

k = The cap rate observed in the property market (initial yield)

T = The typical lease term in years

Although this formula looks complicated, you can see that it is simply a double application of the basic geometric sum formula described in Chapter 8 ($PV = a/[1 - d]$) and can be programmed easily into a calculator or typed into a computer spreadsheet. More important, this formula provides a useful practical result. The variables on the right-hand side of the equation can often be estimated rather accurately by direct empirical observation of the property market. In contrast, the interlease discount rate on the left-hand side is more difficult to observe directly. Thus, the preceding procedure enables the interlease discount rate to be estimated from the variables observable in the marketplace.

*10.24. **a.** Overall total IRR   =   7.77%

    b. Initial yield component (=(6)IRR)   =   8.00%

    c. CF growth component* (=(8)IRR − (6)IRR)   =   0.19%

    d. Yield change component** (=(10IRR − (6)IRR)   =   −0.41%

    e. Interaction effect (−(3)IRR-sum(components))   =   −0.01%

CHAPTER 11

11.1.   The NOI is the operating revenue minus the operating expenses. Apart from extraordinary capital improvement expenditures or partial sales proceeds, the NOI represents the net cash flow spun off by the property. This cash flow is distributed first to any debt holders (mortgage payments), second to the government for income tax obligations, and third to the equity investor.

11.2.   The difference between NOI and net cash flow is capital improvement expenditures: $PBTCF = NOI − CI$.

11.3.   **a.** Normally, the going-out cap rate should be either equal to or greater than the going-in cap rate (i.e., the terminal price/earnings ratio would be equal to or lower than the initial price/earnings ratio at the time of purchase).

    b. This is because the building will be older at the time of sale and hence usually perceived to be at least as risky as it was at the time of purchase, with no more (and perhaps less) further growth opportunities for the rents it can charge.

    c. The more money projected to be spent on capital improvements prior to the end of the holding period, the less need for future capital expenditures by those purchasing the building in the resale, and the greater the possibility for the building to continue to grow the rents it can charge beyond the end of the holding period. So greater capital improvement expenditures during the holding period will justify expectations of a lower going-out cap rate (higher terminal price/earnings ratio) than would otherwise be the case.

    d. The going-in cap rate is inversely related to the state of the property market at the time of property purchase. If the property market is very strong at that time, the going-in cap rate might be abnormally low, and vice versa—if the market is depressed, the going-in rate might be abnormally high. This latter situation could conceivably justify a going-out rate projection lower than the going-in rate projection.

11.5.   You should include the opportunity cost of property management as an operating expense subtracted from the property NOI even if you are going to manage the property yourself, because the NOI should reflect the net earning potential of the property, per se, not your earning potential as a property manager. You should not confuse return on property capital with return on your human capital or labor as a property manager. The opportunity cost can be determined as the cost to hire a professional property manager to manage the property for you.

11.6.

Year	1	2	3	4	5	6	7	8	9	10
Rent roll	$10,800	$11,124	$11,458	$11,801	$12,155	$12,520	$12,896	$13,283	$13,681	$14,092
Vacancy	$831	$856	$881	$908	$935	$963	$992	$1,022	$1,052	$1,084
Oper. exp.	$4,500	$4,635	$4,774	$4,917	$5,065	$5,217	$5,373	$5,534	$5,700	$5,871
NOI	$5,469	$5,633	$5,802	$5,976	$6,156	$6,340	$6,531	$6,726	$6,928	$7,136
Cap. impr.	$0	$0	$3,000	$0	$2,500	$0	$0	$0	$0	$0
PBTCF	$5,469	$5,633	$2,802	$5,976	$3,656	$6,340	$6,531	$6,726	$6,928	$7,136

11.7.

Year	Market Net Rent	Building Expected Rent	Vacancy Allowance	Capital Expenditures (TI Cost)	Reversion	Cash Flow per SF	Building Cash Flow
0						($200.00)	($30,000,000)
1	$22.55	$20.00	$0.00	$0.00		$20.00	$3,000,000
2	$23.11	$20.00	$0.00	$0.00		$20.00	$3,000,000
3	$23.69	$20.00	$0.00	$0.00		$20.00	$3,000,000
4	$24.28	$20.00	$0.00	$0.00		$20.00	$3,000,000
5	$24.89	$20.00	$0.00	$0.00		$20.00	$3,000,000
6	$25.51	$25.51	($12.76)	($10.00)		$2.76	$413,494
7	$26.15	$25.51	$0.00	$0.00		$25.51	$3,826,988
8	$26.80	$25.51	$0.00	$0.00		$25.51	$3,826,988
9	$27.47	$25.51	$0.00	$0.00		$25.51	$3,826,988
10	$28.16	$25.51	$0.00	$0.00	$281.62	$307.13	$46,069,778
					PV =	$203.43	$30,513,895
					NPV =		$513,895
					Asking IRR =		12.27%
					Asking Cap Rate =		10.00%
					Market Cap Rate =		9.83%

11.8.

Year	Market Net Rent	Building Expected Rent	Vacancy Allowance	Capital Expenditures (TI Cost)	Reversion	Cash Flow per SF	Building Cash Flow
0						($200.00)	($30,000,000)
1	$18.00	$20.00	$0.00	$0.00		$20.00	$3,000,000
2	$18.45	$18.45	($9.23)	($10.00)		($0.77)	($116,250)
3	$18.91	$18.45	$0.00	$0.00		$18.45	$2,767,500
4	$19.38	$18.45	$0.00	$0.00		$18.45	$2,767,500
5	$19.87	$18.45	$0.00	$0.00		$18.45	$2,767,500
6	$20.37	$18.45	$0.00	$0.00		$18.45	$2,767,500
7	$20.87	$20.87	($10.44)	($10.00)		$0.44	$65,586
8	$21.40	$20.87	$0.00	$0.00		$20.87	$3,131,172
9	$21.93	$20.87	$0.00	$0.00		$20.87	$3,131,172
10	$22.48	$20.87	$0.00	$0.00	$224.80	$245.67	$36,850,472
					PV =	$137.17	$23,575,295
					NPV =		($6,424,705)
					Asking IRR =		8.42%
					Asking Cap Rate =		10.00%
					Market Cap Rate =		12.73%

Note that the two buildings (or scenarios) described in questions 11.7 and 11.8 have very different market values and very different market-value-based cap rates (9.83% versus 12.73%) even though they have the same initial cash flow (and a seller might attempt to catch an unwary buyer by offering both buildings at the same asking cap rate). That is, to make the investment have a zero NPV, the building in question 11.7 should sell at a cap rate of 9.83%, while the building in question 11.8 should sell at a cap rate of 12.73%. The difference in this case is caused by the difference in the lease structures (the pattern of lease expiration dates), combined with a different relationship between the existing ("vintage") lease rents and the current market rents in the space market in which the buildings are situated. This is a case in which simple application of direct capitalization could give a misleading result. Perhaps the building in question 11.7 is in the more typical situation, and so one observes most buildings selling in this asset market at a cap rate of around 10%. But if the building you are looking at is in the situation of that in question 11.8, the typical 10% rate is not appropriate for it. A full-blown multiyear DCF analysis will tend to catch this type of error.

CHAPTER 12

12.1. MV is important because it represents the opportunity cost (or opportunity value) of buying or holding the real estate asset. It is the most likely amount of present cash the investor must give up in order to purchase or retain the asset.

12.3. a. Market value = $40,000/0.10 = $400,000, before arch demolition cost, $380,000 if buyer has to pay that cost.

   b. Investment value to McDonald's = $50,000/0.10 = $500,000.

12.4. a. The expected (ex ante) NPV to McDonald's (or anyone) from a MV perspective is zero, by definition. As the seller, McDonald's would face an NPV of P − V, which from the MV perspective simply equals MV − MV, ex ante.

   b. The expected (ex ante) NPV to McDonald's from an IV perspective is negative $120,000. As the seller, their NPV = P − V = MV − IV = $380,000 − $500,000 = −$120,000. (If the buyer does not have to pay the arch-demolition cost, then the MV = $400,000, but in that case McDonald's would have to pay the $20,000 demolition cost as part of the deal, so either way, McDonald's faces an NPV of −$120,000.)

12.5 a. As the seller, Bob's expected NPV from the sale is P − V, which from a MV perspective ex ante simply equals MV − MV = 0.

   b. From an IV perspective, Bob's ex ante NPV as seller is P − V = MV − IV. As Bob is a "typical" (i.e., marginal) investor, IV = MV for Bob, so his IV-based NPV is also zero: MV − IV = MV − MV = 0.

   c. Because of the uniqueness of the property, there is a chance that Bob can extract some positive NPV by selling the property to McDonald's. This depends on Bob's and McDonald's' relative negotiating skill and information, and on the number of alternative equivalent sites available to McDonald's. There is no guarantee that Bob could get any more than $380,000 from McDonald's (or perhaps $400,000, since the building already has arches that McDonald's may not have to tear down), if McDonald's has done their homework and realizes that this is the MV of the property. On the other hand, from McDonald's' perspective, if they fail to do the deal with Bob, they will be walking away from a transaction that for them as buyer would potentially have an NPV from an IV perspective equal to NPV = V − P = IV − MV = 500,000 − 380,000 = +$120,000 (but only if they do not have any nearly equivalent alternatives in the form of other suitable sites). If Bob is able to know what McDonald's' IV for the site is, then he may be able to extract some of this positive NPV through the negotiation process.

12.6. Marginal participants in an asset market (on both the buy and sell sides) have investment values approximately equal to market value (IV = MV), resulting in near-zero NPV from investment transactions (buying and selling), when the NPVs are measured correctly.

12.7. When the market is in equilibrium, we would expect to see at least one major "type" of investor on *both* sides of the market. Investor types are defined here by their income tax and real estate operational abilities. For example, REITs, wealthy individuals, pension funds, and profitable taxed corporations are all examples of different types of investors. If one or more of these types are observed to be significantly engaged on both sides of the market (buying and selling), then this is a good indication that the market is currently in equilibrium.

12.9. a. $MV = \$1,000,000 = (50\%)\$900,000 + (50\%)\$1,100,000$

   b. $\pm10\% = STDEVP(900,1100)/1,000$

   c. $NPV(Seller) = P - MV = \$900,000 - \$1,000,000 = -\$100,000.$
      $NPV(Buyer) = MV - P = \$1,000,000 - \$900,000 = +\$100,000.$

   d. $NPV(Seller) = P - MV = \$1,100,000 - \$1,000,000 = +\$100,000.$
      $NPV(Buyer) = MV - P = \$1,000,000 - \$1,100,000 = -\$100,000.$

   e. $E(NPV) = (50\%)(-100,000) + (50\%)(+100,000) = 0$

12.10. Differences between the two parties in (a) information availability, (b) negotiating skills, and (c) motivation to close the deal (e.g., duress or pressure, possible existence of nonzero NPV from an investment value perspective for one or both parties)

12.11. a.

Time	Property A Value	Property B Value
Period 0	$1,000	$1,000
Period 1	$1,050	$1,100
Period 2	$1,100	$1,100

   b. Period 0: Borrow $1,000 and buy B, net zero ($1,000 − $1,000 = 0). Period 1: Sell B and buy A, net $50 ($1,100 − $1,050 = $50). Period 2: Sell A and pay back loan, net $50 ($1,100 − $1,050 = $50). Total profit over all transactions: 0 + $50 + $50 = $100.

   c. Period 0: Borrow $1000 and buy B, lose $30 transaction cost ($1,000 − $1,000 − (0.03)($1,000) = −$30). Period 1: Sell B and buy A, net loss of $14.50 after transaction costs ($1,100 − $1,050 − (0.03)($1,100) − (0.03)(1,050) = −$14.50). Period 2: Sell A and pay back loan, net $17 ($1,100 − $1,050 − (0.03)($1,100) = $17). Total profit over all transactions: −$30 − $14.50 + $17 = −$27.50, i.e., a loss of $27.50.

*12.13. If there is true (widespread, or systematic) differential valuation between the private property market and the REIT market, we would expect to see REITs very active in the private property market, and only on *one side* of that market (either only buying or only selling). By definition, differential valuation implies that IV for REITs differs from the MV in the property market, which makes REITs intramarginal participants in the property market and gives them positive-NPV opportunities from dealing on the appropriate side of that market.

*12.14. a. Fundamentally, differential valuation must result either from differential cash flow expectations or a different opportunity cost of capital (different expected total return requirements by investors).

   b. Apart from idiosyncratic abilities of individual REITs, it is not clear how REITs in general can systematically alter property cash flows. Some possibilities might include economies of scale in property management, brand name recognition or franchise value, externalities and synergistic spillover effects across properties, and perhaps the ability to dominate selected space markets effectively through shear size. While these abilities may not derive from REIT status per se, the benefits of access to public capital markets may lead large and successful real estate firms to widely go public as REITs.

c. The stock market functions differently from the direct private property market, and this affects the liquidity and volatility faced by the average investor, especially in the short run. Furthermore, the investor population in the stock market differs from the investor population active in the direct private property market. There are more small individual investors and mutual funds dealing in the stock market, for example. These investors may have different risk perceptions and preferences regarding real estate than the typical direct investor in the private property market. This could impact the expected returns in the marketplace, at least temporarily.

CHAPTER 13

13.7. a. If the property is bought at fair market value and the loan is unsubsidized, leverage does not affect the equity investor's ex ante risk-adjusted return or expected risk premium per unit of risk.

b. Leverage does not affect the NPV of the equity investment provided the loan is unsubsidized and the investor's supply of equity capital is effectively unconstrained for the purpose of the relevant investment.

13.9. a. None.

b. $100,000

13.10. The underlying conceptual basis of the WACC formula is the definition of the simple holding period return ($HPR = (CF + \Delta V)/V$) plus the combination of the value additivity principle: (*Assets = Liabilities + Owner's Equity*) and the income accounting identity (*Property cash flow = Debt cash flow + Equity cash flow*).

13.11. This statement is usually true on an ex ante basis, given that the expected total return to the mortgage is usually lower than the going-in property IRR. However, nothing requires that the mortgage must *necessarily* be less risky (as perceived by the capital markets) than the underlying property. Hence, it is possible, at least in principle, for mortgage interest rates to exceed property returns, resulting in negative leverage in the total return. Furthermore, if the equity investor overpays for the property, then the realistic expected return on the property is less than the market rate (unlevered), which could result in negative leverage.

13.12. Positive leverage will occur when the property cap rate exceeds the mortgage constant on the loan. Negative leverage will occur when the mortgage constant exceeds the cap rate.

13.18. If $E[g_D] \approx 0$ then the WACC implies $E[g_E] = (LR)E[g_P] - (LR - 1)E[g_D] \approx (LR)E[g_P]$, that the ex ante appreciation return is approximately directly proportional to the leverage ratio. But if $E[y_D] \approx E[y_P]$ then the WACC implies $E[y_E] = (LR)E[y_P] - (LR - 1)E[y_D] \approx E[y_D] \approx E[y_P]$. No matter what the value of LR, the income return will be approximately invariant with the leverage. Thus, leverage will tend to increase the appreciation component relatively.

13.19. With riskless debt the equity risk is directly proportional to the leverage ratio: $LR = 1/(1 - LTV)$. Thus, with $LTV = 60\%$: $LR = 1/(1 - 0.6) = 1/0.4 = 2.5$; with $LTV = 80\%$, $LR = 1/(1 - 0.8) = 1/0.2 = 5$. So there is twice as much risk in the equity with the 80% LTV as compared to the 60% LTV (assuming riskless debt in both cases, i.e., ignoring the increase in the default risk for the debt holder). This would suggest twice the equity volatility or potential ex post return range ($\pm 40\%$ instead of $\pm 20\%$), and this would require twice the risk premium in the equity return ex ante.

13.20. Unlevered, the property has a 3% risk premium, but the target risk premium is 7%. Apply the WACC formula:

$$r_P = (LTV)r_D + [1 - (LTV)]r_E$$

Collect terms:

$$r_P = (LTV)(r_D - r_E) + r_E$$
$$-(r_E - r_P) = -(LTV)(r_E - r_D)$$

Divide to solve for LTV:

$$LTV = (r_E - r_P)/(r_E - r_D)$$

Note, the above is a general way to express the WACC implications for LTV. Expand total returns to reveal risk premium components:

$$LTV = [(r_f + RP_E) - (r_f + RP_P)]/[(r_f + RP_E) - (r_f + RP_D)]$$

Eliminate redundant terms:

$$LTV = (RP_E - RP_P)/(RP_E - RP_D)$$

Note, the above is the general WACC-based relationship between LTV and risk premiums.

Substitute data:

$$RP_P = 3\%$$

We want $RP_E = 7\%$

Riskless debt $\rightarrow RP_D = 0$.

Therefore:

$$LTV = (7\% - 3\%)/(7\% - 0)$$
$$LTV = 4\%/7\% = 57\%$$

13.21. Apply the LTV-based WACC risk-premium formulation from equation (2):

$$LTV = (RP_E - RP_P)/(RP_E - RP_D)$$

Substitute data:

$$RP_P = 3\%$$
$$RP_D = r_D - r_f = 7\% - 5\% = 2\%$$

Target $RP_E = 7\%$.

$$LTV = (7\% - 3\%)/(7\% - 2\%)$$
$$LTV = 4\%/5\% = 80\%$$

13.22. Obviously a job for the equity yield formula (WACC):

a. Equity cash-on-cash:

$$E[y_E] = E[y_D] + (LR)(E[y_P] - E[y_D])$$
$$= 11\% + [1/(1 - 80\%)](12\% - 11\%)$$
$$= 11\% + 5 \times 1\% = 16\%$$

The equity yield increases to 16% from 12% as a result of the 80% LTV leverage ($LR = 5$). This is a case of positive leverage.

b. Similarly the yield would be 13% with 50% leverage.

13.23. a. With a property cap rate ($E[y_P]$) of 12% and expected total return of 10% ($E[r_P]$), the property's expected growth is $E[g_P] = 10\% - 12\% = -2\%$ (remember, $g = r - y$). The mortgage growth rate must be -1%, as this is the difference between the interest rate ($r_D = 10\%$) and mortgage constant ($y_D = 11\%$). Thus, by the WACC:

$$E[g_E] = E[g_D] + (LR)(E[g_P] - E[g_D])$$
$$= (-1\%) + [1/(1 - 80\%)][(-2\%) - (-1\%)]$$
$$= (-1\%) + 5 \times (-1\%) = -6\%$$

b. If the property cap rate were 9% and all else remained the same, the property would have expected growth of +1% (as $g = r - y = 10\% - 9\%$), so the equity growth would be

$$E[g_E] = E[g_D] + (LR)(E[g_P] - E[g_D])$$
$$= (-1\%) + [1/(1 - 80\%)][1\% - (-1\%)]$$
$$= (-1\%) + 5 \times (2\%) = 9\%$$

CHAPTER 14

14.1. The difference between the PBTCF and the EBTCF is the debt service payments (e.g., mortgage payment).

14.2. After-tax cash flow will exceed before-tax cash flow if there is a negative before-tax net taxable income in the property (accrual based), that is, if depreciation expenses plus interest expenses exceed the net operating income: $DE + IE > NOI$.

14.4.
NOI:	850,000
DS:	−600,000
EBTCF:	250,000

14.5.

850,000 NOI	$0.35 \times 850,000 = 297,500$	Tax without shields
−600,000 DS	$-0.35 \times 350,000 = 122,500$	DTS
	$-0.35 \times 550,000 = 192,500$	ITS
250,000 EBTCF		
−(−17,500) Tax	− 17,500	Tax
267,500 EATCF		

In traditional accrual accounting format:

NOI:	850,000
− depreciation expense of:	350,000
= net income (BTI):	500,000
− interest expense of:	550,000
= net income before tax:	(−50,000)
− income tax @ 35% of:	(−17,500) (negative = tax shelter*)
= net income after tax:	(−32,500)
− debt amortization CFs of:	50,000 (600,000 − 550,000)
+ depreciation expense (not CFs) of:	350,000
= equity-after-tax cash flow:	267,500

*Note: Tax shelter can only be applied against other passive income, which would include income from other property holdings, but not income from ordinary earnings. Alternatively, passive income losses can be carried forward to reduce positive taxable passive earnings in subsequent years.

14.6. For nonresidential commercial properties the rate is straight-line over a 39-year life, and the land value component is not depreciable. So, the annual depreciation expense (DE) is $500,000 \times 0.7/39 = \$8,974$.

14.7. Annual depreciation expense $= \$300,000/27.5 = \$10,909$.

Annual tax savings due to depreciation expense $= (0.39) \times \$10,909 = \$4,255$.

These savings will occur each year as regular cash inflows (due to income tax savings) at the end of each of the next five years. The after-tax borrowing rate is appropriate to apply as the opportunity cost of capital for these (virtually) riskless cash flows. (Note that they are based on the historical cost of the property, not its volatile current market value.) Thus, we have a level annuity in arrears, the PV of which is $(\$4,255/0.05)[1 - (1/1.05)^5] = \$18,422$.

At the end of five years there will be $5 \times 10,909 = \$54,545$ accumulated depreciation in the book value of the property. If the property sells for at least the historical cost, then all of this accumulated depreciation will become part of the capital gain income from the sale of the property, taxable at the CGT rate of 28%. This will be a cash outflow at the end of year 5 equal to $0.28 \times \$54,545 = \$15,273$. The PV of this future single sum, discounted over five years at 5% per year is $\$15,273/1.05^5 = \$11,967$. Thus, the overall NPV of the depreciation tax shields in the five-year holding period ownership cycle is $\$18,422 - \$11,967 = \$6,455$.

14.8. a. The NPV(Property) component of the APV would be zero from a market value perspective; however, the NPV(Financing) component would have a positive value due to the subsidized loan:

$$NPV = \$1,500,000 - \left(\sum_{n-1}^{7} \frac{\$90,000}{(1.07)^n} + \frac{\$1,500,000}{(1.07)^7} \right) = +\$80,839$$

Thus, the APV from a market value perspective is $80,839.

b. The NPV(Property) component of the APV is still zero even from the IV perspective because the subject investor is typical of the marginal investors in the property market (for whom MV = IV, by definition). However, on an after-tax (IV) basis, the value of the subsidized loan is:

$$NPV = \$1,500,000 - \left(\sum_{n=1}^{7} \frac{(1-0.35)(\$90,000)}{[1+(1-0.35)(0.07)]^n} + \frac{\$1,500,000}{[1+(1-0.35)(0.07)]^7} \right)$$
$$= +\$57,349$$

Thus, the APV from an investment value perspective is $57,349.

14.10. The market's levered equity going-in IRR is 12.75%, computed as the before-tax IRR of the equity cash flows, under the assumption that the equity investment is zero NPV because the property is bought at market value and the financing is a market-rate loan.

14.11. Calculation of typical value of depreciation tax shield (DTS) in 10-year horizon, levered income property investment:

Apprec. Rate   = 2.50%   Bldg. Val/Prop. Val = 80.00%   Loan = 0.75

Yield   = 9.00%   Depreciable Life   = 39.0 years   Int. = 0.1

Income Tax Rate = 40.00%   CG Tax Rate   = 28.00%

	(1)	(2)	(3)	(4)	(5) Tax w/out	(6)	(7) (4)−(5)+(6)	(8) Loan	(9)	(10) (4)−(8)	(11) (7)−(8)+(9)
Year	Prop. Val	NOI	CI	PBTCF	shields	DTS	PATCF	DS	ITS	EBTCF	EATCF
0	1.0000			−1.0000			−1.0000	−0.7500		−0.2500	−0.2500
1	1.0250	0.0900	0	0.0900	0.0360	0.0082	0.0622	0.0750	0.03	0.0150	0.0172
2	1.0506	0.0923	0	0.0923	0.0369	0.0082	0.0636	0.0750	0.03	0.0173	0.0186
3	1.0769	0.0946	0	0.0946	0.0378	0.0082	0.0649	0.0750	0.03	0.0196	0.0199
4	1.1038	0.0969	0	0.0969	0.0388	0.0082	0.0664	0.0750	0.03	0.0219	0.0214
5	1.1314	0.0993	0	0.0993	0.0397	0.0082	0.0678	0.0750	0.03	0.0243	0.0228
6	1.1597	0.1018	0	0.1018	0.0407	0.0082	0.0693	0.0750	0.03	0.0268	0.0243
7	1.1887	0.1044	0	0.1044	0.0417	0.0082	0.0708	0.0750	0.03	0.0294	0.0258
8	1.2184	0.1070	0	0.1070	0.0428	0.0082	0.0724	0.0750	0.03	0.0320	0.0274
9	1.2489	0.1097	0	0.1097	0.0439	0.0082	0.0740	0.0750	0.03	0.0347	0.0290
10	1.2801	0.1124	0	1.3925	0.1234	−0.0492	1.2199	0.8250	0.03	0.5675	0.4249

IRR of above CF stream =   11.50%   7.78%   14.81%   12.19%

Answers:

a. 11.50%

b. 7.78%

c. $(778/1150) \times 10\% = 6.765\%$

d. $28,414 = PV(DTS, @6.765\%)$

e. $43,546 = (1.025^{10})(\$28,414)/[(1.0778^{10}) - (1.025^{10})]$

f. $71,910 = 7.2\%$ of property value (would be more for apartment buildings)

g. 14.81%

h. 12.19%

i. $(1219/1481) = 82\% = (1 - T) \rightarrow$ Effective $T = 18\%$, as opposed to $(778/1150) = 68\% \rightarrow$ Effective $T = 32\%$ unleveraged.

However, this is not really an argument for debt financing, as such financing increases the equity investor's risk, and the after-tax price of risk (and hence required risk premium) is greater than the before-tax risk premium.

See cash flow worksheet on following page

14.11. Cash flow expansion:
        Traditional Format
        Property (before-debt) proforma:

Operating Items	1	2	3	4	5	6	7	8	9	Oper. Yr. 10	Reversion Item	Reversion Yr. 10	Total Yr. 10
NOI	$90.00	$92.25	$94.56	$96.92	$99.34	$101.83	$104.37	$106.98	$109.66	$112.40	Sale price	$1,280.08	
− DE	$20.51	$20.51	$20.51	$20.51	$20.51	$20.51	$20.51	$20.51	$20.51	$20.51	− Book Val.	$794.87	
= PNIBT	$69.49	$71.74	$74.04	$76.41	$78.83	$81.31	$83.86	$86.47	$89.14	$91.88	= Gain	$485.21	$577.10
− Inc. tax	$27.79	$28.69	$29.62	$30.56	$31.53	$32.53	$33.54	$34.59	$35.66	$36.75	− CGT	$135.86	
= PNIAT	$41.69	$43.04	$44.43	$45.84	$47.30	$48.79	$50.32	$51.88	$53.49	$55.13	= Gain AT	$349.35	$404.48

Adjusting accrual to reflect cash flow:

	1	2	3	4	5	6	7	8	9	Oper. Yr. 10	Reversion Item	Reversion Yr. 10	Total Yr. 10
− CI	$0.00	$0.00	$0.00	$0.00	$0.00	$0.00	$0.00	$0.00	$0.00	$0.00			
+ DE	$20.51	$20.51	$20.51	$20.51	$20.51	$20.51	$20.51	$20.51	$20.51	$20.51	+ Book Val.	$794.87	
= PATCF	$62.21	$63.56	$64.94	$66.36	$67.81	$69.30	$70.83	$72.39	$74.00	$75.64	PATCF	$1,144.22	$1,219.87
+ Inc. tax	$27.79	$28.69	$29.62	$30.56	$31.53	$32.53	$33.54	$34.59	$35.66	$36.75	+ CGT	$135.86	
= PBTCF	$90.00	$92.25	$94.56	$96.92	$99.34	$101.83	$104.37	$106.98	$109.66	$112.40	= PBTCF	$1,280.08	$1,392.48

Equity (after-debt) proforma:

Operating Accrual Items	1	2	3	4	5	6	7	8	9	Oper. Yr. 10	Reversion Item	Reversion Yr. 10	Total Yr. 10
NOI	$90.00	$92.25	$94.56	$96.92	$99.34	$101.83	$104.37	$106.98	$109.66	$112.40	Sale price	$1,280.08	
− DE	$20.51	$20.51	$20.51	$20.51	$20.51	$20.51	$20.51	$20.51	$20.51	$20.51	− Book Val.	$794.87	
− IE	$75.00	$75.00	$75.00	$75.00	$75.00	$75.00	$75.00	$75.00	$75.00	$75.00			
= ENIBT	($5.51)	($3.26)	($0.96)	$1.41	$3.83	$6.31	$8.86	$11.47	$14.14	$16.88	= Gain	$485.21	$502.10
− Inc. tax	($2.21)	($1.31)	($0.38)	$0.56	$1.53	$2.53	$3.54	$4.59	$5.66	$6.75	− CGT	$135.86	
= ENIAT	($3.31)	($1.96)	($0.57)	$0.84	$2.30	$3.79	$5.32	$6.88	$8.49	$10.13	= Gain AT	$349.35	$359.48

Adjusting accrual to reflect cash flow:

	1	2	3	4	5	6	7	8	9	Oper. Yr. 10	Reversion Item	Reversion Yr. 10	Total Yr. 10
− CI	$0.00	$0.00	$0.00	$0.00	$0.00	$0.00	$0.00	$0.00	$0.00	$0.00			
+ DE	$20.51	$20.51	$20.51	$20.51	$20.51	$20.51	$20.51	$20.51	$20.51	$20.51	+ Book Val.	$794.87	
− PP	$0.00	$0.00	$0.00	$0.00	$0.00	$0.00	$0.00	$0.00	$0.00	$0.00	− PP	$750.00	
= EATCF	$17.21	$18.56	$19.94	$21.36	$22.81	$24.30	$25.83	$27.39	$29.00	$30.64	= EATCF	$394.22	$424.87
+ Inc. tax	($2.21)	($1.31)	($0.38)	$0.56	$1.53	$2.53	$3.54	$4.59	$5.66	$6.75	+ CGT	$135.86	
= EBTCF	$15.00	$17.25	$19.56	$21.92	$24.34	$26.83	$29.37	$31.98	$34.66	$37.40	= PBTCF	$530.08	$567.48

CHAPTER 15

15.1. Based on the WACC formula (2), Bob's optimal LR is

$$LR = (r_E - r_D)/(r_P - r_D) = (10\% - 6\%)/(8\% - 6\%) = 4\%/2\% = 2.$$

This implies that his optimal LTV would be $1 - 1/LR = 1 - \frac{1}{2} = 50\%$.

15.2. Optimal $LR = (r_E - r_D)/(r_P - r_D) = (7\% - 6\%)/(8\% - 6\%) = 1\%/2\% = \frac{1}{2} = 50\%$. As the LR is defined as V/E, the gross value of Bob's property holdings divided by the value of Bob's overall net wealth, $LR = 0.5$, suggests that Bob should put half his wealth into property investments (with no borrowing) and the other half of his wealth into Treasury Bonds. This will give Bob the target return of 7%, as $7\% = (50\%)6\% + (50\%)8\%$.

15.3. At the level of the ultimate investor's overall net wealth investment, leverage argues for the use of debt for some investors, and against for others, depending on their risk preferences, so it is neither for nor against for all investors generally. Less risk-averse investors would want to take a more aggressive and riskier position employing the use of debt financing (borrowing), while more risk-averse investors would want to take a more conservative and less risky position avoiding debt financing and perhaps even investing in debtlike assets such as bonds and mortgages. Furthermore, it is not clear that investors' optimal overall debt positions need to be implemented separately within the real estate portion of their overall investment portfolios. At the investment entity level, there may be less need to even consider the relationship between leverage and risk preferences, as the ultimate investor/owners may have varying risk preferences, and they may be able to implement their optimal leverage positions on their own accounts.

15.4. Leverage affects risk and return and also (usually) the breakdown between the income and growth components of the return. These things matter to investors in view of their investment preferences. They also matter to investment entities because they carry implications about the management and strategy of the firm, and possibly about the type of investors (or clientele) that will want to invest in the firm.

15.5. a. No value is added by Bob's ability to borrow money to finance his real estate purchases. He has more than sufficient equity capital of his own to purchase enough properties to fully exhaust his profitable property management capacity. He could allocate $50 million to purchase 1,000,000 SF of property and still have more than half his wealth left over for other investments.

b. For every 100,000 SF of property Bob buys and holds he can make a positive NPV of $200,000 due to his unique property management expertise. Using all of his own $10 million of capital with no borrowing, he could only buy two buildings at a price of $5 million each, totaling 200,000 SF, which would give him a positive-NPV increment to his wealth of $400,000 (in terms of present investment value return on his human capital). If he could borrow up to a 60% LTV, then he could buy five buildings, which would cost $25 million in all (of which he would borrow $15 million), amounting to 500,000 SF under management, which would provide Bob with an NPV of $1 million. This is a $600,000 increment over the $400,000 NPV he could obtain without the use of debt, so the value of Bob's ability to borrow up to an 60% LTV is $600,000. If he could borrow up to a 80% LTV, then he could more than double this increment, buying 10 buildings worth $50 million ($40 million borrowed) encompassing altogether 1,000,000 SF, fully exhausting his management capacity, giving him a positive NPV from property management equal to $2,000,000. This is a $1,600,000 increment over the $400,000 NPV he could obtain without the use of debt. Therefore, the value of Bob's ability to borrow up to an 80% LTV is $1,600,000, almost three times the value to him of being able to borrow only up to a 60% LTV, given his constraints and initial endowment.

CHAPTER 16

16.11. a. Expenses first, then penalties, interest, and principal last.

b. The interest due on the mortgage is $800,000 (10% × 8,000,000), so the payment is applied first to this interest obligation, leaving $200,000 to pay down the principal balance, resulting in a remaining balance of $7,800,000.

c. The late penalty of $10,000 would have to be paid first, resulting in a remaining balance of $7,810,000.

16.15. Bob sells the property to Sue for $10,000,000 and lends her $8,000,000 for five years at 7% in a second mortgage secured by the property, while maintaining his first mortgage in effect, thereby taking in $2,000,000 in cash. Bob uses Sue's annual $560,000 payment to him (7% × $8,000,000) to cover his annual $300,000 obligation on his first mortgage, with $260,000 left over. As Bob's $2,000,000 received from Sue is $3,000,000 less than he would have received if he had sold the property to her for $10,000,000 and paid off his $5,000,000 loan, he has, in effect, invested this $3,000,000 difference in the second mortgage to Sue. (This is known as the "new money" in the wrap loan.) His net cash flow of $260,000 from Sue will provide him with an 8.67% return (260,000/3,000,000) on this investment for the next five years, well above the 8% rate prevailing in the current market. At the end of the five years, he will use his $8,000,000 from Sue to pay off his $5,000,000 debt on the first mortgage, with the remaining $3,000,000 returning his net investment in the second mortgage.

16.25. $10,600,000 − $9,000,000 = $1,600,000

16.26. Expected return = 6% + 1% = 7%. Expected cash flows = (0.7)10,600,000 + (0.2)9,800,000 + (0.1)9,000,000 = 10,280,000. Loan value = $10,280,000/(1.07) = $9,607,477. The loan's nominal yield would be ($10,600,000 − $9,607,477)/ $9,607,477 = 10.33%. The cost of the credit risk is the difference between the PV of a U.S. government bond of equivalent future cash flow, and the PV of the subject loan. The government bond would sell for 10,600,000/1.06 = $10,000,000, so the cost of the credit risk is 10,000,000 − $9,607,477 $392,523, or 3.92% of an equivalent riskless loan's value.

CHAPTER 17

17.20. a. The fact that interest rates may fall further in the near future raises the possibility that the NPV of refinancing could be substantially greater in the near future than it is today. This possibility could make it worthwhile to wait.

b. The classical NPV decision criterion requires maximizing the NPV across all mutually exclusive alternatives. Refinancing today versus waiting and possibly refinancing in the future are mutually exclusive alternatives. The latter alternative may have the greater NPV, even evaluated at its present value today and considering the risk involved. If so, then one would choose to wait. Another possibility is that the market value of the old loan can be observed. Such a market value would incorporate the prepayment option value. In this case, the sign of the NPV defined as the old loan's current market value minus the cost to pay off the old loan today will correctly indicate whether refinancing is optimal.

17.22. a.

Month	OLB (Beg)	PMT	INT	AMORT	OLB (End)
0					$2,000,000.00
1	$2,000,000.00	$13,333.33	$13,333.33	$0.00	$2,000,000.00
2	$2,000,000.00	$13,333.33	$13,333.33	$0.00	$2,000,000.00
3	$2,000,000.00	$13,333.33	$13,333.33	$0.00	$2,000,000.00

b.

Month	OLB (Beg)	PMT	INT	AMORT	OLB (End)
0					$2,000,000.00
1	$2,000,000.00	$18,888.89	$13,333.33	$5,555.56	$1,994,444.44
2	$1,994,444.44	$18,851.85	$13,296.30	$5,555.56	$1,988,888.89
3	$1,988,888.89	$18,814.81	$13,259.26	$5,555.56	$1,983,333.33

c.

Month	OLB (Beg)	PMT	INT	AMORT	OLB (End)
0					$2,000,000.00
1	$2,000,000.00	$14,675.29	$13,333.33	$1,341.96	$1,998,658.04
2	$1,998,658.04	$14,675.29	$13,324.39	$1,350.90	$1,997,307.14
3	$1,997,307.14	$14,675.29	$13,315.38	$1,359.91	$1,995,947.23

17.23. a. $12,397.62

b. $15,001.12

The first payment is computed using the following formula:

$2,000,000/PV(0.08/12,12,1) + 1.1 \times PV(0.08/12,12,1)/(1 + 0.08/12)^{12} + 1.1^2 \times PV(0.08/12,336,1)/(1 + 0.08/12)^{24}$

17.24. a. Yes, 6.0% is less than the fully indexed rate of 5.5% + 2.5% = 8.0%.

b. 8.0% = 5.5% + 2.5%

c. $11,991.01

d. $14,617.18, computed as: $14617.48 = PMT(0.08/12,29*12,1975440)$, where $1975440 = PV(0.06/12,30*12,2000000)$.

e. 7.80%, computed as the IRR of the projected cash flow stream:

$$\$2,000,000 = \sum_{t=1}^{12} \frac{\$11,991.01}{[1 + (0.0780/12)]^t} + \sum_{t=13}^{360} \frac{\$14,617.18}{[1 + (0.0780/12)]^t}$$

17.25. a. $PMT = \$15,436.32$; $FV = 0$

b. $PMT = \$15,436.32$; $FV = \$1,615,266$

c. $PMT = \$19,113.04$; $FV = \$942,625$

d. The faster-amortizing loan has higher regular payments, but a lower balloon payment at the end.

17.26. a. 7.5% (obviously)

b. 7.71%, with $N = 360$; $i = 7.5\%$; $PV = 2,000,000$; $FV = 0$; compute $PMT = 13,984.29$; finally, change PV to 1,960,000 (to reflect points) just before computing $i = 7.71\%$

c. 7.85%, with $N = 360$; $i = 7.5\%$; $PV = 2,000,000$; $FV = 0$; compute $PMT = 13,984.29$; then change N to 96 and compute $FV = 1,805,565$; finally, change PV to 1,960,000 before computing $i = 7.85\%$

17.27. **a.** 7.5% (obviously)

    b. 7.67%

    c. 7.85%

    d. 7.94% [Hint: Don't forget to include the prepayment penalty amount in the *FV* register before you change the *PV* amount.]

17.28. **a.** $2,056,358. The 7.125% BEY equates to 7.02% MEY, as $12\{[(1 + .07125/2)^2]^{1/12} - 1\} = 7.02\%$. Applying this discount rate to the 96 monthly payments of $13,984.29 and the balloon of $1,805,565 gives a *PV* of $2,056,358.

    b. The 7.875% BEY equates to 7.75% MEY, which gives the loan a PV of $1,971,401, which is $28,599 less than the contractual principal of $2,000,000. Thus, the loan requires 1.43 points (as 28,599/2,000,000 = 0.0143).

17.29. **a.** 1.44 points, with $N = 360$; $i = 7.25\%$; $PV = 1$; $FV = 0$; compute $PMT = 0.006822$; then change N to 96 to compute $FV = 0.898909$, and finally, change i to 7.5% before computing PV=0.9856. Subtract 1 from this to arrive at 0.0144. The lender must discount the principal by this fraction to arrive at a disbursement amount that will give the 7.5% yield.

    b. 2.88 points

17.30. **a.** With the longer prepayment horizon, choose the lower-interest loan, as it has an effective rate of 6.36% versus 7.10% for the higher-interest loan.

    b. With the shorter prepayment horizon choose the lower-points loan, as it has an effective interest rate of 6.69% versus 6.81% for the 6%/three-point loan.

*17.31. **a.** *NPV* = $6,048,772 − $5,839,965 − $150,000 − $60,000 = −$1,194. This is based on a current opportunity cost of capital (yield on the new loan) of 8.26% over a five-year maturity.

    b. Yes, as the NPV would be positive including consideration of the prepayment option value in the old loan.

*17.32. **a.** The old loan has a current OLB (after three years) of $5,669,869. So the new money invested in the wrap loan is $8,000,000 − 5,669,869 = $2,330,131. The monthly payment on the old loan is $57,901.30, and on the wrap it is $79,223.31, so the net monthly payment you receive over the remaining 60 months is $79,223.31 − $57,901.30 = $21,322.01. The balloon on the old loan at its maturity in five years (after eight years of the original loan) is $4,844,980, while the OLB on the wrap after five years would be $7,793,973. So the net balloon in the 60th month would be $7,793,973 − $4,844,980 = $2,948,993. These payments give the new money in the wrap investment a yield of 14.62%, as

$$\$2,330,131 = \sum_{t=1}^{60} \frac{\$21,322.01}{[1 + (0.1462/12)]^t} + \frac{\$2,948,993}{\{1 + (0.1462/12)\}^{60}}$$

    b. The excess return is obtainable because the existing loan has a contract interest rate below the current market interest rate. This gives the existing loan a positive value to the borrower. The wrap loan converts this value into a supernormal return on the seller's incremental investment represented by the new money in the wrap loan. In fact, by extending a below-market rate to the wrap borrower (11.5% instead of 12%), the seller is giving at least a portion of the old loan's excess value to the wrap borrower (in return, perhaps, for a higher price on the property). Although 14.62% is probably a supernormal return on the new money, it is certainly not 262 basis points (14.62% − 12%) greater than the normal return. Twelve percent is a normal return for an 80% LTV loan, but the new money in the wrap represents the riskiest component of the 80% LTV, the part that is most exposed to credit loss. If the property value should dip below $8,000,000, the wrap borrower might default, and the deficit in property value below $8,000,000 would come off the wrap loan new money first, as the wrap lender will still owe his entire liability on the first mortgage. Thus, the normal (market rate) expected yield on the new money would be substantially greater than 12%.

*17.33. The 8% MEY equates to 8.1345% BEY:

$$2\{[(1 + .08/12)^{12}]^{(1/2)} - 1\}.$$

This is the yield the lender must be able to get on the loan's OLB invested for three years in the T-bonds. For every $100 invested in the T-bonds, the lender will receive half the stated coupon rate (6%) every half year, thus, six semiannual payments of $3 each, plus the par value of $100 at the end. Discounting these payments at the required 8.1345% BEY yield (8.00% MEY) gives a PV of $94.417557 for every $100 invested. Thus (utilizing the homogeneity property of the present value equation), for every $1 of OLB, the lender must be able to invest $100/$94.417557 = $1.059125 into the T-bonds. Therefore, the required prepayment penalty is 5.9125 points. The 8%, $1 million, 30-year-amortization mortgage would have an OLB after seven years of $924,774. Thus, the required prepayment penalty would be 0.059125 × 924,774 = $54,677. The total liquidating payment received by the lender would be $924,774 + $54,677 = $979,451, which could be invested in the three-year, 6% T-bond to obtain an 8.1345% (BEY, or 8.00% MEY) yield on the $924,774 OLB.

*17.34. The $1 million 8%, 30-year loan has monthly payments of $7,337.66 and a balloon at year 10 of $877,247. The OLB on this loan after seven years (with 36 payments remaining) is $924,774 at the original 8% interest rate. However, discounting the 36 monthly payments of $7,337.66 plus the one balloon payment of $877,247 at 6% (5.50% T-bond rate + 0.50% margin) gives a PV of $974,263. This is the liquidating payment required of the borrower. Thus, the yield-maintenance prepayment penalty is $49,489 = $974,263 − $924,774, or 5.35% of the OLB.

CHAPTER 18

18.3. 9.5% (equation [1])

18.4. a. 1%, 5%, 5%
   b. 4.95%
   c. 10.65%

18.5. 6.61%

18.10. Assuming monthly payments on the mortgage:
   $400,000/1.25 = $320,000; $320,000/12 = $26,667/month = Maximum PMT
   $7 + 1.75 = 8.75\%$ CEY = $(1.04375)^2 - 1 = 8.9414\%$ EAY → $[(1.089414)^{(1/12)} - 1]$ × 12 = 8.59% MEY
   $360 \to N$; $8.59 \to I/YR$; $26667 \to PMT$; $0 \to FV$; PV = $3,439,568

18.11. With calculator set for $1 \to P/YR$:
   $0 \to CF_0$; $1 \to CF_1$; $1.1 \to CF_2$; $3 \to N_2$; $1.5 \to CF_3$; $5 \to N_3$; $12 \to CF_4$; $11.5 \to I/YR$;
   $NPV = \$10.8695$ million $\times 0.70$ $LTV = \$7.60865$ million = Maximum loan

18.15. a. 9.97%
   b. 8.00%
   c. 8.00%
   d. 14.35%
   e. 14.55%

*18.16. As noted in the text box, assuming a 2% drift rate (expected annual appreciation) gives an expected seven-year property value of 115% the current value. The 15% annual volatility and random walk assumption gives a 40% standard deviation in the seven-year value. Thus, two-standard-deviations is 80%. The ex ante two standard deviation range around the seven-year mean is thus 115% ± 80% = 35% to 195% of the current property value. There is a 5% chance that the seven-year value will lie beyond this range, hence, a 2.5% chance that the value will be at or below 35% of the current property value. By the reasoning presented in the text box, this suggests that a 35% LTV ratio criterion would be associated with a 2.5% default probability.

CHAPTER 19

19.13. Volatility in ex post periodic returns reflects the realization of risk (in this case, it is mostly interest rate risk). Ex ante returns are investors' expectations about future returns. Risk is observed in statistical time-series second moments of ex post returns (such as the volatility), while ex ante returns are estimates of only the first moment in those returns.

19.15. Mortgages' lower correlation with inflation and higher correlations with stocks and bonds mean that mortgages (as an investment, that is, long positions in mortgages) provide less inflation protection (indeed, they provide considerable inflation risk exposure) in the mixed-asset portfolio as compared to property equity, and mortgages provide less diversification benefit. This suggests that short positions in mortgages (in the form of levered property equity investments) would improve the inflation protection and diversification benefits of property equity in the mixed-asset portfolio.

19.18. Macaulay duration = 5.54 years; Modified duration = 5.03 years.

19.19. The modified-duration-based prediction would be for a 5.03% increase in mortgage value, while the actual increase in value would be 5.69%.

*19.20. $1 + r_5 = (1 + YTMZ_5)^5/(1 + YTMZ_4)^4 = 1.065^5/1.0625^4 = 1.370087/1.274429 = 1.075$. Thus, the expected year-5 short-term rate (the year-5 forward rate) is $r_5 = 1.075 - 1 = 0.075 = 7.5\%$.

19.21. $dur_E \approx (dur_A - dur_L)(A/E) = (5 - 1.5)(1/0.05) = (3.5)(20) = 70$ years

19.22. Ten years, the same as the average duration of their liabilities.

CHAPTER 20

20.6. $(1 - 0.35)(0.75) = 48.75\%$ LTV ratio in a first mortgage whole loan

20.7. The A tranche was issued with $700 million in par value. The B tranche was issued with $50 million in par value ([30% − 25%]1 billion).

a. Neither tranche loses any par value.

b. The B tranche loses $20 billion par value ([(27% − 25%] 1 billion), or 40% of its original par value.

c. The B tranche loses all of its value while the A tranche loses $30 million, or 4.3% of its original par value.

20.8. The pool underlying these two tranches pays $600 × 10% = $60 million in interest. The senior tranche takes $500 × 7% = $35 million. The mezzanine tranche takes another $100 × 9% = $9 million. This leaves $60 million − $35 million − $9 million = $16 million available to pay the IO tranche, assuming no other par-valued tranches have any claim on this underlying pool.

CHAPTER 21

21.7. Portfolio A's Sharpe ratio is (10% − 5%)/8% = 0.625. Portfolio B's Sharpe ratio is (9% − 5%)/7% = 0.571. Thus, portfolio B cannot possibly be the Sharpe-maximizing portfolio (its Sharpe ratio is not as high as A's). Thus, portfolio B cannot possibly be on the efficient frontier.

21.8. $(0.5)10\% + (0.5)9\% = 9.5\%$

21.9. Portfolio C's volatility will be less than 7.5%.

CHAPTER 22

22.10. $E[r] = r_f + \beta(RP_M) = 5\% + (0.5)(6\%) = 5\% + 3\% = 8\%$

*22.11. **CAPM-Based Risk and Return Expectations**

	Stocks	Bonds	Real Estate
Expected return ($E[r]$)	14.6%	8.6%	6.8%
Volatility	20.0%	10.0%	8.0%
Correlation with:			
Stocks	100.00%	60.00%	30.00%
Bonds		100.00%	−10.00%
Real Estate			100.00%

Calculated as follows. Based on the given data, the covariance table for the three asset classes is

0.04	0.012	0.0048
0.012	0.01	−0.0008
0.0048	−0.0008	0.0064

(e.g., the real estate and stock covariance is $0.0048 = [0.3][0.08][0.2]$.)

The weighted covariance table is just $(1/3)^2$ times each of these values:

0.004444	0.001333333	0.000533333
0.001333	0.001111111	−0.000088889
0.000533	−0.000088889	0.000711111

The market portfolio variance is the sum over all nine of the above cells, equal to 0.009822.

The individual asset class covariances with the market portfolio are found as $(1/3)$ times the sum of the individual covariances. For example, for stocks:

$$COV(r_S, r_M) = (1/3)(0.04 + 0.012 + 0.0048) = 0.018933$$

Similarly for bonds:

$$COV(r_B, r_M) = (1/3)(0.012 + 0.01 - 0.0008) = 0.007067$$

And for real estate:

$$COV(r_{RE}, r_M) = (1/3)(0.0048 - 0.0008 + 0.0064) = 0.003467$$

Thus, the national wealth betas are

$$BETA(Stocks) = 0.018933/0.0098922 = 1.9276$$

$$BETA(Bonds) = 0.007067/0.0098922 = 0.7195$$

$$BETA(Real\ Estate) = 0.003467/0.0098922 = 0.3529$$

Given that the market portfolio has a 10% return, and the riskfree rate is 5%, the market price of risk (RP_M) is thus 5% ($E[r_M] - r_f = 10\% - 5\%$). Thus, the expected returns for each asset class, according to the CAPM are

$$\text{Stocks: } E[r_S] = r_f + \beta_S RP_M = 5\% + (1.9276)(5\%) = 5\% + 9.6\% = 14.6\%$$

$$\text{Bonds: } E[r_B] = r_f + \beta_B RP_M = 5\% + (0.7195)(5\%) = 5\% + 3.6\% = 8.6\%$$

$$\text{Real Estate: } E[r_{RE}] = r_f + \beta_{RE} RP_M = 5\% + (0.3529)(5\%) = 5\% + 1.8\% = 6.8\%$$

CHAPTER 23

23.2. **a.** Best estimate of $C = V^* = (\$2,650,000 + \$2,450,000 + \$2,400,000)/3 = \$2,500,000$

b. Best estimate of $C = V^* = (\$2,650,000 + \$2,450,000 + \$2,400,000 + \$2,550,000)/4 = \$2,512,500$

c. Market value is unobservable, so nobody can know for certain what the fourth property's market value was as of the date it sold, but our best guess is $2,512,500, calculated as in (b).

d. $e_1 = \$2,650,000 - \$2,512,500 = +\$137,500$

$e_2 = \$2,450,000 - \$2,512,500 = -\$62,500$

$e_3 = \$2,400,000 - \$2,512,500 = -\$112,000$

$e_4 = \$2,550,000 - \$2,512,500 = +\$37,500$

23.3. The additional observation reduced our standard error to 87% of what it was with only three comps:

$$V_t^* = 0.2\overline{V}_t + 0.16\overline{V}_{t-1} + 0.128\overline{V}_{t-2} + 0.1024\overline{V}_{t-3} + \cdots$$

23.6. $\alpha = (0.05)^2/[(0.05)^2 + (0.10)^2] = 0.0025/(0.0025 + 0.01) = 0.0025/0.0125 = 0.20$. This would make the Q2 Model for quarter t's valuation as follows:

$$V_t^* = 0.2\overline{V}_t + 0.8V_{t-1}^*$$

23.7.

$$V_t^* = 0.2\overline{V}_t + 0.16\overline{V}_{t-1} + 0.128\overline{V}_{t-2} + 0.1024\overline{V}_{t-3} + \cdots$$

23.9.

Bldg. 1: $100(500000)   + \$5000000(0) - \$2000000(5)$ = \$ 40,000,000
Bldg. 2: $100(1000000) + \$5000000(1) - \$2000000(10)$ = \$ 85,000,000
Bldg. 3: $100(750000)   + \$5000000(0) - \$2000000(7)$ = \$ 61,000,000

Portfolio: = $186,000,000

CHAPTER 24

24.2. **a.** $r = y + g = 7.2\% + 10\% = 17.2\%$

b. $r = y + g = 7.2\% + 5.3\% = 12.5\%$

c. $RP = r - r_f = 12.5\% - 5.5\% = 7\%$

d. If the true long-run growth expectation were $(0.5)5.3\% + (0.5)10\% = 7.65\%$, then, assuming the market's required return expectation was 12.5%, the implied value of General Growth equity shares according to the GGM would have been

$$E = \frac{\$2.04}{12.5\% - 7.65\%} = \frac{\$2.04}{0.0485} = \$42.06$$

This is almost 48% percent above their then-current market price of $28.50 (as $42.06/ $28.50 = 1.48).

24.3. **a.** The equity average cost of capital is given to be 13%.

b. The overall firm-level average cost of capital is 10.8%, found as $(0.4)7.5\% + (1 - 0.4)13\% = 3.0\% + 7.8\% = 10.8\%$.

24.4. **a.** BSR's plowback ratio is zero. Their price/earnings ratio is 12.5, which implies an earnings/price ratio of $1/12.5 = 8\%$, which exactly equals their current dividend yield, which is their dividend/price ratio. As both these ratios are the same, they must be paying all their earnings out as dividends.

b. BSR's firm-level average cost of capital is 13%, found as $r = y + g = 8\% + 5\% = 13\%$.

24.5. **a.** Rentleg OCC $= 10\% + 1.0\% = 11\%$

b. Rentleg value $= \$2,500,000/(11\% - 1\%) = \$2,500,000/0.10 = \$25,000,000$

c. Same as (b). Use the marginal OCC of acquisition, not the average OCC of the firm.

d. NPV $= \$25,000,000 - \$24,000,000 = +\$1,000,000$

24.8. **a.** General Growth 1999 FFO was $289,731,000, computed as follows:

GAAP net income:	$ 78,806,000
+ Depreciation:	$147,746,000
+ Preferred Stock Dividends:	$ 24,468,000
+ Operating Partnership distribution:	$ 26,983,000
– Net gain asset sales:	$ 2,058,000
+ Extraordinary loss:	$ 13,786,000
= FFO:	$289,731,000

b. General Growth's 1999 FAD was $247,612,000, computed as follows:

FFO:	$289,731,000
– Straight-line rent adjustment	$ 14,619,000
– Capital expenditures:	$ 27,500,000
= FAD:	$247,612,000

c. General Growth's 1999 FAD/GAAP net income ratio was $247,612/78,806 = 3.14$.

d. General Growth's 1999 dividend/FFO ratio was $143,826/289,731 = 0.50 = 50\%$.

e. General Growth's 1999 plowback ratio based on FAD was 21%, computed as follows. General Growth's equity distributions were $195,277,000 (including $143,826,000 common share dividends, $24,468,000 preferred dividends, and $26,693,000 unit holder distributions). This left $247,612,000 − $195,277,000 = $52,335,000 plowed back into the firm, or $52,335/247,612 = 0.21 = 21\%$.

f. They exceeded their 90% GAAP income minimum payout requirement by: $\$143,826,000/[(\$78,806,000)(0.9)] - 1 = 1.028 = 102.8\%$; or by $\$143,826,000 - (\$78,806,000)(0.9) = \$72,900,600$.

CHAPTER 25

*25.3. The best estimate of the long-run beta would be

$$\hat{\beta} = 0.05 + 0.15 + 0.10 = 0.30$$

*25.7. The appraisal behavior model in returns is the same as the model in log levels:

$$g_t^* = 0.3g_t + 0.7g_{t-1}^*$$

where g_t is the transaction-price-based appreciation return (here assumed to be noise-free, hence, like Index 3). Inverting this model to solve for the transaction-based return, we have

$$g_t = (g_t^* - 0.7g_{t-1}^*) / 0.3$$

Applying this reverse-engineering model, we recover the current period's Index 3 appreciation return:

$$g_t = [1\% - (0.7)1.5\%] / 0.3 = (1\% - 1.05\%) / 0.3 = -0.05\% / 0.3 = -0.167\%$$

25.8. $g_{97} = (g_{97}^* - 0.6g_{96}^*)/(0.4)$

$= [4.54\% - (0.6)1.34\%]/0.4$

$= 3.74\%/0.4$

$= 9.34\%$

$g_{98} = (g_{98}^* - 0.6g_{97}^*)/(0.4)$

$= [7.01\% - (0.6)4.54\%]/0.4$

$= 4.29\%/0.4$

$= 10.72\%$

CHAPTER 26   No answers are provided for this chapter's questions.

CHAPTER 27   *27.5.   **Piet-Tony Attributes**

	Conditional on Order of Computation		Unconditional
Attribute:	(a) Allocation 1st	(b) Selection 1st	(c)
Allocation	−0.75%	−0.50%	−0.50%
Selection	1.75%	1.50%	1.75%
Interaction			−0.25%
Total differential	1.00%	1.00%	1.00%

27.6.   The appropriate customized benchmark would consist of Tony's within-region (property-level) performance weighted at Piet's mandated 50/50 allocation weights. This gives a benchmark performance of $r_B = (0.5)8\% + (0.5)10\% = 9.00\%$. Piet's performance differential with respect to this benchmark is +150 basis points, computed as the difference between Piet's 10.50% performance ($r_P = [0.5]9\% + [0.5]12\% = 10.50\%$) and that of his custom benchmark (9.00%).

*27.12.   The quarterly standard deviation of the differential between the manager and her benchmark is

$$\sigma_{i-B} = (\sigma_i^2 + \sigma_B^2 - 2C\sigma_i\sigma_B)^{(1/2)}$$

$$= [0.03^2 + 0.03^2 - 2(0.75)(0.03)(0.03)]^{(1/2)}$$

$$= 2.12\%$$

The five-year evaluation interval includes 20 quarters, so the standard error of the observed five-year differential is

$$\text{Standard error} = \sigma_{i-B}/[(20 - 1)^{(1/2)}]$$

$$= 2.12\%/4.36$$

$$= 0.486\%$$

Therefore, the required quarterly average performance differential (in the arithmetic time-weighted means) is approximately $2 \times 0.486\% = 0.972\%$, or 97 basis points.

CHAPTER 28

*28.8. a. $\eta = \{0.09 - 0.06 + (0.2)^2/2 + [(0.06 - 0.09 - (0.2)^2/2)^2 + 2(0.06)(0.2)^2]^{1/2}\}/(0.2)^2$
= 3.386

$RP_{LAND} = \eta RP_P = 3.386 \times 5.00\% = 16.93\%$

So the expected total return on land is $6.00\% + 16.93\% = 22.93\%$.

b. $V* = K\eta/(\eta - 1) = \$800,000 \times (3.386/2.386) = \$1,135,289$

Land Value = $(\$1,135,289 - \$800,000) \times (\$1,000,000/\$1,135,289)^{3.386} = \$218,187$

c. Hurdle B/C ratio = $\eta/(\eta - 1) = 3.386/2.386 = 1.42$

d. $V* = K\eta/(\eta - 1) = \$800,000 \times (3.386/2.386) = \$1,135,289$

This is the hurdle value for the built property to trigger immediate development.

e. It's better to wait because the newly developed property would only be worth $1,000,000, which is less than the $1,135,289 required hurdle value.

CHAPTER 29

29.3.
Potential gross revenue (20,000 × $15):	$ 300,000
− Vacancy at 5%:	$ 15,000
= Effective gross income:	$ 285,000
− Operating expenses not passed on:	$ 100,000
= Net operating income:	$ 185,000
÷ 1.20 (Required debt service):	$ 154,167
÷ 12 (Monthly debt serviced):	$ 12,847
→ Supportable mortgage amount:	$1,244,637
÷ 0.75 LTV (Minimum required value):	$1,659,516
− Construction cost:	$1,030,075
→ Supportable site acquisition cost:	$ 629,441

29.4.
Site and construction costs:	$1,300,000
× Lender-required LTV:	75%
= Permanent mortgage amount:	$ 975,000
× Annualized mortgage constant:[1]	0.123863
= Cash required for debt service:	$ 120,766
× Lender-required DCR:	1.20
= Required NOI:	$ 144,919
+ Estimated operating expenses (landlord):	$ 100,000
= Required EGI:	$ 244,919
÷ Projected occupancy (1-vac):	0.95
= Required PGI:	$ 257,809
÷ Rentable area:	20,000 SF
= Required rent/SF:	$12.89/SF

29.6. The projected NOI in the completed building is $185,000, which, based on the 10% projected cap rate, gives a projected built project value of $1,850,000 one year from now. If the projected construction loan balance due at that time is $1,030,075, then the projected construction project NPV as of the time of completion is $NPV(cons)_1$

[1]From Chapter 8 and 17 we have the monthly mortgage constant: $(0.11/12)/[1 - 1/(1 - 0.11/12)^{240}] = 0.010322$. Multiplying by 12 gives the annual constant: $0.010322 \times 12 = 0.123863$.

= $1,850,000 − $1,030,075 = $819,925. If the development phase opportunity cost of capital is 15%, then the time-zero value of the construction project NPV is

B_0 = $819,925/1.15 = $712,978. This is the maximum land acquisition cost that can be supported at time zero (less any other up-front development costs or fees).

29.7. Growing the $700,000 time-zero investment at the development phase OCC to the time of completion (one year) gives a require $NPV(cons)_1$ of $700,000 × 1.15 = $805,000. Adding the projected construction loan balance due gives a required year-1 stabilized building value of $1,030,075 + $805,000 = $1,835,075. Multiplying by the expected cap rate of 10% gives a required stabilized NOI of $183,508. Adding the projected operating expenses to be borne by the landlord gives a required effective gross income of $183,508 + $100,000 = $283,508. Dividing by the projected stabilized occupancy rate gives a required potential gross income of $283,508/0.95 = $298,429. Dividing by the 20,000 rentable SF gives a required market rent of $298,429/20,000 = $14.92.

29.8. The projected balance at the end of month 4 is $7,130,108.

Month	Direct Cost	Interest Rate	EOM Balance	Interest Accrual	BOM Loan Draw
1	$1,000,000	10.00%	$1,008,333	$8,333	$1,000,000
2	$2,000,000	10.00%	$3,033,403	$25,069	$2,008,333
3	$1,500,000	10.00%	$4,571,181	$37,778	$1,525,069
4	$2,500,000	10.00%	$7,130,108	$58,927	$2,537,778

*29.9. a. Grow the projected construction cost draws at the unconditional expected return on the construction loan:

$10,000,000(1.06)^2 + $20,000,000(1.06) + $10,000,000 = $42,436,000$

Therefore,

$NPV(cons)_2$ = $65,000,000 − $42,436,000 = $22,564,000

b. The 300-basis-point risk premium combined with the 5.5% T-bill yield implies r_P = 5.5% + 3.0% = 8.5%. The question gives the OCC of the construction costs as being 6%. From (a) we can compute the LTV ratio implied by the operational leverage in the development project as L_T/V_T = $42,436,000/$65,000,000 = 0.65. Applying formula (3), we estimate the OCC for the development phase of this project as

$E[r_C]$ = [8.5% − (0.65)6.0%)]/[1 − (0.65)] = 4.6%/0.35 = 13.1%

c. Discount the $NPV(cons)_2$ value computed in (a) for two years at the OCC computed in (b), and subtract the time-zero land cost:

$$NPV_0 = B_0 - C_0 = \frac{\$22,564,000}{1.131^2} - \$15,000,000$$

$$= \$17,640,000 - \$15,000,000 = +\$2,640,000$$

d. The maximum feasible land price would be

$15,000,000 + $2,640,000 − $1,000,000 = $16,640,000

e. The market value of the land reflects the investment value NPV that could be earned by the "second-best" developer of the site. If the subject developer can afford to pay as much as \$16,640,000 for this site with the \$40,000,000 construction project still making financial sense, then the subject developer must be the "first-best" developer. This developer must have some unique ability to maximize the profitability of the development of this site. Otherwise, the market value of the land would be at least \$16,640,00, not \$15,000,000.

f. Waiting to develop later is generally an alternative that is feasible and mutually-exclusive with immediate development (i.e., you cannot develop the same site now, and again in a year or two). In this case, if the land is not already owned by the developer, it can be presumably purchased for \$15,000,000, thereby giving the developer the ability to wait and develop the site later. If the subject developer is the first-best developer of this site, then it is possible that waiting to build later would have sufficiently greater expectations of future profit so that immediate construction would be a suboptimal decision for this developer. This possibility has not been explicitly considered in the above NPV analysis.

CHAPTER 30

30.5. a. $0 + \dfrac{15}{1.10} + \dfrac{15}{1.10^2} + \dfrac{15}{1.10^3} + \dfrac{15}{1.10^4} = \$47.54$

$(.10)\,47.54\,/\{1.10[1 - 1/(1.10)^5]\} = \$11.40 =$ Effective rent

b. $10 + \dfrac{11}{1.10} + \dfrac{12}{1.10^2} + \dfrac{13}{1.10^3} + \dfrac{14}{1.10^4} = \$49.25$

$(.10)\,49.25\,/\{1.10[1 - 1/(1.10)^5]\} = \$11.81 =$ Effective rent

c. $10 + \dfrac{10.25}{1.10} + \dfrac{10.51}{1.10^2} + \dfrac{10.77}{1.10^3} + \dfrac{11.04}{1.10^4} = \$43.63$

$(.10)\,43.63\,/\{1.10[1 - 1/(1.10)^5]\} = \$10.46 =$ Effective rent

d. $12 + \dfrac{11.76}{1.10} + \dfrac{11.51}{1.10^2} + \dfrac{11.26}{1.10^3} + \dfrac{11.00}{1.10^4} = \$48.18$

$(.10)\,48.18\,/\{1.10[1 - 1/(1.10)^5]\} = \$11.55 =$ Effective rent

e. $12 + \dfrac{12}{1.10} + \dfrac{12}{1.10^2} + \dfrac{12}{1.10^3} + \dfrac{12}{1.10^4} = \$50.04$

$(.10)\,50.04\,/\{1.10[1 - 1/(1.10)^5]\} = \$12.00 =$ Effective rent

f. $-5 + \dfrac{15}{1.10} + \dfrac{15}{1.10^2} + \dfrac{15}{1.10^3} + \dfrac{15}{1.10^4} + \dfrac{15}{1.10^5} = \$51.86$

$(.10)\,51.86\,/\{1.10[1 - 1/(1.10)^6]\} = \$10.83 =$ Effective rent

Index